New Media Research Resources

Whether students want to investigate the ideas behind a thought-provoking topic or conduct in-depth research for a paper, our new media research resources online and on CD-ROM can help them refine their research skills, find what they need in the library or on the Web, and then use and document their sources effectively.

DocLinks

bedfordstmartins.com/doclinks

A database of over 750 annotated Web links to primary documents online for the study of American history. Document links include speeches, legislation, United States Supreme Court decisions, treaties, social commentary, newspaper articles, visual artifacts, songs, and poems.

History Links Library

bedfordstmartins.com/historylinks

A database of more than 350 carefully reviewed and annotated American history Web sites containing material on historical archeology, primary documents collections, photograph and illustration galleries, map collections, secondary readings, and audio sources.

Research and Documentation Online

bedfordstmartins.com/resdoc

Diana Hacker, *Prince George's Community College*

This online version of Diana Hacker's popular booklet provides clear advice across the disciplines on how to find, evaluate, and integrate outside material into a paper, how to cite sources correctly, and how to format in MLA, APA, CBE, and *Chicago* styles.

Research Assistant Hyperfolio

Delivered on CD-ROM, this intelligent tool for conducting research helps students collect, evaluate, and cite sources found both online and off.

bedfordstmartins.com/history

FIFTH EDITION

America's History

Volume 1: To 1877

James A. Henretta

University of Maryland

David Brody

University of California, Davis

Lynn Dumenil

Occidental College

Susan Ware

Radcliffe Institute for Advanced Study

Bedford / St. Martin's

Boston • New York

For Bedford / St. Martin's

Publisher for History: Patricia A. Rossi
Director of Development for History: Jane Knetzger
Executive Editor for History: Elizabeth M. Welch
Developmental Editors: Jessica N. Angell and William J. Lombardo
Production Editor: Lori Chong Roncka
Production Assistants: Tina Lai, Kristen Merrill
Senior Production Supervisor: Joe Ford
Marketing Manager: Jenna Bookin Barry
Art Director: Donna Lee Dennison
Text Design: Gretchen Tolles for Anna George Design
Cover Design: Billy Boardman and Donna Lee Dennison
Copy Editors: Barbara G. Flanagan; Susan M. Free of Reap 'n Sow
Indexer: EdIndex
Photo Research: Pembroke Herbert/Picture Research Consultants & Archives
Advisory Editor for Cartography: Gerald A. Danzer
Map Development and Coordination: Tina Samaha
Cartography: Mapping Specialists Limited
Composition: TechBooks
Printing and Binding: R.R. Donnelley & Sons Company

President: Joan E. Feinberg
Editorial Director: Denise B. Wydra
Director of Editing, Design, and Production: Marcia Cohen
Managing Editor: Elizabeth M. Schaaf

Library of Congress Control Number: 2003101705

Manufactured in the United States of America.

8   7   6   5   4   3
f   e   d   c   b   a

For information, write: Bedford / St. Martin's, 75 Arlington Street, Boston, MA 02116 (617–399–4000)

ISBN: 0–312–39879–4 (hardcover)
ISBN: 0–312–40934–6 (paperback Vol. 1)
ISBN: 0–312–40958–3 (paperback Vol. 2)

Cover and title page art: Southeast Prospect of the City of New York, c. 1756–57. The New-York Historical Society / Bridgeman Art Library.

For Emily and Rebecca;
Siena, Cameron, Alex, Lea, and Eleanor;
Norman

In this, the fifth edition, *America's History* makes its debut as a book of the twenty-first century. When we first embarked on this edition, the country was at peace, the economy seemed invincible, and presidential candidate George W. Bush was advocating a "humble" foreign policy and no more "nation-building." The destruction of New York's World Trade Center on September 11, 2001, put an end to most Americans' hopes for a new age of normalcy; instead the nation finds itself plunged into a global war on terrorism, a war without end and without borders. As if on cue, many of our certitudes—about enduring prosperity, about the integrity of our business institutions, about an unsullied Catholic Church, about worldwide enthusiasm for America as global superpower—came crashing down. As the world becomes a threatening place, even those college students who don't think much about America's past or today's news have to wonder: How did that happen?

This question is at the heart of historical inquiry. And in asking it, the student is thinking historically. In *America's History* we aspire to satisfy that student's curiosity. We try to ask the right questions—the big ones and the not-so-big—and then write narrative history that illuminates the answers. The story, we hope, tells not only what happened, but *why*. We exclude no student from our potential audience of readers. How could we, when we hold the conviction that every student, bar none, wants to understand the world in which she lives?

From the very inception of *America's History*, we set out to write a *democratic* history, one that would convey the experiences of ordinary people even as it recorded the accomplishments of the great and powerful. We focus not only on the marvelous diversity of peoples who became American but also on the institutions—political, economic, cultural, and social—that forged a common national identity. And we present these historical trajectories in an integrated way, using each perspective to make better sense of the others. In our discussion of government and politics, diplomacy and war, we show how they affected—and were affected by—ethnic groups and economic conditions, intellectual beliefs and social changes, and the religious and moral values of the times. Just as important, we place the American experience in a global context. We trace aspects of American society to their origins in European and African cultures, consider the American Industrial Revolution within the framework of the world economy, and plot the foreign relations of the United States as part of an ever-shifting international system of impe-rial expansion, financial exchange, and diplomatic alliances.

In emphasizing the global context, however, we had something more in mind. We wanted to remind students that America never existed alone in the world; that other nations experienced developments comparable to our own; and that, knowing this, we can better understand what was distinctive and particular to the American experience. At opportune junctures, we pause for a comparative discussion, for example about the abolition of slavery in different nineteenth-century plantation economies. This discussion enables us to explain why, in the universal struggle by emancipated slaves for economic freedom, the freedmen of the American South became sharecropping tenants in a market economy and not, as in the Caribbean, gang laborers or subsistence farmers. The operative word is *explain* and, insofar as we can make it so, explaining the past is what we intend *America's History* to do. The challenge is to write a text that has explanatory power and yet is immediately accessible to every student who enrolls in the survey course.

Organization

Accomplishing these goals means first of all grounding *America's History* in a strong conceptual framework and a clear chronology. The nation's history is divided into six **parts**, corresponding to the major phases of American development. Each part begins at a crucial turning point, such as the American Revolution or the cold war, and emphasizes the dynamic forces that unleashed it and that symbolized the era. We want to show how people of all classes and groups make their own history, but also how people's choices are influenced and constrained by circumstances: the customs and institutions inherited from the past and the distribution of power in the present. We are writing narrative history, but harnessed to historical argument, not simply a retelling of "this happened, then that happened."

To aid student comprehension, each part begins with a two-page overview. First, a **thematic timeline** highlights the key developments in politics, the economy, society, culture, and foreign affairs; then these themes are fleshed out in a corresponding **part essay**. Each part essay focuses on the crucial engines of historical change—in some eras primarily economic, in others political or diplomatic—that created new conditions of life and transformed social relations. The part organization, encapsulated in the thematic timelines and opening essays, helps students understand the major themes and periods of American history, to see how bits and pieces of historical data acquire significance as part of a larger pattern of development.

The individual chapters are similarly constructed with student comprehension in mind. A **chapter outline** gives readers an overview of the text discussion, followed by a **thematic introduction** that orients them to the central issues and ideas of the chapter. Then, at the end of the chapter, we reiterate the themes in an **analytic summary** and remind students of important events in a **chapter timeline**. A **new glossary** defines the **key concepts** boldfaced in the text where first mentioned. **Suggested references** for each chapter, now united at the back of the book and expanded to include Web sites, are annotated for students and, in another measure to facilitate research, are divided into sections corresponding to those of the chapter.

Features

The fifth edition of *America's History* contains a wealth of special features, offered not with an eye to embellishing the book but as essential components of the text's pedagogical mission. Each chapter includes two **American Voices**—excerpts from letters, diaries, autobiographies, and public testimony that convey the experience of ordinary Americans in their own words. Exciting new selections include "Red Jacket: A Seneca Chief's Understanding of Religion," "Spotswood Rice: 'Freeing My Children from Slavery,'" and "Susana Archuleta: A Chicana Youth Gets New Deal Work." In keeping with our global focus, **Voices from Abroad** similarly offers first-person testimony by foreign visitors and observers in every chapter. "Louis Antonine De Bougainville: The Defense of Canada," "The Ford Miracle: 'Slaves' to the Assembly Line," and "Fei Xiaotong: America's Crisis of Faith" are a few of the new Voices from Abroad selections in this edition. Recognizing the centrality of technology in American life, we offer in each part two **New Technology** essays in which we describe key technical innovations and their impact on American history. Examples range from the cultivation of corn and the mechanization of spinning to rural electrification and the biotech revolution. We retain our vivid **American Lives** feature—incisive biographies in every chapter of well-known, representative American figures such as founder of the African Methodist Episcopal Church Richard Allen, social reformer Dorothea Dix, newspaperman William Randolph Hearst, and Mexican American labor organizer Bert Corona.

In this fifth edition, we add a new part feature, concluding essays we entitle **Thinking about History**. In these essays we take up a major theme discussed in the preceding chapters and examine how it is currently being reconsidered by historians. The particular dynamic on which we focus is the relationship between past and present. The Thinking about History essay for Part Four, for example, deals with the Great Plains, whose settlement after the Civil War is treated in Chapter 16 as the final stage in the westward movement. This is an unexceptional perspective, with an air of the inevitable about it. But today the Great Plains are emptying out. The attempt at taming this semiarid, fragile land is increasingly seen as an ecological disaster, a terrible misstep in the nation's development. As they assimilate that knowledge, the essay asks, how are scholars rethinking the history of Great Plains settlement? And how, as a result, is that history likely to be rewritten in the future? Other Thinking about History essays deal with the tripartite colonial legacy of slavery, racism, and republicanism; the renewed scholarly debate over federalism prompted by the "Reagan Revolution" of the 1980s; the recent controversy over the words "under God" in the Pledge of Allegiance; and the role of gender in explaining the origins and character of the U.S. welfare system. We offer these new essays in hopes of alerting students to the excitement and vitality of historical inquiry and, just as important, in hopes of revealing that the past they are studying is essential to understanding the world in which they live.

Those aims similarly prompt us to offer at the close of the book an **Epilogue** subtitled "Thinking about Contemporary History." Here, however, the argument moves in a direction opposite to the earlier Thinking about History essays—not how the present influences our reading of the past, but how knowledge of the past enables us to understand the present. While we were preparing the fourth edition, the approach of the millennium suggested to us the idea of a historically reflective Epilogue on America in 2000. The Epilogue in this fifth edition, while also reflective about the uses of history, is more concerned with applying that knowledge to the fraught world that college students currently face, most particularly in the wake of September 11.

We revised with equal care the text's illustration program. *America's History* has always been noted for the rich collection of maps, figures, and pictures that help students so much to visualize the past. There is, however, always room for improvement. **One-quarter of the pictures are new** to this edition, selected to reflect changes in the text and to underscore chapter themes. Most appear in full color, with unusually **substantive captions** that actively engage students with the image and encourage them to analyze artwork as primary sources. A **new design** complements the illustrations while drawing attention to our most significant revision of the text's visual aids: a **thoroughly revised and expanded map program**. To oversee the new map program we have enlisted Professor Gerald A. Danzer of the University of Illinois at Chicago, a specialist in geographic literacy. He has worked assiduously to make our maps better teaching tools, reworking many of them, enhancing the topography, and adding map annotations that call out key points. The map program is also much expanded, with over forty new maps, covering every aspect of American life that can be captured geographically. New maps on the Ice Age, the Columbian Exchange, the National Parks and Forests, the Dust Bowl, public works projects of the New Deal, and nuclear weapons testing consider the environmental ramifications of historical events and policies. Creating new maps is an opportunity to further reinforce for students how America's history is indeed part of a broader global history, and to this end we have added maps on the settling of the Americas, fifteenth-century West Africa and the Mediterranean, European immigration to the United States at the turn of the twentieth century, and the Great Powers in East Asia in 1910. We have added new elections maps and have added map series into the narrative that show change over time, depicting, for example, Eurasian trade systems in 1500, 1650, and 1770.

This new map program is well supported by tools that teach students how to extract as much information from a map as possible and to make connections beyond the map to the narrative. The text's introduction now contains a **map primer** that walks students through a map step-by-step, offering guidance and tips on how to "read" and analyze the map. **Cross-references to online map activities**, which appear at the bottom of a key map in each chapter, encourage students to test and improve upon these skills. A **map workbook**, also written by Professor Danzer, provides skill-building exercises for a map in each chapter, effectively teaching students how to use maps to enrich their understanding of American history.

Taken together, these documents, essays, pictures, and maps offer instructors a trove of teaching materials and supply students with rich fare for experiencing the world of the American past.

Textual Changes

Of all the reasons for a new edition, of course, the most compelling is to improve the text itself—a task we have found to be never finished and yet, to our surprise, always gratifying. In this fifth edition, we are spurred on by a shift in authorial responsibility, which always brings forth much rewriting. Marilynn Johnson retires with this edition, and Lynn Dumenil of Occidental College assumes responsibility for the modern era (Chapters 22–30). Professor Dumenil is not, however, new to this project. She joined us when we undertook a concise version, assuming responsibility for the same set of chapters that are now in her charge for *America's History*. It was an opportune meeting for us because Professor Dumenil's work on the concise version makes her a seasoned practitioner of the arts of concision and clarity that, more than anything else, we hope distinguishes the writing of *America's History*.

Ask students taking the U.S. survey—or their instructors, for that matter—what's the biggest problem with the course and they're likely to answer, "Too much to cover!" They have a point. After all, every passing year brings more American history to write about and read about. Consider the issue from a generational perspective. When the most senior of the authors of *America's History* was taking the U.S. survey in 1948–1949, most of Part Six had not yet happened! The intervening years, moreover, have seen an explosion of research into areas of our past that were invisible to earlier generations of historians—from women's history and gender roles to race and ethnicity to family life, popular culture, and work. No one, of course, would want to go back to the days when American history was essentially a chronicle of politics, diplomacy, and white men. But the inclusive, multifaceted history that we celebrate does make life harder for textbook writers. We have to resist the creep, the extra pages, that bulk up our books as we strive to incorporate what's new in the field and in contemporary America. In the fourth edition, we mounted a counteroffensive, cutting two chapters and reducing chapter length by 10 percent. In this edition, we declare victory, with even leaner chapters, 15 percent shorter than in the previous edition, so that, in effect, three words are doing the work originally of four. Our aim is to achieve a clearer, more sharply delineated narrative. Brevity, we have learned all over again, is the best antidote to imprecise language and murky argument. As textbook authors, we have always contended that if written with enough clarity and skill, the introductory survey can be made accessible to students at all levels without simplifying the story or skimping on explanation. In this fifth edition, we have enlisted the power of brevity to reach that goal.

While streamlining the narrative, we also took full advantage of the opportunity that revision affords to integrate new scholarship into our text. In the first chapter, the collision of societies now encompasses Africa as well as Europe and Native America. Our treatment of Native Americans in the colonial era incorporates recent anthropologically influenced work showing how Indian peoples maintained elements of their traditional culture in the face of European domination. We draw on new work dealing with the role of women and gender in eighteenth-century religion and antebellum politics and recent scholarship on the crisis over slavery after Independence. We offer an expanded treatment of the role of state policy during the antebellum Market Revolution, and we draw on recent Reconstruction scholarship that sees the transition from slavery to freedom as largely a battle over labor systems. We continue to incorporate more about the Far West into the nation's historical narrative, relying on the new western history for insight into the interactions among environment, peoples, and economic development. Advances in gender history enable us to offer a new discussion of bachelorhood and masculinity in the late nineteenth century and to temper our treatment of progressive welfare policy as we become aware of its patriarchal underpinnings. New scholarship on ethnic minorities similarly enables us to amplify our discussion of Native Americans during World War I and the New Deal, Asian Americans during the Great Depression, and black women during the 1920s and the later civil rights struggles. Recent scholarship based on hitherto closed Soviet and U.S. archives continues to inform our treatment of the cold war, and analysis of the turbulent 2000 presidential election and the advent of a new Republican administration bring the book to a thoughtful close. In these ways, and others, we strive to maintain the reputation of *America's History* as a fresh and timely text.

Supplements

Readers of *America's History* often cite its ancillary package as a key to the book's success in the classroom. Hence we have revised and expanded with care our array of print and electronic ancillaries for students and teachers.

For Students

Print Resources

Documents to Accompany *America's History*. Volume 1 by Melvin Yazawa (University of New Mexico), Volume 2 by Kevin Fernlund (University of Missouri, St. Louis). Revised for the fifth edition of *America's History*, this affordable documents collection offers students over 350 primary-source readings on topics covered in the main textbook, arranged to match the book's organization. One-quarter of the documents in the collection are new to this edition, giving emphasis to contested issues in American history that will spark critical thinking and class discussions. More than thirty visuals, meant to be "read" and analyzed like written sources, have been added. With many new documents emphasizing the environment, the West, and America in the context of the larger world, the collection remains a balanced assortment of political, economic, social, and cultural sources. Each document is preceded by a brief introduction and followed by questions for further thought, both of which help students analyze the documents and place them in historical context.

Maps in Context: A Workbook for American History. By Gerald A. Danzer (University of Illinois, Chicago). Published in two volumes and written by an expert in geographic literacy, these skill-building workbooks (approximately 100 pages each) correspond to the organization of *America's History* and offer instructors a powerful tool to help their students understand the essential connections between geography and history. Organized into three sections—Basic Geography, Mapping America's History, and One-Minute Quizzes—*Maps in Context* presents a wealth of in-class or take-home projects and convenient pop quizzes that give students hands-on experience working with maps from all areas of American history.

The Bedford Series in History and Culture. Natalie Zemon Davis (Princeton University); Ernest R. May (Harvard University); David W. Blight (Yale University); and Lynn Hunt (University of California at Los Angeles), advisory editors.

Over 65 American titles in this highly praised series combine first-rate scholarship, historical narrative, and important primary documents for undergraduate courses. Each book is brief, inexpensive, and focused on a specific topic or period. Package discounts are available.

Historians at Work Series. Edward Countryman (Southern Methodist University), advisory editor. Each volume in this series combines the best thinking about an important historical issue with helpful learning aids. Unabridged selections by distinguished historians, each with a differing perspective, provide a unique structure within which to examine a single question. With headnotes and questions to guide their reading and complete, original footnotes, students are able to engage in discussion that captures the intellectual excitement of historical research and interpretation. Package discounts are available.

New Media Resources

Online Study Guide at bedfordstmartins.com /henretta The *Online Study Guide* features up-to-date technology to present students with attractive and highly effective presentations and learning tools with unique self-assessment capabilities. As a student completes a practice test, the *Online Study Guide* immediately assesses his performance, targets the subject areas that need review, and refers the student back to the appropriate portions of the text. Through a series of multiple-choice, fill-in-the-blank, short-answer, and essay questions, students can gauge how well they have mastered the chapter's key events and themes. Multimedia activities on maps, visuals, and primary sources engage all types of learners and encourage critical thinking.

DocLinks at bedfordstmartins.com/doclinks DocLinks is a new, extensive database of over 750 annotated Web links to primary documents online for the study of American history. Links to speeches, legislation, U.S. Supreme Court decisions, narratives and testimony, treaties, essays, political manifestos, visual artifacts, songs, and poems provide students with a comprehensive understanding of critical events and trends in U.S. history and society. Documents are searchable by topic and date and are indexed to the chapters of *America's History*.

History Links Library at bedfordstmartins.com /historylinks Links Library is a searchable database of more than 200 carefully reviewed and annotated links to Web sites on American history. The links can be searched by topic or by specific chapters in *America's History*. Teachers can assign these links as the basis for homework assignments or research projects, or students can use them as a point of departure for their own history research.

Research and Documentation Online at bedfordstmartins.com/resdoc By Diana Hacker (Prince George's Community College). This online version of Hacker's popular booklet provides clear advice across the disciplines on how to integrate outside material into a paper, how to cite sources correctly, and how to format in MLA, APA, *Chicago*, or CBE style.

Research Assistant Hyperfolio. Delivered on CD-ROM, this intelligent tool for conducting research helps students collect, evaluate, and cite sources found both online and off.

After September 11: An Online Reader for Writers

bedfordstmartins.com/september11 This free collection of more than 100 annotated links provides social, political, economic, and cultural commentary based on the terrorist attacks of September 11, 2001, on the United States. Thoughtful discussion questions and ideas for research and writing projects are included.

For Instructors

Print Resources

Instructor's Resource Manual. By Bradley T. Gericke (U.S. Army Command and General Staff College). The *Instructor's Resource Manual*, provided free of charge with adoption of the textbook, offers an extensive collection of tools to aid both the first-time and the experienced teacher in structuring and customizing the American history course. Paralleling the textbook organization, this resource includes instructional objectives, annotated chapter outlines to guide lectures, and a chapter summary for each of the book's chapters. Lecture strategies and ideas for class discussion offer possible approaches to teaching each chapter and to presenting potentially difficult topics. A set of exercises for students includes both discussion questions and writing assignments for maps and special features. The manual also offers instructional objectives for each of the book's six parts to help instructors tie together larger sections of the book and provides critical thinking questions to pair with the part-closing Thinking about History essays. Additionally, each chapter of the manual gives an outline of supplementary material (books from the Bedford Series in History and Culture, particular selections from *Documents to Accompany* AMERICA'S HISTORY, activities from the *Online Study Guide*) that pertains to the chapter's content.

Transparencies. A newly expanded set of over 150 full-color acetate transparencies, free to adopters, includes all the maps and many images from the text.

New Media Resources

Computerized Test Bank. A fully updated Test Bank CD-ROM offers over 80 exercises for each chapter, allowing instructors to pick and choose from a collection of multiple-choice, fill-in, map, and short and long essay questions. To aid instructors in tailoring their tests to suit their classes, every question is labeled by topic according to chapter headings and includes a textbook page number so instructors can direct students to a particular page for correct answers. Also, the software allows instructors to edit both questions and answers to further customize their tests. Correct answers are included.

Instructor's Resource CD-ROM. This easy-to-operate disc provides instructors with the resources to build engaging multimedia classroom presentations around a variety of art, photos, maps, and figures from the text. These visuals are provided in two formats: chapter-based PowerPoint files that are fully customizable and individual JPEG files.

Map Central at bedfordstmartins.com/mapcentral Map central is a searchable database of over 700 maps from Bedford/St. Martin's history survey texts that can be used to create visually striking classroom lectures.

Using the Bedford Series in the U.S. History Survey

bedfordstmartins.com/usingseries This short online guide by Scott Hovey gives practical suggestions for using the more than 65 volumes from the Bedford Series in History and Culture with *America's History* in the survey classroom. The guide not only supplies links between the text and these supplements but also provides ideas for starting discussions focused on the primary sources featured in the volumes.

Videos and multimedia. A wide assortment of videos and CD-ROMs on various topics in American history is available to qualified adopters.

Book Companion Site at bedfordstmartins.com /henretta The companion Web site for *America's History*, Fifth Edition, uses the dynamic nature of the

Web to extend the goals of the textbook and offers a convenient home base for students and instructors by gathering all the electronic resources for the text at a single Web address.

Acknowledgments

We are very grateful to the following scholars and teachers who reported on their experiences with the third edition or reviewed chapters of the fourth edition. Their comments often challenged us to rethink or justify our interpretations and always provided a check on accuracy down to the smallest detail.

Ruth M. Alexander, *Colorado State University*
Robert J. Allison, *Suffolk University*
Robin F. Bachin, *University of Miami*
Albert I. Berger, *University of North Dakota*
Neal A. Brooks, *Essex Community College (Maryland)*
Thomas Bryan, *Alvin Community College*
Montgomery Buell, *Walla Walla College*
Markus C. Cachia-Riedl, *University of California, Berkeley*
Kay J. Carr, *Southern Illinois University at Carbondale*
William Carrigan, *Rowan University*
Myles L. Clowers, *San Diego City College*
Curtis Cole, *Huron University College*
Rory T. L. Cornish, *University of Louisiana, Monroe*
John P. Daly, *Louisiana Tech University*
Thomas S. Dicke, *Southwest Missouri State University*
Jonathan Earle, *University of Kansas*
Bradley T. Gericke, *United States Military Academy*
Sally Hadden, *Florida State University*
Paul Harvey, *University of Colorado*
Lybeth Hodges, *Texas Women's University*
Nita S. Howard, *Clovis Community College*
Jen A. Huntley-Smith, *University of Nevada—Reno*
Davis D. Joyce, *East Central University (Oklahoma)*
Louisa Kilgroe, *North Carolina State University*
Keith L. King, *Houston Community College Southeast*
Norman D. Love, *El Paso Community College*
John Lyons, *Joliet Junior College*
John R. McKivigan, *West Virginia University*
Samuel T. McSeveney, *Vanderbilt University*
Rick Malmström, *The Ellis School*
M. Catherine Miller, *Texas Tech University*
Carl H. Moneyhon, *University of Arkansas—Little Rock*

Max Page, *Yale University*
Charles K. Piehl, *Mankato State University*
Edwin G. Quattlebaum III, *Phillips Academy*
Dona Reaser, *Columbus State Community College*
Steven D. Reschly, *Truman State University*
Leonard Riforgiato, *Penn State University—Shenango*
Howard B. Rock, *Florida International University*
Neil Sapper, *Amarillo College*
Timothy Shannon, *Gettysburg College*
Peter H. Shattuck, *California State University—Sacramento*
Anthony J. Springer, *Dallas Christian College*
April Summitt, *Andrews University*
Emily J. Teipe, *Fullerton College*
Suzanne R. Thurman, *Mesa State College*
Benson Tong, *Wichita State University*
Diane Tuinstra, *Kansas State University*
Ken L. Weatherbie, *Del Mar College*
Cecil E. Weller Jr., *San Jacinto College South*
Arthur J. Worrall, *Colorado State University*

As the authors of *America's History*, we know better than anyone else how much of this book is the work of other hands and other minds. We are grateful to the many scholars whose books and articles we have enjoyed and used in writing this narrative and to the editors and production staff who have provided invaluable assistance in previous editions of our text. With advice and support from Elizabeth Welch, Gretchen Boger, Louise Townsend, and Amy Langlais, Jessica Angell expertly edited our text. Charles Christensen, Joan Feinberg, Denise Wydra, Tisha Rossi, Jane Knetzger, and Marcia Cohen have been generous in providing the resources we needed to produce the fifth edition. Special thanks are due to many other individuals: Pembroke Herbert and her staff at Picture Research Associates; our project editor, Lori Chong Roncka; William Lombardo and Tina Samaha, who directed our map program, and Professor Gerald A. Danzer, a distinguished geographer and our map consultant; the fine copyeditors who worked closely with us—Barbara Flanagan and Susan M. Free; Anna George and Gretchen Tolles, who crafted our new design; our cover designers, Billy Boardman and Donna Dennison; our marketing manager, Jenna Bookin Barry; and managing editor Elizabeth Schaaf. Bradley T. Gericke diligently wrote many of the supplements for *America's History*, and Jennifer Blanksteen, Corinne McCutchen, Elizabeth Harrison, Coleen O'Hanley, and Stuart Holdsworth were of great assistance in editing and producing them. We also want to express our thanks for the valuable assistance provided by Norman S. Cohen, Michael Cohen, and Patricia Deveneau.

From the very beginning we have considered this book a joint intellectual venture, and with each edition our collaborative effort has grown. We are proud to acknowledge our collective authorship of *America's History*.

Understanding History through Maps:
An Introduction for Students

Maps and historical studies have much in common: both use art and science to create representations of things we cannot experience directly. In the case of maps, most spaces are too vast and too complex to be understood with a single look. History has an additional challenge: the past has forever slipped away and we need devices to help us recover and understand it. Both the cartographer (or mapmaker) and the historian start by gathering facts, but they are quickly overwhelmed with data, and faced with the need to select, shorten, and clarify their portrayals. The cartographer turns to symbols and visual images while the historian depends primarily on words and concepts. Working together, the historian and the cartographer combine their talents to craft a coherent narrative about the past. Their primary subjects—people, places, and times—are intimately connected. Every historical map needs a title and date, both suggested by human experience. Similarly, every historical account happened in a specific location; events, as we say, "take place."

People, places, and times are the building blocks of all history textbooks. The authors of *America's History*, Fifth Edition, selected over 150 maps designed to establish the geographic context of their story. Combined with the illustrations, figures, and narrative, the maps help readers make connections with the past and get a feel for the setting in which events happened. As in all history textbooks, the maps in *America's History* do double duty. First, they function as shorthand geography, giving readers a picture of a place. Second, maps call attention to human events that

The Common Map Projections: Orthographic, Azimuthal Equidistant, Mercator, and Gall-Peters Equal-Area

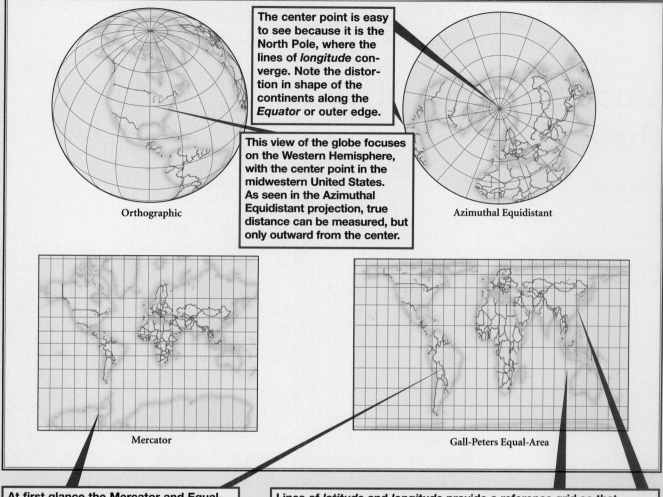

The center point is easy to see because it is the North Pole, where the lines of *longitude* converge. Note the distortion in shape of the continents along the *Equator* or outer edge.

This view of the globe focuses on the Western Hemisphere, with the center point in the midwestern United States. As seen in the Azimuthal Equidistant projection, true distance can be measured, but only outward from the center.

Orthographic

Azimuthal Equidistant

Mercator

Gall-Peters Equal-Area

At first glance the Mercator and Equal-Area projections look similar, but a close examination reveals different degrees of geographic distortion.

Lines of *latitude* and *longitude* provide a reference grid so that points on the map can be easily connected to a global position. Lines of latitude circle the globe east to west and are called *parallels*. Lines of longitude circle the globe north to south and are called *meridians*.

Figure A provides examples of several common map projections: Orthographic, Azimuthal Equidistant, Mercator, and Gall-Peters Equal-Area. All are considered world maps because they seek to depict the entire globe, or as much of it as possible. Because presenting a round image on a flat sheet of paper necessarily distorts area, shape, direction, and distance, over the years cartographers have developed numerous strategies to make their maps. Each projection is useful for a different purpose, and no single projection is the "right" one.

The Orthographic and Azimuthal Equidistant projections show the world as a globe—a three-dimensional object—but the viewer can only see two dimensions of it from any one point in space. The rounded look of the planet is retained, but only half the world can be depicted. The Orthographic projection most resembles a globe. Although it exhibits distortions in shape and area near the edges, the viewer mentally corrects these because of her familiarity with the view. Here, the shape and area of North America is relatively accurate, but to the east, across the Atlantic Ocean, western Europe is not. The Azimuthal Equidistant projection takes the skin off the globe and flattens it out to produce a two-dimensional circle. Like the Orthographic projection, it depicts half the

earth—here, the Northern Hemisphere is shown with the outer edge being the Equator. Its advantage is that it shows correct direction and distance, either of a country or continent, but only measured from the center point (in this case the North Pole). Its disadvantage is that because of the flattening and stretching, it significantly distorts (increases) the size of land forms and bodies of water near the edges.

The Mercator and Gall-Peters Equal-Area projections allow the viewer to see the entire world at a single glance. The Mercator projection accurately depicts the relative size and position of continents, countries, and bodies of water at the Equator, and fairly accurately until 45 degrees north and south latitude. Above and below these latitudes areas become distorted, as you can see from looking at Greenland, which becomes enlarged to look almost as big as North America, and Antarctica, which fills the entire bottom of the map. To correct this distortion problem, geographers developed the Gall-Peters Equal-Area projection. Its great advantage is that it depicts the areas of the continents in accurate proportion. However, its disadvantage is that it significantly distorts their shapes, as shown by the elongated views of Africa and South America.

are historically significant because they help explain change over time. To derive full benefit from the historical maps in *America's History*, readers need to view them with bifocal vision—with one eye on the physical environment and the other on the event or process depicted. A successfully read map mixes the two images, allowing for an appreciation of the human-environmental interaction that is at the root of all our experiences.

Beginning to Read Historical Maps

Readers face three challenges when looking at a map in a history textbook. First, we must discern the event being portrayed. What is the purpose of the map? Second, we must see the geography on the image, to turn the lines and symbols on the map into a picture of the physical environment in which the event took place. What area of the world are we looking at? What did it look like at the time represented? Third, maps place a major demand on our powers of understanding: How did the event and the place interact with each other? What opportunities and constraints did the environment provide? How did topography, climate, resources, or other elements of the geographic situation influence the course of events? Conversely, how did people have an impact on their environment? How did they perceive it and use it? How did a knowledge of, or attitudes toward, the physical environment differ between individuals and groups? Did these attitudes change over time? And, finally, what does it all mean? What does some insight into the experiences of people on earth tell us about who we are and where we have been?

Maps cannot tell us everything about history, and some maps are more complex than others. They have limitations as well as possibilities, and they function best when, as in *America's History*, they are accompanied by graphic aids and are integrated into the narrative flow. Maps also depend on an active reader, one who knows how to use maps and has some facility in integrating all the elements of a textbook into a meaningful educational experience. The ability to understand the strengths and limitations of maps is the core of cartographic literacy.

Developing Cartographic Literacy

The best way to start developing cartographic literacy is to review the three major shortcomings of maps. First, maps change the outer face of a globe, or a portion of it, into a flat surface. This transformation has less effect on maps that have a large scale and hence portray only a small portion of the globe. But on world maps and other small-scale portrayals the distortion created by projecting a sphere onto a plane becomes serious. The process produces exaggerations and inconsistencies of shape, direction, and/or area (Figure A).

Second, maps have a difficult time showing the irregularities on the earth's surface that are important in real life. How are mountains and valleys, plains and plateaus, hills and canyons to be indicated on a flat sheet of paper? Maps, after all, take a vantage point in the sky rather than a view toward the horizon. As Figure B illustrates, to indicate topography the cartographer must use a bag of tricks—symbols, contour lines, and suggestive shading. All of these devices rely on the reader to interpret their meaning and to translate them into landscapes.

The third limitation of maps is that they must be selective. Reducing the size of reality demands simplification, and the cartographer must focus on a few points while excluding the vast majority of details. What should be emphasized? Where should the presentation end? These choices turn any map into a very selective instrument, fashioned for a particular purpose. All maps present an argument advocating a point of view, and good maps raise more questions than they answer. Maps should not be thought of as final steps in the learning process. Instead, consider them as catalysts provided to spur active thought and raise additional issues.

These limitations of maps are directly linked to their strengths and advantages. A world map is the only way we can see all of the earth's surface at a glance. Even a round globe, a much more accurate representation of the planet, can present only a portion of its subject at one time. Paradoxically, if we want to picture the global dimension of something, only a flat world map will do. Maps help us comprehend places we cannot actually see because the distances are too vast. An ocean, a continent, a nation, a state, even a city or a town cannot be taken in by one look. Only its representation on a map enables us to see it whole.

Maps also clarify the world for us. As models of reality, they extract certain features for emphasis to make the world intelligible. Maps are instructional devices, and the cartographer always follows a lesson plan. One way to begin reading a map is to figure out the purpose of the lesson. What is the basic message the map is intended to convey? The title of the map is a good place to start, especially any dates that might be provided. Dates help readers connect the map with the narrative, placing the event described into a sequence of happenings and connecting the incident to other developments occurring at the same time. The alert reader will connect the map's title to its caption. The word *caption* is derived from the same root as the word *capture*. The sentences in every map caption in *America's History* are designed to help the reader seize the purpose of the map—and thus turn it into a valuable possession.

Working with maps also deepens our understanding of the basic themes of geography and how they relate to

FIGURE B

MAP 16.7 The Settlement of the Pacific Slope, 1860–1890

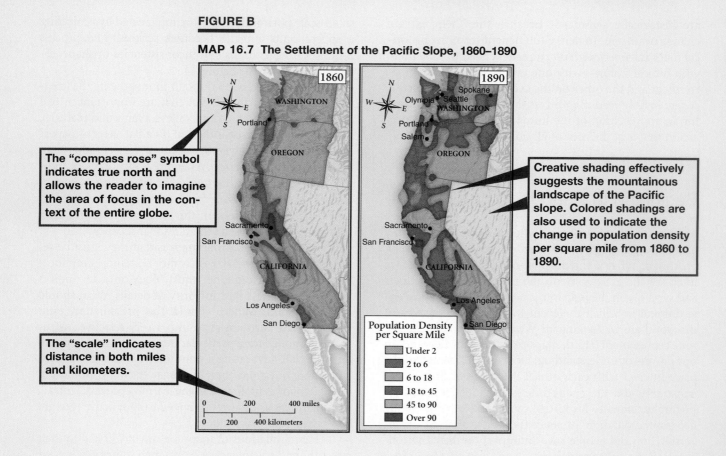

The "compass rose" symbol indicates true north and allows the reader to imagine the area of focus in the context of the entire globe.

Creative shading effectively suggests the mountainous landscape of the Pacific slope. Colored shadings are also used to indicate the change in population density per square mile from 1860 to 1890.

The "scale" indicates distance in both miles and kilometers.

Population Density per Square Mile
- Under 2
- 2 to 6
- 6 to 18
- 18 to 45
- 45 to 90
- Over 90

historical studies. Five of these themes—location, place, region, movement, and interaction—are presented as questions on the following pages, with several maps provided to illustrate how each particular theme might enrich a reader's understanding of the map and the historical situation it depicts. All of the maps reappear later in the text, and all of the questions might be called upon to enhance the value of any individual map. In the end, attention to these basic themes will fortify the reader's cartographic literacy, as well as foster her historical understanding.

Location: Where Is This Place?

"When?" and "Where?" are the first questions asked by historians and cartographers. Every event is connected to a place, and every place needs to be identified by a date. Maps are the best devices to show location, and in the final analysis any place on a map is located in reference to the earth as a whole. Location depends, in an absolute sense, on a reference to global position, most conveniently cited in terms of latitude and longitude (see Figure A).

In a relative sense, however, location can depend on the distance, direction, or travel time from one place to another. As Figure C indicates, in 1817 Pittsburgh, Pennsylvania, was more than ten days' travel from New York City, a distance of roughly 370 miles. By 1841 improvements in travel made the trip possible in about five or six days. Relative location is also at the heart of Figure D, showing the Japanese relocation camps during World War II. Note that latitude and longitude are not used on this map because absolute location is not the point. Instead, this map is intended to show how far the Japanese Americans were forced to relocate—within the same state, several states away, or halfway across the nation. It is not necessary to show all of the states, since only those west of the Mississippi River were primarily involved. The cartographer assumes that the map reader will realize that a portion of the country is not shown and will, if needed, fill in the missing part from her mental map.

FIGURE C

MAP 10.4 The Speed of News in 1817 and 1841

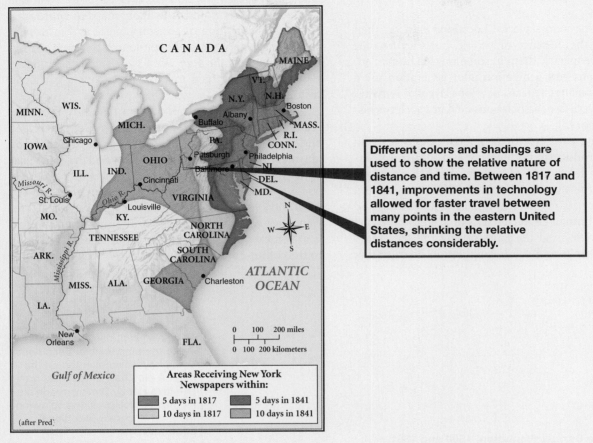

Different colors and shadings are used to show the relative nature of distance and time. Between 1817 and 1841, improvements in technology allowed for faster travel between many points in the eastern United States, shrinking the relative distances considerably.

Areas Receiving New York Newspapers within:

5 days in 1817	5 days in 1841
10 days in 1817	10 days in 1841

(after Pred)

FIGURE D

MAP 26.2 Japanese Relocation Camps

Inset maps allow the cartographer to use a large-scale map to depict the main subject area (here, the continental United States) and still show additional areas relevant to the topic. Alaska and Hawaii were territories, not states, during World War II and are included here because Japanese Americans lived in both.

This national map appears to float free of its location on the planet. Neither oceans nor continents are used to suggest a global position. The boundaries of the United States serve as the boundaries of the map, isolating the nation from its geographical position but allowing for greater focus.

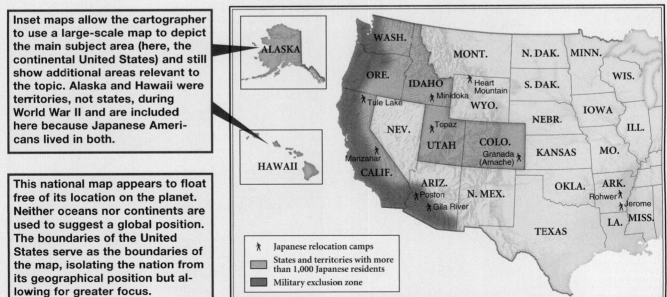

Japanese relocation camps

States and territories with more than 1,000 Japanese residents

Military exclusion zone

Place: How Did This Location Become a Place?

Human activity creates places. Locations exist on their own without the presence of people, but they become places when people use them in some way. As human enterprise thickens and generation after generation use a place, it accumulates artifacts, develops layers of remains, and creates a variety of associations held in a society's history and memory.

Places have two sets of characteristics: physical and human, the products of both nature and culture. A complete physical description of a place would show the topography of the site, identify any bodies of water, and then inventory its climate, minerals, soils, plants, and animals. The human characteristics of a site would start with how people used the land, noting the settlement patterns, buildings and roads, population distribution, economic activities, social organization, language, and culture. The historian takes an additional step and considers how these have changed over time and what that change means. It would take many maps to approach a complete description of a historic place and to unravel all the characteristics and experiences that make it significant. Indeed, the very word *place* suggests a uniqueness that has emerged in large part from a particular history.

Figure E presents a pair of maps that show the settlement pattern of the Barrow plantation in Georgia in 1860 and in 1881. These illustrate how important the date is on any map. The passing of a slave society and the emergence of a sharecropping economy transformed the Barrow landscape. Only the big house remained in place between 1860 and 1881. The tight organization of a controlled society gave way to a dispersed community, but one that gained focal points on a church and a school in addition to the cotton-gin house.

FIGURE E

MAP 15.2 The Barrow Plantation, 1860 and 1881

The "key" includes symbols that make the map legible. Each item in the key is represented on the map. A pie chart that shows how ex-slave Handy Barrow made his income is also provided, allowing the map to convey additional information.

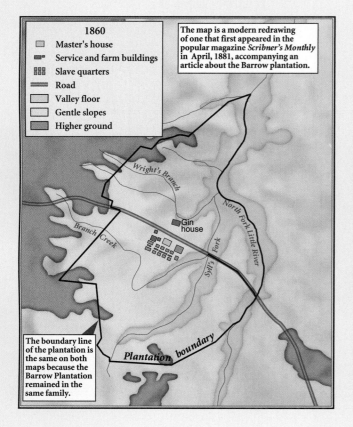

1860

- Master's house
- Service and farm buildings
- Slave quarters
- Road
- Valley floor
- Gentle slopes
- Higher ground

The map is a modern redrawing of one that first appeared in the popular magazine *Scribner's Monthly* in April, 1881, accompanying an article about the Barrow plantation.

Wright's Branch

North Fork Little River

Gin house

Branch Creek

Syll's Fork

The boundary line of the plantation is the same on both maps because the Barrow Plantation remained in the same family.

Plantation boundary

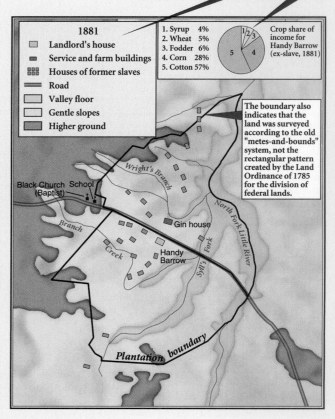

1881

- Landlord's house
- Service and farm buildings
- Houses of former slaves
- Road
- Valley floor
- Gentle slopes
- Higher ground

1. Syrup 4%
2. Wheat 5%
3. Fodder 6%
4. Corn 28%
5. Cotton 57%

Crop share of income for Handy Barrow (ex-slave, 1881)

The boundary also indicates that the land was surveyed according to the old "metes-and-bounds" system, not the rectangular pattern created by the Land Ordinance of 1785 for the division of federal lands.

Black Church School (Baptist)

Wright's Branch

North Fork Little River

Branch Creek

Gin house

Handy Barrow

Syll's Fork

Plantation boundary

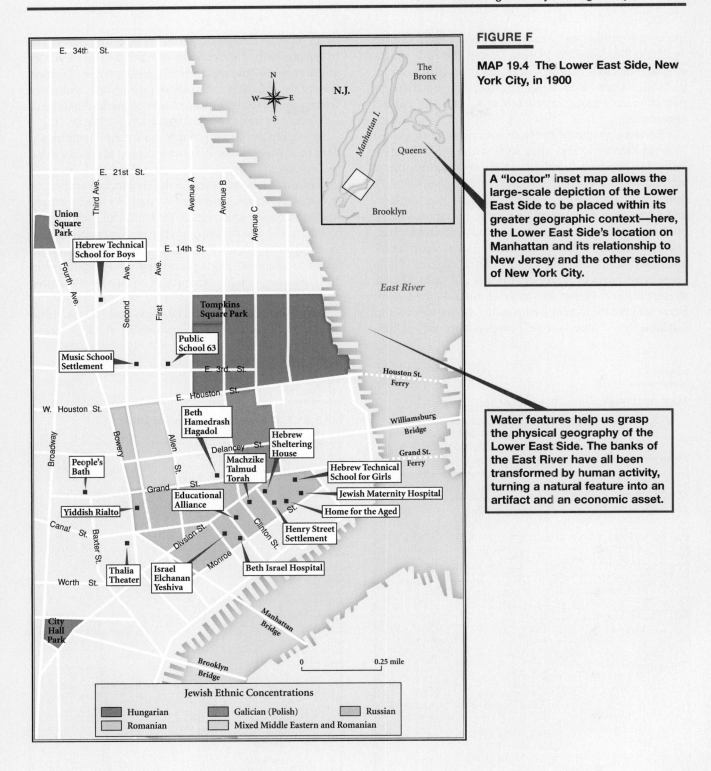

MAP 19.4 The Lower East Side, New York City, in 1900

A "locator" inset map allows the large-scale depiction of the Lower East Side to be placed within its greater geographic context—here, the Lower East Side's location on Manhattan and its relationship to New Jersey and the other sections of New York City.

Water features help us grasp the physical geography of the Lower East Side. The banks of the East River have all been transformed by human activity, turning a natural feature into an artifact and an economic asset.

Figure F maps neighborhood institutions in an urban environment. Again the date is essential to note because the Lower East Side of New York surely had a different mix of institutions in 1850 or 1950 than it did in 1900, the time of the map. In larger terms, the sense of place created here results from its waterfront location, the concentrations of ethnic groups, and the variety of neighborhood institutions.

Region: What Does a Place Have in Common with Its Surroundings?

The concept of place highlights the unique elements of every location. By contrast, the idea of a region highlights elements in common, tying certain places together as a group distinguishable from other places. New England, the cotton-producing South, the Phoenix metropolitan area, and the Columbia Plateau suggest the wide variety of groupings that help us understand the integration of particular places into larger regions. Every location is part of many regions, only a few of which share natural boundaries.

Perceiving regional ties is a great help to the reader of historical maps because they suggest the forces binding individual interests together and encouraging people to act in common. The United States could be considered a political region in which like values, shared institutions, and a common heritage create a sense of national unity. Such a region is a human construction; in contrast, physical characteristics like landforms, climate, ecosystems, and geological structures create natural regions. These often cross national boundaries. Thus the United States shares the Great Plains, the Rocky Mountains, the canyon lands, and the Pacific slope with its neighbors Mexico and Canada. Every state can be grouped with others into larger regional entities like the Midwest or the Gulf States. Internally each state can be divided into a variety of smaller regions that represent differing interests. Upstate, downstate, urban, rural, inner city, suburban, and so on are regularly used regional concepts in analyzing political developments and historical trends.

Geographers often point to an internal pattern evident in many regions. A historical core marks a central place or point of origin for a region. Toward the edges of the region the dominance of the defining characteristic thins out, creating a periphery or frontier marking a transition zone to another region. To this useful construct the historian adds the dynamic of change over time. One way to engage the maps of the many presidential elections found in *America's History* is to apply the regional concept and then look for evidence of change by comparing maps.

Consider, for example, Figures G and H, which illuminate the importance of regions in thinking about

FIGURE G

MAP 28.3 Presidential Election of 1960

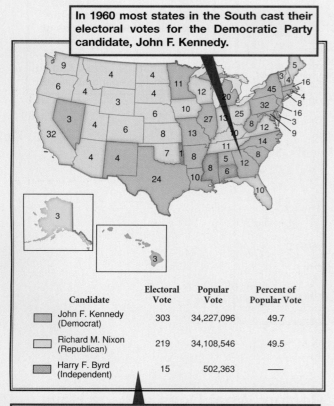

In 1960 most states in the South cast their electoral votes for the Democratic Party candidate, John F. Kennedy.

Candidate	Electoral Vote	Popular Vote	Percent of Popular Vote
John F. Kennedy (Democrat)	303	34,227,096	49.7
Richard M. Nixon (Republican)	219	34,108,546	49.5
Harry F. Byrd (Independent)	15	502,363	—

The presidential election maps in *America's History* allow the reader to quickly see the national distribution of electoral votes on a regional and state basis. Another way to depict election results graphically would be to show the winner of the popular vote per county. By shifting the focus, the results might look very different and raise further questions.

FIGURE H

MAP 31.7 Presidential Election of 2000

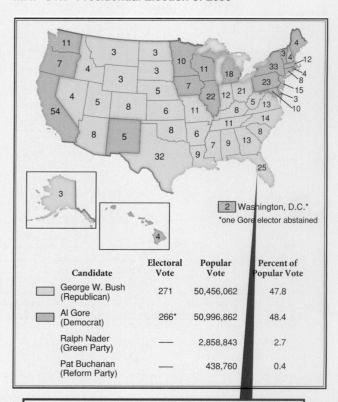

2 Washington, D.C.*
*one Gore elector abstained

Candidate	Electoral Vote	Popular Vote	Percent of Popular Vote
George W. Bush (Republican)	271	50,456,062	47.8
Al Gore (Democrat)	266*	50,996,862	48.4
Ralph Nader (Green Party)	—	2,858,843	2.7
Pat Buchanan (Reform Party)	—	438,760	0.4

Forty years later in the 2000 presidential election, the southern states cast their electoral votes for the Republican Party candidate, George W. Bush. In Alabama, Georgia, Mississippi, North and South Carolina, and Texas, Bush won easily with 55–59 percent of the popular vote; only in Florida was his victory razor-thin.

American politics. In 1960, as Figure G indicates, the South voted solidly Democratic. In 2000, the South voted just as solidly Republican, as shown by Figure H. How can such a fundamental political shift be explained? Understanding regional histories and identities explains a great deal, and presidential election maps like those placed throughout *America's History* are powerful tools that help readers focus on regional patterns and other shifts in voting behavior.

Figure I shows how a particular place—here, the Tennessee Valley—can be considered part of several overlapping regions, the significance of which changes depending on the interest of the viewer. Emerging out of the politics of the New Deal, in the 1930s the Tennessee Valley area became, for the first time, clearly defined. Figure I uses two sets of data to describe the Tennessee Valley Authority: the area served by TVA electric power (an example of a cultural region) and the actual watershed of the river (a natural region).

Movement: What Is Happening Here?

All change involves movement. People move in their daily activities, in seasonal patterns, and in migration to new places of residence. In the process they cross many boundaries. People also use products that move from one place to another through the economic system. An important type of movement is "diffusion," a concept used by geographers to describe the process by which people, animals, goods, services, ideas, and information move from a point of origin to other locations. Diffusion is sometimes a planned, purposeful activity, but it can also be accidental, like the spread of disease. To understand a map fully, the reader must always envision it as one part of a sequence, not unlike a "still" excerpted from a motion picture. To capture all of this activity on a map is a difficult undertaking. To understand the map,

FIGURE I

Map 25.4 The Tennessee Valley Authority, 1933–1952

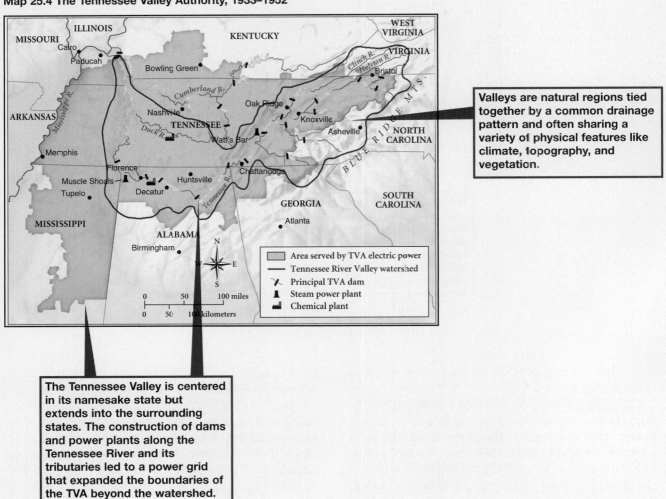

Valleys are natural regions tied together by a common drainage pattern and often sharing a variety of physical features like climate, topography, and vegetation.

The Tennessee Valley is centered in its namesake state but extends into the surrounding states. The construction of dams and power plants along the Tennessee River and its tributaries led to a power grid that expanded the boundaries of the TVA beyond the watershed.

FIGURE J

MAP 8.2 Regional Cultures Move West, 1790–1820

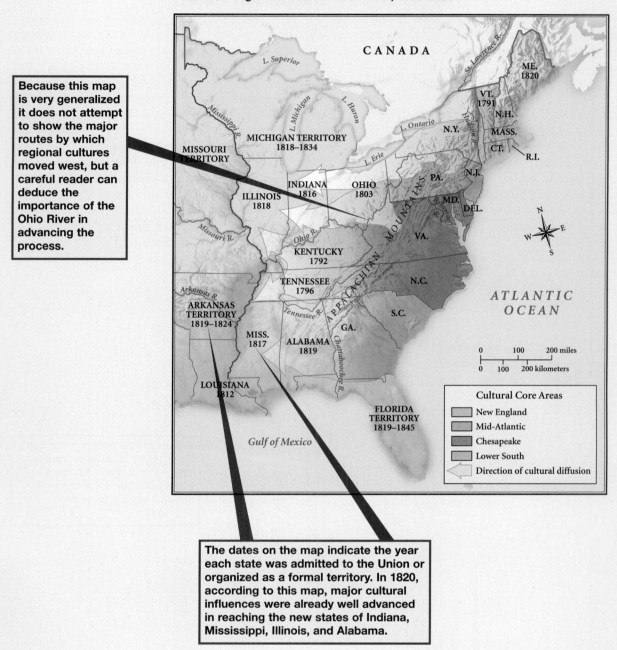

Because this map is very generalized it does not attempt to show the major routes by which regional cultures moved west, but a careful reader can deduce the importance of the Ohio River in advancing the process.

The dates on the map indicate the year each state was admitted to the Union or organized as a formal territory. In 1820, according to this map, major cultural influences were already well advanced in reaching the new states of Indiana, Mississippi, Illinois, and Alabama.

the viewer must perceive that the silent sheet of paper depicts commotion.

Cartographers employ a range of strategies to emphasize movement on maps. One way is to show, usually through color and shading, the routes along which the movement is channeled. Another device, favored in historical cartography to show military campaigns, is to provide dramatic arrows indicating the course of action. Often the width of the arrows represents the size of the army on the march, giving maps with arrows the qualities of graphs and charts.

Figure J uses both arrows and shading to provide a very generalized idea of the way cultural traits such as religious identity, speech patterns, and housing types moved from core areas along the Atlantic coast to the American interior. The large arrows show the general direction of these movements, while the shading indicates the density of the process up to 1820. The large arrows

FIGURE K

MAP 18.2 The Diffusion of the Australian Ballot

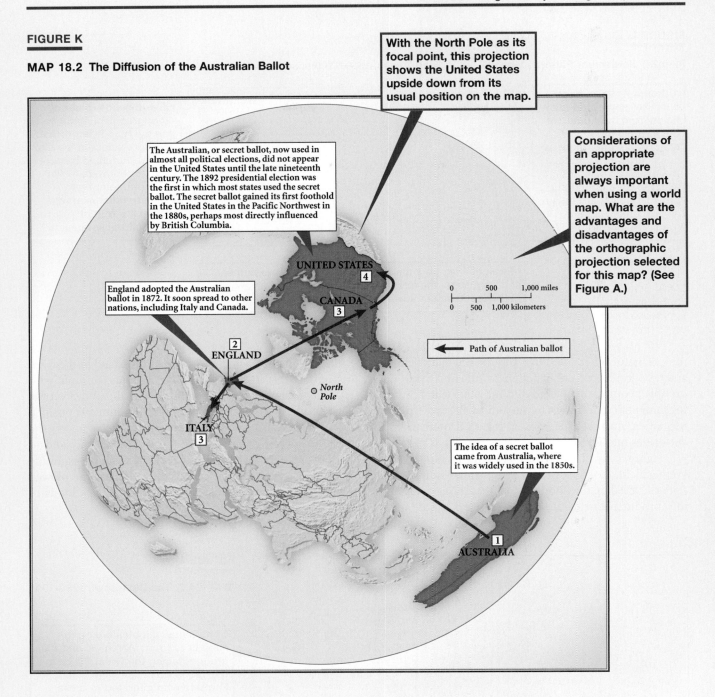

With the North Pole as its focal point, this projection shows the United States upside down from its usual position on the map.

The Australian, or secret ballot, now used in almost all political elections, did not appear in the United States until the late nineteenth century. The 1892 presidential election was the first in which most states used the secret ballot. The secret ballot gained its first foothold in the United States in the Pacific Northwest in the 1880s, perhaps most directly influenced by British Columbia.

Considerations of an appropriate projection are always important when using a world map. What are the advantages and disadvantages of the orthographic projection selected for this map? (See Figure A.)

England adopted the Australian ballot in 1872. It soon spread to other nations, including Italy and Canada.

UNITED STATES [4]

CANADA [3]

[2] ENGLAND

North Pole

ITALY [3]

The idea of a secret ballot came from Australia, where it was widely used in the 1850s.

[1] AUSTRALIA

| 0 | 500 | 1,000 miles |
| 0 | 500 | 1,000 kilometers |

← Path of Australian ballot

also indicate that the movement continued into the future. A creative use of cartographic symbols makes this example very dynamic.

The diffusion of a key idea in modern democratic governance—the Australian, or secret, ballot—is featured in Figure K. Note that a world map is needed for this process because the practice started in Australia in the 1850s and then spread to England. From there it was adopted in several other countries, including Italy and Canada. By the 1880s the secret ballot had gained a foothold in the United States in the Pacific Northwest. In 1892 most states used the Australian ballot for presidential elections.

Interaction: How Do People and Their Environment Influence Each Other?

The interaction between people and the environment divides into two major categories. First, people change their environment to suit their needs. The pioneer era in American history records the chopping down of great trees, followed by the clearing of land to raise crops and animals largely brought from Europe and Africa. Second, opportunities and constraints of the environment force people to change their behavior and culture as they adapt

FIGURE L

Map 2.6 Settlement Patterns within New England Towns, 1630–1700 (inset)

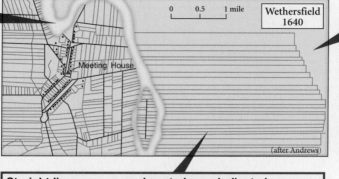

Although the Connecticut River separated many fields from the homes of the farmers along the major road, and might be considered a hindrance, the river was also an asset to the community, providing a water supply as well as a means of transportation.

The absence of strong topographical features on the map is important. Settlers selected the site for Wethersfield because the level terrain, fertile soil, and temperate climate combined to make it a fruitful agricultural settlement.

Straight lines on a map almost always indicate human activity. Here, the lots and fields are carefully arranged to take maximum advantage of the site.

to their natural surroundings. On the one hand, climate and topography present major environmental constraints on how people use the land. On the other hand, human ingenuity has found ways to put almost all places to some use, often turning elements of the environment from curiosities into valuable resources.

Figure L, a plan of the agricultural settlement of Wethersfield, Connecticut, in 1640, shows how Puritan settlers carved up the flood plain of the Connecticut River into productive fields. It seems as if every bit of land in

the settlement was put to use, even the island in the river. Contrast this image, spelling out human triumph, with the situation shown in Figure M. The dust bowl on the Great Plains in the 1930s resulted from humans pushing too hard against environmental constraints, removing the grasses of the American West and plowing the land to plant crops. In the extended period of drought beginning in 1930 crops died and winds ripped apart the plowed landscape, blowing the topsoil away in huge clouds of dust.

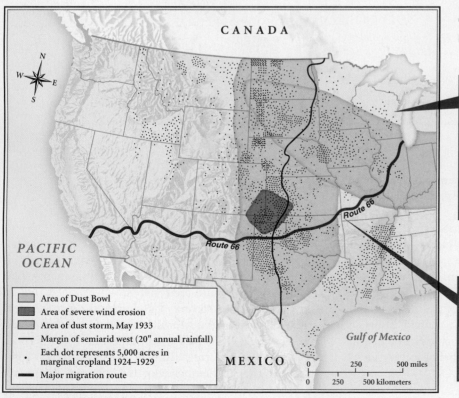

FIGURE M

MAP 24.3 The Dust Bowl, 1930–1941

Continental climates are often subject to great extremes, and the drought facing the Great Plains in the 1930s was especially severe. Farmers who migrated to these marginal lands beginning in the 1880s did not take these extremes into consideration, and the result was financial disaster and environmental catastrophe.

A human construction project, Route 66, is placed on this map of cropland to indicate what many people did when they faced ruin on their farms. Thousands moved to other areas, especially southern California, at the end of the road.

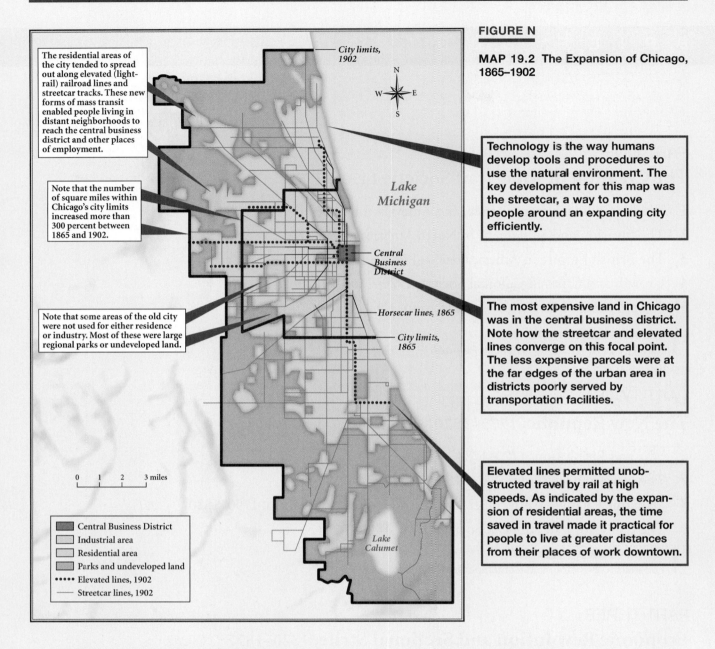

FIGURE N

MAP 19.2 The Expansion of Chicago, 1865–1902

The residential areas of the city tended to spread out along elevated (light-rail) railroad lines and streetcar tracks. These new forms of mass transit enabled people living in distant neighborhoods to reach the central business district and other places of employment.

Note that the number of square miles within Chicago's city limits increased more than 300 percent between 1865 and 1902.

Note that some areas of the old city were not used for either residence or industry. Most of these were large regional parks or undeveloped land.

Technology is the way humans develop tools and procedures to use the natural environment. The key development for this map was the streetcar, a way to move people around an expanding city efficiently.

The most expensive land in Chicago was in the central business district. Note how the streetcar and elevated lines converge on this focal point. The less expensive parcels were at the far edges of the urban area in districts poorly served by transportation facilities.

Elevated lines permitted unobstructed travel by rail at high speeds. As indicated by the expansion of residential areas, the time saved in travel made it practical for people to live at greater distances from their places of work downtown.

City limits, 1902

Lake Michigan

Central Business District

Horsecar lines, 1865

City limits, 1865

Lake Calumet

0   1   2   3 miles

- Central Business District
- Industrial area
- Residential area
- Parks and undeveloped land
- •••• Elevated lines, 1902
- — Streetcar lines, 1902

Figure N details the expansion of a major city, showing that human-environmental concerns operate in urban areas as well as in the countryside. In the case of Chicago, a wet, low-lying former lake bed became the site for a metropolis, which numbered about two million residents by 1900. The flat topography enabled the city to be laid out on straight lines but created sanitation and drainage problems, eventually addressed only by major human efforts, which included reversing the flow of the Chicago River.

Conclusion

Every time you encounter a map in *America's History*, ask yourself the following eight questions. With practice, you will improve your cartographic literacy, thereby deepening your historical understanding.

1. What is the purpose of the map?

2. What date is represented on the map and why is this date historically significant?

3. How does the map help explain the narrative?

4. What additional information does the caption provide?

5. What elements are emphasized on the map?

6. How does the map represent the actual landscape?

7. In what ways does the map show change over time?

8. How do the basic themes of geography—location, place, region, movement, and human-environmental interaction—help unlock the theme of the map?

—Gerald A. Danzer,
University of Illinois at Chicago

BRIEF CONTENTS

CONTENTS

PART ONE

The Creation of American Society, 1450–1775   2

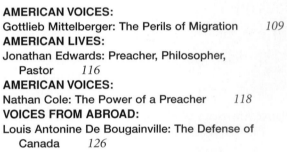

PART TWO
The New Republic,
1775–1820   *162*

Chapter 6
War and Revolution, 1775–1783   *165*

Chapter 7
The New Political Order, 1776–1800   *193*

Chapter 14

Two Societies at War, 1861–1865   *397*

Chapter 15

Reconstruction, 1865–1877   *429*

M A P S

An asterisk (∗) indicates a map annotated to highlight key points and to promote map-reading skills.

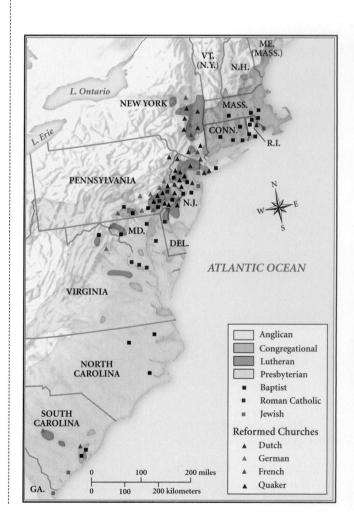

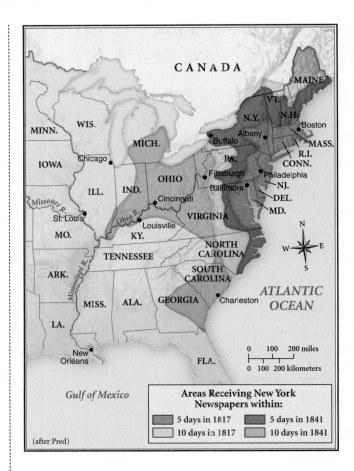

Figures

Tables

SPECIAL FEATURES

New Technology

JAMES A. HENRETTA is Priscilla Alden Burke Professor of American History at the University of Maryland, College Park. He received his undergraduate education at Swarthmore College and his Ph.D. from Harvard University. He has taught at the University of Sussex, England; Princeton University; UCLA; Boston University; as a Fulbright lecturer in Australia at the University of New England; and at Oxford University as the Harmsworth Professor of American History. His publications include *The Evolution of American Society, 1700–1815: An Interdisciplinary Analysis; "Salutary Neglect": Colonial Administration under the Duke of Newcastle; Evolution and Revolution: American Society, 1600–1820;* and *The Origins of American Capitalism.* Recently he coedited and contributed to a collection of original essays, *Republicanism and Liberalism in America and the German States, 1750–1850,* as part of his larger research project on "The Liberal State in America: New York, 1820–1975." In 2002–2003, he held the John Hope Franklin Fellowship at the National Humanities Center in North Carolina.

DAVID BRODY is Professor Emeritus of History at the University of California, Davis. He received his B.A., M.A., and Ph.D. from Harvard University. He has taught at the University of Warwick in England, at Moscow State University in the former Soviet Union, and at Sydney University in Australia. He is the author of *Steelworkers in America; Workers in Industrial America: Essays on the 20th Century Struggle;* and *In Labor's Cause: Main Themes on the History of the American Worker.* He has been awarded fellowships from the Social Science Research Council, the Guggenheim Foundation, and the National Endowment for the Humanities. He is past president (1991–1992) of the Pacific Coast branch of the American Historical Association. His current research is on labor law and workplace regimes during the Great Depression.

LYNN DUMENIL is Robert Glass Cleland Professor of American History at Occidental College in Los Angeles. She is a graduate of the University of Southern California and received her Ph.D. from the University of California, Berkeley. She has written *The Modern Temper: American Culture and Society in the 1920s* and *Freemasonry and American Culture: 1880–1930.* Her articles and reviews have appeared in the *Journal of American History;* the *Journal of American Ethnic History: Reviews in American History;* and the *American Historical Review.* She has been a historical consultant to several documentary film projects and is on the Pelzer Prize Committee of the Organization of American Historians. Her current work, for which she received a National Endowment for the Humanities Fellowship, is on World War I, citizenship, and the state. In 2001–2002 she was the Bicentennial Fulbright Chair in American Studies at the University of Helsinki.

SUSAN WARE specializes in twentieth-century U.S. history and the history of American women. She is affiliated with the Radcliffe Institute for Advanced Study, Harvard University, where she is editing the next volume of the noted biographical dictionary *Notable American Women.* Ware received her undergraduate degree from Wellesley College and her Ph.D. from Harvard University and from 1986 to 1995 taught in the history department at New York University. Her publications include *Beyond Suffrage: Women in the New Deal; Holding Their Own: American Women in the 1930s; Partner and I: Molly Dewson, Feminism, and New Deal Politics; Modern American Women: A Documentary History; Still Missing: Amelia Earhart and the Search for Modern Feminism;* and *Letter to the World: Seven Women Who Shaped the American Century.* She has served on the national advisory boards of the Franklin and Eleanor Roosevelt Institute and the Schlesinger Library at Radcliffe and has been a historical consultant to numerous documentary film projects. Her most recent project is a biography of radio talk show pioneer Mary Margaret McBride.

America's History

Volume 1: To 1877

The Creation of American Society

1450–1775

ECONOMY	SOCIETY	GOVERNMENT	RELIGION	CULTURE
From Staple Crops to Internal Growth	Ethnic, Racial, and Class Divisions	From Monarchy to Republic	From Hierarchy to Pluralism	The Creation of American Identity
1450 ▶ Native American subsistence economy Europeans fish off North American coast	▶ Sporadic warfare among Indian peoples Spanish conquest of Mexico (1519–1521)	▶ Rise of monarchical nation-states in Europe	▶ Protestant Reformation begins (1517)	▶ Diverse Native American cultures in eastern woodlands
1600 ▶ First staple export crops: furs and tobacco	▶ English-Indian warfare African servitude begins in Virginia (1619)	▶ James I claims divine right to rule England Virginia House of Burgesses (1619)	▶ Persecuted English Puritans and Catholics migrate to America	▶ Puritans implant Calvinism, education, and freehold ideal
1640 ▶ New England trade with sugar islands Mercantilist regulations: first Navigation Act (1651)	▶ White indentured servitude in Chesapeake Indians retreat inland	▶ Puritan Revolution Stuart restoration (1660) Bacon's Rebellion in Virginia (1675)	▶ Religious liberty in Rhode Island	▶ Aristocratic aspirations in the Chesapeake
1680 ▶ Tobacco trade stagnates Rice cultivation expands	▶ Indian slavery in the Carolinas Ethnic rebellion in New York (1689)	▶ Dominion of New England (1686–1689) Glorious Revolution ousts James II (1688–1689)	▶ Rise of toleration	▶ Emergence of African American language and culture
1720 ▶ Mature yeoman farm economy in North Imports from Britain increase	▶ Scots-Irish and German migration Growing rural inequality	▶ Rise of the colonial representative assemblies Challenge to "deferential" politics	▶ German and Scots-Irish Pietists in Middle Atlantic region Great Awakening	▶ Expansion of colleges, newspapers, and magazines Franklin and the American Enlightenment
1760 ▶ Trade boycotts encourage domestic manufacturing	▶ Uprisings by tenants and backcountry farmers Artisan protests	▶ Ideas of popular sovereignty Battles of Lexington and Concord (1775)	▶ Evangelical Baptists in Virginia Quebec Act allows Catholicism (1774)	▶ First signs of an American identity Republican innovations in political theory

Societies are made, not born. They are the creation of decades, even centuries, of human endeavor and experience. The first American societies were formed by hunting and gathering peoples who migrated to the Western Hemisphere from Asia many centuries ago. Over many generations these migrants—the Native Americans—came to live in a wide variety of environments and cultures. In much of North America they developed kinship-based societies that relied on farming and hunting. But in the lower Mississippi Valley, Native Americans developed a hierarchical social order similar to that of the great civilizations of the Aztecs, Mayas, and Incas of Mesoamerica. The coming of Europeans and their diseases tore the fabric of most Native American cultures into shreds. Native Americans increasingly confronted a new American society, one dominated by men and women of European origins.

The Europeans who settled America sought to transplant their traditional societies to the New World—their farming practices, their social hierarchies, their culture and heritage, and their religious ideas. But in learning to live in the new land, the Europeans who came to England's North American colonies eventually created societies that were distinctly different from those of their homelands in their economies, social character, political systems, religion, and culture.

ECONOMY Many European settlements were very successful in economic terms. Traditional Europe was made up of poor, overcrowded, and unequal societies that periodically suffered devastating famines. But with few people and a bountiful natural environment, the settlers in North America replaced poverty with plenty, creating a bustling economy and, in the northern mainland colonies, prosperous communities of independent farm families. Indeed, this region became know as "the best poor man's country" for migrants from the British Isles and Germany.

SOCIETY However, some of the European settlements became places of oppressive captivity for Africans. Aided by African slave traders, Europeans transported hundreds of thousands of workers, from many African regions, to the West Indies and the southern mainland colonies and forced them to labor as slaves on sugar, tobacco, and rice plantations. Slowly and with great effort, they and their descendants created an African American culture within a social order dominated by Europeans.

GOVERNMENT In the meantime, whites in the emerging American societies created an increasingly free and competitive political system. The first English settlers transplanted authoritarian institutions to America, and the English government continued to manage their lives. But after 1689 traditional controls gradually gave way to governments based in part on representative assemblies. Eventually, the growth of self-rule would lead to demands for political independence from England.

RELIGION The American experience profoundly changed religious institutions and values. Many migrants left Europe because of the conflicts of the Protestant Reformation and came to America seeking to practice their religion without interference. The societies they created became increasingly religious, especially after the evangelical revivals of the 1740s. By this time many Americans had rejected the harshest tenets of Calvinism (a strict Protestant faith), and others had embraced the rationalist view of the European Enlightenment. As a result, American Protestant Christianity became increasingly tolerant, democratic, and optimistic.

CULTURE The new American society witnessed the appearance of new forms of family and community life. The first English settlers lived in patriarchal families ruled by dominant fathers and in communities controlled by men of high status. By 1750, however, many American fathers no longer strictly managed their children's lives. As these communities became more diverse and open, many men and some women began to enjoy greater personal independence. This new American society was increasingly pluralistic, composed of migrants from many European ethnic groups—English, Scots, Scots-Irish, Dutch, and Germans—as well as enslaved West Africans and many different Native American peoples. Distinct regional cultures developed in New England, the Middle Atlantic colonies, and the Chesapeake and Carolina areas. Consequently, an overarching American identity based on the English language, British legal and political institutions, and shared experiences emerged very slowly.

The story of the colonial experience is thus both tragic and exciting. The settlers created a new American world but one that warred with Native Americans and condemned most African Americans to bondage even as it offered Europeans rich opportunities for economic security, political freedom, and spiritual fulfillment.

OCEANVS OCCIDENTALIS

GROWLAND

Noruegia Datia

Dania

Saxonia
Germania

Hibernia

Anglia

Gallia

Hispania

Mare

Isabella

Spagnolla

Fortunata

Gigant

Brasil

Baccalai

Canibalus

Caput
s. crucis

AMERICA

Archipelago
de s. paulo

Tropicus Capricorni

Equinoctialis Circulus

AFRICA

Libia interior

Regnum
melli

manfa
de ginoa

Rio de
ſado

Ethiopia

Guida

Clupi

angradelsinceps

Ethio
pia

Mons Lune
Rio de magni
congo

mons niger

bona spe
ranza

Caboco

Fuetia

Liuonia

Littouia

Prutenia
Polonia
Ioania

Valachia Ruſſia

Tartaria

Tar
taria
p rotu

Tartaria

Colchis

albania

Mare magor

Venetia

Grecia

Mediterranei

Tuneſe

Cirene

Alcayr

Egip
tus

arabia deserta

Nilus

Mare
minor

Asia
minor

Armenia
maior

Tigris fl.

meso
potonia

Iudea

Caldea

Ifar tuſa

Mare hircanu

Hircania
Parthia

Oriaſtus

Babilonia

Persia

Arabia felix

Rudiana

Sin9
Persi

Carmani

Cambai

Perimo
ianus

Mare
Rubru

Gaſa

Fela

uoga
daſa

Melinda

mon
bala
qui
loa

mon ſanbiqui

Madaga
ſcar

CHAPTER 1

Worlds Collide: Europe, Africa, and America

1450–1620

"**B**EFORE THE FRENCH CAME AMONG US," an elder of the Natchez people of Mississippi exclaimed, "we were men . . . and we walked with boldness every road, but now we walk like slaves, which we shall soon be, since the French already treat us . . . as they do their black slaves." Before the 1490s the Indian peoples of the Western Hemisphere knew absolutely nothing about the light-skinned inhabitants of Europe and the dark-complexioned peoples of Africa. However, Europeans hungry for the trade and riches of Asia had already sailed along the west coast of Africa and were deeply involved in the long-established trade in African slaves. When Christopher Columbus, another European searching for a sea route to Asia, encountered the lands and peoples of the Americas, the destinies of four continents quickly became intertwined. On his second voyage to the Western Hemisphere, Columbus carried a cargo of enslaved Africans, beginning the centuries-long process that created a multitude of triracial societies in the Americas.

◀ **Orbis Typus Universalis**
This map of 1507, drawn by the German cartographer Martin Waldseemüller, is one of the first to use "America" as the name of the western continents. Only the northwestern area of present-day Brazil and a few (mislocated) Caribbean islands appear on Waldseemüller's map. Europeans had not yet comprehended the size and shape of the New World.
John Carter Brown Library, Brown University.

As the Natchez elder knew well, the resulting mixture of peoples from the far-flung continents was based not on equality but on exploitation. By the time he urged his people to resist the invaders, the Europeans were too numerous and too well positioned to be dislodged. The French and their Indian allies killed hundreds of those who joined the Natchez uprising and sold many of the survivors into slavery on the sugar plantations of the West Indies.

5

The fate of the Natchez was hardly unique. Over the course of the three centuries following Columbus's voyage, many Native American peoples came under the domination of the various Europeans—Spanish, Portuguese, French, English, Dutch—who colonized the Western Hemisphere and imported enslaved Africans to work on agricultural plantations. In the new societies—new to all their inhabitants—race became a prime determinant of people's status and lives. How did this happen? How did Europeans become leaders in world trade and extend their influence across the Atlantic? What was the character of the Native Americans' life and culture, and what made their societies vulnerable to conquest by European adventurers? And what led to the transatlantic trade in African slaves? In the answers to these questions lie the origins of the United States and, beyond that, the dominant position of people of European descent in the modern world.

Native American Worlds

When the Europeans arrived, the great majority of Native Americans—about 40 million—lived in Mesoamerica (present-day Mexico and Guatemala), and another 15 million resided in lands to the north (present-day United States and Canada). Some lived in simple hunter-gatherer or agricultural communities governed by kin ties, but the majority resided in societies ruled by warrior-kings and priests. In Mesoamerica and Peru, Indian peoples created

civilizations whose art, religion, society, and economy were as complex as those of Europe and the Mediterranean (Table 1.1).

The First Americans

According to the elders of the Navajo people, history began when their ancestors emerged from under the earth (see American Voices, "A Navajo Emergence Story," p. 7); for the Iroquois, the story of their Five Nations began when people fell from the sky. However, most twenty-first-century anthropologists and historians believe that the first people to live in the Western Hemisphere were migrants from Asia. Some migrants came by water, but most probably came by land. Strong archaeological and genetic evidence suggests that late in the last Ice Age, which lasted from 25,000 B.C. until 11,000 B.C., small bands of hunters—residents of Siberia—followed herds of game across a hundred-mile-wide land bridge between Siberia and Alaska. An oral history of the Tuscarora Indians, who lived in present-day North Carolina, tells of a famine in the old world and a journey over ice toward where "the sun rises," a trek that brought their ancestors to a lush forest with abundant food and game.

Most anthropologists believe that the main migratory stream from Asia lasted from about 13,000 B.C. to 11,000 B.C., until the glaciers melted and the rising ocean waters submerged the land bridge and created the

TABLE 1.1 Important Native American Cultures

| Time Period | Mesoamerica | | Andes | | North America | |
	Coastal Lowlands	Highlands	Coastal Lowlands	Highlands	Southwest	Mississippi & Ohio Valleys
Pre–Classic Era 900 B.C.–A.D. 300	Olmec			Chavin		Hopewell
Classic Era A.D. 300–900	Mayan (Tikal)	Teotihuacán	Mochica	Tiwanaku	Mogollon Hohokam Anasazi	
Post–Classic Era A.D. 900–1500	Mayan (Chichén Itzá)	Toltec Aztec	Nazca	Inca (Cuzco)		Mississippian (Cahokia)

The Olmec were the "mother culture" to the Mayans and the Teotihuacáns, and the Chavin to the Mochica and Tiwanaku, influencing subsequent cultures in both the coastal lowlands and the highlands of the Classic and post–Classic Eras. These subsequent cultures drew additional influences from the surrounding Native American groups.

A Navajo Emergence Story

Every culture has a story—part factual, part mythical—that expresses the meaning of its past. This story was told to Sandoval, whose Navajo name was Hastin Tlo'tsi hee, by his grandmother, herself the descendant of a long line of medicine women. It locates the homeland of the Navajo people in the Plateau country of northwestern Arizona near Abalone Shell Mountain (San Francisco Peak), where the tribe apparently settled sometime between A.D. 1200 and 1500.

Here are the stories of the Four Worlds that had no sun, and of the Fifth, the world we live in. . . . The First World, Ni'hodilquil, was black as black wool. It had four corners and over these appeared four clouds. These four clouds contained within themselves the elements of the First World. They were in color, black, white, blue, and yellow.

The Black Cloud represented the Female Being or Substance. For as a child sleeps when being nursed, so life slept in the darkness of the Female Being. The white Cloud represented the Male Being or Substance. He was the Dawn, the Light-Which-Awakens, of the First World.

In the East, at the place where the Black Cloud and the White Cloud met, First Man, Atse'hastqin, was formed; and with him was formed the white corn, perfect in shape, with kernels covering the whole ear. . . . The First World was small in size, a floating island in mist or water. On it there grew one tree, a pine tree, which was later brought to the present world for firewood. . . . The creatures of the First World are thought of as the Mist People; they had no definite form, but were to change to men, beasts, birds, and reptiles of this world.

Now on the western side of the First World, in a place that later was to become the Land of Sunset, there appeared the Blue Cloud, and opposite it there appeared the Yellow Cloud. Where they came together, First Woman was formed, and with her the yellow corn. This ear of corn was also perfect. With First Woman there came the white shell and the turquoise and the yucca. . . .

Because of the strife in the First World, First Man, First Woman . . . climbed up from the world of Darkness and Dampness to the Second or Blue World. They found a number of people already living there: blue birds, blue hawks, blue jays, blue herons, and all the blue-feathered beings. The powerful swallow people lived there also, and these people made the Second World unpleasant. . . . There was fighting and killing. . . .

The bluebird was the first to reach the Third or Yellow World. After him came . . . all the others. There were six mountains in the Third World. . . . In the West . . . Dichi'li dzil, the Abalone Shell Mountain. . . .

[After climbing to the Fourth World, which was filled with other animals] First Man and his people saw four dark clouds and four white clouds pass, and then they sent the badger up the reed. This time when the badger returned he said he had come out on solid earth. So First Man and First Woman led the people to the Fifth World, which some call the Many Colored Earth and some the Changeable Earth. They emerged through a lake [said to be near Pagosa Springs, Colorado] surrounded by four mountains. The water bubbles in this lake when anyone goes near. . . .

Some medicine men tell us that there are two worlds above us, the first is the World of the Spirits of Living Things, the second is the Place of Melting into One.

Source: Aileen O'Bryan, "The Diné: Origin Myths of the Navaho Indians," *Bureau of American Ethnology*, Bulletin 163 (Washington, D.C.: U.S. Government Printing Office, 1956), 1–13.

Bering Strait. A second movement of peoples around 6000 B.C., now traveling by water across the narrow strait, brought the ancestors of the Navajo and the Apaches to North America, while a third migration around 3000 B.C. introduced the forebears of the Aleut and Inuit peoples—the "Eskimos." Subsequently, the people of the Western Hemisphere, who by that time had moved as far south as the tip of South America and as far east as the Atlantic coast of North America, were largely cut off from the rest of the world for three hundred generations (Map 1.1).

For many centuries the first Americans lived as hunter-gatherers, subsisting on the abundant vegetation and wildlife. Over time, many of the larger species of animals—mammoths, giant beaver, and horses—died out, victims of overhunting and climatic change; their demise forced hunters to become adept at killing more elusive and faster rabbits, deer, and elk. About

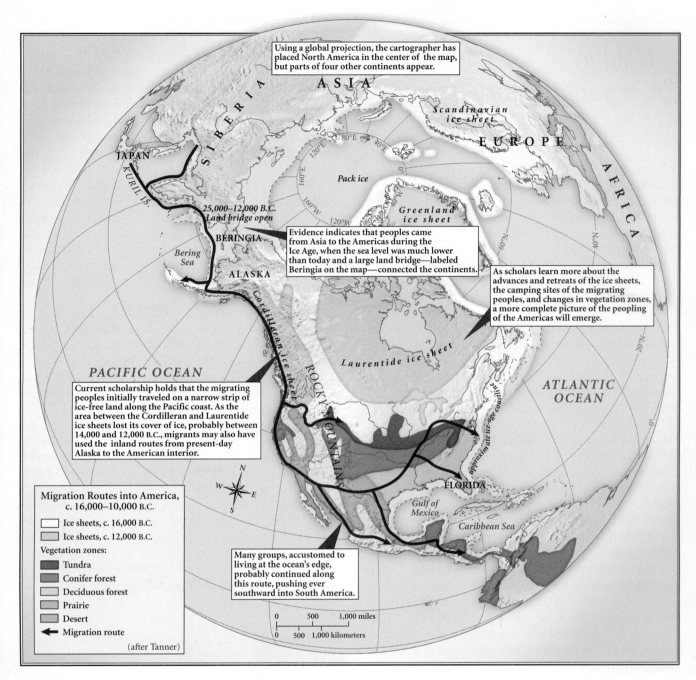

Using a global projection, the cartographer has placed North America in the center of the map, but parts of four other continents appear.

Evidence indicates that peoples came from Asia to the Americas during the Ice Age, when the sea level was much lower than today and a large land bridge—labeled Beringia on the map—connected the continents.

As scholars learn more about the advances and retreats of the ice sheets, the camping sites of the migrating peoples, and changes in vegetation zones, a more complete picture of the peopling of the Americas will emerge.

Current scholarship holds that the migrating peoples initially traveled on a narrow strip of ice-free land along the Pacific coast. As the area between the Cordilleran and Laurentide ice sheets lost its cover of ice, probably between 14,000 and 12,000 B.C., migrants may also have used the inland routes from present-day Alaska to the American interior.

Many groups, accustomed to living at the ocean's edge, probably continued along this route, pushing ever southward into South America.

**Migration Routes into America,
c. 16,000–10,000 B.C.**

- Ice sheets, c. 16,000 B.C.
- Ice sheets, c. 12,000 B.C.

Vegetation zones:
- Tundra
- Conifer forest
- Deciduous forest
- Prairie
- Desert
- → Migration route

(after Tanner)

ASIA

SIBERIA

Scandinavian ice sheet

EUROPE

AFRICA

JAPAN

KURIL IS.

80°E

120°E

160°E

40°E

Pack ice

Greenland ice sheet

25,000–12,000 B.C. Land bridge open

BERINGIA

120°W

60°N

ALASKA

Bering Sea

Cordilleran ice sheet

Laurentide ice sheet

40°N

PACIFIC OCEAN

ROCKY MOUNTAINS

approximate ice-age coastline

ATLANTIC OCEAN

20°N

FLORIDA

Gulf of Mexico

Caribbean Sea

0°

N
W · E
S

0   500   1,000 miles
0   500   1,000 kilometers

MAP 1.1 The Ice Age and the Settling of the Americas

Some sixteen thousand years ago, a sheet of ice covered much of Europe and North America. Taking advantage of a broad bridge of land connecting Siberia and Alaska, hunting peoples from Asia migrated into North America, searching for large game animals, such as woolly mammoths, and ice-free habitats. By 10,000 B.C. the descendants of the migrant peoples had moved as far south as present-day Florida and central Mexico.

3000 B.C. some Native American peoples began to develop horticulture, most notably in the region near present-day Mexico. These inventive farmers planted beans, squashes, and cotton and learned how to breed maize, or Indian corn, as well as tomatoes, potatoes, and manioc—crops that would eventually enrich the food supply of the entire world. Over the centuries the Indian peoples bred maize into a much larger, extremely nutritious plant that was hardier and had more varieties and a higher yield per acre than wheat, barley, and rye, the staple cereals of Europe. They also learned to cultivate beans and squash and plant them together with corn, creating a mix of crops that provided a nutritious diet, preserved soil fertility, and produced intensive farming and high yields. The resulting agricultural surplus laid the economic foundation for populous and wealthy societies in Mexico, Peru, and the Mississippi River Valley.

The Mayas and the Aztecs

The flowering of civilization in Mesoamerica began among the Mayan peoples of the Yucatán Peninsula of Mexico and the neighboring rain forests of Guatemala during the long Olmec era (900 B.C.–A.D. 300). The Mayas built large religious centers, urban communities with elaborate systems of water storage and irrigation. By A.D. 300 the Mayan city of Tikal had at least 20,000 inhabitants, mostly farmers who worked the nearby fields and whose labor was used to build huge stone temples. An elite class claiming descent from the gods ruled Mayan society, living in splendor on goods and taxes extracted from peasant families. Drawing on religious and artistic traditions that stretched back to the Olmec people, who had lived along the Gulf of Mexico around 700 B.C., skilled Mayan artisans decorated temples and palaces with art depicting warrior-gods and complex religious rituals. Mayan astronomers created a calendar that recorded historical events and predicted eclipses of the sun and the moon with remarkable accuracy. The Mayas also developed hieroglyphic writing to record royal lineages and noteworthy events, including wars. These skills in calculation and writing facilitated the movement of goods and ideas, allowing the creation of complex society.

Beginning around A.D. 800, Mayan civilization went into decline. Some evidence suggests that a two-century-long dry period caused a loss in population and an economic crisis that prompted overtaxed peasants to desert the temple cities and retreat into the countryside. By A.D. 900 many religious centers had been abandoned, but some Mayan city-states lasted until the Spanish invasion in the 1520s.

As the Mayan peoples flourished in the Yucatán region, a second major Mesoamerican civilization

Gold Piece from Peru
Skilled Inca artisans created gold jewelry and artifacts of striking beauty. Found in a tomb, this figurine may be a stylized image of the dead man, who was undoubtedly a noble of considerable status. Note the intricate detail on the man's headdress and garment.
Dumbarton Oaks Research Library and Collections, Washington, DC.

developed in the central highlands of Mexico around the city of Teotihuacán, with its magnificent Pyramid of the Sun. At its zenith about A.D. 500, Teotihuacán had more than one hundred temples, about four thousand apartment buildings, and a population of at least 100,000. By A.D. 800 Teotihuacán had also declined, probably because of a long-term drop in rainfall and recurrent invasions by seminomadic warrior peoples. Eventually one of these peoples, the Aztecs, established an even more extensive empire.

The Aztecs entered the highlands of Mexico from the north and settled on an island in Lake Texcoco. There, in A.D. 1325, they began to build a new city, Tenochtitlán (present-day Mexico City). They learned the settled ways of the resident peoples, mastered their complex irrigation systems and written language, and established an elaborate culture with a hierarchical social order. Priests and warrior-nobles ruled over twenty clans of free Aztec commoners who farmed communally owned land, and the nobles used huge numbers of non-Aztec slaves and serfs to labor on their private estates. Artisans worked in stone, pottery, cloth, leather, and

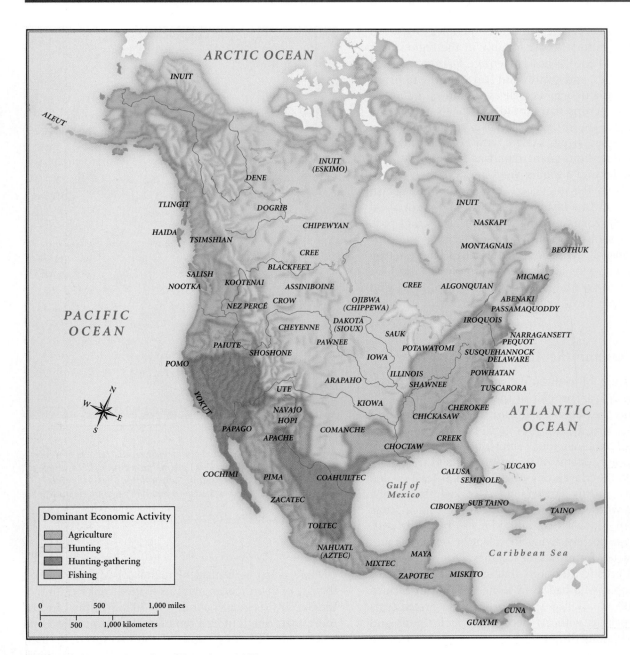

MAP 1.2 Native American Peoples, 1492

Native Americans populated the entire Western Hemisphere at the time of Columbus's arrival, having learned how to live in many environments. They created diverse cultures that ranged from the centralized agriculture-based empires of the Mayas and the Aztecs to seminomadic tribes of hunter-gatherers. The sheer diversity among Indians—of culture, language, tribal identity—usually prevented united resistance to the European invaders.

especially obsidian (hard volcanic glass used to make sharp-edged weapons and tools).

The Aztecs remained an aggressive tribe and soon subjugated most of central Mexico. Their rulers demanded both economic and human tribute from scores of subject tribes, gruesomely sacrificing untold thousands of men and women to ensure agricultural fertility and the daily return of the sun. Aztec merchants created far-flung trading routes and imported furs, gold, textiles, food, and obsidian. By A.D. 1500, Tenochtitlán had grown into a great metropolis with splendid palaces and temples and over 200,000 inhabitants, dazzling the first Spanish soldiers who saw it: "These great towns and pyramids and buildings arising from the water, all made of stone, seemed like an enchanted vision." The Aztecs' wealth, strong institutions, and military power posed a formidable challenge to any adversary, at home or from afar.

The Indians of the North

The Indians who resided north of the Rio Grande were fewer in number and lived in less coercive societies than those to the south. In A.D. 1500 these Indians lived in dispersed communities of a few thousand people and spoke many different languages—no fewer than sixty-eight east of the Mississippi River (Map 1.2). Most were organized in self-governing tribes composed of **clans**—groups of related families that had a common identity and a real or legendary common ancestor. Tribal members lived in scattered settlements composed of various clans and led by a local chief, who, aided by the clan elders, conducted ceremonies and regulated personal life. For example, elders encouraged individuals to share food and other scarce goods, promoting an ethic of reciprocity rather than one of accumulation. "You are covetous, and neither generous nor kind," the Micmac Indians of Nova Scotia told acquisitive-minded French fur traders around 1600. "As for us, if we have a morsel of bread, we share it with our neighbor." The individual ownership of land was virtually unknown in Indian culture; as a French missionary among the Iroquois noted, they "possess hardly anything except in common." However, Indian elders granted families exclusive use-rights over certain planting grounds and hunting areas. Clan leaders also resolved personal feuds, disciplined individuals who violated customs, decided whether to go to war, and banned marriage between members of the same clan, a rule that helped prevent inbreeding. Nonetheless, the elders' and chiefs' power was far less than that of the Mayan and Aztec nobles because their kinship system of government was locally based and worked by consensus, not by coercion.

The Hopewell Culture. Over the centuries some Indian peoples exerted influence over their immediate neighbors through trade or conquest. The earliest expansive Indian cultures appeared in the eastern woodlands of North America as the inhabitants increased the food supply by domesticating plants and were thus able to settle in large villages. By A.D. 100 the vigorous Hopewell people in the area of present-day Ohio had spread their influence through trade from Wisconsin to Louisiana, importing obsidian from the Yellowstone region of the Rocky Mountains, copper from the Great Lakes, and pottery and marine shells from the Gulf of Mexico. They built large burial mounds and surrounded them with extensive circular, rectangular, or octagonal earthworks that in some cases still survive. The Hopewell people buried their dead with striking ornaments fashioned by their craftsmen: copper beaten into intricate artistic designs, crystals of quartz, mica cut into the shapes of serpents and human hands, and stone pipes carved to represent frogs, hawks, bears, and other animals—figurines evidently representing spiritually

powerful beings. For unknown reasons, the elaborate trading network of the Hopewell gradually collapsed around A.D. 400.

The Peoples of the Southwest. A second complex culture developed among the Pueblo peoples of the Southwest—the Hohokams, Mogollons, and Anasazis. By A.D. 600 Hohokam peoples in the highland region along the border of present-day Arizona and New Mexico were using irrigation to grow two crops a year, fashioning fine pottery with red-on-buff designs, and, under Mesoamerican influence, worshiping their gods on platform mounds; by A.D. 1000, they were living in elaborate multiroom stone structures (or pueblos). To the east, in the Mimbres Valley of New Mexico, the Mogollon peoples developed a distinctive black-on-white pottery. In the north of present-day New Mexico, the Anasazi culture developed around A.D. 900. The Anasazis were master architects, building residential-ceremonial villages in steep cliffs and a pueblo in Chaco Canyon that housed 1,000 people. Over four hundred miles of straight roads radiated out of Chaco Canyon, making it

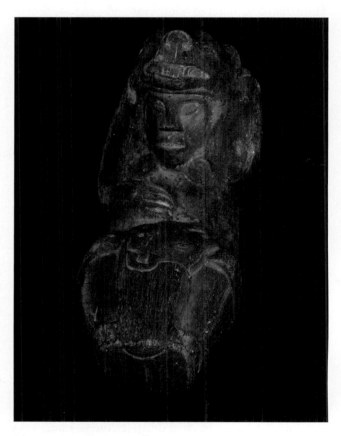

Hopewell Artifact

The Wray figurine is one of the rare representations of a person from the Hopewell mound-building culture. It may depict a noble or a priest or, if the two circles below the chin are stylized breasts, may be a female fertility icon. Note the wolf mask atop the human head and the clawlike fingers of the right hand.
Ohio Historical Society.

a center for trade. However, the culture of the Anasazis, Mogollons, and Hohokams gradually collapsed after A.D. 1150 as long periods of drought and soil exhaustion disrupted maize production and prompted the abandonment of Chaco Canyon and other long-established communities. The descendants of these Pueblo peoples—including the Zunis and the Hopis—later built strong but smaller and more dispersed village societies.

Mississippian Civilization. The last large-scale culture to emerge north of the Rio Grande was the Mississippian civilization. Beginning about A.D. 800, the advanced farming technology of Mesoamerica spread into the Mississippi River Valley, perhaps carried by emigrants fleeing across the Gulf of Mexico from warfare among the Mayas in the Yucatán Peninsula. The Mississippian peoples planted new strains of maize and beans on fertile river bottomland, providing a protein-rich diet and creating an agricultural surplus. A robust culture based on small, fortified temple cities quickly emerged. By A.D. 1150 the largest city, Cahokia (near present-day St. Louis), had a population of 15,000 to 20,000 and more than one hundred temple mounds, one of them as large as the great Egyptian pyramids. As in Mesoamerica, the tribute paid by peasant cultivators supported a privileged class of nobles and priests who waged war against neighboring chiefdoms, patronized skilled artisans, and may have been worshiped as quasi-sacred beings related to the sun god.

However, by A.D. 1350 this six-hundred-year-old Mississippian civilization was in rapid decline, undermined by overpopulation, warfare over fertile bottomlands, and urban diseases such as tuberculosis. Nonetheless, the values and institutions of this culture endured for centuries east of the Mississippi River. When the Spanish adventurer Hernán de Soto invaded the region in the 1540s, he found the Apalachee and Timucua Indians living in permanent settlements, harvesting their fields twice a year, and fiercely resistant to his commands. "If you desire to see me, come where I am," a paramount chief told de Soto, "neither for you, nor for any man, will I set back one foot." A century and a half later French traders and priests who encountered the Natchez people in the area of present-day Mississippi found a society rigidly divided among hereditary chiefs, two groups of nobles and honored people, and a bottom class of peasants. Undoubtedly influenced by Mayan or Aztec rituals, the Natchez practiced human sacrifice; the death of a chief called for the sacrifice of his wives and the enlargement of a ceremonial mound to bury their remains (see Voices from Abroad, "Father le Petite: The Customs of the Natchez," p. 13).

Other peoples in the region retained some Mesoamerican practices and also exhibited traces of the earlier mound-building Hopewell culture. Thus, the

Casa Grande Pot

The artistically and architecturally talented Mogollon and Anasazi peoples of Arizona and New Mexico took utilitarian objects—such as this ordinary pot—and decorated them with black-on-white designs. Their cultures flourished from 1000 to 1250, after which they slowly declined, probably because the climate became increasingly arid.

Courtesy, The Amerind Foundation, Inc., Dragoon, AZ / Photo by Robin Stancliff.

Choctaws regarded a mound in present-day Winston County, Mississippi, as *ishki chito*, the "great mother." There, according to a Choctaw legend, "the Great Spirit created the first Choctaws, and through a hole or cave, they crawled forth into the light of day." However, the Choctaws and others peoples of this region (such as the Creeks, Chickasaws, Cherokees, and Seminoles) lived in small and dispersed agricultural communities and thus escaped the devastating environmental damage and disease that destroyed the impressive city-states of the Mississippian peoples.

The Eastern Woodland Peoples. Although farming in Mesoamerica was the province of both sexes, among eastern Woodland Indians it was the work of women. Over the centuries North American Indian women became adept horticulturists, using flint hoes and more productive strains of corn, squash, and beans to reduce the dependence of their peoples on gathering and hunting (see New Technology, "Indian Women and Agriculture," p. 14). Because of the importance of farming, a matrilineal inheritance system developed among many eastern Indian peoples, including the Five Nations of the Iroquois. Women cultivated the fields around semipermanent settlements, passing the right to use them to their daughters. In these matrilineal societies, fathers stood outside the main lines of kinship, and the main responsibility for childraising fell upon the mother and her brothers, who lived with her. The ritual lives of these

Father le Petite

The Customs of the Natchez

Beliefs and institutions from the earlier Mississippian culture (A.D. 1000–1450) lasted for centuries among the Natchez, who lived in present-day Mississippi. This letter was written around 1730 by Father le Petite, one of the hundreds of Jesuits who lived among the Indians in the French colonies of Louisiana and Canada and wrote detailed accounts of what they saw. Father le Petite accurately describes many Indian customs but misinterprets the rules governing the succession of the chief, which simply followed the normal practice of descent and inheritance in a matrilineal society.

My Reverend Father, The peace of Our Lord.

This Nation of Savages inhabits one of the most beautiful and fertile countries in the World, and is the only one on this continent which appears to have any regular worship. Their Religion in certain points is very similar to that of the ancient Romans. They have a Temple filled with Idols, which are different figures of men and of animals, and for which they have the most profound veneration. Their Temple in shape resembles an earthen oven, a hundred feet in circumference. They enter it by a little door about four feet high, and not more than three in breadth. Above on the outside are three figures of eagles made of wood, and painted red, yellow, and white. Before the door is a kind of shed with folding-doors, where the Guardian of the Temple is lodged; all around it runs a circle of palisades, on which are seen exposed the skulls of all the heads which their Warriors had brought back from the battles in which they had been engaged with the enemies of their Nation. . . .

The Sun is the principal object of veneration to these people; as they cannot conceive of anything which can be above this heavenly body, nothing else appears to them more worthy of their homage. It is for the same reason that the great Chief of this Nation, who knows nothing on the earth more dignified than himself, takes the title of brother of the Sun, and the credulity of the people maintains him in the despotic authority which he claims. To enable them better to converse together, they raise a mound of artificial soil, on which they build his cabin, which is of the same construction as the Temple.

The old men prescribe the Laws for the rest of the people, and one of their principles is . . . the immortality of the soul, and when they leave this world they go, they say, to live in another, there to be recompensed or punished.

In former times the Nation of the *Natchez* was very large. It counted sixty Villages and eight hundred Suns or Princes; now it is reduced to six little Villages and eleven Suns. [Its] Government is hereditary; it is not, however, the son of the reigning Chief who succeeds his father, but the son of his sister, or the first Princess of the blood. This policy is founded on the knowledge they have of the licentiousness of their women. They are not sure, they say, that the children of the chief's wife may be of the blood Royal, whereas the son of the sister of the great Chief must be, at least on the side of the mother.

Source: *The Jesuit Relations and Allied Documents*, ed. Reuben Gold Thwaites (Cleveland: Murrow Brothers, 1900). 68:121–35.

farming peoples focused on religious ceremonies related to the agricultural cycle, such as the Iroquois green corn and strawberry festivals. Indian peoples ate better because of women's labor and long-term advances in their farming practices, but they enjoyed few material comforts, and their populations grew slowly.

In A.D. 1500 most Indians north of the Rio Grande had resided on the same lands for generations, but the elaborate civilizations and strong city-states that had once flourished in the Southwest and in the great river valleys in the heart of the continent had vanished.

Consequently, when the European adventurers, traders, and settlers came ashore from the Atlantic, there were no great Indian empires or religious centers that could lead a campaign of military and spiritual resistance. "When you command, all the French obey and go to war," the Chippewa chief Chigabe told a European general, but "I shall not be heeded and obeyed by my nation." Because household and lineage were the basis of his society, Chigabe explained, "I cannot answer except for myself and for those immediately allied to me."

Indian Women and Agriculture

Corn was the dietary staple of most Native Americans, and its cultivation shaped their vision of the natural world. The Agawam Indians of Massachusetts began their year with the month of Squannikesas, a word that meant "when they set Indian corn," and subsequent months had names that referred to the weeding, hilling, and ripening of corn. To appease the spirit forces in nature and ensure a bountiful harvest, the Seneca Indians of New York held a corn-planting ceremony. They asked the Thunderers, "our grandfathers," to water their crops and beseeched the sun, "our older brother," not to burn them.

Among the eastern Woodland tribes, growing corn was women's work. The French priest Gabriel Sagard spoke of Huron women doing "more work than the men. . . . They have the care of the household, of sowing and gathering corn, grinding flour, . . . and providing the necessary wood." Indian women prepared the ground for planting with wooden hoes tipped with bone, flint, or clamshells. According to a Dutch traveler, they made "heaps like molehills, each about two and a half feet from the others" and planted "in each heap five or six grains." As the tall slender plants appeared, the women piled on more dirt to support the roots. They also "put in each hill three or four Brazilian [kidney] beans. When they grow up, they interlace with the corn, which reaches to a height of from five to six feet; and they keep the ground free of weeds."

The planting of corn and beans together represented a major technological advance, dramatically increasing total yields and human nutrition. The beans fixed nitrogen in the soil, preserving fertility, and conserved moisture, preventing erosion. Beans and corn provided a diet rich in vegetable proteins. By intensively cultivating two acres, an Indian woman typically harvested sixty bushels of shelled corn—half the calories required by five persons for a year.

This economic contribution enhanced the political influence of women in some tribes, especially those in which names and inheritance rights passed through women (matrilinealism). Thus, among the matrilineal Iroquois, women chose the clan leaders. To preserve their status, women jealously guarded their productive role. A Quaker missionary reported as late as 1809 that "if a man took hold of a hoe to use it, the Women would get down his gun by way of derision & laugh and say such a Warrior is a timid woman."

In seventeenth-century America, English farmers appropriated Indian corn technology and made it part of their own culture. Now Protestant ministers (as well as Indian shamans) prayed for a bountiful harvest of corn. After clearing their fields of tree stumps, English farmers

Traditional European Society in 1450

In A.D. 1450 few observers would have predicted that the European peoples would become the overlords of the Western Hemisphere. A thousand years after the fall of the magnificent Roman empire, Europe had become a backward society, devastated around 1350 by a vicious epidemic from the subcontinent of India—the Black Death—that killed one-third of its peoples. Other areas of the world were much more economically advanced and were expanding their seaborne trade. Indeed, the ruling dynasty in China had recently dispatched a major commercial fleet to the eastern coast of Africa.

The Peasantry

There were only a few large cities in Western Europe before A.D. 1450—only Paris, London, and Naples had 100,000 residents and thus equaled the size of Teotihuacán at its zenith. More than 90 percent of the European population consisted of **peasants** living in small rural communities. Peasant families usually owned or leased a small dwelling in the village center and had the right to farm strips of land in the surrounding fields. The fields were "open"—not divided by fences or hedges—making cooperative farming a necessity. The village community decided which crops would be grown, and every family followed its dictates. Because there were few merchants or good roads to carry goods to distant markets, most families exchanged surplus grain and meat with their neighbors or bartered their farm products for the services of local millers, weavers, and blacksmiths. Most peasants yearned to live in a **yeoman** family—a household that was under no obligation to a landlord and owned enough land to support its members in comfort—but relatively few achieved that goal.

plowed furrows at three-foot intervals from north to south. Then they cut east-west furrows, heaping up the soil into Indian-style cornhills at the intersecting points. English planting methods were less labor-intensive than Indian techniques and far less productive, averaging from ten to fifteen bushels per acre, not thirty.

Equally significant, among European settlers men—not women—planted, tended, and harvested the crop. In combination with patrilineal naming and inheritance practices, the dominance of men in agriculture confined colonial women to a subordinate role in economic and political life.

Among Europeans as well as Indians, corn soon became the premier crop, and with good reason. As a Welsh migrant to Pennsylvania noted, corn "produced more increase than any other Graine whatsoever." Pigs and chickens ate its kernels, and cows munched its stalks and leaves. Ground into flour and made into bread, cakes, or porridge, corn became the dietary staple of poor people in the northern English colonies and of white tenant farmers and enslaved blacks in the South and the West Indies.

Iroquois Women at Work, 1724

As this European engraving suggests, Iroquois women took the major responsibility for growing food crops. The women in the background are hoeing the soil into small hillocks, in which they are planting corn and beans. Most of the other workers are tapping sugar maples and boiling the sweet sap to create maple syrup. However, the woman at the left is probably grinding corn into flour and, by adding water, making flat patties for baking. Newberry Library.

The Seasonal Cycle. As among the Native Americans, many aspects of European peasant life followed a seasonal pattern (Figure 1.1). The agricultural year began in March or April, when the ground thawed and dried and the villagers began the exhausting work of spring plowing and the planting of wheat, rye, and oats. During these busy months men sheared the thick winter wool of their sheep, which the women washed and spun into yarn. Peasants cut the first crop of hay in June and stored it as winter fodder for their livestock. In the summer, life became more relaxed, and families mended their fences or repaired their barns. August and September often were marked by grief as infants and old people succumbed to epidemics of flyborne dysentery. Fall brought the strenuous harvest time, followed by solemn feasts of thanksgiving and riotous bouts of merrymaking. As winter approached, peasants slaughtered excess livestock and salted or smoked the meat. During the cold months peasants completed the tasks of threshing grain and weaving textiles and had time to visit friends and relatives in nearby villages. Just before the farming cycle began again in the spring, rural residents held carnivals to celebrate with drink and dance the end of the long winter night.

Many rural people died in January and February, victims of viral diseases and the cold. More mysteriously, in European villages (and later in rural British America), the greatest numbers of babies were born in February and March, with a smaller peak in September and October. The precise causes of this pattern are unknown. Religious practices, such as the abstention from sexual intercourse by devout Christians during Lent, might have increased the number of conceptions in the months following the Easter holy day. Even more likely, seasonal fluctuations in female work patterns or the food supply might have altered a woman's ability to carry a child to full term. One thing is certain. This

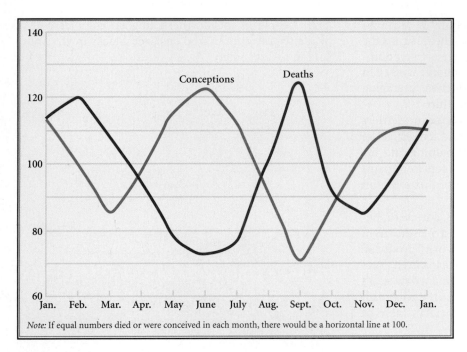

FIGURE 1.1 The Yearly Rhythm of Rural Life and Death

The annual cycle of nature profoundly affected life in the traditional agricultural world. The death rate soared by 20 percent in February and September. Summer was the healthiest season, with the fewest deaths and the greatest number of successful conceptions (as measured by births nine months later).

pattern of births does not exist in modern urban societies, so it must have been a reflection of the rigors of the traditional agriculture cycle.

The Peasant's Lot. For most peasants survival required unremitting labor. Horses and oxen strained to break the soil with primitive wooden plows, while workers harvested hay, wheat, rye, and barley with hand sickles. Because of the lack of high-quality seeds, chemical fertilizers, and pesticides, output was pitifully small—less than one-tenth of present-day yields. The margin of existence was thin, corroding family relations. Malnourished mothers fed their babies sparingly, calling them "greedy and gluttonous," and many newborn girls were "helped to die" so that their older brothers would have enough to eat. About half of all peasant children died before the age of twenty-one. Violence—assault, murder, rape—was much more prevalent than in most modern industrialized societies, and hunger and disease were constant companions. "I have seen the latest epoch of misery," a French doctor reported as famine and plague struck. "The inhabitants . . . lie down in a meadow to eat grass, and share the food of wild beasts."

Often destitute, usually exploited and dominated by landlords and aristocrats, many peasants simply accepted their condition, but others did not. It would be the deprived rural classes of Britain, Spain, and Germany, hoping for a better life for themselves and their children, who would supply the majority of white migrants to the Western Hemisphere.

Hierarchy and Authority

In the traditional European social order, as among the Aztec and Mayan peoples, authority came from above. Kings and princes owned vast tracts of land, conscripted men for military service, and lived in splendor off the labor of the peasantry. Yet rulers were far from supreme, given the power of the nobles, each of whom also owned large estates and controlled hundreds of peasant families. Collectively, these noblemen had the power to challenge royal authority. They had their own legislative institutions, such as the French *parlements* and the English House of Lords, and enjoyed special privileges, such as the right to a trial before a jury of other noblemen. However, after 1450 kings began to undermine the power of the nobility and to create more centralized states, laying the administrative basis for overseas expansion.

Just as kings and nobles ruled the state, so the men in peasant families ruled their women and children. The man was the head of the house, his power justified by the teachings of the Christian Church. As one English clergyman put it, "The woman is a weak creature not embued with like strength and constancy of mind"; law and custom consequently "subjected her to the power of man." On marriage, an English woman assumed her husband's surname and was required (under the threat of legally sanctioned physical "correction") to submit to his orders. Moreover, she surrendered to her husband the legal right to all her property; on his death she received a **dower**, usually the use during her lifetime of one-third of the family's land and goods.

A father controlled the lives of his children with equal authority, demanding that they work for him until their middle or late twenties. Then a landowning peasant would try to provide land to sons and dowries to daughters and choose marriage partners of appropriate wealth and status for them. In many regions fathers bestowed most of the land on the eldest son, an inheritance practice known as "primogeniture," which forced many younger children to join the ranks of the roaming poor. In such a society few men—and even fewer women—had much personal freedom or individual identity.

Hierarchy and authority prevailed in traditional European society both because of the power of established institutions and because, in a violent and unpredictable world, they offered ordinary people a measure of security. These values of order and security, which migrants carried with them to America, would shape the character of family life and the social order there well into the eighteenth century.

The Power of Religion

The Roman Catholic Church served as one of the great unifying forces in Western European society. By A.D. 1000 Christian priests had converted most of pagan Europe. The pope, as head of the Catholic Church, directed a vast hierarchy of cardinals, bishops, and priests. Latin, the great language of classical scholarship, was preserved by Catholic institutions, and Christian dogma provided a common understanding of God, the world, and human history. Equally important, the Church provided another bulwark of authority and discipline in society. Every village had a church, and holy shrines dotted the byways of Europe.

Christian doctrine penetrated deeply into the everyday lives of peasants. Over the centuries the Church had devised a religious calendar that followed the agricultural cycle and transformed pagan festivals into Christian holy days. The pagans of Europe, like many of the Indians of North America, were animists who believed that the entire natural world contained unpredictable spiritual forces that had to be paid ritual honor. Conversely, Christian priests taught that spiritual power came from outside nature, from a great God located above the earth who had sent his divine son, Jesus Christ, into the world to save humanity from its sins. They turned the winter solstice, which for pagans marked the return of the sun, into the feast of Christmas, to mark the coming of the Savior. Likewise the feast of Easter, celebrating Christ's resurrection from the dead, imparted a new meaning to the pagans' spring fertility festivals. To avert famine and plague, Christian peasants did not make ritual offerings to nature but

Artisan Family

Work was slow and output was limited in the preindustrial world, and survival required the efforts of all family members. Here a fifteenth-century French woodworker planes a panel of wood while his wife twists flax fibers into linen yarn for the family's clothes and their son fashions a basket out of reeds.
Giraudon / Art Resource, NY.

turned to priests for spiritual guidance and offered prayers to Christ and the saints.

The Church also taught that Satan, a lesser and evil supernatural being, constantly challenged God by tempting people into sin and wrongdoing. If prophets spread unusual doctrines, or **heresies**, they were surely the tools of Satan. If a devout Christian fell mysteriously ill, the sickness might be the result of an evil spell cast by a witch in league with Satan. Combating other religions and suppressing false doctrines among Christians became an obligation of rulers and a principal task of the new orders of Christian knights. In the centuries after the death in A.D. 632 of the prophet Muhammad, the founder of Islam, the newly converted peoples of the Mediterranean used force and persuasion to spread the Islamic faith and Arab civilization into sub-Saharan Africa, India, and Indonesia and deep into Spain and the Balkan region of eastern Europe. Between 1096 and 1291 successive armies of Christians, led by European kings and nobles, embarked on a series of Crusades to halt the advance of Islam and expel Arab Muslims from the Holy Land in the eastern Mediterranean, where Jesus had lived. Within Europe, Crusader armies crushed heretical Christian sects, such as the Albigensians of southern France.

The crusaders temporarily gained control of much of Palestine, but the impact of the Crusades on Europe was more profound. Religious warfare reinforced and intensified its Christian identity, resulting in renewed persecution of Jews and their expulsion from many European countries. The Crusades also broadened the intellectual and economic horizons of the privileged classes of Western Europe, bringing them into contact with the Mediterranean region of North Africa and its Arabic-speaking peoples. Arab Muslims led the world in scholarship, and their language and merchants dominated the trade routes that stretched from Mongolia to Constantinople and from the East Indies to the Mediterranean.

Europe Encounters Africa and the Americas, 1450–1550

Around A.D. 1400 Europeans shook off the lethargy of their traditional agricultural society with a major revival of learning—the Renaissance (from the French word for "rebirth"). Drawing inspiration from classical Greek and Roman (rather than Christian) sources, Renaissance intellectuals were optimistic in their view of human

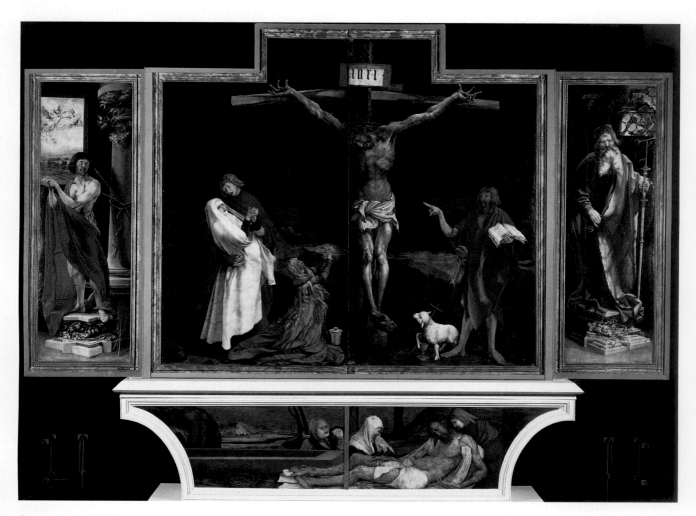

Christ's Crucifixion
This graphic portrayal by the German painter Grünewald of Christ's death on the cross and subsequent burial reminded believers not only of Christ's sacrifice but also of the ever-present prospect of their own death. The panel to the left depicts the martyr St. Sebastian, killed by dozens of arrows, while that to the right probably portrays the abbot of the monastery in Isenheim, Germany, that commissioned the altarpiece.
Colmar, Musée Unterlinden, Colmar-Giraudon/Art Resource.

nature and celebrated individual potential. They saw themselves not as prisoners of blind fate or victims of the forces of nature but as many-sided individuals with the capacity to change the world. Inspired by new knowledge and a new optimism, the rulers of Portugal and Spain commissioned Italian navigators to find new trade routes to India and China. These maritime adventurers soon brought Europeans into direct contact with the peoples of Africa, Asia, and the Americas, beginning a new era in world history.

The Renaissance

Stimulated by the wealth and learning of the Arab world, first Italy and then the countries of northern Europe experienced the rebirth of learning and cultural life now known as the Renaissance. Arab traders had access to the fabulous treasures of the East, such as silks and spices, and Arab societies had acquired magnetic compasses, water-powered mills, and mechanical clocks. In great cultural centers such as Alexandria and Cairo in Egypt, Arab scholars carried on the legacy of Christian Byzantine civilization, which had preserved the great achievements of the Greeks and Romans in religion, medicine, philosophy, mathematics, astronomy, and geography. Through Arab learning, the peoples of Europe reacquainted themselves with their own classical heritage.

Innovations in Economics, Art, and Politics. The Renaissance had the most profound impact on the upper classes. Merchants from the Italian city-states of Venice, Genoa, and Pisa dispatched ships to Alexandria, Beirut, and other eastern Mediterranean ports, where they purchased goods from China, India, Persia, and Arabia and sold them throughout Europe. The enormous profits from this commerce created a new class of merchants, bankers, and textile manufacturers who conducted trade, lent vast sums of money, and spurred technological innovation in silk and wool production. This moneyed elite ruled the republican city-states of Italy and created the concept of **civic humanism**, an ideology that celebrated public virtue and service to the state and would profoundly influence European and American conceptions of government.

In addition to new civic ideals, perhaps no other age in European history has produced such a flowering of artistic genius. Michelangelo, Andrea Palladio, and Filippo Brunelleschi designed and built great architectural masterpieces, while Leonardo da Vinci and Raphael produced magnificent religious paintings, creating styles and setting standards that have endured into the modern era.

This creative energy inspired Renaissance rulers. In *The Prince* (1513), Niccolò Machiavelli provided unsentimental advice on how monarchs could increase their political power. The kings of Western Europe followed his advice, creating royal law courts and bureaucracies to reduce the power of the landed classes and seeking alliances with merchants and urban artisans. Monarchs allowed merchants to trade throughout their realms and granted privileges to artisan guilds, encouraging both domestic manufacturing and foreign trade. In return, these rulers extracted taxes from towns and loans from merchants to support their armies and officials. This alliance of monarchs, merchants, and royal bureaucrats (which eventually became known as **mercantilism**) challenged the power of the agrarian nobility, while the increasing wealth of monarchical nation-states such as Spain and Portugal propelled Europe into its first age of overseas expansion.

Astronomers at Istanbul, 1581
Arab and Turkish scholars transmitted ancient texts and learning to Europeans during the Middle Ages and provided much of the geographical and astronomical knowledge used by European explorers during the sixteenth century, the great Age of Discovery. Ergun Cagutay, Istanbul.

Maritime Expansion. Under the direction of Prince Henry (1394–1460), Portugal led the great surge of

Renaissance Architecture

In the painting The Ideal City, *the Renaissance artist Piero della Francesca uses columned buildings to recall the classical world of Greece and Rome and emphasizes symmetrical forms to create a world of ordered beauty.* Scala/Art Resource.

maritime commercial expansion. Henry was at once a Christian warrior and a Renaissance humanist. As a general of the Crusading Order of Christ, he had fought the Muslims in North Africa, an experience that reinforced his desire to extend the bounds of Christendom—and Portuguese power. As a humanist, Henry patronized Renaissance thinkers; as an explorer, he relied on Arab and Italian geographers for the latest knowledge about the shape and size of the continents. Imbued with the spirit of the Renaissance, he tried to fulfill the mission assigned to him by an astrologer: "to engage in great and noble conquests and to attempt the discovery of things hidden from other men."

Because Arab and Italian merchants dominated trade in the Mediterranean, Henry sought an alternative oceanic route to the wealth of Asia. In the 1420s he established a center for exploration and ocean mapping near Lisbon and sent newly developed, strongly constructed three-masted ships (caravels) to sail the African coast. His seamen soon discovered and settled three sets of islands—the Madeiras, Canaries, and the Azores. By 1435 Portuguese sea captains were roaming the coast of West Africa, seeking ivory and gold in exchange for salt, wine, and fish. By the 1440s they were trading in humans as well, the first Europeans to engage in the long-established African slave trade.

West African Society and Slavery

Vast and diverse, West Africa stretches along the coast from present-day Senegal to Angola. In the 1400s tropical rain forest covered much of the coast, but a series of great rivers—the Senegal, Gambia, Volta, Niger, and Congo—provided relatively easy access to the woodlands, plains, and savanna of the interior (Map 1.3).

West African Life. Most of the people of West Africa farmed modest plots and lived in extended families in small villages. Normally, men cleared the land and women planted and harvested the crops. On the plains of the savanna, millet, cotton, and livestock were the primary products, while the forest peoples grew yams and harvested oil-rich palm nuts. Forest dwellers exchanged palm oil and kola nuts, a mild stimulant, for the textiles and leather goods produced by savanna dwellers. Similarly, salt produced along the seacoast was traded for iron or gold mined in the hills of the interior.

West Africans spoke many different languages and lived in hundreds of distinct cultural and political groups. A majority of the people resided in hierarchical, socially stratified societies ruled by princes. Other West Africans dwelled in stateless societies organized by household and lineage (much like those of the Woodland Indians of eastern North America). Most peoples had secret societies, such as the Poro for men and the Sande for women, that united people from different lineages and clans and exercised political influence by checking the powers of rulers in princely states. These societies provided sexual education for the young, conducted adult initiation ceremonies, and, by shaming individuals and officials, enforced codes of public conduct and private morality.

Spiritual beliefs varied greatly. Although some West Africans had been converted by Arab missionaries from the north to the Muslim faith and believed in a single god, most recognized a variety of deities—ranging from a remote creator-god who seldom interfered in human affairs to numerous animistic spirits that lived in the earth, animals, and plants. Africans viewed their ancestors with great respect, believing that they inhabited a spiritual world from which they could intercede on behalf of their descendants. Royal families in particular paid elaborate homage to their ancestors, hoping to give themselves an aura of divinity.

At first European traders had a positive impact on life in West Africa by introducing new plants and animals. Portuguese merchants carried coconuts from East Africa, oranges and lemons from the Mediterranean, pigs from Western Europe, and (after 1500) maize, manioc, and tomatoes from the Americas. Portuguese merchants also expanded existing African trade networks, stimulating the economy. From small, fortified trading posts on the coast, iron bars and metal products joined kola nuts and salt moving inland; in return, grain, gold, ivory, pepper, cotton textiles, and, eventually, slaves flowed down the rivers to oceangoing ships. Because of disease, the inland trade remained in the hands of Africans; Europeans who lived in the interior of West Africa were quickly

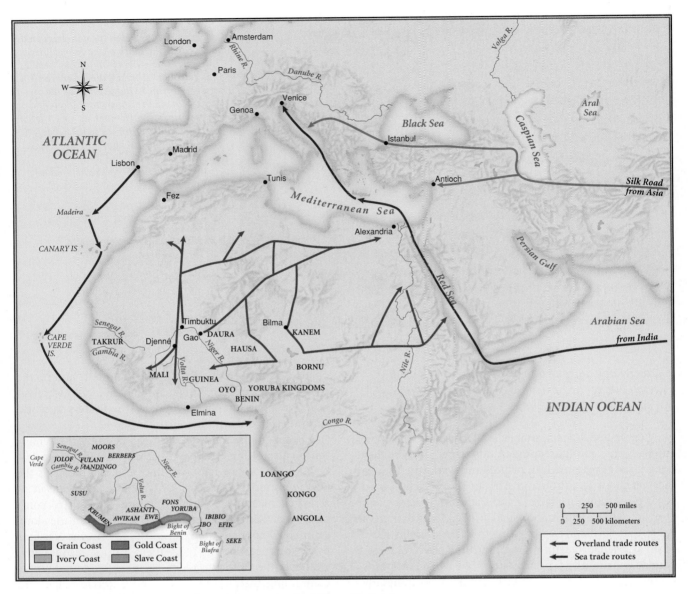

MAP 1.3 West Africa and the Mediterranean in the Fifteenth Century

Trade routes across the Sahara Desert had long connected West Africa with the Mediterranean region. Gold, ivory, and slaves moved northward; fine textiles, spices, and the Muslim faith traveled to the south. Beginning in the 1430s, the Portuguese opened up a maritime trade with the coastal regions of West Africa, which were home to many peoples and dozens of large and small states.

stricken by yellow fever, malaria, and dysentery, and their death rate often reached 50 percent a year.

The Slave Trade.   Europeans soon joined in the trade in humans. Unfree status had existed for many centuries in West Africa. Some people were held in bondage as security for debts; others had been sold into servitude by their kin, often in exchange for food in times of famine; still others were war captives. Although treated as property and exploited as agricultural laborers, slaves usually were considered members of the society that had enslaved them and sometimes were treated as kin. Most retained the right to marry, and their children were

often free. A small proportion of unfree West Africans were **trade slaves**, mostly war captives and criminals sold from one kingdom to another or carried overland in caravans by Arab traders to the Mediterranean region. Thus, the first Portuguese in Senegambia found that the Wolof king there had created a slave-trading society:

[The king] supports himself by raids which result in many slaves from his own as well as neighboring countries. He employs these slaves in cultivating the land allotted to him; but he also sells many to the Azanaghi [Arab]

Fulani Village in West Africa

Around 1550 the Fulani people conquered the lands to the south of the Senegal River. To protect themselves from subject peoples and neighboring tribes, the Fulani constructed fortified villages, such as the one depicted here. Previously the Fulani had been nomadic herders and, as the enclosed pasture shows, continued to keep livestock. Note the cylindrical houses of mud brick, surmounted by thatched roofs.

Frederic Shoberl, ed., *The World in Miniature*, 1821.

For more help analyzing this image, see the ONLINE STUDY GUIDE at bedfordstmartins.com/henretta.

merchants in return for horses and other goods, and also to the Christians, since they have begun to trade with these blacks.

Portuguese traders established "forts" at small port cities—Gorée, Elmina, Mpinda, and Loango—where they bought slaves from African princes and warlords. Initially they carried a few thousand African slaves each year to sugar plantations in Madeira and the Canary Islands and also to Lisbon, which soon had a black population of 9,000, and Seville in Spain, home to 6,000 slaves in 1550. From this small beginning the maritime slave trade expanded enormously, especially after 1550 when Europeans set up sugar plantations in Brazil and the West Indies. By 1700 slave traders were carrying hundreds of thousands of slaves to toil and die on American plantations.

[handwritten: false exaggeration]

Europe Reaches the Americas

As they traded with Africans, Portuguese adventurers continued to look for a direct ocean route to Asia. In 1488 Bartholomeu Dias rounded the Cape of Good Hope, the southern tip of Africa, and ten years later Vasco da Gama reached India. Although the Arab, Indian, and Jewish merchants who controlled the trade along India's Malabar Coast tried to exclude him, da Gama acquired a highly profitable cargo of cinnamon and pepper—spices that were especially valuable because they could be used to flavor and preserve meat. To capture the trade in spices and Indian textiles for Portugal, da Gama returned to India in 1502 with twenty-one fighting vessels, which outmaneuvered and outgunned the Arab fleets. Soon the Portuguese government set up fortified trading posts for its merchants at key points around the Indian Ocean and

opened trade routes from Africa to Indonesia and up the coast of Asia to China and Japan. In a momentous transition, Portuguese replaced Arabs as the leaders in world commerce and the trade in African slaves.

Spain quickly followed Portugal's example. As Renaissance rulers, King Ferdinand of Aragon and Queen Isabella of Castile saw national unity and commerce as the keys to power and prosperity. Married in their teens in an arranged match, the young rulers (r. 1474–1516) combined their kingdoms and completed the centuries-long campaign known as the ***reconquista*** to oust the Muslims from their realm. In 1492 their armies reconquered Granada, the last outpost of Islam in Western Europe. Continuing their effort to use the Catholic religion to build a sense of "Spanishness," Ferdinand and Isabella launched a brutal Inquisition against suspected Christian heretics and expelled or forcibly converted thousands of Jews. Simultaneously they sought new opportunities for trade and empire (Map 1.4).

Because Portugal controlled the southern, or African, approach to Asia, Isabella and Ferdinand listened with interest to proposals for an alternative, western route to

▶ **MAP 1.4 The Eurasian Trade System and European Maritime Ventures, 1500**

For centuries the Mediterranean port cities of Antioch and Alexandria served as the western termini of the great Eurasian trading routes—the silk route from China and the spice trade from India and Indonesia. Between 1480 and 1550, European explorers subsidized by the monarchs and merchants of Portugal, Spain, and Holland opened new maritime connections to Africa, India, and the Americas, challenging the primacy of the Arab-dominated routes through the lands and waterways of the eastern Mediterranean. (To trace changes in trade and empires over time, see also Map 2.2 on p. 46 and Map 5.1 on p. 134.)

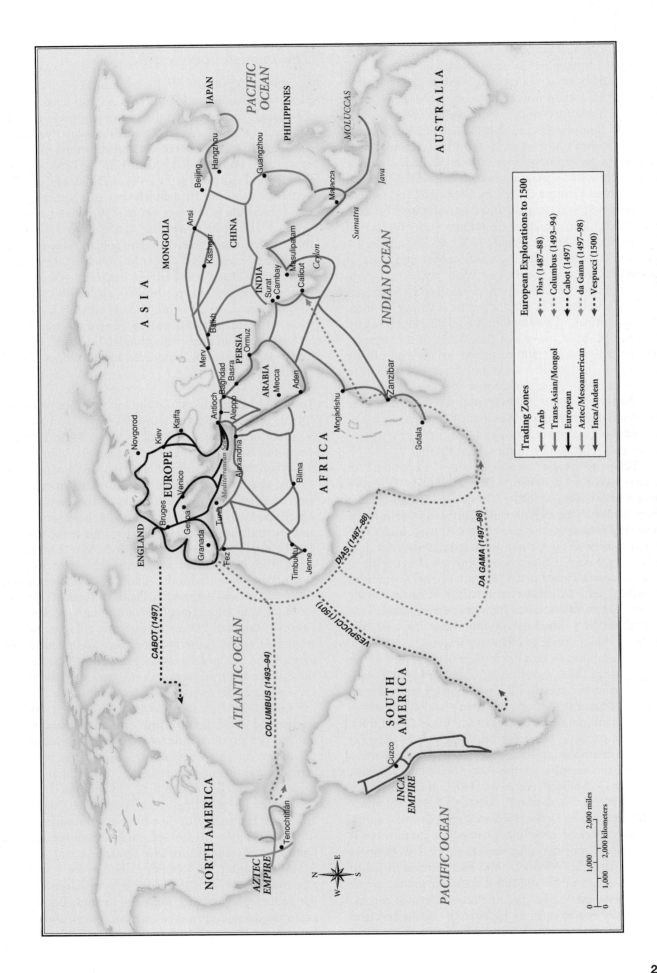

Trading Zones

Arab
Trans-Asian/Mongol
European
Aztec/Mesoamerican
Inca/Andean

European Explorations to 1500

— — — Dias (1487–88)
— ·· — Columbus (1493–94)
— — — Cabot (1497)
— ·· — da Gama (1497–98)
— ·· — Vespucci (1500)

the riches of the East. The main advocate for such a route was Christopher Columbus, a devout Catholic and a struggling Genoese sea captain who was determined to become rich and to convert the peoples of Asia to Christianity. Misinterpreting the findings of Italian geographers, Columbus believed that the Atlantic Ocean, long feared by Arab sailors as a ten-thousand-mile-wide "green sea of darkness," was little more than a narrow channel of water separating Europe from Asia. Dubious at first about Columbus's theory, Ferdinand and Isabella finally agreed to arrange financial backing from Spanish merchants. They charged Columbus with the task of discovering a new trade route to China and, in an expression of the crusading mentality of the *reconquista*, of carrying Christianity to the peoples of Asia.

Columbus set sail with three small ships in August 1492. Six weeks later, after a perilous voyage of three thousand miles, he finally found land, disembarking on October 12, 1492, on one of the islands of the present-day Bahamas. Although surprised by the rude living conditions of the natives, Columbus expected them to "easily be made Christians, for it appeared to me that they had no religion." With ceremony and solemnity, he bestowed the names of the Spanish royal family and Catholic holy days on the islands, intending thereby to claim them for Spain and for Christendom.

Believing he had reached Asia—"the Indies," in fifteenth-century parlance—Columbus called the native inhabitants Indians and the islands the West Indies. He then explored the neighboring Caribbean islands, demanding gold from the local Taino, Arawak, and Carib peoples. Buoyed by the natives' stories of rivers of gold lying "to the west," Columbus left forty men on the island of Hispaniola (present-day Haiti and the Dominican Republic) and returned triumphantly to Spain, taking several Tainos to display to Isabella and Ferdinand.

Although Columbus brought back no gold, the Spanish monarchs were sufficiently impressed by his discovery to support three more voyages over the next twelve years. During those expeditions Columbus began the colonization of the West Indies, transporting more than a thousand Spanish settlers—all men—and hundreds of domestic animals. He also began the transatlantic trade in slaves, carrying hundreds of Indians to bondage in Europe and importing black slaves from Africa to work as artisans and farmers in the new Spanish settlements. However, Columbus failed to find either golden treasures or great kingdoms, so that his death in 1506 went virtually unrecognized. Other explorers soon followed Columbus, and a German geographer named the continents not after their European discoverer but after a Genoese mariner, Amerigo Vespucci, who had traveled to South America around 1500 and called it a *nuevo mundo*, a new world: America. For its part, the Spanish crown continued to call the new lands Las Indias (the Indies) and determined to make them a Spanish world.

The Spanish Conquest

Columbus and other Spanish adventurers ruled the peoples of the Caribbean islands with an iron hand, seizing their goods and exploiting their labor to grow sugarcane. After subduing the Arawaks and Tainos on Hispaniola, the Spanish probed coastal settlements on the mainland in search of booty. In 1513 Juan Ponce de León searched for gold and slaves along the coast of Florida and gave the peninsula its name. That same year Vasco Núñez de Balboa crossed the Isthmus of Darien (Panama), becoming the first European to see the Pacific Ocean. Although these greedy adventurers found no gold, rumors of riches to the west encouraged others to launch an invasion of the interior. These men were not explorers or merchants but hardened veterans of the wars against the Muslims who were eager to do battle and get rich. To encourage these adventurers to expand its American empire, the Spanish crown offered them plunder, landed estates and Indian laborers in the conquered territory, and titles of nobility.

The Fall of the Aztecs and the Incas.   The first great success of the Spanish **conquistadors** (conquerors) occurred in present-day Mexico (Map 1.5). In 1519 the ambitious and charismatic adventurer Hernán Cortés landed on the Mexican coast with 600 men and marched toward the Aztec capital of Tenochtitlán. Fortuitously for the Spaniards, Cortés arrived in the very year in which Aztec mythology had predicted the return of the god Quetzalcoatl to his earthly kingdom. Believing that Cortés might be the returning god, Moctezuma, the Aztec ruler, acted indecisively. After an Aztec ambush against the conquistadors failed, Moctezuma allowed Cortés to proceed without challenge to Tenochtitlán and received him with great ceremony, only to become Cortés's captive. When Moctezuma's forces finally attempted to expel the invaders, they were confronted by superior European military technology. The sight of the Spaniards in full armor, with guns that shook the heavens and inflicted devastating wounds, made a deep impression on the Aztecs, who had learned how to purify gold and fashion it into ornate religious objects but did not produce iron tools or weapons. Moreover, the Aztecs had no wheeled carts or cavalry, and their warriors, fighting on foot with flint- or obsidian-tipped spears and arrows, were no match for mounted Spanish conquistadors wielding steel swords and aided by vicious attack dogs. Although heavily outnumbered and suffering great losses, Cortés and his men were able to fight their way out of the Aztec capital.

At this point, the vast population of the Aztec empire could easily have crushed the European invaders if the Indian peoples had remained united. But Cortés exploited the widespread resentment against the Aztecs, forming military alliances and raising thousands of

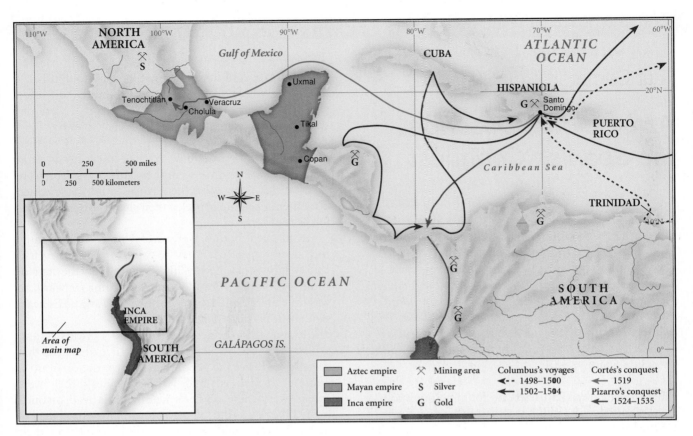

MAP 1.5 The Spanish Conquest of the Great Indian Civilizations

The Spanish first invaded the islands of the Caribbean. Rumors of a magnificent golden civilization led to Cortés's invasion of the Aztec empire in 1519. By 1535 other Spanish conquistadors had conquered the Mayan temple cities and the Inca empire in Peru, completing one of the great conquests in world history.

troops from subject peoples who had seen their wealth expropriated by Aztec nobles and their people sacrificed to the Aztec sun god. The Aztec empire collapsed, the victim not of superior Spanish military technology but of a vast internal rebellion of Indian peoples (see American Voices, "Aztec Elders Describe the Spanish Conquest," p. 26).

As the Spanish sought to impose their dominion over the peoples of the Aztec empire, they had a silent ally—disease. Separated from Eurasia for thousands of years, the inhabitants of the Western Hemisphere had no immunities to common European diseases. A massive smallpox epidemic lasting seventy days ravaged Tenochtitlán following the Spanish exodus, "striking everywhere in the city," according to an Aztec source, killing Moctezuma's brother and many others. "They could not move, they could not stir. . . . Covered, mantled with pustules, very many people died of them." Subsequent outbreaks of smallpox, influenza, and measles killed hundreds of thousands of Aztecs and their subject peoples and sapped the morale of the survivors. Exploiting this demographic weakness, Cortés quickly extended Spanish rule over the entire Aztec

empire, and his lieutenants then moved against the Mayan city-states in the Yucatán Peninsula, eventually conquering them as well (see American Lives, "Cortés and Malinche: The Dynamics of Conquest," p. 30).

In 1524 the Spanish conquest entered a new phase, when Francisco Pizarro led a military expedition to the mountains of Peru, home of the rich and powerful Inca empire that stretched 2,000 miles along the Pacific coast of South America. To govern this far-flung empire, the Inca rulers built 24,000 miles of roads and dozens of carefully placed administrative centers, which were constructed of finely crafted stone. A semidivine Inca king ruled the empire, assisted by a hierarchical bureaucracy staffed by noblemen, many of whom were his relatives. By the time Pizarro and his small force of 168 men and 67 horses reached Peru, half of the Inca population had died from European diseases, which had been spread by Indian traders. Weakened militarily and fighting over succession to the throne, the Inca nobility was easy prey for Pizarro's army. In little more than a decade Spain had become the master of the wealthiest and most populous regions of the Western Hemisphere.

Friar Bernardino de Sahagún

Aztec Elders Describe the Spanish Conquest

During the 1550s Friar Bernardino de Sahagún published the Florentine Codex: General History of New Spain. *According to Sahagún, the authors of the Codex were Aztec elders who lived through the conquest. Here the elders describe their reaction to the invading Europeans and the devastating impact of smallpox. They told their stories to Sahagún in a repetitive style, using the conventions of Aztec oral histories, and he translated them into Spanish.*

Moctezuma enjoyed no sleep, no food, no one spoke to him. Whatsoever he did, it was as if he were in torment. Ofttimes it was as if he sighed, became weak, felt weak. . . . Wherefore he said, "What will now befall us? Who indeed stands [in charge]? Alas, until now, I. In great torment is my heart; as if it were washed in chili water it indeed burns." . . .

And when he had so heard what the messengers reported, he was terrified, he was astounded. . . . Especially did it cause him to faint away when he heard how the gun, at [the Spaniards'] command, discharged: how it resounded as if it thundered when it went off. It indeed bereft one of strength; it shut off one's ears. And when it discharged, something like a round pebble came forth from within. Fire went showering forth; sparks went blazing forth. And its smoke smelled very foul; it had a fetid odor which verily wounded the head. And when [the shot] struck a mountain, it was as if it were destroyed, dissolved . . . as if someone blew it away.

All iron was their war array. In iron they clothed themselves. With iron they covered their heads. Iron were their swords. Iron were their crossbows. Iron were their shields. Iron were their lances. And those which bore them upon their backs, their deer [horses], were as tall as roof terraces.

And their bodies were everywhere covered; only their faces appeared. They were very white; they had chalky faces; they had yellow hair, though the hair of some was black. . . . And when Moctezuma so heard, he was much terrified. It was as if he fainted away. His heart saddened; his heart failed him. . . .

[Soon] there came to be prevalent a great sickness, a plague. It was in Tepeilhuitl that it originated, that there spread over the people a great destruction of men. Some it indeed covered [with pustules]; they were spread everywhere, on one's face, on one's head, on one's breast. There was indeed perishing; many indeed died of it. No longer could they walk; they only lay in their abodes, in their beds. No longer could they move. . . . And when they bestirred themselves, much did they cry out. There was much perishing. Like a covering, covering-like, were the pustules. Indeed, many people died of them, and many just died of hunger. There was death from hunger; there was no one to take care of another; there was no one to attend to another.

Source: Friar Bernardino de Sahagún, *Florentine Codex: General History of New Spain,* trans. Arthur J. O. Anderson and Charles E. Dibble (Santa Fe and Salt Lake City: School of American Research and University of Utah Press, 1975), 12:17–20, 26, 83.

The Legacy of the Conquest. The Spanish invasion and European diseases changed life forever throughout the Americas. Virtually all the Indians of Hispaniola—at least 300,000 people—were wiped out by disease and warfare. In Peru the population plummeted from 9 million in 1530 to fewer than half a million a century later. Likewise, diseases unintentionally introduced by early Spanish expeditions in the present-day United States inflicted equally catastrophic losses on the Pueblo peoples of the Southwest and the Mississippian chiefdoms of the Southeast. In 1500 Mesoamerica as a whole had probably 40 million Indians; by 1650 its Native American population had fallen to a mere 3 million people—one of the greatest demographic disasters in world history.

Once the conquistadors had triumphed, the Spanish government quickly created an elaborate bureaucratic empire, headed in Madrid by the Council of the Indies, which issued laws and decrees to viceroys and other Spanish-born officials in America. However, the conquistadors remained powerful because they held grants (***encomiendas***) from the crown giving them legal

Premonition of Disaster

In 1570 Fray Diego Durán, a Spanish Dominican monk, recorded the history of Aztec people. This leaf from his manuscript captures the moment when Moctezuma first hears of the arrival of white-skinned strangers on the coast of the empire that he ruled. The watercolor shows the comet that Moctezuma reportedly saw plunging to the earth, an event that according to Aztec belief was a harbinger of disaster. Library of Congress.

control of the native population. They ruthlessly exploited the surviving Native Americans, forcing them to work on vast plantations to raise crops and cattle for local consumption and export to Europe. The Spaniards also altered the natural environment by introducing grains and grasses that supplanted the native flora. Horses, first brought to the mainland by Cortés, gradually spread throughout the Western Hemisphere and in the following centuries dramatically changed the way of life of many Indian peoples, especially on the Great Plains of the United States.

The Spanish invasion of the Americas had a significant impact on life in Europe and Africa as well. In a process of transfer known as the **Columbian Exchange**, the food products of the Western Hemisphere—especially maize, potatoes, and cassava (manioc)—became available to the peoples of other continents, significantly increasing agricultural yields and stimulating the growth of population (Map 1.6). Similarly, the livestock and crops—and weeds and human diseases—of African and Eurasian lands became part of the lives of residents

of the Americas. Nor was that all. In addition to this ecological revolution, the gold and silver that had honored Aztec gods flowed into the countinghouses of Spain and into the treasury of its monarchs, making that nation the most powerful in Europe.

By 1550 the once magnificent civilizations of Mexico and Peru lay in ruins. "Of all these wonders"—the great city of Tenochtitlán, rich orchards, overflowing markets—"all is overthrown and lost, nothing left standing," recalled the Spanish chronicler Bernal Díaz, who had been a young soldier in Cortés's army. Moreover, those Native Americans who survived had lost vital parts of their cultural identity. Spanish priests suppressed their worship of traditional gods and converted them to Catholicism. As early as 1531 an Indian convert reported a vision of a dark-skinned Virgin Mary, later known as the Virgin of Guadalupe, a Christian version of the "corn mother" who traditionally protected the maize crop.

Soon Spanish bureaucrats imposed taxes and supervised the lives of the Indians, as no fewer than 350,000

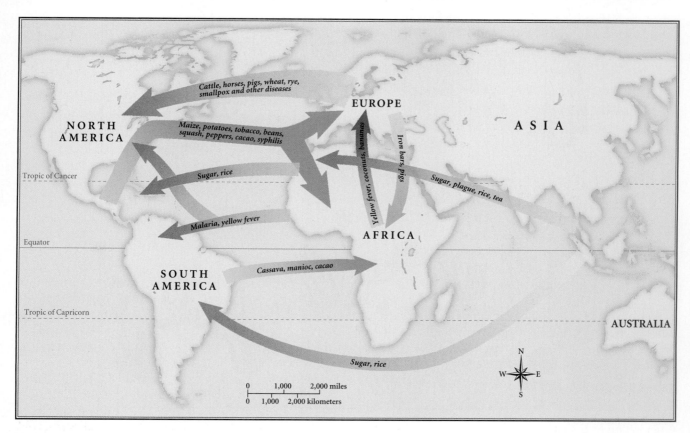

MAP 1.6 The Columbian Exchange

As European traders and adventurers traveled to Africa, the Americas, and Asia between 1430 and 1600, they began what historians call the "Columbian Exchange," a vast intercontinental movement of the plants, animals, and diseases that changed the course of historical development. As the nutritious, high-yielding American crops of corn and potatoes enriched the diets of Europeans and Africans, the Eurasian and African diseases of smallpox, diphtheria, malaria, and yellow fever nearly wiped out the native inhabitants of the Western Hemisphere and virtually ensured that they would lose control of their lands.

For more help analyzing this map, see the ONLINE STUDY GUIDE at **bedfordstmartins.com/henretta.**

Spanish migrants settled between 1500 and 1650 on lands previously occupied by the native peoples of Mesoamerica and South America. Because nearly 90 percent of the Spanish settlers were men who took Indian women as wives or mistresses, the result was a substantial **mestizo** (mixed-race) population and an elaborate system of race-based caste distinctions. Around 1800, at the end of the colonial era, Spanish America had about 17 million people: 7.5 million Indians, 3.2 million Europeans, 1 million enslaved Africans, and 5.5 million people of mixed race and cultural heritage.

Some Indians resisted assimilation by retreating into the mountains, but they lacked the numbers or the power to oust the Spanish invaders or their descendants. Today only a single Indian tongue, Guarani in Paraguay, is a recognized national language, and no Native American state has representation in the United Nations. For

the original Americans the consequences of the European intrusion in 1492 were tragic and irreversible.

The Protestant Reformation and the Rise of England

Religion was a central aspect of European life and, because of a major crisis in Western Christendom, played a crucial role in the settlement of America. Even as Christian fervor drove Portugal and Spain to expel Muslims and Jews from their nations and to convert the peoples of Mesoamerica to Catholicism, Christianity ceased to be a unifying force in European society. New religious doctrines preached by Martin Luther and other reformers divided Christians into armed ideological camps of

TABLE 1.2 Spanish Monarchs, 1474–1598

Monarch	Dates of Reign	Achievements
Ferdinand and Isabella	1474–1516	Expelled Muslims from Spain; dispatched Columbus
Charles I	1516–1556	Holy Roman Emperor, 1519–1556
Philip II	1556–1598	Attacked Protestantism; mounted Spanish Armada

Catholics and Protestants and plunged the continent into religious wars that lasted for decades.

These struggles set the stage for Protestant dominance of North America. In the 1560s a Protestant rebellion in the Spanish Netherlands led to Holland's emergence as a separate nation and a major commercial power in both Asia and the Americas. England likewise experienced a religious revolution and a major economic transformation that gave it the physical resources and spiritual energy to establish Protestant settlements in North America.

The Protestant Movement

Over the centuries the Catholic Church had become a large and wealthy institution, controlling vast resources throughout Europe. Renaissance popes and cardinals were among the leading patrons of the arts, but some also misused the Church's wealth. Pope Leo X (r. 1513–1521) was the most notorious, receiving half a million ducats a year from the sale of religious offices. Ordinary priests and monks regularly used their authority to obtain economic or sexual favors. One English reformer denounced the clergy as a "gang of scoundrels" who should be "rid of their vices or stripped of their authority," but he was ignored. Other reformers, such as Jan Hus of Bohemia, were tried and executed as heretics.

Martin Luther's Attack on Church Doctrine. In 1517 Martin Luther, a German monk and professor at the university in Wittenberg, nailed his famous Ninety-five Theses to the door of the castle church. That widely reprinted document condemned the sale of **indulgences**—church certificates that purportedly pardoned a sinner from punishments in the afterlife. Luther argued that heavenly salvation could come only from God through grace, not from the Church for a fee. He was excommunicated by the pope and threatened with punishment by King Charles I of Spain (r. 1516–1556), the head of the Holy Roman Empire, which included most of Germany (Table 1.2). Northern German princes, who were resisting the emperor's authority for political reasons, embraced Luther's

teachings and protected him from arrest, thus allowing the Protestant movement to flourish.

Luther broadened his attack, articulating positions that differed from Roman Catholic doctrine in three major respects. First, Luther rejected the doctrine that Christians could win salvation through good deeds, arguing that people could be saved only by grace, which came as a free gift from God. Second, he downplayed the role of clergy and the pope as mediators between God and the people, proclaiming, "Our baptism consecrates us all without exception and makes us all priests." Third, Luther said that believers must look to the Bible (not Church doctrine) as the ultimate authority in matters of faith. So that every German-speaking believer could read the Bible, he translated it from Latin into German.

Peasants as well as princes heeded Luther's attack on authority and, to his dismay, mounted social protests of their own. In 1524 some German peasants rebelled against their manorial lords and were ruthlessly suppressed. Fearing social revolution, Luther urged obedience to established political institutions and condemned the teachings of new groups of religious dissidents, such as the Anabaptists (so called because they rejected infant baptism).

Embracing Luther's views, most princes in northern Germany broke from Rome, in part because they wanted the power to appoint bishops and control the Church's property within their own domains. In response, Emperor Charles dispatched armies to Germany to restore Catholic doctrine and his political authority, unleashing a generation of warfare. Eventually the Peace of Augsburg (1555) restored order by allowing princes to decide the religion of their subjects. Most southern German rulers installed Catholicism as the official religion, while those in the north made Lutheranism the state creed (Map 1.7).

The Teachings of John Calvin. The most rigorous Protestant doctrine was established in Geneva, Switzerland, under the leadership of the French theologian John Calvin. Even more than Luther, Calvin stressed the omnipotence of God and the corruption of human nature. His *Institutes of the Christian Religion* (1536) depicted God as an awesome and absolute sovereign who

Cortés and Malinche: The Dynamics of Conquest

Hernán Cortés conquered an empire and destroyed a civilization, an achievement that was both magnificent and tragic. The immensity of Cortés's dual triumph was partly accidental, owing to the rebellion of the non-Aztec peoples and the extraordinarily devastating impact of European diseases, but it also reflected his burning ambition and political vision. Unlike most other gold-hungry Spanish adventurers, Cortés had a sense of politics and of history. Once he learned from the Maya, in whose territory he first landed, of the existence of Moctezuma and his kingdom, Cortés's priority became the pursuit of power rather than of plunder. As Bernal Díaz del Castillo, one of his soldiers, reported in the *History of the Conquest of New Spain*, Cortés immediately declared his intention "to serve God and the king" by subjugating the Aztec king and his great empire.

Could this be done? Six hundred Spanish troops might plunder the lands at the far reaches of an empire of millions, but what chance did they stand against an Aztec army of tens of thousands? The odds of conquering the Aztec empire were so low that a less audacious man would not even have tried. But Cortés was no ordinary man. A person of great presence—intelligent and ruthless, courageous yet prudent, decisive yet flexible—the Spanish chieftain inspired fear and respect among his enemies and unthinking loyalty among his followers, who time and again risked their lives at his command. No one was more loyal to Cortés—and, at crucial points in the conquest of Mexico, more important—than the native woman known as La Malinche, who became his interpreter and mistress. Had he not conquered her affections, he might have failed to conquer the empire.

As a child, the girl who became Malinche was called Malinali, the name of the twelfth month in the Nahuatl language spoken by the Aztec and other Mexican peoples. Her father was the local lord of Painala, a village near the Gulf of Mexico in the far southern reaches of the Aztec empire, and her mother was the ruler of Xatipan, a small nearby settlement. As the daughter of minor nobles, Malinali lived in comfort and no doubt developed the sense of confidence that would serve her so well in the future. But she lived her adolescent years as a mere slave. Following the death of her father and the remarriage of her mother, Malinali was sold into bondage by her mother and stepfather, who wanted to enhance the succession rights of their newborn son. Owned first by merchants, she ended up as an enslaved worker in the Mayan settlement of Potonchan on the Gulf of Mexico. There, in March 1519 when she was about seventeen years old, Malinali had her rendezvous with destiny.

Initially the confrontation between Spaniards and Native Americans took place with gestures and misunderstandings, for the two peoples could not comprehend each other's language, intentions, and values. But Cortés was lucky, for his expedition had chanced upon Father Gerónimo de Aguilar, a shipwrecked Spanish priest who had lived for a decade as a slave among the Mayas and knew their language. And he was doubly lucky when the Mayas of Potonchan, whom he had defeated in battle, presented him with twenty slave women, one of whom was Malinali. Cortés treated these women as servants and concubines, assigning them to his commanders; and because Malinali was "of pleasing appearance and sharp-witted and outward-going" (according to Díaz del Castillo), she was given to his chief lieutenant, Alonso Puertocarrero. Learning that the young woman could speak Nahuatl, Cortés soon took her as his own servant and mistress. At his command she conversed with Nahuatl-speaking peoples and then used Mayan to convey what she had learned to Aguilar, who translated it into Spanish. The process was cumbersome, but it worked. Now Cortés could negotiate directly with both Moctezuma's officials and the leaders of the non-Aztec peoples whose help he needed to conquer the empire.

Of Malinali's motives in providing aid to the Spanish invaders there is no record. Like other Mexican peoples, including Moctezuma, at first she may have viewed Cortés as a returning god. Or, like his Spanish followers, she may have been dazzled by his powerful presence and personality. Or, quite likely, Malinali may have calculated that Cortés was her best hope of escaping slavery and reclaiming a noble status. Whatever the reasons, Malinali's loyalty to her new master was complete and unbending. Rejecting an opportunity to betray the Spanish on their march to the Aztec capital of Tenochtitlán in 1519, she risked her life by warning Cortés of a surprise attack by the Cholulans. In 1520 she stood by him when the Spanish cause seemed lost following the disastrous retreat from Tenochtitlán. And in 1524 and 1525 she helped him survive a catastrophic military campaign in the jungles of present-day Honduras.

Malinche and Cortés

In this Aztec pictograph (c. 1540) Cortés is shown with his Nahuatl-speaking interpreter, mistress, and advisor Malinche (or Marina in Spanish). Signifying her dual identity as an Indian and a European, Malinche wears native clothes while holding up the Christian rosary. Bibliothèque Nationale.

There is no question about Malinali's importance to the Spanish cause. As Bernal Díaz del Castillo concluded, "without her we never should have understood the Mexican language and, upon the whole, [would] have been unable to surmount many difficulties." The Aztecs likewise acknowledged her eminence. They called her Malinche, addressing her with respect by adding the suffix *-che* to her original name, and they often referred to Cortés as "the captain of Malinche," defining the Spaniard in terms of the interpreter through whom he spoke.

Yet there is no evidence that Cortés felt indebted to Malinche or developed a deep emotional bond with the young woman. In 1522 or 1523 she bore him a son (whom he named Martín after his father), but by then he had taken many other mistresses, including the daughters of Moctezuma, and in succeeding years sired numerous illegitimate children by other Mexican women. Moreover, in 1525 Cortés again gave the services of Malinali, now known by the respectful Spanish name of Doña Marina, to one of his commanders, Juan Jaramillo, with whom she lived in marriage until her death in 1551. A mere native woman was not what the great conqueror had in mind as a wife. To solidify his achievement and lay the foundation for a great family dynasty, in 1528 Cortés won entry into the ranks of the Spanish nobility, taking as his wife Juana, daughter of the count of Aguilar and a niece of the duke of Béjar, one of the richest and most politically powerful men in Spain. After living with Juana in Mexico for a decade Cortés returned to his native land, where he died in 1647 at the age of sixty-two, a respected and colossally wealthy man.

Malinche fared less well than her former master did, in death as well as in life. Because she was among the first native women to bear mixed-race (mestizo) children, Malinche has sometimes been celebrated as the symbolic mother of the post-conquest Mexican people. More often, she has seemed to subsequent generations of Mexicans as a traitor to her people, a mere instrument in the hands of greedy invaders who subjugated a society and destroyed a civilization. Within the dynamics of sexual and military conquest, both views are correct.

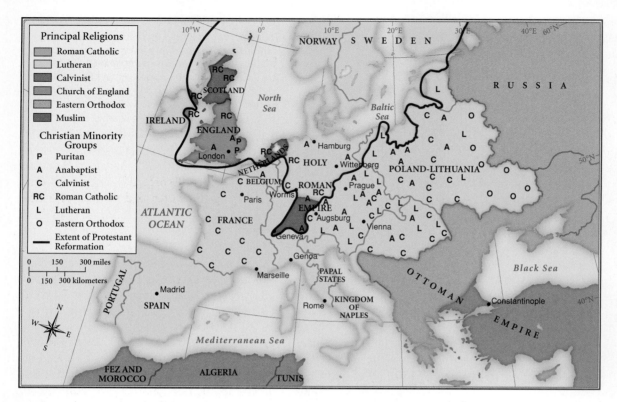

MAP 1.7 Religious Diversity in Europe, 1600

By 1600 Europe was permanently divided. Catholicism remained dominant in the south, but Lutheran princes and monarchs ruled northern Europe, and Calvinism had strongholds in Switzerland, Holland, and Scotland. Radical sects were persecuted by legally established Protestant churches as well as by Catholic clergy and monarchs. These religious conflicts encouraged the migration of minority sects to America.

governed the "wills of men so as to move precisely to that end directed by him." Calvin preached the doctrine of **predestination**—the idea that God had chosen certain people for salvation even before they were born, condemning the rest to eternal damnation. In Geneva he set up a model Christian community, eliminating bishops and placing spiritual power in the hands of ministers chosen by the members of each congregation. These ministers and pious laymen ruled the city, prohibiting frivolity and luxury and imposing religious discipline on the entire society. "We know," wrote Calvin, "that man is of so perverse and crooked a nature, that everyone would scratch out his neighbor's eyes if there were no bridle to hold them in." Despite widespread persecution, Calvinists won converts all over Europe. Calvinism was adopted by the Huguenots in France, by the Protestant (or Reformed) churches in Belgium and Holland, and by Presbyterians and Puritans in Scotland and England.

Protestantism in England. In England, King Henry VIII (r. 1509–1547) initially opposed the spread of Protestantism in his kingdom. But when the pope denied his request for an annulment of his marriage to Catherine of Aragon, Henry broke with Rome in 1534 and made

himself the head of a national Church of England (which promptly granted the annulment). Although Henry made few changes in Church doctrine, organization, and ritual, his daughter Queen Elizabeth I (r. 1558–1603) approved a Protestant confession of faith that incorporated both the Lutheran doctrine of salvation by grace and the Calvinist belief in predes-tination. To mollify traditionalists Elizabeth retained the Catholic ritual of Holy Communion—now conducted in English rather than in Latin—as well as the hierarchy of bishops and archbishops.

Elizabeth's compromises angered radical Protestants, who condemned the power of bishops as "anti-Christian and devilish and contrary to the Scriptures" and demanded major changes in Church organization. Many of these reformers took inspiration from the Presbyterian system pioneered in Calvin's Geneva and developed fully by John Knox for the Church of Scotland; in Scotland local congregations elected lay elders (presbyters), who assisted ministers in running the Church, and sent delegates to synods (councils) that decided Church doctrine. By 1600, at least five hundred ministers in the Church of England wanted to eliminate bishops and install a Presbyterian form of church government.

feminist Profs.

Self righteous

Other radical English Protestants were calling themselves "unspotted lambs of the Lord" or "Puritans." More intensely than most Protestants they wanted to "purify" the Church of "false" Catholic teachings and practices. Following radical Calvinist principles, Puritans condemned many traditional religious rites as magical or idolatrous. Puritan services avoided appeals to dead saints or the burning of incense and instead focused on a carefully argued sermon on ethics or dogma. Puritans also placed special emphasis on the idea of a "calling," the duty to serve God in one's work. To ensure that all men and women had access to God's commands, they encouraged everyone to read the Bible, thus promoting widespread literacy. Finally, most Puritans wanted authority over spiritual and financial matters to rest primarily with the local congregation, not with bishops or even Presbyterian synods (church councils). Eventually thousands of Puritan migrants would establish churches in North America based on these radical Protestant doctrines. *reject Apostolic Authority!*

The Dutch and the English Challenge Spain

Luther's challenge to Catholicism in 1517 came just two years before Cortés conquered the Aztec empire, and the two events remained linked. Gold and silver from Mexico and Peru made Spain the wealthiest nation in Europe and King Philip II (r. 1556–1598), the successor to Charles I, its most powerful ruler. In addition to Spain, Philip presided over wealthy city-states in Italy, the commercial and manufacturing provinces of the Spanish Netherlands (present-day Holland and Belgium), and, after 1580, Portugal and all its possessions in America, Africa, and the East Indies. "If the Romans were able to rule the world simply by ruling the Mediterranean," a Spanish priest boasted, "what of the man who rules the Atlantic and Pacific oceans, since they surround the world?"

Philip, an ardent Catholic, tried to root out Protestantism in the Netherlands, which had become wealthy from trade with the vast Portuguese empire and from the weaving of wool and linen. To protect their Calvinist faith and political liberties, the Dutch and Flemish provinces revolted in 1566, and in 1581 the seven northern provinces declared their independence, becoming the Dutch Republic (or Holland). When Elizabeth I of England dispatched 6,000 troops to assist the Dutch cause, Philip found a new enemy. In 1588 he sent the Spanish Armada—130 ships and 30,000 men—against England. Philip planned to reimpose Catholicism in England and then wipe out Calvinism in Holland. However, the Armada failed utterly, as English ships and a fierce storm destroyed the Spanish fleet. Philip continued to spend his American gold on foreign wars, undermining the Spanish economy and prompting the migration of hundreds of thousands of Spaniards to America. By the time of his death in 1598, Spain was in serious decline.

As Spain faltered, Holland prospered, the economic miracle of the seventeenth century. Amsterdam emerged as the financial capital of northern Europe, and the Dutch Republic became the leading commercial power of Europe, replacing Portugal as the dominant trader in

Dutch Merchant Family
This painting of Pierre de Moucheron and his family by the Dutch artist Cornelius de Zeeuw captures the prosperity and the severe Calvinist ethos of Holland in the sixteenth century. It also suggests the character of the traditional patriarchal family, in which status reflected a rigid hierarchy of gender and age. Rijksmuseum, Amsterdam.

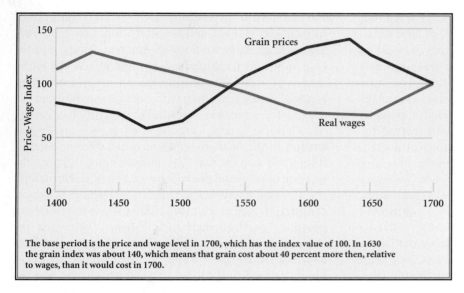

FIGURE 1.2 The Great Price Inflation and Living Standards in Europe

As American gold and silver poured into Europe after 1520, there was more money in circulation and people used it to bid up the price of grain. Grain prices also rose because of increasing demand; the result of growth in Europe's population. Because prices rose faster than wages living standards fell from a high point about 1430 to a low point about 1630. As "real wages" rose after 1630, people lived better.

The base period is the price and wage level in 1700, which has the index value of 100. In 1630 the grain index was about 140, which means that grain cost about 40 percent more then, relative to wages, than it would cost in 1700.

Asia and coastal Africa. The Dutch also looked across the Atlantic, creating the West India Company, which invested in sugar plantations in Brazil and the Caribbean and established the fur-trading colony of New Netherland in North America.

England also emerged as an important European state, its economy stimulated by a rise in population from 3 million in 1500 to 5 million in 1630. An equally important factor was the state-supported expansion of the merchant community. English merchants had long supplied high-quality wool to European weavers, and around 1500 they created their own system of textile production. In this **outwork** (or putting-out) system merchants bought wool from the owners of great estates and provided it to landless peasants, who spun and wove the wool into cloth. The merchants then sold the finished product in English and foreign markets. The government helped manufacturers to expand production by setting low rates for wages and assisted merchants to increase exports by granting special monopoly privileges to the Levant Company (Turkey) in

Elizabeth I (r. 1558–1603)

Attired in richly decorated clothes that symbolize her power, Queen Elizabeth I relishes the destruction of the Spanish Armada (pictured in background) and proclaims her nation's imperial ambitions. The queen's hand rests on a globe, asserting England's claims in the Western Hemisphere.

Woburn Abbey Collection, by permission of the Marquess of Tavistock and the Trustees of the Bedford Estates.

1581, the Guinea Company (Africa) in 1588, and the East India Company in 1600.

This system of state-assisted manufacturing and trade became known as mercantilism. Mercantilist-minded monarchs like Elizabeth I encouraged merchants to invest in domestic manufacturing, thereby increasing exports and reducing imports, in order to give England a favorable balance of trade. The queen and her advisors wanted gold and silver to flow into the country in payment for English manufactures, stimulating further economic expansion and enriching the merchant community. Increased trade also meant higher revenues from import duties, which swelled the royal treasury and enhanced the power of the national government. By 1600 the success of these merchant-oriented policies had laid the foundations for overseas colonization. The English (as well as the Dutch) now had the merchant fleets and economic wealth needed to challenge Spain's monopoly in the Western Hemisphere.

The Social Causes of English Colonization

England's monarchs and ministers of state had long been interested in America. Now economic changes in England (as well as continuing religious conflict) provided a large body of settlers willing to go to America. The massive expenditure of American gold and silver by Philip II and the Spanish conquistadors had doubled the money supply of Europe and sparked a major inflation between 1530 and 1600—known today as the Price Revolution—that brought about profound social changes in the English countryside (Figure 1.2).

The Decline of the Nobility.   In England the nobility was the first casualty of the **Price Revolution**. Aristocrats had customarily rented out their estates on long leases for fixed rents, gaining a secure income and plenty of leisure. As one English nobleman put it, "We eat and drink and rise up to play and this is to live like a gentleman." Then inflation struck. In less than two generations the price of goods more than tripled while the nobility's income from the rents on its farmlands barely increased. As the wealth and status of the aristocracy declined in relative terms, that of the **gentry** and the yeomen rose. The gentry (nonnoble landholders with substantial estates) kept pace with inflation by renting land on short leases at higher rates. Yeomen, described by a European traveler as "middle people of a condition between gentlemen and peasants," owned small farms that they worked with family help. As wheat prices tripled, yeomen used the profits to build larger houses and provide their children with land.

Economics influenced politics. As aristocrats lost wealth, their branch of Parliament, the House of Lords, declined in influence. At the same time, members of the rising gentry entered the House of Commons, the political voice of the propertied classes. Supported by the yeomen, the gentry demanded new rights and powers for the Commons, such as control of taxation. Thus the Price Revolution encouraged the rise of governing institutions in which rich commoners and small property owners had a voice, a development with profound consequences for English—and American—political history.

The Dispossession of the Peasantry.   Peasants and landless farm laborers made up three-fourths of the population of England (Figure 1.3), and their lives also were transformed by the Price Revolution. Many of these rural folk lived in open-field settlements, but the rise of domestic manufacturing increased the demand for wool, prompting profit-minded landlords and wool merchants to persuade Parliament to pass **enclosure acts**. These acts allowed owners to fence in open fields and put sheep to graze on them. Thus dispossessed of their land, peasant families lived on the brink of poverty, spinning and weaving wool or working as wage laborers on large estates. Wealthy men had "taken farms into their hands," an observer noted in 1600, "and rent them to those that will give most, whereby the

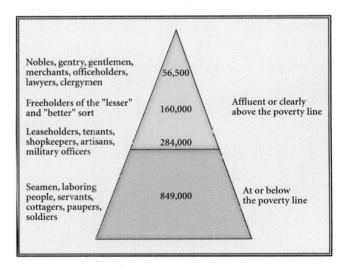

FIGURE 1.3 The Structure of English Society, 1688
This famous table, the work of Gregory King, an early statistician, shows the result of centuries of aristocratic rule. It depicts a social structure shaped like a thin pyramid, with a small privileged elite at the top and a mass of poor working people at the bottom. The majority of English families (some 849,000, according to King) lived at or below the poverty line and, he thought, were "Decreasing the Wealth of the Kingdom." In fact, the labor of the poor produced much of the wealth owned by the 500,500 families at the middle and the top of the social scale.

peasantry of England is decayed and become servants to gentlemen."

These changes, and a series of crop failures caused by cold weather between 1590 and 1640, set the stage for a substantial migration to America. As the danger of starvation increased and land prices continued to rise, thousands of yeomen families looked across the Atlantic for land for their children. Dispossessed peasants and weavers, their livelihoods threatened by a decline in the cloth trade, were likewise on the move. "Thieves and rogues do swarm the highways," warned Justice of the Peace William Lamparde, "and bastards be multiplied in parishes." Seeking food and security, tens of thousands of young propertyless laborers contracted to go to America in the lowly condition of indentured servants. This massive migration of English yeomen families and impoverished laborers would bring about a new collision between the European and Native American worlds.

FOR FURTHER EXPLORATION

▶ For definitions of key terms boldfaced in this chapter, see the glossary at the end of the book.

▶ To assess your mastery of the material covered in this chapter, see the Online Study Guide at **bedfordstmartins.com/henretta**.

▶ For suggested references, including Web sites, see page SR-1 at the end of the book.

▶ For map resources and primary documents, see **bedfordstmartins.com/henretta**.

The first inhabitants of the Western Hemisphere were hunter-gatherers who migrated from Asia some thirty thousand years ago. Their descendants settled throughout the Americas, establishing a great variety of cultures. In Mesoamerica, the Mayan and Aztec peoples created populous agricultural societies with sophisticated systems of art, religion, and politics, while the Incas set up an empire along the western coast of South America. In North America, the Hopewell and Mississippian peoples created elaborate ceremonial and urban sites, as did the Pueblo peoples of the Southwest. However, in 1500 most Indians north of the Rio Grande lived in small-scale communities of hunters and farmers.

The Europeans who invaded America came from a traditional agricultural society ruled by a privileged elite. Christianity provided unity and spiritual meaning to European civilization. Both church and state endorsed hierarchy and authority, demanding that peasants submit to strict discipline. Carried by settlers to America, these values of order and security strongly influenced colonial life.

The Crusades exposed Europeans to the learning of the Arab Muslim world, while the Italian Renaissance and the rise of monarchical nation-states imparted dynamism to European society. Portugal sent explorers and merchants to Africa and Asia and sold enslaved West Africans to sugar planters in the Mediterranean and later in Brazil. Spain conquered Mexico and Peru, the wealthiest areas of the "new world" found by Christopher Columbus. The coming of Europeans—and their diseases, crops, horses, government, and religion—brought death to millions of Native Americans and altered the ecology of Western Hemisphere. Likewise, the Columbian exchange and mass emigration of Europeans and enslaved Africans to the Americas changed the character of the "old world."

Thus, gold and silver from America disrupted Europe's economy and society, which was already reeling from the Protestant Reformation. Religious warfare and the Price Revolution undermined Catholic Spain while assisting the rise of Holland, France, and England. In England, monarchs used mercantilist policies to promote domestic manufacturing and foreign trade, while the enclosure acts and religious conflicts prompted a mass migration to America.

English migrants carried both traditional and modern ideas and institutions across the Atlantic—a contrast between old and new that was sharpened in America: in England's Chesapeake colonies a new form of aristocratic rule would emerge, based first on white indentured servitude and then on African slavery, while in New England the settlers would establish a yeoman society that had few European antecedents.

13,000–3000 B.C.	Main settlement of North America
3000–2000 B.C.	Cultivation of crops begins in Mesoamerica
100–400	Flourishing of Hopewell culture
300	Rise of Mayan civilization
500	Zenith of Teotihuacán civilization
600	Emergence of Pueblo cultures
700–1100	Spread of Arab Muslim civilization
800–1350	Development of Mississippian culture
1096–1291	Crusades link Europe with Arab learning
1300–1450	Italian Renaissance
1325	Aztecs establish capital at Tenochtitlán
1440s	Portugal enters trade in African slaves
1492	Christopher Columbus's first voyage to America
1513	Juan Ponce de León explores Florida
1517	Martin Luther begins Protestant Reformation
1519–1521	Hernán Cortés conquers Aztec empire
1531–1538	Francisco Pizarro vanquishes Incas in Peru
1534	Henry VIII establishes Church of England
1536	John Calvin, *Institutes of Christian Religion*
1550–1630	Price Revolution English mercantilism Enclosure acts
1556–1598	Philip I, king of Spain
1558–1603	Elizabeth I, queen of England
1560s	English Puritan movement begins

Jewish bankers decide to double value of money through paper money. Real cause of disruption!

37

The manner of their fishing.

CHAPTER 2

The Invasion and Settlement of North America

1550–1700

ESTABLISHING COLONIES IN THE DISTANT LAND OF NORTH AMERICA was not for the faint of heart. First came a long voyage in small ships over stormy, dangerous waters. Then the migrants, weakened by weeks of travel, spoiled food, and shipboard diseases, faced the challenges of life in an alien land inhabited by potentially hostile Indian peoples. "We neither fear them or trust them," declared Puritan settler Francis Higginson, but rely for protection on "our musketeers." Although the risks were great and the rewards uncertain, tens of thousands of Europeans crossed the Atlantic during the seventeenth century, driven by poverty and persecution at home or drawn by the lures of the New World: land, gold, and—as another Puritan migrant put it—the hope of "propagating the Gospel to these poor barbarous people."

For Native Americans, the European invasion was nothing short of catastrophic. "Our fathers had plenty of deer and skins, . . . and our coves were full of fish and fowl," the Narragansett chief Miantonomi warned the neighboring Montauk people in 1642, "but these English having gotten our land . . . their cows and horses eat the grass, and their hogs spoil our clam banks, and we shall all be starved." Whether they came as settlers or missionaries or fur traders, the white-skinned

◀ **Carolina Indians Fishing, 1585**

The artist John White was one of the English settlers in Sir Walter Raleigh's ill-fated colony on Roanoke Island, and his watercolors provide a rich visual record of Native American life. Here the Indians who resided near present-day Albemarle Sound in North Carolina are harvesting a protein-rich diet of fish from its shallow waters.
Trustees of the British Museum.

people spread havoc, bringing new diseases and religions and threatening Indian peoples with the loss of their cultures, lands, and lives. The stakes of the contest were enormous and demanded united resistance. "We [are] all Indians," Miantonomi continued, and must "say brother to one another, . . . otherwise we shall all be gone shortly." The first century of cultural contact foretold the course of North American history: the advance of the European invaders and the dispossession of the Indian peoples.

Imperial Conflicts and Rival Colonial Models

In Mesoamerica the Spanish colonial regime forced the Indians to convert to Catholicism and to work digging gold and farming large estates. But in the sparsely populated Indian lands north of the Rio Grande, other Europeans founded different types of colonies (Table 2.1). In the fur-trading empires created by the French and the Dutch, the native peoples retained their lands and political autonomy, while in the English colonies the rapidly multiplying settlers expelled the resident Indians, who were pushed ever farther to the west. Despite the differing goals of these colonial regimes—the exploitation of native labor by the Spanish, the trading of furs by the French and the Dutch, the creation of farming communities by

the English—nearly everywhere the Indian peoples eventually rose in revolt.

New Spain: Colonization and Conversion

In their ceaseless quest for gold, Spanish adventurers became the first Europeans to explore the southern and western United States. In the 1540s Francisco Vásquez de Coronado searched in vain for Cíbola, the fabled seven golden cities said to lie north of present-day Albuquerque. Continuing his search, Coronado dispatched expeditions that discovered the Grand Canyon in Arizona, the Pueblo peoples of New Mexico, and the grasslands of central Kansas. Simultaneously, Hernán de Soto and a force of 600 adventurers cut a bloody swath across the densely populated Southeast, doing battle with the Apalachees of northern Florida and the Coosas of northern Alabama but finding no gold and few other riches (Map 2.1).

By the 1560s few Spanish officials still dreamed of finding rich Indian empires north of Mexico. Now their main goal was to prevent other European nations from establishing settlements. Roving English "sea dogs" were already plundering Spanish possessions in the Caribbean, and French corsairs were attacking Spanish treasure ships, halving the Spanish crown's revenue. Equally ominously, French Protestants began to settle in Florida, long claimed by Spain. In response King Philip II ordered that the Frenchmen in Florida be "cast . . . out by the best

TABLE 2.1 European Colonies in North America before 1660

	Date	First Settlement	Type	Religion	Chief Export or Economic Activity
New France	1608	Quebec	Royal	Catholic	Furs
New Netherland	1613	New Amsterdam	Corporate	Dutch Reformed	Furs
New Sweden	1628	Fort Christina	Corporate	Lutheran	Furs; farming
English Colonies					
Virginia	1607	Jamestown	Corporate (Merchant)	Anglican	Tobacco
Plymouth	1620	Plymouth	Corporate (Religious)	Separatist-Puritan	Mixed farming; livestock
Massachusetts Bay	1630	Boston	Corporate (Religious)	Puritan	Mixed farming
Maryland	1634	St. Mary's	Proprietary	Catholic	Tobacco; grain
Connecticut	1635	Hartford	Corporate (Religious)	Puritan	Mixed farming; livestock
Rhode Island	1636	Providence	Corporate (Religious)	Separatist-Puritan	Mixed farming; livestock

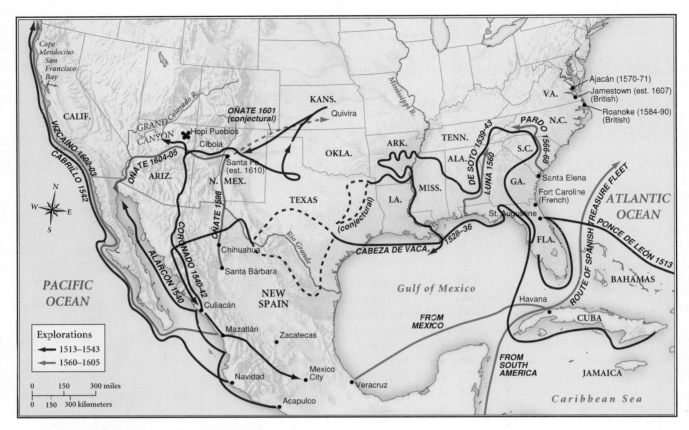

MAP 2.1 New Spain Looks North, 1513–1610

The quest for gold drew Spanish adventurers first to Florida and then deep into the present-day United States. When the wide-ranging expeditions of Hernán de Soto and Francisco Vásquez de Coronado failed to find gold or flourishing Indian civilizations, authorities in New Spain confined northern settlements to St. Augustine in Florida (to protect the treasure fleet) and Santa Fe in the upper Rio Grande Valley.

For more help analyzing this map, see the ONLINE STUDY GUIDE at bedfordstmartins.com/henretta.

means," and Spanish troops massacred 300 members of the "evil Lutheran sect."

To safeguard Florida, in 1565 Spain established a fort at St. Augustine, the first permanent European settlement in the future United States (see American Lives, "Luis de Velasco/Opechancanough/Massatamohtnock: A Case of Possible Multiple Identities," p. 42). It also founded a dozen other military outposts and religious missions, one as far north as Chesapeake Bay, but these were soon destroyed by Indian attacks. Spain also confronted a new threat from the Atlantic. In 1586 the English sea captain Sir Francis Drake sacked the important port city of Cartagena (in present-day Colombia) and nearly wiped out St. Augustine.

Franciscan Missions. Military setbacks at the hands of Native Americans prompted the Spanish crown to adopt a new policy toward the Indian peoples. The Comprehensive Orders for New Discoveries, issued in 1573, placed the "pacification" of new lands primarily in

the hands of missionaries, not conquistadors. Franciscan friars promptly established missions in the Pueblo world visited by Coronado two generations before, naming the area Nuevo México (Map 2.1). The friars built their missions and churches near existing Indian pueblos and farming villages and often learned Indian languages. Protected by Spanish soldiers, the robed and sandaled Franciscans smashed the religious idols of the Native Americans and, to win their allegiance to the Christian God, dazzled them with rich vestments, gold crosses, and silver chalices.

For the Franciscans, religious conversion and cultural assimilation went hand in hand. They introduced the European practice of having men instead of women grow most of the crops and encouraged the Indians to talk, cook, dress, and walk like Spaniards. The friars' rule was hardly benevolent. Sexual sinners and spirit worshipers were whipped, and monks generally ignored Spanish laws intended to protect the native peoples from coerced labor. This neglect allowed privileged Spanish landowners

Luis de Velasco/ Opechancanough/ Massatamohtnock: A Case of Possible Multiple Identities

Long before the Chesapeake Bay took its present name, it was known as the Bahía de Santa María (the Bay of Saint Mary), claimed by Spain and part of the giant colony of Florida that stretched from present-day Texas to Newfoundland. And long before the first English adventurers set foot in the colony they called Virginia, Spanish Jesuits established a mission there (in 1571) at Ajacán; they came to convert the local Algonquian inhabitants—the Powhatan people—to the Catholic faith.

For eighty years, from the 1560s to the 1640s, this land would be contested ground, as Spanish conquistadors, English adventurers, and native chiefs vied with one another for control of the land and its people. Strong but not conclusive evidence suggests that the life of one man spanned this eighty-year struggle and shaped its course. The Spanish knew him as Don Luis de Velasco, a young Indian cacique (chief) who had lived in Spain for a time and had apparently become a pious convert to the Catholic faith. A generation later the English probably encountered the same man as Opechancanough, a local chief, "the King of the Pamaunches" (Pamunkeys), and an astute negotiator who seemed to favor interracial peace. Finally, when Opechancanough succeeded his elder brother as the Powhatan, or main chief, in 1621, he assumed a new name, Massatamohtnock, and a new role: a diplomat-warrior who led two Indian uprisings.

Spanish Catholic convert, pacific leader and diplomat, zealous Native American patriot: Was this a case of several individuals or was there only one man? If so, what accounts for his multiple identities? A confused response to contradictory cultural pressures? Simple deception?

John Smith and Chief Opechancanough
The powerful Indian chief Opechancanough towers over the English adventurer John Smith in this engraving of their confrontation in 1609 over English access to Indian supplies of food. Library of Congress.

This puzzle has its origins in 1561, when two vessels commanded by the Spanish mariner and adventurer Pedro Menéndez de Avilés sailed into the Bahía de Santa María. Like other conquistadors Menéndez came looking for gold and plunder, but he also sought good harbors for naval garrisons to protect Spanish treasure ships from pirates. Menéndez went away without riches but bearing the youthful son of a local chief, an Indian "of fine presence and bearing," whom he promised to take to Europe "that the King of Spain, his lord, might see him." King Philip II was equally impressed by the imposing young cacique, who stood more than six feet tall. He granted the young Indian an allowance and had

Dominican friars teach him the Spanish language and the principles of the Catholic faith.

Three years later the young man was in Mexico, where he acquired a new patron, Don Luis de Velasco, the viceroy of New Spain, who became his godfather and gave the Indian his own name. Eager to return to his people, in 1566 the Indian Don Luis accompanied an expedition to the Bahía de Santa María that was blown off course, and he found himself once again in Spain. Under Jesuit instruction, a contemporary chronicler noted, "he was made ready and they gave him the holy sacraments of the altar and Confirmation." For his part, the Indian Don Luis convinced the Jesuit father Juan Baptista de Segura of his "plan and determination . . . of converting his parents, relatives, and countrymen to the faith of Jesus Christ, and baptizing them and making them Christians as he was."

Thus it was that the young Christianized Indian and eight Jesuit missionaries landed in 1571 in Ajacán, five miles from the later site of Jamestown. Once restored to the land of his childhood, Don Luis readopted its customs, taking a number of wives. Publicly chastised for adultery by Father Segura, he took refuge in his native village. When three missionaries came to fetch him, Don Luis had them killed with a "shower of arrows"; then, according to one account, he murdered Father Segura and the rest of the Jesuits by his own hand. The massacre brought quick retribution. In 1572 Menéndez personally led a punitive expedition that killed dozens of Indians, but his former protégé escaped his wrath.

At this point the historical record becomes cloudy, but there is strong circumstantial evidence that the young cacique, Don Luis, now took the name Opechancanough and became chief of the Pamunkeys. Both chiefs are described in the records as imposing in size, much taller than most Indians and most Europeans. And there is a chronological fit between their lives. When Don Luis returned to America in 1571, he was about twenty-five years old; in 1621, when Opechancanough succeeded Powhatan as chief, he was an elderly man. Finally, there is the translation of Opechancanough's name: "He whose soul is white"—perhaps a reference to his life as a Christian Indian or his remorse about Father Segura's fate.

As Spanish dreams of an eastern North American empire faded in the face of fierce Native American resistance, England dispatched its own adventurers to search for gold and promote "the Christian religion to such People as yet live in Darkness." Opechancanough first confronted the new invaders in December 1607, when he captured Captain John Smith but spared his life. Two years later, after Smith grabbed Opechancanough "by the long lock of his head; and with my pistol at his breast . . . made him fill our bark with twenty tuns of corn," the chief did not seek revenge. Instead, for the next decade, the Pamunkeys' leader pursued a complicated diplomatic strategy: he "stood aloof" from the English and "would not be drawn to any Treaty." In particular, he strongly resisted proposals to take Indian children from their parents so that they might be "brought upp in Christianytie." At the same time, Opechancanough promoted interracial peace by accepting the marriage of his niece Pocahontas to John Rolfe and by arranging a treaty between the English and a Chesapeake tribe. The chief's allegiance may have been divided between two worlds: Algonquian and European. An Indian in culture and outlook, he was also a person whose soul was "white."

Then, in 1621, this man assumed a new identity, taking the name Massatamohtnock. And he took up a new cause. The number of English migrants had greatly increased, leading many Algonquians to believe that the English would soon take up "all their lands and would drive them out the country." To prevent this, the aging Massatamohtnock played a double game. While assuring Governor Wyatt of Virginia that "the Skye should sooner falle than Peace be broken, on his parte," he secretly mobilized the Pamunkeys and more than two dozen other Indian peoples. In 1622 these tribes launched a surprise attack that took the lives of 347 English men, women, and children. Urging the chief of the Potomacks to continue the onslaught, Massatamohtnock declared his goal: "before the end of two Moons there should not be an Englishman in all their Countries."

Finally defeated in the late 1620s when the English systematically burned Indian cornfields, the old chief reappeared in 1644, orchestrating another surprise assault that took the lives of "near five hundred Christians." Now a hundred years old, "so decrepit that he was not able to walk alone but was carried about by his men," Massatamohtnock was captured by the English and taken to Jamestown. There, an English official reported, an angry soldier "basely shot him through the back . . . of which wound he died."

The absence of Algonquian sources makes it unlikely that we will ever know the complete history or the real motives of this remarkable man. But the violent treatment Don Luis meted out to Father Segura and the uprisings Massatamohtnock instigated in 1622 and 1644 suggest that ultimately he defined himself as an Indian patriot, a resolute enemy of the European invaders and their Christian religion.

Conversion in New Mexico

Franciscan friars introduced Catholicism to the Indian peoples north of the Rio Grande, assisted by nuns of various religious orders. This 1631 engraving shows one of those nuns, María de Jesús de Agreda, preaching to a nomadic people (los chichimecos) in New Mexico.

Nettie Lee Benson Latin American Collection, University of Texas at Austin.

[handwritten: She did this by bi location She never left Spain!]

(**encomenderos**) who lived near the missions to collect tribute from the native population, both in goods and in forced labor. The Franciscan missions also depended on Indian workers, who grew the crops and carried them to market, often on their backs. Most Native Americans tolerated the Franciscans out of fear of military reprisals or in hopes of learning their spiritual secrets. But when Christian prayers failed to prevent European diseases, extended droughts, and Apache raids from devastating their communities, many Indians returned to their ancestral religions and began to blame Spanish rule for their ills. Thus, the chief and people of Hawikuh refused to become "wet-heads" (as Indians called baptized Christians) "because with the water of baptism they would have to die."

Indian Revolts. In 1598 the already tense relations between Indians and Spaniards deteriorated when Juan de Oñate led an expedition of 500 Spanish soldiers and settlers into New Mexico to establish a fort and a trading

villa. Oñate's men seized corn and clothing from the Pueblo peoples and murdered or raped those who resisted. When Indians of the Acoma pueblo killed 11 soldiers, the remaining troops destroyed the pueblo, killing 500 men and 300 women and children. Faced by now-hostile Indian peoples, most of the settlers withdrew. In 1610 the Spanish returned, founding the town of Santa Fe and reestablishing the system of missions and forced labor.

By 1680 nearly a hundred years of European diseases, forced tribute, and raids by Navajos and Apaches threatened many pueblos in New Mexico with extinction. Their population, which had once numbered 60,000, had declined to a mere 17,000. In desperation the Indian shaman (priest) Popé led the peoples of two dozen pueblos in a carefully coordinated rebellion, killing over 400 Spaniards and forcing the remaining 2,000 colonists to flee three hundred miles down the Rio Grande to El Paso. Repudiating Christianity, the Pueblo peoples desecrated churches and tortured and killed twenty-one missionaries. Reconquered a decade later, the Indians rebelled again in 1696, only to be subdued. Exhausted by war but having won the right to practice their own religion and avoid forced labor, the Pueblo peoples accepted their dependent position, joining with the Spanish to defend their lands against attacks by nomadic Indians.

Spain had managed to maintain its northern empire but had largely failed to achieve its goals of religious conversion and cultural assimilation. Taken aback by the military costs of expansion, Spanish officials decided not to undertake the settlement of the distant region of California, delaying until 1769 the permanent European occupation of that area. For the time being, Florida and New Mexico stood as the defensive outposts of Spain's American empire.

New France: Furs and Souls

Far to the northeast the French likewise tried to convert the native peoples to Catholicism. In the 1530s Jacques Cartier had claimed the lands bordered by the Gulf of St. Lawrence for France, but the first permanent French settlement came only in 1608, when Samuel de Champlain founded Quebec. Despite a series of brutal famines in northwestern France and the availability of attractive leaseholds in the fertile St. Lawrence Valley, few peasants migrated to America. Government policy was partly to blame. France's Catholic monarchs wanted an ample supply of military recruits at home. They also barred Huguenots (French Protestants) from settling in Quebec, fearing they would not be loyal to the crown. Moreover, the French peasantry held strong legal rights to their village lands and feared the short growing seasons and long bitter winters in Quebec. As one official remarked in 1684, Canada was "regarded as a country at the end of the world," a virtual sentence of "civil death." Of the 27,000 French men and women who migrated to Quebec, nearly

Samuel de Champlain

Going to War with the Hurons

Best known as the founder of Quebec, Samuel de Champlain was primarily a soldier and an adventurer. After fighting in the French religious wars, Champlain joined the Company of New France, determined to create a French empire in North America. In 1603 he traveled down the St. Lawrence River as far as Quebec, lived for three years in the company's failed settlement in Maine, and in 1608 returned to Quebec. To ensure French access to western fur trade, the following year Champlain joined the Hurons in a raid against the Iroquois, which he later described in a book of his American adventures.

Pursuing our route, I met some two or three hundred savages, who were encamped in huts near a little island called St. Eloi.... We made a reconnaissance, and found that they were tribes of savages called Ochasteguins [Hurons] and Algonquins, on their way to Quebec to assist us in exploring the territory of the Iroquois, with whom they are in deadly hostility.... [We joined with them and] went to the mouth of the River of the Iroquois [the Richelieu River, where it joins the St. Lawrence], where we stayed two days, refreshing ourselves with good venison, birds, and fish, which the savages gave us.

In all their encampments, they have their Pilotois, or Ostemoy, a class of persons who play the part of soothsayers, in whom these people have faith. One of these builds a cabin, surrounds it with small pieces of wood and covers it with his robe: after it is built, he places himself inside, so as not to be seen at all, when he seizes and shakes one of the posts of his cabin, muttering some words between his teeth, by which he says he invokes the devil, who appears to him in the form of a stone, and tells them whether they will meet their enemies and kill many of them.... They frequently told me that the shaking of the cabin, which I saw, proceeded from the devil, who made it move, and not the man inside, although I could see the contrary.... They told me also that I should see fire come out from the top, which I did not see at all.

Now, as we began to approach within two or three days' journey of the abode of our enemies, we advanced only at night.... By day, they withdraw into the interior of the woods, where they rest, without straying off, neither making any noise, even for the sake of cooking, so as not to be noticed in case their enemies should by accident pass by. They make no fire, except in smoking, which amounts to almost nothing. They eat baked Indian meal, which they soak in water, when it becomes a kind of porridge....

In order to ascertain what was to be the result of their undertaking, they often asked me if I had had a dream, and seen their enemies, to which I replied in the negative.... [Then one night] while sleeping, I dreamed that I saw our enemies, the Iroquois, drowning near a mountain, within sight. When I expressed a wish to help them, our allies, the savages, told me we must let them all die.... This, upon being related [to our allies], gave them so much confidence that they did not doubt any longer that good was to happen to them....

[After our victory over the Iroquois] they took one of the prisoners, to whom they made a harangue, enumerating the cruelties which he and his men had already practiced toward them without any mercy, and that, in like manner, he ought to make up his mind to receive as much. They commanded him to sing, if he had courage, which he did; but it was a very sad song.

Meanwhile, our men kindled a fire; and, when it was well burning, they brand, and burned this poor creature gradually, so as to make him suffer greater torment. Sometimes they stopped, and threw water on his back. Then they tore out his nails, and applied fire to the extremities of his fingers and private member. Afterwards, they flayed the top of his head, and had a kind of gum poured all hot upon it....

Source: Samuel de Champlain, *Voyages of Samuel de Champlain, 1604–1618,* ed. W. L. Grant (New York: Charles Scribner's Sons, 1907), 79–86.

---

two-thirds eventually returned to their homeland. In 1698 the European population of New France was only 15,200, compared with 100,000 settlers in the English colonies.

Rather than developing as a settler colony, New France instead became a vast fur-trading enterprise, and French explorers traveled deep into the continent to seek new suppliers. In return for French support against the Five Nations of the Iroquois, the Huron Indians (who lived just to the north of the Great Lakes) allowed Champlain and his fur traders into their territory (see Voices from Abroad, "Samuel de Champlain: Going to War with the Hurons," above). By 1673 another French explorer,

Jacques Marquette, reached the Mississippi River in present-day Wisconsin and traveled as far south as Arkansas. Seeking fortune as well as fame, in 1681 Robert de La Salle traveled down the Mississippi to the Gulf of Mexico, completing exploration of the majestic river. As a French priest noted with disgust, La Salle's expedition hoped "to buy all the Furs and Skins of the remotest Savages, who, as they thought, did not know their Value; and so enrich themselves in one single voyage." To honor Louis XIV, the Sun King, La Salle named the region he explored Louisiana; soon it included the small but thriving port of New Orleans on the Gulf of Mexico.

Despite their small numbers, French traders had a disastrous impact on Native Americans living near the Great Lakes. By introducing European diseases, they unwittingly triggered epidemics that killed 25 to 90 percent of the residents of many Indian villages, including those of their Huron allies. Moreover, by providing a market for deerskins and beaver pelts, the French set in motion a devastating series of Indian wars. Beginning in the 1640s, the New York Iroquois seized control of the fur trade by launching aggressive expeditions against the Hurons, forcing them to migrate to the north and west.

While French traders amassed furs, French priests sought converts among both the defeated Hurons and the belligerent Iroquois. Between 1625 and 1763 hundreds of Jesuit priests lived among the Indians and, to a greater extent than the Spanish Franciscans, came to understand their values. One Jesuit reported a Huron belief that "our souls have desires which are inborn and concealed, yet are made known by means of dreams"; he then used this belief to explain the Christian doctrines of immortality and salvation to the native peoples. At first many Indians welcomed the French "Black Robes" as powerful spiritual beings with magical secrets, such as the ability to forge iron, but, as in New Mexico, skepticism grew when prayers to the Christian God did not protect them from disease and enemy attack. A Peoria chief charged that the priest's "fables are good only in his own country; we have our own [religious beliefs], which do not make us die as his do."

Unlike the Spanish Franciscans, the French Jesuits did not use Indians for forced labor and tried to keep alcoholic beverages, which wreaked havoc among Indian peoples, from becoming a bargaining item in the French fur trade. Moreover, the French Jesuits won converts by addressing Indian needs. In the 1690s young women of the Illinois people in the Mississippi River Valley embraced the cult of the Virgin Mary, using its emphasis on chastity to assert the Algonquian belief that unmarried women were "masters of their own body."

Still, the French fur-trading system brought war and cultural devastation to the Indian peoples of eastern North America. According to an oral history of the Iroquois, "Everywhere there was peril and everywhere mourning. Feuds with outer nations, feuds with brother nations,

feuds of . . . sister towns and feuds of families and of clans made every warrior a stealthy man who liked to kill."

New Netherland: Commerce

Unlike the French and Spanish, the Dutch in North America had little interest in religious conversion. Their eyes were fastened on commerce, for the Dutch Republic was the trading hub of Europe. In 1609 Henry Hudson, an Englishman employed by the Dutch East India Company, found and named the Hudson River in the area of present-day New York, and a few years later the Dutch established fur-trading posts on Manhattan Island and at Fort Orange (present-day Albany). In 1621 the Dutch government chartered the West India Company, giving it a trade monopoly in West Africa and exclusive authority to establish outposts in America. Three years later the company founded the town of New Amsterdam on Manhattan Island, the capital of New Netherland (Map 2.2).

The wilderness fur-trading posts attracted few Dutch settlers, and their small size made them vulnerable to invasion by rival European nations. To encourage migration of permanent settlers, the West India Company granted huge estates along the Hudson River to wealthy Dutchmen, stipulating that each proprietor settle fifty tenants on his land within four years or lose it; by 1646 only one proprietor, Kiliaen Van Rensselaer, had succeeded. The population in Dutch North America remained small, reaching only 1,500 in 1664.

Although New Netherland failed as a settler colony, it flourished briefly as a fur-trading enterprise. In 1633 Dutch traders at Fort Orange exported thirty thousand beaver and otter pelts. Subsequently, the Dutch seized prime farming land from the Algonquian-speaking peoples and took over their trading network, in which corn and wampum from Long Island were exchanged for furs from Maine. The Algonquians responded with force. By the end of a bloody two-year war more than 200 Dutch residents and 1,000 Indians had been killed, many in brutal massacres of women, children, and elderly men. After the war the Dutch traders expanded their profitable links with the Mohawks, one of the Iroquois Nations of New York and a long-time foe of the Algonquians, exchanging guns and other manufactures

▶ **MAP 2.2 The Eurasian Trade System and Overseas Spheres of Influence, 1650**
Between 1550 and 1650 Spanish, Portuguese, and Dutch merchants took control of the maritime trade of the Southern Hemisphere, carrying goods to Europe from China, the Philippines, Indonesia, and India. They also created the South Atlantic system (see Chapter 3), transporting African slaves to European-run plantations in Brazil and the Caribbean and returning to Europe with valuable cargoes of sugar. After 1600 the Spanish and the Dutch began to settle and trade in North America as well. (To trace changes in trade and empires over time, see also Map 1.4 on p. 22 and Map 5.1 on p. 134.)

Cathlic France is leftout of this map!

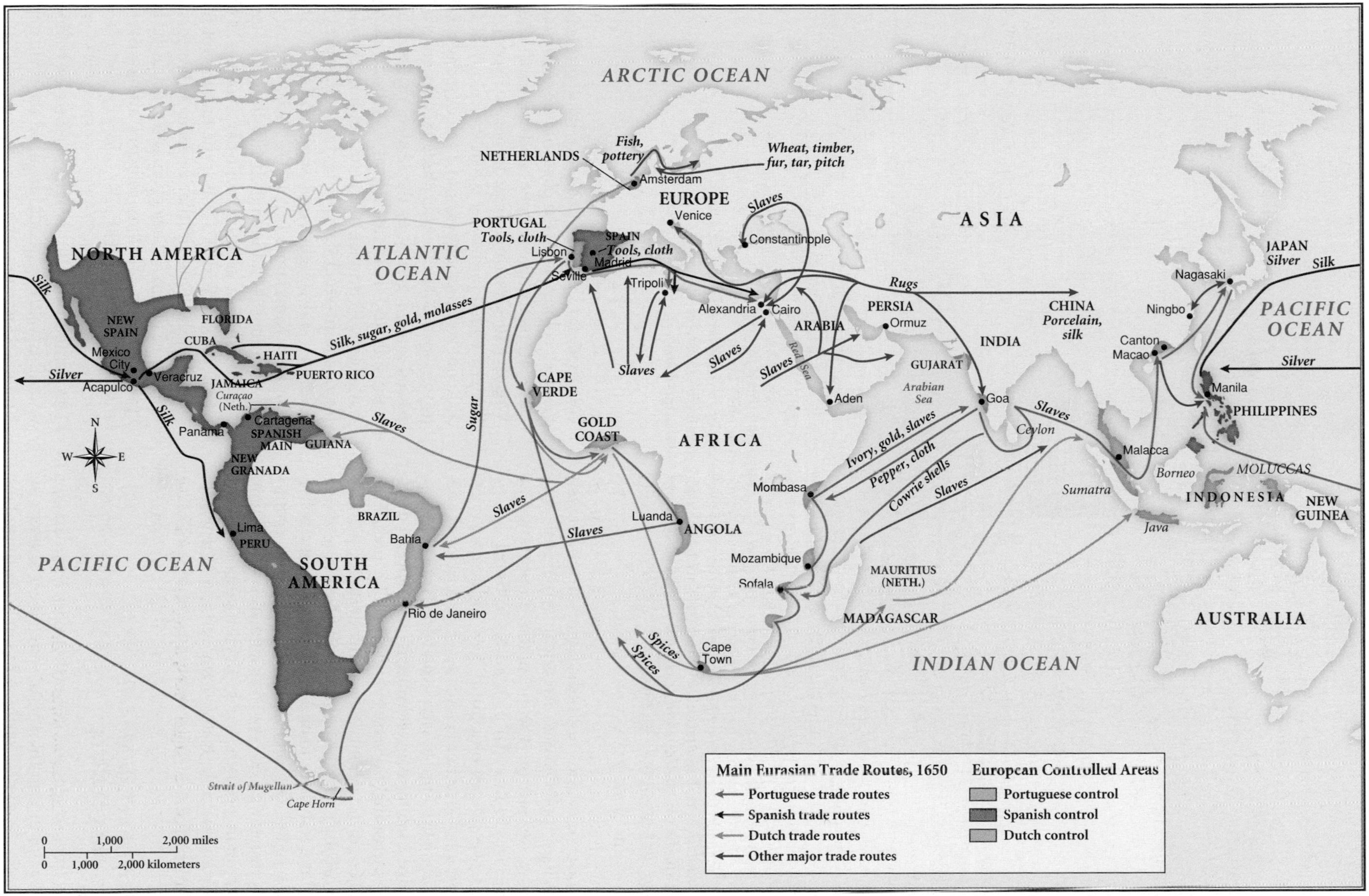

Main Eurasian Trade Routes, 1650

ARCTIC OCEAN

PACIFIC OCEAN

NORTH AMERICA

NEW SPAIN

Mexico City
Veracruz
Acapulco

FLORIDA
CUBA
HAITI
JAMAICA
PUERTO RICO
Curaçao (Neth.)
Cartagena
Panama
SPANISH MAIN
NEW GRANADA
GUIANA

SOUTH AMERICA

PERU
Lima

BRAZIL
Bahia
Rio de Janeiro

Strait of Magellan
Cape Horn

ATLANTIC OCEAN

Silk
Silver
Silk, sugar, gold, molasses
Silver
Silk
Sugar
Slaves

EUROPE
Amsterdam
NETHERLANDS
PORTUGAL
Tools, cloth
Lisbon
SPAIN
Madrid
Seville
Tools, cloth

Venice
Constantinople
Tripoli
Alexandria
Cairo
ARABIA
Red Sea
Aden
PERSIA
Ormuz

Fish, pottery
Wheat, timber, fur, tar, pitch
Slaves
Slaves
Slaves
Rugs

AFRICA
CAPE VERDE
GOLD COAST
ANGOLA
Luanda
Mombasa
Mozambique
Sofala
Cape Town

Slaves
Slaves
Slaves
Slaves
Spices
Spices
Ivory, gold, slaves
Cowrie shells
Pepper, cloth
Cowrie shells, slaves

ASIA
INDIA
GUJARAT
Goa
Ceylon
Arabian Sea

CHINA
Porcelain, silk
JAPAN
Silver
Silk
Nagasaki
Ningbo
Canton
Macao

PHILIPPINES
Manila
MOLUCCAS
NEW GUINEA
INDONESIA
Borneo
Sumatra
Java
Malacca

MAURITIUS (NETH.)
MADAGASCAR

INDIAN OCEAN

PACIFIC OCEAN

AUSTRALIA

European Controlled Areas
- Portuguese control
- Spanish control
- Dutch control

Portuguese trade routes
Spanish trade routes
Dutch trade routes
Other major trade routes

N E S W
0   1,000   2,000 miles
0   1,000   2,000 kilometers

47

New Amsterdam, c. 1640
As the wooden palisade surrounding the town indicates, New Amsterdam was a frontier settlement, a fortlike trading post at the edge of vast lands populated by alien Indian peoples. The first settlers, remembering the architecture and waterways of Amsterdam and other Dutch cities, built houses in the Dutch style, with their gable ends facing the street (note the middle two houses), and excavated a canal across lower Manhattan Island, connecting the Hudson and East Rivers. Library of Congress.

for furs. However, the West India Company now largely ignored its crippled North American settlement, concentrating instead on the profitable importation of African slaves to its sugar plantations in Brazil.

Moreover, Dutch officials in New Amsterdam ruled shortsightedly. Governor Peter Stuyvesant rejected the demands of English Puritan settlers on Long Island for a representative system of government and alienated the colony's increasingly diverse population of Dutch, English, and Swedish migrants. Consequently, in 1664, during an Anglo-Dutch war, the population of New Amsterdam offered little resistance to an English invasion and subsequently accepted English rule. For the rest of the century the renamed towns of New York and Albany remained small fur-trading centers, Dutch-English outposts in a region still dominated by Native Americans. In Albany, Mohawk remained the language of business until the 1720s.

The First English Model: Tobacco and Settlers

The first English ventures in North America, undertaken by minor nobility in the 1580s, were abject failures. Sir Humphrey Gilbert's settlement in Newfoundland

collapsed for lack of financing, and Sir Ferdinando Gorges's colony along the coast of Maine foundered because of inadequate supplies and the harsh climate. Sir Walter Raleigh's three expeditions to North Carolina likewise ended in disaster when the colony he financed at Roanoke vanished without a trace (today it is known as the "lost" colony). After these failures, merchants replaced landed gentry as the leaders of English expansion; initially, their main goal was trade rather than settlement. To provide adequate funding, the merchants formed **joint-stock companies** that sold shares to many investors and sought royal support. In 1606 the new monarch, King James I (r. 1603–1625), granted a group of ambitious London merchants the right to exploit North America from present-day North Carolina to southern New York. To honor the memory of Elizabeth I, the "Virgin Queen," the company's directors named the region Virginia. They promised to settle the land and "propagate the *Christian* religion" among the "infidels and Savages" (Map 2.3).

The Jamestown Settlement.   However, trade for gold and other valuable goods remained the main goal of the Virginia Company, and the first expedition in 1607

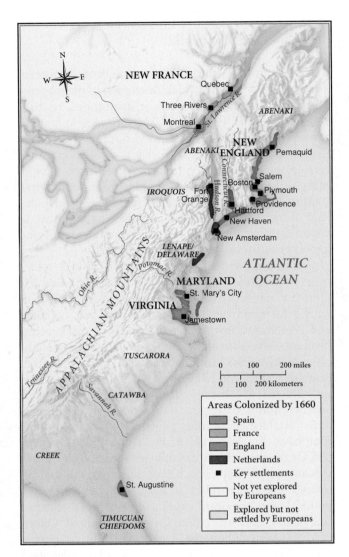

MAP 2.3 Eastern North America in 1650

Four European nations had permanent settlements in eastern North America by 1650, but only England had substantial numbers of settlers, some 25,000 in New England and another 15,000 in the Chesapeake region. However, the European presence extended into the interior, as colonial authorities established diplomatic and commercial relations with neighboring Indian peoples and as French and Dutch fur traders carried European goods and diseases to distant tribes.

included only traders and adventurers—no settlers, ministers, or women. The company retained ownership of all the land and appointed a governor and a small council to direct the adventurers, who were its employees or "servants." They were expected to procure their own food and ship anything of value to England— gold, exotic crops, and Indian merchandise. Some of the employees were young gentlemen with personal ties to the shareholders of the company but no experience in living off the land: a bunch of "unruly Sparks, packed off by their Friends to escape worse Destinies at home." The rest were cynical adventurers bent on seizing gold from the Indians or turning a quick profit from trade in

English cloth and metalware. All they wanted, as one of them said, was to "dig gold, refine gold, load gold."

Unfortunately, such traders were unprepared for the challenges of the new environment. Arriving in Virginia after a hazardous four-month voyage, the newcomers settled on a swampy peninsula on a river. They named both their new home (Jamestown) and the waterway (James River) after the king. Because the adventurers had chosen an unhealthful location with little fresh water and refused to plant crops, their fate was sealed. Of the 120 Englishmen who embarked on the expedition, only 38 were alive nine months later, and death continued to take a high toll. By 1611 the Virginia Company had sent 1,200 settlers to Jamestown, but fewer than half had survived. "Our men were destroyed with cruell diseases, as Swellings, Fluxes, Burning Fevers, and by warres," reported one of the leaders, "but for the most part they died of meere famine."

Native American hostility was a major threat to the survival of the settlement. Upon their arrival, the traders had been immediately confronted by the Pamunkey chief Powhatan, the leader of the Algonquian-speaking tribes of the region, some 14,000 people in all. Powhatan, whom the adventurer John Smith described as a "grave majestical man," allowed his followers to exchange their corn for English cloth and iron hatchets but treated the English as one of the dependent peoples of his chiefdom.

As conflicts over food and land increased, Powhatan threatened war, accusing the English of coming "not to trade but to invade my people and possess my country." In 1614 the Indian leader tried another strategy to integrate the newcomers into his chiefdom, allowing the marriage of his daughter Pocahontas to the adventurer John Rolfe. This tactic also failed, in part because Rolfe imported tobacco seeds from the West Indies and began to cultivate the crop, which was already popular in England. Tobacco quickly became the basis of economic life in Virginia, setting in motion the creation of a settler society.

New Political Institutions. To attract migrants to its increasingly valuable colony, the Virginia Company instituted a new and far-reaching set of policies. In 1617 it allowed individual settlers to own land, granting one hundred acres to every freeman in Virginia, and established a **headright** system giving every incoming head of a household a right to fifty acres of land and fifty additional acres for every servant. The following year the company issued a "great Charter" that swept away the military-style regime of Governor Sir Thomas Dale, laying the basis for a system of representative government. The House of Burgesses, which first convened in Jamestown in 1619, had the authority to make laws and levy taxes, although the governor or the company council in England could veto its legislative acts. By 1622 these incentives of land ownership for ordinary settlers, self-government by local leaders, and a court system based on "the lawes of the realme of England" had attracted about 4,500 new recruits. Virginia was on the verge of becoming an established colony.

However, the influx of settlers sparked all-out war with the Indians. Land-hungry farmers demanded access to land that the Native Americans had cleared and were using, alarming Opechancanough, Powhatan's brother and successor. Mobilizing the peoples of many Chesapeake tribes, in 1622 Opechancanough launched a surprise attack, killing nearly a third of the white population and vowing to drive the rest into the ocean. The English retaliated by harvesting the Indians' cornfields, providing food for themselves while depriving their enemies of sustenance, a strategy that gradually secured the safety of the colony.

The cost of the war was high for both sides. The Indians killed many settlers and destroyed much property, but Opechancanough's strategy had failed; rather than ending the English invasion, the uprising accelerated it. As one English militiaman put it, "[We now felt we could] by right of Warre, and law of Nations, invade the Country, and destroy them who sought to destroy us; whereby wee shall enjoy their cultivated places . . . possessing the fruits of others' labour." The invaders sold captured warriors into slavery and took control of huge areas of land. By 1630 the colonists in Virginia had created a flourishing tobacco economy and a stable English-style local polity, controlled by landed gentlemen sitting as justices of the peace.

The Chesapeake Experience

The English colonies in the Chesapeake brought wealth to some people but poverty and moral degradation to many more. Settlers forcefully dispossessed Indians of their lands, and prominent families ruthlessly pursued their dreams of wealth by exploiting the labor of English indentured servants and enslaved African laborers.

Settling the Tobacco Colonies

Distressed by the Indian uprising of 1622, James I dissolved the Virginia Company, accusing its directors of mismanagement, and created a royal colony in 1624. Under the terms of the charter, the king and his ministers appointed the governor and a small advisory council. The king allowed the House of Burgesses to remain, but any legislation it enacted required ratification by his Privy Council. James also legally established the Church of England in Virginia, so that all property owners had to pay taxes to support the clergy. These institutions—a royal governor, an elected assembly, and an established Anglican church—became the model for royal colonies throughout English America.

Catholics in Maryland. However, a second tobacco-growing settler colony, which developed in neighboring Maryland, had a different set of institutions. In 1632 King Charles I (r. 1625–1649), the successor to James I, conveyed most of the territory bordering the vast Chesapeake Bay to Cecilius Calvert, an aristocrat who carried the title Lord Baltimore. As the proprietor of Maryland (named in honor of Queen Henrietta Maria, Charles's wife), Baltimore could sell, lease, or give this land away as he wished. He also had the authority to appoint public officials and to found churches and appoint ministers.

Baltimore wanted Maryland to become a refuge from persecution for his fellow English Catholics. He therefore devised a policy of religious toleration intended to minimize confrontations between Catholics and Protestants, instructing the governor (his brother, Leonard Calvert) to allow "no scandall nor offence to be given to any of the Protestants" and to "cause All Acts of Romane Catholicque Religion to be done as privately as may be." In 1634, twenty gentlemen (mostly Catholics) and two hundred artisans and laborers (mostly Protestants) established St. Mary's City, which overlooked the mouth of the Potomac River. The population grew quickly, for the Calverts carefully planned and supervised the colony's development, hiring skilled artisans and offering ample grants of land to wealthy migrants. However, political and religious conflict constantly threatened Maryland's stability. When Governor Leonard Calvert tried to govern without the "Advice, Assent, and Approbation" of the freemen of the colony, as the charter specified, a representative assembly elected by the freemen insisted on the right to initiate legislation, which Lord Baltimore grudgingly granted. Uprisings by Protestant settlers also endangered Maryland's religious mission. To protect his Catholic coreligionists, who remained a minority, Lord Baltimore persuaded the assembly to enact a Toleration Act (1649) granting religious freedom to all Christians.

Tobacco and Disease. In Maryland, as in Virginia, tobacco was the basis of the economy. Indians had long used tobacco, a substance unknown in Europe before the Columbian Exchange, as a medicine and a stimulant. By the 1620s English men and women were craving tobacco and the nicotine it contained, smoking, chewing, and snorting it with abandon. Initially James I condemned the use of this "vile Weed" and warned that its "black stinking fumes" were "baleful to the nose, harmful to the brain, and dangerous to the lungs." But the king's attitude changed as revenues from an import tax on tobacco filled the royal treasury.

European demand for tobacco set off a forty-year economic boom in the Chesapeake, attracting thousands

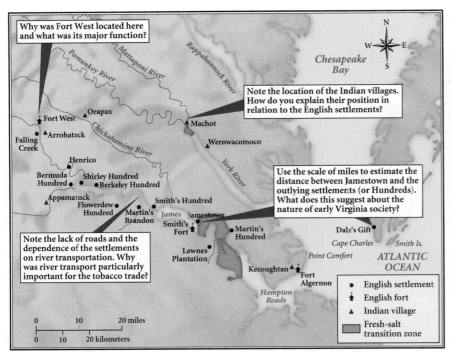

MAP 2.4 River Plantations in Virginia, c. 1640

The first migrants settled in widely dispersed plantations—and different disease environments—along the James River. The growth of the tobacco economy continued this pattern as wealthy planter-merchants traded with English ship captains from their riverfront plantations. Consequently, few substantial towns or trading centers developed in the Chesapeake region.

of profit-hungry migrants. "All our riches for the present do consist in tobacco," a planter remarked in 1630. Exports rose from about 3 million pounds in 1640 to 10 million pounds in 1660. Planters moved up the river valleys, establishing large farms (plantations) that were distant from one another but easily reached by water (Map 2.4). The scarcity of towns meant a much weaker sense of community than existed in the open-field villages of rural England.

For most of the seventeenth century life in the Chesapeake colonies remained harsh, brutish, and short. Most men never married because there were few women settlers, and families were often disrupted by early death. Mosquitoes as well as tobacco flourished in the mild Chesapeake climate, spreading malaria and weakening people's resistance to other diseases (Table 2.2). Pregnant women were especially hard hit. Many died after bearing a first or second child. In Middlesex County, Virginia, more than 60 percent of children lost one or both of their parents by the time they were thirteen. Orphaned children and unmarried young men constituted a large fraction of the society,

TABLE 2.2 Environment, Disease, and Death in Virginia, 1618–1624

Zone of James River Estuary	Percentage of Colony Population in Zone	Annual Mortality in Zone	Percentage of All Deaths in Colony
Freshwater	28.5%	16.7%	16.9%
Freshwater/Saltwater Mix	49.3%	37.1%	64.6%
Saltwater	22.2%	23.3%	18.4%
Estimated Annual Mortality Rate for Virginia: 28.3%			

Early Virginia was a deadly place, with no less than 28 percent of the population dying *each and every* year, mostly from typhoid fever and dysentery (the "bloody flux"). Only a constant stream of migrants allowed slow population growth. Most settlers lived along the James River estuary, and their place of residence determined their chances of survival. The most dangerous environment was the zone of water that was fresh in the spring, when the river ran fast, and mixed fresh and salt in the summer—when the inflow of saltwater from the Atlantic Ocean trapped human and animal waste from upriver and contaminated the water and its fish, oysters, and crabs. The year-round saltwater zone was the next most deadly, because of both fecal contamination and salt poisoning from drinking "brackish" well water.

Source: Adapted from Carville V. Earle, "Environment, Disease, and Mortality in Early Virginia," in *The Chesapeake in the Seventeenth Century,* ed. Thad W. Tate and David L. Ammerman (New York: W. W. Norton, 1979), Table 3.

The Tobacco Economy

Most poor farmers raised tobacco, for it grew just as well in small fields as on vast plantations. Large-scale operations, such as the one pictured here, used indentured servants and slaves to grow and process the crop. The workers cured the tobacco stalks by hanging them for several months in a well-ventilated shed; then they stripped the leaves and packed them tightly into large plantation-made barrels, or "hogsheads," for shipment to Europe. Library of Congress.

For more help analyzing this image, see the ONLINE STUDY GUIDE at bedfordstmartins.com/henretta.

inhibiting population growth. Although 15,000 settlers arrived in Virginia between 1622 and 1640, the number of English settlers rose only from 2,000 to 8,000.

Masters, Servants, and Slaves

Despite the dangers, the prospect of owning land continued to lure migrants to the Chesapeake region. By

1700 more than 80,000 English settlers had moved to Virginia, and another 20,000 had arrived in Maryland, the great majority not as free men and women but as indentured servants.

Indentured Servants. English shipping registers provide insight into the background of these servants. Three-quarters of the 5,000 servants who embarked from the port of Bristol were young men, many of whom had traveled hundreds of miles searching for work. Once in Bristol, these penniless wanderers were persuaded by merchants and sea captains to sign labor contracts called **indentures** and embark for the Chesapeake. The indentures bound them to work in return for room and board for a period of four or five years, after which they would be free, able to marry and work for themselves, planting corn for sustenance and tobacco for sale.

For merchants, servants represented valuable cargo because their contracts fetched high prices from Chesapeake planters. For the plantation owners, they were an incredible bargain. During the tobacco boom a male indentured servant could produce five times his purchase price in a year. Furthermore, imported servants were counted as household members, and so planters in Virginia received fifty acres of land for each one.

Most masters ruled their servants with an iron hand, beating them for bad behavior and withholding permission to marry. If a servant ran away or became pregnant, a master went to court to increase the term of service. Female servants were especially vulnerable to abuse, from both male servants and their owners. As a Virginia law of 1692 stated, "dissolute masters have gotten their maids with child; and yet claim the benefit of their service." Planters got rid of uncooperative servants by selling their contracts to new masters. As an Englishman remarked in disgust, in Virginia "servants were sold up and down like horses."

For most indentured servants this ordeal did not provide the escape from poverty they had sought (see American Voices, "Richard Frethorne: Hard Times in Early Virginia," p. 53). Half the men died before receiving their freedom, and another quarter remained poor. The remaining quarter benefited from their ordeal, acquiring property and respectability (Table 2.3). If they survived, female servants generally fared better because men in the Chesapeake had grown "very sensible of the Misfortune of Wanting Wives." Many such servants married their masters or other well-established men. By migrating to the Chesapeake, these few—and very fortunate—men and women escaped a life of landless poverty in England.

African Laborers. The first African workers fared worse. In 1619 John Rolfe noted that "a Dutch man of warre . . . sold us twenty Negars," but for a generation the numbers of Africans remained small. About 400 Africans lived in the Chesapeake colonies in 1649,

Richard Frethorne

Hard Times in Early Virginia

The lot of an indentured servant in Virginia was always hard, especially before 1630, when food was scarce and Indians were a constant danger. In 1623 Richard Frethorne wrote a letter to his parents begging them to buy out the remaining years of his labor contract so that he could return to England. Richard Frethorne's fate is unknown, but documentary evidence indicates that more than half of the English men and women who went to Virginia as indentured servants died during their four years of service.

Loving and kind father and mother . . . this is to let you understand that I your child am in a most heavy case by reason of the nature of the country . . . it causes much sickness, as the scurvy and the bloody flux [severe dysentery], and diverse other diseases, which make the body very poor and weak, and when we are sick there is nothing to comfort us. For since I came out of the ship, I never ate anything but peas and loblollie [gruel]. As for deer or venison I never saw any since I came into this land. There is indeed some fowl, but we are not allowed to go and get it, but must work hard both early and late for a mess of water gruel and a mouthful of bread and beef.

People cry out day and night, Oh that they were in England without their limbs and would not care to lose any limb to be in England again . . . we live in fear of the enemy every hour. . . . We are in great danger, for our plantation is very weak, by reason of the dearth, and sickness of our company. . . .

I have nothing to comfort me, nor there is nothing to be gotten here but sickness and death, except that one had money to lay out in some things for profit; but I have nothing at all, no not a shirt to my back, but two rags nor no clothes, but one poor suit, nor but one pair of shoes . . . my cloak is stolen by one of my own fellows, and to his dying hours would not tell me what he did with it, but some of my fellows saw him have butter and beef out of a ship, which my cloak [no] doubt paid for. . . .

I am not half, a quarter, so strong as I was in England, and all is for want of victuals, for I do protest unto you, that I have eaten more in a day at home than [is] allowed me here for a week. . . . Good father, do not forget me, but have mercy and pity my miserable case. I know if you did but see me you would weep. . . . The answer of this letter will be life or death to me; therefore, good father, send as soon as you can. . . .

Source: Susan M. Kingsbury, ed., *The Records of the Virginia Company of London* (Washington, D.C.: Library of Congress, 1935), 4:58–60.

---

making up 2 percent of the population, and by 1670 the proportion of blacks had reached only 5 percent. Although many Africans served their masters for life, they were not legally enslaved. English common law acknowledged indentured servitude but not chattel slavery—the ownership as property of one human being by another. Moreover, many of these early workers had labored as slaves in African seaports and had some knowledge of European traders and Atlantic commerce. By cunning calculation, hard work, or conversion to Christianity many of them escaped bondage. Some ambitious African Christian freemen even purchased slaves, bought the labor contracts of white servants, or married English women, suggesting that at this time religion and personal initiative were as important as race in determining social status. By becoming a Christian and a planter, an enterprising African could aspire to near equality with the English settlers.

This mobility came to end in the 1660s because legislatures in the Chesapeake colonies enacted laws that lowered the status of Africans. The motives for these laws are not clear. Perhaps the English-born elite grew more conscious of race as the number of Africans increased or, with the end of the tobacco boom, used race to divide workers. By 1671 the Virginia House of Burgesses had forbidden Africans to own guns or join the militia. It had also barred them—"tho baptized and enjoying their own Freedom"—from buying the labor contracts of white servants and specified that conversion to Christianity did not qualify Africans for eventual freedom. Being black was becoming a mark of inferior legal status, and slavery was becoming a permanent and hereditary condition. As an English clergyman observed around 1680, "These two words, Negro and Slave had by custom grown Homogeneous and convertible."

The Seeds of Social Revolt

By the 1660s the growing size of the Chesapeake tobacco crop triggered a collapse of the market. During the boom years of the 1620s tobacco sold for 24 pence a pound; forty years later it was fetching barely one-tenth as much. As the economic boom turned into a "bust," long-standing social conflicts flared up in political turmoil.

Political decisions in England had a lot to do with the decline of tobacco prices. In 1651, in an effort to exclude Dutch ships and merchants from England's overseas possessions, Parliament passed an Act of Trade and Navigation. Revised and extended in 1660 and 1663, the Navigation Acts permitted only English or colonial-owned ships to enter American ports. They also required the colonists to ship certain "enumerated articles," including tobacco, only to England. Chesapeake planters could no longer legally trade with Dutch merchants, who paid the highest prices. Moreover, to increase royal revenues the English monarchs continually raised the import duty on tobacco, thereby increasing the price to consumers and stifling growth of the market. By the 1670s planters were getting only one penny a pound for their crop.

Nonetheless, the number of planters in Virginia and Maryland grew, and tobacco exports doubled from 20 million pounds annually in the 1670s to 41 million pounds between 1690 and 1720. Profit margins were now thin, and the Chesapeake ceased to offer upward social mobility to whites as well as to blacks. Yeomen families painstakingly raised about 10,000 tobacco plants each year but earned just enough to scrape by, and many fell into debt. Even worse off were newly freed indentured servants. Low tobacco prices made it nearly impossible for them to pay the necessary fees to claim the 50 acres of land to which they were entitled and buy the tools and seed needed to plant it. Many former servants had to sell their labor again, signing new indentures or becoming wageworkers or tenant farmers.

Gradually the Chesapeake colonies came to be dominated by an elite of planter-landlords and merchants. Landowners prospered by dividing their ample estates and leasing small plots to the growing army of former servants. They also lent money at high interest rates to hard-pressed yeomen families. Some well-to-do planters became commercial middlemen, setting up small retail stores or charging a commission for storing the tobacco of their poorer neighbors and selling it to English merchants. In Virginia this elite accumulated nearly half the land by soliciting favors from royal governors; on average, the 215 justices of the peace in four counties owned more than 1,000 acres apiece. In Maryland well-connected Catholic planters were equally dominant; by 1720 Charles Carroll owned 47,000 acres of land, farmed by scores of tenants, indentured servants, and slaves.

As these aggressive planter-entrepreneurs confronted a growing number of young, landless laborers, social divisions intensified, reaching a breaking point in Virginia during the corrupt regime of Governor William Berkeley. Berkeley first served as governor between 1642 and 1652, winning fame in 1644 by putting down the second major Indian revolt led by Opechancanough. Serving as governor again beginning in 1660, he made large land grants to himself and to members of his council, who promptly exempted their own lands from taxation and appointed friends as local justices of the peace and county judges. Berkeley suppressed dissent in the House of Burgesses by assigning land grants to friendly legislators and appointing their relatives to lucrative positions that charged fees for services, such as sheriffs, tax collectors, constables, and estate appraisers. Social and political unrest increased

---

TABLE 2.3   Indentured Servants in the Chesapeake Labor Force

Decade Ending	White Population	Percent of Population in Labor Force	White Labor Force	White Servant Population	Servants as Percent of Labor Force
1640	8,000	75	6,000	1,790	29.6
1660	24,000	66	15,800	4,300	27.2
1680	55,600	58	32,300	5,500	17.0
1700	85,200	46	38,900	3,800	9.7

The population of the Chesapeake increased tenfold between 1640 and 1700, and its character changed significantly. As more women migrated to Virginia and bore children, the percentage of the population in the labor force declined dramatically. The importance of indentured servants also declined; before 1660 white servants formed about 30 percent of the labor force but by 1700 accounted for only 10 percent of the workers.

Source: Adapted from Christopher Tomlins, "Reconsidered Indentured Servitude" (unpublished paper, 2001), Table 3.

when the corrupt Burgesses changed the voting system to exclude landless freemen, who constituted half of all adult white men. Property-holding yeomen retained the vote but—distressed by tobacco prices, rising taxes, and political corruption—were no longer willing to support the rule of increasingly corrupt and power-hungry landed gentry.

Bacon's Rebellion

An Indian conflict suddenly sparked the flame of social rebellion. By 1675 the native inhabitants of Virginia were few and weak, their numbers having dwindled from 30,000 in 1607 to a mere 3,500, as compared to 38,000 Europeans and about 2,500 Africans. Although most Indians now lived along the frontier, their presence remained controversial among English settlers. Hundreds of impoverished English free-holders and aspiring tenants wanted cheap land and insisted that the natives be expelled from their treaty-guaranteed lands or simply exterminated. Wealthy planters on the seacoast, who wanted a ready supply of white labor, opposed expansion into Indian territory, as did the planter-merchants who traded with the Native Americans for furs.

Fighting broke out when a band of Virginia militiamen murdered 30 Indians. Defying orders from Governor Berkeley, a larger force of 1,000 militiamen then surrounded a fortified Susquehannock village and killed five chiefs who had come out to negotiate. The militarily strong Susquehannocks, who had recently migrated from present-day northern Pennsylvania, retaliated by raiding outlying plantations and killing 300 whites. Berkeley did not want war, which would disrupt the fur trade, and proposed a defensive military policy, asking the House of Burgesses in March 1676 to raise taxes for a series of frontier forts. Western settlers dismissed this strategy as useless, a plot by planters and merchants to impose high taxes and, in the words of one yeoman, to take "all our tobacco into their own hands."

Nathaniel Bacon emerged as the leader of the protesters. A bold and wealthy man, he had recently arrived from England and settled on a frontier estate. Although he was only twenty-eight, Bacon commanded the respect of his neighbors because of his vigor and his English connections, which had made him a member of the governor's council. When Berkeley refused to grant Bacon a military commission, the headstrong planter marched his frontiersmen against the Indians anyway, slaughtering some of the peaceful Doeg people and triggering a political upheaval. Condemning the frontiersmen as "rebels and mutineers," Berkeley expelled Bacon from the council and placed him under arrest. When Bacon's followers threatened to free their leader by force, the governor quickly changed course, agreeing to legislative elections that brought many new men into

Nathaniel Bacon

Reviled as a rebel and a traitor in his own time, Nathaniel Bacon emerged in the late nineteenth century as an American hero, a harbinger of the Patriots of 1776. This stained-glass window, possibly the creation of the famed jeweler and glassmaker Tiffany & Co. of New York, was installed in a church, endowing Bacon with a semisacred status.
The Association for the Preservation of Virginia Antiquities.

government. The new House of Burgesses promptly enacted far-reaching political reforms that curbed the powers of the governor and the council and restored voting rights to landless freemen.

These much-needed reforms failed to end the rebellion. Bacon was bitter about Berkeley's arbitrary actions, and the poor farmers and indentured servants in his army resented years of exploitation by arrogant justices of the peace and politically well-connected families. As one yeoman rebel put it, "A poor man who has only his labour to maintain himself and his family pays as much [in taxes] as a man who has 20,000 acres." Backed by 400 armed men, Bacon seized control of the colony and issued a "Manifesto and Declaration of the People," demanding the death or removal of all Indians and an end to the rule of wealthy "parasites." "All the power and sway is got into the hands of the rich," Bacon proclaimed, as his army burned Jamestown to the ground and plundered the plantations of Berkeley's allies. When Bacon died suddenly from dysentery in October 1676, the governor took his revenge, dispersing the rebel army, seizing the estates of well-to-do rebels, and hanging 23 men.

Bacon's Rebellion was a pivotal event in the history of Virginia. Although landed planters continued to dominate the economy and polity, they curbed corruption and found public positions for politically ambitious yeomen. The planter-merchant elite appeased the lower social orders by cutting their taxes and supporting the expansion of settlement onto Indian lands. The uprising also contributed to the expansion of African slavery. To forestall another rebellion by poor whites, planters in Virginia and Maryland turned away from indentured servitude. To provide labor for their expanding plantations, they explicitly legalized slavery and imported thousands of Africans, committing their descendants to a social system based on racial exploitation.

Puritan New England

The Puritan exodus from England from 1620 to 1640 was both a worldly quest for land and a spiritual effort to preserve the "pure" Christian faith. By creating a "holy commonwealth" in America, these pious migrants hoped to promote reform within the established Church of England. By distributing land broadly, they tried to build a society of independent property-owning farm families. And by defining their mission in spiritual terms, the Puritans gave a moral dimension to American history.

The Puritan Migration

From the beginning New England differed from other European settlements. New Spain and Jamestown were populated initially by unruly male adventurers, New France and New Netherland by commercial-minded fur traders. By contrast, women and children as well as men settled Plymouth, the first permanent community in New England, and its leaders were pious Protestants—the Pilgrims.

The Pilgrims.   The Pilgrims were Puritans who had left the Church of England, thus earning the name "Separatists." When King James I embraced hierarchical religious policies in the 1610s and threatened to harry Puritans "out of the land, or else do worse," the Pilgrims left England and settled among like-minded Dutch Calvinists in Holland. Subsequently, 35 of these exiles

resolved to migrate to America to maintain their English identity. Led by William Bradford and joined by 67 other migrants from England, they sailed to America aboard the *Mayflower* in 1620 (Map 2.5).

Before departing, the Pilgrims organized themselves into a joint-stock corporation with backing from sympathetic Puritan merchants. Arriving in America without a royal charter, they created their own covenant of government, the Mayflower Compact, to "combine ourselves together into a civill body politick." This document was the first "constitution" adopted in North America and used the Puritan model of a self-governing religious congregation as the blueprint for political society.

The first winter in America tested the Pilgrims. As in Virginia, hunger and disease took a heavy toll; of the 102 migrants who arrived in November, only half survived until the spring. Thereafter the Plymouth colony—unlike Virginia—became a healthy and thriving community. The cold climate inhibited the spread of mosquito-borne diseases, and the Pilgrims' religious discipline established a strong work ethic. Moreover, because a severe smallpox epidemic in 1618 had killed 90 percent of the local Wampanoag people, the migrants faced few external threats. The Pilgrims quickly built solid houses, planted ample crops, and entered the fur trade. Their numbers grew rapidly to 3,000 by 1640, prompting the creation of ten new self-governing towns. A legal code embodied their social ethics, providing for a colonywide system of representative self-government, broad political rights, and a prohibition of government interference in spiritual matters.

Meanwhile, England was plunging deeper into religious turmoil. King Charles I supported the Church of England but personally repudiated some Protestant doctrines, such as the role of grace in salvation. English Puritans, who had gained many seats in Parliament, accused the king of "popery"—holding Catholic beliefs. Charles's response was to dissolve Parliament in 1629, claiming that he ruled by "divine right." He began to raise money through royal edicts, customs duties, and the sale of monopolies. The king's arbitrary rule struck at the power of the landed gentry, who expected to exercise authority through the House of Commons, and cut away at the profits of the merchant community, a stronghold of Puritanism. Then in 1633 the king chose William Laud, who loathed Puritans, to head the Church of England. Laud removed hundreds of Puritan ministers and forced Anglican rituals on their congregations, prompting thousands to seek refuge in America.

The Massachusetts Bay Colony.   The exodus began in 1630, when 900 Puritans boarded eleven ships and sailed across the Atlantic under the leadership of John Winthrop, a well-educated country squire. Calling England morally corrupt and "overburdened with people," Winthrop sought land and opportunity for his

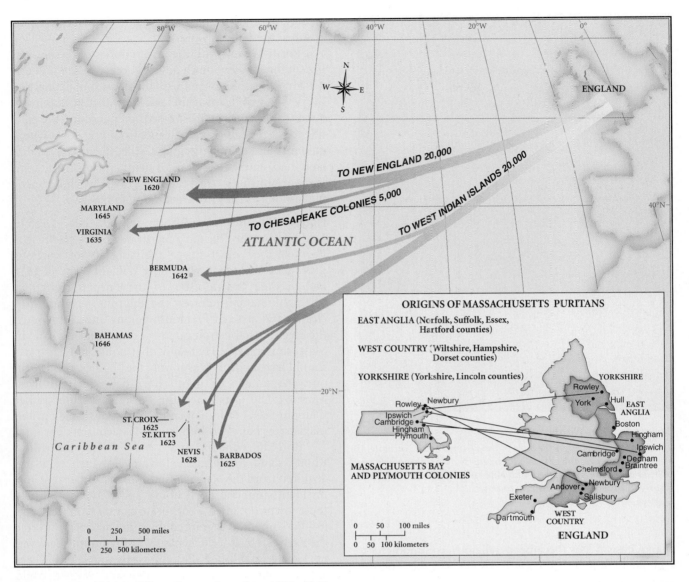

MAP 2.5 The Puritan Migration to America, 1620–1640

Nearly fifty thousand Puritans left England between 1620 and 1640, but they managed to create Puritan-dominated societies only in the New England colonies of Plymouth, Massachusetts Bay, and Connecticut. Within New England, migrants from the three major areas of English Puritanism—Yorkshire, East Anglia, and the West Country—commonly settled among those from their own region. They named American communities after their English towns of origin and transplanted regional customs to New England, such as the open-field agriculture practiced in Rowley in Yorkshire and Rowley in Massachusetts Bay.

children and a place in Christian history for his people. "We must consider that we shall be as a City upon a Hill," Winthrop told his fellow passengers aboard the ship *Arbella* in 1630. "The eyes of all people are upon us." Like the Pilgrims, this larger wave of Puritans envisioned a reformed Christian society, a genuinely "New" England. They saw themselves as a "saving remnant" chosen by God to preserve the true faith in America and inspire religious change in England.

Winthrop and his associates established the Massachusetts Bay colony in the area around Boston and transformed their joint-stock business corporation, the

General Court of shareholders, into a colonial legislature. Over the next decade about 10,000 Puritans migrated to the Massachusetts Bay colony, along with 10,000 others fleeing hard times in England. The Puritans created representative political institutions that were locally based, with the governor as well as the assembly and council elected by the colony's freemen. However, to ensure rule by the godly, the Puritans limited the right to vote and hold office to men who were church members. Eschewing the religious toleration of the Pilgrims, they established Puritanism as the state-supported religion and barred members of other faiths from conducting services.

Governor John Winthrop

This portrait, painted in the style of the Flemish artist Anthony Van Dyke, captures the gravity and intensity of Winthrop, whose policies of religious orthodoxy and elite rule shaped the early history of the Massachusetts Bay colony.

Courtesy, American Antiquarian Society.

Massachusetts Bay became a religious commonwealth with the Bible as its legal as well as spiritual guide. Following a biblical rule, Massachusetts Bay Puritans divided inheritances among all children in a given family, with a double portion going to the oldest son. "Where there is no Law," the colony's government advised local magistrates, they should rule "as near the law of God as they can."

Religion and Society, 1630–1670

In establishing their churches, the Puritans in New England tried to re-create the simplicity of the first Christians. They eliminated bishops and devised a democratic church structure controlled by the laity, or the ordinary members of the congregation—hence their name, Congregationalists. Influenced by John Calvin, Puritans embraced **predestination**, the doctrine that God had decided, or "predestined," the fates of all people before they were born and chosen a few "elect" men and women (the Saints) for salvation and condemned the rest to damnation. Most congregations set extraordinarily high standards for church membership, rigorously examining those who applied. Even so, many Saints lived in great anxiety, for they could never be sure that God had predestined them for salvation.

Puritans dealt with the uncertainties of divine election in three ways. Some congregations stressed the conversion experience: when God infused a soul with grace, the person was "born again" and knew that salvation was at hand. Other Puritans stressed "preparation," the confidence in redemption that came from years of spiritual guidance and church discipline. Still others believed that God had entered into a covenant, or contract, with them, promising to treat them as a divinely "chosen people" as long as they lived according to his laws.

Roger Williams and Rhode Island. To maintain God's favor, the Puritan magistrates of Massachusetts Bay felt they must purge their society of religious dissidents. One target was Roger Williams, who in 1634 had become the minister of the Puritan church in Salem. Williams preferred the Pilgrims' separation of church and state in Plymouth colony and condemned the legal establishment of Congregationalism in Massachusetts Bay. He taught that political magistrates should have authority over only the "bodies, goods, and outward estates of men," not their spiritual lives. Moreover, he questioned the Puritans' seizure (rather than purchase) of Indian lands. In response, the Puritan magistrates banished him from Massachusetts Bay.

In 1636 Williams and his followers resettled in Rhode Island, founding the town of Providence on land acquired from the Narragansett Indians. Other religious dissidents founded Portsmouth and Newport. In 1644 these towns obtained a corporate charter from the English Parliament that granted them full authority "to rule themselves." In Rhode Island as in Plymouth there was no legally established church; every congregation was autonomous, and individual men and women could worship God as they pleased.

Anne Hutchinson. Puritan magistrates in Massachusetts Bay also felt threatened by Anne Hutchinson, the wife of a merchant and a mother of seven who worked as a midwife. Hutchinson held weekly prayer meetings in her house—attended by as many as sixty women—in which she accused certain Boston clergymen of placing undue emphasis on church laws and good behavior. In words that recalled Martin Luther's rejection of indulgences, Hutchinson argued that salvation could not be earned through good deeds; there was no "covenant of works." Rather, God bestowed salvation through the "covenant of grace." Hutchinson stressed the importance of revelation: God directly revealing truth to the individual believer. Since the doctrine of revelation diminished the role of ministers and, indeed, of all established authority, Puritan magistrates found it heretical.

The magistrates also resented Hutchinson because of her sex. Like other Christians, Puritans believed in the

Changing Images of Death

Death—sudden and arbitrary—was a constant presence in the preindustrial world, but it was given various cultural meanings. In the Calvinistic world of pre-1700 New England, gravestones often depicted death as a frightening skull, warning sinners to repent of their sins. After 1700, a smiling cherub adorned many gravestones, suggesting that later generations of Puritans held a more optimistic view of the afterlife. Peabody & Essex Museum.

equality of souls: both men and women could be saved. When it came to the governance of church and state, however, women were seen as being clearly inferior to men. As the Pilgrim minister John Robinson put it, women "are debarred by their sex from ordinary prophesying, and from any other dealing in the church wherein they take authority over the man." Puritan women could never be ministers, lay preachers, or even voting members of the congregation.

In 1637 the Massachusetts Bay magistrates put Hutchinson on trial for heresy, accusing her of believing that inward grace freed an individual from the rules of the church. Hutchinson defended her views with great skill and tenacity, and even Winthrop admitted that she was "a woman of fierce and haughty courage." But the judges found her guilty and berated her for not attend-

ing to "her household affairs, and such things as belong to women." Banished, she followed Roger Williams into exile in Rhode Island.

The coercive policies of the magistrates, along with the desire for better land, prompted some Puritans to leave Massachusetts Bay. In 1636 Thomas Hooker led a hundred settlers to the Connecticut River Valley, where they established the town of Hartford. Others followed, settling along the river at Wethersfield and Windsor. In 1639 the Connecticut Puritans adopted the Fundamental Orders, a plan of government that included a representative assembly and a popularly elected governor. Connecticut was patterned after Massachusetts Bay, with a firm union of church and state and a congregational system of church government, but voting rights were extended to most property-owning men—not just church members.

The English Puritan Revolution. As Puritans established themselves in America, England fell into a religious war. When Archbishop Laud imposed a Church of England prayer book on Presbyterian Scotland in 1642, a Scottish army invaded England. Thousands of English Puritans joined the revolt, demanding greater authority for Parliament and reform of the established church, and hundreds more Puritans returned from America to join the conflict. After four years of civil war the Parliamentary forces led by Oliver Cromwell were victorious. In 1649 Parliament executed Charles I, proclaimed a republican commonwealth, and banished bishops and elaborate rituals from the Church of England.

The Puritan triumph was short-lived. Popular support for the Commonwealth ebbed, especially after 1653 when Cromwell took dictatorial control of the government. Following Cromwell's death, moderate Protestants and a resurgent aristocracy summoned the son of Charles I from Europe, restoring the monarchy and the power of bishops in the Church of England. For many Puritans, Charles II's accession in 1660 represented the victory of the Antichrist—the false prophet described in the last book of the New Testament.

For the Puritans in Massachusetts Bay, the restoration of the monarchy began a new phase of their "errand into the wilderness." They had come to New England to preserve the "pure" Christian church, expecting to return to Europe in triumph. When that sacred mission was dashed by the failure of the English Revolution, Puritan ministers articulated a new vision: they exhorted their congregations to create a permanent new society in America based on their faith and ideals.

The Puritan Imagination and Witchcraft

Like the Native Americans they encountered in New England, the Puritans thought that the physical world was full of supernatural forces. This belief in "spirits" stemmed in part from Christian teachings, such as the Catholic belief in miracles and the Protestant faith in the powers of "grace." Devout Christians saw signs of God's (or Satan's) power in blazing stars, birth defects, and other unusual events. Noting that "more Ministers' Houses than others proportionally had been smitten with Lightning," Cotton Mather, a prominent Massachusetts minister, wondered "what the meaning of God should be in it."

The Puritans' respect for spiritual forces also reflected certain pagan assumptions shared by nearly everyone. When Samuel Sewall, a well-educated Puritan merchant and judge, moved into a new house, he tried to fend off evil spirits by driving a metal pin into the floor. Thousands of ordinary Puritan farmers followed the pagan astrological charts printed in almanacs to determine the best times to plant crops, marry, and make other important decisions.

Zealous ministers attacked many of these beliefs and practices as "superstition" and condemned "cunning" individuals who claimed to have special powers as healers or prophets. Indeed, many Christians looked on folk doctors or conjurers as "wizards" or "witches" who acted at the command of Satan. The people of Andover, Massachusetts, "were much addicted to sorcery," claimed one observer, and "there were forty men in it that could raise the Devil as well as any astrologer." Between 1647 and 1662 civil authorities in Massachusetts and Connecticut hanged 14 people for witchcraft, mostly older women who, their accusers claimed, were "double-tongued" or "had an unruly spirit."

The most dramatic episode of witch-hunting took place in Salem, Massachusetts, in 1692. Initially, a few young girls experienced strange seizures and accused various neighbors of bewitching them. When judges allowed the introduction of "spectral" evidence—visions seen only by the young accusers—the number of accusations spun out of control. Eventually, Massachusetts authorities arrested 175 people and executed 20 of them. The causes of this mass hysteria were complex and are still hard to fathom. Some historians stress group rivalries, pointing out that many of the accusers were the daughters and young female servants of poor farmers in a rural area of Salem, whereas many of the accused witches were wealthier church members or their friends. Because 19 of those executed were women, other historians view the witchcraft trials as part of a broader attempt to keep women, especially those who had inherited property, as subordinate "helpmates" to their husbands. Still other scholars focus on the fears raised by recent Indian attacks in nearby Maine, raids that killed the parents of the young girls whose accusations sparked the Salem prosecutions.

Whatever the cause, the Salem episode marked a turning point for New England. Popular revulsion against the executions weakened the ties between state and church; there would be no more legal prosecutions for

An Affluent Puritan Woman
This well-known painting (c. 1671) of Elizabeth Freake and her daughter Mary is perhaps the finest portrait of a seventeenth-century American. The skill of the artist, probably a visiting English portraitist, and the finery of Mrs. Freake's dress and bonnet suggest the growing cosmopolitanism and prosperity of Boston's merchant community. Worcester Art Museum.

witchcraft or heresy. The European Enlightenment, a major intellectual movement that began around 1675, also helped to limit the number of witchcraft accusations by promoting a more rational view of the world. Increasingly, educated people explained accidents and sudden deaths through theories that drew upon the "laws of nature," not through religion, astrology, or witchcraft. In contrast to Cotton Mather (d. 1728), who believed that lightning might be a supernatural sign, well-read men of the next generation—such as Benjamin Franklin—would conceive of lightning as a natural phenomenon.

A Yeoman Society, 1630–1700

In creating their communities in New England, Puritans consciously shunned the worst features of traditional Europe. They had no wish to live in towns dominated by a few wealthy landowners or controlled by a distant government that levied oppressive taxes. Consequently, they devised land-distribution policies that created self-governing towns and encouraged broad property ownership. Instead of granting thousands of acres to wealthy planters (as occurred in the Chesapeake colonies), the

General Courts of Massachusetts Bay and Connecticut bestowed the title to a township on a group of settlers, or **proprietors**, who distributed the land among themselves. Legal title passed in **fee simple**, which meant that the proprietors' families held the land outright, free from manorial obligations or feudal dues; they could sell, lease, or rent it as they pleased.

Widespread ownership of land did not mean equality of wealth or status. Like most seventeenth-century Europeans, Puritans believed in a social and economic hierarchy. "God had Ordained different degrees and orders of men," proclaimed the wealthy Boston merchant John Saffin, "some to be Masters and Commanders, others to be Subjects, and to be commanded." Town proprietors normally bestowed the largest plots of land on men of high social status, who often became selectmen and justices of the peace. However, all male heads of families received some land, laying the basis for a society of independent yeomen, and landowners had a voice in the town meeting, the main institution of local government (Map 2.6).

Consequently, ordinary farmers in New England communities had much more political power than did most peasants in European villages and most yeomen in the planter-dominated local governments of the Chesapeake colonies. Each year the town meeting chose selectmen to manage its affairs. The meeting also levied taxes; enacted ordinances regarding fencing, lot sizes, and road building; and regulated the use of common fields for grazing livestock and cutting firewood. Beginning in 1634 each town in Massachusetts Bay elected its own representatives to the General Court, a political innovation that gradually shifted authority away from the governor and into the hands of the towns' representatives in the General Court.

As one generation gave way to the next, the farming communities of New England became more socially divided. The larger proprietors owned enough land to divide among all their sons, who usually numbered three or four. Smallholding farmers could provide land for only some of their sons, forcing the rest to begin adult life as propertyless laborers. Newcomers who lacked the rights of proprietors were the least well off, for they had to buy land or work as tenants or laborers. By 1702 in Windsor, Connecticut, landless sons and newcomers accounted for 30 percent of the male taxpayers. It would take years of saving or migration to a new town for these men and their families to become freeholders.

Despite these inequalities, nearly all New Englanders had an opportunity to acquire property, and even those at the bottom of the social scale enjoyed some economic security. When he died in the 1690s, Nathaniel Fish was one of the poorest men in Barnstable, Massachusetts, yet he owned a two-room cottage, eight acres of land, an ox, and a cow. For him and thousands of other settlers, New England had proved to be the promised land, a new world of opportunity.

The Indians' New World

Native Americans along the Atlantic coast were also living in a new world, but for them it was a bleak, dangerous, and conflict-ridden place. Some Indian peoples, like the Pequots, resisted the invaders by force. Others retreated into the Appalachian Mountains to preserve their traditional culture or to band together in new tribes.

Puritans and Pequots

Seeing themselves as God's chosen people, the Puritans justified their intrusions on Native American lands on moral grounds. "By what right or warrant can we enter into the land of the Savages," they asked themselves while still in England, "and take away their rightfull inheritance from them?" John Winthrop provided a clear answer by seeing God's hand in a disastrous smallpox epidemic that reduced the Indian population from 13,000 to 3,000. "If God were not pleased with our inheriting these parts," he asked, "why doth he still make roome for us by diminishing them as we increase?" Citing the Book of Genesis, the magistrates of Massachusetts Bay declared that the Indians had not "subdued" their land and therefore had no "just right" to it.

Imbued with moral righteousness, the Puritans often treated Native Americans with a brutality equal to that of the Spanish conquistadors and Nathaniel Bacon's frontiersmen. When Pequot warriors attacked English farmers who had intruded onto their lands in 1636, Puritan militiamen and their Indian allies led a surprise attack on a Pequot village and massacred about 500 men, women, and children. "God laughed at the Enemies of his People," one soldier boasted, "filling the Place with Dead Bodies." Many of the survivors were ruthlessly tracked down and sold into slavery in the Caribbean.

Like most Europeans, English Puritans viewed the Indians as "savages," culturally inferior people who did not deserve civilized treatment. But the Puritans were not racist as the term is understood today. To them, Native Americans were not genetically inferior—they were white people with sun-darkened skins—and "sin" or Satan, rather than race, accounted for their degenerate condition. "Probably the devil" delivered these "miserable savages" to America, wrote the Puritan minister Cotton Mather, "in hopes that the gospel of the Lord Jesus Christ would never come here to destroy or disturb his absolute empire over them."

This interpretation of the Indians' history inspired the Puritan minister John Eliot to convert them to Christianity. Eliot translated the Bible into Algonquian and undertook numerous missions to Indian villages in eastern Massachusetts. Because Puritans demanded that Indians understand the complexities of Protestant

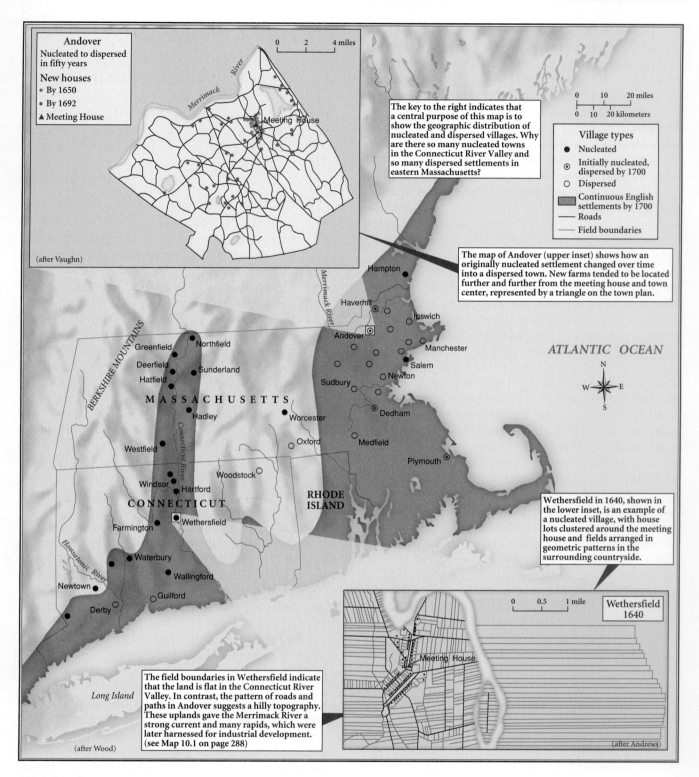

The key to the right indicates that a central purpose of this map is to show the geographic distribution of nucleated and dispersed villages. Why are there so many nucleated towns in the Connecticut River Valley and so many dispersed settlements in eastern Massachusetts?

The map of Andover (upper inset) shows how an originally nucleated settlement changed over time into a dispersed town. New farms tended to be located further and further from the meeting house and town center, represented by a triangle on the town plan.

Wethersfield in 1640, shown in the lower inset, is an example of a nucleated village, with house lots clustered around the meeting house and fields arranged in geometric patterns in the surrounding countryside.

The field boundaries in Wethersfield indicate that the land is flat in the Connecticut River Valley. In contrast, the pattern of roads and paths in Andover suggests a hilly topography. These uplands gave the Merrimack River a strong current and many rapids, which were later harnessed for industrial development. (see Map 10.1 on page 288)

Andover
Nucleated to dispersed in fifty years
New houses
● By 1650
● By 1692
▲ Meeting House

Village types
● Nucleated
◉ Initially nucleated, dispersed by 1700
○ Dispersed
▨ Continuous English settlements by 1700
— Roads
— Field boundaries

MAP 2.6 Settlement Patterns within New England Towns, 1630–1700

Initially, most Puritan towns were compact; regardless of the local topography (hills or plains), families lived close to one another in the nucleated village center and traveled daily to work in the surrounding fields. This pattern is clearly apparent in the 1640 map of Wethersfield, Connecticut, which is situated on the broad plains of the Connecticut River Valley. The first settlers of Andover, Massachusetts, also chose to live in the village center. However, the rugged topography of eastern Massachusetts encouraged a dispersed form of settlement, and by 1692 many residents of Andover lived on their own farms.

theology to become full members of Puritan congregations, only a few Native Americans did so. However, the Puritans created "**praying towns**" that, like the Spanish Franciscans' missions in New Mexico, supervised the Indian population; more than 1,000 Indians lived in fourteen special mission towns. By 1670 the combination of European diseases, military force, and Christianization had pacified most of the Algonquian-speaking peoples who lived along the seacoast of New England, guaranteeing, at least temporarily, the safety of the white settlers.

Metacom's Rebellion

By the 1670s there were three times as many whites as Indians in New England. As the English population grew from 20,000 in 1640 to 55,000, the number of Indians plummeted: from an estimated 120,000 in 1570, to 70,000 in 1620, to barely 16,000. To Metacom, leader of the Wampanoags, the future looked grim. When his people copied English ways, raising hogs and selling pork in Boston, Puritan officials accused them of selling at "an under rate" and placed restrictions on their trade. When they killed wandering livestock that damaged their cornfields, authorities denounced them for violating English property rights. Like Opechancanough in Virginia and Popé in New Mexico, Metacom finally concluded that only military resistance could save Indian lands and culture. So in 1675 Metacom (whom the English called King Philip) forged a military alliance with the Narragansetts and Nipmucks and attacked white settlements throughout New England. Bitter fighting continued into 1676, ending only when Indian warriors ran short of guns and powder, and Mohegans and Mohawks allied with the Massachusetts Bay government ambushed and killed Metacom.

The rebellion was a deadly affair. The Indians burned 20 percent of the English towns in Massachusetts and Rhode Island and killed 1,000 whites, about 5 percent of the adult population. Almost every day, recalled settler William Harris, he had heard new reports of the Indians' "burneing houses, takeing cattell, killing men & women & Children: & carrying others captive." But the Indians' own losses—from famine and disease as well as battle—were much larger: as many as 4,500, or 25 percent of an already diminished population. Many survivors were sold into slavery in the Caribbean, including Metacom's wife and nine-year-old son.

Other members of the defeated Algonquian peoples migrated farther into the New England backcountry, where they intermarried with tribes tied to the French. They had suffered a double tragedy, losing both their land and the integrity of their traditional cultures. Over the next century, these displaced peoples would take their revenge, allying with the French to attack their Puritan enemies (see American Voices, "Mary Rowlandson: A Captivity Narrative," p. 64).

Metacom (King Philip), Chief of the Wampanoag
The Indian uprising of 1675 left an indelible mark on the historical memory of New England. This painting from the 1850s, done on semitransparent cloth and lit from behind for dramatic effect, was used by traveling performers during the 1850s to tell the story of King Philip's War. Note that Metacom is not depicted as a savage but as a dignified man; freed from fear of Indian attack, nineteenth-century New England whites could adopt a romanticized version of their region's often brutal history. Shelburne Museum.

The Fur Trade and the Inland Peoples

As English settlers slowly advanced up the river valleys from the Atlantic coast, the Indians who lived near the Appalachian Mountains and in the great forested areas beyond remained independent. Yet even these distant Indian peoples felt the European presence, as they entered the fur trade to obtain guns and manufactures. Partly because of their location in present-day central New York, the militarily aggressive and diplomatically astute Iroquois peoples were the most successful. Iroquois warriors moved quickly to the east and south along the Mohawk, Hudson, Delaware, and Susquehanna Rivers to exchange goods with (or threaten) the English and Dutch colonies. They traveled north via Lake Champlain and the Richelieu River to French traders in Quebec and west by means

Mary Rowlandson

A Captivity Narrative

Mary Rowlandson, a minister's wife in Lancaster, Massachusetts, was one of many settlers taken captive by the Indians during Metacom's war. Mrs. Rowlandson spent twelve weeks in captivity, traveling constantly, until her family ransomed her for the considerable sum of £20. Her account of this ordeal, The Sovereignty and Goodness of God, *published in 1682, became one of the most popular prose works of its time.*

On the tenth of February 1675, came the Indians with great numbers upon Lancaster: their first coming was about sunrising; hearing the noise of some guns, we looked out; several houses were burning, and the smoke ascending to heaven. . . . [T]he Indians laid hold of us, pulling me one way, and the children another, and said, "Come go along with us"; I told them they would kill me: they answered, if I were willing to go along with them, they would not hurt me. . . .

The first week of my being among them I hardly ate any thing; the second week I found my stomach grow very faint for want of something; and yet it was very hard to get down their filthy trash; but the third week . . . they were sweet and savory to my taste. I was at this time knitting a pair of white cotton stockings for my [Indian] mistress; and had not yet wrought upon a sabbath day. When the sabbath came they bade me go to work. I told them it was the sabbath-day, and desired them to let me rest, and told them I would do as much more tomorrow; to which they answered me they would break my face. . . .

During my abode in this place, Philip [Metacom] spake to me to make a shirt for his boy, which I did, for which he gave me a shilling. I offered the money to my master, but he bade me keep it; and with it I bought a piece of horse flesh. Afterwards he asked me to make a cap for his boy, for which he invited me to dinner. I went, and he gave me a pancake, about as big as two fingers. It was made of parched wheat, beaten, and fried in bear's grease, but I thought I never tasted pleasanter meat in my life. . . .

Hearing that my son was come to this place, I went to see him. . . . He told me also, that awhile before, his master (together with other Indians) were going to the French for powder; but by the way the Mohawks met with them, and killed four of their company, which made the rest turn back again, for which I desire that myself and he may bless the Lord; for it might have been worse with him, had he been sold to the French, than it proved to be in his remaining with the Indians. . . .

My master had three squaws, living sometimes with one, and sometimes with another one. . . . [It] was Weetamoo with whom I had lived and served all this while. A severe and proud dame she was, bestowing every day in dressing herself near as much time as any of the gentry of the land: powdering her hair, and painting her face, going with necklaces, with jewels in her ears, and bracelets upon her hands. When she had dressed herself, her work was to make girdles of wampom and beads. . . .

On Tuesday morning they called their general court (as they call it) to consult and determine, whether I should go home or no. And they all as one man did seemingly consent to it, that I should go home. . . .

Source: C. H. Lincoln, ed., *Original Narratives of Early American History: Narratives of Indian Wars, 1675–1699* (New York: Barnes and Noble, 1952), 14: 139–41.

---

of the Great Lakes and the Allegheny-Ohio river system to the rich fur-bearing lands of the Mississippi Valley.

The rise of the Iroquois was breathtakingly rapid, just as their subsequent decline was tragically sobering. In 1600 the Iroquois in New York numbered about 30,000 and lived in large towns of 500 to 2,000 inhabitants. Two decades later they had organized themselves in a great "longhouse" confederation of the Five Nations: the Senecas, Cayugas, Onondagas, Oneidas, and Mohawks.

Although a virulent smallpox epidemic in 1633 cut their numbers by a third, the Iroquois waged a successful series of wars against the Iroquoian-speaking Hurons (1649), Neutrals (1651), Eries (1657), and Susquehannocks. The victorious Iroquois warriors carried hundreds of captives to New York, where villagers tortured them with firebrands to atone for those lost in battle.

These triumphs gave the Iroquois control of the fur trade with the French in Quebec and the Dutch in New

York. Equally important, it replenished the populations of villages hard hit by epidemics and wartime losses. Taking control of those war captives that were not tortured and killed, Iroquois families conducted "requickening" ceremonies that transferred to them their dead relatives' names, along with social roles and duties. By 1667 half of the population of many Mohawk towns consisted of adopted prisoners. The cultural diversity within Iroquoia further increased as the Five Nations made peace with their traditional French foes and allowed Jesuit missionaries to live among them. Soon about 20 percent of the Iroquois were Catholics, some living under French protection in separate mission-towns.

In 1680 the Iroquois repudiated the treaty with the French. To obtain furs to trade for guns and goods with the English and Dutch merchants in New York, they embarked on a new series of western wars. Warriors of the Five Nations pushed a dozen Algonquian-speaking peoples allied with the French—the Ottawas, Foxes, Sauks, Kickapoos, Miamis, and Illinois—out of their traditional lands north of the Ohio River and into a newly formed multitribal region (present-day Wisconsin) west of Lake Michigan. The cost of these victories was high;

Algonquian Beaver Bowl

In part because of the importance to the fur trade, the beaver played a significant role in Native American cultural life. This beaver-shaped bowl, carved from the root of an ash tree, was the work of an eighteenth-century Algonquian artisan in present-day Ohio or Illinois.

Peabody Museum, Harvard University. Photo by Hillel Burger.

Ætatis suæ 21. Aº. 1616.

An English View of Pocahontas

By depicting the Indian princess Pocahontas as a well-dressed European woman, the artist casts her as a symbol of peaceful assimilation to English culture. In actuality, marriages between white men (often fur traders) and Indian women usually created bilingual families that absorbed elements from both cultures.

National Portrait Gallery, Smithsonian Institution / Art Resource, NY.

after losing about 2,200 warriors, in 1701 the Iroquois again made peace with the French, bringing peace to the inland region for two generations.

However, the character of Indian society in the eastern woodlands had been permanently altered. Most tribes had become smaller as the fighting and European diseases devastated their peoples and as the rum and corn liquor sold by fur traders took their toll. "Strong spirits . . . Causes our men to get very sick," a Catawba leader protested, "and many of our people has Lately Died by the Effects of that Strong Drink." Many Indian peoples also lost their economic and cultural independence. As they exchanged furs for European-made iron utensils and cloth blankets, they neglected traditional artisan skills—each year making fewer flint hoes, clay pots, and skin garments. As a Cherokee chief complained in the 1750s, "Every necessity of life we must have from the white people." Moreover, as French missionaries won converts among the Hurons, Iroquois, and inland peoples, they divided communities into hostile religious factions.

The commitment to constant warfare altered tribal politics. Most strikingly, it increased the influence of those who made war, shifting political power from cautious elders, the sachems, to headstrong young warriors. The sachems, one group of Seneca warriors said with scorn, "were a parcell of Old People who say much but who Mean or Act very little." Equally important, the position and status of women changed in complex and contradictory ways. Traditionally, eastern Woodland women had asserted authority as the chief providers of food and handcrafted goods. As a French Jesuit noted of the Iroquois, "The women are always the first to deliberate . . . on private or community matters. They hold their councils apart and . . . advise the chiefs . . . , so that the latter may deliberate on them in their turn." The influx of European goods and the disruptive impact of warfare on agricultural production threatened the economic basis of women's power. At the same time, the influence of women in victorious tribes increased as they assumed responsibility for assimilating hundreds of captive peoples into the culture.

Finally, the sheer extent of the fur industry—the trapping and killing of hundreds of thousands of beaver, deer, otter, and other animals—profoundly altered the environment. Streams ran faster because there were fewer beaver dams, and the winter hunt for food became more arduous and less fruitful. Death from trapping and hunting severely depleted the animal population of North America, just as death from disease and warfare cut down its Indian inhabitants. The native animals as well as the native peoples now lived in a new American world.

FOR FURTHER EXPLORATION

▶ For definitions of key terms boldfaced in this chapter, see the glossary at the end of the book.

▶ To assess your mastery of the material covered in this chapter, see the Online Study Guide at **bedfordstmartins.com/henretta**.

▶ For suggested references, including Web sites, see page SR-2 at the end of the book.

▶ For map resources and primary documents, see **bedfordstmartins.com/henretta**.

[handwritten: NOT!]

[handwritten left margin: Virginia georgia "carolinas Texas]

Beginning in 1565, first Spain and then England, France, and Holland established permanent settlements in North America. Spain claimed most of the continent, but settled military garrisons and Franciscan missions only in present-day Florida and New Mexico. Both soldiers and friars exploited native laborers, prompting Indian revolts that by 1700 had temporarily expelled most Spaniards from New Mexico. The fur trade became the lifeblood of the Dutch colony of New Netherland and the far-flung French settlements in Canada and Louisiana, where Jesuit priests extended France's influence among the native peoples. The English came primarily as settlers, and their relentless quest for land led to frequent conflict with the Indian peoples.

The English created two types of colonies in North America. Settlers in the Chesapeake region created plantation societies that raised tobacco for export to Europe and were controlled by wealthy planters who exploited the labor of thousands of white indentured servants. In Virginia, economic hardship and political corruption by Governor Berkeley prompted Nathaniel Bacon's unsuccessful rebellion of 1675–1676. Subsequently, Chesapeake planters turned increasingly to slave labor from Africa, creating full-scale slave societies.

The Puritan migrants to New England created a society of freehold farmers who raised crops mostly for their own consumption. Reacting against hierarchical institutions in England, the Puritans set up self-governing churches and towns. At first Puritan magistrates in Boston enforced religious orthodoxy, banishing Roger Williams, Anne Hutchinson, and other religious dissidents, but they gradually relinquished power to a town-based representative assembly.

Wherever Europeans intruded, native peoples died from epidemic diseases, fur-trade-related wars, and political revolts. The Pueblo peoples rose against the Spanish in 1598 and 1680, the Chesapeake Indians nearly wiped out the Virginia colony in 1622, and Metacom's forces dealt New England a devastating blow in 1675–1676. However, by 1700 many Indian communities in New Mexico and along the Atlantic seaboard had been nearly annihilated by disease and warfare, and native peoples in the Ohio and Mississippi Valleys had experienced grave cultural damage.

1539–1543	Coronado and de Soto explore northern lands
1565	Spain establishes St. Augustine, Florida *[handwritten: in Virginia – Carolinas first]*
1598	Acoma rebellion in New Mexico
1603–1625	James I, king of England
1607	English adventurers settle Jamestown, Virginia
1608	Samuel de Champlain founds Quebec *[handwritten: French Jesuits in Maine, N.Y.]*
1613	Dutch set up fur-trading post on Manhattan Island
1619	First Africans arrive in the Chesapeake region / Virginia House of Burgesses convened
1620	Pilgrims found Plymouth colony
1620–1660	Tobacco boom in Chesapeake colonies
1621	Dutch West India Company chartered
1622	Opechancanough's uprising
1624	Virginia becomes a royal colony
1625–1649	Charles I, king of England
1630	Puritans found Massachusetts Bay colony
1634	Maryland settled
1636–1637	Pequot war / Roger Williams and Anne Hutchinson banished
1640s	Puritan revolution in England / Iroquois go to war over fur trade
1651	First Navigation Act
1660	Restoration of English monarchy / Poor tobacco market begins
1664	English conquer New Netherland
1675–1676	Bacon's Rebellion / Metacom's uprising / Expansion of African slavery in the Chesapeake region
1680	Popé's rebellion in New Mexico
1692	Salem witchcraft trials

CHAPTER 3

The British Empire in America

1660–1750

BETWEEN 1660 AND 1750 BRITAIN CREATED A DYNAMIC COMMERCIAL EMPIRE IN AMERICA. When Charles II came to the throne in 1660 England was a second-class trading country, picking up the crumbs left by Dutch merchants who dominated the Atlantic. "What we want is more of the trade the Dutch now have," declared the duke of Albemarle. To win commercial power the English government passed the Acts of Trade and Navigation, which excluded Dutch merchants from its growing American colonies, and then went to war first against the Dutch and then against the French to enforce the new legislation. By the 1720s the newly unified kingdom of Great Britain (comprising England and Scotland) controlled the North Atlantic trade. "We have within ourselves and in our colonies in America," a British pamphleteer boasted, "an inexhaustible fund to supply ourselves, and perhaps Europe." A generation later British officials celebrated the American trade as a leading source of the nation's prosperity. As the ardent imperialist Malachy Postlethwayt proclaimed in 1745, the British empire "was a magnificent superstructure of American commerce and naval power on an African foundation."

As Postlethwayt observed, the wealth of the empire stemmed primarily from the predatory trade in African slaves and the profits generated by slave labor, mainly on the sugar plantations of the West Indies. To protect Britain's increasingly valuable sugar colonies from European rivals—the Dutch in New Netherland, the French in Quebec and the

◄ **Power and Race in the Chesapeake**
Lord Baltimore holds a map of his proprietary colony, Maryland, in this 1670 painting by Gerard Soest. The colony will soon belong to his grandson Cecil Calvert, who points to his magnificent inheritance. The presence of an African servant foreshadows the importance of slave labor in the post-1700 Chesapeake economy.
Enoch Pratt Free Library of Baltimore.

West Indies, and the Spanish in Florida—British officials expanded the navy and repeatedly went to war. Increasingly, economic power came from the barrels of its naval guns and calculated diplomatic policies. Boasted one English pamphleteer, "We are, of any nation, the best situated for trade, . . . capable of giving maritime laws to the world."

To solidify these commercial gains, the British government extended financial and political control over its American settlements. Beginning in the 1660s it successfully controlled the course of colonial commerce through the Navigation Acts and, with less success, tried to subordinate colonial political institutions to imperial direction. These initiatives made Britain a dominant power in Europe and the Western Hemisphere, bringing modest prosperity to most of the white colonists on the North American mainland while condemning thousands of enslaved Africans to brutal work and early death.

The Politics of Empire, 1660–1713

In the first decades of settlement England governed its Chesapeake and New England colonies in a haphazard fashion. Taking advantage of this laxity and the upheaval produced by religious conflict and civil war in England, local oligarchies of Puritan magistrates and tobacco-growing planters ran their societies as they wished. However, with the restoration of the monarchy in 1660 royal bureaucrats imposed order on the unruly settlements and, with the aid of Indian allies, went to war against rival European powers. *Because they were there in several settlements*

The Restoration Colonies

In 1660 Charles II ascended the English throne and promptly gave away millions of acres of American land. A generous but extravagant man who was always in debt, Charles rewarded eight aristocrats who had supported his return to power with a gift of the Carolinas, an area long claimed by Spain and populated by thousands of Indians. Then in 1664 he granted all the territory between the Delaware and Connecticut Rivers to his brother James, the duke of York. That same year James took possession of the conquered Dutch province of New Netherland, renaming it New York, and conveyed the ownership of the adjacent province of New Jersey to two of the Carolina proprietors (Table 3.1).

In one of the great land grabs in history, a few English aristocrats had taken title to vast provinces. Like Lord Baltimore's Maryland, their new colonies were proprietorships; the aristocrats owned all the land and could rule as they wished as long as the laws conformed broadly to those of England. Most proprietors envisioned a traditional social order presided over by a

Maryland—Catholic left out of this list! 1st religious freedom before Penn

TABLE 3.1 English Colonies Created in North America, 1660–1750					
	Date	Type	Religion	Status in 1775	Chief Export or Economic Activity
Carolinas	1663	Proprietary	Church of England	Royal	
North	1691				Mixed farming; naval stores
South	1691				Rice; indigo
New Jersey	1664	Proprietary	Church of England	Royal	Wheat
New York	1664	Proprietary	Church of England	Royal	Wheat
Pennsylvania	1681	Proprietary	No established church	Proprietary	Wheat
Georgia	1732	Trustees	Church of England	Royal	Rice
New Hampshire (separated from Massachusetts)	1739	Royal	Congregationalist	Royal	Mixed farming; lumber; naval stores
Nova Scotia	1749	Royal	Church of England	Royal	Fishing; mixed farming; naval stores

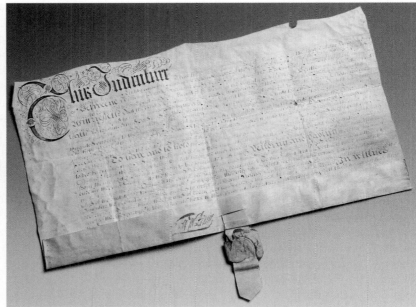

William Penn, Quaker Proprietor
As a member of the Society of Friends, Penn dressed in a plain and simple style, as this portrait shows. However, because of his proprietorship, the young Quaker was a wealthy man, the sole owner of millions of acres of land. This 1685 indenture, or contract, authorized the sale of five hundred acres of land along the Delaware River to John Dwight, a "Gentleman" of Fulham in England. Historical Society of Pennsylvania / Jonathan Horne.

gentry class and a legally established Church of England. Thus, the Fundamental Constitutions of Carolina (1669) prescribed a manorial system with a powerful nobility and a mass of serfs.

The Carolinas. This aristocratic scheme proved to be a pure fantasy. The first settlers in North Carolina, poor families from Virginia, refused to work on large manors and chose to live on modest family farms, raising grain and tobacco. Indeed, farmers in Albemarle County, inspired by Bacon's Rebellion in Virginia and angered by taxes on tobacco exports, rebelled in 1677. They deposed the governor and forced the proprietors to abandon most of their financial claims.

The colonists of South Carolina refused to accept the Fundamental Constitutions and created their own version of the hierarchical social order of Europe. White settlers, many of them migrants from the overcrowded sugar-producing island of Barbados, imported enslaved African workers and used them to raise cattle and food crops for export to the West Indies. They also opened a lucrative trade with Native Americans, exchanging English manufactured goods for furs and Indian slaves. Because of the Carolinians' growing reliance on Indian slaves, they encouraged their native allies to take captives from Indian settlements in Florida, raising the threat of war with Spain. In 1715 these slave raids prompted a brutal war with the Yamasee people, which took the lives

of four hundred settlers. Until the 1720s South Carolina remained an ill-governed, violence-ridden frontier settlement.

William Penn and Pennsylvania. In dramatic contrast to the Carolinas, the new proprietary colony of Pennsylvania (which included present-day Delaware) pursued a pacifistic policy toward Native Americans and quickly became prosperous. In 1681 Charles II bestowed the colony on William Penn in payment of a large debt owed to Penn's father. Born to wealth and seemingly destined for courtly pursuits, the younger Penn had converted to the Society of Friends (Quakers), a radical Protestant sect, and used his wealth and prestige to spread its influence. He designed Pennsylvania as a refuge for Quakers, who were persecuted in England because they refused to serve in the army and would not pay taxes to support the Church of England.

Like the Puritans, the Quakers wanted to restore the simplicity and spirituality of early Christianity. However, the Quakers rejected the pessimistic religious doctrines of Puritans or other Calvinists, who restricted salvation to a small elect. Rather, Quakers followed the teachings of the English visionaries George Fox and Margaret Fell, who argued that all men and women had been imbued by God with an inner "light" of grace or understanding that opened salvation to everyone. Quakers did not have ministers, and when they met for worship there were no sermons; members sat in silence until moved to speak by the inner light.

Penn's Frame of Government (1681) extended Quaker radicalism into politics. In a world dominated by established churches, Penn's constitution guaranteed religious freedom to Christians of all denominations and allowed all property-owning men to vote and hold office. Thousands of Quakers, primarily from the ranks of middling farmers in northwestern England, flocked to Pennsylvania, settling along the Delaware River in or near the city of Philadelphia, which Penn himself laid out in a rational grid pattern of main streets and back alleys. The proprietor sold land at low prices and, to attract Protestant settlers from Europe, published pamphlets in Dutch and German advertising the advantages of his colony. In 1683 migrants from the German province of Saxony founded Germantown (just outside Philadelphia) and thousands of other Germans soon joined them, attracted by cheap, fertile land and the prospect of freedom from religious warfare and persecution. Ethnic diversity, pacifism, and freedom of conscience made Pennsylvania the most open and democratic of the Restoration colonies.

From Mercantilism to Dominion

Since the 1560s, Elizabeth I and her successors had used government subsidies and charters to stimulate English manufacturing and foreign trade. Beginning in the 1650s, the English government extended these policies—known as **mercantilism**—to its American colonies, where they created a generation of political controversy.

The Navigation Acts. The new mercantilist policies regulated colonial commerce and manufacturing. According to mercantilist theory, the American colonies were to produce agricultural goods and raw materials, which English merchants would carry to the home country, where they would be reexported or manufactured into finished products. Consequently, the Navigation Act of 1651 prohibited Dutch merchants from the colonial trade and gave English traders a monopoly by requiring that goods imported into England or its American settlements be carried on English-owned ships. New parliamentary acts in 1660 and 1663 strengthened the ban on foreign merchants and stipulated that colonial sugar, tobacco, and indigo could be shipped only to England. To provide even more business for English merchants, the acts also required that European exports to America pass through England. To enforce these mercantilist laws and raise money, the Revenue Act of 1673 imposed a "plantation duty" on sugar and tobacco exports and created a staff of customs officials to collect the duty (Table 3.2).

The English government backed its mercantilist policy with the force of arms. In three commercial wars between 1652 and 1674 the English navy drove the Dutch from New Netherland and ended Dutch supremacy in the West African slave trade. Meanwhile, English merchants expanded their fleets and dominated Atlantic commerce.

Many Americans resisted these mercantilist laws as burdensome and intrusive. Edward Randolph, an English customs official in Massachusetts, reported that the colony's Puritan-dominated government took

TABLE 3.2 Navigation Acts, 1651–1751

	Date	Purpose	Result
Act of 1651	1651	Cut Dutch trade	Mostly ignored
Act of 1660	1660	Ban foreign shipping; enumerated goods only to England	Partially obeyed
Act of 1663	1663	Require European imports to pass only through England	Partially obeyed
Staple Act	1663	Require enumerated goods to pass through England	Mostly obeyed
Revenue Act	1673	Impose "plantation duty"; create customs system	Mostly obeyed
Act of 1696	1696	Prevent frauds; create Vice-Admiralty Courts	Mostly obeyed
Woolen Act	1699	Prevent export or intercolonial sale of textiles	Partially obeyed
Hat Act	1732	Prevent export or intercolonial sale of hats	Partially obeyed
Molasses Act	1733	Cut American imports of molasses from French West Indies	Extensively violated
Iron Act	1750	Prevent manufacture of finished iron products	Extensively violated
Currency Act	1751	End use of paper currency as legal tender in New England	Mostly obeyed

"no notice of the laws of trade," welcoming Dutch merchants, importing goods from the French sugar islands, and claiming that its royal charter exempted it from most of the new regulations. Outraged, Randolph called for English troops to "reduce Massachusetts to obedience." Instead of using force, the Lords of Trade—the administrative body charged with colonial affairs—pursued a punitive legal strategy. In 1679 they denied the claim of Massachusetts Bay to the adjoining province of New Hampshire and created a separate colony there with a royal governor. To bring the Puritans in Massachusetts Bay directly under their control, in 1684 English officials persuaded the English Court of Chancery to annul the colony's charter on the grounds that the Puritan government had violated the Navigation Acts and virtually outlawed the Church of England.

The Dominion of New England. The accession to the throne of James II (r. 1685–1688), who had grown up in France during the reign of Oliver Cromwell, brought new demands for imperial reform. An admirer of France's authoritarian Louis XIV and of "divine-right" monarchy, James instructed the Lords of Trade to create a centralized imperial system in America. Backed by the king, in 1686 they revoked the corporate charters of Connecticut and Rhode Island and merged them with the Massachusetts Bay and Plymouth colonies to form a new royal province, the Dominion of New England. Two years later the home government added New York and New Jersey to the Dominion, creating a single colony that stretched from the Delaware River to Maine (Map 3.1).

This administrative innovation went far beyond mercantilism, which had respected the political autonomy of the various colonies while regulating their trade, and extended to America the authoritarian model of colonial rule imposed on Catholic Ireland. When James II had taken control of New York in 1674, he had refused to allow an elective assembly and ruled by decree. Now he extended absolutist rule to the entire Dominion, appointing Sir Edmund Andros, a former military officer, as governor and empowering him to abolish the existing colonial legislative assemblies. In Massachusetts, Andros immediately banned town meetings, angering villagers who prized local self-rule, and advocated public worship in the Church of England, offending Puritan Congregationalists. Even worse from the colonists' perspective, the governor imposed new taxes and challenged all land titles granted under the original Massachusetts charter. Andros offered to provide new deeds but only if the colonists would agree to pay an annual fee (or quitrent). The Puritans protested to the king, but James was determined to impose absolutist rule and refused to restore the old charter.

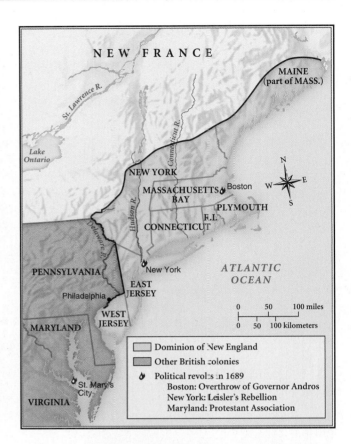

MAP 3.1 The Dominion of New England, 1686–1689

The Dominion created a vast new royal colony stretching nearly five hundred miles along the Atlantic coast. After the Glorious Revolution in England, revolts led or instigated by local politicians and ministers in Boston and New York City ousted royal officials, effectively ending the Dominion. In Maryland, a Protestant association mounted a third revolt, deposing the Catholic proprietary governor. The new governments instituted by King William III balanced the power held by imperial authorities and local political institutions.

The Glorious Revolution of 1688

Fortunately for the colonists, James II angered English political leaders as much as Andros alienated the Americans. The king revoked the charters of many English towns, rejected the advice of Parliament, and aroused popular opposition by openly practicing Roman Catholicism. Then in 1688 James's foreign-born Catholic wife gave birth to a son, raising the prospect of a Catholic heir to the throne. Fearing political persecution similar to that inflicted by King Louis XIV on French Protestants (the Huguenots) in France in 1685, English parliamentary leaders supported the quick and bloodless coup known as the Glorious Revolution. Backed by popular protests and the army, they forced James into exile and enthroned Mary, his Protestant daughter by his first wife, and her Protestant Dutch husband, William of Orange. Queen Mary II and King William III agreed to rule as constitutional monarchs, accepting a bill of rights that limited

A Prosperous Dutch Farmstead

Many Dutch farmers in the Hudson River Valley prospered because of easy access to market and their exploitation of black slaves, which they owned in much greater numbers than their neighbors of English ancestry did. To record his good fortune, Martin Van Bergen of Leeds, New York, had this mural painted over his mantelpiece.
New York State Historical Association, Cooperstown, NY.

royal prerogatives and increased personal liberties and parliamentary powers.

To justify their coup, parliamentary leaders relied on the political philosopher John Locke. In his *Two Treatises on Government* (1690) Locke rejected divine-right theories of monarchical rule; he argued that the legitimacy of government rests on the consent of the governed and that individuals have inalienable natural rights to life, liberty, and property. Locke's celebration of individual rights and representative government had a lasting influence in America, where many political leaders wanted to expand the powers of the colonial assemblies.

More immediately, the Glorious Revolution sparked rebellions by colonists in Massachusetts, Maryland, and New York in 1689. When the news of the coup reached Boston in April 1689, Puritan leaders seized Governor Andros and shipped him back to England. Responding to American protests, the new monarchs broke up the

Dominion of New England. However, they refused to restore the old Puritan-dominated government, creating instead a new royal colony of Massachusetts (which included Plymouth and Maine). According to the new charter of 1692, the king would appoint the governor (as well as naval officers who were charged with enforcing customs regulations), and members of the Church of England would enjoy religious freedom. The charter restored the Massachusetts assembly but stipulated that it be elected by all male property owners (not just Puritan church members).

The uprising in Maryland had both economic and religious causes. Since 1660 tobacco prices had been falling, threatening the livelihoods of small holders, tenant farmers, and former indentured servants, most of whom were Protestants. They resented the rising taxes and the high fees imposed by wealthy proprietary officials, who were primarily Catholics. When Parliament ousted James II, a Protestant association in Maryland quickly removed the Catholic officials appointed by Lord Baltimore. The Lords of Trade suspended Baltimore's proprietorship, imposed royal government, and established the Church of England as the colony's official church. This arrangement lasted until 1715, when Benedict Calvert, the fourth Lord Baltimore, renounced Catholicism and converted to the Anglican faith, prompting the crown to restore the proprietorship to the Calvert family.

In New York the rebellion against the Dominion of New England began a decade of violence and political conflict. New England settlers on Long Island, angered by James's prohibition of representative institutions, began the uprising, and they quickly won the support of Dutch Protestant artisans in New York City, who welcomed the succession of Queen Mary and her Dutch husband. The Dutch militia ousted Lieutenant Governor Nicholson, an Andros appointee and an alleged Catholic sympathizer, and rallied behind a new government led by Jacob Leisler, a militant Protestant merchant and former army officer who had married into a prominent New York Dutch family. Leisler hoped to win the support of all classes and ethnic groups, but his outbursts of religious rage, as he denounced his political rivals as "popish dogs" and "Roages, Rascalls, and Devills," alienated many New Yorkers. When Leisler imprisoned his opponents, imposed new taxes, and championed the interests of Dutch artisans, the wealthy merchants who had traditionally controlled the city government condemned his rule. In 1691 the merchants won the support of a newly appointed royal governor, who instituted a representative assembly and supported a merchant-dominated Board of Aldermen that lowered artisans' wages. The governor had Leisler indicted for treason. He was convicted by a jury, hanged, and then decapitated, an act of political violence that corrupted New York politics for a generation.

In both America and England the Glorious Revolution of 1688 and 1689 began a new phase in imperial history. The uprisings in Boston and New York toppled the authoritarian Dominion of New England and, because William I wanted colonial support for a war against France, won the restoration of internal self-government. In England, the new constitutional monarchs promoted an empire based on commerce, launching a period of "salutary neglect" that gave free rein to enterprising merchants and financiers who developed the American colonies as a source of trade. Although Parliament created a new Board of Trade (1696) to supervise the American settlements, it had little success. Settlers and proprietors resisted the board's attempt to install royal governments in every colony, as did many English political leaders, who feared an increase in monarchical power. Consequently, the empire remained diverse. Colonies that were of minor economic and political importance retained their corporate governments (Connecticut and Rhode Island) or proprietary institutions (Pennsylvania, Maryland, and the Carolinas) while royal governors ruled the lucrative staple-producing settlements in the West Indies and Virginia.

Imperial Wars and Native Peoples

Between 1689 and 1815 Britain vied with France for dominance in western Europe. Prompted by this series of wars, British political leaders created a powerful state that devoted three-quarters of its revenue to military expenses. As these wars spread to the Western Hemisphere, they involved increasing numbers of Native American warriors, who were now armed with European guns and steel knives and hatchets (Table 3.3). By this time many Indian peoples were familiar enough with European goals and diplomacy to turn the fighting to their own advantage.

TABLE 3.3 English Wars, 1650–1750			
	Date	Purpose	Result
Anglo-Dutch	1652–1654	Develop commercial markets	Stalemate
Anglo-Dutch	1664	Acquire markets—conquest	England conquers New Netherland
Anglo-Dutch	1673	Develop commercial markets	England makes maritime gains
King William's (War of the League of Augsburg)	1689–1697	Maintain European balance of power	Stalemate in North America
Queen Anne's (War of the Spanish Succession)	1702–1713	Maintain European balance of power	British acquire Hudson Bay, Nova Scotia, and strategic sites in Europe
Jenkins' Ear	1739	Expand markets in Spanish America	Stalemate
King George's (War of Austrian Succession)	1740–1748	Maintain European balance of power	British capture and return Louisbourg (on Cape Breton Island)

The first significant fighting in North America occurred during the War of the Spanish Succession (1702–1713), which pitted Britain against France and Spain. Taking advantage of this European conflict, English settlers in the Carolinas tried to protect their growing settlements by launching an attack against Spanish Florida. Seeking military allies, the Carolinians armed the Creeks, a 15,000-member agrarian people who lived in matrilineal clans on the fertile lands along the present-day Georgia-Alabama border. A joint English-Creek expedition burned the Spanish town of St. Augustine but failed to capture the nearby fort. Fearing that future Carolinian-backed Indian raids would endanger its colony of Florida and pose a threat to Havana in nearby Cuba, the Spanish reinforced St. Augustine and launched unsuccessful attacks against Charleston, South Carolina.

The Creeks had their own quarrels to settle with the pro-French Choctaws to the west and the Spanish-allied Apalachees to the south, and they took this opportunity to become the dominant tribe in the region. Beginning in 1704 a force of Creek and Yamasee warriors destroyed the remaining Franciscan missions in northern Florida, attacked the Spanish settlement at Pensacola, and massacred the Apalachees, selling 1,000 Apalachee prisoners to South Carolinian traders, who carried most of them to slavery in the West Indies. "In all these extensive dominions and provinces," a Spanish official lamented, "the law of God and the preaching of the Holy Gospel have now ceased." Simultaneously, a Carolina-supplied and Creek-led army attacked the Iroquois-speaking Tuscarora people of North Carolina, killing hundreds, executing 160 male captives, and sending 400 women and children into slavery. The Tuscaroras who survived migrated to the north and joined the New York Iroquois, who now became the Six Nations. Having ruled by the guns and hatchets of their Indian allies, the Carolinians now died by them. In 1715, when traders demanded the payment of debts, the Yamasee and Creek revolted, killing 400 colonists before being overwhelmed by the Carolinians and their new Cherokee allies.

Native Americans also played a central role in the fighting in the Northeast, where French Catholics from Canada confronted English Puritans from New England. Aided by the French, Abenaki and Mohawk warriors took revenge on their Puritan enemies. They destroyed English settlements along the coast of Maine and in 1704 attacked the western Massachusetts town of Deerfield, where they killed 48 residents and carried 112 into captivity. New England responded to these raids by launching attacks against French settlements, joining with British naval forces and troops in 1710 to seize Port Royal in French Acadia (Nova Scotia). However, in the following year a major British-American expedition against the French stronghold at Quebec failed miserably.

The New York frontier remained quiet because France and England did not want to disrupt the lucrative fur trade and because most of the Iroquois Nations had adopted a new policy of "aggressive neutrality." In 1701, after a decade of heavy losses, the Iroquois concluded a peace with France and its Indian allies. Simultaneously, they reinterpreted their "covenant chain" of military alliances with the English governors of New York and the Algonquian tribes of New England. For the next half-century the Iroquois exploited their central geographic location by trading with the English and the French but refusing to fight for either side. The Delaware leader Teedyuscung explained this strategy by showing his people a pictorial message from the Iroquois: "You see a Square in the Middle, meaning the Lands of the Indians; and at one End, the Figure of a Man, indicating the English; and at the other End, another, meaning the French. Let us join together to defend our land against both."

Despite the military stalemate in the colonies, Britain used victories in Europe to win major territorial and commercial concessions in the Americas in the Treaty of Utrecht (1713). From France, Britain obtained Newfoundland, Acadia, the Hudson Bay region of northern Canada, and access to the western Indian trade. From Spain, Britain acquired the strategic fortress of Gibraltar at the entrance to the Mediterranean and a thirty-year contract to supply slaves to Spanish America. These gains solidified Britain's commercial supremacy and brought peace to eastern North America for a generation (Map 3.2).

The Imperial Slave Economy

Britain's increasing administrative and military interest in American affairs reflected the growing importance of its Atlantic trade in slaves and staple crops. European merchants had created a new agricultural and commercial order—the South Atlantic system, as historians call it—that produced sugar, tobacco, rice, and other subtropical products. At the core of the new productive regime stood plantations staffed by enslaved labor from Africa (Table 3.4).

The South Atlantic System

The South Atlantic system had three major components: fertile lands seized from Indians, enslaved laborers purchased from Africans, and capital and ships provided by Europeans. In Brazil and the West Indies—the core of the South Atlantic system—European adventurers and settlers used Indian lands to produce sugar. Before 1500 Europeans had few sweeteners—mostly honey and apple juice—and quickly developed a craving for the

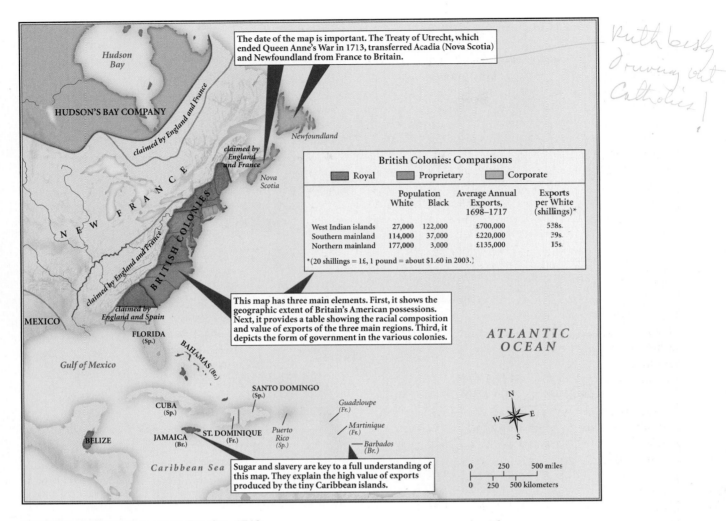

Ruthlessly driving out Catholics!

The date of the map is important. The Treaty of Utrecht, which ended Queen Anne's War in 1713, transferred Acadia (Nova Scotia) and Newfoundland from France to Britain.

British Colonies: Comparisons

| | | | | Royal | Proprietary | Corporate |

	Population White	Black	Average Annual Exports, 1698–1717	Exports per White (shillings)*
West Indian islands	27,000	122,000	£700,000	538s.
Southern mainland	114,000	37,000	£220,000	39s.
Northern mainland	177,000	3,000	£135,000	15s.

*(20 shillings = 1£, 1 pound = about $1.60 in 2003.)

This map has three main elements. First, it shows the geographic extent of Britain's American possessions. Next, it provides a table showing the racial composition and value of exports of the three main regions. Third, it depicts the form of government in the various colonies.

Sugar and slavery are key to a full understanding of this map. They explain the high value of exports produced by the tiny Caribbean islands.

MAP 3.2 Britain's American Empire, 1713

Britain's West Indian possessions were small—mere dots on the Caribbean Sea. However, in 1713 they were by far the most valuable parts of the empire. Their sugar crops brought wealth to English merchants, trade to the northern colonies, and a brutal life (and early death) to African workers.

TABLE 3.4 Slave Imports in the Americas, 1520–1810

Destination	Number of Africans Arriving
South America	
Brazil	3,650,000
Dutch America	500,000
West Indies	
British	1,660,000
French	1,660,000
Central America	
Spanish	1,500,000
North America	
British colonies	500,000
Europe	175,000
TOTAL	**9,645,000**

potent new sweetener. Demand for sugar soared, outrunning supply for decades and guaranteeing high profits to producers.

A new agricultural economy quickly sprang into existence in the semitropical lands of the Western Hemisphere. European merchants and investors provided the organizational skill, ships, and money needed to grow and process sugarcane, carry the refined sugar to market, and supply the plantations with European tools and equipment. To provide labor for the sugar plantations, the merchants relied primarily on slaves from Africa. Between 1550 and 1700 Portuguese and Dutch traders annually transported about 10,000 Africans across the Atlantic. Subsequently, British and French merchants took over this commerce, developing African-run slave-catching systems that extended far into the interior of Africa and funneled captives to the slave ports of Elmina, Whydah, Loango, and Cabinda. Between 1700 and 1810 they

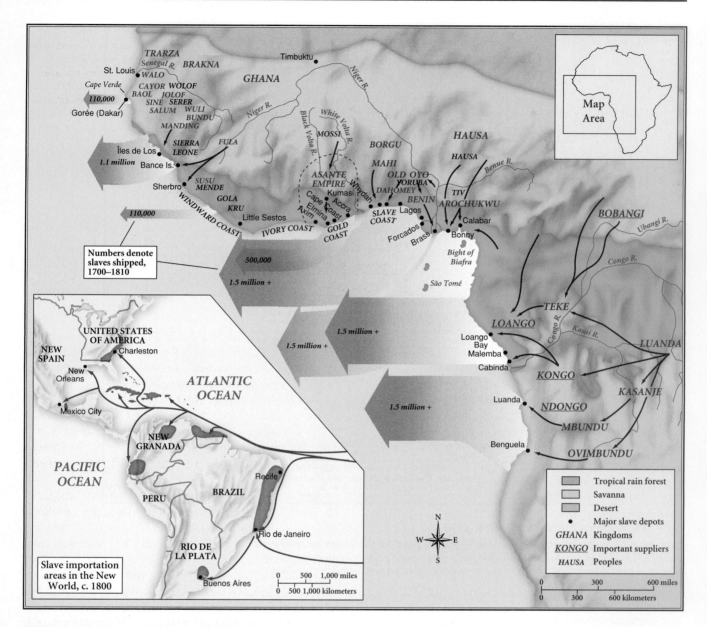

MAP 3.3 Africa and the Atlantic Slave Trade, 1700–1810

The tropical rainforest region of West Africa was home to scores of peoples and dozens of kingdoms. Some kingdoms, such as Dahomey, became aggressive slavers, taking tens of thousands of war captives and funneling them to the seacoast, where they were sold to European traders. About 15 percent of the Africans died on the transatlantic voyage, the grueling Middle Passage, between enslavement in Africa and slavery in the Americas. Most of the survivors labored on sugar plantations in Brazil and the British and French West Indies (see Table 3.4).

For more help analyzing this map, see the ONLINE STUDY GUIDE at bedfordstmartins.com/henretta.

carried about 7 million Africans—800,000 in the 1780s alone—to toil in the Americas (Map 3.3).

Portuguese and Dutch planters developed sugar plantations in Brazil and, beginning in the 1620s, English and French merchants carried the new industry to the subtropical islands of the West Indies. In the 1650s

the island of Barbados had a white population of 30,000, consisting of planters and their indentured servants, who exported tobacco and livestock hides to England. Then came the "sugar revolution," financed initially by Dutch merchants, which quickly converted Barbados into an island of slaves. By 1660 Africans formed a

Shipping Sugar from Antigua

Sugar was a valuable commodity but also a heavy one that was shipped to European markets in giant barrels. Because it was difficult and expensive to build wharves that could accommodate large transports, the barrels were conveyed in small boats to the oceangoing ships, which used winches and pulleys to lift them on board.

National Maritime Museum, London.

majority of the population, and English settlers were departing for the Carolinas. By 1700 English sugar planters were investing heavily in the Leeward Islands and Jamaica, which soon had populations that were 85 to 90 percent African. In 1750, Jamaica—the largest island in the British West Indies—had seven hundred large sugar plantations worked by more than 105,000 slaves, who labored for ten hours a day, slept in flimsy huts, lived on a starchy diet of corn, yams, and dried fish, and were subject to brutal discipline.

Sugar production required fertile land, many laborers to plant and cut the cane, and heavy equipment to process cane into raw sugar and molasses. Because only wealthy merchants or landowners had the capital to outfit a plantation, a planter-merchant elite financed the sugar industry and drew annual profits of more than 10 percent on investments. As the Scottish economist Adam Smith declared in his famous treatise *The Wealth of Nations* (1776), sugar was the most profitable crop in Europe and America.

The South Atlantic system brought wealth to the entire European economy. To take England as an example, the owners of most of the plantations in the British West Indies lived as absentees in England, spending their profits there. Moreover, the British Navigation Acts required that American sugar be sold to English consumers or sent through England to continental markets, thus raising the level of trade. By 1750 reexports of sugar and tobacco from America accounted for half of all British exports. Substantial profits also came from the slave trade, for the Royal African Company and other English traders sold male slaves in the West Indies for three to five times what they paid for them in Africa. Finally, the trade in American sugar and tobacco stimulated manufacturing. To transport slaves (and machinery and settlers) to America, English shipyards

built hundreds of vessels. Thousands of English and Scottish men and women worked in related industries: building port facilities and warehouses, refining sugar and tobacco, distilling rum from molasses (a by-product of sugar), and manufacturing textiles and iron products for the growing markets in Africa and America. Commercial expansion also provided a supply of experienced sailors, helping to make the Royal Navy the most powerful fleet in Europe.

As the South Atlantic system enhanced prosperity in Europe, it brought economic decline, political change, and human tragedy to West Africa and the parts of East Africa, such as Madagascar, where slavers were also active. Between 1550 and 1870 the Atlantic slave trade uprooted about 15 million Africans, diminishing the population and wealth of the continent. Overall, the guns, iron, tinware, rum, cloth, and other European products that entered the African economy in exchange for slaves were worth from one-tenth (in the 1680s) to one-third (by the 1780s) as much as the goods those slaves subsequently produced in America.

Equally important, the slave trade changed the nature of West African society by promoting centralized states and military conquest. In 1739 an observer noted that "whenever the King of Barsally wants Goods or Brandy . . . the King goes and ransacks some of his enemies' towns, seizing the people and selling them." War and slaving became a way of life in Dahomey, where the royal house made the sale of slaves a state monopoly and used the resulting access to European guns to create a regime of military despotism. Dahomey's army, which included a contingent of 5,000 women, systematically raided the interior for captives, and exported thousands of slaves each year (Map 3.3). The Asante kings also used the firearms and wealth acquired through the Atlantic trade to create a bureaucratic empire of 3 million

Olaudah Equiano

This 1780 portrait by an unknown artist in England shows the freed slave and journal writer Olaudah Equiano. Equiano was among the first Africans to develop a consciousness of an African identity that transcended traditional ethnic and national boundaries. Royal Albert Memorial Museum, Exeter, England.

homes, captives were marched in chains to coastal ports such as Elmina on the Gold Coast. From there they made the perilous **Middle Passage** to the New World in hideously overcrowded ships. There was little to eat and drink, and the stench of excrement was nearly unbearable. Some captives jumped overboard, choosing to drown rather than endure more suffering (see Voices from Abroad, "Olaudah Equiano: The Brutal 'Middle Passage,'" p. 81). Nearly a million (15 percent of the 8 million who crossed the Atlantic between 1700 and 1810) died on the journey, mostly from dysentery, smallpox, or scurvy.

For the survivors of the Middle Passage, life only got worse on arrival in northwest Brazil or the West Indies because sugar plantations were based on relentless exploitation and systematic violence. Planting and harvesting sugarcane required intense labor under a tropical sun, with a pace set by the overseer's whip. With sugar prices high and the cost of slaves low, many planters worked slaves to death and then imported more. For example, between 1708 and 1735 about 85,000 Africans were brought into Barbados, but the island's black population increased only from 42,000 to 46,000 during these decades.

Slavery in the Chesapeake and South Carolina

As the British slave trade increased after 1700, planters in Virginia and Maryland imported thousands of Africans into the Chesapeake. In what historian Ira Berlin has termed a "tobacco revolution," leading planters created a slave-based economy and a new plantation regime, buying as many black workers as they could afford and sending them to toil under the direction of overseers on far-flung "quarters." By 1720 Africans numbered 20 percent of the Chesapeake population, and slavery had become a defining principle of the social order, not just one of several forms of labor. Equally important, slavery was increasingly defined in racial terms. A Virginia law of 1692 prohibited sexual intercourse between English and Africans, and in 1705 another statute explicitly defined virtually all resident Africans as slaves: "All servants imported or brought into this country by sea or land who were not Christians in their native country shall be accounted and be slaves" (see American Lives, "From a Piece of Property to a Man of Property: The Odyssey of Robert Pearle," p. 82).

Nonetheless, living conditions for Africans in Maryland and Virginia were much less severe than in the West Indies, and slaves lived relatively long lives. In terms of labor to produce a harvest, tobacco was not as physically demanding a crop as sugar. Slaves planted the young tobacco seedlings in the spring, hoed and weeded the crop throughout the summer, and in the fall picked and hung up the leaves to cure over the winter. Epidemic diseases did not spread easily in the Chesapeake because the plantation quarters were small and dispersed. Also,

to 5 million people. Yet slaving remained a choice for Africans, not a necessity. The old and still powerful kingdom of Benin, famous for its cast bronzes and carved ivory, resolutely opposed the slave trade, prohibiting the export of male slaves for over a century.

The trade in humans produced untold misery—taking tens of thousands of lives and subjecting millions to slavery. In many African societies class divisions hardened as people of noble birth enslaved and sold those of lesser status. Gender relations shifted as well. Men constituted two-thirds of the slaves sent across the Atlantic both because European planters paid more for "men and stout men boys," "none to exceed the years of 25 or under 10," and because African traders directed women captives into local slave markets for sale as agricultural workers and house servants. The resulting imbalance between the sexes in Africa allowed some men to take several wives, changing the nature of marriage. Moreover, the Atlantic trade prompted harsher forms of slavery in Africa, eroding the dignity of human life there as well as in the Western Hemisphere.

But those Africans sold into the heart of the South Atlantic system had the bleakest fate. Torn from their village

Olaudah Equiano

The Brutal "Middle Passage"

Olaudah Equiano, known during his life in London as Gustavus Vassa, claimed to have been born in the ancient kingdom of Benin (in present-day southern Nigeria). However, in separate scholarly articles, two researchers have recently suggested that Equiano was actually born into slavery in America and used information from conversations with African-born slaves to create a fictitious history of an idyllic childhood, kidnapping and enslavement at the age of eleven, and a traumatic Middle Passage across the Atlantic. Whatever the truth of this controversial interpretation, Equiano apparently endured plantation slavery in Barbados and Virginia, where he was purchased by an English sea captain. Buying his freedom in 1766, Equiano lived in London and became an antislavery activist; twenty years later he published the memoir from which this selection has been taken.

My father, besides many slaves, had a numerous family of which seven lived to grow up, including myself and a sister who was the only daughter. . . . I was trained up from my earliest years in the art of war, my daily exercise was shooting and throwing javelins, and my mother adorned me with emblems after the manner of our greatest warriors. One day, when all our people were gone out to their works as usual and only I and my dear sister were left to mind the house, two men and a woman got over our walls, and in a moment seized us both, and without giving us time to cry out or make resistance they stopped our mouths and ran off with us into the nearest wood. . . .

At length, after many days' travelling, during which I had often changed masters, I got into the hands of a chieftain in a very pleasant country. This man had two wives and some children, and they all used me extremely well and did all they could to comfort me, particularly the first wife, who was something like my mother.

Although I was a great many days' journey from my father's house, yet these people spoke exactly the same language with us. This first master of mine, as I may call him, was a smith, and my principal employment was working his bellows.

I was again sold and carried through a number of places till . . . at the end of six or seven months after I had been kidnapped I arrived at the sea coast.

The first object which saluted my eyes when I arrived on the coast was the sea, and a slave ship which was then riding at anchor and waiting for its cargo. I now saw myself deprived of all chance of returning to my native country . . . ; and I even wished for my former slavery in preference to my present situation, which was filled with horrors of every kind. . . . I was soon put down under the decks, and there I received such a salutation in my nostrils as I had never experienced in my life; so that with the loathsomeness of the stench and crying together, I became so sick and low that I was not able to eat, nor had I the least desire to taste any thing. I now wished for the last friend, death, to relieve me; but soon, to my grief, two of the white men offered me eatables, and on my refusing to eat, one of them held me fast by the hands and laid me across I think the windlass, and tied my feet while the other flogged me severely. I had never experienced anything of this kind before, and although, not being used to the water, I naturally feared that element the first time I saw it, yet nevertheless could I have got over the nettings, I would have jumped over the side, but I could not. . . . One day, when we had a smooth sea and moderate wind, two of my wearied countrymen who were chained together (I was near them at the time), preferring death to such a life of misery, somehow made it through the nettings and jumped into the sea.

At last we came in sight of the island of Barbados; the white people got some old slaves from the land to pacify us. They told us we were not to be eaten but to work, and were soon to go on land where we should see many of our country people. This report eased us much; and sure enough soon after we were landed there came to us Africans of all languages.

Source: The Interesting Narrative of the Life of Olaudah Equiano, or Gustavus Vassa, the African, Written by Himself (London, 1789), 15, 22–23, 28–29.

From a Piece of Property to a Man of Property: The Odyssey of Robert Pearle

When Robert Pearle died in 1765 at the age of seventy-five, he owned an extensive estate that included fourteen slaves, whom he divided among his three sons. The father's financial skills apparently rubbed off on his son James. When James Pearle died in 1774, he owned nine slaves, nine thousand pounds of tobacco, and personal goods worth £782, an estate that placed him among the top tenth of all Maryland property owners. Unlike these other wealthy men, the Pearles were not solely European by ancestry. Robert Pearle was a mulatto, "born of a negroe slave" (as a court report put it) and a slave himself until the age of thirty-five. His son James was born free, the son of Nanny Pearle, who was also a mulatto and a former slave.

According to law, Robert Pearle was the product of an illegal union. By 1700 Maryland law strictly prohibited miscegenation, sexual relations between those of European and African descent, labeling such unions "Unnatural and Inordinate Copulations." However, planters handled their human property pretty much as they pleased. For decades planters had flogged the young English indentured servants who worked their lands and had forced themselves on servant women—callously adding a year to the woman's time of service if she became pregnant. The coming of racial slavery only increased this physical and sexual exploitation, as scores of English planters fathered children by enslaved African women. A Maryland census of 1755 listed 42,000 enslaved blacks (28 percent of the total population) and 3,592 mulattos (2 percent), a majority of whom were slaves.

Whatever the brutality of forced interracial sex, it opened the door to freedom. Robert Pearle was undoubtedly the son of his owner, Richard Marsham, a wealthy Catholic planter in Prince George's County who, at his death in 1713, owned thirty-six slaves. Pearle's mother was probably the "Negro woman Sarah" who received special treatment in Marsham's will. Sarah obtained her freedom and the right to receive "good sufficient Dyet and apparill . . . and every year

Robert Pearle's Will, 1765

"In the Name of God Amen." Apart from this ritualistic phrase, Robert Pearle's last Testament—unlike other colonial wills—is completely devoid of religious sentiments, suggesting that he may not have imbibed the Catholic faith of his father and his patrons. In businesslike fashion, the will divides his most valuable property—fourteen slaves—among his sons Daniel, James, and Basill, and provides a token sum of money, a mere five shillings, to each of Pearle's other children—two sons and two daughters.
Maryland Historical Society.

during her natural Life the Sum of two Pounds Sterling." Marsham's will also granted the prospect of freedom to Sarah's mulatto offspring. Robert and his mulatto wife Nanny—perhaps another of Marsham's children—along with their two-year-old son Daniel—were "to be fully discharged and set free" in 1720, provided they remained "vigilent and faithful" to his executors, members of the influential Waring family. In the sins of the white father lay the salvation of the mulatto son and daughter.

Robert Pearle used his freedom wisely. Initially propertyless, he employed his skills as a carpenter to make his way in the world. In 1726 he won a legal suit for a debt against innkeeper Edward Bradshaw, receiving a judgment of 3,200 pounds of tobacco, and collected similar debts from many others: despite Pearle's background, the justices of the Prince George's County court enforced his contractual agreements. On the one occasion when they denied his right to sue, "Considering the Circumstances of the Plaintiff who is a Molatto (born of a Negro slave)," Pearle successfully petitioned the Maryland Assembly for the right "to Recover his Just Debts," eventually winning a substantial judgment of £45.

Something—his carpentry skills, solid character and ambition, or ties to the Marshams and Warings—smoothed Pearle's way through the white world. By 1724 he had acquired 100 acres of land; three years later he owned a white servant; and two years after that he held title to African slaves, mortgaging "negro man Harry" and "negro woman Lucy" to sheriff Richard Lee for 8,400 pounds of tobacco. For the next decade Pearle lived quietly, enjoying his property and raising his children.

Then interracial sex, the source of Robert Pearle's freedom, threatened his family with legal disaster. In 1742 a grand jury indicted William Marshall, a white planter, for marrying a mulatto: Ann Pearle, Robert's daughter. Just as this case was coming to trial, the county court charged Elizabeth Graves, a white woman, with the crime of marrying Daniel Pearle, Robert's mulatto son. For some reason—perhaps a personal vendetta, perhaps increasing racial tension—the Pearles and their spouses found themselves facing severe legal penalties. The justices tried William Marshall, found him guilty of miscegenation, and sentenced him to "Become a Servant for Seven Years"—the fate that awaited Elizabeth Graves as well. If convicted of interracial marriage, the two Pearle children faced a much harsher prospect: to "become a Slave during Life."

Mysteriously, none of these sentences was ever imposed. Marshall successfully appealed his conviction to the Provincial Court, while "by order of [the] Attorney General," the case against Elizabeth Graves was never prosecuted. The young Pearles—Ann and Daniel—were never even indicted. Apparently Robert Pearle's influential white friends had intervened to protect his family. As Pearle's biographer, Mary Jeske, has suggested, their success demonstrated that race relations in the small and intimate world of plantation society were much more fluid and complex than the statutes dictated.

However, the lines of racial caste were steadily hardening. When Robert Pearle won his freedom in 1720, slaves constituted about 20 percent of the population of Prince George's County; by 1740, the proportion was twice as great, and blacks formed the majority in many Tidewater districts. Fearing slave revolts, whites were no longer willing to tolerate free blacks and mulattos, especially those who threatened white supremacy by marrying across racial lines. Aware of this ominous change, in 1744 Robert Pearle, his son Daniel, and his son-in-law William Marshall moved their families west to the Monocacy Valley, a sparsely settled region in what would soon become Frederick County. There, each man took a seventeen-year lease on 100-acre farmsteads on the Carrollton Manor, a vast estate owned by Charles Carroll and populated primarily by German and English tenants. At one stroke the Pearles had escaped the racially charged atmosphere of the Tidewater region and secured a new powerful white Catholic ally. Following in the religious footsteps of his owner-father, Robert Pearle was a Catholic—as were the Warings and the Carrolls. The ties of religion, like those of kinship, counterbalanced the antagonisms of race.

Migration to Carrollton Manor offered the prospect of family cohesion and economic mobility. Land was plentiful, and eventually all of Robert Pearle's sons secured manorial leases. Taking advantage of low rents, high prices for tobacco and wheat, and slave labor, the Pearles attained substantial prosperity.

We can only wonder if the Pearles had any qualms about owning enslaved Africans. Having been raised in a "society with slaves" in which racial boundaries were blurred, the family may have identified with successful planters and regretted only that it did not own more slaves. As biographer Mary Jeske notes: "Had he been the legitimate son of his white father rather than a mulatto bastard, Pearle might well have joined the ranks of the Chesapeake elite." As it was, Robert Pearle had to scrape and struggle for decades, first for freedom, then for economic prosperity, and finally for family security. Racial slavery and the caste system exacted a high price even from those who attained their freedom.

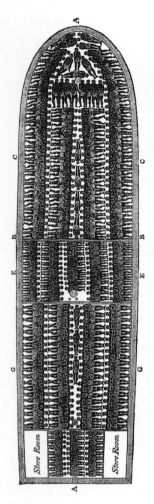

Two Views of the Middle Passage

As the slave trade boomed during the eighteenth century, ship designers packed in more and more human cargo, treating enslaved Africans with no more respect than hogsheads of sugar or tobacco. By contrast, a watercolor of 1846, painted by a ship's officer on a voyage to Brazil, captures the humanity and dignity of the enslaved Africans.
Peabody & Essex Museum / Royal Albert Memorial Museum, Exeter, England / Bridgeman Art Library.

because tobacco profits were low, planters could not afford to buy new slaves and therefore treated those they had less harshly than West Indian planters did. Some tobacco planters attempted to increase their workforce through reproduction, purchasing a high proportion of female slaves and encouraging large families. In 1720 women made up about a third of the African population of Maryland, and the black population had begun to increase naturally. One absentee owner instructed his plantation agent "to be kind and indulgent to the breeding wenches, and not to force them when with child upon any service or hardship that will be injurious to them." And, he added, "the children are to be well looked after." By midcentury slaves made up 40 percent of some parts of the Chesapeake, and over three-quarters of them were American born.

Slaves in South Carolina labored under conditions that were much more oppressive. The colony had grown slowly until 1700, when Africans from rice-growing

societies, who knew how to plant, harvest, and process that nutritious grain, turned it into a profitable export crop (see New Technology, "Rice: Riches, Wretchedness, and Community," p. 86). To expand production, white planters imported tens of thousands of slaves—and a "rice revolution" quickly brought an extraordinary change to the colony (Figure 3.1). By 1720 Africans made up a majority of the population of South Carolina as a whole and constituted 80 percent of the residents of the rice-growing areas, where they lived on plantations of fifty or more slaves. However, many workers met an early death. Growing rice in inland swamp areas required months of work in ankle-deep mud, weeding the crop amidst pools of putrid water. Mosquito-borne epidemic diseases swept through these lowlands, taking thousands of African lives. Overwork killed many more slaves because moving tons of dirt to build irrigation works was brutally hard labor. As a Scottish traveler noted, "the labour required for it is only fit for slaves, and I think the hardest work I have seen them

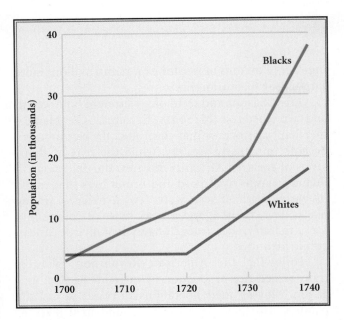

FIGURE 3.1 The Growth of Slavery in South Carolina

To grow more rice, white planters imported thousands of African slaves, giving South Carolina a black majority and prompting the development of an African-influenced language and culture.

engaged in." As in the West Indies, there were many deaths and few births, and the importation of new slaves constantly "re-Africanized" the black population.

African American Community and Resistance

Slaves came from many regions of West Africa. South Carolina slave owners preferred laborers from the Gold Coast and Gambia, who had a reputation as hard workers with farming experience (Map 3.3). However, as African sources of slaves shifted southward after 1730, more than 30 percent of the colony's workforce came from the Congo and Angola. Because of such changes in the trade, no African people or language group formed a majority of the slaves in any American colony (Table 3.5). Moreover, many white planters consciously enhanced this cultural diversity to prevent slave revolts. "The safety of the Plantations," declared a widely read English pamphlet, "depends upon having Negroes from all parts of Guiny, who do not understand each other's languages and Customs and cannot agree to Rebel."

The Emergence of an African American Culture. In fact, slaves initially did not regard each other as "Africans" or "blacks" but as members of a specific family, clan, or people—Mende, Hausa, Ibo, Yoruba—and they associated mostly with those who shared their language or culture. Gradually, however, enslaved peoples found it in their interest to transcend these cultural barriers. Especially in the West Indies and in the lowlands of South Carolina, the largely African-born population created new languages, such as the Gullah dialect in South Carolina, that combined English and African words in an African grammatical structure. "They have a language peculiar to themselves," a missionary reported, "a wild confused medley of Negro and corrupt English, which makes them very unintelligible except to those who have conversed with them for many years." In South Carolina, another missionary complained as late as 1754 that "our negros are so Ignorant of the English Language . . . it is a great while before you can get them to understand . . . the Meaning of

TABLE 3.5 African Slaves Imported into North America, by Ethnicity, 1700–1775

African Region of Departure	Ethnicity	Number	Percent
Senegambia	Mandinka, Fulbe, Serer, Jola, Wolof, and Bambara	47,300	17
Sierra Leone	Vai, Mende, Kpelle, and Kru	33,400	12
Gold Coast	Ashanti and Fanit	19,500	7
Bight of Benin, Bight of Biafra	Ibo and Ibibio	47,300	17
West-Central	Kongo, Tio, and Matamba	44,600	16
Southeast Africa	Unknown	2,800	1
Other or Unknown		83,500	30
TOTAL		**278,400**	**100**

The numbers are estimated from known voyages involving 195,000 Africans. Ethnic origins should be considered as very tentative because slaves from many regions left from the same port and because the ethnic and regional origins of 83,500 slaves (30 percent) are not known.

Source: Aaron S. Fogleman, "From Slaves, Convicts, and Servants to Free Passengers: The Transformation of Immigration in the Era of the American Revolution," *Journal of American History* 85 (June 1998), Table A4.

Rice: Riches, Wretchedness, and Community

Two technological innovations—one African, one European—shaped the evolution of the South Carolina rice industry and black life during the eighteenth century. Because rice was an exotic crop to them, the first English settlers in the Carolinas failed in their attempts to grow the nutritious grain. As one planter recalled, "The people being unacquainted with the manner of cultivating rice, many difficulties attended to the first planting and preparing it, as a vendable commodity."

West Africans soon provided the requisite knowledge. Along the semitropical western coast of Africa, a traveler noted, rice "forms the chief part of the African's sustenance." Eager to have ready access to a familiar food, enslaved blacks in South Carolina took up rice cultivation during the 1690s, teaching their English owners not only how to plant and tend the crop but how to process it. To separate the tough husk of the rice seed from the nutritious grain inside, English settlers had experimented with a "rice mill," a "Pendulum Engine, which doeth much better, and in lesser time and labour, huske rice." When these machines did not prove equal to the task, English planters turned to African women and their traditional husking technology. The women placed the grain in large wooden mortars hollowed from the trunks of pine or cypress trees and then pounded it with long wooden pestles, removing the husks and whitening the grains. Their labor was prodigious. By the 1770s slaves were annually process-

ing 75 million tons of rice for export and millions more for their own consumption.

African labor and technology brought both wealth and wretchedness to South Carolina. The planter-merchant aristocracy that controlled the rice industry became immensely wealthy, while the tens of thousands of enslaved Africans who grew the rice in putrid inland swamps lived hard and brutal lives that ended in early death. There were few marriages among blacks, few children, and a weak sense of community life as the surviving slaves clung to their diverse African ethnic identities.

Following the American Revolution, planters transformed rice production by introducing tidal irrigation. Moving their operations to coastal areas, the planters had their slave laborers build high dikes to keep salt water out of the rice fields and elaborate floodgates and irrigation ditches to admit fresh river water. As the well-irrigated rice grew taller, workers raised the level of the water until the crop had shoots with three leaves (about three weeks after planting). Then they drained the field, hoed away the weeds, and reflooded the fields until harvest time.

The new system was more expensive in terms of initial capital but much more productive. The average yield per acre on a prewar inland swamp plantation was about 800 pounds, while on a postwar tidal plantation it was around 1,300 pounds. Equally important, a worker could now cultivate five times as much rice, dramatically reducing day-to-day labor costs. Finally, planters devised mills that used the tidal flow to power the pestle-and-mortar machines, removing the heavy burden of hulling the rice from slave women.

The new tidal technology permitted the flowering of the task system of labor that was unique to the South Carolina slave economy. Exploiting the weight of their overwhelming numbers, enslaved laborers had gradually won control over their work lives and staged minor rebellions when it was challenged. "All my

Words." In the Chesapeake, where there were more American-born blacks (and in the northern colonies, which had small numbers of slaves), many Africans gradually gave up their native tongues for English. A European visitor to mid-eighteenth-century Virginia reported with surprise that "all the blacks spoke very good English."

The acquisition of a common language, whether Gullah or English, was a prerequisite for the creation of an African American community. A more equal sex ratio,

which would encourage stable families, was another. In South Carolina a high death rate undermined ties of family and kinship, but after 1725 blacks in the Chesapeake colonies created strong nuclear families and extended kin relationships. For example, all but 30 of the 128 slaves on the home quarter of Charles Carroll's estate in Maryland were members of two extended families. These "African Americans" had gradually developed a culture of their own, passing on family names, traditions, and knowledge to the next generation. As one observer noted, blacks had

working Negroes left me last Night," one planter complained in 1786. However, as the carefully laid-out irrigation system on tidal plantations gradually imposed an orderly grid on the landscape, slaves and masters found it easier to negotiate the tasks a worker would perform each day: hoeing a square of 105 feet, digging 75 trenches, harvesting a half-acre. As slaves settled in to a regular work routine, they also lived longer and bore more children, primarily because tidal plantations were less disease-ridden than inland swamps. Even before the end of the Atlantic slave trade in 1808, they had begun to create a cohesive African American community. Technological change had affected the course of cultural life.

Rice Hulling in West Africa and Georgia

The eighteenth-century engraving shows West African women hulling rice using huge wooden mortars and pestles, the same technology employed in the photograph of early-twentieth-century African American women in Georgia.

Library of Congress / Georgia Department of Archives and History, Atlanta.

For more help analyzing these images, see the ONLINE STUDY GUIDE at bedfordstmartins.com/henretta.

created a cultural world of their own, "a Nation within a Nation."

As enslaved blacks forged an identity in an alien land, their lives became a mixture of old African forms and new American experiences. Many Africans arrived in the colonies with filed teeth and ritual scars that white planters called "country markings" or "negro markings." Because slaves could not re-create traditional ethnic-based communities, these marks of tribal or group identity fell into disuse. However, the African heritage took tangible form in wood carvings inspired by traditional motifs, the large wooden mortars and pestles that slaves used to hull rice, and the design of shacks, which often had rooms arranged from front to back in a distinctive "I" pattern (not side by side, as was common in English houses). African values also persisted, as some slaves retained Muslim religious beliefs and many more relied on the spiritual powers of conjurers, who knew the ways of African gods. As an English missionary reported from Georgia in the 1750s, many slaves clung to "the old

African Culture in South Carolina
The dance and the musical instruments are of Yoruba origin, the contribution of Africans from the Niger River–Gold Coast region. This Yoruba-dominated area accounted for one-sixth of the slaves imported into South Carolina. Colonial Williamsburg Foundation.

Superstition of a false Religion." Other slaves adopted Protestant Christianity but reshaped its doctrines, ethics, and rituals to fit their needs and create a spiritually rich and long-lasting religious culture of their own.

Yet there were drastic limits on African American creativity because slaves were denied education and accumulated few material goods. A well-traveled European who visited a slave hut in Virginia in the late eighteenth century found it to be

> *more miserable than the most miserable of the cottages of our peasants. The husband and wife sleep on a mean pallet, the children on the ground; a very bad fireplace, some utensils for cooking. . . . They work all week, not having a single day for themselves except for holidays.*

Oppression and Resistance. Slaves resisted the rigorous work routine at their peril. To punish slaves who disobeyed, refused to work, or ran away, planters resorted to the lash and the amputation of fingers, toes, and ears (see American Voices, "Philip Fithian: Sadism under Slavery," p. 89). Declaring the chronic runaway Ballazore an "incorrigeble rogue," a Virginia planter ordered all his toes cut off: "nothing less than dismembering will reclaim him." Thomas Jefferson, who witnessed such cruelty on his father's plantation in mid-eighteenth-century

Virginia, noted that each generation of whites was "nursed, educated, and daily exercised in tyranny," for the relationship "between master and slave is a perpetual exercise of the most unremitting despotism on the one part, and degrading submission on the other."

The extent of violence by whites depended on the size and density of the slave population. Because their numbers were so small, blacks in rural areas of New York, Pennsylvania, and other northern colonies endured low status but little violence. Conversely, assertive slaves in the predominantly African-populated West Indian islands routinely suffered branding with hot irons. In the lowlands of South Carolina, where Africans outnumbered Europeans eight to one, planters prohibited their black workers from leaving the plantation without special passes and organized their poor white neighbors into armed patrols to police the countryside. Slaves dealt with their plight in a variety of ways. Some newly arrived Africans fled to the frontier, where they tried to establish African villages or, more often, married into Indian tribes. Blacks familiar with white ways, especially those fluent in English, fled to towns, where they tried to pass as free blacks. But the great majority of African Americans worked out their destinies as enslaved laborers on rural plantations, continually bargaining over the terms of their bondage. Some blacks agreed to do extra work in return for better food and clothes; at other times they seized a small privilege

Philip Fithian

Sadism under Slavery

Planters relied on various incentives to get work from their African slaves. A few used rewards, providing cooperative laborers with food, leisure, and relatively good treatment. Many more planters wanted to maximize their profits and relied on force, extracting work by whipping recalcitrant laborers. Some brutal owners and overseers were so determined to demonstrate their power that they went much further, as described by Philip Fithian, a young Princeton College graduate who was employed as a tutor by Robert Carter III, one of the wealthiest Virginia planters.

[1773] This Evening, after I had dismissed the Children, & was sitting in the School-Room cracking Nuts, [I asked] . . . Mr. Carters Clerk, a civil, inoffensive agreeable young Man . . . what their [the slaves' food] allowance is? He told me that, excepting some favourites around the table their weekly allowance is a peck of Corn, & a pound of Meat a Head!—And Mr. Carter is allowed by all . . . [to be] by far the most humane to his Slaves of any in these parts! Good God! are these Christians?

While I am on the Subject, I will relate further, what I heard George Lee's Overseer, one Morgan, say the

other day that he himself had often done to Negroes, and found it useful. He said that whipping of any kind does them no good, for they will laugh at your greatest Severity; But he told us he had invented two things, and by several experiments had proved their success.

For Sullenness, Obstinacy, or Idleness, says he, Take a Negro, strip him, tie him fast to a post; take then a sharp Curry-Comb, and curry him severely till he is well scrap'd; and call a Boy with some dry Hay, and make the Boy rub him down for several Minutes, then salt him, & unlose him. He will attend to his Business (said the inhuman Infidel) afterwards!

But savage Cruelty does not exceed His next diabolical Invention—To get a Secret from a Negro, says he, take the following Method—Lay upon your Floor a large thick plank, having a peg about eighteen inches long, of hard wood, & very Sharp, on the upper end, fixed fast in the plank—then strip the Negro, tie the Cord to a staple in the Ceiling, [and suspend the Negro from that cord] so that his foot may just rest on the sharpened Peg then turn him briskly around, and you would laugh (said our informer) at the Dexterity of the Negro, while he was relieving his Feet on the sharpen'd Peg!

I need say nothing of these seeing there is a righteous God, who will take vengeance on such Inventions.

Source: Philip Vickers Fithian, *Journals and Letters, 1773–1774,* ed. Hunter Dulsingon Farish (Williamsburg, VA: Colonial Williamsburg Press, 1943), 50–51.

and dared the master to revoke it. By such means Sundays became a day free of labor—a right rather than a privilege. When bargaining failed to yield results, slaves protested silently by working slowly or stealing. Other blacks, provoked beyond endurance, attacked their owners or overseers, although such assaults were punishable by mutilation or death. And despite the fact that whites were armed and, outside of coastal South Carolina, more numerous than Africans, some blacks plotted rebellion.

Predictably, South Carolina became the setting for the largest slave uprising of the eighteenth century—the Stono Rebellion of 1739. The governor of the Spanish (and Catholic) colony of Florida helped to instigate the revolt by promising freedom and land to slaves who ran away from their English owners. By February 1739 at least sixty-nine slaves had escaped to St. Augustine, and rumors circulated "that a Conspiracy was formed by Negroes in Carolina to rise and make their way out of the province."

When war between England and Spain broke out later in September, seventy-five Africans—some of them Portuguese-speaking Catholics from the African kingdom of Kongo—rose in revolt and killed a number of whites near the Stono River. Displaying their skills as former soldiers in the war-torn Kongo, the rebels took up arms and marched south toward Florida "with Colours displayed and two Drums beating." Unrest swept the countryside, but the white militia killed many of the Stono rebels and dispersed the rest, preventing a general uprising. Frightened whites imported fewer new slaves and tightened plantation discipline. For Africans the price of active resistance was high.

The Southern Gentry

As the southern colonies became full-fledged slave societies, the character of life changed for whites as well as

blacks. After 1675 settlement in the Chesapeake region moved inland, away from the disease-ridden swampy lowlands, allowing English migrants to live much longer lives and form stable families and communities. Similarly, many white planters in South Carolina improved their health by transferring their residence to Charleston during the hot, mosquito-ridden summer months. As their longevity increased, men reassumed their customary control of family property. When death rates had been high, many husbands had named their wives as executors of their estates and legal guardians of their children and had given their widows large inheritances. After 1700 most wealthy planters named male kin as executors and guardians and again gave priority of inheritance to male children, limiting a widow's portion to the traditional one-third share during her lifetime.

The reappearance of strict patriarchy within the family mirrored broader social developments. The planter and merchant elite now stood at the top of a social hierarchy somewhat like that of Europe, exercising authority over a yeoman class, a larger group of white tenant farmers, and a growing host of enslaved black laborers—the American equivalent of oppressed peasants and serfs. Wealthy planters used Africans to plant orchards and grow food as well as tobacco; build houses, wagons, and tobacco casks; and make shoes and clothes. By increasing the self-sufficiency of their plantations, the planter elite survived the depressed tobacco market between 1660 and 1720. Small-scale planters who used family labor to grow tobacco fared less well, falling deeper into debt to their creditors among the elite.

To prevent another rebellion like Bacon's uprising, which had brought a short military occupation by English troops, the Chesapeake gentry paid attention to the concerns of middling and poor whites. They urged smallholders to invest in land and slaves. By 1770 no fewer than 60 percent of the English families in the Chesapeake owned at least one slave and therefore had a personal stake in this exploitative labor system. In addition, the gentry gradually reduced the taxes paid by poorer whites; in Virginia the annual poll tax paid by every free man fell from 45 pounds of tobacco in 1675 to 5 pounds in 1750. The political elite also allowed poor yeomen and some tenants to vote. The strategy of the leading families—the Carters, Lees, Randolphs, Robinsons—was to curry favor with these voters at election time, bribing them with rum, money, and the promise of favorable legislation and minor offices in county governments. In return, they expected yeomen and tenants to elect them to political office and defer to their authority. This "horse trading" solidified the social position of the planter elite, which used its control of the Virginia House of Burgesses to cut the political power of the royal governor—bargaining with him over patronage and land grants. Hundreds of yeoman farmers benefited as well, tasting political power and garnering substantial fees and salaries as deputy sheriffs, road surveyors, estate appraisers, and grand jurymen.

Even as the expansion of officeholding and slave ownership created new ties between rich planters and yeoman farmers, wealthy Chesapeake gentlemen consciously set themselves apart from their less affluent neighbors. Until the 1720s the ranks of the gentry were filled with boisterous, aggressive men who enjoyed many of the amusements of common folk—from hunting, hard drinking, and gambling on horse races to sharing tales of their manly prowess in seducing female servants and slaves. As time passed, however, affluent

Chesapeake landholders took on the trappings of wealth, modeling themselves after the English aristocracy. Beginning in the 1720s they replaced their modest wooden houses with mansions of brick and mortar. The plantation dwelling of Robert "King" Carter was over seventy-five feet long, forty-four feet wide, and forty feet high. Genteel planters entertained their neighbors in lavish style and sent their sons to London to be educated as lawyers and gentlemen. Most of the southern men who were educated in England returned to America, married well-to-do heiresses, and followed in their fathers' footsteps, managing plantations, socializing with other members of the gentry class, and participating in politics.

Wealthy Chesapeake and South Carolina women also emulated the elegant and refined ways of the English gentry. They read English newspapers and fashionable magazines, wore English clothes, and dined in the English fashion, with an elaborate afternoon tea. To improve their daughters' chances of finding a desirable marriage partner, they hired English tutors to teach them etiquette. Once married, affluent gentry women deferred to their husbands' authority, reared pious children, and maintained elaborate social networks—gradually creating the new ideal of the southern genteel woman. Using the profits of the South Atlantic system, the planter elite formed an increasingly well-educated, refined, and stable ruling class.

The Northern Maritime Economy

The South Atlantic system had a broad geographic reach. As early as the 1640s, New England farmers provided bread, lumber, fish, and meat to the sugar islands. As a West Indian explained in 1647, planters in the islands "had rather buy food at very dear rates than produce it by labour, so infinite is the profit of sugar works." By 1700 the economies of the West Indies and New England were tightly interwoven. After 1720 farmers and merchants in New York, New Jersey, and Pennsylvania entered the West Indian trade, shipping wheat, corn, and bread to the sugar islands.

The South Atlantic system tied the whole British empire together economically. In return for the sugar they exported to England, West Indian planters received bills of exchange (credit slips) from London merchant houses. The planters used those bills to buy slaves from transatlantic slavers and to reimburse North American farmers and merchants for their provisions and shipping services. Farmers and merchants then exchanged the bills for British manufactures, primarily textiles and iron goods, thus completing the cycle.

Urban Development. The West Indian trade created the first American merchant fortunes and the first urban industries (Map 3.4). Merchants in Boston, Newport, Providence, Philadelphia, and New York invested their profits from the West Indian trade in new ships and in factories that refined raw sugar into finished loaves (which previously had been imported from England) and distilled West Indian molasses into rum. By the 1740s Boston distillers were exporting more than half a million gallons of rum annually. In addition, merchants in smaller ports, such as Salem and Marblehead, built a major fishing industry, providing salted mackerel and cod to feed the slaves of the sugar islands and to export to southern Europe. Southern merchants transformed Baltimore into a major port by developing a bustling trade in wheat, while Charleston traders exported deerskins, indigo, and rice to European markets.

The expansion of Atlantic commerce in the eighteenth century fueled rapid growth in American port cities and coastal towns. By 1750 Newport, Rhode Island, and Charleston, South Carolina, had nearly 10,000 residents apiece, Boston had 15,000, and New York had almost 18,000. The largest port was Philadelphia, whose population by 1776 reached 30,000, the size of a large European provincial city. Smaller coastal towns emerged as centers of the shipbuilding and lumber industries. By the 1740s seventy sawmills dotted the Piscataqua River in New Hampshire, providing low-cost wood for homes, warehouses, and especially shipbuilding. Taking advantage of the Navigation Acts, which allowed colonists to build and own trading vessels, scores of shipwrights turned out oceangoing vessels, while hundreds of other artisans made ropes, sails, and metal fittings for the new fleet. Shipyards in Boston and Philadelphia launched about 15,000 tons of oceangoing vessels annually; eventually colonial-built ships made up about one-third of the British merchant fleet.

The impact of the South Atlantic system extended into the interior of North America. A small fleet of trading vessels sailed back and forth between Philadelphia and the villages along the Delaware Bay, exchanging cargoes of European goods for barrels of flour and wheat for sale in both the West Indies and Europe. By the 1750s hundreds of professional teamsters in Maryland moved 370,000 bushels of wheat and corn and 16,000 barrels of flour to market each year—over 10,000 wagon trips. To service this traffic, entrepreneurs and artisans set up taverns, horse stables, and barrel-making shops in small towns along the wagon roads, providing additional jobs. The prosperous interior town of Lancaster, Pennsylvania, boasted more than 200 artisans, both German and English. The South Atlantic system thus provided not only markets for farmers (by far the largest group of northern residents) but also opportunities for merchants, artisans, and workers in country towns and seaport cities.

Seaport Society. At the top of seaport society stood a small group of wealthy landowners and prosperous merchants. By 1750 about forty merchants controlled over

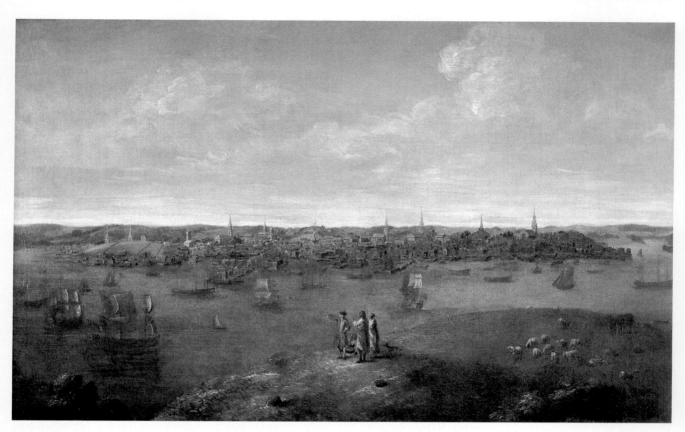

A View of Boston in 1738

In this painting of Boston by John Smibert (1738), church spires dominate the skyline and long wharves extend far into the harbor, offering anchorage for oceangoing vessels. This mixture of religious piety and maritime prosperity gave Boston—and, to a lesser extent, Philadelphia—a distinctive tone, with greater moral discipline than the other large seaport cities of New York, Baltimore, and Charleston. Courtesy, Childs Gallery, Boston.

50 percent of Philadelphia's trade and had taxable assets averaging £10,000, a huge sum at the time (Figure 3.2). Like the Chesapeake gentry, these urban merchants imitated the British upper classes, importing design books from England and building Georgian-style mansions to showcase their wealth. Their wives created a genteel culture, decorating their houses with fine furniture and entertaining guests at elegant dinners.

Artisan and shopkeeper families formed the middle ranks of seaport society and numbered nearly half the population. Innkeepers, butchers, seamstresses, shoemakers, weavers, bakers, carpenters, masons, and dozens of other specialists socialized among themselves, formed mutual self-help societies, and worked to gain a competency—an income sufficient to maintain their families in modest comfort and dignity. Wives and husbands often worked as a team, teaching the "mysteries of the craft" to their children. Some artisans aspired to wealth and status, an entrepreneurial ethic that prompted them to hire apprentices and expand production, and the most prosperous owned their own houses and shops (sometimes run by widows continuing a family business). However, most

craft workers were not well-to-do, and many of them were quite poor. In his entire lifetime a tailor was lucky to accumulate £30 worth of property—far less than the £2,000 owned at death by an ordinary merchant or the £300 listed in the probate inventory of a successful blacksmith.

Laboring men and women formed the lowest ranks of urban society. Merchants needed hundreds of dockworkers to unload manufactured goods and molasses from inbound ships and reload the ships with barrels of wheat, fish, and rice for export. They often filled these demanding jobs with black slaves—who numbered 10 percent of the workforce in Philadelphia and New York City—or they hired unskilled men who worked for wages. Poor women—whether single, married, or widowed—could eke out a living by washing clothes, spinning wool, or working as servants or prostitutes. To make ends meet, most laboring families sent their children out to work at an early age. Indispensable to the economy yet without homes of their own, these urban laborers lived in crowded tenements in back alleys. In good times hard work brought family security or enough money to drink cheap New England rum in waterfront taverns.

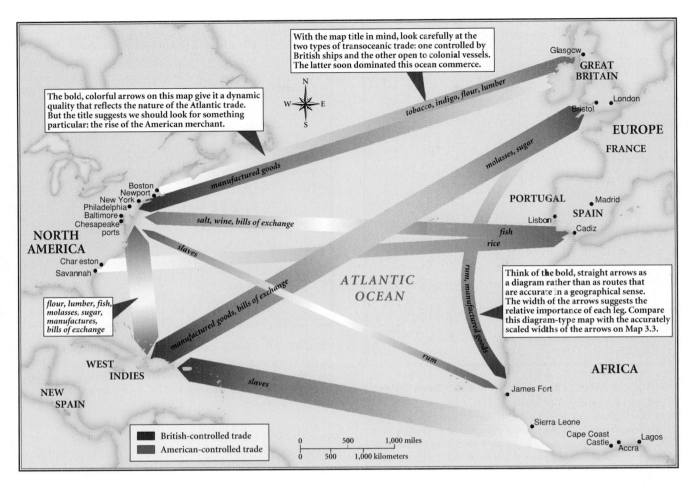

MAP 3.4 The Rise of the American Merchant, 1750

In accordance with mercantilist doctrine, British merchants controlled most of the transatlantic trade in manufactures, sugar, tobacco, and slaves. However, merchants in Boston, New York, and Philadelphia seized control of the West Indian trade, while Newport traders imported some slaves from Africa, and Boston and Charleston merchants carried fish and rice to southern Europe.

Periods of stagnant commerce affected everyone, threatening merchants with bankruptcy and artisans with irregular work. For laborers and seamen, whose household budgets left no margin for sickness or unemployment, depressed trade meant hunger, dependence on charity handed out by town-appointed overseers of the poor, and—for the most desperate—a life of petty thievery. Involvement in the South Atlantic system between 1660 and 1750 brought economic uncertainty as well as jobs and opportunities to northern workers and farmers.

The New Politics of Empire, 1713–1750

The triumph of the South Atlantic system of production and trade changed the politics of empire. British ministers, pleased with the prosperous commerce in staple crops, were content to rule the colonies with a gentle hand. The colonists enjoyed a significant degree of self-government

and economic autonomy, which put them in a position to challenge the rules of the mercantilist system.

The Rise of Colonial Assemblies

Before 1689 the authority of the representative assemblies in most colonies was weak. Political power rested in the hands of proprietors, royal governors, and authoritarian elites, reflecting the traditional view that "Authority should Descend from Kings and Fathers to Sons and Servants," as a royal-minded political philosopher put it. In the Glorious Revolution of 1688 the political faction known as the Whigs challenged that hierarchical outlook in England, winning the fight for a constitutional monarchy that limited the authority of the crown. English Whigs did not advocate democracy but did believe that the substantial property owners represented by the House of Commons should have some political power, especially over the levying of taxes. When Whig politicians forced William and Mary to accept a Declaration of Rights in

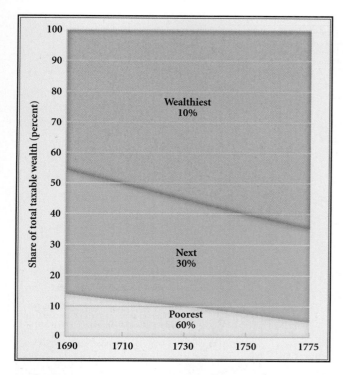

FIGURE 3.2 Wealth Inequality in the Northern Cities
As commerce expanded, the wealth of merchants grew much more rapidly than did that of artisans and laborers. By the 1770s the poorest 60 percent of the taxable inhabitants of Boston, New York, and Philadelphia owned less than 5 percent of the taxable wealth, whereas the top 10 percent—the merchant elite and its allies—controlled 65 percent.

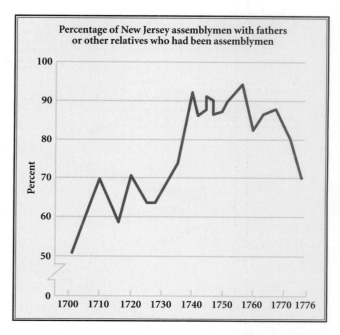

FIGURE 3.3 Family Connections and Political Power
By the 1750s nearly every member of the New Jersey assembly came from a family with a history of political leadership. This is clear testimony to the emergence of an experienced governing elite in the colonies.

1689, they strengthened the powers of the Commons at the expense of the crown.

American representative assemblies also wished to limit the powers of the crown and insisted on maintaining their authority over taxes, refusing to fund military projects and other programs advocated by royal governors. Gradually the colonial legislatures won partial control of the budget and the appointment of local officials, angering imperial bureaucrats and absentee proprietors. "The people in power in America," complained the proprietor William Penn during a struggle with the Pennsylvania Assembly, "think nothing taller than themselves but the Trees." In Massachusetts during the 1720s the assembly refused repeatedly to obey the king's instructions to provide a permanent salary for the royal governor; subsequently legislatures in North Carolina, New Jersey, and Pennsylvania declined to pay their governors any salary for several years.

The rising power of the colonial assemblies created an elitist rather than a democratic political system. Although most property-owning white men had the right to vote after 1700, only men of considerable wealth and status stood for election (Figure 3.3). In Virginia in the 1750s seven members of the influential slave-owning Lee family sat in the House of Burgesses and, along with other powerful families, dominated its major commit-

tees. In New England descendants of the original Puritans had intermarried and formed a core of political leaders. "Go into every village in New England," John Adams said in 1765, "and you will find that the office of justice of the peace, and even the place of representative, have generally descended from generation to generation, in three or four families at most."

However, neither elitist assemblies nor wealthy property owners could impose unpopular edicts on the people. The crowd actions that had overthrown the Dominion of New England in 1689 were a regular part of political life in America and were used to enforce community values. In New York mobs closed houses of prostitution, while in Salem, Massachusetts, they ran people with infectious diseases out of town. In Boston in 1710 crowds prevented merchants from exporting grain during a wartime shortage, and in New Jersey in the 1730s and 1740s angry mobs obstructed proprietors who were forcing tenants from disputed lands. When officials in Boston attempted to restrict the sale of farm produce to a designated public marketplace, a crowd destroyed the building and defied the authorities to arrest them. "If you touch One you shall touch All," an anonymous letter warned the sheriff, "and we will show you a Hundred Men where you can show one." Such expressions of popular power, combined with the growing power of the assemblies, undermined the old authoritarian system. By the 1750s most colonies had representative political institutions that were broadly responsive to popular pressure and increasingly immune to British control.

Salutary Neglect

British colonial policy during the reigns of George I (r. 1714–1727) and George II (r. 1727–1760) contributed significantly to the rise of American self-government. Royal bureaucrats relaxed their supervision of internal colonial affairs, focusing instead on defense and trade. Two generations later the British political philosopher Edmund Burke would praise this strategy as "**salutary** [healthy] **neglect.**"

Salutary neglect was a by-product of the political system developed by Sir Robert Walpole, the leader of the British Whigs in the House of Commons and the king's chief minister between 1720 and 1742. By strategically dispensing appointments and pensions in the name of the king, Walpole won parliamentary support for his policies. However, Walpole's politically driven use of patronage weakened the imperial system by filling the Board of Trade and the royal governorships with men of little talent. When Governor Gabriel Johnson went to North Carolina in the 1730s, he vowed to curb the powers of the assembly and "make a mighty change in the face of affairs." However, Johnson was soon discouraged by the lack of support from the Board of Trade. Forsaking reform, Johnson decided "to do nothing which can be reasonably blamed, and leave the rest to time, and a new set of inhabitants."

Walpole's tactics also weakened the empire by undermining faith in the integrity of the political system. Radical-minded English Whigs were the first to raise the alarm. They argued that Walpole had betrayed the constitutional monarchy established by the Glorious Revolution by using patronage and bribery to create a strong **Court (or Crown) Party**. A Country Party of landed gentlemen likewise warned that Walpole's policies of high taxes and a bloated royal bureaucracy threatened the liberties of the British people. Politically minded colonists adopted these arguments as their own, maintaining that royal governors likewise abused their patronage powers. To preserve American liberty, they tried to enhance the powers of the provincial representative assemblies, thus preparing the way for later demands for political equality within the British empire.

Protecting the Mercantile System of Trade

During the years of salutary neglect Walpole's main preoccupation was to protect British commercial interests in America from the military threats posed by the Spanish and French colonies and from the economic dangers posed by the unwillingness of the American colonists to abide by the acts of Trade and Navigation.

Georgia and War with Spain. Initially, Walpole pursued a cautious foreign policy to allow Britain to

Sir Robert Walpole, the King's Minister
All eyes are on Walpole (left) as he offers advice to the Speaker of the House of Commons. A brilliant politician, Walpole used patronage to command a majority in the Commons and to win the support of George I and George II—the German-speaking monarchs from the duchy of Hanover. Walpole's personal motto, "Let sleeping dogs lie," helps to explain his colonial policy of salutary neglect. © National Trust Photographic Library / John Hammond.

recover from the huge expense of the long wars against Louis XIV of France that finally ended in 1713. However, in 1732 he agreed to provide a subsidy for the new colony of Georgia, a settlement designed by social reformers as a refuge for Britain's poor. Envisioning a society of small farms worked by independent landowners and white indentured servants, the trustees of Georgia limited most land grants to 500 acres and initially outlawed slavery.

Walpole arranged for Parliament to subsidize Georgia because he wanted to protect the valuable rice colony of South Carolina. Spain had long resented the British presence in Carolina and was outraged by the expansion into Georgia, where Spanish Franciscans had Indian missions. In addition, English merchants had steadily increased their trade in slaves and manufactured goods to Spain's colonies in Mesoamerica, eventually controlling two-thirds of that trade. To resist Britain's commercial and geographic expansion, in 1739 Spanish naval forces sparked the so-called War of Jenkins' Ear by mutilating Robert Jenkins, an English

Captain Fayrer Hall

The Impact of the Molasses Act

Before Parliament enacted the Molasses Act of 1733, it conducted a long investigation about its possible effects. One of those testifying was Captain Fayrer Hall, who for many years carried grain, lumber, and horses from the mainland colonies to the West Indies and returned with cargoes of sugar and molasses. Despite considerable evidence that the act would harm the mainland economy and the British export trade, Parliament bowed to the demands of the West Indian Interest—the politically powerful sugar planters and merchants—and passed the legislation.

Capt. Fayrer Hall, you will acquaint the Committee whether you know the Trade between the West-Indies and Northern Colonies?

I have lived in and traded for twenty Years past to the West-Indies, and the Northern Colonies. . . .

What Quantities of Lumber do the French take off from the northern colonies?

Martineco, Gardaloupa, Grand-terre, Marigalant & Granada, these Islands all together, I believe, may take off as much, or more than the British-owned islands do. . . .

Is there a sufficient Quantity of Molasses made at our [British] Sugar Islands to supply the Northern Colonies?

No, they have a Demand for a much greater Quantity than they can make, for they take all that is made at our own [British] islands, and, if I am rightly informed, as much or more from the foreign Settlements; . . . and the Demand is so much increased, that the Northern People could use and vend more, if they knew where to get more, even notwithstanding what they have from the French. . . .

Have our [British] Sugar Islands a demand for all their northern colonial Lumber & Horses?

It is impossible; I have known many losing Voyages from the northern colonies by sending of Lumber and Horses, and they the [British] Islanders have [sent the unsold portions of the goods] to other Islands. The Northern Colonies are capable of selling and sending a thousand Times as much [as the British islands can buy]; the District of Land is Larger than all Europe.

Supposing they were confined only to sell their Lumber and Horses to our [British] Islands?

It would destroy the Employment of three hundred sail of Ships and Vessels; we have three sail to one of any other Nation's. It is not long ago that the Dutch . . . had ten to our one, but the Act of Navigation put an end to that; we are now what the Dutch were at that Time, we have three sail to one, we are the Carriers as they used to be; but if this [Molasses] Act passes, the French will have the far greater Number of Ships, as we have now.

How is the Balance [of payments] in regard to the Northern Colonies? Do they take more Goods [from English merchants] than they send us [from the colonies]?

Yes, they have no other way of paying [English merchants] but by the Remittance of Money which they have from the Dutch & French [trade in the West Indies].

Supposing the Northern Colonies are not suffered to take their Molasses, will not that put a Stop to the Trade of their Lumber and Horses?

Yes. . . . We receive Money from [the French] now, and we never got so much from any of our own [British] Islands; besides, they produce more Sugar, Rum, and Molasses lately, then they used to do. . . .

Source: *New York Gazette*, 17–31 July 1732.

---

sea captain who was trading illegally with the Spanish West Indies.

Yielding to Parliamentary pressure Walpole used this provocation to launch a predatory war against Spain's increasingly vulnerable American empire. In 1740 British regulars commanded by Governor Oglethorpe of Georgia attacked St. Augustine without success, in part because South Carolina whites—still shaken by the Stono revolt—refused to commit militia units to the expedition. In 1741 the governors of the other mainland colonies raised 2,500 volunteers, who joined a British naval force in an assault on the prosperous Spanish seaport of Cartagena (in present-day Colombia). The attack failed and, instead of enriching themselves with Spanish

Bristol Docks and Quay
The triangular trade with Africa, the West Indies, and the mainland colonies made Bristol, in southwest England, into a bustling and prosperous seaport. In this detail from an eighteenth-century painting, horses draw large hogsheads of West Indian sugar to local factories and workers prepare smaller barrels of rum and other goods for export to Africa.
City of Bristol Museum and Art Gallery.

booty, hundreds of colonial troops died of tropical diseases.

The War of Jenkins' Ear quickly became part of a general European conflict, the War of the Austrian Succession (1740–1749), bringing a new threat from France. Massive French armies battled German forces subsidized by Britain in Europe, and French naval forces roamed the West Indies, seeking without success to conquer a British sugar island. However, there were only minor Indian raids along the long frontier between the Anglo-American colonies and French Canada until 1745, when 3,000 New England militiamen, supported by a British naval squadron, captured the powerful French naval fortress of Louisbourg at the entrance to the St. Lawrence River. To the dismay of New England

Puritans, the Treaty of Aix-la-Chapelle (1748) returned Louisbourg to France, but it also secured the territorial integrity of Georgia by reaffirming British military superiority over Spain.

The Politics of Mercantilism. At the same time, Walpole and other British officials confronted an unexpected American threat to British economic ascendancy. According to the mercantilist Navigation Acts, the colonies were expected to produce agricultural goods and other raw materials that British merchants would carry to England and Scotland, where they would be consumed, exported to Europe, or turned into manufactured goods. To enforce the monopoly enjoyed by British manufacturers, Parliament passed a series of acts that prohibited Americans from selling colonial-made textiles (1699), hats (1732), and iron products such as plows, axes, and skillets (1750).

However, the Navigation Acts had a major loophole because they allowed Americans to own ships and transport goods. Colonial merchants exploited those provisions, securing 95 percent of the commerce between the mainland and the West Indies and 75 percent of the trade in manufactures shipped from London and Bristol. Quite unintentionally, the Atlantic trade had created a dynamic community of colonial merchants (see Map 3.4).

Moreover, by the 1720s the British sugar islands could not use all of the flour, fish, and meat produced by the rapidly growing mainland colonies, and so colonial merchants sold them in the French West Indies. These supplies helped French planters produce low-cost sugar, enabling them to capture control of the European sugar market. When American rum distillers began to buy cheap French molasses rather than molasses from the British sugar islands, planters petitioned Parliament for help. The resulting Molasses Act of 1733 permitted the mainland colonies to export fish and farm products to the French islands but—to enhance the competitiveness of British molasses—placed a high tariff on imports of French molasses (see American Voices, "Captain Fayrer Hall: The Impact of the Molasses Act," p. 96).

American merchants and public officials protested that the act would cut farm exports and cripple their distilling industry, making it more difficult for colonists to purchase British goods. When Parliament ignored their petitions, American merchants turned to smuggling, importing French molasses and bribing customs officials to ignore the new tax. Luckily for the Americans, sugar prices rose sharply in the late 1730s, enriching planters in the British West Indies, so the act was not enforced.

The lack of adequate currency in the colonies led to another confrontation. American merchants sent most of the gold and silver coins and **bills of exchange** they earned in the West Indian trade to Britain to pay for manufactured goods, draining the domestic money supply. To remedy this problem, the assemblies of ten colonies established land banks that lent paper money to farmers, taking their land as collateral. Farmers used the paper money to buy tools or livestock or to pay their creditors, thereby stimulating trade. However, some assemblies, such as that of Rhode Island, issued large amounts of currency, causing it to fall in value, and required merchants to accept it as legal tender. Creditors, especially English merchants, rightly complained that they were being forced to accept worthless currency. In 1751 Parliament passed the Currency Act, which prevented all the New England colonies from establishing new land banks and prohibited the use of public currency to pay private debts.

These economic conflicts and the growing assertiveness of the colonial assemblies angered a new generation of British political leaders, who believed that the colonies already had too much autonomy. In 1749 Charles Townshend of the Board of Trade charged that American assemblies had assumed many of the "ancient and established prerogatives wisely preserved in the Crown." Townshend and other officials were determined to replace salutary neglect with a more rigorous system of imperial control.

The wheel of empire had come full circle. In the 1650s England set out to build a centralized colonial empire and, over the course of a century, achieved the economic part of that goal through the use of sweeping mercantilist legislation, warfare against the Dutch, French, and Spanish, and the forced labor of more than a million African slaves. However, as a result of the Glorious Revolution and the era of salutary neglect that followed, the empire unexpectedly devolved into a group of politically self-governing colonies linked together primarily by trade. And so in the 1740s British officials vowed once again to create a politically centralized colonial system.

FOR FURTHER EXPLORATION

▶ For definitions of key terms boldfaced in this chapter, see the glossary at the end of the book.

▶ To assess your mastery of the material covered in this chapter, see the Online Study Guide at **bedfordstmartins.com/henretta**.

▶ For suggested references, including Web sites, see page SR-3 at the end of the book.

▶ For map resources and primary documents, see **bedfordstmartins.com/henretta**.

SUMMARY

Upon becoming king of England in 1660, Charles II pursued contradictory colonial policies. On the one hand, he diminished imperial authority by relinquishing control of Carolina to eight aristocrats, New York to his brother James, and Pennsylvania to William Penn. On the other hand, Charles pursued mercantilist policies, securing the enactment of Navigation Acts that regulated colonial exports and imports. In 1685 his absolutist-minded successor, James II, imposed tighter political controls, abolishing the existing charters of the northern mainland colonies and creating the absolutist Dominion of New England. The Glorious Revolution of 1688 cost James his throne, and revolts in Maryland, Massachusetts, and New York secured the restoration of colonial self-government.

The Navigation Acts ensured that Britain would secure its share of the profits of the South Atlantic system and its valuable commerce in sugar, rice, indigo, and tobacco. To work the sugar plantations of the British West Indies and rice and indigo plantations of South Carolina, planters imported 1.5 million African slaves and brutally exploited their labor. In the Chesapeake colonies, where Africans raised tobacco and grains, the black population grew dramatically through natural increase, resulting in the creation of an African American community. By providing markets for farm products, the South Atlantic system also brought prosperity to farmers and merchants in the northern mainland colonies.

Beginning in the 1690s, the unofficial British policy of salutary neglect allowed American political leaders to strengthen the power of the provincial assemblies. These institutions were dominated by wealthy men but were responsive to the views of ordinary people, who wanted paper money and increased trade with the West Indies. These goals conflicted with British interests and policies and prompted greater imperial scrutiny of American affairs. In 1733, alarmed by the decline of the British sugar industry because of colonial trade with the French West Indies, the British Parliament passed the Molasses Act, which tightened mercantilist controls. By 1750, Parliament had also restricted American manufacturing and regulated the colonists' issue of paper currency. This legislation signaled that the era of salutary neglect was rapidly ending.

TIMELINE

1651	First Navigation Act
1660s	Virginia moves toward slave system
1663	Charles II grants Carolina proprietorship
1664	English capture New Netherland, rename it New York
1681	William Penn founds Pennsylvania
1686–1689	Dominion of New England
1688–1689	Glorious Revolution in England; William and Mary ascend throne
	Revolts in Massachusetts, Maryland, and New York
1689–1713	England, France, and Spain at war
1696	Parliament creates Board of Trade
1705	Virginia enacts slavery legislation
1714–1750	British follow policy of "salutary neglect"
	American assemblies gain power
1720–1742	Sir Robert Walpole serves as chief minister
1720–1750	African American community forms
	Rice exports from Carolina soar
	Planter aristocracy emerges
	Seaport cities expand
1732	Parliament charters Georgia, challenging Spain
	Hat Act
1733	Molasses Act
1739	Stono Rebellion in South Carolina
	War with Spain in the Caribbean
1740	Veto of Massachusetts land bank
1750	Iron Act
1751	Currency Act

CHAPTER 4

Growth and Crisis in Colonial Society

1720–1765

◄ **Young Dutch American Girl, 1730**

This painting of four-year-old Susanna Truax of Albany, New York, was the work of the "Gansevoort Limner," an unknown Dutch portrait painter. Following the artistic conventions of the time, the limner rendered Susanna as a mature young woman adding a lump of sugar to her tea. Born in 1726 (as noted in the upper left corner), Susanna never married; by the time she died in 1805, at age seventy-nine, Albany had lost much of its character as a "Dutch" city.

National Gallery of Art, Washington, DC; gift of Edgar William and Bernice Chrysler Garbisch.

IN 1736 ALEXANDER MACALLISTER LEFT THE HIGHLANDS OF SCOTLAND to settle in the backcountry of North Carolina, where he was soon joined by his wife and three sisters. Over the years MacAllister prospered as a landowner and mill proprietor and had only praise for his new home. Carolina was "the best poor man's country I have heard in this age," he wrote to his brother Hector, urging him to "advise all poor people . . . to take courage and come." In North Carolina there were no landlords to keep "the face of the poor . . . to the grinding stone," and so many Highlanders were arriving that "it will soon be a new Scotland." Here, on the margin of the British empire, people could "breathe the air of liberty, and not want the necessarys of life." Tens of thousands of European migrants—Highland Scots, English, Scots-Irish, Germans—heeded such advice, helping to swell the size of Britain's North American settlements from 400,000 people in 1720 to almost 2 million by 1765.

The rapid and continuous increase in the number of settlers—and slaves—transformed the character of life in every region of British America. Long-settled towns in New England became densely settled and then overcrowded.

Antagonistic ethnic and religious communities jostled uneasily with one another in the Middle Atlantic region, and the influx of the MacAllisters and thousands of other settlers into the southern backcountry altered the traditional dynamics of politics and social conflict in that region as well. Moreover, in every colony the growing influence of a European spiritual movement called Pietism changed the tone of religious life. Finally, and perhaps most important, as the new immigrants and the landless children of long-settled families moved inland, they sparked warfare with the native peoples and with the other European powers contesting for dominance of North America—France and Spain. A generation of growth produced a decade of crisis.

Freehold Society in New England

In the 1630s the Puritans had migrated from a country where a handful of nobles and gentry owned 75 percent of the arable land and farmed it by using servants, leaseholding tenants, and wage laborers. In their new home the Puritans consciously created a yeoman society composed primarily of independent farm families who owned their lands as **freeholders**—without feudal dues or leases. By 1750, however, the rapidly growing population outstripped the supply of easily farmed land, posing a severe challenge to the freehold ideal.

Farm Families: Women's Place

The Puritans' commitment to individual autonomy did not extend to gender relations, and by law and custom men dominated their families. As the Reverend Benjamin Wadsworth of Boston advised women in *The Well-Ordered Family* (1712), being richer, more intelligent, or of higher social status than their husbands mattered little: "Since he is thy Husband, God has made him the head and set him above thee." Therefore, Wadsworth concluded, it was a woman's duty "to love and reverence him." Puritan ideology celebrated the husband as head of the household, according him nearly complete control over his dependents.

Throughout their lives women saw firsthand that their role was a subordinate one. Small girls watched their mothers defer to their fathers. As young women they saw the courts prosecute few men and many women for the crime of fornication, especially those who bore an illegitimate child. And they learned that their marriage portions would be inferior in kind and size to those of their brothers; usually daughters received not highly prized land but rather livestock or household goods. Thus, Ebenezer Chittendon of Guilford, Connecticut, left all his land to his sons, decreeing that "Each Daughter have half so much as Each Son, one half in money and the other half in Cattle." Thanks to the English Statute of Wills of 1540, which eliminated many customary restrictions over the disposition of wealth, fathers had nearly complete freedom to devise their property as they pleased.

In rural New England—indeed, throughout the colonies—women were raised to be dutiful helpmeets (helpmates) to their husbands. Farmwives spun thread and yarn from flax or wool and wove it into shirts and gowns. They knitted sweaters and stockings, made candles and soap, churned milk into butter and pressed curds into cheese, fermented malt for beer, preserved meats, and mastered dozens of other household tasks. The most exemplary or "notable" practitioners of these domestic arts won praise from the community, for their physical labor was crucial to the rural household economy.

Bearing and rearing children were equally central tasks. Most women married in their early twenties; by their early forties many had given birth to six or seven children, usually delivered with the assistance of midwives. A large family sapped the physical and emotional strength of even the most energetic wife, focusing her attention on domestic activities for about twenty of her most active years. A Massachusetts mother explained that she had less time than she would have liked for religious activities because "the care of my Babes takes up so large a portion of my time and attention." Yet more women than men became full members of the Puritan congregations of New England. As the revivalist Jonathan Edwards explained, they joined so "that their children may be baptized" in the church and because they feared the dangers of childbirth.

As the size of farms shrank in long-settled communities, many couples chose to have fewer children. After 1750 women in the typical farm village of Andover, Massachusetts, bore an average of only four children and thus gained the time and energy to pursue other tasks. Farm women made extra yarn, cloth, or cheese to exchange with neighbors or sell to shopkeepers, enhancing their families' standard of living. Or like Susan Huntington of Boston (the wife of a prosperous merchant), they spent more time in "the care & culture of children, and the perusal of necessary books, including the scriptures."

Yet women's lives remained tightly bound by a web of legal and cultural restrictions. While ministers often praised the piety of women, they excluded them from an equal role in the life of the church. When Hannah Heaton grew dissatisfied with her Congregationalist minister, thinking him unconverted and a "blind guide," she sought out Quaker and Baptist churches that welcomed questioning women and allowed them to become spiritual leaders. But by the 1760s even evangelical Baptist congregations were emphasizing traditional male prerogatives. "The government of Church and State must be . . . family government" controlled by its "king,"

The Character of Family Life: The Cheneys

Life in a large colonial-era family was very different from that in a small modern one. Mrs. Cheney's face shows the rigors of having borne many children, a task that has occupied her entire adult life (and may continue still, if the child she holds is her own). Her eldest daughter has married the man standing at the rear and holds two of her own children, who are not much younger than the last of her mother's brood. In such families, the lines between the generations were blurred.

National Gallery of Art, Washington, DC; gift of Edgar William and Bernice Chrysler Garbisch.

declared the Danbury (Connecticut) Baptist Association. Willingly or not, most New England women lived according to the conventional view that, as the essayist Timothy Dwight put it, they should be "employed only in and about the house and in the proper business of the sex."

Farm Property: Inheritance

By contrast, men who migrated to the colonies escaped many traditional constraints of European society, including the curse of landlessness. "The hope of having land of their own & becoming independent of Landlords is what chiefly induces people into America," an official noted in the 1730s. For men who had been peasants in Europe, owning property was a key element of their social identity, justifying their position as heads of the community's households.

Indeed, property ownership and family authority were closely related, because most migrating Europeans wanted farms that were large enough to provide sustenance for the present generation and land for the next one.

Parents with small farms could not provide their children with a start in life and had to adopt a different strategy. Many indentured their sons and daughters as servants and laborers in more prosperous households, where they would have enough to eat. When the indentures ended at age eighteen or twenty-one, their propertyless sons faced the daunting challenge of a ten-to-twenty-year climb up the agricultural ladder, from laborer to tenant and finally to freeholder.

Luckier sons and daughters in successful farm families received a **marriage portion** when they reached the age of twenty-three to twenty-five. The marriage portion—land, livestock, or farm equipment—repaid children for their past labor and allowed parents to choose their children's partners, which they did not hesitate to do. The family's prosperity and the parents' security during old age depended on a wise choice of a wife or husband. Normally, children had the right to refuse an unacceptable match, but they did not have the luxury of "falling in love" with whomever they pleased.

Marriage under English common law was hardly a contract between equals. A bride relinquished to her

Tavern Culture

By the eighteenth century, many taverns were run by women, such as this "Charming Patroness," who needed all her charm to deal with her raucous clientele. It was in taverns, declared puritanical John Adams, that "diseases, vicious habits, bastards, and legislators are frequently begotten."
Connecticut Historical Society.

husband the legal ownership of her land and personal property. After his death, she received her dower right—the right to use (but not to sell) a third of the family's estate. The widow's death or remarriage canceled this use-right, and her portion was divided among the children. In this way the widow's property rights were subordinated to those of the family "line," which stretched, through the children, across the generations.

It was the cultural duty of the father to provide inheritances for his children, and men who failed to do so lost status in the community. Some fathers willed the family farm to a single son, providing their other children with money, apprenticeship contracts, or uncleared land along the frontier or requiring the inheriting son to do so. Alternatively, yeomen moved their families to the New England frontier or to other unsettled regions, where life was hard but land for the children was cheap and abundant. "The Squire's House stands on the Bank

of the Susquehannah," the traveler Philip Fithian reported from the Pennsylvania backcountry in the early 1760s. "He tells me that he will be able to settle all his sons and his fair Daughter Betsy on the Fat of the Earth."

The historic accomplishment of these farmers was the creation of whole communities composed of independent property owners. A French visitor remarked on the sense of personal worth and dignity in this rural world, which contrasted sharply with European peasant life. Throughout the northern colonies, he wrote, he had found "men and women whose features are not marked by poverty, by lifelong deprivation of the necessities of life, or by a feeling that they are insignificant subjects and subservient members of society."

The Crisis of Freehold Society

How long would this happy circumstance last? Because of high rates of natural increase, the population of New England doubled with each generation, a rate of growth that raised the specter of landlessness and poverty. The Puritan colonies had about 100,000 people in 1700, nearly 200,000 in 1725, and almost 400,000 in 1750. In long-settled areas farms had been divided and subdivided and now often consisted of fifty acres or less. Many parents found themselves in a quandary because they could not provide an adequate inheritance. In the 1740s the Reverend Samuel Chandler of Andover, Massachusetts, was "much distressed for land for his children," seven of whom were male. A decade later in the neighboring town of Concord, about 60 percent of farmers owned less land than their fathers had.

Because parents had less to give their sons and daughters, they had less control over their children's lives. The system of arranged marriages broke down as young people engaged in premarital sex and used the urgency of pregnancy to win their fathers' permission to marry. Throughout New England the number of first-born children conceived before marriage rose spectacularly, from about 10 percent in the 1710s to 30 percent or more in the 1740s. Given another chance, young people "would do the same again," an Anglican minister observed, "because otherwise they could not obtain their parents' consent to marry."

New England families met the threat to the freeholder ideal through a variety of strategies. Many parents chose to have smaller families by using primitive methods of birth control. Others joined with neighbors to petition the provincial government for land grants, moving inland and hacking new farms out of the forests of central Massachusetts and western Connecticut—and eventually New Hampshire and the future Vermont. Still other farmers learned to use their small plots more productively, replacing the traditional English crops of wheat and barley with high-yielding potatoes and Indian corn. Corn offered a hearty food for humans, and its leaves furnished feed for cattle and pigs, which in turn provided milk and meat. New England developed a livestock economy, becoming the major supplier of salted and pickled meat to the slave plantations of the West Indies.

Finally, New England farmers made do on their smaller farms by exchanging goods and labor, developing the full potential of what historian Michael Merrill has called the "**household mode of production.**" Men lent each other tools, draft animals, and grazing land. Women and children joined other families in spinning yarn, sewing quilts, and shucking corn. Farmers plowed fields owned by artisans and shopkeepers, who repaid them with shoes, furniture, or store credit. Typically, no money changed hands; instead farmers, artisans, and shopkeepers recorded their debts and credits in personal account books and every few years "balanced" the books by transferring small amounts of cash to one another. The system of community exchange allowed households—and the entire economy—to achieve maximum output, thereby preserving the freehold ideal.

The Middle Atlantic: Toward a New Society, 1720–1765

Unlike New England, which was settled mostly by English Puritans, the Middle Atlantic colonies of New York, New Jersey, and Pennsylvania became home to peoples of differing origins, languages, and religions. These settlers—Scots-Irish Presbyterians, English and Welsh Quakers, German Lutherans, Dutch Reformed Protestants, and others—created ethnic and religious communities that coexisted uneasily with one another. New York was particularly unsettled as a result of a fairly sizable African populace—in 1756 slaves constituted more than 15 percent of its population.

Economic Growth and Social Inequality

Ample fertile land and a long growing season attracted migrants to the Middle Atlantic colonies of New York, New Jersey, and Pennsylvania, and profits from wheat financed their rapid settlement. Between 1720 and 1770 a population explosion in Western Europe doubled the price of wheat; American farmers profited from the growing demand by increasing their exports of wheat, corn, flour, and bread. This boom in exports helped the population of the Middle Atlantic region to surge from 50,000 in 1700 to 120,000 in 1720 and 450,000 in 1765 (Figure 4.1).

Tenancy in New York. As the population rose, so did the demand for land. Nonetheless, many migrants

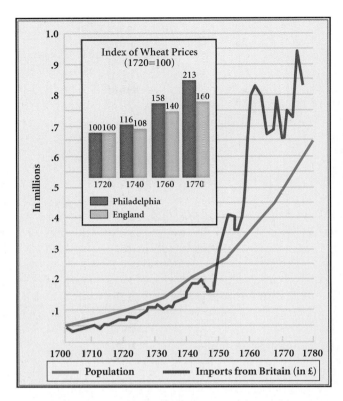

FIGURE 4.1 Population Growth, Wheat Prices, and Imports from Britain in the Middle Colonies
Wheat prices soared in Philadelphia because of demand in the West Indies and Europe. Exports of grain and flour paid for British manufactures, which were imported in large quantities after 1750.

refused to settle in New York's fertile Hudson River Valley. There, Dutch families presided over long-established manors created by the Dutch West India Company and wealthy British families, such as the Clarke and Livingston clans, dominated vast tracts granted by English governors between 1700 and 1714 (Map 4.1). Like the slave-owning planters in the Chesapeake, these landlords tried to live like European gentry, but few migrants wanted to labor as poor and dependent peasants. However, as freehold land became scarce in eastern New York, manorial lords were able to attract tenants, but only by granting them long leases and the right to sell their improvements—their houses and barns—to the next tenant. The number of tenants on the vast Rensselaer estate, for example, rose from 82 in 1714 to 345 in 1752 to nearly 700 by 1765.

Most tenant families hoped that with hard work and luck they could sell enough wheat to buy freehold farmsteads. However, preindustrial technology limited their output, especially during the crucial harvest season. As the wheat ripened, it had to be harvested quickly; any ripe uncut grain promptly sprouted and became useless. Yet a worker with a hand sickle could reap only half an acre a day, limiting the number of acres a family could

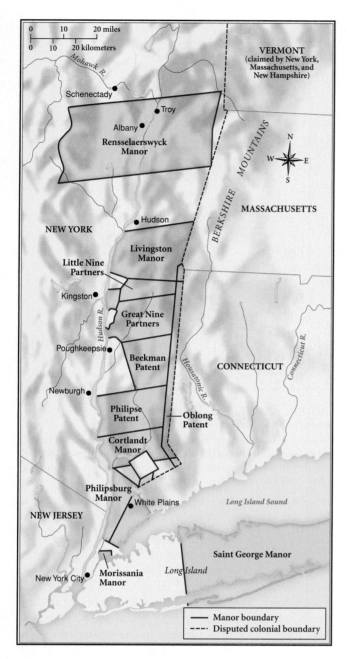

MAP 4.1 The Hudson River Manors

Dutch and English manorial lords dominated the fertile eastern shores of the Hudson River Valley, leasing small farms to German tenant families and refusing to sell land to freehold-seeking migrants from overcrowded New England. This powerful elite produced Patriot leaders, such as Gouverneur Morris (see American Lives, p. 206), and leading American families, such as the Roosevelts.

plant. The **cradle scythe**, an agricultural tool introduced during the 1750s, doubled or tripled the amount of grain a worker could cut. Even so, a family with two adult workers could not reap more than about twelve acres of grain each harvest season, a yield of perhaps 150 to 180 bushels of wheat and rye. After family needs were met, the remaining grain might be worth £15—enough to

buy salt and sugar, tools, and cloth but little else. The road to land ownership was not an easy one.

Quaker Pennsylvania. Unlike New York, rural Pennsylvania and New Jersey were initially marked by relative economic equality because the original Quaker migrants arrived with approximately equal resources (Figure 4.2). The first settlers lived simply in small houses with one or two rooms, a sleeping loft, a few benches or stools, some wooden trenchers (platters), and a few wooden noggins (cups). Only the wealthiest families ate off pewter or ceramic plates imported from England or Holland. However, the rise of the wheat trade and an influx of poor settlers introduced marked social divisions. By the 1760s some farmers in eastern Pennsylvania had grown wealthy by buying slaves and hiring propertyless laborers to raise large quantities of wheat for market sale. Others had bought up land and subdivided it into small farms, which they let out on lease. Still others had become successful commercial entrepreneurs, providing newly arrived settlers with farming equipment, sugar and rum from the West Indies, and financial services. Gradually a new class of wealthy agricultural capitalists—large-scale farmers, rural landlords, speculators, storekeepers, and gristmill operators—accumulated substantial estates that included mahogany tables, four-poster beds, couches, table linen, and imported Dutch dinnerware.

By 1760 there were also many people at the bottom of the Middle Atlantic social order, for half of all white men were propertyless. Some landless men were the sons of property owners and would eventually inherit at least part of the family estate, but just as many were Scots-Irish **inmates**—single men or families "such as live in small cottages and have no taxable property, except a cow." In the predominantly German settlement of Lancaster, Pennsylvania, a merchant noted an "abundance of Poor people" who "maintain their Families with great difficulty by day Labour." Although Scots-Irish and German migrants hoped to become tenants and eventually landowners, sharply rising land prices prevented many from realizing their dreams.

Merchants and artisans took advantage of the ample supply of labor by organizing an outwork system. They bought wool or flax from farmers and paid propertyless workers and land-poor farm families to spin it into yarn or weave it into cloth. In the 1760s an English traveler reported that hundreds of Pennsylvanians had turned "to manufacture, and live upon a small farm, as in many parts of England." Indeed, eastern areas of the Middle Atlantic colonies had become as crowded and socially divided as rural England, and many farm families feared a return to the lowly status of the European peasant. Although some wealthy men heaped abuse on "shitten farmers," a letter to the *Pennsylvania Gazette* celebrated the old Quaker ideal of social equality: it was simply

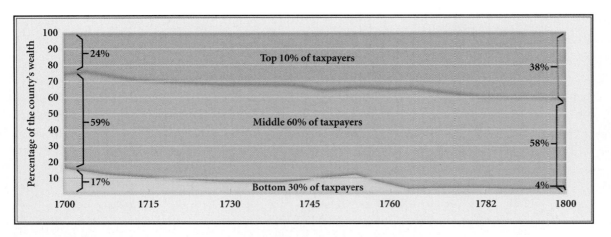

FIGURE 4.2 Increasing Social Inequality in Chester County, Pennsylvania

By renting land and selling goods to a growing population, the county's landed and commercial elite grew rich. Eventually the top 10 percent of taxpayers commanded nearly 40 percent of the wealth, far above the paltry 4 percent owned by the poorest 30 percent.

"impudence to tell another animal like myself that I came into the world his superior; none is born with the right to control another."

Cultural Diversity

The middle colonies were not a melting pot in which European cultures blended into a homogeneous "American" society; rather, they were a patchwork of ethnically and religiously diverse communities (Table 4.1). A traveler in Philadelphia in 1748 found no fewer than twelve religious denominations, including Anglicans, Quakers, Swedish and German Lutherans, Scots-Irish Presbyterians, and even Roman Catholics.

Migrants usually tried to preserve their cultural identities, marrying within their own ethnic groups or maintaining the customs of their native lands. The major exception was the Huguenots—Protestant Calvinists who were expelled from Catholic France. They settled in New York and various seacoast cities and gradually lost their French ethnic identity by intermarrying with other Protestants. More typical were the Welsh Quakers. Seventy percent of the children of the original Welsh migrants to Chester County, Pennsylvania, married other Welsh Quakers, as did 60 percent of the third generation.

Members of the Society of Friends (Quakers) became the dominant social group in Pennsylvania, at first because of their numbers and later because of their wealth and influence. Quakers controlled Pennsylvania's representative assembly until the 1750s and exercised considerable power in New Jersey as well. Because

Period	Germany	Northern Ireland	Southern Ireland	Scotland	England	Wales	Other	Total
1700–1719	4,000	2,000	2,500	700	1,700	1,200	300	12,400
1720–1739	17,900	6,900	10,400	2,800	7,100	4,700	1,000	50,800
1740–1759	52,700	25,400	18,200	6,800	16,300	10,700	2,300	132,400
1760–1779	23,700	36,200	13,400	25,000	19,000	12,400	2,300	132,000
TOTAL	**98,300**	**70,500**	**44,500**	**35,300**	**44,100**	**29,000**	**5,900**	**327,600**

TABLE 4.1 Estimated European Migration to the British Mainland Colonies, 1700–1780

After 1720, European migration to British America increased dramatically, reaching its climax between 1740 and 1780, when over 264,000 settlers arrived in the mainland colonies. Immigration from Germany peaked in the mid-1750s, while that from Ireland, Scotland, England, and Wales continued to increase during the 1760s and early 1770s. Most migrants were Protestants, including those from southern Ireland.

Source: Adapted from Aaron S. Fogleman, "Migrations to the Thirteen British North American Colonies, 1700–1775: New Estimates," *Journal of Interdisciplinary History* 22 (1992).

Quaker Meeting for Worship

Quakers dressed plainly and met in unadorned buildings, sitting in silence until inspired to speak by the "inner light." Women spoke with near-equality to men, a tradition that prepared Quaker women to take a leading part in the nineteenth-century women's rights movement. In this English work, entitled Quaker Meeting, *an elder (his hat on a peg above his head) conveys his thoughts to the congregation.* Museum of Fine Arts, Boston.

Quakers were pacifists, they dealt peaceably with Native Americans, negotiating treaties and buying land rather than seizing it by force. These conciliatory policies enabled Pennsylvania to avoid a major war with the Indian peoples until the 1750s. Some Quakers extended the egalitarian values emphasized by their faith to their relations with blacks. After 1750 many Quaker meetings condemned the institution of slavery, and some expelled members who continued to keep slaves.

The Quaker vision of a "peaceable kingdom" attracted many German settlers who were fleeing their homelands because of war, religious persecution, and poverty. First to arrive, in 1683, was a group of religious dissenters—the Mennonites—attracted by a pamphlet promising religious freedom. In the 1720s religious upheaval and population growth in southwestern Germany and Switzerland stimulated another wave of migrants. "Wages were far better" in Pennsylvania, Heinrich Schneebeli reported to his friends in Zurich after an exploratory trip, and "one also enjoyed there a free unhindered exercise of religion." Beginning in 1749 thousands of Germans and Swiss fled their overcrowded societies; by 1756, nearly 37,000 of these migrants had landed in Philadelphia. Some of these newcomers were redemptioners—a type of indentured servant—but many more were propertied farmers and artisans who

Gottlieb Mittelberger

The Perils of Migration

*G*ottlieb Mittelberger was a Lutheran minister who migrated to Pennsylvania with thousands of other Germans in the 1740s. Dismayed by the lax religious behavior of the colonial population and the lack of state support for religious authority, he returned to his homeland after a few years. In a book published in Germany in 1750, Mittelberger viewed America with a critical eye, warning his readers of the difficulties of migration and of life in a harsh, competitive society.

[The journey from Germany to Pennsylvania via Holland and England] lasts from the beginning of May to the end of October, fully half a year, amid such hardships as no one is able to describe adequately with their misery. Both in Rotterdam and in Amsterdam the people are packed densely, like herrings so to say, in the large sea-vessels. One person receives a place of scarcely 2 feet width and 6 feet length in the bedstead, while many a ship carries four to six hundred souls. . . .

During the journey the ship is full of pitiful signs of distress—smells, fumes, horrors, vomiting, various kinds of sea sickness, fever, dysentery, headaches, heat, constipation, boils, scurvy, cancer, mouth-rot, and similar afflictions, all of them caused by the age and the highly-salted state of the food, especially of the meat, as well as by the very bad and filthy water, which brings about the miserable destruction and death of many. . . .

Children between the ages of one and seven seldom survive the sea voyage; and parents must often watch their offspring suffer miserably, die, and be thrown into the ocean, from want, hunger, thirst, and the like. I myself, alas, saw such a pitiful fate overtake thirty-two children on board our vessel, all of whom were finally thrown into the sea. Their parents grieve all the more, since their children do not find repose in the earth, but are devoured by the predatory fish of the ocean. . . .

When the ships finally arrive in Philadelphia after the long voyage only those are let off who can pay their sea freight or can give good security. The others, who lack the money to pay, have to remain on board until they are purchased and until their purchasers can thus pry them loose from the ship. In this whole process the sick are the worst off, for the healthy are preferred and are more readily paid for. . . . Every day Englishmen, Dutchmen and High-German people select among the healthy persons; . . . adult persons bind themselves in writing to serve 3, 4, 5, or six years for the amount due to them. . . . Many parents must sell and trade away their children like so many head of cattle; for if their children take the debt upon themselves, the parents can leave the ship free and unrestrained. It often happens that whole families, husband, wife, and children, are separated by being sold to different purchasers, especially when they have not paid any part of their passage money. . . .

Thus let him who wants to earn his piece of bread honestly and in a Christian manner and who can only do this by manual labor in his native country stay there rather than come to America.

Source: Gottlieb Mittelberger, *Journey to Pennsylvania* (1756), ed. and trans. Oscar Handlin and John Clive (Cambridge: Harvard University Press, 1960), 11–21.

migrated to secure ample land for their children (American Voices, "Gottlieb Mittelberger: The Perils of Migration," above).

German settlements soon dominated certain districts of eastern Pennsylvania, and thousands of Germans moved down the Shenandoah Valley into the western parts of Maryland, Virginia, and the Carolinas (Map 4.2). The migrants carefully guarded their language and cultural heritage, encouraging their American-born children to marry within the community. A minister in North Carolina admonished his congregation "not to contract any marriages with the English or Irish," explaining that "we owe it to our native country to do our part that German blood and the German language be preserved in America." Well beyond 1800 these settlers spoke German, read German-language newspapers, conducted church services in German, and preserved German agricultural practices, which included women taking an active part in plowing and harvesting. English travelers remarked that German women were "always in the fields, meadows, stables, etc. and do not dislike any work whatsoever." Most German

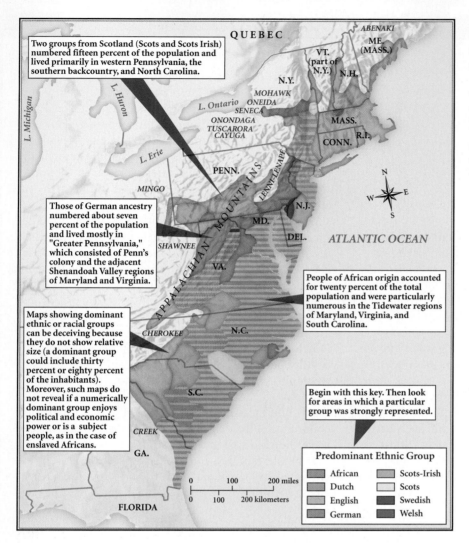

MAP 4.2 Ethnic and Racial Diversity, 1775

In 1700 most colonists in British North America were of English origin, but by 1775 settlers of English descent constituted a minority of the total nonaboriginal population. African Americans now accounted for one-third of the residents of the South, while thousands of Germans and Scots-Irish migrants created ethnic and religious diversity in the Middle Atlantic colonies and southern backcountry (see Table 4.1).

Two groups from Scotland (Scots and Scots Irish) numbered fifteen percent of the population and lived primarily in western Pennsylvania, the southern backcountry, and North Carolina.

Those of German ancestry numbered about seven percent of the population and lived mostly in "Greater Pennsylvania," which consisted of Penn's colony and the adjacent Shenandoah Valley regions of Maryland and Virginia.

Maps showing dominant ethnic or racial groups can be deceiving because they do not show relative size (a dominant group could include thirty percent or eighty percent of the inhabitants). Moreover, such maps do not reveal if a numerically dominant group enjoys political and economic power or is a subject people, as in the case of enslaved Africans.

People of African origin accounted for twenty percent of the total population and were particularly numerous in the Tidewater regions of Maryland, Virginia, and South Carolina.

Begin with this key. Then look for areas in which a particular group was strongly represented.

Predominant Ethnic Group

African	Scots-Irish
Dutch	Scots
English	Swedish
German	Welsh

migrants felt at ease living in a British-controlled colony, for few of them came from the politically active classes and many rejected political involvement on religious grounds. They engaged in politics only to protect their churches and cultural practices—insisting, for example, that as in Germany, married women should have the right to hold property and write wills.

Migrants from Ireland formed the largest group of incoming Europeans, about 150,000 in number. Some were Catholic but most were the descendants of the Presbyterian Scots who had been sent to Ireland between 1608 and 1650 to bolster English control of its Catholic population. In Ireland the Scots faced discrimination and economic regulation from the dominant English. The Irish Test Act of 1704 excluded Scottish Presbyterians as well as Irish Catholics from holding public office; English mercantilist regulations placed heavy import duties on the woolens made by Scots-Irish weavers; and Scots-Irish farmers faced heavy taxes. "Read this letter, Rev. Baptist Boyd," a migrant to New York wrote back to his minister, "and tell all the

poor folk of ye place that God has opened a door for their deliverance . . . all that a man works for is his own; there are no revenue hounds [tax collectors] to take it from us here." Lured by such reports, thousands of Scots-Irish sailed for Philadelphia beginning in the 1720s and then moved to central Pennsylvania and southward down the Shenandoah Valley into the backcountry of Maryland and Virginia. Like the Germans, the Scots-Irish vowed to keep their culture, holding firm to their Presbyterian faith and promoting marriage within the church.

Religious Identity and Political Conflict

In Western Europe the leaders of church and state condemned religious diversity, and some German ministers in Pennsylvania carried these sentiments to America, criticizing the separation of church and state in the colony. "The preachers do not have the power to punish anyone, or to force anyone to go to church," complained

German Farm in Western Maryland

Beginning in the 1730s, wheat became a major export crop in Maryland and Virginia. This engraving probably depicts a German farm, because the harvesters are using oxen, not horses, and women are working in the field alongside men. Using "a new method of reaping" that is possibly of German origin, the harvester cuts only the grain-bearing tip and leaves the wheat stalks in the fields, to be eaten by livestock. Library of Congress.

For more help analyzing this image, see the ONLINE STUDY GUIDE at bedfordstmartins.com/henretta.

the minister Gottlieb Mittelberger. As a result, "Sunday is very badly kept. Many people plough, reap, thresh, hew or split wood and the like." Thus, Mittelberger concluded, "Liberty in Pennsylvania does more harm than good to many people, both in soul and body."

Mittelberger ignored the fact that religious sects in Pennsylvania enforced moral behavior among their members through communal self-discipline. For example, each Quaker family attended a weekly worship meeting and a monthly discipline meeting. Four times a year a committee met with each family to make certain the children were receiving proper religious instruction, a reminder that fathers heeded. "If thou refuse to be obedient to God's teachings," Walter Faucit of Chester admonished his son, "thou will be a fool and a vagabond." The committee also supervised the moral behavior of adults; a Chester County meeting disciplined one of its members "to reclaim him from drinking to excess and keeping vain company." More important, Quaker meetings regulated marriages, granting permission only to couples with land and livestock sufficient to support a family. As a result, the children of well-to-do friends usually married within the sect, while poor Quakers remained unmarried, wed at later ages, or married without permission—in which case they were usually barred

from Quaker meetings. These communal sanctions effectively sustained a self-contained and prosperous Quaker community.

However, in the 1750s Quaker dominance in Pennsylvania came under attack. Scots-Irish Presbyterians living in frontier settlements west of the Susquehanna River challenged the pacifism of the Quaker-dominated assembly by urging a more aggressive Indian policy. Many of the newer German migrants also opposed the Quakers, demanding laws that respected their inheritance customs and fair representation in the provincial assembly. As a European visitor noted, Scots-Irish Presbyterians, German Baptists, and German Lutherans had begun to form "a general confederacy" against the Quakers, but they found it difficult to unite because of "a mutual jealousy, for religious zeal is secretly burning" (Map 4.3).

These ethnic passions embittered the politics of the Middle Atlantic region. In Pennsylvania Benjamin Franklin disparaged the "boorish" character and "swarthy complexion" of German migrants, while in New York a Dutchman declared that he "Valued no English Law no more than a Turd." The Quaker-inspired experiment in cultural and religious diversity prefigured the passionate ethnic and social conflicts that would characterize much of American society in the centuries to come.

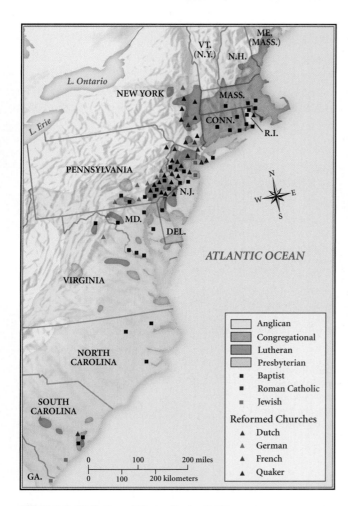

MAP 4.3 Religious Diversity in 1750

By 1750 religious diversity among European Colonists was on the rise and not only in the ethnically disparate Middle Atlantic colonies. Baptists had increased their numbers in New England, long the stronghold of Congregationalism, and would soon be important in Virginia. Already there were good-sized pockets of Presbyterians, Lutherans, and German Reformed in the South, where the Church of England (Anglicanism) was the established religion.

For more help analyzing this map, see the ONLINE STUDY GUIDE at bedfordstmartins.com/henretta.

The Enlightenment and the Great Awakening, 1740–1765

Two great European cultural movements reached America between the 1720s and the 1760s: the Enlightenment and Pietism. The Enlightenment, which emphasized the power of human reason to understand and shape the world, appealed especially to well-educated men and women from merchant or planter families and to urban artisans. **Pietism**, an emotional, evangelical religious movement that stressed a Christian's personal relation to God, attracted many adherents, especially among farmers and urban laborers. The two move-

ments promoted independent thinking in different ways; together they transformed American intellectual and cultural life.

The Enlightenment in America

Most early Americans relied on religious teachings or folk wisdom to explain the workings of the natural world. Thus, Swedish settlers in Pennsylvania attributed medicinal powers to the great white mullein, a common wildflower, tying the leaves around their feet and arms when they had a fever. Even highly educated people believed that events occurred for reasons that today would be considered magical. When a measles epidemic struck Boston in the 1710s, the Puritan minister Cotton Mather thought that only God could end it. Like most Christians of his time, Mather believed that the earth stood at the center of the universe and that God intervened directly in human affairs.

The European Enlightenment. Early Americans held to these beliefs despite the scientific revolution of the sixteenth and seventeenth centuries, which had challenged both traditional Christian and folk worldviews. As early as the 1530s the astronomer Copernicus had observed that the earth traveled around the sun rather than vice versa, implying a more modest place for humans in the universe than had previously been assumed. Other scholars had conducted experiments using empirical methods—actual observed experience—to learn about the natural world. Eventually the English scientist Isaac Newton, in his *Principia Mathematica* (1687), used mathematics to explain the movement of the planets around the sun. Newton's laws of motion and concept of gravity described how the universe could operate without the constant intervention of a supernatural being, undermining traditional Christian explanations of the cosmos.

In the century between the publication of Newton's book and the outbreak of the French Revolution in 1789, the philosophers of the European Enlightenment applied scientific reasoning to all aspects of life, including social institutions and human behavior. Enlightenment thinkers believed that men and women could observe, analyze, and improve their world. They advanced four fundamental principles: the lawlike order of the natural world, the power of human reason, the natural rights of individuals (including the right to self-government), and the progressive improvement of society.

In his *Essay Concerning Human Understanding* (1690), the English philosopher John Locke emphasized the impact of environment, experience, and reason on human behavior, proposing that the character of individuals and societies was not fixed by God's will but could be changed through education and purposeful

Franklin's Influence

Benjamin Franklin's work as a scientist and inventor captivated subsequent generations of Americans. This painted panel (c. 1830) from a fire engine of the Franklin Volunteer Fire Company of Philadelphia depicts Franklin's experiment in 1752 that demonstrated the presence of electricity in lightning. Cigna Museum and Art Collection / Photo by Joseph Painter.

action. Locke's *Two Treatises on Government* (1690) advanced the revolutionary theory that political authority was not given by God to monarchs (as kings such as James II had insisted) but was derived from social compacts that people made to preserve their "natural rights" to life, liberty, and property. In Locke's view, the people should have the right to change government policies— or even their form of government—through the decision of a majority.

The ideas of Locke and other Enlightenment thinkers came to America through books, travelers, and educated migrants and quickly affected the beliefs of influential colonists about religion, science, and politics. As early as the 1710s the Reverend John Wise of Ipswich, Massachusetts, used Locke's political principles to defend the Puritans' decision to vest power in the ordinary members of their churches. Wise argued that just as the social compact formed the basis of political society, the religious covenant made the congregation— not the bishops of the Church of England or even the ministers—the proper interpreter of religious truth. And when a smallpox epidemic threatened Boston in the 1720s, the Puritan minister Cotton Mather sought a scientific rather than a religious remedy, joining with a prominent Boston physician to support the new technique of inoculation.

Franklin in Philadelphia. Benjamin Franklin was the epitome of the American Enlightenment. Born in Boston in 1706 to a devout Calvinist family and apprenticed to a printer as a youth, Franklin was a self-taught, self-made man. While working as a tradesman, printer, and journalist in Philadelphia he formed "a club of mutual improvement" that met weekly to discuss "Morals, Politics, or Natural Philosophy." These dis-cussions and Enlightenment literature, rather than the Bible, shaped Franklin's imagination. As Franklin explained in his *Autobiography*, written in 1771, "from the different books I read, I began to doubt of Revelation [God-revealed truth] itself." Like many urban artisans, wealthy Virginia planters, and affluent seaport merchants, Franklin became a **deist**. Influenced by Enlightenment science, deists believed that God had created the world but allowed it to operate in accordance with the laws of nature. The deists' God was a rational being, a divine "watchmaker" who did not intervene directly in history or in people's lives. Rejecting the authority of the Bible, deists relied on people's "natural reason" to define a moral code. Adherence to the code, they believed, would be rewarded in life and after death. A sometime slave owner himself, Franklin used natural ethics to question the moral legitimacy of racial bondage, eventually repudiating the institution as he became a defender of

Enlightenment Philanthropy: The Philadelphia Hospital

This imposing structure, built in 1753 with public funds and private donations, embodied two Enlightenment principles—that purposeful action could improve society and that the world should express reason and order (exhibited here in the symmetrical facade). Etchings such as this one, drawn about 1761, circulated widely, bolstering Philadelphia's reputation as the center of the American Enlightenment. Historical Society of Pennsylvania.

American freedom from the threat of British political "slavery."

Franklin popularized this practical-minded outlook of the Enlightenment in *Poor Richard's Almanack* (1732–1757), an annual publication read by thousands. In 1743 he helped found the American Philosophical Society, an institution devoted to "the promotion of useful knowledge," and proceeded to invent bifocal lenses for eyeglasses, the Franklin stove, and the lightning rod. Franklin's book on electricity, first published in England in 1751, won praise from the English scientist Joseph Priestley as the greatest contribution to science since Newton. Following in Franklin's footsteps, other ambitious printers in Philadelphia and other American cities published newspapers and gentleman's magazines, the first significant nonreligious publications to appear in the colonies. Thus, the European Enlightenment added a secular dimension to colonial intellectual life, preparing the way for the great American contributions to republican political theory by John Adams, James Madison, and other Patriots during the Revolutionary era.

American Pietism and the Great Awakening

As some influential Americans—merchants and wealthy Virginia planters—and various urban artisans turned to deism, many other colonists embraced the European devotional movement known as Pietism. Pietists emphasized devout, or "pious," behavior, emotional church services, and a striving for a mystical union with God—appealing to the hearts, rather than the minds, of their congregations. Their teachings came to America with German migrants in the 1720s and sparked a religious revival among many farmers, artisans, and laborers. In Pennsylvania and New Jersey the Dutch minister Theodore Jacob Frelinghuysen moved from church to church, preaching rousing, emotional sermons to German settlers. In private prayer meetings he encouraged lay members to carry a message of spiritual urgency to growing congregations. A decade later William Tennent and his son Gilbert, Presbyterian clergymen who copied Frelinghuysen's approach, led revivals among Scots-Irish migrants throughout the Middle Atlantic region.

Simultaneously, a native-born Pietistic movement appeared in Puritan New England. Puritanism had taken root in England as part of a Pietistic upsurge, and the first migrants to America had sustained that intensity. However, over the decades many New England congregations had lost their religious zeal. In the 1730s the minister Jonathan Edwards restored spiritual enthusiasm to the Congregational churches in the Connecticut River Valley. An accomplished philosopher as well as an effective preacher, Edwards urged his hearers—especially young men and women—to commit themselves to a life of piety and prayer (see American Lives, "Jonathan Edwards: Preacher, Philosopher, Pastor," p. 116).

George Whitefield, a young English revivalist with what one historian has called a "flamboyant, highly sexualized style," transformed the local revivals into a "Great Awakening" that spanned the mainland settlements. Whitefield had experienced conversion after reading German Pietistic tracts and became a follower of John Wesley, the founder of English Methodism, who

George Whitefield, c. 1742

No painting captured Whitefield's magical appeal, although this image conveys his open demeanor and religious intensity. When Whitefield spoke to a crowd near Philadelphia, an observer noted, his words were "sharper than a two-edged sword. . . . Some of the people were pale as death; others were wringing their hands . . . and most lifting their eyes to heaven and crying to God for mercy." Courtesy, Trustees of the Boston Public Library.

combined enthusiastic sermons with disciplined "methods" of worship. In 1739 Whitefield carried Wesley's preaching style to America and over the next two years attracted huge crowds of "enthusiasts" from Georgia to Massachusetts. "Religion is become the Subject of most Conversations," the *Pennsylvania Gazette* reported. "No books are in Request but those of Piety and Devotion." The usually skeptical and restrained Benjamin Franklin was so impressed by Whitefield's oratory that when the preacher asked for contributions, Franklin emptied the coins in his pockets "wholly into the collector's dish, gold and all." By the time the evangelist reached Boston, the Reverend Benjamin Colman reported, the people were "ready to receive him as an angel of God."

Whitefield owed his appeal partly to his compelling personal presence. "He looked almost angelical; a young, slim, slender youth . . . cloathed with authority from the Great God," wrote a Connecticut farmer (see American Voices, "Nathan Cole: The Power of a Preacher," p. 118). Like most evangelical preachers, Whitefield did not read his sermons but spoke from memory as if inspired, raising his voice for dramatic effect, gesturing eloquently,

making striking use of biblical metaphors, and even at times assuming a female persona—as a woman in labor struggling to deliver the word of God. The young preacher evoked a deep emotional response, telling his listeners they had all sinned and must seek salvation. Hundreds of men and women suddenly felt the "new light" of God's grace within them. As "the power of god come down," Hannah Heaton recalled, "my knees smote together . . . it seemed to me I was a sinking down into hell . . . but then I resigned my distress and was perfectly easy quiet and calm . . . it seemed as if I had a new soul & body both." Strengthened and self-confident, these "New Lights" were prepared to follow in Whitefield's footsteps.

Religious Upheaval in the North

Like all cultural explosions, the Great Awakening was controversial. Conservative (or "Old Light") ministers such as Charles Chauncy of Boston condemned the "cryings out, faintings and convulsions" produced by emotional preachers. Chauncy denounced the willingness of the New Lights to allow women to speak in public as "a plain breach of that *commandment of the LORD*, where it is said, *Let your* WOMEN *keep silence in the churches.*" In Connecticut the Old Lights persuaded the legislative assembly to prohibit evangelists from speaking to established congregations without the ministers' permission. When Whitefield returned to Connecticut in 1744, he found many pulpits closed to him. But the New Lights resisted attempts by civil officials to silence them. Dozens of farmers, women, and artisans roamed the countryside, condemning the Old Lights as "unconverted" sinners and willingly accepting imprisonment: "I shall bring glory to God in my bonds," a dissident preacher wrote from jail.

As the Awakening proceeded, it undermined support for traditional churches and challenged the authority of governments to impose taxes that supported them. In New England many New Lights left the established Congregational Church. By 1754 they had founded 125 "separatist" churches, supporting their ministers through voluntary contributions. Other religious dissidents joined Baptist congregations, which favored a greater separation of church and state (see Figure 4.3). According to the Baptist preacher Isaac Backus, "God never allowed any civil state upon earth to impose religious taxes." In New York and New Jersey the Dutch Reformed Church split in two, as New Lights resisted conservative church authorities in the Netherlands.

The Awakening also challenged the authority of ministers, whose education and biblical knowledge had traditionally commanded respect. In an influential pamphlet, *The Dangers of an Unconverted Ministry* (1740), Gilbert Tennent maintained that the minister's authority came not from theological training but through the conversion experience. Reasserting Martin

Jonathan Edwards: Preacher, Philosopher, Pastor

Jonathan Edwards did not mince words. Echoing the harsh theology of John Calvin, Edwards preached that men and women were helpless creatures completely dependent on God: "There is Hell's wide gaping mouth open; and you have nothing to stand upon, nor any thing to take hold of: there is nothing between you and Hell but the air; 'tis only the power and mere pleasure of God that holds you up."

Edwards spoke "without much noise of external emotion" and without a single gesture, a listener noted, but his intense "inner fervor" underlined the torments that awaited those who fell into the eternal flames:

> How dismal will it be . . . to know assuredly that you never, never shall be delivered from them; . . . after you shall have endured these torments millions of ages . . . your bodies, which shall have been burning and roasting all this while in these glowing flames, yet shall not have been consumed, but will remain to roast through an eternity yet.

Such was the terrible—and inevitable—fate that Edwards the preacher promised to complacent Christians in his most famous sermon, *Sinners in the Hands of an Angry God* (1742). But Edwards the pastor preached a more hopeful message of personal repentance and spiritual rebirth, telling congregations that this fate awaited only those who "never passed under a great change of heart, by the mighty power of the spirit of God upon your souls; all that were never born again, and made new creatures."

Blending passionate warnings with compassionate forgiveness, Edwards inspired a religious revival in the Connecticut River Valley in the mid-1730s and helped George Whitefield stir up an even greater one in the 1740s. This Connecticut minister, one of the leading revivalists of his age, was also a profound and original philosopher, perhaps the most intellectually brilliant colonial American.

Jonathan Edwards, 1720
This portrait, painted by Joseph Badger when Edwards was seventeen, shows that even as a young man the great preacher and philosopher was grave and dignified.
Yale University Art Gallery, Bequest of Eugene Philips Edwards.

Jonathan Edwards was born in 1703 in East Windsor, Connecticut, the fifth child and only son among the eleven children of Timothy and Esther Stoddard Edwards. His father came from a wealthy family but ended up a poorly paid rural minister who fought constantly with his congregation over his salary and authority, battles that Jonathan would later fight with his own church. His mother was the daughter of Solomon Stoddard, a famous Connecticut preacher and revivalist—a family legacy that would both help and haunt Jonathan Edwards throughout his life.

As a youth Jonathan embraced his grandfather Stoddard's theology, rejecting the Calvinist belief in God's omnipotence over people's lives and labeling it "a horrible doctrine." But at the age of seventeen Edwards became a committed Calvinist, explaining in his *Personal Narrative*, written later in life, that he had then experienced "a delightful conviction" of the Almighty's absolute sovereignty, of "sweetly conversing with Christ, and wrapt and swallowed up in God." In fact, Edwards's autobiography distorted the truth, for he found his Calvinist God only after many years of personal torment and a series of physical and emotional collapses.

The Enlightenment came more easily to the intellectually minded Edwards. While studying for the ministry at Yale College, he read the works of Isaac Newton, John Locke, and other Enlightenment thinkers, beginning a lifetime of philosophical inquiry into the meaning of words and things. He accepted Locke's argument in *An Essay Concerning Human Understanding* (1690) that ideas are not innate at birth but are the product of experience as conveyed through the senses—our ability to see, hear, feel, and taste the world around us. A person who has never tasted a pineapple, said Locke, will never have "the true idea of the relish of that celebrated and delicious fruit."

However, Locke's theory of knowledge was less successful in explaining abstract ideas—such as God, love, salvation—and here Edwards made an original contribution. Locke had suggested that abstract ideas resulted when the mind rationally analyzed various sense experiences. Edwards knew better. He had worked out his theological doctrines through intense personal torment and he knew they had an emotional component. "Love" (whether of God or a fellow human being) was "felt" and not merely understood. It followed that abstract ideas were emotional as well as rational, the product of the passions as well as the senses.

Edwards used his theory of knowledge to justify his style of preaching, arguing that vivid words promoted conversions. As he put it in *A Treatise Concerning Religious Affections* (1746), "true religion, in great part, consists in holy affection." He would save his congregation through powerful sermons: "to fright persons away from Hell." In the end, the philosopher was at one with the preacher.

In 1729 Edwards put these ideas into practice as pastor of the Congregational church in Northampton, Massachusetts, taking over that ministry from his grandfather Solomon Stoddard and matching Stoddard's success as a revivalist. Beginning in 1734, Edwards reported, "the number of true saints multiplied . . . the town seemed to be full of the presence of God," especially among young people. News of the Northampton revival stimulated religious fervor up and down the Connecticut River Valley "till there was a general awakening."

Edwards interpreted his success as "a remarkable Testimony of God's Approbation of the Doctrine . . . that we are justified only by faith in Christ, and not by any manner of virtue or goodness of our own." He maintained that uncompromising Calvinist position during the widespread revivals of the 1740s. Also seeking to restore an older communal order, he took issue with those New Lights who asserted "the absolute Necessity for every Person to act singly . . . as if there was not another human Creature upon earth." Repudiating that spirit of individualism, Edwards insisted that aspiring Saints should heed their pastors, who were "skilful guides," and then make a "credible Relation of their inward Experience" to the congregation, thereby strengthening the covenant bonds that knit members together in a visible church. Edwards extended his critique of individualism to economic affairs, speaking out against "a narrow, private spirit" of greedy merchants and landlords, men who "are not ashamed to hit and bite others [and] grind the faces of the poor."

Edwards's rigorous standards and assault on individualism deeply offended the wealthiest and most influential members of his congregation. In 1750 struggles over his salary and disciplinary authority culminated in a final battle, when Edwards repudiated Stoddard's practice of admitting almost all churchgoers to the sacrament of Communion; he would offer full church membership only to those whom God had chosen as Saints. By a vote of 200 to 20, the Northampton congregation dismissed the great preacher and philosopher from his pastorate. Impoverished and with a family of ten children to support, Edwards moved to Stockbridge, Massachusetts, a small frontier outpost. There he ministered, without great success, to the Housatonic Indians and wrote an impressive philosophical work, *Freedom of the Will* (1752).

In 1757, as Edwards was about to take up the presidency of the College of New Jersey (Princeton), he was inoculated against smallpox, had a severe reaction, and died. He left a pair of spectacles, two wigs, three black coats, and some three hundred books, including twenty-two written by himself—but not much else in the way of earthly goods.

As he lay dying, this turn of fate puzzled America's first great philosopher. Why had God called him to Princeton only to give him no time to undertake his duties? As a preacher and pastor Edwards had always responded to such questions by stressing God's arbitrary power and the "insufficiency of reason" to understand God's purpose. Now he himself had to accept that grim and unsatisfying answer, showing through his personal experience why Calvinism was such a hard faith by which to live . . . and die.

Nathan Cole

The Power of a Preacher

The evangelist George Whitefield transformed the lives of thousands of Americans, such as the Connecticut farmer Nathan Cole, by convincing them of their sinfulness. In his reflections on his life (a short unpublished manuscript now in the archives of the Connecticut Historical Society), Cole described the impact that Whitefield's preaching made on his life in 1741 and his months of agony as he prayed for a sign that he was worthy enough to merit God's grace.

Now it please God to Send Mr. Whitefield into this land; and my hearing of his preaching at Philadelphia, like one of the old apostles, . . . I felt the Spirit of God drawing me by conviction; I longed to see and hear him and wished he would come this way. . . . Then of a sudden, in the morning about 8 or 9 of the clock there came a messenger and said Mr. Whitefield . . . is to preach at Middletown this morning at ten of the clock. I was in my field at work. I dropped my tool that I had in my hand and ran home to my wife, telling her to make ready quickly. . . .

When I saw Mr. Whitefield come upon the scaffold, he looked almost angelical; a young, slim, slender youth before some thousands of people with a bold undaunted countenance. And my hearing how God was with him everywhere as he came, it solemnized my mind and put me into a trembling fear before he began to preach; for he looked as if he was clothed with authority from the Great God, and a sweet solemnity sat upon his brow, and my hearing him preach gave me a heart wound. By God's blessing my old foundation was broken up, and I saw that my righteousness would not save me.

Then I was convinced of the doctrine of Election: and went right to quarrelling with God about it; because that all I could do would not save me, and he had decreed from Eternity who should be saved and who not: I began to think I was not Elected, and that God had made some for heaven and me for hell. And I thought God was not Just in so doing. . . . Now this distress lasted Almost two years—Poor—Me—Miserable me. . . .

Hell fire was most always in my mind; and I have hundreds of times put my fingers into my pipe when I have been smoking to feel how fire felt: And to see how my Body could bear to lye in Hell fire for ever and ever. . . .

And while these thoughts were in my mind God appeared unto me and made me Skringe [cringe]. . . . I seemed to hang in open Air before God, and he seemed to Speak to me in an angry and Sovereign way: What won't you trust your Soul with God? My heart answered Oh yes, yes, yes. I was set free, my distress was gone. . . . Then I began to pray and praise God.

Source: Richard Bushman, *The Great Awakening: Documents on the Revival of Religion, 1740–1745* (Chapel Hill: University of North Carolina Press, 1989), 67–71.

Luther's commitment to the priesthood of all believers, Tennent suggested that anyone who had experienced the saving grace of God could speak with ministerial authority. Not long afterward, Isaac Backus celebrated this spiritual democracy, noting that "the common people now claim as good a right to judge and act in matters of religion as civil rulers or the learned clergy."

Religious revivalism carried a social message, reaffirming the communal ethic of many farm families and questioning the growing competition and pursuit of wealth that accompanied the expansion of the American economy. "In any truly Christian society," Tennent explained, "mutual Love is the Band and Cement"—not the mercenary values of the marketplace. Suspicious of merchants and land speculators and dismayed by the erosion of traditional morality, Jonathan Edwards spoke for many rural Americans when he charged that a "private niggardly [miserly] spirit" was more suitable "for wolves and other beasts of prey, than for human beings."

As religious enthusiasm spread, churches founded new colleges to educate their youth and train ministers. New Light Presbyterians established the College of New Jersey (Princeton) in 1746, and New York Anglicans founded King's College (Columbia) in 1754. Baptists set up the College of Rhode Island (Brown) and the Dutch Reformed Church subsidized Queen's College (Rutgers) in New Jersey (Table 4.2). The true intellectual legacy of the Awakening, however, was not education for the few but a new sense of religious—and ultimately political—authority among the many. As a European visitor to Philadelphia remarked in surprise, "the poorest day-laborer on the bank of the Delaware hold it his right

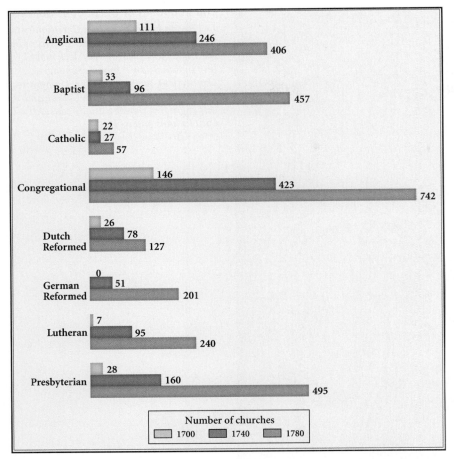

FIGURE 4.3 Church Growth by Denomination, 1700–1780

Some churches, such as the Anglican and Dutch Reformed, grew slowly as parents passed their faith down to their children. After 1740, the fastest-growing denominations were the immigrant churches—German Lutheran, German Reformed, and Scots-Irish Presbyterian— and those with an evangelical message, such as the Baptists.

to advance his opinion, in religious as well as political matters, with as much freedom as the gentleman."

Social and Religious Conflict in the South

In the southern colonies religious enthusiasm also sparked social conflict. In Virginia the Church of England was the legally established religion, supported by public taxes. However, Anglican ministers generally ignored the spiritual needs of African Americans (about 40 percent of the population), and landless whites (another 20 percent) attended irregularly. Middling white freeholders, who accounted for about 35 percent of the population, formed the core of most Anglican congregations. Prominent planters and their families (a mere 5 percent of the

TABLE 4.2 Colonial Colleges

	Date of Founding	Colony	Religious Affiliation
Harvard	1636	Massachusetts	Puritan
William and Mary	1693	Virginia	Church of England
Yale	1701	Connecticut	Puritan
College of New Jersey (Princeton)	1746	New Jersey	Presbyterian
King's (Columbia)	1754	New York	Church of England
College of Philadelphia (University of Pennsylvania)	1755	Pennsylvania	None
College of Rhode Island (Brown)	1764	Rhode Island	Baptist
Queen's (Rutgers)	1766	New Jersey	Dutch Reformed
Dartmouth	1769	New Hampshire	Congregationalist

The Founding of Dartmouth College

In 1769, to bring Protestant Christianity to European settlers and Native Americans in the wilderness, Eleazar Wheelock moved his "Indian School" from Lebanon, Connecticut, to Hanover, New Hampshire. There it became Dartmouth College and, as this engraving shows, initially educated both Indians and whites.

Dartmouth College Library.

population) held real power in the church and used their control of parish finances to discipline Anglican ministers. One clergyman complained that dismissal awaited any minister who "had the courage to preach against any Vices taken into favor by the leading Men of his Parish."

The Presbyterian Revival. The Great Awakening challenged both the Church of England and the power of the southern planter elite. In 1743 the bricklayer Samuel Morris, inspired by his reading of George Whitefield's sermons, led a group of Virginia Anglicans out of the established Church. Seeking a more vital religious experience, Morris and his followers invited New Light Presbyterian ministers from Scots-Irish settlements along the Virginia frontier to lead their prayer meetings. Soon these Presbyterian revivals spread across the backcountry and into the Tidewater region along the Atlantic coast, threatening the social authority of the Virginia gentry. Planters and their well-dressed families were accustomed to arriving at Anglican services in elaborate carriages drawn by well-bred horses, and they often flaunted their power by marching in a body to their

seats in the front pews. These potent reminders of the gentry's social superiority would vanish if freeholders attended New Light Presbyterian rather than Church of England services. Moreover, religious pluralism would threaten the government's ability to tax the population to support the established church.

To prevent the spread of New Light doctrines, Virginia's governor denounced them as "false teachings," and Anglican justices of the peace closed down Presbyterian meetinghouses. This harassment kept most white yeomen families and poor tenants within the Church of England, as did the fact that most Presbyterian ministers were highly educated and sought converts mainly among skilled workers and propertied farmers.

The Baptist Insurgency. Baptists succeeded where Presbyterians failed. The evangelical Baptist preachers who came to Virginia in the 1760s drew their congregations primarily from poor farmers by offering them solace and hope in a troubled world. The Baptists' central ritual was adult baptism, often involving complete immersion in water. Once men and women had experienced the infusion of grace—had been "born again"—they were baptized in an emotional public ceremony that celebrated the Baptists' shared fellowship. During the 1760s thousands of yeomen and tenant farm families in Virginia were drawn to revivalist meetings by the enthusiasm and democratic ways of Baptist preachers.

Even slaves were welcome at Baptist revivals. As early as 1740 George Whitefield had openly condemned the brutality of slaveholders and urged that blacks be brought into the Christian fold. In South Carolina and Georgia a handful of New Light planters took up Whitefield's challenge, but the hostility of the white population and the commitment of many Africans to their ancestral religions kept the number of converts low. Virginia in the 1760s witnessed the first significant conversion of slaves to Christianity, as second- and third-generation African Americans who knew the English language and English ways responded positively to the Baptist message that all people were equal in God's eyes.

The ruling planters reacted violently to the Baptists, viewing them as a threat to social authority and the gentry's way of life. The Baptists emphasized spiritual equality by calling one another "brother" and "sister," and their preachers condemned the customary pleasures of Chesapeake planters—gambling, drinking, whoring, and cockfighting. Hearing Baptist Dutton Lane condemn "the vileness and danger" of drunkenness, planter John Giles took the charge personally: "I know who you mean! and by God I'll demolish you." To maintain traditional practices and Anglican power, sheriffs and justices of the peace broke up Baptist services by force. In Caroline County, Virginia, an Anglican posse attacked a prayer meeting led by Brother John Waller, who, a fellow Baptist reported, "was violently jerked off the stage; they caught him by the back part of his neck, beat his head against the ground, and a gentleman gave him twenty lashes with his horsewhip."

Despite such attacks, Baptist congregations continued to multiply. By 1775 about 20 percent of Virginia's whites and hundreds of enslaved blacks had joined Baptist churches, bringing cultural as well as religious change. To signify their state of grace, some Baptist men "cut off their hair, like Cromwell's round-headed chaplains." Many others refused to attend "a horse race or other unnecessary, unprofitable, sinful assemblies." Still others forged a new ethic of evangelical masculinity, "crying, weeping, lifting up the eyes, groaning" when touched by the Holy Spirit but defending themselves with vigor. "Not able to bear the insults" of heckler Robert Ashby, a group of Baptists "took Ashby by the neck and heels and threw him out of doors," sparking a bloody fray. In the South as in the North, Protestant revivalism was on the way to becoming a powerful American religious movement.

However, the revival in the Chesapeake did not bring radical changes to the social order. Rejecting the requests of evangelical women, Baptist men kept authority within the church in the hands of "free born male members." Anglican slaveholders likewise retained power within the polity. Nonetheless, the Baptist insurgency gave spiritual meaning to the lives of the poor and powerless and influenced some yeomen and tenants to defend their economic interests. Moreover, as Baptist ministers spread Christianity among slaves, the cultural gulf between blacks and whites shrank, undermining one justification for slavery and giving blacks a new sense of religious identity. Within a generation African Americans would develop their own versions of Protestant Christianity.

The Midcentury Challenge: War, Trade, and Social Conflict, 1750–1765

Between 1750 and 1765 colonial life was transformed not only by Pietism and the Enlightenment but also by a major war, a boom-and-bust economy, and brutal frontier violence. First, Britain embarked on a war in America, the French and Indian War, which became a worldwide conflict—the Great War for Empire. Second, a rapid surge in trade boosted colonial prosperity but put Americans deeply in debt to British creditors. Third, a great westward migration sparked new battles with Indian peoples, armed conflicts between settlers and landowners, and frontier rebellions against eastern governments.

The French and Indian War

In 1750 Indian peoples remained dominant throughout the interior regions of eastern North America—the great valleys of the Ohio and Mississippi Rivers. Most Spanish colonists lived far to the west, along the Rio Grande in present-day New Mexico. French settlers lived along the St. Lawrence River, near the fur-trading centers of Montreal and Quebec (see Map 4.4). The more numerous residents of the British colonies inhabited the Atlantic coastal plain. Only a few pioneers had ventured across the Appalachian Mountains, both because there were few natural transportation routes and because of Indian resistance. For more than a generation the Iroquois and other Native Americans had firmly opposed the intrusion of white settlers, using their control of the fur trade to bargain for guns and subsidies from British and French officials.

The Failure of Diplomacy. However, the Iroquois strategy of playing off the French against the British was gradually breaking down as the European governments resisted the rising cost of "gifts" of arms and money.

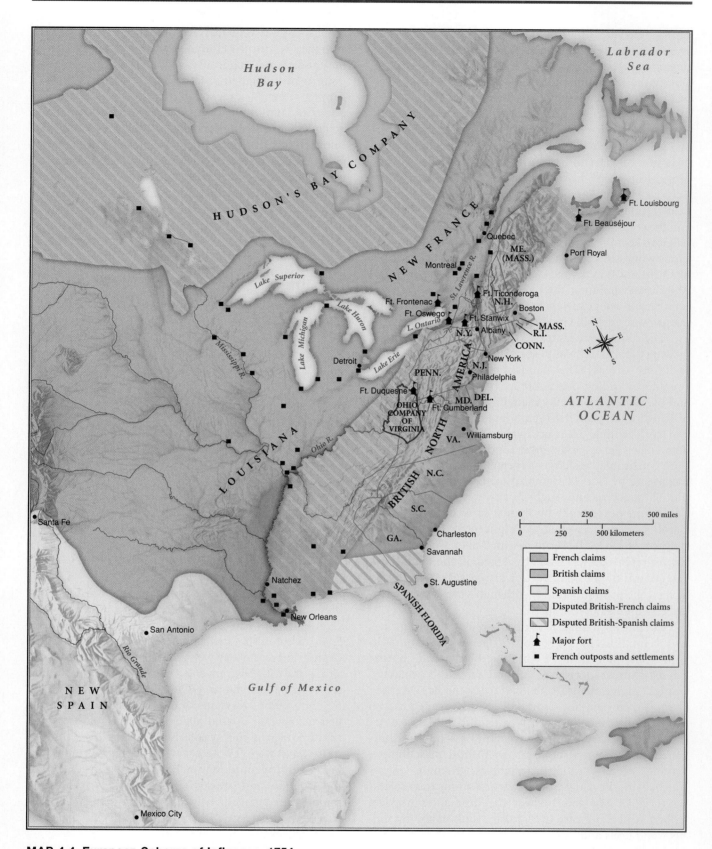

MAP 4.4 European Spheres of Influence, 1754

France and Spain laid claim to vast areas of North America and used their Indian allies to combat the numerical superiority of British settlers. For their part, Native Americans played off one European power against another. As a British official observed: "To preserve the Ballance between us and the French is the great ruling Principle of Modern Indian Politics." By expelling the French from North America, the Great War for Empire disrupted this balance, leaving Indian peoples on their own to resist encroaching Anglo-American settlers.

Equally important, crucial Indian alliances began to crumble. Along the upper Ohio River the Delawares and Shawnees declared that they would no longer abide by Iroquois policies. In part, this Indian discontent stemmed from escalating Anglo-American demand for Indian lands from colonial speculators and recent European migrants. In the late 1740s the Mohawks rebuffed attempts by Sir William Johnson, a British Indian agent and land speculator, to settle Scottish migrants west of Albany. To the south, the Iroquois were infuriated when Governor Dinwiddie of Virginia and a group of prominent planters laid plans for "the Extension of His Majesties Dominions" into the upper Ohio River Valley, an area that they had traditionally controlled. Supported by influential London merchants, the Virginia speculators formed the Ohio Company in 1749 and obtained a royal grant of 200,000 acres along the upper Ohio River. "We don't know what you Christians, English and French intend," the outraged Iroquois complained, "we are so hemmed in by both, that we have hardly a hunting place left."

To shore up the alliance with the Iroquois Nations, the British Board of Trade, the body charged with supervising American affairs, called for a great inter-colonial meeting with the Indians at Albany, New York, in June 1754. At the meeting the American delegates assured the Iroquois that they had no designs on their lands and asked for their assistance against the French. To bolster colonial defenses, Benjamin Franklin proposed a Plan of Union among the colonies with a continental assembly that would manage all western affairs: trade, Indian policy, and defense. But neither the Albany Plan nor a similar proposal by the Board of Trade for a political "union between ye Royal, Proprietary, & Charter Governments" ever materialized because both the provincial assemblies and the imperial government feared that a consolidated colonial government would undermine their authority.

Britain's movement into the Ohio River Valley alarmed the French. They countered by constructing a series of forts, including Fort Duquesne at the point where the Monongahela and Allegheny Rivers join to

The Siege of Louisbourg, 1745

Assisted by British redcoats, blue-coated New England militiamen swarmed ashore on Cape Breton Island in May 1745 and laid siege to the formidable French citadel at Louisbourg. By late June the colonists' artillery had silenced a strategic French battery, allowing British warships to enter the harbor. Faced with a combined assault from land and sea, the French surrendered. Yale University Art Gallery, Mabel Brady Garvan Collection.

Pipe of Peace

In 1760 the Ottawa chief Pontiac welcomed British troops to his territory, offering a pipe of peace to their commander, Major Robert Rogers. Three years later, Pontiac led a coordinated uprising against British troops, traders, and settlers, accusing them of cheating Native American peoples of their furs and lands. Library of Congress.

form the Ohio (present-day Pittsburgh). The confrontation escalated when Governor Dinwiddie dispatched an expedition led by Colonel George Washington, a young planter and Ohio Company stockholder, to support the company's claims. In July 1754 French troops seized Washington and his men and expelled them from the region, prompting expansionists in Virginia and Britain to demand war. The British prime minister, Henry Pelham, urged calm: "There is such a load of debt, and such heavy taxes already laid upon the people, that nothing but an absolute necessity can justifie our engaging in a new War."

Expansionism Triumphant. Pelham could not control the march of events. In Parliament William Pitt, a rising British statesman, and Lord Halifax, the new head of the Board of Trade, strongly advocated a policy of expansionism in the colonies. They persuaded Pelham to dispatch naval and military forces to America, where they joined with colonial militia in attacking French forts. In June 1755 British and New England troops captured Fort Beauséjour in Nova Scotia (Acadia). Equally significant, in a carefully planned military operation of dubious morality, troops from Puritan Massachusetts seized nearly 10,000 French Catholic Acadians, permanently deported them to various destinations—France, Louisiana, the West Indies, South Carolina—and settled English and Scottish Protestants on their farms.

This Anglo-American triumph was quickly offset by a stunning defeat. As 1,400 British regulars and Virginia militiamen advanced on Fort Duquesne in July 1755, they came under attack by a small force of French and a larger group of Delawares and Shawnees, who had decided to side with the French. In the ensuing battle the British commander, General Edward Braddock, lost his life and nearly two-thirds of his troops. "We have been beaten, most shamefully beaten, by a handfull of Men," Washington complained bitterly as he led the militiamen back to Virginia.

The Great War for Empire

By 1756 the fighting in America had spread to Europe, where the conflict aligned Britain and Prussia against France and Austria and was known as the Seven Years' War. When Britain decided to mount major offensives in India and West Africa as well as in North America and the West Indies, the conflict became a "great war for empire." Since 1700 Britain had reaped unprecedented profits from its overseas trading empire and was determined to crush France, the main obstacle to further expansion.

William Pitt, who was appointed secretary of state in 1757, was the grandson of the East Indies merchant "Diamond" Pitt and a committed expansionist. A haughty man, Pitt was constantly at odds with his colleagues. "I know that I can save this country and that I alone can," he declared. Indeed, Pitt was a master of strategy, both commercial and military, and planned to cripple France by attacking its colonies. In designing the critical campaign against New France, Pitt exploited a demographic advantage: on the North American mainland, King George II's 2 million subjects outnumbered the French by 14 to 1. To mobilize the colonists, Pitt agreed to pay half the cost of their troops and supply them with arms and equipment, an expenditure in America of nearly £1 million a year. He then committed

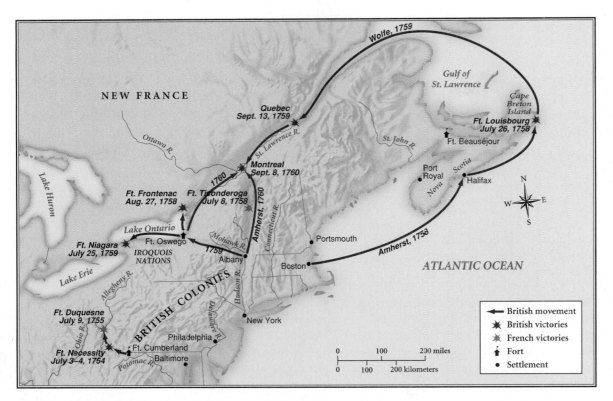

MAP 4.5 The Anglo-American Conquest of New France, 1754–1760

After full-scale war broke out in 1756, it took three years for the British ministry to equip colonial forces and dispatch a British army to America. Then British and colonial troops attacked the heartland of New France, capturing Quebec in 1759 and Montreal in 1760. The conquest both united and divided the allies. Colonists celebrated the great victory—"The Illuminations and Fireworks exceeded any that had been exhibited before," reported the South Carolina Gazette—*but British officers viewed provincial soldiers with disdain: "the dirtiest, most contemptible, cowardly dogs you can conceive."*

a major British fleet and 30,000 British regulars to the American conflict, appointing three young officers— James Wolfe, Jeffrey Amherst, and William Howe—as the top commanders (Map 4.5).

Beginning in 1758 the British moved from one triumph to the next. They forced the French to abandon Fort Duquesne (which they renamed Fort Pitt) and then captured the major fortress of Louisbourg at the mouth of the St. Lawrence (see Voices from Abroad, "Louis Antonine De Bougainville: The Defense of Canada," p. 126). The following year Wolfe sailed down the St. Lawrence to attack Quebec, the heart of France's American empire. After several failed attacks, 4,000 British troops scaled the high cliffs protecting the city and defeated the French. Quebec's fall was the turning point of the war. The Royal Navy prevented French reinforcements from crossing the Atlantic, and when British forces captured Montreal in 1760, the conquest of Canada was complete.

Elsewhere the British also went from success to success. Fulfilling Pitt's dream, the East India Company captured French commercial outposts and took control of trade in large sections of India. British forces seized French

Senegal in West Africa, the French sugar islands of Martinique and Guadeloupe, and the Spanish colonies of Cuba and the Philippine Islands. The Treaty of Paris of 1763 confirmed this triumph, granting Britain sovereignty over half the continent of North America, including French Canada, all French territory east of the Mississippi River, and Spanish Florida. Spain received Louisiana west of the Mississippi, along with the restoration of Cuba and the Philippines. The French empire in North America was reduced to a handful of sugar islands in the West Indies and two rocky islands off the coast of Newfoundland.

As British armies and traders occupied French forts, Indian peoples from New York to Michigan grew increasingly concerned. Fearing an influx of Anglo-American settlers, the Ottawa chief Pontiac hoped for a return of the French, declaring, "I am French, and I want to die French." Neolin, a Delaware prophet, went further, teaching that the suffering of the Indian peoples stemmed from their dependence on the Europeans and their goods, guns, and rum. He called for the expulsion of all Europeans. Inspired by Neolin's vision and his own anti-British sentiments, in 1763 Pontiac led a group of loosely confederated tribes in a major uprising,

Louis Antonine De Bougainville

The Defense of Canada

Following the outbreak of the Seven Years' War in Europe in 1756, the resident French governor in New France mobilized local troops to defend the colony. As Britain poured 11,000 regular troops into the conflict in America, the French government dispatched the marquis de Montcalm and a few thousand soldiers to Quebec. In July 1758 they met an invading British army at Fort Carrillon on Lake Champlain. In his journal Louis Antonine De Bougainville, Montcalm's chief of staff, recorded the following account of the battle. Like most European officers, British as well as French, Bougainville had nothing but contempt for the colonists and their leaders.

July 1, 1758. The Marquis de Montcalm went this morning . . . to reconnoiter the surroundings of Fort Carrillon in order to select a battlefield and the place for an entrenched camp. We lack manpower, and perhaps time is also lacking. Our situation is critical. Action and audacity are our sole resources. . . .

July 2. It has been decided to occupy the heights which dominate Carillon with an entrenched camp, with redoubts and abatis [a defensive line of felled trees and sharpened posts]. . . . But to carry out these works strong arms are needed, as well as the arrival of the colony troops, and time granted us by the enemy. . . .

July 8. Half an hour after noon the English army advanced on us. . . . The left was first attacked by two columns, one of which tried to outflank the defenses and found itself under fire of La Sarre, the other directed its efforts on a salient between [the battalions from] Languedoc and Berry. The center, where Royal Roussillon was, was attacked at almost the same time by a third column, and a fourth carried its attack toward the right between Bearn and La Reine. These different columns were intermingled with their light troops and better marksmen who, protected by trees, delivered a most murderous fire on us. . . . The different attacks, almost all afternoon and almost everywhere, were made with the greatest of vigor. . . .

July 9. The day was devoted to . . . burying our dead and those the enemy had left on the field of battle. Our companies of volunteers went out, advanced up to the falls, and reported that the enemy had abandoned the posts at the falls and even at the portage.

This victory which, for the moment, has saved Canada, is due to the sagacity of the dispositions, to the good maneuvers of our generals before and during the action, and to the unbelievable valor of our troops. . . .

July 29: Certain people [French colonists] are talking a lot of going home. They never made war [European-style] in Canada before 1755. They never had gone into camp. To leave Montreal with a party, to go through the woods, to take a few scalps, to return at full speed once the blow was struck, that is what they called war, a campaign, a success, victory. . . .

Now war is established here on the European basis. Projects for the campaign, for armies, for artillery, for sieges, for battles. It no longer is a matter of making a raid, but of conquering or being conquered. What a revolution! What a change! One would believe that the people of this country, at the novelty of these objects, would ask some time to accustom themselves to it, some more time to reflect on what they have seen. . . . On the contrary, townsmen, bankers, merchants, officers, bishops, parish priests, Jesuits, all plan this [war against English troops], speak of it, discuss it, pronounce on it.

Great misfortune for this country: it will perish, victim of its prejudices, the stupidity or of the roguery of its chiefs.

Source: Adventure in the Wilderness: The American Journals of Louis Antonine De Bougainville, trans. and ed. Edward P. Hamilton (Norman: University of Oklahoma Press, 1964).

capturing nearly every British garrison west of Fort Niagara, besieging the fort at Detroit, and killing or capturing over 2,000 frontier settlers. But the Indian alliance gradually weakened, and British military expeditions defeated the Delawares near Fort Pitt and broke the siege of Detroit. In the peace settlement that followed, Pontiac and his allies accepted the British as their new political "fathers." In return, the British addressed some of the Indians' concerns, temporarily barring Anglo-Americans from settling west of the Appalachians by establishing the Proclamation Line of 1763. Thus, in the aftermath of the Great War for Empire, the British crown took control of Canada and decided not to provide land for the expansion-minded American colonists.

British Economic Growth and the Consumer Revolution

Britain owed its military and diplomatic success in large part to its unprecedented economic resources. Since 1700, when it had wrested control of many oceanic trade routes from the Dutch, Britain had been the dominant commercial power in the Atlantic and Indian Oceans. By 1750 it was becoming the first country to undergo industrialization. Its new technology and work discipline made Britain the first—and for over a century the most powerful—industrial nation in the world.

The new machines and new business practices of the Industrial Revolution allowed Britain to produce more wool and linens, more iron tools, paper, chinaware, and glass than ever before—and to sell those goods at lower prices. British artisans had designed and built water- and steam-driven machines that powered lathes for shaping wood, jennies and looms for spinning and weaving textiles, and hammers for forging iron. The new machines produced goods far more rapidly than human hands could. Furthermore, the entrepreneurs who ran the new factories drove their employees hard, forcing them to keep pace with the machines and work long hours. To market the resulting products, English and Scottish merchants launched aggressive campaigns in the rapidly growing mainland colonies, extending a full year's credit to American traders instead of the traditional six months.

This first "consumer revolution" raised the living standard of many Americans, who soon were purchasing 20 percent of all British exports and paying for them by increasing their exports of wheat, rice, and tobacco (Figure 4.4). For example, Scottish merchants financed the settlement of the Virginia Piedmont, a region of plains and rolling hills just inland from the Tidewater counties. They granted planters and Scots-Irish migrants ample credit to purchase land, slaves, and equipment and took their tobacco crop in payment, exporting it to expanding markets in France and central Europe. In South Carolina planters supported their luxurious lifestyle by using British government subsidies to develop indigo plantations. By the 1760s they were exporting large quantities of the deep blue dye to English textile factories as well as exporting about 65 million pounds of rice a year to Holland and southern Europe. Simultaneously, New York, Pennsylvania, Maryland, and Virginia became the breadbasket of the Atlantic world, supplying Europe's exploding population with wheat at ever-increasing profits. In Philadelphia wheat prices jumped almost 50 percent between 1740 and 1765.

This first American spending binge, like most subsequent splurges, landed many consumers in debt. Even during the boom times of the 1750s and early 1760s exports paid for only 80 percent of imported British goods. The remaining 20 percent—millions of pounds—was financed by Britain, both by the extension of mercantile credit and by Pitt's military expenditures in the colonies. As the war wound down, the loss of military supply contracts and cash subsidies made it more difficult for Americans to purchase British goods. Colonial merchants looked anxiously at their overstocked warehouses and feared bankruptcy. "I think we have a gloomy prospect before us," a Philadelphia trader noted in 1765, "as there are of late some Persons failed, who were in no way suspected." The increase in transatlantic trade had

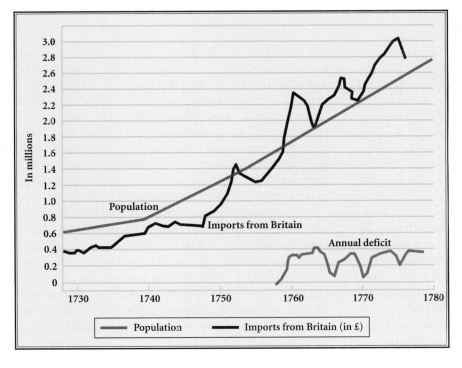

FIGURE 4.4 Colonial Population, Imports from Britain, and the American Trade Deficit

Around 1750 the rate of growth of imports from Britain into the American colonies outpaced the settlers' rate of population growth, indicating that consumption per capita was increasing. The colonists then went into debt to pay for these goods, running an annual deficit with their British suppliers.

New York Manor

The Philipse Manor stretched over ninety thousand acres and included mills and warehouses as well as a grand manor house. In this unattributed painting, the artist garbs the women in the foreground in classical costumes, thereby linking the Philipses to the noble families of the Roman republic. To preserve their aristocratic lifestyle and the quasi-feudal leasehold system of agriculture, the Philipses joined other Hudson River manorial lords in suppressing the tenant uprisings of the 1760s.
Historic Hudson Valley, Tarrytown, New York.

raised living standards but also had made Americans more dependent on overseas creditors and international economic conditions.

Land Conflicts

In good times and bad the colonial population continued to grow, causing increased conflicts over land rights. The families who founded the town of Kent, Connecticut, in 1738 had lived in the colony for a century. Each generation sons and daughters had moved westward to establish new farms, but now they lived at the generally accepted western boundary of the colony. To provide for the next generation, Kent families joined other Connecticut farmers in 1749 to form the Susquehanna Company, a land-speculating venture. Hoping to settle the Wyoming Valley in northeastern Pennsylvania, the company petitioned the legislature to assert jurisdiction

over that region on the basis of Connecticut's "sea-to-sea" royal charter of 1662. But King Charles II had subsequently granted these lands to William Penn, whose family invoked its proprietary rights and issued its own land grants. Soon settlers from Connecticut and Pennsylvania were burning down one another's houses. To avert further violence the two governments referred the dispute to the authorities in London, where it remained undecided at the time of independence (Map 4.6).

Simultaneously, three different land disputes broke out in the Hudson River Valley. First, groups of settlers from Massachusetts moved across the imprecise border with New York and claimed freehold estates on manor lands controlled by the Van Rensselaer and Livingston families. Second, the Wappinger Indians asserted legal claims to their traditional lands, which had been granted by English governors to various manorial lords. Finally, Dutch and German tenants asserted ownership

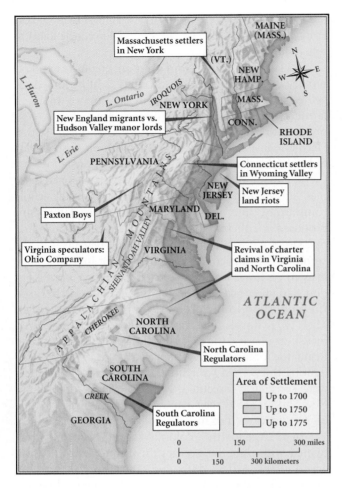

MAP 4.6 Westward Expansion and Land Conflicts, 1750–1775

Between 1750 and 1775 the mainland population doubled— from 1.2 million to 2.5 million—sparking westward migration and legal battles over land, which had become increasingly valuable. Violence broke out in many areas, as tenant farmers and smallholders contested landlord titles in eastern areas and backcountry settlers fought with Indians, rival claimants, and eastern-dominated governments.

rights to farms they had long held by lease and, when the landlords ignored their claims, refused to pay rent. By 1766 the tenants in Westchester, Dutchess, and Albany Counties were in open rebellion against their landlords and used mob violence to close the courts. At the behest of the royal governor, General Thomas Gage and two British regiments joined local sheriffs and manorial bailiffs to suppress the tenant uprising, intimidate the Wappinger Indians, and evict the Massachusetts squatters.

Other land disputes erupted in New Jersey and the southern colonies, where resident landowners and English aristocrats successfully asserted legal claims based on long-dormant seventeenth-century charters. For example, one court decision upheld the right of Lord Granville, an heir of one of the original Carolina

proprietors of 1660, to collect an annual tax on land in North Carolina; another decision awarded ownership of the entire northern neck of Virginia (along the Potomac River) to Lord Fairfax.

This revival of proprietary power underscored the growing strength of the landed gentry and the increasing resemblance between rural societies in Europe and America. High-quality land on the Atlantic coastal plain was getting more expensive, and English aristocrats, manorial landlords, and wealthy speculators had control of much of it. Tenants and even yeomen farmers feared they soon might be reduced to the status of European peasants and searched for cheap freehold land in western regions near the Appalachian Mountains.

Western Uprisings

Movement to the western frontier created new disputes over Indian policy, political representation, and debts. During the war with France, Delaware and Shawnee warriors had attacked farms throughout central and western Pennsylvania, destroying property and killing and capturing hundreds of residents. Subsequently, the Scots-Irish who lived along the frontier wanted to push the Indians out of the colony, but pacifistic Quakers prevented such military action. In 1763 a band of Scots-Irish farmers known as the Paxton Boys took matters into their own hands and massacred twenty members of the peaceful Conestoga tribe. When Governor John Penn tried to bring the murderers to justice, about 250 armed Scots-Irish advanced on Philadelphia, prompting mobilization of the militia. Benjamin Franklin intercepted the angry mob at Lancaster and arranged a truce, narrowly averting a pitched battle. Prosecution of the accused men failed for lack of witnesses. Although the Scots-Irish dropped their demand for the expulsion of the Indians, the episode left a legacy of racial hatred and political resentment.

The South Carolina Regulators.   Violence also broke out in the backcountry of South Carolina, where land-hungry Scottish and Anglo-American settlers had clashed repeatedly with Cherokees during the war with France. After the war ended in 1763, a group of landowning vigilantes, the Regulators, tried to suppress outlaw bands of whites that were roaming the countryside and stealing cattle and other property. The Regulators also wanted greater political rights for their region and demanded that the eastern-controlled government provide them with more local courts, fairer taxes, and greater local representation in the provincial assembly. The South Carolina government, which was dominated by lowland rice planters, decided to compromise with the Regulators because it feared slave revolts if the militia was away in the backcountry. In 1767 the assembly agreed to create locally controlled courts in the western counties of the colony and reduce the fees for legal documents. However, it refused to reapportion the assembly or lower western taxes. Eventually a rival backcountry group, the Moderators, raised an armed force of its own and forced the Regulators to accept the authority of the colonial government. Like the Paxton Boys in Pennsylvania, the South Carolina Regulators attracted attention to western needs but ultimately failed to wrest power from the eastern elite.

Civil Strife in North Carolina.

In 1766 another Regulator movement arose in the newly settled backcountry of North Carolina. After the Great War for Empire tobacco prices plummeted, and many debt-ridden farmers were forced into court. Eastern judges directed sheriffs to seize the property of bankrupt farmers and auction it off to pay creditors and court costs. Backcountry farmers—many of them migrants from Germany—resented merchants' lawsuits, not just because they generated high fees for lawyers and court officials but also because they violated rural custom. In both the Old and New Worlds, smallholding farmers made loans among neighbors on trust and often allowed the loans to remain unpaid for years.

To save their farms from grasping creditors and tax-hungry local officials, North Carolina debtors joined together in a Regulator movement. Disciplined mobs of farmers intimidated judges, closed down courts, and broke into jails to free their comrades. Their leader, Herman Husband, focused his attention on misbehavior of local officials, urging his followers not to vote for "any Clerk, Lawyer, or Scotch merchant. We must make these men subject to the laws or they will enslave the whole community." But the North Carolina Regulators also proposed a coherent program of reforms, demanding passage of a law allowing them to pay their taxes in the "produce of the country" rather than in cash. They insisted on lower legal fees, greater legislative representation, and fairer taxes, proposing that each person be taxed "in proportion to the profits arising from his estate." In May 1771 Royal Governor William Tryon mobilized British troops and the eastern militia and defeated a large Regulator force at the Alamance River; at the end of the fighting thirty men lay dead and seven insurgent leaders were summarily executed. Not since Leisler's revolt in New York in 1689 (see Chapter 3) had a domestic political conflict caused so much bloodshed in America.

In 1770 as in 1689, colonial conflicts became intertwined with imperial politics. In Connecticut the Reverend Ezra Stiles defended the North Carolina Regulators. "What shall an injured & oppressed people do," he asked, when faced with "Oppression and tyranny (under the name of Government)?" Stiles's remarks reflected growing resistance to British imperial control, a result of the profound changes that had occurred in the mainland colonies between 1720 and 1765. America was still a dependent society closely tied to Britain by trade, culture, and politics, but it was also an increasingly complex society with the potential for an independent existence. British policies would determine the direction the maturing colonies would take.

History and Memory

This visually striking highway marker, erected by a government agency in North Carolina, offers an official—and only partially correct—view of the past. Rather than assail the Regulators as extralegal vigilantes or outright lawbreakers (as many observers did at the time), the marker shrouds them in patriotism, as innocent victims of a vengeful British governor.

Alamance Battle Field, photo by Mike Mayse.

FOR FURTHER EXPLORATION

▶ For definitions of key terms boldfaced in this chapter, see the glossary at the end of the book.

▶ To assess your mastery of the material covered in this chapter, see the Online Study Guide at **bedfordstmartins.com/henretta.**

▶ For suggested references, including Web sites, see page SR-4 at the end of the book.

▶ For map resources and primary documents, see **bedfordstmartins.com/henretta.**

Between 1700 and 1760 Britain's mainland colonies grew dramatically in numbers and wealth. A freeholding yeoman society flourished in New England. Men exercised firm authority within families, controlling their wives' property and providing inheritances for their children. As population growth threatened the freehold ideal, New England farmers averted a crisis by planting higher-yielding crops, sharing their labor and goods with one another, or moving to new frontier settlements.

In the Middle Atlantic colonies, farmers prospered because of the rising European demand for wheat. A great influx of Germans and Scots-Irish created an ethnically and religiously diverse society and led to sharp conflicts with the Quakers over Indian policy and access to political power. Economic inequality increased as gentlemen farmers and entrepreneurs grew wealthy and a substantial group of landless workers appeared at the bottom of the social order.

As the American colonies developed closer ties with Europe, they partook of its intellectual life. The rationalism of the European Enlightenment prompted educated Americans such as Benjamin Franklin to become deists and social reformers, while pietistic religion from Germany and England reinvigorated colonial churches. In the 1740s, the preaching of George Whitefield prompted a Great Awakening that brought spiritual renewal and cultural conflict. In the northern colonies enthusiastic New Lights condemned traditional Old Lights, while in Virginia evangelical Baptists converted white tenant farmers and enslaved blacks, challenging the dominance of the Anglican elite.

At midcentury a variety of conflicts disrupted American life. Rival claims to the trans-Appalachian west sparked a major war between Britain and France that ended with the British conquest of Canada. The peace treaty excluded the French from North America, destroying the "playoff system" of the Iroquois and other native American peoples. Within the British colonies, landed proprietors battled with dissident tenants in New York and used the courts to uphold their land claims in Pennsylvania, Virginia, and the Carolinas. In the backcountry of Pennsylvania and the Carolinas yeomen farmers fought with Indians and formed Regulator movements to challenge eastern-controlled governments. Britain's North American settlements had become mature, conflict-ridden provinces.

1700–1714	New Hudson River manors created
1710s–1730s	Enlightenment ideas spread from Europe to America
	Deists rely on "natural reason" to define a moral code
1720s	Germans and Scots-Irish settle in the Middle Atlantic colonies
	Theodore Jacob Frelinghuysen preaches Pietism to German migrants
1730s	William and Gilbert Tennent lead Presbyterian revivals among Scots-Irish
	Jonathan Edwards preaches in New England
1739	George Whitefield sparks the Great Awakening
1740s–1760s	Growing shortage of farmland in New England
	Religious and ethnic pluralism in the Middle Atlantic colonies
	Rising grain and tobacco prices
	Increasing rural inequality
1740s	Great Awakening sparks conflict between Old Lights and New Lights
	Colleges established by religious denominations
1743	Benjamin Franklin founds the American Philosophical Society
1749	Virginia speculators create the Ohio Company
	Connecticut farmers form the Susquehanna Company
1750s	Industrial Revolution begins in England
	Consumer revolution increases American imports and debt to Britain
1754	French and Indian War begins
	Meeting of Iroquois and Americans at Albany; Plan of Union
1756	Britain begins the Great War for Empire
1759	Britain captures Quebec
1760s	Land conflict along the border between New York and New England
	Regulator movements in the Carolinas suppress outlaw bands and seek power
	Baptist revivals in Virginia
1763	Pontiac's uprising leads to the Proclamation of 1763
	Treaty of Paris ends the Great War for Empire
	Scots-Irish Paxton Boys massacre Indians in Pennsylvania

CHAPTER 5

Toward Independence: Years of Decision

1763–1775

As the Great War for Empire ended in 1763, Seth Metcalf and many other American colonists rejoiced over the triumph of British arms. A Massachusetts veteran just returned from the war, Metcalf thanked "the Great Goodness of God" for the "General Peace" that was so "perculary Advantageous to the English Nation." Two years later, Metcalf saw God's dialogue with his chosen Puritan people in very different terms. "God is angry with us of this land," the pious Puritan wrote in his journal, "and is now Smiting [us] with his Rod Especially by the hands of our [British] Rulers."

The rapid disintegration of the bonds uniting Britain and America—events that Metcalf explained in terms of Divine Providence—mystified many Americans. How had it happened, asked the president of King's College in New York in 1775, that such a "happily situated" people had armed themselves and were ready to "hazard their Fortunes, their Lives, and their Souls, in a Rebellion"? Unlike other colonial peoples of the time, the majority of white Americans had enjoyed life in a prosperous and relatively free society with a strong tradition of self-government. They had little to gain and much to lose by rebelling.

◀ **British Troops Occupy Concord**

In April 1775, hundreds of British troops stationed in Boston marched to Lexington and Concord, Massachusetts, searching houses for arms and munitions. The raid prompted a violent and deadly confrontation with the Patriot militia, an outcome prefigured by the unknown artist's depiction of a graveyard in the foreground. Courtesy, Concord Museum.

Britain Triumphant
Celebrating the Great War for Empire, this painting honors George III, "The Best of Kings," and praises two wartime heroes, Prime Minister William Pitt and General James Wolfe, who was killed in the battle of Quebec. The artist also offers a political message with real Whig overtones, warning the king against "Evil and Corrupt Ministers."
Courtesy, American Antiquarian Society.

Or so it seemed in 1765, before the British government attempted to reform the imperial system. The long overdue but disastrous administrative reforms prompted a violent response, beginning a downward spiral of ideological debate and political conflict that ended in civil war. "This year Came an act from England Called the Stamp Act . . . ," Metcalf reflected, "which is thought will be very oppressive to the Inhabitants of North America . . . But Mobbs keep it back." This course of events was far from inevitable. Careful British statecraft and political compromise could have saved the empire. Instead, inflexible negative responses to passionate Patriot agitation brought about its demise.

The Imperial Reform Movement, 1763–1765

The Great War for Empire left a mixed legacy. By driving the French out of Canada, Britain had achieved dominance over eastern North America (Map 5.1). But the cost of the triumph was high: a mountain of debt that prompted the British ministry to impose new taxes on its American possessions. More fundamentally, the war spurred Parliament to redefine the character of the empire, moving from an administrative system based on self-government and trade to one centered on rule by imperial officials.

The Legacy of War

The war fundamentally changed the relationship between Britain and its American colonies. During the fighting, there were major conflicts between colonial leaders and British generals over funding, military appointments, and

policy objectives. Moreover, the massive presence of British troops revealed sharp cultural differences between colonies and the home country. In particular, the arrogance of British officers and their demands for social deference shocked many Americans. A Massachusetts militiaman wrote in his diary that British soldiers "are but little better than slaves to their officers." The disdain was mutual. General James Wolfe complained that colonial troops were drawn from the dregs of society and that "there was no depending on them in action."

Disputes over Trade and Troops. The war also exposed the weak political position of British royal governors and other officials. In theory governors had extensive political powers, including command of the provincial militia; in reality they had to share power with the colonial assemblies, outraging British officials. The Board of Trade complained that in Massachusetts "almost every act of executive and legislative power is ordered and directed by votes and resolves of the General Court." To enhance the authority of the crown in America, British officials began a strict enforcement of

▶ **MAP 5.1 The Eurasian Trade System and European Colonies, c. 1770**
Western European dominance of maritime trade after 1650 spurred the creation of overseas colonies. By 1770 Spain controlled the western halves of North and South America, Portugal dominated Brazil, and Holland ruled Indonesia. Britain, a newcomer on the imperial scene, boasted a far-flung empire, with settler societies in eastern North America, rich Caribbean sugar islands, slave ports in West Africa, and a growing presence on the Indian subcontinent. Only France had failed to sustain a significant colonial empire. (To trace changes in trade and empires over time, see also Map 1.4 on p. 22 and Map 2.2 on p. 46.)

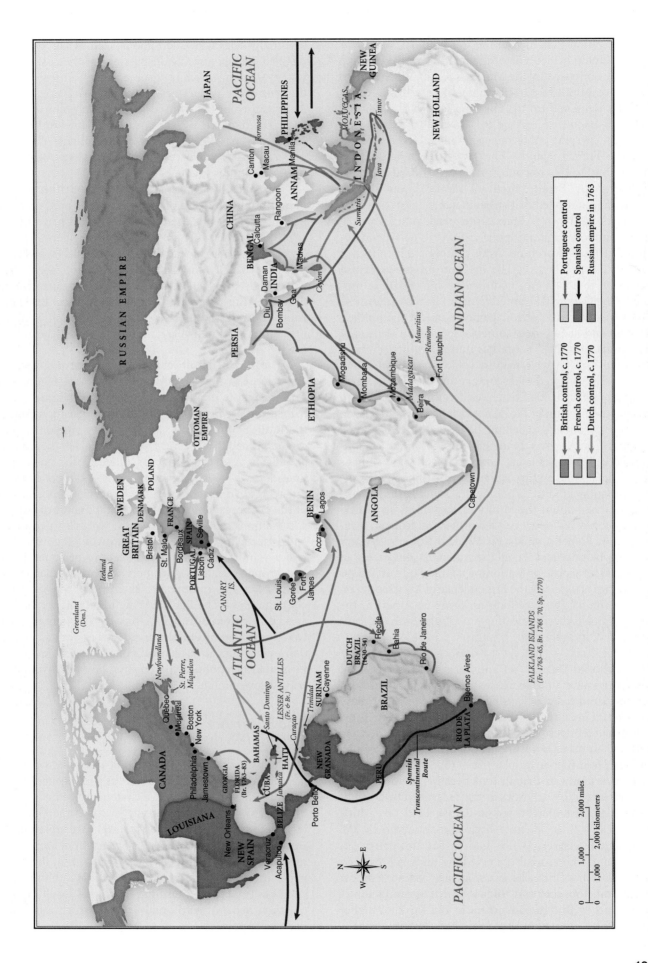

PACIFIC OCEAN

JAPAN

CHINA

Canton
Macau • Formosa

PHILIPPINES

NEW GUINEA

NEW HOLLAND

RUSSIAN EMPIRE

MOLUCCAS

I N D O N E S I A

Timor

ANNAM Manila

Java

Sumatra

Rangoon

Calcutta
BENGAL

Madras

Daman
Diu INDIA
Bombay Goa
Ceylon

PERSIA

Mauritius
Réunion
Fort Dauphin

INDIAN OCEAN

OTTOMAN
EMPIRE

ETHIOPIA

Mogadishu
Mombasa
Mozambique
Madagascar
Beira

SWEDEN
DENMARK
POLAND

GREAT
BRITAIN

Bristol •
St. Malo •
Bordeaux
FRANCE
Lisbon Seville
PORTUGAL SPAIN
Cádiz

CANARY
IS.

Iceland
(Den.)

Greenland
(Den.)

BENIN
Lagos
Accra

St. Louis
Gorée
Fort
James

ANGOLA

Capetown

ATLANTIC
OCEAN

Newfoundland

St. Pierre,
Miquelon

CANADA
Quebec
Montreal
Boston
Philadelphia New York
Jamestown
GEORGIA
FLORIDA
(Br. 1763–83)
New Orleans
LOUISIANA
NEW SPAIN
Veracruz
Acapulco

BAHAMAS
CUBA
Jamaica
HAITI
BELIZE
Porto Bello
NEW
GRANADA
PERU

Santo Domingo
LESSER ANTILLES
(Fr. & Br.)
Trinidad
Curaçao SURINAM
Cayenne

DUTCH
BRAZIL
(1630–54)
Recife
Bahia

BRAZIL

Rio de Janeiro

RIO DE
LA PLATA
Buenos Aires

Spanish
Transcontinental
Route

PACIFIC OCEAN

N
W E
S

0   1,000   2,000 miles
0   1,000   2,000 kilometers

FALKLAND ISLANDS
(Fr. 1763 65, Br. 1765 70, Sp. 1770)

British control, c. 1770
French control, c. 1770
Dutch control, c. 1770

Portuguese control
Spanish control
Russian empire in 1763

135

the Navigation Acts. Before the war colonial merchants had routinely bribed customs officials to avoid paying the duties imposed by the Molasses Act of 1733. To curb such corruption, in 1762 Parliament passed a Revenue Act that tightened up the customs service. In addition, the ministry instructed the Royal Navy to seize vessels that were carrying goods between the mainland colonies and the French islands. The fact that French armies attempting "to Destroy one English province, are actually supported by Bread raised in another" was absurd, declared an outraged British politician.

The victory over France provoked a fundamental shift in imperial military policy, and in 1763 Britain deployed a large peacetime army of about ten thousand men in North America. The decision to station British troops on the mainland stemmed from a variety of motives. King George III wanted to maintain a large army so that he would have patronage positions for his military friends, and he needed someplace to put them—and somebody to pay for them. His ministers worried about the defense of the newly acquired colonies of Quebec and Florida. They wanted to discourage any thought of rebellion among the 60,000 French residents of Canada and to prevent an invasion of Florida, which Spain wanted back. Moreover, Pontiac's rebellion had nearly overwhelmed Britain's frontier forts. It underscored the need for substantial military garrisons both to restrain the Indians and to deter land-hungry whites from settling west of the Proclamation Line of 1763. Finally, some British politicians worried about the loyalty of the American settlers now that they no longer needed protection from an invasion from French Canada. As William Knox, a treasury official who once had served the crown in Georgia, put it: "The main purpose of Stationing a large Body of Troops in America is to secure the Dependence of the Colonys on Great Britain." By stationing an army in America, the British ministry was indicating its willingness to use force to preserve its authority.

The National Debt. Yet another significant result of the war was the rapid increase in Britain's national debt, which soared from £75 million in 1754 to £133 million in 1763. The interest charges on the war debt now consumed 60 percent of the annual budget, forcing cutbacks in other government expenditures. Lord Bute, who became prime minister in 1760, needed to raise taxes—certainly in Britain and perhaps in America as well. However, his advisors in the Treasury Department advised against increasing the British land tax, which was already at an all-time high and was paid by the propertied classes, who had great influence in Parliament. Therefore, Bute taxed the underrepresented poor and middling classes, imposing higher import duties on tobacco and sugar, which manufacturers passed on to British consumers in the form of higher prices. The ministry also increased **excise levies**—

essentially sales taxes—on goods such as salt, beer, and distilled spirits, once again passing on the costs of the war to the king's ordinary subjects. Left unresolved for the moment was the question of imposing taxes on the American colonists, who also had little political power in Parliament. However, ministers knew that free Americans paid only about five shillings a year in imperial taxes, while British taxpayers were liable for nearly five times as much.

To collect these taxes and duties, the British government doubled the size of its bureaucracy and increased its powers. Customs agents and informers patrolled the coasts of southern Britain, arresting smugglers and seizing tons of goods, such as French wines and Flemish textiles, on which import duties had not been paid. Convicted smugglers faced heavy penalties, including death or "transportation" to America as indentured servants. Despite protests by colonial assemblies, nearly fifty thousand English criminals had already been banished to America.

The price of empire abroad had turned out to be debt and a more powerful government at home (Figure 5.1). The emergence of a big and expensive government confirmed the predictions of the British opposition parties, the **Radical Whigs** and Country Party landlords. Both groups argued that the huge war debt had left the treasury at the mercy of the "monied interest," the banks and financiers who were reaping millions of pounds in interest from government bonds. Moreover, the expansion of the tax bureaucracy had created thousands of patronage positions that were filled with "worthless pensioners and placemen." To reverse the growth of government power—and the consequent threats to personal liberty and property rights—reformers demanded that Parliament be made more representative of the property-owning classes. The Radical Whig John Wilkes called for an end to **rotten boroughs**—tiny districts whose voters were controlled by wealthy aristocrats and merchants. In domestic affairs as in colonial policy, the war had transformed British political life, creating a more active and intrusive government.

The Sugar Act and Colonial Rights

The active exercise of government power was particularly apparent in American affairs as a new generation of British officials undertook a systematic reform of the imperial system. The first to act was George Grenville, who became prime minister in 1763. Grenville quickly won Parliamentary approval of a Currency Act (1764) that protected British merchants by banning the use of paper money (which was often worth less than its face value) as legal tender. Ordinary colonists would have to pay their debts in gold or silver coin, which was always in short supply.

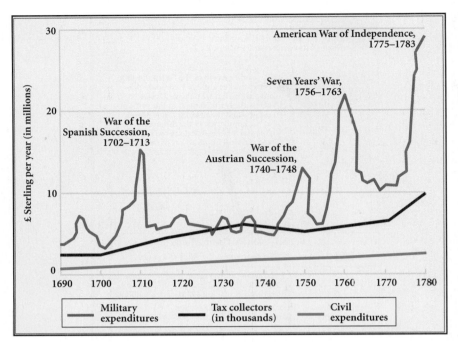

FIGURE 5.1 The Growing Power of the British State

As Britain built a great navy and subsidized the armies of its European allies, the government's military expenditures soared, as did the number of tax collectors. The tax bureaucracy more than doubled in size between 1700 and 1735 and increased sharply again between 1750 and 1780.

The Sugar Act. Then Grenville proposed a new Navigation Act, the Sugar Act of 1764, to replace the widely evaded Molasses Act of 1733. The new legislation was well thought-out. Treasury officials who understood the pattern of colonial trade convinced Grenville that the mainland settlers had to sell some of their wheat, fish, and lumber in the French islands. Without the molasses, sugar, and bills of exchange those sales brought, the officials pointed out, the colonists would lack the funds to buy British manufactured goods. Armed with this knowledge, Grenville resisted demands from British sugar planters for a duty of 6 pence per gallon that would completely cut off colonial imports of French molasses. Instead, he settled on a smaller duty of 3 pence per gallon, arguing that it would allow molasses from the British islands to compete with the cheaper French product without destroying the trade of the North American mainland colonies or their distilling industry (Map 5.2).

This carefully crafted policy garnered little support in America. Many New England merchants, such as John Hancock of Boston, had made their fortunes by smuggling French molasses and thus had never paid the duty. Their profits would be cut severely if the new regulations were enforced. These merchants and New England distillers, who feared a rise in the price of molasses, campaigned publicly against the Sugar Act, claiming that the new tax would wipe out trade with the French islands. Privately, they vowed to evade the duty by smuggling or by bribing officials.

Constitutional Issues. More important, the merchants and their allies raised constitutional objections to the new legislation. The speaker of the Massachusetts

House of Representatives argued that the duties constituted a tax, making the Sugar Act "contrary to a fundamental Principall of our Constitution: That all Taxes ought to originate with the people." The Sugar Act raised other constitutional issues as well. Merchants accused of violating the act would be tried by **vice-admiralty courts**—maritime tribunals composed only of a judge—and not by a local common-law jury. For half a century American legislatures had vigorously opposed vice-admiralty courts, expanding the jurisdiction of colonial courts to cover customs offenses occurring in the seaports. As a result, most merchants charged with violating the Navigation Acts were tried in common-law courts and were often acquitted by friendly local juries. By extending the jurisdiction of vice-admiralty courts to all customs offenses, the Sugar Act closed this loophole.

The new powers given to the vice-admiralty courts revived old American fears and complaints. The influential Virginia planter Richard Bland reminded his fellow settlers that for many decades the colonies had been subject to the Navigation Acts, which restricted their manufactures and commerce. But, he protested, the colonists "were not sent out to be the Slaves but to be the Equals of those that remained behind." John Adams, a young Massachusetts lawyer who was defending merchant John Hancock on a charge of smuggling, similarly condemned the new vice-admiralty courts, saying that they "degrade every American . . . below the rank of an Englishman."

While the logic of these arguments was compelling, some of the facts were wrong. The Navigation Acts certainly discriminated against the colonists; indeed, they were expressly intended to assist British-based merchants

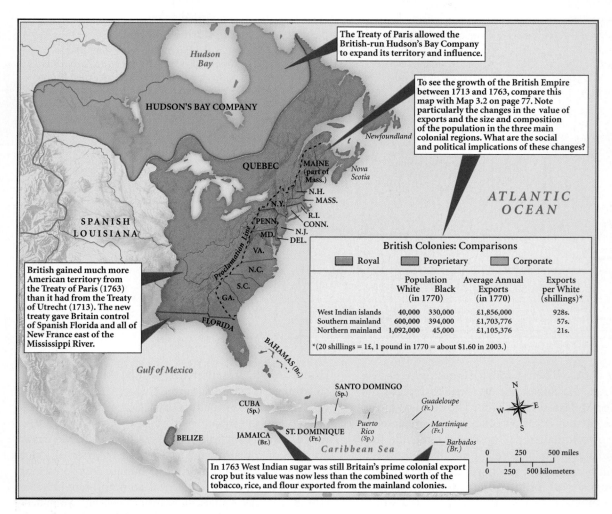

The Treaty of Paris allowed the British-run Hudson's Bay Company to expand its territory and influence.

To see the growth of the British Empire between 1713 and 1763, compare this map with Map 3.2 on page 77. Note particularly the changes in the value of exports and the size and composition of the population in the three main colonial regions. What are the social and political implications of these changes?

British gained much more American territory from the Treaty of Paris (1763) than it had from the Treaty of Utrecht (1713). The new treaty gave Britain control of Spanish Florida and all of New France east of the Mississippi River.

British Colonies: Comparisons

Royal   Proprietary   Corporate

	Population White (in 1770)	Black	Average Annual Exports (in 1770)	Exports per White (shillings)*
West Indian islands	40,000	330,000	£1,856,000	928s.
Southern mainland	600,000	394,000	£1,703,776	57s.
Northern mainland	1,092,000	45,000	£1,105,376	21s.

*(20 shillings = 1£, 1 pound in 1770 = about $1.60 in 2003.)

In 1763 West Indian sugar was still Britain's prime colonial export crop but its value was now less than the combined worth of the tobacco, rice, and flour exported from the mainland colonies.

MAP 5.2 Britain's American Empire in 1763

Following the Great War for Empire and the Treaty of Paris of 1763, Britain held a dominant position in the West Indies and controlled all of eastern North America. British ministers dispatched troops to the conquered colonies of Florida and Quebec and, with the Proclamation Line of 1763, tried to prevent Anglo-American settlement west of the Appalachian Mountains.

and manufacturers. However, the new vice-admiralty legislation did not penalize Americans; those in Britain had long been subject to the same rules. The real issue was the new spirit of imperial reform and the growing administrative power of the British state. Having lived for decades under a policy of "salutary neglect," Americans were quick to charge that the new British policies challenged the existing constitutional structure of the empire. As a committee of the Massachusetts House of Representatives put it, the Sugar Act and other British edicts "have a tendency to deprive the colonies of some of their most essential Rights as British subjects."

For their part, British officials insisted on the supremacy of Parliamentary laws and denied that the colonists were entitled to special privileges or even the traditional legal rights of Englishmen. When Royal Governor Francis Bernard of Massachusetts heard that the Massachusetts House had objected to the Sugar Act,

claiming no taxation without representation, he asserted that Americans did not have that constitutional right. "The rule that a British subject shall not be bound by laws or liable to taxes, but what he has consented to by his representatives," Bernard argued, "must be confined to the inhabitants of Great Britain only." In the eyes of most officials and politicians who now held power in Britain, the Americans were second-class subjects of the king, their rights limited by the Navigation Acts and the interests of the British state, as determined by Parliament.

An Open Challenge: The Stamp Act

The issue of taxation sparked the first great imperial crisis. When Grenville introduced the Sugar Act in 1764, he planned to seek a stamp tax the following

George Grenville, Architect of the Stamp Act
As prime minister from 1764 to 1766, Grenville assumed leadership of the movement for imperial reform and taxation. This portrait of 1763 suggests Grenville's energy and ambition. As events were to show, the new minister was determined to reform the imperial system and ensure that the colonists shared the cost of the empire. The Earl of Halifax, Garrowby, Yorkshire.

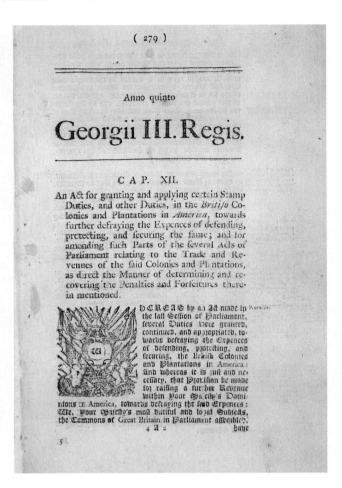

The Stamp Act
The official document that would fan the flames of resistance in America begins in Latin, the ancient language of law and authority: "In the fifth year of the reign of George III. . . ." By imposing a direct tax on the colonists, the new legislation ignited a storm of opposition, much of it violent, and began a decade-long political confrontation between British ministers and American Patriots. Library of Congress.

year. This new levy would cover part of the cost of keeping ten thousand British troops in America—some £200,000 per year (about $20 million today). The tax would raise revenue by requiring small embossed markings (somewhat like today's postage stamps) on all court documents, land titles, contracts, playing cards, newspapers, and other printed items. A similar tax in England was yielding an annual revenue of £290,000; Grenville hoped the American levy would raise at least £60,000 a year. The prime minister knew that some Americans would object to the tax on constitutional grounds, and so he asked explicitly whether any member of the House of Commons doubted "the power and sovereignty of Parliament over every part of the British dominions, for the purpose of raising or collecting any tax." No one rose to object.

Confident of Parliament's support, Grenville vowed to impose a stamp tax in 1765 unless the colonists would tax themselves. This challenge threw the London representatives of the colonial legislatures into confusion because they did not see how the American assemblies could collectively raise and apportion their defense budget. Representatives from the various colonies had met together officially only once, at the Albany Congress of 1754, and not a single assembly had accepted that body's proposals. Benjamin Franklin, who was in Britain as the representative of the Pennsylvania assembly, proposed another solution to Grenville's challenge: American representation in Parliament. "If you chuse to tax us," he suggested to an influential British friend, "give us Members in your Legislature, and let us be one People."

With the exception of William Pitt, British politicians rejected Franklin's radical idea. They argued that the colonists were already **"virtually" represented** in the home legislature by the merchants who sat in Parliament and by other members with interests in America. Colonial leaders were equally skeptical. Americans were "situate at a great Distance from their Mother Country," the Connecticut assembly declared, and therefore "cannot participate in the general Legislature of the Nation." Influential merchants in Philadelphia, worried that a handful of colonial delegates would be powerless in Parliament, warned Franklin "to beware of any measure that might extend to us seats in the Commons."

The way was now clear for Grenville to introduce the Stamp Act. His goal was not only to raise revenue but also to assert a constitutional principle: "the Right of Parliament to lay an internal Tax upon the Colonies," as his chief assistant declared. The ministry's plan worked smoothly. The House of Commons refused to accept American petitions opposing the act and passed the new legislation by an overwhelming vote of 205 to 49. At the request of General Thomas Gage, commander of the British military forces in America, Parliament also passed a Quartering Act directing colonial governments to provide barracks and food for the British troops stationed in the colonies. Finally, Parliament approved Grenville's proposal that violations of the Stamp Act be tried in vice-admiralty courts.

The design was complete. Using the doctrine of Parliamentary supremacy, Grenville had begun to fashion a genuinely imperial administrative system run by British officials without regard for the American assemblies. He thus provoked a constitutional confrontation not only on the specific issues of taxation, jury trials, and quartering of the military but also on the fundamental question of representative self-government.

The Dynamics of Rebellion, 1765–1766

Grenville had thrown down the gauntlet to the Americans. Although the colonists had often opposed unpopular laws and arbitrary governors, they had faced an all-out attack on their institutions only once—in 1686 when James II had arbitrarily imposed the Dominion of New England. Now the danger was even greater, because the new reforms were backed not only by the king and his ministers but also by the Parliament. However, the Patriots—as the defenders of American rights came to be called—took up Grenville's challenge, organizing protest meetings, rioting in the streets, and articulating an ideology of resistance.

The Crowd Rebels

In May 1765 the eloquent young Patrick Henry addressed the Virginia House of Burgesses and blamed the new king, George III (r. 1760–1820) for naming—and supporting—the ministers who designed the new legislation. Comparing George to the tyrannical Charles I who had sparked the Puritan Revolution of the 1640s, Henry seemed to call for a new republican revolution.

The Intensity of Patrick Henry

This portrait, painted in 1795 when Henry was in his sixties, captures his lifelong seriousness and intensity. As an orator, Henry drew on evangelical Protestantism to create a new mode of political oratory. "His figures of speech . . . were often borrowed from the Scriptures," a contemporary noted, and the content of his speeches mirrored "the earnestness depicted in his own features." Mead Art Museum, Amherst College.

Although Henry's remarks against the king (which bordered on treason) dismayed most of the Burgesses, they endorsed his attack on the Stamp Act, declaring that any attempt to tax the colonists without their consent "has a manifest Tendency to Destroy American freedom." In Massachusetts, James Otis, another republican-minded firebrand, persuaded the House of Representatives to call for a general meeting of all the colonies "to implore Relief" from the act.

The Stamp Act Congress.   Nine colonial assemblies sent delegates to the Stamp Act Congress, which met in New York City in October 1765. The Congress issued a set of Resolves protesting against the loss of American "rights and liberties," especially trial by jury. The Resolves also challenged the constitutionality of the Stamp and Sugar Acts, declaring that only the colonists' elected representatives could impose taxes on them (see American Voices, "Samuel Adams: An American View of the Stamp Act," p. 141). However, most of the delegates were moderate men who sought compromise, not confrontation. They concluded by assuring Parliament

Samuel Adams

An American View of the Stamp Act

*T*hanks to his education at Harvard College, distiller *Samuel Adams had impressive intellectual and literary skills. In this private letter to an English friend, Adams presents the various arguments used by British ministers to defend the new measures of imperial taxation and control. Then, in dispassionate, reasoned prose, Adams undertakes to refute them.*

To John Smith
December 19, 1765

Your acquaintance with this country . . . makes you an able advocate on her behalf, at a time when her friends have everything to fear for her. . . . The [British] nation, it seems, groaning under the pressure of a very heavy debt, has thought it reasonable & just that the colonies should bear a part; and over & above the tribute which they have been continually pouring into her lap, in the course of their trade, she now demands an internal tax. The colonists complain that this is both burdensome & unconstitutional. They allege, that while the nation has been contracting this debt solely for her own interest, detached from theirs, they have [been] subduing & settling an uncultivated wilderness, & thereby increasing her power & wealth at their own expense. . . .

But it is said that this tax is to discharge the colonies' proportion of expense in carrying on the [recent] war in America, which was for their defense. To this it is said, that it does by no means appear that the war in America was carried on solely for the defense of the colonies. Had the [British] nation been only on the defensive here, a much less expense would have been sufficient; there was evidently a view of making conquests, [thereby] . . . advancing her dominion & glory. . . .

There are other things which perhaps were not considered when the nation determined this to be a proportionate tax upon the colonies. . . . The [British] nation constantly regulates their trade, & lays it under what restrictions she pleases. The duties upon the goods imported from her & consumed here . . . amount to a very great sum. . . .

There is another consideration which makes the Stamp Act obnoxious to the people here, & that is, that it totally annihilates, as they apprehend, their essential rights as Englishmen. The first settlers . . . immediately after their arrival here . . . solemnly recognized their allegiance to their sovereign in England, & the Crown graciously acknowledged them, granted them charter privileges, & declared them & their heirs forever entitled to all the liberties & immunities of free & natural born subjects of the realm. . . .

The question then is, what the rights of free subjects of Britain are? . . . It is sufficient for the present purpose to say, that the main pillars of the British Constitution are the right of representation & trial by juries, both of which the Colonists lose by this act. Their property may be tried . . . in a court of Admiralty, where there is no jury. [As for representation], no man of common sense can easily be made to believe that the colonies all together have one representative in the House of Commons, *upon their own free election*. If the colonists are free subjects of Britain, which no one denies, it should seem that the Parliament cannot tax them consistent with the Constitution, because they are not represented. . . .

Source: Harry Alonzo Cushing, ed., *The Writings of Samuel Adams* (New York: G. P. Putnam, 1904).

that Americans "glory in being subjects of the best of Kings" and humbly petitioning for repeal of the Stamp Act. Other influential Americans advocated nonviolent resistance through a boycott of British goods.

Popular resentment was not so easily contained. When the act went into effect on November 1, disciplined mobs immediately took action. Led by men who called themselves the **Sons of Liberty**, the mobs demanded the resignation of newly appointed stamp tax collectors, most of whom were native-born colonists. In Boston the Sons of Liberty made an effigy of the collector Andrew Oliver, which they beheaded and burned, and then they destroyed a new brick building he owned. Two weeks later Bostonians attacked the house of Lieutenant Governor Thomas Hutchinson, a defender of social privilege and imperial authority, breaking the furniture, looting the wine cellar, and burning the library.

The BOSTONIAN'S Paying the EXCISE-MAN, or TARRING & FEATHERING
L.   London Printed for Rob.t Sayer & J.Bennett, Map & Printseller. N.53. Fleet Street, as the Act directs 30 Oct.r 1774.

A British View of American Mobs

This satiric view of the Sons of Liberty attacks their brutal treatment of John Malcolm, the commissioner of the customs in Boston, who was threatened with death (note the noose hanging from the tree) and then tarred and feathered and forced to drink huge quantities of tea. See the men in the background, disregarding property rights by pouring tea into Boston Harbor. The presence of a "Liberty Tree" implicitly poses the question Does Liberty mean Anarchy? Courtesy, John Carter Brown Library at Brown University.

The leaders of the mobs were usually middling artisans. "Spent the evening with the Sons of Liberty," John Adams wrote in his diary, "John Smith, the brazier [metalworker], Thomas Crafts, the painter, Edes, the printer, Stephen Cleverly, the brazier; Chase, the distiller; [and] Joseph Field, Master of a vessel." Some of these men had met through their work; more often they were drinking buddies, meeting nightly in the many taverns that dotted the streets and byways of the major port cities and soon became centers of political debate and Patriot agitation.

However, resistance to the Stamp Act spread far beyond the port cities. In nearly every colony crowds of angry people—the "rabble," as their detractors called them—intimidated royal officials. Near Wethersfield, Connecticut, five hundred farmers and artisans held tax collector Jared Ingersoll captive until he resigned his

office. This was "the Cause of the People," shouted one rioter, and he would not "take Directions about it from any Body." In New York nearly three thousand shopkeepers, artisans, laborers, and seamen marched through the streets, breaking street lamps and windows and crying "Liberty!"

The Motives of the Crowd. Although the strength of the Liberty mobs was surprising, such plebeian crowd actions were a fact of life in both Britain and America. Every November 5, Protestant mobs on both sides of the Atlantic marched through the streets celebrating Guy Fawkes Day. They burned effigies of the pope to commemorate the failure in 1605 of a plot by Fawkes and other English Catholics to blow up the Houses of Parliament. Likewise, colonial mobs regularly destroyed houses used as brothels and rioted to protest the impressment of merchant seamen by the Royal Navy.

If rioting was traditional, its political goals were new. The leaders of the Sons of Liberty in New York City were Radical Whigs who feared that reform of the imperial system would undermine political liberty. These men, minor merchants such as Isaac Sears and Alexander McDougall, tried to direct the raw energy of the crowd against the new tax measures. However, the mobs drew support from established artisans, struggling journeymen, and poor laborers and seamen who had different agendas and goals. Some artisans joined the crowds because imports of low-priced British shoes and other manufactured goods threatened their livelihood, and they feared the additional burden of a stamp tax. Unlike "the Common people of England," a well-traveled colonist observed, "the people of America . . . never would submitt to be taxed that a few may be loaded with palaces and Pensions and riot in Luxury and Excess, while they themselves cannot support themselves and their needy offspring with Bread."

Other members of the crowd were stirred by the religious passions of the Great Awakening. As evangelical Protestants who led disciplined, hardworking lives, they resented the arrogance of British military officers and the corruption of royal bureaucrats. In New England, some protesters looked back to the English Puritan Revolution, reviving antimonarchical and prorepublican sentiments of their great-grandparents. A letter sent to a Boston newspaper promising to save "all the Freeborn Sons of America" from "tyrannical ministers" was signed "Oliver Cromwell," the English republican revolutionary of the 1640s. And a masked and costumed figure known as "Joyce, Jr."—named after Cornet George Joyce, who had captured King Charles I—led crowds through the Boston streets. Finally, the mobs in all areas included apprentices, journeymen, day laborers, and unemployed sailors—young men seeking adventure and excitement who, when fortified by drink, were ready to resort to violence.

Throughout the colonies popular resistance nullified the Stamp Act. Fearing a massive assault on Fort George on Guy Fawkes Day (November 5, 1765), New York lieutenant governor Cadwallader Colden called on General Gage to use his small military force to protect the stamps stored in the fort. Gage refused. "Fire from the Fort might disperse the Mob, but it would not quell them," he told Colden, and the result would be "an Insurrection, the Commencement of Civil War." Frightened collectors gave up their stamps, and angry Americans coerced officials into accepting legal documents without them. This popular insurrection gave a democratic cast to the emerging American Patriot movement, extending it far beyond the ranks of merchants, lawyers, and elected officials. "Nothing is wanting but your own Resolution," a New York Son of Liberty declared during the upheaval, "for great is the Authority and Power of the People."

Slow communication across the Atlantic meant that the ministry's response to the Stamp Act Congress and the Liberty mobs would not be known until the spring of 1766. But it was already clear that royal officials could no longer count on the deferential political behavior that had ensured the empire's stability for three generations. As the collector of the customs in Philadelphia lamented, "What can a Governor do without the assistance of the Governed?"

Ideological Roots of Resistance

Initially the American resistance movement had no acknowledged leaders and no central organization. It had arisen spontaneously in the seaport cities because urban residents were directly affected by British policies. The Stamp Act taxed the newspapers sold by printers and the contracts and court documents used by merchants and lawyers, the Sugar Act raised the cost of molasses to distillers, and the flood of British manufactures threatened the livelihood of urban artisans. All in all, an official in Rhode Island reported, the interests of Britain and the colonies were increasingly "deemed by the People almost altogether incompatible in a Commercial View." As urban merchants and crowds protested against the new measures, they found some allies in the colonial assemblies—the traditional defenders of local interests against royal governors—but the movement was slow to develop a coherent outlook and organization.

Consequently, the first protests focused narrowly on particular economic and political matters. One pamphleteer complained that colonists were being compelled to give the British "our money, as oft and in what quantity they please to demand it." Other writers alleged that the British had violated specific "liberties and privileges" embodied in colonial charters. But American Patriot publicists gradually focused the debate by defining "liberty" as an abstract ideal—a natural right of all people—rather than a set of historical privileges. Men trained as lawyers took the lead, in part because merchants hired them to contest the seizure of their goods by customs officials. The lawyers' own professional values and training provided another motive; as practitioners of the common law they opposed extension of vice-admiralty courts and favored trial by juries. Composing pamphlets of remarkable political sophistication, Patriot publicists provided the resistance movement with an intellectual rationale, a political agenda, and a visible cadre of leaders.

Patriot publicists drew on three intellectual traditions. The first was English **common law**—the centuries-old body of legal rules and procedures that protected the king's subjects against arbitrary acts by the government. In 1761 the Boston lawyer James Otis had cited English legal precedent in the famous *Writs of Assistance* case. In that instance Otis disputed the legitimacy of a general search warrant permitting customs officials to inspect the property and possessions of any and all persons. Similarly, in demanding a jury trial for John Hancock, John Adams invoked common-law tradition. "This 29th Chap. of Magna Charta," Adams argued, referring to an ancient English document that had established the right to trial by jury, "has for many Centuries been esteemed by Englishmen, as one of the . . . firmest Bulwarks of their Liberties." Other lawyers protested when the terms of appointment for colonial judges were altered from "during good behavior" to "at the pleasure" of the royal governor, arguing that the change in wording compromised the independence of the judiciary.

A second major intellectual resource for educated Americans was the rationalist thought of the Enlightenment. Unlike American common-law attorneys, who used legal precedents to criticize British measures, the Virginia planter Thomas Jefferson invoked Enlightenment philosophers, such as David Hume and Francis Hutcheson, who questioned the past and relied on reason to discover and correct social ills. Jefferson and other Patriot authors also drew on the political philosopher John Locke, who argued that all individuals possessed certain "natural rights," such as life, liberty, and property, which government was responsible for protecting. And they celebrated the French theorist Montesquieu, who praised institutional curbs, such as the separation of powers among government departments, to prevent the arbitrary exercise of political power.

The republican and Whig strands of the English political tradition provided the third ideological basis for the American Patriot movement. In some places, particularly Puritan New England, Americans had long venerated the Commonwealth era—the brief period between 1649 and 1660 when England was a republic. After the Glorious Revolution of 1688, many colonists had welcomed the constitutional restrictions placed on the monarchy by English Whigs, such as the ban on royally imposed taxes. Later, educated Americans such as Samuel Adams of Boston absorbed the arguments of

Sam Adams, Boston Agitator

This painting by John Singleton Copley (c. 1772) shows the radical Patriot pointing to the Massachusetts Charter of 1692, suggesting that "charter rights" accounted for Samuel Adams's opposition to British policies. But Adams also was influenced by the natural rights tradition.

Deposited by the City of Boston. Courtesy, Museum of Fine Arts, Boston.

Radical Whig spokesmen who denounced political corruption. "Bribery is so common," John Dickinson of Pennsylvania had complained during a visit to London in the 1750s, "that there is not a borough in England where it is not practiced." These republican and Radical Whig sentiments made many Americans suspicious of royal officials. Joseph Warren, a physician and Patriot, reported that many Bostonians believed the Stamp Act

was part of a well-planned political conspiracy. They alleged that the new tax was intended "to force the colonies into rebellion," after which the ministry would use "military power to reduce them to servitude." As historian Alan Taylor has noted, the colonists "were quick to speak of 'slavery' because they knew from their own practice on Africans where unchecked dominion ultimately led."

These writings—swiftly disseminated thanks to the presence of a well-developed colonial printing industry and regularly published newspapers—provided the developing Patriot movement with a sense of identity and an ideological agenda, turning a series of impromptu riots and tax protests into a coherent political coalition.

Parliament Compromises, 1766

In Britain, Parliament was in turmoil, with different political factions advocating radically different responses to the American challenge. George III had replaced Grenville with a new prime minister, Lord Rockingham, who was allied with the Old Whigs and opposed Grenville's tough policies toward the colonies (Table 5.1). But hard-liners in Parliament, outraged by the popular rebellion in America, demanded that imperial reform continue. After listening to Benjamin Franklin tell Parliament that Americans would "never" pay a stamp tax "unless compelled by force of arms," they wanted to dispatch British soldiers to suppress the riots and compel the colonists to submit to the constitutional supremacy of Parliament. "The British legislature," declared Chief Justice Sir James Mansfield, "has authority to bind every part and every subject, whether such subjects have a right to vote or not."

Three factions were willing to repeal the Stamp Act, but for different reasons. The Old Whigs advocated repeal for reasons of policy: they believed that America was more important for its "flourishing and increasing trade" than for its tax revenues. Some Old Whigs even agreed with the colonists that the new tax was unconstitutional. British merchants favored repeal out of self-interest because the American boycott of British goods had caused a

TABLE 5.1 Ministerial Instability in Britain		
Leading Minister	Dates of Ministry	American Policy
Lord Bute	1760–1763	Mildly reformist
George Grenville	1763–1765	Ardently reformist
Lord Rockingham	1765–1766	Accommodationist
William Pitt/Charles Townshend	1766–1770	Ardently reformist
Lord North	1770–1782	Coercive

drastic fall in their sales. A committee of "London Merchants trading to America" mobilized support for repeal in the capital, and in January 1766 the leading commercial centers of Liverpool, Bristol, and Glasgow deluged Parliament with petitions, pointing out the threat to their prosperity. "The Avenues of Trade are all shut up," a Bristol merchant with large inventories on hand complained. "We have no Remittances and are at our Witts End for want of Money to fulfill our Engagements with our Tradesmen." Finally, former prime minister William Pitt demanded that "the Stamp Act be repealed absolutely, totally, and immediately" as a failed policy. Pitt's view of the constitutional issues was confusing. On the one hand, he argued that Parliament could not tax the colonies; on the other hand, he maintained that British authority over America was "sovereign and supreme, in every circumstance of government and legislation whatsoever." The Americans' challenge had raised new and difficult constitutional questions, to which there were few clear answers.

Rockingham gave each group just enough to feel satisfied. To assist British merchants and mollify colonial opinion, he repealed the Stamp Act and ruled out the use of troops against colonial crowds. He also modified the Sugar Act, reducing the duty on French molasses from 3 pence to 1 penny a gallon but extending it to British molasses as well. Thus, the revised Sugar Act regulated foreign trade, which most American officials accepted, but it also taxed a British product, which some colonists saw as unconstitutional. Finally, Rockingham pacified imperial reformers and hard-liners with the Declaratory Act of 1766, which explicitly reaffirmed the British Parliament's "full power and authority to make laws and statutes . . . to bind the colonies and people of America . . . in all cases whatsoever."

Because the Stamp Act crisis ended quickly, it might have been forgotten just as quickly. As of 1766 political positions had not yet hardened. Leaders of goodwill could still hope to work out an imperial relationship that was acceptable to British officials and American colonists.

The Growing Confrontation, 1767–1770

The compromise of 1766 was short lived. Within a year political rivalries in Britain sparked a new and more prolonged struggle with the American provinces, reviving the passions of 1765. The newfound ideological rigidity of key British ministers and American officials aggravated the conflict and dashed prospects for a quick resolution.

The Townshend Initiatives

Often the course of history is changed by a small event—a leader's illness, a personal grudge, a chance remark. So it was in 1767, when Rockingham's Old Whig

ministry collapsed and George III named William Pitt to head the new ministry. Pitt, the master strategist of the Great War for Empire, was chronically ill with gout and frequently missed Parliamentary debates, leaving Chancellor of the Exchequer Charles Townshend in command. Pitt was sympathetic toward America; Townshend was not. Indeed, as a member of the Board of Trade in the 1750s, he had backed measures restricting the power of the colonial assemblies. So when Grenville attacked Townshend's military budget in 1767, demanding that the colonists pay for the British troops in America, Townshend made an unplanned, fateful policy decision. Long convinced of the necessity of imperial reform and eager to reduce the English land tax, he promised that he would find a new source of revenue in America.

The Townshend Act.   The new tax legislation, known as the Townshend Act of 1767, had a political as well as a financial goal. The legislation imposed duties on paper, paint, glass, and tea imported into the colonies and was expected to raise about £40,000 a year. To pacify Grenville, part of this revenue would defray military expenses in America. However, the act reserved the major part of the new tax revenue to create a colonial civil list—a fund to pay the salaries of royal governors, judges, and other imperial officials. Once freed from financial dependence on the American legislatures, royal officials would be able to enforce Parliamentary laws and the king's instructions.

To increase royal power still further, Townshend also devised the Revenue Act of 1767. This act created a Board of American Customs Commissioners in Boston and vice-admiralty courts in Halifax, Boston, Philadelphia, and Charleston. These administrative innovations posed a greater threat to the autonomy of American political institutions than did the small sums raised by the import duties.

The Restraining Act.   The full implications of Townshend's policies became clear in New York, where the assembly refused to comply with the Quartering Act of 1765, which required Americans to house and feed British troops. Fearing an unlimited drain on its treasury, the New York legislature first denied General Gage's requests for barracks and supplies and then limited its assistance. Pointing out that most British troops were in New York to protect against raids by hostile Indians, the ministry instructed the colony to comply fully with the Quartering Act. If the assembly refused, some members of Parliament threatened to impose a special duty on New York's imports and exports. The earl of Shelburne, the new secretary of state, was prepared to go even further. He proposed the appointment of a military governor with authority to seize funds from New York's treasury to pay for quartering the troops and "to act with Force or Gentleness as circumstances might make necessary." Townshend decided on a less provocative but equally coercive measure, the Restraining Act of 1767, which suspended the New York assembly until it submitted to the Quartering Act. Faced with the loss of self-government, New Yorkers reluctantly appropriated the required funds.

The Restraining Act was of great significance because it threatened to deprive the American colonies of their representative governments. The British Privy Council had always supervised the assemblies; over the decades the council invalidated about 5 percent of all colonial laws, such as those establishing land banks or vesting new powers in the assemblies. Townshend's Restraining Act went much further by declaring American government institutions to be completely dependent on Parliamentary favor.

America Again Debates and Resists

The Townshend duties revived the constitutional debate over taxation. During the Stamp Act crisis some Americans, including Benjamin Franklin, had raised a distinction between "external" and "internal" taxes. They suggested that "external" duties on trade, which Britain had long regulated through the Navigation Acts, were acceptable to Americans but that direct or "internal" taxes, which had never before been levied, were not. Townshend thought this distinction between internal and external taxes "perfect nonsense" but told Parliament that "since Americans were pleased to make that distinction, he was willing to indulge them [and] . . . to confine himself to regulations of Trade."

A Second Boycott. However, most colonial leaders refused to accept the legitimacy of Townshend's measures. They agreed with John Dickinson, author of *Letters from a Farmer in Pennsylvania* (1768), that the real issue was not whether the tax was internal or external but the intention of the legislation. These Americans argued that the Townshend duties were really designed to raise the revenue of the imperial government, and therefore were taxes imposed without consent.

Townshend's measures revived American resistance, which now took more organized forms. In February 1768 the Massachusetts House of Representatives sent a letter to the other assemblies condemning the Townshend Act, and by the summer Boston and New York merchants had begun a new boycott of British goods. Philadelphia merchants, sailors, and dockworkers refused to join the boycott because they were heavily involved in direct trade with Britain and believed they had too much to lose. Nonetheless, public support for

nonimportation quickly emerged in the smaller port cities of Salem, Newport, and Baltimore and in some rural areas. In Puritan New England, ministers and public officials supported the boycott by condemning the use of "foreign superfluities" and promoting the domestic manufacture of necessities such as cloth (see Table 5.2).

The Daughters of Liberty. American women, ordinarily excluded from public affairs, became crucial to the nonimportation movement through their production of **homespun** textiles. During the Stamp Act boycott of English manufactured goods, the wives and daughters of Patriot leaders had increased their output of yarn and cloth. Resistance to the Townshend duties mobilized a much broader group of women, including pious farmwives who assembled to spin yarn at the homes of their ministers. Some gatherings of women were openly patriotic, such as one in Berwick, Maine, where "true Daughters of Liberty" celebrated American goods, "drinking rye coffee and dining on bear venison." Many more women's groups combined support for nonimportation with charitable work by spinning flax and wool to donate to the needy. Just as the tradition of crowd actions influenced men's response to the imperial crisis, so women's concerns with the well-being of their communities guided their efforts.

Newspapers celebrated these women as Patriots, prompting thousands to redouble their efforts at the spinning wheel and loom. One Massachusetts town proudly claimed an annual output of thirty thousand yards of cloth; East Hartford, Connecticut, reported seventeen thousand yards. Although this surge in domestic production did not compensate for the loss of British imports, which had averaged about ten million yards of cloth each year, it inspired support for nonimportation in hundreds of communities.

Indeed, the boycott united thousands of Americans, especially those in the seaport cities, in a common political movement. The Sons of Liberty published the names of merchants who imported British goods, broke their store windows, and harassed their employees. By March 1769 most Philadelphia merchants finally responded to public pressure and joined the nonimportation movement. Two months later the members of the Virginia House of Burgesses declared their support for the boycott, vowing not to buy duted articles, luxury goods, or slaves imported by British merchants. "The whole continent from New England to Georgia seems firmly fixed," the *Massachusetts Gazette* proudly announced. "Like a strong, well-constructed arch, the more weight there is laid upon it, the firmer it stands; and thus with America, the more we are loaded, the more we are united." Reflecting colonial self-confidence, Benjamin Franklin called for a return to the pre-1763 mercantilist system and proposed a "plan of conciliation" that was really a demand for British capitulation: "repeal the laws, renounce the

WILLIAM JACKSON,

an IMPORTER; at the

BRAZEN HEAD,

North Side of the TOWN-HOUSE,

and *Oppofite the Town-Pump, i*

Corn-hill, BOSTON.

It is defired that the Sons and
Daughters of *LIBERTY,*
would not buy any one thing of
him, for in fo doing they will bring
Difgrace upon *themfelves,* and their
Pofterity, for *ever* and *ever,* AMEN.

A Nonimportation Broadside
*To punish merchants who defied the boycott against the
Townshend duties, Patriots in Boston and other seaports posted
simply worded broadsides urging residents not to patronize their
businesses. Some Sons and Daughters of Liberty resorted to more
violent tactics, harassing customers and vandalizing buildings.*
Massachusetts Historical Society.

John Wilkes, British Radical
*Wilkes won fame in the colonies as the author of the pamphlet
North Briton, Number 45 (depicted on the left), which called
for major reforms in the British political system. At a dinner
in Boston, Radical Whigs raised their wineglasses to Wilkes—
toasting him forty-five times! However, Wilkes had many
enemies in Britain, including the creator of this image, who
depicts him as a cunning demagogue, wearing the cap of Liberty
in order to curry favor with the mob.*
Miriam and Ira D. Wallach Division of Art, Prints and Photographs, the
New York Public Library. Astor, Lenox and Tilden Foundations.

right, recall the troops, refund the money, and return to
the old method of requisition."

Britain Responds.   American resistance only increased
British determination. When a copy of the Massachusetts
House's letter opposing the Townshend duties reached
London in the late spring of 1768, it sparked an angry
response. Lord Hillsborough, the secretary of state for
American affairs, branded the assembly's action as
"unjustifiable opposition to the constitutional authority
of Parliament." To strengthen the "Hand of Government"
in Massachusetts and assist the Commissioners of the
Customs, who had been forced by a mob to take refuge on
a British naval vessel, Hillsborough dispatched four
regiments of troops to Boston. By the end of 1768, more
than four thousand British regulars were encamped in
Boston, and military coercion was a very real prospect.
General Gage accused public leaders in Massachusetts of

"Treasonable and desperate Resolves" and advised the
ministry to "Quash this Spirit at a Blow." Parliament responded by threatening to appoint a special commission to
hear evidence of treason, and Hillsborough tried to win
support for a plan that would isolate Massachusetts
from the other colonies and then use the British army to
bring the rebellious New Englanders to their knees
(Map 5.3).

The stakes of the conflict had risen. In 1765 American resistance to taxation had provoked a Parliamentary
debate. In 1768 it produced a plan for military coercion.

Lord North Compromises, 1770

At this critical moment the British ministry's resolve faltered. In Scotland and northern England, thousands of

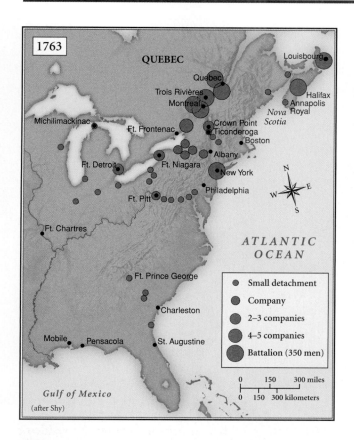

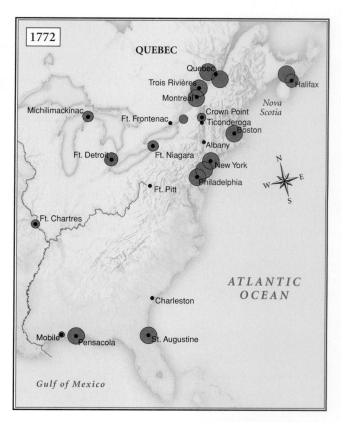

MAP 5.3 British Troop Deployments, 1763–1775

As the imperial crisis deepened, British military priorities changed. In 1763 most British battalions were stationed in Canada to deter Indian uprisings and French-Canadian revolts. After the Stamp Act riots of 1765, the British established larger garrisons in New York and Philadelphia. By 1775 eleven battalions of British regulars occupied Boston, the center of the American Patriot movement.

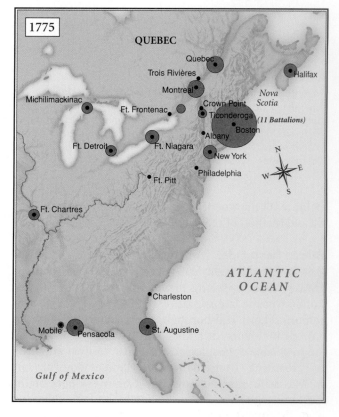

tenants deserted their farms and sought landed independence in America, aggravating a series of natural disasters that cut grain production. As food shortages mounted, riots spread across the English countryside. In

the highly publicized Massacre of Saint George Fields, troops killed seven demonstrators. The Radical Whig John Wilkes, supported by associations of merchants, tradesmen, and artisans, stepped up his attacks on

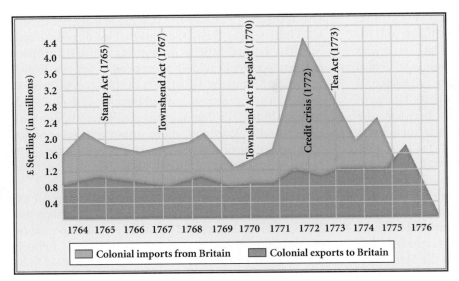

FIGURE 5.2 Trade as a Political Weapon, 1763–1776

Political upheaval did not affect the mainland colonies' exports to Britain, which remained steady (and rose slightly) over the period, but imports fluctuated greatly. The American boycott of 1768–1769 brought a sharp decline in the importation of British manufactures, which then soared after the repeal of the Townshend duties.

government corruption and won election to Parliament. Overjoyed, American Patriots drank toasts in Wilkes's honor and purchased thousands of teapots and drinking mugs emblazoned with his picture. Riots in Ireland over the growing military budget there added to the ministry's difficulties.

Nonimportation Succeeds. The American trade boycott also began to hurt the British economy. Normally the colonies had an annual trade deficit with the home country of £500,000, but in 1768 they imported less from Great Britain, cutting the deficit to £230,000. In 1769 the boycott had a major economic impact. By continuing to export tobacco, rice, fish, and other goods to Britain while refusing to buy its manufactured goods, Americans accumulated a trade surplus of £816,000 (Figure 5.2). To revive their flagging fortunes, British merchants and manufacturers petitioned Parliament for repeal of the Townshend duties. British government revenues, which were heavily dependent on excise taxes and duties on imported goods, had also suffered. By late 1769 merchants' petitions had persuaded some ministers that the Townshend duties were a mistake, and the king had withdrawn his support for Hillsborough's plan to coerce the colonies with military force.

Early in 1770 Lord North became prime minister and arranged a new compromise. Arguing that it was foolish to tax British exports to America, raising their price and decreasing consumption, North persuaded Parliament to repeal the duties on glass, paper, paint, and other manufactured items. However, he retained the tax on tea as a symbol of Parliament's supremacy. Gratified by North's initiative, merchants in New York and Philadelphia rejected pleas from Patriots in Boston to continue the boycott. Rather than contesting the symbolic levy on tea, most Americans simply avoided the tax by drinking smuggled tea provided by Dutch merchants.

Even the outbreak of violence in New York City and Boston did not rupture the compromise. During the boycott New York artisans and workers had taunted British troops, mostly with words but occasionally with stones and fists. In retaliation the soldiers tore down a Liberty Pole (a Patriot flagpole), setting off a week of street fighting. In Boston friction between the residents and British soldiers over constitutional principles and everyday issues, such as competition for part-time jobs, sparked the Boston Massacre. In March 1770, a group of soldiers fired into a rowdy crowd, killing five men, including one of the leaders, Crispus Attucks, an escaped slave who was working as a seaman. Reviving fears of a ministerial conspiracy against liberty, a Radical Whig pamphlet accused the British of deliberately planning the massacre.

Sovereignty Debated. Although most Americans ignored such charges and remained loyal to the empire, five years of conflict over taxes and constitutional principles had taken its toll. In 1765 American leaders had accepted Parliament's authority; the Stamp Act Resolves had opposed only certain "unconstitutional" legislation. By 1770 the most outspoken Patriots—Benjamin Franklin in Pennsylvania, Patrick Henry in Virginia, and Samuel Adams in Massachusetts—had repudiated Parliamentary supremacy, claiming equality for the American assemblies. Beginning from this premise, Franklin looked for a way to redefine the imperial relationship so that the colonies would have political equality within the empire. Perhaps thinking of various European "composite monarchies" (in which kings ruled far-distant and semiautonomous provinces acquired by inheritance or conquest), Franklin suggested that the colonies were now "distinct and separate states" but ones that had "the same Head, or Sovereign, the King."

Franklin's proposal horrified Thomas Hutchinson, the American-born royal governor of Massachusetts, who rejected the idea of "two independent legislatures in one and the same state." For Hutchinson, the British empire was a single whole, its sovereignty indivisible. "I know of no line," he told the Massachusetts House of Representatives, "that can be drawn between the supreme authority of Parliament and the total independence of the colonies."

There the matter rested. The British had twice tried to impose taxes on the colonies, and American Patriots had twice forced them to retreat. If Parliament or the king insisted on exercising Britain's claim to sovereign power, at least some Americans were prepared to resist by force. Nor did they flinch when reminded that George III condemned their agitation. As the Massachusetts House told Hutchinson, "There is more reason to dread the consequences of absolute uncontrolled supreme power, whether of a nation or a monarch, than those of total independence." Fearful of civil war, the ministry hesitated to take the final fateful step.

The Road to War, 1771–1775

The repeal of the Townshend duties in 1770 restored harmony to the British empire. For the next three years most disputes were resolved peacefully. Yet below the surface lay strong fears and passions and mutual distrust. Suddenly, in 1773 those undercurrents erupted, overwhelming any hope for compromise. In less than two years the Americans and the British stood on the brink of war.

The Compromise Ignored

Once roused, political passions were not easily quelled. Radical Boston Patriots who wanted greater rights for the colonies continued to warn Americans of the dangers of imperial domination. In November 1772 Samuel Adams persuaded the Boston town meeting to establish a Committee of Correspondence to urge Patriots in other towns "to state the Rights of the Colonists of this Province." Within a few months eighty Massachusetts towns had similar committees, all in communication with one another. Other colonies organized similar networks when the British government set up a royal commission to investigate the burning of the *Gaspée*, a British customs vessel, in Rhode Island. The commission's broad powers, particularly its authority to send Americans to Britain for trial, aroused the Virginia House of Burgesses to set up a Committee of Correspondence "to communicate with the other colonies" about the situation in Rhode Island. By July 1773 committees had sprung up in Connecticut, New Hampshire, and South Carolina.

The Tea Act.   Parliament's passage of a Tea Act in May 1773 initiated the chain of events that led directly to civil war. The act had little to do with America. Its primary purpose was to provide financial relief for the British East India Company, which was deeply in debt because of military expeditions undertaken to extend British trade in India. The Tea Act provided the company with a government loan and, more important, relieved the company of paying tariffs on the tea it imported into Britain or exported to the colonies. Only the American consumers would pay the duty.

Lord North failed to understand how unpopular the Tea Act would be in America. Since 1768, when the Townshend Act had placed a duty of 3 pence a pound on tea, the colonies had evaded the tax by illegally importing tea from Dutch sources. By relieving the East India Company of English tariffs, the Tea Act gave its tea a competitive price advantage over that sold by Dutch merchants. In this way the act encouraged Americans to drink East India tea—and in the process pay the Townshend duty. Radical Patriots smelled a plot and accused the ministry of bribing Americans to give up their principled opposition to British taxation. As an anonymous woman wrote in the *Massachusetts Spy*, "the use of [British] tea is considered not as a private but as a public evil . . . a handle to introduce a variety of . . . oppressions amongst us." American merchants also voiced their opposition because the East India Company planned to distribute its tea directly to shopkeepers, excluding most colonial merchants from the profits of the trade. "The fear of an Introduction of a Monopoly in this Country," General Haldimand reported from New York, "has induced the mercantile part of the Inhabitants to be very industrious in opposing this Step and added Strength to a Spirit of Independence already too prevalent."

The newly formed Committees of Correspondence took the lead in organizing resistance to the Tea Act. They held public bonfires at which they persuaded their fellow citizens (sometimes gently, sometimes not) to consign British tea to the flames. The Sons of Liberty patrolled the harbors, preventing East India Company ships from landing new supplies. By forcing the company's captains to return the tea to Britain or store it in public warehouses, the Patriots effectively nullified the legislation.

The Tea Party and the Coercive Act.   Governor Thomas Hutchinson of Massachusetts was determined to uphold the Tea Act and hatched a scheme to land the tea and collect the tax. When a shipment of tea arrived on the *Dartmouth*, Hutchinson had the ship passed through customs immediately so that the Sons of Liberty could not prevent its landing. If necessary, he was prepared to use the British army to unload the tea and supervise its sale by auction. But Patriots foiled the governor's plan by raiding the *Dartmouth*: a group of artisans and laborers disguised as Indians boarded the ship, broke open the 342 chests of tea (valued at about £10,000, or roughly $800,000 today), and threw them into the harbor (see American Lives, "George R. T. Hewes and the Meaning of the Revolution," p. 152). "This destruction of the Tea is so bold and it must have so important Consequences," John Adams wrote in his diary, "that I cannot but consider it as an Epoch in History."

The British Privy Council was outraged, as was the king. "Concessions have made matters worse," George III declared. "The time has come for compulsion." Early in 1774 Parliament decisively rejected a proposal to repeal the duty on American tea; instead, it enacted four Coercive Acts to force Massachusetts into submission. A Port Bill closed Boston Harbor until the East India Company received payment for the destroyed tea. A Government Act annulled the Massachusetts charter and prohibited most local town meetings. A new Quartering Act required the colony to build barracks or accommodate soldiers in private houses. Finally, to protect royal officials from Patriot-dominated juries in Massachusetts, a Justice Act allowed the transfer of trials for capital crimes to other colonies or to Britain.

Patriot leaders throughout the mainland colonies condemned these measures, branding them as the "Intolerable Acts" and rallying support for Massachusetts. In far-off Georgia, a Patriot warned the "Freemen of the Province" that "every privilege you at present claim as a birthright, may be wrested from you by the same authority that blockades the town of Boston." "The cause of Boston," George Washington declared from Virginia, "now is and ever will be considered as the cause of America." The activities of the Committees of Correspondence had created a firm sense of unity among those with Patriot sympathies.

In 1774 Parliament passed the Quebec Act, which heightened the sense of common danger among Americans of European Protestant descent who lived in the seaboard colonies. The law extended the boundaries of Quebec into the Ohio River Valley, thus restricting the western boundaries of Virginia and other coastal colonies and angering influential land speculators and politicians with western land claims (Map 5.4). The act also gave legal recognition in Quebec to Roman Catholicism. This humane concession to the predominantly Catholic population aroused latent religious hatreds, especially in New England, where Puritans associated Catholicism with arbitrary royal government and popish superstition. Although the ministry had not intended the Quebec Act as

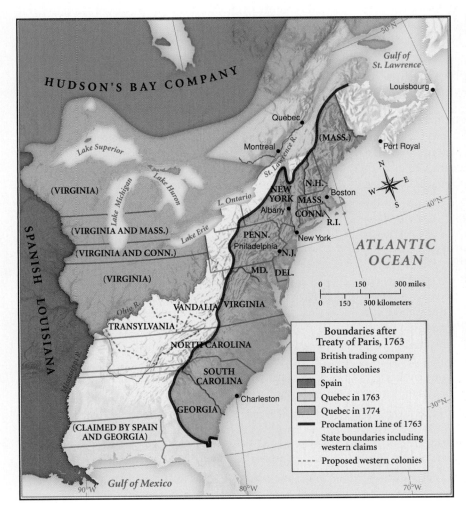

MAP 5.4 British Western Policy, 1763–1774

The Proclamation Line of 1763 restricted white settlement west of the Appalachian Mountains, but colonial land speculators and resident settlers proposed the new colonies of Vandalia and Transylvania. However, the Quebec Act of 1774 designated most western lands as Indian reserves and, by vastly enlarging the boundaries of Quebec, eliminated the sea-to-sea land claims of many seaboard colonies. The act, which also allowed French residents to practice Catholicism, angered many Americans: settlers and land speculators who wanted easy access to the West, New England Protestants who had long feared Catholicism, and colonial political leaders who condemned its failure to provide a representative assembly in Quebec.

For more help analyzing this map, see the ONLINE STUDY GUIDE at bedfordstmartins.com/henretta.

George R. T. Hewes and the Meaning of the Revolution

George Hewes

In this portrait (c. 1835) Joseph Cole presents the elderly Hewes as a dignified gentleman, not the impoverished shoemaker and farmer that he actually was. Bostonian Society / Old State House.

George Robert Twelves Hewes was born in Boston in 1742. He was named George for his father, Robert for a paternal uncle, and Twelves for his maternal grandmother, whose family name was Twelves. Apart from his long name, Hewes received little from his parents—not size, for he was unusually short, at five feet, one inch; not wealth, for his father, a failed leather tanner, died a poor soap boiler when Hewes was seven years old; not even love, for Hewes spoke of his mother only as someone who whipped him for disobedience. When he was fourteen she apprenticed him to a shoemaker, one of the lower trades.

This harsh upbringing shaped Hewes's outlook on life. As an adult he spoke out against all brutality, even the tarring and feathering of a Loyalist who had almost killed him. And throughout his life he was extremely sensitive about his class status. He was "neither a rascal nor a vagabond," Hewes retorted to a Boston gentleman who pulled rank on him, "and though a poor man was in as good credit in town as he [the gentleman] was."

In 1768 the occupation of Boston by four thousand British soldiers drew the twenty-six-year-old Hewes into the resistance movement. At first his concerns were personal: he took offense when British sentries challenged him and when a soldier refused to pay for a pair of shoes. Then they became political: Hewes grew angry when some of the poorly paid British soldiers moonlighted, taking jobs away from Bostonians, and even angrier when a Loyalist merchant fired into a crowd of apprentices who were picketing his shop, killing one of them. So on March 5, 1770, when British soldiers came out in force to clear the streets of rowdy civilians, Hewes joined his fellow townspeople: "They were in the king's highway, and had as good a right to be there" as the British troops, he said.

Fate—and his growing political consciousness—placed Hewes in the middle of the Boston Massacre. He claimed to know four of the five workingmen shot down that night by British troops, and one of them, James Caldwell, was standing by his side. Hewes caught him as he fell. Outraged, Hewes armed himself with a cane, only to be confronted by Sergeant Chambers of the 29th British Regiment and eight or nine soldiers, "all with

very large clubs or cutlasses." Chambers seized his cane, but as Hewes stated in a legal deposition, "I told him I had as good a right to carry a cane as they had to carry clubs." This deposition, which told of the soldiers' threats to kill more civilians, was included in *A Short Narrative of the Horrid Massacre in Boston* (1770), published by a group of Boston Patriots.

Hewes had chosen sides, and his political radicalism did not go unpunished. His deposition roused the ire of one of his creditors, a Loyalist merchant tailor. Hewes had never really made a go of it as a shoemaker and lived on the brink of poverty. When he was unable to make good on a two-year-old debt of 6 pounds, 8 shillings, 3 pence in Massachusetts currency, about $300 today, for "a sappled coat & breeches of fine cloth," the merchant sent him to debtors' prison for over a month. Hewes's extravagance was not in character; his purchase of the suit had been the desperate ploy of a propertyless artisan to win the hand of Sally Summer, the daughter of the sexton of the First Baptist Church, whom Hewes married in 1768.

Prison did not blunt Hewes's enthusiasm for the Patriot cause. On the night of December 16, 1773, he volunteered for the raid on the British tea ship being organized by the radical Patriots of Boston. He "daubed his face and hands with coal dust in the shop of a blacksmith" and then found, to his surprise, that "the commander of the division to which I belonged, as soon as we were on board the ship, appointed me boatswain, and ordered me to go to the captain and demand of him the keys to the hatches."

Hewes had been singled out and made a minor leader, and he must have played the part well. Thompson Maxwell, a volunteer sent to the raid by John Hancock, recalled that "I went accordingly, joined the band under one Captain Hewes; we mounted the ships and made tea in a trice." In the heat of conflict the small man with the large name had been elevated from a poor shoemaker to "Captain Hewes."

A man of greater ability or ambition might have seized the moment, using his reputation as a Patriot to win fame or fortune, but that was not Hewes's destiny. During the War of Independence he fought as an ordinary sailor and soldier, shipping out twice on privateering voyages and enlisting at least four times in the militia, about twenty months of military service in all. He did not win riches as a privateer (although, with four children to support, that was his hope). Nor did he find glory in battle or even adequate pay: "we received nothing of the government but paper money, of very little value, and continually depreciating." Indeed, the war cost Hewes his small stake in society: "The shop which I had built in Boston, I lost"; it was pulled down and burned by British troops.

In material terms, the American Revolution did about as much for Hewes as his parents had. When a journalist found the shoemaker in New York State in the 1830s, he was still "pressed down by the iron hand of poverty." The spiritual reward was greater. As his biographer, Alfred Young, aptly put it: "He was a nobody who briefly became a somebody in the Revolution and, for a moment near the end of his life, a hero." Because Americans had begun to celebrate the memory of the Revolution, in 1835 Hewes was brought back to Boston in triumph as one of the last surviving participants in the Tea Party—the guest of honor on Independence Day.

But an even more fundamental spiritual reward had come to Hewes when he became a revolutionary, casting off the deferential status of a "subject" in a monarchy and becoming a proud and equal "citizen" in a republic. What this meant to Hewes, and to thousands of other poor and obscure Patriots, appeared in his relationship—both real and fictitious—with John Hancock. As a young man Hewes had sat rapt and tongue-tied in the rich merchant's presence. But when he related his story of the Tea Party, Hewes elevated himself to the same level as Hancock, placing the merchant at the scene (which was almost certainly not the case) and claiming that he "was himself at one time engaged with him [Hancock] in the demolition of the same chest of tea." In this lessening of social distance—this declaration of equality—lay one of the profound meanings of the American Revolution.

The Boston "Tea Party"

Led by radical Patriots disguised as Mohawk Indians, Bostonians dump taxed British tea into the harbor. The rioters underlined their "pure" political motives by punishing those who sought personal gain; a Son of Liberty who stole some of the tea was "stripped of his booty and his clothes together, and sent home naked." Library of Congress.

a coercive measure, many colonial leaders saw it as another demonstration of Parliament's power to intervene in American domestic affairs.

The Continental Congress Responds

American leaders called for a new all-colony assembly, the Continental Congress. The newer colonies—Florida, Quebec, Nova Scotia, and Newfoundland—did not attend, nor did Georgia, whose legislature was effectively controlled by a royal governor. But delegates chosen by the other twelve mainland assemblies met in Philadelphia in September 1774. The stakes were high, and understandably the delegates were divided. Southern leaders, fearing a British plot "to overturn the constitution and introduce a system of arbitrary government," favored a new economic boycott. Representatives of the New England colonies wanted to go further, advocating political union and defensive military preparations. But many delegates from the middle colonies wanted to seek a political compromise with the British ministry.

Led by Joseph Galloway of Pennsylvania, these men of "loyal principles" outlined a scheme for a new imperial system that resembled the Albany Plan of Union of 1754. Under Galloway's proposal, America would have a legislative council selected by the colonial assemblies and a president-general appointed by the king. The new council would have veto power over Parliamentary legislation that affected America. Despite this feature, however, the delegates refused to endorse Galloway's plan. With British troops occupying Boston, the majority thought it was too conciliatory.

Instead, the First Continental Congress passed a Declaration of Rights and Grievances that condemned the Coercive Acts and demanded their repeal. It also repudiated the Declaratory Act of 1766, which had proclaimed Parliament's supremacy over the colonies, and demanded that Britain restrict its supervision of American affairs to matters of external trade. Finally, the Congress approved a program of economic retaliation, beginning with nonimportation and nonconsumption agreements that would take effect in December 1774. If Parliament did not repeal the Intolerable Acts by September 1775, the Congress vowed to cut off virtually all colonial exports to Britain, Ireland, and the British West Indies. Ten years of constitutional conflict had culminated in a threat of all-out commercial warfare.

Even at this late date a few British leaders hoped for compromise. In January 1775 William Pitt, now sitting in the House of Lords as the earl of Chatham, asked Parliament to give up its claim to tax the colonies and recognize the Continental Congress as a lawful body. In return for these and other concessions, he suggested, the Congress should acknowledge Parliamentary supremacy and grant a continuing revenue to help defray the British national debt.

The British ministry rejected Chatham's plan. Twice it had backed down in the face of colonial resistance; a third retreat was impossible. The honor of the nation was at stake. Branding the Continental Congress an illegal assembly, the ministry also ruled out Lord Dartmouth's proposal to send commissioners to America to negotiate a settlement. Instead, Lord North set stringent terms: Americans must pay for their own defense and administration and acknowledge Parliament's authority to tax them. To put teeth in these demands, North imposed a naval blockade on American trade with foreign nations and ordered General Gage to suppress dissent in Massachusetts. At this crucial juncture the British ministry did not fear war, confident that its military forces could overwhelm any colonial rebellion. "Now the case seemed desperate," the prime minister told former Massachusetts governor Thomas Hutchinson, who had been forced by Patriot agitation to live in exile in London. "Parliament would not—could not—concede. For aught he could see it must come to violence."

The Rising of the Countryside

Ultimately, the success of the urban-led Patriot movement would depend on the actions of the large rural population. At first most farmers had little interest in imperial issues. Their lives were deeply rooted in the soil, and their prime allegiance was to family and community. But the French and Indian War intruded into their lives, taking their sons for military duty and raising their taxes. In Newtown, Long Island, farmers had paid an average of 10 shillings a year in taxes until 1754; by 1756 their wartime taxes had jumped to 30 shillings. Peace brought only slight relief, for in 1771 the British-imposed Quartering Act cost each Newtown resident 20 shillings in taxes. These levies angered rural Americans, though in fact they paid much lower taxes than did most Britons.

The Expansion of the Patriot Movement. The urban-led nonimportation movements of 1765 and 1769 also raised the political consciousness of many rural Americans. When the Continental Congress declared a new economic boycott of British goods in 1774, it easily established a network of local Committees of Safety and Inspection to support it. Appealing to rural thriftiness, the Congress condemned those who wore expensive imported clothes to funerals, approving only "a black crape or ribbon on the arm or hat for gentlemen, and a black ribbon and necklace for ladies." In Concord, Massachusetts, 80 percent of male heads of families and a number of single women signed a Solemn League and Covenant vowing support for nonimportation. In other towns men who blacked their faces and wrapped themselves in blankets "like Indians" gathered in the streets to express "uneasiness with those that trade in rum, molasses, & Sugar, &c." in violation of the boycott.

TABLE 5.2 Patriot Resistance, 1762–1775

British Action	Date	Patriot Response
Revenue Act	1762	Merchants complain privately
Proclamation Line	1763	Land speculators voice discontent
Sugar Act	1764	Protests by merchants and Massachusetts House
Stamp Act	1765	Riots by Sons of Liberty Stamp Act Congress First nonimportation movement
Quartering Act	1765	New York assembly refuses to implement until 1767
Townshend duties	1767	Second nonimportation movement Harassment of pro-British merchants
Troops occupy Boston	1768	Boston Massacre of 1770
Gaspée affair	1772	Committees of Correspondence created
Tea Act	1773	Widespread resistance Boston Tea Party
Coercive Acts and Quebec Act	1774	First Continental Congress Third nonimportation movement
British raids on Lexington and Concord	1775	Armed resistance by Minutemen Second Continental Congress

Patriots also appealed to the yeoman tradition of agricultural independence, which was everywhere under attack. Arable land had become scarce and expensive in long-settled regions; in many new communities merchants were seizing farmsteads for delinquent debts. The new demands of the British government would further drain "this People of the Fruits of their Toil," complained the town meeting of Petersham, Massachusetts. "The duty on tea," added a Patriot pamphlet, "was only a prelude to a window-tax, hearth-tax, land-tax, and poll-tax, and these were only paving the way for reducing the country to lordships." By the 1770s many northern yeomen felt personally threatened by British imperial policy (Table 5.2).

Despite their much higher standard of living, southern slave owners had similar fears. Many influential Virginia Patriots—including Patrick Henry, George Washington, and Thomas Jefferson—were speculators in western lands and reacted angrily when first the Proclamation Line of 1763 and then the Quebec Act of 1774 invalidated their claims and their hopes of great fortunes. Moreover, many Chesapeake planters had fallen deeply into debt to British merchants; in 1766 one planter observed that a debt of £1,000 had once been considered excessive, but "ten times that sum is now spoke of with indifference and thought no great burthen on Some Estates." In fact, extravagant spending threatened many planters with financial disaster.

"I must return again to a low and less expensive Prudence," Landon Carter vowed unsuccessfully in 1771. As Washington noted, Carter and other planters wanted to live "genteely and hospitably" and were "ashamed" to adopt frugal ways. Accustomed to being masters on their plantations, they resented their financial dependence on British merchants and feared the prospect of political dependence on British ministers. Once Parliament used the Coercive Acts to subdue Massachusetts, the planters feared, it might seize control of Virginia's county courts and House of Burgesses, depriving the gentry of its political power. This threat moved Patriot planters to action, closing the courts so that yeomen could bargain with Scottish merchants over tobacco prices without risking suits for debt. "The spark of liberty is not yet extinct among our people," one planter declared, "and if properly fanned by the Gentlemen of influence will, I make no doubt, burst out again into a flame."

The Loyalists. While many wealthy planters and affluent merchants supported the Patriot cause, other prominent Americans worried that resistance to Britain would destroy respect for all political institutions, ending in mob rule (see American Voices, "Anonymous Broadside, May 18, 1775: 'To the Associators of the City of Philadelphia,'" p. 156). Their fears increased when the Sons of Liberty turned to violence to enforce

Anonymous Broadside, May 18, 1775

"To the Associators of the City of Philadelphia"

Loyalist fears that the "lower sort" would seize power during the conflict with Britain had a basis in fact. When the republican Patriots of Philadelphia mobilized laborers, sailors, and other workers into a military "Association" to take control of the city, they unleashed democratic aspirations for respect and equality. At first this quest took the form of protests against concrete grievances, as in the following broadside by a well-educated Philadelphian who supported the demands of ordinary Associators for an inexpensive uniform. These aspirations soon turned into appeals for political rights, and they partly account for the radically democratic character of the Pennsylvania Constitution of 1776 (see Chapter 7).

A Considerable number of the Associators of this city, on considering the plan of an uniform recommended by a Committee of the Officers, at a late meeting are of opinion that it will be found too expensive for the generality, as well as inconvenient to them; that the aforesaid Officers could not, with propriety, take upon them to adopt of themselves an uniform for the whole city, without the approbation of the people, who are entitled to an equal consultation.

That by adopting the cheapest uniform, such as that of a HUNTING SHIRT, as it will level all distinctions, answers the end of coat and jacket, and is within the compass of almost every person's ability, not costing at the utmost above ten shillings. The officers say that they did not mean to impose any particular uniform upon the people, but then they should have given the privates an opportunity of making known their sentiments. An uniform is granted by all to be absolutely necessary, but let it be something cheap, which the generality can afford.

A very material advantage which the HUNTING SHIRTS have above [over] the present uniform recommended, is that they will answer all seasons of the year, as a person may wear neither coat nor jacket in warm weather, and in winter he may cloath under them as warm as he pleases.

Had the hunting shirts been recommended by the Officers, it would have met the approbation of ninety-nine out of an hundred. A meeting of the Associators ought to be called immediately, that each man may have a voice in what so nearly concerns himself. The author is informed that some of the Captains of the different companies have proposed, that any of the men, who think they are not able to buy uniforms, may be supplied by them; now there are hundreds who could not afford it, yet would never submit to ask any man for a coat, neither would they appear in the ranks to be pointed at by those who had uniforms.

The author [hopes] . . . those gentlemen, who have partly fixed upon an expensive uniform, to concur in sentiment with him.

Source: Pennsylvania History 52 (October 1985): 255–56.

---

nonimportation. As a well-to-do New Yorker complained, "No man can be in a more abject state of bondage than he whose Reputation, Property and Life are exposed to the discretionary violence . . . of the community." As the crisis continued, these men rallied to the support of the royal governors.

Other social groups also refused to support the resistance movement. In regions where many wealthy landowners became Patriots, such as the Hudson Valley of New York, tenant farmers supported the crown because they hated their landlords. Similar social divisions prompted some Regulators in the North Carolina backcountry and many farmers on the eastern shore of Chesapeake Bay in Maryland to oppose the policies advocated by the local Patriot gentry and to welcome imperial intervention. Enslaved blacks had even less reason to support the cause of their Patriot masters. A group of Virginia slaves, James Madison reported in November 1774, planned to flee from their Patriot owners and had chosen "a leader who was to conduct them when the English troops should arrive." Many Quakers and Germans in Pennsylvania and New Jersey tried to remain neutral because of pacifist religious principles and fear of political change.

Beginning in 1774, prominent Americans of "loyal principles"—mostly royal officials, merchants with military contracts, clergy of the Church of England, and

close the royal courts of justice and transfer their political allegiance to the popularly elected House of Representatives. Following the congress, armed crowds harassed Loyalists and ensured Patriot rule in most of New England.

General Thomas Gage, by then the military governor of Massachusetts, tried desperately to maintain imperial power. In September 1774 he ordered British troops in Boston to seize Patriot armories and storehouses at Charlestown and Cambridge. In response, twenty thousand colonial militiamen mobilized to safeguard military supply depots in Concord and Worcester. The Concord town meeting voted to raise a defensive force, the famous **Minutemen**, to "Stand at a minutes warning in Case of alarm." Increasingly, Gage's authority was limited to Boston, where it rested primarily on the bayonets of his thirty-five hundred troops. Meanwhile, the Massachusetts House met on its own authority, issued regulations for the collection of taxes, strengthened the militia, and assumed the responsibilities of government.

Even before the news of Massachusetts's defiance reached London, the colonial secretary, Lord Dartmouth, had proclaimed the colony to be in a state of "open rebellion." Declaring that "force should be repelled by force," he ordered Gage to march quickly against the "rude rabble." On the night of April 18, 1775, Gage dispatched seven hundred soldiers to capture colonial leaders and supplies at Concord. But Paul Revere and two other Bostonians warned the Patriots, and at dawn on April 19 local

Political Propaganda: The Empire Strikes Back

A British cartoon attacks the women of Edenton, North Carolina, for supporting the boycott of British trade, hinting at their sexual lasciviousness and—by showing an enslaved black woman holding an inkstand for these supposed advocates of liberty— their moral hypocrisy. Library of Congress.

For more help analyzing this image, see the ONLINE STUDY GUIDE at bedfordstmartins.com/henretta.

well-established lawyers—denounced the Patriot movement, accusing it of seeking independence. They formed an articulate pro-British party, but one that remained small and ineffective. A Tory Association started by Governor Wentworth of New Hampshire drew only fifty-nine members, fourteen of whom were the governor's relatives. At this crucial juncture Americans who favored resistance to British rule commanded the allegiance—or at least the acquiescence—of the majority of white Americans.

The Failure of Compromise

When the Continental Congress met in September 1774, New England was already in open defiance of British authority. In August 150 delegates had gathered in Concord, Massachusetts, for a Middlesex County Congress. This illegal convention had advised Patriots to

Drum Commemorating the Battle of Lexington

This old drum, its wooden sides cracking and its head split, honors the Patriot militia who opposed the British on April 17, 1775 (note date at lower right). Beaten by drummers at militia musters in the decades after the war, it linked these mundane training exercises to the exploits of the heroes of the Revolutionary generation.

Lexington Historical Society / © Rob Huntley for Chromographics, Inc.

Lieutenant Colonel Francis Smith

A British View of Lexington and Concord

The past vanishes as soon as it occurs, and must be reconstructed by historians from written or oral accounts of the event. On April 26, 1775, a week after British troops marched on Lexington and Concord, the Patriot-controlled Massachusetts assembly (now called the Provincial Congress) issued what it called a "true, and authentic account" of the resulting hostilities. The Congress alleged that at Lexington "the regulars rushed on with great violence and first began the hostilities" and that in the subsequent retreat of the British troops from Concord "houses on the road were plundered, . . . women in child-bed were driven by soldiery naked in the streets, old men peaceably in their houses were shot dead, and such scenes exhibited as would disgrace the annals of the most uncivilized nation." Four days earlier, in his official report to General Gage, British lieutenant colonel Francis Smith offered a very different account of those events, one with a much more favorable view of British actions. Which version should the historian find more "true, and authentic"?

Sir,—In obedience to your Excellency's commands, I marched on the evening of the 18th inst. with the corps of grenadiers and light infantry for Concord, . . . to destroy all ammunition, artillery, tents &c. . . . Notwithstanding we marched with the utmost expedition and secrecy, we found the country had intelligence or strong suspicion of our coming, and fired many signal guns. . . .

At Lexington . . . [we] found on a green close to the road a body of the country people drawn up in military order, with arms and accoutrements, and, as appeared afterward, loaded. . . . Our troops advanced towards them, without any intention of injuring them . . . ; but they in confusion went off, principally to the left, only one of them fired before he went off, and three or four more jumped over a wall and fired from behind it among the soldiers; on which the troops returned it, and killed several of them. They likewise fired on the soldiers from the Meeting[house] and dwelling-houses. . . .

While at Concord we saw vast numbers assembling in many parts; at one of the bridges they marched down, with a very considerable body, on the light infantry posted there. On their coming pretty near, one of our men fired on them, which they returned; on which an action ensued and some few were killed and wounded. In this affair, it appears that, after the bridge was quitted, they scalped and otherwise ill treated one or two of [our] men who were either killed or severely wounded. . . .

On our leaving Concord to return to Boston they began to fire on us from behind walls, ditches, trees, &c., which, as we marched, increased to a very great degree, and continued . . . for, I believe, upwards of eighteen miles; so that I can't think but it must have been a preconcerted scheme in them, to attack the King's troops the first favorable opportunity that offered; otherwise, I think they could not, in such a short a time from our marching out, have raised such a numerous body. . . .

Source: Massachusetts Historical Society, *Proceedings, 1876* (Boston, 1876), 350ff.

militiamen met the British first at Lexington and then at Concord. The skirmishes took a dozen lives. As the British retreated along the narrow roads to Boston, they were repeatedly ambushed by militiamen from neighboring towns. By the end of the day, 73 British soldiers were dead, 174 wounded, and 26 missing. British fire had killed 49 American militiamen and wounded 39 (see Voices from Abroad, "Lieutenant Colonel Francis Smith: A British View of Lexington and Concord," above). The extent of the fighting in Massachusetts settled the issue. Too much blood had now been spilled to allow another compromise. Twelve years of economic conflict and constitutional debate had ended in civil war.

FOR FURTHER EXPLORATION

► For definitions of key terms boldfaced in this chapter, see the glossary at the end of the book.

► To assess your mastery of the material covered in this chapter, see the Online Study Guide at **bedfordstmartins.com/henretta**.

► For suggested references, including Web sites, see page SR-5 at the end of the book.

► For map resources and primary documents, see **bedfordstmartins.com/henretta**.

The Great War for Empire brought a decisive end to the era of salutary neglect and began an era of imperial reform. The war had exposed the weakness of Britain's control over its American colonies and had left that nation with a crushing load of debt. When George Grenville became prime minister in 1763, he embraced the cause of reform. To raise money—and reassert British authority—he enacted the Sugar Act, which extended the jurisdiction of vice-admiralty courts, and the Stamp Act, which for the first time imposed a direct tax on the colonists.

Because they had long taxed and governed themselves, the colonists resisted reform, protesting against the stamp duty through mob violence, a trade boycott, and an extralegal Stamp Act Congress. Well-read colonists based their arguments for American rights on English common law, Enlightenment thought, and the writings of Radical Whigs, while the thousands of less-educated people who served as Sons and Daughters of Liberty opposed the new British legislation out of economic self-interest or a commitment (because of evangelical Protestant beliefs or residence in Puritan New England) to a republican form of government. To assist British merchants and manufacturers, Parliament repealed the Stamp Act in 1766, but it explicitly reaffirmed its complete authority over the colonies.

In 1767 Chancellor of the Exchequer Charles Townshend undermined this first political compromise by imposing a new tax on trade goods and attempting to create a colonial civil list to pay the salaries of royal officials. Americans responded with a second boycott and new constitutional arguments proclaiming the authority of their assemblies over provincial affairs. When the British ministry devised a plan to crush American resistance by force, domestic problems caused its abandonment. By 1770 Lord North had implemented a second compromise, repealing most of the Townshend duties but retaining a tax on tea.

North personally disrupted this second informal agreement by passing the Tea Act in 1773. When Bostonians resisted the new law, the British imposed coercive measures on Massachusetts in order to destroy the Patriot movement there. By 1774 the Patriots were well organized and American political leaders met in the First Continental Congress, which supported Massachusetts and mandated a new program of economic warfare. The Congress had the backing of a majority of American farmers and planters, who were now prepared to resist British rule. The failure to find a new compromise resulted in bloodshed at Lexington and Concord in April 1775 and then in war between Patriot forces and British troops attempting to put down the American rebellion.

1754–1763	Great War for Empire
	British national debt doubles
1760	George III becomes king
1762	Revenue Act reforms customs service
	Royal Navy arrests smugglers
1763	Treaty of Paris ends war
	Proclamation Line restricts settlement west of Appalachians
	George Grenville becomes British prime minister
	John Wilkes demands reform in England
1764	Currency Act protects British merchants
	Sugar Act places duty on French molasses
	Colonists oppose vice-admiralty courts
1765	Stamp Act imposes direct tax on colonists
	Quartering Act provides for British troops
	Riots by Sons of Liberty
	Stamp Act Congress
	First nonimportation movement
1766	First compromise: Stamp Act repealed and Declaratory Act passed
1767	Townshend duties on certain colonial imports
	Restraining Act in New York temporarily suspends colonial assembly there
	Daughters of Liberty make "homespun" cloth
1768	Second nonimportation movement
	British army occupies Boston
1770	Second compromise: Townshend duties repealed
	Boston Massacre
1772	Committees of Correspondence formed
1773	Tea Act passed to assist British East India Company
	Boston Tea Party
1774	Coercive Acts punish Massachusetts
	Quebec Act offends Patriots
	First Continental Congress
	Third nonimportation movement
	Loyalists organize
1775	General Thomas Gage marches to Lexington and Concord

PART ONE

Slavery, Racism, and the American Republic

The creation in British North America of racially based slave-labor societies was one of the most significant—and lasting—legacies of the colonial era. In 1775, what historian Ira Berlin has called "societies with slaves" existed throughout the northern colonies, from the Puritan settlements of New England to the Quaker colonies of Pennsylvania and Delaware. Farther south, in the Chesapeake and the Carolinas, were "slave societies," colonies whose character was shaped by slavery and the sheer number of Africans. The "best poor man's country" for many whites, British North America—like the rest of the Western Hemisphere—was a land of oppression for most blacks.

Patriot demands for freedom from British rule exposed the moral flaw in the colonial social order. "How is it that we hear the loudest yelps for liberty among the drivers of Negroes?" asked British author Samuel Johnson. Many Americans, especially in the North but also in the South, recognized the contradiction between their pursuit of republican freedom and the institution of slavery. Consequently, one northern state after another abolished slavery or provided for gradual emancipation. This outcome was also a legacy of the North's colonial heritage, which had produced a relatively egalitarian society. Most whites enjoyed extensive liberties. They worshiped in the Christian church of their choice. They owned their own farms, paid low taxes, and resided in self-governing communities. Because there was no powerful landowning gentry demanding deference, no impoverished peasantry or sizable slave population threatening chaos, the dominant yeoman and artisan classes could confidently legislate an end to slave labor (see figure).

Drawing inspiration from the North's relatively egalitarian rural world of independent farm families, Thomas Jefferson declared that "the small land holders are the most precious part of a state." But in 1775, Jefferson's own colony of Virginia—and every colony from Maryland to Georgia—was a "slave society," one based on inequality and racial bondage. Throughout the South, Anglican ministers and gentry demanded allegiance to the established Church of England, suppressing the more egalitarian Presbyterian and Baptist churches. Politically influential landlords monopolized thousands of acres of land, grew rich by leasing farms to poor tenant families, and worked vast plantations with slave labor. Some 500,000 Africans and African Americans—over one-third of the region's

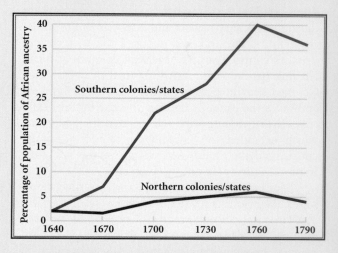

Percentage of Population of African Ancestry, 1640–1790

As enslaved Africans replaced English indentured servants in the tobacco and rice fields after 1680, the Chesapeake and Carolina colonies became "slave societies." The northern colonies remained "societies with slaves," facilitating emancipation there after 1776.
Source: U.S. Bureau of the Census, *Historical Statistics of the United States: Colonial Times to 1970* (Washington, DC, 1975), A:195–209, Z:1–19.

population—labored on tobacco, corn, and rice plantations, receiving only their subsistence in return. In this slave-based society, powerful plantation-owning families—roughly 5 to 10 percent of the population—dominated the new republican institutions of government and refused to end the slave system that made them rich.

These divergent social and political orders shaped the character of American history. Between 1800 and 1860 the North and the South engaged in increasingly bitter battles over economic policy, westward expansion, and the extension of slavery to new territories, culminating in a devastating Civil War that took the lives of over 600,000 soldiers.

The Union victory in 1865 preserved the nation and ended slavery for four million African Americans, but it did not end racial discrimination—either in the North or in the South—until another century had passed. Only in the aftermath of World War II, a struggle waged by the United States and its allies against Nazi Germany and its ideology of racial superiority, would most white Americans begin to reconsider their nation's history of racism. Only then—and only grudgingly—were they prepared to make good on what historian C. Vann Woodward in 1960 called "The Deferred Commitment" of the Civil War: the promise of full equality for black citizens. "Equality was a far more revolutionary aim than freedom," Woodward explained, because it required fundamental alterations in racial attitudes that had deep colonial roots. As the civil rights movement gathered force, scholars probed the early history of American racism in such works as Winthrop Jordan's *White over Black: American Attitudes toward the Negro,*

1550–1812 (1968). Indeed, in 1975 the distinguished historian Edmund Morgan argued in *American Slavery, American Freedom: The Ordeal of Colonial Virginia* that the gentlemen planters who led that colony into the American Revolution were ardent republicans in part *because* they were ardent racists and slave owners.

To understand this paradox—how slavery for blacks enhanced freedom for whites—Morgan turned to the history of republican ideology. Beginning around 1600, Morgan pointed out, radical thinkers and members of the English middling classes began to embrace republicanism and its promise of a popularly elected representative government. However, because a majority of the people were either propertyless or poor, republicanism based on popular sovereignty had a fatal weakness. To grant suffrage to the poor would threaten the entire social order—not only the inherited wealth and privileges of the gentry and aristocracy but also the modest possessions and social status enjoyed by hardworking yeomen farmers and shopkeepers. Events during the English Puritan Revolution of the 1640s confirmed the danger. During that social upheaval, radical Christian Levelers demanded not only equal political rights for all men but also an end to private property. In Virginia itself, during Bacon's Rebellion of 1676, discontented white freemen and rebellious indentured servants spoke from the barrels of their guns, demanding an end to rule by wealthy "parasites." Only bloody repression quelled that uprising. For the Virginia planter-gentry to give votes to this "rabble" would be social suicide.

And, yet exactly a century later, the great leaders of the Virginia gentry—George Mason, Thomas Jefferson, Landon Carter, George Washington—became firm Patriots and ardent republicans, committed to the doctrine of popular sovereignty. What had changed? According to Morgan, the answer lay in the rise of a slave-based society. In 1676, men and women of African origin or descent had numbered about 5 percent of Virginia's population, and most poor people were English indentured servants and free laborers. A century later enslaved blacks formed nearly 40 percent of the population, changing the color of Virginia's poor. More important, racial slavery effectively excluded a majority of the propertyless from the political system and made republicanism a possibility. As antiblack prejudice united rich and poor whites, it laid the social foundation for what historian George Frederickson has called a *herrenvolk* (or master-race) republic.

Was Morgan right? Did slavery for blacks bring freedom for whites? Does the nation owe its heritage of republican liberty to its history of racial oppression?

The answers to these questions, like those to most historical puzzles, are complex. It is certainly true that slavery shaped the contours of southern politics, making the region "safe" for gentry-republicanism before 1775 and for white men's democracy thereafter. However, the social landscape of the northern colonies was far different. There, the number of slaves—and of poor whites—was too small to determine the course of eighteenth-century politics, and the broad ownership of property formed the foundations for a democratic republican society. Morgan had it half-right. Whatever the role of slavery in the South, it was freehold farming that enabled northern whites to embrace a regime of republican liberty—for blacks as well as whites.

But not republican equality. For the colonial era imbued most white northerners with a racial ideology that repudiated political equality for African Americans. As Stephen Douglas, a leading northern politician and future presidential candidate, put it in 1858, "this government was made by our fathers, by white men for the benefit of white men and their posterity forever." That colonial legacy of racial superiority would remain strong—in the North as well as the South—until the mid-twentieth century, and is not yet extinguished.

Plantation Overseer, Mississippi, 1936

This well-known photograph by Dorothea Lange captures the persistence of racial inequality long after the end of slavery. Standing with one foot on his car, the white overseer dominates the visual image, just as he dominates the working lives of the blacks whose jobs depend on his whim.
Courtesy, Hallmark Photographic Collection, Hallmark Cards, Inc., Kansas City, MO.

The New Republic

1775–1820

GOVERNMENT	DIPLOMACY	ECONOMY	SOCIETY	CULTURE
Creating Republican Institutions	European Entanglements	Expanding Commerce and Manufacturing	Defining Liberty and Equality	Pluralism and National Identity
1775 ▶ States constitutions devised and implemented	▶ Independence declared (1776) French alliance (1778)	▶ Wartime expansion of manufacturing	▶ Emancipation of slaves in the North Judith Sargent Murray, *On the Equality of the Sexes* (1779)	▶ Thomas Paine's *Common Sense* calls for a republic
1780 ▶ Articles of Confederation ratified (1781) Legislative supremacy in states Philadelphia convention drafts U.S. Constitution (1787)	▶ Treaty of Paris (1783) British trade restrictions in West Indies U.S. government signs treaties with Indian peoples	▶ Bank of North America (1781) Commercial recession (1783–1789) Western land speculation	▶ Virginia Statute of Religious Freedom (1786) Idea of republican motherhood French Revolution sparks ideological debate	▶ Land ordinances create a national domain in the West German settlers preserve own language Noah Webster defines American English
1790 ▶ Bill of Rights ratified (1791) First national parties: Federalists and Republicans	▶ Wars of the French Revolution Jay's and Pinckney's Treaties (1795) Undeclared war with France (1798)	▶ First Bank of the United States (1792–1812) States charter business corporations Outwork system grows	▶ Sedition Act limits freedom of the press (1798)	▶ Indians form Western Confederacy Sectional divisions emerge between South and North
1800 ▶ Revolution of 1800 Activist state legislatures Chief Justice Marshall asserts judicial power	▶ Napoleonic wars (1802–1815) Louisiana Purchase (1803) Embargo of 1807	▶ Cotton expands into Old Southwest Farm productivity improves Embargo encourages U.S. manufacturing	▶ Youth choose own marriage partners New Jersey decrees male-only suffrage (1807) Atlantic slave trade legally ended (1808)	▶ African Americans absorb Protestant Christianity Tenskwatawa and Tecumseh revive Indian identity
1810 ▶ Triumph of Republican Party State constitutions democratized	▶ War of 1812 Treaty of Ghent (1816) ends war Monroe Doctrine (1823)	▶ Second Bank of the United States (1816–1836) Supreme Court protects business Emergence of a national economy	▶ Expansion of suffrage for white men New England abolishes established churches (1820s)	▶ War of 1812 tests national unity Second Great Awakening shapes American culture

"The American war is over," the Philadelphia Patriot Benjamin Rush declared in 1787, "but this is far from being the case with the American Revolution. On the contrary, nothing but the first act of the great drama is closed. It remains yet to establish and perfect our new forms of government." The job was even greater than Rush imagined, for the republican revolution of 1776 challenged nearly all the values and institutions of the colonial social order, forcing changes not only in politics but also in economic, religious, and cultural life.

GOVERNMENT The first and most fundamental task was to devise a republican system of government. In 1775, no one in America knew how the governments in the new republican states should be organized and if there should be a permanent central authority along the lines of the Continental Congress. It would take time and experience to find out. It would take even longer to assimilate a new institution—the political party—into the workings of government. By 1820 these years of constitutional experiment and party strife had produced a successful republican system on both the state and national levels. This system of political authority had three striking characteristics: popular sovereignty: government of the people; activist legislatures that pursued the public good: government for the people; and democratic decision making by most white adult men: government by the people.

DIPLOMACY To create and preserve their new republic, Americans of European descent had to fight two wars against Great Britain, an undeclared war against France, and many battles with Indian peoples and confederations. The wars against Britain divided the country into bitter factions—Patriots against Loyalists in 1776, and prowar Republicans against antiwar Federalists in 1812—and expended much blood and treasure. Tragically, the extension of American sovereignty and settlement into the trans-Appalachian West brought cultural disaster to many Indian peoples, as their lives were cut short by European diseases and alcohol and their lands were seized by white settlers. Despite the costs, by 1820 the United States had emerged as a strong independent state, free from a half century of entanglement in the wars and diplomacy of Europe and prepared to exploit the riches of the continent.

ECONOMY By this time the expansion of commerce and the market system had established the foundations for a strong national economy. Beginning in the 1780s northern merchants financed a banking system and organized a rural-based system of manufacturing, while state governments used charters and legal incentives to assist business entrepreneurs and provide improved transportation. Simultaneously, southern planters carried slavery westward to Alabama and Mississippi and grew rich by exporting a new staple crop—cotton—to markets in Europe and the North. Some yeoman farm families migrated to the West while others diversified, producing raw materials such as leather and wool for the burgeoning manufacturing enterprises and working part-time as handicraft workers. As a result of these efforts, by 1820 the young American republic had begun to achieve economic as well as political independence.

SOCIETY As Americans defined the character of their new republican society, they divided along lines of gender, race, religion, and class, disagreeing on fundamental issues: legal equality for women, the status of slavery, the meaning of free speech and religious liberty, and the extent of public responsibility for social inequality. They resolved some of these disputes, extinguishing slavery in the North and broadening religious liberty by allowing freedom of conscience and (except in New England) ending the system of established churches. However, they continued to argue over social equality, in part because their republican creed placed authority in the family and society in the hands of men of property and thus denied power not only to slaves but also to free blacks, women, and poor white men.

CULTURE The efforts of political and intellectual leaders to define a distinct American culture and identity was complicated by the diversity of peoples and regions. Native Americans still lived in their own clans and nations, while black Americans, one-fifth of the enumerated population, were developing a new, African American culture. The white inhabitants created vigorous regional cultures and preserved parts of their ancestral heritage—English, Scottish, Scots-Irish, German, and Dutch. Nevertheless, political institutions began to unite Americans, as did their increasing participation in the market economy and in evangelical Protestant churches. By 1820 to be an American meant, for many members of the dominant white population, being a republican, a Protestant, and an enterprising individual in a capitalist-run market system.

CHAPTER 6

War and Revolution

1775–1783

WHEN THE PATRIOTS OF FREDERICK COUNTY, MARYLAND, demanded allegiance to the American cause in 1776, Robert Gassaway would have none of it. "It was better for the poor people to lay down their arms and pay the duties and taxes laid upon them by King and Parliament," he told the local Council of Safety, "than to be brought into slavery and commanded and ordered about as they were." The story was much the same in Farmington, Connecticut, where the Patriot officials imprisoned Nathaniel Jones and seventeen other men for a month for "remaining neutral" and failing to join their militia unit in opposing a British raid. Everywhere, the logic of events was forcing families to choose sides between the Loyalists and the Patriots.

In this battle for the hearts and minds of ordinary men and women, the Patriots' control of local governments gave them an edge. Combining physical threats with monetary incentives, they organized some of their neighbors into Patriot militia units and recruited others for service in the Continental army. Gradually the Patriots forged an army that, despite its ragged appearance and diverse origins, held its own on the field of battle. "I admire the American troops tremendously!" exclaimed a French officer toward the end of the war.

◄ **Washington at Verplank's Point**

Arrayed in the ceremonial uniform of the Continental army (in the traditional Whig colors of buff and blue), General Washington watches the reunion of the American and French armies in New York in 1782, following their victory the previous September over Cornwallis at Yorktown, Virginia. The artist, John Trumbull (1756–1843), served as an aide-de-camp to Washington during the war, then studied painting in London with the American-born artist Benjamin West, and executed this picture in 1790.
Courtesy, Winterthur Museum.

"It is incredible that soldiers composed of every age, even children of fifteen, of whites and blacks, almost naked, unpaid, and rather poorly fed, can march so well and withstand fire so steadfastly."

Military mobilization created political commitment. To encourage ordinary Americans to support the war—as soldiers, taxpayers, and hardworking citizens—the Patriot leadership prompted them to participate actively in forming and maintaining the new republican governments. The locus of power shifted, as common men became the rulers rather than the ruled. "From subjects to citizens the difference is immense," remarked the South Carolina physician and Patriot David Ramsay. "Each citizen of a free state contains . . . as much of the common sovereignty as another." By repudiating aristocratic and monarchical rule and raising a democratic army, the Patriots placed sovereignty in the people, launching the age of democratic revolutions.

Toward Independence, 1775–1776

The Battle of Concord took place on April 19, 1775, but fourteen months would elapse before the rebels formally broke with Britain. In the meantime Patriot legislators in most of the thirteen colonies stretching from New Hampshire to Georgia threw out their royal governors and created the two essentials for independence: a government and an army.

The Second Continental Congress and Civil War

Armed struggle in Massachusetts lent urgency to the deliberations of the Second Continental Congress, which met in Philadelphia in May 1775. Soon after the Congress opened, more than 3,000 British troops attacked new American fortifications on Breed's Hill and Bunker Hill overlooking Boston. After three assaults and 1,000 casualties they finally dislodged the Patriot militia. Inspired by his countrymen's valor, John Adams exhorted the Congress to rise to the "defense of American liberty" by creating a Continental army and nominated George Washington of Virginia to lead it. More cautious delegates and those with Loyalist sympathies warned that these measures would commit the colonists irretrievably to rebellion. After bitter debate Congress approved the proposals—but as Adams lamented, only "by bare majorities."

Congress versus the King. Despite the blood that had been shed, a majority in Congress still hoped for reconciliation with Britain. Led by John Dickinson of Pennsylvania, these moderates passed a proposal known as the Olive Branch petition, expressing loyalty to

George III, 1771

This portrait of George III was painted by Johann Zoffany in 1771. Like George Washington (b. 1732), King George III (b. 1738) was a young man when the American troubles began in 1765. A headstrong monarch, he tried to impose his will on Parliament, sparking political confusion and contributing to the inept policymaking that led to war. But George III strongly supported Parliament's attempts to tax the colonies and continued the war long after most of his ministers agreed that it had been lost. The Royal Collection. © Her Majesty Queen Elizabeth II.

George III and requesting the repeal of oppressive Parliamentary legislation. But zealous Patriots such as Samuel Adams of Massachusetts and Patrick Henry of Virginia mobilized anti-imperial sentiment and won passage of the Declaration of the Causes and Necessities of Taking Up Arms. Americans dreaded the "calamities of civil war," the declaration asserted, but were "resolved to die Freemen rather than to live [as] slaves." George III chose not to exploit these divisions among the Patriots, refusing even to receive the moderates' petition. Instead, in August 1775 he issued the Proclamation for Suppressing Rebellion and Sedition.

Even before the king's proclamation reached America, the radicals in Congress had won support for an invasion of Canada that they hoped would unleash a popular uprising and add a fourteenth colony to the rebellion. Patriot forces easily took Montreal, but in December 1775 they failed to capture Quebec City. To aid the Patriot cause American merchants waged financial warfare, implementing the resolution of the First Continental Congress to cut off all exports to Britain and its West Indian sugar islands. By ending the tobacco trade and disrupting sugar production, they hoped to undermine the British economy. Parliament retaliated at the end of 1775 with the Prohibitory Act, which outlawed all trade with the rebellious colonies.

Rebellion in the South. Meanwhile, skirmishes between Patriots and Loyalists broke out in many colonies. Acting with great purpose, Patriot militia forcibly disarmed hundreds of Loyalist sympathizers in Delaware, southern New Jersey, and Queens County, New York. In June 1775 the Patriot-dominated House of Burgesses in Virginia forced the royal governor, Lord Dunmore, to take refuge on a British warship in Chesapeake Bay. Branding the Patriots "traitors," the governor organized two military forces—one white, the Queen's Own Loyal Virginians, and one black, the **Ethiopian Regiment**, which enlisted about 1,000 slaves who had fled from their Patriot owners and were eager to fight for their freedom. In November 1775 Dunmore issued a controversial proclamation, offering to emancipate all slaves and indentured servants who joined the Loyalist cause. White planters denounced Dunmore's "Diabolical scheme" as "pointing a dagger to their Throats, thru the hands of their slaves." Faced with black unrest and pressed by yeoman and tenant farmers demanding independence, Patriot planters called for a final break with Britain.

In North Carolina, military conflict likewise prompted demands for independence. Early in 1776 North Carolina's royal governor, Josiah Martin, raised a force of 1,500 Scottish Highlanders from the Carolina backcountry. In response, low-country Patriots mobilized the militia and in February defeated Martin's army at the Battle of Moore's Creek Bridge, capturing more than 800 Highlanders. By April radical Patriots had transformed the North Carolina assembly into an independent Provincial Congress, which instructed its representatives in Philadelphia "to concur with the Delegates of other Colonies in declaring Independency, and forming foreign alliances." Virginia followed suit. In May, led by James Madison, Edmund Pendleton, and Patrick Henry, Virginia Patriots met in convention and resolved unanimously to support independence.

Common Sense

Americans moved slowly toward independence because many colonists retained a deep loyalty to the crown. Joyous crowds had toasted the health of George III when he ascended the throne in 1760 and when he appointed a new ministry that repealed the Stamp Act. Even as the imperial crisis worsened, Benjamin Franklin had proposed that the king rule over autonomous American assemblies. The very structure of society supported this loyalty to the crown, because Americans used the same metaphors of age and family to describe both social authority and imperial rule. According to the Stoning-

ton (Connecticut) Baptist Association, a father should act "as a king, and governor in his family." Just as the settlers followed the lead of respected male elders in town meetings, churches, and families, so they should obey the king as the father of his people. Denial of the king's legitimacy might threaten all paternal authority and disrupt the hierarchical social order.

Nonetheless, by 1775 many Americans had turned against the monarch. Responding to the escalating military conflict, they accused George III of supporting oppressive legislation and ordering armed retaliation against them. Surprisingly, agitation against the king became especially intense in Philadelphia, the largest but hardly the most tumultuous and Patriot-minded seaport city. Because many Philadelphia merchants harbored Loyalist sympathies, the city had been slow to join the boycott against the Townshend duties. But artisans, who accounted for about half the city's population, had become a powerful force in the Patriot movement. Worried that British imports threatened their small-scale manufacturing enterprises, they organized a Mechanics Association to protect America's "just Rights and Privileges." By February 1776 forty artisans sat with forty-seven merchants on the Philadelphia Committee of Resistance, the extralegal body that enforced the latest trade boycott.

Many Scots-Irish artisans and laborers in Philadelphia became Patriots for cultural and religious reasons. They came from Presbyterian families who had fled British-controlled northern Ireland to escape economic and religious discrimination. Moreover, many of them had embraced the egalitarian message preached by Gilbert Tennent and other New Light ministers. As pastor of Philadelphia's Second Presbyterian Church, Tennent had told his congregation that all men and women were equal before God. Applying that idea to politics, New Light Presbyterians shouted in street demonstrations that they had "no king but King Jesus." Republican ideas derived from the European Enlightenment also circulated freely in Pennsylvania. Well-educated scientists and political leaders such as Benjamin Franklin and Benjamin Rush questioned not only the wisdom of George III but also the idea of monarchy itself.

With popular sentiment in flux, a single pamphlet tipped the balance toward the Patriot side. In January 1776 Thomas Paine published *Common Sense*, a call for independence and republicanism phrased in language that aroused the public. Paine had been a minor bureaucrat in the Customs Service in England when he was fired for protesting low wages. He found his way to London, where he wangled a meeting with Benjamin Franklin. In 1774, armed with a letter of introduction from Franklin, Paine migrated to Philadelphia, where he met Benjamin Rush and other Patriots who shared his republican sentiments. In *Common Sense* Paine launched a direct assault on the traditional political order in language that the public could understand and respond to.

Thomas Paine

Common Sense

Thomas Paine was a sharp critic and an acute observer. Before arriving in Philadelphia from his native England in mid-1774, Paine had already rejected the legitimacy of monarchical rule. And he quickly came to understand that the existing system of American politics was republican in spirit and localist in character. In the widely read political pamphlet Common Sense *(1776), he showed the colonists that their customary practices of self-rule had intellectual validity and could easily be adapted to create independent republican governments.*

I draw my idea of the form of government from a principle in nature, which no art can overturn, viz. [that is] that the more simple any thing is, the less liable it is to be disordered, and the easier repaired when disordered; and with this maxim in view, I offer a few remarks on the much boasted constitution of England. . . .

If we will suffer ourselves to examine the component parts of the English constitution, we shall find them to be the base remains of two ancient tyrannies, compounded with some new republican materials.

First.—The remains of monarchical tyranny in the person of the king.

Secondly.—The remains of aristocratical tyranny in the person of the peers.

Thirdly.—The new republican materials in the persons of the commons, on whose virtue depends the freedom of England. . . .

The plain truth is, that it is wholly owing to the constitution of the people, and not to the constitution of the government, that the crown is not as oppressive in England as in Turkey. . . . For it is the republican and not the monarchical part of the constitution of England which Englishmen glory in, viz. the liberty of choosing a house of commons from out of their own body—and it is easy to see that when republican virtue fails, slavery ensues. . . .

If there is any true cause of fear respecting independence, it is because no plan is yet laid down. Men do not see their way out—Wherefore, . . . I offer the following hints. . . .

Let the assemblies [in all of the former colonies] be annual, with a President only . . . their business wholly domestic, and subject to the authority of a Continental Congress.

Let each colony be divided into six, eight, or ten convenient districts, each district to send a proper number of delegates to Congress, so that each colony send at least thirty. The whole number in Congress will be at least 390. . . .

But where, say some, is the King of America? I'll tell you. Friend, he reigns above, and doth not make havoc of mankind like the Royal Brute of Britain. Yet that we may not appear to be defective even in earthly honors, let a day be solemnly set apart for proclaiming the charter [of the new Continental republic]; let it be brought forth placed on the divine law, the word of God; let a crown be placed thereon, by which the world may know . . . that in America THE LAW IS KING. For as in absolute governments the King is law, so in free countries the law ought to be King; and there ought to be no other. . . . Let the crown at the conclusion of the ceremony, be demolished, and scattered among the people whose right it is.

Source: Thomas Paine, *Common Sense* (Philadelphia: W. & T. Bradford, 1776), n.p.

"Monarchy and hereditary succession have laid the world in blood and ashes," Paine proclaimed, leveling a personal attack against George III, "the hard hearted sullen Pharaoh of England." Mixing insults with biblical quotations, Paine blasted the British system of "mixed government" among the three estates of king, lords, and commoners. "That it was noble for the dark and slavish times in which it was created," Paine granted, but now this system of governance yielded only "monarchical tyranny in the person of the king" and "aristocratical tyranny in the persons of the peers" (see Voices from Abroad, "Thomas Paine: *Common Sense*," above).

Paine also made a compelling case for American independence. Suggesting that it was absurd for the small island of England to rule a great continent, he turned the traditional metaphor of patriarchal authority on its head: "Is it the interest of a man to be a boy all his life?" Within six months *Common Sense* went through twenty-five editions and reached hundreds of thousands of people throughout the colonies. "There is great talk of independence," a worried New York Loyalist wrote in March 1776, "and the unthinking multitude are mad for it. . . . A pamphlet called Common Sense has carried off . . . thousands." Paine's message was not only popular but also clear: reject the arbitrary powers of king and Parliament and create independent republican states. "A government of our own is our natural right, 'TIS TIME TO PART."

Independence Declared

Throughout the colonies Patriot conventions, inspired by Paine's arguments and beset by armed Loyalists, called urgently for a break from Britain. In June 1776 Richard Henry Lee presented the Virginia Convention's resolution to the Continental Congress: "That these United Colonies are, and of right ought to be, free and independent states . . . absolved from all allegiance to the British Crown." Faced with certain defeat, staunch Loyalists and anti-independence moderates withdrew from the Congress, leaving committed Patriots to take the fateful step. On July 4, 1776, the Congress approved a Declaration of Independence (see Documents, p. D-1).

The main author of the Declaration was Thomas Jefferson, a young Virginia planter and legislative leader who had mobilized resistance to the Coercive Acts with the pamphlet *A Summary View of the Rights of British America*. To persuade Americans and foreign observers of the need to create an independent republic, Jefferson justified the revolt by blaming the rupture on George III rather than on Parliament: "He has plundered our seas, ravaged our coasts, burned our towns, and destroyed the lives of our people. . . . A prince, whose character is thus marked by every act which may define a tyrant," Jefferson concluded, conveniently ignoring his own actions as a slave owner, "is unfit to be the ruler of a free people."

Jefferson, who was steeped in the ideas and rhetoric of the European Enlightenment, preceded these accusations with a proclamation of "self-evident" truths: "that all men are created equal"; that they possess the "unalienable rights" of "Life, Liberty, and the pursuit of Happiness";

Independence Declared

In this painting by John Trumbull, Thomas Jefferson and the other drafters (John Adams of Massachusetts, Roger Sherman of Connecticut, Robert Livingston of New York, and Benjamin Franklin of Pennsylvania) present the Declaration of Independence to John Hancock, the president of the Continental Congress. When the Declaration was read at a public meeting in New York City on July 10, Patriot Lieutenant Isaac Bangs reported, a massive statue of George III was "pulled down by the Populace" and its four thousand pounds of lead melted down to make "Musquet balls" for use against the British troops massed on Staten Island. Yale University Art Gallery, Mabel Brady Garven Collection.

that government derives its "just powers from the consent of the governed" and can rightly be overthrown if it "becomes destructive of these ends." By linking these doctrines of individual liberty and popular sovereignty with independence, Jefferson established revolutionary republicanism as a defining value of the new nation.

For Jefferson as for Paine the pen proved mightier than the sword. In rural hamlets and seaport cities crowds celebrated the Declaration by burning George III in effigy and toppling statues of the king. These acts of destruction broke the Patriots' psychological ties to the father monarch and established the legitimacy of republican state governments that derived their authority from the people. On July 8, 1776, a "great number of spectators" heard a reading of the Declaration at Easton, Pennsylvania, and "gave their hearty assent with three loud huzzahs, and cried out, 'May God long preserve and unite the Free and Independent States of America.'"

The Trials of War, 1776–1778

The Declaration of Independence coincided with Britain's decision to launch a full-scale military assault against the Patriots. For the next two years British forces outfought the Continental army commanded by George Washington, winning nearly every battle. A few inspiring American victories kept the rebellion alive, but in late 1776 and during the winter of 1777 at Valley Forge the Patriot cause hung in the balance.

War in the North

When the British resorted to military force to crush the American revolt, few European observers gave the rebels a chance. Great Britain had 11 million people, compared with the colonies' 2.5 million, nearly 20 percent of whom were enslaved Africans. The British also had a profound economic advantage in the immense profits created by the South Atlantic system and the emerging Industrial Revolution. These financial resources paid for the most powerful navy in the world, a standing army of 48,000 men, and thousands of German mercenaries, soldiers hired to fight for the British cause. British military officers had been tested in combat during the Seven Years' War, and their soldiers were well armed. Finally, the imperial government had the support of tens of thousands of American Loyalists as well as many Indian tribes. The Cherokees in the Carolinas had long opposed the expansion of white settlement and were firmly committed to the British side. So also were four of the six Iroquois Nations of New York—the Mohawks, Senecas, Cayugas and Onondagas—who were led by the pro-British Mohawk chief Joseph Brant; only the Oneida and Tuscarora peoples supported the rebel side (Map 6.1).

By contrast, the rebellious Americans were militarily weak. They had no navy, and General Washington's poorly trained army consisted of about 18,000 troops, mostly short-term recruits hastily assembled by state governments in Virginia and New England. The Patriots could field thousands more militiamen but only for short periods and only near their own farms and towns. Although many American officers had fought during the French and Indian War, even the most experienced had never commanded a large force or faced a disciplined army skilled in the intricate maneuvers of European warfare.

To exploit this military advantage Britain's prime minister, Lord North, responded quickly to the unexpected American invasion of Canada in 1775. Assembling a large invasion force, he selected General William Howe, who had served in the colonies during the French and Indian War, to lead it. North ordered Howe to capture New York City and seize control of the Hudson River, thereby isolating the radical Patriots in New England

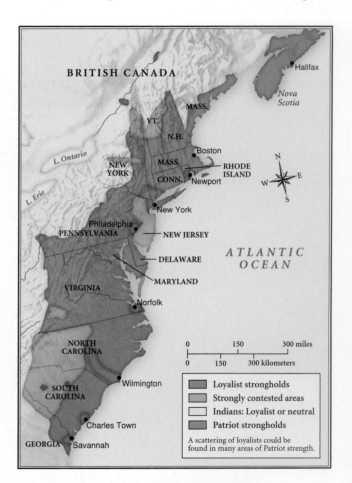

MAP 6.1 Patriot and Loyalist Strongholds

Patriot supporters formed the dominant faction throughout most of the thirteen colonies and used their control of local governments to funnel men, money, and supplies to the rebel cause. Loyalists were powerful only in Nova Scotia, eastern New York, and New Jersey and in certain areas in the South. However, most Native Americans favored the British cause and joined with Loyalist militia to fight Patriot forces in the backcountry of the Carolinas and in central New York (see Map 6.3).

For more help analyzing this map, see the ONLINE STUDY GUIDE at bedfordstmartins.com/henretta.

from the other colonies. In July 1776, as the Continental Congress was declaring independence in Philadelphia, Howe was beginning to land 32,000 troops—British regulars and German **mercenaries**—outside New York City.

British superiority was immediately apparent. In August 1776 Howe attacked the Americans in the Battle of Long Island and forced their retreat to Manhattan Island. There Howe outflanked Washington's troops, nearly trapping them on several occasions. Outgunned and outmaneuvered, the Continental army again retreated, first to Harlem Heights, then to White Plains, and finally across the Hudson River to New Jersey. By December the British army had pushed the rebels out of New Jersey and across the Delaware River into Pennsylvania, forcing Congress to flee from Philadelphia to Baltimore (Map 6.2).

From the Patriots' perspective winter came just in time, for the British halted their campaign for the cold months, according to eighteenth-century military custom. The respite allowed the Americans to catch them off guard and score a few triumphs. On Christmas night in 1776 Washington crossed the Delaware River and staged a surprise attack on Trenton, New Jersey, forcing the surrender of 1,000 German mercenaries. In early January 1777 the Continental army won another victory in a small engagement at nearby Princeton, raising Patriot morale and allowing the Continental Congress to return to Philadelphia. Bright stars in a dark night, these minor triumphs could not mask British military superiority. These are the times, wrote Tom Paine, that "try men's souls."

Armies and Strategies

British superiority did not break the will of the Continental army and, partly because of Howe's tactical decisions

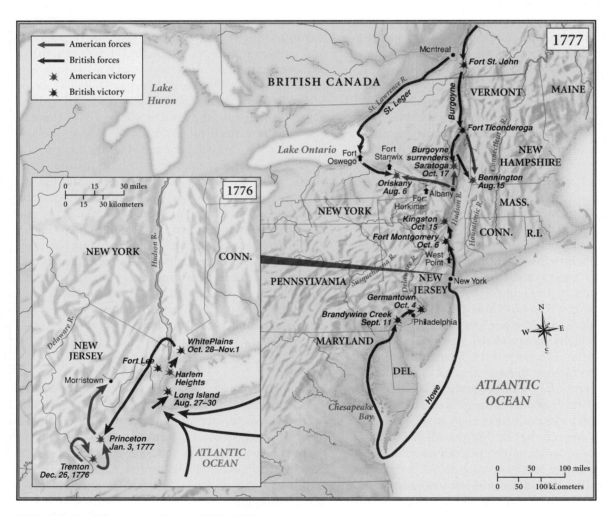

MAP 6.2 The War in the North, 1776–1777

In 1776 the British army drove Washington's forces across New Jersey into Pennsylvania. The Americans counterattacked successfully at Trenton and Princeton and then set up winter headquarters at Morristown. In 1777 British forces stayed on the offensive. General Howe attacked the Patriot capital of Philadelphia from the south, capturing it in early October. Meanwhile, General Burgoyne and Colonel St. Leger launched simultaneous invasions from Canada. Aided by thousands of New England militia, American troops commanded by General Horatio Gates defeated Burgoyne at Bennington, Vermont, and then in October at Saratoga, New York, the military turning point of the war.

A British Camp, c. 1778
While American troops at Valley Forge huddled from the cold in thin tents, British troops stationed just outside New York City (on upper Manhattan Island) lived in simple but well-constructed and warm log cabins. Each hut housed either a few officers or as many as ten soldiers of the 17th Regiment of Foot. This painting, based on careful archaeological fieldwork, was executed in 1915 by John Ward Dunsmore. New-York Historical Society.

and mistakes, the rebellion continued. Howe had opposed the Coercive Acts of 1774, and as the British military commander he still hoped for a political compromise—indeed, he had authority from Lord North to negotiate with the rebels and allow them to surrender on honorable terms. Consequently, instead of following up his early victories with a ruthless pursuit of the retreating American army, Howe was content to show his superior power and tactics, hoping to convince the Continental Congress that resistance was futile. Howe's caution also reflected the conventions of eighteenth-century warfare, which prescribed outmaneuvering the opposing forces and winning their surrender rather than destroying them. Moreover, the British general knew that his troops were 3,000 miles from supplies and reinforcements. In case of a major defeat, replenishing his force would take six months. Although Howe's prudent tactics were understandable, they cost the British the opportunity to nip the rebellion in the bud.

Howe's failure to win a decisive victory was paralleled by Washington's success in avoiding a major defeat. He too was cautious, challenging Howe on occasion but retreating in the face of superior strength. As Washington advised Congress, "On our Side the War should be defensive." His strategy was to draw the British away from the seacoast, extend their lines of supply, and sap their morale while keeping the Continental army intact as a symbol and instrument of American resistance.

Congress had promised Washington a regular force of 75,000 men, but the Continental army never reached a third of that number. Yeomen preferred to serve in the local militia, and so the regular army drew most of its recruits from the lower ranks of society. General William Smallwood of Maryland commanded soldiers who were either poor American-born youths or older foreign-born men—often British ex-convicts and former indentured servants. Such men enlisted not out of patriotism but for a bonus of $20 in cash (about $2,000 today) and the promise of 100 acres of land. Molding such recruits into a fighting force took time. In the face of a British artillery bombardment or flank attack many men panicked; hundreds of others deserted, unwilling to submit to the discipline and danger of military life. The soldiers who stayed resented the contemptuous way Washington and other American officers treated the "camp followers," the women who fed and cared for the troops.

Such personal support was crucial, for the Continental army was poorly supplied and faintly praised. Radical Whig Patriots had long viewed a peacetime standing army as a threat to liberty, and even in wartime they preferred the militia to a professional force. General Philip Schuyler of New York complained that his troops were "weak in numbers, dispirited, naked, destitute of provisions, without camp equipage, with little ammunition, and not a single piece of cannon." Given these handicaps, Washington was fortunate to have escaped an overwhelming defeat in the first year of the war.

Victory at Saratoga

Howe's failure to achieve a quick victory dismayed Lord North and his colonial secretary, Lord George Germain. Accepting the challenge of a long-term military commitment, the British leaders increased the land tax to finance the war and prepared to mount a major campaign in 1777.

The isolation of New England remained the primary British goal and was to be achieved by a three-pronged attack converging on Albany, New York. General John Burgoyne was to lead a large contingent of British regulars from Quebec to Albany. A second, smaller force of Iroquois warriors, who had allied themselves with the British to protect their land from American settlers, would attack from the west under Colonel Barry St. Leger. To assist Burgoyne from the south, Germain ordered Howe to dispatch a force northward from New York City (see Map 6.2).

Wahrhafte Abbildung der Soldaten des Congreßes in Nordamerica, nach der Zeichnung eines Deutschen Officiers. Die Mütze ist von Leder, mit der Aufschrift Congreß. Die ganze Kleidung von Zwillich überall mit weissen Franzen besetzt, die Beinkleider gehen bis auf die Knöchel herunter. Die Meisten laufen barfuß. Jarre Feuer-gewehr sind mit sehr langen Payonets versehen, welche Sie auch Stat eines Seiten gewehrs gebrauchen.
C.B. Henning. exc. Nürnberg.

American Militiamen

Because of the shortage of cloth, the Patriot army dressed in a variety of fashions that used many different kinds of fabrics. This German engraving, based on a drawing by a German officer, shows two barefoot American militiamen arrayed in hunting shirts and trousers made of ticking, a strong woven linen fabric that was often used as the coverings for mattresses and pillows.
Anne S. K. Brown Military Collection, Brown University.

Joseph Brant

The Mohawk chief Thayendanegea, known to the whites as Joseph Brant, was a devout member of the Church of England who had helped to translate the Bible into the Iroquois language. An influential leader, Brant secured the support of four of the six Iroquois Nations for the British. In 1778 and 1779, he led Iroquois warriors and Tory Rangers in devastating attacks on American settlements in the Wyoming Valley of Pennsylvania and Cherry Valley in New York. This portrait by Charles Willson Peale was painted in 1797. Independence National Historic Park.

For more help analyzing this image, see the ONLINE STUDY GUIDE at **bedfordstmartins.com/henretta.**

Howe had a different scheme and it led to a disastrous result. Howe wanted to attack Philadelphia, the home of the Continental Congress, and end the rebellion with a single victory over Washington's army. With Germain's apparent approval, the British commander set his plan in motion—but only very slowly. Rather than march quickly through New Jersey, British troops sailed south from New York, then up the Chesapeake Bay. Approaching Philadelphia from the south, Howe's troops easily outflanked the American positions along Brandywine Creek in Delaware and forced Washington to withdraw. On September 26 the British marched triumphantly into Philadelphia, hoping that the capture of the rebels' capital would end the uprising. But the Continental Congress fled into the interior, determined to continue the struggle.

The British paid a high price for Howe's victory in Philadelphia, for it contributed directly to the defeat of Burgoyne's army from Canada. Initially Burgoyne's troops had sped across Lake Champlain, overwhelming the American defenses at Fort Ticonderoga and driving toward the upper reaches of the Hudson River. Then they stalled, for Burgoyne—"Gentleman Johnny," as he was called—fought with style, not speed, weighed down by comfortable tents and ample stocks of food and wine. The American troops led by General Horatio Gates further impeded Burgoyne's progress by felling huge trees across the crude wagon trail used by Burgoyne and by raiding his long supply lines to Canada.

By the end of the summer Burgoyne's army—6,000 regulars (half of them German mercenaries) and 600 Loyalists and Indians—was in trouble, bogged down in the wilderness near Saratoga, New York. In August 2,000 American militiamen left their farms to fight a bitter battle at nearby Bennington, Vermont, that cost Burgoyne 900 casualties and deprived him of much-needed supplies of food and horses. Meanwhile, Patriot forces in the Mohawk Valley forced St. Leger and the Iroquois to retreat. To make matters worse, the British commander in New York City recalled the 4,000 troops he had sent toward Albany and dispatched them instead to bolster Howe's force in Philadelphia. While Burgoyne waited in vain for help, thousands of Patriot militiamen from Massachusetts, New Hampshire, and New York joined Gates's forces. They "swarmed around the army like birds of prey," an alarmed English sergeant wrote in his journal, and in October 1777 forced Burgoyne to surrender.

The battle at Saratoga proved to be the turning point of the war. The Americans captured more than 5,000 British troops and their equipment. Their victory virtually ensured the success of American diplomats in Paris, who were seeking a military alliance with France. Patriots on the home front were delighted, though their joy was muted by wartime difficulties.

Social and Financial Perils

The war exposed tens of thousands of civilians to deprivation, displacement, and death. "An army, even a friendly one, are a dreadful scourge to any people," a Connecticut soldier wrote from Pennsylvania. "You cannot imagine what devastation and distress mark their steps." New Jersey was particularly hard hit by the fighting, as British and American armies marched back and forth across the state. Families with reputations as Patriots or Loyalists fled their homes to escape arrest—or worse. Soldiers and partisans looted farms, seeking food or political revenge. Wherever the armies went, drunk and disorderly troops harassed and raped women and girls. Families lived in fear of their approach. When British warships sailed up the Potomac River, women and children fled from Alexandria, Virginia, and "stowed themselves into every Hut they can get, out of the reach of the Enemys canon."

In some areas, the War of Independence became a bloody partisan conflict. In New England mobs of Patriot farmers beat suspected Tories or destroyed their property. "Every Body submitted to our Sovereign Lord the Mob," a Loyalist preacher lamented. Patriots organized local Committees of Safety to collect taxes, send food and clothing to the Continental army, and impose fines or jail sentences on those who failed to support the cause. But in some areas of Maryland, the number of "non-associators"—those who refused to join either side—was so large that they successfully defied Patriot organizers. "Stand off you dammed rebel sons of bitches," Robert Davis of Anne Arundel County shouted, "I will shoot you if you come any nearer."

Financial Crisis. Such defiance reflected the weakness of the new state governments, which teetered on the brink of bankruptcy. To feed, clothe, and pay their troops, state officials borrowed gold, silver, or British currency from wealthy individuals. When those funds ran out, Patriot officials were afraid to raise taxes, knowing how unpopular that would be. Instead, individual states printed paper money, issuing $260 million in currency and transferable bonds. Theoretically, the new notes could be redeemed in gold or silver, but since they were printed in huge quantities and were not backed by tax revenues or mortgages on land, many Americans refused to accept them at face value. North Carolina's paper money came to be worth so little that even the state government's tax collectors refused it.

The finances of the Continental Congress collapsed too, despite the efforts of the Philadelphia merchant Robert Morris, the government's chief treasury official.

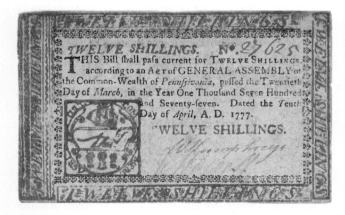

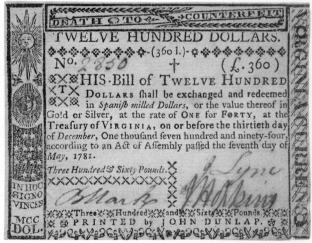

Paper Currency

To symbolize their independent status, the new state governments printed their own currency. Initially Pennsylvania retained the British system of pounds and shillings; Virginia chose the Spanish gold dollar as the basic unit of currency but included the equivalent in pounds ($1,200 was £360, a ratio of 3.3 to 1). By 1781, Virginia had printed so much paper money to pay its soldiers and wartime expenses that the value of the currency had depreciated. It now took 40 Virginia paper dollars to buy the same amount of goods as one Spanish gold dollar (a 40 to 1 ratio).
American Numismatic Society.

The Congress lacked the authority to impose taxes and so depended on funds requisitioned from the states, which frequently paid late or not at all. The Congress therefore borrowed $6 million in specie from France, using it as security to encourage wealthy Americans to purchase Continental loan certificates. When those funds and other French and Dutch loans were exhausted, the Congress followed the lead of the states and printed currency and bills of credit. Between 1775 and 1779 it issued notes with a face value of $191 million, but when funds received from the states retired only $3 million, the actual value of the bills fell dramatically.

Indeed, the excess of currency helped to spark the worst inflation in American history. The amount of goods available for purchase—both domestic foodstuffs and foreign manufactures—had shrunk significantly because of the fighting and the British naval blockade, while the money in circulation had multiplied. Because more currency was chasing fewer goods, prices rose rapidly. In Maryland a bag of salt that had cost $1 in 1776 sold for $3,900 in currency a few years later. Unwilling to accept nearly worthless currency, farmers refused to sell their crops, even to the Continental army. Instead, merchants and farmers turned to barter—trading wheat for tools or clothes—or sold goods only to those who could pay in gold or silver. The result was social upheaval. In Boston a mob of women accused merchant Thomas Boyleston of hoarding goods, "seazd him by his Neck," and forced him to sell—at the traditional prices. In rural Ulster County, New York, women surrounded the Patriot Committee of Safety, demanding steps to end the food shortages; otherwise, they said, "their husbands and sons shall fight no more." Civilian morale and social cohesion crumbled, causing some Patriot leaders to doubt that the rebellion could succeed.

Valley Forge. Fears reached their peak during the winter of 1777–78. Howe camped in Philadelphia and with his officers partook of the finest wines, foods, and entertainment the city could offer. Washington's army retreated to Valley Forge, some twenty miles to the west, where about 12,000 soldiers and hundreds of camp followers suffered horribly. "The army . . . now begins to grow sickly," a surgeon confided to his diary. "Poor food—hard lodging—cold weather—fatigue—nasty clothes—nasty cookery. . . . Why are we sent here to starve and freeze?" Nearby farmers refused to help. Some were pacifists—Quakers and German sectarians—unwilling to support either side. Others pursued the self-interest of their families, hoarding their grain in hopes of higher prices in the spring or willing to accept only the gold and silver offered by British quartermasters. "Such a dearth of public spirit, and want of public virtue," Washington complained—but to no effect. By spring 1,000 of his hungry soldiers had vanished into the countryside and another 3,000 had died from malnutrition and disease.

One winter at Valley Forge took as many American lives as had two years of fighting against General Howe.

In this dark hour Baron von Steuben raised the self-respect and readiness of the American army at Valley Forge. A former Prussian military officer, von Steuben was one of a handful of foreigners who had volunteered their services to the American cause. To counter falling morale, he instituted a standardized system of drill and maneuver and encouraged officers to become more professional in their demeanor and behavior. Thanks to von Steuben, the smaller Continental army that emerged from Valley Forge in the spring was a much tougher and better-disciplined force with a renewed sense of purpose.

The Path to Victory, 1778–1783

Wars are often won as much by astute diplomacy as by sheer firepower, and the War of Independence was no exception. The Patriots' prospects for victory improved dramatically in 1778, when the United States formed a military alliance with France, the most powerful European nation. The alliance brought the Americans money, troops, and supplies and changed the conflict from a colonial rebellion to an international war.

The French Alliance

France and America were unlikely partners. France was Catholic and a monarchy; the United States, largely Protestant and a federation of republics. Moreover, the two peoples had been on opposite sides in wars from 1689 to 1763, and New Englanders had just inflicted enormous suffering on the French population of Acadia (Nova Scotia). But France was intent on avenging its loss of Canada to Britain in the French and Indian War. In 1776 the Comte de Vergennes, the French foreign minister, persuaded King Louis XVI to extend a secret loan to the rebellious colonies and, equally important, to supply them with much-needed gunpowder. Early in 1777 Vergennes opened official commercial and military negotiations with Benjamin Franklin and two other American diplomats, Arthur Lee and Silas Deane. When news of the American victory at Saratoga reached Paris in December 1777, Vergennes sought a formal alliance with the Continental Congress.

Negotiating the Treaty. Franklin and his associates craftily exploited the rivalry between France and Britain, using the threat of a negotiated settlement with Britain to win an explicit French commitment to American independence. The Treaty of Alliance of February 1778 specified that once France had entered the war against Great Britain, neither partner would sign a separate peace before the "liberty, sovereignty, and independence" of the United States were ensured. In return, the American

Marion Crossing the Pedee, **William T. Ranney, 1851**
In 1780 the war in the South went badly for the Patriots. General Lincoln surrendered one American army at Charleston, South Carolina, in May and General Gates lost another at Camden, South Carolina, in August. Then the tide turned, thanks in part to Patriot guerrilla forces led by Francis Marion, known as the "Swamp Fox," whose raids on enemy forts and supply lines forced the British to withdraw from the interior of South Carolina. Here Marion (on the chestnut horse) and his men cross the Pee Dee River on their way to a raid. Amos Carter Museum of Western Art.

diplomats pledged that their government would recognize any French conquests in the West Indies.

The alliance with France gave new life to the Patriots' cause. With access to military supplies and European loans, the American army soon strengthened and hopes soared. "There has been a great change in this state since the news from France," a Patriot soldier reported from Pennsylvania. Farmers—"mercenary wretches," he called them—"were as eager for Continental Money now as they were a few weeks ago for British gold."

The alliance also bolstered the resources and confidence of the Continental Congress. Acting with energy and purpose the Congress addressed the continuing demands of the officer corps for military pensions. Most officers came from the upper ranks of society and had used their own funds to equip themselves and sometimes their men as well. In return they demanded lifetime military pensions at half pay. John Adams condemned the petitioners for "scrambling for rank and pay like apes for nuts," but General Washington urged Congress to grant the pensions, warning the lawmakers that "the salvation of the cause depends upon it." Congress reluctantly agreed to grant the officers half pay after the war, but only for seven years.

The British Response. Meanwhile, the war was becoming increasingly unpopular in Britain. Radical agitators and republican-minded artisans supported American demands for greater rights and campaigned for political reform at home, including broadened voting rights and more equitable representation for cities in Parliament. The landed gentry and urban merchants protested increases in the land tax and new levies on carriages, wine, and imported goods. "It seemed we were to be taxed and stamped ourselves instead of inflicting taxes and stamps on others," a British politician complained.

But George III remained determined to crush the rebellion, afraid it would lead to the collapse of the empire. If America won independence, he warned Lord North, "the West Indies must follow them. Ireland would soon follow the same plan and be a separate state, then this island would be reduced to itself, and soon would be a poor island indeed." Following the British defeat at Saratoga the king assumed a more pragmatic attitude. To head off an American alliance with France, the king authorized North to seek a negotiated settlement. In February 1778 North persuaded Parliament to repeal the Tea and Prohibitory Acts and, in an amazing concession, to renounce its power to tax the colonies. The prime minister then opened discussions with the Continental Congress, offering a return to the constitutional "condition of 1763," before the Sugar and Stamp Acts. But the Patriots, now allied with France, rejected the overture.

War in the South

The French alliance expanded the war but did not rapidly conclude it. When France entered the conflict in June 1778, it hoped to capture a rich sugar island and therefore concentrated its naval forces in the West Indies. Spain, which joined the war in 1779, also had its own agenda: in return for naval assistance to France, it wanted to regain Florida and Gibraltar. The Patriot cause had become enmeshed in a web of European territorial quarrels and complex diplomatic intrigue.

Britain's Southern Strategy. The British ministry, by 1778 beset by many enemies on many fronts, settled on a modest strategy in North America. It decided to use its army to recapture the rich tobacco- and rice-growing colonies of Virginia, the Carolinas, and Georgia and rely on local Loyalists to hold and administer them. The British knew that Scottish Highlanders in North Carolina retained a strong allegiance to the crown and hoped to recruit other Loyalists from the ranks of the Regulators, the enemies of the low-country Patriot planters. The ministry also hoped to take advantage of racial divisions in the plantation regions of the South and potential Indian allies in the backcountry (Map 6.3). In 1776 over 1,000 slaves had fought for Lord Dunmore under the banner "Liberty to Slaves!"; a British military offensive might prompt thousands more to flee from their Patriot owners.

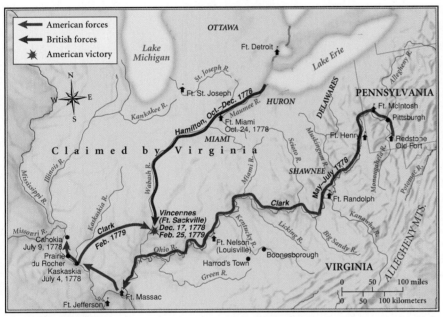

MAP 6.3 Native Americans and the War in the West, 1778–1779

Most Indian peoples remained neutral or, fearing land-hungry Patriot farmers, used British guns to raid American settlements. To thwart attacks on the southern backcountry by militant groups of Shawnees, Cherokees, and Delawares, George Rogers Clark and Patriot militia captured the British fort and supply depot at Vincennes in the Illinois country in late 1778 and again in early 1779. To the north, Patriot Generals John Sullivan and James Clinton defeated pro-British Indian forces near Tioga in August 1779 and then systematically destroyed villages throughout Iroquoia.

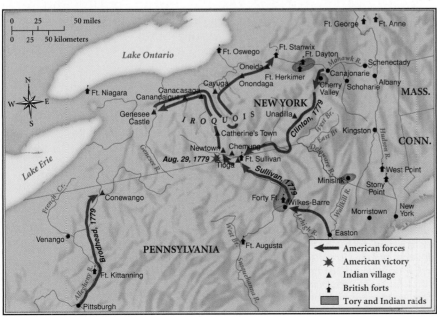

In fact, because African Americans formed 30 to 50 percent of the population, Patriot planters refused to allow their sons or white overseers to leave the plantations and join the Patriot forces. South Carolina could not defend itself, its representative told the Continental Congress, "by reason of the great proportion of citizens necessary to remain at home to prevent insurrection among the Negroes." The policy was a wise one. Whenever British

warships appeared along the coast, blacks would row out to sell provisions and many stayed as volunteers.

Implementing Britain's southern military strategy became the responsibility of Sir Henry Clinton. In June 1778 Clinton moved the main British army from Philadelphia to more secure quarters in New York. In December he launched his southern campaign, capturing Savannah, Georgia, and mobilizing hundreds of blacks to build

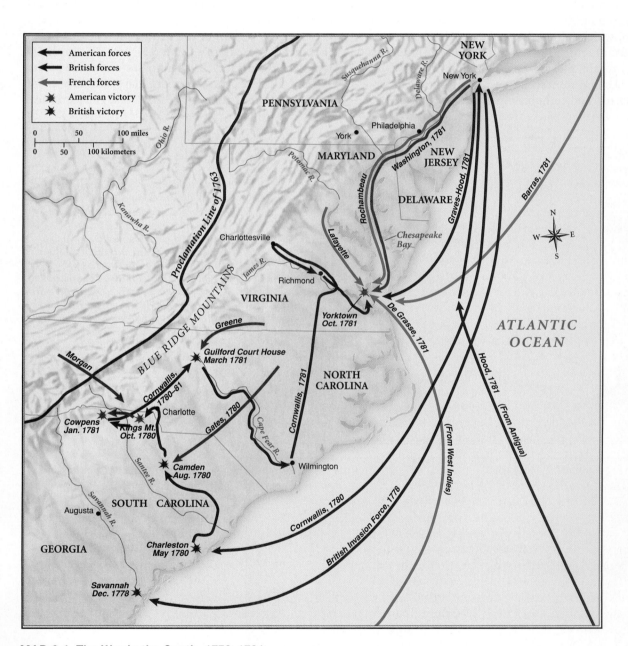

MAP 6.4 The War in the South, 1778–1781

The British ministry's southern strategy started well. British forces captured Savannah in December 1778 and Charleston in May 1780. Brutal warfare raged in the interior over the next eighteen months, fought more by small bands of irregulars than by disciplined armies, and ended in a stalemate between British forces and their Loyalist supporters and the American army and militia. Hoping to break the deadlock, in 1781 British General Charles Cornwallis carried the battle into Virginia. A Franco-American army led by Washington and Lafayette, aided by the French fleet under Admiral de Grasse, surrounded Cornwallis's forces on the Yorktown peninsula and forced their surrender.

barricades and unload supplies. Then Clinton moved inland, capturing Augusta early in 1779. By the end of the year, with the help of local Loyalists, Clinton's forces had taken control of Georgia, and 10,000 troops were poised for an assault on South Carolina. To counter this threat the Continental Congress suggested that South Carolina raise 3,000 black troops, but the state assembly overwhelmingly rejected the proposal.

During most of 1780 British forces marched from victory to victory (Map 6.4). In May Clinton surrounded the city of Charleston, South Carolina, forcing the surrender of General Benjamin Lincoln and his garrison of 5,000 troops. Then Lord Cornwallis assumed control of the British forces and sent out expeditions to secure the countryside. In August Cornwallis defeated an American force at Camden, South Carolina, commanded by General Horatio Gates, the hero of Saratoga. Only about 1,200 Patriot militiamen joined Gates at the battle in Camden—a fifth of the number at Saratoga—and many of them panicked, handing the British control of South Carolina. Hundreds of African Americans fled to freedom in British-controlled Florida, while hundreds more found refuge with the British army, providing labor in return for their liberty.

Then the tide of battle turned. The Dutch declared war against Britain, and France finally dispatched troops to America. The French decision was partly the work of the Marquis de Lafayette, a republican-minded aristocrat who had long supported the American cause. In 1780 Lafayette persuaded Louis XVI to send General Comte de Rochambeau and 5,500 men to Newport, Rhode Island, where they posed a threat to the British forces in New York City.

Partisan Warfare in the Carolinas. Meanwhile, Washington dispatched General Nathanael Greene to recapture the Carolinas. There the fighting had led to social anarchy, making it difficult to distinguish military units from criminal gangs. The words of a Patriot soldier captured the confusion: "Heard of a party of tories on the Sandy River, we killed three and wounded three most notorious villains." Given this social disarray, Greene faced a difficult task. His troops, he reported, "are almost naked and we subsist by daily collections and in a country that has been ravaged and plundered by both friends and enemies." To make use of local militiamen, who were "without discipline and addicted to plundering," Greene devised a new military strategy. He divided the militia into small groups with strong leaders and directed them to harass less-mobile British forces. In October 1780 a militia force of Patriot farmers defeated a regiment of Loyalists at King's Mountain, South Carolina, taking about 1,000 prisoners. Led by the "Swamp Fox," General Francis Marion, American guerrillas won a series of small but fierce battles in South Carolina, while General Daniel Morgan led another band to a bloody victory at Cowpens, South Carolina, in January 1781. But Loyalist

garrisons and militia units remained powerful, assisted by the well-organized Cherokees, who protected their lands by attacking American settlers and troops. "We fight, get beaten, and fight again," General Greene declared doggedly. In March 1781 Greene's soldiers fought Cornwallis's seasoned army to a draw at North Carolina's Guilford Court House.

Weakened by this war of attrition and Patriot successes in restoring authority, Cornwallis decided to concede the southernmost states to Greene and seek a decisive victory in Virginia. Aided by reinforcements from New York, the British general invaded Virginia's Tidewater region. There Benedict Arnold, the infamous traitor to the Patriot cause (see American Lives, "The Enigma of Benedict Arnold, p. 180), led British troops in raids up and down the James River, where they met only slight resistance from an American force commanded by Lafayette. Then in May 1781, as the two armies sparred near the York Peninsula, France ordered its large fleet from the West Indies to North America.

Emboldened by the naval forces at his disposal, Washington launched a well-coordinated attack. Feinting

Lafayette at Yorktown

This painting, executed by the French artist J. B. Le Paon in 1780, shows Lafayette and James Armistead, an enslaved African American who served as a spy for the Patriot army commanded by the French general. Receiving his freedom as a reward for his exploits, James took Lafayette's surname, becoming James Lafayette. The two Lafayettes met again in 1824, when the Frenchman visited the United States.

Lafayette College Art Collection, Easton, PA. Gift of Mrs. John Hubbard.

The Enigma of Benedict Arnold

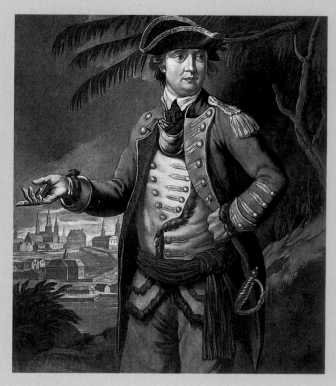

Benedict Arnold, 1776

This engraving depicts Arnold prior to the American assault on Quebec City (pictured in the background). Arnold's portrait is an imaginary representation, issued by a London bookseller to capitalize on British interest in the American revolt.
Anne S. K. Brown Military Collection, Brown University.

Benedict Arnold was an exceptional man, and so too was his military career. During the American War of Independence, Arnold became a hero for both the Patriot and the Loyalist sides.

Arnold began his military exploits as an American Patriot. In May 1775 he devised a plan to capture Fort Ticonderoga on Lake Champlain and then joined with Ethan Allen and the Green Mountain Boys of Vermont to do it. Arnold's heroics continued in September when he led an expedition of 1,150 riflemen against Quebec City, the capital of British Canada. He drove his men hard through the Maine wilderness, overcoming leaky boats, spoiled provisions, treacherous rivers, and near starvation to arrive at Quebec in November, his force reduced to 650 men. These losses did not deter Arnold. Joined by General Richard Montgomery, who had arrived with 300 troops after capturing Montreal, Arnold's forces attacked the strongly fortified city, only to have the assault end in disaster. The British defenders killed 100 Americans, including Montgomery; captured 400 more; and wounded many others—among them Arnold, who fell as he stormed over a barricade, a musket ball through his leg.

Ticonderoga and Quebec were only the beginning. For the next five years Arnold served the Patriot side with distinction, including a dangerous assault against the center of the British line at Saratoga, where he was again wounded in the leg. No general was more imaginative than Arnold, no field officer more daring, no soldier more courageous.

Yet Arnold has become immortalized not as a Patriot hero but as a villain, a military traitor who, as commander of the American fort at West Point, New York, in 1780, schemed to hand it over to the British. Of his role in this conspiracy there is no doubt. His British contact, Major John André, was caught with incriminating documents in Arnold's handwriting, including routes of access to the fort. Fleeing down the Hudson River on a British ship, Arnold defended his conduct in a letter to George Washington, declaring that "love to my country actuates my present conduct, however it may appear inconsistent to the world, who very seldom judge right of any man's actions."

But judge we must. Why did Arnold desert the cause for which he had fought so gallantly and twice been wounded? Was there any justification for his conduct?

Arnold grew up in modest circumstances, a member of a respectable Puritan family, and served in a Connecticut regiment during the French and Indian War. When the fighting began at Lexington and Concord in April 1775, he was thirty-four years old, a minor merchant in New Haven, Connecticut, and a militia captain. Eager to support the Patriot rebellion, Arnold marched off with his militiamen to besiege the British forces in Boston. Along the way he remembered seeing the cannon at Fort Ticonderoga during the French war and realized the Patriots could seize these weapons in order to bombard General Thomas Gage's army. Once his ingenious plan forced the British out of Boston, Arnold submitted an inflated claim for expenses (£1,060 in Massachusetts currency, or about $60,000 today), then protested vehemently when suspicious legislators closely examined each item.

This adventure revealed Arnold's great strengths and equally great flaws. Bold and creative, he thought quickly and acted decisively. Ambitious and thin-skinned, he craved power and money but reacted badly to criticism. Intrepid and ruthless, he risked his life—and the lives of others—to get what he wanted.

Such larger-than-life figures are often resented as much as they are admired, and so it was with Benedict Arnold. At Quebec some New England officers accused him of arrogance, but Congress rewarded the colonel's bravery by making him a brigadier general. When Arnold again distinguished himself in battle in early 1777—having his horse shot out from under him—Congress promoted him to major general "as a token of their admiration of his gallant conduct." Then, in the middle of the struggle at Saratoga, General Horatio Gates relieved Arnold of his command, partly for insubordination and partly because the American commander considered him a "pompous little fellow." Nonetheless, George Washington rewarded Arnold, appointing him commandant at Philadelphia following the British evacuation of the city in July 1778.

By then Arnold was an embittered man, disdainful of his fellow officers and resentful toward Congress for not promoting him more quickly and to even higher rank. A widower, he threw himself into the social life of Philadelphia, courting and marrying Margaret Shippen—a much younger woman from a wealthy merchant family—and falling deeply into debt. Arnold's financial extravagance drew him into shady schemes and into disrepute with Congress, which investigated his accounts and recommended a court-martial—which Arnold managed to dodge. "Having . . . become a cripple in the service of my country, I little expected to meet [such] ungrateful returns," he complained to Washington.

Faced with financial ruin, uncertain of future promotion, and disgusted with congressional politics, Arnold made a fateful decision: he would seek fortune and fame in the service of Great Britain. With cool calculation Arnold initiated correspondence with Sir Henry Clinton, the British commander, promising to deliver West Point and its 3,000 defenders for £20,000 sterling (about $1 million today), a momentous act that he hoped would spark the collapse of the American cause. Persuading Washington to place the fort under his command, in September 1780 Arnold began to execute his audacious plan, only to see it fail when André was captured and executed as a spy. The British ministry nonetheless rewarded Arnold, giving him £6,000 and appointment as a brigadier general.

Arnold served George III with the same skill and daring he had shown in the Patriot cause. In 1781 in Virginia he led an army that looted Richmond and destroyed munitions and grain intended for the American army opposing Lord Cornwallis. Then he fell upon Connecticut, the colony of his birth, burning ships, warehouses, and much of the town of New London, a major port for Patriot privateers.

In the end, Benedict Arnold's moral failure lay not in his disenchantment with the Patriot cause—for many other American officers left the army in disgust. Nor did his infamy result from his decision to join the British side—for other Patriots chose to become Loyalists, sometimes out of principle but just as often for personal gain. Arnold's treason lay in the abuse of his position of authority: he would betray West Point and its garrison to secure his own success. His treachery was not that of a principled man but of a selfish one, and he never lived that down. Hated in America as a consort of "Beelzebub . . . the Devil," after the war Arnold was treated with coldness and even contempt in Britain. He died as he lived—a man without a country.

Major John André Executed as a British Spy
Unable to catch the traitor Benedict Arnold, the American army executed his British accomplice, whose elegance, intelligence, and dignity won the hearts of his captors. "He died universally esteemed and universally regretted," noted Alexander Hamilton.
Library of Congress.

an assault on New York City, he secretly marched General Rochambeau's army from Rhode Island to Virginia, where it joined his Continental army. Simultaneously, the French fleet massed off the coast, establishing control of Chesapeake Bay. By the time the British discovered Washington's audacious plan, Cornwallis was surrounded, his 9,500-man army outnumbered two to one on land and cut off from reinforcement or retreat by sea. Abandoned by the British navy, Cornwallis surrendered at Yorktown in October 1781.

The Franco-American victory at Yorktown broke the resolve of the British government. "Oh God! It is all over!" Lord North exclaimed when he heard the news. The combined French and Spanish fleet was menacing the British sugar islands, Dutch merchants were capturing European markets from British traders, and a group of European states—the League of Armed Neutrality—was demanding an end to Britain's commercial blockade of France. Isolated diplomatically in Europe, stymied militarily in America, and lacking public support at home, the British ministry gave up active prosecution of the war.

The Patriot Advantage

Angry members of Parliament demanded an explanation. How could mighty Britain, victorious in the Great War for Empire, be defeated by a motley group of colonists? The ministry blamed the military leadership, pointing with some justification to a series of blunders. Why had Howe not been more ruthless in pursuing Washington's army in 1776? How could Howe and Burgoyne have failed to coordinate the movement of their armies in 1777? Why had Cornwallis marched deep into the Patriot-dominated state of Virginia in 1781?

Historians have also criticized these blunders while emphasizing the high odds against British success, given broad-based American support for the rebel cause. Although only a third of the white colonists were zealous Patriots, another third were supportive enough to pay the taxes imposed by state governments. Unlike most revolutionaries the Patriots were led by experienced politicians who commanded public support. The more than 55,000 Tories and thousands of Native Americans who joined the British side could not offset these advantages. Once the rebels had the financial and military support of France, they could reasonably hope for victory. While Britain suffered mediocre generals, Americans had the inspired leadership of George Washington as commander of the Continental army. An astute politician, Washington deferred to the civil authorities, winning respect and support from the Congress and the state governments alike. Confident of his own abilities, he recruited outstanding military officers to instill discipline in the ranks of the fledgling Continental army. Thanks to their efforts, the Continental army emerged as a respectable fighting force that was crucial to the American success. Alone, the Patriot militia lacked the organization necessary to defeat the British army. However, in combination with the Continental forces, it proved potent, providing the margin of victory at Saratoga and other important battles. Militarily flexible, Washington came to understand that warfare in a lightly governed agricultural society required the deft use of rural militia units.

But Washington also had a greater margin for error than the British generals did because Patriots controlled local governments and at crucial moments could mobilize the militia to assist his Continental army. Thousands of militiamen had besieged General Gage in Boston in 1775, surrounded Burgoyne at Saratoga in 1777, and forced Cornwallis from the Carolinas in 1781. In the end the American people decided the outcome of the conflict. Preferring Patriot rule, they refused to support Loyalist forces or accept imperial control in British-occupied areas. Consequently, while the British won many military victories, they achieved little, and their defeats at Saratoga and Yorktown proved catastrophic.

Diplomatic Triumph

After Yorktown diplomats took two years to conclude the war. Peace talks began in Paris in April 1782, but the French and Spanish stalled for time, hoping for a major naval victory or territorial conquest. Their delaying tactics infuriated the American diplomats—Benjamin Franklin, John Adams, and John Jay—who feared that France might sacrifice American interests (see American Voices, "John Adams: Making Peace with Stubborn Enemies and Crafty Allies," p. 183). For this reason the Americans negotiated secretly with the British, prepared if necessary to cut their ties to France and sign a separate peace. The British ministry was also eager to obtain a quick settlement, for the war had little support in Parliament and officials feared the loss to France of a rich West Indian sugar island.

Exploiting the rivalry between Britain and France, the American diplomats finally secured peace on very favorable terms. In the Treaty of Paris, signed in September 1783, Great Britain formally recognized the independence of its seaboard colonies and, while retaining Canada, also relinquished its claims to all the lands south of the Great Lakes between the Appalachian Mountains and the Mississippi River—the domain of undefeated, pro-British Indian peoples. Leaving the Native Americans to their fate, the British negotiators did not insist on a separate Indian territory and promised to withdraw their garrisons "with all convenient speed." "In endeavouring to assist you," a Wea Indian complained to a British general, "it seems we have wrought our own ruin."

Other treaty provisions were equally favorable to the American side. They granted Americans fishing rights off Newfoundland and Nova Scotia, forbade the British from "carrying away any negroes or other property," and guaranteed freedom of navigation on the Mississippi to

John Adams

Making Peace with Stubborn Enemies and Crafty Allies

Making peace proved to be as difficult as winning the war. Negotiations commenced following the Franco-American victory at Yorktown in October 1781, but a year later American diplomats Benjamin Franklin, John Jay, and John Adams were still haggling with their British counterparts (Richard Oswald and Richard Strachey) over control of the fisheries off Nova Scotia, navigation of the Mississippi, reparations for confiscated Loyalist property, and prewar American debts owed to British merchants. As the following entries from John Adams's diary show, the Americans could not rely on their Spanish and French allies, who were pursuing their own diplomatic agendas.

September 14, 1782. The Hague [The Netherlands]. Fell into conversation naturally with Don Joas Theolomico de Almeida, Envoy extraordinary of Portugal. He said to me, "The peace is yet a good way off; there will be no peace this winter. . . . Spain will be the most difficult to satisfy of all the powers. Her pretensions will be the hardest for England to agree to. As to the independence of America, that is decided."

November 2. [Paris]. Almost every moment of this week has been employed in negotiation with the English gentlemen concerning peace. . . .

November 3. I proposed to them [Jay and Franklin] that we should agree, that Congress should recommend to the States to open their courts of justice for the recovery of all just debts. They gradually fell into this opinion, and we all expressed these sentiments to the English gentlemen, who were much pleased with it; and with reason, because it silences the clamors of all the British [merchant] creditors against the peace, and prevents them from making common cause with the [Tory] refugees. . . .

November 4. Mr. Strachey is as artful and insinuating a man as they could send; he pushes and presses every point as far as it can possibly go. . . .

November 5. Mr. Jay likes Frenchmen as little as Mr. Lee and Mr. Izard did. He says they are not a moral people; they know not what it is. . . . Our allies don't play fair, he told me; they were endeavoring to deprive us of the fishery, the western lands, and the navigation of the Mississippi; they would even bargain with the English to deprive us of them; they want to play the western lands, Mississippi, and the whole Gulf of Mexico into the hands of Spain.

November 18. I returned Mr. Oswald's visit. We went over the old ground concerning the Tories. . . . I told him he . . . must bend all his thoughts to convince and persuade his Court to give it up; that if the terms now before his Court were not accepted, the whole negotiation would be broken up. "You are afraid," says Mr. Oswald today, "of being made the tools of the powers of Europe." "Indeed I am," says I.

November 20. Dr. Franklin came in [and said] that the fisheries and Mississippi could not be given up; that nothing was clearer to him than that the fisheries were essential to the Northern States, and the Mississippi to the Southern. . . .

November 25. Strachey told us he had been to London, and waited personally on every one of the King's Cabinet Council, and . . . every one of them, unanimously condemned [our proposal] respecting the Tories. . . .

November 26. The rest of the day was spent in endless discussions about the Tories. Dr. Franklin is very staunch against them. . . .

November 29. Strachey [said that] he had determined to advise Mr. Oswald to strike with us, according to the terms we had proposed as our ultimatum respecting the fisheries and the loyalists. Accordingly, we . . . read over the whole treaty, and corrected it, and agreed to meet tomorrow, at Mr. Oswald's house, to sign and seal the treaties.

November 30. The unravelling of the plot has been to me the most affecting and astonishing part of the whole piece. As soon as I arrived in Paris I waited on Mr. Jay, and learned from him the rise and progress of negotiations. Nothing that has happened since the beginning of the controversy [with Britain] in 1761, has ever struck me more forcibly, or affected me more intimately, than that entire coincidence of principles and opinions between him and me.

Source: Charles Francis Adams, ed., *The Works of John Adams, Second President of the United States* (Boston: Little, Brown, 1850), 2: 227–35.

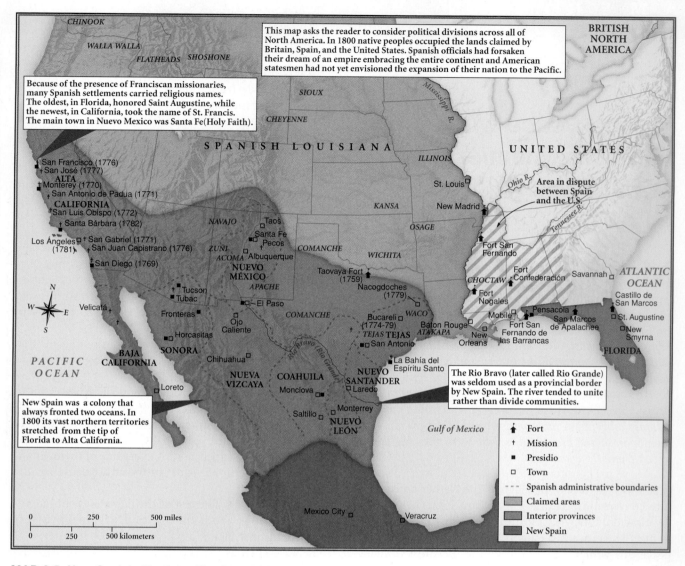

MAP 6.5 New Spain's Northern Empire, 1763–1800

Following its acquisition of Louisiana from France in 1763, Spain tried to create a great northern empire. It established missions and forts in California (such as that at Monterey), expanded its settlements in New Mexico, and, by joining in the American War of Independence, won the return of Florida from Britain. By the early nineteenth century, this dream had been shattered by Indian uprisings in California and Texas, Napoleon's seizure of Louisiana, and an imminent American takeover of Florida.

both British subjects and American citizens "forever." In its only concessions the American government promised to allow British merchants to recover prewar debts and to encourage the state legislatures to return confiscated property to Loyalists and grant them citizenship.

In the Treaty of Versailles, signed at the same time as the Treaty of Paris, Britain made peace with France and Spain. Neither American ally gained very much. Spain reclaimed Florida from Britain but failed in its main objective of regaining the fortress of Gibraltar (Map 6.5). France had the pleasure of reducing British power, but its only territorial gain was the Caribbean island of To-bago. Moreover, the war had quadrupled France's national debt; only six years later cries for tax relief and political liberty would spark the French Revolution. Only Americans

profited handsomely from the treaties, which gave them independence from Britain and opened up the interior of the North American continent for settlement.

Republicanism Defined and Challenged

From the moment they became revolutionary republicans, Americans began to define the character of their new social order. In the Declaration of Independence Thomas Jefferson had turned to John Locke, the philosopher of private liberty, when he declared a universal human right to "Life, Liberty, and the pursuit of Happiness." But Jefferson and many other Americans also lauded "republican virtue," an enlightened quest for the public good. As the New Hampshire constitution phrased it, "Government [was] instituted for the common benefits, protection, and security of the whole community." The tension between individual self-interest and the public interest would shape the future of the new nation.

Republican Ideals under Wartime Pressures

Simply put, a **republic** is a state without a monarch and with a representative system of government. For many Americans republicanism was also a social philosophy. "The word republic" in Latin, wrote Thomas Paine, "means the public good," which citizens have a duty to secure. "Every man in a republic is public property," asserted the Philadelphia Patriot Benjamin Rush, who eventually extended the notion to include women as well. "His time and talents—his youth—his manhood—his old age—nay more, life, all belong to his country." Reflecting this sense of community, members of the Continental Congress praised the militiamen who fought and fell at Lexington and Concord, Saratoga and Camden. And they applauded Henry Laurens of South Carolina, who condemned as a "total loss of virtue" the wartime demand by Continental officers for lifetime pensions. Raised as gentlemen, officers were supposed to be exemplars of virtue who gave freely to the republic.

Republican Ideals Tested. However, the hardships of war undermined selfless idealism, and during the war Patriot military forces became increasingly restive and unruly. Continental troops stationed at Morristown, New Jersey, in the winters of 1779 and 1780 mutinied, unwilling any longer to endure low pay and sparse rations. To restore military authority Washington ordered the execution of several leaders of the revolt but urged Congress to pacify the soldiers with back pay and new clothing. Later in the war unrest among officers erupted at Newburgh, New York, and Washington had to use his personal authority to thwart a dangerous challenge to the Congress's policies.

Economic distress tested the republican virtue of ordinary citizens. The British naval blockade disrupted the New England fishing industry and cut the supply of European manufactures. British occupation of Boston, New York, and Philadelphia also trimmed domestic trade and manufacturing. As unemployed shipwrights, dock laborers, masons, coopers, and bakers deserted the cities and drifted into the countryside, New York City's population declined from 21,000 residents in 1774 to less than half that number by the war's end. In the Chesapeake the British blockade deprived tobacco planters of European markets, forcing them to cultivate grain, which could be sold to the contending armies. All across the land the character of commercial activity changed as farmers and artisans adapted to a war economy.

Mobilizing for War

This 1779 woodcut illustrated a poem by Molly Guttridge, a Daughter of Liberty in Marblehead, Massachusetts, and symbolized the many different wartime contributions of American women. A few Patriot women disguised themselves as men and fought in the war, and thousands more traveled with the Continental army, providing the troops with food and support. Many others took over the farm chores of their soldier-husbands. New-York Historical Society.

Women and Household Production. Faced with a shortage of goods and constantly rising prices, government officials found it necessary to requisition goods directly from the people. In 1776 Connecticut officials called on the citizens of Hartford to provide 1,000 coats and 1,600 shirts and assessed smaller towns on a proportional basis. In 1777 Connecticut officials again pressed the citizenry to provide shirts, stockings, and shoes for their men serving in the Continental army. Soldiers added personal pleas. During the Battle of Long Island in 1776, Captain Edward Rogers lost "all the shirts except the one on my back." "The making of cloath," he wrote to his wife, " . . . must go on. . . . I must have shirts and stockings & a jacket sent me as soon as possible & a blankit."

In those difficult times Patriot women contributed to the war effort by increasing production of homespun cloth. One Massachusetts town produced 30,000 yards of homespun, while women in Elizabeth, New Jersey, promised "upwards of 100,000 yards of linnen and woolen cloth." Other women assumed the burdens of farm production while their men were away at war.

Some went into the fields, plowing, harvesting, and loading grain, while others supervised hired laborers or slaves, in the process acquiring a taste for decision making. "We have sow'd our oats as you desired," Sarah Cobb Paine wrote to her absent husband. "Had I been master I should have planted it to Corn." Taught from childhood to value the welfare of their fathers, brothers, and husbands above their own, women were expected to act "virtuously" and often did so. Their wartime efforts not only increased farm household productivity but also boosted self-esteem, prompting some women to claim greater rights in the new republican society.

Inflation and Regulation. Despite the women's efforts, goods remained in short supply, bringing a sharp rise in prices and widespread appeals for government regulation. Hard-pressed consumers decried merchants and traders as "enemies, extortioners, and monopolizers." But in 1777, when a convention of New England states limited price increases to 75 percent, many farmers and artisans refused to sell their goods at the set prices. In the end, a government official admitted, consumers had to pay the much higher market price "or submit to starving."

The struggle over regulation came to a head in Philadelphia. Following the British withdrawal in 1778, food shortages led to soaring prices and demands by the city's artisans and laborers to establish a Committee on Prices. In May 1779 the committee set prices for thirty-two commodities, invoking the traditional concept of the "just price" and urging citizens to act with "republican virtue." Patriot financier Robert Morris and the merchant community condemned the price controls and espoused "classical liberal" ideas of free trade. They argued that regulation would encourage farmers to hoard their crops, whereas allowing prices to rise would bring more goods to market. Most farmers agreed with Morris, as did Benjamin Franklin, who condemned price controls as "contrary to the nature of commerce."

Nonetheless, most Philadelphians favored "fair" trade rather than "free" trade—at least in principle. At a town meeting in August 1779, over 2,000 Philadelphians voted for regulation, and fewer than 300 opposed it. In practice, however, many artisan-republicans—shoemakers, tanners, and bakers—found that they could not support their families on fixed prices and so refused to abide by them. In civilian life as in the military, self-interest tended to triumph over republican virtue.

Spiraling inflation posed a severe challenge to American families. By 1778 so much currency had been printed that a family needed $7 in Continental bills to buy goods worth $1 in gold or silver. The ratio steadily escalated—to 42 to 1 in 1779, 100 to 1 in 1780, and 146 to 1 in 1781, when not even the most dedicated Patriots would accept paper money. To restore the value of Continental currency, the Congress asked the states to accept tax payments in depreciated Continental bills (with $40 in paper money counting as $1 in specie). This plan redeemed $120 million in Continental bills, but at the end of the war speculators still held $71 million in currency, hoping they could eventually redeem it at face value. "Private Interest seemed to predominate over the public weal," a leading Patriot complained.

Ultimately, this currency inflation transferred most of the costs of the war to ordinary Americans. The tens of thousands of farmers and artisans who received Continental bills as payment for supplies and the soldiers who took them as pay found that the currency literally depreciated in their pockets. Every time they received a paper dollar and kept it for a week, the money lost value and could buy less, thus imposing a hidden currency tax on them. Each individual "tax" was small—a few pennies on each dollar they handled. But taken together—as millions of dollars changed hands multiple times—these currency taxes paid the huge cost of the war.

The Loyalist Exodus

As the war turned in favor of the Patriots, more than 100,000 Loyalists, fearing for their lives, emigrated to the West Indies, Canada, and Britain. Among the more prominent refugees only a few found happiness in exile in England; the majority felt out of place and complained of "their uneasy abode in this country of aliens." Many suffered severe financial losses. John Tabor Kempe, the last royal attorney general of New York,

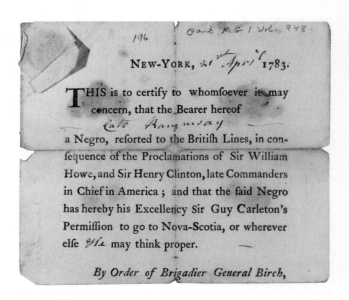

A Black Loyalist Pass, 1783
White Patriots claimed their freedom by fighting against the British, while thousands of black slaves won liberty by fighting for them. This pass certifies that Cato Rammsay, "a Negro," supported the Loyalist cause in New York and is now a free man, able to migrate to British Nova Scotia "or wherever else He may think proper." Nova Scotia Archives and Record Management.

sought £65,000 sterling (about $5 million today) in compensation from the British government but received only £5,000. The great mass of Loyalist refugees received nothing and tried desperately to create new lives. Watching "sails disappear in the distance," an exiled Loyalist woman in Nova Scotia had "such a feeling of loneliness come over me that . . . I sat down on the damp moss with my baby on my lap and cried bitterly."

The Loyalist exodus disrupted the social hierarchy in many communities because, like Kempe, a significant minority of Loyalists came from the ranks of wealthy officials, merchants, and landowners. Although some angry Patriots demanded that the state governments seize the property of these "traitors," most public officials argued that confiscation would be contrary to Patriot principles. In Massachusetts officials cited the state's constitution of 1780, which declared that every citizen should be protected "in the enjoyment of his life, liberty, and property, according to the standing laws."

Consequently, the new republican governments did not seek to change the existing social order. Most states seized only a limited amount of Loyalist property and usually sold it to the highest bidder, who was often a wealthy Patriot rather than a yeoman or a propertyless foot soldier. But in a few cases confiscations did produce a democratic result. In North Carolina about half the new owners of Loyalist lands were small-scale farmers. And on the former Philipse manor in New York many Patriot tenants used their hard-earned savings to buy the seized land and become fee-simple owners. When Philipse tried to reclaim his land, former tenants told him they had "purchased it with the price of their best blood" and "will never become your vassals again." But in general the revolutionary upheaval did not drastically alter the structure of rural society.

Social turmoil was greater in the cities, as Patriot merchants replaced Tories at the top of the economic ladder. In Massachusetts the Lowell, Higginson, Jackson, and Cabot families moved their trading enterprises to Boston to fill the vacuum created by the departure of the Loyalist Hutchinson and Apthorp clans. In Philadelphia, small-scale traders stepped into the vacancies created by the collapse of Anglican and Quaker mercantile firms. In the countinghouses as on the battlefield, Patriots emerged triumphant. The War of Independence replaced a tradition-oriented economic elite—one that invested its profits from trade in real estate, becoming landlords—with a group of entrepreneurial-minded republican merchants who promoted new trading ventures and domestic manufacturing.

The Problem of Slavery

Slavery revealed a contradiction in the Patriots' republican ideology. "How is it that we hear the loudest yelps for liberty among the drivers of Negroes?" the British

Symbols of Slavery—and Freedom

The scar on the forehead of this black woman, who was widely known as "Mumbet," underlined the cruelty of slavery. Winning emancipation through a legal suit in Massachusetts, she chose a name befitting her new status: Elizabeth Freeman. This watercolor, by Susan Sedgwick, was painted in 1811.
Massachusetts Historical Society.

author Samuel Johnson chided the rebellious white Americans, a point some Patriots took to heart. "I wish most sincerely there was not a Slave in the province," Abigail Adams confessed to her husband, John, as Massachusetts went to war. "It always appeared a most iniquitous Scheme to me—to fight ourselves for what we are daily robbing and plundering from those who have as good a right to freedom as we have."

In fact, the struggle of white Patriots for independence raised the prospect of freedom for enslaved Africans. Many slaves hoped for a British invasion that would free them. As the war began, a black preacher in Georgia told his fellow slaves that King George III "came up with the Book [the Bible], and was about to alter the World, and set the Negroes free." Similar rumors circulated among slaves in Virginia and the Carolinas, prompting thousands of African Americans to seek freedom by fleeing behind British lines. Two neighbors of Richard Henry Lee, the Virginia Patriot, lost "every slave they had in the world," as did many other planters. When the British army evacuated Charleston, more than 6,000 former slaves went with them; another 4,000 left from Savannah. All told, some 30,000 blacks may have fled their owners. Hundreds of black Loyalists settled permanently in Canada. Over 1,000 others, poorly treated by British officials and settled on inferior land in Nova Scotia, sought a better life in the abolitionist settlement in Sierra Leone, West Africa (see Chapter 9, American Lives, "Richard Allen and the African American Identity," p. 270).

Benjamin Banneker

On Jefferson and Natural Rights

In his Notes on Virginia *(1785), Thomas Jefferson suggested the inherent inferiority of the black race. In 1791 Benjamin Banneker, a free African American farmer and mathematician who helped to survey the District of Columbia, sent Jefferson a manuscript copy of his forthcoming* Almanac, *an annotated and illustrated guide to the coming agricultural year. In the accompanying letter Banneker asks Jefferson, now the secretary of state in the new federal government, to reconsider his view of Africans, pointing out the contradiction between Jefferson's racial beliefs and the doctrine of natural rights that he had articulated in the* Declaration of Independence.

I suppose it is a truth too well attested to you, to need a proof here, that we are a race of Beings who have long laboured under the abuse and censure of the world . . . considered rather as brutish than human, and Scarcely capable of mental endowments. . . .

Sir, I hope . . . that you are a man far less inflexible in Sentiments of this nature, than many others. . . . Now, Sir, if this is founded in truth, I apprehend you will readily embrace every opportunity to eradicate that train of absurd and false ideas and opinions which so prevail with respect to us, and that your Sentiments are concurrent with mine, which are that the one universal Father has given to us all, and that he hath not only made us all of one flesh, but that he hath also without partiality afforded us all the Same Sensations, and imbued us all with the same faculties, and that however diversified in Situation or colour, we are all of the Same Family, and Stand in the Same relation to him. . . .

Sir, Suffer me to recall to your mind that time in which the Arms and tyranny of the British Crown were exerted with very powerful effort in order to reduce you to a State of Servitude. . . . This, Sir, was a time in which you clearly saw into the injustice of a State of Slavery [and] . . . that you publickly held forth this true and invaluable doctrine . . . : "We hold these truths to be Self evident, that all men are created equal . . ."; but Sir, how pitiable it is to reflect, that . . . in detaining by fraud and violence so numerous a part of my brethren under groaning captivity and cruel oppression that you should at the Same time be found guilty of that most criminal act, which you professedly detested in others, with respect to yourselves.

Source: John J. Patrick, ed., *Founding the Republic: A Documentary History* (Westport, CT: Greenwood Press, 1995), 102–5.

Gradual Emancipation in the North.   For a variety of reasons thousands of African Americans decided to serve the Patriot cause. Knowing firsthand the meaning of slavery and eager to raise their status in society, free blacks in New England volunteered for military service in the First Rhode Island Company and the Massachusetts "Bucks." In Maryland a large number of slaves also took up arms for the Patriot cause in return for a promise of freedom. Elsewhere in the South slaves struck informal bargains with their Patriot masters, trading loyalty in wartime for a promise of eventual liberty. In 1782 the Virginia assembly passed an act allowing **manumission** (liberation); within a decade planters had freed 10,000 slaves.

The Quakers, whose belief in religious and social equality had made them sharp critics of many inequities, took the lead in condemning slavery. Beginning in the 1750s the Quaker evangelist John Woolman had urged Friends to free their slaves, and during the war many did so. Other rapidly growing pietistic groups, notably the Methodists and the Baptists, also advocated emancipation and admitted both enslaved and free blacks to their congregations. In 1784 a conference of Virginia Methodists declared that slavery was "contrary to the Golden Law of God on which hang all the Law and Prophets."

Enlightenment philosophy also worked to undermine slavery and racism. John Locke had argued that ideas were not innate but stemmed from a person's experiences in the world. Accordingly, Enlightenment thinkers suggested that the oppressive conditions of slavery, not inherent inferiority, accounted for the debased situation of Africans in the Western Hemisphere. As one American put it, "A state of slavery has a mighty tendency to shrink and contract the minds of men." Anthony Benezet, a Quaker philanthropist who funded a school for blacks in Philadelphia, defied popular opinion in declaring that African Americans were "as capable of improvement as White People" (see American Voices, "Benjamin Banneker: On Jefferson and Natural Rights," above).

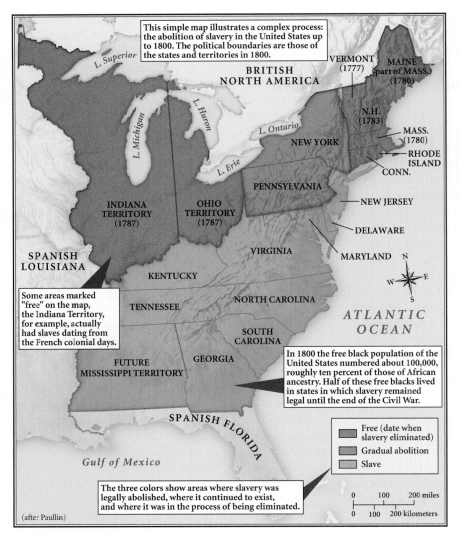

This simple map illustrates a complex process: the abolition of slavery in the United States up to 1800. The political boundaries are those of the states and territories in 1800.

Some areas marked "free" on the map, the Indiana Territory, for example, actually had slaves dating from the French colonial days.

In 1800 the free black population of the United States numbered about 100,000, roughly ten percent of those of African ancestry. Half of these free blacks lived in states in which slavery remained legal until the end of the Civil War.

The three colors show areas where slavery was legally abolished, where it continued to exist, and where it was in the process of being eliminated.

Free (date when slavery eliminated)
Gradual abolition
Slave

(after Paullin)

MAP 6.6 The Status of Slavery, 1800

In 1775 racial slavery was legal in every British American colony. By the time the American states achieved their independence in 1783, most African Americans in New England had also become free. By 1800 nearly all of the states north of Maryland had provided for the gradual abolition of slavery, a slow process that was not completed until the 1830s. After the Revolution, some slave owners in the Chesapeake region had also manumitted their slaves, leaving only the whites of the Lower South firmly committed to racial bondage.

By 1784 Massachusetts abolished slavery outright, and three other states—Pennsylvania, Connecticut, and Rhode Island—provided for its gradual termination. Within another twenty years every state north of Delaware had enacted similar laws (Map 6.6). Gradual emancipation laws compensated white owners by requiring more years—even decades—of servitude; the New York Emancipation Act of 1799 granted freedom to slave children only when they reached the age of twenty-five. As late as 1810, almost 30,000 blacks in the northern states—nearly a fourth of their African American residents—were still enslaved. Emancipation came slowly because whites feared competition for jobs and housing and the prospect of race melding. To keep the races separate, in 1786 Massachusetts reenacted an old law prohibiting whites from marrying blacks, Indians, or mulattos.

The White South Grapples with Slavery. The tension between the republican values of liberty and property was greatest in the South, where slaves made up 30 to 60 percent of the population and represented a huge financial investment. Some planters, moved by religious principles or oversupplied with workers on declining tobacco plantations, allowed blacks to buy their freedom through paid work as artisans or laborers. In Maryland, manumission and self-purchase gradually brought freedom to a third of its African American residents, but in 1792 in Virginia the legislature made manumission more difficult. Following the lead of Thomas Jefferson, who owned more than 100 slaves, the Chesapeake gentry argued that slavery was a "necessary evil" required to maintain white supremacy and the luxurious planter lifestyle. Resistance to freedom for blacks was even greater in North Carolina, where the legislature condemned Quaker manumissions as "highly criminal and reprehensible." The rice-growing states of South Carolina and Georgia rejected emancipation out of hand.

The debate over emancipation among southern whites ended in 1800, when Virginia authorities thwarted an uprising planned by the enslaved artisan Gabriel Prosser and hanged him and thirty of his followers. "Liberty and equality have brought the evil upon us," a letter to the *Virginia Herald* proclaimed, for such doctrines are "dangerous and extremely wicked in this country, where every white man is a master, and every black man is a slave." To preserve their privileged social position, whites redefined republicanism so that it applied only to the "master race."

A Republican Religious Order

Political revolution broadened the appeal of religious liberty, forcing Patriot lawmakers to devise a new relationship between church and state. During the colonial era only the Quaker- and Baptist-controlled governments of Pennsylvania and Rhode Island had repudiated the idea of an established church. Then in 1776 James Madison and George Mason used Enlightenment principles to undermine the traditional commitment to a single state-supported church in Virginia. They persuaded the state's constitutional convention to issue a Declaration of Rights guaranteeing all Christians the "free exercise of religion." To win broad support for the war, the Virginia Anglican elite put this doctrine into practice, accepting the legitimacy of the dissenting Presbyterian and Baptist churches that they had previously persecuted. In 1778 Virginia Anglicans launched their own religious revolution by severing ties with the hierarchy of the Church of England in London and creating the Protestant Episcopal Church of America.

After the Revolution an established church and compulsory religious taxes were no longer the norm in the United States. Baptists in particular opposed the use of taxes to support religion. In Virginia their political influence prompted lawmakers to reject a bill supported by George Washington and Patrick Henry, which would have imposed a general tax to fund all Christian churches. Instead, in 1786 the Virginia legislature enacted Thomas Jefferson's Bill for Establishing Religious Freedom, which made all churches equal before the law and granted direct financial support to none. In New York and New Jersey the sheer number of churches—Episcopalian, Presbyterian, Dutch Reformed, Lutheran, and Quaker, among others—prevented legislative agreement on an established church or compulsory religious taxes. In New England Congregationalism remained the official state church until the 1830s, but state law allowed Baptists and Methodists to pay religious taxes to their own churches.

However, even in Virginia, the separation of church and state was never complete. Many Americans still believed that firm connections between church and state were necessary to promote morality and respect for authority. "Pure religion and civil liberty are inseparable companions," a group of North Carolinians advised their minister. "It is your particular duty to enlighten mankind with the unerring principles of truth and justice, the main props of all civil government." Accepting this premise, most state governments provided churches with indirect aid by exempting their property and ministers from taxation.

Freedom of conscience proved equally difficult to achieve. In Virginia Jefferson's Bill for Establishing Religious Freedom instituted the principle of liberty of conscience by outlawing religious requirements for political and civil officeholding. But many states enforced religious criteria for voting and officeholding, penalizing individuals who dissented from the doctrines of Protestant Christianity. The North Carolina constitution of 1776 disqualified from public office any citizen "who shall deny the being of God, or the Truth of the Protestant Religion, or the Divine Authority of the Old or New Testament." New Hampshire's constitution contained a similar provision until 1868.

Americans influenced by the Enlightenment and by evangelical Protestantism condemned such restrictions on freedom of conscience, but for different reasons. Leading American intellectuals, including Thomas Jefferson and Benjamin Franklin, argued that God had given humans the power of reason so that they could determine moral truths for themselves. To protect society from "ecclesiastical tyranny," they demanded complete freedom of expression. Many evangelical Protestants also wanted religious liberty, but their goal was to protect their churches from the government. The New England minister Isaac Backus warned Baptists not to incorporate their churches under the law or accept public funds because that might lead to state control. In Connecticut a devout Congregationalist welcomed voluntarism (the voluntary funding of churches by their members) for another reason: it allowed the laity to control the clergy, thereby furthering "the principles of republicanism."

In religion as in politics, independence provided Americans with the opportunity to fashion a new institutional order. In each case they repudiated the hierarchical ways of the past—monarchy and establishment—in favor of a republican alternative. These choices reflected the outlook and increased influence of ordinary citizens, who had fought and financed the long, difficult military struggle. True to the prediction of a wealthy Virginia planter in April 1776, independence and revolution had allowed yeomen to promote "their darling Democracy."

FOR FURTHER EXPLORATION

▶ For definitions of key terms boldfaced in this chapter, see the glossary at the end of the book.

▶ To assess your mastery of the material covered in this chapter, see the Online Study Guide at **bedfordstmartins.com/henretta**.

▶ For suggested references, including Web sites, see page SR-6 at the end of the book.

▶ For map resources and primary documents, see **bedfordstmartins.com/henretta**.

The War of Independence changed the course of American history by creating the United States as a separate nation with a republican system of government. This dramatic change gathered momentum in April 1775, when the American colonists challenged British authority with military force. Thomas Paine's *Common Sense* attacked the monarchical system and persuaded many Americans to support republicanism and independence, which was formally declared by the Continental Congress on July 4, 1776.

The British ministry dispatched a large British army under General Howe to put down the rebellion. Howe's force defeated Washington's Continental army in a series of battles during 1776, but Patriot triumphs at Trenton and Princeton revived American morale. Howe captured Philadelphia, the Patriots' capital, in the summer of 1777, but the rebels won a major victory at Saratoga, New York, in October. The Patriots nearly lost their main army to cold and hunger at Valley Forge, Pennsylvania, during the winter of 1777–78. Simultaneously, a severe inflation caused by an excess of paper money undermined public support for the new republican governments.

The tide turned in February 1778, when an alliance with France aided the Patriot cause. Congress rejected British overtures for a negotiated settlement, and Lord North embarked on a southern military strategy. British troops won important victories in Georgia and the Carolinas during 1779 and 1780, but Patriot troops finally forced General Cornwallis and his army into Virginia, where they suffered a stinging defeat at Yorktown in October 1781. The Treaty of Paris in 1783 acknowledged the independence of the United States and defined its western boundary at the Mississippi River. Thousands of Loyalists fled to various parts of the British empire, and thousands of slaves won their freedom by assisting the British or escaping to Spanish Florida.

Some Patriots defined republicanism as pursuit of the common good, while others embraced the liberal outlook inspired by John Locke and celebrated the pursuit of individual self-interest. Wartime hardships—such as currency inflation, the hidden tax that paid for the Patriots' military effort—increased the tension between these republican and liberal ideals.

Long after the war ended, Americans continued to debate the social and cultural implications of republicanism. State governments in the North began the gradual abolition of slavery, but those in the South refused to extend freedom to most African Americans. However, throughout the new nation there was growing commitment to freedom of religious worship and the separation of church and state.

1775 Second Continental Congress meets in Philadelphia (May)

Battle of Bunker Hill

Congressional moderates submit Olive Branch petition; King rejects it

Lord Dunmore's proclamation offers freedom to slaves and servants (November)

American invasion of Canada

1776 Patriots and Loyalists skirmish in the South

Thomas Paine publishes *Common Sense* (January)

Declaration of Independence (July 4)

Howe forces Washington to retreat from New York and New Jersey

Virginia Declaration of Rights

1777 Patriot women become important in war economy

Howe occupies Philadelphia (September)

Gates defeats Burgoyne at Saratoga (October)

Continental army suffers at Valley Forge during winter

Severe inflation of paper currency begins

1778 Franco-American alliance (February)

Lord North seeks political settlement; Congress rejects negotiations

British begin southern strategy; capture Savannah (December)

1780 Sir Henry Clinton seizes Charleston (May)

French army lands in Rhode Island

1781 Lord Cornwallis invades Virginia (April); surrenders at Yorktown (October)

Large-scale Loyalist emigration

Partial redemption of Continental currency at 40 to 1

1782 Virginia passes law allowing slave manumission (reversed in 1792)

1783 Treaty of Paris (September 3) officially ends war

1786 Virginia enacts Bill for Establishing Religious Freedom

1800 Gabriel Prosser organizes slave rebellion in Virginia

CHAPTER 7

The New Political Order

1776–1800

LIKE AN EARTHQUAKE THE AMERICAN REVOLUTION SHOOK the foundations of the traditional European political order, and its aftershocks were felt far into the nineteenth century. By "creating a new republic based on the rights of [the] individual, the North Americans introduced a new force into the world," the eminent German historian Leopold von Ranke explained to the king of Bavaria in a private lecture in 1854, warning that the ideology of republicanism might cost the monarch his throne:

> This was a revolution of principle. Up to this point, a king who ruled by the grace of God had been the center around which everything turned. Now the idea emerged that power should come from below [from the people]. . . . These two principles are like opposite poles, and it is the conflict between them that determines the course of the modern world.

◀ **Congress Hall, Philadelphia**
As the elegant Georgian edifice depicted (left foreground) in William Birch's 1800 painting suggests, Philadelphia boasted the most distinguished architecture of all the American port cities. Between 1790 and 1800, the Quaker city served as the home of the national government. Huntington Library.

Previous republican revolutions—such as that of the Puritan Commonwealth in England in the 1650s—had ended in political chaos and military rule, and many Europeans expected the new American states to experience the same fate. But General George Washington stunned the world in 1783 when he voluntarily left public life to return to his plantation.

"Tis a Conduct so novel," the American painter John Trumbull reported from London, "so inconceivable to People [here], who, far from giving up powers they possess, are willing to convulse the empire to acquire more." Washington's retirement bolstered the authority of elected Patriot leaders, who were firmly committed to representative government.

Fashioning republican institutions absorbed the energy and intellect of an entire generation. Between 1776 and 1800 Americans wrote new state and federal constitutions and devised a system of politics that was responsive to the popular will. Controversies arose at every step in the process. When a bill was introduced into a state legislature, conservative Ezra Stiles grumbled that every elected official "instantly thinks how it will affect his constituents" rather than what its impact would be on the welfare of the public as a whole. What Stiles criticized as an excess of democracy, most ordinary Americans welcomed. For the first time the interests of middling citizens were represented in the halls of government, and the monarchs of Europe trembled.

Creating Republican Institutions, 1776–1787

Once independence had been won, Patriots had to allocate political power among themselves. "Which of us shall be the rulers?" asked a Philadelphia newspaper. The question was complex: Where would power reside, in the national government or the states? Who would control the new republican institutions, traditional elites or average citizens?

The State Constitutions: How Much Democracy?

In May 1776 the Continental Congress had urged Americans to suppress royal authority and establish new governing institutions. Most states quickly complied. Within six months Virginia, Maryland, North Carolina, New Jersey, Delaware, and Pennsylvania had written new constitutions, and Connecticut and Rhode Island had transformed their colonial charters into republican documents by deleting references to the king. "Constitutions employ every pen," an observer noted.

The Meaning of Popular Sovereignty. However, republicanism meant more than ousting the king. The Declaration of Independence had stated the principle of popular sovereignty: that governments derive "their just powers from the consent of the governed." In the heat of revolution many Patriots gave this clause a democratic twist. In North Carolina the backcountry farmers of Mecklenburg County instructed their delegates to the state's constitutional convention to "oppose everything that leans to aristocracy or power in the hands of the rich and chief men exercised to the oppression of the poor." In Virginia voters elected a new assembly that, an observer remarked, "was composed of men not quite so well dressed, nor so politely educated, nor so highly born," while Delaware's constitution declared that "the Right of the People to participate in the Legislature, is the Foundation of Liberty and of all free government."

This democratic outlook received its fullest expression in Pennsylvania, thanks to a coalition of Scots-Irish farmers, Philadelphia artisans, and Enlightenment-influenced intellectuals. Pennsylvania's constitution abolished property owning as a test of citizenship and granted all men who paid taxes the right to vote and hold office. It also created a **unicameral** (one-house) legislature with complete power. No council or upper house was reserved for the wealthy, and no governor exercised veto power. Other constitutional provisions mandated an extensive system of elementary education, protected citizens from imprisonment for debt, and called for a society of economically independent freemen. Pennsylvania's democratic constitution alarmed many leading Patriots, who believed that voting and especially office-holding should be restricted to "men of learning, leisure and easy circumstances." From Boston John Adams denounced Pennsylvania's unicameral legislature as "so democratical that it must produce confusion and every evil work." "Remember," Adams continued, "democracy never lasts long. It soon wastes, exhausts, and murders itself." He and other conservative Patriots feared that popular rule would lead to ordinary citizens using their numerical advantage to tax the rich: "If you give [democrats] the command or preponderance in the . . . legislature, they will vote all property out of the hands of you aristocrats. . . ."

To counter the appeal of the Pennsylvania constitution, Adams published his *Thoughts on Government* (1776) and sent the treatise to friends at constitutional conventions in other states. In his treatise Adams adapted the British Whig theory of **mixed government** (in which power was shared by the king, lords, and commons) to a republican society. To preserve liberty his system dispersed authority by assigning the different functions of government—lawmaking, administering, and judging—to separate branches. Thus, legislatures would make the laws and the executive and the judiciary would enforce them. Adams also called for a **bicameral** (two-house) legislature in which the upper house would be restricted to men who owned substantial property; its role would be to check the power of popular majorities in the lower house. As a further curb on democracy, he proposed an elected governor with the power to veto laws and an appointed—not elected—judiciary to review them. Adams argued that his plan was republican because the people would elect both the chief executive and the legislature.

Leading Patriots endorsed Adams's scheme because it preserved representative government while restricting popular power. Consequently, they wrote state constitutions providing for bicameral legislatures in which membership in both houses was elective. However, only three constitutions gave the veto power to governors; many Patriots recalled the arbitrary conduct of royal governors and had no wish to enhance the power of the executive. In line with Adams's suggestions, many states also retained traditional property qualifications for voting. In New York 90 percent of white men could vote in elections for the assembly, but only 40 percent could vote for the governor and the upper house. The most flagrant use of property to maintain the power of the elite occurred in South Carolina, where the 1778 constitution required candidates for governor to have a debt-free estate of £10,000 (about $600,000 today), senators to be worth £2,000, and assemblymen to own property valued at £1,000. These provisions ruled out officeholding for about 90 percent of white men.

Nonetheless, post-Revolutionary politics had a distinctly democratic tinge (Figure 7.1). The legislature emerged as the dominant branch of government, and state constitutions apportioned seats on the basis of population, giving farmers in rapidly growing western areas the fair representation they had long demanded. Indeed, because of backcountry pressure some legislatures moved the state capital from merchant-dominated seaports such as New York City and Philadelphia to inland cities such as Albany and Harrisburg. Even conservative South Carolina moved its seat of government inland, from Charleston to Columbia.

Moreover, most of the state legislatures were filled by new sorts of political leaders. Rather than electing their social "betters" to office, ordinary citizens increasingly chose men of "middling circumstances" who knew "the wants of the poor." By the mid-1780s middling farmers and urban artisans controlled the lower houses in most northern states and formed a sizable minority in southern assemblies. These middling men took the lead in opposing the collection of back taxes and other measures that tended "toward the oppression of the people."

The political legacy of the Revolution was complex. Only in Pennsylvania and Vermont were radical Patriots able to take power and create democratic institutions. Yet everywhere representative legislatures had more power, and the day-to-day politics of electioneering and interest-group bargaining became much more responsive to the demands of average citizens.

The Political Status of Women.   The extraordinary excitement of the Revolutionary era also tested the dictum that only men could engage in politics. While men continued to control all public institutions—legislatures, juries, government offices—upper-class women entered into political debate, filling their letters and diaries (and undoubtedly their conversations) with opinions on public issues. "The men say we have no business [with politics]," Eliza Wilkinson of South Carolina complained in 1783. "They won't even allow us liberty of thought, and that is all I want" (see American Voices, "Abigail and John Adams: The Status of Women," p. 197).

These American women did not insist on complete civic equality with men, but they wanted to eliminate certain restrictive customs and laws. Abigail Adams demanded equal legal rights for married women, pointing out that under existing common law wives could not own most forms of property and could not enter into a contract or initiate a lawsuit without their husbands' action. "Men would be tyrants" if they continued to hold such power over women, Adams declared to her husband, criticizing him and other Patriots for "emancipating all nations" from monarchical despotism while "retaining absolute power over Wives."

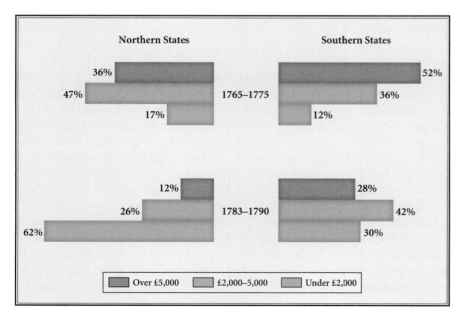

FIGURE 7.1 Middling Men Enter the Halls of Government, 1765–1790

Before the Revolution, wealthy men dominated the colonial assemblies. In the new republic, the proportion of men of middling property (as measured by tax lists and probate records) increased dramatically, especially in the northern states.

Source: Adapted from Jackson T. Main, "Government by the People: The American Revolution and the Democratization of the Legislatures," *William and Mary Quarterly*, 3rd ser., vol. 23 (1966).

John and Abigail Adams

Both Adamses had strong personalities and often disagreed in private about political and social issues. In 1794 John playfully accused his wife of being a "Disciple of Wollstonecraft," but (as the American Voices selection on p. 197 shows) Abigail's commitment to legal equality for women long predated Wollstonecraft's A Vindication of the Rights of Woman *(1792).*

Boston Athenaeum / New York State Historical Association, Cooperstown, NY.

Most men paid little attention to women's requests, and most husbands remained patriarchs, dominating their households. Even young men who embraced the republican ideal of "companionate" marriage did not support reform of the common law or a public role for their wives and daughters. With the partial exception of New Jersey, which until 1807 granted the vote to unmarried and widowed women of property, women remained second-class citizens, unable to participate directly in American political and economic life.

The republican quest for an educated citizenry provided the avenue for the most important advances made by American women. In her 1779 essay "On the Equality of the Sexes" (published in 1790), Judith Sargent Murray compared the intellectual faculties of men and women, arguing that women had an equal capacity for memory and superior imagination. Murray conceded that most women were inferior to men in judgment and reasoning, but only because of a lack of training: "We can only reason from what we know," she argued, and most women had been denied "the opportunity of acquiring knowledge." To remedy this situation, the attorney general in Massachusetts persuaded a jury in the 1790s that girls had an equal right to schooling under the state constitution.

With greater access to public elementary schools and the rapid creation of girls' academies (private high schools), many young women became literate and knowledgeable. By 1850 as many women as men in the northeastern states would be able to read and write, and literate women would again challenge their subordinate legal and political status.

The Articles of Confederation

As the Patriots moved toward independence in 1776, they envisioned a central government with limited powers. Carter Braxton of Virginia thought the Continental Congress should have the power to "regulate the affairs of trade, war, peace, alliances, &c." but "should by no means have authority to interfere with the internal police [governance] or domestic concerns of any Colony."

This intensely state-focused outlook informed the Articles of Confederation, passed by Congress in November 1777. As the first national constitution, the Articles provided for a loose confederation in which "each state retains its sovereignty, freedom, and independence" as well as all powers and rights not "expressly delegated" to the United States. The Articles gave the

Abigail and John Adams

The Status of Women

*M*ost American women of European descent accepted the subordinate status of their sex; it was the way life had always been and, many believed, the way God intended it to be. Yet the rhetoric of liberty and equality prompted a few women, including Abigail Adams, the wife of the prominent Massachusetts Patriot John Adams, to challenge men's dominant position. However, as this exchange between the Adamses suggests, most of these challenges were very tentative and very brief.

March 31, 1776 Abigail Adams to John Adams
I long to hear that you have declared an independancy—and by the way in the new Code of Law . . . be more generous and favorable to [the Ladies] than your ancestors. Do not put such unlimited power into the hands of Husbands. Remember all Men would be tyrants if they could. If perticuliar care and attention is not paid to the Ladies we are determined to foment a Rebellion, and will not hold ourselves bound by any Laws in which we have no voice, or Representation. . . . Men of Sense in all Ages abhor those customs which treat us only as the vassals of your Sex. Regard us then as Beings placed by providence under your protection. . . .

April 14, 1776 John Adams to Abigail Adams
As to your extraordinary Code of Laws, I cannot but laugh. We have been told that our Struggle [for independence] has loosened the bonds of Government every where. That Children and Apprentices were disobedient—that schools and Colledges were grown turbulent—that

Indians slighted their Guardians and Negroes grew insolent to their Masters. But your letter was the first Intimation that another Tribe more numerous and powerful than all the rest were grown discontented. . . .

Depend on it, We know better than to repeal our Masculine System. Altho they are in full Force, you know they are little more than Theory. We dare not exert our Power in its full Latitude. We are obliged to go fair, and softly, and in Practice you know We are the subjects. We have only the Name of Masters, and rather than give up this, which would compleatly subject Us to the Despotism of the Peticoat, I hope General Washington, and all our brave Heroes would fight. . . .

May 7 and August 14, 1776 Abigail Adams to John Adams
Notwithstanding all your wise Laws and Maxims we have it in our power not only to free ourselves but to subdue our Masters, and without violence to throw both your natural and legal authority at our feet—

"Charm by accepting, by submitting sway
Ye have our Humour most when we obey."

I most sincerely wish that some more liberal plan might be laid or executed for the Benefit of the rising Generation, and that our new constitution may be distinguished for Learning and Virtue. If we mean to have Heroes, Statesmen and Philosophers, we should have learned women. The world would laugh at me, and accuse me of vanity, But you I know have a mind too enlarged and liberal. . . . If much depends as is allowed upon the early Education of youth and the first principles which are instilld take the deepest root, great benifit must arise from litirary accomplishments in women.

Source: Lyman H. Butterfield, ed., *Adams Family Correspondence*, 4 vols. (Cambridge: Harvard University Press, 1963), 1: 370, 382–83, 402–3; 2: 94.

confederation government considerable authority; it could declare war and peace, make treaties with foreign nations, adjudicate disputes between the states, borrow and print money, and requisition funds from the states "for the common defense or general welfare." These powers were to be exercised by a central legislature, Congress, in which each state had one vote regardless of its wealth or population. Important laws needed approval by at least nine of the thirteen states, and changes in the

Articles required unanimous consent. In the new national government there was no separate executive branch or judiciary.

Because of disputes over western lands, some states did not ratify the Articles until 1781. Some states, such as Virginia, Massachusetts, and Connecticut, invoked their royal charters to claim boundaries that stretched to the Pacific Ocean. States with no claims to land in the West, such as Maryland and Pennsylvania, refused to accept the

Judith Sargent (Murray), Age Nineteen

The well-educated daughter of a wealthy Massachusetts merchant, Judith Sargent enjoyed a privileged childhood. She endured a difficult seventeen-year marriage to John Stevens, who ultimately went bankrupt, fled from his creditors, and died in the West Indies. In 1788 she wed the Reverend John Murray, who became a leading American Universalist. Her portrait, painted around 1771 by the renowned artist John Singleton Copley, captures Sargent's skeptical view of the world, an outlook that enabled her to question customary gender roles. Terra Museum of American Art, Chicago, Illinois. Daniel J. Terra Collection.

Articles until the land-rich states relinquished their claims and allowed Congress to create a common national domain. Threatened by Cornwallis's army in 1781, Virginia finally agreed to give up its land claims, and Maryland, the last holdout, then ratified the Articles (Map 7.1).

Ongoing Fiscal Crisis. Formal approval of the Articles was anticlimactic. Congress had been exercising de facto constitutional authority for four years, raising the Continental army and negotiating with foreign nations. Despite its successes, the Confederation government had a major weakness. Congress lacked the authority to impose taxes and therefore had to requisition funds from the state legislatures and hope they would pay, which they usually failed to do. Indeed, by 1780 the Confederation was nearly bankrupt. Facing imminent disaster, General Washington called urgently for a national system of taxation, warning Patriot leaders that otherwise "our cause is lost."

In response, nationalist-minded members of Congress tried to expand the Confederation's authority. Robert Morris, who became superintendent of finance in 1781, persuaded Congress to charter the Bank of North America, a private institution in Philadelphia, hoping to use its notes to stabilize the inflated Continental currency. Morris also developed a comprehensive financial plan that apportioned some war expenses among the states while centralizing control of army expenditures and foreign debt. He hoped that the existence of a national debt would underline the Confederation's need for an import duty. But some state legislatures refused to support an increase in the Confederation's powers, which required the unanimous consent of the states. In 1781 Rhode Island rejected Morris's proposal for an import duty of 5 percent, and two years later New York refused to accept a similar plan, pointing out that it had opposed British-imposed import duties and would not accept them from Congress.

The Northwest Ordinance. Despite its limited powers, Congress successfully planned the settlement of the trans-Appalachian West. In fact, Congress strongly asserted the Confederation's title to the lands in the West in part because it wanted to sell them to farmers and speculators and thereby raise revenue for the government. In 1783 Congress began to negotiate with Indian tribes, hoping to persuade them that the Treaty of Paris had extinguished their land rights. Congress also bargained with white squatters—"white savages," John Jay called them—who had illegally settled on unoccupied land, allowing them to stay only if they paid for the property. Given the natural barrier of the Appalachian Mountains, many members of Congress also feared that an uncontrolled surge of settlers into the West might result in the creation of separate republics. Such governments might then ally themselves with Spain in order to export their crops via the Mississippi River and Spanish-controlled Louisiana. The danger was real: in 1784 settlers in what is now eastern Tennessee organized the new state of Franklin and the worry about Spanish influence increased. To preserve its authority over the West, Congress refused to recognize Franklin or consider its application to join the Confederation. Instead, the delegates directed the states of Virginia, North Carolina, and Georgia to administer the process of creating new states south of the Ohio River, a decision that indirectly encouraged the expansion of slavery into that vast region.

To the north of the Ohio River, Congress established the Northwest Territory and issued three ordinances affecting the settlement and administration of western lands. The Ordinance of 1784, written by Thomas Jefferson, called for the admission of states as soon as the population of a territory equaled that of the smallest existing state. To deter squatters the Land Ordinance of 1785

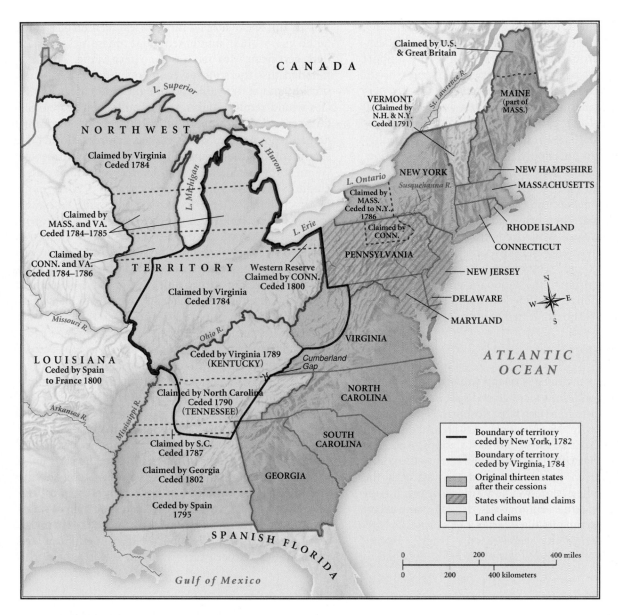

MAP 7.1 The Confederation and Western Land Claims

The Confederation Congress resolved the conflicting land claims of the states by creating a "national domain" west of the Appalachian Mountains. Between 1781 and 1802 all of the seaboard states with western land claims ceded them to the national government. In the Northwest Ordinances, the Confederation Congress laid out rules for establishing territories with democratic political institutions in this domain and declared that all territories were open to settlement by citizens from all the states.

For more help analyzing this map, see the ONLINE STUDY GUIDE at
bedfordstmartins.com/henretta.

required that the lands be surveyed before settlement and mandated a grid surveying system that would allow the work to be done quickly (although without attention to the contours and characteristics of the environment). The ordinance also specified a minimum price of $1 per acre and required that 50 percent of the townships be sold in single blocks of 23,040 acres each, which only large-scale investors and speculators could afford, and the rest in parcels of 640 acres each, which only well-to-do farmers could manage to buy (see Map 8.3).

Finally, the Northwest Ordinance of 1787 provided for the creation of three to five territories that would eventually become the states of Ohio, Indiana, Illinois, Michigan, and Wisconsin. Reflecting the Enlightenment social philosophy of Jefferson and other Patriots, the ordinance prohibited slavery in those territories and earmarked funds from the sale of some land for the support of schools. It also specified that initially Congress should appoint a governor and judges to administer a new territory. Once the number of free adult men reached 5,000 settlers could elect their own legislature. When the population grew to 60,000 residents could write a republican constitution and apply to join the Confederation. On admission a new state would enjoy all the rights and privileges of the existing states.

The ordinances of the 1780s were a great and enduring achievement. They provided for the orderly settlement of the West while reducing the prospect of secessionist movements and preventing the emergence of dependent "colonies." The ordinances also added a new "western" dimension to the national identity. The United States was no longer confined to thirteen governments on the eastern seaboard. It had space to expand.

Shays's Rebellion

However bright the futures of the western states, in the East postwar conditions were grim. Peace had brought a recession rather than a return to prosperity. The war had destroyed many American merchant ships and disrupted the export of tobacco and other farm goods. And now the British Navigation Acts, which had nurtured colonial commerce, barred Americans from trading with the British West Indies. Moreover, low-priced British manufactures flooded American markets, driving many urban artisans and wartime textile firms out of business.

State governments were equally fragile, having emerged from the war with large debts that now had to be paid off. Speculators—mostly wealthy merchants and landowners—had purchased huge quantities of state debt certificates for far less than face value. They demanded that the state governments redeem the bonds quickly, and at full value, despite the fact that such policies would require high taxes. Simultaneously, yeomen farmers and artisans, hard hit by the postwar recession, demanded tax relief. Most state legislatures followed the sentiments of the farmer-majority. To assist indebted yeomen, they enacted laws allowing debtors to pay their creditors in installments. Other states printed more paper currency in an effort to extend credit. Although wealthy men deplored these actions as destructive of "the just rights of creditors," these stopgap measures probably prevented a major social upheaval.

In Massachusetts the lack of debtor-relief legislation provoked the first armed uprising in the new nation. Merchants and creditors had persuaded the Massachusetts legislature to impose taxes to repay the state's war debt and not to issue more paper currency. When cash-strapped farmers could not pay their private debts, creditors threatened them with court suits and high legal fees. Debtor Ephraim Wetmore heard that merchant Stephan Salisbury threatened that he "would have my Body Dead or Alive in case I did not pay." In 1786 residents of central and western counties called extralegal meetings not only to protest the taxes and property seizures but also to demand abolition of imprisonment for debt, property qualifications for officeholding, and the upper house of the state legislature. To back up these radical political demands, bands of angry farmers—including men of status and substance—closed the courts by force. "[I] had no Intensions to Destroy the Publick Government," declared Captain Adam Wheeler, a former town selectman; rather,

History and Memory: Shays's Rebellion

Unlike the North Carolina Regulators (see the illustration on p. 130), the debt-ridden farmers who joined Daniel Shays have not won a place in the pantheon of American heroes. Only a worn, tilting stone hidden away at the side of a field marks the final battle of their struggle against creditor lawsuits, high taxes, and an unresponsive state government. While some Americans have viewed the Shaysites as fighters for freedom, many more have seen them as dangerous political radicals. As Sam Adams, a onetime Patriot radical put it, "The man who dares to rebel against the laws of a republic ought to suffer death." To escape the gallows, Shays fled to New York State, where he died in 1821, still a poor farmer.

Jim Abell, National Geographic Image Collection.

he had rioted to prevent "Valuable and Industrious members of Society [being] dragged from their families to prison [because of their debts], to the great damage . . . [of] the Community at large." The resistance gradually grew into a full-scale revolt led by Captain Daniel Shays, a former Continental army officer who had received a sword for gallant service during the war.

As a struggle against taxes imposed by the distant state government in Boston, Shays's Rebellion resembled colonial resistance to the British Stamp Act. To drive home that point, members of Shays's army placed twigs from pine trees in their hats, just as the Continental army had done. "The people have turned against their teachers the doctrines which were inculcated to effect the late revolution," complained the conservative Massachusetts political leader Fisher Ames. But even the Radical Patriots of 1776 condemned the Shaysites as antirepublican. "Those Men, who . . . would lessen the Weight of Government lawfully exercised must be Enemies to our happy Revolution and Common Liberty," charged onetime revolutionary Samuel Adams. To preserve its authority the Massachusetts legislature passed a Riot Act outlawing illegal assemblies. Governor James Bowdoin, supported by eastern merchants, equipped a formidable fighting force to put down the rebellion and called for additional troops from the Continental Congress. But Shays's army dwindled during the winter of 1786–87, falling victim to freezing weather and inadequate supplies, and Bowdoin's military force easily dispersed the rebels.

The collapsed rebellion provided graphic proof that the costs of war and the fruits of independence were not being shared evenly. Many middling families who had suffered while supporting the struggle for independence felt they had exchanged one tyranny for another. Angry Massachusetts voters turned Governor Bowdoin out of office, and debt-ridden farmers in New York, northern Pennsylvania, Connecticut, and New Hampshire closed courthouses, demanding economic relief. As British officials in Canada predicted the imminent demise of the United States, many Americans feared for the fate of their republican experiment. At this dire moment nationalists redoubled their efforts to create a central government equal to the challenges facing the new republic. Events in Massachusetts, declared Henry Knox, formed "the strongest arguments possible" for the creation of "a strong general government."

The Constitution of 1787

From the moment of its creation, the Constitution was a controversial document, praised by advocates as a solution to the nation's economic woes and condemned by critics as a perversion of republicanism. Simply put, the issue was whether the institutions of self-government were suited only to relatively small states or could be extended across a vast nation. This debate, begun in 1787, would not be finally resolved until the Civil War.

The Rise of a Nationalist Faction

Money questions—debts, taxes, and tariffs—dominated the postwar political agenda, and men who had served the Confederation government during the war as military officers, diplomats, and officials looked at them from a "national" rather than a "state" perspective. National leaders such as General Washington, financier Robert Morris, and diplomats Benjamin Franklin, John Jay, and John Adams became advocates of a stronger central government with the power to control foreign commerce and impose tariffs. They knew that without tariff revenue Congress would be unable to pay the interest on the foreign debt and the nation's credit would collapse. However, key commercial states in the North— New York, Massachusetts, Pennsylvania—resisted national tariffs because they already had trade policies that subsidized local merchants and imposed state taxes on imported goods. Most southern planters also opposed tariffs because they were eager to import British textiles and ironware at the lowest possible prices.

However, some southern planters took a strong nationalist stance because they were deeply worried about the financial policies of the state governments. Legislatures in Virginia and other southern states had responded to the economic hard times of the 1780s by lowering taxes and granting tax relief to various groups of citizens. Such measures troubled wealthy creditors because they diminished public revenue and delayed the redemption of state debts. Taxpayers were being led to believe they would "never be compelled to pay" the public debt, lamented Charles Lee of Virginia, a wealthy bondholder. Private creditors had similar complaints against debtors who persuaded state governments to enact laws that stayed (delayed) the payment of debts. "While men are madly accumulating enormous debts, their legislators are making provisions for their nonpayment," a South Carolina creditor complained. To these nationalists, the democratic majorities in the state legislatures constituted a grave threat to republican government.

In 1786 nationalists took an important initiative when James Madison persuaded the Virginia legislature to ask states to attend a special commercial convention to discuss tariff and taxation policies. Only five state governments responded, sending twelve delegates to a meeting in Annapolis, Maryland; undeterred by their small numbers, the delegates called for another meeting in Philadelphia to undertake an even broader review of the Confederation government. Spurred on by Shays's

Rebellion, nationalists in Congress secured a resolution supporting the Philadelphia convention and calling for a revision of the Articles of Confederation "adequate to the exigencies of government and the preservation of the Union." "Nothing but the adoption of some efficient plan from the Convention," a fellow nationalist wrote to James Madison, "can prevent anarchy first & civil convulsions afterwards."

The Philadelphia Convention

In May 1787 fifty-five delegates arrived in Philadelphia, representing every state except Rhode Island, whose legislature opposed any increase in central authority. Some delegates, such as Benjamin Franklin of Pennsylvania, had been early leaders of the independence movement. Others, including George Washington and Robert Morris, had become prominent during the war. Several famous Patriots missed the convention. John Adams and Thomas Jefferson were in Europe, serving as the American ministers to Britain and France, respectively. The radical Samuel Adams had not been chosen as a delegate by the Massachusetts legislature, while the firebrand Patrick Henry refused to attend because he favored a strictly limited national government and "smelt a rat." Their places were taken by capable young nationalists such as James Madison and Alexander Hamilton; both believed that the decisions of the convention would "decide for ever the fate of Republican Government."

Most delegates to the Philadelphia convention were men of property: merchants, slaveholding planters, or "monied men." There were no artisans, backcountry settlers, or tenants and only a single yeoman farmer. Consequently, most delegates supported the property rights of creditors. The majority also favored a stronger central government that would protect the republic from "the imprudence of democracy," as Hamilton put it.

The Virginia and New Jersey Plans.   The delegates elected Washington as the presiding officer and, to forestall popular opposition, decided to deliberate behind closed doors (in fact, Americans learned of the proceedings only in the 1840s, when Madison's notebooks were published). They agreed that each state would have one vote, as in the Confederation, and that a majority of states would decide an issue. Then the delegates exceeded their mandate to revise the Articles of Confederation and considered the Virginia Plan, a scheme for a truly national government devised by James Madison. Madison had arrived in Philadelphia determined to fashion a new political order run by men of high character. A graduate of Princeton, he had read classical and modern political theory and served in both the Confederation Congress and the Virginia assembly. Once an optimistic Patriot and republican, Madison had grown increasingly pessimistic. His experience in the

Virginia legislature had convinced him of the "narrow ambition" and lack of public virtue of many state political leaders. He wanted to design a national government that would inhibit petty factional disputes, what he called the "Vices of the Political System."

Madison's Virginia Plan differed from the Articles of Confederation in three crucial respects. First, it rejected state sovereignty in favor of the "supremacy of national authority." The central government would have the power not only to "legislate in all cases to which the separate States are incompetent" but also to overturn state laws. Second, the plan called for a national republic that drew its authority directly from all the people and had direct power over them. As Madison explained, the new central government would bypass the states, operating directly "on the individuals composing them." Third, the plan created a three-tier national government with a lower house elected by voters, an upper house elected by the lower house, and an executive and judiciary chosen by the entire legislature.

From a political perspective Madison's plan had two fatal flaws. First, state politicians and many ordinary citizens would strongly oppose the provision allowing the national government to veto laws enacted by state legislatures. Second, by assigning great power to the lower house, whose composition was based on population, Madison's plan would increase the influence of voters who lived in the large states. Consequently, delegates from the less populous states rejected the plan out of hand, fearing, as a Delaware delegate put it, that the states with many inhabitants would "crush the small ones whenever they stand in the way of their ambitious or interested views."

Delegates from the smaller states rallied behind a plan devised by William Paterson, a delegate from New Jersey. The New Jersey Plan, as it came to be called, strengthened the Confederation by giving the central government the power to raise revenue, control commerce, and make binding requisitions on the states. But it preserved the states' control over their own laws and guaranteed their equality: each state would have one vote in a unicameral legislature, as in the Confederation. Delegates from the populous states rejected this provision of Paterson's plan and, after a month of debate, mustered a bare majority in favor of the principles of the Virginia Plan.

This decision raised the prospect of a dramatically new constitutional system and prompted two New York representatives—Robert Yates and John Lansing—to accuse the delegates of exceeding their mandate and to leave the convention (see American Voices, "Robert Yates and John Lansing: A Protest against the Philadelphia Convention," p. 203). During the hot, humid summer of 1787 the remaining delegates met six days a week, debating high principles and discussing a multitude of technical details. Experienced and realistic

Robert Yates and John Lansing

A Protest against the Philadelphia Convention

Robert Yates and John Lansing attended the Philadelphia convention as delegates from New York but left in protest when the Virginia Plan became the basis for a new constitutional order. In a letter to the governor of New York, Yates and Lansing explained their reasons: the convention lacked the authority to create the "consolidated" government implicit in the Virginia Plan, and a centralized system of rule would undermine civil liberties and republican principles of representative government. These Antifederalist arguments failed to prevent ratification of the Constitution, but they remained powerful and were restated by hundreds of American politicians—from the North as well as the South—for the next seventy years and beyond.

We beg leave, briefly, to state some cogent reasons, which, among others, influenced us to decide against a consolidation of the states. . . .

Our powers were explicit, and confined to the sole and express purpose of revising the Articles of Confederation. . . . [We believed] that a system of consolidated government could not, in the remotest degree, have been in contemplation of the legislature of this state; for that so important a trust, as adopting measures which tended to deprive the state government of its most essential rights of sovereignty, could not have been confided by implication. . . .

Reasoning in this manner, we were of opinion that the leading feature of every amendment ought to be the preservation of the individual states in their uncontrolled constitutional rights, and that, in reserving these, a mode might have been devised of granting to the Confederacy, the moneys arising from a general system of revenue, the power of regulating commerce and enforcing the observance of foreign treaties, and other necessary matters of less moment.

[We also] entertained an opinion that a general government, however guarded by declarations of rights, or cautionary provisions, must unavoidably, in a short time, be productive of the destruction of the civil liberty of such citizens who could be coerced by it, by reason of the extensive territory of the United States, the dispersed situation of its inhabitants, and the insuperable difficulty of controlling or counteracting the views of a set of men (however unconstitutional and oppressive their acts might be) possessed of all the power of government, and who [were remote] . . . from their constituents. . . . [Moreover, we believed] that however wise and energetic the principles of the general government might be, the extremities of the United States could not be kept in due submission and obedience to its laws, at the distance of so many hundred miles from the seat of government;

[And finally] that, if the general legislature was composed of so numerous a body of men as to represent the interests of all the inhabitants of the United States, in the usual and true ideas of representation, the expense of supporting it would become intolerably burdensome; and that, if a few only were vested with a power of legislation, the interests of a great majority of the inhabitants of the United States must necessarily be unknown. . . . These reasons were, in our opinion, conclusive against any system of consolidated government.

Source: J. Elliot, ed., *Debates in the Several State Conventions on the Adoption of the Constitution* (New York, 1861), 1: 480–83.

politicians, they knew that their final plan had to be acceptable to existing political interests and powerful social groups. Pierce Butler of South Carolina invoked a classical Greek precedent: "We must follow the example of Solon, who gave the Athenians not the best government he could devise but the best they would receive."

The Great Compromise. Representation remained the central problem. To satisfy both large and small states the Connecticut delegates suggested amending the Virginia Plan so that the upper house, the Senate, would always have two members from each state, while seats in the lower chamber, the House of Representatives, would be apportioned on the basis of population. In addition, the size of the states' delegations would be altered every ten years on the basis of a national census. After bitter debate, this "Great Compromise" was accepted, but only reluctantly; to some delegates from populous states it seemed less a compromise than a victory for the smaller states.

Other issues that would directly affect the interests of the existing states were quickly settled by restricting (or leaving ambiguous) the extent of central authority. Some delegates opposed establishing national courts within the states, warning that "the states will revolt at such encroachments." The convention therefore defined the judicial power of the United States in broad terms, vesting it "in one supreme Court" and leaving the new national legislature to decide whether to establish lower courts within the states. The convention also decided against requiring voters in national elections to own a certain amount of land. "Eight or nine states have extended the right of **suffrage** beyond the freeholders [landowners]," George Mason of Virginia pointed out. "What will people there say if they should be disfranchised?" The convention also curried favor with the existing state governments by placing the selection of the president in an **electoral college** chosen on a state-by-state basis and specifying that state legislatures, not the voters at large, would elect members of the U.S. Senate. By giving states an important role in the new constitutional system, the delegates encouraged their citizens to accept a reduction in state sovereignty.

Slavery hovered in the background of the delegates' debates, rarely discussed but always a factor. When the issue came to the fore, speakers divided along regional lines. Speaking for many northerners Gouverneur Morris of New York condemned slavery as "a nefarious institution" and hoped for its eventual demise (see American Lives, "Gouverneur Morris: An Elitist Liberal in a Republican Age," p. 206). Reflecting the outlook of many Chesapeake planters, who wanted to retain the institution but already owned ample numbers of slaves, George Mason of Virginia advocated an end to the Atlantic slave trade. However, delegates from the rice-growing states of South Carolina and Georgia insisted that slave imports must continue, warning that otherwise their states "shall not be parties to the Union." At their insistence the delegates denied Congress the power to regulate slave imports for twenty years; thereafter the slave trade could be abolished by legislative action (which Congress proceeded to do in 1808).

For the sake of national unity, the delegates likewise treated other slavery-related issues as political rather than moral questions. To protect the property of southern slave owners, they agreed to a "fugitive" clause that allowed masters to reclaim enslaved blacks (or white indentured servants) who took refuge in other states. To mollify the northern states the delegates did not mention slavery explicitly in the Constitution (referring instead to citizens and "all other Persons"), thus denying the institution national legal status. They also refused southern demands to count slaves and citizens equally in determining states' representation in Congress, accepting a compromise proposal in which a slave would be counted as three-fifths of a free person for purposes of representation and taxation.

National Power. Having allayed the concerns of small states and slave states, the delegates proceeded to create a powerful national government that favored the interests of creditors over those of debtors. The finished document declared that the Constitution and all national legislation and treaties made under its authority would be the "supreme" law of the land. It gave the national government broad powers over taxation, military defense, and external commerce as well as the authority to make all laws "necessary and proper" to implement those and other provisions. To protect creditors and establish the fiscal integrity of the new government, the Constitution mandated that the United States honor the existing national debt. Finally, it restricted the ability of state governments to assist debtors by forbidding the states to issue money or enact "any Law impairing the Obligation of Contracts."

The proposed Constitution was not a "perfect production," Benjamin Franklin admitted on September 17, 1787, as he urged the forty-one delegates still present to sign it. Yet the great diplomat confessed his astonishment at finding "this system approaching so near to perfection as it does." His colleagues apparently agreed; all but three signed the document.

The People Debate Ratification

The procedures for ratifying the new Constitution were as controversial as its political proposals. The delegates hesitated to submit the Constitution to the state legislatures for their unanimous consent, as required by the Articles of Confederation, because they knew that Rhode Island (and perhaps a few other states) would reject it. So they specified that the Constitution would go into effect on ratification by special conventions in at least nine of the thirteen states. Because of its nationalist sympathies the Confederation Congress winked at this extralegal procedure; surprisingly, so too did most state legislatures, which promptly called the ratification conventions.

As a great national debate began, the nationalists seized the initiative with two bold moves. First, they called themselves Federalists, a term that suggested a loose, decentralized system of government and partially obscured their quest for a strong central authority. Second, they launched a coordinated political campaign, publishing dozens of pamphlets and newspaper articles supporting the proposed Constitution.

The Antifederalists. The opponents of the Constitution, who became known as Antifederalists, had diverse backgrounds and motives. Some, like

Governor George Clinton of New York, feared losing their power at the state level. Others were rural democrats who predicted that a powerful central government controlled by merchants and creditors would produce a new aristocracy. "These lawyers and men of learning and monied men expect to be managers of this Constitution," worried a Massachusetts farmer, "and get all the power and all the money into their own hands and then they will swallow up all of us little folks . . . just as the whale swallowed up Jonah." Melancton Smith of New York warned that the large electoral districts prescribed by the Constitution would encourage the election of a few wealthy upper-class men, whereas the smaller state districts produced "a representative body, composed principally of respectable yeomanry." Smith and other Antifederalists pointed out that the Constitution, unlike most state constitutions, lacked a declaration of individual rights.

Well-educated Americans with a traditional republican outlook also opposed the new system. To keep government "close to the people," they wanted the nation to remain a collection of small sovereign republics tied together only for trade and defense—not the "United States" but the "States United." Citing the French political philosopher Montesquieu, Antifederalists argued that republican institutions were best suited to cities or small states—a localist outlook that shaped American political thinking well into the twentieth century. "No extensive empire can be governed on republican principles," James Winthrop of Massachusetts declared. Patrick Henry predicted the Constitution would re-create the worst features of British rule: high taxes, an oppressive bureaucracy, a standing army, and a "great and mighty President . . . supported in extravagant munificence."

In New York, where ratification was hotly contested, James Madison, John Jay, and Alexander Hamilton countered these arguments in a series of eighty-five essays collectively called *The Federalist*. Although not widely read at the time outside of New York City (as only a few of the essays were reprinted in newspapers elsewhere), *The Federalist* was subsequently recognized as a classic work of republican political theory. Its authors stressed the need for a strong government to conduct foreign affairs and denied that it would foster domestic tyranny. Citing Montesquieu's praise for mixed government (and drawing on John Adams's *Thoughts on Government*), Madison, Jay, and Hamilton pointed out that national authority would be divided among a president, a bicameral legislature, and a judiciary. Each branch of government would check and balance the others, thus preserving liberty.

Indeed, in *The Federalist*, No. 10, Madison made a significant contribution to the theory of republicanism by denying it was suited only to small states. It was "sown in the nature of man," Madison wrote, that individuals would seek power and form factions to advance their interests. Indeed, "a landed interest, a manufacturing interest, a mercantile interest, a moneyed interest, with many lesser interests, grow up of necessity in civilized nations." He argued that a free society should not suppress those groups but simply prevent any one of them from becoming dominant—an end best achieved in a large republic. "Extend the sphere," Madison concluded, "and you take in a greater variety of parties and interests; you make it less probable that a majority of the whole will have a common motive to invade the rights of other citizens."

The Ratification Conventions. The delegates who met at the state ratifying conventions between December 1787 and June 1788 represented a wide spectrum of Americans, from untutored farmers and middling artisans to well-educated gentlemen. Generally, delegates from the backcountry were Antifederalists, whereas those from the seacoast were Federalists. Thus, a coalition of merchants, artisans, and commercial farmers from Philadelphia and its vicinity spearheaded an easy Federalist victory in Pennsylvania. Other early Federalist successes came in the less populous states of Delaware, New Jersey, Georgia, and Connecticut, where delegates counted on a strong national government to offset the power of their larger neighbors.

The Constitution's first real test came in January 1788 in Massachusetts, one of the most populous states and a hotbed of Antifederalist sentiment (Map 7.2). Influential Patriots, including Samuel Adams and Governor John Hancock, opposed the new constitution, as did Shaysite sympathizers in the western part of the state. But Boston artisans, who wanted tariff protection from British imports, supported ratification. Astute Federalist politicians finally persuaded wavering delegates by promising that the new government would consider a national guarantee of individual rights. By a close vote of 187 to 168, the Federalists carried the day.

Spring brought new Federalist victories in Maryland and South Carolina. When New Hampshire ratified by the narrow margin of 57 to 47 in June, the required nine states had approved the Constitution. Still, the essential states of Virginia and New York had not yet acted. Writing in *The Federalist*, Madison, Jay, and Hamilton used their superb rhetorical skills to win support in those states. Addressing a powerful Antifederalist argument, leading Federalists reiterated their promise to amend the Constitution with a bill of rights. In the end the Federalists won narrowly in Virginia, 89 to 79, and that success carried them to victory in New York by the even smaller margin of 30 to 27. Suspicious of centralized power, the yeomen of North Carolina and Rhode Island ratified only in 1789 and 1790, respectively.

Ratification of the Constitution brought an end to the Antifederalist agitation and marked a temporary

Gouverneur Morris: An Elitist Liberal in a Republican Age

The life of Gouverneur Morris (1752–1814) reveals the personal and ideological complexity of the American Revolution. Morris was born into the comfortable world of the New York aristocracy and quickly imbibed its values. Even as a young man he understood the dangers to his class posed by a "democratic" revolution supported by social nobodies such as George Robert Twelves Hewes (see Chapter 5, American Lives, p. 154). Responding to agitation for independence in 1774, Morris advised New York's political elite "to seek for reunion with the parent state." Otherwise, "I see, and I see it with fear and trembling, that . . . we shall be under the worst of all possible dominions . . . the domination of a riotous mob." "The mob begin to think and reason," he warned again in 1775, and soon "they will bite, depend on it."

His family situation had a lot to do with Morris's fear and disdain of ordinary men and women. His grandfather Lewis Morris was the first lord of Morrisania, a large estate in Westchester County, New York, and the king's governor of New Jersey. His father, Lewis Jr., was also a royal official, a judge of the vice-admiralty court, who vowed on his deathbed that Gouverneur should have "the best Education that is to be had in Europe or America." In fact, education was a consolation prize, provided to younger sons who had no prospects of a valuable landed inheritance. So Gouverneur studied at King's College in New York and then took up an apprenticeship with William Smith Jr., an eminent New York lawyer. Socially privileged yet economically deprived, Morris feared downward mobility and hurled abuse on his social inferiors.

The sharpening struggle with Britain forced Gouverneur Morris to make a fateful decision. Breaking with his mother, many relatives, and his legal mentor, all of whom remained loyal to the crown, Morris became a Patriot—of the most conservative stripe. At the Provincial Convention that drafted the New York State constitution of 1777, Morris argued strenuously for maintaining the old aristocratic method of voting by public declaration, but more republican-minded members mandated voting by ballot. Still, the convention heeded Morris's call to impose high property qualifications for voting: a freehold worth £20 to vote for the assembly and one valued at £100 to vote for the senate or governor.

Morris was equally conservative—but much more innovative—in Patriot politics at the national level. As one of New York's delegates to the Continental Congress, Morris worked hard to remedy the financial weaknesses of the Confederation. As early as 1778 Morris proposed the elimination of state currencies, the creation of a national domain in the West, and national tariffs to pay off the growing war debt. Three years later he happily enlisted as the assistant to the new superintendent of finance, the merchant Robert Morris. Together the Morrises (who were not related) devised measures to restore the government's credit. In 1781 they won approval for the Bank of North America and then issued a "Report on Public Credit" that called for the Confederation government to assume the entire national debt, issue new interest-bearing debt certificates, and impose tariffs and internal taxes to pay the interest costs. Here in outline was the fiscal program implemented a decade later by Alexander Hamilton.

Like Hamilton, Gouverneur Morris was a man of "spirit and nerve" who never doubted his own judgment and rarely respected that of others. George Washington chastised Morris for displaying his "brilliant imagination" too quickly and recklessly. Never humbled, not even by an accident in 1780 that left him with a wooden leg, Morris used his personal charm and intellectual brilliance to compensate for these flaws in his character. He played a prominent role at the Philadelphia convention in 1787, insisting that "property was the sole or primary object of Government & Society." To protect property rights, Morris demanded an elitist Senate whose members would serve for life, a national freehold property qualification for voting, and a strong president with the power of the veto.

Nevertheless, Morris rejected the legitimacy of two traditional types of property rights—the feudal dues paid by tenants to landowners and the ownership of slaves. In debates over the New York constitution Morris called for the end of "domestic slavery . . . so that in future ages, every human being who breathes the air of the State, shall enjoy the privileges of a freeman," a proposition he reiterated with great force at the Philadelphia convention.

Morris's defense of freedom for individuals—in their personal lives, their property rights, and their ability to form legal contracts—aligned him with those Patriots who gave a "classical liberal" definition to the American Revolution (rather than the Patriots who gave greater weight to "classical republican" values of public virtue and the public good). Valuing individual liberty more highly than majority rule, liberal Patriots such as Morris hoped the new Constitution would protect property rights from popularly elected state legislatures and encourage economic growth.

Indeed, Morris's outlook—and increasingly his life—reflected the emergent principles of a free-market capitalism. After serving as Robert Morris's assistant, Gouverneur became his business partner. The two men invested jointly in land in New York and Pennsylvania, a maritime venture in Massachusetts, and the sale of tobacco to the French tobacco monopoly. Such speculations landed Robert Morris in debtors' prison but made Gouverneur Morris a rich man, able at last to live in the elegant style to which he had been bred.

Beginning in 1788, Morris resided in Europe for ten years, first as a speculating merchant, then as the American minister to France (1792–1794), and finally as a cultured man of independent wealth. Fluent in French, polished in manners, confident of his talents, Morris fit easily into Parisian high society. He took as his mistress the young wife of an aging aristocrat, formed a lifelong friendship with the formidable Madame de Staël (a leading figure in Paris society), and came to share the hopes and fears of the endangered French monarch and his aristocratic supporters. While disparaging the French nobility for "Hugging the Privileges of Centuries long elapsed," Morris refused to support the constitutional monarchy proposed by the Marquis de Lafayette and other republican-minded French reformers. Indeed, as republicans seized control of France in 1792, Morris joined an unsuccessful aristocratic plot to smuggle King Louis XVI out of Paris.

In the end Gouverneur Morris stands forth as an elitist classical liberal, an American precursor of Alexis de Tocqueville (see Chapter 8, Voices from Abroad, p. 247). Patrician in manners and fearful of mob rule, Morris was a political conservative, "opposed to the Democracy from Regard to Liberty." More egalitarian in his economic views, he celebrated the classical liberal principles of personal freedom, entrepreneurial enterprise, and equal opportunity.

Gouverneur Morris, Federalist Statesman
Morris almost became a Loyalist because he was a snob who liked privilege and feared the people. ("The mob begins to think and reason," he once noted with disdain.) He became a Federalist for similar reasons, helping to write the Philadelphia Constitution and, after 1793, strongly supporting the Federalist Party.
National Portrait Gallery, Smithsonian Institution / Art Resource, NY.

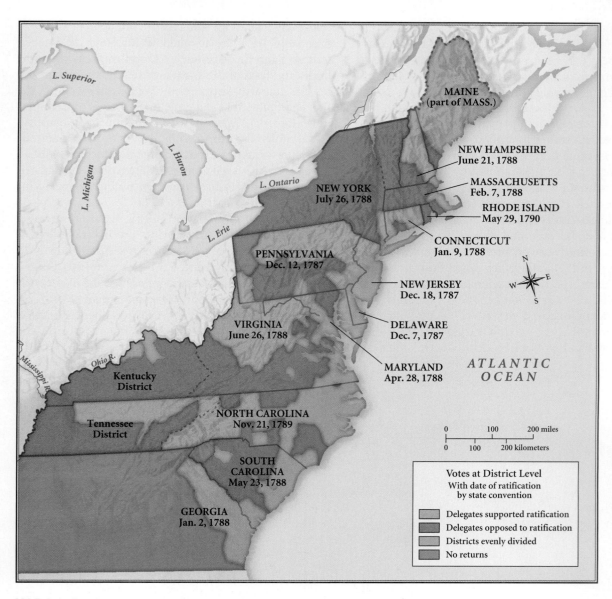

MAP 7.2 Ratifying the Constitution of 1787

In 1907 the geographer Owen Libby mapped the votes of members of the state ratification conventions. His map shows that most delegates from seaboard or commercial farming districts favored the Constitution, while those from backcountry areas opposed it. Subsequent research has confirmed Libby's socioeconomic interpretation in North and South Carolina and Massachusetts; however, other factors influenced delegates in some states with frontier districts, such as Georgia, where the Constitution was ratified unanimously.

decline in ascendancy of the democratically inclined state legislatures. "A decided majority" of the New Hampshire General Assembly had long opposed the "new system" of centralized authority, reported Joshua Atherton, but had now bowed to the inevitable, saying, "It is adopted, let us try it." In Virginia, Antifederalist firebrand Patrick Henry likewise vowed to "submit as a quiet citizen" and fight for amendments "in a constitutional way."

Working against great odds the Federalists had created a national republic that restored the political authority of established leaders. To celebrate their victory Federalists organized great processions in the seaport cities. By marching in an orderly fashion—in a conscious effort to contrast themselves to the riotous Revolutionary mobs—Federalist-minded citizens affirmed their commitment to a self-governing republican community based on law. Floats carried a copy of the Constitution on an "altar of liberty," using sacred symbols to endow the new national regime with moral legitimacy and lay the foundations for a secular "civil religion."

The Federalists Implement the Constitution

The Constitution expanded the dimensions of American political life, allowing voters to fill national as well as local and state offices. The Federalists swept the election of 1788, placing forty-four supporters in the first Congress; only eight Antifederalists won election. As expected, members of the electoral college chose George Washington as president. John Adams received the second highest number of electoral votes and became vice president. The two men took up their posts in New York City, the temporary home of the national government.

Devising the New Government. Washington, the military savior of his country, became its political father as well. At fifty-seven he was a man of great personal dignity and influence. Instinctively cautious, he generally followed the administrative practices of the Confederation, asking Congress to reestablish the existing executive departments: Foreign Affairs (State), Finance (Treasury), and War. However, he made one important innovation. The Constitution gave the president the power to appoint major officials with the consent of the Senate, but Washington insisted that only he—and not the Senate—could remove them, thus ensuring the chief executive's control over the bureaucracy. To head the Department of State Washington chose Thomas Jefferson, a fellow Virginian and an experienced diplomat. For secretary of the treasury he turned to Alexander Hamilton, a lawyer and wartime military aide. The new president designated Jefferson, Hamilton, and Secretary of War Henry Knox as his **cabinet**, or advisory body.

The Constitution had created a Supreme Court but left the establishment of the court system to Congress. Because the Federalists wanted national institutions to act directly on individual citizens within the various states, they enacted a far-reaching Judiciary Act in 1789. The act created a hierarchical federal court system with thirteen district courts, one for each state, and three circuit courts to hear appeals from the districts, with the Supreme Court having the final say. Moreover, the Judiciary Act permitted appeals to the Supreme Court of federal legal issues that arose in state-run courts, ensuring that national (and not state) judges would decide the meaning of the Constitution.

The Bill of Rights. The Federalists kept their promise to add a declaration of rights to the Constitution. Drawing on proposed lists of rights submitted by the states' ratifying conventions, James Madison, who had been elected to the House of Representatives, submitted nineteen amendments to the first Congress, and ten of them were approved by that Congress and ratified by the

The First "White House"

In 1790 New York City became the home of the new national government. To keep the capital at New York, the city began to build an imposing mansion for the president. To symbolize the nation's commitment to republicanism, the architects gave the residence a classical columned facade like those of the Roman Republic, creating a sharp contrast with nearby Dutch-influenced buildings. Shortly before the completion of the mansion, the national government moved to the District of Columbia, a federal territory created by cessions from Maryland and Virginia. New-York Historical Society.

states in 1791. These ten amendments, which became known as the Bill of Rights, safeguarded certain fundamental personal rights, such as freedom of speech and religion, and mandated certain legal procedures that protected the individual, such as trial by jury. The Second Amendment gave the people the right to bear arms so that they might serve in the militia and defend their liberties, while the Tenth Amendment limited the authority of the national government by reserving powers not otherwise addressed to the states or the people.

As a safeguard against improper governmental authority, the amendments have had a complex history. Like all constitutional clauses and ordinary laws, they are subject to judicial interpretation, which has changed with time and circumstance. For example, the Second Amendment, which gives the people the right "to keep and bear Arms," has been interpreted by most twentieth-century courts to allow the states and Congress to forbid citizens from owning certain types of guns (such as automatic weapons) and to require the registration of others (such as handguns in cities). Moreover, in 1833 the Supreme Court (in the important case of *Barron v. Baltimore*) declared that the amendments safeguarded rights only from infringement by the national government; for protection from state authorities, citizens would have to rely on the state constitutions. But nearly a century later, in the 1920s, federal courts began to enforce the Fourteenth Amendment (1868), which prohibited the states from depriving "any person of life, liberty, or property, without due process of law," against state and local governments.

Whatever their ultimate fate, the amendments addressed Antifederalists' concerns, securing the legitimacy of the new government and ensuring broad political support for the Constitution.

The Political Crisis of the 1790s

The final decade of the century brought fresh political challenges. The Federalists divided into two irreconcilable factions over financial policy, and the ideological impact of the French Revolution widened this split. In the course of these struggles Alexander Hamilton and Thomas Jefferson offered contrasting ideological visions of the American future.

Hamilton's Financial Program

One of George Washington's most important decisions was his choice of Alexander Hamilton as secretary of the treasury. An ambitious self-made man of great charm and intelligence, Hamilton had served as Washington's personal aide during the war. He married into the rich and influential Schuyler family of Hudson River landowners and during the 1780s became a leading lawyer in New York City. At the Philadelphia convention Hamilton condemned the "amazing violence and turbulence of the democratic spirit," calling for an authoritarian government headed by a president with nearly monarchical powers.

As treasury secretary Hamilton devised bold policies to enhance the authority of the national government and favor wealthy financiers and seaport merchants (Figure 7.2). He outlined his plans in three path-breaking and interrelated reports to Congress: on public credit (January 1790), a national bank (December 1790), and manufactures (December 1791).

Public Credit.   The financial and social implications of Hamilton's "Report on the Public Credit" made it instantly controversial. The report called for Congress to buy ("redeem") at face value the millions of dollars in securities issued by the Confederation, a plan that would bolster the government's credit but also provide windfall profits to speculators. For example, the Massachusetts merchant firm of Burrell & Burrell had paid about $600 for Confederation notes with a face value of $2,500; their redemption at full value would bring the firm an enormous profit of $1,900. Equally controversial, Hamilton proposed to create a permanent **national debt** to pay the Burrells and other note holders. Their Confederation notes would not be paid off in gold or silver coins but with new government-issued securities bearing the relatively high annual interest rate of 6 percent.

Hamilton's plan for a permanent national debt owned by wealthy families reawakened Radical Whig and republican fears of scheming British financiers. Speaking for the Virginia House of Burgesses Patrick Henry condemned the plan, arguing that "in an agricultural country like this, to erect, and concentrate, and perpetuate a large monied interest [must prove] . . . fatal to the existence of American liberty." Challenging the morality of Hamilton's proposal, James Madison asked Congress to assist the thousands of shopkeepers, farmers, and soldiers who had accepted Confederation securities during the dark days of the war and then been forced by hard times to sell them to speculators. Madison proposed giving the present bondholders only "the highest price which has prevailed in the market" and distributing the remaining funds to the original owners. But finding the original owners would have been difficult; moreover, nearly half the members of the House of Representatives owned Confederation securities and would personally profit from Hamilton's plan. Melding practicality with self-interest the House rejected Madison's innovative proposal. By way of protest, an angry citizen composed an ode, "On the Rejection of Mr. Madison's Motion":

> *A soldier's pay are rags and fame,*
> *A wooden leg—a deathless name.*
> *To specs, both in and out of Cong.*
> *The four and six per cents belong.*

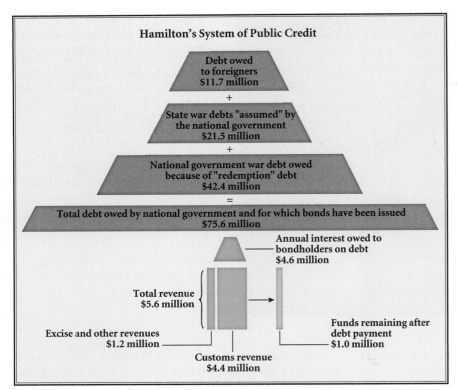

Hamilton's System of Public Credit

Debt owed
to foreigners
$11.7 million

+

State war debts "assumed" by
the national government
$21.5 million

+

National government war debt owed
because of "redemption" debt
$42.4 million

=

Total debt owed by national government and for which bonds have been issued
$75.6 million

Annual interest owed to
bondholders on debt
$4.6 million

Total revenue
$5.6 million

Excise and other revenues
$1.2 million

Customs revenue
$4.4 million

Funds remaining after
debt payment
$1.0 million

FIGURE 7.2 Hamilton's Fiscal Structure, 1792

Alexander Hamilton used the revenue from excise taxes and customs duties to defray the annual interest on the national debt. He did not pay off the debt because he wanted to tie wealthy American bondholders to the new national government.

Hamilton then advanced a second proposal that favored wealthy creditors, a plan by which the national government would take over ("assume") the war debts of the states. Rumors of this plan unleashed a flurry of speculation and some governmental corruption. Before Hamilton's announcement, Assistant Secretary of the Treasury William Duer used insider knowledge to buy up the depreciated war bonds of southern states; if Congress approved the assumption plan, Duer and his speculator associates would reap an enormous profit. Concerned members of Congress condemned such speculation and pointed out that some state legislatures had already levied high taxes to pay off their states' war debts. Responding to that argument, Hamilton modified his plan to reimburse those states. Other representatives, particularly those from Virginia and Maryland, argued that assumption would further enhance the already excessive powers of the national government. To quiet their fears about a runaway central government, the treasury chief backed their bid to locate the national capital (which the Constitution specified would consist of a special "district") along the banks of the Potomac—where they could easily watch its operations. Such astute political bargaining gave Hamilton the votes he needed in the House of Representatives to enact his assumption plan.

A National Bank. In December 1790 Hamilton issued a second report, asking Congress to charter a national financial institution, the Bank of the United States. The bank would be jointly owned by private stockholders and the national government. Hamilton argued that the bank, by making loans to merchants, handling government funds, and issuing financial notes, would provide a respected currency for the specie-starved American economy and make the new national debt easier to fund. These benefits persuaded Congress to enact Hamilton's bill and send it to the president for approval.

At this critical juncture Secretary of State Thomas Jefferson joined ranks with Madison against Hamilton. Jefferson had condemned the shady dealings in southern war bonds and the "corrupt squadron of paper dealers" who had arranged them. Now he charged that Hamilton's scheme for a national bank was unconstitutional. "The incorporation of a Bank," Jefferson told President Washington, was not a power "delegated to the United States by the Constitution." Giving a *strict* interpretation to the national charter, Jefferson maintained that the central government had only the limited powers explicitly assigned to it. In response, Hamilton articulated a *loose* interpretation, noting that Article 1, Section 8, empowered Congress to make "all Laws which shall be necessary and proper" to carry out the Constitution's provisions. Washington agreed with his treasury secretary and signed the legislation creating the bank.

Revenue and Tariffs. Hamilton turned now to the final element of his financial system: a national revenue that would be used to pay the annual interest on the permanent debt. In 1792, at Hamilton's insistence, Congress imposed a variety of domestic excise taxes, including a duty on whiskey distilled in the United States.

Two Visions of America

Thomas Jefferson and Alexander Hamilton confront each other in these portraits, as they did during the political battles of the 1790s. Jefferson was pro-French, Hamilton pro-British. Jefferson favored farmers and artisans; Hamilton supported merchants and financiers. Jefferson believed in democracy and rule by legislative majorities; Hamilton argued for a strong executive and for judicial review. But in 1800 Hamilton's timely support for Jefferson in his postelection struggle with Aaron Burr, whom Hamilton detested, secured the presidency for his longtime political foe.

Jefferson, by Rembrandt Peale, © White House Historical Association / Photo by National Geographic Society; Yale University Art Gallery, Mabel Brady Garven Collection.

But the revenue from those taxes was small, a mere $1 million a year. To raise another $4–5 million the treasury secretary proposed to raise tariffs on foreign imports. Although his "Report on Manufactures" (1791) called for a nation that was self-sufficient in manufactured goods, he did not ask Congress to impose high protective tariffs that would exclude foreign products. Such **tariffs** would inhibit foreign commerce, and so Hamilton settled for a modest increase in customs duties, a tariff that would allow trade and provide revenue for the national government.

Hamilton's carefully designed plan worked brilliantly. As American trade increased, customs revenue rose steadily (providing about 90 percent of the U.S. government's income from 1790 to 1820), allowing the treasury to pay for the redemption and **assumption** programs. In less than two years Hamilton had devised a strikingly modern fiscal system that provided the new national government with financial stability.

Jefferson's Agrarian Vision

Hamilton paid a high price for this success. By the time Washington began his second four-year term in 1793, Hamilton's financial measures had split the Federalists who wrote and ratified the Constitution into two irreconcilable factions. Most northern Federalists adhered to the political alliance led by Hamilton, and most southerners to a rival group headed by Madison and Jefferson. By the elections of 1794 the two **factions** had acquired names. Hamilton's supporters retained their original name: Federalists; Madison and Jefferson's supporters called themselves Democratic-Republicans or simply Republicans.

The southern planters and western farmers who became Republicans rejected Hamilton's economic and social philosophy. Thomas Jefferson, a man of great learning as well as an able politician and diplomat, spoke for them. Well read in architecture, natural history, scientific farming, and political theory, Jefferson embraced the optimistic spirit of the Enlightenment, declaring his belief in the "improvability of the human race." But he knew that progress was not inevitable and deplored both the long-standing speculative practices of merchants and financiers and the emerging social divisions of an urban industrial economy. Having seen the masses of propertyless laborers in the manufacturing regions in Britain, Jefferson had concluded that workers who depended on wages lacked the economic independence required to sustain a republic (see New Technology, "Machine Technology and Republican Values," p. 214).

Jefferson's vision of the American future was agrarian and democratic. Although he had grown up (and remained) a privileged slave owner, he understood the needs of yeomen farmers and other ordinary white Americans. When Jefferson drafted the Ordinance of 1784, he pictured a West settled by productive yeomen farm families. His vision took form in his *Notes on the State of Virginia* (1785): "Those who labor in the earth are the chosen people of God," he wrote. Their grain and meat would feed European nations, which "would manufacture and send us in exchange our clothes and other comforts" in an international division of labor similar to that proposed by the Scottish economist Adam Smith in *The Wealth of Nations* (1776).

Turmoil in Europe created new opportunities for American farmers, bringing Jefferson's vision closer to reality. The French Revolution began in 1789, and four years later France's new republican government went to war against a British-led coalition of monarchical states. As warfare disrupted European farming, wheat prices

Urban Affluence

Beginning in the 1790s, New York merchants built large town houses and furnished them with fine pieces of furniture. This detail of John Rubens Smith's watercolor The Shop and Warehouse of Duncan Phyfe *(c. 1816) illustrates the success of America's most skillful furniture designer and manufacturer. Phyfe employed more than a hundred skilled joiners and carvers in his New York factory.*
Metropolitan Museum of Art, Rogers Fund, 1922.

leaped from 5 to 8 shillings a bushel and remained high for twenty years, bringing substantial profits to export-minded Chesapeake and Middle Atlantic farmers. Simultaneously, a boom in the export of raw cotton, fueled by the invention of the cotton gin and mechanization of cloth production in Britain, boosted the economy of Georgia and South Carolina. As Jefferson had hoped, European markets brought prosperity to American farmers and planters.

The French Revolution Divides Americans

American merchants profited even more handsomely from the European war. President Washington issued a Proclamation of Neutrality, which allowed U.S. citizens to trade with both sides. As neutral carriers, American ships claimed the right to pass through the British naval blockade along the French coastline and soon took over the lucrative sugar trade between France and its West Indian islands. The American merchant fleet became one of the largest in the world, increasing from 355,000 tons in 1790 to more than 1.1 million tons in 1808. Commercial earnings rose spectacularly, averaging $20 million annually in the 1790s—twice the value of cotton and tobacco exports. To keep up with demand, northern shipowners invested in new vessels, providing work for thousands of shipwrights, sail makers, laborers, and seamen. Hundreds of carpenters, masons, and cabinetmakers in Boston, New York, and Philadelphia found work building warehouses and fashionable town houses,

in what became known as the Federal style, for newly affluent merchants. In Philadelphia, a European visitor reported, "a great number of private houses have marble steps to the street door, and in other respects are finished in a style of elegance."

Ideological Conflict and Rebellion. Even as they prospered from the European struggle, Americans argued passionately over its ideologies. Most Americans had welcomed the French Revolution of 1789 because it abolished feudalism and established a constitutional monarchy. But the creation of the democratic French republic in 1792 and the execution of King Louis XVI the following year divided public opinion. Many American artisans praised the egalitarianism of the radical French Jacobins and followed their example, addressing each other as "citizen" and founding political clubs modeled on the radical democratic societies in Paris—the controversial Jacobin clubs. But Americans with strong religious beliefs condemned the new French regime for abandoning Christianity in favor of atheism. Wealthy Americans likewise denounced Robespierre and his radical republican followers for executing King Louis XVI, 3,000 of his aristocratic supporters, and 14,000 other citizens (see Voices from Abroad, "William Cobbett: Peter Porcupine Attacks Pro-French Americans," p. 217).

These ideological conflicts sharpened the debate over Hamilton's economic policies and even helped foment a domestic insurrection. In 1794 farmers in western Pennsylvania mounted the Whiskey Rebellion

Machine Technology and Republican Values

Household Industry

This woodcut by Alexander Anderson shows the home as a small-scale factory. Unlike the traditional artisan households (see the illustration on p. 17), these domestic workers produced goods—textiles and baskets—that were sold in regional or national (rather than local) markets.

Miriam and Ira D. Wallach Division of Art, Prints and Photographs, the New York Public Library, Astor, Lenox and Tilden Foundations.

In 1805 the young American scientist Benjamin Silliman visited the industrial city of Manchester, England. He was impressed by the great factories, "the wonder of the world and the pride of England," but troubled by the degraded character of the workers—"at best an imbecile people," he wrote—and the unhealthy conditions in which they lived and worked. "Heaps of dung, rubble from buildings, putrid, stagnant pools are found here and there among the houses, and a sort of black smoke covers the city," another visitor reported. "Under this half daylight 300,000 human beings are ceaselessly at work. . . . The crunching wheels of machinery, the shriek of steam from boilers, the regular beat of the looms, the heavy rumble of the carts, these are the noises from which you can never escape."

Silliman contrasted this dismal scene of early industrialization with a peaceful image of rural America: "fields and forests, in which pure air . . . and simple manners, give vigour to the limbs, and a healthful aspect to the face." Were the wonders of British technology, he asked, worth "the physical and . . . moral evils which they produce?"

No American struggled harder with this question than Thomas Jefferson. "Those who labour in the earth are the chosen people of God," Jefferson wrote in his *Notes on the State of Virginia* (1785), and he remained committed to the moral superiority of a society of yeomen farm families. Yet Jefferson knew that "a people who are entirely dependent upon foreigners for food or clothes, must always be subject to them." Even before the embargo of 1807 and the War of 1812 (see Chapter 8) convinced him of the necessity of American manufacturing, Jefferson advocated the use of advanced technology. He introduced cast-iron plows and improved threshing machines on his plantation at Monticello, Virginia, and rotated crops in accordance with the latest scientific theory.

Jefferson championed manufacturing on the plantation as well. As early as 1796 he bought an iron-cutting machine to make nails and, by employing a dozen slave men, made ten thousand nails a day. By 1812 Jefferson had built two water-powered mills at another plantation and had equipped his Monticello slaves

---

to protest Hamilton's excise tax on spirits, which had raised the price—and thus cut the demand—for the corn whiskey they sold locally and bartered for eastern manufactures. Like the Sons of Liberty of 1765 and the Shaysites of 1786, the Whiskey rebels attacked both local tax collectors and the authority of a distant government. But these protesters also waved banners proclaiming the French revolutionary slogan "Liberty, Equality, and Fraternity!" To uphold national authority (and deter secessionist movements along the frontier) President Washington raised an army of 12,000 troops that soon suppressed the rebels.

Jay's Treaty. Britain's maritime strategy also widened the growing political divisions in the United States. In November 1793 the Royal Navy began to prey on American ships bound for France from the West Indies, seizing more than 250 vessels and confiscating their

to manufacture textiles. He and other Americans, the former president boasted to a European friend, "have reduced the large and expensive machinery for most things to the compass of a private family. . . . I need 2,000 yards of linen, cotton and woolen yearly, to cloth my family [of slaves], which this machinery, costing $150 only, and worked by two women and two girls, will more than furnish."

Here, then, was Jefferson's way of avoiding the "dark Satanic mills" of Manchester. Each American household would become a small factory, using the labor of "women, children, and invalids" to enhance the prosperity and independence of American freehold farmers. For Jefferson, the key was democratic ownership of the means of agricultural and industrial production.

This dream was noble and not at all unrealistic. The United States did become a nation of household producers between 1790 and 1820 (see Chapter 8). Hundreds of rural men made nails as a wintertime employment, thousands of farm women made butter and cheese for market sale, and tens of thousands of families worked in their homes manufacturing shoes, textiles, and other goods for merchant entrepreneurs. Particularly in the Northeast, the American countryside became a vast workshop.

Yet Jefferson's vision concealed important aspects of American rural life and was flawed by internal contradictions. Many families in the Northeast were driven to home manufacture by the threat of poverty; their subdivided farms yielded only a bare subsistence. The situation in the southern states was even more problematic. Was the enslaved labor that produced Jefferson's nails and textiles more compatible with republican moral and economic principles than was the waged labor in Manchester factories? And, over the long run, could household producers compete successfully with the water- and steam-driven factories owned by wealthy capitalists?

A candid observer must answer "No" to these questions. With his customary skill, Jefferson had identified the crucial issues: how the means of production should be owned and organized, and who should benefit financially from the new technology. He was unable, however, to show how the technological advances and social conditions of his age could be made compatible with the republican value of liberty and the democratic ideal of equality. That question remains unresolved to this day.

Coalbrookdale by Night
This painting by Philip James de Louterbourg depicts an iron smelter, which poet William Blake called one of the "dark Satanic mills" of industrial England.
The Science Museum, London.

cargoes of sugar. To avoid war President Washington sent John Jay to Britain. Jay returned in 1795 with a controversial treaty requiring the U.S. government to make "full and complete compensation" to British merchants for all pre–Revolutionary War debts owed by American citizens. The treaty also acknowledged Britain's right to remove French property from neutral ships, overturning the American merchants' claim that "free ships make free goods." In return, the agreement allowed American merchants to submit claims of illegal seizure to arbitration and required the British to remove their military garrisons from the Northwest Territory and to end their aid to the Indians there. Jefferson and other Republicans attacked Jay's Treaty as too conciliatory, and the Senate ratified it only by the bare two-thirds majority required by the Constitution. As long as Hamilton and his Federalist allies were in power, the United States would have a pro-British foreign policy.

Federalist Gentry

A prominent New England Federalist, Oliver Ellsworth served as chief justice of the United States (1796–1800). His wife, Abigail Wolcott Ellsworth, was the daughter of a Connecticut governor. In 1792 the portraitist Ralph Earl captured the aspirations of the Ellsworths by giving them an aristocratic demeanor and prominently displaying their mansion (in the window). Like other Federalists who tried to reconcile their wealth and social authority with republican values, Ellsworth dressed with restraint, and his manners, remarked Timothy Dwight, were "wholly destitute of haughtiness and arrogance." Wadsworth Atheneum, Hartford.

The Rise of Political Parties

The appearance of Federalists and Republicans marked a new stage in American politics. Although colonial legislatures had often divided into temporary factions based on family alliances, ethnicity, or region, they lacked well-organized parties. The new state and national constitutions made no provision for organized political bodies; indeed, most politically minded Americans considered parties unnecessary and dangerous. Following classical republican principles, they wanted voters and legislators to act independently and in the interest of the public—not a party. Thus, Senator Pierce Butler of South Carolina criticized his colleagues in Congress as "men scrambling for partial advantage, State interests, and in short, a train of narrow, impolitic measures."

However, the revolutionary ideology of popular sovereignty drew average citizens into politics and created a contest for their votes. Simultaneously, the financial and ideological conflicts of the 1790s divided the political elite. The result was a competitive—and potentially destructive—**party system**. Merchants, creditors, and urban artisans favored Federalist policies, as did wheat-exporting slaveholders in the Tidewater districts of the Chesapeake. The emerging Republican coalition was more diverse and drew supporters from across the social spectrum. It included not only southern tobacco and rice planters and debt-conscious western farmers but also German and Scots-Irish in the southern backcountry, and subsistence-oriented eastern farmers.

Party identity crystallized during the election of 1796. To prepare for the election Federalist and Republican leaders called legislative caucuses in Congress and conventions in the states to discuss policies and nominate candidates. To mobilize the citizenry the parties organized public festivals and processions, with the Federalists celebrating Washington's achievements and the Republicans invoking the egalitarian principles of the Declaration of Independence.

Federalist candidates triumphed in the 1796 election, winning a majority in Congress and electing John Adams as the new president. Adams continued Hamilton's pro-British foreign policy and reacted sharply when the French navy seized American merchant ships. When the French foreign minister Talleyrand solicited a loan and a bribe from American diplomats to stop the seizures, Adams urged Congress to prepare for war. He charged that Talleyrand's agents, whom he dubbed X, Y, and Z, had insulted the honor of the United States. Responding to the "XYZ Affair," the Federalist-controlled Congress cut off trade with France in 1798 and authorized American privateers to seize French ships. Party conflict, which had begun over Hamilton's financial policies, now extended to foreign affairs.

Constitutional Crisis, 1798–1800

For the first time in American history (but not the last) a controversial foreign policy prompted domestic protest and governmental repression. As the United States

William Cobbett

Peter Porcupine Attacks Pro-French Americans

The Democratic-Republican followers of Thomas Jefferson declared that "he who is an enemy to the French Revolution, cannot be a firm republican." William Cobbett, a British journalist who settled in Philadelphia and wrote under the pen name "Peter Porcupine," contested this definition of republicanism. A strong supporter of the Federalist Party, Cobbett was eager to attack its opponents and did so frequently in caustic and widely read pamphlets and newspaper articles. Here he evokes the horrors of the Terror in France, during which thousands of aristocrats and ordinary citizens were executed, and warns that the triumph of Radical Republicanism would bring the same fate to the United States.

France is a republic, and the decrees of the Legislators were necessary to maintain it a republic. This word outweighs, in the estimation of some persons (I wish I could say they were few in number), all the horrors that have been and that can be committed in that country. One of these modern republicans will tell you that he does not deny that hundreds of thousands of innocent persons have been murdered in France; that the people have neither religion nor morals; that all the ties of nature are rent asunder; . . . that its riches, along with millions of the best of the people, are gone to enrich and aggrandize its enemies; that its commerce, its manufactures, its sciences, its arts, and its honour, are no more; but at the end of all this, he will tell you that it must be happy, because it is a republic. I have heard more than one of these republican zealots declare, that he would sooner see the last of the French exterminated, than see them adopt any other form of government. Such a sentiment is characteristic of a mind locked up in a savage ignorance.

Shall we say that these things never can take place among us? . . . We are not what we were before the French revolution. Political projectors from every corner of Europe, troublers of society of every description, from the whining philosophical hypocrite to the daring rebel, and more daring blasphemer, have taken shelter in these States.

We have seen the guillotine toasted to three times three cheers. . . . And what would the reader say, were I to tell him of a Member of Congress, who wished to see one of these murderous machines employed for lopping off the heads of the French, permanent in the Statehouse yard of the city of Philadelphia?

If these men of blood had succeeded in plunging us into a war; if they had once got the sword into their hands, they would have mowed us down like stubble. The word Aristocrat would have been employed to as good account here, as ever it had been in France. We might, ere this, have seen our places of worship turned into stables; we might have seen the banks of the Delaware, like those of the Loire, covered with human carcasses, and its waters tinged with blood: ere this we might have seen our parents butchered, and even the head of our admired and beloved President rolling on a scaffold.

I know the reader will start back with horror. His heart will tell him that it is impossible. But, once more, let him look at the example before us. The attacks on the character and conduct of the aged Washington, have been as bold, if not bolder, than those which led to the downfall of the unfortunate French Monarch [Louis XVI, executed in 1793]. Can it then be imagined, that, had they possessed the power, they wanted the will to dip their hands in his blood?

Source: William Cobbett, *Peter Porcupine in America,* ed. David A. Wilson (Ithaca: Cornell University Press, 1994), 150–54.

---

fought an undeclared maritime war against France, pro-Republican and anti-British immigrants from Ireland vehemently attacked Adams's foreign policy. Some Federalists responded in kind: "Were I president, I would hang them for otherwise they would murder me," declared a Philadelphia Federalist pamphleteer. To silence its critics, in 1798 the administration enacted coercive measures. The Naturalization Act increased the residency requirement for American citizenship from five to fourteen years; the Alien Act authorized the deportation of foreigners; and the Sedition Act prohibited the publication of ungrounded or malicious attacks on the president or Congress. "He that is not for us is against us," thundered the Federalist *Gazette of the United States.* Prosecutors arrested more than twenty Republican newspaper editors and politicians, accused them of sedition, and won convictions and jail sentences against some of them.

The Federalists' repressive actions created a constitutional crisis. Republicans charged that the Sedition Act violated the First Amendment's prohibition against "abridging the freedom of speech, or of the press." However, they did not appeal to the Supreme Court, both because the Court's power to review congressional legislation had not been established and because the Court was packed with Federalists. Instead Madison and Jefferson looked to the federal system—and the state legislatures—to remedy unconstitutional laws. "The powers of the federal government" resulted "from the compact to which the states are parties," Madison declared. At Jefferson's urging, in 1798 the Kentucky legislature declared the Alien and Sedition Acts to be "unauthoritative, void, and of no force," arguing that the states had a "right to judge" the constitutionality of national laws. The Virginia legislature passed a similar resolution that also followed Madison's "**states' rights**" interpretation of the Constitution.

The debate over the Sedition Act set the stage for the election of 1800. Jefferson, once opposed in principle to political parties, now saw them as a valuable way "to watch and relate to the people" the activities of an oppressive government. Republicans strongly supported Jefferson's bid for the presidency, pointing to the wrongful imprisonment of newspaper editors and championing states' rights. President Adams responded to these attacks by reevaluating his foreign policy. Adams was a complicated man who was dogmatic and easily offended, but he also possessed great personal strength and determination. Rejecting the advice of Hamilton and other belligerent-minded Federalists to declare war against France (and benefit from an upsurge in patriotism), Adams put country ahead of party and entered into diplomatic negotiations that brought an end to the fighting.

Nonetheless, the election of 1800 was the first "dirty" political campaign. The Federalists attacked Jefferson's character, branding him as an irresponsible pro-French radical, "the arch-apostle of irreligion and free thought," and both parties forced changes in state election laws to favor their candidates. A low Federalist turnout in Virginia and Pennsylvania and the three-fifths rule for slave representation (which boosted the number of electoral votes in the southern states) gave Jefferson a narrow 73 to 65 victory in the electoral college. But the Republican electors unexpectedly also gave seventy-three votes to Aaron Burr of New York (Jefferson's choice for vice president), throwing the presidential election into the House of Representatives. (The Twelfth Amendment, ratified in 1804, would remedy this constitutional defect by requiring electors to vote separately for president and vice president.)

Ironically, as the era of Federalism and its aristocratic outlook came to an end, Alexander Hamilton ushered in a more democratic era. For thirty-five ballots, Federalists in the House of Representatives blocked Jefferson's election. Then Hamilton intervened. Calling Burr an "embryo Caesar" and the "most unfit man in the United States for the office of president," he persuaded key Federalists to permit Jefferson's selection. The Federalists' concern for political stability also played a role. As Senator James Bayard of Delaware explained, "It was admitted on all hands that we must risk the Constitution and a Civil War or take Mr. Jefferson."

Jefferson called the election the "Revolution of 1800," and so it was. The bloodless transfer of power demonstrated that governments elected by the people could be changed in an orderly way, even in times of bitter partisan conflict and foreign crisis. In his inaugural address in 1801 Jefferson praised this achievement, declaring: "We are all Republicans, we are all Federalists." Despite the predictions of European conservatives, the new republican constitutional order of 1776 had survived a quarter century of economic and political turmoil.

FOR FURTHER EXPLORATION

▶ For definitions of key terms boldfaced in this chapter, see the glossary at the end of the book.

▶ To assess your mastery of the material covered in this chapter, see the Online Study Guide at **bedfordstmartins.com/henretta**.

▶ For suggested references, including Web sites, see page SR-8 at the end of the book.

▶ For map resources and primary documents, see **bedfordstmartins.com/henretta**.

The republican revolution began in the states, which between 1776 and 1780 wrote new constitutions. Most states established property qualifications for voting and a separation of powers that inhibited popular rule. The Pennsylvania and Vermont constitutions were more democratic, with a powerful one-house legislature and voting rights for most free men. The New Jersey constitution allowed property-owning women to vote, but most American women were excluded from the political sphere. A few women asserted claims of intellectual and social equality and sought greater legal rights, mostly without success. On the national level the government created by the Articles of Confederation began the orderly settlement of the trans-Appalachian West, but it lacked the authority to regulate foreign trade or raise enough revenue to pay off wartime debts. Clashes over debts and taxes also disrupted the state governments and culminated in 1786 in Shays's Rebellion, an uprising of indebted farmers in Massachusetts.

The perceived weaknesses of the Confederation led nationalists and creditors to convene a constitutional convention in Philadelphia in 1787. The delegates devised a new constitution that derived its authority not from the states but from the people, who were directly represented in the lower house of the legislature. The delegates created a strong national government with the power to levy taxes, issue money, and control trade. Its legislation was to be the supreme law of the land. In several important states the Constitution was ratified by narrow margins because it diminished the sovereignty of the states and seemed to create a potentially oppressive central government immune from popular control.

In 1789 George Washington became the first president under the new government and, working with the first Congress, established the executive and judicial departments. The economic policies of Washington's secretary of the treasury, Alexander Hamilton, favored northern merchants and financiers and led to the creation of the Federalist Party. Thomas Jefferson and James Madison organized farmers, planters, and artisans into a rival Republican Party. The French Revolution prompted bitter ideological struggles in the United States and, during an undeclared war with France, political repression in the form of the Alien and Sedition Acts of 1798. The peaceful transfer of power to Jefferson and the Republicans in 1800 ended a decade of political strife.

1776	Pennsylvania approves a democratic constitution
	John Adams, *Thoughts on Government*
	Propertied women allowed to vote in New Jersey (retracted in 1807)
1777	Articles of Confederation (ratified 1781)
1779	Judith Sargent Murray, "On the Equality of the Sexes" (published in 1790)
1780s	Postwar commercial recession increases creditor-debtor conflicts in the states
1781	Confederation Congress charters Bank of North America
1784–1785	Political and Land Ordinances outline settlement policy for new states
1785	Thomas Jefferson, *Notes on the State of Virginia*
1786	Commercial convention in Annapolis, Maryland
	Shays's Rebellion roils Massachusetts
1787	Northwest Ordinance
	Constitutional convention in Philadelphia
1787–1788	States hold ratification conventions
	John Jay, James Madison, and Alexander Hamilton write the *Federalist* essays
1789	George Washington inaugurated as first president
	Judiciary Act establishes federal court system
	Outbreak of French Revolution
1790	Hamilton wins Congress's approval of redemption and assumption
1791	Bill of Rights ratified
1792	Mary Wollstonecraft, *A Vindication of the Rights of Woman*
1793	French create Republic and execute King Louis XVI
	Madison and Jefferson found Republican Party
	War between Britain and France; Washington's Proclamation of Neutrality
1794	Whiskey Rebellion in western Pennsylvania
1795	Jay's Treaty with Great Britain
1798	XYZ Affair (1797) prompts war with France
	Alien, Sedition, and Naturalization Acts
	Kentucky and Virginia Resolutions contest federal authority
1800	Jefferson elected president in "Revolution of 1800"

CHAPTER 8

Dynamic Change: Western Settlement and Eastern Capitalism

1790–1820

"IT IS A COUNTRY IN FLUX," a French aristocrat observed of the United States in 1799, "that which is true today as regards its population, its establishments, its prices, its commerce will not be true six months from now." Indeed, the coming of the nineteenth century would produce a dramatic change in American society and politics. In 1800, the American republic stood on the edge of a period of dynamic westward expansion and eastern economic development that would soon change its very character. "If movement and the quick succession of sensations and ideas constitute life," another French observer wrote a few decades later, "here one lives a hundred fold more than elsewhere; here, all is circulation, motion, and boiling agitation."

◄ **The Fairview Inn**, by Thomas Cole Ruckle (detail)
Scores of inns dotted the roads of the new republic, providing food, accommodations, and livery services for settlers moving west and for cattle drovers and teamsters carrying western produce to eastern markets. Although executed in 1889, this painting accurately depicts the architecture of an early-nineteenth-century Maryland inn and captures the character of its workforce—with free and enslaved African Americans driving cattle and tending to horses. Maryland Historical Society.

Circulation and motion were especially evident along the western frontier. Standing on the eastern edge of the continent in 1766, a white observer noted that "the thirst after Indian lands, is become almost universal." When the Treaty of Paris in 1783 gave the United States access to the trans-Appalachian West, hundreds of thousands of extraordinarily self-confident Americans trekked into the interior to farm its rich soils with a nearly complete disregard for Indian property rights. As George Washington put it, members of the Sons of Liberty in the East became "the lords and proprietors of a vast tract of continent" in the West.

221

Unfortunately for Washington's Federalist Party, the votes of these western farmers helped to ensure the political ascendancy of Republican president Thomas Jefferson and his western-oriented policies. To provide even more land for American farmers, Jefferson doubled the country's size through the Louisiana Purchase in 1803. "[No] territory can be too large," declared Dr. David Ramsay of South Carolina, "for a people, who multiply with such unequalled rapidity."

While Republican policy encouraged homesteading in the West, state legislatures in the East promoted banking, manufacturing, and commercial growth. This governmental stimulus unleashed a cumulative process of capitalist-financed economic growth. "Experiment follows experiment; enterprise follows enterprise," a European traveler noted, and "riches and poverty follow." Of the two, riches were the more apparent. Beginning around 1800 per capita income in the United States increased by more than 1 percent per year—over 30 percent in a single generation. By the 1820s the nation was well on its way to becoming a republic that was continental in scope and capitalist in character.

Westward Expansion

In 1803 Shawnee diplomats told American officials that long ago their ancestors had stood on the shores of the Atlantic Ocean and seen a strange object. "At first they took it for a great bird, but they soon found it to be a monstrous canoe filled with . . . white people." Soon thereafter, the Indian emissaries continued, the white people robbed the Shawnees of their wisdom and then "usurped their land," purchasing it with goods that "were more the property of the Indians than the white people because the knowledge which enabled them to manufacture these goods actually belonged to the Shawnees."

Whatever the truth of this legend, by 1803 the expansionist-minded American republic clearly threatened the Shawnees and other native peoples. The first national census in 1790 counted 3.9 million people, both white and black, with 200,000 of them living west of the Appalachian Mountains. By 1820 there were 9.6 million white and black Americans, and no fewer than 2 million inhabited nine new states and three new territories west of the Appalachians. The country was moving west at an astonishing pace.

Native American Resistance

In the Treaty of Paris of 1783 Great Britain relinquished its claims to the trans-Appalachian region and, as one British statesman put it, left the Indian nations "to the care of their [American] neighbours." "Care" was hardly the right term, for some influential Americans wanted to exterminate the native peoples. "Cut up every Indian Cornfield and burn every Indian town," proclaimed William Henry Drayton of South Carolina, so that their "nation be extirpated and the lands become the property of the public." Many others, including Henry Knox, President Washington's first secretary of war, favored assimilating the Indians into American society. Knox wanted commonly held tribal lands to become the private property of individual Indian families, who would become citizens of the various states. Most Indians rejected these policies out of hand and continued to view themselves as members of a particular clan or tribe. Without much success, a few Native American leaders raised the notion of a broader, pan-Indian identity.

Conflict over Land Rights. Not surprisingly, the major struggle between Indians and whites concerned

Red Jacket or Sagoyewatha, c. 1758–1830
Like most Senecas, Sagoyewatha fought for the British during the American War for Independence, acquiring his English name from the coat given him by a British officer. In 1792 Red Jacket journeyed to Philadelphia as a member of a delegation that ceded Iroquois lands to the United States. There he met with President Washington, who presented him with the silver peace medal depicted in this painting by an unknown artist (based on a portrait by Robert W. Weir, c. 1828). Subsequently, Red Jacket became the leader of the Seneca faction that opposed Christian missionary efforts and called for a return to the traditional Indian way of life.
Fenimore Art Museum / © New York State Historical Association, Cooperstown, NY.

land rights. Invoking the Paris treaty and claiming that pro-British Indians were conquered peoples, the United States government asserted ownership over all Indian lands in the West. Native Americans rejected this claim, pointing out that they had not signed the treaty and had never been conquered. The Confederation Congress and the state governments brushed aside those arguments. In 1784 U.S. commissioners used military threats to force pro-British Iroquois peoples— the Mohawks, Onondagas, Cayugas, and Senecas—to sign the Treaty of Fort Stanwix and relinquish much of their land in New York and Pennsylvania. New York officials and land speculators used liquor and bribes to take title to additional millions of acres. By 1800 the once powerful Iroquois were confined to relatively small reservations.

American negotiators employed similar tactics farther to the west. In 1785 they induced the Chipewyans, Delawares, Ottawas, and Wyandots to sign away most of the future state of Ohio. The tribes quickly repudiated the agreements, claiming—justifiably—that they were made under duress. Those peoples, along with the Shawnees, Miamis, and Potawatomis, formed a Western Confederacy to defend themselves against aggressive

settlers. Led by Little Turtle, a Miami chief, they defeated American armies in 1790 and again in 1791.

Fearing an alliance between the Western Confederacy and the British in Canada, President Washington doubled the size of the U.S. Army and ordered General "Mad Anthony" Wayne to lead a new expedition. In August 1794 Wayne defeated the Indians in the Battle of Fallen Timbers (near present-day Toledo, Ohio). Nevertheless, the Western Confederacy remained strong, forcing a compromise peace in the Treaty of Greenville (Ohio) in 1795. American negotiators acknowledged Indian ownership of the lands of the trans-Appalachian West, while the members of the confederacy accepted American political sovereignty and agreed to place themselves "under the protection of the United States, and no other Power whatever." In practice this agreement encouraged American officials and settlers to pressure Native Americans to give up their lands but allowed Indian peoples to demand money or goods in return. Indeed, during the Greenville negotiations the Indians ceded ownership of most of Ohio and certain strategic areas along the Great Lakes, including Detroit and the future site of Chicago (Map 8.1). Recognizing the gains made by the United States, Britain cut some of

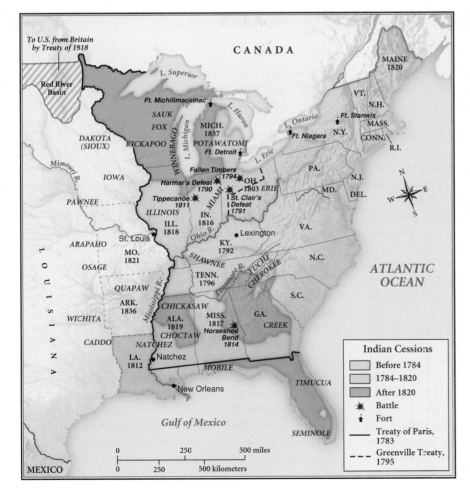

MAP 8.1 Indian Cessions and State Formation, to 1840

By virtue of the Treaty of 1783 with Britain, the United States claimed sovereignty over the entire trans-Appalachian West. The Western Indian Confederacy contested this claim, which the U.S. government upheld by military force. As Native American peoples were coerced by armed diplomacy to cede most of their domain, white settlers occupied the land, formed territorial governments, and eventually entered the Union as members of separate—and equal—states. Gradually, the new western region emerged as an important economic and political force.

Red Jacket

A Seneca Chief's Understanding of Religion

The Seneca chief Red Jacket (c. 1758–1830) acquired his name during the Revolutionary War, when he fought for the British "redcoats" to protect his people from the threat posed by American settlers. Although reconciled to American rule, Red Jacket strongly adhered to Indian values and rejected Christianity. In 1805 he explained why to a group of missionaries, whom he addressed as "Brother."

Brother: Continue to listen. You say that you are sent to instruct us how to worship the Great Spirit agreeably to his mind; and, if we do not take hold of the religion which you white people teach, we shall be unhappy hereafter. You say that you are right, and we are lost. How do we know this to be true? We understand that your religion is written in a book. If it was intended for us as well as you, why has not the Great Spirit given to us, and not only to us, but why did He not give to our forefathers, the knowledge of the book, with the means of understanding it rightly?

Brother: The Great Spirit has made us all, but he has made a great difference between his white and red children. He has given us different complexions and different customs. To you He has given the arts [i.e., manufacturing]. To these He has not opened our eyes. We know these things to be true. Since He has made a great difference between us in other things, why may we not conclude that He has given us different religion according to our understanding? The Great Spirit does right. He knows what is best for his children; we are satisfied.

Source: David J. Rothman and Sheila Rothman, eds., *Sources of the American Social Tradition* (New York: Basic Books, 1975), 182.

---

its trading ties with the Indians and, in Jay's Treaty of 1795, reaffirmed its (still unfulfilled) obligation under the Treaty of Paris to remove its military garrisons from the region.

American westward migration increased as soon as the fighting ended. In 1805 the two-year-old state of Ohio had more than 100,000 residents. Thousands more farm families moved into the future states of Indiana and Illinois, sparking new conflicts with native peoples over land and hunting rights. As a Delaware Indian declared, "The Elks are our horses, the buffaloes are our cows, the deer are our sheep, & the whites shan't have them."

Attempts at Assimilation. To alleviate these tensions the U.S. government encouraged Native Americans to become farmers and assimilate into white society. The goal, as one Kentucky Protestant minister put it, was to make the Indian "a farmer, a citizen of the United States, and a Christian." Most Native Americans resisted these efforts. As a Munsee prophet put it, "There are two ways to God, one for the whites and one for the Indians." To preserve their traditional cultures, many Indian peoples drove out white missionaries and forced Christianized Indians to participate in tribal rites. A few Indian leaders tried to find a middle path between ancestral ways and European practices. Among the Senecas of New York the prophet Handsome Lake promoted traditional Iroquois ceremonies that gave thanks to the earth, plants, animals, water, and sun. But he also incorporated some Christian beliefs, such as heaven and hell, into his teachings and used them to deter his followers from drinking alcohol, gambling, and practicing witchcraft. Handsome Lake's rejection of some Indian beliefs and his support of Quaker missionaries divided the tribe into hostile religious factions. More conservative Senecas, led by Chief Red Jacket, condemned Indians who accepted white ways and beliefs and demanded a return to ancestral customs (see American Voices, "Red Jacket: A Seneca Chief's Understanding of Religion," above).

Most Indian women also rejected European farming practices. Among the Iroquois and many other Eastern Woodland peoples, women had long been responsible for growing staple foods; partly as a result, they controlled the inheritance of cultivation rights and exercised considerable political power. Shawnee women had even more authority, because women "war" chiefs decided whether to dispatch a war party or to torture captives. Even those Indians who embraced Christian teachings retained many traditional values. To view themselves as individuals, as the Europeans demanded, meant repudiating the clan, the essence of Indian life.

Migration and the Changing Farm Economy

Native American resistance did not deter the advance of white farmers and planters, who poured across the Appalachians and moved along the Atlantic coastal plain in search of fertile lands. This migratory upsurge brought financial rewards to many settlers and an increasing diversity of crops to the American farm economy.

Movement Out of the South.   Between 1790 and 1820 two great streams of migrants moved out of the southern states. One stream of migrants, composed primarily of white tenant farmers and struggling yeomen families, flocked through the Cumberland Gap into Kentucky and Tennessee. They were fleeing the depleted soils and planter elite of the Chesapeake region, confident that they would prosper by growing cotton and hemp, which were in great demand. The second stream, dominated by slave-owning planters and their enslaved workers, moved along the coastal plain of the Gulf of Mexico into the future states of Alabama and Mississippi. A worried eastern landlord lamented the massive loss of farm labor, writing to the *Maryland Gazette* that "boundless settlements open a door for our citizens to run off and leave us, depreciating all our landed property and disabling us from paying taxes."

Many migrants to Kentucky and Tennessee were poor, without ready cash to buy land. To gain title to farmland, they relied upon "the ancient cultivation law" governing frontier tracts. Invoking the argument of the North Carolina Regulators (see Chapter 4), they argued that poor settlers had a customary right "from time out of Mind" to occupy "back waste vacant Lands" sufficient "to provide a subsistence for themselves and their posterity." The Virginia government, which administered the Kentucky Territory, had a more elitist vision. While it allowed poorer settlers to purchase up to 1,400 acres of land at reduced prices, it also sold or granted estates of 20,000 to 200,000 acres to scores of wealthy individuals and partnerships. Consequently, when Kentucky became a state in 1792, a handful of **speculators** owned one-fourth of the state, while half the adult white men owned no land and lived as **squatters** or tenant farmers.

Slave Auction in Charleston, South Carolina, 1833
As one slave departs with his new master (far right), the auctioneer tries to interest the assembled planters in his next sale item, a black family. The artist, a British Canadian named Henry Byam Martin, showed his disdain for these proceedings in the sketch itself (compare the family's dignified bearing with the planters' slouching postures) and in its sarcastic title: The Land of the Free and the Home of the Brave.
National Archives of Canada.

The rest of the southern frontier became a stronghold of racial slavery. Until the 1810s, wealthy planters and up-and-coming young white men from the Chesapeake and the Lower South set up new slave plantations in the interior of Georgia and South Carolina and then they moved into the Old Southwest—the future states of Alabama, Mississippi, and Louisiana. They carried some slaves with them and imported more from Africa. Between 1776 and 1809, when Congress cut off the Atlantic slave trade, these planters bought about 115,000 African slaves. The black population also grew through reproduction, increasing from half a million in 1775 to 1.8 million in 1820.

Although many enslaved African Americans still toiled in tobacco and rice fields of the Chesapeake and South Carolina, a new crop—cotton—financed the expansion of slavery into the Old Southwest. After 1750 technological breakthroughs such as water-powered spinning jennies and weaving mules boosted European textile production and greatly increased the demand for raw wool and cotton. By the 1790s American inventors—including Connecticut-born Eli Whitney—had developed machines (called gins) that efficiently extracted the seeds from the strands of cotton, and thousands of white planters in South Carolina and Georgia began growing the crop. Expansion-minded planters—and their slaves—carried cotton production into Alabama and Mississippi, which entered the Union in 1817 and 1819, respectively. In a single year a government land office in Huntsville, Alabama, sold $7 million of uncleared land. The expression "doing a land-office business"—a metaphor for rapid commercial expansion—dates from this time.

Exodus from New England. As southern whites and blacks moved into the trans-Appalachian West and the Gulf Coast, a third stream of migrants flowed out of New England (Map 8.2). Previous generations of yeomen farm families had left the overcrowded communities of Massachusetts and Connecticut and moved north and east, settling New Hampshire, Vermont, and Maine. Now farmers throughout New England were on the move, this time to the West. To provide land for the four or five children who survived to adulthood, thousands of parents packed their wagons with tools and household goods and migrated into New York. By 1820 nearly

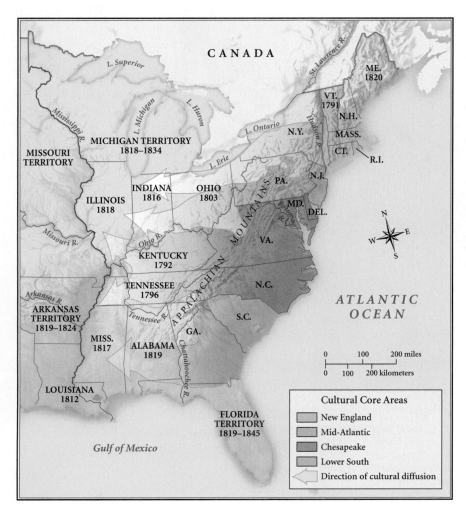

MAP 8.2 Regional Cultures Move West, 1790–1820

By 1790 four distinct "core" cultures had developed in the long-settled states along the Atlantic seaboard. Then, between 1790 and 1820, residents of these four regions migrated into the trans-Appalachian West, carrying their cultures with them. New England customs and institutions exercised a dominant influence in upstate New York and along the Great Lakes, while the Lower South's hierarchical system of slavery and heavy concentration of African Americans shaped the culture of the new states along the Gulf of Mexico. The pattern of cultural diffusion was more complex in the Ohio and Tennessee River Valleys, which were settled by migrants from various core regions.

800,000 New England migrants lived in a string of settlements that stretched from Albany to Buffalo. Thousands more moved on to Ohio and Indiana.

This vast migration was organized not by governments or joint-stock companies but by the settlers themselves, who often moved in large groups linked by family and religion. As a traveler reported from central New York, "The town of Herkimer is entirely populated by families come from Connecticut. We stayed at Mr. Snow's who came from New London with about ten male and female cousins." When 176 residents of Granville, Massachusetts, moved to Ohio, they transplanted their Congregational ministers and elders along with their system of **freehold** agriculture. Throughout this region—known as the Old Northwest—many "new" communities were actually old communities that had moved inland.

In New York, as in Kentucky, well-connected speculators snapped up much of the best land. In the 1780s the financier Robert Morris acquired 1.3 million acres in the Genesee region of central New York, where the Wadsworth family also bought thousands of acres of prime land and created leasehold farms similar to those on Hudson River Valley manors. To attract tenants the Wadsworths leased farms rent-free for the first seven years, after which they charged rents. Many New England yeomen preferred to sign agreements with a Dutch-owned syndicate of speculators: the Holland Land Company. Holland Land contracts allowed settlers to buy the land as they worked it, but high interest rates and the lack of markets mired thousands of these aspiring freeholders deeply in debt. As one pioneer recalled, "In the early years, there was none but a home market and that was mostly barter—it was so many bushels of wheat for a cow; so many bushels for a yoke of oxen." Fleeing declining prospects in the East these farmers found themselves at the bottom of the economic ladder in the West.

Agricultural Change in the East.   The settlement of western lands prompted changes in eastern agriculture. As low-cost western wheat began to flow to eastern markets, farmers in New England planted different crops, such as potatoes, which were nutritious and high yielding. To compensate for the lost labor of sons and daughters, Middle Atlantic farmers replaced metal-tipped wooden plows with cast-iron models that dug deeper and required a single yoke of oxen instead of two or three. These improvements allowed them to maintain production levels even with fewer laborers.

Easterners also took advantage of the progressive farming methods recently publicized by wealthy British agricultural reformers. "Improvers" rotated their crops to maintain soil fertility, planting nitrogen-rich clover to offset nutrient-hungry crops of wheat and corn. In Pennsylvania crop rotation doubled the average wheat yield per acre. Yeomen diversified production, raising sheep and selling the wool to textile manufacturers. Many farmers adopted a year-round planting cycle, sowing wheat in the winter for market and corn in the spring for animal fodder. Women and girls milked the family cows and sold butter and cheese in the growing towns and cities.

In this new agricultural economy families worked harder and longer, but their efforts were rewarded with higher output and a better standard of living. Whether hacking fields out of western forests or carting manure

Hop Picking, by Lucy Sheldon, 1801
Work was nothing new for rural women and children, who had always labored about the farm. What was different in the early nineteenth century was the growing number of landless families who worked for employers such as shopkeepers and manufacturers. In this watercolor by a schoolgirl at the Litchfield Female Academy in Connecticut, a young couple and their children pick hops, which they will sell to a storekeeper or local brewer to be made into beer. Litchfield Historical Society.

to replenish eastern soils, farm families increased their productivity. Westward migration had boosted the entire American economy.

The Transportation Bottleneck

American geography threatened to cut short this economic advance: water transport was the quickest and cheapest way to get goods to market, but no rivers cut through the Appalachian Mountains. It cost Pennsylvania farmers as much to send crops fifty miles by road to Philadelphia as to ship them from Philadelphia to London. Without access to waterways or other cheap means of transportation, settlers west of the Appalachian Mountains would be unable to send goods to markets in the East, Europe, and the West Indies (see American Voices, "Noah M. Ludlow: Traveling to Kentucky, 1815," p. 229).

Improved inland trade therefore became a high priority for the new state governments, which actively encouraged transportation ventures. Between 1793 and 1812 the Pennsylvania legislature granted fifty-five corporate charters to private turnpike companies, and Massachusetts chartered over a hundred. Turnpike companies built level gravel roads that significantly reduced travel time and transport costs and charged tolls for their use. State governments and private entrepreneurs constructed even more cost-efficient inland waterways, dredging rivers to make them navigable and constructing short canals to bypass waterfalls or rapids. By 1816 the United States had about 100 miles of canals, but only three of these artificial waterways were more than 2 miles long and none breached the great Appalachian barrier. Only after 1819, when the Erie Canal began to connect the central and western counties of New York to the Hudson River, could inland farmers sell their produce in eastern markets (see Chapter 10).

For farmers farther west the great streams that connected to the Mississippi River represented the great hope. Western settlers paid premium prices for land along navigable rivers, while speculators bought up property in growing towns—such as Cincinnati, Louisville, Chattanooga, and St. Louis—along the Ohio, Tennessee, and Mississippi Rivers. Western farmers and merchants built barges to float cotton, surplus grain, and meat down this great interconnected river system to the port of New Orleans, which by 1815 was processing about $5 million in agricultural products yearly.

But many western settlers in the trans-Appalachian West lacked access to these waterways and had no choice but to be self-sufficient. "A noble field of Indian corn

View of Cincinnati, by John Casper Wild, c. 1835
Thanks to its location on the Ohio River, Cincinnati quickly became one of the major commercial cities of the trans-Appalachian West. By the 1820s passenger steamboats as well as freight barges connected the city with Pittsburgh to the north and the ocean port of New Orleans to the far south. Museum of Fine Arts, Boston.

Noah M. Ludlow

Traveling to Kentucky, 1815

In 1815, Noah Ludlow (1795–1886) was an actor in a traveling theatrical troupe headed by Samuel Drake, one of the first cultural entrepreneurs to bring entertainment to the trans-Appalachian West. As Ludlow ventured from Albany, New York, to Frankfort, Kentucky, he encountered firsthand the hazards of water transportation and the slow and difficult course of travel by land—adventures he recounted in a memoir published in 1880.

With the commencement of the year 1815, Mr. Drake was looking around for some actors and actresses bold and adventurous enough to risk their lives and fortunes in a Western wilderness. . . . His course was to travel northwest in the State of New York, until he should reach Canandaigua; then to deflect to the south-west, strike the head waters of the Allegheny river, descend by boat to Pittsburgh, and perform there until the assembling of the State Legislature of Kentucky, early in December. . . .

Sometime about the latter part of July, 1815, our party started from Canandaigua for the head waters of the Allegheny River. Our means of transportation were a road wagon, drawn by two horses, owned by Mr. Drake, and a light spring-wagon . . . [for the] comfort of his wife. . . . The other portions of the company . . . were expected to walk the greater part of the way . . . [to] Olean, a settlement on the Allegheny . . . about one hundred and fifty miles south-west.

Olean . . . was a wild-looking place. . . . Mr. Drake immediately made a trade, disposing of his wagons and horses, and purchasing a flat-bottomed boat, known in those days as an "Ark," or "broad-horn." It was about twenty-five feet long by fifteen wide, boarded up at the sides, and covered with an elliptical roof about high enough to allow a man . . . to stand erect. . . . In one end of this boat were two rooms, partitioned off as bedrooms, one for Mr. Lewis and wife; the other for the three single young ladies. . . . The men . . . were expected to "rough it." . . .

The good "broadhorn" wended her slow but steady way wherever it pleased the current of old Allegheny to carry her . . . [until] an alarming cry that the boat was going over a waterfall. Five [men] . . . plunged into the river . . . and . . . succeeded in getting the boat safely to shore. After resting a little, we set to work to retrace the course we had come, until we should reach that point at which . . . the boat had taken the wrong "chute," or fork of the river. This we effected with much labor by passing a rope to the shore . . . [and] those on shore pulled it along. . . .

At Pittsburgh another "broad-horn" boat had been purchased, larger and more conveniently arranged [and] . . . we commenced our voyage down the Ohio. . . . There was a great sameness in this water journey of about four hundred miles. . . . [We reached] Maysville, on the Kentucky side of the river . . . about a week from the time we left Pittsburgh. . . .

I do not recollect how many days we were journeying to Frankfort, but it was . . . a very slow method of travelling. We did not make more than from twenty to twenty-five miles each day.

Source: Noah M. Ludlow, *Dramatic Life as I Found It* (St. Louis: G. I. Jones and Company, 1880), 5–14, 17–21, 76–78.

stretched away into the forest on one side," an English visitor to an isolated Ohio farm in the 1820s noted,

and immediately before the house was a small potato garden, with a few peach and apple trees. The woman told me that they spun and wove all the cotton and woollen garments of the family, and knit all the stockings; her husband, though not a shoemaker by trade, made all the shoes. She manufactured all the soap and candles they use.

Self-sufficiency meant a low standard of living. As late as 1840 per capita income in states formed out of the Northwest Territory was only 70 percent of the national average.

Despite these financial hardships and transportation bottlenecks white Americans continued to migrate westward. They knew it would take a generation to clear land, build houses, barns, and roads and plant orchards, and yet they were confident that their sacrifices and the expansion of the canal and road system would yield future security for themselves and their children. The humble achievements of thousands of yeomen and tenant families slowly transformed the landscape of the interior of the continent, turning forests into farms and crossroads into communities.

The Republicans' Political Revolution

Agricultural expansion was a central policy of the Republican Party and accounted for much of its appeal. From 1801 to 1825 three Republicans from Virginia—Thomas Jefferson, James Madison, and James Monroe—served two terms each as president. Supported by voters in the new western states and strong majorities in Congress, this "Virginia Dynasty" reversed many Federalist policies, completing what Jefferson called the Revolution of 1800. Western issues such as Indian policy and territorial disputes with Spain and Britain occupied the attention of politicians and, together with maritime disputes in the Atlantic, precipitated the War of 1812.

The Jeffersonian Presidency

Thomas Jefferson was an accomplished statesman, an insightful political philosopher, and a superb politician. On assuming the presidency in 1801 Jefferson became the first chief executive to hold office in the District of Columbia, the new national capital. However, his administration did not begin with a clean slate. After a dozen years of Federalist presidents the federal judiciary was filled with their appointees. The most important was the formidable John Marshall of Virginia, who presided over the Supreme Court. Moreover, in 1801 the outgoing Federalist-controlled Congress had passed a Judiciary Act. It created sixteen new judgeships and six additional circuit courts, which, along with a variety of existing patronage posts, President Adams had filled with "midnight appointments" just before he left office. The Federalists "have retired into the judiciary as a stronghold," Jefferson complained, "and from that battery all the works of Republicanism are to be beaten down and destroyed."

Jefferson's fears were quickly realized. In 1798, during the dispute over the Alien and Sedition Acts, Republican-dominated legislatures in Kentucky and Virginia had asserted their authority to determine the constitutionality of national laws. However, the Constitution stated that "the judicial Power shall extend to all Cases . . . arising under this Constitution [and] the Laws of the United States," implying that the Supreme Court held the final power of **judicial review**. This important political and constitutional issue came to the fore when James Madison, the new secretary of state, refused to deliver the commission appointing William Marbury, one of Adams's midnight appointees, as a justice of the peace in the District of Columbia. Marbury petitioned the Supreme Court to compel delivery, arguing that the Judiciary Act of 1789 gave the Court jurisdiction. However, in *Marbury v. Madison* (1803), Chief Justice Marshall ruled that while Marbury had a right to his commission, the Court did not have power under the Constitution to enforce that particular right. By using this reasoning Marshall cleverly condemned Madison's action while avoiding a direct confrontation with the Republican administration. More important, in ruling that the section of the Judiciary Act extending the Court's jurisdiction violated the Constitution, Marshall asserted the Court's power to overturn a national law and to exercise the power of judicial review. "It is emphatically the province and duty of the judicial department to say what the law is," Marshall declared, directly repudiating the Republican view that the state legislatures had that power.

Ignoring Marshall's challenge, Jefferson and the Republicans used their newfound national power to reverse many Federalist policies. Charging the Federalists with grossly expanding the national government's size and power, Jefferson mobilized the Republican Congress to shrink it back. "The President has only to act and the Majority will approve," an observer noted. When the Alien and Sedition Acts expired in 1801, the Congress refused to reenact them, branding the acts as politically motivated and unconstitutional. It also amended the Naturalization Act to permit resident aliens to become citizens after five years. But the new president governed tactfully. Although Jefferson secured repeal of the Judiciary Act, thereby ousting forty of Adams's "midnight appointees," he appointed some Federalists to government posts and allowed competent Federalist bureaucrats to remain in their jobs. Apart from the midnight appointees, during eight years as chief executive he removed only 69 of 433 Federalist officeholders.

In foreign affairs Jefferson faced an immediate crisis. In the 1790s the Barbary States of North Africa had systematically raided American merchant ships, and Federalist officials had paid an annual bribe ("tribute") to buy their protection. Initially Jefferson reversed this policy, declaring in 1801 that the United States would no longer pay tribute. When the Barbary "pirates" renewed their assaults, he ordered the U.S. Navy to retaliate. But Jefferson wanted to avoid all-out war, which would increase taxes and the national debt. So he accepted a diplomatic solution that granted a reduced tribute.

In domestic matters Jefferson set a clearly Republican course. He abolished all internal taxes, including the excise tax that had sparked the Whiskey Rebellion of 1794. Addressing his party's fears of a military takeover, Jefferson reduced the size of the permanent army. He tolerated the economically important Bank of the United States (which he had condemned as unconstitutional in 1791), but as his secretary of the treasury Jefferson chose

Albert Gallatin, a fiscal conservative who believed that the national debt was "an evil of the first magnitude." By carefully controlling government expenditures and using customs revenues to redeem government bonds, Gallatin reduced the debt from $83 million in 1801 to $45 million in 1808. With Jefferson and Gallatin at the helm the nation was no longer run in the interests of northeastern creditors and merchants.

Jefferson and the West

Long before he became president, Jefferson championed the settlement of the West. He celebrated the yeoman farmer in *Notes on the State of Virginia* (1785), helped compose the Confederation's western land ordinances and strongly supported Pinckney's Treaty of 1795, which allowed settlers in the interior to ship crops down the Mississippi River for export through the Spanish-held port of New Orleans.

As president, Jefferson seized the opportunity to increase the flow of settlers to the West. During the 1790s the Federalist-dominated Congresses had refused to make it easier for migrating families to buy a farm in the national domain. In fact, the Federalist Land Act of 1796 doubled the minimum price to $2 per acre. Because Jefferson wanted to see the West populated with yeomen farm families, the Republicans in Congress passed laws in 1800 and 1804 reducing the minimum allotment first to 320 and then to 160 acres. Eventually the Land Act of 1820 cut the minimum purchase to 80 acres and the price to $1.25 per acre, enabling a farmer with only $100 in cash to buy a western farm (Table 8.1; Map 8.3).

The Louisiana Purchase. International events challenged Jefferson's vision for the West. In 1799 Napoleon Bonaparte seized power in France and began an ambitious campaign to establish a French empire both in Europe and in America. In 1801 Napoleon coerced Spain into signing a secret treaty that returned to France its former colony of Louisiana. A year later he directed Spanish officials in Louisiana to restrict American access to New Orleans, thus violating the terms of Pinckney's Treaty. Meanwhile, Napoleon planned an invasion to restore French rule in Haiti (then called Saint-Domingue), a rich sugar island seized in 1793 by rebellious black slaves led by Toussaint L'Ouverture.

Napoleon's aggressive actions prompted Jefferson to question his party's traditionally pro-French foreign policy. Any nation that denied Americans access to the port of New Orleans, Jefferson declared, must be "our natural and habitual enemy." To avoid hostilities with France Jefferson instructed Robert R. Livingston, the American minister in Paris, to negotiate the purchase of New Orleans. Simultaneously, Jefferson sent James Monroe to Britain to seek its assistance in case of war. "The day that France takes possession of New Orleans," the president warned, "we must marry ourselves to the British fleet and nation."

Jefferson's diplomacy yielded a magnificent prize: the entire territory of Louisiana. By 1802 the French invasion of Haiti was faltering in the face of disease and determined resistance, a new war threatened in Europe, and Napoleon feared an American invasion of Louisiana. Acting with characteristic decisiveness, the French ruler offered to sell not only New Orleans but also the entire territory of Louisiana. For about $15 million ($450 million today), Livingston and Monroe concluded what became known

TABLE 8.1 Major Acts Involving Land Sales of National Domain, 1785–1862

Date of Act	Minimum Purchase (Acres)	Minimum Auction Price Per Acre	Terms of Sale
1785	640	$1.00	Cash
1796	640	2.00	$\frac{1}{2}$ cash; $\frac{1}{2}$ credit for 1 yr.
1800	320	2.00	$\frac{1}{4}$ cash; rest over 3 yrs.
1804	160	2.00	Same as 1800
1820	80	1.25	Cash
1832	40	1.25	Cash
1841	None	NA	Pre-emption Act gives purchase rights to squatters
1854	40	None	Graduation Act allows purchase of unsold lands at low price
1862	160	None	Homestead Act gives land for free if cultivated for 5 yrs.

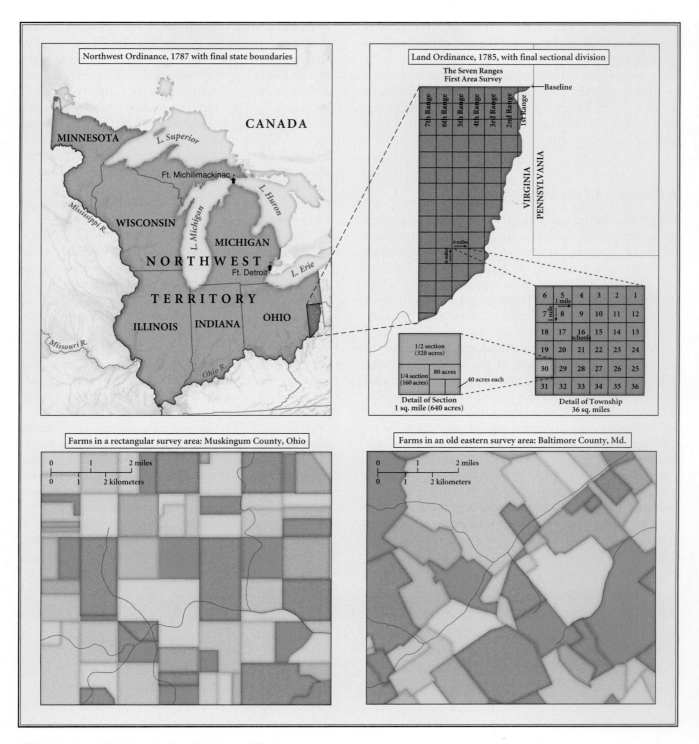

MAP 8.3 Land Division in the Northwest Territory

Throughout the Northwest Territory, government surveyors imposed a rectangular grid on the landscape, regardless of the local topography, so that farmers bought neatly defined properties. The right-angled property lines in Muskingum County, Ohio (lower left), contrasted sharply with those in Baltimore County, Maryland (lower right), where—as in most of the eastern and southern states—boundaries followed the contours of the land.

A scientist as well as a statesman, Jefferson wanted detailed information about the physical features of the new territory and its plant and animal life. In 1804 he sent his personal secretary, Meriwether Lewis, to explore the region with William Clark, an army officer. Aided by Indian guides Lewis and Clark and their group of American soldiers and frontiersmen traveled up the Missouri River, across the Rocky Mountains, and (venturing beyond the bounds of the Louisiana Purchase) down the Columbia River to the Pacific Ocean. After two years they returned with the first maps of the immense wilderness and vivid accounts of its natural resources and inhabitants (Map 8.4).

Threats to the Union.   The Louisiana Purchase was a stunning accomplishment, doubling the size of the nation at a single stroke, but it brought a new threat. New England Federalists, fearing that western expansion would diminish the power of their states and their party, talked openly of leaving the Union. When Alexander Hamilton refused to support their plan for a separate Northern Confederacy, the secessionists turned to Aaron Burr, the ambitious vice president, who was seeking election as governor of New York. In July 1804 Hamilton accused Burr of participating in a conspiracy to destroy the Union, and Burr challenged him to a pistol duel. Hamilton died by gunshot in the illegal confrontation, and state courts in New York and New Jersey indicted Burr for murder.

This tragic event propelled Burr into yet another secessionist scheme. After his vice presidential term ended early in 1805, Burr moved west to avoid prosecution. There he conspired with General James Wilkinson, the military governor of the Louisiana Territory. Their plan remains a mystery, but it probably involved either the capture of territory in New Spain or a rebellion to establish Louisiana as a separate nation headed by Burr. Wilkinson betrayed Burr, however, and arrested him for treason as the former vice president led an armed force down the Ohio River. In a highly politicized trial presided over by Chief Justice John Marshall, the jury acquitted Burr of treason. The verdict was less important than the dangers to national unity that it revealed. The Republicans' policy of western expansion had increased sectional tension and party conflict, generating states' rights sentiment in New England and secessionist schemes in the West.

Conflict with Britain and France

As the Napoleonic Wars ravaged Europe between 1802 and 1815, they threatened the commercial interests of the American republic. Great Britain and France, the major belligerents, refused to respect the neutrality of American merchant vessels. Napoleon imposed the "Continental System" on European ports under French

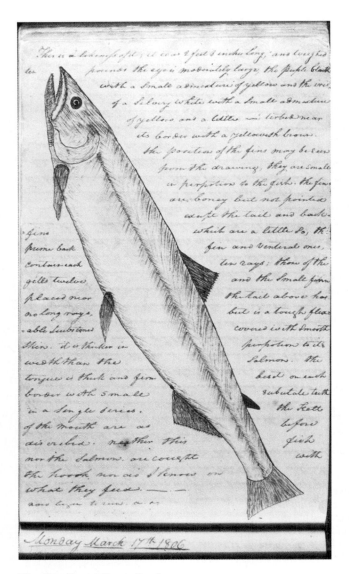

The Continent Described

Meriwether Lewis and William Clark fulfilled Jefferson's injunction to explore the trans-Mississippi West by filling their journals with drawings and descriptions of its topography, plants, and animals. Clark drew this picture of the white salmon trout along the Columbia River (in present-day Washington State) in his diary in March 1806.
Missouri Historical Society, Voorhis Number 2, William Clark Papers.

as the Louisiana Purchase. "We have lived long," Livingston remarked to Monroe, "but this is the noblest work of our lives."

The Louisiana Purchase forced the president to reconsider his interpretation of the Constitution. Jefferson had always been a strict constructionist, maintaining that the national government possessed only the powers "expressly" delegated to it in the Constitution. There was no provision in the Constitution for adding new territory, however, so to fulfill his dreams for the West Jefferson pragmatically accepted a loose interpretation of the treaty-making powers granted by the Constitution to complete the deal with France.

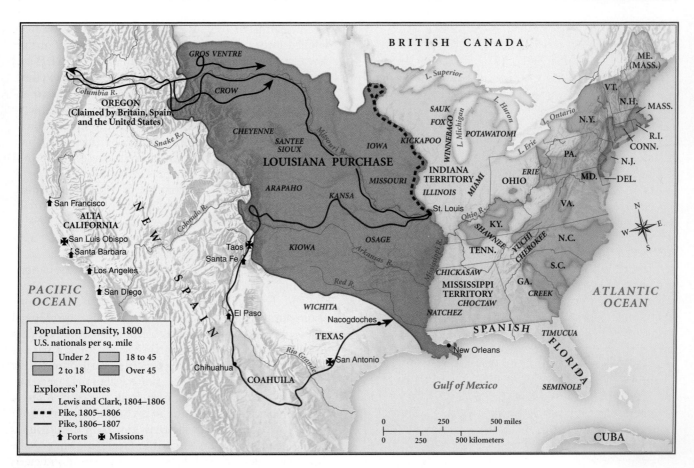

MAP 8.4 U.S. Population Density in 1803 and the Louisiana Purchase

When the United States purchased Louisiana from France in 1803, much of the land between the Appalachian Mountains and the Mississippi River remained in Indian hands, with only a few residents of European or African descent. The vast lands beyond the Mississippi were virtually unknown, even after the epic explorations of Zebulon Pike and Meriwether Lewis and William Clark. Nonetheless, President Jefferson predicted (quite accurately, as it turned out) that the vast Mississippi Valley "from its fertility . . . will ere long yield half of our whole produce, and contain half of our whole population."

control, requiring customs officials to seize neutral ships that had stopped in Britain. For its part, the British ministry set up a naval blockade, seizing ships carrying goods to Europe, including American vessels filled with sugar and molasses from the French West Indies. The British navy also searched American ships for British deserters and **impressed** (forced) them back into service. Between 1802 and 1811 British officers seized nearly eight thousand sailors, many of whom were American citizens. American resentment turned to outrage in 1807, when a British warship attacked the U.S. Navy vessel *Chesapeake*, killing or wounding twenty-one men and seizing four alleged deserters. "Never since the battle of Lexington have I seen this country in such a state of exasperation as at present," Jefferson declared.

The Embargo. To protect American interests while avoiding war Jefferson pursued a policy of **peaceful coercion**. Working closely with Secretary of State James

Madison, the president devised the Embargo Act of 1807, which prohibited American ships from leaving their home ports until Britain and France repealed their restrictions on U.S. trade. Though the embargo was a creative diplomatic measure—an economic weapon similar to the nonimportation movements between 1765 and 1775—it overestimated the dependence of France and Britain on American shipping and underestimated resistance from New England merchants, who feared it would ruin them.

The embargo was a disaster for the American economy. Exports plunged from $108 million in 1806 to $22 million in 1808, hurting farmers as well as merchants and prompting Federalists to demand its repeal. When the Republican Congress passed a Force Act giving customs officials extraordinary powers to prevent smuggling into Canada, Federalists railed against government tyranny. "Would to God," exclaimed one Federalist, "that the Embargo had done as little evil to ourselves as it has done to foreign nations."

Despite discontent over the embargo voters elected James Madison, one of its authors, to the presidency in 1808. As the main architect of the Constitution, an advocate of the Bill of Rights, and a prominent congressman and party leader, Madison had served the nation well. But as John Beckley, a loyal Republican, complained in 1806, he had performed poorly as secretary of state: "Madison is deemed by many too timid and indecisive as a statesman." Thus, at a crucial juncture in foreign affairs, a man with little understanding of the devious, cutthroat world of international politics became president. Madison quickly acknowledged the embargo's failure and replaced it with a series of new economic restrictions, none of which succeeded in persuading France and Britain to respect America's neutral rights. "The Devil himself could not tell which government, England or France, is the most wicked," an exasperated congressman declared.

Republican War Hawks. Republican congressmen from the West—the future "war hawks" of 1812—thought Britain was the major offender, pointing in particular to its assistance to the Indians in the Ohio River Valley. Bolstered by British guns and supplies, in 1809 the Shawnee chief Tecumseh, assisted by his brother, the prophet Tenskwatawa, had revived the Western Confederacy of the 1790s (see American Lives, "Tenskwatawa: Shawnee Prophet," p. 236). Their goal was to exclude whites from all lands west of the Appalachian Mountains. Responding to this threat, expansionists in Congress condemned British support of Tecumseh and threatened to invade Canada. In 1811, following a series of clashes between settlers and the Confederacy, William Henry Harrison, the governor of the Indiana Territory, led an army against Tenskwatawa's village of Prophetstown (on the Wabash River in present-day Indiana). After fending off the confederacy's warriors at the Battle of Tippecanoe, Harrison burned the village to the ground.

Henry Clay of Kentucky, the new Speaker of the House of Representatives, and John C. Calhoun, a rising young congressman from South Carolina, pushed Madison toward war with Great Britain. Southern and western Republican congressmen eyed new territory in British Canada and Spanish Florida, part of which had already been seized by American militia. They also hoped that war would discredit the Federalists, who had long pursued a pro-British foreign policy. With national elections approaching, Madison demanded British respect for American sovereignty in the West and neutral rights on the Atlantic. When the British did not respond quickly, Madison asked Congress for a declaration of war. In June 1812 a sharply divided Senate voted 19 to 13 for war, and the House of Representatives concurred, 79 to 49. To mobilize support for the war, Republicans emphasized Britain's disregard for American rights. As President Madison put it, "National honor is national property of the highest value."

The underlying causes of the War of 1812 have been much debated. Officially, the United States went to war because of violations of its neutral rights: the seizure of merchant ships and the impressment of their sailors. But the Federalists who represented merchants' and seamen's interests in Congress voted against the war declaration, and in the subsequent election voters in New England and the Middle Atlantic states cast their ballots (and 89 electoral votes) for the Federalist candidate for president, De Witt Clinton of New York. Madison amassed most of his 128 electoral votes in the South and West, where Republican congressmen and their constituents supported the war. Because of this regional split, more than one historian has argued that the conflict was "a western war with eastern labels."

The War of 1812

The War of 1812 was a near disaster for the United States, both militarily and politically. Predictions of an easy victory over British forces in Canada ended when a first invasion resulted in a hasty American retreat back to Detroit. But Americans stayed on the offensive in the West, as Commodore Oliver Hazard Perry defeated a small British flotilla on Lake Erie. Then in October 1813 General William Henry Harrison triumphed over a combined British and Indian force at the Battle of the Thames, killing Tecumseh, who had become a general in the British army. Another American expedition burned York (present-day Toronto) but lacking sufficient men and supplies quickly withdrew.

Political divisions in the United States prevented a major invasion of Canada in the East. New Englanders opposed the war and prohibited their militias from fighting outside their states. Boston merchants and banks declined to lend money to the federal government, making the war difficult to finance. In Congress Daniel Webster, a dynamic young representative from New Hampshire, led Federalist opposition to higher taxes and tariffs and to the national conscription of state militiamen.

Partly because of these domestic conflicts, the tide of battle gradually began to turn in Britain's favor. Initially the British had lost scores of merchant vessels to American privateers, but the Royal Navy redeployed its forces and British commerce moved in relative safety. By 1813 a flotilla of British warships moved up and down the American coastline, harassing American shipping and threatening seaport cities. In 1814 a British fleet sailed up Chesapeake Bay and British troops stormed ashore to attack the District of Columbia, burning government buildings. Then the troops advanced on Baltimore, where they were finally repulsed at Fort McHenry. After two years of sporadic warfare the United States had made little military progress along the Canadian frontier and was on the defensive along the Atlantic,

Tenskwatawa: Shawnee Prophet

By 1800 Indian peoples in the interior of North America were in a state of crisis—their warriors dying at the hands of aggressive frontiersmen, their communities disintegrating from the violence and sexual promiscuity that flowed from the white man's whiskey, their very existence threatened by the European diseases of influenza, measles, and smallpox. War, alcoholism, disease—the trilogy of social disasters that had virtually wiped out the eastern Indian peoples—now ravaged the tribes of the American heartland.

Everywhere along the frontier new Indian leaders arose to explain these disastrous happenings and to prescribe solutions. The religious prophet Handsome Lake urged the Senecas of New York to abstain from alcohol and revive traditional Indian spiritual beliefs. Eight hundred miles to the west, the eloquent shaman Main Poc denounced whites for disrupting Indian life and spread his message of Indian renewal not only among his fellow Potawatomis in Illinois and Wisconsin but also among the neighboring Sac, Winnebago, and Chippewa peoples.

The most important Indian prophet was Tenskwatawa (pronounced *Tens-qua-ta-wa*). He was born in 1775 at Old Piqua, a Shawnee village on the Mad River in western Ohio. His father, a prominent Shawnee warrior, had died four months before his birth, killed in battle against the Virginia militia; four years later his Creek mother abandoned the village, leaving her young children to be raised by kinfolk. As a young man the future prophet was known as Lalawethika ("Rattle" or "Noisemaker") because of his boastful ways, blatant alcoholism, and flagrant disrespect for sacred Shawnee laws. Then in 1805, at age thirty, he had a profound emotional experience, lapsing for hours into an unconscious state resembling death.

Upon awakening Lalawethika claimed to have died and to have visited the Master of Life, the Good Spirit and main Shawnee god, who allowed him a glimpse of heaven: "a rich fertile country, abounding in game, fish, pleasant hunting grounds and fine corn fields," where virtuous Shawnee would go after death. He also observed the spirits of sinful Indians suffering fiery tortures (similar to those described by the Puritan preacher Jonathan Edwards). Transformed by this experience, Lalawethika renounced his wicked ways and old identity, taking the name Tenskwatawa ("The One That Opens the Door"). He settled at Greenville in western Ohio, where he lived as a holy man, vowing to deliver the Shawnees from their present woes.

Like other Indian prophets, Tenskwatawa preached a nativist message, urging his followers to shun Americans, "the children of the Evil Spirit . . . who have taken away your lands." He denounced the consumption of alcohol, a "poison and accursed" drink, and called for a return to traditional food and clothes: "You must not dress like the White Man . . . you must go naked Excepting the Breach cloth, and when you are clothed, it must be in skins or leather." To spread these teachings, Tenskwatawa founded a new religion, deriving some of its rituals from Catholicism, which French Jesuits had spread among the Indian peoples of the region. Converts were to confess their sins and then to worship an effigy of Tenskwatawa, fingering a string of beads (similar to a rosary) and thereby "shaking hands with the Prophet."

The new religion spread like wildfire among the Delawares of Indiana, who in 1806 showed their zeal by burning alive six suspected Indian witches. Shocked by these deaths, William Henry Harrison, the American governor of the Indiana Territory, denounced Tenskwatawa as a "pretended prophet" who was leading the Shawnees down "a dark, crooked, and thorny road." "If he is really a prophet," Harrison told the Indians, "ask of him to cause the sun to stand still . . . or the dead to rise from their graves." Harrison soon regretted these words. Learning from visiting American astronomers of an imminent eclipse of the sun in Indiana and Illinois, Tenskwatawa announced that on June 16 he would darken the sun at midday. "Did I not speak the truth?" he asked those—Delawares and Wyandots as well as Shawnees—who gathered at Greenville at the appointed time. "See, the sun is dark." As reports of this "miracle" circulated, warriors and wise men from many western tribes—Kickapoo, Potawatomi, Winnebago, Ottawa, Chippewa—journeyed to Greenville to learn the Prophet's teachings.

In 1808 the new religion took on a political cast. Fearing attacks by Americans and seeking closer proximity to his western followers, Tenskwatawa founded a new holy village, Prophetstown, near the juncture of the Tippecanoe and Wabash Rivers. There, he said, "they would be able to watch the Boundary Line between the Indians and white people—and if a white man put his foot over it [the Wabash River] then the warriors could easily put him back." To defend this newly defined boundary, the Prophet dispatched his older brother Tecumseh to Canada, where he secured food, manufactures, and guns from British officials. The determination of the Shawnee brothers stiffened in September 1809 when "government

Tenskwatawa, "The Prophet," 1836
Tenskwatawa added a spiritual dimension to Native American resistance, urging a holy war against the invading whites. His religious message transcended differences among Indian peoples, helping to create a formidable political and military alliance.
Smithsonian American Art Musuem, Washington, D.C. / Art Resource, NY.

chiefs" (Miami, Delaware, and Potawatomi leaders who received annuities from U.S. officials) ceded more than 3 million acres of land in Indiana and Illinois to the United States. Arguing that the land belonged to all Indians, Tenskwatawa declared that "no sale was good unless made by all the Tribes." Tecumseh demanded that the governor "restore the land"; otherwise he would "kill all the chiefs that sold you this land" and form a great confederation that would unite with the British to expel American invaders. What had begun as a movement of religious revitalization had become a crusade for Indian political unity and land rights.

As the movement changed its focus, Tecumseh seized the reins of leadership. After meeting Tecumseh in August 1811, Harrison reported to the secretary of war that he was "really the efficient man—the Moses of the family . . . a bold, active, sensible man, daring in the extreme and capable of any undertaking." When Tecumseh left for the South (to persuade the Chickasaws, Choctaws, and Creeks to join the Indian Confederation), Harrison took advantage of his absence, quickly mobilizing an army of 1,000 men and marching on Prophetstown. Ignoring his

brother's instructions to avoid conflict, Tenskwatawa assured his force of 600 warriors that the Master of Life would make them invulnerable and attacked Harrison's camp near the Tippecanoe River. In a bitter but inconclusive battle, the Americans suffered 62 dead and 124 wounded while the Indians lost 50 dead and 80 wounded. But the victory went to Harrison. Shocked by their losses, Tenskwatawa's followers now scoffed at his claims of religious power, threatened him with death, and melted away, allowing the American troops to burn Prophetstown.

The Prophet's religion suffered a severe wound on the battlefield at Tippecanoe, and it died during the War of 1812, as American bullets took the lives of Tecumseh and many of Tenskwatawa's remaining followers. After a decade of exile in British Canada, Tenskwatawa returned to the United States in 1824 as one of the "government chiefs" he had long despised, working for U.S. officials and persuading hundreds of Shawnees to leave Indiana and move with him to a reservation on the plains of eastern Kansas. He died there in 1836, without power, influence, or followers.

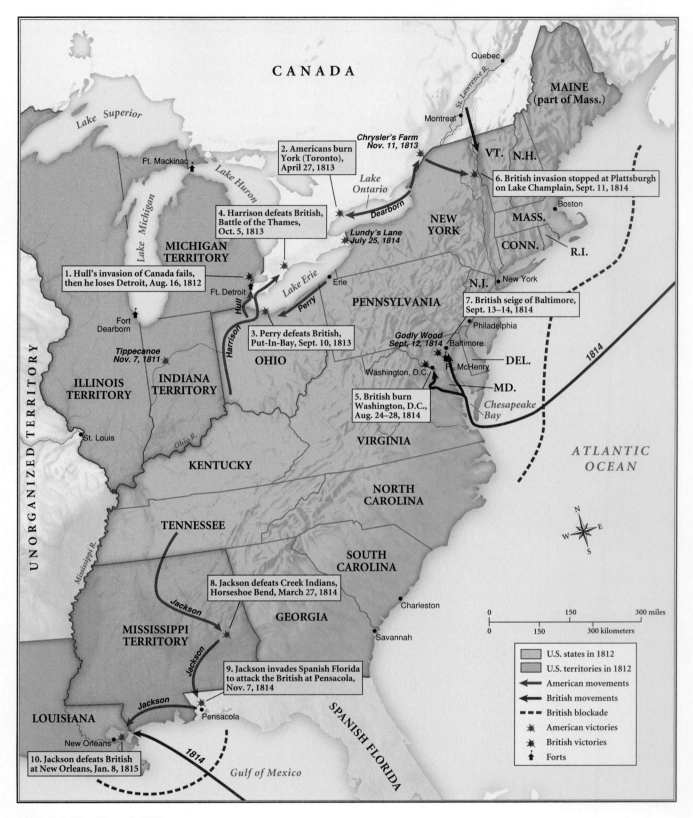

MAP 8.5 The War of 1812

Unlike the War for Independence, the War of 1812 had few large-scale military campaigns. The most extensive fighting took place along the Canadian border. In 1812 and 1813, American armies led by Generals Hull, Harrison, and Dearborn and a naval force commanded by Commodore Perry attacked British targets with mixed success. The British took the offensive in 1814, launching a successful raid on Washington and Baltimore but suffering heavy losses when they invaded the United States along Lake Champlain. Near the Gulf of Mexico, American forces moved from one success to another, as General Andrew Jackson defeated the pro-British Creek Indians at the Battle of Horseshoe Bend and, in the major battle of the war, an invading British army at New Orleans.

with its new capital city in ruins. The only positive news came from the Southwest. There a rugged slave-owning planter named Andrew Jackson led an army of militiamen from Tennessee to victory over the British-supported Creek Indians in the Battle of Horseshoe Bend (1814), forcing the Indians to cede 23 million acres of land (Map 8.5).

American military setbacks strengthened opposition to the war, especially in New England. In 1814 Federalists in the Massachusetts legislature called for a convention "to lay the foundation for a radical reform in the National Compact," and New England Federalists met in Hartford, Connecticut, to discuss strategy. Some delegates to the Hartford convention proposed secession by their states, but the majority favored revising the Constitution. To end domination of the presidency by Virginians the delegates proposed a constitutional amendment that would limit the office to a single four-year term and require it to rotate among citizens from different states. Other delegates suggested amendments restricting commercial embargoes to sixty days and requiring a two-thirds majority in Congress to declare war, prohibit trade, or admit a new state to the Union.

As a minority party in Congress and the nation, the Federalists could prevail only if the war continued to go badly—a very real prospect. In late summer of 1814 a planned British invasion of the Hudson River Valley was narrowly averted by an American naval victory at the Battle of Lake Champlain. Then while the Federalists were meeting in Hartford in December, thousands of seasoned British troops landed at New Orleans, threatening to cut off the access of western settlers to the sea. The United States was under military pressure from both north and south.

Fortunately for the young American republic, Britain wanted peace. The twenty-year struggle against France had sapped its wealth and energy, and so it entered into negotiations with the United States in Ghent, Belgium. At

***Battle of New Orleans,* by Jean Hyacinthe de Laclotte (detail)**

As their artillery (right center) bombarded the American lines, British troops attacked the center of General Andrew Jackson's troops while a column of redcoats (foreground) tried to turn the right flank of the American fortifications. Secure behind their battlements, Jackson's forces repelled the assaults, leaving the ground littered with British casualties and taking thousands of prisoners.

New Orleans Museum of Art, gift of Edgar William and Bernice Chrysler Garbisch.

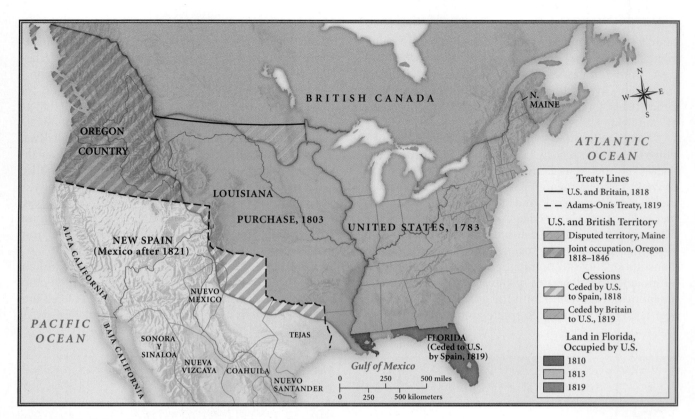

MAP 8.6 Defining the National Boundaries, 1800–1820

After the War of 1812 American diplomats negotiated treaties with Great Britain and Spain that defined the boundaries of the Louisiana Purchase with British Canada to the north and New Spain (which in 1821 became the independent nation of Mexico) to the south and west. These treaties eliminated the threat of border wars with neighboring states for a generation, providing the United States with a much-needed period of peace and security.

For more help analyzing this map, see the ONLINE STUDY GUIDE at bedfordstmartins.com/henretta.

first the American commissioners—John Quincy Adams, Albert Gallatin, and Henry Clay—demanded territory in Canada and Florida, and British diplomats insisted on an Indian buffer state between the United States and Canada. Ultimately, both sides realized that small concessions won at the bargaining table were not worth the costs of prolonged warfare. The Treaty of Ghent, signed on Christmas Eve 1814, restored the prewar borders of the United States.

This result hardly justified three years of fighting, but a final victory in combat lifted Americans' morale. Before news of the Treaty of Ghent reached the United States, newspaper headlines proclaimed an "ALMOST INCREDIBLE VICTORY!! GLORIOUS NEWS": on January 8, 1815, General Andrew Jackson's troops (including a contingent of French-speaking black Americans, the Corps d'Afrique) crushed the British forces attacking New Orleans. The Americans fought from carefully constructed breastworks and were amply supplied with cannon, which rained "grapeshot and cannister bombs" on the massed British formations. The British lost some of

their finest troops, with seven hundred dead and two thousand wounded or taken prisoner. By contrast the Americans sustained only thirteen dead and fifty-eight wounded. The victory made Jackson a national hero and a symbol of the emerging West. It also redeemed the nation's battered pride and, together with the coming of peace, undercut the Hartford convention's demands for a significant revision of the Constitution.

Just as Jackson emerged as a war hero, John Quincy Adams rose to national prominence for his diplomatic efforts at Ghent and his subsequent success in resolving boundary disputes. The son of Federalist president John Adams, John Quincy had joined the Republican Party before the war and in 1817 became secretary of state under President James Monroe (1817–1825). In 1817 Adams negotiated the Rush-Bagot Treaty with Great Britain, which limited both nations' naval forces on the Great Lakes; the following year he concluded another agreement that set the border between the Louisiana Purchase and British Canada at the forty-ninth parallel. Then in 1819

Adams persuaded Spain to cede Florida to the United States in the Adams-Onís Treaty. In return the American government took responsibility for its citizens' financial claims against Spain, renounced Jefferson's earlier claim that Spanish Texas was part of the Louisiana Purchase, and agreed on a compromise boundary between New Spain and the state of Louisiana, which had entered the Union in 1812 (Map 8.6). As a result of Adams's efforts the United States gained undisputed possession of nearly all the land south of the forty-ninth parallel and between the Mississippi River and the Rocky Mountains.

The Capitalist Commonwealth

The increasing size of the American republic was paralleled by the growth of its economic institutions and wealth. Before 1790 the United States was an agricultural society, dependent on Great Britain for markets, credit, and manufactured goods. Over the next generation the nation gradually developed a more diverse economy as some rural Americans became manufacturers, bankers supplied credit to expand trade, merchants developed regional markets, and state governments actively encouraged economic development.

The emerging American economic order was capitalist in character because it was based on private property and market exchanges and because capitalists—investors, bankers, and wealthy entrepreneurs—shaped many of its political and financial policies. But this capitalist political economy was still influenced by the political ideology of the republican commonwealth, which elevated the public good over private gain.

A Merchant-Based Economy: Banks, Manufacturing, and Markets

America was "a Nation of Merchants," a British visitor reported from Philadelphia in 1798, "always alive to their interests; and keen in the pursuit of wealth in all the various modes of acquiring it." And acquire it they did, especially during the European wars that lasted from 1792 to 1815 and provided opportunities for spectacular profits. Entrepreneurs such as the fur trader John Jacob Astor and the merchant Robert Oliver became the nation's first millionaires. Migrating from Germany to New York in 1784, Astor became wealthy by carrying furs from the Pacific Northwest to markets in China. He soon became the largest landowner in New York City. Oliver started in Baltimore as an agent for Irish linen merchants and then opened his own mercantile firm. Exploiting the wartime shipping boom, he reaped enormous profits in the West Indian coffee and sugar trade.

Banking and Credit. To finance such enterprises Americans needed a banking system. Before 1776

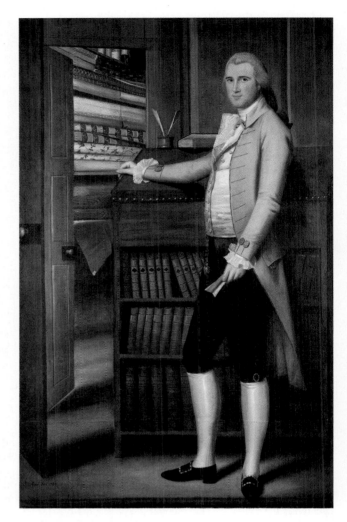

Cloth Merchant
Elijah Boardman (1760–1832) was a prosperous storekeeper in New Milford, Connecticut, who eventually became a United States senator. Along with other American traders, he imported huge quantities of cloth from Britain. When war cut off trade, some merchants financed the domestic production of textiles. Others, including Boardman, turned to speculation in western lands; in 1795 he joined the Connecticut Land Company and bought huge tracts in Connecticut's "Western Reserve," including the present towns of Medina, Palmyra, and Boardman, Ohio. Ralph Earl painted this portrait of Boardman in 1789.
Metropolitan Museum of Art, bequest of Susan W. Tyler, 1979.

ambitious colonists found it difficult to secure loans. Farmers relied on government-sponsored land banks, while merchants arranged partnerships, borrowed funds from other merchants, or obtained credit from British suppliers. Then in 1781 Philadelphia merchants persuaded the Confederation Congress to charter the Bank of North America to provide short-term commercial loans; traders in Boston and New York founded similar banks in 1784. Those institutions provided merchants with the credit they needed to finance their transactions. "Our monied capital has so much increased from the Introduction of Banks, & the

Circulation of the Funds," the Philadelphia merchant William Bingham boasted as early as 1791, "that the Necessity of Soliciting Credits from England will no longer exist, & the Means will be provided for putting in Motion every Specie of Industry."

In 1791, on Alexander Hamilton's initiative, Congress chartered the First Bank of the United States. The bank had the power to issue notes and make commercial loans, and although the bank's managers used their lending powers cautiously, profits still averaged a handsome 8 percent annually. By 1805, in response to the continuing demand for commercial credit, the bank had branches in eight major cities. Despite this success the First Bank of the United States did not survive. Jeffersonians, who were suspicious of corruption by monied men, accused the bank of encouraging "a consolidated, energetic government supported by public creditors, speculators, and other insidious men lacking in public spirit of any kind." When the bank's charter expired in 1811, President Madison did not seek renewal, forcing merchants, artisans, and farmers to ask their state legislatures to charter new banks. By 1816, when Madison adopted a more "national" stance with respect to economic policy and signed the congressional legislation creating the Second Bank of the United States, there were 246 state-chartered banks with $68 million in banknotes in circulation.

Many state banks were shady operations, issuing notes without adequate specie reserves and making ill-advised loans to insiders. Such poorly managed state banks were one cause of the Panic of 1819, a credit crisis sparked by a sharp drop in world agricultural prices. As farm income plummeted by one-third, many farmers could not pay their bills, causing bankruptcies among local storekeepers, wholesale merchants, and overextended state banks. By 1821, those state banks that were still solvent had only $45 million in circulation and court dockets were crowded with thousands of cases, as creditors tried to save their own businesses by taking possession of the devalued property of their debtors. The panic gave Americans their first taste of the business cycle—the periodic expansion and contraction of profits and employment that is an inherent part of a market economy.

Rural Manufacturing.   The panic also revealed that artisans and yeomen as well as merchants now depended on regional or national markets. Before 1790 most artisans in New England and the Middle Atlantic region sold their handicrafts locally or bartered them with neighbors. For example, John Hoff of Lancaster, Pennsylvania, sold his fine wooden-cased clocks locally and bartered them with his neighbors for such things as a dining table, a bedstead, and labor on his small farm. But others—shipbuilders in seacoast towns, iron smelters in Pennsylvania and Maryland, and shoemakers in Lynn, Massachusetts—already sold their products in far-flung markets. Indeed, merchant-entrepreneurs were hard at work developing a rural-based manufacturing system similar to the European outwork, or putting-out, system (see Chapter 1) and selling its products in all parts of the nation. Merchants stood at the center of this system, buying raw materials, organizing workers to make goods, and selling finished products. At the periphery were hundreds of thousands of farm families that supplied the labor. When a French traveler visited central Massachusetts in 1795, he found "almost all these houses . . . inhabited by men who are both cultivators and artisans; one is a tanner, another a shoemaker, another sells goods, but all are farmers."

By the 1820s thousands of New England farm families produced shoes, brooms, palm-leaf hats, and tinware—baking pans, cups, utensils, lanterns. Merchants shipped these products to cities and slave plantations, while New England peddlers, equipped "with a horse and a cart covered with a box or with a wagon," blanketed the South and acquired a reputation as crafty, hard-bargaining "Yankees." The success of these peddlers and merchants expanded the commercial sector of the American domestic economy.

This economic advance stemmed initially from innovations in organization and marketing rather than in technology. Water-powered machines—the product of the Industrial Revolution in Britain—were adopted slowly in America, beginning in the textile industry. In the 1780s merchants built small mills along the waterways of New England and the Middle Atlantic states. They installed water-powered machines and hired workers to card and comb wool—and later cotton—into long strands. For several decades the next steps in the manufacturing process were accomplished under the outwork system rather than in water-powered factories. Wage-earning farm women and children spun the strands into yarn by hand, and men in other households used foot-powered looms to weave the yarn into cloth. In his *Letter on Manufactures* (1810) Secretary of the Treasury Albert Gallatin estimated that there were 2,500 outwork weavers in New England. A decade later more than 12,000 household workers in that region wove woolen cloth, which then went to water-powered fulling mills to be pounded flat and finished smooth. Thus, even before textile production was centralized in factories, the nation had a profitable and expanding preindustrial outwork system of manufacturing.

Toward a Market Economy.   The penetration of the market economy into rural areas motivated farmers to produce more goods. Ambitious farm families switched from mixed-crop agriculture to raising cattle, in order to sell their hides to the booming shoe industry, and to keeping dairy cows to provide milk for cheese making. As a Polish traveler in central Massachusetts reported in 1798, "Along the whole road from Boston, we saw women engaged in making cheese" for sale in cities. Hatmaking emerged as another new industry. "Straw hats and

The Yankee Peddler, c. 1830

Even in 1830 most Americans lived too far from market towns to go there regularly to buy needed goods. Instead, farm families, such as this relatively prosperous one depicted by an unknown artist, purchased most of their tinware, clocks, textiles, and other manufactures from peddlers, often from New England, who traveled far and wide in small horse-drawn vans such as that pictured in the doorway. Collection IBM Corporation, Armonk, NY.

For more help analyzing this image, see the ONLINE STUDY GUIDE at bedfordstmartins.com/henretta.

Bonnets are manufactured by many families," a Maine official commented, while another observer noted that "probably 8,000 females" in the vicinity of Foxborough, Massachusetts, braided rye straw into hats for market sale. Other farm families began to raise sheep and sold raw wool to textile manufacturers. Processing these raw materials brought new businesses to many farming towns. In 1792 Concord, Massachusetts, had one slaughterhouse and five small tanneries; a decade later the town had eleven slaughterhouses and six large tanneries.

As the rural economy produced more goods, it also produced significant changes in the environment. For example, foul odors from stockyards and tanning pits now wafted over Concord and many other leather-producing towns. Moreover, the multiplication of livestock—dairy cows, cattle, and especially sheep—created a new landscape as farmers cut down hundreds of thousands of acres of trees to provide pasturage. By the mid-nineteenth century, most of the forests in southern New England were

gone, leaving a barren visual landscape. Likewise, New England's rivers were now dotted with scores of textile milldams that altered the flow of rivers, and made it difficult if not impossible for fish to reach their upriver spawning grounds. Even as the income of many farmers rose, the quality of their natural environment deteriorated.

At first, barter transactions were a central feature of the emergent market system. When Ebenezer and Daniel Merriam of Brookfield, Massachusetts, began publishing books in the 1810s and distributing them to booksellers and publishers in New York City, Philadelphia, and Boston, they received neither cash nor credit in return. Rather, they received other books, which they had to exchange with local storekeepers to get supplies for their business. The Merriams also paid their employees on a barter basis; a journeyman printer received a third of his "wages" in books, which he had to peddle himself. Gradually a cash economy replaced this complex barter system. As farm families sold more and more goods in the market,

Voting Box

Elections in Pennsylvania were often contentious affairs, marred by riots and fistfights as rival political groups tried to keep their opponents from the polls. Once safely inside the voting place, citizens deposited their ballots in containers such as this nicely crafted late-eighteenth-century walnut box from the Delaware Valley. Independence National Historic Park.

they stopped making their own textiles and shoes and bought them instead, using the cash or store credit they had earned.

The new capitalist-run market economy had some drawbacks. Rural parents and their children now worked longer and harder, making specialized products during the winter in addition to their regular farming chores during the warmer seasons. Perhaps more important, they lost some of their economic independence. Instead of working solely for themselves as yeomen farm families, they toiled as part-time wage earners for merchants and manufacturers. The new market system decreased the self-sufficiency of families and communities even as it made them more productive. But the tide of change was unstoppable.

Public Policy: The Commonwealth System

Throughout the nineteenth century state governments were the most important political institutions in the United States and were the leading lawmaking bodies. They enacted legislation governing criminal and civil affairs, established taxation systems, and oversaw county, city, and town officials. Consequently, state governments had a much greater impact on the day-to-day lives of Americans than did the national government.

As early as the 1790s many state legislatures devised an American plan of mercantilism, known to historians as the commonwealth system (because its goal was to increase the common wealth, or common good, of the society). Just as the British Parliament had promoted the imperial economy through the Navigation Acts

(1651–1696), state legislatures enacted measures to stimulate commerce and economic development. In particular, they granted hundreds of corporate charters to private businesses to build roads, bridges, and canals, enterprises that were intended to be "of great public utility," as the act establishing the Massachusetts Bank put it. For example, in 1794 the Pennsylvania assembly chartered the Lancaster Turnpike Company to lay a graded gravel road between Lancaster and Philadelphia, a distance of sixty-five miles. The venture was expensive—nearly $500,000 (about $8 million today)—but the road made a modest profit for the investors and greatly enhanced the regional economy by allowing a rapid movement of goods and people. "The turnpike is finished," noted a farm woman, "and we can now go to town at all times and in all weather." A boom in turnpike construction soon connected dozens of inland market centers to seaport cities.

By 1800 state governments had granted more than three hundred corporate charters. Incorporation often included a grant of **limited liability** that made it easier to attract investors; in the event the business failed, the personal assets of the shareholders could not be seized to pay the corporation's debts. Most transportation charters also included the power of **eminent domain**, giving turnpike, bridge, and canal corporations the use of the judicial system to force the sale of privately owned land along proposed routes. State legislatures also came to the aid of capitalist flour millers or textile manufacturers whose dams flooded adjacent land, thereby infringing on the property rights of farmers or constituting a public "nuisance" under **common law**. In Massachusetts, the

Mill Dam Act of 1795 overrode common law and required farmers to accept "fair compensation" for their lost acreage.

To some critics such uses of state power by private companies ran contrary to republicanism, "which does not admit of granting peculiar privileges to any body of men." Charters not only violated the "equal rights" of all citizens, opponents argued, but also restricted the sovereignty of the people. As a Pennsylvanian put it, "Whatever power is given to a corporation, is just so much power taken from the State" and therefore the citizenry. Nonetheless, state courts consistently upheld corporate charters and routinely approved grants of eminent domain to private corporations. "The opening of good and easy internal communications is one of the highest duties of government," a New Jersey court declared.

State mercantilism soon encompassed much more than transportation. Following the embargo of 1807, which cut off goods and credit from Europe, New England states awarded charters to two hundred iron-mining, textile-manufacturing, and banking firms, and the Pennsylvania legislature granted more than eleven hundred. Thus by 1820 innovative state governments had created a new political economy: the commonwealth system. The use of state incentives to encourage business and improve the general welfare would continue for another generation.

Federalist Law: John Marshall and the Supreme Court

Both Federalists and Republicans endorsed the commonwealth idea but in different ways. Federalists looked

***John Marshall*, by Chester Harding, c. 1830**
Even at age seventy-five, John Marshall (1755–1835) had a commanding personal presence. Upon becoming chief justice of the U.S. Supreme Court in 1801, Marshall elevated the Court from a minor department of the national government to a major institution in American legal and political life. His constitutional decisions dealing with judicial review, contract rights, the regulation of commerce, and national banking permanently shaped the character of American law. Boston Athenaeum.

to the national government for economic leadership and supported Alexander Hamilton's program of national mercantilism: a funded debt, tariffs, and a central bank. Jeffersonian Republicans generally opposed such policies, preferring state-based initiatives, but following the War of 1812 some Republicans began to support national economic policies. As Speaker of the House of Representatives, Republican Henry Clay of Kentucky supported the creation of the Second Bank of the United States in 1816. In the following year Clay won passage of the Bonus Bill, sponsored by Representative John C. Calhoun of South Carolina, to establish a national fund for roads and other internal improvements. But most Republicans still believed that such policies exceeded the powers delegated to the national government by the Constitution. They welcomed President Madison's veto of the Bonus Bill and urged state legislatures to take the lead in promoting economic development. This fundamental disagreement over the role of the national government remained a key issue of political debate for the next thirty years (see Chapter 11).

The difference between Federalist and Jeffersonian Republican conceptions of public policy emerged during John Marshall's tenure on the Supreme Court. Appointed chief justice by President John Adams in January 1801, Marshall was a committed Federalist from Virginia who dominated the Court until 1822 and upheld nationalist principles on the Court until his death in 1835. His success stemmed not from a mastery of legal principles and doctrines but from the power of his logic and the force of his personality. By winning the support of Joseph Story and other nationalist-minded Republican judges on the Court, Marshall shaped the evolution of the Constitution. Three principles formed the basis of his jurisprudence: a commitment to judicial authority, the supremacy of national over state legislation, and a traditional, static view of property rights (Table 8.2).

After Marshall proclaimed the power of judicial review in *Marbury v. Madison* (see Chapter 7), the doctrine evolved slowly. During the first half of the nineteenth century the Supreme Court and the state courts used it sparingly and then only to overturn state laws that clearly conflicted with constitutional principles. Not until the *Dred Scott* decision of 1857 would the Supreme Court void another law passed by Congress (see Chapter 13).

Federal-State Relations. The position of the Marshall Court on federal-state relations was most eloquently expressed in *McCulloch v. Maryland* (1819). In 1816 Congress created the Second Bank of the United States, giving it authority to handle the notes of state-chartered banks and thus to monitor their financial reserves. To preserve the competitive position of its state-chartered banks, the Maryland legislature imposed an annual tax of $15,000 on notes issued by the Baltimore branch office of the Second Bank. In response, the Second Bank contested the constitutionality of the Maryland law, claiming that it infringed on the powers of the national government. To make their case, lawyers for the state of Maryland adopted Jefferson's argument against the First Bank of the United States, maintaining that Congress lacked the constitutional authority to charter a national bank. Even if such a bank could be created, the lawyers argued, Maryland had a right to tax its activities within the state.

Marshall and the nationalist-minded Republicans on the Court firmly rejected both arguments. The Second Bank was constitutional, said the chief justice, because it was "necessary and proper," given the national government's responsibility to control currency and credit. Like Alexander Hamilton and other Federalists, Marshall preferred a loose construction of the Constitution. If the goal of a law is "legitimate [and] . . . within the scope of the Constitution," he wrote, then "all means which are appropriate" to secure that goal are also constitutional, even if they are not explicitly mentioned. As for Maryland's right to tax the national bank, the chief justice stated that "the power to tax involves the power to destroy," suggesting that Maryland's bank tax would render the national government "dependent on the states"—an outcome that "was not intended by the American people" who ratified the Constitution.

TABLE 8.2 Major Decisions of the Marshall Court

Date	Case	Significance of Decision
1803	*Marbury v. Madison*	Asserts principle of judicial review
1810	*Fletcher v. Peck*	Protects property rights by a broad reading of "contract" clause
1819	*Dartmouth College v. Woodward*	Safeguards property rights of chartered corporations
1819	*McCulloch v. Maryland*	Interprets Constitution to give broad powers to national government
1824	*Gibbons v. Ogden*	Gives national government jurisdiction over interstate commerce

The Marshall Court asserted the dominance of national statutes over state legislation again in *Gibbons v. Ogden* (1824), which struck down a monopoly that the New York legislature had granted to Aaron Ogden for steamboat passenger service across the Hudson River to New Jersey. Asserting that the Constitution gave the federal government the authority to regulate interstate commerce, the chief justice sided with Thomas Gibbons, who held a federal license to transport people and goods between the two states.

Property Rights. Marshall also turned to the Constitution to uphold his view of property rights. During the 1790s Thomas Jefferson and other Republicans had celebrated the primacy of statute (or "positive") law enacted by representatives of the people. As a Republican jurist put it, a magistrate "should be governed himself by positive law" while executing and enforcing "the will of the supreme power, which is the will of THE PEOPLE." In response, Federalist judges and politicians warned that popular sovereignty had to be curbed to prevent the "tyranny of the majority"—the passage of statutes that would infringe on the property rights of individual citizens. To prevent state legislatures from overriding property rights, Federalist lawyers asserted that judges had the power to void laws that violated traditional common-law principles or were contrary to "natural law" or "natural rights" (see Chapter 4).

Marshall shared the goal of protecting individuals' property from government interference but used another legal strategy. He seized on the contract clause of the Constitution (Article 1, Section 10; see Documents, p. D-9), which prohibits the states from passing any law "impairing the obligation of contracts." Delegates at the 1787 Philadelphia convention had included this clause primarily to allow creditors to overturn state laws that prevented them from seizing the lands and goods of debtors, but Marshall expanded it to defend other property rights.

To extend the reach of this constitutional provision, Marshall gave an exceedingly broad definition to the term *contract*, enlarging it to embrace grants and charters made by the state governments. The case of *Fletcher v. Peck* (1810) involved a large grant of land made by the Georgia legislature to the Yazoo Land Company. A newly elected state legislature canceled the grant, alleging it had been obtained through fraud and bribery; in response, speculators who had already purchased Yazoo lands appealed to the Supreme Court to uphold their titles. Marshall ruled that the legislative grant to Yazoo Land Company was a contract that could not subsequently be abridged by the state. The property rights of the company and the purchasers had become "vested" in the new owners. This far-reaching decision not only gave constitutional protection to those who purchased state-owned lands but also promoted the development of a national capitalist economy by protecting out-of-state investors.

The court extended its defense of vested property rights even further in *Dartmouth College v. Woodward* (1819). Dartmouth College was a private institution established by a charter granted by King George III. In 1816 the Republican-dominated legislature of New Hampshire tried to convert the college into a public university that would educate more of the state's citizens, thereby enhancing the commonwealth. The Dartmouth trustees resisted the legislature and engaged Daniel Webster, a renowned constitutional lawyer as well as a leading Federalist politician, to plead their case. Citing the Court's decision in *Fletcher v. Peck*, Webster argued that the royal charter constituted a contract and therefore could not be tampered with by the New Hampshire legislature. Marshall and Story agreed, upholding the rights of the college. Marshall's triumph seemed complete. Many Federalist principles, such as judicial review and corporate property rights, had been permanently incorporated into the American legal system (see Voices from Abroad, "Alexis de Tocqueville: Law and Lawyers in the United States," p. 248).

The "Era of Good Feeling." Yet even as Marshall announced the *Dartmouth* and *McCulloch* decisions in 1819, the political fortunes of his Federalist Party were in severe decline. Nationalist-minded Republicans had won the allegiance of many Federalist voters in the East, while the pro-agrarian policies of Jeffersonian Republicans commanded the support of most western farmers and southern planters. "No Federal character can run with success," Gouverneur Morris of New York lamented, and the election results of 1818 bore out his pessimism. Following the election Republicans outnumbered Federalists 37 to 7 in the Senate and 156 to 27 in the House of Representatives. Westward expansion and the transformation in American government begun by Jefferson's Revolution of 1800 had brought the tumultuous era of Federalist-Republican conflict to an end.

The decline of political controversy prompted contemporary observers to dub James Monroe's two terms as president (1817–1825) the "Era of Good Feeling." Actually, national political harmony was more apparent than real, for the Republican Party was now divided into a National faction and a Jeffersonian (or "state"-oriented) faction. The two groups fought bitterly over patronage and policy, especially the issue of federal support for internal improvement projects such as roads and canals. As the aging Jefferson himself complained about the National Republicans, "You see so many of these new republicans maintaining in Congress the rankest doctrines of the old federalists." This division in the ranks of the Republican Party would soon produce a second party system—in which Whigs faced off against Democrats. One cycle of American politics and economic debate had ended and another was about to begin.

Alexis de Tocqueville

Law and Lawyers in the United States

A French aristocrat and lawyer, Alexis de Tocqueville came to the United States to study its innovative prison system but ended up writing Democracy in America *(1835), a comprehensive and astute analysis of its dynamic society. Here argues that the raw vigor of American democracy was restrained by the ingrained conservatism of men of the law, who dominated the political system.*

The political activity that pervades the United States must be seen in order to be understood. No sooner do you set foot upon American ground than you are stunned by a kind of tumult . . . everything is in motion around you; here the people of one quarter of a town are met to decide upon the building of a church; there the election of a representative is going on; . . . in another place, the laborers of a village quit their plows to deliberate upon the project of a road or a public school. . . .

The political agitation of American legislative bodies, which is the only one that attracts the attention of foreigners, is a mere episode, or a sort of continuation, of that universal movement which originates in the lowest classes of the people and extends successively to all the ranks of society. . . .

In visiting the Americans and studying their laws, we perceive that the authority they have entrusted to the members of the legal profession, and the influence that these individuals exercise in the government, are the most powerful existing security against the excesses of democracy. This effect seems to me to result from a general cause, which it is useful to investigate. . . . Men who have made a special study of the laws derive from [that] occupation certain habits of order, a taste for formalities, and a kind of instinctive regard for the regular connection of ideas, which naturally render them very hostile to the revolutionary spirit and the unreflecting passions of the multitude. . . .

[Moreover,] the government of democracy is favorable to the political power of lawyers; for when the wealthy, the noble, and the prince are excluded from the government, the lawyers take possession of it, in their own right, as it were, since they are the only men of information and sagacity, beyond the sphere of the people, who can be the object of popular choice. . . .

The people in democratic states do not mistrust the members of the legal profession, because it is known that they are interested to serve the popular cause. . . . Lawyers belong to the people by birth and interest, and to the aristocracy by habit and taste; they may be looked upon as the connecting link between the two great classes of society. . . . When the American people are intoxicated by passion or carried away by the impetuosity of their ideas, they are checked and stopped by the almost invisible influence of their legal counselors.

As most public men are legal practitioners, they introduce the customs and technicalities of their profession into the management of public affairs. The jury extends this habit to all classes. The language of the law thus becomes, in some measure, a vulgar tongue . . . so that at last the whole people contract the habits and the tastes of the judicial magistrate.

Source: Alexis de Tocqueville, Democracy in America, ed. Philip Bradley (New York: Vintage, 1945), 1: 283–90.

FOR FURTHER EXPLORATION

- For definitions of key terms boldfaced in this chapter, see the glossary at the end of the book.

- To assess your mastery of the material covered in this chapter, see the Online Study Guide at **bedfordstmartins.com/henretta**.

- For suggested references, including Web sites, see page SR-9 at the end of the book.

- For map resources and primary documents, see **bedfordstmartins.com/henretta**.

Between 1790 and 1820 the United States acquired immense new lands in the West and developed a capitalist economy in the East. The pace of westward expansion was rapid despite determined resistance by Indian peoples, the difficulties of transport and trade across the Appalachian Mountains, and the high price of land sold by both the U.S. government and speculators. Nonetheless, by 1820, fully 2 million Americans, white and black, were living west of the Appalachians.

Led by Thomas Jefferson, who strongly favored westward expansion, the Republicans wrested political power from the Federalists. While retaining the Bank of the United States and many Federalist officeholders, Jefferson eliminated excise taxes, reduced the national debt, cut the size of the army, and lowered the price of national lands in the West. Faced with British and French seizures of American ships and sailors, he devised the embargo of 1807, but it failed to change the policies of the warring nations. Eventually, Indian uprisings and expansionist demands by western Republicans led President James Madison into the War of 1812 against Britain. The war split the nation, prompting a secessionist movement in New England, but a negotiated peace ended the military conflict and Andrew Jackson's victory at New Orleans preserved American honor. The diplomacy of John Quincy Adams won the annexation of Florida to the United States in 1819 and the settlement of boundaries with British Canada and Spanish Texas. Western expansion helped to seal the fate of the Federalist Party, which faded from the scene, leaving a divided Republican Party in charge of the affairs of the nation.

As white Americans imposed European agricultural practices and private property rights on the lands of the West, they developed a capitalist economy in the East. Beginning in the 1790s merchant capitalists created a flourishing outwork system of rural manufacturing, and state governments devised the commonwealth system—awarding corporate charters and subsidies to assist transportation companies, manufacturers, and banks. Republican-minded state legislatures enacted statutes that promoted economic development by redefining common-law property rights. Led by the Federalist John Marshall, the Supreme Court protected the vested rights of property owners and the charter privileges of business corporations. Entrepreneurs took advantage of state legislation and judicial protection to create new business enterprises, strong regional economies, and the beginnings of a national market system.

1783	Treaty of Paris gives Americans access to the trans-Appalachian West
1787	Northwest Ordinance
1790s	State mercantilism: states grant corporation charters
	Entrepreneurs build turnpikes and short canals
	Merchants create a rural outwork system
1790–1791	Little Turtle defeats American armies in Northwest Territory
1791	First Bank of the United States founded; charter expires in 1811
1792	Kentucky joins Union; Tennessee follows (1796)
1794	Battle of Fallen Timbers
1795	Treaty of Greenville recognizes Indian land rights
	Massachusetts Mill Dam Act promotes textile industry
	Pinckney's Treaty with Spain allows U.S. use of Mississippi River
1801	Spain restores Louisiana to France
	John Marshall becomes chief justice of the Supreme Court
1801–1807	Treasury Secretary Albert Gallatin reduces national debt
	Seizures of American ships by France and Britain
1803	Louisiana Purchase; Lewis and Clark expedition
	Marshall asserts judicial review in *Marbury v. Madison*
1807	Embargo Act cripples American shipping
	Congress bans importation of slaves
1809	Tecumseh and Tenskwatawa mobilize Indians
1810	*Fletcher v. Peck* extends contract clause
1810s	Expansion of slavery into Old Southwest
1811	Battle of Tippecanoe
1812–1815	War of 1812
1817–1825	Era of Good Feeling during Monroe's presidency
1819	Adams-Onís Treaty annexes Florida and defines Texas boundary
	McCulloch v. Maryland enhances power of national government
	Dartmouth College v. Woodward protects property rights

The Quest for a Republican Society

1790–1820

B Y THE 1820S A SENSE OF OPTIMISM pervaded white American society. "The temperate zone of North America already exhibits many signs that it is the promised land of civil liberty, and of institutions designed to liberate and exalt the human race," a Kentucky judge declared in a Fourth of July speech. Not even the deaths on July 4, 1826, of both John Adams and Thomas Jefferson shook people's optimism. Rather, most took it as a divine sign. Two great founding fathers had died, but the republic lived on.

There were good reasons for this enthusiasm. A half century after independence, white Americans lived in a self-governing society that was free from both arbitrary taxes and a dogmatic, established church. Moreover, many citizens had come to consider themselves "republicans" not simply in their legal order and their constitutional system of representative government but also in their political behavior, social outlook, and cultural habits.

However, Americans defined republicanism in different ways. Many white Americans in the North subscribed to "democratic republicanism," an ideology that encouraged individuals to aspire to greater equality in politics and within the family. However, they often failed to achieve this goal because of the strength of entrenched cultural values and economic interests.

◀ **The Fourth of July in Philadelphia, c. 1811**

By the early nineteenth century July Fourth had become a popular holiday, a time for political speeches, leisurely conversations, and youthful revelry. This detail from a painting by J. Krimmel shows a crowd celebrating the holiday. The young man buying an alcoholic drink from a street vendor (left side) may well engage in some rowdy behavior before Independence Day is over.

Pennsylvania Academy of the Fine Arts, Philadelphia. Pennsylvania Academy Purchase (from the estate of Paul Beck Jr.).

In the South many whites shared these democratic aspirations, but their society was so sharply divided along the lines of class and race that such ideals were impossible to sustain. Consequently, southern leaders gradually devised an aristocratic-republican ideology that better represented the hierarchical character and deferential values of their society. Yet a third vision of American republican society took shape in the wake of the massive religious revival that swept through the nation during the first half of the nineteenth century. For the many Americans—white and black, southern and northern—who embraced this vision, the United States was both a great experiment in republican government and the seedbed of a new Christian civilization that would redeem the world.

Democratic Republicanism

After independence, leading Americans developed a political system based on the principle of "ordered liberty," which in practice meant rule by the traditional elite. Gradually, white men of modest means deserted these patrician political leaders and embraced the republican doctrines of political equality and social mobility. Many citizens also reorganized traditional institutions such as families and schools, pursuing more egalitarian marriages and more affectionate ways of rearing and educating their children.

Social and Political Equality for White Men

Between 1780 and 1820 hundreds of well-educated Europeans visited the United States. Coming from countries with monarchical governments, established churches, patriarchal families, and profound divisions between social classes, they thought that the American republic represented a genuinely different and more just social order. In his famous *Letters from an American Farmer* (1782) the French-born essayist St. Jean de Crèvecoeur wrote that European society was composed "of great lords who possess everything, and of a herd of people who have nothing." America, by contrast, had "no aristocratical families, no courts, no kings, no bishops."

Social Mobility. This absence of a hereditary aristocracy encouraged Americans to condemn inherited social privilege, and republican ideology proclaimed legal equality for all free men. "The law is the same for everyone both as it protects and as it punishes," noted one European traveler. Yet Americans willingly accepted social divisions if they were based on personal achievement. As one letter to a newspaper put it, people should be valued not for their "wealth, titles, or connections" but for their "talents, integrity, and virtue."

As individuals amassed wealth, they gained a higher social standing, a result that astounded some Europeans. "In Europe to say of someone that he rose from nothing is a disgrace and a reproach," remarked an aristocratic Polish visitor. "It is the opposite here. To be the architect of your own fortune is honorable. It is the highest recommendation."

Changes in the legal profession exemplify the popular belief in the superiority of a competitive, achievement-oriented society. During the Revolutionary era American attorneys had won legislation that prevented untrained lawyers from practicing law. By 1800 most states required at least three years of formal schooling or a long apprenticeship in a law firm, training available only to young men from well-established families. As legal rules and the legal profession became more central to American life, republican-minded critics attacked what they called the "professional aristocracy" of lawyers. They demanded that legislatures regulate attorneys' fees, create small-claims courts in which ordinary citizens could represent themselves, and lower educational requirements for admission to the bar. Legislatures met many of these demands; by the 1820s only eleven of the twenty-six states required lawyers to complete a fixed period of legal education. These changes lowered the intellectual quality of the legal profession even as they made it more democratic in composition and spirit (Table 9.1).

Some Americans from long-distinguished families questioned the morality of a social order based on mobility and financial success. "The aristocracy of Kingston [New York] is more one of money than any village I have ever seen," complained Nathaniel Booth, whose family had once ruled Kingston but had lost its prominence. "Man is estimated by dollars," he lamented; "what he is worth determines his character and his position at once." For most white men such a system meant the opportunity to better themselves.

A Wider Franchise for Men. By the 1810s republicanism also meant voting rights for all free white men. As early as 1776 the state constitutions of Pennsylvania and Vermont allowed all taxpayers to vote, which opened up political participation to propertyless young men who paid a "poll" (or head) tax and artisans who did not own land but paid an occupational tax. By 1810 Maryland and South Carolina had extended the vote to all adult white men, and the new states of Indiana (1816), Illinois (1818), and Alabama (1819) provided for a broad male franchise in their constitutions. Within another decade fifteen states allowed all white male taxpayers to vote, and another seven instituted universal white manhood suffrage, leaving only three states with property qualifications (Map 9.1).

This expansion of suffrage changed the tone of politics. Most conservative politicians accepted popular

TABLE 9.1   Number of Lawyers in Three Selected States, to 1820

	Number of Lawyers	Lawyers per 10,000 Population
Massachusetts (including Maine)		
1740	15	10
1775	71	24
1780	34	11
1785	92	24
1790	112	24
1800	200	35
1810	492	70
1820	710	87
Connecticut		
1790	129	54
1800	169	67
1820	248	90
South Carolina		
1771	24	19
1820	200	40

Source: George Dargo, *Law in the New Republic: Private Law and the Public Estate* (New York: Knopf, 1983), 49. Reprinted by permission of McGraw-Hill, Inc.

suffrage but insisted upon an elite-dominated political system. As Samuel Stone put it, the Federalist ideal was "a speaking aristocracy in the face of a silent democracy." However, Americans increasingly rejected this hierarchical system. They refused to vote for politicians who flaunted their high social status by wearing "top boots, breeches, and shoe buckles," their hair in "powder and queues." Instead, voters elected politicians who dressed simply and endorsed democracy, even if those leaders still favored policies that benefited those with substantial wealth.

As the political power of middling and poor white men grew, the rights and status of white women and free blacks declined. In 1802 Ohio disfranchised African Americans, and in 1821 New York kept property-holding requirements for black voters while eliminating them for whites. The most striking case of racial and sexual discrimination occurred in New Jersey, where the state constitution of 1776 had granted suffrage to all property holders. As Federalists and Republicans competed for votes after 1800, they challenged political custom by encouraging property-owning blacks and unmarried women and widows to vote. Sensing a threat to the polit-

ical dominance of white men, in 1807 the New Jersey legislature enacted legislation that defined full citizenship (and therefore voting rights) as an attribute of white men only. To justify the exclusion of women, legislators invoked both biology and custom. As one letter to a newspaper put it, "Women, generally, are neither by nature, nor habit, nor education, nor by their necessary condition in society fitted to perform this duty with credit to themselves or advantage to the public."

Toward a Republican Marriage System

European and American husbands had long dominated their wives and controlled the family's property. However, as John Adams had lamented on behalf of husbands in 1776, the revolutionary doctrine of political equality had "spread where it was not intended," encouraging some white women to demand the right to control their inheritances or speak out on public matters. These women maintained that the subordination of women was at odds with a belief in equal natural rights. Patriarchy was not "natural," the Patriot author and historian Mercy Otis

MAP 9.1 The Expansion of Voting Rights for White Men, 1800–1830

Between 1800 and 1830 the United States moved steadily toward political democracy for white men. Many existing states revised their constitutions, replacing property ownership with taxpaying or militia service as a qualification for voting. Some new states in the West extended the suffrage to all adult white men. As parties sought votes from a broader electorate, the tone of politics became more open and competitive—swayed by the interests and values of ordinary people.

Warren argued; making men the heads of households could be justified only "for the sake of order in families."

Economic and cultural changes also eroded customary paternal authority. Traditionally, landowning fathers had arranged their children's marriages to ensure the economic well-being of themselves and their wives during old age. As land holdings shrank in long-settled rural communities, yeomen fathers could no longer bequeath substantial farms—the economic incentives they had used to influence their children's selection of a spouse. Young men and women began to choose their own partners, influenced by the new cultural attitude of **sentimentalism**.

The Effects of Sentimentalism.   Sentimentalism was an outlook that originated in Europe during the Romantic movement of the late eighteenth century and spread quickly among all classes of American society. Sentimentalism celebrated the importance of "feeling"— that is, a physical, sensuous appreciation of God, nature, and other human beings. This new sensibility found many forms of expression. It dripped from the pages of German and English literary works, fell from the lips of

actors in popular tear-jerking melodramas, and infused the emotional rhetoric of revivalist preachers.

As the passions of the heart overwhelmed the cool logic of the mind, a new marriage system appeared. Parents had always considered physical attraction and emotional compatibility as they arranged marriages for their children, but they were primarily concerned with the personal character and financial resources of a prospective son- or daughter-in-law. Now magazines encouraged marriages "contracted from motives of affection, rather than of interest." Many young people began to seek a spouse who was, as Eliza Southgate of Maine put it, "calculated to promote my happiness."

As young people arranged their own marriages, fathers gave up the goal of complete patriarchal control and instead became paternalists, protecting the interests of their children. To guard against free-spending sons-in-law, wealthy fathers placed their daughters' inheritances in legal trust—out of their husbands' control. As a Virginia planter wrote to his lawyer, "I rely on you to see the property settlement properly drawn before the marriage, for I by no means consent that Polly shall be left to the Vicissitudes of Life."

The Wedding, 1805
The unknown artist who painted this watercolor depicts the bride and groom staring intently into each other's eyes as they exchange marriage vows, suggesting that their union stems more from love than from economic calculation. Given the plain costumes of the assembled guests and the sparse furnishing of the room, this may be a rural Quaker wedding. Philadelphia Museum of Art.

Companionate Marriages.   Theoretically the new republican ideal of **"companionate" marriage** gave wives "true equality, both of rank and fortune," with their husbands, as one Boston man suggested. However, husbands continued to occupy a privileged position because of deeply ingrained habits and laws that gave them control of the family's property. The new marriage system also discouraged parents from becoming too involved in their children's married lives, making young wives more dependent on their husbands than their mothers had been. In addition, governments accepted no obligation to prevent domestic abuse; as a lawyer noted, women who would rather "starve than submit" to the orders of their husbands were left to their fate. The marriage contract "is so much more important in its consequences to females than to males," a young man at the Litchfield Law School in Connecticut concluded in 1820, "for besides leaving everything else to unite themselves to one man, they subject themselves to his authority. He is their all—their only relative—their only hope."

Young adults who chose partners unwisely were severely disappointed when their spouses failed as providers or faithful companions, and a few sought divorces. Before 1800 most petitioners for divorce had charged their spouses with neglect, abandonment, or adultery—serious offenses against the moral order of society. After 1800 emotional grounds dominated divorce petitions. One woman complained that her husband had "ceased to cherish her," while a man grieved that his wife had "almost broke his heart." Reflecting these changed cultural values, some states expanded the legal grounds for divorce to include personal cruelty and drunkenness.

Republican Motherhood

In all societies, marriage has many purposes: it channels sexuality, facilitates the inheritance of property, and, by creating strong family and kinship ties, eases the rearing of children. Traditionally, most American women had focused their lives on family duties: work in the home or farm and the bearing and nurture of children. However, by the 1790s the birthrate in the northern seaboard states was dropping dramatically. In the farm village of Sturbridge, Massachusetts, women who had married around 1750 gave birth on average to eight or nine children, whereas women who married around 1810 had only about six. An even greater decline occurred in urban areas, where native-born white women bore an average of only four children.

Women's Health and Fertility: From Folk Remedies to Pharmacies

"**I** once was verry Bad with a violent pain in my Back and Bowells and three months Gone with Child," Philadelphia shopkeeper Elizabeth Coates Pascall noted in her Receipt Book around 1760. As her condition steadily worsened from this "violent Chollick Pain," Pascall consulted medical professionals, who advised an abortion. "It was Judged Both By the Doctor and midwife that if I was not Speedily Delivered I should Dye." The midwife "tryed to Deliver me butt found it impossible," so Pascall turned to a folk healer, "an Elderly woman [who] proposed Giving me a Glister [an herbal potion]. . . . I took it and Lay Still Near an hour after it: Being presently Eased and the Child came from me [and] the after Birth all together and with very Little pain."

Like most American women in the eighteenth century, Elizabeth Pascall was not trying to control her fertility or restrict the number of her offspring. She would bear and rear the number of children that her husband and her God gave her. However, to do so she needed to protect her health, and like countless other Americans of her time she turned to folk medicine.

The general state of medical knowledge was low. Most women understood that the lack of menstruation might be a sign of conception. As Dr. Samuel Jennings's *The Married Lady's Companion* (1808) put it, "An entire suppression of the menses attends almost every case of pregnancy." But they also believed that the absence of menstruation might simply be a sign of illness, either "mental despondency" that took the form of "Grief and Distress," or "hysteria," characterized by "lowness of spirits, oppression and anxiety" as well as by stomach pains that caused "inflation, sickness and sometimes vomiting." In 1805 Lydia Tallender "had not had the female customs for 2 mos [months], and had been unwell," so she took medicines to cure her "illness."

In popular discourse, Lydia Tallender had "taken a cold"—the absence of "hot" menstrual blood indicated that a cold "humor" had taken control of her body. To restore her flow, an afflicted woman normally drank a medicine made of water suffused with herbs and minerals such as savin (a variety of juniper), red cedar, rue, aloes, or seneca snakeroot. When Elizabeth Drinker found her daughter Molly Rhoads "disorder'd and in pain . . . oweing to takeing colds," she administered "mint water," probably peppermint and magnesia.

Health manuals and diaries written in English did not mention the abortive qualities of such potions, but German publications were more forthright. *The Small*

The United States was one of the first countries in the world to experience this sharp decline in the birthrate—what historians have termed "demographic transition." There were several causes. Beginning in the 1790s thousands of young men migrated to the trans-Appalachian West, leaving some women without partners and delaying the marriage of many more. Women who married later in life had fewer children. Also, thousands of white American couples in the emerging middle class deliberately limited the size of their families. After having four or five children, they used birth control or abstained from sexual intercourse. Fathers wanted to provide each of their children with an adequate inheritance and so favored smaller families; mothers, affected by new ideas of individualism and self-achievement, were no longer willing to spend all of their active years bearing and rearing children (see New Technology, "Women's Health and Fertility: From Folk Remedies to Pharmacies," above).

As women looked for new opportunities, they found support from changes in Christian thought. Traditionally, most religious writers had viewed women as morally inferior to men—as sexual temptresses or witches—but by 1800 Protestant ministers, probably influenced by the numerical dominance of women in their congregations, had begun to place responsibility for sexual misconduct primarily on men. In fact, Christian moralists now claimed that modesty and purity were inherent in women's nature, making women uniquely qualified to educate the spirit.

Reflecting this sentiment, political leaders called on women to become "republican wives" and "republican mothers" who would correctly shape the characters of American men. In his *Thoughts on Female Education* (1787) the Philadelphia physician Benjamin Rush argued that a young woman should receive intellectual training so that she would be "an agreeable companion for a sensible man" and ensure "his perseverance in the

Herbal of Little Cost, printed in Germantown, Pennsylvania, between 1762 and 1778 by Christopher Sauer, provided women with recipes "to expel the dead fruit," and German midwifery manuals explained that such tonics would expel the fetus, "be it dead or alive." However, English women clearly understood the potions' effect. Nursing mothers commonly drank savin tea to delay a new pregnancy—both to preserve their own health and to ensure a supply of milk for their nursing babies. However, the cost of taking such tonics was high, for they caused physical pain and might identify a woman as weak, dependent, and "hysterical."

By the late eighteenth century, American women no longer had to turn to folk healers for such medicines. Pharmacists in England and America had learned how to make pills and tonics to promote menstruation (or induce abortions), and energetic entrepreneurs quickly marketed them. One of the most popular was Hooper's Female Pills, which were composed of Barbados aloes, iron sulfate, hellebore, and myrrh. Such patent medicines—including rosemary-laced Hungary Water, Dr. Ryans's Sugar Plums, and Fraunce's Female Elixir—were advertised in newspapers as "highly serviceable to the Female Sex" and, by the beginning of the nineteenth century, were widely available in rural shops as well as urban pharmacies.

This advance in technology, along with the importation in the 1790s of French syringes (a douche used to clean the vagina that could be used to prevent conception), assisted some American women in limiting their fertility. Previously, women had used folk remedies to preserve their health or lengthen the interval between births. Now some upper-class women and Quaker women in Pennsylvania used patent medicines and other means in a conscious program of family planning. "It gives me great pleasure to hear of your prudent resolution of not increasing your family," Margaret Shippen Arnold of Philadelphia wrote to her sister around 1790. "I have determined upon the same plan; and when our Sisters have had five or six [children], we will likewise recommend it to them."

Dr. Hooper's Female Pills

As early as the 1740s English women had access to patent medicines that, the makers alleged, would address their special needs. Within a few decades, these medicines (and competing American brands) were widely available in the United States. Science, Medicine, and Society Division, National Museum of American History, Smithsonian.

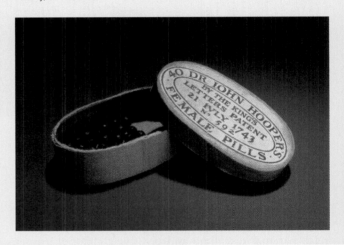

paths of rectitude." Rush also called for loyal "republican mothers" who would instruct "their sons in the principles of liberty and government." As the author of a list of "Maxims for Republics" commented, "Some of the first patriots of ancient times were formed by their mothers."

Christian ministers readily embraced the idea of **republican motherhood**. "Preserving virtue and instructing the young are not the fancied, but the real 'Rights of Women,'" the Reverend Thomas Bernard told the Female Charitable Society of Salem, Massachusetts. He urged his audience to dismiss the public roles for women advocated by English activist Mary Wollstonecraft and others. Instead, women should be content to care for their children, a responsibility that gave them "an extensive power over the fortunes of man in every generation." Although Bernard wanted women to remain in their traditional domestic sphere, he campaigned to enhance its value. A few ministers went further and envisioned a public role for women based on their domestic virtues. As South Carolina minister Thomas Grimké asserted, "Give me a host of educated pious mothers and sisters and I will revolutionize a country, in moral and religious taste."

Raising and Educating Republican Children

Republican social thought also altered assumptions about inheritance and childrearing. Under English common law, property owned by a father who died without a will passed to his eldest son, a practice known as **primogeniture**. However, legislators in most American states enacted statutes that required such estates to be divided equally among all the offspring. Most American parents supported these statutes because they had already begun to treat all of their children as equals and to

Republican Motherhood

Art often reveals much of the cultural values of the time. In this 1795 painting, the artist James Peale, brother of the famous portraitist Charles Willson Peale, depicts himself with his wife and children. The mother stands in the foreground, offering advice to her eldest daughter, while her husband stands to the rear, pointing to the other children. The father, previously the center of attention in family portraits during the colonial era (see pp. 33 and 103), now gives pride of place to his wife and offspring.

Pennsylvania Academy of the Fine Arts, Philadelphia.

teach all of them—including the eldest son—how to make their own way in the world.

Encouraging Independence. Foreign visitors believed that republican ideology encouraged American parents to relax parental discipline and give their children greater freedom. Because of the "general ideas of Liberty and Equality engraved on their hearts," suggested a Polish aristocrat who traveled through the United States around 1800, American children had "scant respect" for their parents. Several decades later a British traveler was dumbfounded when an American father excused his son's "resolute disobedience" with a smile and the remark, "a sturdy republican, sir." The traveler guessed that American parents encouraged such independence to assist young people to "go their own way" in the world.

However, these relatively permissive childrearing habits were not universal. Foreign visitors interacted primarily with well-to-do Americans, who were often members of Episcopal or Presbyterian churches. These parents often followed the teachings of rationalist-minded religious writers influenced by John Locke and the Enlightenment. In their minds children were "rational creatures" who should be encouraged to act correctly by means of praise, advice, and reasoned restraint. Training should develop the children's consciences and stress self-discipline so that young people would learn to control their own behavior and to think and act responsibly

(see American Voices, "Lydia Maria Child: Raising Middle-Class Children," p. 259).

By contrast, many yeomen and tenant farmers influenced by the Second Great Awakening followed the precepts of authoritarian-minded writers. These parents, especially those in Calvinist-oriented churches, raised their children using strict rules and harsh discipline. Evangelical Baptists and Methodists believed that infants were "full of the stains and pollution of sin" and needed strict discipline. Fear was a "useful and necessary principle in family government," the minister John Abbott advised parents; a child "should submit to your authority, not to your arguments or persuasions." Abbott told parents to instill humility in children and to teach them to subordinate their personal desires to God's will. Both of these modes of childrearing—the authoritarian and the rationalist—persisted, with the rationalists' emphasis on self-discipline becoming the preference among families in the rapidly expanding middle class.

Expanding Education. The values transmitted within families were crucial because until the 1820s most education still took place within the household. In New England locally funded public schools provided most boys and some girls with basic instruction in reading and writing. In other regions fewer white children and virtually no African American children received schooling; about a quarter of the boys and perhaps 10 percent of the

Lydia Maria Child

Raising Middle-Class Children

Violence was pervasive in traditional Europe and colonial America. Masters whipped servants and slaves and challenged one another to duels; husbands beat wives and cowed children into submission; fistfights and brawls spilled out of taverns and into the streets. Gentry and plebeians alike paid homage to the codes of physical strength and personal honor.

In the late eighteenth century evangelical ministers and middle-class moralists challenged the dominant ethos of violence. Ministers urged believers to "turn the other cheek" if assaulted and respect the bodies of others as temples of God. Mothers taught their children to control their passions and to fight with words rather than fists.

Lydia Maria Child (1802–1880) was a social reformer who combined middle-class values and religious principles. In the following selection from The Mother's Book *(1831), Child accepts John Locke's theory of knowledge that the mind at birth is a "blank slate" ("a vessel empty and pure") and is shaped by its environment. Melding Lockean psychology with religious sentimentalism (the child as "the beautiful little image of God"), she sets forth an affectionate-rationalist approach to childrearing for the emerging middle class.*

I once saw a mother laugh very heartily at the distressed face of a kitten, which a child of two years old was pulling backward by the tail. At last, the kitten, in self-defense, turned and scratched the boy. He screamed, and his mother ran to him, kissed the wound, and beat the poor kitten, saying all the time, "Naughty kitten, to scratch John." . . .

This little incident, trifling as it seems, no doubt had important effects on the character of the child. . . .

In the first place, the child was encouraged in cruelty, by seeing that it gave his mother amusement. . . .

In the next place, the kitten was struck for defending herself; this was injustice to the injured animal, and a lesson of tyranny to the boy. In the third place, striking the kitten because she had scratched him, was teaching him retaliation. . . . The influence upon him is, that it is right to injure when we are injured. . . .

The mind of a child is not like that of a grown person . . . it is a vessel empty and pure—always ready to receive, and always receiving. Every look, every movement, every expression, does something toward forming the character of the little heir to immortal life. . . .

The rule, then, for developing good affections in a child is, that he never be allowed to see or feel the influence of bad passions, even in the most trifling things; and in order to effect this, you must drive evil passions from your own heart. Nothing can be real that has not its home within us. The only sure way, as well as the easiest, to appear good, is to be good.

It is not possible to indulge anger, or any other wrong feeling, and conceal it entirely. If not expressed in words, a child feels the baneful influence. Evil enters into his soul, as the imperceptible atmosphere he breathes enters into his lungs: and the beautiful little image of God is removed farther and farther from his home in heaven.

Source: Lydia Maria Child, *The Mother's Book* (Boston: Carter and Hendee, 1831), 45–46.

girls attended privately funded schools or had personal tutors. Even in New England only a small fraction of the men and almost no women went on to grammar (high) school. Only 1 percent of men graduated from college.

In the 1790s Bostonian Caleb Bingham, an influential textbook author, called for "an equal distribution of knowledge to make us emphatically a 'republic of letters.'" Thomas Jefferson and Benjamin Rush separately proposed ambitious schemes for a comprehensive system of primary and secondary schooling, followed by college attendance for young men. They also advocated the establishment of a university in which distinguished scholars would lecture on law, medicine, theology, and political economy.

To ordinary citizens such educational proposals smacked of elitism. Farmers, artisans, and laborers looked to schools for basic instruction in the "three Rs": reading, 'riting, and 'rithmetic. They supported public funding for primary schools but not for secondary schools or colleges, because their own teenage children had already joined the workforce. "Let anybody show what advantage the poor man receives from colleges," an anonymous "Old Soldier" wrote to the Maryland *Gazette.* "Why should they support them, unless it is to serve those who are in affluent circumstances, whose children can be spared from labor, and receive the benefits?"

The Battle over Education
The artist pokes fun at a tyrannical schoolmaster and, indirectly, at the evangelicals' strict approach to childrearing. The students' faces reflect the rationalist outlook of the artist. As one Enlightenment-influenced minister put it, we see in their eyes "the first dawn of reason, beaming forth its immortal rays."
Copyright, The Frick Collection.

Although many state constitutions encouraged the use of public resources to fund primary schools, there was not much progress until the 1820s. Then a new generation of reformers, led primarily by merchants and manufacturers, successfully campaigned to raise standards by certifying qualified teachers and appointing state superintendents of education. To encourage self-discipline and individual enterprise in the students, the reformers chose textbooks, such as *The Life of George Washington* by "Parson" Mason Weems, that praised honesty and hard work while condemning gambling, drinking, and laziness. They also required the study of American history, believing that patriotic instruction would foster shared cultural ideals. As Thomas Low, a New Hampshire schoolboy, recalled, "We were taught every day and in every way that ours was the freest, the happiest, and soon to be the greatest and most powerful country of the world."

Promoting Cultural Independence. The author Noah Webster had long championed the goal of American intellectual greatness. Asserting that "America must be as independent in *literature* as she is in politics," he called on his fellow citizens to detach themselves "from the dependence on foreign opinions and manners, which is fatal to the efforts of genius in this country."

Webster's *Dissertation on the English Language* (1789) introduced American spelling (such as *labor* for the British *labour*) and defined words according to American usage. His "blue-backed speller," first published in 1783, sold 60 million copies over the next half century and helped give Americans of all backgrounds a common vocabulary and grammar. "None of us was 'lowed to see a book," an enslaved African American recalled, "but we gits hold of that Webster's old blue-back speller and we . . . studies [it]."

Though Webster and others promoted an independent, republican literary culture, it was slow to develop. Ironically, the most accomplished and successful writer in the new republic was Washington Irving, an elitist-minded Federalist in politics and an expatriate. His essays and histories, including *Salmagundi* (1807) and *Diedrich Knickerbocker's History of New York* (1809), had substantial American sales and won fame abroad. Impatient with the slow pace of American literary development, Irving lived in Europe for seventeen years, drawn to its aristocratic manners and intense intellectual life.

Apart from Irving no American author was well known in Europe, partly because most American writers followed primary careers as planters, merchants, or lawyers. "Literature is not yet a distinct profession with

Women's Education

Even in education-conscious New England, few girls attended the free public primary school for more than a few years. After 1800, as this scene from A Seminary for Young Ladies (c. 1810–1820) indicates, some girls stayed in school into their teenage years and were exposed to a wide variety of subjects, such as geography. Many of the graduates of these female academies became teachers, entering a new field of employment for women.
St. Louis Art Museum.

us," Thomas Jefferson told an English friend. "Now and then a strong mind arises, and at its intervals from business emits a flash of light. But the first object of young societies is bread and covering." Not until the 1830s and 1840s, in the works of Ralph Waldo Emerson and novelists of the American Renaissance, would American-born authors make a significant contribution to the great literature of the Western world (see Chapter 12).

Aristocratic Republicanism and Slavery, 1780–1820

Both in theory and in practice, republicanism in the South differed significantly from that in the North. Republican theorists had traditionally defined governmental tyranny as the greatest political evil and slave-owning planters, fearing political attacks on their landed wealth or slave property, were in full agreement. To prevent despotic rule by tyrants or demagogues, they wanted to place authority in the hands of independent and incorruptible men of "virtue." Indeed, planters came to see themselves as the practical embodiment of this ideal, men whose private wealth from slave owning freed them from dependence on government favors and whose education and training equipped them to discern and protect the welfare of the entire white community. Some consciously cast themselves as republican aristocrats. "The planters here are essentially what the nobility are in other countries," declared John Henry Hammond of South Carolina. "They stand at the head of society & politics . . . [and form] an aristocracy of talents, of virtue, of generosity and courage."

The North and South Grow Apart

European visitors to the new American republic commonly noted profound social differences among the regions. New England was home to religious "fanaticism," according to a British observer, but "the lower orders of citizens" there had "a better education, are more intelligent, and better informed" than those he met in the South. "The state of poverty in which a great number of white people live in Virginia" surprised the Marquis de Chastellux, and other visitors to the South commented on the rude manners, heavy drinking, and lack of a strong work ethic they found there. White tenant farmers and small freeholders seemed only to have a "passion for gaming at the billiard table, a cock-fight or cards."

Some southerners felt that slavery was a major cause of the ignorance and poverty of their region. The wealthy planters who controlled southern society wanted a compliant labor force, content with the drudgery of agricultural work. Consequently, they trained most of their slaves as field hands (allowing only a few to learn the arts of the blacksmith, carpenter, or bricklayer), and they made little or no effort to provide ordinary whites with elementary instruction in reading or arithmetic. In 1800 the leadership of Essex County, Virginia, spent about twenty-five cents per person for local government, including schooling, while their counterparts in Acton, Massachusetts, expended about one dollar per person. As a result, over one-third of white southerners could not read or write, compared with less than 1 percent of New Englanders. A South Carolina merchant likewise linked slavery to a weak work ethic: "Where there are Negroes a White Man despises to work, saying what, will you have me a Slave and work like a Negroe?"

Slavery and National Politics. Slavery quickly found its way into national politics. At the Philadelphia Convention in 1787 most delegates accepted slavery as a fact of American life that, like the state governments, would have to be accommodated to secure approval of the new national constitution. To assure the accession of

Georgia and South Carolina to the Union, they inserted a clause that prevented Congress from restricting the importation of people (including enslaved workers) for twenty years. The delegates also included a fugitive clause that prevented state governments from offering a safe haven to runaway slaves and indentured servants. Southerners sought additional protection for slavery in the second session of the new national legislature, winning approval of James Madison's resolution that "Congress have no authority to interfere in the emancipation of slaves, or in the treatment of them within any of the States."

Slavery remained a contested issue nationally. The slave revolts in Haiti and other French sugar islands during the 1790s brought a flood of white refugees to the United States and prompted congressional debates about diplomatic relations with the new black-run government of Haiti. Simultaneously, northern political leaders attacked the British impressment of American sailors as "to all intents and purposes a practice as unjust, as immoral, as base, as oppressive and tyrannical as the slave trade," and called for the end of both. When Congress ended legal American participation in the Atlantic slave trade in 1807, northern representatives tried to regulate the coastal trade in slaves and provide for the emancipation of illegally imported slaves. In response, the southern congressmen asserted a strong defense of their labor system. "A large majority of people in the Southern states do not consider slavery as even an evil," declared one congressman, and the South's political clout—its domination of the presidency and the Senate—ensured that the national government would protect its central institution. American diplomats vigorously—and successfully—demanded compensation for slaves freed by the British during the War of 1812, and Congress secured the existence of slavery in the District of Columbia by enforcing the property rights of slave owners who lived there.

Political conflict over slavery increased as the northern states emancipated more and more of their African American laborers and the South expanded its slave-based agricultural economy into new territories and states in the lower Mississippi Valley. Antislavery advocates grew increasingly concerned as Louisiana (1812), Mississippi (1816), and Alabama (1818) joined the Union with state constitutions permitting slavery. They had hoped that African bondage would "die a natural death" following the demise of the Atlantic slave trade and the decline of the tobacco economy.

Colonization.   In 1817 the founders of the American Colonization Society, who included President James Monroe and Speaker of the House Henry Clay, proposed another means of ending slavery. The society would encourage southern planters to emancipate their slaves—who now numbered nearly 1.5 million people—and the society would arrange for their resettlement in Africa. The society's leaders believed, as Clay put it, that racial bondage had placed his state of Kentucky and the other

slaveholding states "in the rear of our neighbors . . . in the state of agriculture, the progress of manufactures, the advance of improvement, and the general prosperity of society." Slavery had to go, as did the freed slaves. Emancipation without colonization, the Kentucky congressman predicted, "would be followed by instantaneous collisions between the two races, which would break out into a civil war that would end in the extermination or subjugation of the one race or the other." Northerners who joined the Colonization Society had much the same outlook. They regarded the 250,000 free blacks in the northern states as "notoriously ignorant, degraded and miserable, mentally diseased, brokenspirited," as one society report put it. Hoping to create a "white man's country," what they wanted was "African removal."

The American Colonization Society was a dismal failure. Despite appeals to wealthy individuals, churches, and state governments, the society raised enough money to purchase freedom for only a few hundred slaves. Moreover, most free blacks rejected colonization, agreeing with Bishop Richard Allen of the African Methodist Episcopal Church that "this land which we have watered with our tears and our blood is now our mother country." Three thousand African Americans met in Philadelphia's Bethel Church to condemn colonization, declaring that their goal was to advance in American society using "those opportunities . . . which the Constitution and the laws allow to all." Lacking significant support from either blacks or whites, the society transported only 6,000 African Americans to Liberia, a colony it established on the west coast of Africa.

Toward a New Southern Social Order

Colonization failed in part because the South was changing in a dramatic fashion—and in ways that encouraged the expansion of slavery. In 1780 the western boundary of the plantation system ran through the middle of Georgia; by 1820 the plantation frontier stretched through the middle of Louisiana. That jump of six hundred miles had doubled the geographic area cultivated by slave labor. Moreover, many of the workers on those plantations were African-born slaves who had been imported into the United States between 1780 and 1808, when the Atlantic slave trade legally ended. During those three decades nearly 250,000 Africans had been added to the workforce—a total that equaled the number of slaves imported into Britain's mainland settlements during the entire colonial period. Most of these Africans labored on cotton and sugar plantations in the newly settled southwestern states and territories.

Despite this influx of new slaves, the demand for labor in the Southwest far exceeded the supply. "The Negro business is a great object with us," one merchant declared, because "the Planter will as far in his power sacrifice every thing to attain Negroes." To acquire workers for their plantations, white owners purchased or moved

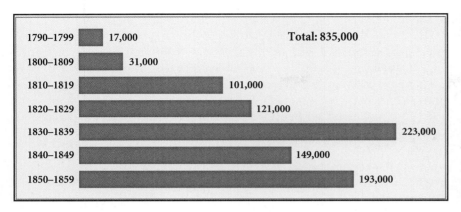

1790–1799	17,000
1800–1809	31,000
1810–1819	101,000
1820–1829	121,000
1830–1839	223,000
1840–1849	149,000
1850–1859	193,000

Total: 835,000

FIGURE 9.1 Movement of Slaves from Upper South to Lower South, 1790–1860

The cotton boom that began in the 1810s set in motion a great redistribution of the African American population. Between 1810 and 1860 white planters moved or sold nearly 800,000 slaves from the Upper to the Lower South, a process that broke up families and long-established black communities.

Source: Adapted from Robert William Fogel and Stanley Engerman, *Time on the Cross* (Boston: Little, Brown, 1974), figure 12.

African American workers from long-settled regions that had a surplus of labor. Between 1790 and 1820 whites relocated more than 150,000 African Americans from Maryland, Virginia, and parts of North and South Carolina (Figure 9.1). Some of these forced migrants—perhaps as many as one-half—moved with relatives and friends when their owners sold their old plantations and began anew on the fertile plains of Alabama, Mississippi, and Louisiana (Map 9.2). Thousands of others were sold, and separation became a common experience for black families. "I am Sold to a man by the name of Peterson a trader," lamented a Georgia slave. "My Dear wife for you and my Children my pen cannot Express the griffe I feel to be parted from you all." Some of these slaves forever lost touch with their families. "Dey sole [sold] my sister Kate," Anna Harris remembered decades later, ". . . and I ain't seed or heard of her since." Planters who remained on their estates in Maryland, Virginia, the Carolinas, and Georgia reaped impressive profits by selling their "surplus" blacks to slave traders. The profits to be gained by planting cotton in the Southwest and selling enslaved laborers from the Southeast doomed both the colonization movement and many well-established African American communities.

Westward movement also changed the character of white society. Following the tobacco and rice revolutions of the early eighteenth century (see Chapter 3), a wealthy planter elite exercised considerable political power in much of the South. However, particularly in tobacco-growing areas, slave owning remained broadly diffused. During the 1770s about 60 percent of the white families in the Chesapeake region owned at least one African American worker and benefited directly from slavery. By 1820 a much smaller proportion of white families in all regions of the South owned slaves, and the percentage continued to fall. For example, in Alabama in 1830 only 30 percent of the voters owned slaves. Among those 30 percent were the owners of the new cotton plantations that, like the rice-growing plantations in South Carolina and Georgia, were large-scale operations using dozens of enslaved black workers. Their wealthy and influential owners dominated society and gave an aristocratic republican definition to politics. In Alabama a majority of the legislators owned more than 20 African Americans, and one-quarter held more than 50. "Inequality is the fundamental law of the universe," proclaimed one southern politician. "Slavery does indeed create an aristocracy."

The Internal Slave Trade

Mounted whites escort a convoy of slaves from Virginia to Tennessee in Lewis Miller's Slave Trader, Sold to Tennessee *(1853). For white planters, the trade was a lucrative one, pumping money into the declining Chesapeake economy and providing workers for the expanding plantations of the cotton belt. For blacks it was a traumatic journey, a new Middle Passage that broke up families and long-settled slave communities.*

Abby Aldrich Rockefeller Folk Art Center.

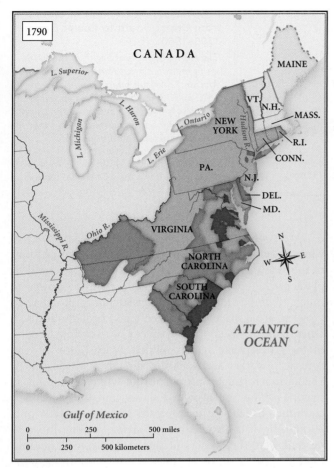

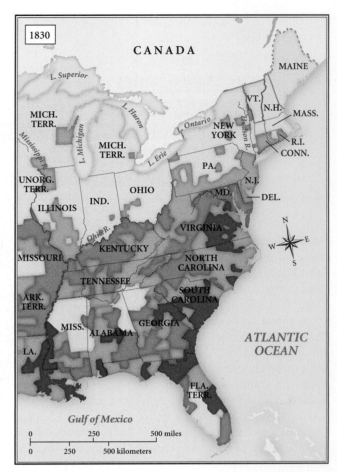

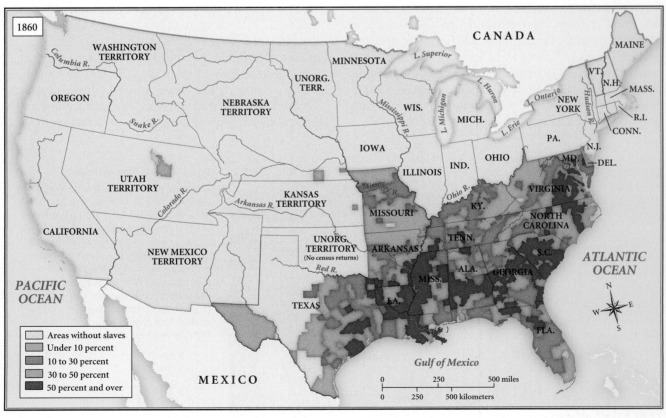

Areas without slaves
Under 10 percent
10 to 30 percent
30 to 50 percent
50 percent and over

◀ **MAP 9.2 Distribution of the Slave Population in 1790, 1830, and 1860**

The cotton boom shifted enslaved African Americans to the Old Southwest. In 1790 most slaves lived and worked on the tobacco plantations of the Chesapeake and in the rice and indigo areas of South Carolina. By 1830, tens of thousands were laboring on the cotton and sugar lands of the lower Mississippi Valley and on cotton plantations in Georgia and Florida. Three decades later, the centers of slavery lay along the Mississippi River and in an arc of fertile cotton land—the "black belt"—sweeping from Mississippi through Georgia.

For more help analyzing this map, see the ONLINE STUDY GUIDE at bedfordstmartins.com/henretta.

As cotton production consolidated in fewer and fewer hands, some white yeomen in plantation regions became the tenants of wealthy landlords. Other white families scraped by on small farms, growing foodstuffs for sustenance and a few bales of cotton for cash. Influenced by the patriarchal ideology of the planter class, the husbands in these households asserted traditional male authority over their wives and children, ruling their small worlds with a firm hand. Other yeomen families retreated into the backcountry near the Appalachian Mountains, hoping to maintain their economic independence and to control local county governments. Owning hilly farms of fifty to one hundred acres, these families grew some cotton but primarily raised corn and livestock, especially hogs. Their goal was modest: to preserve their holdings and secure enough new land or goods to set up all of their children as small-scale farmers.

In the new southwestern economy, prosperity was limited primarily to the shrinking minority of the white population that owned plantations and slaves. The prospect of a more equal political and social order raised by the democratic impulses of the Revolutionary era had been counterbalanced by an expanding aristocratic republican plantation society based on cotton and sugar.

Slave Society and Culture

As planters ruled over a class-divided white social order, African Americans created a distinct and relatively unified rural culture. A major cause was the end of the transatlantic slave trade in 1808, which gradually created an entirely American-born black population. Even in South Carolina—the point of entry of most of the slaves imported since independence—in 1820 only about 20 percent of the black inhabitants had been born in Africa. Second, the rapid movement of slavery into the Mississippi Valley reduced cultural differences among slaves. For example, the Gullah dialect spoken by slaves from the Carolina low country gradually died out on the cotton plantations of Alabama and Mississippi, replaced by the black English spoken by slaves from the Chesapeake.

African Influences. Even as the black population became more homogeneous, African cultural elements remained important. At least one-third of the slaves who entered the United States between 1776 and 1809 were from the Congo region of west-central Africa, and they brought their culture with them (Table 9.2). As the traveler Isaac Holmes reported in 1821, "In Louisiana,

TABLE 9.2 African Slaves Imported into North America by Ethnicity, 1776–1809

African Region of Departure	Ethnicity	Number	Percentage of Imported Slaves
Senegambia	Mandinka, Fulbe, Serer, Jola, Wolof, and Bambara	8,000	7
Sierra Leone	Via, Mende, Kpelle, and Kru	18,300	16
Gold Coast	Ashanti and Fanit	15,000	13
Bight of Benin; Bight of Biafra	Ibo and Ibibio	5,700	5
West Central Africa	Kongo, Tio, and Matamba	37,800	33
Southeast Africa	Unknown	1,100	1
Other or Unknown		28,700	25
TOTAL		**114,600**	**100**

Note: The numbers are estimated from known voyages involving 65,000 Africans. Ethnic origins should be considered as very tentative because slaves from many regions left from the same port and because the ethnic and regional origins of 28,700 slaves (25 percent) are not known.

Source: Aaron S. Fogleman, "From Slaves, Convicts, and Servants to Free Passengers: The Transformation of Immigration in the Era of the American Revolution," *Journal of American History* (June 1998): table A.6.

Sugar Harvest in Louisiana
In Louisiana, as in the West Indies, cultivating and harvesting sugarcane was backbreaking work that took the lives of many workers. Throughout the nineteenth century, death rates in sugar-growing areas of Louisiana rivaled those in the crowded, disease-ridden immigrant districts in northern cities. This watercolor, by an unknown artist, shows that enslaved women joined men in the fields during harvest time.
Glenbow Museum, Calgary, Alberta, Canada.

and the state of Mississippi, the slaves . . . dance for several hours during Sunday afternoon. The general movement is in what they call the Congo dance." Similar descriptions of blacks who "danced the Congo and sang a purely African song to the accompaniment of . . . a drum" appeared as late as 1890.

Enslaved blacks in South Carolina and elsewhere continued to respect African incest taboos, shunning marriage between cousins. On the Good Hope plantation in South Carolina nearly half of the slave children born between 1800 and 1857 were related by blood to one another, yet only one marriage had taken place between cousins. By contrast, many wealthy planter families in South Carolina and Georgia encouraged marriage between cousins to keep inherited property in the family.

However, southern state legislatures and law courts prohibited legal marriages between slaves, so that they could be sold without breaking a legal bond. African Americans therefore devised their own marriage rituals, first asking their parents' consent to marry and then seeking their owner's permission to live together. Following African custom, many couples symbolized their married state by jumping over a broomstick together in a public ceremony. Christian slaves often had a religious service performed by a white or black preacher, but these rites never ended with the customary phrase "until death do you part." Everyone knew that black marriages could end with the sale of one or both of the spouses. To maintain their cultural identity, recently imported slaves often gave their children African names. Males born on Friday were often called Cuffee—the name of that day in several West African languages. Most Chesapeake slaves chose names of British origin and named sons after fathers, uncles, or grandfathers and daughters after grandmothers. Like incest rules and marriage rituals, these

naming patterns solidified kinship ties, creating order in a harsh and arbitrary world.

A World of Limited Choices. By forming stable families and strong communities, African Americans were better able to control their own lives. In the rice-growing lowlands of South Carolina blacks won the right to labor by the **task** rather than work under constant supervision. Each day a worker had to complete a precisely defined task—for example, turn over a quarter acre of land, hoe half an acre, or pound seven mortars of rice. By working hard, many finished their tasks "by one or two o'clock in the afternoon," a Methodist preacher reported, and had "the rest of the day for themselves, which they spend in working their own private fields . . . planting rice, corn, potatoes, tobacco &c. for their own use and profit." These private efforts provided slaves with better clothes and food, and on some large plantations planters gave decent health care to children, the sick, and the elderly. But few enslaved African Americans enjoyed a comfortable standard of living, and slaves clearly understood that planters gave them material favors not out of benevolence but to protect their investment (see American Voices, "Jacob Stroyer: A Child Learns the Meaning of Slavery," p. 267).

A few blacks, such as Gabriel and Martin Prosser in Virginia (1800), definitely plotted mass uprisings and murders, and others, such as Denmark Vesey in South Carolina (1822), may have done so. But in most areas blacks accounted for less than half the population, and everywhere they lacked the strong institutions—such as the communes of free peasants or serfs in Europe— needed to organize a successful rebellion. Moreover, whites were well armed, unified, and militant. Escape was equally problematic. Blacks in the Lower South

Jacob Stroyer

A Child Learns the Meaning of Slavery

Jacob Stroyer, born into slavery in South Carolina, was emancipated and became a minister in Salem, Massachusetts, and an abolitionist. In My Life in the South *(1885), he relates a dramatic incident that revealed his family's subordinate and powerless status as slaves.*

Father had a surname, Stroyer, which he could not use in public, as the surname Stroyer would be against the law; he was known only by the name of William Singleton, because that was his master's name. . . . Mother's name was Chloe. She belonged to Colonel M. R. Singleton too; she was a field hand, and was never sold, but her parents once were. . . .

Father . . . used to take care of horses and mules. I was around with him in the barnyard when but a small boy; of course that gave me an early relish for the occupation of hostler, and soon I made known my preference to Colonel Singleton, who was a sportsman and had fine horses. . . . Hence I was allowed to be numbered among those who took care of the fine horses, and learned to ride. . . .

It was not long after I had entered my new work before they put me upon the back of a horse which threw me to the ground almost as soon as I reached his back. . . .

When I got up there was a man standing near with a switch in hand, and he immediately began to beat me. . . . This was the first time I had been whipped by anyone except Mother and Father, so I cried out in a tone of voice as if I would say, this is the first and last whipping you will give me when Father gets hold of you.

When I got away from him I ran to Father with all my might, but soon my expectation was blasted, as Father very coolly said to me, "Go back to your work and be a good boy, for I cannot do anything for you." But that did not satisfy me, so I went on to Mother with my complaint and she came out to the man who whipped me. He was a groom, a white man whom master hired to train his horses . . . [and] he took a whip and started for her, and she ran from him, talking all the time. . . .

Then the idea first came to me that I, with my dear father and mother and the rest of my fellow Negroes, was doomed to cruel treatment through life and was defenseless. . . .

One day, about two weeks after Boney Young and Mother had the conflict, he . . . gave me a first-class flogging. That evening when I went home to Father and Mother, I said to them, "Mr. Young is whipping me too much now; I shall not stand it. I shall fight him." Father said to me, "You must not do that, because if you do he will say that your mother and I advised you to do it, and it will make it hard for your mother and me, as well as yourself. You must do as I told you my son. . . . I can do nothing more than pray to the Lord to hasten the time when these things shall be done away."

Source: Linda R. Monk, ed., *Ordinary Americans: U.S. History through the Eyes of Everyday People* (Alexandria, VA: Close Up Publications, 1994), 71–72.

could seek freedom in Spanish Florida until 1819, when the United States annexed the territory.

Even then, hundreds of blacks continued to flee to Florida, where they intermarried with the Seminole Indians. Elsewhere in the South small groups of escaped slaves eked out a living in deserted marshy areas or in mountain valleys, hoping that they would not be killed, enslaved, or returned by Indian warriors. Given these limited options most slaves had no choice but to build the best possible lives for themselves on the plantations where they lived.

The Free Black Population

Between 1790 and 1820 the number of free blacks rose steadily from 8 percent of the total African American population to about 13 percent, but few of them were truly free. One-third of all free blacks—some 50,000 in 1810—lived in the North, where they performed the most menial and low-paying work and were treated as second-class citizens. In rural areas of the North free blacks worked as farm laborers or tenant farmers; in towns and cities, as domestic servants, laundresses, or day laborers. Only a small minority of free African Americans owned land. "You do not see one out of a hundred . . . that can make a comfortable living, own a cow, or a horse," a traveler in New Jersey noted. In addition, blacks were usually forbidden to vote, attend public schools, or sit next to whites in churches. Of the states admitted to the Union between 1790 and 1821 only Vermont and Maine extended the vote to free blacks,

CLASS No. 1.

Comprises those prisoners who were found guilty and executed.

Prisoners Names.	Owners' Names.	Time of Commit.	How Disposed of.
Peter	James Poyas	June 18	Hanged on Tuesday the 2d July, 1822, on Blake's lands, near Charleston.
Ned	Gov. T. Bennett,	do.	
Rolla	do.	do	
Batteau	do.	do.	
Denmark Vesey	A free black man	22	
Jessy	Thos. Blackwood	23	
John	Elias Horry	July 5	Do. on the Lines near Ch.; Friday July 12.
Gullah Jack	Paul Pritchard	do.	
Mingo	Wm. Harth	June 21	
Lot	Forrester	27	
Joe	P. L. Jore	July 6	
Julius	Thos. Forrest	8	
Tom	Mrs. Russell	10	
Smart	Robt. Anderson	do.	
John	John Robertson	11	
Robert	do.	do.	
Adam	do.	do.	
Polydore	Mrs. Faber	do.	Hanged on the Lines near Charleston, on Friday, 26th July.
Bacchus	Benj. Hammet	do.	
Dick	Wm. Sims	13	
Pharaoh	— Thompson	do.	
Jemmy	Mrs. Clement	18	
Mauidore	Mordecai Cohen	19	
Dean	— Mitchell	do.	
Jack	Mrs. Purcell	12	
Bellisle	Est. of Jos. Yates	18	
Naphur	do.	do.	
Adam	do.	do.	
Jacob	John S. Glen	16	
Charles	John Billings	18	
Jack	N. McNeill	22	
Cæsar	Miss Smith	do.	
Jacob Stagg	Jacob Lankester	23	Do. Tues. July 30.
Tom	Wm. M. Scott	24	
William	Mrs. Garner	Aug. 2	Do. Friday, Aug. 9.

"An Account of the Late Intended Insurrection, Charleston, South Carolina"

In 1822 Charleston had a free black population of 1,500, which boasted an array of its own institutions, including a Brown Fellowship Society (for those of mixed racial ancestry) and an African Methodist Episcopal (AME) church. Historians have long thought that one of these free African Americans, Denmark Vesey, organized a conspiracy to free the city's slaves. However, recent studies have suggested that the prospect of slave rebellion reflected white fears rather than historical fact. In any event, South Carolina authorities hanged Vesey and thirty-four co-conspirators and tore down the AME church where they had allegedly plotted the insurrection.
Rare Book, Manuscript & Special Collections, Duke University Library.

Captain Absalom Boston
Absalom Boston was born in 1785 on the island of Nantucket, the heart of the American whaling industry. A member of a community of free black whalers manumitted from slavery by their Quaker owners, Boston went to sea at age fifteen. By the age of thirty he had used his earnings to become the proprietor of a public inn. In 1822 Boston became the first black master with an all-black crew to undertake a whaling voyage from Nantucket. In later years he became an important leader of the island's black community, serving as a trustee of the African School.
Nantucket Historical Association.

and they could testify against whites in court only in Massachusetts. The federal government did not allow free African Americans to work for the postal service, claim public lands, or hold a U.S. passport.

Nonetheless, a few free blacks in the North were able to make full use of their talents, and some achieved great distinction. The mathematician and surveyor Benjamin Banneker published an almanac and helped lay out the new national capital in the District of Columbia. Joshua Johnston, a skilled painter, won praise for his portraiture, and merchant Robert Sheridan acquired a small fortune from his business enterprises. More impressive and enduring were the community institutions created by this first generation of free African Americans. In many northern communities they founded schools, mutual-benefit organizations, and fellowship groups, often with the title Free African Society. Discriminated against in white Protestant churches, they also formed their own congregations and an independent religious denomination—the African Methodist Episcopal (AME) Church. These institutions gave free African Americans a sense of cultural, if not political, autonomy (see American Lives, "Richard Allen and African American Identity," p. 270).

Most free blacks who lived in slave states resided in the Upper South—some 110,000 in 1810. In Maryland a quarter of the black population was free; in Delaware free blacks outnumbered slaves by three to one. Free blacks accused of crimes were often denied a jury trial, and many others had to contend with vagrancy and apprenticeship laws intended to force them back into slavery. To prove their free status blacks had to carry manumission documents and in some states needed official permission to travel across county lines. Even with valid papers free African Americans in the South had to be careful; kidnapping and sale were constant threats. Yet the shortage of skilled workers in southern cities created opportunities for many blacks, who became the backbone of the region's urban workforce. Trained African American carpenters, blacksmiths, barbers, butchers, and shopkeepers in Baltimore, Richmond, Charleston, and New Orleans formed benevolent societies and churches, providing education, recreation, and social welfare programs for their communities.

As a privileged group among African Americans, free blacks felt both loyalty to the welfare of their families, which often meant assimilating white culture, and loyalty to their race, which meant identifying with the great mass of enslaved African Americans. Some wealthier free blacks, particularly the mulatto children of white masters and black women, drew apart from common laborers and field hands and adopted the outlook of the planter class. In Charleston and New Orleans a few free African Americans even owned slaves.

Generally, however, both free and enslaved African Americans saw themselves as one people. "We's different [from whites] in color, in talk and in 'ligion and beliefs," as one put it. Knowing their own freedom was not secure as long as slavery existed, free blacks sought to win freedom for all those of African ancestry. Free blacks in the South aided fugitive slaves, while free black northerners supported the antislavery movement. In the rigid caste system of American race relations, free blacks stood as symbols of hope to enslaved African Americans and as omens of danger to the majority of whites.

The Missouri Crisis

White society was increasingly divided over the question of the wisdom and morality of a republican society based on slave labor. The rapid advance of plantation society into the Southwest heightened the tension and added a new dimension to the debate. In a speech opposing nationally financed internal improvements in 1818, Congressman Nathaniel Macon of North Carolina warned that radical-minded members of the "colonizing bible and peace societies" wanted to increase the federal power in order "to try the question of emancipation." Indeed, a major conflict over emancipation came even more quickly than Macon had anticipated. When Missouri applied for admission to the Union as a slave state in 1819, Congressman James Tallmadge of New York proposed a ban on the importation of slaves into Missouri and the gradual emancipation of its black inhabitants. When Missouri whites rejected those conditions, the northern majority in the House of Representatives blocked the territory's admission to the Union.

Southerners were horrified. "It is believed by some, & feared by others," Alabama Senator John Walker reported from Washington, that Tallmadge's amendment was "merely the entering wedge and that it points already to a total emancipation of the blacks." The outlook was grim. "You conduct us to an awful precipice, and hold us over it," Mississippi Congressman Christopher Rankin warned his northern colleagues. To underline their determination to protect slavery, southerners used their power in the Senate (where they held half the seats) to withhold statehood from Maine, which was seeking to separate itself from Massachusetts.

In the ensuing debate, southerners advanced three constitutional arguments. First, they raised the principle of "equal rights," arguing that Congress could not impose conditions for statehood on the citizens of Missouri that it had not imposed on other new states. Second, they argued that slavery was purely an internal affair, a matter that fell under the sovereignty of the state government. Finally, they maintained that Congress had no authority to infringe on the property rights of slaveholders. Going beyond these constitutional issues, southern leaders abandoned the traditional argument that slavery was a "necessary evil" and now championed the institution as a "positive good." "Christ himself gave a sanction to slavery," declared Senator William Smith of South Carolina, and many southern religious leaders agreed. "If it be offensive and sinful to own slaves," a prominent Mississippi Methodist remarked, "I wish someone would just put his finger on the place in Holy Writ."

Controversy raged for two years before Henry Clay of Kentucky put together a series of political agreements known collectively as the Missouri Compromise. A series of legislative measures allowed Maine to enter the Union as a free state in 1820 and Missouri to be admitted as a slave state in 1821. By admitting both states, the compromise preserved the existing balance between North and South in the Senate and set a precedent for the future admission of states in pairs—one free and one slave. To mollify northern antislavery activists in the House of Representatives, southern congressmen accepted legislation that prohibited slavery in the rest of the Louisiana Purchase north of latitude 36°30', the southern boundary of Missouri (Map 9.3).

Just as in the Constitutional Convention of 1787, white leaders in both the North and the South had given first priority to the Union, finding complex but workable ways to reconcile regional interests. But the task had become more difficult. The Philadelphia delegates had resolved sectional and other differences in two months. Congress took two years to work out the Missouri Compromise, with no guarantee that it would work. The fate of the western lands, the Union, and the black race had become inextricably intertwined and the specter of civil war lurked in the background. As the aging Thomas Jefferson exclaimed in the midst of the Missouri crisis,

Richard Allen and African American Identity

Richard Allen lived a full life. Born into slavery in Philadelphia in 1760 and sold with his family as a child to a farmer in Delaware, he died in 1831 not only free but influential, a founder of the African Methodist Episcopal Church and its first bishop. Allen's rise to fame is a classic American success story, but it bears a larger significance: As one of the first African Americans to be emancipated during the Revolutionary era, Allen worked to forge an identity for his people as well as for himself.

Allen began his ascent in 1777, when Freeborn Garretson, an itinerant preacher, converted him to Methodism. A powerful foe of slavery, Garretson also converted Allen's master and convinced him that on Judgment Day slaveholders would be "weighted in the balance, and . . . found wanting." Allowed by his repentant owner to buy his freedom, Allen earned a living sawing cordwood and driving a wagon during the Revolutionary War. After the war he enlisted in the Methodist cause, becoming a "licensed exhorter" and preaching to blacks and whites from New York to South Carolina.

Allen's success as a preacher attracted the attention of white Methodist leaders, including Francis Asbury, the first American bishop of the Methodist Church. In 1786 Allen won appointment as an assistant minister in Philadelphia, serving the racially mixed congregation of St. George's Methodist Church. The following year he and Absalom Jones, another black preacher, joined other former slaves and Quaker philanthropists to establish the Free African Society, a benevolent organization that offered fellowship and mutual aid to "free Africans and their descendants."

Allen remained a staunch Methodist throughout his life. In 1789, when the Free African Society adopted the Quaker custom of having fifteen minutes of silence at its meetings, Allen led a withdrawal of those who preferred more enthusiastic Methodist practices. Five years later he rejected an offer to become the pastor of St. Thomas's African Church, the Episcopal-affiliated church that the Free African Society had built and that a majority of its members had joined. "I informed them that I could not be anything else but a Methodist, as I was born and awakened under them," Allen recalled.

Now Allen confronted a more difficult challenge: reconciling his Methodist faith with the fact that many white Methodists were prejudiced against African Americans. Allen's solution was to form a separate congregation. Gathering a group of ten black Methodists, Allen formed the Bethel African Methodist Episcopal Church in the increasingly black southern section of Philadelphia. There its tiny congregation worshiped "separate from our white brethren." A few years later Allen helped to found another all-black institution, the Society of Free People of Colour for Promoting the Instruction and School Education of Children of African Descent. By 1811 there were no fewer than eleven black schools in the city.

Allen's decision to found separate black institutions was partly a response to white racism. Although most white Methodists in the 1790s favored emancipation, they did not treat free blacks as social equals. They refused to allow African Americans to be buried in the regular Methodist cemetery and, in a famous incident in 1792, segregated black worshipers in a newly built gallery of St. George's Methodist Church. Allen's initiative also reflected a desire among African Americans to control their religious lives, "to call any brother that appears to us adequate to the task to preach or exhort as a local preacher." By 1795 the congregation of Allen's Bethel Church numbered 121; a decade later it had grown to 457, and by 1813 it had reached 1,272.

Bethel's rapid expansion reflected that of Philadelphia's free black population, which numbered nearly 10,000 by 1810, as well as the appeal of Methodist practices. Blacks welcomed Methodist "love feasts," which allowed the full expression of emotions repressed under slavery, and the church's strict system of discipline—its communal sanctions against drinking, gambling, and marital infidelity—which helped them bring order to their lives.

Nonetheless, Allen and his congregation grew dissatisfied with Methodism, as white ministers retreated from their antislavery principles and the Church hierarchy curbed the autonomy of African American congregations. In 1807 the Bethel Church added an "African Supplement" to its articles of incorporation, and in 1816 it won legal recognition as an independent church. In the same year Allen and representatives from four other black Methodist congregations (in Baltimore, Maryland; Wilmington, Delaware; Salem, New Jersey; and Attleboro, Pennsylvania) organized a new denomination—the African Methodist Episcopal Church. The delegates chose Allen as the first bishop of the church, the first fully independent black denomination in America.

But where did Allen think "free people of colour" should look for their future? This question had arisen in Philadelphia as early as 1787, in a debate over a plan to settle free American and West Indian blacks in Sierra Leone, a settlement on the west coast of Africa founded

The Mount Bethel African Methodist Episcopal Church and Its First Minister, the Reverend Richard Allen

During the 1790s Allen founded a separate congregation for Philadelphia's African American Methodists, who eventually established the Mount Bethel Church. In 1816 Allen invited ministers from other black Methodist congregations to Mount Bethel where they founded the first independent black denomination in the United States: the African Methodist Episcopal Church. Library of Congress; Mount Bethel A.M.E. Church, Philadelphia.

For more help analyzing these images, see the ONLINE STUDY GUIDE at bedfordstmartins.com/henretta.

by British abolitionists. Many blacks in Boston and Newport had endorsed this scheme, but the members of Philadelphia's Free African Society had rejected it. While acknowledging the racism that kept blacks in a subordinate position, they declared their intention to seek advancement in America.

To pursue their goal, Philadelphia's blacks adopted a dual strategy. As a social group, they embraced their ancestry by forming "African" churches and benevolent societies. However, as individuals they asserted their American identity by taking English names (although virtually never those of their former owners). Although these efforts yielded few significant gains in wealth or status, Philadelphia's African Americans again rejected colonization when the issue was revived around 1800. Only four people signed up for immigration to Sierra Leone.

Instead, the city's black community turned to political action to improve the social and legal condition of the race. Hundreds of African Americans signed petitions asking Congress to end the Atlantic slave trade and to repeal the Fugitive Slave Act of 1793, which allowed slave owners to seize blacks without a warrant. Underlining the importance of the latter issue, in 1806 Allen himself was held temporarily as a fugitive slave, showing that even the most prominent northern blacks could not be sure of their freedom.

Allen's brush with slavery may account for his initial support for the American Colonization Society. But a mass meeting of nearly 3,000 Philadelphia blacks condemned the society's plan to settle free blacks in Africa. Instead, it set forth a different vision of the African American future: "Whereas our ancestors (not of choice) were the first successful cultivators of the wilds of America, we their descendants feel ourselves entitled to participate in the blessings of her luxuriant soil."

Philadelphia's black community, including Allen, was more favorably inclined toward the Haitian Emigration Society, founded in 1824 to help African Americans settle in the black-run republic of Haiti. When this venture failed in 1827, Allen forcefully urged blacks to remain in the United States, writing in *Freedom's Journal*, the nation's first black newspaper: "This land which we have watered with our tears and our blood is now our mother country."

Born a slave of African ancestry, Allen had won freedom for himself and had helped to fashion an African American religious identity for his people. Tempted by emigration but ultimately rejecting that option, Allen cast his lot and that of his descendants with a society pervaded by racism. It was a brave decision, characteristic of the man who made it, but indicative of the very limited choices available to men and women freed from the bonds of slavery.

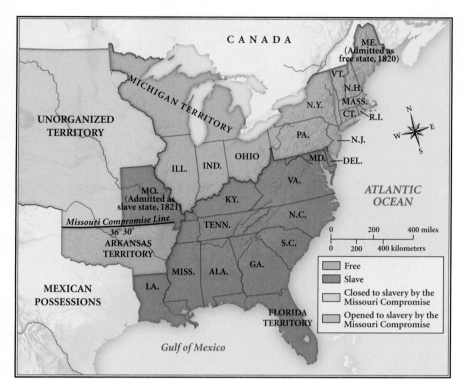

MAP 9.3 The Missouri Compromise, 1820–1821

The Missouri Compromise resolved for a generation the issue of slavery in the lands of the Louisiana Purchase. The agreement prohibited slavery north of the Missouri Compromise line (36°30′ north latitude), with the exception of the state of Missouri. To maintain an equal number of senators from free and slave states in the U.S. Congress, the compromise provided for the nearly simultaneous admission to the Union of Maine and Missouri.

"This momentous question, like a fire-bell in the night, awakened and filled me with terror."

Protestant Christianity as a Social Force

Religion had always been a significant part of American life. However, beginning in 1790 a series of religious revivals planted the values of Protestant Christianity deep in the national character and gave a spiritual definition to American republicanism. The revivals also changed African American life. Free and enslaved blacks became Christians, absorbing the faith of white Baptists and Methodists and creating a distinctive and powerful institution—the black church. Evangelical Christianity also created new public roles for women, especially in the North, and set in motion a long-lasting movement for social reform.

The Second Great Awakening

The revivals that began around 1790 were much more complex than those of the First Great Awakening. In the 1740s most revivals had occurred in existing congregations; fifty years later they took place in frontier camp meetings as well and often involved the creation of new churches and denominations. More striking, the Second Great Awakening spawned new organizations dedicated to social and political reform.

Republican Churches and Revivalism. Churches that prospered in the new nation were those that adopted a republican outlook, proclaiming the spiritual equality of all believers and creating relatively democratic church organizations (Table 9.3). Because the Roman Catholic Church was dominated by bishops and priests, it attracted few converts among Protestants, who adhered to Luther's doctrine of the priesthood of all believers, or among the unchurched—the great number of Americans who had never belonged to churches and who feared clerical power. The number of Catholic congregations grew primarily through immigration. Likewise, few ordinary native-born Americans joined the Episcopal Church (created by former members of the Church of England), which had a hierarchical structure similar to that of Catholicism and was dominated by its wealthiest members. The Presbyterian Church was more popular, in part because the membership elected laymen to the synods (congresses) where doctrine and practice were formulated. The Methodist and Baptist Churches attracted even more Americans because most of their preachers were fervent evangelists and promoted an egalitarian religious culture, encouraging lay preaching and communal singing.

A continuous wave of revivalism fueled the expansion of Protestant Christianity. Beginning in the 1790s Baptists and Methodists evangelized the cities and the backcountry of New England. A new sect of Universalists, who repudiated the Calvinist doctrine of predestination and preached universal salvation, attracted thousands of converts, especially in Massachusetts and

TABLE 9.3 Number of Church Congregations by Denomination, 1780 and 1860

	1780	1860	Increase
Anglican / Episcopalian	406	2,100	5-fold
Baptist	457	12,150	26-fold
Catholic	50	2,500	50-fold
Congregational	742	2,200	3-fold
Lutheran	240	2,100	8-fold
Methodist	50	20,000	400-fold
Presbyterian	495	6,400	13-fold

northern New England. After 1800 enthusiastic camp meeting revivals swept the frontier regions of South Carolina, Kentucky, Tennessee, and Ohio (Map 9.4).

When frontier preachers got together at a revival meeting, they were electrifying. James McGready, a Scots-Irish Presbyterian preacher, "could so array hell before the wicked," an eyewitness reported, "that they would tremble and Quake, imagining a lake of fire and brimstone yawning to overwhelm them." James Finley described the Cane Ridge, Kentucky, revival of 1802:

> *The noise was like the roar of Niagara. The vast sea of human beings seemed to be agitated as if by a storm. I counted seven ministers, all preaching at one time, some on stumps, others on wagons. . . . Some of the people were singing, others praying, some crying for mercy.*

Through such revivals, Baptist and Methodist preachers reshaped the spiritual landscape of the South and the Old Southwest. Because of their emotional message, revivalists were particularly successful in attracting the unchurched. The evangelicals' promise of religious fellowship also appealed to young men and women and geographically mobile families who had few social ties in their new communities. With the assistance of black ministers, they began to implant evangelical Protestant Christianity among African Americans as well (see Voices from Abroad, "Frances Trollope: A Camp Meeting in Indiana," p. 276).

The Second Great Awakening changed the denominational base of American religion. The leading churches of the colonial period—the Congregationalists, Episcopalians, and Quakers—declined in relative membership because they were content to maintain existing congregations or to grow slowly through natural increase. Because of their evangelical activities and democratic outlook, Methodist and Baptist churches grew

spectacularly. By the early nineteenth century they had become the largest religious denominations in the United States. In New England and the Middle Atlantic states, pious women supplemented the work of preachers and lay elders by holding prayer meetings and providing material aid and spiritual comfort to poorer members of the congregation, doubling the amount of organized spiritual energy. In the South and West, Baptist and Methodist preachers traveled constantly. A Methodist minister followed a circuit, "riding a hardy pony or horse . . . with his Bible, hymn-book, and Discipline." These "circuit riders" established new churches by searching out devout families, bringing them together for worship, and then appointing lay elders to lead the congregation and enforce moral discipline until the circuit rider returned.

Evangelical ministers copied the techniques of George Whitefield and other eighteenth-century revivalists, codifying their methods in manuals on "practical preaching." To attract converts, preachers were advised to adopt theatrical gestures and a flamboyant style, to throw away their precise but stodgy written sermons and to speak extemporaneously. "Preach without papers" and emphasize piety rather than theology, advised one minister, "seem earnest & serious; & you will be listened to with Patience, & Wonder; both of your hands will be seized, & almost shook off as soon as you are out of the Church."

In the South evangelical religion became increasingly important. Initially revivalism was a disruptive force; by proclaiming the spiritual equality of all people—women and blacks as well as white men—it threatened the traditional authority wielded by husbands and planters and incurred their wrath. In response Methodist and Baptist preachers adapted the social content of their religious message so that it supported the rule of yeomen patriarchs and slave-owning planters. "We hold that a Christian slave must be submissive,

A Baptist Ceremony

Unlike many other Christian churches, which practiced infant baptism, Baptists reserved this sacred ceremony for adults who had been born again by the infusion of God's grace. Some Baptist congregations, such as the one depicted in this 1819 painting, required complete immersion in water, symbolizing the cleansing of all sins. Such communal practices, along with an egalitarian atmosphere and an intense religiosity, attracted tens of thousands of converts and quickly made the Baptists one of the largest American denominations. Chicago Historical Society.

faithful, and obedient," a Methodist conference proclaimed, while a Baptist minister declared that a man was naturally at "the head of the woman." Ultimately Christian republicanism in the South added a sacred dimension to the ideology of aristocratic republicanism, while in the North it pushed forward the movement toward a democratic republican society.

Black Protestantism.   After the family, the religious community played the most important role in the lives of enslaved African Americans. Initially most blacks maintained the practices of their African homeland. "At the time I first went to Carolina," remembered Charles Ball, an escaped slave, "there were a great many African slaves in the country. . . . Many of them believed there were several gods [and] I knew several . . . Mohamedans [Muslims]."

When the First Great Awakening swept through the Upper South in the 1750s and 1760s, some blacks joined

Christian churches, but the first major wave of conversions began along the James River in Virginia in the mid-1780s. Evangelical white Baptists and Methodists won the conversion of hundreds of slaves and free blacks, who absorbed the white churches' teachings and adapted them to their needs. Black Christians generally preferred to envision God as a warrior who had liberated the Jews, his chosen people. Their cause was similar to the Israelites', Martin Prosser told his fellow slave conspirators as they plotted rebellion in Virginia in 1800. "I have read in my Bible where God says, if we worship him, we should have peace in all our land and five of you shall conquer a hundred and a hundred of you a hundred thousand of our enemies." Confident of their special relationship with God, the slaves prepared themselves spiritually for emancipation, which they saw as deliverance to the Promised Land.

Blacks generally ignored the doctrines of original sin and predestination as well as biblical passages that encouraged unthinking obedience to authority or

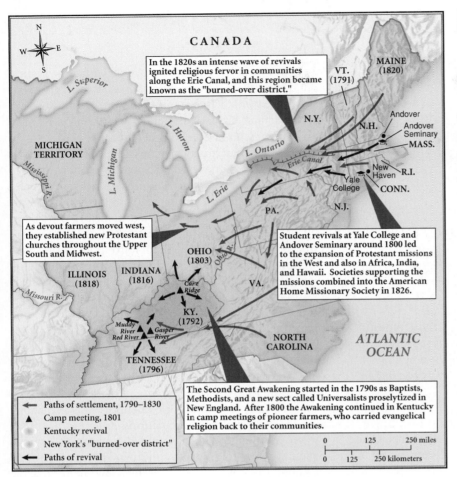

In the 1820s an intense wave of revivals ignited religious fervor in communities along the Erie Canal, and this region became known as the "burned-over district."

As devout farmers moved west, they established new Protestant churches throughout the Upper South and Midwest.

Student revivals at Yale College and Andover Seminary around 1800 led to the expansion of Protestant missions in the West and also in Africa, India, and Hawaii. Societies supporting the missions combined into the American Home Missionary Society in 1826.

The Second Great Awakening started in the 1790s as Baptists, Methodists, and a new sect called Universalists proselytized in New England. After 1800 the Awakening continued in Kentucky in camp meetings of pioneer farmers, who carried evangelical religion back to their communities.

← Paths of settlement, 1790–1830
▲ Camp meeting, 1801
● Kentucky revival
● New York's "burned-over district"
← Paths of revival

MAP 9.4 The Second Great Awakening, 1790–1860

The awakening lasted for decades and invigorated churches in every part of the nation. However, the revivals in Kentucky and in New York State were particularly intense and influential. As thousands of farm families migrated to the South and West (see Map 8.2), they carried with them the fervor generated by the Cane Ridge revival in Kentucky in 1802 and the religious wildfires that swept through the "burned-over district" along the Erie Canal in New York between 1825 and 1835.

portrayed the church as a lawgiver. When a white minister urged slaves in Liberty County, Georgia, to obey their masters, he noted that "one half of my audience deliberately rose up and walked off." Slaves identified not only with the powerful Father-God but also with his persecuted Savior-Son, who had suffered and died so that his followers might gain salvation. By offering eventual liberation from life's sorrows, the Christian message helped many slaves endure their bondage. Amid the manifest injustice of their own lives African Americans used Christian principles to affirm their spiritual equality with whites and to hope for ultimate justice in the afterlife. Black Christianity thus developed as a religion of emotional fervor and stoical endurance.

New Religious Thought and Institutions.
Like African Americans, whites responded more positively to certain Christian doctrines than to others. The Calvinist preoccupation with human depravity and weakness had shaped the thinking of many colonial-era writers, teachers, and statesmen. By the early nineteenth century, ministers (whether or not they were revivalists) placed greater stress on human ability and individual free will, making the religious culture of the United States more optimistic and more compatible with republican doctrines of liberty and equality.

In New England many educated, well-off Congregationalists reacted against the emotionalism of Methodist and Baptist services by stressing the power of human reason. Rejecting the concept of the Trinity—God the Father, Son, and Holy Spirit—they worshiped an indivisible and "united" God; hence their name: Unitarians. "The ultimate reliance of a human being is, and must be, on his own mind," argued the famous Unitarian minister William Ellery Channing, "for the idea of God is the idea of our own spiritual nature, purified and enlarged to infinity." This emphasis on a believer's reason, a legacy of the Enlightenment, gave Unitarianism a humanistic and individualistic aspect.

Lyman Beecher, the preeminent New England Congregationalist clergyman, accepted the doctrine of universal salvation. Although Beecher continued to believe that humans had a natural tendency to sin, he retreated from the Calvinist doctrine of predestination still held by many ministers, declaring that men and women had the capacity to choose God. In emphasizing choice—the free will of the believer—Beecher testified to the growing confidence in the power of human action.

Frances Trollope

A Camp Meeting in Indiana

*F*rances Trollope, a successful English author and the mother of novelist Anthony Trollope, resided in the United States during the late 1820s. She lived for a time in Cincinnati, where she owned a bazaar that sold imported goods from Europe. Unsuccessful as a storekeeper, she won great acclaim as a social commentator. Her critical and at times acerbic Domestic Manners of the Americans *(1832) was a best-seller in both Europe and the United States. Here she provides her readers with a vivid description of a revivalist meeting in Indiana around 1830.*

We reached the ground about an hour before midnight, and the approach to it was highly picturesque. The spot chosen was the verge of an unbroken forest, where a space of about twenty acres appeared to have been partially cleared for the purpose. Tents of different sizes were pitched very near together in a circle round the cleared space. . . .

Four high frames, constructed in the form of altars, were placed at the four corners of the inclosure; on these were supported layers of earth and sod, on which burned immense fires of blazing pine-wood. On one side a rude platform was erected to accommodate the preachers, fifteen of whom attended this meeting, and with very short intervals for necessary refreshment and private devotion, preached in rotation, day and night, from Tuesday to Saturday.

When we arrived, the preachers were silent; but we heard issuing from nearly every tent mingled sounds of praying, preaching, singing, and lamentation. . . . The floor [of one of the tents] was covered with straw, which round the sides was heaped in masses, that might serve as seats, but which at that moment were used to support the heads and arms of the close-packed circle of men and women who knelt on the floor.

Out of about thirty persons thus placed, perhaps half a dozen were men. One of these [was] a handsome-looking youth of eighteen or twenty. . . . His arm was encircling the neck of a young girl who knelt beside him, with her hair hanging dishevelled upon her shoulders, and her features working with the most violent agitation; soon after they both fell forward on the straw, as if unable to endure in any other attitude the burning eloquence of a tall grim figure in black, who, standing erect in the center, was uttering with incredible vehemence an oration that seemed to hover between praying and preaching. . . .

One tent was occupied exclusively by Negroes. They were all full-dressed, and looked exactly as if they were performing a scene on a stage. . . . The men were in snow white pantaloons, with gay colored linen jackets. One of these, a youth of coal-black comeliness, was preaching with the most violent gesticulations. . . .

At midnight, a horn sounded through the camp, which, we were told, was to call the people from private to public worship; and we presently saw them flocking from all sides to the front of the preacher's stand. . . . There were about two thousand persons assembled.

One of the preachers began in a low nasal tone, and, like all other Methodist preachers, assured us of the enormous depravity of man. . . . Above a hundred persons, nearly all females, came forward, uttering howlings and groans so terrible that I shall never cease to shudder when I recall them. They appeared to drag each other forward, and on the word being given, "let us pray," they fell on their knees . . . and they were soon all lying on the ground in an indescribable confusion of heads and legs.

Source: Frances Trollope, *Domestic Manners of the Americans* (London: Whittaker, Treacher and Co., 1832), 139–42.

Reflecting this optimistic outlook, the minister Samuel Hopkins linked individual salvation with social reform through the concept of religious benevolence. Benevolence was the practice of disinterested virtue, to be undertaken by those who had received God's sanctifying grace. According to the New York Presbyterian minister John Rodgers, fortunate individuals who had received God's grace had a duty "to dole out charity to their poorer brothers and sisters." Heeding this message pious merchants founded the New York Humane Society and other charitable organizations. By the 1820s some conservative church leaders were complaining that lay men and women were devoting themselves to secular reforms, such as the prevention of pauperism, to the neglect of spiritual goals. Their criticism underlined a key element of the new religious outlook: its emphasis on improving society. It was her belief, the social reformer Lydia Maria Child later recalled, that "the only true church organization [is] when heads and hearts unite in working for the welfare of the human-race."

Unlike the First Great Awakening of the 1740s, which split churches into factions, the Second Great Awakening fostered cooperation among the denominations. Five interdenominational societies were founded between 1815 and 1826: the American Education Society (1815), the American Bible Society (1816), the American Sunday School Union (1824), the American Tract Society (1824), and the American Home Missionary Society (1826). The new organizations were based in New York, Boston, and Philadelphia, but they ministered to a national congregation. Each year these societies dispatched hundreds of missionaries to small towns and rural villages and distributed tens of thousands of religious pamphlets, organizing thousands of church members in a great collective undertaking and diminishing the importance of differences over religious doctrine. Many congregations abandoned books and pamphlets that took controversial stances on old theological debates over predestination and replaced them, a layman explained, with publications that would not give "offense to the serious Christians of any denomination."

This unity among Protestants had a galvanizing effect, as men and women scattered across the expanding nation saw themselves as part of a single religious movement that could change the course of history. "I want to see our state evangelized," declared one pious New York layman: "Suppose the great State of New York in all its physical, political, moral, commercial, and pecuniary resources should come over to the Lord's side. Why it would turn the scale and could convert the world. I shall have no rest until it is done."

As a result of the Second Awakening, religion became a central force in American political life. On July 4, 1827, the Reverend Ezra Stiles Ely called on the members of the Seventh Presbyterian Church in Philadelphia to begin a "Christian party in politics." In his sermon, entitled "The Duty of Christian Freemen to Elect Christian Rulers," Ely set out for the American republic a new religious goal—one that the recently deceased Thomas Jefferson and John Adams would have found strange if not troubling. The two founders had believed that America's mission was to spread political republicanism. In contrast Ely urged the United States to become an evangelical Christian nation, dedicated to religious conversion at home and abroad. As Ely put it, "All our rulers ought in their official capacity to serve the Lord Jesus Christ."

Women's New Religious Roles

Pious women assumed a new leading role in many Protestant churches in the North and even founded new sects. Mother Ann Lee organized the Shaker sect in Britain and migrated in 1774 to America, where she and a handful of followers attracted numerous recruits; by the 1820s Shaker communities dotted the American countryside from New Hampshire to Kentucky and Indiana (see Chapter 12). In 1776 in Rhode Island, Jemima Wilkinson, a young Quaker woman stirred by reading the sermons of George Whitefield, had a vision that she had died and been reincarnated as the second coming of Christ:

> The heavens were open'd and she saw [two] Archangels descending from the east . . . and the Angels said, the Spirit of Life from God had descended to earth. . . . And according to the declaration of the Angels, the Spirit took full possession of the Body it now Animates.

Repudiating her birth name, Wilkinson declared herself to be the Publick Universal Friend and won scores of converts to her new religion, which blended the Calvinist warning of "a lost and guilty, gossiping, dying World" with Quaker-inspired plain dress, pacifism, and abolitionism.

Increasing Public Activities. Far more important were the activities undertaken by women in mainstream churches. To give but a few examples, in New Hampshire women managed more than fifty local "cent" societies to raise funds for the Society for Promoting Christian Knowledge. Evangelical women in New York City founded the Society for the Relief of Poor Widows. And young Quaker women in Philadelphia ran the Society for the Free Instruction of African Females.

Women became active in religion and charitable work partly because they were excluded from other spheres of public life and partly because ministers were forced to rely on female members, who formed a substantial majority in some denominations, to do the work of the church. After 1800 over 70 percent of the members of New England Congregational churches were female. Ministers acknowledged their presence by changing long-standing practices such as gender-segregated seating at services and separate prayer meetings for each sex, while evangelical Methodist and Baptist preachers actively encouraged mixed seating and praying. "Our prayer meetings have been one of the greatest means of the conversion of souls," a minister in central New York reported in the 1820s, "especially those in which brothers and sisters have prayed together."

Far from promoting promiscuity, as critics feared, these new practices were accompanied by greater moral self-discipline. Absorbing the principle of female virtue, many young women and the men who courted them postponed sexual intercourse until after marriage—a form of self-restraint uncommon in the eighteenth century. In Hingham, Massachusetts, and many other New England towns, about 30 percent of the women who married between 1750 and 1800 had borne a child within eight months of their wedding day. By the 1820s the proportion had dropped to 15 percent.

Nevertheless, as women exercised their new spiritual authority, men scrutinized their behavior and tried to curb their power. Evangelical Baptist churches that had once stressed spiritual equality now denied women the right to vote on church affairs or to offer testimonies of faith before the congregation. Such activities, declared one layman, were "directly opposite to the apostolic command in Cor[inthians] xiv, 34, 35, 'Let your women learn to keep silence in the churches.'" "Women have a different *calling*," claimed another, "That they *be chaste, keepers at home* is the Apostle's direction." Seizing on that role, by the 1820s mothers throughout the United States had founded local maternal associations to encourage Christian childrearing. Newsletters such as *Mother's Magazine* were widely read in hundreds of small towns and villages, giving women a sense of shared purpose and identity as women.

Women's Education. Religious activism also advanced female education. Churches established scores of seminaries and academies where girls from the middling classes received sound intellectual training and moral instruction. Emma Willard, the first American to advocate higher education for women, opened the Middlebury Female Seminary in Vermont in 1814 and later founded girls' schools in Waterford and Troy, New York. Women educated in these seminaries and academies gradually displaced men as public-school teachers. By the 1820s women taught the summer session in many schools; in the following decade they took on the more demanding winter term as well. Women were able to usurp these formerly male roles because women had few other opportunities and would therefore accept lower pay than men. Female schoolteachers earned from $12 to $14 per month with room and board—less than a farm laborer. However, as schoolteachers women had an acknowledged place in public life, one that had been beyond their reach in colonial and Revolutionary times. Here too, the Second Great Awakening had transformed the scope of women's lives. Just as the ideology of democratic republicanism had expanded voting rights and the political influence of ordinary men in the North, so the values of Christian republicanism had encouraged women to take a more active role in the affairs of their communities.

FOR FURTHER EXPLORATION

▶ For definitions of key terms boldfaced in this chapter, see the glossary at the end of the book.

▶ To assess your mastery of the material covered in this chapter, see the Online Study Guide at **bedfordstmartins.com/henretta**.

▶ For suggested references, including Web sites, see page SR-10 at the end of the book.

▶ For map resources and primary documents, see **bedfordstmartins.com/henretta**.

Three variants of republican society developed in the United States in the early nineteenth century: democratic republicanism in the North, aristocratic republicanism in the South, and an evangelical Protestant vision of republicanism that was embraced by many people in both regions. In the North the ideals of liberty and equality encouraged the emergence of a white male citizenry that demanded voting rights, pursued social mobility, and looked with suspicion on those with aristocratic pretensions. Political and religious leaders promoted a different path for women, developing the notion of a separate sphere consisting primarily of domestic responsibilities. Republicanism and sentimentalism encouraged young people to marry for love as well as for economic security and prompted parents to rear their children using reason as well as authority.

White society in the South changed as southern planters extended the slave regime into the Old Southwest in response to the demand for cotton. Ownership of slaves became concentrated in fewer hands, and smallholding white farmers moved into the hilly backcountry. Southern society developed an aristocratic republican system of politics dominated by slaveholders. Distressed by the rapid geographic growth of plantation society, northern representatives in Congress delayed for two years the entry of Missouri into the Union. Finally, the Missouri Compromise temporarily resolved the crisis, by dividing the lands of the Louisiana Purchase into free and slave territory.

Enslaved blacks gradually forged a distinct African American culture, melding together various African traditions with the English language and Christian religious practices. Slaves developed increasingly strong family, community, and religious values, which helped them survive the forced migration to the cotton South and the relentless work of carving new plantations out of the wilderness. In the northern cities, free blacks founded independent churches and benevolent institutions.

The Second Great Awakening made Americans a fervently Protestant people and dramatically increased the influence of the evangelical Baptist and Methodist Churches. Religious revivalism also enhanced the status of women, whose moral activism broadened their sphere to encompass teaching in public schools and managing charitable groups and religious societies. The shared religious experience of hundreds of thousands of Americans between the 1770s and the 1820s formed the core of an emerging national identity, even as the citizens of the North and the South defined republicanism in distinctly different ways.

1782   St. Jean de Crèvecoeur publishes *Letters from an American Farmer*

1787   Benjamin Rush, *Thoughts on Female Education*

1790s   Parents limit family size as farms shrink

Second Great Awakening expands church membership

Ministers encourage "Republican motherhood"

1800   Gabriel Prosser plots a slave rebellion in Virginia

1800s   Rise of sentimentalism and republican marriage system

Women's religious activism; founding of female academies

Spread of evangelical Baptists and Methodists

Religious benevolence sparks social reform

Chesapeake blacks adopt Protestant beliefs

1807   New Jersey excludes propertied women from suffrage

1810s   Expansion of suffrage for men

Slavery defended as a "necessary evil"

Expansion of cotton South and domestic slave trade

1819–1821   Conflict over admission of Missouri as a slave state ends with Missouri Compromise

1820s   Reform of public education

Women become schoolteachers

PART TWO

Federalism as History and Contemporary Politics

People sometimes wonder why they need to know about what seems like ancient history—events that took place, as in Part Two, hundreds of years ago or more. Not politicians. They root around avidly in the nation's past to find traditions and precedents to justify their policies. No era is more heavily exploited than the nation-building decades recounted in the chapters you have just read. Take, for example, the "Reagan Revolution" of the 1980s. President Ronald Reagan (1981–1989) was bent on diminishing the power of the national government by cutting its tax revenue and transferring policymaking and spending authority to the state and local levels. In 1987 he issued Executive Order 12612 instructing all executive departments and agencies to "refrain, to the maximum extent possible, from establishing uniform, national standards for programs and . . . defer to the States to establish standards." Entitled "Federalism," Order 12612 laid down some of the general principles underlying the Reagan Revolution, including its basic premise that "our political liberties are best assured by limiting the size and scope of the national government." As the historical grounding for this argument, the order quoted the words of none other than the author of the Declaration of Independence, Thomas Jefferson, that the states are "the most competent administrations for our domestic concerns and the surest bulwarks against antirepublican tendencies."

In appealing to Jefferson, Reagan was setting himself against the reigning scholarly consensus. Historians had long debated the merits of the Antifederalists—those who had opposed the U.S. Constitution of 1789 and defended states' rights—as against those of the Federalists—supporters of the Constitution and activist national policies. By Reagan's time, most historians thought that the Federalists had the stronger case. In a famous article of 1955, the highly respected constitutional historian Cecilia Kenyon had denigrated the Antifederalists as "men of little faith" who had misread the course of history and the meaning of the American experiment by refusing to support a strong national government. Influenced by the New Deal, a wide-ranging set of federal programs that had rescued the nation from the Great Depression of the 1930s, many other historians—and especially those with a "liberal" outlook—likewise praised activist governments. During the 1940s historians Oscar Handlin, Louis Hartz, and Carter

Goodrich celebrated those state governments that had actively subsidized economic development between 1790 and 1840; subsequently, scholars of the Progressive Era (1890–1914) praised reformers who strengthened regulatory powers on the state and national levels. In their eyes, stronger government was the wave of the future.

The actual results of the Reagan Revolution would seem to have sustained the interpretation of these liberal historians. For all his rhetoric of states' rights and personal liberty, Reagan failed to reverse the centralizing tendencies of American government. The anti-Communist crusade of his administration was too vigorous, the entitlements of federal programs were too valued, even by his own conservative constituents, to allow Reagan to dismantle the powerful national regulatory, Social Security, and military bureaucracies created during the New Deal and the cold war.

If the Reagan Revolution fell short of its political objectives, it succeeded remarkably as an intellectual movement. The Antifederalists have again become respectable in scholarly circles. In part this result has been the fruit of a sustained effort by Reagan's followers to breathe new life into conservative American thought by means of think tanks like the Heritage Foundation and the Cato Institute. Conservative and libertarian scholars such as Gary L. McDowell (*Reason and Republicanism: Thomas Jefferson's Legacy of Liberty,* 1997) and David A. J. Richards (*Foundations of American Constitutionalism,* 1989) reinvigorated the study of the Antifederalists and the doctrines of state-based federalism, individualism, and limited government. They have been joined by such mainstream scholars as Saul Cornell, who explains in *The Other Founders: Anti-Federalism and the Dissenting Tradition in America, 1788–1828* (1999) how Jeffersonian Republicans embraced the strong localist impulses represented by the Antifederalists and devised a new constitutional doctrine, the "compact" or "states' rights" theory of federalism. Even on the left the values of the Antifederalists have drawn sympathy. In *The Transformation of American Law, 1780–1860* (1976), legal scholar Morton Horwitz shows how activist state government systematically favored entrepreneurs and capitalists in the nineteenth century, throwing the costs of economic development on workers and taxpayers.

Once they began to explore, moreover, historians had no difficulty identifying the long-standing strength—and political integrity—of the traditions of limited government and local self-rule. Consider the following examples from the period covered in Part Two, The New Republic, 1775–1820:

▸ In theory and law, the British Constitution declared the supremacy of central authority: the king-in-

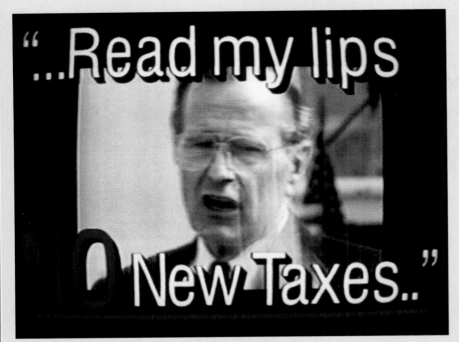

"...Read my lips NO New Taxes.."

Parliament. However, many American political leaders rejected the primacy of imperial law, for they had long governed according to what John Phillip Reid (*In a Defiant Stance*, 1977) has called "Whig Law," rules enacted by local institutions and enforced by local officials. Why should we be governed by "strangers *ignorant* of the interests and laws of the Colonies?" asked William Henry Drayton of South Carolina, a future leader of the Patriot localist revolt against British centralized authority.

▶ Having vanquished a distant, powerful government in London, the Antifederalists were determined not to allow a new one in America. Their leaders subjected the centralizing Constitution of 1787 to thorough, coherent criticism. Massachusetts Antifederalist James Winthrop spoke for them when supporting the existing system of "Whig Law": "It is necessary that there should be local laws and institutions," he argued, "for a people inhabiting various climates will unavoidably have local habits and different modes of life."

▶ When the Antifederalists failed to block ratification of the Constitution of 1787, they limited its authority by insisting on a Bill of Rights to protect individual liberty. Subsequently, when Alexander Hamilton as secretary of the treasury expanded the powers of the new national government, former Antifederalists joined James Madison and Thomas Jefferson in the Democratic Republican Party, which in turn adopted their localist outlook (see Chapter 7) and articulated a new interpretation of the Constitution, a compact theory of federalism. In the Kentucky Resolution of 1798, Jefferson suggested that each state had "an equal right to judge for itself" whether an act of the national government was unconstitutional. In addition to this ideological contribution to the theory of federalism, Jefferson laid the institutional foundations for a limited central government. As president from 1801 to 1809, he systematically dismantled the energetic national government created by Hamilton.

As in the contest between Jefferson and Hamilton, President Reagan's ideologically charged statement of administrative policy inevitably evoked a political counterresponse. Speaking for those who favored an activist central government, in 1998 President William Jefferson Clinton (1993–2001) issued Executive Order 13083, also entitled "Federalism," which offered a nationalist reading of American constitutional history. "Preserving the supremacy of Federal law," it asserted, "provides an essential balance to the power of the States. "Clinton's executive order justified national action in many circumstances, including those in which "there is a need for uniform national standards" and in which "States have not adequately protected individual rights and liberties."

What are we to make of these political and historical controversies? In the first place they remind us that the established facts of "history" were once the contested terrain of "politics." In seeking to reverse Hamilton's policies, Jefferson was just as much a politician as Clinton. Second, these episodes warn us about the frequent abuse of the historical record by self-interested politicians. In celebrating Jefferson's ideology and achievements, Reagan consciously ignored Hamilton's great contributions to the American political tradition. Finally, the struggle over federalism shows us the intimate connection between contemporary politics and historians' views of the past. If history is always more complex than political rhetoric suggests, historians' interpretations often reflect the political wisdom of the moment.

Economic Revolution and Sectional Strife

1820–1877

ECONOMY	SOCIETY	GOVERNMENT	CULTURE	SECTIONALISM
The Economic Revolution Begins	A New Class Structure Emerges	Creating a Democratic Polity	Reforming People and Institutions	From Compromise to Civil War and Reconstruction
1820 ▸ Waltham textile factory (1814) Erie Canal completed (1825); market economy expands	▸ Business class emerges Rural women and girls recruited as factory workers	▸ Spread of universal white male suffrage Rise of Jackson and Democratic Party	▸ American Colonization Society (1817) Benevolent Reform Movements Revivalist Charles Finney	▸ Missouri Compromise (1820) David Walker's *Appeal to the Colored Race* (1829)
1830 ▸ Protective tariffs aid owners and workers Panic of 1837 U.S. textile makers outcompete British	▸ Mechanics form craft unions Depression shatters labor movement	▸ Anti-Masonic movement Whig Party formed (1834); Second Party System emerges	▸ Joseph Smith founds Mormonism Female Moral Reform Society (1834) Temperance Crusade expands	▸ Nullification crisis (1832) W. L. Garrison forms American Anti-Slavery Society (1833)
1840 ▸ Irish join labor force *Commonwealth v. Hunt* (1842) legalizes unions Manufacturing grows	▸ Working-class districts emerge in cities Irish immigration accelerates	▸ Log Cabin campaign mobilizes voters Antislavery parties: Liberty and Free Soil	▸ Fourierist and other communal settlements founded Seneca Falls convention (1848)	▸ Texas annexation, Mexican War, and Wilmot Proviso (1846) increase sectional conflict
1850 ▸ Growth of cotton output in South and railroads in the North and Midwest Panic of 1857	▸ Expansion of farm society into Midwest and Far West Free labor ideology justifies inequality	▸ Whig Party disintegrates; Republican Party founded (1854): Third Party System begins	▸ Harriet Beecher Stowe's *Uncle Tom's Cabin* (1852) Anti-immigrant nativist movement	▸ Compromise of 1850 Kansas-Nebraska Act (1854) and Bleeding Kansas *Dred Scott* decision (1857)
1860 ▸ Republicans enact agenda: Homestead Act, railroad aid, high tariffs, national banking	▸ Emancipation Proclamation (1863) Free blacks struggle for control of land	▸ Thirteenth Amendment (1865) ends slavery; Fourteenth Amendment (1868) extends legal and political rights	▸ U.S. Sanitary Commission and American Red Cross founded	▸ South Carolina leads secession movement (1860) Confederate States of America (1861–1865)
1870 ▸ Panic of 1873	▸ Rise of sharecropping in the South	▸ Fifteenth Amendment extends vote to black men (1870)	▸ Freed African Americans create schools and churches	▸ Compromise of 1877 ends Reconstruction

Between 1820 and 1877 the United States changed from a predominantly agricultural society into one of the world's most powerful manufacturing economies. This profound transformation began slowly in the Northeast and then accelerated after 1830, affecting every aspect of life in the northern and midwestern states and bringing important changes to the South as well.

ECONOMY Two revolutions in industrial production and the market system transformed the nation's economy. Factory owners used high-speed machines and a new system of labor discipline to boost production, and enterprising merchants employed a newly built network of canals and railroads to create a vast national market. The manufacturing sector produced an ever-increasing share of the country's wealth: from less than 5 percent in 1820 to more than 30 percent in 1877.

SOCIETY The new economic system spurred the creation of a class-based society. A wealthy elite of merchants, manufacturers, bankers, and other entrepreneurs emerged at the top of the social order and tried to maintain social stability through a paternalistic program of religious reform. However, an urban middle class with a distinct material and religious culture grew in size and political importance. Equally striking was the increasing number of propertyless workers, many of them immigrants from Germany and Ireland, who labored for wages in the new factories and built the new canals and railroads. By 1860 half the nation's free workers labored for wages, and wealth had become concentrated in the hands of relatively few families.

GOVERNMENT Economic growth and social diversity facilitated the development of political parties and a more open, democratic polity. To enhance their economic prospects, farmers, workers, and entrepreneurs turned to politics, seeking improved transportation, shorter work days, and special corporate charters. Catholic immigrants from Ireland and Germany also entered the political arena in order to protect their religion and culture from attacks by nativists and reformers. Led by Andrew Jackson, the Democratic party took the lead in advancing the interests of southern planters, farmers, and urban workers. It did so primarily by carrying through a democratic political and constitutional revolution that cut governmental aid to financiers, merchants, and business corporations. To compete with the Democrats, the Whig party (and, beginning in the 1850s, the Republican party) promoted reform and a vision of a society with few class barriers and a high rate of individual social mobility. The result was a two-party system that engaged the energies of the vast majority of the electorate and unified the fragmented social order.

CULTURE During these decades, a series of reform movements, many with religious roots and goals, swept across America. Dedicated men and women preached the gospel of temperance, observance of Sunday, prison reform, and dozens of other causes. Some Americans pursued their social dreams in utopian communities in the Midwestern states, but most reformers worked within society. Two interrelated groups—abolitionists and women's rights activists—called for radical changes in the social order, the immediate end of slavery and reform of the patriarchal legal and cultural order. Abolitionist attacks prompted southern leaders to defend slavery as beneficial to slaves as well as planters. During the 1840s and 1850s, antislavery advocates turned to political action, campaigning for free soil in the western territories and alleging that the southern slave power threatened free labor and republican values.

SECTIONALISM These economic, political, and cultural changes combined to sharpen sectional divisions: the North developed into an urbanizing and industrializing society based on free labor, whereas the South remained a rural, slaveholding society dependent on the production and export of cotton. Following the conquest of vast areas of the West during the Mexican War (1846–1848), northern and southern politicians argued vigorously over the issue of permitting slavery in these newly acquired territories. These conflicts could not be resolved by political compromise, leading in 1861 to the secession of the South from the Union and, thereafter, civil war. The conflict became a total war, a struggle between two societies as well as two armies. Because of new technology and the mass mobilization of armies, the two sides endured unprecedented casualties and costs before the North emerged victorious.

The fruits of victory were substantial. During Reconstruction, the Republican Party ended slavery, imposed its economic policies and constitutional doctrines on the nation, and began to extend full democratic rights to the former slaves. Faced by massive resistance from white southerners, northern leaders lacked the will to undertake the fundamental transformation of the economic and political order of the South that was required to provide African Americans with the full benefits of freedom.

ART IS THE HANDMAID OF HUMAN GOOD. · LOWELL. ·

CHAPTER 10

The Economic Revolution

1820–1860

◄ **Technology Celebrated**

Artists joined with manufacturers in praising the new industrial age. In this 1836 emblem, a proposed seal for the city of Lowell, Massachusetts, a cornucopia (horn of plenty) spreads its bounty over the community, as bales of raw cotton (in the foreground) await their transformation in the city's textile factories into smooth cloth for shipment to far-flung markets via the new railroad system. The image of prosperity was deceptive; two years earlier, 2,000 women textile workers had gone on strike in Lowell, claiming that their wages were too low to provide a decent standard of living. Private collection.

For more help analyzing this image, see the ONLINE STUDY GUIDE at bedfordstmartins.com/henretta.

IN 1804 LIFE SUDDENLY TURNED GRIM for eleven-year-old Chauncey Jerome. Following the death of his farmer-blacksmith father, Jerome was hired out as an indentured servant to a farmer. Aware that few farmers "would treat a poor boy like a human being," Jerome bought out his indenture by finding a job making dials for clocks and eventually ended up working as a journeyman for clockmaker Eli Terry. A manufacturing wizard, Terry had turned Litchfield, Connecticut, into the clock-making center of the United States by designing an enormously popular desk-model clock with brass parts. Jerome followed in Terry's footsteps, setting up his own clock business in 1816. By organizing work more efficiently and using new machines to make interchangeable metal parts, Jerome drove down the price of a simple clock from $20 to $5 and then to less than $2. By the 1840s he was selling his clocks in England, the center of the Industrial Revolution; two decades later his workers were turning out 200,000 clocks a year, testimony to American industrial enterprise. By 1860 the United States was not only the world's leading exporter of cotton and wheat but also the third-ranking manufacturing nation, behind only Great Britain and France.

The French aristocrat Alexis de Tocqueville captured a key feature of Chauncey Jerome's experience and the American economic revolution in his treatise *Democracy in America* (1835). "What most astonishes me," Tocqueville remarked after a two-year stay in the United States, "is not so much the marvelous grandeur of some undertakings, as the innumerable magnitude of small ones." The individual efforts of tens of thousands of artisan-inventors like Eli Terry and Chauncey Jerome had propelled the country into a new economic era. As the editor of *Niles' Weekly Register* in Baltimore put it, there was an "almost universal ambition to get forward."

Not all Americans embraced the new ethic of enterprise, and many who did failed to share in the new prosperity. The Industrial Revolution and the Market Revolution created a class-divided society that challenged the founders' vision of an agricultural republic with few distinctions of wealth or power. As the philosopher Ralph Waldo Emerson warned in 1839, "The invasion of Nature by Trade with its Money, its Credit, its Steam, [and] its Railroad threatens to . . . establish a new, universal Monarchy."

The Coming of Industry: Northeastern Manufacturing

Together the Industrial Revolution and the Market Revolution created a new economy. Industrialization came to the United States after 1790 as American merchants and manufacturers increased the output of goods by reorganizing work and building factories. The rapid construction of turnpikes, canals, and railroads by state governments and private entrepreneurs allowed manufactured goods and farm products from many regions to be sold throughout the land. Thanks to these innovations in production and transportation, the average per capita wealth of Americans increased by nearly 1 percent per year—30 percent over the course of a generation. Goods that once had been luxury items became part of everyday life (Table 10.1).

Division of Labor and the Factory

This impressive gain in living standards stemmed initially from changes in the organization of production. Consider the shoe industry. Traditionally New England shoemakers worked in small wooden shacks called "ten-footers," where they turned leather hides into finished shoes and boots. During the 1820s and 1830s merchants and manufacturers centered in Lynn, Massachusetts, took over the shoe industry and increased output through a **division of labor**. The employers hired semiskilled journeymen and set them to work in large central shops cutting the leather into soles and uppers. They then sent out the upper sections to shoe binders, women in dozens of Massachusetts towns who worked at home sewing in fabric linings. Finally, the manufacturers had other journeymen assemble the shoes and return them to the central shop for inspection and packing. The new system made the manufacturer into a powerful "shoe boss" and eroded the workers' control over the pace and conditions of labor. "I guess you won't catch me to do that little thing again," vowed one Massachusetts binder. Whatever the cost to workers, the division of labor dramatically increased the output of shoes while cutting their price.

For tasks that were not suited to the outwork system, entrepreneurs created an even more important new organization, the modern **factory**, which concentrated production under one roof and divided the work into

TABLE 10.1 Leading Branches of Manufacture, 1860

Item	Number of Workers	Value of Product	Value Added by Manufacture	Rank by Value Added
Cotton Textiles	115,000	$107.3 million	$54.7 million	1
Lumber	75,600	104.9 million	53.8 million	2
Boots and Shoes	123,000	91.9 million	49.2 million	3
Flour and Meal	27,700	248.6 million	40.1 million	4
Men's Clothing	114,800	80.8 million	36.7 million	5
Iron (cast, forged, etc.)	49,000	73.1 million	35.7 million	6
Machinery	41,200	52.0 million	32.5 million	7
Woolen Goods	40,600	60.7 million	25.0 million	8
Leather	22,700	67.3 million	22.8 million	9
Liquors	12,700	56.6 million	32.5 million	10

Source: Adapted from Douglass C. North, *Growth and Welfare in the American Past,* 2nd ed. (Paramus, NJ: Prentice-Hall, 1974), table 6.1.

specialized tasks performed under supervision by different individuals. For example, in the 1830s Cincinnati merchants built slaughterhouses that rationalized the process of butchering hogs—that is, subdivided the process into a series of specific tasks. A simple system of overhead rails moved the hog carcasses past workers who split the animals, removed various organs, and trimmed the carcasses into pieces. Then packers stuffed the cuts of pork into barrels and pickled them to prevent spoilage. The system was efficient and quick—sixty hogs per hour—and by the 1840s Cincinnati was butchering so many hogs that the city became known as "Porkopolis."

Some factories boasted impressive new technology. The prolific Delaware inventor Oliver Evans built a highly automated flour mill driven by waterpower. His machinery lifted the grain to the top of the mill, cleaned the grain as it fell into hoppers, ground it into flour, conveyed the flour back to the top of the mill, and then cooled the flour during its descent into barrels. Evans's factory, remarked one observer, "was as full of machinery as the case of a watch." It needed only six men to mill 100,000 bushels of grain a year.

Subsequently, factory owners used newly improved stationary steam engines to power their mills and began to

Pork Packing in Cincinnati

The only form of modern technology in this Cincinnati pork-packing plant was the overhead pulley system that carried hog carcasses past the workers. The plant's efficiency came from organization, a division of labor in which each worker performed a specific task. Such plants pioneered the design of the moving assembly lines that reached a high level of sophistication in the early-twentieth-century automobile factories of Henry Ford.
Cincinnati Historical Society.

manufacture new types of products. Before 1830 power-driven machines and assembly lines mainly processed agricultural goods—pork, leather, wool, and cotton; subsequently they were used to fabricate goods and machines made of metal. Cyrus McCormick of Chicago developed power-driven conveyor belts to assemble reaping machines, and Samuel Colt built an assembly-line factory in Hartford, Connecticut, to produce his invention—the "six-shooter" revolver, as it became known. As a team of British observers noted apprehensively, "The contriving and making of machinery has become so common in this country, and so many heads and hands are at work with extraordinary energy, that . . . it is to be feared that American manufacturers will become exporters not only to foreign countries, but even to England."

The Textile Industry and British Competition

British textile manufacturers were particularly worried about American competition. To protect its industrial leadership, the British government prohibited the export of textile machinery and the emigration of mechanics who knew how to build it. However, lured by high wages or offers of partnerships, thousands of British mechanics disguised themselves as ordinary laborers and set sail for the United States. By 1812 there were more than 300 British mechanics at work in the Philadelphia area alone.

Samuel Slater was the most important of the immigrants. Slater came to America in 1789 after working for Richard Arkwright, the inventor and operator of the most advanced British machinery for spinning cotton. Having memorized the design of Arkwright's machinery, the young Slater introduced his innovations in merchant Moses Brown's cotton mill in Providence, Rhode Island. The opening of Slater's factory in 1790 marks the advent of the American Industrial Revolution (see New Technology, "Cotton Spinning: From Spinsters to Machines," p. 289).

American and British Advantages. In competing with British mills, American manufacturers had one major advantage: an abundance of natural resources. America's rich agriculture produced a wealth of cotton and wool, and from Maine to Delaware its rivers provided a cheap source of energy. As rivers cascaded downhill from the Appalachian foothills to the Atlantic coastal plain, they were easily harnessed to run power machinery. Industrial villages and towns sprang up along these waterways, dominated by massive textile mills—150 feet long, 40 feet wide, and four stories high (Map 10.1).

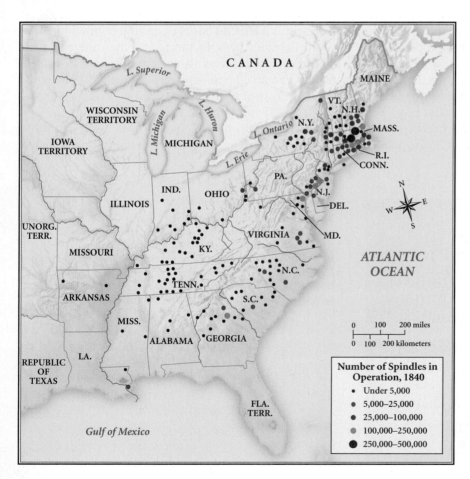

MAP 10.1 New England's Dominance in Cotton Spinning, 1840

Although the South grew the nation's cotton, Boston and Rhode Island entrepreneurs built most of the factories for spinning and weaving the cotton into cloth in New England, using the abundant waterpower of the region. The new factories relied on the labor of young farm women and, later, of immigrants from Ireland and French-speaking regions of Canada.

Number of Spindles in Operation, 1840
- Under 5,000
- 5,000–25,000
- 25,000–100,000
- 100,000–250,000
- 250,000–500,000

Cotton Spinning: From Spinsters to Machines

For centuries the making of cloth had been slow and laborious work, mostly done by women. Taking raw wool or cotton, women pulled out burrs and seeds and separated the fibers into strands by running over them with a comb or "card," a flat paddle studded with twigs or nails. Next they began the even more time-consuming task of spinning the fibers into cotton or woolen thread (or more bulky woolen yarn) by using hand- or foot-powered spinning machines. Finally, the women fitted hundreds of these threads into hand-powered looms so that they could be woven into cloth, sometimes by women but more often by men.

Despite its importance in cloth making, spinning had a low social value, in part because it was drudge work—slow, repetitive, and uninteresting. It became the work of women without power: young girls, grandmothers, and especially unmarried women. Living in the households of their fathers or brothers, unmarried women sat at the bottom of the family hierarchy, condemned to the menial tasks of cleaning, mending, and especially spinning. Indeed, the connection between spinning and never-married older women was so close that such women became (and remain) known as "spinsters."

The name should not have survived the Industrial Revolution, which transformed the processing of cotton and wool and made spinsters obsolete. By 1800 carding was no longer handwork, as water- or hand-powered carding machines turned raw cotton into clean fibers. Consisting of two or more cylinders covered with wire pins, the machines combed the fibers into parallel strands and fed them into other machines that wound the carded cotton into a long, loose rope called "roving."

Mechanization also revolutionized the technology of spinning. The key tool in spinning had always been the spindle, which first elongated the strands of fiber and then twisted them together to make strong threads or yarn. In 1765 the British inventor James Hargreaves devised a "spinning jenny" that imitated the function of spinning wheels. The jenny's operator manually turned a wheel that spun a series of spindles—from twenty-four to one hundred—each of which simultaneously drew out the roving and twisted it into thread. Using a jenny, one person could now do the work of dozens of spinsters, and in less time.

However, American textile manufacturers preferred another British invention—the spinning frame, patented by Richard Arkwright in 1769 and pirated to the United States by Samuel Slater. The spinning frame separated the functions of drawing and twisting. After two pairs of rollers had elongated the roving, it was passed down the arm of a flier, a device attached to a spindle. The flier twisted the roving into thread and wound it onto a bobbin attached to the spindle.

The spinning frame lowered production costs dramatically. The machine ran hundreds of spindles continuously on inexpensive waterpower and produced threads and yarn that were strong enough to be woven on the fast-moving, waterpowered looms that came into use during the 1820s. Most important from the manufacturers' perspective, the spinning frame required only low-skilled and low-priced labor. The operative had only to affix the roving to the frame and tie any threads that broke. In many American factories, tending spinning frames became the ill-paid work of young women and girls—such as the two hundred girls between the ages of six and thirteen employed at the Union Manufactory and McKim's Cotton Factory in Baltimore in 1820.

By a cruel twist of fate, spinning had once again become drudge work—repetitive, uninteresting, and low-paid. But now it was the work not of family-dependent "spinsters" but of wage-dependent juvenile "proletarians" (workers who had nothing to sell but their labor). In myriad such small transformations, the Industrial Revolution changed the character of American economic—and social—life.

Samuel Slater's Spinning Frame

Samuel Slater's frame for spinning wool was powered by water and could spin thread simultaneously onto ninety-six bobbins (forty-eight on each side of the lower part of the machine). The introduction of the spinning frame revolutionized textile manufacturing by dramatically increasing the output of a single worker.
Museum of History and Technology, Smithsonian Institution, Washington, DC.

Nevertheless, the British producers easily under-sold their American competitors. Thanks to cheap shipping and lower interest rates in Britain, they could import raw cotton from the United States, manufacture it into cloth, and sell it in America at a low price. Moreover, because British companies were better established, they could engage in cutthroat competition, cutting prices briefly but sharply to drive the newer American firms out of business. The most important British advantage was cheap labor. Britain had a larger population—about 12.6 million in 1810 compared with 7.3 million Americans—and thousands of landless laborers who were willing to take low-paying factory jobs. Since unskilled American workers could obtain good pay for farm or construction work, American manufacturers had to pay them higher wages.

To offset these British advantages American entrepreneurs sought assistance from the federal government. In 1816 Congress passed a tariff that gave manufacturers protection from low-cost imports of cotton cloth. New protective legislation in 1824 levied a tax of 35 percent on imported iron products, higher-grade woolen and cotton textiles, and various agricultural products, and the rate rose to 50 percent in 1828. But in 1833, under pressure from southern planters, western farmers, and urban consumers—who wanted to buy inexpensive imported manufactures—Congress began to reduce tariffs (see Chapter 11), causing some American textile firms to go out of business.

Improved Technology and Women Workers.

American producers adopted two other strategies to compete with their British rivals. First, they improved on British technology. In 1811 Francis Cabot Lowell, a wealthy Boston merchant, spent a holiday touring British textile mills. A well-educated and charming young man, he flattered his hosts by asking many questions, but his easy manner hid a serious purpose. Lowell secretly made detailed drawings of power machinery, and Paul Moody, an experienced American mechanic, then copied the machines and made improvements. In 1814 Lowell joined two other merchants, Nathan Appleton and Patrick Tracy Jackson, to form the Boston Manufacturing Company. Raising the staggering sum of $400,000, they built a textile plant on the Charles River in Waltham, Massachusetts. The Waltham factory was the first in America to perform all the operations of cloth making under one roof. Thanks to Moody's improvements, Waltham's power looms operated at higher speeds than British looms and needed fewer workers.

The second American strategy was to find less expensive workers. In the 1820s the Boston Manufacturing Company pioneered a labor system that became known as the "Waltham plan." The company recruited thousands of farm girls and women, who would work at low wages, as textile operatives. To attract these workers,

the company provided boardinghouses and cultural activities such as evening lectures. The mill owners reassured anxious parents by enforcing strict curfews, prohibiting alcoholic beverages, and requiring regular church attendance. At Lowell (1822), Chicopee (1823), and other sites in Massachusetts and New Hampshire, the company built new cotton factories on the Waltham plan; other Boston-owned firms quickly followed suit.

By the early 1830s more than 40,000 New England women were working in textile mills. Lucy Larcom became an operative when she was eleven so that she would not be "a trouble or burden or expense" to her widowed mother. Other women sent their savings home to help their fathers pay off farm mortgages, defray the cost of schooling for their brothers, or accumulate a dowry for themselves. A few just had a good time. Susan Brown, who worked as a Lowell weaver, spent half of her earnings on food and lodging and much of the rest for entertainment—attending fifteen plays, concerts, and

Mill Girl, c. 1850
This fine daguerreotype (an early form of photography) shows a neatly dressed textile worker about twelve years old. The harsh working conditions in the mill have taken a toll on her spirit and body: the young girl's eyes and mouth show little joy or life and her hands are rough and swollen. She probably worked either as a knotter, tying broken threads on spinning jennies, or a warper, straightening out the strands of cotton or wool as they entered the loom. Jack Naylor Collection.

Lucy Larcom

Early Days at Lowell

Lucy Larcom (1824–1893) went to work in a textile mill in Lowell, Massachusetts, when she was eleven years old and remained there for a decade. She then migrated to Illinois with her sisters and a great tide of other New Englanders. In later life Larcom became a teacher and a writer; in her autobiography she decribed the impact of industrial labor on the lives and outlook of women from farms and rural villages.

I never cared much for machinery. The buzzing and hissing and whizzing of pulleys and rollers and spindles and flyers around me often grew tiresome. I could not see into their complications, or feel interested in them. But in a room below us we were sometimes allowed to peer in through a sort of blind door at the great water-wheel that carried the works of the whole mill. It was so huge we could only watch a few of its spokes at a time, and part of its dripping rim, moving with a slow, measured strength through the darkness that shut it in. It impressed me with something of the awe which comes to us in thinking of the great Power which keeps the mechanism of the universe in motion. . . .

We did not call ourselves ladies. We did not forget that we were working girls, wearing coarse aprons suitable to our work, and that there was some danger of our becoming drudges. I know that sometimes the confinement of the mill became very wearisome to me. In the sweet June weather I would lean far out of the window, and try not to hear the unceasing clash of sound inside.

Looking away to the hills, my whole stifled being would cry out

> *Oh, that I had wings!*

Still I was there from choice, and

> *The prison unto which we doom ourselves,*
> *No prison is.*

I regard it as one of the privileges of my youth that I was permitted to grow up among these active, interesting girls, whose lives were not mere echoes of other lives, but had principle and purpose distinctly their own. Their vigor of character was a natural development. The New Hampshire girls who came to Lowell were descendants of the sturdy backwoodsmen who settled that State scarcely a hundred years before. Their grandmothers had suffered the hardships of frontier life. . . . Those young women did justice to their inheritance. They were earnest and capable; ready to undertake anything that was worth doing. My dreamy, indolent nature was shamed into activity among them. They gave me a larger, firmer ideal of womanhood. . . .

Country girls were naturally independent, and the feeling that at this new work the few hours they had of every-day leisure were entirely their own was a satisfaction to them. They preferred it to going out as "hired help." It was like a young man's pleasure in entering upon business for himself. Girls had never tried that experiment before, and they liked it. It brought out in them a dormant strength of character which the world did not previously see.

Source: Lucy Larcom, *A New England Girlhood* (Boston: Houghton Mifflin, 1889), 153–55, 181–83, 196–200.

---

lectures and taking a two-day excursion to Boston. Like many other textile operatives, Brown's spirits were gradually ground down by the monotony and never-ending rigor of factory labor—twelve hours a day, six days a week. After eight months she quit, probably to take a break at home and then to move to another mill. Whatever the hardships, waged work gave many young women a new sense of freedom and autonomy. "Don't I feel independent!" a mill worker wrote to her sister in the 1840s. "The thought that I am living on no one is a happy one indeed to me" (see American Voices, "Lucy Larcom: Early Days at Lowell," above).

The owners of the Boston Manufacturing Company were even happier. By combining improved technology, female labor, and **tariff** protection, they could sell cheap textiles for a lower price than their British rivals could. They also had an advantage over textile manufacturers in New York and Pennsylvania, where farmworkers were better paid than in New England and textile wages consequently were higher. Manufacturers in those states pursued a different strategy, modifying traditional technology to produce higher-quality cloth, also with good results. In 1825 Thomas Jefferson, once a critic of industrialization, expressed his pride in the American achievement: "Our manufacturers are now very nearly on a footing with those of England."

American Mechanics and Technological Innovation

By the 1820s American-born craftsmen had replaced British immigrants at the cutting edge of technological innovation. Although few of these mechanics had a formal education and once had been viewed as "mean" or even "servile" workers, they now claimed respect as "men professing an ingenious art." In 1837 one such inventor, Richard Garsed, experimented with improvements on power looms in his father's factory and in three years nearly doubled their speed. By 1846 Garsed had patented a cam and harness device that allowed fabrics such as damask (which contains elaborate designs) to be woven by machine.

In the Philadelphia region the most important inventors came from the remarkable Sellars family. Samuel Sellars Jr. invented a machine for twisting worsted woolen yarn. His son John devised more efficient ways of using waterpower to run the family's sawmills and built a machine to weave wire sieves. John's sons and grandsons built machine shops that turned out a variety of new products: riveted leather fire hoses, papermaking equipment, and eventually locomotives. In 1824 the Sellars family and other mechanics founded the Franklin Institute in Philadelphia. Named after Benjamin Franklin, whom the mechanics admired for his scientific accomplishments and idealization of hard work, the institute fostered a sense of professional identity. The Franklin Institute published a journal; provided high-school-level instruction in mechanics, chemistry, mathematics, and mechanical drawing; and organized annual fairs to exhibit new products. Craftsmen in Ohio and other states soon established their own mechanics institutes, which played a crucial role in disseminating technical knowledge and encouraging innovation. Around 1820 the United States Patent Office had issued about two hundred patents on new inventions each year, mostly to gentlemen and merchants. By 1850 it was awarding a thousand patents annually, mostly to mechanics from modest backgrounds, and by 1860 more than four thousand.

During these years American craftsmen pioneered the development of **machine tools**—machines for making other machines—thus facilitating the rapid spread of the Industrial Revolution. **Mechanics** in the textile industry invented lathes, planers, and boring machines that turned out standardized parts, making it possible to manufacture new spinning jennies and weaving looms at a low cost and to repair broken machines. Moreover, this machinery was precise enough in design and construction to operate at higher speeds than British equipment.

Technological innovation swept through the rest of American manufacturing. For example, in 1832 the mechanics employed by Samuel W. Collins in his Connecticut ax-making company built a vastly improved die-forging machine—a device that pressed and hammered hot metal into dies, or cutting forms. Using the improved machine, a skilled worker could increase the production of ax heads from twelve to three hundred a day. In the South, Welsh- and American-born mechanics at the Tredegar Iron Works helped to make Richmond, Virginia, a regional manufacturing center. Especially important technical advances came in the firearms industry. To fill large-scale contracts for guns from the federal government, Eli Whitney and his coworkers in Connecticut developed machine tools that produced interchangeable, precision-crafted parts (see American Lives, "Eli Whitney: Machine Builder and Promoter," p. 294). After Whitney's death his partner, John H. Hall, an engineer at the federal armory at Harpers Ferry, Virginia, built a series of sixteen special-purpose lathes to make a gun stock out of sawn lumber and an array of machine tools to work metal: turret lathes, milling machines, and precision grinders. Thereafter, manufacturers could use those machine tools to produce complicated machinery with great speed, at low cost, and in large quantities.

With this expansion in the availability of machines, the American Industrial Revolution came of age. The sheer volume of output caused some products—Remington rifles, Singer sewing machines, and Yale locks—to become household names in the United States and abroad. After showing their machine-tooled goods at the Crystal Palace Exhibition in London in 1851 (the first major international display of industrial goods), Remington, Singer, and other American businesses built factories in Great Britain and soon dominated many European markets.

Wage Workers and the Labor Movement

As the Industrial Revolution gathered momentum, it changed the nature of work and of workers' lives. Each decade, more and more white Americans ceased to be self-employed and took jobs as wage-earning workers. They had little security of employment or control over their working conditions.

The Emergence of Unions. Some wageworkers labored as journeymen, having acquired some of the skills of a traditional artisan craft. These carpenters,

Woodworker, c. 1850

Skilled cabinetmakers took great pride in their work, which was often intricately designed and beautifully executed. To underline the dignity of his occupation, this woodworker poses in formal dress and proudly displays the tools of his craft. A belief in the value of labor was an important ingredient of the artisan-republican ideology held by many workers. Library of Congress.

house painters, stonecutters, masons, nailers, and cabinetmakers had both valuable skills and a strong sense of craft identity. Consequently, they were able to form unions and bargain with the master artisans who employed them. The journeymen's main concern was the increasing length of the workday, which deprived them of time to spend with their families or improve their education. During the eighteenth century the workday for apprentices and journeymen workers in the building trades had averaged about twelve hours, including breaks for meals. By the 1820s masters were demanding a longer day during the summer, when it stayed light longer, while paying journeymen the old daily rate. In response, 600 carpenters in Boston went on strike in 1825, demanding a ten-hour workday, 6 A.M. to 6 P.M., with an hour each for breakfast and a noontime meal. Although the Boston protest failed, two years later journeymen carpenters in Philadelphia won a similar strike and then helped found the Mechanics' Union of Trade Associations. This citywide organization of fifty unions and 10,000 Philadelphia wage earners set forth a broad program of reform, demanding "a just balance of power . . . between all the various classes." To secure this

goal, in 1828 the Philadelphia artisans founded the Working Men's Party, which campaigned for the abolition of banks, equal taxation, and a universal system of public education. By the mid-1830s skilled building-trades workers had forced many urban employers to accept a ten-hour workday and persuaded President Andrew Jackson to set a similar standard at the Philadelphia navy yard.

Artisans whose occupations were threatened by industrialization were less successful in controlling their work lives. As aggressive entrepreneurs and machine technology changed the nature of work, shoemakers, hatters, printers, furniture makers, and weavers faced declining incomes, unemployment, and loss of status. To avoid the regimentation of factory work some artisans in these trades moved to small towns or set up specialized shops. In New York City, 800 highly skilled cabinetmakers worked in artisan-like shops that made fashionable or custom-made furniture. In status and income they outranked a much larger group of 3,200 semitrained workers—derogatively called "botches"—who labored in factories and turned out cheap, mass-produced tables and chairs. The coming of the new industrial system had divided the traditional artisan class into two groups: self-employed craftsmen and wage-earning workers.

In many industries these wage-earning workers banded together to form unions and bargain for higher wages. However, under English and American common law, workers' organizations for raising wages were illegal—"a government unto themselves," in the words of a Philadelphia judge—because they prevented other workers from hiring out for whatever wages they wished. Despite such legal obstacles, unions sprang up whenever wages fell and working conditions became intolerable. In 1830 in Lynn, Massachusetts, journeymen shoemakers founded a Mutual Benefit Society, which quickly spread to other shoemaking centers. "The division of society into the producing and nonproducing classes," the journeymen explained, had made workers like themselves into a mere "commodity" whose labor could be bought and sold without regard for their welfare. As another group of workers put it, "The capitalist has no other interest in us, than to get as much labor out of us as possible. We are hired men, and hired men, like hired horses, have no souls." In 1834 local unions from Boston to Philadelphia combined their resources in the National Trades' Union, the first regional union of different trades.

Labor Ideology and Strikes. Union leaders mounted a critique of the new industrial order, devising an artisan-republican ideology that celebrated the labor and autonomy of working people. Worried that waged workers were becoming "slaves to a monied aristocracy," they condemned the new outwork and factory systems in

Eli Whitney: Machine Builder and Promoter

Eli Whitney (1765–1825) thought life was "a Lottery in which many draw blanks," but thanks to the opportunities offered by the Industrial Revolution, that was not to be his fate. Whitney's luck, combined with intense social ambition and exceptional talents for self-advertisement and mechanical innovation, allowed him to rise in the world and to exert a significant influence on the development of industry in America.

Born into a middling farm family in Massachusetts, Eli Whitney found routine farming chores boring and even depressing. As often as he could, the young lad fled to the farm's workshop to repair household furniture and farm tools. As his sister recalled, Eli "possessed a great measure of affability" and enjoyed talking with his family's neighbors. Those conversations sharpened Whitney's awareness of the limits of New England's mature farm economy—how its poor soil and overcrowded towns condemned most young people to lives of unrelenting labor and meager economic rewards.

The outbreak of the American Revolution opened new doors for the restless youth. In 1779, when he was fourteen, Eli went into business for himself. Persuading his father to install a forge in the workshop, he manufactured nails and knife blades. This enterprise flourished during the war, but peace brought an avalanche of cheap nails from Britain, ruining Eli's market. So the young entrepreneur began producing women's hatpins and men's walking sticks.

Despite his success, Whitney realized that his workshop and his father's small farm would not provide a living for himself, two younger brothers, and four sisters. Moreover, the young man aspired to wealth and high social status, ambitious goals that would be facilitated by a college education—then the privileged preserve of a mere 1 percent of American men. To acquire the necessary training in English grammar, classics, and mathematics, Eli enrolled at Leicester Academy, financing his studies by teaching primary school. By 1789, at age twenty-four, Whitney finally had the skills and the social connections necessary to win admission to Yale College.

At Yale, Whitney pursued a traditional curriculum, with a heavy emphasis on ancient languages, history, rhetoric, and religion. The absence of courses in science

Eli Whitney

Eli Whitney posed for this portrait in the 1820s, when he had achieved both prosperity and social standing. Whitney's success as an inventor prompted the artist, his young New Haven neighbor Samuel F. B. Morse, to turn his creative energies from painting to industrial technology. By the 1840s Morse had devised the first successful commercial telegraph.
Yale University Art Gallery, gift of George Hoadley, B.A. 1801.

or engineering was of little concern because Eli wanted to exploit the social advantages of his college education. Upon Whitney's graduation in 1792, the president of Yale found him a position as a tutor on a Georgia plantation. In traveling south Whitney met Catherine Greene, the young widow of the Revolutionary War general Nathanael Greene, who was charmed by Whitney's "affability" and Yale-bred manners. When Whitney's tutoring position fell through, she invited him for an extended visit to her Georgia plantation, Mulberry Grove.

The exclusive social world of the southern planters fascinated the young New Englander and he paid close attention to their efforts to expand cotton production. Encouraged by Catherine Greene, he set up a workshop and built a simple machine to separate cottonseeds from the delicate fibers that surrounded them. Applying techniques learned in producing women's hatpins, Whitney fashioned thin tines of metal and arrayed them in ranks to

An Early Cotton Gin

As the worker turned the crank of the gin, brushes at the back of the machine pushed the bolls of cotton through an array of wire teeth, which separated the seeds in the bolls from the cotton fiber. The gin processed cotton rapidly and cheaply, and its efficiency facilitated the dramatic expansion of the cotton textile industry. Smithsonian Institution.

create a rudimentary cotton gin, the machine that would revolutionize the processing of cotton. In 1793 Whitney returned to New Haven and began manufacturing gins in quantity. "One of the most Respectable Gentlemen in N. Haven," the young manufacturer proudly reported to his father, said "he would rather be the author of the [my] Invention than the prime minister of England."

If the cotton gin brought prestige, it did not yield wealth. Although Whitney had patented his invention in 1794, he was unable to control the market. Exploiting Whitney's ideas, numerous planters built their own gins, while other manufacturers made slight improvements on his design and competed with him for sales. In a futile bid to assert his patent rights and collect royalties, Whitney filed scores of lawsuits, using up the profits from the sales of his own gins and falling into debt.

To restore his finances, Whitney decided to manufacture military weapons—a product with a guaranteed government market. His Yale connections again served him well. While patenting his cotton gin, he had formed a friendship with a Yale alumnus, Oliver Wolcott, who had become secretary of the treasury. In 1798 Whitney convinced Wolcott that he could mechanize the production of firearms and turn out guns at an unprecedented

scale and pace. Whitney's timing was superb. The new national government had established two armories— in Springfield, Massachusetts, and Harpers Ferry, Virginia—but their production was dismal. To prepare for a possible war with France, Congress had just authorized the Treasury Department to contract for arms with private parties. Almost immediately Wolcott engaged Whitney to manufacture ten thousand muskets within twenty-eight months.

Whitney knew little about muskets, but he had a clear understanding of machine tools and was confident that his tools could produce interchangeable musket parts. As he wrote to Wolcott, "[I will] form the tools so that the tools themselves shall fashion the work and give to every part its just proportion." The young inventor quickly devised improved forms and jigs to guide the hands of mechanics; crafted the first milling machine, which used sharp teeth on a gearlike wheel to cut metal; and achieved a greater interchangeability of parts than previous manufacturers.

Despite these technical advances, Whitney was unable to fulfill his original contract on time. It took ten years—not twenty-eight months—to produce the ten thousand muskets, and even then some components had to be made by hand. But Wolcott continued to support the young inventor, as did the government inspector in New Haven, yet another Yale alumnus, and a group of ten prominent citizens of New Haven, including Pierpont Edwards, the wealthy son of the preacher and philosopher Jonathan Edwards (see Chapter 4).

Whitney also won the backing of Thomas Jefferson, who had been interested in interchangeable parts since the 1780s. Because of his curiosity about science, Jefferson knew of Whitney's cotton gin and in 1800 had witnessed his dramatic public demonstration of interchangeability. Understanding that these techniques would vastly increase the productivity of American manufacturers, Jefferson helped Whitney to win new contracts for military weapons during the War of 1812. These contracts, along with shrewd investment advice from Oliver Wolcott, gave Eli the wealth and social position that he had long craved. Yale awarded him an honorary master's degree and in 1817 he joined one of New England's most respected families, marrying Henrietta Edwards, the daughter of Pierpont Edwards.

When Whitney died in 1825, he had still not achieved his goal of mass production. But his revolutionary technical advances in the design of machine tools had provided a great stimulus to industrial production in the United States. By midcentury American manufacturers led the world in the output of goods that used standardized, interchangeable parts. As a team of British observers noted with admiration, many American products were made "with machinery applied to almost every process . . . all reduced to an almost perfect system of manufacture."

which "capital and labor stand opposed." To restore a just society, they devised a **labor theory of value**, arguing that the price of a product should reflect the labor required to make it. Moreover, they wanted artisans and farmers (and not merchants and factory owners) to reap most of the profit from the sales of products, to enable them "to live as comfortably as others." Appealing to the spirit of the American Revolution, which had destroyed the aristocracy of birth, they called for a new revolution to destroy the aristocracy of capital. Armed with this artisan-republican ideology, in 1836 union men organized nearly fifty strikes for higher wages.

Women textile operatives were equally active. Competition in the cotton textile industry was fierce as output grew (at 5 percent per year) and prices fell (about 1 percent per year). As prices and profits declined, employers reduced workers' wages and imposed more stringent work rules. In 1828 women mill workers in Dover, New Hampshire, struck against new rules, winning some relief; six years later more than 800 Dover women walked out to protest wage cuts. In Lowell, Massachusetts, 2,000 women operatives backed a strike by withdrawing their savings from an employer-owned bank. The Boston *Transcript* reported that "one of the leaders mounted a pump, and made a flaming . . . speech on the rights of women and the iniquities of the 'monied aristocracy.'" When conditions did not improve, young New England women refused to enter the mills, and impoverished Irish (and later French Canadian) immigrants took their places. Many of the new textile workers were men, foreshadowing the emergence of a predominantly male system of factory labor (see Chapter 17).

By the 1850s workers faced yet another threat to their jobs. As machines produced more goods, the supply of manufactures exceeded the demand for them, prompting employers to lay off or dismiss workers. One episode of overproduction preceded the Panic of 1857—a financial crisis sparked by excess railroad investments—and resulted in a major recession. Unemployment rose to 10 percent, reminding Americans of the social costs of the new—and otherwise very successful—system of industrial production.

The Expansion of Markets

As American factories and farms turned out more goods, merchants and legislators created faster and cheaper ways to get those products to consumers—setting in motion a **Market Revolution**. Beginning in the 1820s they promoted the construction of a massive system of canals and roads to link the Atlantic coast states with one another and with the new states in the trans-Appalachian West. By 1860 nearly one-third of the nation's people lived in the Midwest (the five states carved out of the Northwest Territory—Ohio, Indiana,

Illinois, Michigan, and Wisconsin—along with Missouri, Iowa, and Minnesota), where they created a complex society and economy that increasingly resembled that of the Northeast.

Migration to the Southwest and the Midwest

After 1820 vast numbers of men and women migrated to the West, following in the footsteps of the thousands who had already left the seaboard states (Map 10.2). Abandoned farms and homes dotted the countryside of the Carolinas, Vermont, and New Hampshire. "It is useless to seek to excite patriotic emotions" for one's state of birth, complained an easterner, "when self-interest speaks so loudly." Some migrant families wanted to acquire enough land to settle their children on nearby farms, recreating traditional rural communities. Others were more entrepreneurial and hoped for greater profits from the fertile soil of the western territories. By 1840 about 5 million people lived west of the Appalachians.

As in the past the new pioneers migrated in three great streams. In the South plantation owners encouraged by the voracious demand for raw cotton moved more slaves into the Old Southwest (see Chapter 9), expanding the cotton kingdom in Louisiana, Mississippi, and Alabama and pushing on to Missouri (1821) and Arkansas (1836). "The Alabama Feaver rages here with great violence," a North Carolina planter remarked, "and has carried off vast numbers of our Citizens."

Small-scale farmers from the Upper South, especially Virginia and Kentucky, created a second stream as they crossed the Ohio River into the Northwest Territory. Some of these migrants were fleeing planter-dominated slave states. In a free community, thought Peter Cartwright, a Methodist lay preacher from southwestern Kentucky, "I would be entirely clear of the evil of slavery . . . [and] could raise my children to work where work was not thought a degradation." These southerners introduced corn and hog farming to the southern regions of Ohio, Indiana, and Illinois.

A third stream of migrants continued to pour out of the overcrowded farming communities of New England. Thousands of settlers flowed first into upstate New York and then into the fertile farmlands of the Old Northwest, establishing wheat farms throughout the Great Lakes Basin: northern Ohio, northern Illinois, Michigan (admitted in 1837), Iowa (1846), and Wisconsin (1848).

To meet the demand for cheap farmsteads, in 1820 Congress reduced the price of federal land from $2.00 an acre to $1.25—just enough to cover the cost of the survey and sale. For $100 a farmer could buy eighty acres, the minimum required under federal law. Many American families saved enough in a few years to make the minimum purchase and used money from the sale of an old farm to finance the move. By 1860 the

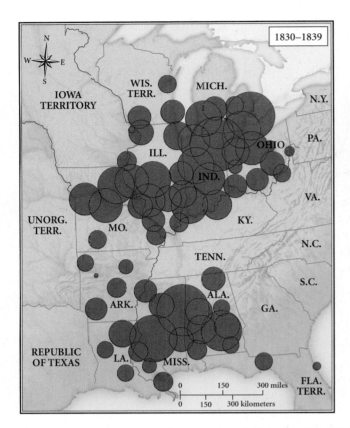

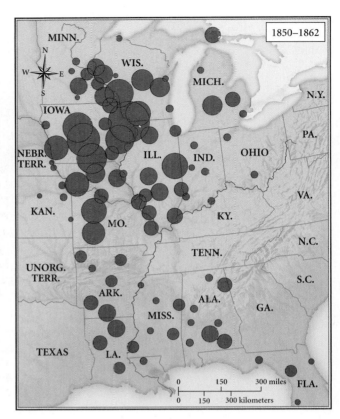

MAP 10.2 Western Land Sales, 1830–1839 and 1850–1862

The federal government set up land offices to sell farmland to western settlers. During the 1830s the offices sold huge amounts of land in the corn and wheat belt of the Old Northwest (Ohio, Indiana, Illinois, and Michigan) and the cotton belt of the Old Southwest (especially Alabama and Mississippi). By the 1850s most government land sales were in the upper Mississippi River Valley (particularly Iowa and Wisconsin). Each circle centers on a government land office and depicts the relative amount of land sold at that office.

population center of American society had shifted significantly to the west.

The Transportation Revolution Forges Regional Ties

To enhance the "common wealth" of their citizens, the federal and state governments took measures to create a larger market. Beginning in the 1790s they chartered private companies to build toll-charging turnpikes in well-populated areas and subsidized road construction in the West. The most significant feat was the National Road, which started in Cumberland, Maryland, passed Wheeling (then in Virginia) in 1818, crossed the Ohio River in 1833, and reached Vandalia, Illinois, in 1839 (Map 10.3). The National Road and other interregional highways carried migrants and their heavily loaded wagons to the West, where they passed herds of livestock being driven to eastern markets. However, such long-distance road travel was too slow and expensive to transport manufactured goods and heavy farm crops.

Canals and Steamboats. To carry wheat, corn, and manufactured goods to far-flung markets, Americans developed a water-borne transportation system of unprecedented size, complexity, and cost, beginning with the Erie Canal. When the New York legislature approved the building of the canal in 1817, no artificial waterway in the United States was longer than 28 miles—a reflection of their huge capital cost and the lack of American engineering expertise. The New York project had three things in its favor: the vigorous support of New York City merchants, who wanted access to western markets; the backing of New York's governor, DeWitt Clinton, who persuaded the legislature to finance the waterway from tax revenues, tolls, and bond sales to foreign investors; and the relative gentleness of the terrain west of Albany. Even so, the task was enormous. Workers—many of them Irish immigrants—had to dig out millions of cubic yards of soil, quarry thousands of tons of rock to build huge locks to raise and lower boats, and construct vast reservoirs to ensure a steady supply of water.

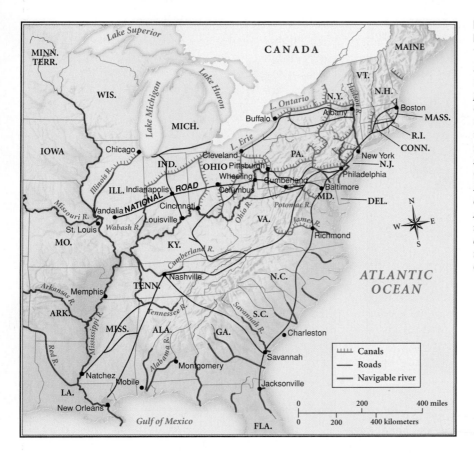

MAP 10.3 The Transportation Revolution: Roads and Canals, 1820–1850

By 1850 the United States had an efficient transportation system with three distinct parts. One system, composed of short canals and navigable rivers, carried cotton, tobacco, and other products from the upcountry of the southern seaboard states into the Atlantic commercial system. A second system, centered on the Erie, Chesapeake and Ohio, and Pennsylvania Mainline Canals, linked the major seaport cities of the Northeast to the vast trans-Appalachian region. Finally, a set of regional canals in the Old Northwest connected most of the Great Lakes region to the Ohio and Mississippi Rivers and New Orleans.

The first great engineering project in American history, the Erie Canal altered the ecology and the economy of an entire region. Hundreds of streams and rivers soon flowed into the canal, depriving some areas of the water needed to sustain wildlife and settlers. As towns and farming communities sprang up along the waterway, millions of trees were cut down to provide wood for building and land for growing wheat and corn. Cows and pigs now foraged in forests where deer and bears had once held sway.

Building the Erie Canal

The success of the Erie Canal prompted the construction by 1860 of a vast canal system, a precursor of the national railroad network of the late nineteenth century and the interstate highway system of the mid- to late twentieth century. Tens of thousands of workers—many of them Irish immigrants and free blacks—dug out thousands of miles of canals by hand and, with the aid of the simple hoists shown here, built hundreds of stone locks. The unknown artist who sketched this scene was more interested in the scale of the project than in the personalities of the faceless laborers who undertook this dangerous work. In the marshes near Syracuse, New York, a thousand workers fell ill with fever and many died.

Miriam and Ira D. Wallach Division of Art, Prints and Photographs. The New York Public Library. Astor, Lenox and Tilden Foundations.

The Erie Canal was an instant success. The first section, a stretch of 75 miles, opened in 1819, and immediately generated enough revenue to repay its cost. When the canal was completed in 1825, a 40-foot-wide ribbon of water stretched 364 miles from the Lake Erie port of Buffalo to Albany, where it joined the Hudson River for a 150-mile trip to New York City. One-hundred-ton freight barges pulled by two horses moved along the canal at a steady 30 miles a day, greatly accelerating the flow of goods and cutting transportation costs. On New York's roads it took four horses to pull a one-ton wagon 12 miles in a day.

The Erie Canal brought prosperity to central and western New York, carrying wheat and meat from farming communities in the interior to eastern cities and foreign markets. In 1818 the mills in Rochester had processed 26,000 barrels of flour from the wheat grown by nearby farmers; ten years later their output soared to 200,000 barrels, and in 1840 to 500,000 barrels. After a trip on the canal the novelist Nathaniel Hawthorne suggested that its water "must be the most fertilizing of all fluids, for it causes towns with their masses of brick and stone, their churches and theaters, their business and hubbub, their luxury and refinement, their gay dames and polished citizens, to spring up." The canal also linked the economies of the Northeast and the Midwest. Northeastern manufacturers provided clothing, boots, and agricultural equipment to farm families throughout the Great Lakes Basin and the Ohio Valley. In payment the farmers sent grain, cattle, and hogs as well as raw materials (such as leather, wool, and hemp) to the East (Table 10.2).

The spectacular benefits of the Erie Canal prompted a national canal boom (see Map 10.3). Civic and business leaders in Philadelphia and Baltimore proposed their own waterways to compete for the trade of the West. Copying New York's fiscal innovations, they persuaded their state governments to invest directly in canal companies or force state-chartered banks to do so. They also won state guarantees for their bonds, thereby encouraging British and Dutch investors to buy them. Indeed, foreign investors provided almost three-quarters of the $400 million invested in canals by 1840. Soon these waterways connected the Midwest with the

TABLE 10.2 Government Investment in Canals in Three States		
State	Canal	Cost
1. Successful: *Income Pays Capital Cost = Great Economic Benefit*		
New York	Erie Canal	$7.1 million
New York	Champlain Canal	.9 million
New York	Oswego Canal	2.5 million
Ohio	Ohio Canal	4.2 million
Pennsylvania	Delaware Division Canal	1.5 million
	TOTAL: Successful Canals	**$16.2 million**
2. Unsuccessful: *Cost Exceeds Income = Marginal Economic Benefit*		
New York	Black River Canal	$3.2 million
New York	Genesee Valley Canal	5.7 million
New York	Chenango Canal	3.1 million
Ohio	Miami and Erie Canal	5.9 million
Ohio	Hocking Canal	.9 million
Ohio	Two short canals	1.1 million
Pennsylvania	Mainland Canal	16.5 million
Pennsylvania	Five Lateral Canals	15.0 million
	TOTAL: Unsuccessful Canals	**$51.4 million**

Source: Adapted from Roger Ransom, "Canals and Development," *American Economic Review* 54 (1964): 365–76, table 1.

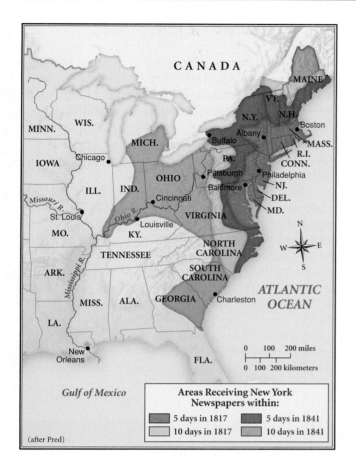

MAP 10.4 The Speed of News in 1817 and 1841

The transportation revolution increased the speed of trade and communication between the Atlantic seaports and the towns of the interior. Aggressive entrepreneurs provided for the national circulation of daily New York City newspapers, and by 1841 many parts of the country received economic and other news from New York in less than ten days. By 1860 telegraph lines ran between major cities in the Northeast, allowing for instantaneous communication.

For more help analyzing this map, see the ONLINE STUDY GUIDE at bedfordstmartins.com/henretta.

great port cities of New York and Philadelphia (via the Erie and Pennsylvania Canals) and New Orleans (via the Ohio and Mississippi Rivers).

The steamboat, another product of the industrial age, ensured the success of this vast transportation system. The engineer-inventor Robert Fulton had built the first American steamboat, the *Clermont*, which he navigated up the Hudson River in 1807. However, the first steamboats consumed huge amounts of wood or coal and could not navigate shallow western rivers. During the 1820s engineers broadened the hulls of these boats, thereby enlarging their cargo capacity and giving them a shallower draft. The improved design cut the cost of upstream river transport in half and dramatically increased the flow of goods, people, and news into the

interior. In 1830 a traveler or a letter from New York could go by water to Buffalo or Pittsburgh in less than a week and to Detroit or St. Louis in two weeks. Thirty years earlier the same journeys, by road or sail, had taken twice as long (Map 10.4).

Various agencies of the national government played key roles in the creation of this interregional system of transportation. Following the passage of the Post Office Act of 1792, the mail network grew rapidly—to eight hundred post offices by 1800 and more than eight thousand by 1830—and safely carried thousands of letters and millions of dollars of banknotes from one end of the country to the other. The Supreme Court, headed by John Marshall, likewise encouraged interstate communication and trade by striking down state restrictions on commerce. In the crucial case of *Gibbons v. Ogden* (1824) the Court voided a New York law that created a monopoly on steamboat travel into New York City, ruling that the federal government had paramount authority over interstate commerce (see Chapter 8). This decision meant that no local or state monopolies—or tariffs—would impede the flow of goods and services across the nation.

Railroads and Regional Ties. Another product of industrial technology—the railroad—created close ties between the Northeast and the Midwest (Map 10.5). As late as 1852 canals were carrying twice the tonnage of railroads, but over the next six years track mileage increased dramatically and railroads became the nation's main carriers of freight. Serviced by a vast network of locomotive and freight-car repair shops, the Erie Railroad, the Pennsylvania Railroad, and other major long-distance railroad lines connected the Atlantic ports—New York, Philadelphia, and Boston—with the Great Lakes cities of Cleveland and Chicago. Each year more and more midwestern grain moved east by rail rather than south by barge down the Ohio and Mississippi Rivers.

Tied together by the steel rails that ran along the route of New England migration, the Midwest and the Northeast increasingly resembled each other in ethnic composition, cultural values, and technical skills. The first migrants to the Midwest had relied on manufactured goods made in Britain or in the Northeast. They bought high-quality shovels and spades fabricated at the Delaware Iron Works, axes forged in Connecticut factories, and steel horseshoes manufactured in Troy, New York. By the 1830s midwestern entrepreneurs were producing many of these goods. As a blacksmith in Grand Detour, Illinois, John Deere made his first steel plow out of old saws in 1837; ten years later he opened a factory in Moline, Illinois, that used mass-production techniques. His steel plows, superior in strength to the cast-iron model developed earlier in New York by Jethro Wood, soon dominated the midwestern market. Other midwestern companies—McCormick and Hussey—mass-produced self-raking reapers that allowed a farmer

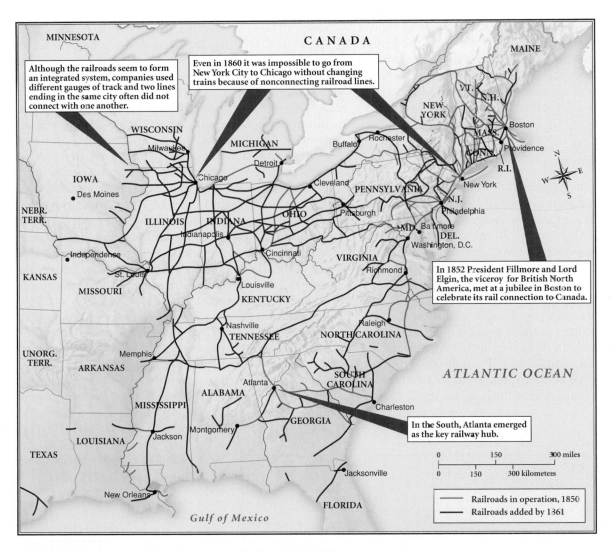

MAP 10.5 Railroads of the North and South, 1850–1860

In the decade before the Civil War, entrepreneurs in the Northeast and the Midwest laid thousands of miles of new railroad lines, providing those regions with extensive and dense transportation systems that stimulated economic development. The South built a much simpler system. In all regions, railroad companies used different track gauges, which hindered the efficient flow of traffic.

to harvest twelve acres of grain a day (rather than the two or three acres he could cut by hand).

The maritime trade that linked northeastern cotton brokers and textile plants with southern planters increased the wealth of these two regions as well but did not produce a similar social and economic order. Southern investors continued to concentrate their capital in the plantation economy, investing in land and slaves, with impressive economic results. By the 1840s the South was producing more than two-thirds of the world's cotton and accounted for almost two-thirds of the total value of American exports. Except in Richmond, Virginia, planters did not invest the profits from the cotton trade in local industries but continued to buy manufactures from the Northeast and Britain. Moreover, the

South did not develop a well-educated workforce. Planters wanted compliant workers who would be content with the drudgery of agricultural work, so they trained most of their slaves as field hands (allowing only a few to learn the arts of the blacksmith, carpenter, or bricklayer). Likewise, they made few efforts to provide blacks or ordinary whites with elementary instruction in reading or arithmetic. At the height of the prosperity of the slave regime, most African Americans and about 20 percent of white southerners could not read or write (as compared with less than 1 percent in New England). Lacking cities, factories, and highly trained workers, the South remained an agricultural economy that brought higher living standards only to the 25 percent of the white population who owned plantations and slaves. By

1860 the southern economy generated an average annual per capita income of $103, while the more productive economic system of the North created an average income of $141. The national system of commerce had accentuated the agricultural character of the South even as it helped to create a diversified economy in the Midwest.

The Growth of Cities and Towns

The expansion of industry and trade led to a dramatic increase in the urban population. In 1820 there were only 58 towns in the nation with more than 2,500 inhabitants; by 1840 there were 126 urban centers, located mostly in the Northeast and Midwest. During those two decades the total number of city dwellers grew fourfold, from 443,000 to 1,844,000.

The most rapid growth occurred in the new industrial towns that sprang up along rivers at the fall line (the point at which the rivers began a rapid descent to the coastal plain). In 1822 the Boston Manufacturing Company built a complex of mills in the sleepy Merrimack River village of East Chelmsford, Massachusetts, quickly transforming it into the bustling textile factory town of Lowell. Hartford, Connecticut; Trenton, New Jersey; and Wilmington, Delaware, also became urban centers as mill owners exploited the waterpower of the nearby rivers and recruited workers from the surrounding countryside.

Western commercial cities such as New Orleans, Pittsburgh, Cincinnati, and Louisville grew almost as rapidly. The initial expansion of these cities resulted from their location at points where goods were transferred from one mode of transport, such as canal boats or farmers' wagons, to another, such as steamboats or sailing vessels. As the midwestern population grew during the 1830s and 1840s, St. Louis, Rochester, Buffalo, and Detroit emerged as dynamic centers of commerce. Merchants and bankers settled in those cities, developing the marketing, provisioning, and financial services that were essential to farmers and small-town merchants in the hinterland (Map 10.6).

Within a few decades these midwestern commercial hubs—joined by Cleveland and Chicago—became manufacturing centers as well. Exploiting these cities' locations as key junctions for railroad lines and steamboats, entrepreneurs established flour mills, packing plants, and docks and provided work for hundreds of

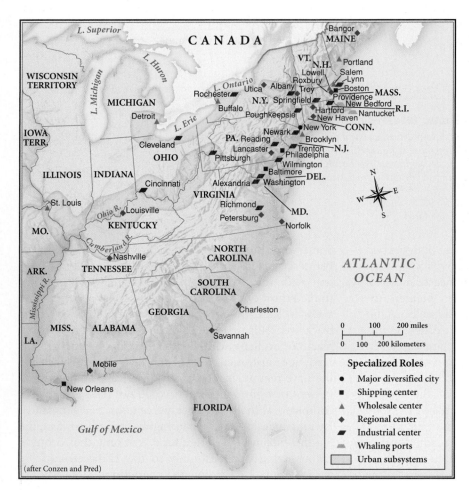

MAP 10.6 The Nation's Major Cities in 1840

By 1840 the United States boasted three major networks of cities. The string of port cities on the Atlantic—from Boston to Baltimore—served as centers for import merchants, banks, insurance companies, ready-made clothing manufacturers, and many other businesses, and their reach extended far into the interior—nationwide in the case of New York City. A second group of cities stretched along Lake Erie and included the wholesale distribution hubs of Buffalo and Detroit and the manufacturing center of Cleveland. A third urban system extended along the Ohio River, comprising the industrial cities of Cincinnati and Pittsburgh and the wholesale hubs of Louisville and St. Louis.

artisans and laborers. In 1846 Cyrus McCormick moved his reaper factory from western Virginia to Chicago to be closer to his midwestern customers. St. Louis and Chicago were the fastest-growing boom towns and by 1860 had become the nation's third and fourth largest cities, respectively, after New York and Philadelphia.

Yet the old Atlantic seaports—Boston, Philadelphia, Baltimore, Charleston, and especially New York—remained important for their foreign commerce and increasingly as centers of finance and manufacturing. In 1817 New York merchants founded the New York Stock Exchange, which soon became the nation's chief market for securities. The New York metropolis grew at a phenomenal rate; between 1820 and 1860 the population quadrupled to more than 800,000 as tens of thousands of German and Irish immigrants poured into the city. Drawing on the abundant supply of labor, New York became a center of small-scale manufacturing. Entrepreneurs also developed the ready-made clothing industry, which relied on the labor of thousands of low-paid seamstresses, both native- and foreign-born. "The wholesale clothing establishments are . . . absorbing the business of the country," a "Country Tailor" complained to the New York *Tribune*, "casting many an honest and hardworking man out of employment [and allowing] . . . the large cities to swallow up the small towns."

New York's growth stemmed primarily from its dominant position in foreign trade. It had the best harbor in the United States, and oceangoing vessels could sail or steam up the Hudson River to Albany and the Erie Canal. The city's merchants exploited these natural advantages. In 1818 four Quaker merchants founded the Black Ball Line, a service that operated on a regular schedule and carried cargo, people, and mail between New York and the European ports of Liverpool, London, and Le Havre. New York merchants likewise gained an unassailable lead in commerce with the newly independent Latin American nations of Brazil, Peru, and Venezuela. New York–based traders also took over the cotton trade by offering finance, insurance, and shipping to cotton exporters in southern ports. And by persuading the state government to build the Erie Canal, the city's merchants acquired a dominant position in the export of western grain to European markets. By 1840 the port of New York handled almost two-thirds of foreign imports into the United States, almost half of all foreign trade, and much of the immigrant traffic.

Changes in the Social Structure

The Industrial and Market Revolutions transformed the material lives of many Americans, allowing them to live in larger houses, cook on iron stoves, and wear better-made clothes. But the new economic order created distinct social classes: a wealthy industrial and commercial elite, a substantial urban middle class, and a mass of propertyless wage earners. By creating a class-divided society, industrialization posed a momentous challenge to American republican ideals.

The Business Elite

Before industrialization white American society had been divided into various ranks, with "notables" ruling over the "lower orders." But in rural society the different ranks shared a common culture: gentlemen farmers talked easily with yeomen about crop yields, while their wives conversed about the art of quilting. In the South humble tenants and aristocratic slave owners shared the same amusements: gambling, cockfighting, and horse racing. Rich and poor attended the same Quaker meetinghouse or Presbyterian church. "Almost everyone eats, drinks, and dresses in the same way," a European visitor to Hartford, Connecticut, reported in 1798, "and one can see the most obvious inequality only in the dwellings."

The Industrial Revolution shattered this traditional order and created a society of classes, each with its own culture. The new economic system pulled many Americans into cities and made a few of them—the business elite of merchants, manufacturers, bankers, and landlords—very rich. In 1800 the top 10 percent of the nation's families owned about 40 percent of the wealth; by 1860 the wealthiest 10 percent owned nearly 70 percent. In large cities—New York, Chicago, Baltimore, New Orleans—the richest 1 percent of the population held more than 40 percent of all tangible property—such as land and buildings—and an even higher share of intangible property—such as stocks and bonds.

Government tax policies allowed this accumulation of wealth. The U.S. Treasury raised most of its revenue from tariffs—taxes on imported goods such as textiles that were purchased mostly by ordinary citizens. State and local governments also favored the wealthier classes. They usually taxed real estate (farms, city lots, and buildings) and tangible personal property (such as furniture, tools, and machinery) but almost never taxed the stocks and bonds owned by the rich or the inheritances they passed on to their children.

Over time the wealthiest families consciously set themselves apart from the rest of the population. They dressed in well-tailored clothes, rode around town in fancy carriages pulled by fine horses, and lived in expensively furnished houses tended by butlers, cooks, coachmen, and other servants. The women of the family no longer socialized with those of lesser wealth, and the men no longer labored side by side with their journeymen. Instead, they became managers and directors, issuing orders through trusted subordinates to hundreds of factory operatives. Increasingly merchants, manufacturers, and bankers chose to live in separate residential areas, turning away from traditional practices such as boarding unmarried workers in their own homes. By the 1830s most employers had moved their families to distinct upper-class enclaves, often at the edge of the city. The desire for greater privacy by privileged families and the massive flow of immigrants into many cities created fragmented communities, divided geographically along the lines of class, race, and ethnicity.

The Middle Class

Standing between wealthy owners and entrepreneurs at one end of the social spectrum and nonpropertied wage earners at the other was a growing middle class—the product of the Market Revolution. As a Boston printer and publisher explained, the "middling class" was made up of "the farmers, the mechanics, the manufacturers, the traders, who carry on professionally the ordinary operations of buying, selling, and exchanging merchandize." The growth of cities likewise fostered the rise of various professional groups—building contractors, lawyers, and surveyors—who suddenly found their services in great demand and financially profitable. Middle-class business owners, employees, and professionals were most numerous in the Northeast, where they numbered about 30 percent of the population in 1840, but they could be found in every American town and village, even in the agrarian South. In the boom town of Oglethorpe, Georgia (population 2,500), in 1854, there were no fewer than eighty "business houses" and eight hotels.

The size, wealth, and cultural influence of the middle class continued to grow, fueled by a dramatic rise in prosperity. Between 1830 and the Panic of 1857, the per capita income of Americans increased by about 2.5 percent a year, a remarkable rate that the United States has never since matched. This surge in income, along with the availability of inexpensive mass-produced goods, facilitated the creation of a distinct middle-class culture, especially in urban areas of the Northeast. Middle-class husbands had sufficient earnings so that their wives did not have to seek paid work. Typically these men saved about 15 percent of their income, depositing it in banks and then using it to buy a well-built house in a "respectable part of town." They purchased handsome clothes for themselves and their families and drove about town in smart carriages. Their wives and daughters were literate and accomplished, buying books and pianos as well as commodious furniture for their front parlors. Rather than hiring servants to perform menial tasks, they turned to the new industrial technology, outfitting their residences with furnaces that heated water for bathing and radiators that warmed entire rooms; stoves with ovens, including broilers and movable grates; treadle-operated sewing machines; and iceboxes, which ice company wagons filled periodically, to preserve perishable food. They also bought packaged goods: as early as 1825 the Underwood Company of Boston was marketing well-preserved Atlantic salmon in jars. Following the introduction of the airtight Mason jar in 1858, housewives bought perishable farm produce when it was cheap and preserved it, thereby providing their families with a varied diet even in winter.

If material comfort was one distinguishing mark of the middle class, moral and mental discipline was another. Seeking to pass on their status to their children, successful parents usually provided them with a high school education (in an era when most white children

Middle-Class Family Life, 1836
The family of Azariah Caverly boasted many of the amenities of middle-class life—handsome clothes, finely decorated furniture, and a striking floor covering. Underlining the social conventions of the time, the husband and his son hold a newspaper and a square, symbolizing the worlds of commerce and industry, while the wife and her daughter are pictured next to a Bible, indicating their domestic and moral vocations.
New York State Historical Association, Cooperstown, NY.

received only five years of schooling). Ambitious parents were equally concerned with their children's character and stressed discipline, morality, and hard work. Puritans and other American Protestants had long believed that work in an earthly "calling" was a duty people owed to God. Now the business elite and the middle class gave this idea a secular twist: they celebrated work as socially beneficial, the key to a higher standard of living for the nation and social mobility for the individual.

Benjamin Franklin gave classical expression to the secular work ethic in his *Autobiography*, which was published in full in 1818 and immediately found a huge audience. Heeding Franklin's suggestion that an industrious man would become a rich one, tens of thousands of young American men worked hard, saved their money, adopted temperate habits, and practiced honesty in their business dealings. Countless magazines, children's books, self-help manuals, and novels taught the same lessons. The ideal of the "**self-made man**" became a central theme of American popular culture. Just as a rural-producer ethic had united the social ranks in pre-1800 America, this new goal of personal achievement and social mobility tied together the upper and middle classes of the new industrializing society. Knowing that many affluent families had risen from modest beginnings, middle-class men and women took them as models and shunned the rapidly increasing numbers of working families who owned nothing and had to struggle just to survive.

The New Urban Poor

As thoughtful business leaders surveyed the emerging social landscape, they concluded that the old yeoman society of independent families no longer seemed possible or even advisable. "Entire independence ought not to be wished for," Ithamar A. Beard, the paymaster of the Hamilton Manufacturing Company, told a mechanics' association in 1827. "In large manufacturing towns, many more must fill subordinate stations and must be under the immediate direction and control of a master or superintendent, than in the farming towns."

Beard had a point. In 1840 all of the nation's slaves and about half of its native-born free workers were laboring for others rather than for themselves. The bottom 10 percent of this wage-earning labor force consisted of casual workers—those hired on a short-term basis for the most arduous jobs. Poor women washed clothes, while their husbands and sons carried lumber and bricks for construction projects, loaded ships and wagons, and dug out dirt and stones to build canals. When they could find work, these men earned "their dollar *per diem*," an "Old Inhabitant" wrote to the *Baltimore American,* but he reminded readers that most workers could never save enough "to pay rent, buy fire wood and eatables" for their families when the harbor froze up. During business depressions they bore the brunt of unemployment, and even in the best of times their jobs were unpredictable, seasonal, and dangerous.

Other laborers had greater security of employment, but few were prospering. In Massachusetts in 1825 the daily wage of an unskilled worker was about two-thirds that of a mechanic; two decades later it was less than half as much. The 18,000 native-born and immigrant women who made men's clothing in New York City in the 1850s were even worse off, averaging less than $80 a year. These meager wages paid for food and rent and not much more, so many wage earners were unable to take advantage of the rapidly falling prices of manufactured goods. Only the most fortunate working families could afford to educate their children, pay the fees required for an apprenticeship, or accumulate small dowries so that their daughters could marry men with better prospects. Most families sent their children out to work, and the death of one of the parents often threw the survivors into dire poverty. As a charity worker noted, "What can a bereaved widow do, with 5 or 6 little children, destitute of every means of support but what her own hands can furnish (which in a general way does not amount to more than 25 cents a day)."

By the 1830s most urban factory workers and unskilled laborers resided in well-defined neighborhoods. Single men and women lived in large, crowded boardinghouses, while families inhabited tiny apartments carved out of the living quarters, basements, and attics of small houses. As immigrants poured into the nation after 1840, urban populations soared and developers squeezed more and more buildings onto a single lot, interspersed with outhouses and connected by foul-smelling courtyards. Venturing into the slums of New York City in the 1850s, state legislators were shocked to find gaunt, shivering people with "wild ghastly faces" living amid "hideous squalour and deadly effluvia, the dim, undrained courts oozing with pollution, the dark, narrow stairways, decayed with age, reeking with filth, overrun with vermin."

Living in such distressing conditions, many wage earners turned to the dubious solace of alcohol. Alcohol had long been an integral part of American life; beer and rum had lubricated ceremonies, work breaks, barn raisings, and games. But during the 1820s native-born urban wage earners led Americans to new heights of alcohol consumption. Aiding them were western farmers, who distilled corn and rye into gin and whiskey as a low-cost way to get their grain to market. By 1830 drinkers consumed enormous amounts of liquor every year—enough to provide every man, woman, and child in the United States with five gallons, more than three times present-day levels (see Voices from Abroad, "Frances Trollope: American Workers and Their Wives," p. 307).

Drinking patterns changed as well. Workers in many craft unions "swore off" liquor, convinced that it would undermine their skilled work as well as their health and finances. But other workers began to drink on the job—

The Eastern State Penitentiary, Philadelphia, 1836

Today it is unusual to see prisons celebrated on postcards or, as here, in a color lithograph meant to be hung on a living room wall. However, in the 1820s and 1830s, American penitentiaries were world famous, their physical layout and methods of discipline studied by Alexis de Tocqueville and hundreds of other foreign observers and penal experts. Benevolent reformers pledged that the new institutions would turn criminals into model citizens by using methods of mental conditioning rather than physical punishment. In fact, most prisons quickly became places of incarceration rather than reform.
Paul Eisenhauer.

and not just during the traditional 11 A.M. and 4 P.M. "refreshers." Journeymen used apprentices to smuggle whiskey into shops, and then, as one baker recalled, "One man was stationed at the window to watch, while the rest drank." Even before the appearance of spirit-drinking Irish and beer-drinking German immigrants, grogshops and tippling houses had appeared on almost every block in working-class districts. The saloons became focal points for crimes and urban disorder. Fueled by unrestrained drinking, a fistfight among young men one night could turn into a brawl the second night and a full-scale riot the third. The urban police forces, consisting of low-paid watchmen and untrained constables, were unable to contain the lawlessness.

The Benevolent Empire

The disorder among native-born urban wage earners sparked concern among well-to-do Americans. Inspired by the religious ideal of benevolence—doing good for the less fortunate—they created a number of organizations that historians refer to collectively as the "**Benevolent Empire.**" During the 1820s Congregational and Presbyterian ministers united with like-minded merchants and their wives to launch a program of social reform and regulation. Their purpose, announced leading Presbyterian minister Lyman Beecher, was to restore "the moral government of God." The reformers introduced new forms of moral discipline into their own lives and tried to infuse them into the lives of working people as well. They would regulate popular behavior—by persuasion if possible, by law if necessary.

Although the Benevolent Empire targeted age-old evils such as drunkenness, prostitution, and crime, its methods were new. Instead of relying on church sermons and moral suasion by community leaders, the reformers set out in a systematic fashion to institutionalize charity and combat evil. They established large-scale organizations, such as the Prison Discipline Society and the American Society for the Promotion of Temperance, among

Frances Trollope

American Workers and Their Wives

During her four-year stay in the United States, British businesswoman Frances Trollope traveled widely and proved to be an acute social commentator. Her book Domestic Manners of the Americans *(1832)* was a best-seller on both sides of the Atlantic. She frequently compared life in America with that in Britain, as in this discussion of the living conditions and habits of working people.

Mohawk [in southern Ohio], as our little village was called, gave us an excellent opportunity of comparing the peasants of the United States with those of England, and of judging the average degree of comfort enjoyed by each. . . .

Mechanics, if good workmen, are certain of employment, and good wages, rather higher than with us; the average wages of a labourer throughout the Union is ten dollars a month, with lodging, boarding, washing, and mending; if he lives at his own expense he has a dollar a day. It appears to me that the necessaries of life, that is to say, meat, bread, butter, tea, and coffee (not to mention whiskey), are within the reach of every sober, industrious, and healthy man who chooses to have them; and yet I think that an English peasant, with the same qualifications, would, in coming to the United States, change for the worse [because American men indulge in various vices that consume their money and their health]. . . .

Tobacco grows at their doors, and is not taxed: yet this too costs something, and the air of heaven is not in more general use among the men of America than chewing tobacco. . . . Ardent spirits, though lamentably cheap, still cost something, and the use of them among the men . . . is universal. . . . I am not now pointing out the evils of dram-drinking, but it is evident, that where this practice prevails universally, and often to the most frightful excess, the consequence must be, that the money spent to obtain the dram [a small glass of whiskey] is less than the money lost by the time consumed in drinking it.

Long, disabling, and expensive fits of sickness are incontestably more frequent in every part of America than in England, and the sufferers have no aid to look to, but what they have saved, or what they may be enabled to sell. I have never seen misery exceeded what I have witnessed in an American cottage where disease has entered.

But if the condition of the labourer be not superior to that of the English peasant, that of his wife and daughters is incomparably worse. It is they who are indeed the slaves of the soil. One has but to look at the wife of an American cottager, and ask her age, to be convinced that the life she leads is one of hardship, privation, and labour. It is rare to see a woman in this station who has reached the age of thirty, without losing every trace of youth and beauty.

Even the young girls, though often with lovely features, look pale, thin, and haggard. . . . The horror of domestic service, which the reality of slavery, and the fable of equality, have generated, excludes the young women from that sure and most comfortable resource of decent English girls; and the consequence is . . . the daughters are, to the full extent of the word, domestic slaves.

Source: Frances Trollope, *Domestic Manners of the Americans* (New York: Whittaker, Treacher & Co., 1832), n.p.

---

many others. Each organization had a managing staff, a network of volunteers and chapters, and a newspaper.

Often working in concert, these benevolent groups set out to improve society. First they encouraged people to lead well-disciplined lives, campaigning for temperance in drinking habits and an end to prostitution. To encourage orderly behavior, they persuaded local governments to ban carnivals of drink and dancing, such as Negro Election Day (mock festivities in which African Americans symbolically took over the government), which had been enjoyed by whites as well as blacks. Second, they devised new institutions to control people who were threats to society and to assist those who were unable to handle their own affairs. Reformers provided homes of refuge for the abandoned children of the poor and removed the insane from isolation in attics and cellars and placed them in newly built asylums. They also campaigned to end corporal punishment for criminals, advocating instead their confinement and moral rehabilitation in penitentiaries—a largely unsuccessful experiment in social engineering.

Women played an increasingly active role in the Benevolent Empire. Since the 1790s upper-class women had sponsored a number of charitable organizations, such as the Society for the Relief of Poor Widows with Small Children, founded in New York by Isabella Graham, a devout Presbyterian widow. By the 1820s Graham's society was assisting hundreds of widows and their children in New York City. Her daughter Joanna Bethune set up other charitable institutions, including the Orphan Asylum Society and the Society for the Promotion of Industry, which found hundreds of poor women jobs as spinners and seamstresses.

Some reformers came to believe that one of the greatest threats to the "moral government of God" was the decline of the traditional Sabbath. As the pace of commercial activity accelerated, merchants and shippers began to conduct business on Sunday, since they did not want their goods and equipment to lie idle one day in every seven. To restore traditional values, in 1828 Lyman Beecher and other ministers formed the General Union for Promoting the Observance of the Christian Sabbath. General Union chapters—usually with women's auxiliaries—sprang up from Maine to the Ohio Valley. Seeking a symbolic issue to rally Christians to their cause, the General Union focused on a law Congress had enacted in 1810 allowing mail to be transported—though not delivered—on Sunday. To secure its repeal the Union adopted the tactics of a political party, organizing rallies and circulating petitions. Its members also boycotted shipping companies that did business on the Sabbath and campaigned for municipal laws forbidding games and festivals on the Lord's day.

Not everyone agreed with the program of the Benevolent Empire. Men who labored twelve or fourteen hours a day for six days a week refused to spend their one day of leisure in meditation and prayer. Shipping company managers demanded that the Erie Canal provide lockkeepers on Sundays and joined those Americans who argued that using boycotts and laws to enforce morality was "contrary to the free spirit of our institutions." And when the evangelical reformers proposed to teach Christianity to slaves, many white southerners were outraged. Such popular resistance or indifference limited the success of the Benevolent Empire. A different kind of message was required if religious reformers were to do more than preach to the already converted and discipline the already disciplined.

Revivalism and Reform

The Presbyterian minister Charles Grandison Finney brought just such a message to Americans. Finney was not part of the traditional religious elite. Born into a poor farming family in Connecticut, he hoped to join the new middle class as a lawyer. But in 1823 Finney underwent an intense conversion experience and decided

Charles Finney, Evangelist (1792–1875)
When this portrait was painted in 1834, Finney was forty-two years old and at the height of his career as an evangelist. Handsome and charismatic, Finney had just led a series of enormously successful revivals in Rochester, New York, and other cities along the Erie Canal. In 1835 he established a theology department at the newly founded Oberlin College in Ohio, where he helped train a generation of ministers and served as its president from 1851 to 1866. Oberlin College Archives.

to become a minister. Beginning in towns along the Erie Canal, the young minister conducted emotional revival meetings that stressed conversion rather than instruction; what counted for Finney was the will to be saved. Repudiating traditional Calvinist beliefs, he maintained that God would welcome any sinner who submitted to the Holy Spirit. Finney's ministry drew on—and greatly accelerated—the Second Great Awakening, the wave of Protestant revivalism that had begun after the Revolution (see Chapter 9).

Evangelical Ideology. Finney's message that "God has made man a moral free agent" who could choose salvation was particularly attractive to members of the new middle class, who had already chosen to improve their material lives. But he became famous for converting those at the ends of the social spectrum: the haughty rich, who had placed themselves above God, and the abject poor, who seemed lost to drink, sloth, and misbehavior. To humble the pride of the rich and relieve the shame of the poor, Finney celebrated their common fellowship in Christ and identified them spiritually with earnest, pious middle-class respectability.

Finney's most spectacular triumph came in 1830, when he moved his revivals from small towns to Rochester, New York, now a major milling and commercial city on the Erie Canal. Preaching every day for six months he won over the influential merchants and manufacturers of Rochester, who pledged to reform their lives and those of their workers. They promised to attend church, join the Cold Water movement by giving up intoxicating beverages, and work steady hours. To encourage their employees to follow suit, wealthy businessmen founded a new Free Presbyterian Church— "free" because members did not have to pay for pew space. Other evangelical Protestants founded two similar churches to serve canal laborers, transients, and the settled poor. To reinforce the work of the churches, Rochester's business elite established a savings bank to encourage thrift, Sunday schools to instruct poor children, and the Female Charitable Society to provide relief for the families of the unemployed.

However, these initiatives to create a harmonious community of morally disciplined Christians were not altogether effective. To reach as many nonbelievers as possible, Finney added a new tactic—group prayer meetings in family homes—in which women played an active role. Finney's wife, Lydia, and other pious middle-class women carried the Christian message to the wives of the unconverted, often while their husbands were at work. But skilled workers who belonged to strong crafts organizations—bootmakers, carpenters, stonemasons, and boat builders—resisted the message, arguing that workers needed higher wages and schools more urgently than sermons and prayers. And Finney's revival seldom moved poor people, especially the Irish Catholic immigrants who had recently begun arriving in American cities, including Rochester, and who thought of Protestants as religious heretics and as their political oppressors in Ireland.

Ignoring these setbacks, revivalists in cities and towns from New England to the Midwest duplicated Finney's evangelical message and techniques. In New York City, the wealthy silk merchants Arthur and Lewis Tappan founded a magazine, *The Christian Evangelist*,

"The Drunkard's Progress: From the First Glass to the Grave"

This lithograph of 1846, published by the firm of N. Currier, depicts the inevitable fate of those who partake of alcoholic beverages. The drunkard's descent into "Poverty and Disease" ends with "Death by Suicide," leaving a grieving and destitute wife and child. Temperance reformers urged Americans to take the "Cold Water Cure," drinking water instead of liquor. To promote abstinence among the young, the Reverend Thomas Hunt founded the Cold Water Army, an organization that grew to embrace several hundred thousand children, all of whom pledged "perpetual hate to all that can Intoxicate."

Library of Congress.

John Gough

The Vice of Intemperance

John Gough (1817–1886) was twelve years old when his impoverished English parents shipped him to New York City, where he found work as a bookbinder—and eventually turned to drink. In 1842, at age twenty-five, Gough converted to temperance. For the next four decades he used his eloquence as a lecturer—and his considerable talents as an actor—to command high fees and persuade thousands to join the temperance movement. The following selection is taken from his Autobiography *(1869).*

Will it be believed that I again sought refuge in rum? Yet so it was. Scarcely had I recovered from the fright, than I sent out, procured a pint of rum, and drank it all in less than an hour. And now came upon me many terrible sensations. Cramps attacked me in my limbs, which racked me with agony; and my temples throbbed as if they would burst. . . . Then came on the drunkard's remorseless torturer—delirium tremens, in all its terrors, attacked me. For three days I endured more agony than pen could describe, even were it guided by the mind of Dante. . . . I was at one time surrounded by millions of monstrous spiders, that crawled slowly over every limb, whilst the beaded drops of perspiration would start to my brow, and my limbs would shiver until the bed rattled. . . . All at once, whilst gazing at a frightful creation of my distempered mind, I seemed struck with sudden blindness. I knew a candle was burning in the room, but I could not see it—all was so pitchy dark. . . . And then the scene would change: I was falling—falling swiftly as an arrow—far down into some terrible abyss. . . .

By the mercy of God, I survived this awful seizure; and when I rose, a weak, broken-down man, and surveyed my ghastly features in the glass, I thought of my mother, and asked myself how I had obeyed the instructions received from her lips, and to what advantage I had turned the lessons she taught me. I remembered her countless prayers and tears. . . . Oh! how keen were my rebukes; and, in the excitement of the moment, I resolved to lead a better life, and abstain from the accursed cup.

For about a month, terrified by what I had suffered, I adhered to my resolution; then my wife came home, and, in my joy at her return, I flung my good resolutions to the wind, and, foolishly fancying that I could now restrain my appetite, which had a whole month remained in subjugation, I took a glass of brandy. That glass aroused the slumbering demon, who would not be satisfied by so tiny a libation. Another and another succeeded, until I was again far advanced in the career of intemperance. The night of my wife's return, I went to bed intoxicated.

Source: David Brion Davis, ed., *Antebellum American Culture: An Interpretive Anthology* (Lexington, MA: Heath, 1979), 402–3.

which promoted Finney's ideas across the country. Soon converts in towns in many states—North Carolina, Tennessee, Indiana, Pennsylvania—reported that "You could not go upon the street and hear any conversation, except upon religion." The success of the revival "has been so general and thorough," concluded a General Assembly of Presbyterians, "that the whole customs of society have changed."

Temperance. The temperance movement proved to be the most effective arena for national evangelical reform. In 1832 evangelicals gained control of the American Temperance Society; within a few years it had grown to two thousand chapters with more than 200,000 members. The society adapted the methods that had worked so well in the revivals—group confession and prayer, a focus on the family and the spiritual role of women, and sudden, emotional conversion—and took them into virtually every town in the North and rural hamlet in the South. On one day in New York City in 1841, more than 4,000 people took the temperance "pledge." The average annual consumption of spirits fell from about five gallons per person in 1830 to about two gallons in 1845 (see American Voices, "John Gough: The Vice of Intemperance," above).

Evangelical reformers used religion to reinforce the traditional moral foundations of the American work ethic. Laziness and drinking could not be cured by following Benjamin Franklin's method of self-discipline, they argued; rather, people had to experience the profound change of heart achieved through religious conversion. As this evangelical message spread, it fostered a commitment to individual enterprise and moral discipline not only among middle-class Americans but also among many wage earners. Religion and the ideology of social mobility served as powerful cement, holding society together in the face of the massive changes brought by the spread of industrial enterprise and the market economy.

Immigration and Cultural Conflict

Between 1840 and 1860 about 2 million Irish immigrants, 1.5 million Germans, and 750,000 Britons poured into the United States, placing new strains on the American social order. Most immigrants avoided the South because they opposed slavery, shunned blacks, or feared competition from enslaved workers. Many German migrants settled on farms or in the growing cities of the midwestern states of Wisconsin, Iowa, and Missouri, often comprising a majority of the local residents. Other Germans and most of the Irish settled in the Northeast, where by 1860 they accounted for nearly one-third of white adults.

Irish Poverty. The most prosperous immigrants were the British, many of whom were professionals, propertied farmers, and skilled workers. The majority of German immigrants also came from farming and artisan families and could afford to buy land in America. The poorest migrants were Irish peasants and laborers, fleeing a widespread famine caused by severe overpopulation and a devastating blight on the potato crop. Arriving in dire poverty the Irish found new homes in the cities of New England and New York and took low-skilled, low-paying jobs as laborers in factories and on construction projects and as servants in private residences. Many Irish immigrants lived in crowded tenements with primitive sanitation systems and were the first to die when epidemics swept through American cities. In the summer of 1849 a cholera epidemic took the lives of thousands of poor immigrants in St. Louis and New York.

In times of hardship and sorrow immigrants turned to their churches. Many Germans and virtually all the Irish were Catholics, and they fueled the growth of the Catholic Church. In the 1840s there were sixteen Catholic dioceses and seven hundred churches in the United States; by 1860 the number had increased to forty-five dioceses and twenty-five hundred churches. Under the guidance of their priests and bishops the Irish built an impressive network of institutions—charitable societies, orphanages, militia companies, parochial schools, and political organizations—that helped them maintain their cultural identity.

Nativism. Owing in part to the religious fervor raised by the Second Great Awakening, the immigrants' Catholic beliefs and institutions stirred up fear and distaste among native-born citizens. A rash of anti-Catholic publications greeted the first Irish immigrants in the 1830s. One of the most militant critics of Catholicism was Samuel F. B. Morse (who would later make the first commercial adaptation of the telegraph). In 1834 Morse published *Foreign Conspiracy against the Liberties of the United States*, which warned of a Catholic threat to American republican institutions. Morse believed that Catholic immigrants would obey the dictates of Pope Pius IX, who had condemned republicanism as a false political ideology based on the sovereignty of the people rather than on the sovereignty of God. Republican-minded Protestants of

An Anti-Catholic Riot

When riots against Irish Catholics broke out in Philadelphia in 1844, the governor of Pennsylvania called out the militia to protect Catholic churches and residential neighborhoods. In the foreground, two Protestant rioters, depicted by the artist as well-dressed gentlemen, attack an Irish family with sticks, while in the background the militia exchanges musket fire with other members of the mob. Library Company of Philadelphia.

many denominations shared Morse's fears, and *Foreign Conspiracy* became their textbook.

The social tensions stemming from industrialization intensified anti-Catholic sentiment. Unemployed Protestant mechanics and factory workers joined mobs that attacked Catholics, accusing them of taking jobs and driving down wages; other Protestants organized Native American Clubs, which called for limits on immigration, the restriction of public office to native-born citizens, and the exclusive use of the Protestant version of the Bible in public schools. Many reformers supported the anti-Catholic movement for reasons of public policy—to prevent the diversion of tax resources to Catholic schools and to oppose alcohol abuse by many Irish men. These cultural conflicts also inhibited the growth of a strong labor movement because Protestant wage earners felt they had more in common with their Protestant employers than with their Catholic co-workers.

In almost every large northeastern city religious and cultural conflicts led to violence. In 1834 in Charlestown, Massachusetts, a quarrel between Catholic laborers repairing a convent owned by the Ursuline order of nuns and Protestant workers in a neighboring brickyard turned into a full-scale riot and the burning of the convent. In Philadelphia the violence peaked in 1844 when the Catholic bishop persuaded public school officials to use the Catholic as well as the Protestant version of the Bible. Anti-Irish rioting incited by the city's Native American Clubs lasted for two months and escalated into open warfare between Protestants and the Pennsylvania militia.

Thus, even as economic revolution brought prosperity to many Americans, it divided the society along the lines of class and, by encouraging the influx of immigrants, created new ethnic and religious tensions. Differences of class and culture now split the North in much the same way that race and class had long divided the South. Yet overall the majority of white Americans shared a common commitment to a dynamic economic system based on private property and a vibrant political culture of democratic republicanism.

FOR FURTHER EXPLORATION

▶ For definitions of key terms boldfaced in this chapter, see the glossary at the end of the book.

▶ To assess your mastery of the material covered in this chapter, see the Online Study Guide at **bedfordstmartins.com/henretta**.

▶ For suggested references, including Web sites, see page SR–11 at the end of the book.

▶ For map resources and primary documents, see **bedfordstmartins.com/henretta**.

Between 1820 and 1860 the United States experienced an "industrial" and a "market" revolution that created a new economic structure. Merchants and manufacturers organized increasingly efficient systems of production and, aided by skilled mechanics, introduced water- and steam-powered machines to turn out huge quantities of goods. Simultaneously merchants, traders, and shopkeepers created a vast market system in which they exchanged these manufactures for grain, meat, cotton, leather, and wool produced by a rapidly growing—and westward-moving—farm population.

Three streams of migrants transplanted the cultures of the plantation South, the Middle Atlantic, and yeoman New England into the Old Southwest, the Ohio River Valley, and the Old Northwest. State governments promoted this westward movement— and the creation of regional and national markets— by subsidizing the building of roads, canals, and railroads and creating a transportation system that was unprecedented in size and complexity. As domestic markets and production grew, urbanization accelerated in the Northeast, where industrial towns dotted the landscape, and New York City became the nation's largest city and leading trading center.

Economic growth fostered the creation of new social classes: a wealthy urban business elite of merchants and manufacturers; a prosperous, educated, and well-housed middle class; and a mass of wage-earning laborers with little or no property. Some artisans and workers formed trade unions in generally unsuccessful efforts to improve their economic welfare; other working people lived in poverty and sought solace in drink.

To improve the living conditions and the morals of the poor, upper-class Americans formed benevolent reform societies that promoted temperance, dispensed charity, and encouraged respect for the Christian Sabbath. Simultaneously, Charles Grandison Finney and other evangelical clergymen gave new life to the Second Great Awakening, enlisting millions of propertied farmers and middle-class Americans in a massive religious revival. Preaching the doctrine of "free moral agency," Finney urged Americans both to assist in their own salvation and to reform the world in which they lived.

Protestant evangelicalism heightened the cultural conflict between native-born Americans and millions of Catholic immigrants from Ireland and Germany. Nativist writers attacked Irish Catholics as antirepublican, and American workers blamed immigrant labor for their economic woes—attitudes that led to ethnic riots in many northern cities. By 1860 the United States was a more prosperous society than ever before, and a more socially divided one.

1782	Oliver Evans develops automated flour mill
1790	Samuel Slater opens spinning mill in Providence, Rhode Island
1793	Eli Whitney manufactures cotton gins
1807	Robert Fulton launches the *Clermont,* the first American steamboat
1810s	Cotton kingdom begins in Old Southwest
1814	Boston Manufacturing Company opens cotton mill in Waltham, Massachusetts
1817	Erie Canal begun; completed in 1825
1820	Minimum federal land price reduced to $1.25 per acre
1820s	New England women become textile operatives
	Building-trade workers seek ten-hour workday
	Rise of Benevolent Empire
1821	End of Panic of 1819; fifteen-year boom begins
1824	Congress raises tariffs; increased again in 1828
	Gibbons v. Ogden promotes interstate trade
1830s	Expansion of western commercial cities
	Labor movement gains strength
	Class-segregated cities
	Growth of temperance movement
	Creation of middle-class culture
1830	Charles Grandison Finney begins Rochester revival
1837	Panic of 1837
	John Deere invents steel plow
1839	European financial crisis begins four-year depression in United States
1840s	Irish and German immigration; ethnic riots
1850s	Expansion of railroads
	Rise of machine-tool industry
1857	Financial panic after fourteen-year boom

CHAPTER 11

A Democratic Revolution

1820–1844

I F AMERICANS BELIEVED their political institutions were ordained by God, visiting Europeans thought them the work of the Devil. "The gentlemen spit, talk of elections and the price of produce, and spit again," Mrs. Frances Trollope reported in *Domestic Manners of the Americans* (1832). In her view American politics was the sport of party hacks who reeked of "whiskey and onions." Other European visitors used more refined language but likewise found little to celebrate. Harriet Martineau was "deeply disgusted" by the "clap-trap of praise and pathos" uttered by a leading Massachusetts politician, while Basil Hall could only shake his head in astonishment at the shallow arguments, the "conclusions in which nothing was concluded," that were advanced by the inept "farmers, shopkeepers, and country lawyers" who sat in the New York assembly.

◀ **The Inauguration of President William Henry Harrison, March 4, 1841 (detail)**

After being sworn into office, President Harrison stands on the steps of the U.S. Capitol reviewing a parade of military units. Despite the fact that they could not vote, many women attended the ceremony not only to enjoy the festivities but also because the Whig Party actively solicited their support for its policies of moral reform.

Anne S. K. Brown Military Collection, Brown University.

The verdict was unanimous and negative. As the French aristocrat Alexis de Tocqueville put it in *Democracy in America* (1835): "The most able men in the United States are very rarely placed at the head of affairs," a result he ascribed to the character of democracy itself. Ordinary citizens were jealous of their intellectual superiors and so refused to elect them to office; moreover, because most voters had little time to consider important policy issues, they assented to "the clamor of a mountebank [charlatan] who knows the secret of stimulating [their] tastes."

The European visitors were witnesses to the unfolding of the American democratic revolution. In the early years of the nation the ruling ideology had been *republicanism*, rule by property-owning "men of TALENTS and VIRTUE." By the 1820s and 1830s the watchword was becoming *democracy*, which in the nineteenth-century United States meant power exercised by party politicians elected by the people as a whole. "That the majority should govern was a fundamental maxim in all free governments," declared Martin Van Buren, the most talented of the new breed of middle-class professional politicians who had taken over the halls of government. The new party politicians were often crude and usually self-interested, but by uniting ordinary Americans in "election fever," they held together an increasingly fragmented social order.

The Rise of Popular Politics, 1820–1829

Expansion of the **franchise** was the most dramatic expression of the democratic revolution. Beginning in the late 1810s many states revised their constitutions to eliminate property qualifications, giving the franchise to nearly every farmer and wage earner. Nowhere else in the world did ordinary men have so much political power; in England, even after passage of the Reform Bill of 1832, only 600,000 out of 6 million men—a mere 10 percent—had the right to vote.

The Decline of the Notables and the Rise of Parties

In America's traditional agricultural society, people from the low and middle ranks of society deferred to their "betters," and wealthy notable men—northern landlords, slave-owning planters, and seaport merchants—dominated the political system. As former Supreme Court justice John Jay—himself a notable—put it in 1810, "Those who own the country are the most fit persons to participate in the government of it." The notables managed local elections by building up an "interest": lending money to small farmers, giving business to storekeepers and artisans, and treating their workers and tenants to rum at election time. An outlay of $20 for refreshments, according to an experienced poll watcher, "may produce about 100 votes." Martin Van Buren, whose father was a tavern keeper, knew from personal experience that this gentry-dominated system excluded men of modest means who lacked wealth and "the aid of powerful family connections" from running for office.

The Rise of Democracy. The first assaults on the traditional political order came in the Midwest and Southwest. As smallholding farmers and ambitious laborers settled the trans-Appalachian region, they broke free of control by the notables. In Ohio, a traveler

reported, "no white man or woman will bear being called a servant." Influenced by this social egalitarianism, the constitutions of the new states of Indiana (1816), Illinois (1818), and Alabama (1819) prescribed a broad male franchise. Once armed with the vote, ordinary citizens in the western states usually elected middling men to local and state offices. A well-to-do migrant in Illinois noted with surprise that the man who plowed his fields "was a colonel of militia, and a member of the legislature." Once in public office, men from modest backgrounds listened to the demands of their ordinary constituents, enacting laws that restricted imprisonment for debt, kept taxes low, and allowed farmers to claim "squatters' rights" to unoccupied land.

To deter migration to the western states and unrest at home, the notables who ran most eastern legislatures grudgingly accepted a broader franchise. Responding to reformers who condemned property qualifications as a "tyranny" that endowed "one class of men with privileges which are denied to another," in 1810 the Maryland legislature extended the vote to all adult white men. By the mid-1820s only a few states—North Carolina, Virginia, Rhode Island—required the ownership of freehold property for voting. A solid majority of the states had instituted universal white manhood suffrage, and most of the others, such as Ohio and Louisiana, excluded only the relatively few men who did not pay taxes (on their property, persons, or occupations) or serve in the militia. Moreover, between 1818 and 1821 the eastern states of Connecticut, Massachusetts, and New York revised their entire constitutions, reapportioning the representation of legislative districts on the basis of population and instituting more democratic forms of local government, such as the election (rather than the appointment) of judges and justices of the peace.

The politics of the new democracy was more complex and contentious than the traditional politics of deference. Powerful entrepreneurs and speculators—whether they were notables or self-made men—demanded government assistance for their business enterprises and paid bribes to legislators to get it. Bankers sought charters from the state and opposed laws that placed limits on interest rates, while land speculators demanded the eviction of squatters and the building of roads and canals to enhance the value of their holdings. Other Americans turned to politics to advance religious and cultural causes. In 1828 evangelical Presbyterians in Utica, New York, campaigned for a town ordinance to restrict secular activities on Sunday. In response a member of the local Universalist Church (a free-thinking Protestant denomination) attacked this effort at coercive reform and called for "Religious Liberty."

Parties Take Command. Political parties allowed the voices of diverse interest groups—and even individual voters—to be heard. The founders of the American republic had condemned political "factions" and "parties" as antirepublican and therefore refused to give parties a role in the new constitutional system. But as the power of notables declined, the political party emerged as the central organizing force in the American system of government. The new parties were disciplined groups run by professional politicians from middle-class backgrounds, especially lawyers and journalists. To some observers the parties resembled the mechanical innovations of the Industrial Revolution, **political "machines"** that, like a well-designed textile loom, wove the diverse threads of social groups and economic interests into an elaborate tapestry—a coherent legislative program.

Martin Van Buren of New York was the chief architect—and advocate—of the emerging system of party government. Between 1817 and 1821 the "Little Magician" created the first statewide political machine, the Albany Regency; a few years later he organized the first nationwide political party, the Jacksonian Democrats. Van Buren repudiated the republican principle that political parties were dangerous to the commonwealth. Indeed, he argued, the opposite was true: "All men of sense know that political parties are inseparable from free government" because they checked the government's "disposition to abuse power . . . [and curbed] the passions, the ambition, and the usurpations" of potential tyrants.

One key to Van Buren's success as a politician in New York was his systematic use of the *Albany Argus* and other party newspapers to promote a platform and drum up the vote. **Patronage** was even more important to the success of Van Buren's party because the Albany Regency's control of the legislature gave Van Buren and his followers a greater "interest" than any landed notable—some six thousand appointments to the legal bureaucracy of New York (judges, justices of the peace, sheriffs, deed commissioners, and coroners) carrying salaries and fees worth $1 million. Finally, Van Buren insisted on party discipline, requiring state legislators to follow the majority decisions of a party meeting, or **caucus**. On one crucial occasion, Van Buren pleaded with seventeen legislators to "magnanimously sacrifice individual preferences for the general good" and rewarded their party loyalty with patronage and a formal banquet where, an observer wrote, they were treated with "something approaching divine honors."

The Election of 1824

The advance of political democracy disrupted the old system of national politics and undermined the power of the leading notables who ran it. The aristocratic Federalist Party virtually disappeared, and the Republican Party broke up into competing factions. As the election of 1824 approached, no fewer than five candidates, all calling themselves Republicans, campaigned for the presidency. Three were veterans of President James Monroe's cabinet: Secretary of State John Quincy Adams, the son of former president John Adams; Secretary of War John C. Calhoun; and Secretary of the

John Quincy Adams (1767–1848)
This famous daguerreotype of the former president, taken about 1843 by Philip Haas, conveys his rigid personality and high moral standards. These personal attributes hindered Adams's effectiveness as the nation's chief executive but contributed to his success as an antislavery congressman from Massachusetts in the 1830s and 1840s.
Metropolitan Museum of Art. Gift of I. N. Phelps Stokes, Edward S. Hawes, Alice Mary Hawes, Marion Augusta Hawes.

Treasury William H. Crawford. The fourth candidate was Henry Clay of Kentucky, the dynamic Speaker of the House of Representatives, and the fifth was General Andrew Jackson, now a senator from Tennessee. Although a caucus of the Republicans in Congress had selected Crawford as the "official" nominee, the other candidates refused to accept that result.

Instead they introduced democracy to national politics by seeking support among ordinary voters. As a result of democratic reforms, eighteen of the twenty-four states used popular elections (rather than a vote of the state legislature) to choose members of the electoral college. Thus in three-quarters of the states the contest for the presidency depended directly on the votes of ordinary men.

The battle was closely fought. Thanks to his diplomatic successes as secretary of state (see Chapter 10), John Quincy Adams enjoyed national recognition and, because of his Massachusetts origins, commanded most of the electoral votes of the New England states. Henry Clay framed his candidacy around domestic issues.

During his many years in Congress, Clay had gradually articulated a program known as the **American System**, a plan for economic development in which the national government would use the Second Bank of the United States to regulate state banks and would spend tariff revenues to subsidize internal improvements such as roads and canals. Clay's nationalistic program won him great popularity in the West, where such transportation improvements would have a strong impact, and equally great criticism in the South, which could rely on rivers to carry its cotton to market and did not have manufacturing industries to protect. William Crawford of Georgia led a strong southern contingent of "Old Republicans," heirs of the political principles of Thomas Jefferson. Fearing the "consolidation" of all political power in Washington, the Old Republicans attacked the American System as a danger to the authority and powers of the state governments. Recognizing Crawford's strength in his home region, John C. Calhoun of South Carolina withdrew his candidacy, endorsing Andrew Jackson for the presidency and seeking the vice presidency for himself.

As the hero of the Battle of New Orleans, Jackson surged to prominence on the wave of nationalistic pride that flowed from the War of 1812. Born in the Carolina backcountry, Jackson had settled in Nashville, Tennessee, where he formed ties to influential families through marriage and his career as an attorney and slave-owning cotton planter. His reputation as a man of civic virtue and "plain solid republican utility" attracted many voters, and his rise from common origins fit the tenor of the new democratic age. Nominated for the presidency by the Tennessee legislature, Jackson soon commanded nationwide support.

Still, Jackson's strong showing in the election surprised most political leaders, who had predicted a dead heat among Adams, Jackson, and Crawford. The Tennessee senator received 99 votes in the electoral college; Adams garnered 84 votes; Crawford, who suffered a stroke during the campaign, won 41; and Clay finished with 37 (Map 11.1). Since no candidate had received an absolute majority, the Constitution specified that the House of Representatives would choose the president from among the three leading contenders. Throwing the election into the House hurt Jackson, because many congressmen rebelled at the thought of a rough-hewn westerner in the White House and feared that this "military chieftain" might become a political tyrant. Personally out of the race, Henry Clay used his powers as Speaker to thwart Jackson's election. By the time the House met in February 1825, Clay had assembled a coalition of congressmen from New England and the Ohio Valley that voted Adams into the presidency. Adams showed his gratitude by appointing Clay as secretary of state, the traditional steppingstone to the presidency.

Clay's appointment was a fatal mistake for both men. Convinced Adams and Clay had made a deal before the election was decided, John C. Calhoun

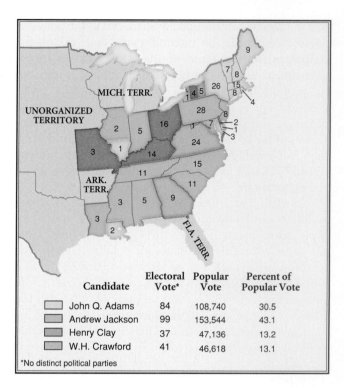

Candidate	Electoral Vote*	Popular Vote	Percent of Popular Vote
John Q. Adams	84	108,740	30.5
Andrew Jackson	99	153,544	43.1
Henry Clay	37	47,136	13.2
W.H. Crawford	41	46,618	13.1

*No distinct political parties

MAP 11.1 Presidential Election of 1824
Regional ties decided the presidential election of 1824. John Quincy Adams captured every electoral vote in New England and most of those in New York. Henry Clay carried Ohio and Kentucky, the most populous trans-Appalachian states, and William Crawford took the southern states of Virginia and Georgia. Only Andrew Jackson claimed a national constituency, winning Pennsylvania and New Jersey in the East, Indiana and Illinois in the Midwest, and most of the South. Only about 356,000 Americans voted, about 27 percent of the eligible electorate.

accused Adams of subverting the popular will by using "the power and patronage of the Executive" to select his successor. It was, he wrote, "the most dangerous stab, which the liberty of this country has yet received." Jackson's many supporters in Congress likewise suspected that Clay had made a preelection deal to become secretary of state. Condemning this "corrupt bargain," they vowed that Clay would never become president.

The Last Notable President: John Quincy Adams

As president, Adams called for a government based on "talent and virtue alone" and bold national leadership. "The moral purpose of the Creator," he told Congress, was to use the president and every other public official to "improve the conditions of himself and his fellow men." Adams called for the establishment of a national university in Washington, extensive scientific explorations in the Far West, and the adoption of a uniform standard of weights and measures. Most important of all, he embraced the American System of national economic development proposed by Henry Clay: (1) a protective tariff to stimulate manufacturing, (2) federally subsidized internal improvements (roads and canals) to aid commerce, and (3) a national bank to provide a uniform currency and control credit.

Internal Improvements Rejected.   Adams's policies favored the business elite of the Northeast and also assisted entrepreneurs and commercial farmers in the Midwest. They won little support among southern planters, who opposed protective tariffs, and among smallholding farmers, who feared powerful banks. From his deathbed Thomas Jefferson condemned Adams for promoting "a single and splendid government of [a monied] aristocracy . . . riding and ruling over the plundered ploughman and beggared yeomanry." Other politicians objected to the American System on constitutional grounds. In 1817 President Madison had vetoed a Bonus Bill, proposed by Henry Clay and John C. Calhoun, that would have used the federal government's income from the Second Bank of the United States to fund internal improvement projects in the various states. In his veto message Madison had argued that such projects fell into the province of the states and exceeded the national government's constitutional powers, a sentiment that was widely shared. Declaring his allegiance on "Constitutional questions . . . with the doctrines of the Jefferson School," Martin Van Buren joined with the Old Republicans in voting against federal subsidies for roads and canals and proposed constitutional amendments to limit them. A hostile Congress defeated most of Adams's ambitious proposals for a nationally financed system of economic development, approving only a few navigation improvements and a short extension of the National Road from Wheeling, Virginia, into Ohio.

The Tariff Battle.   The most far-reaching battle of the Adams administration came over tariffs. The Tariff of 1816 effectively excluded imports of cheap English cotton cloth, giving control of that market to New England textile producers. In 1824 a new tariff had imposed a protective tax of 35 percent on more expensive types of woolen and cotton cloth as well as iron goods. Adams and Clay now demanded even higher duties to protect the iron and textile industries in Pennsylvania and New England. When Van Buren and his Jacksonian allies took control of Congress in 1826, they also supported higher tariffs but for different reasons. By imposing tariffs on imported raw materials, such as wool and hemp, Van Buren hoped to win the support of farmers in New York, Ohio, and Kentucky for Jackson's presidential candidacy in 1828. The tariff had become a prisoner of politics. "I fear this tariff thing," remarked Thomas Cooper of South Carolina, "by some strange mechanical contrivance . . . it will be changed into a machine for manufacturing Presidents, instead of broadcloths, and bed blankets." Disregarding southern opposition, northern Jacksonians joined with the supporters of Adams and Clay to enact the Tariff of 1828, which raised duties on both raw materials and manufactures.

A CARTOON COMPARING CONDITIONS UNDER FREE TRADE AND
PROTECTIVE TARIFF
From "The United States Weekly Telegram," November 5, 1832.

The Tariff of Abominations

Political cartoons were widely used in eighteenth-century England and became popular in the United States during the political battles of the First Party System (1794–1815). By the 1820s newspapers, most of which were subsidized by political parties, published daily cartoons. This political cartoon of 1828 attacks the new tariff as hostile to the interests and prosperity of the South. The gaunt figure on the left represents a southern planter, starved by exactions of the tariff, while the northern textile manufacturer on the right has grown stout by feasting on the bounty of protection. Corbis-Bettmann.

The new tariff enraged the South, which gained nothing from the legislation. As the world's cheapest producer of raw cotton, the South did not need a protective tariff, and by raising the price of British manufactures, the tariff cost southern planters about $100 million a year. Now they had to buy either higher-cost American textiles and iron goods, thus enriching northeastern businesses and workers, or highly taxed British goods, thus paying the cost of the national government. The new tariff was "little less than legalized pillage" declared an Alabama legislator, a "Tariff of Abominations."

"The Democracy" and the Election of 1828

Despite the Jacksonians' support for the tariff, most southerners blamed President Adams for the new act and, also offended by his Indian policy, refused to support Adams's bid for a second term. A deeply moralistic man, Adams had supported the land rights of Native Americans against expansionist-minded southern whites. In 1825 U.S. commissioners had secured a treaty from one faction of Creeks that ceded the remaining Creek lands in Georgia to the United States. When the Creek National Council repudiated the treaty as fraudulent, Adams called for new negotiations. In response Governor George M. Troup vowed to take the lands by force. Troup attacked the president as a "public enemy . . . the unblushing ally of the savages" and persuaded Congress to pass legislation that extinguished the Creeks' land titles, forcing most Creeks to leave the state.

Elsewhere in the nation Adams's primary weakness was political. He was the last notable to serve in the White House, and he acted the part: aloof, moralistic, paternalistic. When Congress rejected his activist economic policies, Adams questioned the wisdom of the people and advised elected officials not to be "palsied by the will of our constituents." Ignoring his waning popularity, the president failed to use patronage to reward his supporters; indeed, he allowed hostile federal officeholders to keep their appointed positions as long as they were competent. As the election of 1828 approached, Adams did not mount a full-scale campaign. Rather than "run" for reelection, he "stood" for it, telling supporters, "If my country wants my services, she must ask for them."

Martin Van Buren and the professional politicians handling Andrew Jackson's campaign for the presidency had no reservations about "running" for office. Now a U.S. senator from New York, Van Buren began to fashion the first national campaign organization. His goal was to re-create the old Jeffersonian coalition, uniting northern farmers and artisans (the "plain Republicans of the North") with the southern slave owners and smallholding farmers who had voted Jefferson, Madison, and Monroe into the presidency. John C. Calhoun, Jackson's semiofficial running mate, brought his South Carolina allies into Van Buren's party, and Jackson's close friends in Tennessee rallied voters in the Old Southwest to the cause. Directed by Van Buren, state politicians orchestrated a massive newspaper campaign; in New York fifty newspapers declared their support for Jackson on the same day. Local Jacksonians organized mass meetings, torchlight parades, and barbecues to excite public interest. They celebrated Jackson's frontier origins and his rise to fame without the advantages of birth, education, or political intrigue. Old Hickory—the nickname came from the toughest American hardwood tree—was a "natural" aristocrat, a self-made man. "Jackson for ever!" was their cry.

Initially the Jacksonians called themselves Democratic Republicans, but as the campaign wore on, they became Democrats or "the Democracy." The name conveyed their message. The American republic had been corrupted by "special privilege" and corporate interests that, as Jacksonian Thomas Morris told the Ohio legislature, gave "a few individuals rights and privileges not enjoyed by the citizens at large." Morris promised that his party would destroy "artificial distinction in society" and ensure rule by the majority—the Democracy. As Jackson himself declared, "Equality among the people in the rights conferred by government" was the "great radical principle of freedom."

Jackson's message of equal rights and popular rule appealed to a variety of social groups. His hostility to special privileges for business corporations and to Clay's American System won support among urban workers

and artisans in the Northeast who felt threatened by industrialization. In the Southeast and the Midwest Old Hickory's well-known animus toward Native Americans reassured white farmers who favored Indian removal. On the controversial Tariff of Abominations, Jackson benefited from the financial boost it gave to Pennsylvania ironworkers and New York farmers, but he declared his personal preference for a "judicious" tariff, thus appealing for southern votes by suggesting that the existing rates were too high.

The Democrats' strategy of seeking votes from a variety of social and economic groups worked like a charm. In 1824 only about a fourth of the eligible electorate had voted; in 1828 more than half went to the polls, and they voted overwhelmingly for Jackson (Figure 11.1). The senator from Tennessee received 178 of 261 electoral votes and became the first president from a western state, indeed from any state other than Virginia and Massachusetts (Map 11.2). As Jackson traveled to Washington to take up the reins of government, an English visitor noted, he "wore his hair carelessly but not ungracefully arranged, and in spite of his harsh, gaunt features looked like a gentleman and a soldier." However, the massive outpouring of popular support for Jackson had frightened men of wealth and influence. As the ex-Federalist and corporate lawyer Daniel Webster warned his clients, the new president would "bring a breeze with him. Which way it will blow, I cannot tell [but]. . . my fear is stronger than my hope." Watching an unruly crowd clamber over the elegant furniture in the White House to shake the hand of the newly inaugurated president, Supreme Court

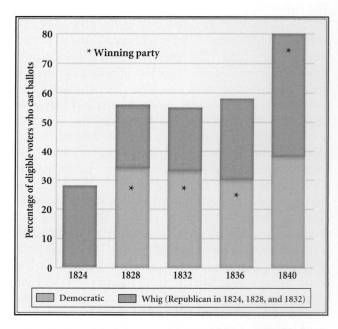

FIGURE 11.1 Changes in Voting Patterns, 1824–1840
Because of the return of two-party competition, voter participation soared in the critical presidential elections of 1828 and 1840.

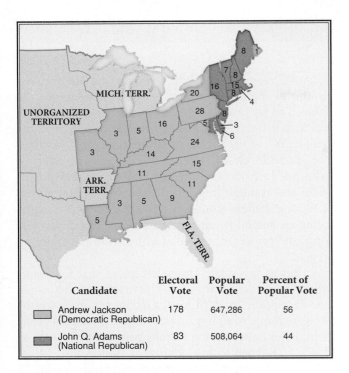

MAP 11.2 Presidential Election of 1828

As in 1824, John Quincy Adams carried all of New England and some of the Middle Atlantic states. However, Andrew Jackson swept the rest of the nation and won a resounding victory in the electoral college. Nearly 1.2 million American men cast ballots in 1828, three times the number who voted in 1824.

Candidate	Electoral Vote	Popular Vote	Percent of Popular Vote
Andrew Jackson (Democratic Republican)	178	647,286	56
John Q. Adams (National Republican)	83	508,064	44

Justice Joseph Story thought he knew the answer, lamenting that "the reign of King 'Mob' seemed triumphant" (see American Voices, "Margaret Bayard Smith: Republican Majesty and Mobs," p. 322).

The Jacksonian Presidency, 1829–1837

Political democracy—a broad franchise, a disciplined political party, and policies tailored to specific social groups—had carried Andrew Jackson to the presidency. Jackson used his popular mandate to enhance the authority of the president over that of Congress, destroy the nationalistic American System of Adams and Clay, and ordain a new ideology for the Democracy. An Ohio supporter outlined Jackson's vision: "the Sovereignty of the People, the Rights of the States, and a Light and Simple Government."

Jackson's Agenda: Patronage and Policy

To decide policy, Jackson relied primarily on an informal group of advisors, his so-called Kitchen Cabinet. Its most influential members were Francis Preston Blair of Kentucky, who edited the *Washington Globe*; Amos Kendall, also from Kentucky, who helped Jackson write

his public addresses; Roger B. Taney of Maryland, who became attorney general and then chief justice of the United States; and, the most influential, Secretary of State Martin Van Buren.

Following Van Buren's example in New York, Jackson used patronage to create a loyal and disciplined national party. He insisted on rotation in office: when a new administration came to power, bureaucrats would have to leave government service and return "to making a living as other people do." Dismissing the argument that forced rotation would eliminate expertise, Jackson suggested that most public duties were "so plain and simple that men of intelligence may readily qualify themselves for their performance." William L. Marcy, a New York Jacksonian, put it more bluntly: government jobs were like the spoils of war, and there was "nothing wrong in the rule that to the victor belong the spoils of the enemy." Using the **spoils system**, Jackson dispensed government jobs to aid his friends and win support for his legislative program.

Jackson's main priority was to destroy the American System. As Henry Clay noted apprehensively, the new president wanted "to cry down old constructions of the Constitution . . . to make all Jefferson's opinions the articles of faith of the new Church." Declaring that the "voice of the people" called for "economy in the expenditures of the Government," Jackson rejected federal support for transportation projects, which he also opposed on constitutional grounds. In 1830 he vetoed four internal improvement bills, including an extension of the National Road, arguing in part that the proposed extension would lie entirely within Kentucky and therefore amounted to "an infringement of the reserved powers of states." Then Jackson turned his attention to two complex and equally politically-charged parts of the American System: protective tariffs and the national bank.

The Tariff and Nullification

The Tariff of 1828 had helped Jackson win the presidency, but it saddled him with a major political crisis. Fierce opposition to the tariff arose in South Carolina, where slave owners faced the prospect of slave rebellion and suffered from chronic insecurity. South Carolina was the only state with an African American majority— 56 percent of the population in 1830—and, like the white planters in the predominantly black sugar islands of the West Indies, its slave owners lived in fear of a black rebellion. They also worried about the legal abolition of slavery. The British Parliament had promised to end slavery in the West Indies (and did so in August 1833), and South Carolina planters worried that the U.S. government might do the same. "If the general government shall continue to stretch their powers," a southern congressman had warned as early as 1818, antislavery societies "will undoubtedly put them to try the question of emancipation." To rule out this

Margaret Bayard Smith

Republican Majesty and Mobs

As Andrew Jackson ascended to the presidency in 1829, he threatened the established political and social system by questioning the legitimacy of a powerful central government and calling for democracy and "equal rights." Writing to her son, the Washington socialite Margaret Bayard Smith revealed a mixture of pride and anxiety about the new president and the coming of popular democracy.

The inauguration . . . was one grand whole—an imposing and majestic spectacle. . . . Thousands and thousands of people, without distinction of rank, collected in an immense mass around the Capitol, silent, orderly, and tranquil, with their eyes fixed on the front of the Capitol, waiting the appearance of the president. . . . The door from the Rotunda opens, preceded by the marshall surrounded by the judges of the Supreme Court, the old man [President Jackson] with his grey hair, that crown of glory, advances, bows to the people, who greet him with a shout that rends the air. The cannon, from the heights around from Alexandria and Fort Washington, proclaim the [oath of office] he has taken and all the hills around reverberate the sound. It was grand; it was sublime! An almost breathless silence succeeded and the multitude was still—listening to catch the sound of his voice, though it was so low as to be heard only by those nearest to him.

After reading his speech, the oath was administered to him by the chief justice. The marshall presented the Bible. The president took it from his hand, pressed his lips to it, laid it reverently down, then bowed again to the people. Yes, to the people in all their majesty—and had the spectacle closed here, even Europeans must have acknowledged that a free people, collected in their might, silent and tranquil, restrained solely by a moral power, without a shadow around of military force, was majesty, rising to sublimity, and far surpassing the majesty of kings and princes, surrounded with armies and glittering in gold. . . .

[But at the White House reception that followed,] what a scene did we witness!! The majesty of the people had disappeared, and [instead] a rabble, a mob . . . scrambling, fighting, romping . . . [crowded around] the president, [who,] after having literally been nearly pressed to death . . . escaped to his lodgings at Gadsby's. Cut glass and bone china to the amount of several thousand dollars had been broken in the struggle to get refreshments. . . . Ladies fainted, men were seen with bloody noses. . . . Ladies and gentlemen only had been expected at this [reception], not the people en masse. . . . But it was the people's day, and the people's president. . . .

God grant the people do not put down all rule and rulers. I fear . . . as they have been found in all ages and countries where they get power in their hands, that of all tyrants, they are the most ferocious, cruel, and despotic. The . . . rabble in the president's house brought to my mind descriptions I had read of the mobs in the Tuileries and at Versailles [during the French Revolution].

Source: M. B. Smith to J. B. H. Smith, March 1829, Smith Family Correspondence, Library of Congress, in Linda R. Monk, ed., *Ordinary Americans: U.S. History through the Eyes of Ordinary People* (Alexandria, VA: Close Up Foundation, 1993), 49–50.

possibility, South Carolina politicians tried to limit the power of the central government and chose the tariff as their target.

The crisis began in 1832, when high-tariff congressmen ignored southern warnings that they were "endangering the Union" and passed legislation retaining the duties imposed by the Tariff of Abominations. In November leading South Carolinians called a state convention, which boldly adopted an Ordinance of Nullification. The ordinance declared the tariffs of 1828 and 1832 null and void, forbade the collection of those duties in the state after February 1, 1833, and threatened secession if federal bureaucrats tried to collect them.

South Carolina's act of **nullification** rested on the constitutional arguments developed in a tract published in 1828, *The South Carolina Exposition and Protest*. Written anonymously by Vice President John C. Calhoun, the *Exposition* denied that majority rule lay at the heart of republican government. "Constitutional government and the government of a majority are utterly incompatible," Calhoun wrote. "An unchecked majority is a despotism." To devise a mechanism to check congressional

Fashion and Fear in South Carolina, c. 1831

This painting, executed by South Carolina artist S. Bernard around the time of the nullification crisis, shows fashionably dressed whites strolling along the East Battery of Charleston. To the left, two African Americans resort to fisticuffs, while other blacks sit and watch. Although the scene is tranquil, many whites feared an uprising by enslaved blacks, who formed a majority of the state's population. Yale University Art Gallery.

majorities, Calhoun turned to the arguments advanced by Jefferson and Madison in the Kentucky and Virginia Resolutions of 1798. Developing a constitutional theory that states' rights advocates would use well into the twentieth century, Calhoun maintained that the U.S. Constitution had been ratified by the people in state conventions. Consequently, he argued, a state convention could determine whether a congressional law was unconstitutional and declare it null and void within the state's borders.

Although Jackson wanted to limit the powers of the national government, he believed it should be done through the existing constitutional system. Confronting Calhoun at a banquet in 1830, Jackson publicly repudiated his vice president's ideas by proposing a formal toast: "Our Federal Union—it must be preserved." Two years later the president's response to South Carolina's Nullification Ordinance was equally forthright. "Disunion by armed force is treason," he declared in December 1832. Appealing to patriotism, Jackson asserted that

nullification violated the Constitution and was "unauthorized by its spirit, inconsistent with every principle on which it is founded, and destructive of the great object for which it was formed." At Jackson's request, Congress passed a Force Bill early in 1833 authorizing him to use the army and navy to compel South Carolina to obey national laws. Simultaneously, Jackson met the South's objections to high import duties by winning passage of a compromise Tariff Act that provided for a gradual reduction in rates. By 1842 import taxes would revert to the modest levels set in 1816, eliminating another part of Clay's American System.

The compromise worked. Having won a gradual reduction in duties, the South Carolina convention rescinded its nullification of the tariff (while defiantly nullifying the now meaningless Force Act). Jackson was satisfied. He had upheld the principle that no state could nullify a law of the United States, a position that Abraham Lincoln would embrace in defense of the Union during the secession crisis of 1861.

The Bank War

In the middle of the tariff crisis Jackson faced another major challenge, this one from the supporters of the Second Bank of the United States. The Second Bank stood at the center of the American financial system. A privately managed entity, it had operated since 1816 under a twenty-year charter from the federal government, which owned 20 percent of its stock. The bank's most important role was to stabilize the nation's money supply. Most American money consisted of notes and bills of credit—in effect, paper money—issued by state-chartered banks. The banks promised to redeem the notes on demand with "hard" money—that is, gold or silver coins (also known as **specie**). By collecting those notes and regularly demanding specie, the Second Bank kept the state banks from issuing too much paper money and thereby prevented monetary inflation and higher prices.

During the prosperous 1820s the Second Bank had maintained monetary stability by restraining some expansion-minded banks in the western states and forcing others to close. This tight-money policy pleased bankers and entrepreneurs in Boston, New York, and Philadelphia, whose capital investments were underwriting economic development, but aroused considerable popular hostility. Most Americans did not understand the regulatory role of the Second Bank and feared its ability to force bank closures, which left ordinary citizens holding worthless paper notes. Some wealthy Americans also opposed the Second Bank because they resented the financial clout wielded by its arrogant president, Nicholas Biddle. "As to mere power," Biddle wrote to a friend, "I have been for years in the daily exercise of more personal authority than any President habitually enjoys." Fearing Biddle's power, New York bankers wanted the specie owned by the federal government to be deposited in their institutions rather than in the Second Bank. Likewise, expansion-minded bankers in western cities, including friends of Jackson in Nashville, wanted to escape supervision by a central bank.

Jackson Vetoes the Rechartering Bill.
However, it was a political miscalculation by the supporters of the Second Bank that brought about its downfall. In 1832 Jackson's opponents in Congress, led by Henry Clay and Daniel Webster, persuaded Biddle to request an early recharter of the bank. They had the votes to get a rechartering bill through Congress and hoped to lure Jackson into a veto that would split the Democrats just before the 1832 elections.

Jackson turned the tables on Clay and Webster. He vetoed the bill that rechartered the bank and became a public hero by justifying his action in a masterful public statement. His veto message blended constitutional arguments with class rhetoric and patriotic fervor. Adopting the position that Jefferson had taken in 1792, Jackson declared that Congress had no constitutional authority to charter a national bank, which was "subversive of the rights of the States." Then, using the populist republican rhetoric of the American Revolution, he attacked the Second Bank as "dangerous to the liberties of the people," a nest of special privilege and monopoly power that promoted "the advancement of the few at the expense of the many . . . the farmers, mechanics, and laborers." Finally, the president evoked national patriotism by pointing out that British aristocrats owned much of the bank's stock; any such powerful institution should be "purely American," he declared.

Jackson's attack on the bank carried him to victory in the presidential election of 1832. He jettisoned Calhoun as a running mate because of the South Carolinian's support for nullification and Calhoun's refusal to welcome Peggy Eaton, a cabinet wife accused of sexual improprieties, into Washington society. As his new vice president, Jackson chose his longtime political ally and advisor Martin Van Buren. Together Old Hickory and Little Van overwhelmed Henry Clay, who headed the National Republican ticket, by 219 to 49 electoral votes. Jackson's most fervent supporters were eastern workers and western farmers, whose lives had been disrupted by falling wages or price fluctuations and who blamed their fate on the Second Bank. "All the flourishing cities of the West are mortgaged to this money power," charged Senator Thomas Hart Benton of Missouri. "They may be devoured by it at any moment. They are in the jaws of the monster." But just as many Jacksonians were the beneficiaries of a decade of strong economic growth and rising living standards and wanted more of the same. Expansion-minded state bankers hoped to benefit from the demise of the Second Bank, and thousands of middle-class Americans—lawyers, clerks, shopkeepers, artisans—cheered Jackson's attacks on privileged corporations. They wanted equal opportunity to rise in the world (see Voices from Abroad, "Alexis de Tocqueville: Parties in the United States," p. 325).

The Bank Destroyed.
Shortly after his reelection and in the midst of the tariff struggle with South Carolina, Jackson launched a new assault on the Second Bank, which still had four years left on its charter. He appointed Roger B. Taney, a strong opponent of corporate privilege, as secretary of the treasury and directed Taney to withdraw the government's gold and silver from the bank and deposit it in state institutions, which critics called his "pet banks." To justify this abrupt (and probably illegal) act Jackson claimed that his own reelection represented "the decision of the people against the bank," giving him a mandate to destroy it. This was the first time a president had claimed that victory at the polls allowed him to act independently of Congress.

The "bank war" escalated. In March 1834 Jackson's opponents in the Senate passed a resolution written by

Alexis de Tocqueville

Parties in the United States

*I*n the late 1820s Alexis de Tocqueville visited the United States to inspect its innovative system of prisons and ended up writing a brilliant memoir. In Democracy in America (1835) Tocqueville presented both a philosophical analysis of the society of the United States and an astute description of its political institutions. Here the republican-minded French aristocrat explains why "great political parties" are not to be found in the United States and how regional interests and individual ambitions threaten the stability of the political system.

The political parties that I style great are those which cling to principles rather than to their consequences; to general and not to special cases; to ideas and not to men. . . . In them private interest, which always plays the chief part in political passions, is more studiously veiled under the pretext of the public good. . . .

Great political parties . . . are not to be met with in the United States at the present time. Parties, indeed, may be found which threaten the future of the Union; but there is none which seems to contest the present form of government or the present course of society. The parties by which the Union is menaced do not rest upon principles, but upon material interests. These interests constitute, in the different provinces of so vast an empire, rival nations rather than parties. Thus, upon a recent occasion [the Tariff of 1832 and the nullification crisis] the North contended for the system of commercial prohibition, and the South took up arms in favor of free trade, simply because the North is a manufacturing and the South an agricultural community; and the restrictive system that was profitable to the one was prejudicial to the other.

In the absence of great parties the United States swarms with lesser controversies. . . . The pains that are taken to create parties are inconceivable, and at the present day it is no easy task. In the United States there is no religious animosity, . . . no jealousy of rank, . . . no public misery. . . . Nevertheless, ambitious men will succeed in creating parties. . . . A political aspirant in the United States begins by discerning his own interest . . . [and] then contrives to find out some doctrine or principle that may suit the purposes of this new organization, which he adopts in order to bring forward his party and secure its popularity. . . .

The deeper we penetrate into the inmost thought of these parties, the more we perceive that the object of the one is to limit and that of the other to extend the authority of the people. I do not assert that the ostensible purpose or even that the secret aim of American parties is to promote the rule of aristocracy or democracy in the country; but I affirm that aristocratic or democratic passions may easily be detected at the bottom of all parties. . . .

To quote a recent example, when President Jackson attacked the Bank of the United States, the country was excited, and parties were formed; the well-informed classes rallied round the bank, the common people round the President. But it must not be imagined that the people had formed a rational opinion upon a question which offers so many difficulties to the most experienced statesmen. By no means. The bank is a great establishment, which has an independent existence; and the people . . . are startled to meet with this obstacle to their authority [and are] led to attack it, in order to see whether it can be shaken, like everything else.

Source: Alexis de Tocqueville, *Democracy in America* (1835; New York: Random House, 1981), 1:94–99.

Henry Clay censuring the president and warning of executive tyranny: "We are in the midst of a revolution, hitherto bloodless, but rapidly descending towards a total change of the pure republican character of the Government, and the concentration of all power in the hands of one man." Jackson was not deterred by widespread congressional opposition and was determined to succeed, "regardless of who goes with me." As he vowed to Van Buren, "The Bank is trying to kill me but I will kill it!" And so he did. In 1836 the Second Bank lost its national charter and became a state bank in Pennsylvania, still a wealthy institution but one without public responsibilities.

Jackson had destroyed both national banking—the creation of Alexander Hamilton—and the American System of protective tariffs and internal improvements favored by John Quincy Adams and Henry Clay. The result was a profound change in the policies and powers of the national government. "All is gone," observed a Washington newspaper correspondent. "All is gone,

Jackson Destroys the Bank
In this political cartoon Jackson proudly orders the withdrawal of "Public Money" from the privately run Second Bank of the United States. Crushed by the subsequent collapse of the bank are its director Nicholas Biddle, depicted as the Devil, wealthy British and American investors, and the newspapers that supported Biddle during the bank war. Standing behind the president is "Major Jack Downing," the pseudonym for Seba Smith, a pro-Jackson humorist. Library of Congress.

For more help analyzing this image, see the ONLINE STUDY GUIDE at bedfordstmartins.com/henretta.

which the General Government was instituted to create and preserve."

Indian Removal

The status of the Native American peoples was as difficult a political issue as the tariff and the bank, and it also raised issues of national versus state power. In the late 1820s white voices throughout the western states and territories called for the resettlement of Indians to the west of the Mississippi River (Map 11.3). Many easterners also favored removal. Even to those whites who were sympathetic to the Native American peoples, resettlement seemed the only way to protect Indians from alcoholic degradation and economic sharp dealing and to preserve their traditional cultures.

Most Indians had no wish to leave their ancestral lands. The Old Southwest was the home of the so-called Five Civilized Tribes: the Cherokees and Creeks in Georgia, Tennessee, and Alabama; the Chickasaws and Choctaws in Mississippi and Alabama; and the Seminoles in Florida. During the War of 1812 Jackson's military expeditions had forced the Creeks to relinquish millions of acres. But Indian peoples still controlled vast tracts of land and, led by the mixed-blood descendants of white traders and Indian women, strongly resisted removal. Growing up in a bicultural world, mixed-blood Indians had learned the political ways of whites and some of them emulated the lifestyle of southern planters. James Vann, a Georgia Cherokee, owned more than twenty black slaves, two trading posts, and a gristmill. Forty other Cherokee mixed-blood families owned a total of more than a thousand slaves. To protect their property and the lands of their people, the mixed-bloods attempted to forge a strong national identity. Sequoyah, a mixed-blood, developed a system of writing for the Cherokee language, and the tribe published a newspaper. In 1827 the Cherokees introduced a new

charter of government modeled directly on the U.S. Constitution. Full-blooded Cherokees, who made up 90 percent of the population, resisted many of the mixed-bloods' cultural and political innovations but were equally determined to retain their ancestral lands. "We would not receive money for land in which our fathers and friends are buried," one chief declared. "We love our land; it is our mother."

The Cherokees' preferences carried no weight with the Georgia legislature. In 1802 Georgia had given up its land claims in the West in return for a federal promise to extinguish Indian landholdings in the state. Now it demanded the fulfillment of that promise, declaring that the Cherokees were merely tenants on state-owned land. Having spent most of his military life fighting Indians and seizing their lands, Jackson gave full support to Georgia. On assuming the presidency, he withdrew the federal troops that had protected Indian enclaves there and in Alabama and Mississippi. The states, he argued, were sovereign within their borders.

Jackson then pushed through Congress the Indian Removal Act of 1830, which provided territory in present-day Oklahoma and Kansas to Native Americans who would give up their ancestral holdings. To persuade Indians to move, government officials promised that they could live on the new lands, "they and all their children, as long as grass grows and water runs." When Chief Black Hawk and his Sauk and Fox followers refused to move from rich farmland along the Mississippi River in western Illinois in 1832, Jackson sent troops to expel them (see American Voices, "Black Hawk: A Sacred Reverence for Our Lands," p. 329). Rejecting Black Hawk's offer to surrender, the American army pursued him into the Wisconsin Territory and, in the brutal eight-hour Bad Axe Massacre, killed 850 of Black Hawk's 1,000 warriors. Over the next five years diplomatic pressure and military power forced seventy Indian peoples to sign treaties and move west of the Mississippi. Those

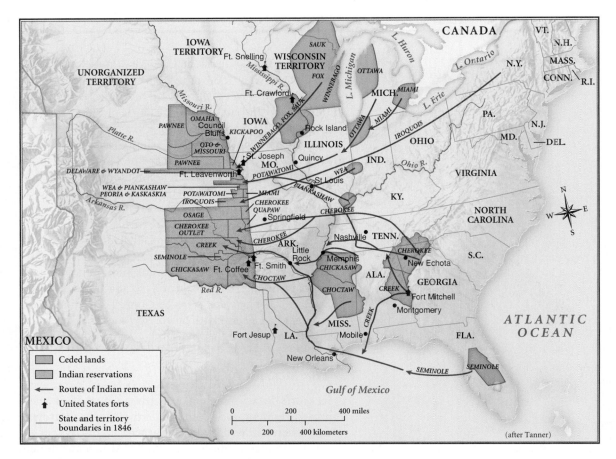

MAP 11.3 The Removal of Native Americans, 1820–1843

Beginning in the 1820s the U.S. government coerced scores of Native American peoples to sign treaties that exchanged Indian lands in the East for money and designated tracts west of the Mississippi River. During the 1830s the government used military force to expel the Cherokees, Chickasaws, Choctaws, Creeks, and many Seminoles from their ancestral homes in the Old Southeast and resettle them on reservations in the Indian Territory in the present-day states of Oklahoma and Kansas.

Raising Public Opinion against the Seminoles

During the eighteenth century hundreds of enslaved Africans from South Carolina and Georgia sought refuge in Spanish Florida, where they lived among and intermarried with the Seminole people. This graphic color engraving of the 1830s, intended to bolster political support for the forced removal of the Seminoles to the Indian Territory, shows red and black Seminoles butchering respectable white families. By the mid-1840s, after a decade of warfare, the U.S. Army had forced 2,500 Seminoles—about half the total number—to migrate to Oklahoma; the remainder continued to live in Florida, protected by a new treaty. Granger Collection.

Black Hawk (1767–1838)

This portrait of Black Hawk, by Charles Bird King, shows the Indian leader as a young warrior, wearing a medal commemorating an early-nineteenth-century agreement with the U.S. government. Later, in 1830, when Congress approved Andrew Jackson's Indian Removal Act, Black Hawk mobilized Sauk and Fox warriors to protect ancestral lands in Illinois. "It was here, that I was born—and here lie the bones of many friends and relatives," the aging chief declared, "I . . . never could consent to leave it." Newberry Library.

agreements exchanged 100 million acres of land in the East for $68 million and 32 million acres in the West.

In the meantime the Cherokees had carried their case to the Supreme Court, claiming the status of a "foreign nation" under the U.S. Constitution. In *Cherokee Nation v. Georgia* (1831) Chief Justice John Marshall denied their claim to national independence. Speaking for a majority of the justices Marshall declared that Indian peoples enjoyed only partial autonomy and were "domestic dependent nations." However, in *Worcester v. Georgia* (1832) Marshall sided with the Cherokees, voiding Georgia's extension of state law over them and holding that Indian nations were "distinct political communities, having territorial boundaries, within which their authority is exclusive . . . [and this is] guaranteed by the United States." When Jackson heard the outcome, he reputedly responded, "John Marshall has made his decision; now let him enforce it."

Rather than guaranteeing the Cherokees' territory, Jackson moved purposefully to take it from them. U.S. commissioners signed a removal treaty with a minority

faction and insisted that all Cherokees abide by it. By the deadline in May 1838 only 2,000 of the 17,000 Cherokees had departed. During the summer, Martin Van Buren, who had succeeded Jackson as president, ordered General Winfield Scott to enforce the treaty. Scott's army rounded up about 14,000 Cherokees and forcibly marched them 1,200 miles to the new Indian Territory, an arduous journey they remembered as the Trail of Tears (see Map 11.3). Along the way 3,000 Indians died of starvation and exposure. After the Creeks, Chickasaws, and Choctaws moved west of the Mississippi, the only remaining Indian people in the Old Southwest were the Seminoles in Florida. Aided by runaway slaves who had married into the tribe, a portion of the Seminoles fought a successful guerrilla war during the 1840s and remained in Florida. They were the exceptions. The national government had asserted its control over most eastern Indian peoples and forced their removal.

The Jacksonian Impact

Jackson's legacy as chief executive, like that of every great president, was complex and rich. By destroying the American System, he disrupted the movement toward stronger central direction of American life and reinvigorated the Jeffersonian tradition of a limited, frugal national government. Having restrained the reach of the Union government, the president firmly defended it during the nullification crisis, threatening the use of military force to uphold laws enacted by the national legislature. Finally, Jackson permanently expanded the authority of the nation's chief executive, using the rhetoric of popular sovereignty to declare that "the President is the direct representative of the American people."

The Taney Court.   Jackson and his Democratic Party used their political predominance to infuse American institutions with their principles. Following the death in 1835 of John Marshall, Jackson appointed Roger B. Taney as chief justice of the Supreme Court. During his long tenure (1835–1864), Taney persuaded the Court to give constitutional legitimacy to Jackson's policies of antimonopoly and states' rights. Writing for a majority of the Court in the landmark case *Charles River Bridge Co. v. Warren Bridge Co.* (1837) Taney declared that the legislative charter held by the Charles River Bridge Company in Massachusetts did not convey a monopoly because an exclusive right was not explicitly stated in the charter. Consequently, the legislature retained the power to charter a competing bridge company. As Taney put it: "While the rights of private property are sacredly guarded, we must not forget that the community also has rights." This decision qualified John Marshall's interpretation of the contract clause of the Constitution in *Dartmouth College v. Woodward* (1819), which had emphasized the binding nature of public charters and

AMERICAN VOICES

Black Hawk

A Sacred Reverence for Our Lands

Black Hawk (1767–1838), or Makataimeshekiakiak in the language of his people, was a chief of the Sauk and Fox. In 1833 he dictated his life story to a government interpreter, and a young newspaper editor published it. Here Black Hawk describes the coming of white settlers to his village, near present-day Rock Island, Illinois, and his decision to resist removal to lands west of the Mississippi River.

We had about eight hundred acres in cultivation. The land around our village . . . was covered with bluegrass, which made excellent pasture for our horses. . . . The rapids of Rock river furnished us with an abundance of excellent fish, and the land, being good, never failed to produce good crops of corn, beans, pumpkins, and squashes. We always had plenty—our children never cried with hunger, nor our people were never in want. Here our village had stood for more than a hundred years.

[In 1828] Nothing was now talked of but leaving our village. Ke-o-kuck [the principal chief] had been persuaded to consent to . . . remove to the west side of the Mississippi. . . . [I] raised the standard of opposition to Ke-o-kuck, with full determination not to leave my village. . . . I was of the opinion that the white people had plenty of land and would never take our village from us. . . .

During the [following] winter, I received information that three families of whites had arrived at our village and destroyed some of our lodges, and were making fences and dividing our corn-fields for their own use. . . . I requested them [to remove, but some weeks later] we came up to our village, and found that the whites had not left it—but that others had come, and that the greater part of our corn-fields had been enclosed. . . . Some of the whites permitted us to plant small patches in the fields they had fenced, keeping all the best ground for themselves. . . . The white people brought whiskey into our village, made people drunk, and cheated them out of their homes, guns, and [beaver] traps!

That fall [1829] I paid a visit to the agent, before we started to our hunting grounds. . . . He said that the land on which our village stood was now ordered to be sold to individuals; and that, when sold, our right to remain, by treaty, would be at an end, and that if we returned next spring, we would be forced to remove! I refused . . . to quit my village. It was here, that I was born—and here lie the bones of many friends and relatives. For this spot I felt a sacred reverence, and never could consent to leave it, without being forced therefrom.

[In the spring of 1831] I directed my village crier to proclaim, that my orders were, in the event of the [Indian] war chief coming to our village to remove us [to honor the treaty], that not a gun should be fired, nor any resistance offered. That if he determined to fight, for them to remain quietly in their lodges, and let them kill them if he chose.

Source: David Jackson, ed., Black Hawk: An Autobiography (Urbana: University of Illinois Press, 1964), 88–90, 95–97, 111–13.

had limited the power of states to alter or repeal them (see Chapter 8). Taney's decision encouraged competitive enterprise, opening the way for legislatures to charter railroads that would vie for business with existing canal and turnpike companies.

Other decisions by the Taney Court refused to broaden Marshall's nationalistic interpretation of the commerce clause. Instead, it enhanced the regulatory role of state governments. For example, in *Mayor of New York v. Miln* (1837) the Taney Court ruled that New York State could use its "police power" to inspect the health of arriving immigrants. The new Jacksonian Court also restored to the states some of the economic powers they had exercised before 1787. In *Briscoe v. Bank of Kentucky*

(1837) the Court approved the issuance of currency by a bank owned and controlled by the state of Kentucky, ruling that it did not violate the provision (in Article 1, Section 10, of the U.S. Constitution; see p. D-9) that forbade states from issuing "bills of credit."

State Government Reform. Jacksonian Democrats in the various states mounted their own constitutional revolution. Between 1830 and 1860 twenty states called conventions to revise their basic charters. Most states extended the vote to all white men and reapportioned their legislatures on the basis of population. The revised constitutions also brought government "near to the people" by mandating the election, rather than the appointment, of most public officials—including sheriffs, justices of the peace, and judges.

By inserting Jacksonian ideals into the new constitutions, the delegates changed their character from "republican" governments that undertook public projects to "liberal" regimes that limited the power of the state. Thus most Jacksonian-era constitutions prohibited states from granting exclusive charters to corporations or extending loans or credit guarantees to private businesses. "If there is any danger to be feared in . . . government," declared a New Jersey Democrat, "it is the danger of associated wealth, with special privileges." The revised state constitutions also protected taxpayers by setting strict limits on state debts and encouraging judges to enforce them. As a New York reformer put it, "We will not trust the legislature with the power of creating indefinite mortgages on the people's property." Just as Jackson had destroyed the American System's program of government subsidies on the national level, so his disciples in the states undermined the "commonwealth" philosophy of using chartered corporations and state funds to promote economic development. Declaring that "the world is governed too much," Jacksonians attacked government-granted special privileges and embraced a small-government, laissez-faire outlook. The first American "populists," they celebrated the power of ordinary people to make decisions in the marketplace and the voting booth.

Class, Culture, and the Second Party System

The rise of the Democracy and Jackson's tumultuous presidency sparked the creation in the mid-1830s of a second national party—the Whigs. For the next two decades Whigs and Democrats dominated American politics, forming what historians call the Second Party System. Many evangelical Protestants became Whigs, while most Catholics and nonevangelical Protestants joined the Democrats. The two parties competed fiercely for votes, debating issues of economic policy, class power, and moral reform and offering Americans a clear choice between political programs.

The Whig Worldview

The Whig Party began in Congress in 1834, when opponents of Andrew Jackson banded together to protest his policies and high-handed "kinglike" actions. They took the name **Whigs** to identify themselves with the pre-Revolutionary American and British parties—also called Whigs—that had opposed the arbitrary actions of British monarchs. The congressional Whigs charged that "King Andrew I" had violated the Constitution by creating a "spoils system" and increasing presidential authority, an "executive usurpation" that had undermined

government by elected legislators, the true representatives of the sovereign people.

Whig Ideology. The Whigs were a diverse group, a "heterogeneous mass of old National Republicans and former Jackson men; Masons and Antimasons; abolitionists and proslavery men; bank men and antibank men," according to Whig congressman Millard Fillmore. However, led by Senators Webster of Massachusetts, Clay of Kentucky, and Calhoun of South Carolina, the Whigs gradually elaborated a distinct political vision. Beginning in the congressional elections of 1834 they sought votes especially among evangelical Protestants and upwardly mobile middle- and working-class citizens in the North. Their goal, like that of the Federalists of the 1790s, was a political world dominated by men of ability and wealth;

A Whig Cartoon

Attacking the president as "KING ANDREW THE FIRST," this political cartoon accuses Andrew Jackson of acting arbitrarily, like a monarch, and trampling on the principles of the Constitution. It emphasizes Jackson's contempt for Congress, expressed in his vetoes of legislation on banking and internal improvements. Seeking to turn democratic fervor to the advantage of the Whig Party, the caption asked: "Shall he reign over us, or shall the PEOPLE RULE?" New-York Historical Society.

unlike the Federalists, the Whig elite would be chosen by talent, not birth.

The Whigs celebrated the role played by enterprising entrepreneurs. "This is a country of self-made men," they boasted, pointing to the relative absence of permanent distinctions of class and status among white citizens of the United States. Arguing that the Industrial Revolution had increased social harmony, they welcomed the investments of "moneyed capitalists" as providing the poor with jobs, "bread, clothing and homes" and stressed the role of activist governments in increasing the nation's wealth. Whig congressman Edward Everett told a Fourth of July crowd in Lowell, Massachusetts, that there was a "holy alliance" among laborers, owners, and governments. Many workers agreed, especially those holding jobs in the New England textile factories and Pennsylvania iron mills that benefited from state subsidies and protective tariffs. To ensure continued economic progress, Everett and northern Whigs called for a return to the American System of Henry Clay and John Quincy Adams.

Support for the Whigs in the South was fragmentary and rested on the appeal of specific policies rather than agreement with the Whigs' social vision. Some southern Whigs were wealthy planters who invested in railroads and banks or sold their cotton to New York merchants. The majority were yeomen whites in the backcountry who wanted to break the grip over state politics held by low-country planters, most of whom were Democrats. In addition, some states' rights Democrats in Virginia and South Carolina became Whigs because, like John C. Calhoun, they condemned Andrew Jackson's crusade against nullification. Like Calhoun, most southern Whigs did not share their party's enthusiasm for high tariffs and social mobility. Indeed, Calhoun argued that the northern Whig ideal of equal opportunity was contradicted not only by slavery, which he considered a fundamental American institution, but also by the wage-labor system of industrial capitalism. "There is and always has been in an advanced state of wealth and civilization a conflict between labor and capital," he argued in 1837, urging southern slave owners and northern factory owners to unite in a defensive alliance against their common foe: the working class composed of enslaved blacks and propertyless whites.

Most Whig leaders rejected Calhoun's class-conscious vision. "A clear and well-defined line between capital and labor" might fit the slave South or class-ridden Europe, Daniel Webster conceded, but in the North "this distinction grows less and less definite as commerce advances." Webster focused on the growing size and affluence of the northern middle class. Indeed, in the election of 1834 the Whigs won a majority in the House of Representatives by appealing to middling groups—the prosperous farmers, small-town merchants, and skilled industrial workers in New England, New York, and the new communities along the Great Lakes.

Anti-Masonry Influence. Many Whig voters had previously been Anti-Masons, members of a powerful but short-lived political movement of the late 1820s. As their name implies, Anti-Masons opposed the Order of Freemasonry, a secret deistic and republican organization that began in eighteenth-century Europe. Spreading rapidly to America it attracted leading political leaders—including George Washington, Henry Clay, and Andrew Jackson—and ambitious businessmen. By the mid-1820s there were 20,000 Masons in New York State alone, organized into 450 local lodges. Following the kidnapping and murder of William Morgan, a New York Mason who had threatened to reveal the order's secrets, Thurlow Weed, a Rochester newspaper editor, spearheaded an Anti-Masonic political party. Attacking Masonry as a secret aristocratic fraternity, the Anti-Masons drove its members from local and state offices. Having achieved its goals, the movement collapsed.

Picking up on Anti-Masonic themes—temperance, equality of opportunity, evangelical religious values—the Whigs recruited Anti-Masons by advocating legal curbs on the sale of alcohol and local bylaws that preserved Sunday as a day of worship. The Whigs also won congressional seats in the Ohio and Mississippi Valleys, where farmers, bankers, and shopkeepers favored Henry Clay's policies for governmental subsidies for roads, canals, and bridges.

The Election of 1836. In the election of 1836 the Whig Party faced Martin Van Buren, the architect of the Democratic Party and Jackson's handpicked successor. Van Buren emphasized his opposition to the American System, declaring its revival would undermine the rights of the states and create an oppressive system of "consolidated government." Positioning himself as a defender of individual rights, Van Buren likewise opposed the plans of Whigs and moral reformers to use governmental power to impose temperance, evangelical religious values, and the abolition of slavery. "The government is best which governs least" became his motto.

To oppose Van Buren the Whigs ran four regional candidates, hoping to garner enough electoral votes to throw the contest into the House of Representatives, which they controlled. The plan failed. The Whig tally—73 electoral votes collected by William Henry Harrison of Ohio, 26 by Hugh L. White of Tennessee, 14 by Daniel Webster of New Hampshire, and 11 by W. P. Magnum of Georgia—fell far short of Van Buren's 170 votes. Still, the size of the popular vote for the four Whig candidates—49 percent of the total—showed that the party's message of economic improvement and moral uplift appealed not only to middle-class Americans but

Celebrating a Political Triumph, 1836
To commemorate Martin Van Buren's election to the presidency and to reward friends for their support, the Democratic Party distributed thousands of snuffboxes inscribed with his portrait. By using such innovative measures to enlist the loyalty of voters, Van Buren and his allies transformed American politics from an upper-class avocation to a democratic contest for votes and power. Collection of Janice L. and David J. Frent.

also to farmers and workers with little or no property. Most important, the election of 1836 witnessed the creation of the Second Party System, a closely fought struggle between Whigs and Democrats that would define American political life for the next two decades.

Labor Politics and the Depression of 1837–1843

As the Democratic and Whig Parties battled for power, they faced challenges from new worker-based political parties. Moreover, a set of sudden catastrophic financial upheavals threw the American economy into a sustained depression, which further increased class tensions and political conflicts.

Working Men's Parties and the Rise of Unions. In seeking the votes of workers, the established parties had to compete with radical reformers, such as Frances Wright (see American Lives, "Frances Wright: Radical Reformer," p. 336) and the Working Men's Parties that had sprung up in fifteen states between 1827 and 1833. Rising prices and stagnant wages had lowered the standard of living of many urban artisans and wage earners, who feared what they called "the glaring inequality of society" and began to organize politically.

"Past experience teaches us that we have nothing to hope from the aristocratic orders of society," declared the New York Working Men's Party, which vowed "to send men of our own description, if we can, to the Legislature at Albany." It called for the end to private banks, chartered monopolies, and imprisonment for debt. The Philadelphia Working Men's Party demanded higher taxes on the wealthy and in 1834 persuaded the Pennsylvania legislature to authorize free, tax-supported schools so that workers' children could advance into the ranks of the propertied classes.

The Working Men's Parties embraced the ideology of artisan republicanism. Their goal was a society in which (as the radical thinker Orestes Brownson put it) there would be no dependent wage earners and "all men will be independent proprietors, working on their own capitals, on their own farms, or in their own shops." This vision led the Working Men's Parties to join the Jacksonians in demanding equal rights and attacking chartered corporations and monopolistic banks. "The only safeguard against oppression," argued William Leggett, a leading member of the New York Loco-Foco (Equal Rights) Party, "is a system of legislation which leaves to all the free exercise of their talents and industry." At first the Working Men's Parties prospered at the polls, but divisions over policy and voter apathy soon took a toll. By the mid-1830s most politically active workers had joined the Democratic Party, urging it to oppose protective tariffs and to tax the stocks and bonds owned by wealthy capitalists.

Taking advantage of the economic boom of the early 1830s, which increased the demand for skilled labor, workers formed unions to bargain for higher wages. Employers responded by attacking the union movement. In 1836 clothing manufacturers in New York City agreed not to hire workers belonging to the Union Trade Society of Journeymen Tailors and circulated a list—a so-called **blacklist**—of its members. The employers also brought lawsuits to overturn **closed-shop agreements** that required them to hire only union members. They argued that such contracts violated both the common law and legislative statutes that prohibited "conspiracies" in restraint of trade.

Judges usually agreed. In 1835 the New York Supreme Court found that a shoemakers' union in Geneva had illegally caused "an industrious man" to be "driven out of employment." "It is important to the best interests of society that the price of labor be left to regulate itself," the Court declared. When a court in New York City upheld a conspiracy verdict against a tailors' union, a crowd of 27,000 people demonstrated outside city hall, and tailors circulated handbills proclaiming that the "Freemen of the North are now on a level with the slaves of the South." In 1836 popular demonstrations prompted local juries to acquit shoemakers in Hudson, New York, carpet makers in Thompsonville, Connecticut, and plasterers in Philadelphia of similar conspiracy charges.

The Panic and the Depression. At this juncture the Panic of 1837 threw the American economy into disarray. The panic began early in the year, when the Bank of England, hoping to boost the faltering British economy, sharply curtailed the flow of money and credit to the United States. For the previous decade and a half British manufacturers and investors had stimulated the American economy, providing southern planters with credit to expand cotton production and purchasing millions of dollars of the canal bonds issued by northern states. Suddenly deprived of British funds, American planters, merchants, and canal corporations had to withdraw specie from domestic banks to pay their foreign loans and commercial debts. Moreover, because the Bank of England refused to advance credit to American cotton brokers, the price of raw cotton in the South collapsed from 20 cents a pound to 10 cents or less.

Falling cotton prices and the drain of gold and silver set off a general financial crisis. On May 8 the Dry Dock Bank of New York City closed its doors, and panicked depositors withdrew more than $2 million in gold and silver coins from other city banks, forcing them to suspend all payments in specie. Within two weeks every bank in the United States had followed suit, shocking high-flying entrepreneurs and ordinary citizens and sending the economy into a steep decline (Map 11.4). "This sudden overthrow of the commercial credit and honor of the nation" had a "stunning effect," observed Henry Fox, the British minister in Washington. "The conquest of the land by a foreign power could hardly have produced a more general sense of humiliation and grief."

A second, longer-lasting economic downturn began in 1839. Following the Panic of 1837, state governments had increased their investments in canals and other transportation ventures. As more and more bonds to finance these ventures were sold in Europe, their prices fell sharply, sparking an international financial crisis in 1839 that lasted for four years. The crisis soon engulfed state governments, which were unable to meet the substantial interest payments on their bonds. Nine states defaulted on their obligations to foreign creditors; other states declared a moratorium on debt payments, undermining the confidence of British investors and cutting the flow of capital. Bumper crops drove down cotton prices even further, bringing more bankruptcies.

The American economy fell into a deep depression. By 1843 canal construction had dropped 90 percent and prices nearly 50 percent. Unemployment reached almost 20 percent of the workforce in seaports and industrial centers. From his pulpit, minister Henry Ward Beecher described a land "filled with lamentation . . . its inhabitants wandering like bereaved citizens among the ruins of an earthquake, mourning for children, for houses crushed, and property buried forever."

By creating a surplus of unemployed workers the depression devastated the labor movement. In 1837, six thousand masons, carpenters, and other building-trades workers lost their jobs in New York City, depleting union membership and destroying unions' bargaining power. By 1843 most local unions and all the national labor organizations had disappeared, along with their newspapers.

However, two events during the depression years improved the long-term prospects of the labor movement. One was a major legal victory. In *Commonwealth v. Hunt* (1842), a case decided by the Massachusetts Supreme Judicial Court, Chief Justice Lemuel Shaw upheld the rights of workers to form unions and enforce a closed shop. Shaw, one of the great jurists of the nineteenth century, overturned common-law precedents by making two critical rulings: (1) a union was not an inherently illegal organization, and (2) union members could legally attempt to enforce a closed shop, even by striking. Courts in other states generally accepted Shaw's opinion, but judges (who were mostly Whigs) found other methods, such as court injunctions, to restrict strikes and boycotts. Labor's second success was political. Continuing Jackson's effort to attract workers to the Democratic Party, in 1840 President Van Buren signed an executive order establishing a ten-hour day for all federal employees. Significantly, this achievement came after the unions had been defeated in the marketplace, underlining the fact that the outcome of workers' struggles—like conflicts over tariffs, banks, and internal improvements—would depend not only on economic factors but also on political decisions.

"Tippecanoe and Tyler Too!"

The depression had a major impact on American politics. Few people understood the complex workings of the international economy, and thus many Americans blamed the Democrats for their economic woes. In particular, they derided Jackson for destroying the Second Bank and for issuing the Specie Circular of 1836, which required western settlers to use gold and silver coins to pay for land purchases. Not realizing that shipment of specie to Britain (to pay off past debts) was the main cause of the financial panic, the Whigs blamed Jackson's policies.

The public turned its anger on Van Buren, who entered office just as the panic began. Ignoring the pleas of influential bankers, the new president refused to revoke the Specie Circular or take other actions that might reverse the downturn. Holding to his philosophy of limited government, Van Buren advised Congress that "the less government interferes with private pursuits the better for the general prosperity." As a major depression settled upon the nation in 1839, this laissez-faire outlook commanded less and less political support. Worse, Van Buren's major piece of economic legislation, the Independent Treasury Act of 1840, actually delayed recovery. The act pulled federal specie out of Jackson's "pet banks" (which had used it to back loans) and placed it in government vaults (where it did no economic good at

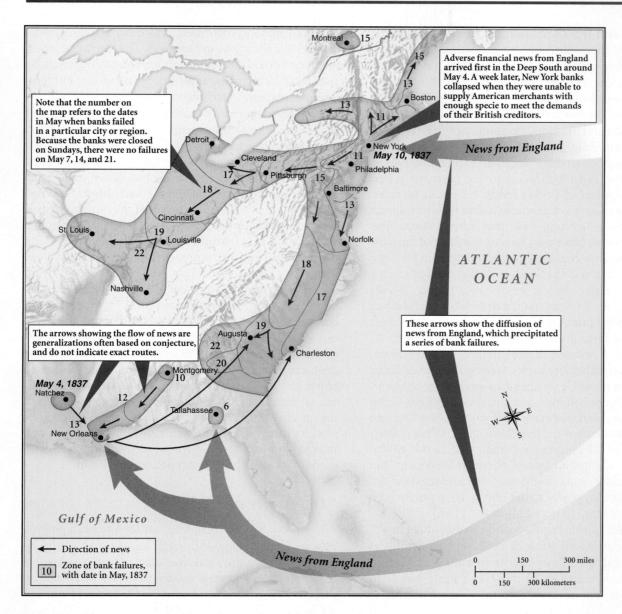

MAP 11.4 Anatomy of a Panic: Bank Suspensions in May 1837

The first failures occurred in cotton belt banks (Natchez, Tallahassee, Montgomery), prompted by news that the Bank of England would no longer advance credit to American cotton brokers. A few days later, when British bankers and creditors demanded repayment of loans in specie, New York City merchants withdrew millions of dollars in gold from the city's banks, forcing them to close. This collapse precipitated a chain reaction; within twelve days most banks along the Atlantic coast, the Erie Canal, and the Ohio River had shut their doors. This pattern of bank failures clearly reveals the central importance of New York in the economic nerve system of the nation. (See Map 10.4, on p. 300, for an additional illustration of New York's growing importance.)

For more help analyzing this map, see the ONLINE STUDY GUIDE at **bedfordstmartins.com/henretta**.

all). Whatever its value in placing the nation's financial reserves above politics, the Independent Treasury Act did little to enhance Van Buren's popularity.

The Election of 1840. Determined to exploit Van Buren's weakness, in 1840 the Whigs organized their first national convention and nominated William Henry

Harrison of Ohio for president and John Tyler of Virginia for vice president. A military hero of the Battle of Tippecanoe and the War of 1812, Harrison was well advanced in age (sixty-eight) and had little political experience. But the Whig leaders in Congress, Clay and Webster, did not want a strong president; they planned to have Harrison rubber-stamp their program for protective tariffs and a national bank. Party strategists such as Thurlow Weed of New York had chosen Harrison primarily because of his military record and western background, promoting him as the Whig version of Andrew Jackson. An unpretentious, amiable man, Harrison warmed to that task, telling voters that Whig policies were "the only means, under Heaven, by which a poor industrious man may become a rich man without bowing to colossal wealth."

Panic and depression stacked the political cards against Van Buren, but the contest itself turned as much on style as on substance. It became the great "log cabin" campaign—the first occasion on which two well-organized parties competed for the loyalties of a mass electorate by projecting vivid images of their candidates and creating a new style of festive political celebrations. Whig pamphleteering, songfests, parades, and well-orchestrated mass meetings dominated the contest, drawing new voters and new social groups into the political arena. Whig speakers assailed "Martin Van Ruin" as a manipulative politician with aristocratic tastes—a devotee of fancy wines and elegant clothes, as indeed he was. With less candor they praised Harrison, actually the son of a wealthy planter who had signed the Declaration of Independence, as a self-made soldier and statesman who lived in a simple log cabin and enjoyed hard cider, a drink of the common man.

The Whigs boosted their electoral hopes by welcoming women to their festivities. Previously women had been systematically excluded not only from voting and jury duty but also from nearly every other aspect of political life, even marching in July 4 and Washington's Birthday parades. Jacksonian Democrats celebrated politics as a "manly" affair, likening the women who ventured into the political arena to the ordinary run of "public" women—the prostitutes who plied their trade in theaters and other public places. However, the Whigs recognized that women from Yankee families, a core Whig constituency, were deeply involved in American public life through religious revivalism, the temperance movement, and other benevolent activities. So in October 1840 Daniel Webster addressed a special meeting of 1,200 Whig women, perhaps the first mass meeting of women in American politics. Noting women's benevolent efforts, Webster praised their moral perceptions as "both quicker and juster" than those of men and identified their concerns with the Whig programs for moral reform. "This way of making politicians of their women is something new under the sun," noted one Democrat, worried that it would bring more Whig men to the polls. Whatever the cause, more than 80 percent of the eligible male voters cast ballots in 1840 (up from less than 60 percent in 1832 and 1836). Heeding the Whig slogan "Tippecanoe and Tyler Too," they voted Harrison into the White House as

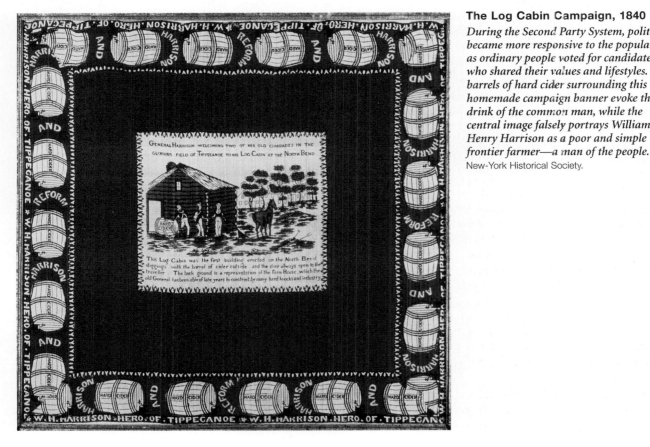

The Log Cabin Campaign, 1840
During the Second Party System, politics became more responsive to the popular will as ordinary people voted for candidates who shared their values and lifestyles. The barrels of hard cider surrounding this homemade campaign banner evoke the drink of the common man, while the central image falsely portrays William Henry Harrison as a poor and simple frontier farmer—a man of the people.
New-York Historical Society.

Frances Wright:
Radical Reformer

Frances Wright (1795–1852) arrived in New York City on January 1, 1829, intending to begin the New Year with a new life and a new message. Born into a wealthy, republican-minded merchant family in Glasgow, Scotland, Wright had first learned about America at age sixteen. "From that moment on," she recalled, "my attention became rivetted on this country as upon the theatre where man might first awake to the full knowledge and exercise of his powers." Of the many Europeans drawn to the United States by the egalitarian doctrines of the Declaration of Independence, Wright was among the most radical and controversial. She was an advocate of deism, black emancipation, the abolition of private property, and women's rights.

In 1818 Wright first crossed the Atlantic to her promised land. Returning to Britain three years later, she published an enthusiastic account of republican society, *Views of Society and Manners in America* (1821), which was translated into three languages. Among her readers was the Marquis de Lafayette, the French hero of the American Revolution, who became Wright's friend and patron. She and her sister moved to France, residing at the country estate of the sixty-four-year-old widower. Ignoring the objections of Lafayette's family, Wright stayed with the aging aristocrat for almost two years, at one point begging him either to marry her or adopt her as a daughter.

Wright's tie to Lafayette provided a new link to the United States. In 1824 she accompanied the French general on his triumphal tour of the United States and exploited his social contacts. During a six-week stay with Thomas Jefferson at Monticello, the young Scotswoman outlined a bold plan to set up a community of whites and freed slaves who would live together in full equality. Like other visionaries who believed in human perfectibility, Wright had great ambitions.

Encouraged by Jefferson, in 1825 Wright founded her utopian community, called Nashoba, in the wilderness of western Tennessee. Joined by young white idealists, Wright purchased about thirty enslaved African Americans. Believing in the dignity of labor and self-reliance, she required the slaves to earn their freedom by working the land. While the slaves labored in the fields, the Nashoba community educated their children. A genuine egalitarian, Wright joined in the arduous task of clearing and ditching the marshy land. But she soon lost the willing support of the black workers, who saw little improvement in their lives.

Wright remained undaunted. She embraced the ideals of Robert Owen, a Scottish manufacturer and philanthropist who in 1824 had founded his own utopian community in New Harmony, Indiana. Endorsing Owen's criticism of marriage, organized religion, and private property, Wright called on those at Nashoba to form a society "where affection shall form the only marriage, kind feelings and kind action the only religion, . . . and reunion of interest the bond of peace and security." However, the rude conditions at Nashoba repelled potential recruits, and its numbers dwindled.

By 1828 Wright had concluded that the solution to society's ills required a general campaign to reform the "collective body politic." Forsaking Nashoba, Wright joined forces with Owen's son Robert Dale Owen who had become infatuated with her. Together they launched a lecture campaign that brought her to New York, the high temple of the emerging American capitalist system and a center of trade unionism.

Wright took New York by storm. Preceded by rumors of free love and racial mixing at Nashoba, she attracted large audiences and lived up to her advance billing. Sweeping onto the stage with a group of women apostles, Wright would throw off her cloak to reveal her unorthodox attire—a tunic of white muslin. Then she would wave a copy of the Declaration of Independence and elaborate on its ideals in a resonant, musical voice. The poet Walt Whitman, who heard Wright lecture when he was a young lad, remembered that "we all loved her; fell down before her: her very appearance seemed to enthrall us." Echoing Robert Dale Owen's socialist ideas, Wright told her listeners that a "monied aristocracy" of bankers and a "professional aristocracy" of ministers, lawyers, and politicians was oppressing the "laboring class." She lashed out at evangelical ministers, describing the Benevolent Empire of religious-minded social reformers as the "would-be Christian Party in politics."

Wright preached peaceful reform, not violent revolution. To promote the gradual transition to a better society, she called for the compulsory training in boarding schools of all children between the ages of two and sixteen. Such an educational system would encourage social equality, insulate children from organized religion, and benefit young women, who would learn to break their "mental chains" and seek equality under the law. To nurture a radical culture, Wright and Owen took over an abandoned church in a working-class neighborhood and

Frances Wright

Wright not only preached radical doctrine but also lived by its precepts. This portrait, painted in 1826 at the Nashoba community in Tennessee, broadcasts a culturally subversive message. Wright dresses in masculine attire, wearing the simple and practical costume for women adopted by Robert Owen's socialist community at New Harmony, Indiana— pantaloons covered by a tunic. She also poses next to a horse, a traditional symbol of masculine virility; note the similarity between Wright's pose and that of General George Washington on page 164.
Miriam and Ira D. Wallach Division of Art, Prints and Photographs. The New York Public Library. Astor, Lenox and Tilden Foundations.

transformed it into a "Hall of Science." They established a newspaper, *The Free Enquirer*, a reading room and lecture auditorium, a free medical dispensary, and a deist Sunday school. The two reformers hoped that rationalist science—the religion of the Enlightenment—would displace Protestant dogma as the guiding principle of workers' lives. Wright won a significant following among artisans and journeymen, some of whom turned to politics and energized the Working Men's Party. In 1829 twenty devotees wrote her name on their ballots for the New York assembly.

But most New York workers rejected Wright's message. They believed that a skewed distribution of wealth and opportunity—not traditional religion—was the primary cause of their poverty and powerlessness. Disheartened, in 1831 Wright and Owen sold the Hall of Science to a Methodist congregation and went their separate ways. Owen returned to New Harmony and became a Jacksonian politician. Wright transported the African Americans at Nashoba to the black-run nation of Haiti and then sailed for Paris, where she married a French reformer.

Wright never abandoned her dreams. Inspired by Andrew Jackson's war against the Second Bank, she returned to America in 1835. But her time had passed. Audiences greeted her lectures and her speeches for presidential candidate Martin Van Buren with indifference or hostility. Newspaper editors labeled her the "Red Harlot of Infidelity" (a phrase that simultaneously condemned her socialism, feminism, and deism), and Christian parents compared her to Satan, invoking her name to frighten their children.

Wright settled in Cincinnati, where she lived out her life in obscurity. She became increasingly pessimistic about the American republic, which appeared to have squandered its republican ideals in a mad quest for wealth. Wright no longer felt at home in her chosen land. It seemed, she mused, as if she had "fallen from a strange planet among a race whose sense and perceptions are all different from my own."

the nation's first Whig president and gave the Whigs a majority in Congress.

The Tyler Administration. The Whig triumph was short-lived. One month after his inauguration Harrison died of pneumonia, and the nation got "Tyler Too." Vice President John Tyler of Virginia, who became president, had joined the Whig Party primarily because he opposed Jackson's stance against nullification. On economic issues Tyler was really a Democrat, sharing Jackson's hostility to the Second Bank and the American System. Consequently, he vetoed bills that would have raised tariffs and created a new national bank. Also like Jackson, Tyler favored the common man and the rapid settlement of the West. He approved the Preemption Act of 1841, which allowed cash-poor settlers to stake a free claim to 160 acres of federal land. By building a house and farming the land, they could buy the property later at a set price of $1.25 an acre.

The split between Tyler and the Whigs allowed the Democrats to regroup. The party vigorously recruited supporters among subsistence farmers in the North and smallholding planters in the South. It cultivated the votes of the urban working class and was particularly successful among Irish and German Catholic immigrants— whose numbers had increased rapidly during the 1830s—supporting their demands for religious and cultural freedom (Figure 11.2). Thanks to these recruits, the Democrats remained the majority party in most parts of the nation. Their program of equal rights, states' rights, and cultural liberty was more attractive than the Whig platform of economic nationalism, moral reform, and individual mobility.

The continuing struggle between Whigs and Democrats, each claiming to speak for "the people," completed the democratic revolution that European visitors found so troubling. The new system perpetuated many problematic political customs—denying women, Indians, and most African Americans an effective voice in public life— and introduced a few more dubious practices, such as the spoils system and a coarser standard of public debate. Yet the United States now boasted universal suffrage for white men as well as a highly organized system of representative government that was responsive to ordinary citizens. In their scope and significance these political initiatives matched the economic advances of the Industrial and Market Revolutions.

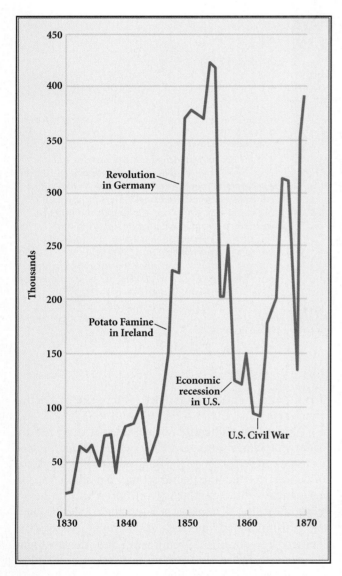

FIGURE 11.2 The Surge in Immigration, 1842–1855

The failure of the potato crop prompted a wholesale migration of peasants from the overcrowded farms of western Ireland. Population pressure likewise spurred the migration of tens of thousands of German peasants, while the failure of the liberal political revolution of 1848 prompted hundreds of prominent German politicians and intellectuals to settle in the United States. Source: David M. Potter, *Division and the Stresses of Reunion, 1845–1876.* Copyright © 1973 Scott, Foresman and Company. Reprinted by permission.

FOR FURTHER EXPLORATION

► For definitions of key terms boldfaced in this chapter, see the glossary at the end of the book.

► To assess your mastery of the material covered in this chapter, see the Online Study Guide at **bedfordstmartins.com/henretta**.

► For suggested references, including Web sites, see page SR-12 at the end of the book.

► For map resources and primary documents, see **bedfordstmartins.com/henretta**.

With the rise of popular politics in the states, the power of notable men declined, and political parties and professional politicians assumed control of American public life. Martin Van Buren and other party leaders used patronage to enact legislation favorable to powerful social groups.

Political democracy came to national politics in 1824, as John Quincy Adams, Henry Clay, William Crawford, and Andrew Jackson competed for the presidency. Jackson received the most electoral votes but, because he lacked a majority, the House of Representatives decided the contest. A "corrupt bargain" between Adams and Clay elevated Adams to the presidency and made Clay his secretary of state. As president, Adams failed to win congressional approval for the American System because many citizens opposed the expansion of federal power. The high rates imposed by the Tariff of 1828 caused many southerners to oppose Adams's reelection, and Andrew Jackson won an overwhelming victory in 1828.

During his eight years as president, Jackson carried through a political revolution, dramatically reducing the economic agenda of the national government. He ended federal subsidies for internal improvements and won a gradual reduction in tariff rates. Jackson likewise eliminated national banking by refusing to recharter the Second Bank of the United States. However, Jackson used the military power of the national government to carry through his policy of Indian removal and to coerce South Carolina to renounce nullification. He was the first "modern" president, in claiming that his victory at the polls gave him a political mandate.

Charging that "King Andrew I" had abused his powers, Henry Clay, Daniel Webster, and John C. Calhoun formed the Whig Party. It drew support from the growing middle class and from former Anti-Masons, who were attracted by the Whigs' ideology of social mobility, and moral reform. For the next two decades Whigs and Democrats struggled for dominance in the Second Party System.

The Panic of 1837 and the depression of 1839 destroyed the workingmen's parties and most labor unions. The depression helped the Whigs to victory in the log cabin campaign of 1840, but when the new president, William Henry Harrison, suddenly died, President John Tyler pursued Democrat-like policies that prevented the Whigs from instituting Clay's American System. By the early 1840s the American democratic revolution was complete, and the new political system was about to be tested by the growing conflict over slavery.

1810s Revision of state constitutions and expansion of voting rights for men

Martin Van Buren creates a disciplined party in New York

1825 John Quincy Adams elected president by House; advocates Henry Clay's American System

1827 Philadelphia Working Men's Party organized

1828 "Tariff of Abominations" raises duties on imported materials and manufactures

The South Carolina Exposition and Protest challenges idea of majority rule

1830 Andrew Jackson vetoes extension of National Road

Congress enacts Jackson's Indian Removal Act

1831 *Cherokee Nation v. Georgia* denies Indians' claim of national independence

1832 Expulsion of Sauk and Fox peoples; Bad Axe Massacre by American troops

Jackson vetoes the rechartering of the Second Bank

South Carolina nullifies Tariff of 1832

Worcester v. Georgia upholds political autonomy of Indian peoples

1833 Force Bill and compromise Tariff Act

1834 Whig Party formed by Henry Clay, John C. Calhoun, and Daniel Webster

1835 Roger Taney named Supreme Court chief justice

1837 *Charles River Bridge Co. v. Warren Bridge Co.* weakens legal position of chartered monopolies

Panic of 1837 ends long period of economic expansion.

1838 Trail of Tears: thousands of Cherokees die on forced march to new Indian Territory

1839 American borrowings spark international financial crisis and four-year economic depression

1840 Van Buren finally wins Independent Treasury Act

Whig victory in "log cabin" campaign

1841 John Tyler succeeds William Henry Harrison as president

Preemption Act promotes purchase of federal land

1842 *Commonwealth v. Hunt* legitimates trade unions

Little acts of kindness
Little words of love

Make our earthly eden
like our Heaven above

Is our
Home a
Heaven

Heaven
is our
Home

Be still Peace

Kind
Words
Never
Die

Forgive
as you
hope to be
forgiven

Earth has
no sorrow
Heaven
cannot
heal

Be still
and know
that I am
God

No Cross No Crown

Let thy will be done

Oh sacred
Patience
with my
soul abide

There is a
magic in
kindness
that springs
from above

Maria
Cadman
Hubbard
aged 79

If you can
not be a
Golden pipp
and don't turn
crab apple

abide with us

Love one
another

1848

CHAPTER 12

Religion and Reform

1820–1860

"THE SPIRIT OF REFORM IS IN EVERY PLACE," the children of legal reformer David Dudley Field wrote in their handwritten monthly *Gazette* in 1842:

the labourer with a family says "reform the common schools"; the merchant and the planter say, "reform the tariff"; the lawyer "reform the laws," the politician "reform the government," the abolitionist "reform the slave laws," the moralist "reform intemperance," . . . the ladies wish their legal privileges extended, and in short, the whole country is wanting reform.

◀ **"Pieties Quilt," by Maria Cadman Hubbard, 1848**

Maria Hubbard may have been a Quaker because "No Cross, No Crown" (an inscription on the far right) was the title of William Penn's pamphlet of the 1670s attacking the Church of England. Whatever Hubbard's affiliation, she used her skills as a quilt maker to express deeply held religious beliefs. By inscribing her name and age on the quilt, Maria Cadman Hubbard also created an artifact of material culture that would perpetuate her memory among descendants and provide a historical document for future generations. Unlike most women of her time, she would not vanish from the record of the past.

Collection of the American Folk Art Museum, New York. Gift of Cyril Irwin Nelson in loving memory of his parents, Cyril Arthur and Elise Macy Nelson.

Like many Americans, the young Field children sensed that a whirlwind of political change in the 1830s had transformed the way people thought about themselves as individuals and as a society. It encouraged men and women to believe that they could improve not just their personal lives but society as a whole. Some people dedicated themselves to societal reform. Beginning as an antislavery advocate, William Lloyd Garrison went on to embrace women's rights, pacifism, and the abolition of prisons. Such individuals, the Unitarian minister Henry W. Bellows warned, were obsessed, pursuing "an object, which in its very nature is unattainable—the perpetual improvement of the outward condition."

Many obstacles stood in the way of the reformers' quest for a better society. The American social order was still rigidly divided by race and gender as well as by wealth and religious belief. Moreover, recent social changes brought hardships to some individuals even as they enhanced the standard of living for many others. Most strikingly, the emergent economic system imposed greater discipline on many workers, as slave owners compelled enslaved African Americans to work in labor gangs and factory managers prescribed strict routines for factory operatives. In fact, the first wave of American "improvers," the benevolent reformers of the 1820s, seized on social discipline as the answer to the nation's ills, championing regular church attendance, temperance, and the strict moral codes of the evangelical churches.

Then in the 1830s and 1840s a more powerful wave of reform spilled out of these conservative religious channels and washed over American society, threatening to submerge traditional values and institutions. Mostly middle-class northerners and midwesterners in origin, the new reformers propounded a bewildering assortment of radical ideals—extreme individualism, common ownership of property, the immediate emancipation of slaves, and sexual equality—and demanded immediate action to satisfy their visions. Although they formed a small minority of the American population, the reformers launched a far-reaching intellectual and cultural debate that challenged the premises of the social order and won the attention, but not the respect, of the majority. As a fearful southerner saw it, the goal of the reformers was a world in which there would be "No-Marriage, No-Religion, No-Private Property, No-Law and No Government."

The Founder of Transcendentalism

As this painting of Ralph Waldo Emerson by an unknown artist indicates, the young New England philosopher was an attractive man, his face brimming with confidence and optimism. Because of his radiant personality and incisive intellect, Emerson deeply influenced dozens of influential writers, artists, and scholars and enjoyed great success as a lecturer among the emerging middle class.
The Metropolitan Museum of Art, bequest of Chester Dale, 1962 [64.97.4].

Individualism

The reform movement reflected the social conditions and intellectual currents of American life. In 1835 Alexis de Tocqueville coined a new word, **individualism**, to describe the condition and values of native-born white Americans. He argued that Americans lived a more solitary existence than their European ancestors, "no longer attached to each other by any tie of caste, class, association, or family." Unlike Tocqueville, an aristocrat who feared the disintegration of society, the New England transcendentalist Ralph Waldo Emerson (1803–1882) celebrated this liberation of the individual from traditional social and institutional constraints. Emerson's vision of individual freedom—balanced by a strong sense of personal responsibility—influenced thousands of ordinary Americans and a generation of important artists and writers.

Emerson and Transcendentalism

Emerson was the leading spokesman for **transcendentalism**, an intellectual movement rooted in the religious soil of New England. Its first advocates were spiritually inclined young men, often Unitarian ministers from well-to-do New England families, who questioned the constraints imposed by their Puritan heritage. For inspiration they turned to Europe, drawing on a new conception of self and society known as *Romanticism*. Romantic thinkers, such as the English poet Samuel Taylor Coleridge, rejected the ordered, rational world of the eighteenth-century Enlightenment. Instead they tried to capture the passionate character of the human spirit and sought deeper insights into the mysteries of existence. Drawing on ideas borrowed from the German philosopher Immanuel Kant, English Romantics and Unitarian radicals believed that behind the concrete world of the senses was an ideal world. To reach this deeper reality people had to "transcend," or go beyond, the rational ways in which they normally comprehended the world. By tapping mysterious intuitive powers people could soar beyond the limits of ordinary experience and gain mystical knowledge of ultimate and eternal things.

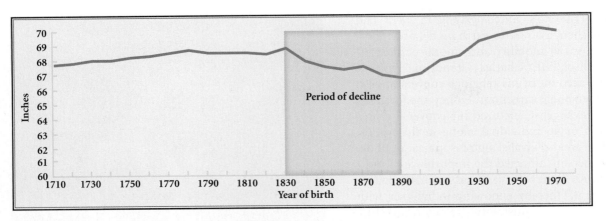

FIGURE 12.1 Environment and Health: Heights of Native-born Men, by Year of Birth

The Transcendentalists sensed that the new commercial and industrial economy would bring a decline in living standards, and modern research suggests they were right. Military records and other sources show that men born in America from the 1830s to the 1890s had average heights as adults that were significantly lower than those of men born between 1710 and 1830. Important causes seem to be a decline in the quality of childhood nutrition and an increase in diseases, especially in urban areas. Better nutrition, public health regulations, and higher living standards in the twentieth century ushered in a rise in the average height of men.

Source: Richard Steckel, "Health and Nutrition in the Preindustrial Era," National Bureau of Economic Research, Working Paper 8452 (2001), figure 3.

Emerson had followed in the footsteps of his father and had become a Unitarian minister, thus placing himself outside the religious mainstream. Unlike most Christians, Unitarians held that God was a single being and not a trinity of Father, Son, and Holy Spirit. In 1832 Emerson moved still further from orthodox Christianity, resigning his Boston pulpit and rejecting organized religion. Moving to Concord, Massachusetts, he gradually articulated the philosophy of transcendentalism in a series of influential essays. His focus was what he called "the infinitude of the private man," the idea of the radically free individual.

The young philosopher saw people as being trapped in inherited customs and institutions. They wore the ideas of people from earlier times—the tenets of New England Calvinism, for example—as a kind of "faded masquerade" and needed to shed those values and practices. "What is a man born for but to be a Reformer, a Remaker of what man has made?" he asked. For Emerson an individual's re-making depended on the discovery of his or her own "original relation with Nature," an insight that would lead to a mystical private union with the "currents of Universal Being." The ideal setting for such a discovery was solitude under an open sky, among nature's rocks and trees.

Emerson's genius lay in his capacity to translate such abstract ideas into examples that made sense to ordinary middle-class Americans. His essays and lectures conveyed the message that all nature was saturated with the presence of God—a pantheistic spiritual outlook that departed from traditional Christian doctrine and underlay his attack on organized religion. Emerson also criticized the new industrial society, predicting that a preoccupation with work, profits, and the consumption of factory-made goods would drain the nation's spiritual energy (Figure 12.1). "Things are in the saddle," Emerson wrote, "and ride mankind."

The transcendentalist message of inner change and self-realization reached hundreds of thousands of people, primarily through Emerson's writings and lectures. Public lectures had become a spectacularly successful way of spreading information and fostering discussion among the middle classes. Beginning in 1826 the **American Lyceum** undertook to "promote the general diffusion of knowledge." Named in honor of the place where the ancient Greek philosopher Aristotle taught, the Lyceum organized lecture tours by all sorts of speakers—poets, preachers, scientists, reformers—and soon achieved great popularity, especially in the North and Midwest. In 1839, nearly 150 local Lyceums in Massachusetts invited lecturers to their towns to speak to more than 33,000 subscribers. Among the hundreds of lecturers on the Lyceum circuit, Emerson was the most popular. Between 1833 and 1860 he gave 1,500 lectures in more than 300 towns in twenty states.

Emerson celebrated individuals who rejected traditional social restraints but were self-disciplined and responsible members of society. His outlook tapped currents that already ran deep in the predominantly middle-class members of his audience, because many of them had made their own way in the world. The publication of Benjamin Franklin's *Autobiography* in 1818 had given many of them a down-to-earth model of an individual seeking social mobility and "moral perfection" through self-discipline. Charles Grandison Finney's widely known account of his religious conversion also pointed in Emersonian directions. Finney, the foremost business-class evangelist, pictured his conversion as a mystical union of an individual, alone in the woods, with God. The great revivalist's philosophical outlook, like that of Emerson, affirmed the importance of individual action. As Finney put it, "God has made man a moral free agent," thereby endowing individuals with the ability—and the responsibility—to determine their spiritual fate.

Emerson's Literary Influence

Emerson took as one of his tasks the remaking of American literature. In an address entitled "The American Scholar" (1837) the philosopher issued a literary declaration of independence from the "courtly muse" of Old Europe. He urged American writers to celebrate democracy and individual freedom and find inspiration not in the doings and sayings of aristocratic courts but in the "familiar, the low . . . the milk in the pan; the ballad in the street; the news of the boat; the glance of the eye; the form and gait of the body."

Henry David Thoreau and Margaret Fuller. A young New England intellectual, Henry David Thoreau (1817–1862), heeded Emerson's call by turning to the American environment for inspiration. In 1845, depressed by his beloved brother's death, Thoreau turned away from society and embraced self-reliance and the natural world, building a cabin at the edge of Walden Pond near Concord, Massachusetts, and living alone there for two years. In 1854 he published *Walden, or Life in the Woods*, an account of his spiritual search for meaning beyond the artificiality of "civilized" life:

> I went to the woods because I wished to live deliberately, to front only the essential facts of life, and see if I could not learn what it had to teach, and not, when I came to die, discover that I had not lived.

Although Thoreau's book had little impact outside transcendentalist circles during his lifetime, *Walden* has become an essential text of American literature and an inspiration to those who reject the dictates of society. Its most famous metaphor provides an enduring justification for independent thinking: "If a man does not keep pace with his companions, perhaps it is because he hears a different drummer." Beginning from this premise, Thoreau became an advocate of social nonconformity and civil disobedience against unjust laws.

Margaret Fuller, by Thomas Hicks, 1848
At the age of thirty-eight, Fuller moved to Italy, where she worked as a correspondent for a New York newspaper reporting on the Italian Revolution of 1848. There Fuller became enamored of Thomas Hicks (1823–1890), a much younger American artist. Hicks rebuffed Fuller's advances but painted this rather flattering portrait, softening her features and giving her a pensive look. Fuller married a Roman nobleman, Giovanni Angelo, Marchese d'Ossoli, and gave birth to a son in September 1848. Constance Fuller Threinen.

As Thoreau sought independence and self-realization for men, Margaret Fuller (1810–1850) explored the possibilities of freedom for women. Born into a wealthy Boston family, Fuller mastered six languages, read broadly in the classic works of literature, and educated her four siblings. While teaching in a school for girls, she became interested in Emerson's ideas and in 1839 began a transcendental "conversation," or discussion group, for educated Boston women. Soon Fuller was editing the leading transcendentalist journal, the *Dial*, and in 1844 she published *Woman in the Nineteenth Century*, which proclaimed that a "new era" was coming in the relations between men and women.

Fuller's philosophy began with the transcendental belief that women, like men, had a mystical relationship with God that gave them identity and dignity. It followed that every woman deserved psychological and social independence—the ability "to grow, as an intellect to discern, as a soul to live freely and unimpeded." Thus, she declared, "We would have every arbitrary barrier thrown down" and "every path laid open to Woman as freely as to Man." Embracing that vision, Fuller became the literary critic of the *New York Tribune* and went to Italy to report on the Revolution of 1848. Her adventurous life led to an early death; returning to the United States at the age of forty, she drowned in a shipwreck. Nonetheless, Fuller's example and writings inspired a rising generation of women writers and reformers.

Walt Whitman. Another writer who responded to Emerson's call was the poet Walt Whitman (1819–1892). When Whitman first encountered Emerson, he later recalled, he had been "simmering, simmering." Then Emerson "brought me to a boil." Whitman had been a teacher, a journalist, an editor of the *Brooklyn Eagle* and other newspapers, and an active publicist for the Democratic Party. But poetry was the "direction of his dreams." In *Leaves of Grass*, first published in 1855 and constantly revised and expanded for almost four decades afterward, he recorded in verse his attempt to pass a number of "invisible boundaries": between solitude and community, between prose and poetry, and even between the living and the dead. It was a wild, exuberant poem in both form and content, self-consciously violating every poetic rule and every canon of respectable taste. Unlike the cautious Emerson, Whitman dared readers to shut the book in revulsion or accept his idiosyncratic vision.

At the center of *Leaves of Grass* is the individual—the figure of the poet, "I, Walt." He begins alone: "I celebrate myself, and sing myself." But because he has what Emerson called an "original relation" with nature, Whitman claims not solitude but perfect communion with others: "For every atom belonging to me as good belongs to you." Whitman celebrates democracy as well as himself, arguing that a poet can claim a profoundly intimate, mystical relationship with a mass audience. For Emerson, Thoreau, and Fuller the individual had a divine spark. For Whitman the individual had expanded to become divine, and democracy assumed a sacred character.

The transcendentalists were not naive optimists. Whitman wrote about human suffering with passion, and Emerson's accounts of the exhilaration that could come in natural settings were tinged with anxiety. "I am glad," he once said, "to the brink of fear." Thoreau's gloomy judgment of everyday life is well known: "The mass of men lead lives of quiet desperation." Still, such dark murmurings were muted in their work, woven into triumphant and expansive assertions that nothing was impossible for an individual who could break free from tradition, law, and other social restraints and discover an "original relation with Nature."

Darker Visions. Emerson's writings also influenced two great novelists, Nathaniel Hawthorne and Herman Melville, who had more pessimistic outlooks. They addressed the opposition between individual transcendence and the legitimate requirements of social order, discipline, and responsibility. Both sounded powerful warnings that unfettered egoism could destroy individuals and those around them. Hawthorne's most brilliant exploration of the theme of excessive individualism appeared in his novel *The Scarlet Letter* (1850). The two main characters, Hester Prynne and Arthur Dimmesdale, challenge their seventeenth-century New England community in the most blatant way—by committing adultery and producing a child. The result of their assertion of individual freedom from social discipline is not liberation but degradation—a profound sense of personal guilt and condemnation by the community.

Herman Melville explored the limits of individualism in even more extreme and tragic terms and emerged as a scathing critic of transcendentalism. He made his most powerful statement in *Moby Dick* (1851), the story of Captain Ahab's obsessive hunt for a mysterious white whale that ends in death not only for Ahab but for all but one member of his crew. Here the quest for spiritual meaning in nature brings death, not transcendence, because Ahab, the liberated individual, lacks inner discipline and self-restraint.

Moby Dick was a commercial failure. The middle-class audience that was the primary target of American publishers refused to follow Melville into the dark, dangerous realms of individualism gone mad. Readers also were unenthusiastic about Thoreau's advocacy of civil disobedience and Whitman's boundless claims for a mystical union between the man of genius and the democratic masses. What American readers emphatically preferred were the more modest examples of individualism offered by Emerson—personal improvement through spiritual awareness and self-discipline.

Brook Farm

To escape the constraints of life in America's emerging market society, transcendentalists and other radical reformers created ideal communities, or **utopias**. They hoped that these planned societies, which organized life in new ways, would allow members to realize their spiritual and moral potential. The most important communal experiment of the transcendentalists was Brook Farm, founded in 1841. Once freed from the tension and demands of an urban, competitive society, its members hoped to develop their minds and souls and uplift society through inspiration. The Brook Farmers supported themselves by selling milk, vegetables, and hay for cash but organized their farming so that they could remain relatively independent of the market, with its unpredictable cycles of boom and bust. Residents who did not work on the farm made cash payments—in effect, tuition for what was virtually a transcendentalist boarding school.

The intellectual life at Brook Farm was electric. Hawthorne lived there for a time and later used the setting for his novel *The Blithedale Romance* (1852). All the major transcendentalists, including Emerson, Thoreau, and Fuller, were residents or frequent visitors. A former member recalled that they "inspired the young with a passion for study, and the middle-aged with deference and admiration, while we all breathed the intellectual grace that pervaded the atmosphere." Music, dancing, games, plays, parties, picnics, and dramatic readings filled the leisure hours.

If Brook Farm offered intellectual bliss, it failed to prosper economically. At first most of its members were ministers, teachers, writers, and students who had few productive skills; to succeed as a farming enterprise it needed practical men and women. A reorganization in 1844 attracted more farmers and artisans but yielded only marginal economic gains. And these changes resulted in a more disciplined routine that, as one resident put it, suppressed "the joyous spirit of youth." After a devastating fire in 1846 the organizers disbanded and sold the farm.

After the failure of Brook Farm the transcendentalists abandoned their attempts to fashion a new system of social organization. Most accepted the brute reality of the coming industrial order and tried to reform it, especially through the education of workers. However, the passion of the transcendentalists for individual freedom and social progress lived on in the movement to abolish slavery, which many of them actively supported.

Communalism

Even as Brook Farm faded, thousands of Americans joined other communal settlements during the 1840s, primarily in the rural areas of the Northeast and Midwest (Map 12.1). Most communalists were ordinary farmers and artisans seeking refuge and security from the seven-year economic depression that had begun with the Panic of 1837. These rural utopias were also symbols of social protest. By organizing themselves along socialist lines with common ownership of property or by experimenting with unconventional forms of marriage and family life, the members questioned acquisitive capitalist values and traditional gender roles.

The Shakers

The Shakers, whose origins dated back to the Revolutionary era, were the first successful American communal movement. In 1770 Ann Lee Stanley (Mother Ann), a young cook in Manchester, England, had a vision that she was an incarnation of Christ and that Adam and Eve had been banished from the Garden of Eden because of their sexual lust. Four years later she led a band of eight followers to America, where they established a church near Albany, New York. Because of the ecstatic dances that became part of their worship, the sect became known as "Shaking Quakers" or, more simply, "Shakers." After Mother Ann's death in 1784, the Shakers venerated her as the Second Coming of Christ and decided to withdraw

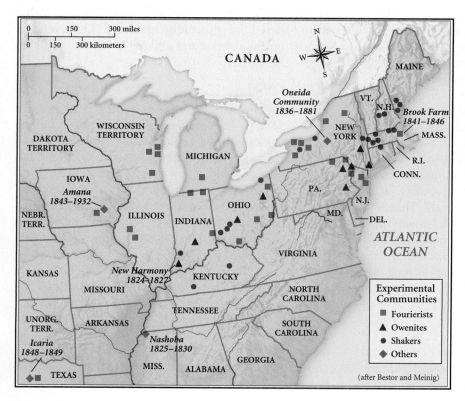

MAP 12.1 Major Communal Experiments before 1860

Some experimental communities settled along the frontier, but the vast majority chose relatively secluded areas in well-settled regions of the North and West. Because of their opposition to slavery, communalists avoided the South. Most secular experiments failed within a few decades, as the founders lost their reformist enthusiasm or died off; religious communities—such as the Shakers and the Mormons—were longer-lived.

The Shaker Community at Poland Hill, Maine (detail)
Like all Shaker communities, the settlement at Poland Hill, Maine, painted by Joshua H. Bussell around 1850, was built on a regular gridlike plan. There was a large dwelling for communal living, surrounded by various workshops and farm buildings. The design of the architecture, like that of Shaker furniture, was plain and sparse.
Collection of the United Society of Shakers, Sabbathday Lake, ME.

For more help analyzing this image, see the ONLINE STUDY GUIDE at bedfordstmartins.com/henretta.

agriculture and crafts, especially furniture making, acquired a reputation for quality that enabled most of these communities to become self-sustaining and even comfortable. Thanks to this economic success and their ideology of sexual equality, Shaker communities attracted more than three thousand converts during the 1830s, with women outnumbering men more than two to one. They welcomed blacks as well as whites; to Rebecca Cox Jackson, an African American seamstress from Philadelphia who joined their community, the Shakers seemed to be "loving to live forever." Because the Shakers had no children of their own, they had to rely on converts and the adoption of young orphans to replenish their numbers. As these sources dried up in the 1840s and 1850s, the communities stopped growing and eventually began to decline (see Voices from Abroad, "Charles Dickens Assails the Shakers," p. 348). By the end of the nineteenth century most Shaker communities had virtually disappeared, leaving as their material legacy a distinctive and much-imitated furniture style.

The Fourierist Phalanxes

The rise of the American Fourierist movement in the 1840s was one cause of the Shakers' decline. Charles Fourier (1777–1837) was a French utopian reformer who devised an eight-stage theory of social evolution, predicting the imminent decline of individualism and capitalism. As interpreted by his idealistic American disciple Arthur Brisbane, Fourierism would complete "our great political movement of 1776" through new social institutions that would end the "menial and slavish system of Hired Labor or Labor for Wages." In the place of capitalist waged labor there would be cooperative work in communities called **phalanxes**. The members of a phalanx would be its shareholders; they would own all its property in common, including stores and a bank as well as a school and a library.

Fourier and Brisbane saw the phalanx as a practical, more humane alternative to a society based on private property and capitalist values, and one that would liberate women as well as men. "In society as it is now constituted," Brisbane wrote, "Woman is subjected to unremitting and slavish domestic duties"; in the "new Social Order . . . based upon Associated households" women's domestic labor would be shared with men.

Brisbane skillfully promoted Fourier's ideas in his influential book *The Social Destiny of Man* (1840), a regular column in Horace Greeley's *New York Tribune*, and hundreds of lectures, many of them in towns along the Erie Canal. These ideas found a receptive audience among educated farmers and craftsmen, who yearned for economic stability and communal solidarity in the wake of the Panic of 1837. In the 1840s Brisbane and his followers started nearly one hundred cooperative communities, mostly in western New York and the midwestern states of Ohio, Michigan, and Wisconsin, but almost all were unable to

from the evils of the world into strictly run communities of believers. They embraced the common ownership of property, accepted strict government by the church, and pledged to abstain from alcohol, tobacco, politics, and war. Shakers also eliminated marriage and made a commitment to celibacy, in accordance with Mother Ann's testimony against "the lustful gratifications of the flesh as the source and foundation of human corruption."

The Shakers believed that God was "a dual person, male and female," and that Mother Ann represented God's female element. These doctrines provided the underpinning for their attempt to eliminate distinctions between the sexes. Community governance was the dual responsibility of women and men, the Eldresses and Elders, but in other respects Shakers maintained a traditional division of labor between men and women.

Beginning in 1787 Shakers founded twenty communities, mostly in New England, New York, and Ohio. Their

Charles Dickens Assails the Shakers

The English novelist Charles Dickens enjoyed a meteoric rise to fame and by 1837, at the age of twenty-five, was a major literary figure in his home country. Five years later he ventured to the United States intending, like Alexis de Tocqueville, to investigate the prison system. Unlike his French predecessor, Dickens showed little sympathy for Americans and their institutions. In this excerpt from his American Notes, *the English novelist recounts his visit to the Shaker community in New Lebanon, New York, and assails the sect's way of life, which he views as grim and repressive.*

As we rode along, we passed a party of Shakers, who were at work upon the road; who wore the broadest of all broad brimmed hats; and were in all visible respects such very wooden men, that I felt about as much sympathy for them, and as much interest in them, as if they had been so many figure-heads of ships. Presently we came to the beginning of the village, and . . . requested permission to see the Shaker worship.

Pending the conveyance of this request to some person in authority, we walked into a grim room, where several grim hats were hanging on grim pegs, and the time was grimly told by a grim clock which uttered every tick with a kind of struggle, as if it broke the grim silence reluctantly, and under protest. Ranged against the wall were six or eight stiff high-backed chairs. . . .

Presently, there stalked into this apartment, a grim old Shaker, with eyes as hard, and dull, and cold, as the great round metal buttons on his coat and waistcoat; a sort of calm goblin. Being informed of our desire, he [informed us] . . . that in consequence of certain unseemly interruptions which their worship had received from strangers, their chapel was closed to the public for the space of one year. . . .

All the possessions and revenues of the [Shaker] settlement are thrown into a common stock, which is managed by the elders. As they have made converts among people who were well to do in the world, and are frugal and thrifty, it is understood that this fund prospers. . . .

They eat and drink together, after the Spartan model, at a great public table. There is no union of the sexes, and every Shaker, male and female, is devoted to a life of celibacy. . . .

This is well enough, but nevertheless I cannot, I confess, incline towards the Shakers; view them with much favour, or extend towards them any very lenient construction. I so abhor, and from my soul detest that bad spirit, no matter by what class or sect it may be entertained, which would strip life of its healthful graces, rob youth of its innocent pleasures, pluck from maturity and age their pleasant ornaments, and make existence but a narrow path towards the grave: that odious spirit which, if it could have had full scope and sway upon the earth, must have blasted and made barren the imaginations of the greatest men, and left them . . . no better than the beasts: that, in these very broad brimmed hats and very sombre coats, in [their] stiff-necked solemn visaged piety . . . I recognise the worst among the enemies of Heaven and Earth, who turn the water at the marriage-feasts of this poor world, not into wine, but gall. . . .

Source: Charles Dickens, *American Notes* (New York: Harper & Brothers, 1842), 71–72.

---

support themselves and quickly collapsed. Despite its failure to establish viable communities, the Fourierist movement underscored both the extent of the social dislocation caused by the economic depression and the difficulty of establishing a utopian community in the absence of charismatic leaders or a compelling religious vision.

John Humphrey Noyes and the Oneida Community

The radical minister John Humphrey Noyes (1811–1886) was both charismatic and deeply religious. He believed that the Fourierists had failed because their communities lacked the strong religious ethic required for sustained altruism and cooperation and pointed to the success of the Shakers, praising them as the true "pioneers of modern Socialism." Noyes was also attracted by the Shakers' marriageless society and set about creating a community that defined sexuality and gender roles in radically new ways.

Noyes was a well-to-do graduate of Dartmouth College in New Hampshire who was inspired to join the ministry by the preaching of Charles Finney. When Noyes was expelled from his Congregational church for holding unorthodox beliefs, he became a leader of **perfectionism**. Perfectionism was an evangelical movement that attracted thousands of followers during the 1830s, primarily among religiously minded New Englanders who had settled in New York. Perfectionists believed that the Second Coming of Christ had already occurred and that people could therefore aspire to perfection in their earthly lives, attaining complete freedom from sin. Unlike most perfectionists (who lived conventional personal lives), Noyes believed that the major barrier to achieving this ideal state was marriage, which did not exist in heaven and should not exist on earth. "Exclusiveness, jealousy, quarreling have no place at the marriage supper of the Lamb," Noyes wrote. Like the Shakers, Noyes wanted to liberate individuals from sin by reforming relations between men and women. However, his solution was dramatically different: instead of Shaker celibacy, Noyes and his followers embraced **complex marriage**—all the members of his community were married to one another.

Complex marriage was a complex doctrine designed to attain various social goals. Noyes rejected monogamy partly because he wished to free women from being regarded as the property of their husbands, as they were by custom and by common law. To give women even more freedom, he sought to limit childbirth by urging men to have intercourse without orgasm. For those children they did have, Noyes set up communal nurseries. By freeing women from endless childbearing and childraising, Noyes gave them the time and energy to become full and equal members of the community. To symbolize their equality with men the women cut their hair short and wore pantaloons under their calf-length skirts.

In the 1830s Noyes established a community in his hometown of Putney, Vermont. In 1848, as local opposition to the practice of complex marriage grew increasingly intense, Noyes moved his followers to an isolated settlement in Oneida, New York. By the mid-1850s more than two hundred people were living at Oneida, and it became financially self-sufficient when the inventor of a highly successful steel animal trap joined the community. With the profits from the production of traps Oneida diversified into making silverware. After Noyes fled to Canada in 1879 to avoid prosecution for adultery, the community abandoned complex marriage and founded a joint-stock silver manufacturing company, the Oneida Community, Ltd., which survived as an independent business well into the twentieth century.

As with the Shakers and Fourierists, the historical significance of Noyes and his followers does not lie in their numbers, which were small, or in their fine crafts. Rather, these alternative communities were important because, in an even more radical way than Emerson, they questioned traditional customs and repudiated the class divisions and sexual norms of the emergent capitalist society. They stood as countercultural blueprints for a more egalitarian social order.

The Mormon Experience

The Shakers and the Oneidians challenged marriage and family life—two of the most deeply rooted institutions in American society—but their small communities aroused little hostility. The Mormons, or the Church of Jesus Christ of Latter-day Saints, provoked much more animosity because of their equally controversial doctrines and their success in attracting thousands of members.

Joseph Smith.   Like many social movements of the era, Mormonism emerged from the religious ferment

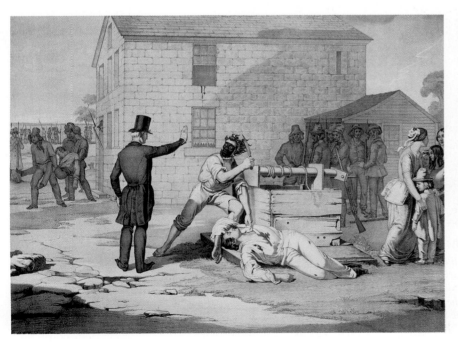

Mob Violence against Mormons
In this lithograph, Martyrdom of Joseph and Hiram Smith in Carthage Jail, June 27, 1844, *the artist G. N. Fasel after C. G. Crehen evokes sympathy for the fallen Mormon leader by depicting an assailant as a masked ruffian, prevented from mutilating the corpse only by the intervention of a gentleman. In fact, many leading Illinois politicians and businessmen feared Smith and welcomed the mob's action. The murders prompted Brigham Young, the leader of a large group of Mormons, to move his followers into territory claimed by Mexico, where they hoped to escape religious persecution.*
Library of Congress.

among families of Puritan descent who lived along the Erie Canal. The founder of the Mormon Church was Joseph Smith (1805–1844), a vigorous, powerful individual. Born in Vermont, he moved at the age of ten with his very religious but rather poor farming and shopkeeping family to Palmyra in central New York. In a series of religious experiences that began in 1820, Smith came to believe that God had singled him out to receive a special revelation of divine truth. In 1830 he published *The Book of Mormon*, claiming he had translated it from ancient hieroglyphics on gold plates shown to him by an angel named Moroni. *The Book of Mormon* told the story of ancient civilizations from the Middle East that had migrated to the Western Hemisphere and of the visit of Jesus Christ, soon after the Resurrection, to one of them.

Smith proceeded to organize the Church of Jesus Christ of Latter-day Saints. Seeing himself as a prophet to a sinful, excessively individualistic society, Smith affirmed traditional patriarchal authority within the family and Church control over many aspects of life. Like many Protestant ministers, he encouraged his followers to work hard, save their earnings, and become entrepreneurs—practices central to success in the age of capitalist markets and factories. Unlike other ministers, Smith placed equal emphasis on a communal framework that would protect the Mormon "New Jerusalem" from individualism and outside threats. His goal was a Church-directed society that would inspire moral perfection.

Smith struggled for years to establish a secure home for his new religion. Facing persecution from anti-Mormons, Smith and his growing congregation trekked west, eventually settling in Nauvoo, Illinois, a town they founded on the Mississippi River (Map 12.2). By the early 1840s Nauvoo had become the largest utopian community in the United States, with 30,000 inhabitants. The rigid discipline and secret rituals of the Mormons, along with their prosperity, hostility to other

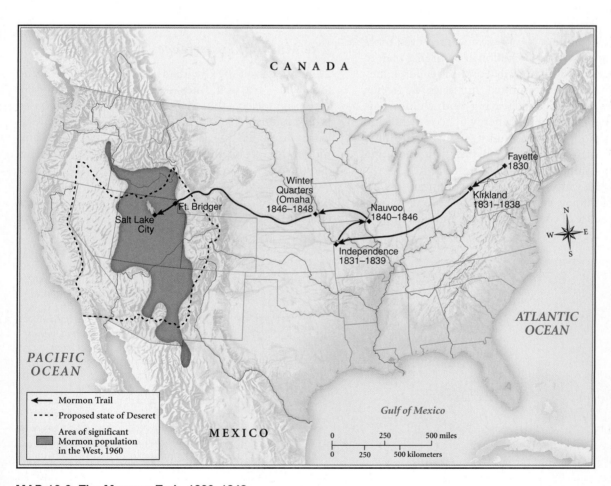

MAP 12.2 The Mormon Trek, 1830–1848

Because of their unorthodox religious views and communal solidarity, Mormons faced hostility first in New York and then in Missouri and Illinois. Following the murder of Joseph Smith, Brigham Young led the polygamist faction of Mormons into lands thinly populated by Native American peoples. From Omaha, the migrants followed the path of the Oregon Trail to Fort Bridger and then struck off to the Southwest, settling in Mexican territory along the Wasatch Mountains in the basin of the Great Salt Lake in present-day Utah.

An Illinois "Jeffersonian" Attacks the Mormons

The corporate solidarity of the Mormon community enraged many Illinois residents, who feared both the political power wielded by the Mormons' large and nearly independent city-state at Nauvoo and the military might of the two-thousand-strong "Legion" commanded by Joseph Smith. In 1844 a mob led by "respectable citizens" assassinated Smith and his brother, and some Illinois residents—such as the author of this letter to the Warsaw Signal, *a newspaper in a town near Nauvoo—called for the forcible expulsion of the Mormons from the state.*

Mr. Editor,

. . . It is a low pitiable contemptable kind of electioneering, that old Tom Jefferson would have been ashamed of—when a body of men acting under the garb of religion (as the Mormons themselves say they are) shall decide our elections and act together as a body politically, we might as well bid a final farewell to our liberties and the common rights of man.

Now Sir, under all these circumstances, it is high time that every individual should come out and clearly define the position that he occupies. I too am an Anti-Mormon both in principle and in practice. . . . Mr. Editor when I speak harshly of the Mormons, I wish it to be perfectly understood I do not mean every individual that advocates the Mormon cause. By no means; that

there are some good, law-abiding peaceable citizens belonging to the Mormon profession I verily believe . . . but I am opposed to them because of the unprincipled manner in which the leaders of that fanatical sect, set at defiance the laws of the land . . . (as was the case in Missouri) claiming to be the chosen people of God; not subject to the laws of the state in any respect whatever, and receiving revelations direct from Heaven almost daily commanding them to take the property of the older citizens of the county and confiscate it to the use of the Mormon church. . . .

It was for the commission of such deeds together with deeds ten fold more dark and damning in their nature that finally led to their expulsion from that state, and one of the brightest pages in the history of Missouri is that, on which is written "Governor Boggs's exterminating order" directing that the lawless rabble should be driven beyond the limits of the state, or exterminated at their own option. They chose the former, [which was] a most unfortunate thing for the state of Illinois.

Strange to tell, yet such is the fact, they have commenced nearly the same operation here that they did in Missouri . . . they have attempted to subsidize the press, thereby attempting to corrupt the very fountains of public virtue,—they have went [*sic*] into the legislative halls and attempted to bribe the representatives of the people in their seats and made them their tools.

They have in short, by a long series of high handed outrages . . . forfeited all claims (if any they ever had) to confidence and respect, and ought justly to receive the condemnation of every individual, not only in this community, but in this nation.

Source: David Brion Davis, *Antebellum America: An Interpretive Anthology* (University Park: Pennsylvania State University Press, 1997), 226–27.

---

sects, and bloc voting in Illinois elections, fueled resentment among their neighbors. This resentment turned to overt hostility when Smith refused to abide by any Illinois law that he did not approve of, asked Congress to turn Nauvoo into a separate federal territory, and in 1844 declared himself a candidate for president of the United States (see American Voices, "An Illinois 'Jeffersonian' Attacks the Mormons," above).

Moreover, Smith had received a new revelation that justified **polygamy**—the practice of a man having more than one wife at one time. A few leading Mormon men began to practice polygamy, dividing the community,

while Christian outrage encouraged assaults from outside the Mormon Church. In 1844 Illinois officials arrested Smith and charged him with treason for allegedly conspiring with foreign powers to create a Mormon colony in Mexican territory. An anti-Mormon mob stormed the jail in Carthage, Illinois, where Smith and his brother were being held and murdered them.

Brigham Young and Utah. Now led by Brigham Young, a large contingent of Mormons sought religious freedom by leaving the United States. In 1846 Young led a phased migration of more than 10,000 people across the Great Plains into Mexican territory. Eventually the settlers reached their destination, the Great Salt Lake Valley in present-day Utah. Using communal labor and an elaborate irrigation system based on communal water rights, the Mormon pioneers transformed the region. They quickly spread planned agricultural communities along the base of the Wasatch Range.

Most Mormons who did not support polygamy remained in the United States rather than travel to Utah. Led by Smith's son Joseph Smith III, they formed the Reorganized Church of Jesus Christ of Latter-day Saints and settled throughout the Midwest.

When the United States acquired Mexico's northern territories in 1848 (see Chapter 13), the Mormons petitioned Congress to create a vast new state, Deseret, stretching from present-day Utah to the Pacific coast. Instead, Congress tried to confine Mormon influence, setting up the much smaller Utah Territory in 1850 and naming Brigham Young as territorial governor. In 1858 President James Buchanan removed Young from the governorship and, responding to pressure from Protestant Christian churches to eliminate polygamy, sent a small army to Salt Lake City. However, the "Mormon War" proved bloodless. Fearing that the forced abolition of the "domestic institution" of polygamy would serve as a precedent for the ending of slavery, Buchanan pursued a pro-southern policy and withdrew the troops. The national government did not succeed in pressuring the Utah Mormons to make polygamy illegal until 1890, six years before Utah became a state.

Mormons had succeeded where other social experiments and utopian communities had failed. By endorsing the private ownership of property and encouraging individualistic economic enterprise, they became prosperous contributors to the new market society. However, Mormon leaders resolutely used strict religious controls to create disciplined communities and patriarchal families, reaffirming traditional values inherited from the eighteenth century. This blend of economic innovation, social conservatism, and hierarchical leadership created a wealthy church with a strong missionary impulse.

Abolitionism

In most cities and farm villages, the communalists attracted far less attention than the abolitionists, whose demand for the immediate end to racial slavery led to fierce political debates, riots, and sectional conflict. Like other reform movements, abolitionism drew on the religious energy and ideas generated by the Second Great Awakening, which altered the attitude of many northern and midwestern whites toward the South's "peculiar institution." Early-nineteenth-century reformers had criticized human bondage as contrary to the tenets of republicanism and liberty. Now abolitionists condemned slavery as a sin and saw it as their moral duty to end this violation of God's law.

Slave Rebellion

During the first decades of the nineteenth century, African American leaders in the North had encouraged free blacks to "elevate" themselves. They hoped that a majority of free blacks, by securing "respectability"—through education, temperance, moral discipline, and hard work—could rise to a position of equality with the white citizenry. To promote that goal, black leaders such as James Forten, a Philadelphia sail maker; Prince Hall, a Boston barber; and ministers Hosea Easton and James Allen founded an array of churches, schools, and self-help associations. Testifying to the success of these efforts, in 1827 John Russwurm and Samuel D. Cornish published the first African American newspaper, *Freedom's Journal*, in New York.

However, the black quest for respectability threatened many whites, who organized antiblack mobs in Boston, Pittsburgh, and other northern cities during the 1820s. White mobs in Cincinnati were so violent and destructive that they prompted several hundred African Americans to flee to Canada.

Partly in response to these attacks, in 1829 David Walker published a stirring pamphlet entitled *An Appeal . . . to the Colored Citizens of the World*. Walker was a free black from North Carolina who had moved to Boston, where he sold secondhand clothes and served as the agent for *Freedom's Journal*. A self-educated man, Walker studied the speeches of Thomas Jefferson and other slave owners and devoured volumes of history, seeking to place racial slavery within a coherent historical context. His pamphlet ridiculed the religious pretensions of slaveholders, justified slave rebellion, and in biblical language warned white Americans that the slaves would revolt if justice was delayed. "We must and shall be free," he told white Americans. "And woe, woe, will be it to you if we have to obtain our freedom by fighting. . . . Your DESTRUCTION is at hand, and will be speedily consummated unless you REPENT." Within a year Walker's *Appeal* had gone through three printings and, carried by black merchant seamen, had begun to reach free African Americans in the South.

In 1830 Walker and other African American activists called a national convention in Philadelphia. The delegates did not adopt Walker's radical call for revolt but made collective equality for all blacks—enslaved as well as free—their fundamental demand. Stressing "race-equality" rather than individual uplift and respectability, a new generation of African American leaders such as Martin Delaney urged free blacks to use every legal means to improve the condition of their race and asked for divine assistance in breaking "the shackles of slavery."

As Walker was predicting violent black rebellion from Boston, Nat Turner, a slave in Southampton County, Virginia, staged a bloody revolt—a coincidence

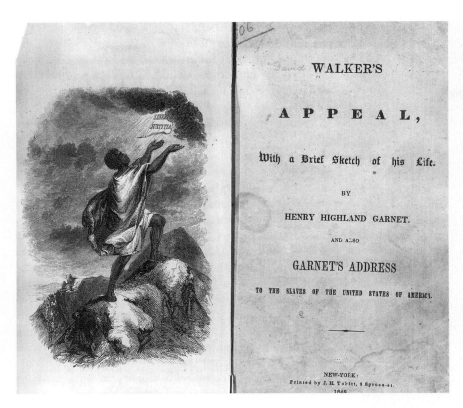

A Call for Revolution

David Walker (1785–1830), who ran a used-clothing shop in Boston, Massachusetts, spent his own savings to issue An Appeal . . . to the Colored Citizens of the World, *a learned and passionate attack against racial slavery. In the* Appeal, *published in 1829, Walker depicts Christ as an avenging "God of justice and of armies" and raises the banner of slave rebellion. A year later he was found in his shop, dead from unknown causes.* Library of Congress.

that had far-reaching consequences. As a child Turner had taught himself to read and had hoped to be emancipated, but a new master forced him into field work and another master separated him from his wife. Turner became deeply spiritual and had considerable success as a preacher. Then, in a religious vision, "the Spirit" told him that "Christ had laid down the yoke he had borne for the sins of men, and that I should take it on and fight against the Serpent, for the time was fast approaching when the first should be last and the last should be first." Taking an eclipse of the sun as an omen, Turner and a handful of relatives and close friends plotted to meet the masters' terror with a terror of their own. In August 1831 Turner and his followers rose in rebellion and killed almost sixty whites, in many cases dismembering and decapitating them. Turner hoped that a vast army of slaves would rally to his cause, but he had mustered only sixty men by the time a white militia dispersed his poorly armed and exhausted force. Vengeful whites now took slaves' lives at random. One company of cavalry killed forty blacks in two days, putting the heads of fifteen on poles to warn "all those who should undertake a similar plot." Fifty slaves were prosecuted, and twenty were hanged. After hiding for nearly two months Turner was captured and hanged, still identifying his mission with that of the Savior. "Was not Christ crucified?" he asked.

Deeply shaken by Turner's Rebellion, the Virginia legislature debated a bill providing for gradual emancipation and colonization. When the bill was rejected in 1832 by a vote of 73 to 58, the possibility that southern planters would legislate an end to slavery faded forever. Instead, the southern states marched down another path, toughening their slave codes, limiting the movement of slaves, and prohibiting anyone from teaching them to read. They would meet Walker's radical *Appeal* with radical measures of their own.

Garrison and Evangelical Abolitionism

The prospect of a bloody racial revolution mobilized a dedicated cadre of northern and midwestern whites who belonged to evangelical churches. Inspired by the antislavery efforts of free blacks, they launched a moral crusade to abolish slavery. Previously many Quakers—and some pious Methodists and Baptists—had freed their own slaves and campaigned for the gradual emancipation of all blacks. Now radical Christian abolitionists demanded that southerners free their slaves immediately. The evangelical abolitionists believed the issue was absolute: if the slave owners did not repent and allow slaves their God-given status as free moral agents, they faced the prospect of revolution in this world and damnation in the next. "The conviction that SLAVERY IS A SIN is the Gibraltar of our cause," declared abolitionist Wendell Phillips.

William Lloyd Garrison, Theodore Weld, and Angelina and Sarah Grimké.   The most uncompromising leader of the abolitionist movement was William Lloyd Garrison (1805–1879). A Massachusetts-born printer, Garrison had

William Lloyd Garrison, c. 1835

As this portrait suggests, William Lloyd Garrison was an intense and righteous man. In 1831, his hatred of slavery prompted Garrison to demand its immediate end, thereby beginning the abolitionist movement. His attack on slavery led him eventually on a passionate quest to destroy all institutions and cultural practices that prevented individuals—whites as well as blacks, women as well as men—from discovering their full potential. Garrison demanded civic equality for women and, believing it upheld slavery, publicly burned the U.S. Constitution, declaring: "So perish all compromises with tyranny."

worked in Baltimore during the 1820s with a Quaker, Benjamin Lundy, the publisher of the *Genius of Universal Emancipation*, the leading antislavery newspaper of the decade. In 1830 Garrison went to jail, convicted of writing and publishing an article that libeled a New England merchant engaged in the domestic slave trade; after seven weeks he was released when a wealthy moral reformer paid his fine. In 1831 Garrison moved to Boston and founded his own antislavery weekly, *The Liberator*, which attracted many free-black subscribers. The next year he spearheaded the formation of the New England Anti-Slavery Society.

From the outset *The Liberator* took a radical stance, demanding the immediate abolition of slavery without reimbursement to slaveholders. In pursuing this goal, Garrison declared, "I *will be* as harsh as truth, and as uncompromising as justice . . . I will not retreat a single

inch—AND I WILL BE HEARD." He lived up to his word, condemning the American Colonization Society and charging that its real aim was to strengthen slavery by removing troublesome African Americans who were already free. He assailed the U.S. Constitution for its implicit acceptance of racial bondage, labeling it "a covenant with death, an agreement with Hell." As time went on, Garrison concluded that slavery was a sign of deep corruption infesting all American institutions and called for comprehensive reform of society. He demanded not only the equality of women but also the repudiation of all governments because their rule, like that of slave owners, rested ultimately on force.

Theodore Dwight Weld, who joined Garrison as a leading abolitionist, came to the movement from the religious revivals of the 1830s. The son of a Congregationalist minister and inspired by Charles Finney, Weld became an advocate of temperance and educational reform. Turning to abolitionism, he worked in northern Presbyterian and Congregational churches, preaching the moral responsibility of all Americans for the denial of liberty to slaves. In 1834 Weld inspired a group of students at Lane Theological Seminary in Cincinnati to form an antislavery society. Weld's crusade gathered force, buttressed by the theological arguments he advanced in *The Bible against Slavery* (1837). Collaborating closely with Weld were Angelina Grimké, whom he married in 1838, and her sister, Sarah. The Grimkés had left their father's South Carolina slave plantation and converted to Quakerism and taken up the cause of abolitionism in Philadelphia.

Weld and the Grimkés provided the abolitionist movement with a mass of evidence in *American Slavery as It Is: Testimony of a Thousand Witnesses* (1839). The book set out to answer a simple question—"What is the actual condition of the slaves in the United States?"—with evidence from southern newspapers and firsthand testimonies. In one account Angelina Grimké told of a treadmill that slave owners used for punishment: "One poor girl, [who was] sent there to be flogged, and who was accordingly stripped naked and whipped, showed me the deep gashes on her back—I might have laid my whole finger in them—large pieces of flesh had actually been cut out by the torturing lash." The book sold over 100,000 copies in its first year alone.

The American Anti-Slavery Society. In 1833 Weld and Garrison met in Philadelphia with sixty delegates, black and white, from local abolitionist groups and established the American Anti-Slavery Society. The society received financial support from Arthur and Lewis Tappan, wealthy silk merchants in New York City. Women abolitionists quickly established separate organizations, such as the Philadelphia Female Anti-Slavery Society, founded by Lucretia Mott in 1833, and the Anti-Slavery Conventions of American Women,

No. 4

THE PARTING "Buy us too."

Antislavery Card

"Buy us too," cries the enslaved mother with her child, as a trader leads her husband away in chains. This card was one of a series of twelve issued in 1863 by H. T. Helmbold, a drug and chemical company, to promote its products (such as "Helmbold's Rose Wash") while also mobilizing support among its customers for abolition. Scenes showing the breakup of African American families were among the most effective antislavery images, because the spread of sentimentalism had enhanced the importance of family ties for many middle-class northerners.
Library of Congress.

formed by a network of local societies in the late 1830s. The women's societies raised money for *The Liberator* and were a major force in the movement, especially in the farm villages and rural areas of the Midwest, distributing abolitionist literature and collecting tens of thousands of signatures on antislavery petitions.

Abolitionist leaders developed a three-pronged plan of attack, beginning with an appeal to public opinion. To foster intense public condemnation of slavery they adopted the tactics of the religious revivalists: large rallies led by stirring speakers, constant agitation by local antislavery chapters, and home visits by agents of the movement. The abolitionists also used the latest techniques of mass communication. Assisted by new steam-powered printing presses, the American Anti-Slavery Society distributed more than 100,000 pieces of literature in 1834. In 1835 the society launched its "great postal campaign," which flooded the nation, including the South, with a million abolitionist pamphlets. In July 1835 alone abolitionists mailed more than 175,000 items at the New York City post office.

The abolitionists' second strategy was to assist the African Americans who fled from slavery. Those blacks who lived near a free state had the greatest chance of success, but fugitives from plantations deeper in the South received aid from the "underground railroad," an informal network of whites and free blacks in Richmond, Charleston, and other southern cities (Map 12.3). In Baltimore a free African American sailor lent his identification papers to the future abolitionist Frederick Douglass, who used them to escape to New York. Many escaped slaves, such as Harriet Tubman, returned repeatedly to the South, risking reenslavement or death to help others escape. As Tubman wrote, "I should fight for . . . liberty as long as my strength lasted, and when the time came for me to go, the Lord would let them take me." Thanks to the "railroad," by the 1840s about a thousand African Americans reached freedom in the North each year.

There they faced an uncertain future. Whites in the northern and midwestern states did not support civic equality for free blacks. Five New England states extended suffrage to African American men, but six northern and midwestern states changed their constitutions to deny the franchise to free blacks. Moreover, the Fugitive Slave Law (1793) allowed masters and hired slave catchers to capture suspected fugitives and carry them back to bondage. To thwart these efforts, white abolitionists in northern cities joined with crowds of free blacks to seize recaptured slaves and drive slave catchers out of town.

The third element of the abolitionists' program was to seek support among state and national legislators. In 1835 the American Anti-Slavery Society encouraged local chapters and members to bombard Congress with petitions demanding the abolition of slavery in the District of Columbia, an end to the domestic slave trade, and a ban on the admission of new slave states. By 1838 petitions with nearly 500,000 signatures had arrived in Washington.

This agitation drew thousands of deeply religious people to abolitionism—farmers, wage earners, and small proprietors, many of whom lived in rural villages and small towns. During the 1830s the number of local abolitionist societies grew swiftly, from about two hundred in 1835 to more than five hundred in 1836 and nearly two thousand by 1840—when they had nearly 200,000 members, including many leading transcendentalists. Emerson condemned American society for tolerating slavery;

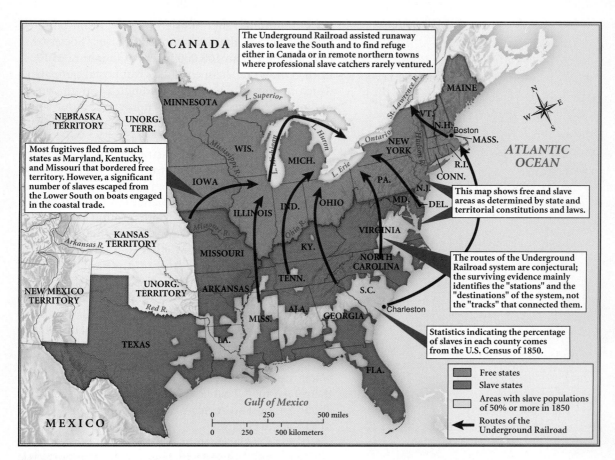

The Underground Railroad assisted runaway slaves to leave the South and to find refuge either in Canada or in remote northern towns where professional slave catchers rarely ventured.

Most fugitives fled from such states as Maryland, Kentucky, and Missouri that bordered free territory. However, a significant number of slaves escaped from the Lower South on boats engaged in the coastal trade.

This map shows free and slave areas as determined by state and territorial constitutions and laws.

The routes of the Underground Railroad system are conjectural; the surviving evidence mainly identifies the "stations" and the "destinations" of the system, not the "tracks" that connected them.

Statistics indicating the percentage of slaves in each county comes from the U.S. Census of 1850.

Free states
Slave states
Areas with slave populations of 50% or more in 1850
Routes of the Underground Railroad

MAP 12.3 The Underground Railroad in the 1850s

Before 1840, most blacks who fled slavery did so on their own or with the aid of their family and friends. Thereafter, they could count on support from members of the underground railroad, a loose network of black and white antislavery activists. Provided with food, directions, and guides by free blacks in the South, fugitive slaves crossed into free states, where they received protection and shelter from sympathetic whites and blacks, who arranged for their transportation to Canada or to "safe" American cities and towns.

Thoreau was even more assertive. Seeing the Mexican War (see Chapter 13) as an attempt to extend slavery, in 1846 he refused to pay his taxes and submitted to arrest. Two years later he published an anonymous essay entitled "Civil Disobedience," which outlined how individuals, by resisting governments because of loyalty to a higher moral law, could redeem themselves and the state. "A minority is powerless while it conforms to the majority," Thoreau declared, but it becomes "irresistible when it clogs by its whole weight."

Opposition and Internal Conflict

As Thoreau recognized, despite the thousands drawn to its cause, the abolitionist crusade had won the wholehearted allegiance of only a small minority of white Americans. Perhaps 10 percent of northerners and midwesterners strongly supported the movement; another 20 percent were sympathetic to its goals. Its opponents were

much more numerous and no less aggressive. Men of wealth feared that the abolitionist attack on slave property might become a general assault on all property rights; tradition-minded clergymen condemned the public roles assumed by abolitionist women; and northern merchants and textile manufacturers rallied to the support of the southern planters who supplied them with cotton. Northern wage earners feared that freed slaves would work for subsistence wages and take their jobs. Finally, whites almost universally opposed the prospect of "amalgamation"—racial mixing and intermarriage—that Garrison seemed to support by encouraging joint meetings of black and white abolitionists of both sexes.

Attacks on Abolitionism. Moved by such sentiments, northern opponents of abolitionism turned to violence, often led or instigated by "gentlemen of property and standing." In 1833 an antiabolitionist mob of fifteen hundred New Yorkers stormed a church in search of

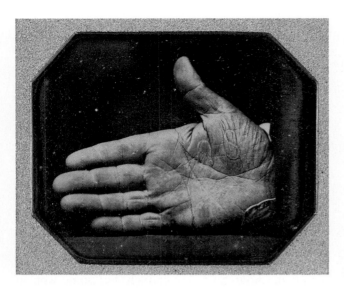

Retribution, Southern Style

Jonathan Walker, a Massachusetts shipwright, paid a high price for his abolitionist activities by being branded, as this daguerreotype shows. Captured off the coast of Florida in 1844 while trying to smuggle seven slaves to freedom in the Bahama islands, Walker had the initials "SS" (for "slave stealer") burned into his hand. Massachusetts Historical Society.

Garrison and Arthur Tappan, and in 1834 a group of laborers vandalized and set fire to Lewis Tappan's house. Another white mob swept through Philadelphia's African American neighborhoods, clubbing and stoning residents, destroying homes and churches, and forcing crowds of black women and children to flee the city. In 1835 in Utica, New York, a group of lawyers, local politicians, merchants, and bankers broke up an abolitionist convention and beat several delegates. Two years later in Alton, Illinois, a mob shot and killed an abolitionist editor, Elijah P. Lovejoy. By pressing the issues of emancipation and equality, the abolitionists had exposed the extent of racial prejudice and the near-impossibility of creating in the North a biracial middle class of "respectable" whites and blacks. Indeed, their initiative had heightened race consciousness, encouraging whites—and blacks—to identify across class lines with those of their own race.

Racial solidarity was particularly strong in the South, where whites reacted to abolitionism with fury. Southern legislatures banned the movement and passed resolutions demanding that northern states follow suit. The Georgia legislature offered a $5,000 reward to anyone who would kidnap Garrison and bring him south to be tried for inciting rebellion. In Nashville vigilantes whipped a northern college student for distributing abolitionist pamphlets, and a mob in Charleston attacked the post office and destroyed sacks of abolitionist mail. After 1835 southern postmasters simply refused to deliver mail suspected to be of abolitionist origin.

Politicians joined the fray. President Andrew Jackson, though a radical on many issues, was a longtime

slave owner and a firm supporter of the southern social order. Jackson privately approved of South Carolina's removal of abolitionist pamphlets from the U.S. mail, and in 1835 he asked Congress to restrict the use of the mails by abolitionist groups. Congress did not comply, but in 1836 the House of Representatives adopted the so-called **gag rule**. Under this informal rule, which remained in force until 1844, antislavery petitions were automatically tabled when they were received so that they could not become the subjects of debate in the House.

Internal Divisions.   Assailed by racists from the outside, abolitionists were also divided among themselves. Many antislavery clergymen denounced the public lecturing to mixed audiences by the Grimké sisters and other abolitionist women as "promiscuous" and immoral. Other supporters abandoned the Anti-Slavery Society because of Garrison's advocacy of further social reforms.

Indeed, Garrison had broadened his agenda and now supported pacifism and the abolition of prisons and asylums. Arguing that "our object is universal emancipation, to redeem women as well as men from a servile to an equal condition," he demanded that the American Anti-Slavery Society adopt a broad statement of policy that included support for women's rights. At the convention of the American Anti-Slavery Society in 1840 Garrison precipitated a split with more conservative abolitionists by insisting on equal participation by women and helping to elect Abby Kelley to the organization's business committee. When the movement split, Kelley and fellow women's rights activists Lucretia Mott and Elizabeth Cady Stanton remained with Garrison in the American Anti-Slavery Society. They recruited new women agents, including Lucy Stone, to proclaim the common interests of enslaved blacks and free women.

Garrison's opponents founded a new organization, the American and Foreign Anti-Slavery Society, which received financial backing from Lewis Tappan and focused its energies on ending slavery. Some of its members worked through their churches to win public support while others turned to electoral politics, establishing the Liberty Party and nominating James G. Birney for president in 1840. Birney was a former Alabama slave owner who had been converted to abolitionism by Theodore Weld and had founded an antislavery newspaper in Cincinnati. Birney and the Liberty Party argued that the Constitution did not recognize slavery; that the Fifth Amendment, by barring any congressional deprivation of "life, liberty, or property," prevented the federal government from supporting slavery; and that slaves became automatically free when they entered areas of federal authority, such as the District of Columbia and national territories. However, Birney won few votes in the election of 1840, and the future of the Liberty Party and political abolitionism appeared dim.

Coming hard on the heels of popular violence in the North and governmental suppression in the South, these schisms and electoral failures stunned the abolitionist movement. By melding the energies and ideas of thousands of evangelical Protestants, moral reformers, and transcendentalists, it had raised the banner of antislavery to new heights. Indeed, the very strength of abolitionism had proved its undoing because its radical program had aroused the hostility of a substantial majority of the white population. "When we first unfurled the banner of *The Liberator*," Garrison admitted in 1837, ". . . it did not occur to us that nearly every religious sect, and every political party would side with the oppressor."

The Women's Rights Movement

The prominence of women among the abolitionists was the product of a broad shift in American culture. After the American Revolution women began to play a significant role in public life, joining religious revivals and reform movements such as the temperance crusade. Suddenly issues involving gender—sexual behavior, marriage, family authority—rose to the surface not only among communal groups such as Mormons and Shakers but also among the white citizenry. However, it was the public activities of abolitionist women that created the greatest controversy over gender issues and made some reformers into women's rights activists. They argued that women had rights as individuals and within marriage that were equal to those of men.

Origins of the Women's Movement

"Don't be afraid, not afraid, fight Satan; stand up for Christ; don't be afraid." So spoke Mary Walker Ostram on her deathbed in 1859. Her religious convictions were as firm at the age of fifty-eight as they had been in 1816, when she helped found the first Sabbath School in Utica, New York. Married to a lawyer-politician but childless, Ostram had devoted her life to evangelical Presbyterian religion and the benevolent social reform that it helped spawn. Her minister, the Reverend Philemon Fowler, celebrated her as a "living fountain" of faith, an exemplar of "Women's Sphere of Influence" in the world.

Such a public presence had been won only grudgingly. Even as Reverend Fowler heaped praise on Ostram, he reiterated the precepts of Revolutionary era Patriot leaders that women should limit their political role to that of "republican mothers" who would instruct "their sons in the principles of liberty and government." As Fowler put it, women inhabited a "separate sphere" and had no place in "the markets of trade, the scenes of politics and popular agitation, the courts of justice and the halls of legislation. Home is her peculiar sphere and members of her family her peculiar care."

As Ostram's life suggested, many middle-class women transcended these rigid boundaries, by joining in the Second Great Awakening and becoming guardians of morality. Such spiritual activities bolstered their authority within the household, enabling many wives to enlarge their influence over all areas of family life, including the timing of pregnancies. Publications such as *Godey's Lady's Book* and Catharine Beecher's *Treatise on Domestic Economy* (1841) taught women how to make their homes more efficient and justified a life of middle-class domesticity. To protect their homes and husbands from the evils of alcoholic excess, farm women joined the Independent Order of Good Templars, a temperance organization that granted them full membership and sought to safeguard family life.

For most middle-class women a greater influence within the household was enough, but some women used their newfound religious authority to increase their public activities. Moral reform was among the first of their efforts. In 1834 a group of middle-class women founded the New York Female Moral Reform Society and elected Lydia Finney, the wife of the evangelical minister Charles Finney, as its president. Its goals were to end prostitution, redeem "fallen" women, and protect single women from moral corruption. Eschewing the culturally embedded male double standard, the society advocated a single moral code, demanding chastity for men as well as for women. By 1840 it had grown into a national association, the American Female Moral Reform Society, with 555 chapters and 40,000 members throughout the North and Midwest. Employing only women as its agents, bookkeepers, and staff, the society attempted to provide moral "government" for factory girls, seamstresses, clerks, and servants who lived away from their families. Women reformers even visited brothels, where they sang hymns, offered prayers, searched for runaway girls, and noted the names of clients. They also founded homes of refuge for prostitutes and homeless women and won the passage of laws regulating men's sexual behavior—including making seduction a crime—in Massachusetts in 1846 and New York in 1848.

Women also turned their energies to the reform of social institutions, working to improve conditions in almshouses, asylums, hospitals, and jails, all of which grew in number in the 1830s and 1840s. The Massachusetts reformer Dorothea Dix was a leader in these efforts, persuading legislatures in many states to expand state hospitals to accommodate poor people and mentally ill women rather than jail them with criminals (see American Lives, "Dorothea Dix: Public Woman," p. 360). Other female reformers also enlisted the aid of the government in their projects. In New York in 1849 the Female Guardian Society secured the authority to take charge of the children of "dissipated and vicious parents" and to supervise their upbringing and education.

Both as reformers and as teachers, northern women played a major role in education. From Maine to Wisconsin women vigorously supported the movement led by Horace Mann to increase the number of public elementary schools and improve their quality. As secretary of the newly created Massachusetts Board of Education from 1837 to 1848, Mann lengthened the school year; established teaching standards in reading, writing, and arithmetic; and improved instruction by recruiting well-educated women as teachers. The intellectual leader of the new corps of women educators was Catharine Beecher, who founded academies for young women in Hartford and Cincinnati. In a series of publications Beecher argued that "energetic and benevolent women" were the best qualified to impart moral and intellectual instruction to the young. By the 1850s most teachers were women both because school boards heeded Beecher's arguments and because women could be paid less than men.

Abolitionism and Women

The public accomplishments of moral reformers such as Dix and Beecher inspired other women to assume an active role in the movement to end slavery (Map 12.4). During the Revolutionary era, Quaker women in Philadelphia had established schools for freed slaves, and subsequently many Baptist and Methodist women in the Upper South endorsed religious arguments against slavery. When William Lloyd Garrison began his radical campaign for abolition, a number of women rallied to his cause. One of the first Garrisonian abolitionists was Maria W. Stewart, an African American who spoke to mixed audiences of men and women in Boston in the early 1830s. As the abolitionist movement mushroomed, scores of white women delivered lectures condemning slavery and thousands more conducted home "visitations" to win converts.

Influenced by abolitionist ideas and their own experience of discrimination, a few women challenged the subordinate status of their sex. The most famous were Angelina and Sarah Grimké, who had become antislavery lecturers. When some Congregationalist clergymen demanded in 1836 that they cease lecturing on slavery to mixed male and female audiences, Sarah Grimké turned to the Christian Bible for justification: "The Lord Jesus defines the duties of his followers in his Sermon on the Mount . . . without any reference to sex or condition," she wrote. "Men and women are CREATED EQUAL! They

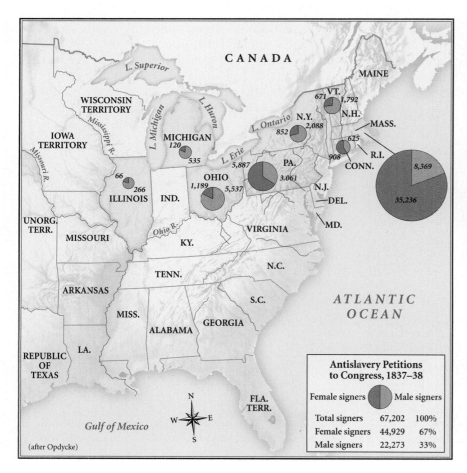

MAP 12.4 Women and Antislavery, 1837–1838

Beginning in the 1830s, abolitionists and antislavery advocates dispatched dozens of petitions to Congress, which, to avoid sectional conflict, refused to discuss them. Women made up two-thirds of the 67,000 people signing the petitions submitted in 1837–1838, suggesting not only their influence in the antislavery movement but also the extent of female organizations and social networks.

For more help analyzing this map, see the ONLINE STUDY GUIDE at **bedfordstmartins.com/henretta**.

Antislavery Petitions to Congress, 1837–38		
Female signers		Male signers
Total signers	67,202	100%
Female signers	44,929	67%
Male signers	22,273	33%

Dorothea Dix: Public Woman

At the time of Dorothea Dix's birth in 1802 women were second-class citizens, excluded by law and custom from voting and from most civic activities. They could not sit on juries, attend secondary school or college, or speak in public about the issues of the day. At her death in 1887 the world had changed significantly. Some women were demanding complete civic equality with men, and many more were already playing active roles in society. Although she never fully endorsed the goals of this social revolution, Dorothea Dix had a lot to do with it—as a teacher, author, moral reformer, and political activist.

"I never knew childhood," Dix once remarked, because she had always been forced to fend for herself. Her paternal grandparents, Elijah and Dorothy Dix, were prominent Bostonians, but her father, Joseph Dix, had dropped out of Harvard and never made much of his life. After marrying an older woman, he moved to Maine to manage his father's land developments. There he suffered one business failure after another, ending up an itinerant (and alcoholic) Methodist minister. For Dorothea and her two brothers, family life meant poverty, frequent moves, and emotional abuse. Dorothea's grandmother came to the rescue, bringing the twelve-year-old girl to Boston. But Grandmother Dix was a rigid and remote person and a poor mentor for a precocious and willful child.

These emotionally scarring early experiences made Dix into a compassionate young woman with a strong sense of moral purpose. At the age of nineteen she set up a school for young children at her grandmother's Boston mansion. Like other "dame" or "marm" schools, it prepared young boys for further education in secondary schools and provided young girls with the only intellectual training most of them would ever get. Drawing again on her grandparents' financial resources, Dorothea opened a "charity school" to "rescue some of America's miserable children from vice," urging them to become responsible adults through individual moral uplift. For the next seventeen years she ran such schools, taking time off only to recover from bouts of physical illness and mental stress.

When she was too weak to teach, Dix would write. In 1824 she published *Conversations on Common Things*, an enormously successful book on natural science and moral improvement that went through sixty editions over the next four decades. By 1832 Dix had published six more books, establishing herself as a public personality. Substantial royalties, along with an inheritance from her grandmother, gave her financial independence.

Dix's literary achievements—and her family background—gave her access to the highest reaches of Boston society. William Ellery Channing, the most prominent Unitarian minister in the nation, invited Dix to teach his children and soon became a close friend. When Dorothea's health and spirits broke again in 1836, she spent eighteen months on the English estate of William Rathbone, a wealthy Unitarian merchant and philanthropist. There she met British reformers who were addressing the maladies of industrial society, and they inspired her to look for similar possibilities in America.

In March 1841 Dix found her cause. Outraged by her discovery that insane women were jailed alongside male criminals, she petitioned the Massachusetts courts for separate facilities for the women. Expanding her goals, Dix spent two years studying the institutions that treated the insane and mentally retarded. She praised reformers for founding new asylums that cared compassionately for mentally ill patients but worried that those institutions served only the families of New England's elite and that poorer patients continued to endure neglect and punishment. In a petition to the Massachusetts legislature in 1843, she presented "the condition of the miserable, the desolate, the outcast" in detail and persuaded the lawmakers to enlarge the state hospital in Worcester to accommodate indigent mental patients.

Exhilarated by this success, Dix began a national movement to establish separate, well-funded state hospitals for the mentally ill. Between 1843 and 1854 she traveled more than thirty thousand miles and visited eighteen state penitentiaries, three hundred county jails and houses of correction, and more than five hundred almshouses in addition to innumerable hospitals. Issuing dozens of reports and memorials, she aroused public support and prompted many states to expand their state hospitals. To secure additional funding, Dix turned to the national legislature, declaring that "the insane poor, through the Providence of God, are wards of the nation." In 1848 she asked Congress to place five million acres of land into a national trust to fund asylums for the mentally ill. If canal and railroad developers could lobby for public lands to subsidize their ventures, "why can I not too, go in with this selfish, struggling throng, and plead for God's poor . . . that they shall not be forgotten?"

Dorothea Dix (1802–1887)

This daguerreotype captures Dix's firm character, which helped her endure emotional abuse as a child and accounted for her great success as a social reformer. Her call for government action to address social problems anticipated twentieth-century reform and social welfare measures. Boston Athenaeum.

At first, Dix's relentless lobbying seemed to work. In 1850 the House of Representatives passed her funding proposal, but the Senate failed to act; the next year her legislation got through the Senate but not the House. On both occasions President Millard Fillmore, a Whig sympathetic to moral reform and Dix's friend, was ready to sign her bill. But when Dix finally persuaded both houses of Congress to pass the measure in 1854, President Franklin Pierce vetoed the bill. A small-government Democrat, Pierce argued that the legislation was unconstitutional because it exceeded the prescribed powers of the national government and encroached on the responsibilities of the states. Amidst the crisis over slavery, Pierce and other pro-southern Democrats feared any measure that might enhance national authority. Although temporarily depressed by this defeat, Dix continued her reform work at the state level and founded an international movement to improve the treatment of the mentally ill.

During the Civil War, Dix accepted a presidential appointment as superintendent of hospital nurses for the entire Union army, making her the highest-ranking woman in the federal government. These responsibilities revealed the limits of Dix's talents and outlook. She was a mediocre administrator, and her old-fashioned expectations about the role and character of "proper" nurses hampered the recruitment of an adequate medical staff. Moreover, Dix quarreled with younger women activists who wanted to press for significant advances in women's rights. Her energy drained and her reputation shattered, Dix returned to private life in 1866. She remained active in reform for another fifteen years and then, as her health deteriorated, retired to the New Jersey state hospital in Trenton, an institution she had helped establish.

Dix's career embodied the temper of her age. During her lifetime, thousands of women became active participants in moral and social reform, and she was in the forefront of that movement, one of the first "public women." If her "proper" views of women's place stamped her as a lady of the early nineteenth century, Dix's political activism placed her far in advance of her time. More politically aware than most women reformers, Dix became a successful legislative lobbyist. Her systematic investigations of social problems were also pathbreaking, making Dix a precursor of the scientific-minded social reformers of the late nineteenth century. Finally, in her campaign for a nationally funded social welfare program, Dorothea Dix was genuinely innovative, anticipating the reform movements of the twentieth century.

are both moral and accountable beings and whatever is right for man to do is right for woman." In a debate with Catharine Beecher (who wanted women to exercise power primarily as wives, mothers, and schoolteachers) Angelina Grimké pushed the argument beyond religion, using Enlightenment principles to claim equal civic rights for women:

> It is a woman's right to have a voice in all the laws and regulations by which she is governed, whether in Church or State. . . . The present arrangements of society, on these points are a violation of human rights, a rank usurpation of power, a violent seizure and confiscation of what is sacredly and inalienably hers.

By 1840 the Grimkés and other female abolitionists were asserting that traditional gender roles amounted to the "domestic slavery" of women. "How can we endure our present marriage relations," asked Elizabeth Cady Stanton, since they give woman "no charter of rights, no individuality of her own?" As another female reformer put it, "the radical difficulty . . . is that women are considered as *belonging* to men" (see American Voices, "Keziah Kendall: A Farm Woman Defends the Grimké Sisters," p. 363).

As abolitionists paid increasing attention to issues of gender during the 1840s and 1850s, they emphasized the special horrors of slavery for women. Apologists for slavery had exalted the sexual purity of white plantation women, contrasting them with stereotypical descriptions of passionately sexual black men and women. Critics pointed out that the reality of plantation life was much more complex and contradictory. Speaking of forced sexual relations with her white owner, the black abolitionist Harriet Jacobs confessed in anguish in her autobiography, *Incidents in the Life of a Slave Girl* (1861), "I cannot tell how much I suffered in the presence of these wrongs." As Jacobs and other former slaves testified, sexual assault by their masters was compounded by cruel treatment at the hands of mistresses enraged by their husbands' promiscuity. In *Uncle Tom's Cabin* (1852), Harriet Beecher Stowe charged that among the greatest moral failings of slavery was its destruction of the slave family and the degradation of slave women. Sojourner Truth, a former slave who lectured to both antislavery and women's rights conventions, hammered home the point that women slaves were denied both basic human rights and the protected separate sphere enjoyed by free women. "I have ploughed and planted and gathered into barns, and no man could head me—and ain't I a woman?" she asked. Drawn into public life by abolitionism, thousands of northern women had become firm advocates of greater rights not only for enslaved African American women but also for themselves.

Sojourner Truth

Few women had as interesting a life as Sojourner Truth. Born as "Isabella" in Dutch-speaking rural New York about 1797, she labored as a slave until 1827. Following a religious vision, Isabella moved to New York City, learned English, and worked for deeply religious—and ultimately fanatical—Christian merchants. In 1843, seeking further spiritual enlightenment, she took the name "Sojourner Truth" and left New York. After briefly joining the Millerites (who believed the world would end in 1844), Truth became famous as a forceful speaker on behalf of abolitionism and women's rights. This illustration, showing Truth addressing an antislavery meeting, suggests her powerful personal presence.

Miriam and Ira D. Wallach Division of Art, Prints and Photographs, the New York Public Library.

The Program of Seneca Falls

The commitment to full civil equality for women emerged during the 1840s as activists devised a pragmatic program of reform. While championing the rights of women, they did not challenge the institution of marriage or even the conventional division of labor within the family. Instead, harking back to the efforts of Abigail Adams and other Revolutionary era women, they tried to strengthen the legal rights of married women, especially with respect to property. This initiative won crucial support from affluent men, who wanted to protect their wives' assets in case their own businesses went into bankruptcy, a constant threat in the volatile economy of mid-nineteenth-century America. By giving property rights to married women, they

Keziah Kendall

A Farm Woman Defends the Grimké Sisters

The Grimké sisters' lecture tour of New England on behalf of abolitionism sparked a huge outcry from orthodox ministers and social conservatives, who questioned the propriety of women taking public roles and speaking to "mixed" audiences of men and women. In a lecture titled "The Legal Rights of Women," Simon Greenleaf, Royall Professor of Law at Harvard College, added his voice to those advocating a restricted role for women. Replying to Greenleaf, Keziah Kendall—possibly the fictional creation of a contemporary women's rights advocate—sent the following letter to her local newspaper.

My name is Keziah Kendall. I live not many miles from Cambridge, on a farm with two sisters, one older, one younger than myself. I am thirty two. Our parents and only brother are dead—we have a good estate—comfortable house—nice barn, garden, orchard &c and money in the bank besides. . . . Under these circumstances the whole responsibility of our property, not less than twenty five thousand dollars rest upon me.

Well—our milkman brought word when he came from market that you were a going to lecture on the legal rights of women, and so I thought I would go and learn. Now I hope you wont think me bold when I say, I did not like that lecture much . . . [because] there was nothing in it but what every body knows. . . .

What I wanted to know, was good reasons for some of those laws that I cant account for. . . . One Lyceum lecture that I heard in C[ambridge] stated that the Americans went to war with the British, because they were taxed without being represented in Parliament. Now we [women] are taxed every year to the full amount of every dollar we possess—town, county, state taxes—taxes for land, for movable [property], for money and all. Now I don't want to [become a legislative] representative . . . any more than I do to be a "constable or a sheriff," but I have no voice about public improvements, and I don't see the justice of being taxed any more than the "revolutionary heroes" did.

Nor do I think we are treated as Christian women ought to be, according to the Bible rule of doing to others as you would others should do unto you. . . . Another thing . . . women have joined the Antislavery societies, and why? Women are kept for slaves as well as men—it is a common cause, deny the justice of it, who can! To be sure I do not wish to go about lecturing like the Misses Grimkie, but I have not the knowledge they have, and I verily believe that if I had been brought up among slaves as they were . . . I should run the venture of your displeasure, and that of a good many others like you.

Source: Dianne Avery and Alfred S. Konefsky, "The Daughters of Job: Property Rights and Women's Lives in Mid-Nineteenth-Century Massachusetts," *Law and History Review* 10 (Fall 1992): 323–56.

also hoped to guard against irresponsible sons-in-law who might waste their daughters' inheritances. Such considerations influenced legislatures in three states—Mississippi, Maine, and Massachusetts—which enacted Married Women's Property Acts between 1839 and 1845. In New York, women activists entered the campaign and won a more comprehensive statute (1848), which gave a woman full legal control over the property she brought to a marriage and became the model for similar laws in fourteen other states.

To advance the nascent women's movement, Elizabeth Cady Stanton and Lucretia Mott, who had become friends at the World Anti-Slavery Convention in London in 1840, organized a gathering in Seneca Falls in central New York in 1848. Seventy women activists and thirty men, mostly from the local area, attended the meeting, which devised a coherent statement of women's equality. Taking the republican ideology of the Declaration of Independence as a starting point, the attendees declared that "all men and women are created equal." "The history of mankind is a history of repeated injuries and usurpations on the part of man toward woman," their Declaration of Sentiments continued, "having in direct object the establishment of an absolute tyranny over her." To persuade Americans to right this long-standing wrong, the activists resolved to "use every instrumentality within our power . . . [to] employ agents, circulate tracts, petition the State and National legislatures, and endeavor to enlist the pulpit and the press on our behalf." By staking out claims for equality for women in public life, the Seneca Falls reformers repudiated the idea that the assignment of separate spheres for men and women was the natural order of society.

Most men dismissed the Seneca Falls Declaration as nonsense, and many women repudiated the activists and their message. Writing in her diary, one small-town mother and housewife lashed out at the female reformer who "aping mannish manners . . . wears absurd and barbarous attire, who talks of her wrongs in harsh tone, who struts and strides, and thinks that she proves herself superior to the rest of her sex."

Nonetheless, the women's rights movement attracted a committed group of female reformers and a few radical men to its ranks. In 1850 the activists convened the first national women's rights convention in Worcester, Massachusetts, and began to hammer out a program. Local and state conventions of women called on churches to revise concepts of female inferiority in their theology. They also proposed legal changes to allow married women to control their property and earnings, guarantee the custody rights of mothers in the event of divorce or the husband's death, and ensure women's rights to sue and testify in court. Finally, and above all else, they began a concerted campaign to win the vote for women. In 1851 the national convention declared that suffrage was "the corner-stone of this enterprise, since we do not seek to protect woman, but rather to place her in a position to protect herself."

The struggle for legislation required leaders who had talents as organizers and lobbyists. The most prominent political operative was Susan B. Anthony (1820–1906). Anthony came from a Quaker family and as a young woman had been active in temperance and antislavery efforts. Her experience in the temperance movement, Anthony explained, had taught her "the great evil of woman's utter dependence on man." In 1851 she joined the movement for women's rights and forged an enduring friendship with Elizabeth Cady Stanton. Anthony created a network of political "captains," all women, who relentlessly lobbied the legislature in New York and other states. In 1860 her efforts culminated in a New York law granting women the right to collect and spend their own wages (which fathers or husbands previously could insist on controlling), bring suit in court, and, if widowed, acquire full control of the property they had brought to the marriage. Such successes would provide the basis for more aggressive reform attempts after the Civil War.

The attack by women's rights activists against the traditional legal and social prerogatives of husbands, like the abolitionists' assault on the power and property of southern slaveholders, prompted many Americans to fear that social reform might not perfect their society but destroy it. The various movements for reform, begun with such confidence and religious zeal, had raised legal and political issues that threatened the fabric of society and the unity of the nation.

FOR FURTHER EXPLORATION

▶ For definitions of key terms boldfaced in this chapter, see the glossary at the end of the book.

▶ To assess your mastery of the material covered in this chapter, see the Online Study Guide at **bedfordstmartins.com/henretta**.

▶ For suggested references, including Web sites, see page SR-13 at the end of the book.

▶ For map resources and primary documents, see **bedfordstmartins.com/henretta**.

After 1820 rapid economic and political change prompted many Americans to question traditional values and to support social reform movements. Ralph Waldo Emerson and other transcendentalists urged men—and women—to reject the outworn ideas of the past and realize their complete potential as individuals. To promote full spiritual growth, transcendentalists founded utopian communities such as Brook Farm. Transcendental thought influenced a generation of American writers, many of whom probed the tensions between individual freedom and social responsibility.

Thousands of other Americans joined utopian communities that questioned traditional gender roles and the acquisitive capitalist values of the market-oriented, industrializing society. Shakers, Fourierists, and members of the Oneida Community endorsed the communal ownership of property and devised various schemes—celibacy, phalanxes, complex marriage—to promote greater equality between men and women.

Joseph Smith and his Mormon followers created the most successful communal enterprise. They encouraged their members to pursue capitalist enterprise but subjected them to strict religious controls. Mormons celebrated the traditional patriarchal family, and some practiced polygamy. The Mormons' unorthodox marriage practices, along with their bloc voting, resulted in mob attacks on their communities and the migration of many Mormons to Utah.

During the 1830s thousands of middle-class white women also questioned traditional social practices. Many women became active in moral reform, attacking the sexual double standard and trying to eliminate prostitution. Other women enlisted in the abolitionist movement and, when denied an equal role, demanded complete political and civil equality for women. In 1848 they issued a "Declaration of Sentiments," beginning the modern women's rights movement.

The most dramatic expression of reform was a new attack on slavery by William Lloyd Garrison, who demanded the immediate, uncompensated emancipation of slaves. His crusade soon attracted the support of thousands of reformers. In 1835 the nationwide postal campaign of the American Anti-Slavery Society prompted widespread mob violence against abolitionists. In 1840 some abolitionists turned to politics, forming the Liberty Party. Over the next two decades, political struggles over slavery would gradually come to dominate the nation's history.

1817	American Colonization Society founded
1829	David Walker's *Appeal . . . to the Colored Citizens* encourages slave rebellion
1830	Joseph Smith publishes *The Book of Mormon*
1831	William Lloyd Garrison founds *The Liberator*
	Nat Turner's uprising in Virginia
1832	Ralph Waldo Emerson rejects organized religion and embraces transcendentalism
1833	American Anti-Slavery Society founded
1834	New York Female Moral Reform Society established
1835	Abolitionists launch mail campaign; antiabolitionists riot against them
1836	House of Representatives adopts gag rule on antislavery petitions
	Grimké sisters defend public roles for women
1840	Liberty Party runs James G. Birney for president
1840s	Fourierist communities founded in Midwest
1841	Transcendentalists found Brook Farm, a utopian community
	Dorothea Dix promotes hospitals for the insane
1844	Margaret Fuller publishes *Woman in the Nineteenth Century*
1845	Henry David Thoreau withdraws to Walden Pond
1846	Mormon followers of Brigham Young trek to Salt Lake
1848	John Humphrey Noyes founds Oneida Community
	Seneca Falls convention proposes women's equality
1850	Nathaniel Hawthorne publishes *The Scarlet Letter*
1851	Herman Melville's *Moby-Dick*
1852	Harriet Beecher Stowe writes *Uncle Tom's Cabin*
	Walt Whitman issues *Leaves of Grass*
1858	The "Mormon War" over polygamy

CHAPTER 13

The Crisis of the Union

1844–1860

◄ War News from Mexico, by Richard Caton Woodville, 1848

In this painting of a crowd gathered on the porch of the "American Hotel" in an unknown town, artist Richard Caton Woodville (1825–1855) captures the public's hunger for news of the Mexican War, the first military conflict with a foreign nation since the War of 1812. As a journalist in Woodville's hometown of Baltimore noted, "People begin to collect every evening, about 5 o'clock at the telegraph and newspaper offices, waiting for extras and despatches, where they continue even to 12 or 1 o'clock at night, discussing the news that may be received." National Gallery of Art, Washington, DC.

DURING THE 1850S THE CRUSADERS in the temperance and antislavery movements faced off against the defenders of traditional rights. The resulting struggle was nowhere more intense than in South Carolina. When local temperance activists demanded a law like that in Maine to prohibit the sale of intoxicants, Randolph Turner was outraged: any such "legislation upon Liquor would cast a shade on my character which as a Caucassian [*sic*] and a white man, I am not willing to bear." A candidate for the South Carolina assembly, Turner vowed to shoulder his musket and, along with "hundreds of men in this district, . . . fight for individual rights, as well as State Rights."

In Washington, Congressman Preston Brooks and other South Carolinians likewise battled against abolitionists to defend "Southern Rights." In an inflammatory speech in 1856, Senator Charles Sumner of Massachusetts denounced the South and accused Senator Andrew P. Butler of South Carolina of having taken "the harlot slavery" as his mistress. Outraged by Sumner's verbal attack on his uncle, Brooks accosted the Massachusetts senator at his desk and beat him unconscious with a walking cane. As Brooks struck down Sumner in Washington in 1856, Axalla Hoole of South Carolina and

367

other proslavery migrants in the Kansas Territory leveled their guns at an armed force of abolitionist settlers. Passion and violence had replaced political compromise as the hallmark of American public life.

The immediate events that sparked the political violence of the 1850s were the admission of Texas to the Union in 1845 and the war with Mexico that followed. The ultimate causes lay much deeper in the process of economic and cultural change that had widened the long-standing differences between North and South. By midcentury these sectional differences were keenly felt, especially in the South. As John C. Calhoun declared explicitly in 1850, white southerners feared the North's wealth, political power, and moral righteousness, especially its "long-continued agitation of the slavery question."

Now a massive surge of westward migration accentuated the importance of those divisions. To many Americans it was the nation's "manifest destiny" to extend republican institutions to the Pacific Ocean. But whose republican institutions: the aristocratic traditions and practices of the slaveholding South or the more democratic customs and culture of the reform-minded North and Midwest? The answer to this question would determine the future of the nation.

Manifest Destiny

Between 1820 and 1860 the white planters in the South grew rich and powerful as they developed a cotton economy. Shaken by the crisis over Missouri (see Chapter 9), the two major political parties prevented another confrontation over slavery by devising programs that were national in appeal. The compromise worked as long as the geographic boundaries of the United States remained unchanged, but by the 1840s the people of the nation were again on the move.

The Mature Cotton Economy, 1820–1860

By 1820 the American South produced more raw cotton than any other country in the world—160 million pounds a year—and by the 1840s grew over two-thirds of the world's supply (Figure 13.1). Family labor by thousands of white families accounted for hundreds of thousands of bales of the prized fiber, but most cotton came from large plantations employing slave labor. To increase output, profit-conscious slave owners in the upland regions of South Carolina and Georgia and in Alabama and Mississippi devised a new gang-labor system. Previously planters had either supervised their workers sporadically while attending to other tasks or assigned them a daily quota and let them work at their own pace. Now masters with twenty or more slaves organized the hands into disciplined teams, or "gangs,"

supervised by black "drivers" or white overseers, and assigned them specific tasks. They instructed drivers and overseers to use the lash to work the gangs at a steady pace, clearing and plowing the land or hoeing and picking cotton. A traveler glimpsed two gangs returning from work in Mississippi:

> *First came, led by an old driver carrying a whip, forty of the largest and strongest women I ever saw together; they were all in a simple uniform dress of a bluish check stuff, the skirts reaching little below the knee; their legs and feet were bare; they carried themselves loftily, each having a hoe over the shoulder, and walking with a free, powerful swing.*

Next marched the plow hands with their mules, "the cavalry, thirty strong, mostly men, but a few of them women." Finally, "a lean and vigilant white overseer, on a brisk pony, brought up the rear." By 1860 nearly two million enslaved African Americans were laboring on the cotton and sugar lands of the lower Mississippi Valley and along an arc of fertile cotton land—the "black belt"—sweeping from Mississippi through Georgia.

The slaveholding elite who owned great plantations and scores of slaves described themselves as natural aristocrats and indulged in displays of conspicuous consumption. They married their children to one another,

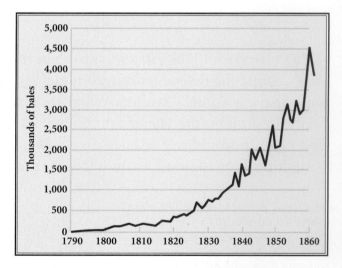

FIGURE 13.1 The Surge in Cotton Production, 1835–1860

Between 1835 and the mid-1840s, southern cotton planters doubled their output from one to two million 500-pound bales per year. Another dramatic rise came in the 1850s, as production doubled again—reaching four million bales per year by the end of the decade. Because the price of raw cotton rose slightly (from about 11 cents a pound in the 1830s to 13 cents in the 1850s), planters reaped substantial profits—reinforcing their commitment to the slave system.

Source: Robert William Fogel and Stanley L. Engerman, *Time on the Cross* (Boston: Little, Brown, 1974), figure 25.

and their sons and daughters became commercial and cultural leaders—the men working as planters, merchants, lawyers, newspaper editors, and ministers and the women hosting plantation balls and church bazaars. John Henry Hammond, a leading South Carolina planter and politician, inhabited a Greek Revival mansion with a center hall fifty-three feet by twenty feet, its floor embellished with stylish Belgian tiles and expensive Brussels carpets. "Once a year, like a great feudal landlord," a guest recounted, Hammond "gave a fete or grand dinner to all the country people."

The planters justified their power by endowing it with moral purpose. Before the Missouri crisis, southern apologists defended slavery as a "necessary evil" to maintain white living standards and prevent racial warfare; subsequently they argued that slavery was a "positive good" that allowed a civilized lifestyle for leading whites and provided tutelage for genetically inferior Africans. Seeking a religious justification, southern ministers pointed out that the Hebrews, God's chosen people, had owned slaves and that Jesus Christ had never condemned slavery. As Hammond told a British abolitionist in 1845: "What God ordains and Christ sanctifies should surely command the respect and toleration of man." Some defenders of slavery also depicted planters and their wives as aristocratic models of "disinterested benevolence" whose workers were adequately fed, housed, and cared for in old age (see American Voices, "Mary Boykin Chesnut: A Slaveholding Woman's Diary," p. 370).

Seeing themselves as a republican aristocracy, the elite planters encouraged ambitious men from modest backgrounds to buy slaves and grow rich as they had. In fact, white politics and society in the South remained deeply divided along the lines of class and region. Slave owners used their political power to exempt their slave property from taxation and to impose land taxes by acreage rather than by value, shifting the tax burden to yeoman farmers in the backcountry. Planters also enacted laws that forced yeomen to "fence in" their livestock, sparing themselves the cost of building fences around their large properties. Finally, legislatures forced all white men—whether they owned slaves or not—to serve in patrols and militias that deterred slaves from running away or rising in rebellion. Warning of race warfare, John Henry Hammond told his poor white neighbors that "in a slave country every freeman is an aristocrat."

Control of enslaved African Americans—a majority of the population throughout the "black belt"—was a matter of overriding concern for planters. In theory masters had virtually unlimited power over their slaves. By law enslaved individuals were personal property, subject to discipline at the will of their owners and bought and sold as if they were horses. As Thomas Ruffin, a justice of the North Carolina Supreme Court, declared in a court decision in 1829, "The power of the master must be absolute to render the submission of the slave perfect." In practice, both social conventions and black resistance limited the power of masters. Especially after 1830, when abolitionists subjected slavery to critical scrutiny, masters resorted less frequently to the lash and searched for positive incentives—food, visiting privileges, specified workloads—to manage their American-born laborers.

To resist the demands of their white masters, slaves used various strategies. They slowed the pace of work by feigning illness and were deliberately careless with the master's property, losing or breaking tools and setting fire to houses and barns. They also challenged the arbitrary breakup of communities, insisting that people be sold "in families" and defying their masters when they were not (see Figure 9.1, p. 263). One Maryland slave, faced with transport to Mississippi and separation from his wife, "neither yields consent to accompany my people, or to be exchanged or sold," his owner reported. Masters ignored such resistance at their peril because a slave's relatives might retaliate with arson, poison, or destruction of crops or equipment. Slavery was never a regime of equality but over the decades many masters and slaves had come to be tied to one another by complex personal—and often biological—bonds that reduced the extent of day-to-day violence. The institution of slavery had become part of the fiber of American life, and white southerners wanted to extend its sway across the entire continent.

The Independence of Texas

Beginning in the 1820s northeastern farmers and European migrants moved by the tens of thousands into the Midwest. Simultaneously thousands of farmers from the Ohio Valley and the South carried both yeoman farming and plantation slavery into Arkansas and Missouri, pushing just beyond their western boundaries to the ninety-fifth meridian. Beyond this north–south line stretched the semiarid Great Plains. An army explorer, Major Stephen H. Long, described the area between the Missouri River and the Rocky Mountains as a Great American Desert, "almost wholly unfit for cultivation." Sharing this assumption, land-hungry southern planters looked toward the west and the Mexican province of Texas (see Map 13.3, p. 374).

American Settlements. Texas had long been a zone of conflict between European nations. During the eighteenth century the Spanish had used Texas as a buffer against the French. After the Louisiana Purchase in 1803, Texas became Spain's buffer against Americans. Although adventurers from the United States did settle in Texas, the Adams-Onís Treaty of 1819 guaranteed Spanish sovereignty over the region.

Mary Boykin Chesnut

A Slaveholding Woman's Diary

During the 1850s, in response to Harriet Beecher Stowe's Uncle Tom's Cabin *and Republican celebrations of free labor, proslavery advocate George Fitzhugh wrote* Sociology for the South; or, the Failure of Free Society. *In this influential book and in his other writings, Fitzhugh contrasted the slave owners' benevolent concern for their enslaved workers with the factory owners' indifference toward the welfare of their wage laborers. Mary Boykin Chesnut (1823–1886), wife of South Carolina senator James Chesnut, held a more complex view. Although believing that blacks were innately inferior and celebrating the benevolence of white women, she hated slavery, in part because she thought that it oppressed the women of both races. Chesnut recorded her views in notes made during the Civil War, later revised into a beautifully written diary.*

March 18, 1861 . . . I wonder if it be a sin to think slavery a curse to any land. [Massachusetts senator Charles] Sumner said not one word of this hated institution which is not true. Men and women are punished when their masters and mistresses are brutes and not when they do wrong—and then we live surrounded by prostitutes. An abandoned woman is sent out of any decent house elsewhere. Who thinks any worse of a negro or mulatto woman for being a thing we can't name? God forgive us, but ours is a monstrous system and wrong. . . . Like the patriarchs of old our men live all in one house with their wives and their concubines, and the mulattoes one sees in every family exactly resemble the white children—and every lady tells you who is the father of all the mulatto children in everybody's household, but those in her own she seems to think drop from the clouds, or pretends so to think. Good women we have . . . the purest women God ever made. Thank God for my countrywomen—alas for the men! No worse than men everywhere, but the lower their mistresses, the more degraded they must be.

November 27, 1861 . . . Now what I have seen of my mother's life, my grandmother's, my mother-in-law's: These people were educated at Northern schools mostly—read the same books as their Northern condemners, the same daily newspapers, the same Bible—have the same ideas of right and wrong—are highbred, lovely, good, pious—doing their duty as they conceive it. They live in negro villages. They do not preach and teach hate as a gospel and the sacred duty of murder and insurrection, but they strive to ameliorate the condition of these Africans in every particular. . . . These women are more troubled by their duty to negroes, have less chance to live their own lives in peace than if they were African missionaries. They have a swarm of blacks about them as children under their care—not as Mrs. Stowe's fancy paints them, but the hard, unpleasant, unromantic, undeveloped savage Africans. And they hate slavery worse than Mrs. Stowe. . . .

We are human beings of the nineteenth century—and slavery has to go, of course. All that has been gained by it goes to the North and to negroes. The slave-owners, when they are good men and women, are the martyrs. And as far as I have seen, the people here are quite as good as anywhere else. I hate slavery.

Source: *C. Vann Woodward,* Mary Chesnut's Civil War *(New Haven: Yale University Press, 1981), 29–30, 245–46.*

After winning independence from Spain in 1821, the Mexican government encouraged the settlement of Texas by both its citizens and migrants from the United States. To win the allegiance of the American settlers, officials granted them some of the best land (Map 13.1). One early grantee was Moses Austin, who moved to Texas to create an aristocratic-like landed estate, occupied by tenants or smallholders: "one great family who are under my care." His son, Stephen F. Austin, later acquired about 180,000 acres, which he sold to new migrants. Most American settlers did not assimilate Mexican culture and in 1829 won special exemption from a law ending slavery in Mexico. By 1835, about 27,000 white Americans and their 3,000 African American slaves were raising cotton and cattle in eastern and central Texas; they far outnumbered the 3,000 Mexican residents, most of whom lived, along with a few Americans, in the southwestern towns of Goliad and San Antonio.

When the Mexican government asserted greater control over Texas in the mid-1830s, the Americans split into two groups. The "peace party," led by Stephen

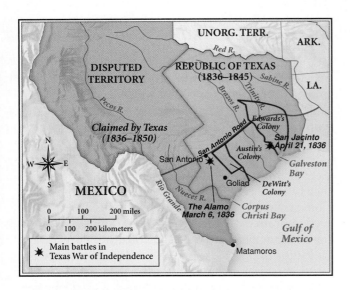

MAP 13.1 American Settlements in Texas, 1821–1836
During the 1820s Mexican authorities granted huge tracts of land in the province of Texas to American empresarios (essentially land entrepreneurs), who were expected to encourage immigration. Stephen F. Austin managed the largest "colony"; by 1835 he had issued land titles to more than 1,000 families, who grew cotton and exported it from Galveston and other Gulf ports. By the mid-1830s, there were nearly 30,000 Americans in Texas, far outnumbering the Mexican settlers, who lived primarily in the town of Goliad and areas south.

Austin and other longtime settlers with substantial interests to protect, worked to win more self-government for the province, while the "war party," led by recent migrants from Georgia, demanded independence. Austin won significant concessions from Mexican authorities, but the new president, General Antonio López de Santa Anna, nullified these measures. A strong nationalist, Santa Anna appointed a military commandant for Texas, prompting the American war party to provoke a rebellion that most of the American settlers ultimately supported. On March 2, 1836, the rebels proclaimed the independence of Texas and adopted a constitution legalizing slavery.

Rebellion and War.   Santa Anna vowed to put down the rebellion. On March 6 his army wiped out the rebel garrison defending the Alamo in San Antonio and soon thereafter captured the settlement of Goliad (see Voices from Abroad, "Colonel José Enrique de la Peña: A Mexican View of the Battle of the Alamo," p. 372). With these victories Santa Anna thought he had crushed the rebellion, but the battle of the Alamo had captured the attention of New Orleans and New York newspapers. Their correspondents romanticized the heroism of the Texans and the deaths at the Alamo of folk heroes Davy Crockett and Jim Bowie. Using strong anti-Catholic rhetoric, the newspapers described the Mexicans as tyrannical butchers in the service of the pope. Hundreds of American adventurers, lured by Texan offers of land bounties, flocked in from neighboring states. Reinforced by the new arrivals and led by General Sam Houston, in April 1836 the rebels routed the Mexicans in the Battle of San Jacinto, establishing de facto independence. The

SIEGE OF THE ALAMO.

Assault on the Alamo
After a thirteen-day siege, on March 6, 1836, a Mexican army of 4,000 stormed the small mission in San Antonio, Texas. "The first to climb were thrown down by bayonets . . . or by pistol fire," reported a Mexican officer. Only a half hour of continuous assaults gave the attackers control of the wall. This contemporary woodcut shows the fierceness of the battle, which took the lives of all 250 American defenders; the Mexicans suffered 1,500 dead or wounded.
Archives Division, Texas State Library.

For more help analyzing this image, see the ONLINE STUDY GUIDE at bedfordstmartins.com/henretta

Colonel José Enrique de la Peña

A Mexican View of the Battle of the Alamo

In February 1836 a Mexican army led by General Antonio López de Santa Anna laid siege to the Alamo, an old San Antonio mission building held by about 250 Texas rebels and some American supporters, all of whom were commanded by William B. Travis. In his personal narrative of the war in Texas, Colonel José Enrique de la Peña offers a dramatic and critical account of the ensuing events, in which he played a prominent role.

Our commander [Santa Anna] became more furious when he saw that the enemy resisted the idea of surrender. He believed as others did that the fame and honor of the army were compromised the longer the enemy lived. . . . But prudent men . . . were of the opinion that victory over a handful of men concentrated in the Alamo did not call for a great sacrifice. In fact, it was necessary only to await the artillery's arrival at Béjar for these to surrender. . . .

Travis's resistance was on the verge of being overcome, for several days his followers had been urging him to surrender, giving the lack of food and the scarcity of munitions as reasons. . . . [O]n the 5th he promised them if no help arrived on that day they would surrender the next day or would try to escape under the cover of darkness. . . . [I]t was said as a fact . . . that the president-general [Santa Anna] knew of Travis's decision, and it was for this reason that he precipitated the assault, because he wanted to create a sensation and would have regretted taking the Alamo without clamor and without bloodshed, for some believed that without these there is no glory. . . .

The columns, bravely storming the fort in the midst of a terrible shower of bullets and cannon-fire, had reached the base of the walls. . . . A lively rifle fire coming from the roof . . . caused painful havoc. . . . [Finally] our soldiers, some stimulated by courage and others by fury, burst into the quarters . . . our losses were grievous. . . . [But our men] turned the enemy's own cannon to bring down the [inner] doors . . . a horrible carnage took place, and some [rebels] were trampled to death. . . . This scene of extermination went on for an hour before the curtain of death covered and ended it. . . .

Some seven men had survived the general carnage and, under the protection of General Castrillon, they were brought before Santa Anna. Among them was one of great stature, well proportioned, with regular features, in whose face there was the imprint of adversity, but in whom one noticed a degree of resignation and nobility that did him honor. He was the naturalist David Crockett, well known in North America for his unusual adventures, who had undertaken to explore the country and who, finding himself at Béjar at the very moment of surprise, had taken refuge in the Alamo, fearing his status as a foreigner might not be respected. Santa Anna answered Castrillon's intervention in Crockett's behalf with a gesture of indignation and . . . ordered his execution. The commanders and officers were outraged at this action and did not support the order. . . . [But several officers] thrust themselves forward, in order to flatter their commander, and with swords in hand, fell upon these unfortunate, defenseless men just as a tiger leaps upon his prey. . . .

To whom was this sacrifice useful and what advantage was derived by increasing the number of victims? . . . [T]he taking of the Alamo was not considered a happy event, but rather a defeat that saddened us all.

Source: José Enrique de la Peña, *With Santa Anna in Texas: A Personal Narrative of the Revolution*, trans. Carmen Perry (College Station: Texas A&M University Press, 1975), 40–57.

Mexican government refused to recognize the new republic but abandoned efforts to reconquer it.

The Texans quickly voted by plebiscite for annexation by the United States, but Presidents Andrew Jackson and Martin Van Buren refused to act. They knew that adding Texas as a slave state would divide the Democratic Party and the nation and almost certainly lead to war with Mexico.

The Push to the Pacific: Oregon and California

The annexation of Texas became a more pressing issue in the 1840s, as American expansionists developed continental ambitions. Those dreams were captured by the term **Manifest Destiny**, coined in 1845 by John L. O'Sullivan, the editor of the *Democratic Review*. As O'Sullivan

***Sam Houston,* by Martin Johnson Heade, 1846**
Military hero, president of the Lone Star Republic of Texas, and senator from the state of Texas: Sam Houston cut an impressive figure and had many admirers both inside and outside politics. According to a Nashville belle who knew the Texan as a young man, "two classes of people pursued Sam Houston all his life—artists and women." Heade's portrait, painted when Houston was a senator, conveys the Texan's flamboyant character and personal charm. Texas State Library and Archives Collection.

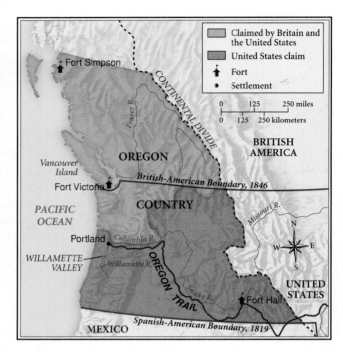

MAP 13.2 Territorial Conflict in Oregon, 1819–1846
As thousands of American settlers poured into the "Oregon Country" in the early 1840s, British authorities tried to confine them south of the Columbia River. But the migrants—and fervent midwestern expansionists—asserted that Americans could settle anywhere in the territory. In 1846 British and American diplomats resolved the dispute by dividing the region at the forty-ninth parallel.

put it, "Our manifest destiny is to overspread the continent allotted by Providence for the free development of our yearly multiplying millions." Behind the rhetoric of Manifest Destiny was a sense of cultural and even racial superiority; "inferior" peoples—Native Americans and Mexicans—were to be brought under American dominion, taught about republican forms of government, and converted to Protestantism.

Oregon. Already many residents of the Ohio River Valley were casting their eyes westward to the fertile valleys of the Oregon Country. This region stretched along the Pacific Coast from the forty-second parallel in the south (the border with Mexican California) to the fifty-fourth parallel in the north (54°40′, the border with Russian Alaska) and was claimed by both Great Britain and the United States. Since 1818 a British-American convention had allowed both the British and Americans to settle anywhere in the disputed region. The British-run Hudson's Bay Company developed a

lucrative fur trade north of the Columbia River, while several hundred Americans settled to the south, mostly in the Willamette Valley. On the basis of this settlement, the United States established a claim to the zone between the forty-second parallel and the Columbia River (Map 13.2).

In 1842 American interest in Oregon increased dramatically. Navy Lieutenant Charles Wilkes published glowing reports of the potential harbors he had found in the area of Puget Sound, news of great interest to New England merchants plying the China trade. In the same year a party of a hundred settlers journeyed along the Oregon Trail that fur traders and explorers had blazed through the Great Plains and the Rocky Mountains (Map 13.3). Their reports from Oregon told of a mild climate and fertile soil.

"Oregon fever" suddenly raged. In May 1843 over a thousand men, women, and children—with more than a hundred wagons and five thousand oxen and cattle—gathered in Independence, Missouri, for the trek to Oregon. The migrants were mostly farming and trading families from Missouri, Kentucky, and Tennessee. With military-style organization, the pioneers overcame flooding streams, dust storms, dying livestock, and encounters with Indians. After a journey of six months they reached the Willamette Valley, more than two

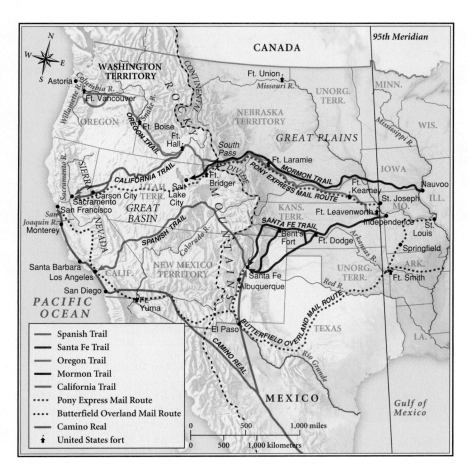

MAP 13.3 Routes to the West, 1835–1860

By the mid- to late 1840s a variety of trails spanned the arid zone west of the ninety-fifth meridian and the Pacific Coast. From the south, El Camino Real linked Mexico City to the California coast, Santa Fe, and the breakaway province of Texas. From the east, the Santa Fe, Oregon, California, and Mormon Trails carried tens of thousands of Americans from departure points on the Mississippi and Missouri Rivers to new communities in Utah and along the Pacific Coast. By the 1860s both the Pony Express and the Butterfield Overland Mail provided reliable communication between the eastern United States and California.

thousand miles across the continent. During the next two seasons another 5,000 people reached Oregon, and numbers continued to grow.

By 1860 about 350,000 Americans had braved the Oregon Trail. More than 34,000 of them died in the effort, mostly from disease and exposure; only 400 deaths came from Indian attacks. The walking migrants wore three-foot-deep paths and their wagons carved five-foot-deep ruts across sandstone formations in southern Wyoming—tracks that are visible today. Women found the trail especially difficult, for it exaggerated the authority of their husbands and added to their traditional chores the labor of driving wagons and animals.

California. Some pioneers ended up in the Mexican province of California. They left the Oregon Trail at the Snake River and struggled southward down the California Trail, settling in the interior valley along the Sacramento River. California had been the remotest corner of Spain's American empire, and Spain had established a significant foothold there only in the 1770s, when it built a chain of religious missions and forts (presidios) along the coast (see Chapter 8). New England merchants soon struck up trade with the settlers in California, buying sea otter pelts that they carried to China. Commerce increased after

Mexico won independence. To promote California's development the new Mexican government took over the Franciscan-run missions, liberating more than 20,000 Indians who worked on them, and promoted large-scale cattle ranching.

The rise of cattle ranching in California created a new society and economy. While some mission Indians joined Native American peoples in the interior, many remained in the coastal region. They intermarried with the local mestizos (Mexicans of mixed Spanish and Indian ancestry) and worked as laborers and cowboys. New England merchants carried the leather and tallow produced on the large California ranches to the booming Massachusetts boot and shoe industry. To handle the increased business, New England firms dispatched dozens of resident agents to California. Unlike the American settlers in Texas, many of those New Englanders assimilated Mexican culture. They married into the families of the elite Mexicans—the Californios—and adopted their dress, manners, outlook, and Catholic religion. A crucial exception was Thomas Oliver Larkin, the most successful merchant in the coastal town of Monterey. Larkin established a close working relationship with Mexican authorities, but he remained an American citizen and plotted for the peaceful annexation of California to the United States.

***The Promised Land—The Grayson Family,* by William S. Jewett, 1850**

For adventurous nineteenth-century Americans, the West symbolized a brighter future. Here Andrew Jackson Grayson (1819–1869) and his family catch their first glimpse of the fertile lands of California's Sacramento Valley. The Graysons had traveled west with the ill-fated migrants who perished in a blizzard at the Donner Pass; fortunately, they had left the main group and made their own way over the Sierra Nevada. To celebrate his family's safe arrival, Andrew Grayson commissioned this painting by William S. Jewett, who executed it at the very spot the Graysons first saw their new home.
Terra Museum of American Art, Chicago, Illinois. Daniel J. Terra Collection.

Like Larkin, American migrants in the Sacramento Valley had no desire to assimilate into Mexican society. Moreover, their legal standing was uncertain; many were squatters and others held land grants of dubious validity. Some of them hoped to emulate the Americans in Texas by colonizing the country, overwhelming what they regarded as an inferior culture and then seeking annexation to the United States. However, these settlers numbered only about 700 in the early 1840s, compared with the coastal population of 7,000 Mexicans and 300 American traders.

The Fateful Election of 1844

The election of 1844 determined the course of the American government's policy toward California, Oregon, and Texas. Since 1836, when Texas requested annexation, some southern leaders had favored territorial expansion to extend the slave system. They had been opposed not only by cautious party politicians and northern abolitionists but also, southerners came to think, by British antislavery advocates. In 1839 Britain and France had intervened in Mexico to force payment of foreign debts, and there were rumors that Britain wanted California as payment. Southern leaders also believed that Britain was encouraging Texas to remain independent and had designs on Spanish Cuba, which some southerners wanted to annex. To thwart any such British schemes southern expansionists demanded the immediate annexation of Texas.

At this crucial moment "Oregon fever" and Manifest Destiny altered the political and diplomatic landscape in the North. In 1843 Americans throughout the Ohio Valley and the Great Lakes states called on the federal government to renounce the joint occupation of Oregon. Democrats and Whigs jointly organized "Oregon conventions," and in July a bipartisan national convention demanded that the United States seize Oregon all the way to 54°40′ north latitude, the southern limit of Russian Alaska.

Now that northern Democrats were demanding expansion, southern Democrats could champion the annexation of Texas without threatening party unity. Moreover, they had the support of President John Tyler. Disowned by the Whigs because of his opposition to Henry Clay's nationalist economic program, Tyler hoped to win reelection in 1844 as a Democrat. To curry favor among expansionists Tyler proposed to annex Texas and seize Oregon to the 54°40′ line. In April 1844 Tyler and John C. Calhoun, his new secretary of state, submitted to the Senate a treaty to annex Texas. Two political leaders with presidential ambitions, Democrat Martin Van Buren and Whig Henry Clay, quickly declared their opposition. They knew that annexation would alienate many northern voters and persuaded Whig and northern Democratic senators to defeat the treaty.

Texas became the central issue in the election of 1844. The Democrats passed over Tyler, whom they did not trust, and Van Buren, whom southern Democrats despised for his opposition to annexation. They selected former Governor James K. Polk of Tennessee, a slave owner who favored annexation and who, as Andrew Jackson's personal favorite, was nicknamed "Young

A Californio Patriarch

The descendant of a Spanish family that had lived—and prospered—in Mexico since the Spanish conquest, Mariano Guadalupe Vallejo served in Mexican California as a military officer. In the 1820s he acquired 270,000 acres of land in the Sonoma Valley north of San Francisco. Vallejo, the father of nine children, presents himself in this photograph as a proud patriarch, surrounded by two daughters and three granddaughters. During the American takeover in 1846, he was imprisoned for a short period and subsequently suffered severe financial setbacks, losing most of his vast landholdings to squatters and rival claimants.

Bancroft Library, University of California, Berkeley.

Hickory." Unimpressive in appearance, Polk was a man of iron will and boundless ambition for the nation. "Fifty-four forty or fight!" became the patriotic cry of his expansionist campaign.

The Whigs nominated Henry Clay, who again championed his American System of internal improvements, high tariffs, and national banking. Initially Clay dodged the issue of Texas, finally suggesting that he might support annexation. His evasive position disappointed thousands of northern Whigs and Democrats who strongly opposed any expansion of slavery. Rather than vote for Clay, some antislavery advocates supported the Liberty Party's candidate, James G. Birney of Kentucky. Birney garnered less than 3 percent of the total vote but probably claimed enough Whig votes in New York to cause Clay to lose that state. By taking New York's 36 electoral votes, Polk won the presidency by a

margin of 170 to 105 in the electoral college (otherwise Clay would have won, by a margin of 141 to 134).

Following Polk's victory, congressional Democrats closed ranks and moved immediately to bring Texas into the Union. Unable to secure a two-thirds majority in the Senate for a treaty with the Republic of Texas, they approved annexation by a joint resolution of Congress, which required only a majority vote in each house. Polk's strategy of linking Texas and Oregon had put him in the White House and Texas in the Union.

War, Expansion, and Slavery, 1846–1850

Polk had even greater territorial ambitions than Texas and Oregon: he wanted all of Mexico between Texas and the Pacific Ocean and was prepared to go to war to get it. What he was not prepared for, though he should have been, was the major crisis over slavery unleashed by the success of his expansionist dreams.

The War with Mexico, 1846–1848

Mexico had not prospered in the twenty-five years since it won independence from Spain in 1821. Its population remained small at 7 million people, and its stagnant economy yielded only modest tax revenue, which was eaten up by interest payments on foreign debts and a bloated government bureaucracy. Consequently, the Mexican government lacked the people and the money to settle its distant northern provinces. The Spanish-speaking population of California and New Mexico remained small—about 75,000 in 1840—and contributed little to the national economy. Still, Mexican officials were determined to retain all their nation's historical territories, and when the breakaway Texas Republic accepted American statehood on July 4, 1845, Mexico broke off diplomatic relations with the United States.

Polk's Expansionist Program. Taking advantage of the rupture, President James Polk put into action a secret plan he had devised to acquire Mexico's far northern provinces. To intimidate the Mexican government he ordered General Zachary Taylor and an American army of 2,000 soldiers to occupy the disputed lands between the Nueces River (the historical boundary of the Mexican province of Texas) and the Rio Grande, which the expansionist-minded Texas Republic had claimed as its southern and western border (see Map 13.1). Then Polk launched a diplomatic initiative, dispatching John Slidell on a secret mission to Mexico City. Slidell was instructed to secure Mexico's acceptance of the Rio Grande boundary and buy the Mexican provinces of New Mexico and California, paying as much as $30 million. When Slidell arrived in December 1845, Mexican officials refused to see him, declaring that the American annexation of Texas was illegal.

Anticipating the failure of Slidell's mission, Polk had already embarked on an alternative plan to take California. The president's strategy was to foment a revolution that, as in Texas, would lead to the creation of an independent republic and a request for annexation. In October 1845 Secretary of State James Buchanan told merchant Thomas O. Larkin, now the U.S. consul in the port of Monterey, to encourage leading Mexican residents to declare independence and support peaceful annexation. To add military muscle to his plan, Polk sent orders to American naval commanders in the Pacific to seize San Francisco Bay and California's coastal towns in

case of war. The president also had the War Department dispatch Captain John C. Frémont and an "exploring" party of heavily armed soldiers deep into Mexican territory. By December 1845 Frémont had reached California's Sacramento Valley.

Events now moved quickly toward war. When Polk learned of the failure of Slidell's mission, he ordered General Taylor to build a fort near the Rio Grande, hoping to incite an armed response by Mexico. As Ulysses S. Grant, a young officer serving with Taylor, said much later, "We were sent to provoke a fight, but it was essential that Mexico should commence it." When Mexican and American forces clashed near the Rio Grande in May 1846, Polk delivered the war message he had drafted long before. Taking liberties with the truth, the president declared that

Street Fighting in the Calle de Iturbide, 1846

The American conquest of Monterrey, which Spain's troops had been unable to capture during Mexico's war for independence in 1820–1821, came after bloody house-to-house fighting. Protected by thick walls and shuttered windows, Mexican defenders pour a withering fire on dark-uniformed American troops and buckskin-clad frontier fighters. A spacious Catholic cathedral looms in the background, its foundations obscured by the smoke from Mexican cannon. West Point Museum, United States Military Academy, West Point, NY.

Mexico "has passed the boundary of the United States, has invaded our territory, and shed American blood upon the American soil." Ignoring Whig pleas for a peaceful resolution of the dispute, the Democratic majority in Congress voted for war with Mexico, unleashing large and almost hysterical demonstrations of popular support. To avoid a simultaneous war with Britain over Oregon, Polk retreated from his campaign pledge of "fifty-four forty or fight" and accepted a British proposal to divide the Oregon region at the forty-ninth parallel.

American Military Success. Following the outbreak of fighting in May 1846, Zachary Taylor's forces in Texas crossed the Rio Grande, occupied Matamoros, and after a fierce six-day battle in September took the interior Mexican town of Monterrey. Two months later a U.S. naval squadron in the Gulf of Mexico seized Tampico, Mexico's second most important port. By the end of 1846 the United States controlled much of northeastern Mexico (Map 13.4).

In the meantime, fighting had broken out in California between American naval forces and Mexican authorities. In June 1846 naval commander John Sloat landed 250 marines and seamen in Monterey and declared that California "henceforward will be a portion of the United States." Almost simultaneously American settlers in the interior staged a revolt and, supported by Frémont's forces, captured the town of Sonoma. To ensure American control of California, Polk ordered army units to capture Santa Fe in New Mexico and march to the Pacific Ocean. Despite stiff resistance from the Mexicans, American forces secured control of all of California early in 1847.

Polk expected that these American victories in Texas, New Mexico, California, and other northern Mexican states would prompt the Mexican government to sue for peace, but he had underrated the Mexicans' national pride and the determination of President Santa Anna. Santa Anna went on the offensive, attacking the depleted units of Zachary Taylor at Buena Vista in February 1847. Only superior artillery enabled Taylor to eke out a victory and hold the American line in northeastern Mexico.

To bring Santa Anna to terms, Polk accepted the plan devised by General Winfield Scott to strike deep

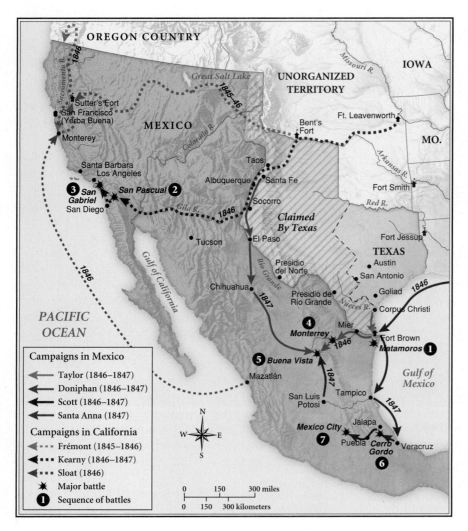

MAP 13.4 The Mexican War, 1846–1848

Departing from Fort Leavenworth in present-day Kansas, American forces commanded by Captain John C. Frémont and General Stephen Kearney defeated Mexican armies in California in 1846 and early 1847. Simultaneously U.S. armies under General Zachary Taylor and Colonel Alfred A. Doniphan won victories over General Santa Anna's forces far to the south of the Rio Grande. Then in mid-1847 General Winfield Scott mounted a successful attack on Mexico City, ending the war.

into the heart of Mexico. In March 1847 Scott captured the port of Veracruz and began the 260-mile march to Mexico City. Leading Scott's 14,000 troops was a cadre of talented West Point officers who would become famous in the Civil War: Robert E. Lee, George Meade, and P. G. T. Beauregard. Scott's troops crushed Santa Anna's attempt to block their march at Cerro Gordo and, after inflicting heavy losses on the Mexican army at the Battle of Churubusco, seized Mexico City in September 1847. Following these decisive defeats Santa Anna lost power, and a new Mexican government agreed to make peace with the United States.

A Divisive Victory

Initially many Americans viewed the war with Mexico as a noble struggle to extend American republican institutions, but the conflict quickly became politically divisive. A few Whigs, such as Charles Francis Adams of Massachusetts and Joshua Giddings of Ohio, had opposed the war from the beginning on moral grounds. Known as "**conscience Whigs**," they viewed the war as a southern conspiracy to add new slave states in the West. They argued that the expansion of slavery would jeopardize the Jeffersonian ideal of a yeoman freeholder society and ensure control of the federal government by slaveholding Democrats. These antislavery Whigs grew bolder after the elections of 1846, which gave their party control of Congress.

The Wilmot Proviso. Polk's expansionist policy split the Democrats into sectional factions. As early as 1839 Senator Thomas Morris of Ohio had warned Congress and the nation that "the power of SLAVERY is aiming to govern the country, its Constitutions and laws." In August 1846 David Wilmot, a Democratic representative from Pennsylvania, took up that refrain. To prevent the South from profiting from the war, Wilmot proposed to prohibit slavery in any new territories acquired from Mexico. This measure, known as the Wilmot Proviso, quickly became a rallying point for antislavery northerners. In the House the northern Democratic supporters of Martin Van Buren joined forces with antislavery Whigs to pass the proviso. The Senate, dominated by southerners and proslavery northern Democrats, killed it.

In this heated atmosphere the most fervent Democratic expansionists became even more aggressive. Polk, Secretary of State Buchanan, and Senators Stephen A. Douglas of Illinois and Jefferson Davis of Mississippi wanted the United States to take at least part of Mexico south of the Rio Grande. However, some southerners worried that the United States could not absorb the Mexicans and feared that a longer war would augment the power of the federal government. John C. Calhoun declared that the United States should take California

and New Mexico, the most sparsely populated areas of Mexico.

To reunify the Democratic Party before the next election Polk and Buchanan abandoned their expansionist dreams in Mexico and accepted Calhoun's policy. In February 1848 Polk signed the Treaty of Guadalupe Hidalgo, in which the United States agreed to pay Mexico $15 million in return for more than one-third of its territory: Texas north of the Rio Grande, New Mexico, and California (Map 13.5). The United States also agreed to assume all the claims of its citizens against the Mexican government. The Senate ratified the treaty in March 1848.

Free Soil. The passions aroused by the war dominated the election of 1848. The Wilmot Proviso had energized abolitionists who had been seeking political action against slavery. Alarmed by the Senate's rejection, antislavery advocates embraced Thomas Morris's charge of a massive "Slave Power" conspiracy. To defeat this alleged plan, thousands of ordinary northerners joined a new "**free-soil**" movement. "The curse of slavery," Abijah Beckwith of Herkimer County in New York wrote to his grandson, "threatens the general and equal distribution of our lands into convenient family farms." To Beckwith, who was an ordinary yeoman farmer, slavery was an institution of "aristocratic men" that threatened "the generally equal distribution of wealth" and the liberties of "the great mass of the people."

The free-soilers abandoned the Liberty Party's focus on the sinfulness of slavery and the natural rights of African Americans. Like Beckwith, they depicted slavery as a threat to republican institutions and yeoman farming. This shift in emphasis—toward keeping the West open for settlement by white families and away from freeing slaves—led the radical abolitionist William Lloyd Garrison to denounce free-soil doctrine as racist "whitemanism." Nonetheless, the Wilmot Proviso's call for free soil was the first antislavery proposal to attract broad popular support. Hundreds of women in the Great Lakes states joined female free-soil organizations formed by the American and Foreign Anti-Slavery Society. Frederick Douglass, the foremost black abolitionist, also endorsed free soil, seeing it as the best way to provoke a political struggle between the North and the South that would overthrow slavery (see American Lives, "Frederick Douglass: Development of an Abolitionist," p. 380).

The conflict over slavery took a toll on Polk and the Democratic Party. Opposed by free-soilers and exhausted by his rigorous dawn-to-midnight work regime, Polk declined to run for a second term and died three months after leaving office. In his place the Democrats nominated Senator Lewis Cass of Michigan, an avid expansionist who had advocated buying Cuba, annexing Mexico's

Frederick Douglass: Development of an Abolitionist

Frederick Douglass, c. 1848

The daguerreotype of Douglass was taken when he was about thirty years old. Describing Douglass, an admirer wrote: "He was more than six feet in height, and his majestic form . . . straight as an arrow, muscular, yet lithe and graceful, his flashing eye, and more than all, his voice, that rivaled Webster's in its richness and in the depth . . . of its cadences, made up such an ideal of an orator as the listeners never forgot."
Chester County Historical Society.

Frederick Douglass was born a slave in 1818. Thirty years later he was a famous man, author of the acclaimed *Narrative of the Life of Frederick Douglass* (1845) and a leading moral abolitionist. Within another five years Douglass had become a political activist, convinced that only the power of the government would end slavery.

His white father's sense of paternity—or guilt—played a crucial role in Frederick Douglass's life, but his own abilities and determination accounted for his rapid ascent to fame: he was a man of remarkable talents. Born on a Maryland plantation, Douglass grew up as Frederick Bailey, having been given his enslaved mother's family name. He never knew the identity of his father, though talk in the slave quarters pointed toward a man Douglass later described as "his master." This rumor was probably true, given the course of Frederick Bailey's early life. In 1827 his owner, Thomas Auld, sent nine-year-old Frederick to Baltimore to live with his brother Hugh Auld.

There were no other slaves in Hugh Auld's household and, quite remarkably, for the next five years Frederick was treated much like the Auld children. He listened to Sophia Auld read the Bible, learned to read from a spelling book, figured out the meaning of abolition from newspapers, and heard about slaves running away to the North. At age twelve he purchased a copy of *The Columbian Orator,* a collection of speeches expounding the virtues of the American republic—including its devotion to "the rights of man." Enthralled, Frederick memorized and recited the speeches to his friends, including the free blacks he sought out at Methodist and Baptist churches. Despite his legal status, the young Frederick Bailey had begun to think and act like a free man.

In 1833 Thomas Auld returned Frederick to the sleepy rural town of St. Michaels, perhaps to keep him

from running away or becoming mixed up in antislavery agitation. Frederick became rebellious, organizing a Sabbath school and refusing to work. So in 1834 Auld hired him out to Edward Covey, a farmer with a reputation for "breaking" unruly slaves. After enduring six months of heavy labor and regular beatings, Frederick reached his own breaking point and had it out with Covey. Their brutal fight "was the turning point in my 'life as a slave,'" Douglass recalled. "I was nothing before; I WAS A MAN NOW." Determined "to be a FREEMAN" as well, Frederick hatched an escape plan. Betrayed by a fellow conspirator, he found himself in jail, faced with being sold into the harsh slavery of the Deep South. Once again Thomas Auld intervened, returning Frederick to his brother's charge in Baltimore and promising him freedom in eight years, at the age of twenty-five. Becoming a journeyman caulker in the shipyards, the young slave soon worked independently, giving Hugh Auld a weekly payment.

Frederick plunged enthusiastically into the life of Baltimore's free African American community, which numbered almost 30,000. He courted a free black woman, Anna Murray, and joined the East Baltimore Mental Improvement Society, a self-help organization set up by free black caulkers. This stimulating life came to an abrupt end when Frederick fell behind in his payments to Hugh Auld. Rather than face the loss of his independence, Frederick decided to run away. In the fall of 1838 he borrowed the identification papers of a free African American sailor and sailed to New York City.

Frederick Bailey began his life of freedom by taking the new name Douglass, marrying Anna Murray, and settling in the seaport town of New Bedford, Massachusetts. Inspired by the lectures of William Lloyd Garrison, he became a public antislavery speaker. Hearing Douglass deliver a powerful address in 1841, Garrison hired him as a lecturer for the American Anti-Slavery Society. Soon Douglass became a celebrity. His partly African origins drew crowds to his lectures, as did his commanding personal presence, dramatic rhetoric, and forceful intellect. He lectured in hundreds of communities in the Northeast, holding audiences spellbound. Hearing Douglass speak in Boston, the future women's rights activist Elizabeth Cady Stanton was deeply impressed:

Around him sat the great antislavery orators of the day watching the effect of his eloquence on that immense audience, that laughed and wept by turns, completely carried away by the wondrous gifts of his pathos and humor. On this occasion, all the other speakers seemed tame after Frederick Douglass.

In his speeches Douglass denounced slavery in the South and racial discrimination in the North. Gradually his views diverged from those of Garrison. To rid America of the sin of slavery, Garrison was prepared to expel the southern states from the Union. To Douglass this policy was madness because it would perpetuate slavery. Following a triumphal British lecturing tour from 1845 and 1847, Douglass founded an antislavery newspaper, the *North Star*. Departing from Garrison's

moral radicalism, the *North Star* gravitated toward political abolitionism. In 1848 Douglass attended the Buffalo convention that established the Free-Soil Party and ignored Garrison's condemnation of the party as a species of "whitemanism," a racist effort to keep the territories white. Douglass also attended the women's rights convention at Seneca Falls, and subsequently he endorsed a wider public role for women. "In respect to political rights," he declared in the *North Star*, "we hold woman to be justly entitled to all we claim for men."

In 1851 Douglass publicly separated himself from Garrison and the American Anti-Slavery Society by defending the Constitution, which Garrison had previously condemned as "a covenant with death." A year later in his influential "Fifth of July" speech, Douglass celebrated the Constitution as a vehicle for black liberation. "In that instrument, I hold there is no warrant, license, nor sanction of the hateful thing [of slavery]; but, interpreted as it ought to be interpreted, the Constitution is a GLORIOUS LIBERTY DOCUMENT."

Douglass's involvement in practical politics deepened during the 1850s. Although he believed that violence would be necessary to abolish slavery, he was cautious in encouraging slave insurrections, declining to join John Brown's raid on Harpers Ferry. Nonetheless, popular suspicion that he was a key conspirator led Douglass to flee to Canada and then to Britain. When he resumed speech making in America in 1860, the victory of the Republican Party and its program of free soil seemed imminent.

During and after the Civil War Douglass remained a respected African American leader. He pressed the Republicans to embrace the abolition of slavery as a war aim, celebrated Lincoln's Emancipation Proclamation, and assisted the War Department in recruiting black soldiers. Throughout Reconstruction he spoke and lobbied effectively for equal treatment for African Americans, especially for the right to vote. Finally rewarding Douglass's service to its cause, the Republican Party secured his appointment in 1888 as the American minister to the black nation of Haiti.

By the time of his death in 1895 Douglass's optimism about race relations had waned, as Jim Crow laws in the southern states fastened new bonds of discrimination on African Americans. In his last major speech he warned that the "presence of eight millions of people . . . constituting an aggrieved class, smarting under terrible wrongs, denied the exercise of the commonest rights of humanity . . . [is] a disgrace and scandal to . . . the whole country."

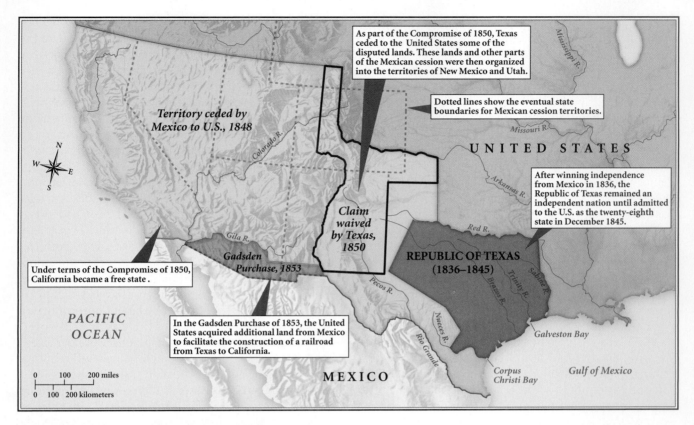

Territory ceded by Mexico to U.S., 1848

As part of the Compromise of 1850, Texas ceded to the United States some of the disputed lands. These lands and other parts of the Mexican cession were then organized into the territories of New Mexico and Utah.

Dotted lines show the eventual state boundaries for Mexican cession territories.

UNITED STATES

After winning independence from Mexico in 1836, the Republic of Texas remained an independent nation until admitted to the U.S. as the twenty-eighth state in December 1845.

Claim waived by Texas, 1850

Gadsden Purchase, 1853

REPUBLIC OF TEXAS (1836–1845)

Under terms of the Compromise of 1850, California became a free state.

In the Gadsden Purchase of 1853, the United States acquired additional land from Mexico to facilitate the construction of a railroad from Texas to California.

PACIFIC OCEAN

MEXICO

Galveston Bay

Corpus Christi Bay

Gulf of Mexico

0 100 200 miles
0 100 200 kilometers

MAP 13.5 The Mexican Cession, 1848–1853

In the Treaty of Guadalupe Hidalgo (1848), Mexico ceded to the United States its vast northern territories—the present-day states of California, Nevada, Utah, Arizona, New Mexico, and half of Colorado and Texas. These new territories, President Polk boasted to Congress, "constitute of themselves a country large enough for a great empire, and the acquisition is second in importance only to that of Louisiana in 1803."

Yucatán Peninsula, and taking all of Oregon. To maintain party unity Cass was deliberately vague on the question of slavery in the West. He promoted a new idea—squatter sovereignty—that would give settlers in each territory the power to determine its status as free or slave.

The Election of 1848.   Cass's political ingenuity failed to hold the party together. Demanding unambiguous opposition to the expansion of slavery, some northern Democrats joined the newly formed Free-Soil Party, which nominated Martin Van Buren for president. Van Buren's conversion to free soil was genuine, but he also wanted to punish southern Democrats for having denied him the presidential nomination in 1844. To attract Whig votes, the Free-Soil Party chose conscience Whig Charles Francis Adams as its candidate for vice president.

To avoid divisions in their ranks, the Whigs nominated General Zachary Taylor. Taylor was a southerner and a Louisiana slave owner, but he had not taken a position on the politically charged issue of slavery in the territories. Equally important, the general's exploits during the war with Mexico had made him a popular hero.

Known as "Old Rough and Ready," Taylor possessed a common touch that had won him the affection of his troops. "Our Commander on the Rio Grande," wrote Walt Whitman, "emulates the Great Commander of our revolution"—George Washington.

In 1848, as in 1840, running a military hero worked for the Whigs. Taylor and his vice presidential running mate, Millard Fillmore, took 47 percent of the popular vote against 42 percent for Cass, but the margin in the electoral college was thin: 163 to 127. The Free-Soil ticket of Van Buren and Adams made the difference in the election. They won 10 percent of the popular vote and, crucially, deprived the Democrats of enough votes in New York to cost Cass that state and the presidency. The bitter debate over the Wilmot Proviso had fractured the Democratic Party in the North and changed the dynamics of American politics.

1850: Crisis and Compromise

Even before President Zachary Taylor took office, events in California sparked a major political crisis that threatened the Union. In January 1848 workmen building a

A General Runs for President

Of the first nine presidents, three—Washington, Jackson, and Harrison—owed their political success to their exploits as military commanders. Fresh from the battlefields of the Mexican War, General Zachary Taylor followed in their footsteps, posing for this daguerreotype campaign portrait in his uniform. In part because of his popular appeal as a military hero, Taylor— running on the Whig ticket—won a narrow victory over Democrat Lewis Cass. Collection of Janice L. and David J. Frent.

mill for John A. Sutter in the Sierra Nevada foothills in northern California discovered flakes of gold. Sutter was a Swiss immigrant who arrived in California in 1839, became a Mexican citizen, and established an estate in the Sacramento Valley. He tried to keep the discovery a secret, but by May Americans from San Francisco were pouring into the foothills. When President Polk confirmed the discovery in December, the gold rush was on. By January 1849 sixty-one crowded ships had departed from northeastern ports to sail around Cape Horn for San Francisco, and by May, nearly twelve thousand wagons had crossed the Missouri River, also bound for the gold fields. In 1849 alone more than 80,000 migrants—the "forty-niners"— arrived in California (Map 13.6).

Statehood for California.   The rapid influx of settlers revived the national debate over free soil. The forty-niners, who lived in crowded, chaotic towns and mining camps, demanded the formation of a territorial government to protect their lives and property. To avoid an extended debate over slavery, President Taylor advised the Californians to apply for statehood immediately, and in November 1849 they ratified a state constitution that prohibited slavery. Few of the many southerners who flocked to the gold fields or to San Francisco owned slaves or wanted to. For his part Taylor wanted to attract Free-Soilers and northern Democrats into the Whig Party and urged Congress to admit California as a free state.

The swift victory of the antislavery forces in California alarmed southern politicians. The admission of California as a free state would not only cut off the expansion of slavery to the Pacific but also threaten the carefully maintained balance in the Senate. In 1845 the entry of Texas and Florida had raised the total of slave states to fifteen, against thirteen free states. However, the entry of Iowa in 1846 and Wisconsin in 1848 had reestablished the balance. Fearing that the South would be placed at a political disadvantage from which it would never recover, southern politicians decided to block California's admission unless the federal government guaranteed the future of slavery.

Constitutional Conflict.   The resulting political impasse produced long and passionate debates in Congress and four different positions with respect to the status of slavery in the territories. As usual John C. Calhoun took an extreme stance. He began by asserting the right of states to secede from the Union and warning that, to protect their slave property, the southern states might exercise that right. To avoid that outcome he proposed a constitutional amendment that would permanently balance power between the sections. Calhoun also advanced the radically new doctrine that Congress had no constitutional authority to regulate slavery in the territories. This argument ran counter to a half century of practice. In 1787 Congress had prohibited slavery in the Northwest Territory, and in the Missouri Compromise of 1821 it had extended this ban to most of the Louisiana Purchase.

Although Calhoun's controversial constitutional doctrine that all the territories were open to slavery won support in the Deep South, many southerners were prepared to accept a second—more moderate—position: an extension of the Missouri Compromise line to the Pacific Ocean. This extension would guarantee slave owners access to some western territory, including a separate state in southern California. Some northern Democrats, including former secretary of state James Buchanan, also favored this plan as a way to resolve the crisis.

A third alternative for resolving the status of slavery in the territories was squatter sovereignty, the plan advanced by Lewis Cass in 1848 and now championed by Democratic senator Stephen Douglas of Illinois. Douglas called his plan "**popular sovereignty**" to emphasize

California Gold Prospectors
Beginning in 1849, thousands of fortune seekers from all parts of the world converged on the California gold fields. By 1852 the state had 200,000 residents, including 25,000 Chinese, many of whom toiled in the gold fields as wage laborers. Working at the head of the Auburn Ravine in 1852, these prospectors are using a primitive technique—panning—to separate gold from sand and gravel. California State Library.

its roots in republican ideology, and it had considerable appeal. Popular sovereignty would place decisions about slavery in the hands of local settlers and their territorial governments, removing the explosive issue from national politics. However, popular sovereignty was a vague and slippery concept. For example, did popular sovereignty mean that residents could accept or ban slavery when a territory was first organized or only when a territory had enough people to frame a constitution and apply for statehood?

For their part, antislavery advocates were unwilling to accept any plan that might involve the expansion of slavery and stood firm for complete exclusion. In 1850 Senator Salmon P. Chase of Ohio, elected by a Democratic–Free-Soil coalition, and Senator William H. Seward, a New York Whig, urged federal authorities to restrict slavery within its existing boundaries and then extinguish it completely. Condemning slavery as "morally unjust, politically unwise, and socially pernicious" and invoking "a higher law than the Constitu-

tion," Seward demanded bold action to protect freedom, "the common heritage of mankind."

A Complex Compromise. Standing on the brink of disaster, senior Whigs and Democrats desperately sought a compromise to preserve the Union. Through a long and complex legislative process, Whig leaders Henry Clay and Daniel Webster and Democrat Stephen A. Douglas organized an interrelated package of six laws known collectively as the Compromise of 1850. To mollify the South, the Compromise included a new Fugitive Slave Act allowing slave owners to demand that federal magistrates in the free states help return runaway slaves. To satisfy the North, the legislation admitted California as a free state, resolved a boundary dispute between New Mexico and Texas in favor of New Mexico, and abolished the slave trade (but not slavery) in the District of Columbia. Finally, the Compromise organized the rest of the lands acquired from Mexico into the territories of New Mexico and Utah on the basis of popular sovereignty (Map 13.7).

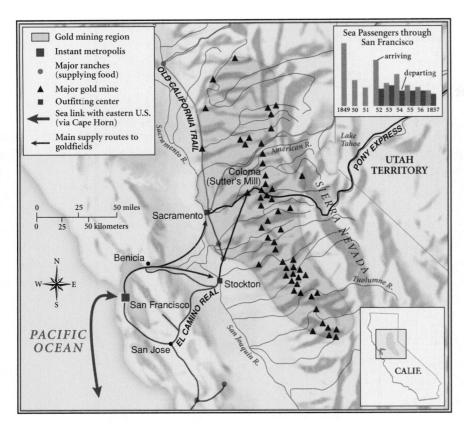

MAP 13.6 The California Gold Rush, 1849–1857

Traveling from all parts of the world—Europe, China, and Australia as well as the eastern United States—hundreds of thousands of bonanza seekers converged on the California gold fields. Miners traveling by sea landed at San Francisco, which became an instant metropolis; many others trekked overland to the gold fields on the Old California Trail. By the mid-1850s the gold rush was over; almost as many people departed by sea from San Francisco each year as arrived to seek their fortune.

The Compromise averted a secession crisis in 1850—but only barely. In the midst of the struggle the governor of South Carolina declared that there was not "the slightest doubt" that his state would secede from the Union. He and other "**fire-eaters**" in Georgia, Mississippi, and Alabama organized special conventions to protect "Southern Rights" and demand secession. To persuade these conventions to support the Compromise, moderate southern politicians agreed to support secession in the future if Congress abolished slavery anywhere or refused to grant statehood to a territory with a proslavery constitution. Lacking sufficient popular support, the "fire-eaters" drew back from secession, averting a constitutional crisis.

The End of the Second Party System, 1850–1858

The architects of the Compromise of 1850 hoped that their agreement would resolve the issue of slavery for a generation. Their hopes were quickly dashed. Demanding freedom for fugitive slaves and free soil in the West, some northerners refused to accept the letter or the spirit of the Compromise. Some southerners were equally hostile to the agreement and plotted to expand slavery in the West and the Caribbean. These resulting disputes destroyed the Second Party System, deepening the crisis of the Union.

Resistance to the Fugitive Slave Act

The most controversial element of the Compromise proved to be the Fugitive Slave Act, which ensured federal protection for slavery and made no concessions to the humanity of African Americans. Under its terms federal judges or special commissioners in the northern states determined the status of blacks who were accused of being runaway slaves. The accused blacks were denied jury trials and even the right to testify. Because federal marshals were legally required to support slave catchers, the new legislation was effective, and about two hundred fugitives (as well as some free northern blacks) were sent to the South and enslaved.

The plight of runaways and the appearance of slave catchers aroused popular hostility in the North and Midwest, and free blacks and abolitionists defied the new law. In October 1850 Boston abolitionists helped two slaves escape to freedom and drove a Georgia slave catcher out of town. The following year rioters in Syracuse, New York, broke into a courthouse to free a fugitive slave. Abandoning his commitment to nonviolence, Frederick Douglass declared that "the only way to make a Fugitive Slave Law a dead letter is to make half a dozen or more dead kidnappers." As if in response, in September 1851 a deadly confrontation took place in the Quaker village of Christiana, Pennsylvania. About twenty African Americans exchanged gunfire with a group of slave catchers from Maryland, killing two of them. Federal

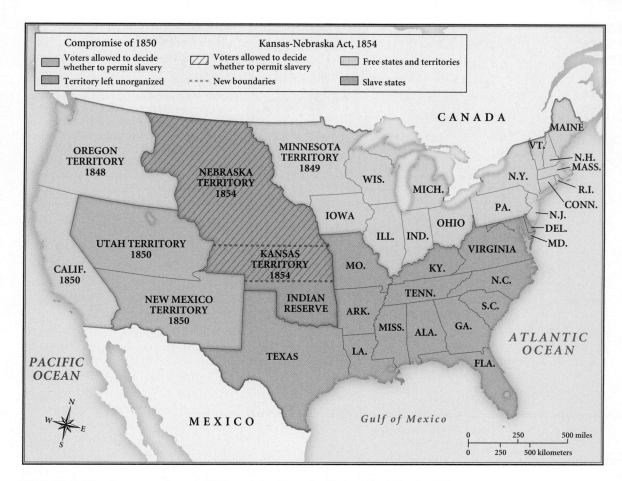

MAP 13.7 The Compromise of 1850 and the Kansas-Nebraska Act of 1854

Vast territories were at stake in the contest over the extension of slavery. The Compromise of 1850 resolved the status of lands in the Far West: California would be a free state, and the settlers of the Utah and New Mexico Territories would decide their own fate by voting for or against slavery. But the implementation of popular sovereignty in Kansas and Nebraska in 1854 sparked a bitter local war between the advocates of free soil and slavery, revealing a fatal flaw in the concept.

For more help analyzing this map, see the ONLINE STUDY GUIDE at bedfordstmartins.com/henretta.

marshals arrested thirty-six blacks and four whites and had them indicted for treason for defying the law. But a Pennsylvania jury acquitted one defendant, and northern public opinion forced the government to drop its charges against the rest.

Harriet Beecher Stowe's abolitionist novel *Uncle Tom's Cabin* (1852) increased northern opposition to the Fugitive Slave Act. By translating the moral principles of abolitionism into heartrending personal situations, Beecher's novel evoked empathy and outrage throughout the North. Members of northern state legislatures were equally outraged that the South was using the federal government as an agent of the slaveholding interest within their states. In response, they enacted **personal-liberty laws** that extended legal rights in their states to accused fugitives. In 1857 the

Wisconsin Supreme Court went even further, ruling in *Ableman v. Booth* that the Fugitive Slave Act was void in Wisconsin because it was contrary to state law and resulted in the illegal federal confinement of a Wisconsin citizen accused of violating it. Continuing to assert a state's rights position, the Wisconsin court rejected the authority of federal courts to review its decision. When the case reached the U.S. Supreme Court in 1859, Chief Justice Roger B. Taney led a unanimous court in affirming the supremacy of federal over state courts—a position that has stood the test of time—and upheld the constitutionality of the Fugitive Slave Act. By that time popular opposition in the North had made it nearly impossible to catch fugitive blacks. As Frederick Douglass had hoped, the act had become a "dead letter."

Uncle Tom's Cabin, 1852

The cover of this "Young Folks Edition" of Uncle Tom's Cabin shows Tom as an old man, worn down by his life as a slave and the brutal punishments of overseer Simon Legree. Little Eva, whom Tom had saved from drowning, rests her hand compassionately on his knee. Like the book's text, this image offered whites a sympathetic view of African Americans, challenging generations of negative stereotypes. Picture Research Consultants & Archives.

The Whigs' Decline and the Democrats' Diplomacy

The conflict over fugitive slaves split the Whig Party, which went into the election of 1852 weakened by the death of Henry Clay, one of its greatest leaders. Rejecting Millard Fillmore, who had become president on the death of Zachary Taylor, the Whigs nominated General Winfield Scott, another hero of the war with Mexico. However, about a third of southern Whigs threw their support to the Democrats, refusing to support Scott because northern members of the Whig Party refused to support slavery.

The Democrats too were divided. Southerners wanted a candidate who would support Calhoun's position that all territories should be open to slavery. But northern and midwestern Democrats advocated the principle of popular sovereignty, as did the three leading candidates—Lewis Cass of Michigan, Stephen Douglas of Illinois, and James Buchanan of Pennsylvania. At the national convention no candidate could secure the necessary two-thirds majority. Exhausted after forty-eight ballots, the convention settled on a compromise nominee, Franklin Pierce of New Hampshire, a congenial man reputed to be sympathetic to the South.

The Democrats' cautious strategy paid off, and they swept the election. Pleased by the admission of California as a free state, Martin Van Buren and many other Free-Soilers voted for Pierce, reuniting the Democratic Party. Conversely, the election fragmented the Whig Party into sectional wings; it would never again wage a national campaign.

As president, Pierce pursued an expansionist foreign policy. To assist northern merchants he sent a mission to Japan to negotiate a commercial treaty. Pierce was even more solicitous of southern interests. To resolve a dispute over the southern boundary of New Mexico, the president revived Polk's plan to annex a large amount of territory south of the Rio Grande and named James Gadsden as his negotiator. Mexican officials rejected Pierce's annexation bid but agreed to sell a small amount of land that Gadsden, a railroad promoter, wanted to construct a southern-based transcontinental railroad to the Pacific (see Map 13.5).

Pierce's most dramatic foreign policy initiative came in the Caribbean. Southern expansionists had previously funded three clandestine military expeditions to Spanish Cuba, where they hoped to prod the slave-owning elite into declaring independence and then joining the United States. In 1853 Pierce covertly supported a new Cuban expedition led by John A. Quitman, a former governor of Mississippi. While Quitman was building up his forces, the Pierce administration threatened war with Spain over the seizure of an American ship, demanding an apology and a large indemnity. When northern Democrats in Congress refused to support this aggressive diplomacy, Pierce and Secretary of State William L. Marcy had to back down. Still determined to seize Cuba, Marcy tried to buy the island from Spain and then prompted American diplomats in Europe to pressure Pierce to seize it. In the Ostend Manifesto (1854), the diplomats sent a message to Pierce declaring that the United States would be justified in seizing Cuba "by every law, human and Divine." Quickly leaked to the press by antiexpansionists, the Ostend Manifesto triggered a new wave of northern resentment against the South and forced Pierce to halt his efforts. But his expansionist policy had already revived northern fears of a "**Slave Power**" conspiracy.

The Kansas-Nebraska Act and the Rise of New Parties

In the wake of the Ostend Manifesto a new struggle over westward expansion inflamed sectional divisions. Because the Missouri Compromise prohibited slavery in the Louisiana Purchase north of 36°30′, southern senators had delayed the political organization of that area. However, westward-looking residents of the Ohio River Valley and the Upper South demanded its settlement. Senator Stephen A. Douglas of Illinois became their spokesman, in part because he supported a northern transcontinental railroad from Chicago to California. In

Presidential Election of 1852

In this cartoon, Franklin Pierce races toward the White House on a fleet Democratic horse while General Winfield Scott futilely beats his stubborn Whig mule, which is pulled by members of the Know-Nothing Party ("Native Americans") and prodded by a group of African Americans. By identifying Scott and the Whigs as anti-foreigner and pro-black (because many Whigs opposed the Fugitive Slave Act of 1850), the cartoonist seeks to garner votes for Pierce and the Democrats from New York's large population of Irish and German immigrants. Collection of Janice L. and David J. Frent.

1854 Douglas introduced a bill to extinguish Native American rights on the central Great Plains and organize a large territory to be called Nebraska. Because Nebraska was north of 36°30', it would be a free territory.

Douglas's bill conflicted with the plans of southern senators and representatives, who wanted to extend slavery throughout the Louisiana Purchase. Moreover, like James Gadsden, southern leaders hoped that one of their cities—New Orleans, Memphis, or St. Louis—would become the eastern terminus of a transcontinental railroad. To win southern support for the organization of Nebraska, Douglas made two major concessions. First, he amended his bill so that it explicitly repealed the Missouri Compromise and organized the region on the basis of popular sovereignty. Second, Douglas agreed to the formation of two new territories, Nebraska and Kansas, giving slaveholders a chance to dominate the settlement of Kansas, the more southern territory (see Map 13.7). To persuade northerners and midwesterners, Douglas argued that Kansas would be settled primarily by nonslaveholders because its climate and terrain were not suited to plantation agriculture.

After weeks of bitter debate, the Senate enacted the Kansas-Nebraska Act, which was strongly supported by President Pierce. However, the House of Representatives initially voted to kill the measure, as sixty-six northern Democrats defied party policy. Using all the powers at his disposal—patronage pressure, newspaper propaganda, floor management—Pierce persuaded twenty-two members to change their votes, and the measure squeaked through.

Republicans and Know-Nothings. The price of this victory was enormous because passage of the Kansas-Nebraska Act completed the destruction of the Whig Party and nearly wrecked the Democratic Party. Abolitionists and Free-Soilers denounced the act, calling it "part of a great scheme for extending and perpetuating supremacy of the slave power," and their message now fell on receptive ears. Antislavery northern Whigs and "anti-Nebraska" Democrats abandoned their respective parties to create a new Republican Party, named after the party headed by Thomas Jefferson. Emphasizing uncompromising opposition to the

"Bleeding Kansas"
The confrontation between North and South in Kansas took many forms. In the spring of 1859 Dr. John Doy (seated) slipped across the border into Missouri and tried to lead thirteen escaped slaves to freedom in Kansas, only to be captured and jailed in St. Joseph, Missouri. This serious-minded band of antislavery men, well armed with guns and Bowie knives, attacked the jail and carried Doy back to Kansas. Kansas State Historical Society.

expansion of slavery, the Republicans ran a slate of candidates in the congressional election of 1854.

Like most American parties, the Republican Party was a coalition of diverse groups—Free-Soilers, antislavery Democrats, conscience Whigs—but most of its founders shared a common philosophy. They opposed slavery because it degraded manual labor, enslaving blacks and thereby driving down the wages and working conditions of free white workers. In contrast, Republicans as diverse as farmer Abijah Beckwith of Herkimer, New York, and Senator Thaddeus Stevens of Pennsylvania celebrated the moral virtues of a society based on "the middling classes who own the soil and work it with their own hands." Abraham Lincoln, an Illinois Whig who became a Republican, articulated the party's vision of social mobility. "There is no permanent class of hired laborers among us," he argued, and every man had a chance to become a property owner. In the face of increasing class divisions in the industrializing North and Midwest, Lincoln and his fellow Republicans asserted the values of republican freedom and individual enterprise.

Competing for Whig and Democratic votes was another new party, the American, or "Know-Nothing," Party. The American Party had its origins in the anti-immigrant and anti-Catholic organizations of the 1840s (see Chapter 10). In 1850 these secret societies banded together as the Order of the Star-Spangled Banner and the following year they formed the American Party. The secrecy-conscious members sometimes answered outsiders' questions by saying, "I know nothing," giving the party its nickname, but its program was far from secret. Know-Nothings hoped to unite native-born Protestants against the "alien menace" of Irish and German Catholics, banning further immigration and instituting literacy tests for voting. In 1854 the Know-Nothings gained control of the state governments of Massachusetts and Pennsylvania and, allied with the Whigs, commanded a majority in the U.S. House of Representatives. The emergence of a

new major party led by nativists suddenly became a real possibility.

"Bleeding Kansas."   At the same time, the Kansas-Nebraska Act had created yet another political crisis. In 1854 thousands of settlers rushed into the Kansas Territory, putting Douglas's theory of popular sovereignty to the test. On the side of slavery Senator David R. Atchison of Missouri organized residents of his state to cross into Kansas and vote in crucial elections there. Opposing him were agents of the abolitionist New England Emigrant Aid Society, which dispatched hundreds of Free-Soilers to Kansas. In March 1855 the Pierce administration stepped into the fray by accepting the legitimacy of the territorial legislature sitting in Lecompton, Kansas, which had been elected primarily by border-crossing Missourians and had adopted proslavery legislation. However, the majority of Kansas residents were Free-Soilers and refused allegiance to the Lecompton government.

In May 1856 both sides turned to violence. A proslavery gang, seven hundred strong, sacked the free-soil town of Lawrence, destroying two newspaper offices, looting stores, and burning down buildings (see American Voices, "Axalla John Hoole: 'Bleeding Kansas': A Southern View," p. 390). The attack enraged John Brown, an abolitionist from New York and Ohio, whose free-state militia force arrived too late to save the town. Brown was a complex man with a checkered past. Born in 1800, he had started more than twenty businesses in six states and had often been sued by his creditors. Despite his record of business failures, Brown had an intelligence and a moral intensity that won the trust of influential people, including leading abolitionists. Taking vengeance for the sack of Lawrence, he and a few followers murdered and mutilated five proslavery settlers. We must "fight fire with fire" and "strike terror in the hearts of the proslavery people," Brown declared. The sack of Lawrence and the "Pottawatomie massacre," as

Axalla John Hoole

"Bleeding Kansas": A Southern View

Early in 1856 Axalla John Hoole and his bride left South Carolina to build a new life in the Kansas Territory (K.T.). These letters from Hoole to his family show that things did not go well from the start and gradually got worse; after eighteen months the Hooles returned to South Carolina. A Confederate militia captain during the Civil War, Axalla Hoole died in the Battle of Chickamauga in September 1863.

Kansas City, Missouri, Apl. 3d., 1856. The Missourians . . . are very sanguine about Kansas being a slave state & I have heard some of them say it shall be . . . but generally speaking, I have not met with the reception which I expected. Everyone seems bent on the Almighty Dollar, and as a general thing that seems to be their only thought. . . . [T]he supper bell has rung and I must close. Give my love to [the family] and all the Negroes. . . .

Lecompton, K.T., Sept. 12, 1856. I have been unwell ever since the 9th of July. . . . I thought of going to work in a few days, when the Abolitionists broke out and I have had to stand guard of nights when I ought to have been in bed, took cold which . . . caused diarrhea. . . . Betsie is well—

You perceive from the heading of this that I am now in Lecompton, almost all of the Proslavery party between this place and Lawrence are here. We brought our families here, as we thought that we would be better able to defend ourselves. . . .

Lane [and a force of abolitionists] came against us last Friday (a week ago to-day). As it happened we had about 400 men with two cannon—we marched out to meet him, though we were under the impression at the time that we had 1,000 men. We came in gunshot of each other, but the regular [U.S. Army] soldiers came and interfered, but not before our party had shot some dozen guns, by which it is reported that five of the Abolitionists had been killed or wounded. We had strict orders . . . not to fire until they made the attack, but some of our boys would not be restrained. I was a rifleman and one of the skirmishers, but did all that I could to restrain our men though I itched all over to shoot myself. . . . [B]ut we were acting on the defensive, and did not think it prudent to commence the engagement. I firmly believe we would have whipped them, though we would have lost a good many men. . . .

July the 5th., 1857. I fear, Sister, that [our] coming here will do no good at last, as I begin to think that this will be made a Free State at last. 'Tis true we have elected Proslavery men to draft a state constitution, but I feel pretty certain, if it is put to a vote of the people, it will be rejected, as I feel pretty confident that they have a majority here at this time. The South has ceased all efforts, while the North is redoubling her exertions. We nominated a candidate for Congress last Friday—Ex-Gov. Ransom of Michigan. I must confess I have not much faith in him, tho he professes to hate the abolitionists bitterly. . . . If we had nominated a Southern man, he would have been sure to have been beaten. . . .

Source: William Stanley Hoole, ed., "A Southerner's Viewpoint of the Kansas Situation, 1856–1857," *Kansas Historical Quarterly* 3 (1934): 43–65, 149–71, passim.

the killings became known, initiated a guerrilla war in Kansas that cost about two hundred lives.

The Election of 1856 and Dred Scott

The violence in Kansas dominated the presidential election of 1856. The two-year-old Republican Party counted on anger over "Bleeding Kansas" to boost its fortunes. The party's platform denounced the Kansas-Nebraska Act and, alleging a "Slave Power" conspiracy, insisted that the federal government prohibit slavery in all the territories. Its platform also called for federal subsidies to transcontinental railroads, reviving the element of the Whig economic program that was most popular among midwestern Democrats. For president the Republicans nominated Colonel John C. Frémont, a Free-Soiler famous for his role in the conquest of California. The American Party entered the election with high hopes, but it quickly split into sectional factions over Kansas. The southern faction of the American Party nominated former Whig President Millard Fillmore. The Republicans cleverly maneuvered the northern faction of the American Party into endorsing Frémont, and they won the support of many Know-Nothing workingmen by adding anti-Catholic nativism to the Republican Party's program of high tariffs on foreign manufactures. As a Pennsylvania Republican declared, "Let our motto be, protection to everything American, against everything foreign." In

New York Republicans likewise shaped their policies "to cement into a harmonious mass . . . all of the Anti-Slavery, Anti-Popery and Anti-Whiskey" voters.

The Democrats reaffirmed their support for popular sovereignty and the Kansas-Nebraska Act and nominated James Buchanan of Pennsylvania. A tall, dignified figure of sixty-four, Buchanan was an experienced but unimaginative and timid politician. Drawing upon his party's organizational strength and the loyalty of Democratic voters, Buchanan won the three-way race, amassing 174 votes in the electoral college and winning the popular vote—1.8 million votes (45 percent) to 1.3 million (33 percent) for Frémont. Nonetheless, Frémont demonstrated the appeal of the new Republican Party in the North by carrying eleven free states with 114 electoral votes. Buchanan took only five free states, and a small shift of the popular vote to Frémont in Illinois and Pennsylvania would have given him the presidency. Fillmore, the candidate of the southern members of the American Party, won 21 percent of the national vote but only 8 electoral votes.

The dramatic restructuring of parties was now apparent (Map 13.8). With the splintering of the Know-Nothings, the Republicans had replaced the Whigs as the second major party. Moreover, because they had no support in the South, a Republican victory in the next presidential election might mean the end of the Union. The fate of the republic hinged on the ability of President Buchanan to defuse the passions of the past decade and achieve a new compromise that would protect free soil in the West and slavery in the South.

Events—and his own values and weaknesses—conspired against Buchanan. Shortly after the election the Supreme Court prepared to render a decision on the case of Dred Scott, which involved the bitterly controversial issue of Congress's constitutional authority to regulate slavery in the territories. Scott was an enslaved African American who had lived for a time with his owner, an army surgeon, in the free state of Illinois and at Fort Snelling, then in the Wisconsin Territory, where the Northwest Ordinance (1787) prohibited slavery. In his suit Scott claimed that his residence in a free state and a free territory had made him free. In March 1857, after Buchanan had pressured several northern justices to vote in tandem with their southern colleagues, the Court announced its decision in *Dred Scott v. Sandford*.

Seven of the nine members of the Court concurred on one critical point: Scott remained a slave. Because they could not agree on the legal issues, each justice wrote a separate opinion. In the most influential opinion, Chief Justice Roger B. Taney of Maryland declared that Negroes, whether enslaved or free, could not be citizens of the United States and that Scott therefore had no right to sue in federal court. That argument was controversial enough, since free blacks could be citizens of a state and therefore presumably had access to the federal courts. But Taney went on to make two even more con-

troversial points. First, he endorsed John C. Calhoun's argument that because the Fifth Amendment prohibited the taking of property without due process of law, Congress could not prevent southern citizens from taking their slave "property" into the territories or owning it there. Consequently, the chief justice concluded, the Northwest Ordinance and the Missouri Compromise—which prohibited slavery in the territories—had never been constitutional. Second, Taney declared that Congress could not give to territorial governments any powers that Congress itself did not possess. Since Congress had no authority to prohibit slavery in a territory, neither did a territorial government. Taney thereby endorsed Calhoun's interpretation of popular sovereignty: only when settlers wrote a constitution and requested statehood could they prohibit slavery. In a single stroke a Democrat-dominated Supreme Court had declared the Republicans' antislavery platform to be unconstitutional, a decision the Republicans could never accept. Led by Senator William H. Seward of New York, they accused the Supreme Court and President Buchanan of participating in the "Slave Power" conspiracy.

Buchanan then added new fuel to the raging constitutional fire. In early 1858 he recommended the admission of Kansas as a slave state under the Lecompton constitution. Many observers—including the influential Democratic senator Stephen Douglas—believed that the constitution had been enacted by fraudulent means. Angered that Buchanan would not permit a referendum in Kansas on the Lecompton constitution, Douglas broke with the president and his southern allies and persuaded Congress to deny statehood to Kansas. (Kansas would enter the Union as a free state in 1861.) By pursuing a proslavery agenda—first in the *Dred Scott* decision and then in Kansas—Buchanan had helped to split his party and the nation.

Abraham Lincoln and the Republican Triumph, 1858–1860

The crisis of the Union intensified as the national Democratic Party fragmented into sectional factions and the Republicans gained the support of a majority of northern voters. During this transition Abraham Lincoln emerged as the pivotal figure in American politics, the only Republican leader whose policies and temperament might have saved the Union. But few southerners trusted Lincoln, and his election threatened to unleash the secessionist movement that had menaced the nation since 1850.

Lincoln's Political Career

The flourishing of the middle class of storekeepers, lawyers, and entrepreneurs in the small towns of the Ohio River Valley shaped Lincoln's early career. He came from an illiterate yeoman farming family that had moved from

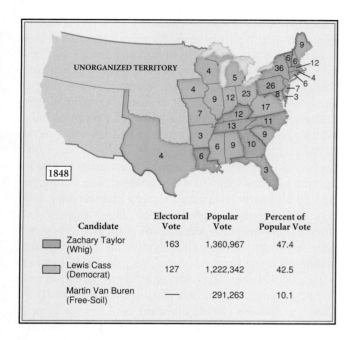

Candidate	Electoral Vote	Popular Vote	Percent of Popular Vote
Zachary Taylor (Whig)	163	1,360,967	47.4
Lewis Cass (Democrat)	127	1,222,342	42.5
Martin Van Buren (Free-Soil)	—	291,263	10.1

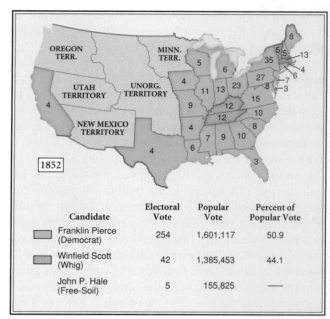

Candidate	Electoral Vote	Popular Vote	Percent of Popular Vote
Franklin Pierce (Democrat)	254	1,601,117	50.9
Winfield Scott (Whig)	42	1,385,453	44.1
John P. Hale (Free-Soil)	5	155,825	—

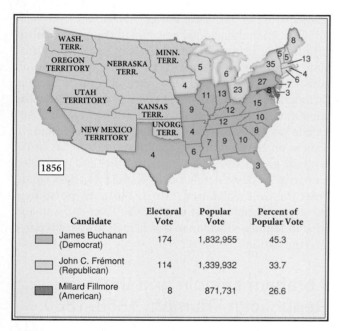

Candidate	Electoral Vote	Popular Vote	Percent of Popular Vote
James Buchanan (Democrat)	174	1,832,955	45.3
John C. Frémont (Republican)	114	1,339,932	33.7
Millard Fillmore (American)	8	871,731	26.6

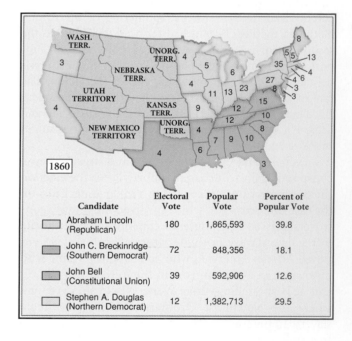

Candidate	Electoral Vote	Popular Vote	Percent of Popular Vote
Abraham Lincoln (Republican)	180	1,865,593	39.8
John C. Breckinridge (Southern Democrat)	72	848,356	18.1
John Bell (Constitutional Union)	39	592,906	12.6
Stephen A. Douglas (Northern Democrat)	12	1,382,713	29.5

MAP 13.8 Political Realignment, 1848–1860

In 1848 both the Whigs and the Democrats boasted national parties, with strong support in most parts of the nation. Then political conflict over slavery and the Compromise of 1850 destroyed the Whig Party in the South, making the Democrats the only nationwide party and giving them an easy victory in 1852. The Democratic supremacy was short-lived: by 1856 the passions aroused by "Bloody Kansas" resulted in the creation of the Republican Party, which carried most of the states of the Northeast and Midwest. By 1860 a new regionally based party system had taken shape and would persist for the next seventy years, with Democrats dominant in the South and Republicans in the Northeast and Midwest.

Kentucky, where Lincoln was born in 1809, to Indiana and then to Illinois. In 1831 Lincoln rejected the farmer's life of his father and became a store clerk in New Salem, Illinois. Socially ambitious, Lincoln sought entry into the middle class, joining the New Salem Debating Society and reading Shakespeare and other literary works.

Lincoln's ambition was "a little engine that knew no rest," his closest associate later remarked. Admitted to the bar in 1837, Lincoln moved to Springfield, the small country town that had become the new state capital. There he met Mary Todd, the cultured daughter of a Kentucky banker; they married in 1842. The couple were a picture in contrasts. Her tastes were aristocratic; his were humble. She was volatile in temperament; he had an easygoing manner but suffered bouts of depression that tried her patience and tested his character. Entering political life, Lincoln served four terms as a Whig in the Illinois assembly, where he promoted education, state banking, and internal improvements such as canals and railroads. In 1846 the rising lawyer-politician won election to Congress.

As a congressman during the war with Mexico, Lincoln had to take a stand on the contentious issue of slavery. He had long felt that slavery was unjust but did not believe that the federal government had the constitutional authority to tamper with slavery in the South. With respect to the war with Mexico, Lincoln took the middle ground. He endorsed military appropriation bills but voted to restrict slavery, throwing his support behind the Wilmot Proviso. He also proposed that Congress follow the lead of the northern states and enact legislation for the gradual (and therefore compensated) emancipation of slaves in the District of Columbia. Lincoln argued that such measures—firm opposition to the expansion of slavery, gradual emancipation, and the colonization of freed slaves in Africa and elsewhere—represented the only practical way to address the issue. In the highly emotional political atmosphere of the time, both abolitionists and proslavery activists derided these pragmatic policies. Dismayed, Lincoln withdrew from politics and devoted his energies to a lucrative legal practice representing railroads and manufacturers.

Lincoln returned to the political fray after the passage of Stephen Douglas's Kansas-Nebraska Act. Attacking Douglas's doctrine of popular sovereignty, Lincoln reaffirmed his position on slavery. He would not threaten the institution in the states where it existed but would use national authority to exclude it from the territories. Confronting the moral issue, Lincoln declared that if the nation was to uphold its republican ideals, then it must eventually cut out slavery like a "cancer."

Abandoning the Whig Party in favor of the Republicans, Lincoln quickly emerged as their leader in Illinois. Campaigning for the U.S. Senate against Stephen Douglas in 1858, Lincoln alerted his audiences to the dangers of the "Slave Power" conspiracy. He warned that the proslavery Supreme Court might soon declare that the Constitution "does not permit a state to exclude slavery from its limits," just as it had decided (in *Dred Scott*) that "neither Congress nor the territorial legislature can do it." In that event, he continued, "we shall awake to the reality . . . that the Supreme Court has made Illinois a slave state." This fear of the spread of slavery into the North informed Lincoln's famous "House Divided" speech. Quoting from the Bible, "A house divided against itself cannot stand," he predicted a constitutional crisis: "I believe this government cannot endure permanently half slave and half free. . . . It will become all one thing, or all the other." The contest in Illinois between Lincoln and Douglas in 1858 attracted

A. Lincoln   *S. A. Douglas*

Abraham Lincoln and Stephen Douglas, 1860
When Douglas and Lincoln squared off in the presidential election of 1860, they distributed thousands of silk campaign ribbons bearing their portraits and signatures. The well-known photographer Matthew Brady took their pictures and retouched the images to make them more flattering—smoothing out Lincoln's gaunt and well-lined face and slimming down Douglas's ample cheeks. Collection of Janice L. and David J. Frent.

national interest because of Douglas's prominence and Lincoln's reputation as a formidable speaker. During a series of seven debates Douglas declared his support for white supremacy and attacked Lincoln for his alleged belief in "negro equality." Put on the defensive by Douglas's racist tactics, Lincoln advocated economic opportunity for blacks (but not equal political rights) and asked Douglas how he could accept the *Dred Scott* decision (which protected slave owners' property in the territories) and at the same time advocate popular sovereignty (which asserted settlers' power to exclude slavery). Douglas responded with the so-called Freeport Doctrine, asserting that the residents of a territory could exclude slavery simply by not adopting local legislation to protect it. Douglas's statement upset both proslavery advocates, who feared they would be denied the victory won in the *Dred Scott* decision, and abolitionists, who were not convinced that local regulations would halt the expansion of slavery. Nonetheless, the Democrats won a narrow victory in Illinois, and the state legislature re-elected Douglas to the U.S. Senate.

The Party System Fragments

The election of 1858 established the Republican Party as a formidable political force, as it won control of the House of Representatives and gave Lincoln a national reputation, making him a potential presidential candidate.

The Rise of Radicalism. In the wake of these Republican gains, southern Democrats divided into two groups. Moderates such as Senator Jefferson Davis of Mississippi, who were known as Southern Rights Democrats, pursued the traditional policy of seeking ironclad commitments to protect slavery in the states and territories. Radical southern leaders, such as Robert Barnwell Rhett of South Carolina and William Lowndes Yancey of Alabama, repudiated the Union and actively promoted secession. Radical antislavery northerners played into their hands. Senator William Seward of New York declared that freedom and slavery were locked in "an irrepressible conflict." That battle, whether inevitable or not, seemed to have begun in October 1859 when the militant abolitionist John Brown led eighteen heavily armed black and white men in an unsuccessful raid on the federal arsenal at Harpers Ferry, Virginia. Brown's announced purpose was to provide arms for a slave rebellion that would establish an African American state in the South.

Republican leaders disavowed Brown's raid, but Democrats called his plot "a natural, logical, inevitable result of the doctrines and teachings of the Republican party." Fueling the Democratic charges were letters that linked six leading abolitionists to the financing of Brown's raid. Brown was charged with treason, sentenced to death, and hanged—only to be praised by reformer Henry David Thoreau as "an angel of light." Slaveholders were horrified by northern admiration of Brown and looked toward the future with fear. "The aim of the present black republican organization is the destruction of the social system of the Southern States, without regard to consequences," warned one newspaper.

Nor could the South count on the Democratic Party to protect its interests. At its April 1860 convention, northern Democrats rejected Jefferson Davis's program to protect slavery in the territories, prompting the delegates from eight southern states to leave the hall. At a second Democratic convention in Baltimore, northern and western delegates nominated Stephen Douglas; southern Democrats met separately and nominated Buchanan's vice president, John C. Breckinridge of Kentucky. At odds with each other since the *Dred Scott* decision, the sectional factions of the Democratic Party now separated into two distinct organizations.

The Election of 1860. The Republicans sensed victory. They courted white voters by opposing both slavery and racial equality: "Missouri for white men and white men for Missouri," declared that state's Republican platform. On the national level the Republican convention chose Lincoln as its presidential candidate. Lincoln's position on

slavery was more moderate than that of the best-known Republicans, Senator William H. Seward of New York and Salmon P. Chase of Ohio, who demanded its abolition. Lincoln also conveyed a compelling egalitarian image that appealed to smallholding farmers and wage earners. And Lincoln's home territory—the rapidly growing Midwest—was crucial in the competition between Democrats and Republicans. The Republican Party's campaign slogan of "free soil, free speech, free labor, and free men" focused on liberty and had radical overtones. However, the party's platform endorsed Lincoln's moderate views, upholding free soil in the West and denying the right of states to secede but ruling out direct interference with slavery in the South. In addition, the platform endorsed the old Whig program of economic development, which had gained increasing support in the Midwest, especially after the economic Panic of 1857.

The Republican strategy was successful. Lincoln received only 40 percent of the popular vote but won every northern and western state except New Jersey, giving him a majority in the electoral college. Douglas took 30 percent of the total vote, drawing support from all regions except the South, but won electoral votes only in Missouri and New Jersey. Breckinridge captured every state in the Deep South as well as Delaware, Maryland, and North Carolina, while John Bell, a former Tennessee Whig who became the nominee of the compromise-seeking Constitutional Union Party, carried the Upper South states where the Whigs had been strongest: Kentucky, Tennessee, and Virginia.

The Republicans had united the Northeast, the Midwest, and the Far West behind free soil and had seized national power. A revolution was in the making. Slavery had permeated the American federal republic for so long and so thoroughly that southerners had come to see it as part of the constitutional order—an order now under siege. To many southerners it seemed time to think carefully about the meaning of Lincoln's words of 1858 that the Union must "become all one thing, or all the other."

FOR FURTHER EXPLORATION

▶ For definitions of key terms boldfaced in this chapter, see the glossary at the end of the book.

▶ To assess your mastery of the material covered in this chapter, see the Online Study Guide at **bedfordstmartins.com/henretta**.

▶ For suggested references, including Web sites, see page SR-14 at the end of the book.

▶ For map resources and primary documents, see **bedfordstmartins.com/henretta**.

Westward expansion carried American settlers into the disputed Oregon Country, parts of California, and the Mexican province of Texas, where they mounted a successful rebellion and petitioned for annexation to the United States. The popular appeal of Manifest Destiny prompted southern leaders such as John Tyler and John C. Calhoun to advocate the immediate annexation of Texas and to support northern politicians who laid claim to all of Oregon. This expansionist program carried Democrat James K. Polk to the presidency in the election of 1844.

Polk's expansionist schemes led the United States into a successful war of conquest against Mexico, but the acquisition of new territory in the West undermined the long-standing political compromise over the spread of slavery and threatened to split the Union. Democratic and Whig leaders joined in framing a political settlement known as the Compromise of 1850; its most important aspects were laws admitting California as a free state and providing federal assistance to planters seeking the return of fugitive slaves.

The Compromise and the Second Party System died in the political conflicts and armed violence of the 1850s. Antislavery northerners defied the Fugitive Slave Act by battling southern slave catchers in the courts and on the streets. When northern Whigs refused to support the act and the westward expansion of slavery, southerners deserted the Whig Party, killing it as a national organization. The Democratic Party also lost support as its leaders conspired to add slave states in northern Mexico and the Caribbean and as Stephen Douglas's doctrine of popular sovereignty failed to allow for the peaceful settlement of Kansas and Nebraska. As a guerrilla war festered in "Bleeding Kansas," northern Whigs and Free-Soilers established the Republican Party, which also attracted anti-Nebraska Democrats and former Know-Nothings. By 1856 the Second Party System of Democrats and Whigs had given way to a new alignment in which proslavery Democrats confronted antislavery Republicans.

The national Democratic Party disintegrated following the Supreme Court's decision in the *Dred Scott* case and President James Buchanan's support for a proslavery constitution in Kansas. Following John Brown's attempt to raise a major black rebellion, southern Democrats unsuccessfully demanded ironclad protection for the institution of slavery. In the 1860 election the Democrats divided along sectional lines, facilitating the election of Abraham Lincoln and the Republican Party. The nation stood poised on the brink of secession and civil war.

1820s	Expansion of cattle raising in Mexican California
1821	Mexico wins independence from Spain
1836	Texas proclaims independence from Mexico
1842	Overland migration to Oregon begins
1844	Fate of Texas and Oregon dominate presidential election
1845	John O'Sullivan coins term *Manifest Destiny*
	Texas admitted to Union as a slave state
	John Slidell's diplomatic mission to Mexico fails
1846	United States declares war on Mexico
	Treaty with Britain divides Oregon Country at forty-ninth parallel
	Wilmot Proviso to prohibit slavery in any territories acquired from Mexico dies in the Senate
1847	General Winfield Scott captures Mexico City
1848	Gold discovered in California
	In Treaty of Guadalupe Hidalgo Mexico cedes its provinces of California, New Mexico, and Texas to the United States
	Free-Soil Party organized
1850	Compromise of 1850 seeks to preserve the Union
	Fugitive Slave Act rejected by northern abolitionists
1851	American (Know-Nothing) Party formed
1852	Harriet Beecher Stowe publishes *Uncle Tom's Cabin*
1854	Ostend Manifesto seeks expansion of slavery in Caribbean
	Kansas-Nebraska Act implements popular sovereignty
	Republican Party formed
1856	"Bleeding Kansas" undermines popular sovereignty
1857	*Dred Scott v. Sandford* allows slavery in the territories
1858	James Buchanan backs Lecompton constitution
	Lincoln-Douglas debates
1860	Abraham Lincoln elected president in four-way contest

CHAPTER 14

Two Societies at War

1861–1865

"WHAT A SCENE IT WAS," the Union soldier Elisha Hunt Rhodes wrote in his diary in July 1863 as the battle of Gettysburg ended. "Oh the dead and the dying on this bloody field." The passions kindled by southern rights and the northern nationalism had inspired thousands of men to die in battle, and the slaughter would continue for two more years. "What is this all about?" asked Confederate lieutenant R. M. Collins at the end of another gruesome battle. "Why is it that 200,000 men of one blood and tongue . . . [should be] seeking one another's lives? We could settle our differences by compromising and all be at home in ten days." But there was no compromise—not in 1861 nor even in 1865.

To explain why Southerners seceded and then fought the war to the bitter end is not simple, but racial slavery is an important part of the answer. For political leaders in the South, the Republican victory in 1860 presented a clear and immediate danger to the slave-owning republic that had existed since 1776. Lincoln was the only president elected without a single electoral vote from the South, and Southerners knew that his Republican Party would prevent the extension of slavery into the territories.

◀ **Fields of Death**
Fought with mass armies and new weapons, the Civil War took a huge toll in human lives, as evidenced by grisly photographs like this one of a battlefield at Antietam, Maryland. At Shiloh, Tennessee, General Ulysses Grant surveyed a field "so covered with dead that it would have been possible to walk . . . in any direction, stepping on dead bodies, without a foot touching the ground." Library of Congress.

Moreover, they refused to believe Lincoln when he said, "I have no purpose, directly or indirectly, to interfere with the institution of slavery in the States where it exists." Soon, a southern senator warned, "cohorts of Federal office-holders, Abolitionists, may be sent into [our] midst" to mobilize the African American population. The result would be waves of bloody slave revolts and racial intermixture—by which was meant relations between black men and white women, as white slave owners had already fathered untold numbers of children by their black women slaves. "Better, far better! [to] endure all horrors of civil war," declared a Confederate recruit from Virginia, "than to see the dusky sons of Ham leading the fair daughters of the South to the altar." To preserve black slavery and the supremacy of white men, radical southern leaders embarked on the dangerous journey of secession.

Lincoln and the North would not let them go in peace. In a world still ruled by kings and princes, northern leaders believed that the dissolution of the American Union might destroy for all time the prospect of a republican government based on majority rule, constitutional procedures, and democratic elections. "We cannot escape history," the new president eloquently declared. "We shall nobly save, or meanly lose, the last best hope of earth." As a young Union army recruit from Ohio put the issue more simply, "If our institutions prove a failure . . . of what value will be house, family, or friends?"

And so came the Civil War. Called the "War between the States" by Southerners and the "War of the Rebellion" by Northerners, the struggle went on until the great issues of the Union and slavery had been resolved once and for all. The cost was incredibly high: more lives lost than in all the nation's subsequent wars put together and a century-long legacy of bitterness between the triumphant North and the vanquished South.

Secession and Military Stalemate, 1861–1862

After Lincoln's election in November 1860, secessionist fervor swept through the Deep South, and the future of the Union appeared dim. Nonetheless, the politicians in Washington—veteran party leaders who had run the country for a generation—did not give up. In the four months between Lincoln's election and his inauguration, they struggled to forge a new compromise that (like those of 1787, 1821, and 1850) would preserve the Union.

Choosing Sides

The movement toward secession was most rapid in South Carolina—the home of John C. Calhoun, nullification, and the southern Radical movement. Robert

Barnwell Rhett and other South Carolina "fire-eaters" had called for secession during the crisis of 1850 and had kept up their campaign for a decade. With Lincoln's election, their goal was suddenly within reach. On December 20 a special state convention voted unanimously to dissolve "the union now subsisting between South Carolina and other States."

Moving quickly, fire-eaters elsewhere in the Deep South called similar conventions and mobilized vigilante groups and militia units to suppress local Unionists and prepare for war. In early January, amid an atmosphere of public celebration, Mississippi enacted a secession ordinance. Within a month Florida, Alabama, Georgia, Louisiana, and Texas had also left the Union (Map 14.1). In early February the jubilant secessionists met in Montgomery, Alabama, to proclaim a new nation—the Confederate States of America. Adopting a provisional constitution, the delegates named Jefferson Davis of Mississippi, a former U.S. senator and secretary of war, as its provisional president.

Secessionist fervor was less intense in the eight slave states of the **Upper South** (Virginia, Delaware, Maryland, North Carolina, Kentucky, Tennessee, Missouri, and Arkansas), where there were fewer slaves and yeomen farmers had greater political power. For decades yeomen had resented the authority claimed by the slave-owning gentry, and some actively opposed it. In the 1850s Hinton Helper of North Carolina roused the "Non-slaveowners of the South! farmers, mechanics and workingmen," warning that "the slaveholders, the arrogant demagogues whom you have elected to offices of honor and profit, have hoodwinked you, . . . used you as mere tools for the consummation of their wicked designs." Influenced by such sentiments, in January 1861 the legislatures of Virginia and Tennessee voted to resist any invasion from the North but refused to join the secessionist movement. Instead, seeking a compromise that would restore the Union, Upper South leaders proposed federal guarantees for slavery in the states where it existed.

Meanwhile, the Union government floundered. In his last message to Congress in December 1860 President Buchanan declared secession illegal but claimed that the federal government lacked the authority to restore the Union by force. South Carolina interpreted Buchanan's message as an implicit recognition of its independence and demanded the surrender of Fort Sumter, a federal garrison in Charleston harbor. Reluctant to turn over federal property, Buchanan tested the secessionists' resolve by ordering an unarmed merchant ship to resupply the fort. When the South Carolinians fired on the ship, Buchanan backed down, refusing to order the navy to escort it into the harbor.

The Crittenden Plan. As the crisis continued, Buchanan urged Congress to find a compromise. The

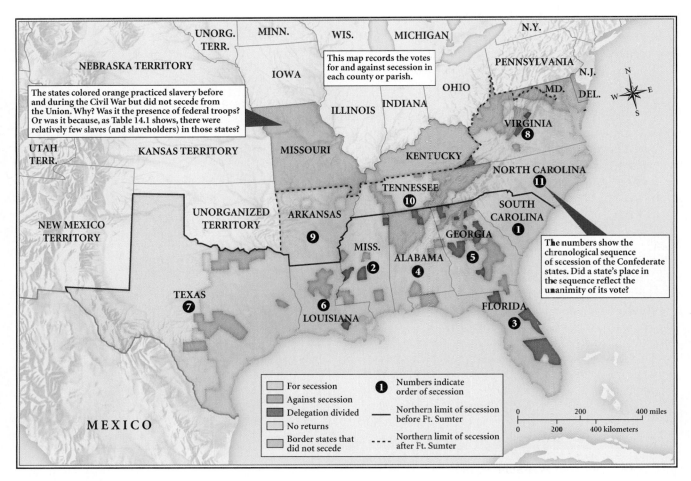

MAP 14.1 The Process of Secession, 1860–1861

The states with the highest concentration of slaves (see Table 14.1) led the secessionist movement. After the attack on Fort Sumter, the states of the Upper South joined the Confederacy. Yeomen farmers in Tennessee and the backcountry of Alabama, Georgia, and Virginia opposed secession but, except in the future state of West Virginia, initially rallied to the Confederate cause. Consequently, the South entered the Civil War with a white population generally opposed to the policies of Lincoln's administration.

scheme proposed by Senator John J. Crittenden of Kentucky, an aging follower of Henry Clay, received the most support. Crittenden's plan had two parts. The first part, which won congressional approval, called for a constitutional amendment that would permanently protect slavery from federal interference in any state where it already existed. To deal with the territories, Crittenden offered a second provision that called for the westward extension of the Missouri Compromise line (36°30′ north latitude) to the California border. Slavery would be barred north of the line and protected to the south, including any territories "hereafter acquired."

Following Lincoln's instructions, congressional Republicans rejected this part of Crittenden's plan. The president-elect was determined to uphold the doctrine of free soil and feared that extending the Missouri Compromise line would encourage the South to embark on new imperialist adventures. Crittenden's plan, Lincoln

charged, would be "a perpetual covenant of war against every people, tribe, and State owning a foot of land between here and Tierra del Fuego [the southern tip of South America]."

In his inaugural address in March 1861, Lincoln carefully balanced a call for reconciliation with a firm commitment to the Union. He promised to permit slavery in states where it existed but stood firm for free soil in the territories. Most important, he stated that the Union was "perpetual"; consequently, the secession of the Confederate states was illegal and acts of violence in support of their action constituted insurrection. He announced equally clearly that he intended to enforce federal law throughout the Union and—of particular relevance to Fort Sumter—to continue to "hold, occupy, and possess" federal property in the seceded states and "to collect duties and imposts." If force was necessary to preserve the Union, Lincoln—like Andrew Jackson

The Bombardment of Fort Sumter, 1861
Currier and Ives, a New York publishing house, brought colorful art into thousands of middle-class homes by printing inexpensive lithographs of pastoral scenes and dramatic historical events. This fairly realistic depiction of the Confederate bombardment of Fort Sumter in Charleston harbor in April 1861 was especially popular in the South.
Library of Congress.

during the nullification crisis—promised to use it. The choice was the South's: return to the Union or face war.

The Seizure of Fort Sumter. The decision came quickly. Within a month of Lincoln's inauguration the garrison at Fort Sumter urgently needed supplies. To maintain his credibility, the new president dispatched a relief expedition, promising that it would not land troops or arms unless the rebels disrupted the delivery of food and medicine. Jefferson Davis and his government welcomed Lincoln's decision, believing that a confrontation would turn the wavering Upper South against the North and win foreign support for the Confederate cause. Resolving to take the fort immediately, Davis demanded its surrender. When Major Robert Anderson refused to comply, the Confederate forces opened fire on April 12, forcing the surrender of the fort two days later. The next day Lincoln called 75,000 state militiamen into federal service for ninety days to put down an insurrection "too powerful to be suppressed by the

ordinary course of judicial proceedings." All talk of compromise was past.

Northerners responded to Lincoln's call to arms with enthusiasm. Asked to provide thirteen regiments of volunteers, Republican Governor William Dennison of Ohio sent twenty. "Our fathers made this country," declared an enlisted man in the 12th Ohio Regiment, "we their children are to save it." Many northern Democrats were equally committed to the Union cause. As Stephen Douglas declared six weeks before his death: "Every man must be for the United States or against it. There can be no neutrals in this war, only patriots—or traitors."

The Contest for the Upper South. The white residents of the Upper South now had to choose between the Union and the Confederacy, and their decision was crucial. Those eight states accounted for two-thirds of the South's white population, more than three-fourths of its industrial production, and well over half of its food and fuel. They were home to many of the nation's best military leaders, including Colonel Robert E. Lee of Virginia, a career officer whom General in Chief Winfield Scott recommended to Lincoln as field commander of the new Union army. And they were geographically strategic. Kentucky, with its 500-mile border on the Ohio River, was essential to the movement of troops and supplies. Maryland was vital to the Union's security because it surrounded the nation's capital on the north.

The weight of history decided the outcome in Virginia, the original home of American slavery. Three days after the fall of Fort Sumter, a Virginia convention passed an ordinance of secession by a vote of 88 to 55. The dissenting votes came mainly from the yeoman-dominated northwestern counties (see Map 14.1); elsewhere in Virginia whites rallied to the Confederate cause. As William Poague, a former Unionist lawyer, explained his decision to enlist in a Virginia artillery unit: "The North was the aggressor. The South resisted her invaders." Refusing Scott's offer to command the Union troops, Robert E. Lee resigned from the army. "Save in defense of my native state," Lee told Scott, "I never desire again to draw my sword." Arkansas, Tennessee, and North Carolina quickly joined Virginia in the Confederacy.

Lincoln moved aggressively to hold the rest of the Upper South. In May he ordered General George B. McClellan to take control of northwestern Virginia, thus securing the railway line between Washington and the Ohio Valley. In October voters in that predominantly yeoman region overwhelmingly approved the creation of a breakaway state, West Virginia, which was admitted to the Union in 1863. The Union cause also triumphed in Delaware but received much less support in Maryland, where slavery was well entrenched. A pro-Confederate mob attacked Massachusetts troops marching between railroad stations in Baltimore, causing the war's first combat deaths: four soldiers and twelve civilians. When other Maryland secessionists destroyed railroad bridges and telegraph lines, Lincoln ordered military occupation of the state and imprisoned suspected secessionists, including members of the state legislature. He released them only in November 1861, after Unionists had gained control of the Maryland legislature.

In Missouri, the key to communications and trade on the Missouri and upper Mississippi Rivers, Lincoln mobilized support among the large German American community. In July a force of German American militia defeated Confederate sympathizers commanded by the governor. Despite continuing raids by Confederate guerrilla bands led by William Quantrill and Jesse and Frank James, the Union retained control of Missouri (see Voices from Abroad, "Ernest Duveyier de Hauranne, German Immigrants and the Civil War within Missouri," p. 402).

In Kentucky secessionist and Unionist sentiment was evenly balanced, so Lincoln moved cautiously. He waited until August, when Unionists took control of the state government, before ordering federal troops to halt Kentucky's thriving trade with the Confederacy in horses, mules, whiskey, and foodstuffs. When the Confederates responded to this cutoff by moving troops into Kentucky, the Unionist legislature asked for federal protection. In September Illinois volunteers under the command of the relatively unknown Brigadier General Ulysses S. Grant crossed the Ohio River and drove out the Confederates. Of the eight states of the Upper South, Lincoln had kept four (Delaware, Maryland, Kentucky, and Missouri) and a portion of a fifth (western Virginia) in the Union (Table 14.1).

Setting Objectives and Devising Strategies

Following the creation of the Confederacy, its leaders called on their people to defend its independence. At his inauguration in February 1861 Jefferson Davis identified the Confederate cause with that of the American Revolution: like their grandfathers, white Southerners were fighting against tyranny and for the "sacred right of

TABLE 14.1 Slavery and Secession		
Group	Percentage of Whites in Slave-owning Families	Percentage of Slaves in Population
Original Confederate States	38%	47%
Border States that Later Joined the Confederacy	24%	32%
Border States that Remained in Union	14%	15%

Ernest Duveyier de Hauranne

German Immigrants and the Civil War within Missouri

Tens of thousands of German immigrants settled in Missouri and other midwestern states in the two decades before the Civil War and, as the following letter by the Frenchman Ernest Duveyier de Hauranne indicates, most of them supported the Union cause. De Hauranne traveled widely, and his letters home offer an intelligent commentary on American politics and society during the Civil War.

St. Louis, September 12, 1864

Missouri is to all intents and purposes a rebel state, an occupied territory where the Federal forces are really nothing but a garrison under siege; even today it is not certain what would happen if the troops were withdrawn. Party quarrels here are poisoned by class hatreds. . . . The old Anglo-French families, attached to Southern institutions, harbor a primitive, superstitious prejudice in favor of slavery. Conquered now, but full of repressed rage, they exhibit the implacable anger peculiar to the defenders of lost causes. . . .

The more recent German population is strongly abolitionist. They have brought to the New World the instincts of European democracy, together with its radical attitudes and all-or-nothing doctrines. Ancient precedents and worn-out laws matter little to them. They have not studied history and have no respect for hallowed injustices; but they do have, to the highest degree, that sense of moral principle which is more or less lacking in American democracy. They aren't afraid of revolution: to destroy a barbarous institution they would, if necessary, take an axe to the foundations of society. Furthermore, their interests coincide with their principles. . . .

The immigrant arrives poor and lives by his work. A newcomer, having nothing to lose and caring little for the interests of established property owners, sees that the subjection of free labor to the ruinous competition of slave labor must be ended. At the same time, his pride rebels against the prejudice attached to work in a land of slavery; he wants to reestablish its value. . . .

There is no mistaking the hatred the two parties, not to say the two peoples, have for each other. . . . As passions were coming to a boil, the Federal government sent General [John C.] Frémont here as army commander and dictator. . . . An abolitionist and a self-made man, he put himself firmly at the head of the German party, determined to crush the friends of slavery. He formed an army of Germans who are completely devoted to their chief. . . .

[However,] bands of guerrillas hold the countryside, where they raid as much as they please; politics serves as a fine pretext for looting. Their leaders are officers from the army of the South who receive their orders from the Confederate government. . . . These "bushwackers," who ordinarily rob indiscriminately, maintain their standing as political raiders by occasionally killing some poor, inoffensive person. Finally, people bent on personal vengeance take advantage of the state of civil war: sometimes one hears of villages divided against themselves so bitterly that massacres are carried on from door to door with incredible ferocity. . . . You can see what emotions are still boiling in this region that is supposed to be pacified.

Source: Ernest Duveyier de Hauranne, *A Frenchman in Lincoln's America* (Chicago: Lakende Press, 1974), 305–9.

self-government." As Davis put it, the Confederacy sought "no conquest, no aggrandizement, no concession of any kind from the states with which we were lately confederated; all we ask is to be let alone." The decision to focus on the defense of the Confederacy and not to conquer western territories gave southern leaders a strong advantage: they needed only a military stalemate to guarantee independence. However, the Confederacy's firm commitment to slavery undermined its support in Europe, where opposition to forced labor was strong. Alexander Stephens of Georgia, the vice president of the Confederacy, ruled out any plan for gradual emancipation, declaring that his nation's "cornerstone rests upon the great truth that the Negro is not equal to the white man, that slavery—subordination to the superior race—is his natural or normal condition."

Lincoln made his first major statement on Union goals and strategy in a speech to Congress on July 4,

1861. He portrayed secession as an attack on popular government, America's great contribution to world history, telling his audience that the issue at stake was "whether a constitutional republic, or a democracy—a government of the people, by the same people—can or cannot maintain its territorial integrity against its domestic foe." Convinced that the nation could preserve its republican principles only by crushing the rebellion, Lincoln rejected General Winfield Scott's plan to use economic sanctions and a naval blockade to persuade the Confederates to return to the Union. Instead, the president insisted on an aggressive military strategy and a policy of unconditional surrender.

The Union Thrust toward Richmond.   The president hoped that a successful strike against the Confederate capital of Richmond, Virginia, would end the rebellion. He therefore dispatched General Irwin McDowell and an army of 30,000 men to attack P. G. T. Beauregard's force of 20,000 troops at Manassas, a major rail junction thirty miles southwest of Washington. In July McDowell launched a strong attack near Manassas Creek (also called Bull Run), but panic swept through his troops during a Confederate counterattack. For the first time Union soldiers heard the hair-raising rebel yell. "The peculiar corkscrew sensation that it sends down your backbone under these circumstances can never be told,"

one Union veteran wrote. "You have to feel it." McDowell's troops retreated in disarray to Washington, along with the many civilians who had come to observe the battle. The victorious Confederate troops also dispersed, confused and without the wagons and supplies they needed to pursue McDowell's army.

The rout of the Union army at Bull Run made it clear that the rebellion would not be easily crushed. To bolster northern morale, Lincoln replaced McDowell with General George B. McClellan and signed bills for the enlistment of an additional million men, who would serve for three years in the newly created Army of the Potomac. A cautious military engineer, McClellan spent the winter of 1861 training raw recruits, and early in 1862 he launched the first major offensive of the war, a thrust toward Richmond. In a maneuver that required skillful logistics, the Union general transported about 100,000 troops by boat down the Potomac River and Chesapeake Bay, putting them ashore on the peninsula between the York and James Rivers (Map 14.2). Ignoring Lincoln's advice to "strike a blow" quickly, McClellan advanced slowly up the peninsula toward the South's capital, tactics that allowed the Confederates to mount a counterstroke. To relieve the pressure on Richmond, a Confederate army under Thomas J. ("Stonewall") Jackson marched rapidly north up the Shenandoah Valley in western Virginia, threatening Washington. Lincoln recalled 30,000 troops from

The Battle of Antietam: The Fight for Burnside's Bridge

Nearly 8,000 soldiers lost their lives at Antietam on September 17, 1862, many of them in the struggle for the Rohrback Bridge, which crossed Antietam Creek. One of those who survived the battle, Captain James Hope of the Second Vermont Volunteers, recorded the event in this painting, giving the bridge the name of the Union general who sacrificed many of his troops trying to capture it.

Antietam National Battlefield, National Park Service, Sharpsburg, Maryland.

McClellan's army to protect the Union's capital, but Jackson, a brilliant general, won a series of small engagements, tying down the larger Union forces. Then Jackson quickly joined the Confederates' formidable commanding general, Robert E. Lee, who had confronted McClellan outside Richmond. Lee launched a ferocious attack that lasted for seven days (June 25–July 1), suffering 20,000 casualties (to the Union's 10,000). McClellan failed to exploit the Confederates' weakness, refusing to renew the offensive unless he received fresh troops. Lincoln ordered the withdrawal of the Army of the Potomac, and Richmond remained secure.

Lee Moves North. Lee promptly went on the offensive, hoping for victories that would humiliate Lincoln's government. Joining with Jackson in northern Virginia, Lee routed Union troops in the Second Battle of Bull Run (August 1862) and then struck north

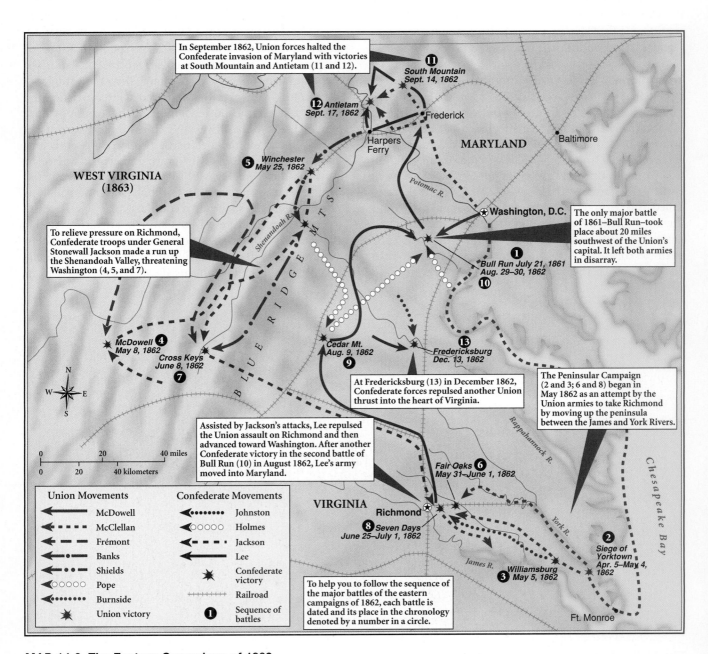

MAP 14.2 The Eastern Campaigns of 1862

Many of the great battles of the Civil War took place in the 125 miles between the Union capital of Washington and the Confederate capital of Richmond. During the eastern campaigns of 1862, Confederate Generals Robert J. "Stonewall" Jackson and Robert E. Lee secured victories that were almost decisive; they also suffered a defeat—at Antietam, in Maryland—that was almost fatal. As was often the case in the Civil War, the victors in these battles were either too bloodied or too timid to exploit their advantage.

through western Maryland, where he met with near disaster. When Lee divided his force—sending Jackson to capture Harpers Ferry in West Virginia—a copy of his orders fell into McClellan's hands. But the Union general again failed to pursue his numerical advantage, delaying his attack against Lee's depleted army and thereby allowing it to occupy a strong defensive position behind Antietam Creek, near Sharpsburg, Maryland. Outnumbered 87,000 to 50,000, Lee desperately fought off McClellan's attacks. Just as Union regiments were about to overwhelm his right flank, Jackson's troops arrived, saving the Confederates from a major defeat. Appalled by the number of Union casualties, McClellan let Lee retreat to Virginia.

The fighting at Antietam was savage. A Wisconsin officer described his men as "loading and firing with demoniacal fury and shouting and laughing hysterically." At a critical point in the battle a sunken road, nicknamed Bloody Lane, was filled with Confederate bodies two and three deep, and the attacking Union troops knelt on "this ghastly flooring" to shoot at the retreating Confederates. The battle at Antietam on September 17, 1862, remains the bloodiest single day in U.S. military history. Together the Confederate and Union dead numbered 4,800 and the wounded 18,500, of whom 3,000 soon died. (In comparison, 6,000 Americans were wounded or killed on D-Day, which began the invasion of Nazi-occupied France in World War II.)

In public Lincoln declared Antietam a victory, but privately he declared that McClellan should have fought Lee to the finish. A masterful organizer of men and supplies, McClellan lacked the stomach for an all-out attack. Dismissing McClellan as commander of the Army of the Potomac, Lincoln began a long search for an effective replacement. His first choice was Ambrose E. Burnside, who proved to be more daring but less competent than his predecessor. In December, after heavy losses in futile attacks against well-entrenched Confederate forces at Fredericksburg, Virginia, Burnside resigned his command and Lincoln replaced him with Joseph ("Fighting Joe") Hooker. As 1862 ended, the Confederates had some reason to be content: the war in the East was a stalemate.

The War in the West.   In the West, Union forces had been more successful. The goal of the Union commanders was to control the Ohio, Mississippi, and Missouri Rivers, dividing the Confederacy and reducing the mobility of its armies (Map 14.3). The decision of Kentucky not to join the rebellion had already given the Union dominance in the Ohio River Valley. In 1862 the Union army launched a series of highly innovative land

Lincoln Visits the Army of the Potomac, 1862
Following the battle of Antietam, President Lincoln journeyed to the headquarters of General McClellan. Supported by his military advisors (standing to his rear), the towering commander in chief vigorously urged his principal general to exploit the opportunity offered by Lee's heavy casualties and launch an all-out attack against Richmond. When McClellan did not undertake this offensive, Lincoln removed him as commander of the Army of the Potomac. Library of Congress.

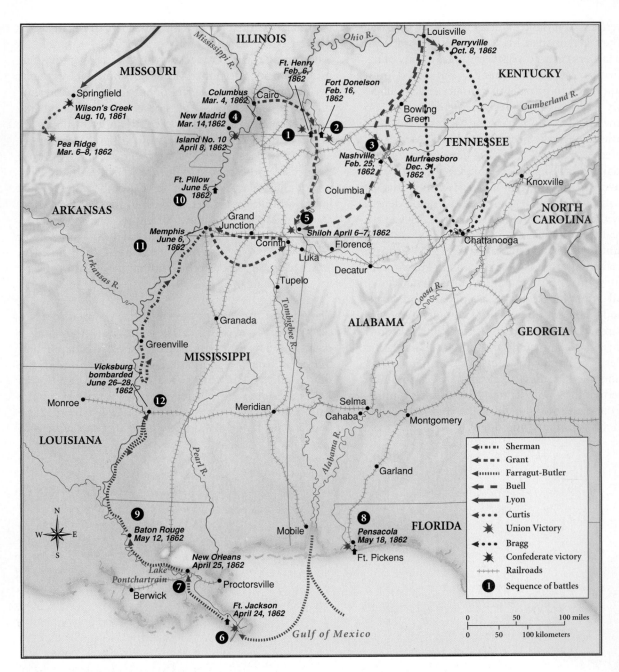

MAP 14.3 The Western Campaigns, 1861–1862

As the Civil War intensified in 1862, Union and Confederate military and naval forces fought to control the great valleys of the Ohio, Tennessee, and Mississippi Rivers. Between February and April, Union armies moved south through western Tennessee (#1, 2, 3, and 5). By the end of June, Union naval forces controlled the Mississippi River north of Memphis (#4, 10, and 11) and from the Gulf of Mexico to Vicksburg (#6, 7, 9, and 12). These victories gave the Union control of crucial transportation routes, kept Missouri in the Union, and carried the war to the borders of the states of the Deep South.

and water operations to gain control of the Tennessee and Mississippi Rivers as well. In the north, General Ulysses S. Grant used riverboats clad with iron plates to take Fort Henry on the Tennessee River and Fort Donelson on the Cumberland. Grant then moved south along the Tennessee to seize critical railroad lines. A Confederate army under Albert Sidney Johnston and P. G. T. Beauregard caught Grant by surprise on April 6 near a small log church named Shiloh. Grant relentlessly threw troops into the battle, forcing a Confederate withdrawal but taking huge casualties. When the fighting ended, Grant looked out over a large field "so covered with dead that it would have been possible to walk over the clearing in any direction, stepping on dead bodies, without a foot touching the ground." The cost in lives was high, but Lincoln was pleased. "What I want . . . is generals who will fight battles and win victories." Grant had done that, creating military momentum for the Union in the West.

Three weeks later Union naval forces commanded by David G. Farragut struck from the south, moving through the Mississippi Delta from the Gulf of Mexico to capture New Orleans. The Union now held the South's financial center and largest city as well as a major base for future naval operations. Union victories in the West had significantly undermined Confederate strength in the Mississippi Valley.

Toward Total War

The carnage at Antietam and Shiloh had made it clear that the war would be long, costly, and fought to the finish. After Shiloh, Grant later noted, he "gave up all idea of saving the Union except by complete conquest." The conflict became a **total war**—arraying the entire resources of the two societies against each other and eventually resulting in warfare against enemy civilians. Aided by a strong party and a talented cabinet, Lincoln skillfully mobilized the North for all-out war, organizing an effective central government. Jefferson Davis was less successful in harnessing the resources of the South because the eleven states of the Confederacy remained deeply suspicious of centralized rule.

Mobilizing Armies and Civilians

Initially, patriotic fervor filled both armies with eager volunteers. The widowed mother of nineteen-year-old Elisha Hunt Rhodes of Pawtuxet, Rhode Island, sent her son to war, saying, "My son, other mothers must make sacrifices and why should not I?" The call for soldiers was especially successful in the South, which had a strong military tradition, an ample supply of trained officers, and a culture that stressed duty and honor. "Would you, My Darling, . . . be willing to leave your Children under such a [despotic Union] government?" James B. Griffin of Edgefield, South Carolina, asked his wife, "No—I know you would sacrifice every comfort on earth, rather than submit to it." However, the initial surge of enlistments fell off as potential recruits learned of the realities of mass warfare: heavy losses to epidemic diseases in the camps and dreadful carnage on the battlefields. Soon both governments faced the necessity of forced enlistment.

The Military Draft. The Confederacy was the first to act. In April 1862, after the bloody defeat at Shiloh, the Confederate Congress imposed the first legally binding draft in American history. One law extended all existing enlistments for the duration of the war; another required three years of military service from all able-bodied men between the ages of eighteen and thirty-five. In September, after the heavy casualties at Antietam, the age limit was raised to forty-five. The Confederate draft had two loopholes, both controversial. First, it exempted one white man—the planter, a son, or an overseer—for each twenty slaves, allowing men on large plantations to avoid military service. Second, drafted men could hire substitutes. Before this provision was repealed in 1864, the price for a substitute had risen to $300 in gold, about three times the annual wages of a skilled worker. Laborers and yeomen farmers angrily complained that it was "a rich man's war and a poor man's fight."

Consequently, some Southerners refused to serve, and the Confederate government lacked the power to compel them. Because the Confederate constitution vested sovereignty in the individual states, strong governors such as Joseph Brown of Georgia and Zebulon Vance of North Carolina simply ignored Davis's first draft call in early 1862. Elsewhere state judges issued writs of **habeas corpus** (a legal process designed to protect people from arbitrary arrest) and ordered the Confederate army to release protesting draftees. Reluctantly the Confederate Congress overrode the judges' authority to free conscripted men, enabling the Confederacy to keep substantial armies in the field well into 1864.

The Union government took a more authoritarian stance toward potential foes and ordinary citizens. To prevent sabotage and concerted resistance to the war effort, Lincoln suspended habeas corpus and over the course of the war imprisoned about 15,000 Confederate sympathizers without trial. The president also extended martial law to civilians who discouraged enlistment or resisted the draft, making them subject to military courts rather than local juries. This firm policy had the desired effect. The Militia Act of 1862 set a quota of volunteers for each state, which was increased by the Enrollment Act of 1863. States and towns enticed volunteers with cash bounties, prompting the enlistment or reenlistment of almost a million men. As in the South, wealthy men could avoid military service by providing a substitute or paying a $300 **commutation**, or exemption, fee.

The Enrollment Act sparked significant opposition, as thousands of recent immigrants from Germany and Ireland refused to serve in the Union army, saying it was not their fight. Northern Democrats exploited this resentment by charging that Lincoln was drafting poor whites to free the slaves and flood the cities with black laborers who would take their jobs. Some northern Democrats opposed the war, believing that the South should be allowed to secede, while others simply wanted to protect the interests of immigrants, most of whom

Draft Riots and Antiblack Violence in New York City

The Enrollment Act of 1863 enraged many workers and recent Irish and German immigrants who did not want to go to war. In July in New York City they took out their anger on free blacks in a week-long series of riots. This engraving depicts the burning by a mob of the Colored Orphan Asylum on Fifth Avenue, home to two hundred African American children. All of the children escaped before the mob set fire to the building; the fire spread to adjoining structures, forcing residents to flee with whatever possessions they could carry. Library of Congress.

which had accounted for three-fourths of the deaths in the recently concluded Crimean War between Britain and Russia. Through its network of 7,000 local auxiliaries, the Sanitary Commission gathered supplies; distributed clothing, food, and medicine to the army; improved the sanitary standards of camp life; and recruited battlefield nurses and doctors for the Union Army Medical Bureau. Despite these measures, epidemic diseases took a fearful toll. Dysentery, typhoid, and malaria spread through the camps, as did childhood viruses such as mumps and measles, to which many rural men had not developed an immunity. Diseases and infections killed about 250,000 Union soldiers, about twice the number who died in combat. Still, better sanitation and high-quality food substantially lowered the mortality rate among Union troops compared with the rate in major nineteenth-century wars in Europe. Confederate soldiers were less fortunate. Although thousands of women volunteered as nurses, the Confederate health system was poorly organized. Thousands of southern soldiers contracted scurvy because of the lack of vitamin C in their diets, and they died from camp diseases at higher rates than did Union soldiers.

Women took a leading role in the Sanitary Commission and other wartime agencies. As superintendent

Hospital Nursing

Working as nurses in battlefront hospitals, thousands of Union and Confederate women gained firsthand experience of the horrors of war. A sense of calm prevails in this behind-the-lines Union hospital in Nashville, Tennessee, as nurse Anne Belle tends to the needs of soldiers recovering from their wounds. Most Civil War nurses served as unpaid volunteers and spent time cooking and cleaning for their patients as well as tending their injuries. U.S. Army Military History Institute.

were Democratic voters. In July 1863 hostility to the draft and to African Americans turned to violence on the streets of New York City. For five days immigrant Irish and German workers ran rampant, burning draft offices, sacking the homes of important Republicans, and attacking the police. The rioters lynched and mutilated a dozen African Americans, drove hundreds of black families from their homes, and burned down the Colored Orphan Asylum. Lincoln rushed in Union troops, fresh from the battle of Gettysburg, who killed more than a hundred rioters and suppressed the insurrection.

The Civilian War Effort. The Union government's determination to wage total war won greater support among native-born middle-class citizens. In 1861 prominent New Yorkers established the United States Sanitary Commission. Its task was to provide medical services and prevent the spread of epidemic diseases,

of female nurses, Dorothea Dix became the first woman to receive a major federal appointment (see Chapter 12, American Lives, "Dorothea Dix: Public Woman," p. 360). Dix used her influence to combat the prejudice against women treating men, opening a new occupation to women. Thousands of educated Union women also joined the war effort as clerks in the expanding government bureaucracy, while in the South women staffed the efficient Confederate postal service. Indeed, in both sections millions of women assumed new economic responsibilities and worked with far greater intensity. They took over many farm tasks previously done by men and filled jobs not only in schools and offices but also in textile, clothing, and shoe factories. A number of women even took on military duties as spies, scouts, and (disguising themselves as men) soldiers. As the nurse Clara Barton, who later founded the American Red Cross, recalled, "At the war's end, woman was at least fifty years in advance of the normal position which continued peace would have assigned her."

Mobilizing Resources

Wars are usually won by the side with superior resources and economic organization, and in this regard the Union entered the war with a distinct advantage. With nearly two-thirds of the American people, about two-thirds of the nation's railroad mileage, and nearly 90 percent of American industrial output, the North's economy was far superior to the South's (Figure 14.1). The North had an especially great advantage in the manufacture of cannon and rifles because many of its arms factories were equipped for mass production.

However, the Confederate position was far from weak. Virginia, North Carolina, and Tennessee had substantial industrial capacity. Richmond, with its Tredegar Iron Works, was an important industrial center, and in 1861 the Confederacy transported to Richmond the gun-making machinery from the U.S. armory at Harpers Ferry. The production of the Richmond armory, the purchase of Enfield rifles from Britain, and the capture of 100,000 Union guns enabled the Confederacy to provide every infantryman with a modern rifle-musket by 1863 (see New Technology, "The Rifle-Musket," p. 410).

Moreover, with 9 million people, the Confederacy could mobilize enormous armies. Although one-third of that number were slaves, their masters kept them in the fields, producing food for the army and cotton for export. In fact, Confederate leaders counted on "**King Cotton**" to provide the revenue to purchase clothes, boots, blankets, and weapons from abroad. They also counted on cotton as a diplomatic weapon, hoping that Britain, which depended on the South to supply its textile factories, would grant diplomatic recognition and provide military aid. Although the British government never

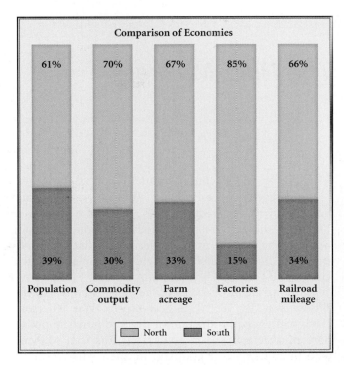

FIGURE 14.1 Economies, North and South, 1860
The military advantages of the North were even greater than this chart suggests because the population figures included slaves whom the South feared to arm and because its commodity output was dominated by farm goods rather than manufactures. Moreover, southern factories were, on average, much smaller than those in the North.
Source: Stanley Engerman, "The Economic Impact of the Civil War," in Robert W. Fogel and Stanley L. Engerman, *The Reinterpretation of American Economic History* (New York: Harper & Row, 1971), U.S. Census data.

recognized the Confederacy as an independent nation, it regarded the conflict as a war (rather than a domestic insurrection), thereby giving the rebels the status of a belligerent power with the right under international law to borrow money and purchase weapons. Thus the odds did not necessarily favor the Union, despite its superior resources.

Forging New Economic Policies. The outcome ultimately depended on the success of the rival governments in mobilizing their societies. To build political support for their fledgling party and boost industrial output, Lincoln and the Republicans enacted the program of national mercantilism previously advocated by Henry Clay and the Whig Party. First the Republicans raised tariffs, winning praise from northeastern manufacturers and laborers who feared competition from cheap foreign goods. Then Secretary of the Treasury Salmon P. Chase created a national banking system—an important element of every modern centralized government—by linking thousands of local banks. This integrated banking system was far more

The Rifle-Musket

"War is the continuation of politics by other means," the Prussian military strategist Karl Von Clauswitz declared in the 1820s, and the American Civil War showed just how bloody that politics would be. The war was the first conflict fought with railroad transport, ironclad ships, and highly efficient and deadly guns.

Among the most deadly of the new weapons was the rifle-musket. By 1855 U.S. Secretary of War Jefferson Davis had ended production of the traditional smooth-bore musket and begun equipping American soldiers with the new type of gun. During the Civil War most Union infantrymen used Springfields, rifle-muskets manufactured by the U.S. armory at Springfield, Massachusetts. Many Confederate soldiers carried Enfields, a similar weapon made in Britain. In many

1861 Springfield Rifle-Musket
Private Collection.

respects, the rifle-musket was a traditional weapon. Like a musket, it had a long barrel (usually forty inches), fired a single shot, and was loaded through the muzzle, a cumbersome process. Before aiming and firing, a soldier had to rip open a paper-wrapped cartridge of gunpowder with his teeth, pour the powder and a bullet down the barrel, jam them tight with a ramrod, half-cock the hammer to insert a percussion cap, and then—finally—cock the hammer. Some soldiers could do all this lying on their backs, but to fire two or three times a minute, most men had to load from a kneeling or standing position, exposing themselves to enemy fire.

That fire was now much more accurate because the rifle-muskets used the advanced technology of eighteenth-century hunting weapons: tapered barrels that were rifled—lined with spiral grooves—to give the bullet greater speed and accuracy. These hunting rifles had given Daniel Boone his reputation as a "Kentucky sharpshooter" but they had not previously been issued to combat soldiers because the grooved barrel quickly accumulated gunpowder and required frequent cleaning.

A technological innovation solved that problem. In the early 1850s James S. Burton, an American mechanic working at the Harpers Ferry armory in Virginia, developed a new bullet based on an earlier French model. Burton's cylindro-conoidal bullet had a radically different shape from the round bullets of the day and was cast with a cavity at its base. When the gunpowder in the barrel exploded, hot gas expanded the soft-metal cavity and forced the bullet to engage the grooves of the rifling, cleaning them as it sped through the barrel.

The rifle-musket revolutionized warfare and military strategy by enormously strengthening defensive forces. Infantrymen could now kill reliably at three hundred yards—triple the previous range—and thus keep attackers from getting close enough for hand-to-hand combat. As a result, bayonets accounted for less than 1 percent of all wounds in the Civil War.

Elaborate entrenchments strengthened defensive positions even more. Firing from deep trenches, infantrymen with rifle-muskets could easily turn back assaults by forces three to four times their size, as the great success of the depleted Confederate forces defending Atlanta and Richmond in 1864 and 1865 clearly showed. Indeed, the grinding trench warfare around Petersburg, Virginia, provided a chilling preview of World War I, when quick-firing breech-loaded rifles and machine guns strengthened defensive positions even more.

The new rifle technology baffled most Civil War commanders, who continued to use the tactics perfected during the heyday of the musket and bayonet. They ordered thousands of infantrymen into dense close-order formations and sent them against enemy positions in successive waves. The result was brutally tragic. In battle after battle charging infantrymen went down like harvested wheat. Finally, the terrible losses at Gettysburg forced officers to search for ways to cope with the rifle-musket—the new and deadly weapon of war.

Industrial Richmond

Exploiting their city's location at the falls of the James River, Richmond entrepreneurs developed a wide range of industries: flour mills, tobacco factories, railroad and port facilities, and, most important, a profitable and substantial iron industry. In 1861 the Tredegar Iron Works employed nearly a thousand workers and, as the only facility in the South that could manufacture large machinery and heavy weapons, made a major contribution to the Confederate war effort. Virginia State Library.

effective in raising capital and controlling inflation than earlier efforts by the First and Second Banks of the United States had been. Finally, the Lincoln administration implemented Clay's program for a nationally financed system of internal improvements. In 1862 the Republican Congress began to build transcontinental railroads, chartering the Union Pacific and Central Pacific Railroads and subsidizing them lavishly. In addition, the Republicans moved aggressively to provide northern farmers with "free land" in the West. The Homestead Act of 1862 gave heads of families or individuals age twenty-one or older the title to 160 acres of public land after five years of residence and improvement. This economic program sustained the allegiance of many Northerners to the Republican Party while bolstering the Union's ability to fight the war.

In contrast, the Confederate government had a much less coherent economic policy. True to its states' rights philosophy, the Confederacy initially left most economic matters in the hands of the state governments. As the realities of total war became clear, the Davis administration took some extraordinary measures: it built and operated shipyards, armories,

foundries, and textile mills; commandeered food and scarce raw materials such as coal, iron, copper, and lead; requisitioned slaves to work on fortifications; and exercised direct control over foreign trade. As the war wore on, ordinary southern citizens resented these measures, especially in areas where Confederate leaders failed to manage wartime shortages. To sustain the war effort, the Confederacy increasingly counted on white solidarity: Jefferson Davis warned whites that a Union victory would destroy slavery "and reduce the whites to the degraded position of the African race."

Raising Money in the North. For both the North and the South the cost of fighting a total war was enormous. In the Union, government spending shot up from less than 2 percent of gross national product to about 15 percent (Table 14.2). To meet those expenses the Republicans established a powerful modern state that raised money in three ways. First, the government increased tariffs on consumer goods and imposed direct taxes on business corporations, large inheritances, and incomes. These levies paid for about 20 percent of the cost of the war. The sale of treasury bonds financed

TABLE 14.2 The Cost of the War: Union Finances, 1860 and 1864

	1860	1864
Income	$56.1 million	$264.6 million
Expenditures	$63.1 million	$865.3 million
General	32.0 million	35.1 million
Army and Navy	27.9 million	776.5 million
Interest on Debt	3.2 million	53.7 million
Total Public Debt	$64.8 million	$1,815.8 million

In 1864, the Union government received five times as much revenue as it had in 1860, but it spent nearly fourteen times as much, mostly to pay soldiers and buy military supplies. In four years the public debt had risen twenty-eight-fold, so that interest payments in 1865 nearly equaled the level of all federal government expenditures in 1860.

another 65 percent of the northern war effort. Led by Jay Cooke, a Philadelphia banker, the treasury used newspaper advertisements and 2,500 subagents to persuade nearly a million northern families to buy war bonds. In addition, the National Banking Acts of 1863 and 1864 forced state banks to accept national charters, which, in turn, required them to purchase treasury bonds and thereby finance the war.

The Union paid the remaining cost of the war by printing paper money. The Legal Tender Act of 1862 authorized the issue of $150 million in treasury notes—which soon became known as **greenbacks**—and required the public to accept them as legal tender. As with the "Continentals" issued during the War of Independence, these treasury notes were backed by faith in the government rather than by specie. Unlike the Continentals, this paper money did not depreciate disastrously in value. Although $450 million in greenbacks had been issued by the end of the war, this paper money funded only 15 percent of wartime expenses (as opposed to 80 percent during the Revolutionary War) and consequently did not spark an inflationary rise in prices. By imposing broad-based taxes, borrowing from the middle classes, and creating a national monetary system, the Union government had created the financial foundations of a modern nation-state.

The South Resorts to Inflation. The financial demands on the South were just as great, but it lacked a powerful central government that could tax and borrow.

The War's Toll on Civilians
Fighting along the Mississippi River in the spring of 1862 and the Union blockade along the Gulf of Mexico disrupted the supply of foodstuffs to New Orleans. By the time Union troops captured the city in May, foodstocks were severely depleted. In June, hungry citizens—men in top hats and fashionably dressed women as well as barefoot children and white and black working people—stormed the stores and emptied them of their last supplies of food. This engraving, titled Starving People of New Orleans, *appeared in* Harper's Weekly, *a prominent New York journal.*
Library of Congress.

The Confederate Congress fiercely opposed taxes on cotton exports and slaves, the most valuable property of wealthy planters. Taxes fell primarily on urban middle-class and nonslaveholding yeomen farm families, who often refused to pay. Consequently, the Confederacy covered less than 5 percent of its expenditures through taxation. The government paid for another 35 percent by borrowing, although many wealthy planters refused to buy large quantities of Confederate bonds, and foreign bankers were equally wary.

Thus the Confederacy was forced to finance about 60 percent of its expenses with unbacked paper money. The flood of currency created a spectacular inflation, which was compounded by the widespread circulation of counterfeit Confederate notes. As the huge supply of money (and shortages of goods) caused food prices to soar, riots broke out in more than a dozen southern cities and towns. In Richmond several hundred women broke into bakeries, crying, "Our children are starving while the rich roll in wealth." By the spring of 1865 prices had risen to ninety-two times their 1861 levels. Inflation not only undermined civilians' morale but also prompted them to refuse Confederate money, sometimes with serious consequences. When South Carolina store clerk Jim Harris refused to accept Confederate notes from a group of soldiers, they raided his storehouse and "robbed it of about five thousand dollars worth of goods." Army supply officers did the same, offering payment in worthless IOUs. Fearful of a strong government and taxation, the Confederacy was forced to violate the property rights of its citizens to sustain the war.

The Turning Point: 1863

By 1863 the Lincoln administration had mobilized northern society, creating a complex war machine and a coherent financial system. "Little by little," the young diplomat Henry Adams noted at his post in London, "one began to feel that, behind the chaos in Washington power was taking shape; that it was massed and guided as it had not been before." Slowly but surely the tide of the struggle shifted toward the Union.

Emancipation

From the beginning of the conflict antislavery Republicans had tried to persuade their party to make abolition—as well as restoration of the Union—a central war aim. They based their argument not just on morality but also on "military necessity," pointing out that slave-grown crops sustained the Confederate war effort. As Frederick Douglass put it, "the very stomach of this rebellion is the Negro in the form of a slave. Arrest that hoe in the hands of the Negro, and you smite the rebellion in

the very seat of its life." Lincoln initially refused to consider the war as a struggle for black freedom, telling Horace Greeley of the *New York Tribune* that "if I could save the Union without freeing any slave, I would do it." As war casualties mounted in 1862, Lincoln and some Republican leaders moved closer to Douglass's position and began to redefine the war as a struggle against slavery—the cornerstone of southern society.

"Contrabands." However, it was enslaved African Americans who forced the issue by seizing freedom for themselves. Exploiting the disorder of wartime, tens of thousands of slaves escaped and sought refuge behind Union lines. The first Union official to confront this issue was General Benjamin Butler. When three slaves reached his army camp on the Virginia coast in May 1861, he labeled them "contraband of war" and refused to return them to their owner. His term stuck, and for the rest of the war slaves behind Union lines were known as **contrabands**. Within a few months a thousand contrabands were camping with Butler's army. To define their status and undermine the Confederate war effort, in August 1861 Congress passed the First Confiscation Act, which authorized the seizure of all property—including slaves—used to support the rebellion.

Radical Republicans, who had long condemned slavery, now saw a way to use the war to end it. By the spring of 1862 leading Radicals—Treasury Secretary Chase; Charles Sumner, chair of the Senate Committee on Foreign Relations; and Thaddeus Stevens, chair of the House Ways and Means Committee—had pushed moderate Republicans toward abolition. A longtime Pennsylvania congressman and an uncompromising foe of slavery, Stevens was a masterful politician, adept at fashioning legislation that commanded majority support. In April 1862 Stevens and his Radical allies persuaded Congress to end slavery in the District of Columbia, with compensation for owners. In June it outlawed slavery in the federal territories, finally enacting into law the Wilmot Proviso and the Republicans' free-soil policy. And in July Congress passed the Second Confiscation Act. This far-reaching legislation overrode the property rights of Confederate slave owners, declaring "forever free" all fugitive slaves and all slaves captured by the Union army. Emancipation had become an instrument of war.

The Emancipation Proclamation. Lincoln now seized the initiative from the Radicals. In July 1862 he prepared a general proclamation of emancipation and, viewing the battle of Antietam as "an indication of the Divine Will," issued it on September 22, 1862. Based on the president's powers as commander in chief, the proclamation declared Lincoln's intention to fight the rebellion by ending slavery in all states that remained out of the Union on January 1, 1863. The rebel states

First Reading of the Emancipation Proclamation, **by Francis Bicknell Carpenter**

Treasury Secretary Salmon P. Chase (far left) and Secretary of State William H. Seward (center foreground) were longtime foes of slavery. As thousands of black contrabands sought freedom behind Union lines, Chase and Seward pressed Lincoln to make abolition one of his war aims. In July 1862 the president drew up a draft proclamation but Seward, himself a successful politician who knew the importance of timing, persuaded Lincoln to "postpone its issue until you can give it to the country supported by military success." On September 21, four days after the battle of Antietam, Lincoln read the Emancipation Proclamation to his cabinet and the next day issued it to the public.
U.S. Capitol Historical Society.

had a hundred days in which to preserve slavery by renouncing secession. None chose to do so.

The proclamation was politically astute. Because Lincoln needed to keep the loyalty of the border states still in the Union, the proclamation left slavery intact there. He also wanted to secure the allegiance of the areas occupied by Union armies—western and central Tennessee, western Virginia, and southern Louisiana, including New Orleans—so he left slavery untouched there. Consequently, the Emancipation Proclamation did not actually free a single slave. Yet, as the abolitionist Wendell Phillips perceived, Lincoln's proclamation had moved the institution of slavery to "the edge of Niagara," where it would soon be swept over the brink, bringing freedom to all enslaved African Americans. Indeed, Union troops soon became agents of liberation, freeing slaves as they advanced into the South. "I became free in 1863, in the summer, when the yankees come by and said I could go work for myself," Jackson Daniel of Maysville, Alabama, recalled. "I was farming after that

[and also] . . . making shoes." The conflict was no longer simply a struggle to preserve the Union but, as Lincoln put it, a war of "subjugation" in which "the old South is to be destroyed and replaced by new propositions and ideas."

As a war aim, emancipation was controversial. In the Confederacy, Jefferson Davis labeled it the "most execrable measure recorded in the history of guilty man," while in the North it produced the backlash among whites that the moderate Republicans had feared. During the congressional election of 1862 the Democrats denounced emancipation as unconstitutional, warned of slave uprisings and massive bloodshed in the South, and claimed that a "black flood" would wash away the jobs of northern workers. Democrat Horatio Seymour won the governorship of New York by declaring that if abolition was the purpose of the war, the South should not be conquered. Other Democrats swept to victory in Pennsylvania, Ohio, and Illinois, and the party gained thirty-four seats in Congress. However, the Republicans still held a twenty-five-seat majority in the House and had gained five seats in the Senate. Lincoln refused to retreat. On New Year's Day 1863 he signed the Emancipation Proclamation. To reassure Northerners who sympathized with the South or feared race warfare, Lincoln urged slaves to "abstain from all violence." He now justified emancipation as an "act of justice." "If my name ever goes into history," he said, "it was for this act."

Vicksburg and Gettysburg

The fate of the proclamation would depend on the success of Union armies and the Republicans' ability to win political support for their war policies. The outlook was not encouraging. Not only had Democrats registered gains in the election of 1862 but there was also increased popular support for Democrats who favored a negotiated peace. Two brilliant victories by Lee, whose army defeated Hooker's forces at Fredericksburg (December 1862) and Chancellorsville, Virginia (May 1863), caused further erosion of northern support for the war, as did rumors of a new draft.

The Crucial July Battles. At this critical juncture General Grant mounted a major offensive in the West designed to split the Confederacy in two. Grant drove south along the west bank of the Mississippi and then moved his troops across the river near Vicksburg, Mississippi, where he defeated two Confederate armies and laid siege to the city. After repelling Union assaults for six weeks, the exhausted and starving Vicksburg garrison surrendered on July 4, 1863. Five days later Union forces took Port Hudson, Louisiana, establishing Union control of the Mississippi River. Grant had taken 31,000 prisoners, cut off Louisiana, Arkansas, and Texas from the rest of the Confederacy, and prompted hundreds of slaves to desert their plantations (see American Voices, "Elizabeth Mary Meade Ingraham: A Vicksburg Diary," p. 416).

Grant's initial advance down the Mississippi had created an argument over strategy within the Confederate leadership. Jefferson Davis and other civilian leaders wanted to throw in reinforcements to defend Vicksburg and send troops to Tennessee to draw Grant out of Mississippi. But Robert E. Lee, buoyed by his recent victories over Hooker, favored a new invasion of the North. He argued that a military thrust into the free states would relieve the pressure on Vicksburg by drawing the Union armies east. Beyond that Lee hoped for a major victory that would undermine northern support for the war.

Lee won out. In June 1863 he maneuvered his army north through Maryland into Pennsylvania. The Union's Army of the Potomac moved along with him, positioning itself between Lee and the federal capital of Washington. Early in July the two great armies met in an accidental but decisive confrontation at Gettysburg, Pennsylvania (Map 14.4). On the first day of battle, July 1, Lee drove the Union's advance guard to the south of town. There General George G. Meade, who had just taken over command of the Union forces from Hooker, placed his troops in well-defended hilltop positions and called up reinforcements. By the morning of the second day Meade had 90,000 troops to Lee's 75,000. Aware that he was outnumbered but bent on victory, Lee attacked both of Meade's flanks but failed to turn them. General Richard B. Ewell, assigned to attack the Union right, was unwilling to risk his men in an all-out assault, and General Longstreet, on the Union left, was unable to dislodge Meade's forces from a hill known as Little Round Top.

On July 3 Lee decided to attempt a frontal assault on the center of the Union lines. He recognized the danger of this tactic but felt this might be his last chance to inflict a crushing defeat on the North. Moreover, he had enormous confidence in his troops. After the heaviest artillery barrage of the war, Lee ordered 14,000 men under General George E. Pickett to take Cemetery Ridge. Anticipating this attack, Meade had reinforced the center of his line with artillery and his best troops. When Pickett's men charged across a mile of open terrain, they were met by massive fire from artillery and rifle-muskets; thousands were killed, wounded, or captured. By the end of the battle Lee had suffered 28,000 casualties, one-third of the Army of Northern Virginia, while 23,000 of Meade's soldiers lay killed or wounded, making Gettysburg the most lethal battle of the Civil War. Shocked by the bloodletting, Meade allowed the remaining Confederate soldiers to escape, thus losing an opportunity to end the war. "As it is," Lincoln brooded, "the war will be prolonged indefinitely."

Political and Diplomatic Effects. Nonetheless, Gettysburg was a great Union victory and, in combination with the triumph at Vicksburg, represented a major turning point in the conflict. Never again would a southern army invade the North. In the fall of 1863 Republicans reaped the political gains from those victories by sweeping state and local elections in Pennsylvania, Ohio, and New York. In the South the military setbacks accentuated war weariness. The Confederate elections of 1863 went sharply against the politicians who supported Jefferson Davis, and a large minority in the new Confederate Congress were outspokenly hostile to his policies. A few advocated peace negotiations, and many more criticized the ineffectiveness of the war effort, with the Confederate vice president, Alexander Stephens, comparing Davis to "my poor old blind and deaf dog."

Vicksburg and Gettysburg also represented a great diplomatic triumph for the North, ending the Confederacy's prospect of winning foreign recognition and acquiring advanced weapons. In 1862 British shipbuilders

Elizabeth Mary Meade Ingraham

A Vicksburg Diary

Elizabeth Mary Meade Ingraham (1806–?) was the sister of Union General George Meade but, having become a plantation mistress, she sided with the Confederacy. In 1831 Ingraham and her husband, who had been an agent of the Second Bank of the United States, moved from Philadelphia to Mississippi and purchased Ashwood Plantation, thirty miles from Vicksburg. Her diary, which covers the six weeks between May 2 and June 13, 1863, describes how Ulysses S. Grant's Vicksburg campaign dramatically changed the relationship between masters and slaves.

May 4. [Union General] Osterhaus' Division, scum of St. Louis, camped in the big field. All the corn ruined in the field, and nearly all consumed in the granaries. . . . Nancy [a slave] sent me a little. Elsy, faithful and true, and Jack and Emma [all slaves] very attentive.

May 8. The last thing Eddens [a slave] did was to save some meat for me. He slept in the spare room Sunday night, and Monday at noon he had quit our service. . . . Parker, Sol, Mordt, Jim Crow, Isaiah, and Wadloo, have quit us, but the rest are here, and very attentive and willing. . . .

May 13. Elsy still faithful, feeds us, and does what she can; Rita Jane too; Bowlegs very attentive. Emma beginning to tire of waiting on me, did not come up at noon; Nancy not true.

May 15. Edward's [Ingraham's son] sash and six pairs of gloves taken out of my wardrobe. I am afraid Emma has done this; don't feel as if I could trust any one but Elsy; she feeds and takes care of me.

May 18. [We] have reason to think the hands will all leave; only a question of time, they are not quite ready; Elsy still true; but Jack doubtful. . . .

May 27. Negro meetings are being held, and the few whites left begin to be very anxious. . . . Powers was burnt out by his own negroes. I fear the blacks more than I do the Yankees. Jack trying to persuade Elsy to leave. . . . She tells him to get her a home and a way of earning a living, and she is ready to go, but [I] told her, if he left here, to move up into the wash-house with her children. I would give her $12 a month and free her four children.

June 3. Our darkeys in great commotion, yesterday, on account of Secesh [secessionists], who, about twenty-five in number, have been going the rounds, and setting the negroes to work; they whipped one fellow . . . and hung another; and we thought last evening all ours but a few meant to go. . . . I wish the Secesh would come [here]. . . .

June 6. Martha with her three children and Emma, left at midnight Friday . . . and the rest are packing to-day. Hays resolved to go, and I dread lest he take his wife with him, for I can hardly get along as it is, and shall die if I have the cooking to do.

June 10. Fanny, John Smith, and the children, Buck and his family, Dave and his, Kate and hers, making in all thirteen who have gone—Dave intending to come back, but the Yankees would not let him. . . . [T]hose who have stayed are utterly demoralized; if they work for you, the job is only half done.

Source: W. Maury Darst, "The Vicksburg Diary of Mrs. Alfred Ingraham," *Journal of Mississippi History* 44 (May 1982): 148–79.

---

had begun to supply armed cruisers to the Confederacy, and one of them, the *Alabama*, had sunk or captured more than a hundred Union merchant ships. Charles Francis Adams, the son of John Quincy Adams and the American minister in London, despaired of preventing the scheduled delivery of two more ironclad cruisers in mid-1863. News of the Union victories changed everything, and Adams persuaded the British government to impound the ships.

Moreover, cotton had not become an effective diplomatic weapon, as the South had hoped. British manufacturers had stockpiled raw cotton before the war, and when those stocks were depleted, they found new sources in Egypt and India. Equally important, the dependence of British consumers on cheap wheat from the North deterred the government from supporting the Confederacy. Finally, British workers and reformers were enthusiastic champions of abolition, which the Emancipation Proclamation had established as a Union war aim. The results at Vicksburg and Gettysburg confirmed British neutrality by demonstrating the military might of the Union. The British did not want to risk Canada or their merchant marine by provoking a strong, well-armed United States.

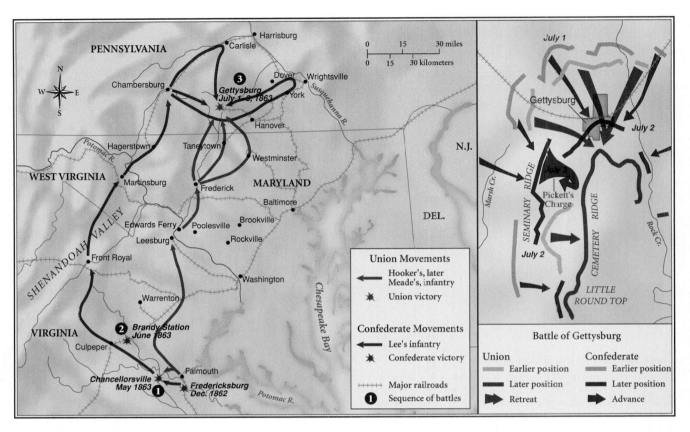

MAP 14.4 Lee Invades the North, 1863

After Lee's victory at Chancellorsville and Brandy Station (#1 and 2), the Confederate forces moved northward, constantly shadowed by the Union army, until the two armies met accidentally near Gettysburg, Pennsylvania, in early July. In the ensuing battle (#3), the Union army, commanded by General George Meade, emerged victorious, primarily because it was much larger than the Confederate force and held well-fortified positions along Cemetery Ridge, which gave its units a major tactical advantage.

The Union Victorious, 1864–1865

The Union victories of 1863 made it clear that the South could not win the war on the battlefield, but the Confederacy still hoped for a military stalemate and a negotiated peace. Lincoln and his generals faced the daunting task of winning a quick and decisive victory; otherwise a majority of northern voters might well desert the Republican Party and its policies.

Soldiers and Strategy

Two developments allowed the Union to prosecute the war with continued vigor and eventually to prevail: the enlistment of African American soldiers and the emergence of generals capable of fighting a modern war.

The Impact of Black Troops. Free African Americans and fugitive slaves had tried to enlist in the Union army as early as 1861, and the black abolitionist Frederick Douglass had embraced their cause: "Once

let the black man get upon his person the brass letters, 'U.S.' . . . a musket on his shoulder and bullets in his pockets, and there is no power on earth which can deny that he has earned the right to citizenship in the United States." The possibility of such an outcome frightened many northern whites, who were determined to keep blacks in a position of political inferiority. Moreover, most Union generals doubted that former slaves would make good soldiers, and so the Lincoln administration initially refused to consider blacks for military service. Nonetheless, by 1862 free and contraband blacks had formed regiments in South Carolina, Louisiana, and Kansas and waited for orders to join the fighting.

The Emancipation Proclamation changed popular thinking and military policy. If blacks were to benefit from a Union victory, some northern whites argued, they should share in the fighting and dying. The valor exhibited by the first African American regiments also influenced northern opinion. In January 1863 Thomas Wentworth Higginson, the white abolitionist commander of the black First South Carolina Volunteers,

Black Soldiers in the Union Army

Determined to end racial slavery, tens of thousands of African Americans volunteered for service in the Union army in 1864 and 1865, boosting the northern war effort at a critical time. These proud soldiers were members of the 107th Colored Infantry, stationed at Fort Corcoran near Washington, D.C. In January 1865 their regiment participated in the daring capture of Fort Fisher, which protected Wilmington, North Carolina, the last Confederate port open to blockade runners. Library of Congress.

wrote a glowing newspaper account of their military prowess: "No officer in this regiment now doubts that the key to the successful prosecution of the war lies in the unlimited employment of black troops." In July the heroic but costly attack on Fort Wagner, South Carolina, by another black regiment, the Fifty-fourth Massachusetts Infantry, convinced many white Northerners, including Union officers, of the value of black soldiers. The War Department authorized the enlistment of free blacks and contraband slaves, and as white resistance to conscription increased, the Lincoln administration recruited as many African Americans as it could. Without black soldiers, the president suggested in the autumn of 1864, "we would be compelled to abandon the war in three weeks." By the spring of 1865 there were nearly 200,000 African American soldiers and sailors.

Military service did not end racial discrimination. Black soldiers served under white officers in segregated regiments and were used primarily to build fortifications, garrison forts, and guard supply lines. At first they were paid less than white soldiers ($7 versus $13 per month) and won equal pay only by threatening to lay down their arms. Despite such treatment African Americans volunteered for military service in disproportionate numbers and diligently served the Union cause. They knew they were fighting for freedom and the possibility of a new social order. "Hello, Massa," said one black

soldier to his former master, who had been taken prisoner. "Bottom rail on top dis time." The worst fears of the secessionists had come true: through the agency of the Union army, blacks had enlisted in a great rebellion against slavery (see American Voices, "Spotswood Rice: Freeing My Children from Slavery," p. 419).

New Generals Take Command. As African Americans joined the ranks, Lincoln finally found a commanding general in whom he had confidence. Impressed with General Ulysses S. Grant's victories in the West, in March 1864 Lincoln placed Grant in charge of all the Union armies and created a command structure appropriate to the large, complex organization that the Union army had become. From then on, the president would determine general strategy and Grant would decide how best to implement it. Lincoln directed Grant to advance simultaneously against all the major Confederate forces, a strategy Grant had long favored. Both the general and the president wanted a decisive victory before the election of 1864.

As the successful western campaigns of mid-1863 showed, Grant understood how to fight a modern war—a war relying on industrial technology and directed at an entire society. At Vicksburg he had besieged an entire city and forced its surrender. Then, in November 1863, he had used the North's superior technology, utilizing railroad

Spotswood Rice

Freeing My Children from Slavery

The face of the war changed in 1864 as tens of thousands of blacks—many of them ex-slaves—joined the Union army, which now began to occupy significant parts of the Confederacy. In February, Spotswood Rice, a tobacco roller and the slave of Benjamin Lewis, fled from his owner near Glasgow, Missouri, and became a Union soldier. In September, although hospitalized with rheumatism, Rice wrote the following letters to his still enslaved children and to Kittey Diggs, who owned one of them.

[Benton Barracks Hospital, St. Louis, Mo., September 3, 1864]

My Children I take my pen in hand to rite you a few lines to let you know that I have not forgot you and that I want to see you as bad as ever. Now my Dear Children . . . be assured that I will have you if it cost me my life.

on the 28th of the mounth, 8 hundred White and 8 hundred blacke solders expects to start up the rivore to Glasgow and [will] . . . be jeneraled by a jeneral that will give me both of you. When they Come I expect to be with them and expect to get you both in return. Dont be uneasy my children I expect to have you.

If Diggs dont give you up this Government will [take you from Diggs] and I feel confident that I will get you Your Miss Kaitty said that I tried to steal you But I'll let her know that god never intended for man to steal his own flesh and blood. . . . If I ever had any Confidence in her I have none now and never expect to have And I want her to remember if she meets me with ten thousand soldiers she [will] meet her enemy I once [thought] that I had some respect for them but now my respects is worn out and have no sympathy for Slaveholders. And as for her cristianantty I expect the Devil has Such in hell. You tell her from me that She is the frist Christian that I ever hard say that a man could Steal his own child especially out of human bondage. . . .

now my Dear children I am a going to close my letter to you. . . . Oh! My Dear children how I do want to see you

[To Kittey Diggs]

I received a leteter from Cariline telling me that you say I tried to steal, to plunder my child away from you now I want you to understand that mary is my Child and she is a God given rite of my own . . . the longor you keep my Child from me the longor you will have to burn in hell and the qwicer [quicker] youll get their

for we are now making up a bout one thoughsand blacke troops to . . . come through Glasgow and when we come wo [woe] be to Copperhood rabbels and to the Slaveholding rebbels for we dont expect to leave them there. . . .

I want you to understand kittey diggs that where ever you and I meets we are enmays to each orthere I offered once to pay you forty dollers for my own Child but I am glad now that you did not accept it. . . . my Children is my own and I expect to get them and . . . to exacute vengencens on them that holds my Child

I have no fears about geting mary out of your hands this whole Government gives chear to me and you cannot help your self

Spotswood Rice

Source: Ira Berlin, Joseph P. Reidy, and Leslie S. Rowland, eds., *Freedom's Soldiers: The Black Military Experience in the Civil War* (New York: Cambridge University Press, 1998), 131–33.

transport to charge to the rescue of a Union army near Chattanooga, Tennessee, and drive an invading Confederate army back into Georgia. Moreover, Grant was willing to accept heavy casualties in assaults on strongly defended positions, abandoning the caution of earlier Union commanders. Their attempts "to conserve life" had in fact prolonged the war, Grant argued. These aggressive tactics earned Grant a reputation as a butcher both of his own men and of enemy armies, which he pursued relentlessly. To crush the South's will to resist, the new Union commander was willing to terrorize the civilian population.

In May 1864 Grant ordered major new offensives on two fronts. Personally taking charge of the 115,000-strong Army of the Potomac, he set out to destroy Lee's force of 75,000 troops in Virginia. Simultaneously he instructed General William Tecumseh Sherman, who shared his views on warfare, to invade Georgia and take Atlanta. As Sherman prepared for battle, he wrote that

Grant Planning an Attack

On June 2, 1864, the day this photograph was taken, Grant moved his headquarters to the Bethesda Church, carried the pews out under the shade of the surrounding trees, and planned the costly attack he would make at Cold Harbor the next day—a frontal assault that resulted in 7,000 Union casualties. While Grant (to the left) leaned over a pew, gesturing at a map, his officers smoked their pipes and read reports of the war in newspapers that had just arrived from New York City. Library of Congress.

"all that has gone before is mere skirmish. The war now begins" (see American Lives, "William Tecumseh Sherman: An Architect of Modern War," p. 422).

Grant advanced toward Richmond, hoping to force Lee to fight in open fields, where the Union's superior manpower and artillery could prevail. Remembering his tactical errors at Gettysburg, Lee remained in strong defensive positions, attacking only when he held an advantage. The Confederate general seized such opportunities twice, winning narrow victories in early May at the battles of the Wilderness and Spotsylvania Court House. Nevertheless Grant drove on toward Richmond (Map 14.5). In early June he attacked Lee at Cold

Harbor but withdrew after losing 7,000 men in a single hour in a frontal assault. Grant had severely eroded Lee's forces, which had suffered 31,000 casualties, but Union losses were even higher at 55,000 men.

The fighting took a heavy psychological toll. "Many a man has gone crazy since this campaign began from the terrible pressure on mind and body," observed a Union captain, Oliver Wendell Holmes Jr. (a future eminent justice of the Supreme Court). Previous battles had lasted only a few days and had been separated by long intervals. In this campaign Grant's relentless advance and Lee's defensive tactics produced sustained fighting and grueling attrition, as the morale and health

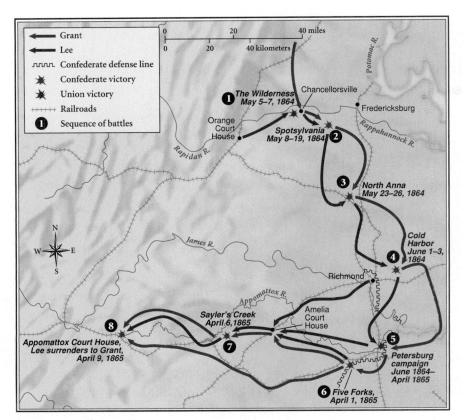

MAP 14.5 The Closing Virginia Campaign, 1864–1865

Beginning in May 1864, General Ulysses Grant launched an all-out campaign against Richmond. By threatening Robert E. Lee's lines of communication, Grant attempted to lure him into open battle. But Lee avoided a major test of strength, falling back and taking defensive positions at the Wilderness, Spotsylvania, North Anna, and Cold Harbor (#1–4) and inflicting heavy casualties on the Union attackers. From June 1864 to April 1865, the two armies faced each other across defensive fortifications outside Petersburg (#5), a protracted siege broken finally by Grant's flanking maneuver at Five Forks (#6). Lee's surrender followed shortly.

of the soldiers declined and some deserted. In June Grant pulled some of his troops away from Richmond to lay siege to Petersburg, an important railroad center. Protracted trench warfare, which foreshadowed that of World War I, made the spade as important as the sword. Union and Confederate soldiers built complex networks of trenches, tunnels, and artillery emplacements for almost fifty miles around Richmond and Petersburg and dared the other side to attack. An officer invoked biblical imagery to describe the continuous artillery firing and sniping as "living night and day within the 'valley of the shadow of death.'" The stress was especially great for the outnumbered Confederate troops, who spent months in the muddy, sickening trenches without rotation to the rear. As time passed, Lincoln and Grant felt pressures of their own; the enormous casualties and continued military stalemate threatened Lincoln with defeat in the November election.

The outlook for the Republicans worsened in July 1864, when a raid by Jubal Early's cavalry near Washington forced Grant to divert his best troops from the Petersburg campaign. To punish farmers in the Shenandoah Valley, who provided a base for Early and food for Lee's army, Grant ordered General Philip H. Sheridan to turn the region into "a barren waste." Through the fall, Sheridan's troops conducted a scorched-earth campaign, destroying grain supplies, barns, farming implements, and gristmills. This terrorism went beyond the military norms of the day, for most officers regarded civilians as

noncombatants and feared that punishing them would erode military discipline. But Grant's decision to carry the war to Confederate civilians had changed the definition of conventional warfare.

The Election of 1864 and Sherman's March to the Sea

As the siege at Petersburg dragged on, some Republicans deserted Lincoln and searched for an alternative candidate. The president's hopes for nomination and reelection now rested on the success or failure of General William Sherman in Georgia. Sherman had gradually penetrated to within about thirty miles of Atlanta, a great railway hub that lay at the heart of the Confederacy. Although his army outnumbered that of General Joseph E. Johnston by 90,000 to 60,000 men, Sherman avoided a direct attack and slowly pried the Confederates out of one defensive position after another. Finally, on June 27 at Kennesaw Mountain, Sherman engaged Johnston in a set battle, only to suffer 3,000 casualties while inflicting only about 600. By late July the Union general had laid siege to Atlanta on the north, but the next month brought little gain. Like Grant, Sherman seemed bogged down in a hopeless campaign.

The Union Party versus the Peace Democrats. Meanwhile, the presidential campaign of 1864 was well under way. In June a Republican convention attended

William Tecumseh Sherman: An Architect of Modern War

The Civil War rescued William Tecumseh Sherman (1820–1891) from a life of disappointment and failure, giving him the opportunity to use his talents as a ruthless soldier and military strategist. By the end of the war Sherman had emerged not only as a major force in the Union victory but also as an important architect of modern warfare.

Disappointment had come early in Sherman's life. He was born into a socially prominent clan in Connecticut, but his immediate family fell on hard times when his parents moved west to Lancaster, Ohio. His father's law practice did not prosper, and his early death in 1829 shattered the family. Able to support only two of her eleven children, Sherman's mother sent the rest to be raised by friends and relatives. The sixth child, Tecumseh (named after the great Indian chief), went to live with Thomas Ewing, a close family friend and a wealthy Lancaster lawyer.

Life with the Ewings brought many privileges but not much pleasure. His foster mother insisted that Tecumseh be baptized into her Catholic faith and take the Christian name William. Embarrassed by his father's financial failure, Sherman never adjusted to his new life. In 1836 he gladly left Ohio to enter the United States Military Academy at West Point, an appointment arranged by Thomas Ewing, who was now a U.S. senator.

Sherman flourished at West Point and adopted the army as his real family, finding in the corps of professional officers the sense of identity, order, and belonging that he had missed as a child. After his graduation in 1840, the young officer used assignments in Florida, Alabama, South Carolina, and Georgia to travel widely. However, the Ewings had grandiose plans for their foster son, approving his marriage to their daughter Ellen and encouraging him to enter the world of business. Sherman refused to leave the army, hoping he would rise in the ranks during the Mexican War. But by the time he reached California in 1847 there was little to do except paperwork. Six years later, he resigned his commission.

Sherman had no more success as a businessman than he had as a soldier. Unstable financial times ruined

William Tecumseh Sherman
Sherman was a nervous man who smoked cigars and talked continuously. When he was seated, he crossed and uncrossed his legs incessantly, and a journalist described his fingers as constantly "twitching his red whiskers—his coat buttons— playing a tattoo on the table—or running through his hair." But Sherman was a decisive general who commanded the loyalty of his troops. This photograph was taken in 1865, after Sherman's devastating march through Georgia and the Carolinas.
Library of Congress.

his budding career as a banker, and he was forced to accept a junior partnership in a business run by two of his foster brothers. Unwilling to remain a dependent of the Ewings, in 1860 Sherman rejoined the army as superintendent of the brand-new Louisiana Military Seminary.

The new superintendent's earlier assignments in the South had made him sympathetic to the planter class and its institutions. In particular, he believed that slavery was necessary to maintain the stability of southern social order. However, Sherman remained a staunch Unionist. A Whig in politics and a soldier by profession, he was convinced that a strong national government was the key to American greatness. In 1861 there was no question on which side William Tecumseh Sherman would stand. When Louisiana troops seized the U.S. arsenal at Baton Rouge in January 1861, Sherman resigned his position.

Secession meant "anarchy," he told his southern friends, and had to be crushed. "There can be no peaceable secession," he continued. "If war comes, as I fear it surely will, I must fight your people whom I best love."

Sherman understood how costly and bloody the war would be, and he doubted that Abraham Lincoln and his administration would pay the price. But his family was firmly committed to the war effort and, urged on by Senator Ewing and his younger brother John Sherman, who had just been elected as a Republican senator from Ohio, William Tecumseh became a colonel in a newly formed Union brigade.

Bull Run was Sherman's first taste of combat, and the rout of the Union army confirmed his long-standing doubts about democratic individualism. "The want of organization and subordination of our people is a more dangerous enemy than the armies of the South," he wrote. By October 1861 Sherman had risen to the rank of brigadier general and had command of the Union forces in Kentucky, but he remained so darkly pessimistic about Union prospects that Lincoln relieved him of his command. Thanks to his military friends and his powerful family, by February 1862 Sherman was back in Kentucky, serving under Ulysses S. Grant. A quiet, confident general, Grant provided the sense of determination that Sherman needed. Moreover, Grant agreed with Sherman's emphasis on strict military discipline and on the swift and decisive deployment of forces. Under Grant's guidance, Sherman enjoyed a string of successes. He distinguished himself at Shiloh, winning a promotion to major general. As military governor of Memphis he pacified a strategic sector along the Mississippi River and then in 1863 joined Grant in the successful campaign against the Confederate stronghold at Vicksburg.

Now experienced and increasingly self-confident, Sherman developed his innovative military ideas. Assuming command of a Union army in Tennessee, he turned his troops loose against prosouthern civilians suspected of assisting anti-Union guerrillas. "When one nation is at war with another, all the people of one are enemies of the other," he declared. After guerrillas fired on a boat with Unionist passengers near Randolph, Tennessee, Sherman sent a regiment to level the town, asserting, "We are justified in treating all inhabitants as combatants."

In March 1864 Sherman assumed command of all military operations in the West and worked closely with Grant on a coordinated plan to destroy the Confederacy. Over the next year, Sherman's army dealt the secessionist cause a series of major blows, taking and burning the strategic railway hub of Atlanta, devastating the countryside as he marched through Georgia to the sea, and then sweeping quickly across the Carolinas. These campaigns demonstrated both his tactical military genius and his understanding of psychological warfare: he would destroy the rebels' army and morale by laying waste to southern society.

Following the Union victory Sherman received international acclaim. His former troops revered him, grateful American businessmen made him wealthy, and world leaders honored him. Unlike Grant and other Union generals who pursued political careers, Sherman remained a military man, leading a war against the Great Plains Indians and serving as commanding general of the army from 1869 to 1883. Contemptuous of democratic politics, Sherman rebuffed all overtures from Democratic and Republican leaders. Asked to run for the presidency in 1883, Sherman replied with the oft-quoted words "If nominated, I will not accept; if elected, I will not serve." A stickler for order and discipline, Sherman had no stomach for the anarchic and increasingly corrupt world of American politics.

Imprisoned Confederate Troops, by Julian Scott
As the Union armies advanced, they captured tens of thousands of Confederate soldiers. This 1873 painting depicts an African American orderly distributing meager rations to Confederate soldiers, who are crowded into a small cell.
West Point Museum, U.S. Military Academy / Photo by Ted Speigel.

For more help analyzing this image, see the ONLINE STUDY GUIDE at bedfordstmartins.com/henretta.

by both Republicans and Unionist Democrats endorsed Lincoln's war measures, demanded the unconditional surrender of the Confederacy, and called for a constitutional amendment to abolish slavery. Attempting to attract border-state voters to their northern- and midwestern-based party and create a genuinely national organization, Lincoln and the Republican leadership took a new name, the National Union Party, and chose as Lincoln's vice presidential running mate Andrew Johnson, a slave owner and a Unionist Democrat from Tennessee.

The Democratic convention met in late August and nominated General George B. McClellan, whom Lincoln had removed from a military command because of his opposition to emancipation. Like McClellan, the Democratic delegates rejected freedom for blacks and condemned Lincoln's uncompromising repression of domestic dissent. Then they split into two camps over the issue of continuing the war. By threatening to bolt the convention, the "Peace Democrats" forced through a platform calling for "a cessation of hostilities" and for a constitutional convention to restore peace "on the basis of the Federal Union." Although personally a "**War Democrat**," McClellan promised if elected to recommend an immediate armistice and a peace convention. Rejoicing in "the first ray of real light I have seen since the war began," Confederate vice president Alexander Stephens declared that if Atlanta and Richmond held out, then Lincoln could be defeated and northern Democrats persuaded to accept an independent Confederacy.

The Fall of Atlanta and Lincoln's Victory.   However, on September 2, 1864, Atlanta fell to Sherman's army. In a stunning move the Union general pulled his troops from the trenches and swept around the city to destroy its roads and rail links to the rest of the Confederacy. Fearing that Sherman would be able to trap and destroy his army, Hood abandoned the city. "Atlanta is ours, and fairly won," Sherman telegraphed Lincoln, sparking 100-gun salutes and wild Republican celebrations in northern cities. A deep pessimism settled over the Confederacy. In her diary Mary Chesnut, a slave-owning plantation mistress, confessed that she "felt as if all were dead within me, forever" and foresaw the end of the Confederacy: "We are going to be wiped off the earth." Acknowledging the dramatic change in the military situation, McClellan repudiated the Democratic peace platform, and dissident Republicans abandoned all efforts to dump Lincoln. Instead, the Republican Party went on the offensive, charging that McClellan was still a peace candidate and attacking Peace Democrats as "copperheads" (poisonous snakes) who were hatching treasonous plots.

Sherman's success in Georgia gave Lincoln a clear-cut victory in November. The president took 212 of 233 electoral votes, winning 55 percent of the popular vote and carrying all of the free states as well as the border states of Maryland, Tennessee, and Missouri. Republicans won 145 of the 185 seats in the House of Representatives and increased their Senate majority to 42 of 52 seats. Many of those victories came from the votes of Union troops, most of whom wanted the war to continue until the Confederacy met every Union demand, including emancipation.

Already legal emancipation was under way at the edges of the Confederacy. In 1864 Maryland and Missouri amended their constitutions to free their slaves, and the three occupied states of Tennessee, Arkansas, and Louisiana followed suit. Abolitionists still worried that the Emancipation Proclamation, based on the president's wartime powers, would lose its force at the end of the war and that southern states would reestablish slavery. Urged on by Lincoln, the Republican-dominated Congress took a major step to guarantee black freedom. On January 31, 1865, it approved the Thirteenth Amendment, which prohibited slavery throughout the United States, and sent it to the states for ratification. Slavery was nearly dead.

Sherman's Total War.   Thanks to William Tecumseh Sherman, the Confederacy was nearly dead as well. After the capture of Atlanta Sherman declined to follow the retreating Confederate army into Tennessee and decided on a bold strategy. Rather than spread his troops dangerously thin by protecting supply lines to the rear, he would "cut a swath through to the sea," living off the land. To persuade Lincoln and Grant to approve this unconventional plan, Sherman pointed out that such a march would devastate Georgia and score a major psychological victory. It would be "a demonstration to the world, foreign and domestic, that we have a power [Jefferson] Davis cannot resist."

Sherman carried out the concept of total war he and Sheridan had pioneered: destruction of the enemy's economic resources and will to resist. "We are not only fighting hostile armies," Sherman wrote, "but a hostile people, and must make old and young, rich and poor, feel the hard hand of war." He left Atlanta in flames and during his three-hundred-mile march to the sea destroyed railroads, property, and supplies (Map 14.6). A Union veteran wrote that "[we] destroyed all we could not eat, stole their niggers, burned their cotton & gins, spilled their sorghum, burned & twisted their R.Roads and raised Hell generally." The havoc so demoralized Confederate soldiers that many deserted their units and fled home to protect their farms and families. When Sherman reached Savannah, Georgia, in mid-December, the 10,000 Confederate defenders left without a fight.

In February 1865 Sherman invaded South Carolina. He planned to link up with Grant at Petersburg and along the way punish the state where secession had begun. "The truth is," Sherman wrote, "the whole army

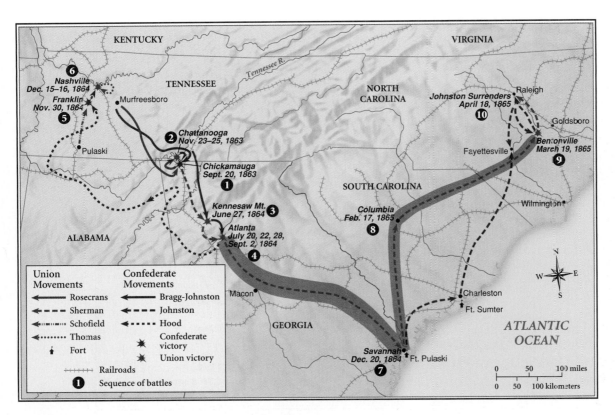

MAP 14.6 Sherman's March through the Confederacy, 1864–1865

The Union victory (#2) in November 1863 at Chattanooga, Tennessee, was almost as critical as the victories in July at Gettysburg and Vicksburg. The Union was now in position to invade the heart of the Confederacy by advancing on the railway hub of Atlanta (#3 and 4). After finally taking the city in September 1864, General William Tecumseh Sherman relied on other Union armies to repulse General John B. Hood's invasion of Tennessee (#5 and 6). Sherman swept on to Savannah in a devastating "March to the Sea" (#7) and then in 1865 cut a swath through the Carolinas (#8, 9, and 10).

For more help analyzing this map, see the ONLINE STUDY GUIDE at bedfordstmartins.com/henretta.

is burning with an insatiable desire to wreak vengeance upon South Carolina." His troops cut a comparatively narrow swath across the state but ravaged the countryside even more thoroughly than they had in Georgia. After capturing South Carolina's capital, Columbia, they burned the business district, most churches, and the wealthiest residential neighborhoods. "This disappointment to me is extremely bitter," lamented Jefferson Davis. By March Sherman had reached North Carolina and was on the verge of linking up with Grant and crushing Lee's army.

The Confederate Collapse. Sherman's march exposed an internal Confederate weakness: rising class resentment on the part of poor whites. Long angered by the "twenty-negro" exemption from military service given to slave owners and fearing that the Confederacy was doomed, ordinary southern farmers resisted

military service. "It is no longer a reproach to be known as a deserter," a Confederate officer in South Carolina complained in late 1863. "I am now going to work instead of to the war," declared David Harris, a backcountry farmer. "I think I will like it the best." By early 1865 the Confederacy was experiencing such a severe manpower crisis that its leaders decided to take an extreme measure: arming the slaves. Urged on by Lee, the Confederate Congress voted to enlist black soldiers; Davis issued an executive order granting freedom to all blacks who served in the Confederate army. But the war ended too soon to reveal whether any slaves would have fought for the Confederacy.

The symbolic end of the war took place in Virginia. In April 1865 Grant finally forced Lee into a showdown by gaining control of the crucial railroad junction at Petersburg and cutting off his supplies. Lee abandoned the defense of Richmond and turned west, hoping to join

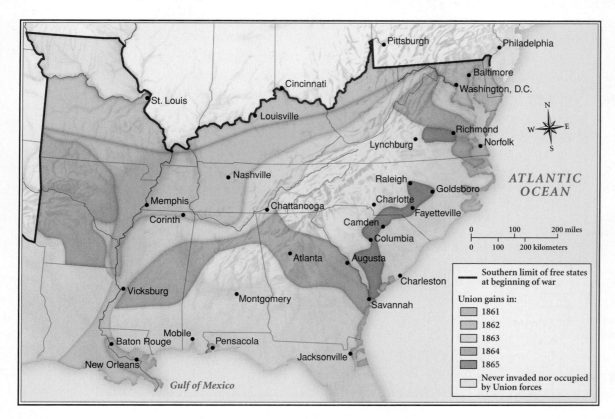

MAP 14.7 The Conquest of the South, 1861–1865

It took four years for the Union armies to defeat those of the Confederacy. Until the last year of the long conflict, most of the South remained in Confederate hands, and even at the end of the war Union armies had never entered many parts of the rebellious states. Most of the Union's territorial gains came on the vast western front, where its control of strategic lines of communication—rivers and railways—gave its forces a decisive advantage.

Confederate forces in North Carolina. While Lincoln visited the ruins of the Confederate capital, mobbed by joyful former slaves, Grant cut off Lee's escape route. On April 9, almost precisely four years after the attack on Fort Sumter, Lee surrendered to Grant at Appomattox Court House, Virginia. In accepting the surrender of the Confederate general, Grant set a tone of generosity, allowing Lee's men to take their horses home for spring planting. By late May all the Confederate generals had ceased to fight, and the Confederate army and government simply dissolved (Map 14.7; see also Map 14.5).

The armies of the Union had destroyed the Confederacy and much of the South's economy. Its factories, warehouses, and railroads were in ruins, as were many of its farms and some of its most important cities. Almost 260,000 Confederate soldiers had paid for secession with their lives. Most significant, the Union had been preserved and slavery destroyed. But the cost of victory was enormous in money, resources, and lives. More than

360,000 Union soldiers were dead, and hundreds of thousands were maimed and crippled. The hard and bitter war was over, and a reunited nation turned to the tasks of peace. These were to be equally hard and bitter.

FOR FURTHER EXPLORATION

▶ For definitions of key terms boldfaced in this chapter, see the glossary at the end of the book.

▶ To assess your mastery of the material covered in this chapter, see the Online Study Guide at **bedfordstmartins.com/henretta**.

▶ For suggested references, including Web sites, see page SR-15 at the end of the book.

▶ For map resources and primary documents, see **bedfordstmartins.com/henretta**.

SUMMARY

Following the victory of Abraham Lincoln and the antislavery Republican Party in the election of 1860, secessionists led the cotton-producing states of the Deep South out of the Union. After fighting began at Fort Sumter, South Carolina, in April 1861, other southern and border states joined the rebellious Confederate states, but owing mainly to Lincoln's efforts, four border states and a portion of a fifth (western Virginia) remained loyal to the United States.

In the East, the first major military battles were inconclusive. In the spring of 1862 Confederate forces commanded by Robert E. Lee repulsed a Union advance on Richmond, and in September northern forces halted Lee's first invasion of the North at Antietam in Maryland. In the West, Union forces under Ulysses S. Grant scored significant victories.

The conflict became a total war, one of unsurpassed cost in lives and resources. To staff their armies, the Union and Confederate governments resorted to a draft, which sparked resistance and riots. The Lincoln administration pursued a coherent economic policy, instituting Henry Clay's American System. It also created an efficient system of taxation and borrowing to finance most of its war effort, whereas Jefferson Davis's Confederate government had to pay its troops and suppliers primarily by printing paper money, which produced a runaway inflation.

The turning point of the war came in 1863, which began with Lincoln's Emancipation Proclamation, establishing abolition as a Union policy. Tens of thousands of African American slaves fled behind Union lines, and many of those eventually enlisted in the northern army. In July 1863 Grant's capture of Vicksburg gave the Union control of the Mississippi and split the Confederacy. Simultaneously, George Meade's victory over Lee at Gettysburg ended the Confederate hope for a military victory.

The war turned into a stalemate, threatening Lincoln's bid for reelection and raising the prospect of a negotiated peace that would give independence to the Confederacy. Then in September 1864 Union forces under William Tecumseh Sherman captured the key city of Atlanta, Georgia, giving military momentum to the North and ensuring Lincoln's reelection. Sherman's devastating "march to the sea" undermined Confederate morale, and Grant's capture of Petersburg in early 1865 led to the surrender of Lee's army.

The Union victory ended the secessionist rebellion and ensured the triumph of nationalist constitutional principles. The Republicans enacted and ratified the Thirteenth Amendment, which ended slavery.

TIMELINE

1861
Confederate States of America formed (February 4)

Abraham Lincoln inaugurated (March 4)

Confederates fire on Fort Sumter (April 12)

Virginia leads Upper South out of Union (April 17)

General Benjamin Butler declares runaway slaves "contraband of war" (May)

Confederates rout Union forces at first Battle of Bull Run (July 21)

1862
Congress passes Legal Tender Act, begins to print greenbacks

Homestead Act provides free land to settlers

Congress extends federal subsidies to transcontinental railroads

Battle of Shiloh advances Union cause in West (April 6–7)

Confederacy introduces first draft

Union halts Confederate offensive at Antietam, Maryland (September 17)

Lincoln issues preliminary Emancipation Proclamation (September 22)

1863
Lincoln signs Emancipation Proclamation (January 1)

Enrollment Act begins draft in North; riots in New York City (July)

Union victories at battles of Gettysburg (July 1–3) and Vicksburg (July 4)

1864
Ulysses S. Grant given command of all Union armies (March)

Grant advances on Richmond and lays seige to Petersburg (May)

William T. Sherman takes Atlanta (September 2)

Lincoln reelected (November)

Sherman marches through Georgia (November and December)

1865
Congress approves Thirteenth Amendment, which outlaws slavery (January)

Robert E. Lee surrenders at Appomattox Court House, Virginia (April 9)

Ratification of Thirteenth Amendment

CHAPTER 15

Reconstruction

1865–1877

IN HIS SECOND INAUGURAL ADDRESS, President Lincoln spoke of the need to "bind up the nation's wounds." No one knew better than Lincoln how daunting a task that would be. Foremost, of course, were the terms on which the rebellious states would be restored to the Union. But America's Civil War had opened more fundamental questions. Slavery was finished. That much was certain. But what system of labor should replace plantation slavery? What rights should the freedmen be accorded beyond emancipation? How far should the federal government go to settle these questions? And who should decide—the president or Congress?

◄ Chloe and Sam (1882)

After the Civil War the country went through the wrenching peacemaking process known as Reconstruction. The struggle between the victorious North and the vanquished South was fought out on a political landscape, but Thomas Hovenden's heartwarming painting reminds us of the deeper meaning of Reconstruction: that Chloe and Sam, after lives spent in slavery, might end their days in the dignity of freedom.

Thomas Colville Fine Art.

The last speech Lincoln delivered, on April 11, 1865, demonstrated his grasp of these issues. Reconstruction, he said, had to be regarded as a practical, not a theoretical, problem. It could be solved only if Republicans remained united, even if that meant compromising on principled differences dividing them, and only if the defeated South gave its consent, even if that meant forgiveness of the South's transgressions. The speech showed, above all, Lincoln's sense of the fluidity of events, of policy toward the South as an evolving, not a fixed, position.

What course Reconstruction might have taken had Lincoln lived is one of the unanswerable questions of American history. On April 14, 1865—five days after Lee's surrender at Appomattox—Lincoln was shot in the head at Ford's Theatre in Washington by a fanatic actor named John Wilkes Booth. Ironically, Lincoln might have been spared if the war had dragged on longer, for Booth and his Confederate associates had originally plotted to kidnap the president to force a negotiated settlement. After Lee's surrender, Booth became bent on revenge. Without regaining consciousness, Lincoln died on April 15.

With one stroke John Wilkes Booth had sent Lincoln to martyrdom, hardened many Northerners against the South, and handed the presidency to a man utterly lacking in Lincoln's moral sense and political judgment, Vice President Andrew Johnson.

Presidential Reconstruction

The procedure for Reconstruction—how to restore rebellious states to the Union—was not addressed by the Founding Fathers. The Constitution does not say which branch of government handles the readmission of rebellious states or, for that matter, even contemplates the possibility of secession. It was an open question whether, on seceding, the Confederate states had legally left the Union. If so, their reentry surely required legislative action by Congress. If not, if even in defeat they retained their constitutional status, then the terms for restoring them to the Union might be defined as an administrative matter best left to the president. The ensuing battle between the White House and Capitol Hill was one of the fault lines in Reconstruction's stormy history.

Lincoln's Approach

Lincoln, as wartime president, had the elbow room to take the initiative, offering in December 1863 a general amnesty to all but high-ranking Confederates willing to pledge loyalty to the Union. When 10 percent of a state's 1860 voters had taken this oath, the state would be restored to the Union, provided that it abolished slavery. The Confederate states (save those like Louisiana and Tennessee that were under Union control) rebuffed Lincoln's generous offer, ensuring that the war would have to be fought to the bitter end.

What the Ten Percent Plan also revealed was the rocky road that lay ahead for Reconstruction. In Louisiana, for example, the Unionist government restored under Lincoln's offer employed curfew laws to restrict the movements of the freed slaves and vagrancy regulations to force them back to work. But the Louisiana freedmen fought back. Led by the free black community of New Orleans, they began to agitate for political rights. No less than their former masters, ex-slaves intended to be actors in the savage drama of Reconstruction.

With the struggle in Louisiana in mind, congressional Republicans proposed a stricter substitute for Lincoln's Ten Percent Plan. The initiative came from the Radical wing of the party—those bent on a stern peace and full rights for the freedmen—but with broad support among more moderate Republicans. The Wade-Davis Bill, passed on July 2, 1864, laid down, as conditions for the restoration of the rebellious states to the Union, an oath of allegiance by a majority of each state's adult white men, new state governments formed only by those who had never carried arms against the Union, and permanent disfranchisement of Confederate leaders. The Wade-Davis bill served notice that the congressional Republicans were not about to hand over Reconstruction policy to the president.

Rather than openly challenging Congress, Lincoln executed a **pocket veto** of the Wade-Davis bill by not signing it before Congress adjourned. At the same time he initiated informal talks with congressional leaders aimed at finding common ground. Lincoln's successor, however, had no such inclinations. Andrew Johnson held the view that Reconstruction was the president's prerogative, and by an accident of timing he was free to act on his convictions: under leisurely rules that went back to the early republic, the 39th Congress elected back in November 1864 was not scheduled to convene until December 1865.

Johnson's Initiative

Andrew Johnson was a self-made man from the hills of eastern Tennessee. A Jacksonian Democrat, he saw himself as the champion of the common man. He hated what he called the "bloated, corrupt aristocracy" of the Northeast, and he was equally disdainful of the southern planters, whom he blamed for the poverty of the South's small farmers. It was the poor whites that he championed; Johnson, a slave owner himself, had little sympathy for the enslaved blacks. Johnson's political career had taken him to the U.S. Senate, where he remained when the war broke out, loyal to the Union. After federal forces captured Nashville, Johnson became Tennessee's military governor. The Republicans nominated him for vice president in 1864 in an effort to promote wartime unity and to court the support of southern Unionists.

In May 1865, just a month after Lincoln's death, Johnson launched his own Reconstruction plan. He offered amnesty to all Southerners who took an oath of allegiance to the Constitution, except for high-ranking Confederate officials and wealthy planters, whom he held responsible for secession. Such persons could be pardoned only by the president. Johnson appointed provisional governors for the southern states and, as conditions for their restoration, required only that they revoke their ordinances of secession, repudiate their Confederate debts, and ratify the Thirteenth Amendment, which abolished slavery. Within months all the former Confederate

Andrew Johnson

The president was not an easy man. This photograph of Andrew Johnson (1808–1875) conveys some of the prickly qualities that contributed so centrally to his failure to reach an agreement with Republicans on a moderate Reconstruction program.
Library of Congress.

states had met Johnson's requirements and had functioning, elected governments.

At first Republicans responded favorably. The moderates among them were sympathetic to Johnson's argument that it was up to the states, not the federal government, to settle what civil and political rights the freedmen should have. Even the Radicals held their fire. They liked the stern treatment of Confederate leaders, and they hoped that the new southern governments would show good faith by generous treatment of the freed slaves.

Nothing of the sort happened. The South lay in ruins (see Voices from Abroad, "David Macrae: The Devastated South," p. 432). But Southerners held fast to the old order. The newly seated legislatures moved to restore slavery in all but name. They enacted laws—known as **Black Codes**—designed to drive the former slaves back to the plantations and deny them elementary civil rights. The new governments had mostly been formed by southern Unionists, but when it came to racial attitudes, little distinguished these loyalists from the Confederates. The latter, moreover, soon filtered back into the corridors of power. Despite his hard words against them, Johnson forgave ex-Confederate leaders easily, so long as he got the satisfaction of humbling them in their appeals to him for pardons.

His perceived indulgence of their efforts to restore white supremacy emboldened the ex-Confederates. They packed the delegations to the new Congress with old comrades—nine members of the Confederate Congress, seven former officials of Confederate state governments, four generals and four colonels, and even the vice president of the Confederacy, Alexander Stephens. This was the last straw for the Republicans.

Under the Constitution Congress is "the judge of the Elections, Returns and Qualifications of its own Members" (Article 1, Section 5; see Documents, p. D-8). With this power the Republican majorities in both houses refused to admit the southern delegations when Congress convened in early December 1865, effectively blocking Johnson's Reconstruction program. Seeking to formulate the terms on which the South would be readmitted to Congress, the Republicans established a House-Senate committee—the Joint Committee on Reconstruction—and began public hearings on conditions in the South.

In response the southern states backed away from the most flagrant of the Black Codes, replacing them with regulatory ordinances silent on race yet not different in effect; in practice they applied to blacks, not to whites. On top of that a wave of violence erupted across the South against the freedmen. In Tennessee a Nashville paper reported that white gangs "are riding about whipping, maiming and killing all negroes who do not obey the orders of their former masters, just as if slavery existed." Listening to the testimony of officials, observers, and victims, Republicans concluded that the South had embarked on a concerted effort to circumvent the Thirteenth Amendment. The only possible response was for the federal government to intervene.

Back in March 1865, before adjourning, the 38th Congress had established the Freedmen's Bureau to provide emergency aid to ex-slaves during the transition from war to peace. Now in early 1866, under the leadership of the moderate Republican Senator Lyman Trumbull, Congress voted to extend the Freedmen's Bureau's life, gave it direct funding for the first time, and authorized its agents to investigate mistreatment of blacks.

More extraordinary was Trumbull's proposal for a Civil Rights Act declaring all persons born in the United States to be citizens and granting them—without regard to race—equal rights of contract, access to the courts, and protection of person and property. Trumbull's bill nullified all state laws depriving citizens of these rights, authorized U.S. attorneys to bring enforcement suits in the federal courts, and provided for fines and imprisonment for violators, including public officials. Provoked by an unrepentant South, Republicans of the most moderate persuasion demanded that the federal government assume responsibility for securing the basic civil rights of the freedmen.

Acting on Freedom

While Congress debated, emancipated slaves acted on their own idea of freedom. News that their bondage was

David Macrae

The Devastated South

In this excerpt from The Americans at Home *(1870), an account of his tour of the United States, the Scottish clergyman David Macrae describes the war-stricken South as he found it in 1867–1868.*

I was struck with a remark made by a Southern gentleman in answer to the assertion that Jefferson Davis [the president of the Confederacy] had culpably continued the war for six months after all hope had been abandoned.

"Sir," he said, "Mr. Davis knew the temper of the South as well as any man in it. He knew if there was to be anything worth calling peace, the South must win; or, if she couldn't win, she wanted to be whipped—well whipped—thoroughly whipped."

The further south I went, the oftener these remarks came back upon me. Evidence was everywhere that the South had maintained the desperate conflict until she was utterly exhausted. . . . Almost every man I met at the South, especially in North Carolina, Georgia, and Virginia, seemed to have been in the army; and it was painful to find many who had returned were mutilated, maimed, or broken in health by exposure. When I remarked this to a young Confederate officer in North Carolina, and said I was glad to see that he had escaped unhurt, he said, "Wait till we get to the office, sir, and I will tell you more about that." When we got there, he pulled up one leg of his trousers, and showed me that he had an iron rod there to strengthen his limb, and enable him to walk without limping, half of his foot being off. He showed me on the other leg a deep scar made by a fragment of a shell; and these were two of but seven wounds which had left their marks upon his body. When he heard me speak of relics, he said, "Try to find a North Carolina gentleman without a Yankee mark on him."

Nearly three years had passed when I travelled through the country, and yet we have seen what traces the war had left in such cities as Richmond, Petersburg, and Columbia. The same spectacle met me at Charleston. Churches and houses had been battered down by heavy shot and shell hurled into the city from Federal batteries at a distance of five miles. Even the valley of desolation made by a great fire in 1861, through the very heart of the city, remained unbuilt. There, after the lapse of seven years, stood the blackened ruins of streets and houses waiting for the coming of a better day. . . . Over the country districts the prostration was equally marked. Along the track of Sherman's army especially, the devastation was fearful—farms laid waste, fences burned, bridges destroyed, houses left in ruins, plantations in many cases turned into wilderness again.

The people had shared in the general wreck, and looked poverty-stricken, careworn, and dejected. Ladies who before the war had lived in affluence, with black servants round them to attend to their every wish, were boarding together in half-furnished houses, cooking their own food and washing their own linen, some of them, I was told, so utterly destitute that they did not know when they finished one meal where they were to find the next. . . . Men who had held commanding positions during the war had fallen out of sight and were filling humble situations—struggling, many of them, to earn a bare subsistence. . . . I remember dining with three cultured Southern gentlemen, one a general, the other, I think, a captain, and the third a lieutenant. They were all living together in a plain little wooden house, such as they would formerly have provided for their servants. Two of them were engaged in a railway office, the third was seeking a situation, frequently, in his vain search, passing the large blinded house where he had lived in luxurious ease before the war.

Source: Allan Nevins, ed., *America through British Eyes* (Gloucester, MA: Peter Smith, 1968), 345–47.

over left them exultant and hopeful (see American Voices, "Jourdon Anderson: Relishing Freedom," p. 434). Freedom meant many things—the end of punishment by the lash, the ability to move around, the reuniting of families, the opportunity to begin schools, to form churches and social clubs, and, not least, to engage in politics. Across the South blacks held mass meetings, paraded, and formed organizations. Topmost among their demands were equality before the law and the right to vote—"an essential and inseparable element of self-government."

Struggling for Economic Independence. First of all, however, came ownership of land, which emancipated blacks believed was the basis for true freedom. During the Civil War they had acted on this assumption whenever

Union armies drew near. In the chaotic final months of the war, as plantation owners fled Union forces, freedmen seized control of land where they could. Most famously, General William T. Sherman reserved large coastal tracts in Georgia and South Carolina—the Sea Islands and abandoned plantations within thirty miles of the coast—for liberated slaves and settled them on forty-acre plots. Sherman only wanted to be rid of the responsibility for the refugees as his army drove across the lower South. But the freedmen assumed that Sherman's order meant that the land would be theirs. When the war ended, resettlement became the responsibility of the Freedmen's Bureau, which was charged with feeding and clothing war refugees, distributing confiscated land to "loyal refugees and freedmen," and regulating labor contracts between freedmen and planters.

Encouraged by the Freedmen's Bureau, blacks across the South occupied confiscated or abandoned land. Many families stayed on their old plantations, awaiting redistribution of the land to them after the war. When the South Carolina planter Thomas Pinckney returned home, his freed slaves told him: "We ain't going nowhere. We are going to work right here on the land where we were born and what belongs to us."

Johnson's amnesty plan, entitling pardoned Confederates to recover property seized during the war, shattered these hopes. In October 1865 Johnson ordered General Oliver O. Howard, head of the Freedmen's Bureau, to tell Sea Islands' blacks that the land they occupied would have to be restored to the white owners. When Howard reluctantly obeyed, the dispossessed farmers protested: "Why do you take away our lands? You take them from us who have always been true, always true to the Government! You give them to our all-time enemies! That is not right!"

In the Sea Islands and elsewhere, former slaves resisted efforts to remove them. Led by black veterans of the Union army, they fought pitched battles with plantation owners and bands of ex-Confederate soldiers. Landowners struck back hard. One black veteran wrote from Maryland: "The returned colard Solgers are in Many cases beten, and their guns taken from them, we darcent walk out of an evening. . . . They beat us badly and Sumtime Shoot us." Often aided by federal troops, the local whites generally prevailed in this land war.

Resisting Wage Labor.   As planters prepared for a new growing season, a great battle took shape over the labor system that would replace slavery. Convinced that blacks needed supervision, planters wanted to retain the gang labor of the past, only now with wages replacing the food, clothing, and shelter their slaves had once received. The Freedmen's Bureau, although watchful against exploitative labor contracts, sided with the planters. The main thing, its designers had always felt, was that the bureau not encourage dependency "in the guise of guardianship." Rely upon your "own efforts and

exertions," an agent told a large crowd of freedmen in North Carolina, "make contracts with the planters" and "respect the rights of property."

This was advice given with little regard for the world in which those North Carolina freedmen lived. It was not only their unequal bargaining power they worried about, or even that their ex-masters' real desire was to re-enslave them under the guise of "free" contracts. In their eyes the condition of wage labor was itself, by definition, debasing. The rural South was not like the North, where working for wages was the norm and qualified a man as independent. In the South, selling one's labor to another—and in particular, selling one's labor to work another's land—implied not freedom, but dependency. To be a "freeman"—a fully empowered citizen—meant heading a household, owning some property, conducting one's own affairs.

So the issue of wage labor cut to the very core of the former slaves' struggle for freedom. Nothing had been more horrifying than that as slaves their persons had been the property of others. When a master cast his eye on a slave woman, her husband had no recourse, nor, for that matter, was rape of a slave a crime. In a famous oration celebrating the anniversary of emancipation, the Reverend Henry M. Turner spoke bitterly of the time when his people had "no security for domestic happiness," when "our wives were sold and husbands bought, children were begotten and enslaved by their fathers," and "we therefore were polygamists by virtue of our condition." That was why formalizing marriage was so urgent a matter after emancipation and why, when hard-pressed planters demanded that freedwomen go back into the fields, they resisted so resolutely. If the ex-slaves were to be free as white folk, then their wives could not, any more than white wives, labor for others. "I seen on some plantations," one freedman recounted, "where the white men would . . . tell colored men that their wives and children could not live on their places unless they work in the fields. The colored men [answered that] whenever they wanted their wives to work they would tell them themselves; and if he could not rule his own domestic affairs on that place he would leave it and go someplace else."

The reader will see the irony in this definition of freedom: it assumed the wife's subordinate role and designated her labor the husband's property. But if that was the price of freedom, freedwomen were prepared to pay it. Far better to take a chance with their own men than with their ex-masters.

Many freedpeople voted with their feet, abandoning their old plantations and seeking better lives and more freedom in the towns and cities of the South. Those who remained in the countryside refused to work the cotton fields under the hated gang-labor system or negotiated tenaciously over the terms of their labor contracts. Whatever system of labor finally might emerge, it was clear that the freedpeople would never settle for anything resembling the old plantation system.

Jourdon Anderson

Relishing Freedom

*F*olklorists *have recorded the sly ways that slaves found, even in bondage, for "puttin' down" their masters. But only in freedom—and beyond reach in a northern state at that—could Anderson's sarcasm be expressed so openly, with the jest that his family might consider returning if they first received the wages due them, calculated to the dollar, for all those years in slavery. Yet intermixed with the bitterness, and the pride in personal dignity, is an admission of affection for "the dear old home" that helps explain why, even after the horror of bondage, ex-slaves often chose to remain in familiar surroundings and even work for their former masters. Anderson's letter, although probably written or edited by a white friend in Dayton, surely is faithful to what the ex-slave wanted to say.*

Dayton, Ohio. August 7, 1865.
To My Old Master, Colonel P. H. Anderson, Big Spring, Tennessee.
Sir:

I got your letter, and was glad to find that you had not forgotten Jourdon, and that you wanted me to come back and live with you again, promising to do better for me than anybody else can. I have often felt uneasy about you. I thought the Yankees would have hung you long before this, for harboring Rebs they found at your house. I suppose they never heard about your going to Colonel Martin's to kill the Union soldier that was left by his company in their stable. Although you shot at me twice before I left you, I did not want to hear of your being hurt, and am glad you are still living. It would do me good to go back to the dear old home again, and see Miss Mary and Miss Martha and Allen, Esther, Green, and Lee. Give my love to them all, and tell them I hope we will meet in the better world, if not in this. I would have gone back to see you all when I was working in the Nashville Hospital, but one of the neighbors told me that Henry intended to shoot me if he ever got a chance.

I want to know particularly what the good chance is you propose to give me. I am doing tolerably well here.

I get twenty-five dollars a month, with victuals and clothing; have a comfortable home for Mandy,—the folks call her Mrs. Anderson,—and the children—Milly, Jane, and Grundy—go to school and are learning well. The teacher says Grundy has a head for a preacher. They go to Sunday school, and Mandy and me attend church regularly. We are kindly treated. Sometimes we overhear others saying, "Them colored people were slaves" down in Tennessee. The children feel hurt when they hear such remarks; but I tell them it was no disgrace in Tennessee to belong to Colonel Anderson. Many darkeys would have been proud, as I used to be, to call you master. Now if you will write and say what wages you will give me, I will be better able to decide whether it would be to my advantage to move back again. . . .

Mandy says she would be afraid to go back without some proof that you were disposed to treat us justly and kindly; and we have concluded to test your sincerity by asking you to send us our wages for the time we served you. This will make us forget and forgive old scores, and rely on your justice and friendship in the future. I served you faithfully for thirty-two years, and Mandy twenty years. At twenty-five dollars a month for me and two dollars a week for Mandy, our earnings would amount to eleven thousand six hundred and eighty dollars. Add to this the interest for the time our wages have been kept back, and deduct what you paid for our clothing, and three doctor's visits to me, and pulling a tooth for Mandy, and the balance will show what we are in justice entitled to. . . .

In answering this letter, please state if there would be any safety for my Milly and Jane, who are now grown up, and both good-looking girls. You know how it was with poor Matilda and Catherine. I would rather stay here and starve—and die, if it come to that—than have my girls brought to shame by the violence and wickedness of their young masters. You will also please state if there has been any schools opened for the colored children in your neighborhood. The great desire of my life now is to give my children an education, and have them form virtuous habits.

Say howdy to George Carter, and thank him for taking the pistol from you when you were shooting at me.

From your old servant,
Jourdon Anderson

Source: Stanley I. Kutler, ed., *Looking for America*, 2nd ed. (New York: W. W. Norton, 1979), 2: 4–6.

Wage Labor of Former Slaves
This photograph, taken in South Carolina shortly after the Civil War, shows former slaves leaving the cotton fields. Ex-slaves were organized into work crews probably not that different from earlier slave gangs, although they now worked for wages and their plug-hatted boss bore little resemblance to the slave drivers of the past.
New-York Historical Society.

The efforts of former slaves to control their own lives challenged deeply entrenched white attitudes. "The destiny of the black race," asserted one Texan, could be summarized "in one sentence—subordination to the white race." Southern whites, a Freedmen's Bureau official observed, could not "conceive of the negro having any rights at all." And when freedmen resisted, white retribution was swift and often terrible. In Pine Bluff, Arkansas, "after some kind of dispute with some freedmen," whites set fire to their cabins and hanged twenty-four of the inhabitants—men, women, and children. The toll of murdered and beaten blacks mounted into untold thousands. The governments established under Johnson's plan only put the stamp of legality on the pervasive efforts to enforce white supremacy. Blacks "would be *just as well* off with no law at all or no Government," concluded a Freedmen's Bureau agent, as with the justice they got under the restored white rule.

In this unequal struggle, blacks turned to Washington. "We stood by the government when it wanted help," a black Mississippian wrote President Johnson. "Now . . . will it stand by us?"

Congress versus President

Andrew Johnson was, alas, not the man to ask. In February 1866 he vetoed the Freedmen's Bureau bill. The bureau, Johnson charged, was an "immense patronage," showering benefits on blacks never granted to "our own people." Republicans could not muster enough votes to

override his veto. A month later, further rebuffing his critics, Johnson vetoed Trumbull's civil rights bill, arguing that federal protection of black civil rights constituted "a stride toward centralization." His racism, hitherto muted, now blazed forth. In his view granting blacks the privileges of citizenship was discriminatory, operating "in favor of the colored and against the white race," and threatening all manner of evil consequences, including racial mixing.

Galvanized by Johnson's attack on the civil rights bill, the Republicans went into action. In early April they got the necessary two-thirds majorities in both houses to override a presidential veto. The enactment of the civil rights bill into law was a truly historic event, the first time Congress had prevailed over a presidential veto on a major piece of legislation. Republican resolve was reinforced by news of mounting violence in the South, culminating in three days of rioting in Memphis. Forty-six blacks and two whites were left dead, and hundreds of black homes, churches, and schools were looted and burned. In July an angry Congress renewed the Freedmen's Bureau over a second Johnson veto.

The Fourteenth Amendment. Eager to consolidate their gains, Republicans moved to enshrine black civil rights in an amendment to the Constitution. The heart of the Fourteenth Amendment was Section 1, which declared that "all persons born or naturalized in the United States" were citizens. No state could abridge "the privileges or immunities of citizens of the United States," deprive "any person of life, liberty, or property, without due process of law," or deny anyone "the equal protection of the laws." These phrases were vague, intentionally so, but they established the constitutionality of the Civil Rights Act and, more important, the basis on which the courts and Congress could establish an enforceable standard of equality before the law in the states.

For the moment, however, the Fourteenth Amendment was most important for its impact on national politics. With the 1866 Congressional elections approaching, Johnson somehow figured he had a winning issue in the Fourteenth Amendment. He urged the states not to ratify it. Months earlier, Johnson had begun to maneuver politically against the Republicans, aiming to build a coalition of white Southerners, northern Democrats, and conservative Republicans under the banner of National Union. Any hope of creating a new party, however, was shattered by Johnson's intemperate behavior and by escalating violence in the South. A dissension-ridden National Union convention in July ended inconclusively, and Johnson's campaign against the Fourteenth Amendment became, effectively, a campaign for the Democratic Party.

Republicans responded furiously, unveiling a practice that would become known as "waving the bloody shirt." The Democrats were traitors, charged Indiana governor Oliver Morton, and their party was "a common sewer and loathesome receptacle, into which is emptied every element of treason North and South, every element of inhumanity and barbarism which has dishonored this age." In late August Johnson embarked on a disastrous "swing around the circle"—a railroad tour from Washington to Chicago and St. Louis and back. It was unprecedented for a president to campaign personally, and Johnson made matters worse by engaging in shouting matches with hecklers and insulting the hostile crowds.

The 1866 Congressional elections inflicted a humiliating defeat on Johnson. The Republicans won a three-to-one majority in Congress, so that, to begin with, the Republicans considered themselves "masters of the situation," free to proceed "entirely regardless of [Johnson's] opinions or wishes." As a referendum on the Fourteenth Amendment, moreover, the election registered overwhelming popular support for the civil rights of the former slaves. The Republican Party emerged with a new sense of unity—a unity coalescing not at the center, but on the left, around the unbending program of the Radical minority.

Radical Republicans.   The Radicals represented the abolitionist strain within the Republican Party. Most of them hailed from New England or from the area of the upper Midwest settled by New Englanders. In the Senate they were led by Charles Sumner of Massachusetts; in the House, by Thaddeus Stevens from Pennsylvania. For them Reconstruction was never primarily about restoring the Union but about remaking southern society. "The foundations of their institutions . . . must be broken up and relaid," declared Stevens, "or all our blood and treasure will have been spent in vain."

Only a handful went as far as Stevens in demanding that the plantations be treated as "forfeited estates of the enemy" and broken up into small farms for the former slaves. About the need to guarantee the freedmen's civil and political rights, however, there was agreement. In this endeavor Radicals had no qualms about expanding the powers of the national government. "The power of the great landed aristocracy in those regions, if unrestrained by power from without, would inevitably reassert itself," warned Congressman George Julian. Radicals were aggressively partisan. They regarded the Republican Party as the instrument of the Lord and black votes as the means by which the party would bring regeneration of the South.

At first, in the months after Appomattox, few but the Radicals themselves imagined that so extreme a program had any chance of enactment. Black suffrage especially seemed beyond reach, since the northern states (excepting in New England) denied blacks the vote at this time. And yet as fury mounted against the intransigent South, Republicans became ever more radicalized until, in the wake of the smashing victory of 1866, they embraced the Radicals' vision of a reconstructed South.

Radical Reconstruction

Afterward, thoughtful Southerners admitted that the South had brought radical Reconstruction on itself. "We had, in 1865, a white man's government in Alabama," remarked the man who had been Johnson's provisional governor, "but we lost it." The state's "great blunder" was not to "have at once taken the negro right under the protection of the laws." Remarkably, the South remained defiant even after the 1866 elections. Every state legislature but Tennessee's rejected the Fourteenth Amendment, mostly by virtual acclamation. It was as if they could not imagine that governments installed under the presidential imprimatur and fully functioning might be swept away. But that, in fact, is just what the Republicans intended to do.

Congress Takes Command

The Reconstruction Act of 1867, enacted in March by the Republican Congress, organized the South as a conquered land, dividing it into five military districts, each under the command of a Union general (Map 15.1). The price for reentering the Union was granting the vote to the freedmen and disfranchising those of the South's prewar leadership class who had participated in the rebellion. Each military commander was ordered to register

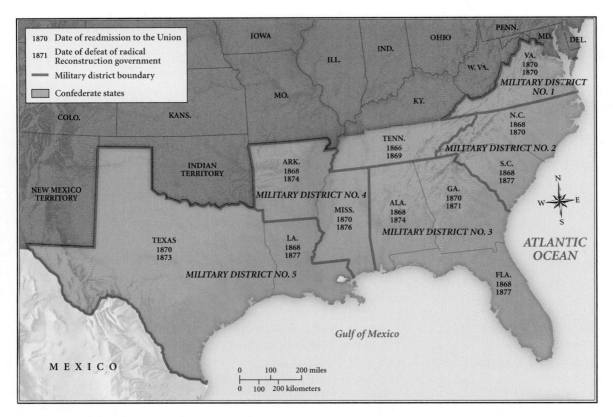

MAP 15.1 Reconstruction

The federal government organized the Confederate states into five military districts during radical Reconstruction. For each state the first date indicates when that state was readmitted to the Union; the second date shows when Radical Republicans lost control of the state government. All the ex-Confederate states rejoined the Union from 1868 to 1870, but the periods of radical rule varied widely. Republicans lasted only a few months in Virginia; they held on until the end of Reconstruction in Louisiana, Florida, and South Carolina.

all eligible adult males (black as well as white), supervise the election of state conventions, and make certain that the new constitutions contained guarantees of black suffrage. Congress would readmit a state to the Union if its voters ratified the constitution, if that document proved acceptable to Congress, and if the new state legislature approved the Fourteenth Amendment (thus insuring the needed ratification by three-fourths of the states). Johnson vetoed the Reconstruction Act, but Congress overrode the veto (Table 15.1).

Impeachment. Republicans also restricted President Johnson's room for maneuver. The Tenure of Office Act, a companion to the Reconstruction Act, required Senate consent for the removal of any official whose appointment had required Senate confirmation. Congress chiefly wanted to protect Secretary of War Edwin M. Stanton, a Lincoln holdover and the only member of Johnson's cabinet who favored radical Reconstruction. In his position Stanton could do much to frustrate Johnson's anticipated efforts to undermine Reconstruction. The law also required the president to issue all orders to the army through its commanding general, Ulysses S. Grant. In effect

Congress was attempting to reconstruct the presidency as well as the South.

Seemingly defeated, Johnson appointed generals recommended by Stanton and Grant to command the five military districts in the South. But he was just biding his time. In August 1867, after Congress had adjourned, he "suspended" Stanton and replaced him with Grant, believing that the general would act like a good soldier and follow orders. Next Johnson replaced four of the commanding generals. Johnson, however, had misjudged Grant, who publicly objected to the president's machinations. When the Senate reconvened in the fall, it overruled Stanton's suspension. Grant, now an open enemy of Johnson's, resigned so that Stanton could resume his office.

On February 21, 1868, Johnson formally dismissed Stanton. The feisty secretary of war, however, barricaded the door of his office and refused to admit the replacement Johnson had appointed. Three days later, House Republicans introduced articles of **impeachment** against the president, employing the power granted the House of Representatives by the Constitution to charge high federal officials with "Treason, Bribery, or other high Crimes and Misdemeanors." The House overwhelmingly approved

TABLE 15.1 Primary Reconstruction Laws and Constitutional Amendments	
Law (Date of Congressional Passage)	**Key Provisions**
Thirteenth Amendment (January 1865*)	Prohibited slavery
Civil Rights Act of 1866 (April 1866)	Defined citizenship rights of freedmen Authorized federal authorities to bring suit against those who violated those rights
Fourteenth Amendment (June 1866†)	Established national citizenship for persons born or naturalized in the United States Prohibited the states from depriving citizens of their civil rights or equal protection under the law Reduced state representation in House of Representatives by the percentage of adult male citizens denied the vote
Reconstruction Act of 1867 (March 1867‡)	Divided the South into five military districts, each under the command of a Union general Established requirements for readmission of ex-Confederate states to the Union
Tenure of Office Act (March 1867)	Required Senate consent for removal of any federal official whose appointment had required Senate confirmation
Fifteenth Amendment (February 1869)	Forbade states to deny citizens the right to vote on the grounds of race, color, or "previous condition of servitude"
Ku Klux Klan Act (April 1871)	Authorized the president to use federal prosecutions and military force to suppress conspiracies to deprive citizens of the right to vote and enjoy the equal protection of the law

*Ratified by three-fourths of all states in December 1868.
†Ratified by three-fourths of all states in July 1868.
‡Ratified by three-fourths of all states in March 1870.

eleven counts of presidential misconduct, nine of which dealt with violations of the Tenure of Office Act.

The case went to the Senate, which acts as the court in impeachment cases, with Chief Justice Salmon P. Chase presiding. After an eleven-week trial, thirty-five senators on May 15 voted for conviction, one vote short of the two-thirds majority required. Seven moderate Republicans broke ranks, voting for acquittal along with twelve Democrats. The dissenting Republicans felt that the Tenure of Office Act was of dubious validity (in fact, the Supreme Court subsequently declared it unconstitutional), that the motives of the impeachers were really political, and that removing a president for defying Congress was too extreme and too threatening to constitutional checks and balances, even for the sake of punishing Johnson.

Despite his acquittal, however, Johnson had been defanged. For the remainder of his term he was powerless to alter the course of Reconstruction.

The Election of 1868. The impeachment controversy made Grant, already the North's war hero, a Republican hero as well, and he easily won the party's presidential nomination in 1868. In the fall campaign he supported radical Reconstruction, but he also urged reconciliation between the sections. His Democratic opponent Horatio Seymour, a former governor of New York, almost declined the nomination because he doubted that the Democrats could overcome the stigma of their ties with the disloyal South.

As Seymour feared, the Republicans "waved the bloody shirt," stirring up old wartime emotions against the Democrats to great effect. Grant won about the same share of the northern vote (55 percent) that Lincoln had won in 1864 and received 214 of 294 electoral votes. The Republicans also retained two-thirds majorities in both houses of Congress.

The Fifteenth Amendment. In the wake of their smashing victory, the Republicans quickly produced the last major piece of Reconstruction legislation—the Fifteenth Amendment, which forbade either the federal government or the states from denying citizens the right to vote on the basis of race, color, or "previous condition of servitude" (see Documents, p. D-17). The amendment left room for **poll taxes** and property or literacy tests that might be used to discourage blacks from voting, which

Resistance in the South

This engraving, entitled "If He Is a Union Man or Freedman: Verdict, Hang the D——— Yankee and Nigger," appeared in Harper's Weekly *on March 23, 1867, just as the Reconstruction Act was being adopted. Thomas Nast's cartoon encapsulated the outrage at the South's murderous intransigence that led even moderate Republicans to support radical Reconstruction.* Library of Congress.

For more help analyzing this image, see the ONLINE STUDY GUIDE at bedfordstmartins.com/henretta.

was necessary because its authors did not want to alienate northern states that already relied on such qualifications to keep immigrants and the "unworthy" poor from the polls. A California senator warned that in his state, with its rabidly anti-Chinese sentiment (see Chapter 16), any restriction on that power would "kill our party as dead as a stone."

Despite grumbling by Radical Republicans, the amendment passed without modification in February 1869. Congress required the states still under federal control—Virginia, Mississippi, Texas, and Georgia—to ratify it as a condition for being readmitted to the Union. A year later the Fifteenth Amendment became part of the Constitution.

Woman Suffrage Denied.   If the Fifteenth Amendment troubled some proponents of black suffrage, this was nothing compared to the outrage felt by women's rights advocates. They had fought the good fight for the abolition

of slavery for so many years, only to be abandoned when the chance finally came to get the vote for women. All it would have taken was one more word in the Fifteenth Amendment so that the protected categories for voting would have read "race, color, *sex,* or previous condition." Leading suffragists such as Susan B. Anthony and Elizabeth Cady Stanton did not want to hear from Radical Republicans that this was "the Negro's hour" and that women would have to wait for another day. How could suffrage be granted to ex-slaves, Stanton demanded to know, but not to them?

In her despair Stanton lashed out in ugly racist terms against "Patrick and Sambo and Hans and Ung Tung," ignorant as they were about the Declaration of Independence, yet entitled to vote, while the best and most accomplished of American women remained voteless. In 1869 the annual meeting of the Equal Rights Association, the champion of both black and woman suffrage, broke up in acrimony, and Stanton and Anthony came out against the Fifteenth Amendment.

At this searing moment a schism opened in the ranks of the women's movement. The majority, led by Lucy Stone and Julia Ward Howe, reconciled themselves to disappointment and accepted the priority of black suffrage. Organized into the American Woman Suffrage Association, these moderates remained allied to the Republican Party, in hopes that once Reconstruction had been settled it would be time for the woman's vote. The Stanton-Anthony group, however, struck out in a new direction. The embittered Stanton declared that woman "must not put her trust in man" in fighting for her rights. The new organization she headed, the New York–based National Woman Suffrage Association, accepted only women, focused exclusively on women's rights, and resolutely took up the battle for a federal woman suffrage amendment.

The fracturing of the women's movement obscured the common ground the two sides shared. Both now realized that a constituency had to be built beyond the narrow confines of abolitionism and evangelical reform. Both elevated suffrage into the preeminent women's issue. And both were energized by a shared anger not evident in earlier times. "If I were to give vent to all my pent-up wrath concerning the subordination of woman," Lydia Maria Child wrote the Republican warhorse Charles Sumner in 1872, "I might frighten *you.* . . . Suffice it, therefore, to say, either the theory of our government is *false,* or women have a right to vote." If radical Reconstruction seemed a barren time for women's rights, in fact it had planted the seeds of the modern feminist movement.

Republican Rule in the South

Between 1868 and 1871 all the southern states met the congressional stipulations and rejoined the Union. Protected by federal troops and encouraged by northern party leaders, state Republican organizations took hold

A Woman Suffrage Quilt

Homemade quilts provided funds and a means of persuasion for the temperance and antislavery movements. Suffragists, however, regarded quilts and needlework as symbols of the domestic subjugation of women, so woman suffrage quilts, such as this one (c. 1860–1880) depicting a women's rights lecture, were rare. Collections of Mrs. Nancy W. Livingston and Mrs. Elizabeth Livingston Jaeger / Photo courtesy, Los Angeles County Museum of Art.

across the South and won control of the newly established Reconstruction governments. These Republican administrations remained in power for periods ranging from a few months in Virginia to nine years in South Carolina, Louisiana, and Florida (see Map 15.1). Their core support came from African Americans, who constituted a majority of registered voters in Alabama, Florida, South Carolina, and Mississippi.

Carpetbaggers and Scalawags. Southern white Republicans faced the scorn of Democratic ex-Confederates, who mocked them as **scalawags**—an ancient Scots-Irish term for runty, worthless animals. Whites who had come from the North they denounced as **carpetbaggers**—self-seeking interlopers who carried all their property in cheap suitcases called carpetbags. Such labels glossed over the actual diversity of these white Republicans.

Some carpetbaggers, while motivated by personal profit, also brought capital and skills. Others were Union army veterans taken with the South—its climate, people, and economic opportunities. And interspersed with the self-seekers were many idealists anxious to advance the cause of emancipation.

The scalawags were even more diverse. Some were former slave owners, ex-Whigs and even ex-Democrats, drawn to Republicanism as the best way to attract

northern capital to southern railroads, mines, and factories. In southwest Texas the large population of Germans was strongly Republican. They sent to Congress Edward Degener, an immigrant San Antonio grocer whom Confederate authorities had imprisoned and whose sons had been executed for treason. But most numerous among the scalawags were yeomen farmers from the backcountry districts who wanted to rid the South of its slaveholding aristocracy. Scalawags had generally fought against, or at least refused to support, the Confederacy; they believed that slavery had victimized whites as well as blacks. "Now is the time," a Georgia scalawag wrote, "for every man to come out and speak his principles publickly [*sic*] and vote for liberty as we have been in bondage long enough."

African American Leadership. The Democrats' scorn for black political leaders as ignorant field hands was just as false as stereotypes about white Republicans. The first African American leaders in the South came from an elite of blacks freed before the Civil War. They were joined by northern blacks who moved south when radical Reconstruction offered the prospect of meaningful freedom. Like their white allies, many were Union army veterans. Some had participated in the antislavery crusade; a number were employed by the Freedmen's Bureau or northern missionary societies. Others had escaped from slavery and were returning home. One of these was Blanche K. Bruce, who had been tutored on the Virginia plantation of his white father. During the war Bruce escaped and established a school for ex-slaves in Missouri. In 1869 he moved to Mississippi, became active in politics, and in 1874 became Mississippi's second black U.S. senator.

As the reconstructed Republican governments of 1867 began to function, this diverse group of ministers, artisans, shopkeepers, and former soldiers reached out to the freedmen. African American speakers, some financed by the Republican Party, fanned out into the old plantation districts and recruited ex-slaves for political roles. Still, few of the new leaders were field hands; most had been preachers or artisans. The literacy of one ex-slave, Thomas Allen, who was a Baptist minister and shoemaker, helped him win election to the Georgia legislature. "In my county," he recalled, "the colored people came to me for instructions, and I gave them the best instructions I could. I took the *New York Tribune* and other papers, and in that way I found out a great deal, and I told them whatever I thought was right."

Although never proportionate to their numbers in the population, black officeholders were prominent across the South. In South Carolina African Americans constituted a majority in the lower house of the legislature in 1868. Three were elected to Congress, another joined the state supreme court. Over the entire course of Reconstruction, twenty African Americans served in

African American Congressional Delegation, 1872

This Currier and Ives lithograph celebrates one of the notable achievements of radical Reconstruction—the representation that ex-slaves won, however briefly, in the U.S. Congress. Hiram Revels of Mississippi, the Senate's first African American member, is seated at the extreme left.

Granger Collection.

state administrations as governor, lieutenant governor, secretary of state, treasurer, or superintendent of education, more than six hundred served as state legislators, and sixteen as congressmen.

The Radical Program. The Republicans who took office had ambitious plans for a reconstructed South. They wanted to end its dependence on cotton agriculture and build an entrepreneurial economy like the North's. They fell far short of achieving this vision but accomplished more than their critics gave them credit for.

The Republicans modernized state constitutions, eliminated property qualification for the vote, and made more offices elective. They attended especially to the personal freedom of the ex-slaves, sweeping out the shadow Black Codes that coerced the freedmen and limited their mobility. Women also benefited from the Republican defense of personal liberty. Nearly all the new constitutions expanded the rights of married women, enabling them to hold property and earnings independent of their husbands—"a wonderful reform," a Georgia woman wrote, for "the cause of Women's Rights." Republican social programs called for hospitals, more humane penitentiaries, and asylums for orphans and the insane. Republican governments built roads in areas where roads had never existed. They poured money into rebuilding the region's railroad network. And they did all this without federal financing.

To pay for their ambitious programs the Republican governments copied taxes that Jacksonian reformers had earlier introduced in the North—in particular, gen-

eral property taxes on both real estate and personal wealth. The goal was to make planters pay their fair share and to broaden the tax base. In many plantation counties, former slaves served as tax assessors and collectors, administering the taxation of their one-time owners.

Higher tax revenues never managed to overtake the burgeoning obligations assumed by the Reconstruction governments. State debts mounted rapidly and, as interest payments on bonds fell into arrears, public credit collapsed. On top of that, much of the spending was wasted or ended in the pockets of state officials. Corruption was endemic to American politics, present in the southern states before the Republicans came on the scene, and rampant everywhere in this era, not least in the Grant administration itself. Still, in the free-spending atmosphere of the southern Republican regimes, corruption was especially luxuriant and damaging to the cause of radical Reconstruction.

Nothing, however, could dim the achievement in public education. Here the South had lagged woefully; only Tennessee had a system of public schooling before the Civil War. Republican state governments vowed to make up for lost time, viewing education as the foundation for a democratic order. African Americans of all ages rushed to attend the newly established schools, even when they had to pay tuition. An elderly man in Mississippi explained his hunger for education: "Ole missus used to read the good book [the Bible] to us . . . on Sunday evenin's, but she mostly read dem places where it says, 'Servants obey your masters.' . . . Now we is free, there's heaps of tings in that old book we is just suffering to learn." By 1875 about half of all the children in Florida, Mississippi, and South Carolina were in school.

The Role of Black Churches.   The building of schools was part of a larger effort by African Americans to fortify the institutions that had sustained their spirit during the days before emancipation. Religious belief had struck deep roots in nineteenth-century slave society. Now, in freedom, the African Americans left their old white-dominated congregations, where they had been relegated to segregated balconies and denied any voice in church governance, and built churches of their own. These churches joined together to form African American versions of the Southern Methodist and Southern Baptist denominations, including, most prominently, the National Baptist Convention and the African Methodist Episcopal Church. Everywhere the robust black churches served not only as places of worship but as schools, social centers, and political meeting halls.

Black clerics were community leaders and often, political leaders as well. As Charles H. Pearce, a Methodist minister in Florida, declared, "A man in this State cannot do his whole duty as a minister except he looks out for the political interests of his people." Calling forth the special destiny of the ex-slaves as the new "Children of Israel," black ministers provided a powerful religious underpinning for the Republican politics of their congregations.

The Quest for Land

In the meantime the freedmen were locked in a great economic struggle with their former owners. In 1869 the Republican government of South Carolina had established a land commission empowered to buy property and resell it on easy terms to the landless. In this way about 14,000 black families acquired farms. South Carolina's land distribution plan showed what was possible, but it was the exception and not the rule. Despite a lot of rhetoric, Republican regimes elsewhere did little to help the freedmen fulfill their dreams of becoming independent farmers. Federal efforts proved equally feeble. The Southern Homestead Act of 1866 offered eighty-acre grants to settlers, limited for the first year to freedmen and southern Unionists. The advantage was strictly symbolic, however, since the public land made available to homesteaders was off the beaten track in swampy, infertile parts of the Lower South. Only about a thousand families succeeded.

Sharecropping.   There was no reversing President Johnson's order restoring confiscated lands to ex-Confederates. Property rights, it seemed, trumped everything else, even for most Radical Republicans. The Freedman's Bureau, which had earlier championed the land claims of the ex-slaves, now devoted itself to teaching them how to be good agricultural laborers.

While they yearned for farms of their own, most freedmen started out landless and with no option but to work for their former owners. But not, they vowed, under the conditions of slavery—no gang work, no overseers, no fines or punishments, no regulation of their private lives. In certain parts of the agricultural South wage work became the norm—for example, on the great sugar plantations of Louisiana taken over after the war by northern investors. The problem was that cotton planters lacked the money to pay wages, at least not until the crop came in, and sometimes, in lieu of a straight wage, they offered a share of the crop. As a wage,

Freedmen's School, c. 1870
This rare photograph shows the interior of one of the 3,000 freedmen's schools established across the South after the Civil War. Although many of these schools were staffed by white missionaries, a main objective of northern educators was to prepare black women to take over the classrooms. The black teacher shown here is surely one of the first. Library of Congress.

this was a bad deal for the freedmen, but if they could be paid in shares for their work, why could they not pay in shares to rent the land they worked?

This form of land tenantry was already familiar in parts of the white South, and the freedmen now seized on it for the independence it offered them. Planters resisted, believing, as one wrote, that "wages are the only successful system of controlling hands." But, in a battle of wills that broke out all across the cotton South, the planters yielded to "the inveterate prejudices of the freedmen, who desire to be masters of their own time."

Thus there sprang up the distinctive laboring system of cotton agriculture—**sharecropping**, in which the freedmen worked as renters, exchanging their labor for the use of land, house, implements, sometimes seed and fertilizer, typically turning over half to two-thirds of their crops to the landlord (Map 15.2). The sharecropping system joined laborers and the owners of land and capital in a common sharing of risks and returns. But it was a very unequal relationship, given the force of southern law and custom on the white landowner's side, and given the sharecroppers' dire economic circumstances. Starting out penniless, they had no way of making it through the first growing season without borrowing for food and supplies.

Country storekeepers stepped in. Bankrolled by their northern suppliers, they "furnished" the sharecropper and took as collateral a **lien** on the crop, effectively assuming ownership of the cropper's share and leaving him only the proceeds that remained after his debts had been paid. Once indebted at one store, the sharecropper was no longer free to shop around and became an easy target for exorbitant prices, unfair interest rates, and crooked bookkeeping. As cotton prices declined during the 1870s, more and more sharecroppers failed to settle accounts and fell into permanent debt.

And if the merchant was also the landowner, or conspired with the landowner, the debt became a pretext for forced labor, or **peonage**, although evidence now suggests that sharecroppers generally managed to pull up stakes and move on once things became hopeless. Sharecroppers always thought twice about moving, however, because part of their "capital" was being known and well reputed in their home communities. Freedmen who lacked that local standing generally found sharecropping hard going and ended up in the ranks of agricultural laborers.

In the face of so much adversity, black families struggled to better themselves. Being that it enabled *family*, struggle was, in truth, the saving advantage of sharecropping because it mobilized husbands and wives in common enterprise while shielding both from personal subordination to whites. Freedwomen were doubly blessed, neither field hands for their ex-masters, nor dependent housewives, but partners laboring side by side with their husbands. The trouble with sharecropping, one planter grumbled, was that "it makes the laborer too independent; he becomes a partner, and has to be consulted." By the end of Reconstruction, about one-quarter of sharecropping families had managed to save enough to rent with cash payments, and eventually black farmers owned about a third of the land they cultivated.

A Comparative Perspective.   The battle between planters and freedmen over the land was by no means unique to the American South. Whenever slavery ended—in Haiti after the slave revolt of 1791, in the British Caribbean by abolition in 1833, in Cuba and Brazil by gradual emancipation during the 1880s—a fierce struggle ensued between planters bent on restoring a gang-labor system and ex-slaves bent on gaining economic autonomy. The outcome of this universal

Sharecroppers

This sharecropping family stands proudly in front of their new cabin and young cotton crop, which is planted nearly up to the cabin door. But the presence of the white landlord in the background casts a shadow on them, suggesting their hard struggle for economic freedom. Brown Brothers.

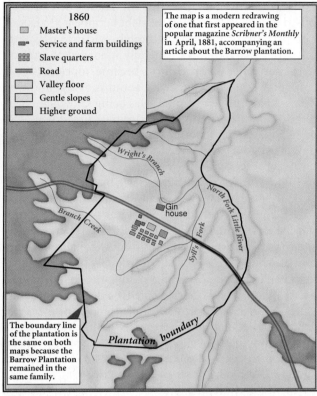

1860

- ☐ Master's house
- ◼ Service and farm buildings
- ▦ Slave quarters
- ═ Road
- ☐ Valley floor
- ☐ Gentle slopes
- ◼ Higher ground

The map is a modern redrawing of one that first appeared in the popular magazine *Scribner's Monthly* in April, 1881, accompanying an article about the Barrow plantation.

Wright's Branch

North Fork Little River

Branch Creek

Syll's Fork

Gin house

The boundary line of the plantation is the same on both maps because the Barrow Plantation remained in the same family.

Plantation boundary

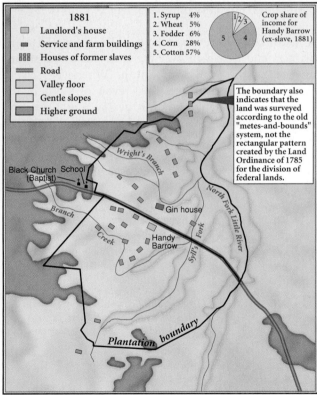

1881

- ☐ Landlord's house
- ◼ Service and farm buildings
- ▦ Houses of former slaves
- ═ Road
- ☐ Valley floor
- ☐ Gentle slopes
- ◼ Higher ground

1. Syrup 4%
2. Wheat 5%
3. Fodder 6%
4. Corn 28%
5. Cotton 57%

Crop share of income for Handy Barrow (ex-slave, 1881)

The boundary also indicates that the land was surveyed according to the old "metes-and-bounds" system, not the rectangular pattern created by the Land Ordinance of 1785 for the division of federal lands.

Black Church School (Baptist)

Wright's Branch

North Fork Little River

Branch Creek

Syll's Fork

Gin house

Handy Barrow

Plantation boundary

◄ **MAP 15.2 The Barrow Plantation, 1860 and 1881**

Comparing the 1860 map of this central Georgia plantation with the 1881 map reveals the impact of sharecropping on patterns of black residence. In 1860 the slave quarters were clustered near the planter's house. The sharecroppers scattered across the plantation's 2,000 acres, building cabins on the ridges of land between the low-lying streams. The name Barrow was common among the sharecropping families, which means almost certainly that they had been slaves on the Barrow plantation who, years after emancipation, still had not moved on. For all the croppers freedom surely meant not only their individual lots and cabins, but the school and church shown on the map.

so by the importation of indentured servants from India and China. Where land could not be had, as in British Barbados or Antigua, the ex-slaves returned to plantation labor as wage workers, although often in some combination with customary rights to housing and garden plots. The cotton South fit neither of these broad patterns. The freedmen did not get the land, but neither did the planters get field hands. What both got was sharecropping.

The reason for this exceptional outcome was ultimately political. Elsewhere, emancipation almost never meant civil or political equality for the freed slaves. Even in the British islands, where substantial self-government existed, high property qualifications effectively disfranchised the ex-slaves. In the United States, however, hard on the heels of emancipation came civil rights, manhood suffrage and, for a brief era, a real measure of political power for the freedmen. Sharecropping took shape during Reconstruction, and there was no going back afterward.

For the freedmen sharecropping was not the worst choice; it certainly beat laboring for their former owners. But for southern agriculture the costs were devastating. Sharecropping committed the South inflexibly to cotton, despite soil depletion and low prices. Crop diversification declined, costing the South its self-sufficiency in grains and livestock. And with farms leased year-to-year, neither tenant nor owner had much incentive to improve the property. The crop-lien system lined merchants' pockets with unearned profits that might otherwise have gone into agricultural improvement. The result was a stagnant farm economy, blighting the South's future and condemning it to economic backwardness—a kind of retribution, in fact, for the fresh injustices visited on the people it had once enslaved.

The Undoing of Reconstruction

Ex-Confederates were blind to the benefits of radical Reconstruction. Indeed, no amount of achievement could have persuaded them that it was anything but an abomination, undertaken without their consent and intended

conflict depended on the ex-slaves' access to land. Where vacant land existed, as in British Guiana, or where plantations could be seized, as in Haiti, the ex-slaves became subsistence farmers, and insofar as the Caribbean plantation economy survived without the ex-slaves, it did

to deny them their rightful place in southern society. Led by the planters, ex-Confederates staged a massive counterrevolution—one designed to "redeem" the South and restore them to political power under the banner of the Democratic Party. But the **Redeemers** could not have succeeded on their own. They needed the complicity of the North. The undoing of Reconstruction is as much about northern acquiescence as it is about southern resistance.

Counterrevolution

Insofar as they could win at the ballot box, southern Democrats took that route. They worked hard to get ex-Confederates restored to the rolls of registered voters, they appealed to racial solidarity and southern patriotism, and they campaigned against black rule as a threat to white supremacy. But force was equally acceptable. Throughout the Deep South, especially where black voters were heavily concentrated, ex-Confederate planters and their supporters organized secret societies and waged campaigns of terrorism against blacks and their white allies.

The Ku Klux Klan. The most widespread of these groups, the Ku Klux Klan, first appeared in 1866 as a Tennessee social club but quickly became a paramilitary force under the aegis of Nathan Bedford Forrest, the Confederacy's most decorated cavalry general (see American Lives, "Nathan Bedford Forrest: Defender of Southern Honor," p. 446). By 1870 the Klan was operating almost everywhere in the South as a terrorist organization serving the Democratic Party. The Klan murdered and whipped Republican politicians, burned black schools and churches, and attacked party gatherings (see American Voices, "Harriet Hernandes: The Intimidation of Black Voters," p. 448). Such terrorist tactics enabled the Democrats to seize power in Georgia and North Carolina in 1870 and make substantial gains elsewhere. An African American politician in North Carolina wrote, "Our former masters are fast taking the reins of government."

Congress responded by passing enforcement legislation, including the Ku Klux Klan Act of 1871, authorizing President Grant to use federal prosecutions, military force, and martial law to suppress conspiracies to deprive citizens of the right to vote, hold office, serve on juries, and enjoy equal protection of the law. In South Carolina, where the Klan was most deeply entrenched, federal troops occupied nine counties, made hundreds of arrests, and drove as many as 2,000 Klansmen from the state.

The Grant administration's assault on the Klan raised the spirits of southern Republicans, but it also emphasized how dependent they were on the federal government. The potency of the Ku Klux Klan Act, a Mississippi Republican wrote, "derived alone from its

Klan Portrait

Two armed Klansmen pose in their disguises, which they donned not only to hide their identity but also to intimidate their black neighbors. Northern audiences saw a lithograph based on this photograph in Harper's Weekly *on December 28, 1868.*
Rutherford B. Hayes Presidential Center.

source" in the federal government. "No such law could be enforced by state authority, the local power being too weak." If they were to prevail over antiblack terrorism, Republicans needed what one carpetbagger described as "steady, unswerving power from without."

The Failure of Federal Enforcement. But northern Republicans were growing weary of Reconstruction and the endless bloodshed it seemed to produce. Prosecuting Klansmen was an uphill battle. U.S. attorneys usually faced all-white juries, and the Justice Department lacked the resources to handle the cases. After 1872 prosecutions began to drop off, and many Klansmen received hasty pardons; few served significant prison terms.

In a kind of self-fulfilling prophecy, the unwillingness of the Grant administration to shore up Reconstruction guaranteed that it would fail. Republican governments that were denied federal help found themselves overwhelmed by the massive resistance of

Nathan Bedford Forrest: Defender of Southern Honor

Nathan Bedford Forrest in Uniform, c. 1865
Library of Congress.

As a boy Nathan Bedford Forrest had little stake in the old plantation order of the South. His father was a blacksmith who followed the frontier to Tennessee, where Nathan, the oldest of eleven children, was born on July 13, 1821. When he was only sixteen, his father died, leaving Forrest the primary breadwinner. With hardly any schooling, the boy took charge of the family's rented Mississippi farm; he also became an adept horse-trader. At age twenty-one, when his mother remarried, Forrest left for Hernando, Mississippi, where his uncle ran a livery business.

Tall and physically imposing, Forrest was normally soft-spoken, the soul of courtesy, but he had a violent temper. When four men attacked his uncle, Forrest leapt to his defense. The uncle died from a bullet meant for his nephew, but the young Forrest had shown his mettle. Admiring his raw courage, Hernando citizens rewarded Forrest by electing him town constable. Equally implacable in love, Forrest so insistently wooed a young lady from a well-connected local family that at their third meeting she agreed to marry him.

For a hard-driving young man like Forrest, the booming cotton economy offered much opportunity. He took over his uncle's business, ran a stagecoach service, traded livestock and—in due course—slaves. In 1851 ambition took him and his family to Memphis, Tennessee, where he became a well-known slave trader. With his profits he purchased a large plantation in Mississippi. By now he had become a man of substance, a leading Memphis citizen. In the sectional crisis brewing in the late 1850s, Forrest fiercely championed southern rights and, of course, slavery.

When war came in 1861, Forrest immediately organized a Tennessee cavalry regiment. In April 1862 he distinguished himself at the bloody battle of Shiloh, where he was badly wounded. Promoted to brigadier general, he began a brilliant career as a cavalry raider, fighting mostly behind Union lines. His warrior spirit often led him into the thick of battle, oblivious to the fact that he was a general and not a trooper. That same explosiveness ignited one of the war's worst atrocities, the slaughter by his men of black troops at Fort Pillow, Tennessee, on April 12, 1864, evidently because of rumors that the Fort Pillow garrison had been harassing local whites loyal to the Confederacy.

The Fort Pillow massacre anticipated the civil strife that would consume Tennessee over the next half-decade. The Republican governor William G. Brownlow, a former Confederate prisoner, was not shy about calling his enemies to account. Elected in March 1865, he disfranchised ex-Confederates, leaving political power in the hands of a minority of Unionist whites and freed slaves. Foreshadowing the reaction to radical Reconstruction a few years later, ex-Confederates around the state concluded that they could regain power only by waging a secret campaign of terror against Brownlow's black supporters. This was the genesis, among other things, of the first den of the Ku Klux Klan in Pulaski, Tennessee, sometime in late 1865 or early 1866.

Home safe from the war, Forrest was absorbed by his own damaged fortunes. The wealth represented by his slaves had been wiped out by emancipation, and he was heavily in debt. With the aid of the Freedmen's Bureau, Forrest managed to put his former slaves back to work on his plantation. But flooding over war-damaged levies wiped out his cotton crop. In August 1866 he gave up, surrendering his plantation to his creditors, swept down, like so many others, by the war-devastated economy. In desperation, he considered leading an expedition of former Confederate comrades to seize the riches of Mexico.

A more promising avenue for Forrest's energies, however, had by now opened up. From its obscure beginnings after the war, the Ku Klux Klan proliferated wildly across Tennessee and into neighboring states. What the Klan needed was a tough, respected figure able to impose order on the Invisible Empire and prevent it from spinning out of control—none other than Nathan Bedford Forrest. At a clandestine meeting in Nashville sometime in late 1866, he accepted the job and donned the robes of Grand Wizard, the Klan's highest office. Forrest's activities are mostly unknown because he worked in secrecy, but there is no mystery about why he gravitated to the Klan. For him, the Klan was politics by other means, the vehicle by which disfranchised former Confederates like himself might strike a blow against the despised Republicans who ran Tennessee.

In many towns, including Memphis, the Klan became virtually identical to the Democratic clubs; in fact, Klan members—including Forrest—dominated the state's delegation to the Democratic national convention of 1868. On the ground the Klan unleashed a murderous campaign of terror against Republican sympathizers. Governor Brownlow responded resolutely, threatening to mobilize the state militia and root out the Klan. If Brownlow tried, answered Forrest, "there will be war, and a bloodier one than we have ever witnessed. . . . If the militia attack us, we will resist to the last; and, if necessary, I think I could raise 40,000 men in five days, ready for the field."

For many months, Tennessee endured a high state of tension. In September 1868 a new law identified membership in the Klan as a felony, and the following February martial law was declared in nine Klan-ridden counties. But it was the Republicans, not the Klan, who cracked. In March 1869 Brownlow retreated to the U.S. Senate. The Democrats were on their way back to power, and the Klan, having served its purpose, was officially disbanded in Tennessee.

Like many other Confederate heroes, Forrest might now have anticipated a comfortable life in politics. But he had too much blood on his hands. He was among the very last to be pardoned by President Johnson. His appearance at the Democratic convention in 1868 brought forth bitter Republican denunciations against "the Fort Pillow Butcher." Physical violence, moreover, still dogged his life, including the killing (he claimed self-defense) of a sharecropper on his plantation. What sealed Forrest's political fate, however, was the Ku Klux Klan. Forrest had regarded the Klan's mission in strictly political terms, its violence calibrated to the task of driving the Republicans from power. In this Forrest only reflected what conservative Southerners generally favored.

KKK Flag

Striking fear in the hearts of its enemies was a favorite tactic of Forrest's Ku Klux Klan—hence this menacing ceremonial flag from Tennessee, with its fierce dragon and mysterious Latin motto, "Because it always is, because it is everywhere, because it is abominable." Chicago Historical Society.

But he could not curb the senseless brutality against blacks done in the Klan's name. Any ruffian, he complained, could put on a white sheet and go after his neighbors. But Forrest was the Grand Wizard, and even after he resigned, his name could not be dissociated from Klan savagery. Celebrated though he might have been, when it came to supporting him for political office, Democratic leaders kept their distance.

So Forrest had to cash in his chips elsewhere, which he did as president and chief promoter of the Memphis & Selma Railroad. Beginning in 1869 he hawked bonds to communities along the proposed right of way and lobbied for state and county subsidies, expending his considerable reputation on an ambitious project linking Memphis by rail to northern Alabama and eastern Mississippi: all in vain. The unfinished Memphis & Selma collapsed after the Panic of 1873, and Forrest was left with nothing. Resilient to the end, he contracted with Selby County for convicts to work 1,700 acres of land he had rented on President's Island, four miles from Memphis. Leasing convicts was a practice notorious for horrendous abuses, but none were reported on President's Island. The swamp-ridden island, however, proved hard on him; he contracted a debilitating intestinal illness that ultimately proved fatal. After so many setbacks, his luck turned at least in this regard: against all odds, Nathan Bedford Forrest died peacefully in his bed on October 29, 1877. The legacy he left, however, gave the South no peace. Racial violence plagued the land, and in 1915 the Ku Klux Klan revived, its victims extending beyond the black community to include Jews, Catholics, and immigrants.

Harriet Hernandes

The Intimidation of Black Voters

T*he following testimony was given in 1871 by Harriet Hernandes, a black resident of Spartanburg, South Carolina, to the Joint Congressional Select Committee investigating conditions in the South. The terrorizing of black women through rape and other forms of physical violence was among the means of oppression used by the Ku Klux Klan.*

Question: How old are you?
Answer: Going on thirty-four years. . . .
Q: Are you married or single?
A: Married.
Q: Did the Ku-Klux come to your house at any time?
A: Yes, sir; twice. . . .
Q: Go on to the second time. . . .
A: They came in; I was lying in bed. Says he, "Come out here, sir; come out here, sir!" They took me out of bed; they would not let me get out, but they took me up in their arms and toted me out—me and my daughter Lucy. He struck me on the forehead with a pistol, and here is the scar above my eye now. Says he, "Damn you, fall." I fell. Says he, "Damn you, get up." I got up. Says he, "Damn you, get over this fence!" and he kicked me over when I went to get over; and then he went on to a brush pile, and they laid us right down there, both together. They laid us down twenty yards apart, I reckon. They had dragged and beat us along. They struck me right on

top of my head, and I thought they had killed me; and I said, "Lord o'mercy, don't, don't kill my child!" He gave me a lick on the head, and it liked to have killed me; I saw stars. He threw my arm over my head so I could not do anything with it for three weeks, and there are great knots on my wrist now.
Q: What did they say this was for?
A: They said, "You can tell your husband that when we see him we are going to kill him. . . . "
Q: Did they say why they wanted to kill him?
A: They said, "He voted the radical ticket [slate of candidates], didn't he?" I said, "Yes," that very way. . . .
Q: When did [your husband] get back home after this whipping? He was not at home, was he?
A: He was lying out; he couldn't stay at home, bless your soul! . . .
Q: Has he been afraid for any length of time?
A: He has been afraid ever since last October. He has been lying out. He has not laid in the house ten nights since October.
Q: Is that the situation of the colored people down there to any extent?
A: That is the way they all have to do—men and women both.
Q: What are they afraid of?
A: Of being killed or whipped to death.
Q: What has made them afraid?
A: Because men that voted radical tickets they took the spite out on the women when they could get at them.
Q: How many colored people have been whipped in that neighborhood?
A: It is all of them, mighty near.

Source: Report of the Joint Congressional Select Committee to Inquire into the Condition of Affairs in the Late Insurrectionary States, House Report, 42nd Cong., 2nd sess. (Washington, DC: U.S. Government Printing Office, 1872), vol. 5, South Carolina, December 19, 1871.

their ex-Confederate enemies. Democrats overthrew Republican governments in Texas in 1873, in Alabama and Arkansas in 1874, and in Mississippi in 1875.

The Mississippi campaign showed all too clearly what the Republicans were up against. As elections neared in 1875, paramilitary groups such as the Rifle Clubs and Red Shirts operated openly. Often local Democrats paraded armed, as if they were militia companies. They identified black leaders in assassination lists called "dead books," broke up Republican meetings, provoked rioting that left hundreds of African Americans dead, and threat-

ened voters. Mississippi's Republican governor, Adelbert Ames, a Congressional Medal of Honor winner from Maine, appealed to President Grant for federal troops, but Grant refused. Ames then contemplated organizing a state militia but ultimately decided against it, believing that only blacks would join and that the state would be plunged into racial war. Brandishing their guns and stuffing the ballot boxes, the Redeemers swept the 1875 elections and took control of Mississippi. Facing impeachment by the new Democratic legislature, Governor Ames resigned his office and returned to the North.

By 1876 Republican governments, backed by token U.S. military units, remained in only three states—Louisiana, South Carolina, and Florida. Elsewhere, the former Confederates were back in the saddle.

The Acquiescent North

The faltering of Reconstruction stemmed from more than discouragement about prosecuting the Klan, however. Sympathy for the freedman began to wane. The North was flooded with one-sided, often racist reports, such as James M. Pike's *The Prostrate State* (1873), describing extravagant, corrupt Republican rule and a South in the grip of "a mass of black barbarism." The impact of this propaganda could be seen in the fate of the civil rights bill, which Charles Sumner introduced in 1870 at the height of radical Reconstruction. Sumner's bill was a remarkable application of federal power against discrimination in the country, guaranteeing citizens equal access to public accommodation, schools, and jury service. By the time the bill passed in 1875, it had been stripped of its key provisions and was of little account as a weapon against discriminatory treatment of African Americans. The Supreme Court finished the demolition job when it declared the remnant Civil Rights Act unconstitutional in 1883.

The political cynicism that overtook the Civil Rights Act signaled the Republican Party's reversion to the practical politics of earlier days. In many states a second generation took over the party—men like Roscoe Conkling of New York, who treated the Manhattan Customs House, with its regiment of political appointees, as an auxiliary of his machine. Conkling and similarly minded politicos had little enthusiasm for Reconstruction, except as it benefited the Republican Party. As the party lost headway in the South, they abandoned any interest in the battle for black rights. In Washington President Grant presided benignly over this transformation of his party, turning a blind eye on corruption even as it began to lap against the White House.

The Liberal Republicans and Election of 1872.
As Grant's administration lapsed into cronyism, a revolt took shape inside the Republican Party, led by an influential collection of intellectuals, journalists, and reform-minded businessmen. The first order of business for them was civil service reform that would replace corrupt patronage with a merit-based system of appointments. The reformers also, however, disliked the government activism spawned by the Civil War crisis. They regarded themselves as liberals—believers in free trade, market competition, and limited government. And, with unabashed elitism, they spoke out against universal suffrage, which "can only mean in plain English the government of ignorance and vice." So it followed that liberal reformers would have little patience with the former slaves. Although mostly veterans

of the antislavery movement, they now became strident critics of radical Reconstruction.

Unable to deny Grant renomination for a second term, the dissidents broke away and formed a new party under the name Liberal Republican. Their candidate was Horace Greeley, longtime editor and publisher of the *New York Tribune* and a warhorse of American reform in all its variety, including antislavery. The Democratic Party, still in disarray, also nominated Greeley, notwithstanding his editorial diatribes against Democrats as "murderers, adulterers, drunkards, liars, thieves." A poor campaigner, Greeley was assailed so bitterly during the campaign that, as he said, "I hardly knew whether I was running for the Presidency or the penitentiary."

Grant won overwhelmingly, capturing 56 percent of the popular vote and every electoral vote. Yet the Liberal Republicans had managed to shift the terms of political debate in the country. The new agenda they had established—civil service reform, limited government, reconciliation with the South—was adopted by the Democrats as they shed their disloyal reputation and reclaimed their place as a legitimate national party. In the 1874 elections the Democrats dealt the Republicans a heavy blow, gaining control of the House of Representatives for the first time since secession and capturing seven normally Republican states.

Scandal and Depression.
Charges of Republican corruption, mounting ever since Grant's reelection, came to a head in 1875. The scandal involved the Whiskey Ring, a network of liquor distillers and treasury agents who defrauded the government of millions of dollars of excise taxes on whiskey. The ringleader was a Grant appointee, and Grant's own private secretary, Orville Babcock, had a hand in the thievery. The others went to prison, but Grant stood by Babcock, possibly perjuring himself to save his secretary from jail. The stench of scandal, however, had engulfed the White House.

On top of this the economy had fallen into a severe depression after 1873. The precipitating event was the bankruptcy of the Northern Pacific Railroad and its main investor, Jay Cooke. Both Cooke's privileged role as financier of the Civil War and the generous federal subsidies to the Northern Pacific suggested to many economically pressed Americans that Republican financial manipulations had caused the depression. Grant's administration responded ineffectually, rebuffing the pleas of debtors for relief by increasing the money supply (see Chapter 18). In 1874 Democrats gained enough Republican support to push through Congress a bill that would have increased the volume of currency in circulation and eased the money pinch. But President Grant vetoed it, fueling Democratic charges that the Republicans served only the business interests.

Among the casualties of the bad economy was the Freedman's Savings and Trust Company, which held the small deposits of thousands of ex-slaves. When the bank failed in 1874, Congress refused to compensate the depositors, and many lost their life savings. In denying their pathetic pleas, Congress was signaling also that Reconstruction had lost its moral claim on the country. National politics had moved on; other concerns absorbed the voter as another presidential election approached in 1876.

The Political Crisis of 1877

Abandoning Grant, the Republicans nominated Rutherford B. Hayes, governor of Ohio, a colorless figure, but untainted by corruption or by strong convictions—in a word, a safe man. His Democratic opponent was Samuel J. Tilden, governor of New York, a wealthy lawyer with ties to Wall Street and a reform reputation for helping to break the grip of the thieving Tweed Ring on New York City politics. The Democrat Tilden, of course, favored "**home rule**" for the South but so, more discreetly, did the Republican Hayes. Reconstruction actually did not figure prominently in the campaign and was mostly subsumed under broader Democratic charges of "corrupt centralism" and "incapacity, waste, and fraud." By now Republicans had essentially written off the South and scarcely campaigned there. Not a lot was said about the states still ruled by Reconstruction governments— Florida, South Carolina, and Louisiana.

Once the returns started coming in on election night, however, those three states began to loom very large indeed. Tilden led in the popular vote and, victorious in key northern states, he seemed headed for the White House. But sleepless politicians at Republican headquarters realized that if they kept Florida, South Carolina, and Louisiana, Hayes would win by a single electoral vote. The campaigns in those states had been bitterly fought, replicating the Democratic assaults on blacks that had overturned Republican regimes everywhere else in the South. But Republicans still controlled the election machinery in those states, and, citing Democratic fraud and intimidation, they certified Republican victories. The audacious announcement came forth from Republican headquarters: Hayes had carried the three southern states and won the election. But, of course, newly elected Democratic officials in the three states also sent in electoral votes for Tilden, and, when Congress met in early 1877, it faced two sets of electoral votes from those states.

The Constitution does not provide for this contingency. All it says is that the President of the Senate (in 1877, a Republican) opens the electoral certificates before the House (Democratic) and the Senate (Republican) and that "the Votes shall then be counted" (Article 2, Section 1; see Documents, p. D-9). An air of crisis gripped the country. There was talk of inside deals, of a new election, even of a violent coup and civil war. Just in case, the commander of the army, General William T. Sherman,

deployed four artillery companies in Washington. Finally, Congress decided to appoint an electoral commission to settle the question. The commission included seven Republicans, seven Democrats, and, as the deciding member, David Davis, a Supreme Court justice not known to have fixed party loyalties. But Davis disqualified himself by accepting an Illinois seat in the Senate. He was replaced by Republican justice Joseph P. Bradley, and by 8 to 7 the commission awarded the disputed votes to Hayes.

Outraged Democrats had one more trick up their sleeves. They controlled the House, and they set about stalling a final count of the electoral votes so as to prevent Hayes's inauguration on March 4. But a week before, secret Washington talks had begun between southern Democrats and Ohio Republicans representing Hayes. Other issues may have been on the table, but the main thing was the situation in South Carolina and Louisiana, where rival governments were encamped at the state capitols, with federal soldiers holding the Democrats at bay. Exactly what deal was struck or how involved Hayes himself was will probably never be known, but on March 1 the House Democrats suddenly ended their filibuster, the ceremonial counting of votes went forward, and Hayes was inaugurated on schedule. He soon ordered the Union troops back to their barracks and the Republican regimes in South Carolina and Louisiana fell. Reconstruction had ended.

In 1877 political leaders on all sides seemed ready to say that what Lincoln had called "the work" was complete. But for the freedpeople, the work had only begun. Reconstruction turned out to have been a magnificent aberration, a leap beyond what most white Americans actually felt was due their black fellow citizens. Redemption represented a sad falling back to the norm. Still, something real had been achieved—three rights-defining amendments to the Constitution, some elbow room to advance economically, and, not least, a stubborn confidence among blacks that, by their own efforts, they could lift themselves up. Things would, in fact, get worse before they got better, but the work of Reconstruction was imperishable and could never be erased.

FOR FURTHER EXPLORATION

▶ For definitions of key terms boldface in this chapter, see the glossary at the end of the book.

▶ To assess your mastery of the material covered in this chapter, see the Online Study Guide at **bedfordstmartins.com/henretta**.

▶ For suggested references, including Web sites, see page SR-17 at the end of the book.

▶ For map resources and primary documents, see **bedfordstmartins.com/henretta**.

When the Civil War ended in 1865, no one could have foreseen the future course of Reconstruction. The slaves had been emancipated, but there was no consensus about their future status as citizens. The South had been defeated, but there was no consensus about its restoration to the Union. Had Abraham Lincoln lived, these great questions might have been settled peaceably, but with his assassination they were left to the mercy of unfolding events.

Without consulting Congress, Lincoln's successor, Andrew Johnson, offered the South easy terms for reentering the Union. This might have succeeded had the South responded with restraint, but instead a concerted effort was made to reenslave the freedmen through the Black Codes. In this opening round of freedom's struggle, the ex-slaves showed their determination to be agents of their own fate, resisting the Black Codes and demanding equal civil and political rights. Infuriated by southern intransigence, congressional Republicans closed ranks behind the Radicals, embraced the freedmen's demand for full equality, placed the South under military rule in 1867, and inaugurated radical Reconstruction.

The new Republican state governments that undertook to reconstruct the South through ambitious programs of economic and educational improvement. No amount of accomplishment, however, could have reconciled the ex-Confederates to Republican rule, and they staged a violent counterrevolution in the name of white supremacy and "redemption."

Despite an initially stern response, the Grant administration had no stomach for a protracted guerrilla war in the South. Northern politics moved on, increasingly absorbed by Republican scandals and, after depression hit in 1873, by the nation's economic problems. By allying with the Liberal Republicans in 1872, the discredited Democrats scrambled back into the political mainstream and began to compete on even terms with the Republicans. So close was the presidential election of 1876 that both parties claimed victory. The constitutional crisis was resolved only by Democratic agreement to accept the Republican Hayes as president in exchange for an end to Republican rule in South Carolina and Louisiana, signaling the conclusion of Reconstruction.

1863 Lincoln announces his Ten Percent Plan

1864 Wade-Davis Bill passed by Congress

Lincoln gives Wade-Davis Bill a "pocket" veto

1865 Freedmen's Bureau established

Lincoln assassinated; Andrew Johnson succeeds as president

Johnson implements his restoration plan

Joint Committee on Reconstruction formed

1866 Civil Rights Act passes over Johnson's veto

Memphis riots

Johnson makes disastrous "swing around the circle"; defeated in congressional elections

1867 Reconstruction Act

Tenure of Office Act

1868 Impeachment crisis

Fourteenth Amendment ratified

Ulysses S. Grant elected president

1870 Ku Klux Klan at peak of power

Fifteenth Amendment ratified

1872 Grant's reelection as president

1873 Panic of 1873 ushers in depression of 1873–1877

1874 Democrats win majority in House of Representatives

1875 Whiskey Ring scandal undermines Grant administration

1877 Compromise of 1877; Rutherford B. Hayes becomes president

Reconstruction ends

PART THREE

Religion in American Public Life

For Americans, reciting the Pledge of Allegiance is the most personal way they have for affirming their national identity. So students must think the words are in the same league with the Declaration of Independence and the Constitution. In fact, the pledge is of much later origin, composed in 1892 by Francis Bellamy, a Boston cleric-turned-social critic, who used its final words to promote his personal philosophy of "liberty and justice for all." Originally, it was an entirely secular document. Only in 1954 did "under God" become part of the pledge, inserted by Congress to further the cold war crusade against "godless Communism." Once in, however, that phrase, like the pledge itself, came to seem timeless and beyond questioning.

It therefore came as a shock in 2002 when a three-judge panel of the 9th U.S. Circuit Court of Appeals declared that a California law requiring students to recite the pledge was unconstitutional because of the words "under God." The political reaction to *Newdow v. U.S. Congress et al.* was quick and harsh. The Republican president George W. Bush denounced the decision, asserting, "America is a nation that values our relationship with an Almighty." Senator Joseph Lieberman, the Democratic vice presidential candidate in 2000 and an orthdox Jew, called for a constitutional amendment to make clear that "we are one nation because of our faith in God."

We have been down this road before. In 1863 the House of Representatives considered amending the Preamble of the Constitution to read: "Acknowledging the Lord Jesus Christ as the Governor among nations, His revealed will as the supreme law of the land, in order to constitute a Christian government, we the people of the United States. . . ." Like Senator Lieberman, living in the shadow of the terrorist attacks on America of September 11, 2001, the U.S. congressmen of 1863 were acting at a time of great national crisis, when Americans were pitted against their fellow citizens in a bloody civil war.

These professions of faith occupy one side of a great fault line in American public life. On the other side stands a secular constitutional tradition that goes back to the Revolutionary era and to the document that founded the national republic, the U.S. Constitution. The Constitution is a thoroughly secular document, containing no reference to God and mentioning religion in Article VI only to prohibit religious tests for federal office. Then came the Bill of Rights, the original ten amendments ratified in 1793. The First Amendment begins: "Congress shall make no law respecting an establishment of religion, or prohibiting the free exercise thereof. . . ." The first of these prohibitions, known as the Establishment Clause, mandates the separation of church and state and is the basis for the decision by the 9th Circuit Court in the *Newdow* case. The second, the "free exercise clause," also is germane, because freedom of conscience seems incompatible with state-mandated expressions of faith—like the phrase "under God" in the Pledge of Allegiance—that touch every citizen. These two provisions are, like freedom of speech and assembly, at the core of American civil liberties protected by the Bill of Rights.

This constitutional triumph was, however, by no means unqualified. The state constitutions of the 1770s and 1780s already in place were far from secular. Most New England states imposed taxes for the support of religion, and various states required elected officials to profess belief in "the Christian religion." Moreover, even at the federal level the secularist triumph was not quite what it seemed. As Akhil Reed Amar argues in *The Bill of Rights* (1998), many churchgoing Americans actually favored the Establishment Clause in hopes that it would shield state support of religion from federal interference. Separation of church and state, if a remarkable achievement, was tempered from the start by an abiding sense that the cohesion of the nation rested on Christian faith.

Ever since those nation-building years, religious belief and constitutional secularism have coexisted in this state of tension. And what determines which has the relative advantage? Primarily, scholars suggest, the varying intensity of religious belief. The Revolutionary era had been an age of rationalism. Thereafter, as the Second Great Awakening took hold, religious enthusiasm again swept the country. In *Southern Cross: The Beginnings of the Bible Belt* (1997), Christine Heyrman estimates that the number of white Southerners who attended evangelical churches jumped from 25 percent in 1776 to 65 percent in 1835. Alexis de Tocqueville remarked in

Democracy in America (1835) that the Great Awakening gave "the Christian religion . . . a greater influence over the souls of men" in the United States than in any other society. Modern scholars concur with Tocqueville. As we have shown in the preceding chapters, religious fervor prompted political activism on many fronts in the antebellum years—from abolitionism to temperance to the condemnation by 8,000 federal postmasters of mail delivery on Sunday, the Christian Sabbath, as "a disgrace to the nation, and an insult to the Supreme Lawgiver."

What this age of faith also revealed, however, was the staying power of constitutional secularism. Americans were coming to regard the Constitution itself as an inviolable document and a model for the states. Even in these fervent years, the bastions of public religion began to fall as churches were disestablished in the New England states and religious tests for officeholders were abandoned. New political realities set in. Irish Catholics arrived in great numbers and, ironically, the Second Great Awakening itself stimulated denominational diversity. Politicians took heed of President Andrew Jackson's warning that religiously inspired public policies would disturb "the security which religion now enjoys in this country in its complete separation from the political concerns of the General Government." Similar concerns sealed the fate of the Civil War amendment seeking to make Christianity the official federal creed.

As religious fervor waned after the Civil War, so did efforts to breach the wall of church/state separation. It is telling that the man who wrote the Pledge of Allegiance without invoking the Almighty was a Baptist minister. Moreover, the Establishment Clause proved not to be the shield for state support for religion that some of its original supporters had hoped for. In the twentieth century the courts began to move aggressively on this front. In *Everson v. Board of Education* (1947), a New Jersey case involving the use of public funds to transport students to Catholic schools, Justice Hugo Black declared that the Constitution erected "a wall of separation between church and state" that the courts would enforce. Then, in the landmark New York case of *Engel v. Vitale* (1962), the Court held that prayer in the public schools was "wholly inconsistent with the Establishment Clause," a decision that was a precedent for the *Newdow* decision and aroused even more controversy.

In each age, as the pendulum swings, a new balance has to be struck between the contradictory traditions of constitutional secularism and religious belief. That, at any rate, is what the history of church/state relations in America suggests. In our own time, a new age of faith, the courts have looked for legal accommodation. Thus laws limiting Sunday activities have been allowed on the secular grounds that they "provide a uniform day of rest for all citizens"; similarly, using a legal theory of "child benefit," judges have approved the use of public taxes to buy textbooks or defray tuition at religious schools. Such a strategy may be in the offing with respect to the pledge. Unlike President Bush and those who proclaim the centrality of faith in American public life, the Department of Justice has sought reconsideration of the *Newdow* case on the grounds that the words "under God" are essentially ritualistic, one of "many ceremonial references to our religious heritage and do not establish a religious faith." Such a legal tactic could well resolve the pledge controversy and satisfy the country. What do *you* think the outcome will be? And if, by the time you read this essay, the Supreme Court has decided this case, what did the judges actually do—and why?

Inculcating . . . What???

Three young children stare reverently at the American flag as they say (or listen to) the Pledge of Allegiance. Intended originally to promote national identity and social justice, during the twentieth century the pledge became a vehicle for inculcating patriotism and religious belief. Should children be required to recite the pledge? If so, what beliefs should it promote? Newsweek.

453

The Declaration of Independence

In Congress, July 4, 1776, The Unanimous Declaration of the Thirteen United States of America

When in the Course of human events, it becomes necessary for one people to dissolve the political bands which have connected them with another, and to assume among the Powers of the earth, the separate and equal station to which the Laws of Nature and of Nature's God entitle them, a decent respect to the opinions of mankind requires that they should declare the causes which impel them to the separation.

We hold these truths to be self-evident, that all men are created equal, that they are endowed by their Creator with certain unalienable rights, that among these are Life, Liberty, and the pursuit of Happiness. That to secure these rights, Governments are instituted among Men, deriving their just powers from the consent of the governed. That whenever any Form of Government becomes destructive of these ends, it is the Right of the People to alter or to abolish it, and to institute new Government, laying its foundation on such principles and organizing its powers in such form, as to them shall seem most likely to effect their Safety and Happiness. Prudence, indeed, will dictate that Governments long established should not be changed for light and transient causes; and accordingly all experience hath shown, that mankind are more disposed to suffer, while evils are sufferable, than to right themselves by abolishing the forms to which they are accustomed. But when a long train of abuses and usurpations, pursuing invariably the same Object evinces a design to reduce them under absolute Despotism, it is their right, it is their duty, to throw off such Government, and to provide new Guards for their future security.—Such has been the patient sufferance of these Colonies; and such is now the necessity which constrains them to alter their former Systems of Government. The history of the present King of Great Britain is a history of repeated injuries and usurpations, all having in direct object the establishment of an absolute Tyranny over these States. To prove this, let Facts be submitted to a candid world.

He has refused his Assent to Laws, the most wholesome and necessary for the public good.

He has forbidden his Governors to pass Laws of immediate and pressing importance, unless suspended in their operation till his Assent should be obtained; and, when so suspended, he has utterly neglected to attend to them.

He has refused to pass other Laws for the accommodation of large districts of people, unless those people would relinquish the right of Representation in the Legislature, a right inestimable to them and formidable to tyrants only.

He has called together legislative bodies at places unusual, uncomfortable, and distant from the depository of their public Records, for the sole purpose of fatiguing them into compliance with his measures.

He has dissolved Representative Houses repeatedly, for opposing with manly firmness his invasions on the rights of the people.

He has refused for a long time, after such dissolutions, to cause others to be elected; whereby the Legislative powers, incapable of Annihilation, have returned to the People at large for their exercise; the State remaining in the mean time exposed to all the dangers of invasion from without and convulsions within.

He has endeavoured to prevent the population of these States; for that purpose obstructing the Laws of Naturalization of Foreigners; refusing to pass others to encourage their migrations hither, and raising the conditions of new Appropriations of Lands.

He has obstructed the Administration of Justice, by refusing his Assent to Laws for establishing Judiciary powers.

He has made Judges dependent on his Will alone, for the tenure of their offices, and the amount and payment of their salaries.

He has erected a multitude of New Offices, and sent hither swarms of Officers to harass our People, and eat out their substance.

He has kept among us, in times of peace, Standing Armies without the Consent of our legislature.

He has combined with others to subject us to a jurisdiction foreign to our constitution, and unacknowledged by our laws; giving his Assent to their Acts of pretended Legislation:

For quartering large bodies of armed troops among us:

For protecting them, by a mock Trial, from Punishment for any Murders which they should commit on the Inhabitants of these States:

For cutting off our Trade with all parts of the world:

For imposing taxes on us without our Consent:

For depriving us, in many cases, of the benefits of Trial by jury:

For transporting us beyond Seas to be tried for pretended offences:

For abolishing the free System of English Laws in a neighbouring Province, establishing therein an Arbitrary government, and enlarging its Boundaries so as to render it at once an example and fit instrument for introducing the same absolute rule into these Colonies:

For taking away our Charters, abolishing our most valuable Laws, and altering fundamentally the Forms of our Governments:

For suspending our own Legislatures, and declaring themselves invested with Power to legislate for us in all cases whatsoever.

He has abdicated Government here, by declaring us out of his Protection and waging War against us.

He has plundered our seas, ravaged our Coasts, burnt our towns, and destroyed the lives of our people.

He is at this time transporting large armies of foreign mercenaries to compleat the works of death, desolation, and tyranny, already begun with circumstances of Cruelty & perfidy scarcely paralleled in the most barbarous ages, and totally unworthy the Head of a civilized nation.

He has constrained our fellow Citizens taken Captive on the high Seas to bear Arms against their Country, to become the executioners of their friends and Brethren, or to fall themselves by their Hands.

He has excited domestic insurrections amongst us, and has endeavoured to bring on the inhabitants of our frontiers, the merciless Indian Savages, whose known rule of warfare, is an undistinguished destruction of all ages, sexes, and conditions.

In every stage of these Oppressions We have Petitioned for Redress in the most humble terms: Our repeated Petitions have been answered only by repeated injury. A Prince, whose character is thus marked by every act which may define a Tyrant, is unfit to be the ruler of a free people.

Nor have We been wanting in attention to our British brethren. We have warned them from time to time of attempts by their legislature to extend an unwarrantable jurisdiction over us. We have reminded them of the circumstances of our emigration and settlement here. We have appealed to their native justice and magnanimity, and we have conjured them by the ties of our common kindred to disavow these usurpations, which would inevitably interrupt our connections and correspondence. They too have been deaf to the voice of justice and of consanguinity. We must, therefore, acquiesce in the necessity, which denounces our Separation, and hold them, as we hold the rest of mankind, Enemies in War, in Peace Friends.

We, therefore, the Representatives of the United States of America, in General Congress, Assembled, appealing to the Supreme Judge of the world for the rectitude of our intentions, do, in the Name, and by Authority of the good People of these Colonies, solemnly publish and declare, That these United Colonies are, and of Right ought to be FREE AND INDEPENDENT STATES; that they are Absolved from all Allegiance to the British Crown, and that all political connection between them and the State of Great Britain, is and ought to be totally dissolved; and that as Free and Independent States, they have full Power to levy War, conclude Peace, contract Alliances, establish Commerce, and to do all other Acts and Things which Independent States may of right do. And for the support of this Declaration, with a firm reliance on the Protection of Divine Providence, we mutually pledge to each other our Lives, our Fortunes, and our sacred Honor.

John Hancock

Button Gwinnett	**George Wythe**	**James Wilson**	**Josiah Bartlett**
Lyman Hall	**Richard Henry Lee**	**Geo. Ross**	**Wm. Whipple**
Geo. Walton	**Th. Jefferson**	**Caesar Rodney**	**Matthew Thornton**
Wm. Hooper	**Benja. Harrison**	**Geo. Read**	**Saml. Adams**
Joseph Hewes	**Thos. Nelson, Jr.**	**Thos. M'Kean**	**John Adams**
John Penn	**Francis Lightfoot Lee**	**Wm. Floyd**	**Robt. Treat Paine**
Edward Rutledge	**Carter Braxton**	**Phil. Livingston**	**Elbridge Gerry**
Thos. Heyward, Junr.	**Robt. Morris**	**Frans. Lewis**	**Step. Hopkins**
Thomas Lynch, Junr.	**Benjamin Rush**	**Lewis Morris**	**William Ellery**
Arthur Middleton	**Benja. Franklin**	**Richd. Stockton**	**Roger Sherman**
Samuel Chase	**John Morton**	**John Witherspoon**	**Sam'el Huntington**
Wm. Paca	**Geo. Clymer**	**Fras. Hopkinson**	**Wm. Williams**
Thos. Stone	**Jas. Smith**	**John Hart**	**Oliver Wolcott**
Charles Carroll of Carrollton	**Geo. Taylor**	**Abra. Clark**	

The Articles of Confederation and Perpetual Union

Agreed to in Congress, November 15, 1777; Ratified March 1781

BETWEEN THE STATES OF NEW HAMPSHIRE, MASSACHUSETTS BAY, RHODE ISLAND AND PROVIDENCE PLANTATIONS, CONNECTICUT, NEW YORK, NEW JERSEY, PENNSYLVANIA, DELAWARE, MARYLAND, VIRGINIA, NORTH CAROLINA, SOUTH CAROLINA, GEORGIA.*

Article 1.

The stile of this confederacy shall be "The United States of America."

Article 2.

Each State retains its sovereignty, freedom and independence, and every power, jurisdiction, and right, which is not by this confederation expressly delegated to the United States, in Congress assembled.

Article 3.

The said states hereby severally enter into a firm league of friendship with each other for their common defence, the security of their liberties and their mutual and general welfare; binding themselves to assist each other against all force offered to, or attacks made upon them, or any of them, on account of religion, sovereignty, trade, or any other pretence whatever.

Article 4.

The better to secure and perpetuate mutual friendship and intercourse among the people of the different states in this union, the free inhabitants of each of these states, paupers, vagabonds, and fugitives from justice excepted, shall be entitled to all privileges and immunities of free citizens in the several states; and the people of each State shall have free ingress and regress to and from any other State, and shall enjoy therein all the privileges of trade and commerce, subject to the same duties, impositions, and restrictions, as the inhabitants thereof respectively; provided, that such restrictions shall not extend so far as to prevent the removal of property, imported into any State, to any

other State of which the owner is an inhabitant; provided also, that no imposition, duties, or restriction, shall be laid by any State on the property of the United States, or either of them.

If any person guilty of, or charged with treason, felony, or other high misdemeanor in any State, shall flee from justice and be found in any of the United States, he shall, upon demand of the governor or executive power of the State from which he fled, be delivered up and removed to the State having jurisdiction of his offence.

Full faith and credit shall be given in each of these states to the records, acts, and judicial proceedings of the courts and magistrates of every other State.

Article 5.

For the more convenient management of the general interests of the United States, delegates shall be annually appointed, in such manner as the legislature of each State shall direct, to meet in Congress, on the 1st Monday in November in every year, with a power reserved to each State to recall its delegates, or any of them, at any time within the year, and to send others in their stead for the remainder of the year.

No State shall be represented in Congress by less than two, nor by more than seven members; and no person shall be capable of being a delegate for more than three years in any term of six years; nor shall any person, being a delegate, be capable of holding any office under the United States, for which he, or any other for his benefit, receives any salary, fees, or emolument of any kind.

Each State shall maintain its own delegates in a meeting of the states, and while they act as members of the committee of the states.

In determining questions in the United States, in Congress assembled, each State shall have one vote.

Freedom of speech and debate in Congress shall not be impeached or questioned in any court or place out of Congress: and the members of Congress shall be protected in their persons from arrests and imprisonments, during the time of their going to and from, and attendance on Congress, except for treason, felony, or breach of the peace.

Article 6.

No State, without the consent of the United States, in Congress assembled, shall send any embassy to, or receive any embassy from, or enter into any conference, agreement, alliance, or treaty with any king, prince, or state; nor shall any person, holding any office of profit or trust under the United States, or any of them, accept of any present, emolument, office or title,

---

*This copy of the final draft of the Articles of Confederation is taken from the *Journals*, 9:907-25, November 15, 1777.

of any kind whatever, from any king, prince, or foreign state; nor shall the United States, in Congress assembled, or any of them, grant any title of nobility.

No two or more states shall enter into any treaty, confederation, or alliance, whatever, between them, without the consent of the United States, in Congress assembled, specifying accurately the purposes for which the same is to be entered into, and how long it shall continue.

No state shall lay any imposts or duties which may interfere with any stipulations in treaties entered into by the United States, in Congress assembled, with any king, prince, or state, in pursuance of any treaties already proposed by Congress to the courts of France and Spain.

No vessels of war shall be kept up in time of peace by any State, except such number only as shall be deemed necessary by the United States, in Congress assembled, for the defence of such State or its trade; nor shall any body of forces be kept up by any State, in time of peace, except such number only as, in the judgment of the United States, in Congress assembled, shall be deemed requisite to garrison the forts necessary for the defence of such State; but every State shall always keep up a well regulated and disciplined militia, sufficiently armed and accoutred, and shall provide, and constantly have ready for use, in public stores, a due number of field pieces and tents, and a proper quantity of arms, ammunition and camp equipage.

No State shall engage in any war without the consent of the United States, in Congress assembled, unless such State be actually invaded by enemies, or shall have received certain advice of a resolution being formed by some nation of Indians to invade such State, and the danger is so imminent as not to admit of a delay till the United States, in Congress assembled, can be consulted; nor shall any State grant commissions to any ships or vessels of war, nor letters of marque or reprisal, except it be after a declaration of war by the United States, in Congress assembled, and then only against the kingdom or state, and the subjects thereof, against which war has been so declared, and under such regulations as shall be established by the United States, in Congress assembled, unless such State be infested by pirates, in which case vessels of war may be fitted out for that occasion, and kept so long as the danger shall continue, or until the United States, in Congress assembled, shall determine otherwise.

Article 7.

When land forces are raised by any State for the common defence, all officers of or under the rank of colonel, shall be appointed by the legislature of each State respectively, by whom such forces shall be raised, or in such manner as such State shall direct; and all vacancies shall be filled up by the State which first made the appointment.

Article 8.

All charges of war and all other expences, that shall be incurred for the common defence or general welfare, and allowed by the United States, in Congress assembled, shall be defrayed out of a common treasury, which shall be supplied by the several states, in proportion to the value of all land within each State, granted to or surveyed for any person, as such land and the buildings and improvements thereon shall be estimated according to such mode as the United States, in Congress assembled, shall, from time to time, direct and appoint.

The taxes for paying that proportion shall be laid and levied by the authority and direction of the legislatures of the several states, within the time agreed upon by the United States, in Congress assembled.

Article 9.

The United States, in Congress assembled, shall have the sole and exclusive right and power of determining on peace and war, except in the cases mentioned in the 6th article; of sending and receiving ambassadors; entering into treaties and alliances, provided that no treaty of commerce shall be made, whereby the legislative power of the respective states shall be restrained from imposing such imposts and duties on foreigners as their own people are subjected to, or from prohibiting the exportation or importation of any species of goods or commodities whatsoever; of establishing rules for deciding, in all cases, what captures on land or water shall be legal, and in what manner prizes, taken by land or naval forces in the service of the United States, shall be divided or appropriated; of granting letters of marque and reprisal in times of peace; appointing courts for the trial of piracies and felonies committed on the high seas, and establishing courts for receiving and determining, finally, appeals in all cases of captures; provided, that no member of Congress shall be appointed a judge of any of the said courts.

The United States, in Congress assembled, shall also be the last resort on appeal in all disputes and differences now subsisting, or that hereafter may arise between two or more states concerning boundary, jurisdiction or any other cause whatever; which authority shall always be exercised in the manner following: whenever the legislative or executive authority, or lawful agent of any State, in controversy with another, shall present a petition to Congress, stating the matter in question, and praying for a hearing, notice thereof shall be given, by order of Congress, to the legislative or executive authority of the other State in controversy, and a day assigned for the appearance of the parties by their lawful agents, who shall then be directed to appoint, by joint consent, commissioners or judges to constitute a court for hearing and determining the matter in question; but, if they cannot agree, Congress shall name three persons out of each of the United States, and from the list of such persons each party shall alternately strike out one, the petitioners beginning, until the number shall be reduced to thirteen; and from that number not less than seven, nor more than nine names, as Congress shall direct, shall, in the presence of Congress, be drawn out by lot; and the persons whose names shall be so drawn, or any five of them, shall be commissioners or judges to hear and finally determine the controversy, so always as a major part of the judges who shall hear the cause shall agree in the determination; and if either party shall neglect to attend at the day appointed, without shewing reasons which Congress shall judge sufficient, or, being present, shall refuse to strike, the Congress shall proceed to nominate three persons out of each State, and the secretary of Congress shall strike in behalf of such party absent or refusing; and the judgment and sentence of the court to be appointed, in the manner before prescribed, shall be final and conclusive; and if any of the parties shall refuse to submit to the authority of such court, or to appear or defend their claim or cause, the court shall nevertheless proceed to pronounce sentence or judgment, which shall, in like manner, be final and decisive, the judgment or sentence and other proceedings begin, in either case, transmitted to Congress, and lodged among the acts of Congress for the security of the parties concerned: provided, that every commissioner, before he sits in judgment, shall take an oath, to be administered by one of the judges of the supreme or superior court of the State where the cause shall be tried, "well and truly to hear and determine the matter in question, according to the best of his judgment, without favour, affection, or hope of reward:" provided, also, that no State shall be deprived of territory for the benefit of the United States.

All controversies concerning the private right of soil, claimed under different grants of two or more states, whose jurisdictions, as they may respect such lands and the states which passed such grants, are adjusted, the said grants, or either of them, being at the same time claimed to have originated antecedent to such settlement of jurisdiction, shall, on the petition of either party to the Congress of the United States, be finally determined, as near as may be, in the same manner as is before prescribed for deciding disputes respecting territorial jurisdiction between different states.

The United States, in Congress assembled, shall also have the sole and exclusive right and power of regulating the alloy and value of coin struck by their own authority, or by that of the respective states; fixing the standard of weights and measures throughout the United States; regulating the trade and managing all affairs with the Indians not members of any of the states; provided that the legislative right of any State within its own limits be not infringed or violated; establishing and regulating post offices from one State to another throughout all the United States, and exacting such postage on the papers passing through the same as may be requisite to defray the expences of the said office; appointing all officers of the land forces in the service of the United States, excepting regimental officers; appointing all the officers of the naval forces, and commissioning all officers whatever in the service of the United States; making rules for the government and regulation of the said land and naval forces, and directing their operations.

The United States, in Congress assembled, shall have authority to appoint a committee to sit in the recess of Congress, to be denominated "a Committee of the States," and to consist of one delegate from each State, and to appoint such other committees and civil officers as may be necessary for managing the general affairs of the United States, under their direction; to appoint one of their number to preside; provided that no person be allowed to serve in the office of president more than one year in any term of three years; to ascertain the necessary sums of money to be raised for the service of the United States, and to appropriate and apply the same for defraying the public expences; to borrow money or emit bills on the credit of the United States, transmitting, every half year, to the respective states, an account of the sums of money so borrowed or emitted; to build and equip a navy; to agree upon the number of land forces, and to make requisitions from each State for its quota, in proportion to the number of white inhabitants in such State; which requisitions shall be binding; and thereupon, the legislature of each State shall appoint the regimental officers, raise the men, and cloathe, arm, and equip them in a soldier-like manner, at the expence of the United States; and the officers and men so cloathed, armed, and equipped, shall march to the place appointed and within the time agreed on by the United States, in Congress assembled;

but if the United States, in Congress assembled, shall, on consideration of circumstances, judge proper that any State should not raise men, or should raise a smaller number than its quota, and that any other State should raise a greater number of men than the quota thereof, such extra number shall be raised, officered, cloathed, armed, and equipped in the same manner as the quota of such State, unless the legislature of such State shall judge that such extra number cannot be safely spared out of the same, in which case they shall raise, officer, cloathe, arm, and equip as many of such extra number as they judge can be safely spared. And the officers and men so cloathed, armed, and equipped, shall march to the place appointed and within the time agreed on by the United States, in Congress assembled.

The United States, in Congress assembled, shall never engage in a war, nor grant letters of marque and reprisal in time of peace, nor enter into any treaties or alliances, nor coin money, nor regulate the value thereof, nor ascertain the sums and expences necessary for the defence and welfare of the United States, or any of them: nor emit bills, nor borrow money on the credit of the United States, nor appropriate money, nor agree upon the number of vessels of war to be built or purchased, or the number of land or sea forces to be raised, nor appoint a commander in chief of the army or navy, unless nine states assent to the same; nor shall a question on any other point, except for adjourning from day to day, be determined, unless by the votes of a majority of the United States, in Congress assembled.

The Congress of the United States shall have power to adjourn to any time within the year, and to any place within the United States, so that no period of adjournment be for a longer duration than the space of six months, and shall publish the journal of their proceedings monthly, except such parts thereof, relating to treaties, alliances or military operations, as, in their judgment, require secrecy; and the yeas and nays of the delegates of each State on any question shall be entered on the journal, when it is desired by any delegate; and the delegates of a State, or any of them, at his, or their request, shall be furnished with a transcript of the said journal, except such parts as are above excepted, to lay before the legislatures of the several states.

Article 10.

The committee of the states, or any nine of them, shall be authorized to execute, in the recess of Congress, such of the powers of Congress as the United States, in Congress assembled, by the consent of nine states, shall, from time to time, think expedient to vest them with; provided, that no power be delegated to the said committee, for the exercise of which, by the articles of confederation, the voice of nine states, in the Congress of the United States assembled, is requisite.

Article 11.

Canada acceding to this confederation, and joining in the measures of the United States, shall be admitted into and entitled to all the advantages of this union; but no other colony shall be admitted into the same, unless such admission be agreed to by nine states.

Article 12.

All bills of credit emitted, monies borrowed and debts contracted by, or under the authority of Congress before the assembling of the United States, in pursuance of the present confederation, shall be deemed and considered as a charge against the United States, for payment and satisfaction whereof the said United States and the public faith are hereby solemnly pledged.

Article 13.

Every State shall abide by the determinations of the United States, in Congress assembled, on all questions which, by this confederation, are submitted to them. And the articles of this confederation shall be inviolably observed by every State, and the union shall be perpetual; nor shall any alteration at any time hereafter be made in any of them, unless such alteration be agreed to in a Congress of the United States, and be afterwards confirmed by the legislatures of every State.

These articles shall be proposed to the legislatures of all the United States, to be considered, and if approved of by them, they are advised to authorize their delegates to ratify the same in the Congress of the United States; which being done, the same shall become conclusive.

The Constitution of the United States of America

Agreed to by Philadelphia Convention, September 17, 1787
Implemented March 4, 1789

We the People of the United States, in Order to form a more perfect Union, establish Justice, insure domestic Tranquility, provide for the common defence, promote the general Welfare, and secure the Blessings of Liberty to ourselves and our Posterity, do ordain and establish this Constitution for the United States of America.

Article I

Section 1. All legislative Powers herein granted shall be vested in a Congress of the United States, which shall consist of a Senate and a House of Representatives.

Section 2. The House of Representatives shall be composed of Members chosen every second Year by the People of the several States, and the Electors in each State shall have the Qualifications requisite for Electors of the most numerous Branch of the State Legislature.

No Person shall be a Representative who shall not have attained to the Age of twenty-five Years, and been seven Years a Citizen of the United States, and who shall not, when elected, be an Inhabitant of that State in which he shall be chosen.

Representatives and direct Taxes shall be apportioned among the several States which may be included within this Union, according to their respective Numbers, *which shall be determined by adding to the whole Number of free Persons, including those bound to Service for a Term of Years, and excluding Indians not taxed, three fifths of all other Persons.*[*] The actual Enumeration shall be made within three Years after the first Meeting of the Congress of the United States, and within every subsequent Term of ten Years, in such Manner as they shall by Law direct. The Number of Representatives shall not exceed one for every thirty Thousand, but each State shall have at Least one Representative; and *until such enumeration shall be made, the State of New Hampshire shall be entitled to chuse three, Massachusetts eight, Rhode Island and Providence Plantations one, Connecticut five, New York six, New Jersey four, Pennsylvania eight, Delaware one, Maryland six, Virginia ten, North Carolina five, South Carolina five, and Georgia three.*

When vacancies happen in the Representation from any State, the Executive Authority thereof shall issue Writs of Election to fill such Vacancies.

The House of Representatives shall chuse their Speaker and other Officers; and shall have the sole Power of Impeachment.

Section 3. The Senate of the United States shall be composed of two Senators from each State, *chosen by the Legislature thereof,*[†] for six Years; and each Senator shall have one Vote.

Immediately after they shall be assembled in Consequence of the first Election, they shall be divided as equally as may be into three Classes. The Seats of the Senators of the first Class shall be vacated at the Expiration of the second Year, of the second Class at the Expiration of the fourth Year, and of the third Class at the Expiration of the sixth Year, so that one-third may be chosen every second Year; and if Vacancies happen by Resignation, or otherwise, during the Recess of the Legislature of any State, the Executive thereof may make temporary Appointments until the next Meeting of the Legislature, which shall then fill such Vacancies.[‡]

No person shall be a Senator who shall not have attained to the Age of thirty Years, and been nine Years a Citizen of the United States, and who shall not, when elected, be an Inhabitant of that State for which he shall be chosen.

The Vice President of the United States shall be President of the Senate, but shall have no Vote, unless they be equally divided.

The Senate shall chuse their other Officers, and also a President pro tempore, in the absence of the Vice President, or when he shall exercise the Office of President of the United States.

The Senate shall have the sole Power to try all Impeachments. When sitting for that Purpose, they shall be on Oath or Affirmation. When the President of the United States is tried, the Chief Justice shall preside: And no Person shall be convicted without the Concurrence of two-thirds of the Members present.

Judgment in Cases of Impeachment shall not extend further than to removal from Office, and disqualification to hold and enjoy any Office of honor, Trust or Profit under the United States: but the Party convicted shall nevertheless be liable and subject to Indictment, Trial, Judgment and Punishment, according to Law.

Section 4. The Times, Places and Manner of holding Elections for Senators and Representatives, shall be prescribed in each State by the Legislature thereof; but the Congress may at any time by Law make or alter such Regulations, except as to the Places of Chusing Senators.

Note: The Constitution became effective March 4, 1789. Provisions in italics are no longer relevant or have been changed by constitutional amendment.

[*]Changed by Section 2 of the Fourteenth Amendment.

[†]Changed by Section 1 of the Seventeenth Amendment.

[‡]Changed by Clause 2 of the Seventeenth Amendment.

The Congress shall assemble at least once in every Year, and such Meeting *shall be on the first Monday in December, unless they shall by Law appoint a different Day.*[*]

Section 5.   Each House shall be the Judge of the Elections, Returns and Qualifications of its own Members, and a Majority of each shall constitute a Quorum to do Business; but a smaller number may adjourn from day to day, and may be authorized to compel the Attendance of absent Members, in such Manner, and under such Penalties, as each House may provide.

Each House may determine the Rules of its Proceedings, punish its Members for disorderly Behavior, and, with the Concurrence of two-thirds, expel a Member.

Each House shall keep a Journal of its Proceedings, and from time to time publish the same, excepting such Parts as may in their Judgment require Secrecy; and the Yeas and Nays of the Members of either House on any question shall, at the Desire of one-fifth of those Present, be entered on the Journal.

Neither House, during the Session of Congress, shall, without the Consent of the other, adjourn for more than three days, nor to any other Place than that in which the two Houses shall be sitting.

Section 6.   The Senators and Representatives shall receive a Compensation for their Services, to be ascertained by Law, and paid out of the Treasury of the United States. They shall in all Cases, except Treason, Felony and Breach of the Peace, be privileged from Arrest during their Attendance at the Session of their respective Houses, and in going to and returning from the same; and for any Speech or Debate in either House, they shall not be questioned in any other Place.

No Senator or Representative shall, during the Time for which he was elected, be appointed to any civil Office under the Authority of the United States, which shall have been created, or the Emoluments whereof shall have been increased, during such time; and no Person holding any Office under the United States, shall be a Member of either House during his Continuance in Office.

Section 7.   All Bills for raising Revenue shall originate in the House of Representatives; but the Senate may propose or concur with Amendments as on other Bills.

Every Bill which shall have passed the House of Representatives and the Senate, shall, before it becomes a Law, be presented to the President of the United States; If he approve he shall sign it, but if not he shall return it, with his Objections to that House in which it shall have originated, who shall enter the Objections at large on their Journal, and proceed to reconsider it. If after such Reconsideration two-thirds of that House shall agree to pass the Bill, it shall be sent, together with the Objections, to the other House, by which it shall likewise be reconsidered, and if approved by two-thirds of that House, it shall become a Law. But in all such Cases the Votes of both Houses shall be determined by Yeas and Nays, and the Names of the Persons voting for and against the Bill shall be entered on the Journal of each House respectively. If any Bill shall not be returned by the President within ten Days (Sundays excepted) after it shall have been presented to him, the Same shall be a Law, in like Manner as if he had signed it, unless the Congress by their Adjournment prevent its Return, in which Case it shall not be a Law.

Every Order, Resolution, or Vote to which the Concurrence of the Senate and the House of Representatives may be necessary (except on a question of Adjournment) shall be presented to the President of the United States; and before the Same shall take Effect, shall be approved by him, or being disapproved by him, shall be repassed by two-thirds of the Senate and House of Representatives, according to the Rules and Limitations prescribed in the Case of a Bill.

Section 8.   The Congress shall have Power To lay and collect Taxes, Duties, Imposts and Excises, to pay the Debts and provide for the common Defence and general Welfare of the United States; but all Duties, Imposts and Excises shall be uniform throughout the United States;

To borrow money on the credit of the United States;

To regulate Commerce with foreign Nations, and among the several States, and with the Indian Tribes;

To establish an uniform Rule of Naturalization, and uniform Laws on the subject of Bankruptcies throughout the United States;

To coin Money, regulate the Value thereof, and of foreign Coin, and fix the Standard of Weights and Measures;

To provide for the Punishment of counterfeiting the Securities and current Coin of the United States;

To establish Post Offices and post Roads;

To promote the Progress of Science and useful Arts, by securing for limited Times to Authors and Inventors the exclusive Right to their respective Writings and Discoveries;

To constitute Tribunals inferior to the supreme Court;

To define and punish Piracies and Felonies committed on the high Seas, and Offenses against the Law of Nations;

To declare War, grant Letters of Marque and Reprisal, and make Rules concerning Captures on Land and Water;

To raise and support Armies, but no Appropriation of Money to that Use shall be for a longer Term than two Years;

To provide and maintain a Navy;

To make Rules for the Government and Regulation of the land and naval Forces;

To provide for calling forth the Militia to execute the Laws of the Union, suppress Insurrections and repel Invasions;

To provide for organizing, arming, and disciplining the Militia, and for governing such Part of them as may be employed in the Service of the United States, reserving to the States respectively, the Appointment of the Officers, and the Authority of training the Militia according to the discipline prescribed by Congress;

To exercise exclusive Legislation in all Cases whatsoever, over such District (not exceeding ten Miles square) as may, by Cession of particular States, and the acceptance of Congress, become the Seat of Government of the United States, and to exercise like Authority over all Places purchased by the Consent of the Legislature of the State in which the Same shall be, for the Erection of Forts, Magazines, Arsenals, dock-Yards, and other needful Buildings;—And

To make all Laws which shall be necessary and proper for carrying into Execution the foregoing Powers, and all other Powers vested by this Constitution in the Government of the United States, or in any Department or Officer thereof.

---

[*]Changed by Section 2 of the Twentieth Amendment.

Section 9. The Migration or Importation of such Persons as any of the States now existing shall think proper to admit, shall not be prohibited by the Congress prior to the Year one thousand eight hundred and eight but a tax or duty may be imposed on such Importation, not exceeding ten dollars for each Person.

The privilege of the Writ of Habeas Corpus shall not be suspended, unless when in Cases of Rebellion or Invasion the public Safety may require it.

No Bill of Attainder or ex post facto Law shall be passed.

No capitation, or other direct, Tax shall be laid, unless in Proportion to the Census or Enumeration herein before directed to be taken.[*]

No Tax or Duty shall be laid on Articles exported from any State.

No Preference shall be given by any Regulation of Commerce or Revenue to the Ports of one State over those of another: nor shall Vessels bound to, or from, one State, be obliged to enter, clear, or pay Duties in another.

No Money shall be drawn from the Treasury, but in Consequence of Appropriations made by law; and a regular Statement and Account of the Receipts and Expenditures of all public Money shall be published from time to time.

No Title of Nobility shall be granted by the United States: And no Person holding any Office of Profit or Trust under them, shall, without the Consent of the Congress, accept of any present, Emolument, Office, or Title, of any kind whatever, from any King, Prince, or foreign State.

Section 10. No State shall enter into any Treaty, Alliance, or Confederation; grant Letters of Marque and Reprisal; coin Money; emit Bills of Credit; make any Thing but gold and silver Coin a Tender in Payment of Debts; pass any Bill of Attainder, ex post facto Law, or Law impairing the Obligation of Contracts, or grant any Title of Nobility.

No State shall, without the Consent of the Congress, lay any Imposts or Duties on Imports or Exports, except what may be absolutely necessary for executing its inspection Laws: and the net Produce of all Duties and Imposts, laid by any State on Imports or Exports, shall be for the Use of the Treasury of the United States; and all such Laws shall be subject to the Revision and Control of the Congress.

No State shall, without the Consent of the Congress, lay any duty of Tonnage, keep Troops, or Ships of War in time of Peace, enter into any Agreement or Compact with another State, or with a foreign Power, or engage in War, unless actually invaded, or in such imminent Danger as will not admit of delay.

Article II

Section 1. The executive Power shall be vested in a President of the United States of America. He shall hold his Office during the Term of four Years, and, together with the Vice President, chosen for the same Term, be elected, as follows:

Each State shall appoint, in such Manner as the Legislature thereof may direct, a Number of Electors, equal to the whole Number of Senators and Representatives to which the State may be entitled in the Congress; but no Senator or Representative, or Person holding an Office of Trust or Profit under the United States, shall be appointed an Elector.

The Electors shall meet in their respective States, and vote by Ballot for two Persons, of whom one at least shall not be an Inhabitant of the same State with themselves. And they shall make a List of all the Persons voted for, and of the Number of Votes for each; which List they shall sign and certify, and transmit sealed to the Seat of the Government of the United States, directed to the President of the Senate. The President of the Senate shall, in the Presence of the Senate and House of Representatives, open all the Certificates, and the Votes shall then be counted. The Person having the greatest Number of Votes shall be the President, if such Number be a Majority of the whole Number of Electors appointed; and if there be more than one who have such Majority, and have an equal Number of Votes, then the House of Representatives shall immediately chuse by Ballot one of them for President; and if no Person have a Majority, then from the five highest on the List the said House shall in like Manner chuse the President. But in chusing the President, the Votes shall be taken by States, the Representation from each State having one Vote; a quorum for this Purpose shall consist of a Member or Members from two thirds of the States, and a Majority of all the States shall be necessary to a Choice. In every Case, after the Choice of the President, the Person having the greatest Number of Votes of the Electors shall be the Vice President. But if there should remain two or more who have equal Votes, the Senate shall chuse from them by Ballot the Vice President.[†]

The Congress may determine the Time of chusing the Electors, and the Day on which they shall give their Votes; which Day shall be the same throughout the United States.

No Person except a natural born Citizen, or a Citizen of the United States, at the time of the Adoption of this Constitution, shall be eligible to the Office of President; neither shall any Person be eligible to that Office who shall not have attained to the Age of thirty five Years, and been fourteen Years a Resident within the United States.

In Case of the Removal of the President from Office, or of his Death, Resignation, or Inability to discharge the Powers and Duties of the said Office, the same shall devolve on the Vice President, and the Congress may by Law provide for the Case of Removal, Death, Resignation, or Inability, both of the President and Vice President, declaring what Officer shall then act as President, and such Officer shall act accordingly, until the Disability be removed, or a President shall be elected.[‡]

The President shall, at stated Times, receive for his Services a Compensation, which shall neither be increased nor diminished during the Period for which he shall have been elected, and he shall not receive within that Period any other Emolument from the United States, or any of them.

Before he enter on the Execution of his Office, he shall take the following Oath or Affirmation:—"I do solemnly swear (or affirm) that I will faithfully execute the Office of President of the United States, and will to the best of my Ability, preserve, protect and defend the Constitution of the United States."

Section 2. The President shall be Commander in Chief of the Army and Navy of the United States, and of the Militia of the several States, when called into the actual Service of the United

---

[*]Changed by the Sixteenth Amendment.

[†]Superseded by the Twelfth Amendment.

[‡]Modified by the Twenty-fifth Amendment.

States; he may require the Opinion, in writing, of the principal Officer in each of the executive Departments, upon any Subject relating to the Duties of their respective Offices, and he shall have Power to Grant Reprieves and Pardons for Offences against the United States, except in Cases of Impeachment.

He shall have Power, by and with the Advice and Consent of the Senate, to make Treaties, provided two thirds of the Senators present concur; and he shall nominate, and by and with the Advice and Consent of the Senate, shall appoint Ambassadors, other public Ministers and Consuls, Judges of the supreme Court, and all other Officers of the United States, whose Appointments are not herein otherwise provided for, and which shall be established by Law: but the Congress may by Law vest the Appointment of such inferior Officers, as they think proper, in the President alone, in the Courts of Law, or in the Heads of Departments.

The President shall have Power to fill up all Vacancies that may happen during the Recess of the Senate, by granting Commissions which shall expire at the End of their next Session.

Section 3.   He shall from time to time give to the Congress Information of the State of the Union, and recommend to their Consideration such Measures as he shall judge necessary and expedient; he may, on extraordinary Occasions, convene both Houses, or either of them, and in Case of Disagreement between them, with Respect to the Time of Adjournment, he may adjourn them to such Time as he shall think proper; he shall receive Ambassadors and other public Ministers; he shall take Care that the Laws be faithfully executed, and shall Commission all the Officers of the United States.

Section 4.   The President, Vice President and all civil Officers of the United States, shall be removed from Office on Impeachment for, and Conviction of, Treason, Bribery, or other high Crimes and Misdemeanors.

Article III

Section 1.   The judicial Power of the United States, shall be vested in one supreme Court, and in such inferior Courts as the Congress may from time to time ordain and establish. The Judges, both of the supreme and inferior Courts, shall hold their Offices during good Behaviour, and shall, at stated Times, receive for their Services a Compensation, which shall not be diminished during their Continuance in Office.

Section 2.   The judicial Power shall extend to all Cases, in Law and Equity, arising under this Constitution, the Laws of the United States, and Treaties made, or which shall be made, under their Authority;—to all Cases affecting Ambassadors, other public Ministers and Consuls;—to all Cases of admiralty and maritime Jurisdiction;—to Controversies to which the United States shall be a Party;—to Controversies between two or more States;—*between a State and Citizens of another State;* *—between Citizens of different States;—between Citizens of the same State claiming Lands under Grants of different States, and between a State, or the Citizens thereof, and foreign States, Citizens or Subjects.

In all Cases affecting Ambassadors, other public Ministers and Consuls, and those in which a State shall be Party, the supreme Court shall have original Jurisdiction. In all the other Cases before mentioned, the supreme Court shall have appellate Jurisdiction, both as to Law and Fact, with such Exceptions, and under such Regulations as the Congress shall make.

The trial of all Crimes, except in Cases of Impeachment, shall be by Jury; and such Trial shall be held in the State where said Crimes shall have been committed; but when not committed within any State, the Trial shall be at such Place or Places as the Congress may by Law have directed.

Section 3.   Treason against the United States, shall consist only in levying War against them, or in adhering to their Enemies, giving them Aid and Comfort. No Person shall be convicted of Treason unless on the Testimony of two Witnesses to the same overt Act, or on Confession in open Court.

The Congress shall have Power to declare the Punishment of Treason, but no Attainder of Treason shall work Corruption of Blood, or Forefeiture except during the Life of the Person attainted.

Article IV

Section 1.   Full Faith and Credit shall be given in each State to the public Acts, Records, and judicial Proceedings of every other State. And the Congress may by general Laws prescribe the Manner in which such Acts, Records, and Proceedings shall be proved, and the Effect thereof.

Section 2.   The Citizens of each State shall be entitled to all Privileges and Immunities of Citizens in the several States.

A Person charged in any State with Treason, Felony, or other Crime, who shall flee from Justice, and be found in another State, shall on demand of the executive Authority of the State from which he fled, be delivered up, to be removed to the State having Jurisdiction of the Crime.

No Person held to Service or Labour in one State, under the Laws thereof, escaping into another, shall, in Consequence of any Law or Regulation therein, be discharged from such Service or Labour, but shall be delivered up on Claim of the Party to whom such Service or Labour may be due.†

Section 3.   New States may be admitted by the Congress into this Union; but no new State shall be formed or erected within the Jurisdiction of any other State; nor any State be formed by the Junction of two or more States, or parts of States, without the Consent of the Legislatures of the States concerned as well as of the Congress.

The Congress shall have Power to dispose of and make all needful Rules and Regulations respecting the Territory or other Property belonging to the United States; and nothing in this Constitution shall be so construed as to Prejudice any Claims of the United States, or of any particular State.

Section 4.   The United States shall guarantee to every State in this Union a Republican Form of Government, and shall

---

*Restricted by the Eleventh Amendment.

†Superseded by the Thirteenth Amendment.

protect each of them against Invasion; and on Application of the Legislature, or of the Executive (when the Legislature cannot be convened) against domestic Violence.

Article V

The Congress, whenever two-thirds of both Houses shall deem it necessary, shall propose Amendments to this Constitution, or, on the Application of the Legislatures of two-thirds of the several States, shall call a Convention for proposing Amendments, which, in either Case, shall be valid to all Intents and Purposes, as Part of this Constitution, when ratified by the Legislatures of three-fourths of the several States, or by Conventions in three-fourths thereof, as the one or the other Mode of Ratification may be proposed by the Congress; Provided that no Amendment which may be made prior to the Year One thousand eight hundred and eight shall in any Manner affect the first and fourth Clauses in the Ninth Section of the first Article; and that no State, without its Consent, shall be deprived of its equal Suffrage in the Senate.

Article VI

All Debts contracted and Engagements entered into, before the Adoption of this Constitution, shall be as valid against the United States under this Constitution, as under the Confederation.

This Constitution, and the Laws of the United States which shall be made in Pursuance thereof; and all Treaties made, or which shall be made, under the Authority of the United States, shall be the supreme Law of the Land; and the Judges in every State shall be bound thereby, any Thing in the Constitution or Laws of any State to the Contrary notwithstanding.

The Senators and Representatives before mentioned, and the Members of the several State Legislatures, and all executive and judicial Officers, both of the United States and of the several States, shall be bound by Oath or Affirmation, to support this Constitution; but no religious Test shall ever be required as a Qualification to any Office or public Trust under the United States.

Article VII

The Ratification of the Conventions of nine States shall be sufficient for the Establishment of this Constitution between the States so ratifying the Same.

Done in Convention by the Unanimous Consent of the States present the Seventeenth Day of September in the Year of our Lord one thousand seven hundred and Eighty seven and of the Independence of the United States of America the Twelfth. In Witness whereof We have hereunto subscribed our Names.

Go. Washington
President and deputy from Virginia

New Hampshire	*New Jersey*	*Delaware*	*North Carolina*
John Langdon	Wil. Livingston	Geo. Read	Wm. Blount
Nicholas Gilman	David Brearley	Gunning Bedford jun	Richd. Dobbs Spaight
	Wm. Paterson	John Dickinson	Hu Williamson
Massachusetts	Jona. Dayton	Richard Bassett	
Nathaniel Gorham		Jaco. Broom	*South Carolina*
Rufus King	*Pennsylvania*		J. Rutledge
	B. Franklin	*Maryland*	Charles Cotesworth Pinckney
Connecticut	Thomas Mifflin	James McHenry	Pierce Butler
Wm. Saml. Johnson	Robt. Morris	Dan. of St. Thos. Jenifer	
Roger Sherman	Geo. Clymer	Danl. Carroll	*Georgia*
	Thos. FitzSimons		William Few
New York	Jared Ingersoll	*Virginia*	Abr. Baldwin
Alexander Hamilton	James Wilson	John Blair	
	Gouv. Morris	James Madison, Jr.	

Amendments to the Constitution with Annotations (Including the Six Unratified Amendments)

In their effort to gain Antifederalists' support for the Constitution, Federalists frequently pointed to the inclusion of Article 5, which provides an orderly method of amending the Constitution. In contrast, the Articles of Confederation, which were universally recognized as seriously flawed, offered no means of amendment. For their part, Antifederalists argued that the amendment process was so "intricate" that one might as easily roll "sixes an hundred times in succession" as change the Constitution.

The system for amendment laid out in the Constitution requires that two-thirds of both houses of Congress agree to a proposed amendment, which must then be ratified by three-quarters of the legislatures of the states. Alternatively, an amendment may be proposed by a convention called by the legislatures of two-thirds of the states. Since 1789, members of Congress have proposed thousands of amendments. Besides the seventeen amendments added since 1791, only the six "unratified" ones included here were approved by two-thirds of both houses but not ratified by the states.

Among the many amendments that never made it out of Congress have been proposals to declare dueling, divorce, and interracial marriage unconstitutional as well as proposals to establish a national university, to acknowledge the sovereignty of Jesus Christ, and to prohibit any person from possessing wealth in excess of $10 million.*

Among the issues facing Americans today that might lead to constitutional amendment are efforts to balance the federal budget, to limit the number of terms elected officials may serve, to limit access to or prohibit abortion, to establish English as the official language of the United States, and to prohibit flag burning. None of these proposed amendments has yet garnered enough support in Congress to be sent to the states for ratification.

Although the first ten amendments to the Constitution are commonly known as the Bill of Rights, only Amendments 1 through 8 provide guarantees of individual rights. Amendments 9 and 10 deal with the structure of power within the constitutional system. The Bill of Rights was promised to appease Antifederalists who refused to ratify the Constitution without guarantees of individual liberties and limitations to federal power. After studying more than two hundred amendments recommended by the ratifying conventions of the states, Federalist James Madison presented a list of seventeen to Congress, which used Madison's list as the foundation for the twelve amendments that were sent to the states for ratification. Ten of the twelve were adopted in 1791. The first on the list of twelve, known as the Reapportionment Amendment, was never adopted (p. D-14). The second proposed amendment was adopted in 1992 as Amendment 27 (p. D-22).

Amendment I [1791]†

Congress shall make no law respecting an establishment of religion, or prohibiting the free exercise thereof; or abridging the freedom of speech, or of the press; or the right of the people peaceably to assemble, and to petition the Government for a redress of grievances.

• • •

The First Amendment is a potent symbol for many Americans. Most are well aware of their rights to free speech, freedom of the press, and freedom of religion and their rights to assemble and to petition, even if they cannot cite the exact words of this amendment.

The First Amendment guarantee of freedom of religion has two clauses: the "free exercise clause," which allows individuals to practice or not practice any religion, and the "establishment clause," which prevents the federal government from discriminating against or favoring any particular religion. This clause was designed to create what Thomas Jefferson referred to as "a wall of separation between church and state." In the 1960s the Supreme Court ruled that the First Amendment prohibits prayer and Bible reading in public schools.

Although the rights to free speech and freedom of the press are established in the First Amendment, it was not until the twentieth century that the Supreme Court began to explore the full meaning of these guarantees. In 1919 the Court ruled in Schenck v. United States that the government could suppress free expression only where it could cite a "clear and present danger." In a decision that continues to raise controversies, the Court ruled in 1990, in Texas v. Johnson, that flag burning is a form of symbolic speech protected by the First Amendment.

Amendment II [1791]

A well regulated Militia, being necessary to the security of a free State, the right of the people to keep and bear Arms shall not be infringed.

• • •

Fear of a standing army under the control of a hostile government made the Second Amendment an important part of the Bill

---

*Richard B. Bernstein, *Amending America* (New York: Times Books, 1993), 177–81.

†The dates in brackets indicate when the amendment was ratified.

of Rights. Advocates of gun ownership claim that the amendment prevents the government from regulating firearms. Proponents of gun control argue that the amendment is designed only to protect the right of the states to maintain militia units.

In 1939 the Supreme Court ruled in United States v. Miller *that the Second Amendment did not protect the right of an individual to own a sawed-off shotgun, which it argued was not ordinary militia equipment. Since then, the Supreme Court has refused to hear Second Amendment cases, whereas lower courts have upheld firearm regulations. Several justices currently on the bench seem to favor a broader interpretation of the Second Amendment, which would affect gun-control legislation. The controversy over the impact of the Second Amendment on gun owners and gun-control legislation will certainly continue.*

Amendment III [1791]

No Soldier shall, in time of peace, be quartered in any house, without the consent of the Owner, nor in time of war, but in a manner to be prescribed by law.

• • •

The Third Amendment was extremely important to the framers of the Constitution, but today it is nearly forgotten. American colonists were especially outraged that they were forced to quarter British troops in the years before and during the American Revolution. The philosophy of the Third Amendment has been viewed by some justices and scholars as the foundation of the modern constitutional right to privacy.

Amendment IV [1791]

The right of the people to be secure in their persons, houses, papers, and effects, against unreasonable searches and seizures, shall not be violated, and no Warrants shall issue, but upon probable cause, supported by Oath or affirmation, and particularly describing the place to be searched, and the persons or things to be seized.

• • •

In the years before the Revolution, the houses, barns, stores, and warehouses of American colonists were ransacked by British authorities under "writs of assistance" or general warrants. The British, thus empowered, searched for seditious material or smuggled goods that could then be used as evidence against colonists who were charged with a crime only after the items were found.

The first part of the Fourth Amendment protects citizens from "unreasonable" searches and seizures. The Supreme Court has interpreted this protection as well as the words search *and* seizure *in different ways at different times. At one time, the Court did not recognize electronic eavesdropping as a form of search and seizure, although it does today. At times, an "unreasonable" search has been almost any search carried out without a warrant, but in the two decades before 1969 the Court sometimes sanctioned warrantless searches that it considered reasonable based on "the total atmosphere of the case."*

The second part of the Fourth Amendment defines the procedure for issuing a search warrant and states the requirement of "probable cause," which is generally viewed as evidence indicating that a suspect has committed an offense.

The Fourth Amendment has been controversial because the Court has sometimes excluded evidence that has been seized in violation of constitutional standards. The justification is that excluding such evidence deters violations of the amendment, but doing so may allow a guilty person to escape punishment.

Amendment V [1791]

No person shall be held to answer for a capital or otherwise infamous crime, unless on a presentment or indictment of a Grand Jury, except in cases arising in the land or naval forces, or in the Militia, when in actual service in time of War or public danger; nor shall any person be subject for the same offence to be twice put in jeopardy of life or limb; nor shall be compelled in any criminal case to be a witness against himself, nor be deprived of life, liberty, or property, without due process of law; nor shall private property be taken for public use, without just compensation.

• • •

The Fifth Amendment protects people against government authority in the prosecution of criminal offenses. It prohibits the state, first, from charging a person with a serious crime without a grand-jury hearing to decide whether there is sufficient evidence to support the charge and, second, from charging a person with the same crime twice. The best-known aspect of the Fifth Amendment is that it prevents a person from being "compelled . . . to be a witness against himself." The last clause, the "takings clause," limits the power of the government to seize property.

Although invoking the Fifth Amendment is popularly viewed as a confession of guilt, a person may be innocent yet still fear prosecution. For example, during the cold war era of the late 1940s and 1950s, many people who had participated in legal activities that were associated with the Communist Party claimed the Fifth Amendment privilege rather than testify before the House Un-American Activities Committee because the mood of the times cast those activities in a negative light. Because "taking the Fifth" was viewed as an admission of guilt, those people often lost their jobs or became unemployable. Nonetheless, the right to protect oneself against self-incrimination plays an important role in guarding against the collective power of the state.

Amendment VI [1791]

In all criminal prosecutions, the accused shall enjoy the right to a speedy and public trial, by an impartial jury of the State and district wherein the crime shall have been committed, which district shall have been previously ascertained by law, and to be informed of the nature and cause of the accusation; to be confronted with the witnesses against him; to have compulsory process for obtaining witnesses in his favor, and to have the Assistance of Counsel for his defence.

• • •

The original Constitution put few limits on the government's power to investigate, prosecute, and punish crime. This process was of great concern to many Antifederalists, and of the twenty-eight rights specified in the first eight amendments, fifteen have to do with it. Seven rights are specified in the Sixth Amendment. These include the right to a speedy trial, a public trial, a jury trial, a notice of accusation, confrontation by opposing witnesses, testimony by favorable witnesses, and the assistance of counsel.

Amendment VII [1791]

In suits at common law, where the value in controversy shall exceed twenty dollars, the right of trial by jury shall be preserved, and no fact tried by a jury, shall be otherwise reexamined in any Court of the United States, than according to the Rules of the common law.

• • •

This amendment guarantees people the same right to a trial by jury as was guaranteed by English common law in 1791. Under common law, in civil trials (those involving money damages) the role of the judge was to settle questions of law and that of the jury was to settle questions of fact. The amendment does not specify the size of the jury or its role in a trial, however. The Supreme Court has generally held that those issues be determined by English common law of 1791, which stated that a jury consists of twelve people, that a trial must be conducted before a judge who instructs the jury on the law and advises it on facts, and that a verdict must be unanimous.

Amendment VIII [1791]

Excessive bail shall not be required, nor excessive fines imposed, nor cruel and unusual punishments inflicted.

• • •

The language used to guarantee the three rights in this amendment was inspired by the English Bill of Rights of 1689. The Supreme Court has not had a lot to say about "excessive fines." In recent years it has agreed that despite the provision against "excessive bail," persons who are believed to be dangerous to others can be held without bail even before they have been convicted.

Although opponents of the death penalty have not succeeded in using the Eighth Amendment to achieve the end of capital punishment, the clause regarding "cruel and unusual punishments" has been used to prohibit capital punishment in certain cases.

Amendment IX [1791]

The enumeration in the Constitution, of certain rights, shall not be construed to deny or disparage others retained by the people.

• • •

Some Federalists feared that inclusion of the Bill of Rights in the Constitution would allow later generations of interpreters to claim that the people had surrendered all rights not specifically enumerated there. To guard against this, James Madison added language that became the Ninth Amendment. Interest in this heretofore largely ignored amendment revived in 1965 when it was used in a concurring opinion in Griswold v. Connecticut *(1965). While Justice William O. Douglas called on the Third Amendment to support the right to privacy in deciding that case, Justice Arthur Goldberg, in the concurring opinion, argued that the right to privacy regarding contraception was an unenumerated right that was protected by the Ninth Amendment.*

In 1980 the Court ruled that the right of the press to attend a public trial was protected by the Ninth Amendment. Although some scholars argue that modern judges cannot identify the unenumerated rights that the framers were trying to protect, others argue that the Ninth Amendment should be read as providing a constitutional "presumption of liberty" that allows people to act in any way that does not violate the rights of others.

Amendment X [1791]

The powers not delegated to the United States by the Constitution, nor prohibited by it to the States, are reserved to the States respectively, or to the people.

• • •

The Antifederalists were especially eager to see a "reserved powers clause" explicitly guaranteeing the states control over their internal affairs. Not surprisingly, the Tenth Amendment has been a frequent battleground in the struggle over states' rights and federal supremacy. Prior to the Civil War, the Jeffersonian Republican Party and Jacksonian Democrats invoked the Tenth Amendment to prohibit the federal government from making decisions about whether people in individual states could own slaves. The Tenth Amendment was virtually suspended during Reconstruction following the Civil War. In 1883, however, the Supreme Court declared the Civil Rights Act of 1875 unconstitutional on the grounds that it violated the Tenth Amendment. Business interests also called on the amendment to block efforts at federal regulation.

The Court was inconsistent over the next several decades as it attempted to resolve the tension between the restrictions of the Tenth Amendment and the powers the Constitution granted to Congress to regulate interstate commerce and levy taxes. The Court upheld the Pure Food and Drug Act (1906), the Meat Inspection Acts (1906 and 1907), and the White Slave Traffic Act (1910), all of which affected the states, but it struck down an act prohibiting interstate shipment of goods produced through child labor. Between 1934 and 1935 a number of New Deal programs created by Franklin D. Roosevelt were declared unconstitutional on the grounds that they violated the Tenth Amendment. As Roosevelt appointees changed the composition of the Court, the Tenth Amendment was declared to have no substantive meaning. Generally, the amendment is held to protect the rights of states to regulate internal matters such as local government, education, commerce, labor, and business as well as matters involving families such as marriage, divorce, and inheritance within the state.

Unratified Amendment

Reapportionment Amendment (proposed by Congress September 25, 1789, along with the Bill of Rights)

After the first enumeration required by the first article of the Constitution, there shall be one Representative for every thirty thousand, until the number shall amount to one hundred, after which the proportion shall be so regulated by Congress, that there shall be not less than one hundred Representatives, nor less than one Representative for every forty thousand persons, until the number of Representatives shall amount to two hundred; after which the proportion shall be so regulated by Congress, that there shall not be less than two hundred Representatives, nor more than one Representative for every fifty thousand persons.

• • •

If the Reapportionment Amendment had passed and remained in effect, the House of Representatives today would have more than 5,000 members rather than 435 to reflect the current U.S. population.

Amendment XI [1798]

The Judicial power of the United States shall not be construed to extend to any suit in law or equity, commenced or prosecuted against one of the United States by Citizens of another State, or by Citizens or subjects of any foreign state.

• • •

In 1793 the Supreme Court ruled in favor of Alexander Chisholm, executor of the estate of a deceased South Carolina merchant. Chisholm was suing the state of Georgia because the merchant had never been paid for provisions he had supplied during the Revolution. Many regarded this Court decision as an error that violated the intent of the Constitution.

Antifederalists and many other Americans feared a powerful federal court system because they worried that it would become like the British courts of this period, which were accountable only to the monarch. Furthermore, Chisholm v. Georgia *prompted a series of suits against state governments by creditors and suppliers who had made loans during the war.*

In addition, state legislators and Congress feared that the shaky economies of the new states, as well as the country as a whole, would be destroyed, especially if Loyalists who had fled to other countries sought reimbursement for land and property that had been seized. The day after the Supreme Court announced its decision, a resolution proposing the Eleventh Amendment, which overturned the decision in Chisholm v. Georgia, *was introduced in the U.S. Senate.*

Amendment XII [1804]

The Electors shall meet in their respective States and vote by ballot for President and Vice-President, one of whom, at least, shall not be an inhabitant of the same State with themselves; they shall name in their ballots the person voted for as President, and in distinct ballots the person voted for as Vice-President, and they shall make distinct lists of all persons voted for as President, and of all persons voted for as Vice-President, and of the number of votes for each, which lists they shall sign and certify, and transmit sealed to the seat of government of the United States, directed to the President of the Senate;—the President of the Senate shall, in the presence of the Senate and House of Representatives, open all the certificates and the votes shall then be counted;—The person having the greatest number of votes for President, shall be the President, if such number be a majority of the whole number of Electors appointed; and if no person have such majority, then from the persons having the highest numbers not exceeding three on the list of those voted for as President, the House of Representatives shall choose immediately, by ballot, the President. But in choosing the President, the votes shall be taken by States, the representation from each State having one vote; a quorum for this purpose shall consist of a member or members from two-thirds of the States, and a majority of all the States shall be necessary to a choice. And if the House of Representatives shall not choose a President whenever the right of choice shall devolve upon them, before *the fourth day of March* next following, then the Vice-President shall act as President, as in the case of the death or other constitutional disability of the President.[*]—The person having the greatest number of votes as Vice-President, shall be the Vice-

President, if such number be a majority of the whole number of Electors appointed; and if no person have a majority, then from the two highest numbers on the list, the Senate shall choose the Vice-President; a quorum for the purpose shall consist of two-thirds of the whole number of Senators, and a majority of the whole number shall be necessary to a choice. But no person constitutionally ineligible to the office of President shall be eligible to that of Vice-President of the United States.

• • •

The framers of the Constitution disliked political parties and assumed that none would ever form. Under the original system, electors chosen by the states would each vote for two candidates. The candidate who won the most votes would become president, and the person who won the second-highest number of votes would become vice president. Rivalries between Federalists and Republicans led to the formation of political parties, however, even before George Washington had left office. In 1796 Federalist John Adams was chosen as president, and his great rival, Thomas Jefferson (whose party was called the Republican Party), became his vice president. In 1800 all the electors cast their two votes as one of two party blocs. Jefferson and his fellow Republican nominee, Aaron Burr, were tied with seventy-three votes each. The contest went to the House of Representatives, which finally elected Jefferson after thirty-six ballots. The Twelfth Amendment prevents these problems by requiring electors to vote separately for the president and vice president.

Unratified Amendment

Titles of Nobility Amendment (proposed by Congress May 1, 1810)

If any citizen of the United States shall accept, claim, receive or retain any title of nobility or honor or shall, without the consent of Congress, accept and retain any present, pension, office or emolument of any kind whatever, from any emperor, king, prince or foreign power, such person shall cease to be a citizen of the United States, and shall be incapable of holding any office of trust or profit under them, or either of them.

• • •

This amendment would have extended Article I, Section 9, Clause 8 of the Constitution, which prevents the awarding of titles by the United States and the acceptance of such awards from foreign powers without congressional consent. Historians speculate that general nervousness about the power of the Emperor Napoleon, who was at that time extending France's empire throughout Europe, may have prompted the proposal. Though it fell one vote short of ratification, Congress and the American people thought the proposal had been ratified, and it was included in many nineteenth-century editions of the Constitution.

The Civil War and Reconstruction Amendments
(Thirteenth, Fourteenth, and Fifteenth Amendments)

In the four months between the election of Abraham Lincoln and his inauguration, more than two hundred proposed constitutional amendments were presented to Congress as part of a desperate attempt to hold the rapidly dissolving Union together. Most of these were efforts to appease the southern states by protecting

---

[*]Superseded by Section 3 of the Twentieth Amendment.

the right to own slaves or by disfranchising African Americans through constitutional amendment. None were able to win the votes required from Congress to send them to the states. Ultimately, the Corwin Amendment seemed to be the only hope for preserving the Union by amending the Constitution.

The northern victors in the Civil War tried to restructure the Constitution just as the war had restructured the nation. Yet they were often divided in their goals. Some wanted to end slavery; others hoped for social and economic equality regardless of race; others hoped that extending the power of the ballot box to former slaves would help create a new political order. The debates over the Thirteenth, Fourteenth, and Fifteenth Amendments were bitter. Few of those who fought for these changes were satisfied with the amendments themselves; fewer still were satisfied with their interpretation. Although the amendments put an end to the legal status of slavery, it was nearly a hundred years after the amendments' passage before most of the descendants of former slaves could begin to experience the economic, social, and political equality the amendments were intended to provide.

Unratified Amendment

Corwin Amendment
(proposed by Congress March 2, 1861)

No amendment shall be made to the Constitution which will authorize or give to Congress the power to abolish or interfere, within any State, with the domestic institutions thereof, including that of persons held to labor or service by the laws of said State.

• • •

Following the election of Abraham Lincoln, Congress scrambled to try to prevent the secession of the slaveholding states. House member Thomas Corwin of Ohio proposed the "unamendable" amendment in the hope that by protecting slavery where it existed, Congress would keep the southern states in the Union. Lincoln indicated his support for the proposed amendment in his first inaugural address. Only Ohio and Maryland ratified the Corwin Amendment before the war caused it to be forgotten.

Amendment XIII [1865]

Section 1. Neither slavery nor involuntary servitude, except as a punishment for crime whereof the party shall have been duly convicted, shall exist within the United States, or any place subject to their jurisdiction.

Section 2. Congress shall have power to enforce this article by appropriate legislation.

• • •

Because the Emancipation Proclamation of 1863 abolished slavery only in the parts of the Confederacy still in rebellion, Republicans proposed a Thirteenth Amendment that would extend abolition to the entire South. In February 1865, when the proposal was approved by the House, the gallery of the House was newly opened to black Americans who had a chance at last to see their government at work. Passage of the proposal was greeted by wild cheers from the gallery as well as tears on the House floor, where congressional representatives openly embraced one another.

The problem of ratification remained, however. The Union position was that the Confederate states were part of the country of thirty-six states. Therefore, twenty-seven states were needed to ratify the amendment. When Kentucky and Delaware rejected it, backers realized that without approval from at least four former Confederate states, the amendment would fail. Lincoln's successor, President Andrew Johnson, made ratification of the Thirteenth Amendment a condition for southern states to rejoin the Union. Under those terms, all the former Confederate states except Mississippi accepted the Thirteenth Amendment, and by the end of 1865 the amendment had become part of the Constitution and slavery had been prohibited in the United States.

Amendment XIV [1868]

Section 1. All persons born or naturalized in the United States, and subject to the jurisdiction thereof, are citizens of the United States and of the State wherein they reside. No State shall make or enforce any law which shall abridge the privileges or immunities of citizens of the United States; nor shall any State deprive any person of life, liberty, or property, without due process of law; nor deny to any person within its jurisdiction the equal protection of the laws.

Section 2. Representatives shall be apportioned among the several States according to their respective numbers, counting the whole number of persons in each State, excluding Indians not taxed. But when the right to vote at any election for the choice of electors for President and Vice-President of the United States, Representatives in Congress, the Executive and Judicial officers of a State, or the members of the Legislature thereof, is denied to any of the male inhabitants of such State, being twenty-one years of age and citizens of the United States, or in any way abridged, except for participation in rebellion, or other crime, the basis of representation therein shall be reduced in the proportion which the number of such male citizens shall bear to the whole number of male citizens twenty-one years of age in such State.

Section 3. No person shall be a Senator or Representative in Congress, or Elector of President and Vice-President, or hold any office, civil or military, under the United States, or under any State, who, having previously taken an oath, as a member of Congress, or as an officer of the United States, or as a member of any State legislature, or as an executive or judicial officer of any State, to support the Constitution of the United States, shall have engaged in insurrection or rebellion against the same, or given aid or comfort to the enemies thereof. Congress may, by a vote of two-thirds of each house, remove such disability.

Section 4. The validity of the public debt of the United States, authorized by law, including debts incurred for payment of pensions and bounties for services in suppressing insurrection or rebellion, shall not be questioned. But neither the United States nor any State shall assume or pay any debt or obligation incurred in aid of insurrection or rebellion against the United States, or any claim for the loss or emancipation of any slave; but all such debts, obligations, and claims shall be held illegal and void.

Section 5. The Congress shall have power to enforce, by appropriate legislation, the provisions of this article.

• • •

Without Lincoln's leadership in the reconstruction of the nation following the Civil War, it soon became clear that the Thirteenth Amendment needed additional constitutional support. Less than a year after Lincoln's assassination, Andrew Johnson was ready to bring the former Confederate states back into the Union with few changes in their governments or politics. Anxious Republicans drafted the Fourteenth Amendment to prevent that from happening. The most important provisions of this complex amendment made all native-born or naturalized persons American citizens and prohibited states from abridging the "privileges or immunities" of citizens; depriving them of "life, liberty, or property, without due process of law"; and denying them "equal protection of the laws." In essence, it made all former slaves citizens and protected the rights of all citizens against violation by their own state governments.

As occurred in the case of the Thirteenth Amendment, former Confederate states were forced to ratify the amendment as a condition of representation in the House and the Senate. The intentions of the Fourteenth Amendment, and how those intentions should be enforced, have been the most debated point of constitutional history. The terms due process *and* equal protection *have been especially troublesome. Was the amendment designed to outlaw racial segregation? Or was the goal simply to prevent the leaders of the rebellious South from gaining political power?*

The framers of the Fourteenth Amendment hoped Section 2 would produce black voters who would increase the power of the Republican Party. The federal government, however, never used its power to punish states for denying blacks their right to vote. Although the Fourteenth Amendment had an immediate impact in giving black Americans citizenship, it did nothing to protect blacks from the vengeance of whites once Reconstruction ended. In the late nineteenth and early twentieth centuries, Section 1 of the Fourteenth Amendment was often used to protect business interests and strike down laws protecting workers on the grounds that the rights of "persons," that is, corporations, were protected by "due process." More recently, the Fourteenth Amendment has been used to justify school desegregation and affirmative action programs, as well as to dismantle such programs.

Amendment XV [1870]

Section 1. The right of citizens of the United States to vote shall not be denied or abridged by the United States or by any State on account of race, color, or previous condition of servitude—

Section 2. The Congress shall have power to enforce this article by appropriate legislation.

• • •

The Fifteenth Amendment was the last major piece of Reconstruction legislation. Although earlier Reconstruction acts had already required black suffrage in the South, the Fifteenth Amendment extended black voting rights to the entire nation. Some Republicans felt morally obligated to do away with the double standard between the North and South because many

northern states had stubbornly refused to enfranchise blacks. Others believed that the freedman's ballot required the extra protection of a constitutional amendment to shield it from white counterattack. But partisan advantage also played an important role in the amendment's passage because Republicans hoped that by giving the ballot to northern blacks, they could lessen their party's political vulnerability.

Many women's rights advocates had fought for the amendment. They had felt betrayed by the inclusion of the word male *in Section 2 of the Fourteenth Amendment and were further angered when the proposed Fifteenth Amendment failed to prohibit denial of the right to vote on the grounds of sex as well as "race, color, or previous condition of servitude." In this amendment, for the first time, the federal government claimed the power to regulate the franchise, or vote. It was also the first time the Constitution placed limits on the power of the states to regulate access to the franchise. Although ratified in 1870, however, the amendment was not enforced until the twentieth century.*

The Progressive Amendments
(Sixteenth–Nineteenth Amendments)

No amendments were added to the Constitution between the Civil War and the Progressive Era. America was changing, however, in fundamental ways. The rapid industrialization of the United States after the Civil War led to many social and economic problems. Hundreds of amendments were proposed, but none received enough support in Congress to be sent to the states. Some scholars believe that regional differences and rivalries were so strong during this period that it was almost impossible to gain a consensus on a constitutional amendment. During the Progressive Era, however, the Constitution was amended four times in seven years.

Amendment XVI [1913]

The Congress shall have power to lay and collect taxes on incomes, from whatever source derived, without apportionment among the several States, and without regard to any census or enumeration.

• • •

Until passage of the Sixteenth Amendment, most of the money used to run the federal government came from customs duties and taxes on specific items, such as liquor. During the Civil War the federal government taxed incomes as an emergency measure. Pressure to enact an income tax came from those who were concerned about the growing gap between rich and poor in the United States. The Populist Party began campaigning for a graduated income tax in 1892, and support continued to grow. By 1909 thirty-three proposed income tax amendments had been presented in Congress, but lobbying by corporate and other special interests had defeated them all. In June 1909 the growing pressure for an income tax, which had been endorsed by Presidents Roosevelt and Taft, finally pushed an amendment through the Senate. The required thirty-six states had ratified the amendment by February 1913.

Amendment XVII [1913]

Section 1. The Senate of the United States shall be composed of two Senators from each State, elected by the people thereof, for six years; and each Senator shall have one vote. The electors in each State shall have the qualifications requisite for electors of [voters for] the most numerous branch of the State legislatures.

Section 2. When vacancies happen in the representation of any State in the Senate, the executive authority of such State shall issue writs of election to fill such vacancies: Provided, that the Legislature of any State may empower the executive thereof to make temporary appointments until the people fill the vacancies by election as the Legislature may direct.

Section 3. This amendment shall not be so construed as to affect the election or term of any Senator chosen before it becomes valid as part of the Constitution.

• • •

The framers of the Constitution saw the members of the House as the representatives of the people and the members of the Senate as the representatives of the states. Originally, senators were to be chosen by the state legislators. According to reform advocates, however, the growth of private industry and transportation conglomerates during the late nineteenth century had created a network of corruption in which wealth and power were exchanged for influence and votes in the Senate. Senator Nelson Aldrich, who represented Rhode Island in this period, for example, was known as "the senator from Standard Oil" because of his open support of special business interests.

Efforts to amend the Constitution to allow direct election of senators had begun in 1826, but because any proposal had to be approved by the Senate, reform seemed impossible. Progressives tried to gain influence in the Senate by instituting party caucuses and primary elections, which gave citizens the chance to express their choice of a senator who could then be officially elected by the state legislature. By 1910 fourteen of the country's thirty senators received popular votes through a state primary before the state legislature made its selection. Despairing of getting a proposal through the Senate, supporters of a direct-election amendment had begun in 1893 to seek a convention of representatives from two-thirds of the states to propose an amendment that could then be ratified. By 1905 thirty-one of forty-five states had endorsed such an amendment. Finally, in 1911, despite extraordinary opposition, a proposed amendment passed the Senate; by 1913 it had been ratified.

Amendment XVIII [1919; repealed 1933 by Amendment XXI]

Section 1. After one year from the ratification of this article the manufacture, sale, or transportation of intoxicating liquors within, the importation thereof into, or the exportation thereof from the United States and all territory subject to the jurisdiction thereof, for beverage purposes, is hereby prohibited.

Section 2. The Congress and the several States shall have concurrent power to enforce this article by appropriate legislation.

Section 3. This article shall be inoperative unless it shall have been ratified as an amendment to the Constitution by the legislatures of the several States, as provided by the Constitution, within seven years from the date of the submission thereof to the States by the Congress.

• • •

The Prohibition Party, formed in 1869, began calling for a constitutional amendment to outlaw alcoholic beverages in 1872. A prohibition amendment was first proposed in the Senate in 1876 and was revived eighteen times before 1913. Between 1913 and 1919 another thirty-nine attempts were made to prohibit liquor in the United States through a constitutional amendment. Prohibition became a key element of the Progressive agenda as reformers linked alcohol and drunkenness to numerous social problems, including the corruption of immigrant voters. Whereas opponents of such an amendment argued that it was undemocratic, supporters claimed that their efforts had widespread public support. The admission of twelve "dry" western states to the Union in the early twentieth century and the spirit of sacrifice during World War I laid the groundwork for passage and ratification of the Eighteenth Amendment in 1919. Opponents added a time limit to the amendment in the hope that they could thereby block ratification, but this effort failed. (See also Amendment XXI.)

Amendment XIX [1920]

Section 1. The right of citizens of the United States to vote shall not be denied or abridged by the United States or by any State on account of sex.

Section 2. Congress shall have the power to enforce this article by appropriate legislation.

• • •

Advocates of women's rights tried and failed to link woman suffrage to the Fourteenth and Fifteenth Amendments. Nonetheless, the effort for woman suffrage continued. Between 1878 and 1912 at least one and sometimes as many as four proposed amendments were introduced in Congress each year to grant women the right to vote. Although over time women won very limited voting rights in some states, at both the state and federal levels opposition to an amendment for woman suffrage remained very strong. President Woodrow Wilson and other officials felt that the federal government should not interfere with the power of the states in this matter. And many people were concerned that giving women the vote would result in their abandoning traditional gender roles. In 1919, following a protracted and often bitter campaign of protest in which women went on hunger strikes and chained themselves to fences, an amendment was introduced with the backing of President Wilson. It narrowly passed the Senate (after efforts to limit the suffrage to white women failed) and was adopted in 1920 after Tennessee became the thirty-sixth state to ratify it.

Unratified Amendment

Child Labor Amendment
(proposed by Congress June 2, 1924)

Section 1.   The Congress shall have power to limit, regulate, and prohibit the labor of persons under eighteen years of age.

Section 2.   The power of the several States is unimpaired by this article except that the operation of State laws shall be suspended to the extent necessary to give effect to legislation enacted by Congress.

• • •

Throughout the late nineteenth and early twentieth centuries, alarm over the condition of child workers grew. Opponents of child labor argued that children worked in dangerous and unhealthy conditions, that they took jobs from adult workers, that they depressed wages in certain industries, and that states that allowed child labor had an economic advantage over those that did not. Defenders of child labor claimed that children provided needed income in many families, that working at a young age helped to develop character, and that the effort to prohibit the practice constituted an invasion of family privacy.

In 1916 Congress passed a law that made it illegal to sell through interstate commerce goods made by children. The Supreme Court, however, ruled that the law violated the limits on the power of Congress to regulate interstate commerce. Congress then tried to penalize industries that used child labor by taxing such goods. This measure was also thrown out by the courts. In response, reformers set out to amend the Constitution. The proposed amendment was ratified by twenty-eight states, but by 1925 thirteen states had rejected it. Passage of the Fair Labor Standards Act in 1938, which was upheld by the Supreme Court in 1941, made the amendment irrelevant.

Amendment XX [1933]

Section 1.   The terms of the President and Vice-President shall end at noon on the 20th day of January, and the terms of Senators and Representatives at noon on the 3rd day of January, of the years in which such terms would have ended if this article had not been ratified; and the terms of their successors shall then begin.

Section 2.   The Congress shall assemble at least once in every year, and such meeting shall begin at noon on the 3rd day of January, unless they shall by law appoint a different day.

Section 3.   If, at the time fixed for the beginning of the term of the President, the President-elect shall have died, the Vice-President-elect shall become President. If a President shall not have been chosen before the time fixed for the beginning of his term, or if the President-elect shall have failed to qualify, then the Vice-President-elect shall act as President until a President shall have qualified; and the Congress may by law provide for the case wherein neither a President-elect nor a Vice-President-elect shall have qualified, declaring who shall then act as President, or the manner in which one who is to act shall be selected, and such person shall act accordingly until a President or Vice-President shall have qualified.

Section 4.   The Congress may by law provide for the case of the death of any of the persons from whom the House of Representatives may choose a President whenever the right of choice shall have devolved upon them, and for the case of the death of any of the persons from whom the Senate may choose a Vice-President whenever the right of choice shall have devolved upon them.

Section 5.   Sections 1 and 2 shall take effect on the 15th day of October following the ratification of this article.

Section 6.   This article shall be inoperative unless it shall have been ratified as an amendment to the Constitution by the Legislatures of three-fourths of the several States within seven years from the date of its submission.

• • •

Until 1933, presidents took office on March 4. Because elections are held in early November and electoral votes are counted in mid-December, this meant that more than three months passed between the time a new president was elected and when he took office. Moving the inauguration to January shortened the transition period and allowed Congress to begin its term closer to the time of the president's inauguration. Although this seems like a minor change, an amendment was required because the Constitution specifies terms of office. This amendment also deals with questions of succession in the event that a president- or vice-president-elect dies before assuming office. Section 3 also clarifies a method for resolving a deadlock in the electoral college.

Amendment XXI [1933]

Section 1.   The eighteenth article of amendment to the Constitution of the United States is hereby repealed.

Section 2.   The transportation or importation into any State, Territory, or Possession of the United States for delivery or use therein of intoxicating liquors, in violation of the laws thereof, is hereby prohibited.

Section 3.   This article shall be inoperative unless it shall have been ratified as an amendment to the Constitution by conventions in the several States, as provided in the Constitution, within seven years from the date of the submission thereof to the States by the Congress.

• • •

Widespread violation of the Volstead Act, the law enacted to enforce prohibition, made the United States a nation of lawbreakers. Prohibition caused more problems than it solved by encouraging crime, bribery, and corruption. Further, a coalition of liquor and beer manufacturers, personal liberty advocates, and constitutional scholars joined forces to challenge the amendment. By 1929 thirty proposed repeal amendments had been introduced in Congress, and the Democratic Party made repeal part of its platform in the 1932 presidential campaign. The Twenty-first Amendment was proposed in February 1933 and ratified less than a year later. The failure of the effort to enforce prohibition through a constitutional amendment has often been cited by opponents of subsequent efforts to shape public virtue and private morality.

Amendment XXII [1951]

Section 1. No person shall be elected to the office of the President more than twice, and no person who has held the office of President, or acted as President, for more than two years of a term to which some other person was elected President shall be elected to the office of President more than once. But this article shall not apply to any person holding the office of President when this Article was proposed by the Congress, and shall not prevent any person who may be holding the office of President, or acting as President, during the term within which this Article becomes operative from holding the office of President or acting as President during the remainder of such term.

Section 2. This article shall be inoperative unless it shall have been ratified as an amendment to the Constitution by the legislatures of three-fourths of the several States within seven years from the date of its submission to the States by the Congress.

• • •

George Washington's refusal to seek a third term of office set a precedent that stood until 1912, when former president Theodore Roosevelt sought, without success, another term as an independent candidate. Democrat Franklin Roosevelt was the only president to seek and win a fourth term, though he did so amid great controversy. Roosevelt died in April 1945, a few months after the beginning of his fourth term. In 1946 Republicans won control of the House and the Senate, and early in 1947 a proposal for an amendment to limit future presidents to two four-year terms was offered to the states for ratification. Democratic critics of the Twenty-second Amendment charged that it was a partisan posthumous jab at Roosevelt.

Since the Twenty-second Amendment was adopted, two of the three presidents who might have been able to seek a third term, had it not existed, were Republicans Dwight Eisenhower and Ronald Reagan. Since 1826, Congress has entertained 160 proposed amendments to limit the president to one six-year term. Such amendments have been backed by fifteen presidents, including Gerald Ford and Jimmy Carter.

Amendment XXIII [1961]

Section 1. The District constituting the seat of Government of the United States shall appoint in such manner as the Congress may direct: A number of electors of President and Vice-President equal to the whole number of Senators and Representatives in Congress to which the District would be entitled if it were a State, but in no event more than the least populous State; they shall be in addition to those appointed by the States, but they shall be considered for the purposes of the election of President and Vice-President, to be electors appointed by a State; and they shall meet in the District and perform such duties as provided by the twelfth article of amendment.

Section 2. The Congress shall have the power to enforce this article by appropriate legislation.

• • •

When Washington, D.C., was established as a federal district, no one expected that a significant number of people would make it their permanent and primary residence. A proposal to allow citizens of the district to vote in presidential elections was approved by Congress in June 1960 and was ratified on March 29, 1961.

Amendment XXIV [1964]

Section 1. The right of citizens of the United States to vote in any primary or other election for President or Vice-President, for electors for President or Vice-President, or for Senator or Representative in Congress, shall not be denied or abridged by the United States or any State by reason of failure to pay any poll tax or other tax.

Section 2. The Congress shall have the power to enforce this article by appropriate legislation.

• • •

In the colonial and Revolutionary eras, financial independence was seen as necessary to political independence, and the poll tax was used as a requirement for voting. By the twentieth century, however, the poll tax was used mostly to bar poor people, especially southern blacks, from voting. Although conservatives complained that the amendment interfered with states' rights, liberals thought that the amendment did not go far enough because it barred the poll tax only in national elections and not in state or local elections. The amendment was ratified in 1964, however, and two years later the Supreme Court ruled that poll taxes in state and local elections also violated the equal protection clause of the Fourteenth Amendment.

Amendment XXV [1967]

Section 1. In case of the removal of the President from office or of his death or resignation, the Vice-President shall become President.

Section 2. Whenever there is a vacancy in the office of the Vice-President, the President shall nominate a Vice-President who shall take office upon confirmation by a majority vote of both Houses of Congress.

Section 3. Whenever the President transmits to the President pro tempore of the Senate and the Speaker of the House of Representatives his written declaration that he is unable to discharge the powers and duties of his office, and until he transmits to them a written declaration to the contrary, such powers and duties shall be discharged by the Vice-President as Acting President.

Section 4. Whenever the Vice-President and a majority of either the principal officers of the executive departments or of such other body as Congress may by law provide, transmit to the President pro tempore of the Senate and the Speaker of the House of Representatives their written declaration that the President is unable to discharge the powers and duties of his office, the Vice-President shall immediately assume the powers and duties of the office as Acting President.

Thereafter, when the President transmits to the President pro tempore of the Senate and the Speaker of the House of Representatives his written declaration that no inability exists, he shall resume the powers and duties of his office unless the Vice-President and a majority of either the principal officers of the executive department[s] or of such other body as Congress may by law provide, transmit within four days to the President pro tempore of the Senate and the Speaker of the House of Representatives their written declaration that the President is unable to discharge the powers and duties of his office. Thereupon Congress shall decide the issue, assembling within forty-eight hours for that purpose if not in session. If the Congress, within twenty-one days after receipt of the latter written declaration, or, if Congress is not in session, within twenty-one days after Congress is required to assemble, determines by two-thirds vote of both Houses that the President is unable to discharge the powers and duties of his office, the Vice-President shall continue to discharge the same as Acting President; otherwise, the President shall resume the powers and duties of his office.

• • •

The framers of the Constitution established the office of vice president because someone was needed to preside over the Senate. The first president to die in office was William Henry Harrison, in 1841. Vice President John Tyler had himself sworn in as president, setting a precedent that was followed when seven later presidents died in office. The assassination of President James A. Garfield in 1881 posed a new problem, however. After he was shot, the president was incapacitated for two months before he died; he was unable to lead the country, and his vice president, Chester A. Arthur, was unable to assume leadership. Efforts to resolve questions of succession in the event of a presidential disability thus began with the death of Garfield.

In 1963 the assassination of President John F. Kennedy galvanized Congress to action. Vice President Lyndon Johnson was a chain-smoker with a history of heart trouble. According to the 1947 Presidential Succession Act, the two men who stood in line to succeed him were the seventy-two-year-old Speaker of the House and the eighty-six-year-old president of the Senate. There were serious concerns that any of these men might become incapacitated while serving as chief executive. The first time the Twenty-fifth Amendment was used, however, was not in the case of presidential death or illness, but during the Watergate crisis. When Vice President Spiro T. Agnew was forced to resign following allegations of bribery and tax violations, President Richard M. Nixon appointed House Minority Leader Gerald R. Ford vice president. Ford became president following Nixon's resignation eight months later and named Nelson A. Rockefeller as his vice president. Thus, for more than two years, the two highest offices in the country were held by people who had not been elected to them.

Amendment XXVI [1971]

Section 1.   The right of citizens of the United States, who are eighteen years of age or older, to vote shall not be denied or abridged by the United States or by any State on account of age.

Section 2.   The Congress shall have power to enforce this article by appropriate legislation.

• • •

Efforts to lower the voting age from twenty-one to eighteen began during World War II. Recognizing that those who were old enough to fight a war should have some say in the government policies that involved them in the war, Presidents Eisenhower, Johnson, and Nixon endorsed the idea. In 1970 the combined pressure of the antiwar movement and the demographic pressure of the baby-boom generation led to a Voting Rights Act lowering the voting age in federal, state, and local elections.

In Oregon v. Mitchell (1970), the state of Oregon challenged the right of Congress to determine the age at which people could vote in state or local elections. The Supreme Court agreed with Oregon. Because the Voting Rights Act was ruled unconstitutional, the Constitution had to be amended to allow passage of a law that would lower the voting age. The amendment was ratified in a little more than three months, making it the most rapidly ratified amendment in U.S. history.

Unratified Amendment

Equal Rights Amendment (proposed by Congress March 22, 1972; seven-year deadline for ratification extended, June 30, 1982)

Section 1.   Equality of rights under the law shall not be denied or abridged by the United States or by any State on account of sex.

Section 2.   The Congress shall have the power to enforce, by appropriate legislation, the provisions of this article.

Section 3.   This amendment shall take effect two years after the date of ratification.

• • •

In 1923, soon after women had won the right to vote, Alice Paul, a leading activist in the woman suffrage movement, proposed an amendment requiring equal treatment of men and women. Opponents of the proposal argued that such an amendment would invalidate laws that protected women and would make women subject to the military draft. After the 1964 Civil Rights Act was adopted, protective workplace legislation was removed anyway.

The renewal of the women's movement, as a by-product of the civil rights and antiwar movements, led to a revival of the Equal Rights Amendment (ERA) in Congress. Disagreements over language held up congressional passage of the proposed amendment, but on March 22, 1972, the Senate approved the ERA by a vote of 84 to 8, and it was sent to the states. Six states ratified the amendment within two days, and by the middle of 1973 the amendment seemed well on its way to adoption, with thirty of the needed thirty-eight states having ratified it. In the mid-1970s, however, a powerful "Stop ERA" campaign developed. The campaign portrayed the ERA as a threat to "family values" and traditional relationships between men and women. Although thirty-five states ratified the ERA, five of those state legislatures voted to rescind ratification, and the amendment was never adopted.

Unratified Amendment

D.C. Statehood Amendment
(proposed by Congress August 22, 1978)

Section 1. For purposes of representation in the Congress, election of the President and Vice President, and article V of this Constitution, the District constituting the seat of government of the United States shall be treated as though it were a State.

Section 2. The exercise of the rights and powers conferred under this article shall be by the people of the District constituting the seat of government, and as shall be provided by Congress.

Section 3. The twenty-third article of amendment to the Constitution of the United States is hereby repealed.

Section 4. This article shall be inoperative, unless it shall have been ratified as an amendment to the Constitution by the legislatures of three-fourths of the several states within seven years from the date of its submission.

• • •

The 1961 ratification of the Twenty-third Amendment, giving residents of the District of Columbia the right to vote for a president and vice president, inspired an effort to give residents of the district full voting rights. In 1966 President Lyndon Johnson appointed a mayor and city council; in 1971 D.C. residents were allowed to name a nonvoting delegate to the House; and in 1981 residents were allowed to elect the mayor and city council. Congress retained the right to overrule laws that might affect commuters, the height of federal buildings, and selection of judges and prosecutors. The district's nonvoting delegate to Congress, Walter Fauntroy, lobbied fiercely for a congressional amendment granting statehood to the district. In 1978 a proposed amendment was approved and sent to the states. A number of states quickly ratified the amendment, but, like the ERA, the D.C. Statehood Amendment ran into trouble. Opponents argued that Section 2 created a separate category of "nominal" statehood. They argued that the federal district should be eliminated and that the territory should be reabsorbed into the state of Maryland. Most scholars believe that the fears of Republicans that the predominantly black population of the city would consistently elect Democratic senators constituted a major factor leading to the defeat of the amendment.

Amendment XXVII [1992]

No law varying the compensation for the services of the Senators and Representatives, shall take effect, until an election of Representatives shall have intervened.

• • •

Whereas the Twenty-sixth Amendment was the most rapidly ratified amendment in U.S. history, the Twenty-seventh Amendment had the longest journey to ratification. First proposed by James Madison in 1789 as part of the package that included the Bill of Rights, this amendment had been ratified by only six states by 1791. In 1873, however, it was ratified by Ohio to protest a massive retroactive salary increase by the federal government. Unlike later proposed amendments, this one came with no time limit on ratification. In the early 1980s Gregory D. Watson, a University of Texas economics major, discovered the "lost" amendment and began a single-handed campaign to get state legislators to introduce it for ratification. In 1983 it was accepted by Maine. In 1984 it passed the Colorado legislature. Ratifications trickled in slowly until May 1992, when Michigan and New Jersey became the thirty-eighth and thirty-ninth states, respectively, to ratify. This amendment prevents members of Congress from raising their own salaries without giving voters a chance to vote them out of office before they can benefit from the raises.

The American Nation

Admission of States into the Union

State	Date of Admission	State	Date of Admission	State	Date of Admission
1. Delaware	December 7, 1787	18. Louisiana	April 30, 1812	35. West Virginia	June 20, 1863
2. Pennsylvania	December 12, 1787	19. Indiana	December 11, 1816	36. Nevada	October 31, 1864
3. New Jersey	December 18, 1787	20. Mississippi	December 10, 1817	37. Nebraska	March 1, 1867
4. Georgia	January 2, 1788	21. Illinois	December 3, 1818	38. Colorado	August 1, 1876
5. Connecticut	January 9, 1788	22. Alabama	December 14, 1819	39. North Dakota	November 2, 1889
6. Massachusetts	February 6, 1788	23. Maine	March 15, 1820	40. South Dakota	November 2, 1889
7. Maryland	April 28, 1788	24. Missouri	August 10, 1821	41. Montana	November 8, 1889
8. South Carolina	May 23, 1788	25. Arkansas	June 15, 1836	42. Washington	November 11, 1889
9. New Hampshire	June 21, 1788	26. Michigan	January 26, 1837	43. Idaho	July 3, 1890
10. Virginia	June 25, 1788	27. Florida	March 3, 1845	44. Wyoming	July 10, 1890
11. New York	July 26, 1788	28. Texas	December 29, 1845	45. Utah	January 4, 1896
12. North Carolina	November 21, 1789	29. Iowa	December 28, 1846	46. Oklahoma	November 16, 1907
13. Rhode Island	May 29, 1790	30. Wisconsin	May 29, 1848	47. New Mexico	January 6, 1912
14. Vermont	March 4, 1791	31. California	September 9, 1850	48. Arizona	February 14, 1912
15. Kentucky	June 1, 1792	32. Minnesota	May 11, 1858	49. Alaska	January 3, 1959
16. Tennessee	June 1, 1796	33. Oregon	February 14, 1859	50. Hawaii	August 21, 1959
17. Ohio	March 1, 1803	34. Kansas	January 29, 1861		

Territorial Expansion

Territory	Date Acquired	Square Miles	How Acquired
Original states and territories	1783	888,685	Treaty of Paris
Louisiana Purchase	1803	827,192	Purchased from France
Florida	1819	72,003	Adams-Onís Treaty
Texas	1845	390,143	Annexation of independent country
Oregon	1846	285,580	Oregon Boundary Treaty
Mexican cession	1848	529,017	Treaty of Guadalupe Hidalgo
Gadsden Purchase	1853	29,640	Purchased from Mexico
Midway Islands	1867	2	Annexation of uninhabited islands
Alaska	1867	589,757	Purchased from Russia
Hawaii	1898	6,450	Annexation of independent country
Wake Island	1898	3	Annexation of uninhabited island
Puerto Rico	1899	3,435	Treaty of Paris
Guam	1899	212	Treaty of Paris
The Philippines	1899–1946	115,600	Treaty of Paris; granted independence
American Samoa	1900	76	Treaty with Germany and Great Britain
Panama Canal Zone	1904–1978	553	Hay–Bunau-Varilla Treaty
U.S. Virgin Islands	1917	133	Purchased from Denmark
Trust Territory of the Pacific Islands*	1947	717	United Nations Trusteeship

*A number of these islands have recently been granted independence: Federated States of Micronesia, 1990; Marshall Islands, 1991; Palau, 1994.

Presidential Elections

Year	Candidates	Parties	Percentage of Popular Vote	Electoral Vote	Percentage of Voter Participation
1789	**George Washington**	No party designations	*	69	
	John Adams†			34	
	Other candidates			35	
1792	**George Washington**	No party designations		132	
	John Adams			77	
	George Clinton			50	
	Other candidates			5	
1796	**John Adams**	Federalist		71	
	Thomas Jefferson	Democratic-Republican		68	
	Thomas Pinckney	Federalist		59	
	Aaron Burr	Democratic-Republican		30	
	Other candidates			48	
1800	**Thomas Jefferson**	Democratic-Republican		73	
	Aaron Burr	Democratic-Republican		73	
	John Adams	Federalist		65	
	Charles C. Pinckney	Federalist		64	
	John Jay	Federalist		1	
1804	**Thomas Jefferson**	Democratic-Republican		162	
	Charles C. Pinckney	Federalist		14	
1808	**James Madison**	Democratic-Republican		122	
	Charles C. Pinckney	Federalist		47	
	George Clinton	Democratic-Republican		6	
1812	**James Madison**	Democratic-Republican		128	
	De Witt Clinton	Federalist		89	
1816	**James Monroe**	Democratic-Republican		183	
	Rufus King	Federalist		34	
1820	**James Monroe**	Democratic-Republican		231	
	John Quincy Adams	Independent Republican		1	
1824	**John Quincy Adams**	Democratic-Republican	30.5	84	26.9
	Andrew Jackson	Democratic-Republican	43.1	99	
	Henry Clay	Democratic-Republican	13.2	37	
	William H. Crawford	Democratic-Republican	13.1	41	
1828	**Andrew Jackson**	Democratic	56.0	178	57.6
	John Quincy Adams	National Republican	44.0	83	
1832	**Andrew Jackson**	Democratic	54.5	219	55.4
	Henry Clay	National Republican	37.5	49	
	William Wirt	Anti-Masonic	8.0	7	
	John Floyd	Democratic	‡	11	
1836	**Martin Van Buren**	Democratic	50.9	170	57.8
	William H. Harrison	Whig		73	
	Hugh L. White	Whig		26	
	Daniel Webster	Whig	49.1	14	
	W. P. Mangum	Whig		11	
1840	**William H. Harrison**	Whig	53.1	234	80.2
	Martin Van Buren	Democratic	46.9	60	
1844	**James K. Polk**	Democratic	49.6	170	78.9
	Henry Clay	Whig	48.1	105	
	James G. Birney	Liberty	2.3		

(*continued on next page*)

*Prior to 1824, most presidential electors were chosen by state legislators rather than by popular vote.

†Before the Twelfth Amendment was passed in 1804, the electoral college voted for two presidential candidates; the runner-up became vice-president.

‡Percentages below 2.5 have been omitted. Hence the percentage of popular vote might not total 100 percent.

Year	Candidates	Parties	Percentage of Popular Vote	Electoral Vote	Percentage of Voter Participation
1848	**Zachary Taylor**	Whig	47.4	163	72.7
	Lewis Cass	Democratic	42.5	127	
	Martin Van Buren	Free Soil	10.1		
1852	**Franklin Pierce**	Democratic	50.9	254	69.6
	Winfield Scott	Whig	44.1	42	
	John P. Hale	Free Soil	5.0		
1856	**James Buchanan**	Democratic	45.3	174	78.9
	John C. Frémont	Republican	33.1	114	
	Millard Fillmore	American	21.6	8	
1860	**Abraham Lincoln**	Republican	39.8	180	81.2
	Stephen A. Douglas	Democratic	29.5	12	
	John C. Breckinridge	Democratic	18.1	72	
	John Bell	Constitutional Union	12.6	39	
1864	**Abraham Lincoln**	Republican	55.0	212	73.8
	George B. McClellan	Democratic	45.0	21	
1868	**Ulysses S. Grant**	Republican	52.7	214	78.1
	Horatio Seymour	Democratic	47.3	80	
1872	**Ulysses S. Grant**	Republican	55.6	286	71.3
	Horace Greeley	Democratic	43.9		
1876	**Rutherford B. Hayes**	Republican	48.0	185	81.8
	Samuel J. Tilden	Democratic	51.0	184	
1880	**James A. Garfield**	Republican	48.5	214	79.4
	Winfield S. Hancock	Democratic	48.1	155	
	James B. Weaver	Greenback-Labor	3.4		
1884	**Grover Cleveland**	Democratic	48.5	219	77.5
	James G. Blaine	Republican	48.2	182	
1888	**Benjamin Harrison**	Republican	47.9	233	79.3
	Grover Cleveland	Democratic	48.6	168	
1892	**Grover Cleveland**	Democratic	46.1	277	74.7
	Benjamin Harrison	Republican	43.0	145	
	James B. Weaver	People's	8.5	22	
1896	**William McKinley**	Republican	51.1	271	79.3
	William J. Bryan	Democratic	47.7	176	
1900	**William McKinley**	Republican	51.7	292	73.2
	William J. Bryan	Democratic; Populist	45.5	155	
1904	**Theodore Roosevelt**	Republican	57.4	336	65.2
	Alton B. Parker	Democratic	37.6	140	
	Eugene V. Debs	Socialist	3.0		
1908	**William H. Taft**	Republican	51.6	321	65.4
	William J. Bryan	Democratic	43.1	162	
	Eugene V. Debs	Socialist	2.8		
1912	**Woodrow Wilson**	Democratic	41.9	435	58.8
	Theodore Roosevelt	Progressive	27.4	88	
	William H. Taft	Republican	23.2	8	
	Eugene V. Debs	Socialist	6.0		
1916	**Woodrow Wilson**	Democratic	49.4	277	61.6
	Charles E. Hughes	Republican	46.2	254	
	A. L. Benson	Socialist	3.2		

(*continued on next page*)

Year	Candidates	Parties	Percentage of Popular Vote	Electoral Vote	Percentage of Voter Participation
1920	**Warren G. Harding**	Republican	60.4	404	49.2
	James M. Cox	Democratic	34.2	127	
	Eugene V. Debs	Socialist	3.4		
1924	**Calvin Coolidge**	Republican	54.0	382	48.9
	John W. Davis	Democratic	28.8	136	
	Robert M. La Follette	Progressive	16.6	13	
1928	**Herbert C. Hoover**	Republican	58.2	444	56.9
	Alfred E. Smith	Democratic	40.9	87	
1932	**Franklin D. Roosevelt**	Democratic	57.4	472	56.9
	Herbert C. Hoover	Republican	39.7	59	
1936	**Franklin D. Roosevelt**	Democratic	60.8	523	61.0
	Alfred M. Landon	Republican	36.5	8	
1940	**Franklin D. Roosevelt**	Democratic	54.8	449	62.5
	Wendell L. Willkie	Republican	44.8	82	
1944	**Franklin D. Roosevelt**	Democratic	53.5	432	55.9
	Thomas E. Dewey	Republican	46.0	99	
1948	**Harry S Truman**	Democratic	49.6	303	53.0
	Thomas E. Dewey	Republican	45.1	189	
1952	**Dwight D. Eisenhower**	Republican	55.1	442	63.3
	Adlai E. Stevenson	Democratic	44.4	89	
1956	**Dwight D. Eisenhower**	Republican	57.6	457	60.6
	Adlai E. Stevenson	Democratic	42.1	73	
1960	**John F. Kennedy**	Democratic	49.7	303	64.0
	Richard M. Nixon	Republican	49.5	219	
1964	**Lyndon B. Johnson**	Democratic	61.1	486	61.7
	Barry M. Goldwater	Republican	38.5	52	
1968	**Richard M. Nixon**	Republican	43.4	301	60.6
	Hubert H. Humphrey	Democratic	42.7	191	
	George C. Wallace	American Independent	13.5	46	
1972	**Richard M. Nixon**	Republican	60.7	520	55.5
	George S. McGovern	Democratic	37.5	17	
1976	**Jimmy Carter**	Democratic	50.1	297	54.3
	Gerald R. Ford	Republican	48.0	240	
1980	**Ronald W. Reagan**	Republican	50.7	489	53.0
	Jimmy Carter	Democratic	41.0	49	
	John B. Anderson	Independent	6.6	0	
1984	**Ronald W. Reagan**	Republican	58.4	525	52.9
	Walter F. Mondale	Democratic	41.6	13	
1988	**George H. W. Bush**	Republican	53.4	426	50.3
	Michael Dukakis	Democratic	45.6	111*	
1992	**Bill Clinton**	Democratic	43.7	370	55.1
	George H. W. Bush	Republican	38.0	168	
	H. Ross Perot	Independent	19.0	0	
1996	**Bill Clinton**	Democratic	49	379	49.0
	Robert J. Dole	Republican	41	159	
	H. Ross Perot	Reform	8	0	
2000	**George W. Bush**	Republican	47.8	271	51.3
	Albert Gore	Democratic	48.4	267	
	Ralph Nader	Green	0.4	0	

*One Dukakis elector cast a vote for Lloyd Bentsen.

Supreme Court Justices

Name	Terms of Service	Appointed by	Name	Terms of Service	Appointed by
John Jay*, N.Y.	1789–1795	Washington	Joseph McKenna, Cal.	1898–1925	McKinley
James Wilson, Pa.	1789–1798	Washington	Oliver W. Holmes, Mass.	1902–1932	T. Roosevelt
John Rutledge, S.C.	1790–1791	Washington	William R. Day, Ohio	1903–1922	T. Roosevelt
William Cushing, Mass.	1790–1810	Washington	William H. Moody, Mass.	1906–1910	T. Roosevelt
John Blair, Va.	1790–1796	Washington	Horace H. Lurton, Tenn.	1910–1914	Taft
James Iredell, N.C.	1790–1799	Washington	Charles E. Hughes, N.Y.	1910–1916	Taft
Thomas Johnson, Md.	1792–1793	Washington	**Edward D. White**, La.	1910–1921	Taft
William Paterson, N.J.	1793–1806	Washington	Willis Van Devanter, Wy.	1911–1937	Taft
John Rutledge, S.C.	1795	Washington	Joseph R. Lamar, Ga.	1911–1916	Taft
Samuel Chase, Md.	1796–1811	Washington	Mahlon Pitney, N.J.	1912–1922	Taft
Oliver Ellsworth, Conn.	1796–1800	Washington	James C. McReynolds, Tenn.	1914–1941	Wilson
Bushrod Washington, Va.	1799–1829	J. Adams	Louis D. Brandeis, Mass.	1916–1939	Wilson
Alfred Moore, N.C.	1800–1804	J. Adams	John H. Clarke, Ohio	1916–1922	Wilson
John Marshall, Va.	1801–1835	J. Adams	**William H. Taft**, Conn.	1921–1930	Harding
William Johnson, S.C.	1804–1834	Jefferson	George Sutherland, Utah	1922–1938	Harding
Brockholst Livingston, N.Y.	1807–1823	Jefferson	Pierce Butler, Minn.	1923–1939	Harding
Thomas Todd, Ky.	1807–1826	Jefferson	Edward T. Sanford, Tenn.	1923–1930	Harding
Gabriel Duvall, Md.	1811–1835	Madison	Harlan F. Stone, N.Y.	1925–1941	Coolidge
Joseph Story, Mass.	1812–1845	Madison	**Charles E. Hughes**, N.Y.	1930–1941	Hoover
Smith Thompson, N.Y.	1823–1843	Monroe	Owen J. Roberts, Pa.	1930–1945	Hoover
Robert Trimble, Ky.	1826–1828	J. Q. Adams	Benjamin N. Cardozo, N.Y.	1932–1938	Hoover
John McLean, Ohio	1830–1861	Jackson	Hugo L. Black, Ala.	1937–1971	F. Roosevelt
Henry Baldwin, Pa.	1830–1844	Jackson	Stanley F. Reed, Ky.	1938–1957	F. Roosevelt
James M. Wayne, Ga.	1835–1867	Jackson	Felix Frankfurter, Mass.	1939–1962	F. Roosevelt
Roger B. Taney, Md.	1836–1864	Jackson	William O. Douglas, Conn.	1939–1975	F. Roosevelt
Philip P. Barbour, Va.	1836–1841	Jackson	Frank Murphy, Mich.	1940–1949	F. Roosevelt
John Cartron, Tenn.	1837–1865	Van Buren	**Harlan F. Stone**, N.Y.	1941–1946	F. Roosevelt
John McKinley, Ala.	1838–1852	Van Buren	James R. Byrnes, S.C.	1941–1942	F. Roosevelt
Peter V. Daniel, Va.	1842–1860	Van Buren	Robert H. Jackson, N.Y.	1941–1954	F. Roosevelt
Samuel Nelson, N.Y.	1845–1872	Tyler	Wiley B. Rutledge, Iowa	1943–1949	F. Roosevelt
Levi Woodbury, N.H.	1845–1851	Polk	Harold H. Burton, Ohio	1945–1958	Truman
Robert C. Grier, Pa.	1846–1870	Polk	**Frederick M. Vinson**, Ky.	1946–1953	Truman
Benjamin R. Curtis, Mass.	1851–1857	Fillmore	Tom C. Clark, Texas	1949–1967	Truman
John A. Campbell, Ala.	1853–1861	Pierce	Sherman Minton, Ind.	1949–1956	Truman
Nathan Clifford, Me.	1858–1881	Buchanan	**Earl Warren**, Cal.	1953–1969	Eisenhower
Noah H. Swayne, Ohio	1862–1881	Lincoln	John Marshall Harlan, N.Y.	1955–1971	Eisenhower
Samuel F. Miller, Iowa	1862–1890	Lincoln	William J. Brennan Jr., N.J.	1956–1990	Eisenhower
David Davis, Ill.	1862–1877	Lincoln	Charles E. Whittaker, Mo.	1957–1962	Eisenhower
Stephen J. Field, Cal.	1863–1897	Lincoln	Potter Stewart, Ohio	1958–1981	Eisenhower
Salmon P. Chase, Ohio	1864–1873	Lincoln	Bryon R. White, Colo.	1962–1993	Kennedy
William Strong, Pa.	1870–1880	Grant	Arthur J. Goldberg, Ill.	1962–1965	Kennedy
Joseph P. Bradley, N.J.	1870–1892	Grant	Abe Fortas, Tenn.	1965–1969	Johnson
Ward Hunt, N.Y.	1873–1882	Grant	Thurgood Marshall, Md.	1967–1991	Johnson
Morrison R. Waite, Ohio	1874–1888	Grant	**Warren E. Burger**, Minn.	1969–1986	Nixon
John M. Harlan, Ky.	1877–1911	Hayes	Harry A. Blackmun, Minn.	1970–1994	Nixon
William B. Woods, Ga.	1881–1887	Hayes	Lewis F. Powell Jr., Va.	1971–1987	Nixon
Stanley Matthews, Ohio	1881–1889	Garfield	William H. Rehnquist, Ariz.	1971–1986	Nixon
Horace Gray, Mass.	1882–1902	Arthur	John Paul Stevens, Ill.	1975–	Ford
Samuel Blatchford, N.Y.	1882–1893	Arthur	Sandra Day O'Connor, Ariz.	1981–	Reagan
Lucius Q. C. Lamar, Miss.	1888–1893	Cleveland	**William H. Rehnquist**, Ariz.	1986–	Reagan
Melville W. Fuller, Ill.	1888–1910	Cleveland	Antonin Scalia, Va.	1986–	Reagan
David J. Brewer, Kan.	1890–1910	B. Harrison	Anthony M. Kennedy, Cal.	1988–	Reagan
Henry B. Brown, Mich.	1891–1906	B. Harrison	David H. Souter, N.H.	1990–	Bush
George Shiras Jr., Pa.	1892–1903	B. Harrison	Clarence Thomas, Ga.	1991–	Bush
Howell E. Jackson, Tenn.	1893–1895	B. Harrison	Ruth Bader Ginsburg, N.Y.	1993–	Clinton
Edward D. White, La.	1894–1910	Cleveland	Stephen G. Breyer, Mass.	1994–	Clinton
Rufus W. Peckham, N.Y.	1896–1909	Cleveland			

*Chief Justices are printed in bold type.

The American People: A Demographic Survey

A Demographic Profile of the American People							
	Life Expectancy from Birth		Average Age at First Marriage		Number of Children Under 5 (per 1,000 Women Aged 20–44)	Percentage of Women in Paid Employment	Percentage of Paid Workers Who Are Women
Year	White	Black	Men	Women			
1820					1,295	6.2	7.3
1830					1,145	6.4	7.4
1840					1,085	8.4	9.6
1850					923	10.1	10.8
1860					929	9.7	10.2
1870					839	13.7	14.8
1880					822	14.7	15.2
1890			26.1	22.0	716	18.2	17.0
1900	47.6	33.0	25.9	21.9	688	21.2	18.1
1910	50.3	35.6	25.1	21.6	643	24.8	20.0
1920	54.9	45.3	24.6	21.2	604	23.9	20.4
1930	61.4	48.1	24.3	21.3	511	24.4	21.9
1940	64.2	53.1	24.3	21.5	429	25.4	24.6
1950	69.1	60.8	22.8	20.3	589	29.1	27.8
1960	70.6	63.6	22.8	20.3	737	34.8	32.3
1970	71.7	65.3	22.5	20.6	530	43.3	38.0
1980	74.4	68.1	24.7	22.0	440	51.5	42.6
1990	76.2	71.4	26.1	23.9	377	57.4	45.2
1999	77.5	72.2	27.0	25.0	375	60.0	46.6

Source: Historical Statistics of the United States, Colonial Times to 1970 (1975); Statistical Abstract of the United States, 2001.

American Population

Year	Population	Percentage Increase	Year	Population	Percentage Increase
1610	350	—	1810	7,239,881	36.4
1620	2,300	557.1	1820	9,638,453	33.1
1630	4,600	100.0	1830	12,866,020	33.5
1640	26,600	478.3	1840	17,069,453	32.7
1650	50,400	90.8	1850	23,191,876	35.9
1660	75,100	49.0	1860	31,443,321	35.6
1670	111,900	49.0	1870	39,818,449	26.6
1680	151,500	35.4	1880	50,155,783	26.0
1690	210,400	38.9	1890	62,947,714	25.5
1700	250,900	19.2	1900	75,994,575	20.7
1710	331,700	32.2	1910	91,972,266	21.0
1720	466,200	40.5	1920	105,710,620	14.9
1730	629,400	35.0	1930	122,775,046	16.1
1740	905,600	43.9	1940	131,669,275	7.2
1750	1,170,800	29.3	1950	150,697,361	14.5
1760	1,593,600	36.1	1960	179,323,175	19.0
1770	2,148,100	34.8	1970	203,235,298	13.3
1780	2,780,400	29.4	1980	226,545,805	11.5
1790	3,929,214	41.3	1990	248,709,873	9.8
1800	5,308,483	35.1	2000	281,421,906	13.2

Note: These figures largely ignore the Native American population. Census takers never made any effort to count the Native American population that lived outside their political jurisdictions and compiled only casual and incomplete enumerations of those living within their jurisdictions until 1890. In that year the federal government attempted a full count of the Indian population: the Census found 125,719 Indians in 1890, compared with only 12,543 in 1870 and 33,985 in 1880.

Source: Historical Statistics of the United States, Colonial Times to 1970 (1975); Statistical Abstract of the United States, 2001.

White/Nonwhite Population

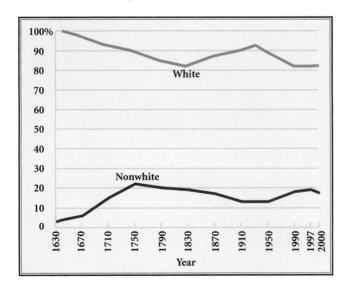

Urban/Rural Population

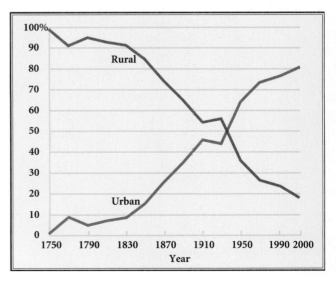

The Ten Largest Cities by Population, 1700–2000

		City	Population			City	Population
1700	1.	Boston	6,700		6.	Cleveland	560,663
	2.	New York	4,937*		7.	Baltimore	558,485
	3.	Philadelphia	4,400†		8.	Pittsburgh	533,905
					9.	Detroit	465,766
1790	1.	Philadelphia	42,520		10.	Buffalo	423,715
	2.	New York	33,131	1930	1.	New York	6,930,446
	3.	Boston	18,038		2.	Chicago	3,376,438
	4.	Charleston, S.C.	16,359		3.	Philadelphia	1,950,961
	5.	Baltimore	13,503		4.	Detroit	1,568,662
	6.	Salem, Mass.	7,921		5.	Los Angeles	1,238,048
	7.	Newport, R.I.	6,716		6.	Cleveland	900,429
	8.	Providence, R.I.	6,380		7.	St. Louis	821,960
	9.	Marblehead, Mass.	5,661		8.	Baltimore	804,874
	10.	Portsmouth, N.H.	4,720		9.	Boston	781,188
1830	1.	New York	197,112		10.	Pittsburgh	669,817
	2.	Philadelphia	161,410	1950	1.	New York	7,891,957
	3.	Baltimore	80,620		2.	Chicago	3,620,962
	4.	Boston	61,392		3.	Philadelphia	2,071,605
	5.	Charleston, S.C.	30,289		4.	Los Angeles	1,970,358
	6.	New Orleans	29,737		5.	Detroit	1,849,568
	7.	Cincinnati	24,831		6.	Baltimore	949,708
	8.	Albany, N.Y.	24,209		7.	Cleveland	914,808
	9.	Brooklyn, N.Y.	20,535		8.	St. Louis	856,796
	10.	Washington, D.C.	18,826		9.	Washington, D.C.	802,178
1850	1.	New York	515,547		10.	Boston	801,444
	2.	Philadelphia	340,045	1970	1.	New York	7,895,563
	3.	Baltimore	169,054		2.	Chicago	3,369,357
	4.	Boston	136,881		3.	Los Angeles	2,811,801
	5.	New Orleans	116,375		4.	Philadelphia	1,949,996
	6.	Cincinnati	115,435		5.	Detroit	1,514,063
	7.	Brooklyn, N.Y.	96,838		6.	Houston	1,233,535
	8.	St. Louis	77,860		7.	Baltimore	905,787
	9.	Albany, N.Y.	50,763		8.	Dallas	844,401
	10.	Pittsburgh	46,601		9.	Washington, D.C.	756,668
1870	1.	New York	942,292		10.	Cleveland	750,879
	2.	Philadelphia	674,022	1990	1.	New York	7,322,564
	3.	Brooklyn, N.Y.	419,921‡		2.	Los Angeles	3,485,398
	4.	St. Louis	310,864		3.	Chicago	2,783,726
	5.	Chicago	298,977		4.	Houston	1,630,553
	6.	Baltimore	267,354		5.	Philadelphia	1,585,577
	7.	Boston	250,526		6.	San Diego	1,110,549
	8.	Cincinnati	216,239		7.	Detroit	1,027,974
	9.	New Orleans	191,418		8.	Dallas	1,006,877
	10.	San Francisco	149,473		9.	Phoenix	983,403
1910	1.	New York	4,766,883		10.	San Antonio	935,933
	2.	Chicago	2,185,283	2000	1.	New York	8,008,278
	3.	Philadelphia	1,549,008		2.	Los Angeles	3,694,820
	4.	St. Louis	687,029		3.	Chicago	2,896,016
	5.	Boston	670,585		4.	Houston	1,953,631
					5.	Philadelphia	1,517,550
					6.	Phoenix	1,321,045
					7.	San Diego	1,223,400
					8.	Dallas	1,188,580
					9.	San Antonio	1,144,646
					10.	Detroit	951,270

*Figure from a census taken in 1698.

†Philadelphia figures include suburbs.

‡Annexed to New York in 1898.

Source: U.S. Census data.

Immigration by Decade

Year	Number	Percentage of Total Population	Year	Number	Percentage of Total Population
1821–1830	151,824	1.6	1921–1930	4,107,209	3.9
1831–1840	599,125	4.6	1931–1940	528,431	0.4
1841–1850	1,713,251	10.0	1941–1950	1,035,039	0.7
1851–1860	2,598,214	11.2	1951–1960	2,515,479	1.6
1861–1870	2,314,824	7.4	1961–1970	3,321,677	1.8
1871–1880	2,812,191	7.1	1971–1980	4,493,000	2.2
1881–1890	5,246,613	10.5	1981–1990	7,338,000	3.0
1891–1900	3,687,546	5.8	1991–2000	9,095,083	3.66
1901–1910	8,795,386	11.6	**Total**	**32,433,918**	
1911–1920	5,735,811	6.2			
Total	**33,654,785**		1821–2000		
			GRAND TOTAL	**66,088,703**	

Sources: U.S. Bureau of the Census, *Historical Statistics of the United States, Colonial Times to 1970* (1975), part 1,105–106; *Statistical Abstract of the United States, 2001.*

Regional Origins

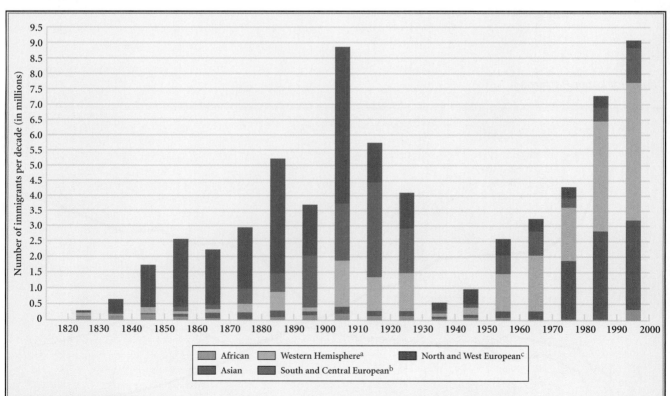

a Canada and all countries in South America and Central America.
b Italy, Spain, Portugal, Greece, Germany (Austria included, 1938–1945), Poland, Czechoslovakia (since 1920), Yugoslavia (since 1920), Hungary (since 1861), Austria (since 1861, except 1938–1945), former USSR (excludes Asian USSR between 1931 and 1963), Latvia, Estonia, Lithuania, Finland, Romania, Bulgaria, Turkey (in Europe), and other European countries not classified elsewhere.
c Great Britain, Ireland, Norway, Sweden, Denmark, Iceland, Netherlands, Belgium, Luxembourg, Switzerland, France.
Source: Stephan Thernstrom, ed., *Harvard Encyclopedia of American Ethnic Groups* (1980), 480; U.S. Bureau of the Census, *Statistical Abstract of the United States, 1991;* U.S. Immigration and Naturalization Service, *Statistical Yearbook, 2000.*

The Labor Force (Thousands of Workers)

Year	Agriculture	Mining	Manufacturing	Construction	Trade	Other	Total
1810	1,950	11	75	—	—	294	2,330
1840	3,570	32	500	290	350	918	5,660
1850	4,520	102	1,200	410	530	1,488	8,250
1860	5,880	176	1,530	520	890	2,114	11,110
1870	6,790	180	2,470	780	1,310	1,400	12,930
1880	8,920	280	3,290	900	1,930	2,070	17,390
1890	9,960	440	4,390	1,510	2,960	4,060	23,320
1900	11,680	637	5,895	1,665	3,970	5,223	29,070
1910	11,770	1,068	8,332	1,949	5,320	9,041	37,480
1920	10,790	1,180	11,190	1,233	5,845	11,372	41,610
1930	10,560	1,009	9,884	1,988	8,122	17,267	48,830
1940	9,575	925	11,309	1,876	9,328	23,277	56,290
1950	7,870	901	15,648	3,029	12,152	25,870	65,470
1960	5,970	709	17,145	3,640	14,051	32,545	74,060
1970	3,463	516	20,746	4,818	15,008	34,127	78,678
1980	3,364	979	21,942	6,215	20,191	46,612	99,303
1990	3,223	724	21,346	7,764	24,622	60,849	118,793
1999	3,281	565	20,070	8,987	27,572	74,733	135,208

Source: Historical Statistics of the United States, Colonial Times to 1970 (1975), 139; Statistical Abstract of the United States, 1998, table 675.

Changing Labor Patterns

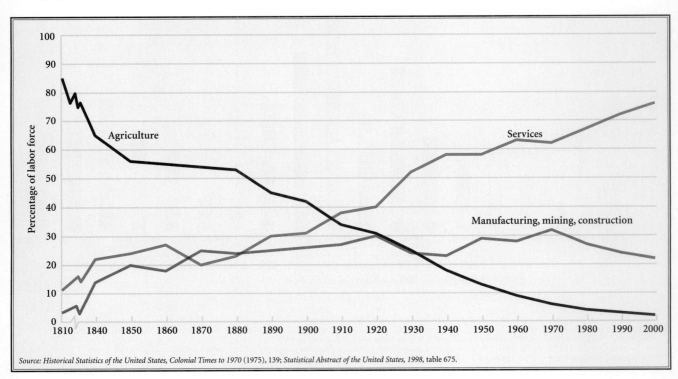

Source: Historical Statistics of the United States, Colonial Times to 1970 (1975), 139; Statistical Abstract of the United States, 1998, table 675.

Birth Rate, 1820–2000

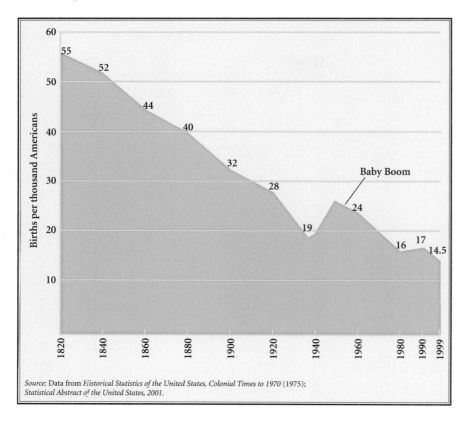

Source: Data from *Historical Statistics of the United States, Colonial Times to 1970* (1975);
Statistical Abstract of the United States, 2001.

Death Rate, 1900–2000

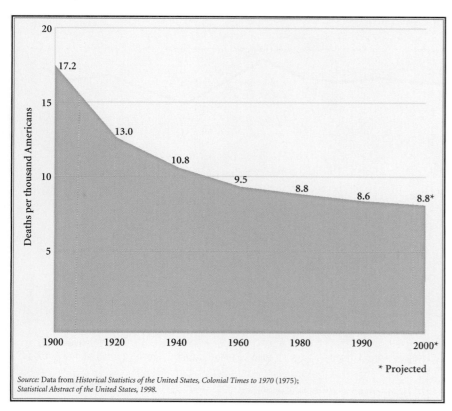

Source: Data from *Historical Statistics of the United States, Colonial Times to 1970* (1975);
Statistical Abstract of the United States, 1998.

Life Expectancy (at birth), 1900–2000

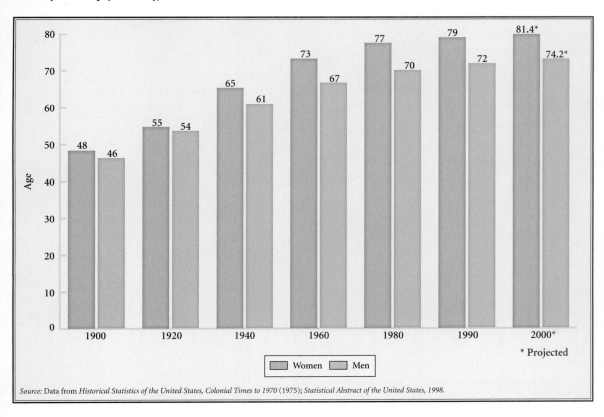

Source: Data from *Historical Statistics of the United States, Colonial Times to 1970* (1975); *Statistical Abstract of the United States, 1998.*

The Aging of the U.S. Population, 1850–1999

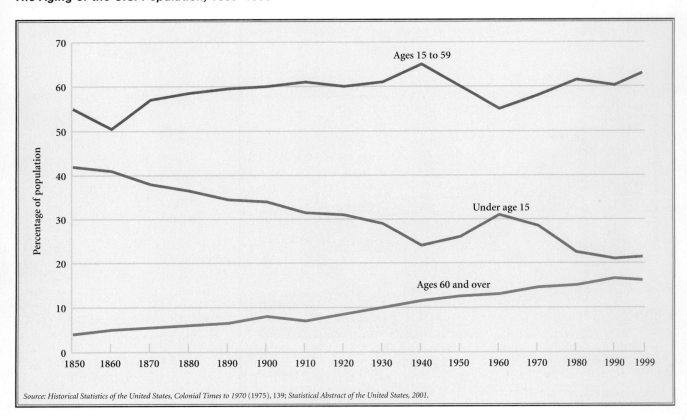

Source: *Historical Statistics of the United States, Colonial Times to 1970* (1975), 139; *Statistical Abstract of the United States, 2001.*

The American Government and Economy

The Growth of the Federal Government

	Employees (millions)		Receipts and Outlays ($ millions)	
Year	Civilian	Military	Receipts	Outlays
1900	0.23	0.12	567	521
1910	0.38	0.13	676	694
1920	0.65	0.34	6,649	6,358
1930	0.61	0.25	4,058	3,320
1940	1.04	0.45	6,900	9,600
1950	1.96	1.46	40,900	43,100
1960	2.38	2.47	92,500	92,200
1970	3.00	3.06	193,700	196,600
1980	2.99	2.05	517,112	590,920
1990	3.13	2.07	1,031,321	1,252,705
2000	2.88	1.38	2,025,200	1,788,800

Source: Statistical Profile of the United States, 1900-1980; Statistical Abstract of the United States, 2001.

Gross Domestic Product, 1840–2000

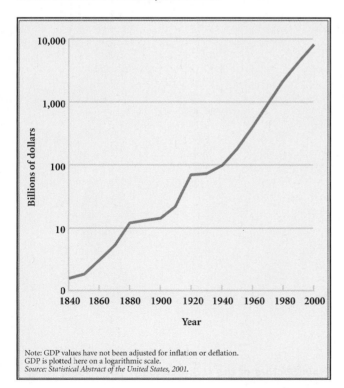

Note: GDP values have not been adjusted for inflation or deflation.
GDP is plotted here on a logarithmic scale.
Source: Statistical Abstract of the United States, 2001.

GDP per Capita, 1840–2000

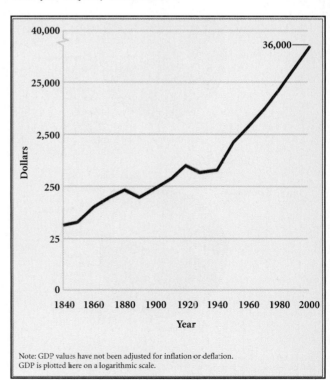

Note: GDP values have not been adjusted for inflation or deflation.
GDP is plotted here on a logarithmic scale.

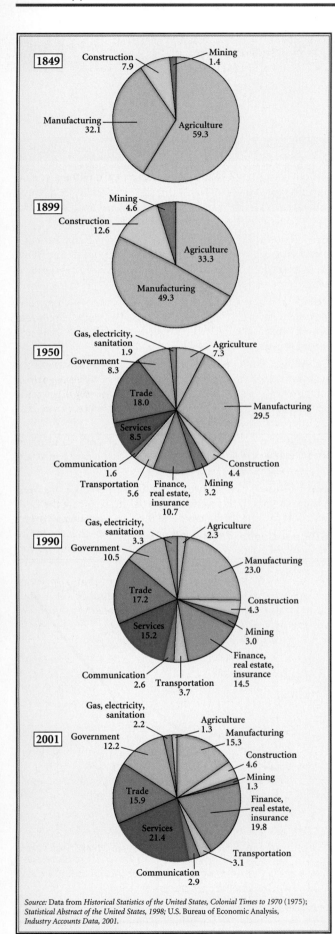

1849
- Construction 7.9
- Mining 1.4
- Manufacturing 32.1
- Agriculture 59.3

1899
- Mining 4.6
- Construction 12.6
- Agriculture 33.3
- Manufacturing 49.3

1950
- Gas, electricity, sanitation 1.9
- Government 8.3
- Agriculture 7.3
- Trade 18.0
- Manufacturing 29.5
- Services 8.5
- Communication 1.6
- Construction 4.4
- Transportation 5.6
- Finance, real estate, insurance 10.7
- Mining 3.2

1990
- Gas, electricity, sanitation 3.3
- Government 10.5
- Agriculture 2.3
- Trade 17.2
- Manufacturing 23.0
- Services 15.2
- Construction 4.3
- Mining 3.0
- Communication 2.6
- Transportation 3.7
- Finance, real estate, insurance 14.5

2001
- Gas, electricity, sanitation 2.2
- Government 12.2
- Agriculture 1.3
- Manufacturing 15.3
- Construction 4.6
- Mining 1.3
- Trade 15.9
- Finance, real estate, insurance 19.8
- Services 21.4
- Transportation 3.1
- Communication 2.9

Source: Data from *Historical Statistics of the United States, Colonial Times to 1970* (1975); *Statistical Abstract of the United States, 1998*; U.S. Bureau of Economic Analysis, *Industry Accounts Data, 2001*.

◄ **Main Sectors of the U.S. Economy: 1849, 1899, 1950, 1990, and 2001**

Consumer Price Index

$100 in the year		is equivalent to		in 2001
	1790		$1,920	
	1800		1,400	
	1810		1,430	
	1820		1,500	
	1830		1,900	
	1840		2,030	
	1850		2,250	
	1860		2,110	
	1870		1,340	
	1880		1,720	
	1890		1,940	
	1900		2,090	
	1910		1,850	
	1920		882	
	1930		1,050	
	1940		1,260	
	1950		735	
	1960		598	
	1970		456	
	1980		215	
	1990		135	

This index provides a very rough guide to the purchasing power of $100 in various periods of American history. For example, in the early 1830s, day laborers earned about $1 a day or about $300 a year. This sum is the equivalent of about $5,700 a year in 2001 (3 × $1,900 = $5,700), or about one-half the gross income of a worker earning the federal government-designated minimum wage of $5.15 per hour.

Source: Samuel H. Williamson, "What Is the Relative Value?" Economic History Services, April 2002, <http://www.eh.net/ hmit/compare/>

American Lyceum A lecture circuit beginning in 1826 that sent ministers, transcendentalists, and scientists all across the north on speaking tours. The Lyceum movement helped to spread transcendentalism and reform ideas in the nineteenth century.

American System Federal government program to expand economic development through federally funded system of internal improvements (roads and canals), tariffs, and a national bank. Brainchild of Henry Clay and supported by John Quincy Adams in 1824.

assumption In 1790 Alexander Hamilton wanted the federal government to take over the war debts of the states and the states' creditors. By doing so, the national government quickly increased its national debt while relieving the state governments of their debts.

Benevolent Empire A broad-ranging campaign of moral and institutional reform inspired by evangelical Christian ideals and created by middle-class men and women in the 1820s. "Benevolence" became a seminal concept in American spiritual thinking during the Second Great Awakening. Promoters of benevolent reform suggested that people who had experienced saving grace should provide charity to the less fortunate.

bicameral A two-house assembly, usually a house of representatives and a senate, suggested by John Adams in his *Thoughts on Government* (1776). Different qualifications, procedures, term lengths, and means of election differentiate the two. Its existence ensures that each piece of legislation is reviewed and debated by two different groups.

bills of exchange Credit slips that British manufacturers, West Indian planters, and American merchants used to trade among themselves in the eighteenth century.

Black Codes After the Civil War, southern states passed these laws to keep African Americans in conditions close to slavery, forcing them back to the plantations and denying them civil rights.

cabinet George Washington organized bureaucratic departments to carry out the work of the executive branch and appointed secretaries to run those departments in 1788. These secretaries formed the cabinet, a small group of the president's closest advisors on matters of policy.

carpetbaggers A derisive name given by Southerners to Northerners who moved to the South during Reconstruction to help develop the region's economic potential. Former Confederates despised these Northerners as transient exploiters. Carpetbaggers included former Union army officers and also educated professionals.

caucus An informal meeting of politicians held by political parties to make majority decisions and enforce party discipline. First put into practice by Martin Van Buren in the early nineteenth century.

civic humanism A concept that stressed service to the state and government in order to promote the good of the community. During the Renaissance, this idea of selfless service was thought to be critical in a republic where control was vested in a politically active and committed citizenry.

clan A group of related families who share a common ancestor. In the sixteenth century many native peoples north of the Rio Grande organized their societies around these groups, which often combined to form tribes.

closed-shop agreement Labor agreement in which an employer agrees to hire only union members. Many employers viewed these agreements as illegal and worked to overturn them in the courts.

Columbian Exchange The sixteenth-century transfer of the agricultural products of the Western Hemisphere—maize, tomatoes, potatoes, manioc—to the people of other continents, and the transfer of African and Eurasian crops and diseases to the Americas.

common law Centuries-old body of English legal rules and procedures that protected the king's subjects against arbitrary acts by the government.

commutation Fees allowed by both northern and southern governments to hire substitutes for the draft during the Civil War. In the North, Democrats and their immigrant supporters attacked the law for favoring the rich at their expense. In the South, poor southern yeomen complained that commutation made it "a rich man's war and a poor man's fight."

companionate marriage Empowered by republican ideas, women in the early nineteenth century pressed for legal equality in matrimony. Even though husbands retained significant power as patriarchs, they increasingly viewed their wives as loving partners rather than as inferiors or dependents.

complex marriage John Humphrey Noyes led his Oneida Community in this practice in the 1830s, based on the belief that all members of the community were wedded to one another. Noyes believed complex marriage was liberating for women.

conquistadors Spanish "conquerors," veterans of the wars against the Muslims, who followed the first Spanish explorers to the Americas in the early sixteenth century. The Spanish crown offered them plunder, estates in the conquered territory, and titles in return for creating an empire.

Conscience Whigs Term used to describe politicians who opposed the Mexican War in the 1840s on moral grounds, arguing that the purpose of the war was to acquire more land for the expansion of slavery. They believed that more slave states would destroy yeoman freeholder society and put slaveholders in charge of the federal government.

contrabands Term for the thousands of slaves who fled the plantations for protection behind Union lines during the Civil

War. General Benjamin Butler refused to return them to their owners, and Congress regularized this policy in the First Confiscation Act, which authorized Union troops to seize all property, including slaves, used on behalf of the Confederacy.

Court (or Crown) Party The select group in eighteenth-century British Parliament that Robert Walpole favored in patronage appointments, leading to charges of corruption from the Whig Party.

deism A religious belief associated with the Enlightenment in which a rational, "watchmaker" God did not intervene directly in history or in people's lives. Deists like Benjamin Franklin rejected the authority of the Bible and relied on people's "natural reason" to define a moral code.

division of labor The separation of tasks in a larger manufacturing process designed to improve efficiency and productivity but which also eroded the workers' control over the conditions of labor. The shoe factories in Lynn, Massachusetts, in the 1820s and 1830s are some of the first places where managers put this method of production into practice.

dower right A legal right originating in medieval Europe and carried to the American colonies that extended to a woman following the death of her husband the use of one-third of the family's land and goods during her lifetime.

electoral college As set forth in the Constitution, the president was to be elected indirectly. A group of electors, chosen state by state, were appointed each election year, to vote for the president and vice president according to the majority of popular votes cast. This was done to give individual states a greater role in the choosing of a president.

eminent domain Under the law, this principle gives a government control of all property within its sovereign jurisdiction, and grants it the power to take and use property for public purposes provided that compensation is given to the owners. In the early nineteenth century, states granted this power to private corporations so that, like the states themselves, they could seize property for public use—for example, to build roads, bridges, and canals.

enclosure acts The laws passed in England in the sixteenth century that gave landowners the right to fence open land for their sheep to graze. This prevented peasants from sharing and farming what traditionally had been open lands and dispossessed many of England's poor.

encomenderos Privileged Spanish landholders in America with land grants from the king. In the sixteenth century they collected tribute from the resident Native American population, both in goods and through forced labor.

encomiendas Land grants in America from the king given to privileged Spanish landholders in the sixteenth century. The *encomiendas* gave the landholders legal control over the native population in the New World.

Ethiopian Regiment Loyalist military unit that consisted of 1,000 escaped slaves, organized by Virginia's royal governor in the 1770s. This action, coupled with the governor's proclamation offering freedom to any slave who joined the Loyalist cause, pushed Virginia slaveholders to support the Patriot cause.

excise levies Taxes imposed on goods such as salt, beer, and distilled spirits in late eighteenth-century Britain. These taxes passed on the cost of imperial management to the king's subjects.

faction A small political group or alliance organized around a single issue or person. Factions often become the basis for political parties. In the eighteenth century, many considered factions dangerous because they were thought to undermine the stability of a community or nation.

factory Manufacturing businesses first created in the late eighteenth century that concentrated all the aspects of production under one roof, reorganized production, and divided work into specialized tasks. Factories made production faster and more efficient, while narrowing the range of worker activities and skills.

fee-simple The legal status of land titles in seventeenth-century Puritan society. This term meant that landowners possessed their land outright, free from manorial obligations or feudal dues.

fire-eaters Southern politicians who sought secession. They organized secession conventions in several southern states in 1850 but backed away because of a lack of support and the promise of moderate southern backing for secession if Congress tried to outlaw slavery in the future.

franchise The right to vote. Extended to all adult white males in the early nineteenth century by most new states and most older states as well.

freehold Ownership of a plot of land and possession of the title or deed. Freeholders have the legal right to improve, transfer, or sell their property. This type of landholding characterized New England in the seventeenth and eighteenth centuries, as its founders attempted to avoid the concentration of land in the hands of an elite—an undesirable characteristic of the England that they had left.

free soil Term describing the belief that slavery should be kept out of the territories because it threatened republican institutions and yeoman farming. In the 1840s, the short-lived Free Soil Party's slogan stated "free soil, free labor, free men."

gag rule Procedure in the House of Representatives from 1836–1844 by which antislavery petitions were automatically tabled when they were received, so that they could not become the subject of debate in the House.

gentry A class of English men and women who were substantial landholders but lacked the social privileges and titles of nobility that marked the aristocracy. During the Price Revolution of the sixteenth century, the wealth and status of the gentry rose while that of the aristocracy declined.

habeas corpus Constitutional right that protects citizens against arbitrary arrest and detention. During the Civil War, Lincoln suspended *habeas corpus* to stop protests against the draft and other disloyal activities. Lincoln also transferred cases of disloyalty from civilian to military jurisdiction, fearing that local juries would have been lenient toward Confederate sympathizers.

headright A program begun by the Virginia Company in 1617 that granted the head of a household 50 acres for himself and 50 additional acres for every adult family member or servant brought into the Virginia colony.

heresies Religious doctrines inconsistent with the teaching of an established, official Christian church. Some of the Crusades between 1096 and 1291 stand as examples of Christians attempting to crush groups spreading these "unauthorized" doctrines.

home rule White southern Democrats referred to their desire to overthrow legitimately elected Reconstruction governments and replace them with white supremacy with this euphemism. By 1876, both national parties favored home rule.

homespun Yarn and cloth produced by American women. During political boycotts in the 1760s it allowed the colonies to escape dependence on British textile manufactures and creating a space for women to make a unique contribution to the colonial resistance.

household mode of production System of exchanging goods and labor that helped eighteenth-century New England freeholders survive on ever-shrinking farms as available land became more scarce.

impeachment First step in the constitutional process for removing the president from office in which charges of wrongdoing (articles of impeachment) are passed by the House of Representatives and then judged in a trial conducted by the Senate.

impressment Forcible, unwilling draft into military service. The British navy forced American merchant sailors into service in the years preceding the War of 1812, greatly increasing tensions between the two nations.

indenture A seventeenth-century labor contract that promised service for a period of time in return for passage to North America. Indentures were typically for a term of four or five years, provided room and board in exchange for labor, and granted free status at the successful completion of the contract period.

individualism Term coined by Alexis de Tocqueville in 1835 that described Americans as people no longer bound by social attachments to classes, castes, associations, and families. Some observers worried that this was a cause of social disorder; others saw it as liberating.

indulgences Catholic Church certificates pardoning a sinner from punishments in the afterlife. In his *Ninety-Five Theses*, written in 1517, Martin Luther condemned the sale of indulgences, a common practice among Catholic clergy.

inmates New class of the poor in the eighteenth century, made up of Scots-Irish single men or families who possessed little property and existed as tenants or day laborers with little hope of earning economic independence.

joint-stock company A financial arrangement established by the British to facilitate the colonization of the New World in the seventeenth century. These agreements allowed merchants to band together as stockholders, raising large amounts of money while sharing the risks and profits in proportion to their part of the total investment.

judicial review The right of the courts to judge the constitutionality of laws passed by Congress and the state legislatures. This power is implicit within the federal Constitution and was first practiced by the Supreme Court in *Marbury v. Madison* in 1803.

King Cotton In the 1860s, many Confederates believed that cotton would not only provide enough money to fight the war, but the potential threat to supplies would convince the British, whose textile industry was dependent on southern cotton, to recognize the South as an independent nation.

labor theory of value The belief that the price of a product should reflect the work that went into making it and should be paid mostly to the person who produced it. This idea was popularized by the National Trades' Union in the mid-nineteenth century.

lien (crop lien) Southern redemption governments passed laws in the late nineteenth century allowing furnishing merchants to assume ownership, or lien, of a borrower's (usually sharecroppers) crops as collateral for loans of seed, tools, and fertilizer. This system trapped farmers in a cycle of debt and prevented economic diversification away from the increasingly unprofitable cotton-based agriculture.

limited liability A contractual clause that ensures that the personal assets of shareholders cannot be seized to cover the debts of a corporation. By 1800, state governments had granted more than three hundred corporate charters, many of which included limited liability.

machine tools Machines that are used to produce other machines with standardized parts at a low cost. The development of machine tools by American inventors in the early nineteenth century facilitated the rapid spread of the Industrial Revolution.

Manifest Destiny Term coined by John L. O'Sullivan in 1845, based on an American sense of cultural and racial superiority. It describes the idea that Americans were fated by Providence to develop the continent from the Atlantic to the Pacific and bring "inferior" peoples under American dominion.

manumission The act of a master liberating a slave. In 1782 the Virginia assembly passed an act allowing manumission; within a decade planters had freed 10,000 slaves.

Market Revolution The combined impact of the rapidly increased production of goods and the development of a transportation network to distribute them. In the early nineteenth century this led to the growth of urban production and distribution centers, western migration, and the construction of a variety of transportation methods including canals, roads, steamboats, and railroads.

marriage portion Parcel of land, livestock, farm equipment, or household goods that eighteenth-century New England parents gave to their children as a marriage gift to help them start life on their own. Parents expected children to repay this gift by caring for them in their old age.

mechanics Class of skilled craftsmen and inventors who built and improved machinery and developed machine tools for industry in the nineteenth century. They developed a professional identity and established institutes to spread their skills and knowledge.

mercantilism A set of policies that regulated colonial commerce and manufacturing for the enrichment of the mother country. These policies insured that the American colonies in the mid-seventeenth century produced agricultural goods and raw materials, which would then be carried to Britain, where they would be reexported or made into finished goods.

mercenary A soldier for hire; one who cares nothing for the principles or values behind the war, but will fight for either side for money. Thousands of German mercenaries joined the British troops during the Revolutionary War in 1776.

mestizo A person of mixed blood, the offspring of inter-marriage or sexual liaison between white Europeans and native people, usually a white man and an Indian woman. In sixteenth-century Mesoamerica, nearly 90 percent of the Spanish settlers were men who took Indian women as wives or mistresses; the result was a substantial mixed-race population.

Middle Passage The brutal sea voyage from Africa to the Americas in the eighteenth and nineteenth centuries in which nearly a million Africans lost their lives.

Minutemen In the 1770s colonists organized into voluntary militia units that would be ready to face British troops in a battle on short notice. These soldiers formed the core of the citizen army that met the British at Lexington.

mixed government John Adams's 1776 plan called for three branches of government, each representing one function: executive, legislative, and judicial. This system of dispersed authority was devised to maintain a balance of power and ensure the legitimacy of governmental procedures.

national debt First created in the late eighteenth century by borrowing money from the wealthy through the sale of bonds. Alexander Hamilton believed that drawing on this source of capital to finance government would create ties of loyalty between the government and the business community.

nullification Idea supported by many southerners starting in the 1820s that a state convention could declare unconstitutional any federal law. John C. Calhoun based this concept on the earlier writings of Jefferson and Madison as published in the Virginia and Kentucky resolutions.

outwork A system of manufacturing, also known as "putting out," used in the English woolen industry. Merchants in the sixteenth and seventeenth centuries bought wool and provided it to landless peasants, who spun and wove it into cloth, which the merchants in turn sold in English and foreign markets.

party (party system) An organized political body with specific ideologies or interests, established with the goal of organizing the electorate and directing the policies of a government. While not part of the Constitution, competitive political parties appeared quickly in the United States during the election of 1796.

patronage The power of elected officials to grant government jobs to party members to create and maintain strong party loyalties. In the United States, patronage was first used extensively by Martin Van Buren in early nineteenth-century New York.

peaceful coercion Thomas Jefferson's strategy designed to force the British and the French to accept the American definition of neutral rights by forbidding American trade with Europe. The centerpiece of this flawed policy was the Embargo Act of 1807.

peasant A farm laborer who often worked land held by a landlord. In 1450 Europe, these laborers sometimes owned or leased a small plot in the town and worked collectively with other village laborers on the landlord's land.

peonage (debt peonage) As cotton prices declined during the 1870s, many sharecroppers fell into permanent debt. Merchants often conspired with landowners to make the debt a pretext for forced labor, or peonage.

perfectionism The religious belief that people could be without flaws, or free from sin, because the Second Coming of

Christ had already occurred. This evangelical movement attracted thousands of followers during the 1830s.

personal-liberty laws Laws passed by northern legislatures in the 1850s to challenge the federal Fugitive Slave Act and extend legal rights to escaped slaves.

phalanxes Cooperative work groups in the 1840s organized as part of the Fourierist movement in which all members were shareholders in a community as an alternative to capitalist wage labor.

pietism A European spiritual outlook emphasizing devout behavior and an emotional effort to achieve a personal, mystical union with God that reached America in the mid-eighteenth century. Unlike Puritans and most other Protestants, adherents avoided debates over theological dogma or doctrine.

pocket veto Presidential way to kill a piece of legislation without issuing a formal veto. When congressional Republicans passed the Wade-Davis Bill in 1864, a harsher alternative to President Lincoln's restoration plan, Lincoln used this method to kill it by simply not signing the bill and letting it expire after Congress adjourned.

political machine Nineteenth-century term for a highly organized political party, which was often compared to new technological innovations because of its efficiency and complexity.

poll tax Legal device used throughout the South beginning during Reconstruction to prevent freedmen from voting. Nationally, the northern states used poll taxes to keep immigrants and others deemed unworthy from the polls.

polygamy The practice of a man having multiple wives. Adopted by some Mormons in the 1840s and practiced until outlawed in 1890 under pressure from the federal government.

popular sovereignty Michigan senator and Democratic presidential candidate Lewis Cass introduced this solution to the problem of slavery in the territories in 1848 by proposing that territorial residents should have the right to determine the status of slavery locally. This policy alienated free-soil Democrats, but it was later adopted by Senator Stephen Douglas of Illinois, who gave it its final name in the Kansas–Nebraska Act.

Praying towns Native American settlements supervised by New England Puritans. In these seventeenth-century settlements, Puritans attempted to Christianize Indians, in part, through an Algonquian-language Bible.

predestination The idea that God had chosen certain people for salvation even before they were born. This strict belief was preached by John Calvin in the sixteenth century and became a fundamental tenet of Puritan theology.

Price Revolution A term that describes the significance of the high rate of inflation in Europe in the mid-1500s resulting from the introduction of American wealth into the European economy by the Spanish, which doubled the money supply in Europe. It brought about profound social changes by reducing the political power of the aristocracy and leaving many peasant families on the brink of poverty, setting the stage for a substantial migration to America.

primogeniture An inheritance practice by which a family's estate was passed on to the eldest son, forcing many younger children into poverty. In the Revolutionary era, republican Americans increasingly felt this was unfair. As a result, most state legislatures rejected the practice by passing laws requiring the equal distribution of estates.

proprietors A group of settlers, in seventeenth-century Puritan society, who determined how the land of a township would be distributed. To guarantee a wide distribution of property, the General Courts of Massachusetts Bay and Connecticut gave the title of a township to a group of proprietors and allowed them to distribute land among the settlers.

Radical Whigs Eighteenth-century opposition party in the British Parliament that challenged the cost of the growing British empire and the subsequent increase in tax collector positions that were used for patronage. They demanded that British government include more representatives of the propertied classes.

reconquista The centuries-long campaign by Spanish Catholics to drive African Moors (Muslims) from the European mainland. After a long effort to recover control of their lands, the Spanish defeated the Moors at the battle of Granada in 1492 and drove them back to Africa.

Reconstruction Post–Civil War policies whereby the freedmen, abolitionists, and radical Republican politicians hoped to make changes in the South that would ensure political equality for the freedmen and grant them greater economic rights.

Redeemers Ex-Confederates who sought to return the political and economic control of the South to white southerners in the decades after the Civil War. They believed that Union support of the freedmen had deprived the South of democratic self-government and organized secret societies and campaigns of terror to regain it, leading to the undoing of Reconstruction.

republic A state without a monarch and with a representative system of government. In Revolutionary America, "republicanism" became a social philosophy that embodied a sense of community and called individuals to act selflessly for the public good.

republican motherhood The idea that American women's moral superiority gave them a special role to play in the new political and social system. In the early-to-mid-nineteenth century, republican mothers were to instill the values of patriotic duty and republican virtue in their children and mold them into exemplary American citizens with moral and religious education.

Restoration The name given to the reign of Charles II, King of England, the monarch whom Parliament crowned in 1660, following a decade of Puritan rule under Oliver Cromwell.

rotten boroughs Tiny electoral districts for Parliament whose voters were controlled by wealthy aristocrats or merchants. In the 1760s Radical Whig John Wilkes called for their elimination to make Parliament more representative of the property-owning classes.

salutary neglect British colonial policy during the reigns of George I (r. 1714–1727) and George II (r. 1727–1760). Relaxed supervision of internal colonial affairs by royal bureaucrats contributed significantly to the rise of American self-government.

scalawags Southern whites who joined the Republicans during Reconstruction and were ridiculed by ex-Confederates as worthless traitors. They included wealthy ex-Whigs and yeomen farmers who had not supported the Confederacy and who believed that an alliance with the Republicans was the best way to attract northern capital to the South.

self-made man This middle-class icon was based on an ideal that became a central theme of American popular culture in the nineteenth century. The ideology of the self-made man held that hard work, temperate habits, and honesty in business was the key to a high standard of living for the nation and social mobility and prosperity for individuals.

sentimentalism European-spawned idea that emphasized feelings and emotions, a physical appreciation of God, nature, and other people, rather than reason and logic. Sentimentalism had an impact on the American people starting in the early nineteenth century, as love became as important in marriage as financial considerations.

sharecropping Labor system developed during Reconstruction by which freedmen agreed to work the land and pay a portion of their harvested crops to the landowner in exchange for land, a house, and tools. A compromise between freedmen and white landowners, this system developed in the cash-strapped South because the freedmen wanted to work their own land but lacked the money to buy it, while the white landowners needed agricultural laborers, but did not have money to pay wages.

slave power Term used by antislavery advocates in the 1850s to describe a suspected conspiracy of southern politicians and their northern business allies. It was believed that these groups planned to expand the bounds of slavery into new territories.

Sons of Liberty Carefully directed and well-disciplined mobs that sought to channel popular discontent against British rule toward terrorizing local British officials and other symbols of colonial authority in the decade of hostilities leading up to the American Revolution.

specie Gold or silver coins used by banks to back paper currency. In the early nineteenth century most American money consisted of notes and bills of credit, which were redeemed on demand with specie by the Second Bank of the United States.

speculator Someone who enters a market to buy and then resell at a higher price with the sole goal of making money. The eighteenth-century western land market was dominated by people who acquired land at a low price through political influence, then sold it for a profit to settlers.

spoils system Andrew Jackson began this practice in 1829 of awarding public jobs to political supporters to fulfill his campaign promise to introduce rotation in office and open public service to his supporters.

squatter Someone who settles on land they do not own. Many eighteenth- and nineteenth-century settlers established themselves on land before it was surveyed and entered for sale, requesting the first right to purchase the land when sales began.

states' rights An interpretation of the Constitution that argues that the states hold the ultimate sovereignty and have power over the federal government. Expressed in the Virginia and Kentucky resolutions of 1798, the states' rights philosophy became the basis for resistance by the South against attempts to control slavery.

suffrage The right to vote. In the early national period suffrage was limited by property restrictions. Gradually state constitutions gave the vote to all white men over the age of twenty-one. Over the course of American history, suffrage has expanded as barriers of race, gender, and age have fallen.

task system Unlike the gang-labor system, the privilege of working unsupervised on an assigned daily task allowed slaves in the nineteenth century the opportunity to pace themselves according to their other obligations. Once the specific job was finished, the slaves could do what they wished, including cultivate their own small plots.

total war Traditionally, armies fought each other and left civilians alone, but as the Civil War progressed, Lincoln and Grant realized that to force the Confederacy to surrender, they would have to break the will of the southern people using this style of warfare. Total war required a struggle that mobilized the nation's entire resources against the whole of southern society, not just against the Confederacy's troops.

trade slaves A small proportion of unfree West Africans who were sold from one African kingdom to another and not considered members of the society that had enslaved them. European traders began buying trade slaves from African princes and warlords in the early sixteenth century.

transcendentalism A nineteenth-century intellectual movement that espoused an ideal world of mystical knowledge and harmony beyond the world of the senses. Proponents included intellectuals such as Emerson and Thoreau, who emphasized individuality, self-reliance, and nonconformity.

unicameral A one-house assembly in which the elected legislators directly represent the people. Considered efficient and democratic, this type of assembly was established in Pennsylvania during the Revolution.

Upper South Eight states of the Union that did not immediately secede following Lincoln's election in 1860. Following the seizure of Fort Sumter, four of these Upper South states (Virginia, North Carolina, Tennessee, Arkansas) joined the Confederacy; the other four remained in the Union.

utopias (utopian communities) Reformers and transcendentalists founded numerous communities to help realize their spiritual and moral potential and to escape from the competition of modern industrial society. The most famous communal experiment was Brook Farm, founded by the transcendentalists outside of Boston, Massachusetts, in 1841.

vice-admiralty courts Military tribunals composed only of a judge with no local common-law jury. The Sugar Act of 1764 required that offenders be tried before this tribunal rather than in local courts, provoking opposition from smugglers accustomed to acquittal before sympathetic local juries.

virtual representation Claim made by British politicians in 1754 that merchants and others in Parliament with interest in the colonies could provide adequate support for colonial concerns, rather than having Americans serve in Parliament.

War Democrats Faction of the northern opposition party that opposed emancipation but backed a policy of continuing with the fighting. George McClellan was part of this faction, but initially, during the 1864 presidential campaign, he backed an immediate cessation of hostilities.

Whigs A British political party with a reputation for supporting liberal principles and reform. They rose in power during the Glorious Revolution of 1688 and favored "mixed government" in which the House of Commons would have a voice in shaping policies, especially the power of taxation.

yeoman In medieval England, a farmer below the level of gentry, but above the peasantry. A freeholder, he owned his own land, which released him from economic obligations to a landlord. In America, Thomas Jefferson envisioned a nation based on democracy and a thriving agrarian society, built on the labor and prosperity of the yeomen.

Chapter 1: Worlds Collide: Europe, Africa, and America, 1450–1620

Two works by Kenneth Pomeranz, *The Great Divergence: Europe, China, and the Making of the Modern World Economy* (2000) and (with Steven Topek) *The World That Trade Created: Society, Culture, and the World Economy* (1999), set the settlement of America in the perspective of world history. A fine study of the interaction of European and Native American peoples is Eric Wolf, *Europe and the People without History* (1982). See also Noble David Cook, *Born to Die: Disease and the New World Conquest (1492–1650)* (1998); Alfred W. Crosby Jr., *Ecological Imperialism: The Biological Expansion of Europe, 900–1900* (1986); G. V. Scammell, *The World Encompassed: The First European Maritime Empires* (1981); and Roger Schlesinger, *In the Wake of Columbus: The Impact of the New World on Europe, 1492–1650* (1996).

Native American Worlds

Brian M. Fagan, *The Great Journey: The People of Ancient America* (1987), synthesizes recent scholarship on prehistoric American Indians, and his *Kingdoms of Gold, Kingdoms of Jade: The Americas before Columbus* (1991) does the same for the Mesoamerican peoples. See also Stuart J. Fiedel, *Prehistory of the Americas* (1992); Inga Clendinnen, *Aztecs: An Interpretation* (1991); John S. Henderson, *The World of the Maya* (1981); and David Carrasco, *Quetzalcoatl and the Irony of Empire* (1982). Two fine supplements are Michael Coe et al., *Atlas of Ancient America* (1986), and Manuel Lucena Salmoral, *America in 1492* (1991), a photographic survey of dress, artifacts, and architecture. Alfred W. Crosby Jr., *The Columbian Exchange: Biological and Cultural Consequences of 1492* (1972), traces the impact of European diseases. See also Russell Thornton, *American Indian Holocaust and Survival: A Population History since 1492* (1987). Two interesting Public Broadcasting Service (PBS) videos examine the ancient civilizations of Mesoamerica: *Odyssey: Maya Lords of the Jungle* (1 hour); *Odyssey: The Incas* (1 hour). For additional information log on to "1492: An Ongoing Voyage" <http://lcweb.loc.gov/exhibits/1492/intro.html>, which provides a survey of the native cultures of the Western Hemisphere, the impact of discovery, and full-color images of artifacts and art.

On North America consult the following general works: *The Cambridge History of the Native Peoples of the Americas, Volume 1: North America*, ed. Bruce G. Trigger and Wilcomb Washburn (1996); Alvin M. Josephy Jr., ed., *America in 1492* (1993); Philip Kopper, *The Smithsonian Book of North American Indians before the Coming of the Europeans* (1986); and Carl Waldman and Molly Braun, *Atlas of the North American Indian* (1985). Good specialized studies include Linda S. Cordell, *Ancient Pueblo Peoples* (1994); Bruce D. Smith, ed., *The Mississippian Emergence* (1990); and Robert Silverberg,

Mound Builders of Ancient America: The Archaeology of a Myth (1968). Roger Kennedy, *Hidden Cities* (1994), surveys the early Indian civilizations of the Mississippi Valley, and Samuel W. Wilson, ed., *The Indigenous People of the Caribbean* (1997), offers important essays on that topic. Material on an early Indian civilization in the southwestern United States is available at "Sipapu: The Anasazi Emergence into the Cyber World" <http://sipapu.gsu.edu>.

Traditional European Society in 1450

Barbara W. Tuchman, *A Distant Mirror: The Calamitous Fourteenth Century* (1978), presents a vivid portrait of the late medieval world. Two wide-ranging studies of subsequent developments are George Huppert, *After the Black Death: A Social History of Modern Europe* (1986), and Henry Kamen, *European Society, 1500–1700* (1984). Illuminating specialized studies include Peter Burke, *Popular Culture in Early Modern Europe* (1978); Pierre Goubert, *The French Peasantry in the Seventeenth Century* (1986); B. H. Slicher Van Bath, *The Agrarian History of Western Europe, A.D. 500–1850* (1963); and Emanuel Le Roy Ladurie, *The Peasants of Languedoc* (1974). See also Joel Mokyr, *The Lever of Riches: Technological Creativity and Economic Progress* (1990), and E. P. Thompson, *Customs in Common: Studies in Traditional Popular Culture* (1991).

Europe Encounters Africa and the Americas, 1450–1550

The preconditions for European expansion are treated in James D. Tracy, ed., *Rise of Merchant Empires: Long Distance Trade in the Early Modern World, 1350–1750* (1990). For southern Europe, read selectively in Fernand Braudel's stimulating *The Mediterranean and the Mediterranean World in the Age of Philip II* (1949).

Paul H. Chapman, *The Norse Discovery of America* (1981), and Boies Penrose, *Travel and Discovery in the Renaissance, 1420–1620* (1952), illuminate the growth of geographical knowledge. For the expansion of Portugal and Spain, see Bailey W. Diffie and George Winius, *Foundations of the Portuguese Empire, 1415–1580* (1977), and Henry Kamen, *Crisis and Change in Early Modern Spain* (1993). A good short biography of Columbus and his times is Felipe Fernández-Armesto, *Columbus* (1991), but also see William D. Phillips Jr. and Carla Rahn Phillips, *The Worlds of Christopher Columbus* (1992).

For the Spanish and Portuguese colonial empires, see Charles R. Boxer, *The Portuguese Seaborne Empire* (1969), and James Lockhart and Stuart B. Schwartz, *Early Latin America: Colonial Spanish America and Brazil* (1984). Fine accounts of the Spanish conquest include the memorable firsthand report by Bernal Díaz del Castillo, *The Discovery and Conquest of Mexico* (ed. I. A. Leonard, 1956); Leon Portilla, *Broken Spears:*

The Aztec Account of the Conquest of Mexico (1962); and Hugh Thomas, *Conquest: Montezuma, Cortés, and the Fall of Old Mexico* (1994). The decline of native society in New Spain is outlined in Daniel T. Reff, *Disease, Depopulation, and Culture Change in Northwestern New Spain, 1518–1764* (1991). Thomas C. Patterson, *The Inca Empire* (1991); Nigel Davies, *The Incas* (1995); and R. Tom Zuidema, *Inca Civilization in Cuzco* (1992), explore the native civilization of Peru. Susan E. Ramírez, *The World Upside Down: Cross-Cultural Contact and Conflict in Sixteenth-Century Peru* (1996), offers a close analysis of Inca life after the conquest.

The Protestant Reformation and the Rise of England

On the European Reformation, consult William J. Bouwsma, *John Calvin* (1987), and De Lamar Jensen, *Reformation Europe: Age of Reform and Revolution* (1981). For England, see Patrick Collinson, *The Religion of the Protestants: The Church in English Society, 1559–1625* (1982), and Susan Doran and Christopher Durston, *Princes, Pastors, and People: The Church and Religion in England, 1529–1689* (1991). "Martin Luther" <http://www.luther.de/e/index.html> offers biographies of the leading figures of the Protestant Reformation and striking images of the era.

On the decline of Spain, consult Henry Kamen, *Spain: A Society in Conflict, 1479–1714* (2nd ed., 1991), and John Lynch, *The Hispanic World in Crisis and Change, 1598–1700* (1992), which also traces the growing economic independence of New Spain.

A brilliant and forceful portrait of English preindustrial society is offered by Peter Laslett, *The World We Have Lost* (3rd ed., 1984). Other important works are Keith Wrightson, *English Society, 1580–1680* (1982), and Lawrence Stone, *The Crisis of the Aristocracy* (1965). On the movement of people, see Ida Altman and James Horn, eds., *"To Make America": European Emigration in the Early Modern Period* (1991).

Chapter 2: The Invasion and Settlement of North America, 1550–1700

David Weber, *The Spanish Frontier in North America* (1992), and Richard White, *The Middle Ground: Indians, Empires, and Republics in the Great Lakes Region, 1650–1815* (1991), are important studies while Bernard Bailyn, *The Peopling of British North America* (1986), and Colin G. Calloway, *New Worlds for All: Indians, Europeans, and the Remaking of Early America* (1997), offer incisive overviews of two important topics.

Imperial Conflicts and Rival Colonial Models

For a discussion of Spain's northern empire in America, see Ramón Gutiérrez, *When Jesus Came, the Corn Mothers Went Away: Marriage, Sexuality, and Power in New Mexico, 1500–1846* (1991). The French threat to Spain's domain is traced by Robert S. Weddle, *The French Thorn: Rival Explorers in the Spanish Sea, 1682–1762* (1991), and Daniel H. Usner Jr., *Indians, Settlers, and Slaves in a Frontier Exchange Economy: The Lower Mississippi Valley before 1783* (1991).

The best general studies of French Canada are by W. J. Eccles: *The Canadian Frontier, 1534–1760* (1983) and *France in America* (rev. ed., 1990). French interaction with Native Americans is covered by Bruce G. Trigger, *The Children of Aataentsic: A History of the Huron People to 1660* (1976); Daniel K. Richter, *The Ordeal of the Long House: The Peoples of the Iroquois League in the Era of European Colonization* (1992); and Olive Patricia Dickason, *Canada's First Nations: A History of the Founding Peoples from Earliest Times* (1992).

Two works by Jonathan I. Israel, *The Dutch Republic: Its Rise, Greatness and Fall* (1995) and *Dutch Primacy in World Trade, 1585–1740* (1989), show the impressive reach of Dutch commerce. For its American component, consult Oliver A. Rink, *Holland on the Hudson: An Economic and Social History of Dutch New York* (1986).

For a discussion of English expansion, see Kenneth Andrews, *Trade, Plunder, and Settlement: Maritime Enterprise and the Genesis of the British Empire, 1480–1630* (1984); Nicholas Canny, *Kingdom and Colony: Ireland in the Atlantic World, 1560–1800* (1988); A. L. Rowse, *Sir Walter Raleigh* (1962); David B. Quinn, *England and the Discovery of America, 1481–1620* (1974); and Karen O. Kupperman, *Roanoke* (1984). The interaction of the English and Dutch with Native Americans can be followed in Gary B. Nash, *Red, White, and Black: The Peoples of Early America* (1982); Francis Jennings, *The Invasion of America* (1975); and two works by James Axtell, *The European and the Indian* (1981) and *The Invasion Within: The Contest of Cultures in Colonial North America* (1985).

The Chesapeake Experience

Alden Vaughan, *American Genesis: Captain John Smith and the Founding of Virginia* (1975), covers the earliest years, while Edmund S. Morgan, *American Slavery, American Freedom: The Ordeal of Colonial Virginia* (1975), provides a brilliant analysis of the rest of the seventeenth century. Important essays appear in Thad W. Tate and David L. Ammerman, eds., *The Chesapeake in the Seventeenth Century* (1979), and Lois Green Carr, Philip D. Morgan, and Jean B. Russo, *Colonial Chesapeake Society* (1989). Other significant studies include Lois Green Carr et al., *Robert Cole's World: Agriculture and Society in Early Maryland* (1991); Kathleen Brown, *Good Wives, Nasty Wenches, and Anxious Patriarchs: Gender, Race, and Power in Colonial Virginia* (1996); and James Horn, *Adapting to a New World: English Society in the Seventeenth-Century Chesapeake* (1994). For a discussion of political institutions, see W. F. Craven, *The Southern Colonies in the Seventeenth Century, 1607–1689* (1949), and David W. Jordan, *Foundations of Representative Government in Maryland, 1632–1715* (1988). Contrasting accounts of Bacon's Rebellion can be found in T. J. Wertenbaker, *Torchbearer of the Revolution* (1940), and Wilcomb B. Washburn, *The Governor and the Rebel* (1958). "Colonial Williamsburg" <http://www.history.org/> offers an extensive collection of documents, illustrations, and secondary texts about colonial life, as well as information about the archeological excavations at Williamsburg.

Puritan New England

For the Puritan migration, see Virginia DeJohn Anderson, *New England's Generation: The Great Migration and the Formation of Society and Culture in the Seventeenth Century* (1991); Edmund Morgan, *The Puritan Dilemma: The Story of*

John Winthrop (1955); David Grayson Allen, *In English Ways: The Movement of Societies and the Transferral of English Local Law and Custom to Massachusetts Bay in the Seventeenth Century* (1981); and David Cressy, *Coming Over: Migration and Communication between England and New England in the Seventeenth Century* (1987). A highly acclaimed site on the Pilgrims at Plymouth is "Caleb Johnson's Mayflower Web Pages" <http://members.aol.com/calebj/mayflower.html>.

Puritanism as an intellectual movement is best explored in the works of Perry Miller; see especially *The New England Mind: The Seventeenth Century* (1939). Charles Hambrick-Stowe, *The Practice of Piety: Puritan Devotional Disciplines* (1982), discusses the emotional dimension of Puritanism, while David D. Hall, *World of Wonder, Days of Judgment: Popular Religious Belief in Early New England* (1989), explores its supernatural aspects. See also Andrew Delbanco, *The Puritan Ordeal* (1989).

For a discussion of dissent in early New England, consult Philip Gura, *A Glimpse of Sion's Glory: Puritan Radicalism in New England, 1620–1660* (1984); Edwin S. Gaustad, *Liberty of Conscience: Roger Williams in America* (1991); Amy Schrager Lang, *Prophetic Woman: Anne Hutchinson and the Problem of Dissent in the Literature of New England* (1987); Paul Boyer and Steven Nissenbaum, *Salem Possessed: The Social Origins of Witchcraft* (1974); and Carol F. Karlsen, *The Devil in the Shape of a Woman: Witchcraft in New England* (1987). Extensive materials on the Salem witchcraft episode can be viewed at <http://etext.lib.virginia.edu/salem/witchcraft/>.

Community studies that describe the lives of ordinary New England men and women include John Demos, *The Little Commonwealth: Family Life in Plymouth Colony* (1971), and Kenneth A. Lockridge, *A New England Town . . . Dedham, Massachusetts, 1636–1736* (1970). See also John Demos, *The Unredeemed Captive: A Family Story from Early America* (1994), and Stephen Innes, *Creating the Commonwealth: The Economic Culture of Puritan New England* (1995).

The Indians' New World

James H. Merrell, *The Indians' New World: Catawbas and Their Neighbors from European Contact through the Era of Removal* (1989), is a pathbreaking study. Alfred Cave, *The Pequot War* (1996), explores the first war in New England. Three fine studies of subsequent conflicts are Jill Lepore, *The Name of War: King Philip's War and the Origins of American Identity* (1998); Patrick M. Malone, *The Skulking Way of War: Technology and Techniques among New England Indians* (1991); and Russell Bourne, *Red King's Rebellion* (1995). See also Karen Ordahl Kupperman, *Settling with the Indians: The Meeting of English and Indian Cultures in America, 1580–1640* (1981); Bernard Sheehan, *Savagism and Civility: Indians and Englishmen in Colonial Virginia* (1980); and Daniel K. Richter and James H. Merrell, *Beyond the Covenant Chain: The Iroquois and Their Neighbors in Indian North America* (1987). A PBS video, *Surviving Columbus* (2 hours), traces the experiences of the Pueblo Indians over 450 years. "First Nations Histories" <http://www.dickshovel.com/Compacts.html> presents short histories of many North American Indian peoples and information on their politics, language, culture, and demography. A fine ecological study is William Cronon, *Changes in the Land: Indians, Colonists, and the Ecology of New England* (1983).

Chapter 3: The British Empire in America, 1660–1750

The best overview of England's empire is Michael Kammen, *Empire and Interest: The American Colonies and the Politics of Mercantilism* (1970); for more recent accounts, see Alison Olson, *Making the Empire Work: London and American Interest Groups, 1690–1790* (1992), and Linda Colley, *Britons: Forging the Nation, 1707–1837* (1992). On Africa, consult Paul Bohannan and Philip Curtin, *Africa and the Africans* (3rd ed., 1988). Two fine syntheses of the African American experience are Philip D. Morgan, *Slave Counterpoint: Black Culture in the Eighteenth-Century Chesapeake and Low Country* (1998), and Ira Berlin, *Many Thousands Gone: The First Two Centuries of Slavery in North America* (1999).

The Politics of Empire, 1660–1713

Jonathan Scott, *England's Troubles* (2000), sets the European context for imperial politics, while Robert Bliss, *Revolution and Empire: English Politics and the American Colonies in the Seventeenth Century* (1990), and Jack M. Sosin, *English America and the Restoration Monarchy of Charles II: Transatlantic Politics, Commerce, and Kinship* (1980), explore their impact in the colonies. See also Stephen S. Webb, *1676: The End of American Independence* (1984).

For the events of 1688–1689, consult W. A. Speck, *Reluctant Revolutionaries: Englishmen and the Revolution of 1688* (1989), and David S. Lovejoy, *The Glorious Revolution in America* (1972). A good case study is Lois Green Carr and David W. Jordan, *Maryland's Revolution of Government, 1689–1692* (1974). Ethnic tension in New York can be traced in Robert C. Ritchie, *The Duke's Province: Politics and Society in New York, 1660–1691* (1977); Donna Merwick, *Possessing Albany, 1630–1710: The Dutch and English Experiences* (1990); and Joyce Goodfriend, *Before the Melting Pot: Society and Culture in Colonial New York City, 1664–1730* (1992). Jack M. Sosin, *English America and Imperial Inconstancy: The Rise of Provincial Autonomy, 1696–1715* (1985), outlines the new imperial system.

The Imperial Slave Economy

For the African background, see John Thornton, *Africa and Africans in the Making of the Atlantic World, 1400–1680* (1992), and Richard Olaniyan, *African History and Culture* (1982). Specialized studies of forced African migration include Patrick Manning, *Slavery and African Life* (1990); Philip Curtin, *The Atlantic Slave Trade: A Census* (1969); Paul Lovejoy, ed., *Africans in Bondage: Studies in Slavery and the Slave Trade* (1986); Hugh Thomas, *The Slave Trade* (1991); and Barbara L. Solow, ed., *Slavery and the Rise of the Atlantic System* (1991).

Richard S. Dunn, *Sugar and Slaves: The Rise of the Planter Class in the English West Indies, 1624–1713* (1972), provides a graphic portrait of the brutal slave-based economy, while Sidney W. Mintz, *Sweetness and Power: The Place of Sugar in Modern History* (1985), explores the impact of the major crop of the slave economy. Winthrop D. Jordan, *White over Black, 1550–1812* (1968), remains the best account of Virginia's decision for slavery, but see also Thomas D. Morris, *Southern Slavery and the Law, 1619–1860* (1996).

Lorena Walsh, *From Calabar to Carter's Grove* (1998), closely examines the lives of Africans in Virginia as does Michael Gomez, *Exchanging Our Country Marks: The Transformation of African Identities in the Colonial and Antebellum South* (1998). Other works exploring the creation of African American society include Allan Kulikoff, *Tobacco and Slaves: Southern Cultures in the Chesapeake, 1680–1800* (1986); Daniel C. Littlefield, *Rice and Slaves: Ethnicity and the Slave Trade in Colonial South Carolina* (1981); Peter H. Wood, *Black Majority: Negroes in Colonial South Carolina through the Stono Rebellion* (1974); and Marvin L. Michael Kay and Lorin Lee Cary, *Slavery in North Carolina, 1748–1775* (1995). See also Richard Price, ed., *Maroon Societies: Rebel Slave Communities in the Americas* (1973); Ira Berlin and Philip D. Morgan, eds., *Cultivation and Culture: Labor and the Shaping of Slave Life in the Americas* (1992); and Mechel Sobel, *The World They Made Together* (1987), which discusses the mingling of cultures in Virginia. The PBS video, *Africans in America*, Part 1: "Terrible Transformation, 1450–1750" (1.5 hours) covers the African American experience in the colonial period; the Web site <http://www.pbs.org/wgbh/aia/part1/title.html> contains a wide variety of pictures, historical documents, and scholarly commentary. "Excerpts from Slave Narratives" <http://vi.uh.edu/pages/mintz/primary.htm> presents materials selected by Steven Mintz from forty-six accounts, arranged in eleven chronological and thematic categories.

On white society in the South, read Richard Bushman, *The Refinement of America* (1992); Daniel Blake Smith, *Inside the Great House: Planter Family Life in Eighteenth-Century Chesapeake Society* (1980); Timothy H. Breen, *Tobacco Culture* (1985); and a fine older study of political practices, Charles Sydnor, *American Revolutionaries in the Making* (1952). Urban society and trade are explored in Gary B. Nash, *The Urban Crucible* (1979); Gary M. Walton and James F. Shepherd, *The Economic Rise of Early America* (1979); and Christine L. Heyrman, *Commerce and Culture: The Maritime Communities of Colonial Massachusetts, 1690–1750* (1984). See also Marcus Rediker, *Between the Devil and the Deep Blue Sea: Merchant Seamen, Pirates, and the Anglo-American Maritime World, 1700–1750* (1987).

The New Politics of Empire, 1713–1750

The appearance of a distinctive American system of politics is traced in Bernard Bailyn, *The Origins of American Politics* (1968). Studies of various colonies include Trevor Burnard, *Creole Gentlemen: The Maryland Elite, 1691–1776* (2000); Jack P. Greene, *The Quest for Power: The Lower Houses of Assembly in the Southern Royal Colonies, 1689–1776* (1963); Patricia U. Bonomi, *A Factious People: Politics and Society in Colonial New York* (1971); A. Roger Ekirch, *"Poor Carolina": Politics and Society in Colonial North Carolina, 1729–1776* (1981); and Richard Bushman, *King and People in Provincial Massachusetts* (1985). John Schutz, *William Shirley* (1961), shows how a competent colonial governor wielded power, while Thomas C. Barrow, *Trade and Empire: The British Customs Service in Colonial America, 1660–1775* (1967), and Alison G. Olson, *Anglo-American Politics, 1660–1775* (1973), explore various aspects of British mercantilism.

Douglas E. Leach, *Roots of Conflict: British Armed Forces and Colonial Americans, 1677–1763* (1986), covers the diplomatic and military conflicts of the period, but this Anglo-American perspective is balanced by Patricia Wood, *French-Indian Relations on the Southern Frontier* (1992); David J. Weber, *The Spanish Frontier in North America* (1992); and Ian K. Steele, *Warpaths: Invasions of North America* (1993).

Chapter 4: Growth and Crisis in Colonial Society, 1720–1765

Two collections of important articles are in Stanley Katz, John Murrin, and Douglas Greenberg, eds., *Colonial America: Essays in Politics and Social Development* (5th ed., 2001), and Bernard Bailyn and Philip D. Morgan, eds., *Strangers within the Realm: Cultural Margins of the First British Empire* (1991). John J. McCusker and Russell R. Menard, *The Economy of British America, 1607–1783* (1985), surveys economic change, and Jon Butler, *Awash in a Sea of Faith: Christianizing the American People* (1990), covers religious developments. Jack P. Greene, *Pursuits of Happiness* (1988), offers a provocative comparative analysis of regional social evolution. See also Allan Kulikoff, *From British Peasants to American Colonial Farmers* (2000), and Christopher L. Tomlins and Bruce H. Mann, eds., *The Many Legalities of Early America* (2001).

Freehold Society in New England

A good local study is Daniel Vickers, *Farmers and Fishermen: Two Centuries of Work in Essex County, Massachusetts, 1630–1830* (1994). Bruce C. Daniels, *The Fragmentation of New England: Comparative Perspectives on Economic, Political, and Social Divisions in the Eighteenth Century* (1988), and Allan Kulikoff, *The Agrarian Origins of American Capitalism* (1992), offer a wider view. See also Robert Gross, *The Minutemen and Their World* (1976), and Richard Bushman, *From Puritan to Yankee: Character and the Social Order in Connecticut, 1690–1765* (1967). On women's lives, see Laurel Thatcher Ulrich, *Good Wives: Image and Reality in the Lives of Women of Northern New England, 1650–1750* (1982); Marylynn Salmon, *Women and the Law of Property in Early America* (1986); Cornelia H. Dayton, *Women before the Bar: Gender, Law, and Society in Connecticut, 1639–1789* (1995); and William J. Scheick, *Authority and Female Authorship in Colonial America* (1998). For insight into the day-to-day lives of women see the PBS video *A Midwife's Tale* (1.5 hours), which tells the story of Martha Ballard, who lived at the end of the eighteenth century; additional materials on Ballard's experiences are available on the Web at <http://www.pbs.org/amex/midwife> and <http://www.DoHistory.org>.

For studies of material culture, see Robert B. St. George, ed., *Material Life in America, 1600–1860* (1988), and Cary Carson et al., eds., *Of Consuming Interest* (1994). For insight into day-to-day economic life, see the "Colonial Currency and Colonial Coin" site <http://www.coins.nd.edu/>, which contains detailed essays as well as pictures of colonial money.

The Middle Atlantic: Toward a New Society, 1720–1765

On Pennsylvania, consult Michael Zuckerman, ed., *Friends and Neighbors: Group Life in America's First Plural Society*

(1982); Barry J. Levy, *Quakers and the American Family* (1988); and James T. Lemon, *The Best Poor Man's Country* (1972). On white indentured servants, see the classic study by Abbot E. Smith, *Colonists in Bondage* (1947).

Important studies of migration include Marilyn C. Baseler, *"Asylum for Mankind": America 1607–1800* (1998); Bernard Bailyn, *Voyagers to the West* (1986); A. G. Roeber, *Palatines, Liberty, and Property: German Lutherans in Colonial British America* (1993); Jon Butler, *The Huguenots in America* (1983); Ned Landsman, *Scotland and Its First American Colony, 1683–1775* (1985); A. Roger Ekirch, *Bound for America: The Transportation of British Convicts to the Colonies, 1718–1775* (1987); Aaron S. Fogleman, *Hopeful Journeys: German Immigration, Settlement, and Political Culture in Colonial America, 1717–1775* (1996); Marianne Wokeck, *Trade in Strangers: The Beginnings of Mass Migration to North America* (1999); and Patrick Griffin, *The People with No Name: Ireland's Ulster Scots, America's Scots Irish, and the Creation of a British Atlantic World, 1689–1764* (2001).

Important studies on Middle Atlantic politics include Benjamin H. Newcomb, *Political Partisanship in the American Middle Colonies, 1700–1776* (1995); Patricia U. Bonomi, *A Factious People: Politics and Society in Colonial New York* (1971); Thomas L. Purvis, *Proprietors, Patronage, and Money: New Jersey, 1703–1776* (1986); and Alan Tully, *Forming American Politics* (1994).

The Enlightenment and the Great Awakening, 1740–1765

Henry F. May, *The Enlightenment in America* (1976), is still the standard treatment, but see also Douglas Anderson, *The Radical Enlightenment of Benjamin Franklin* (1997); Ned Landsman, *From Colonials to Provincials: Thought and Culture in America, 1680–1760* (1998); Michael Warner, *The Letters of the Republic* (1990); and David S. Shields, *Civil Tongues and Polite Letters in British America* (1997). Franklin's life and times are presented at "The Electric Franklin" <http://www.ushistory.org/franklin/>. For medical knowledge, consult Richard Shryock, *Medicine and Society in America, 1660–1860* (1960).

Good studies of the Great Awakening in Europe and America include W. R. Ward, *The Protestant Evangelical Awakening* (1992); David S. Lovejoy, *Religious Enthusiasm in the New World: Heresy to Revolution* (1985); Patricia U. Bonomi, *Under the Cope of Heaven: Religion, Society, and Politics in Colonial America* (1986); and Harry S. Stout, *The New England Soul: Preaching and Religious Culture in Colonial New England* (1986). Three good biographies of New England revivalists are Patricia Tracy, *Jonathan Edwards, Pastor* (1979); W. G. McLoughlin, *Isaac Backus and American Pietistic Tradition* (1957); and Christopher Jedrey, *The World of John Cleaveland* (1979). Harry S. Stout's *The Divine Dramatist* (1991) is a fine biography of George Whitefield. Richard Bushman, ed., *The Great Awakening* (1970), and Rhys Isaac, *The Transformation of Virginia, 1740–1790* (1982), capture the emotions of ordinary participants in the Great Awakening. "Jonathan Edwards On-Line" <http://www.JonathanEdwards.com/> provides access to the writings of the great philosopher and preacher, but note that this site uses Edwards's arguments to advance one side of a present-day theological debate.

The Midcentury Challenge: War, Trade, and Social Conflict, 1750–1765

Fred Anderson, *Crucible of War: The Seven Years' War and the Fate of Empire in British North America, 1754–1766* (2000), is a definitive study. Douglas E. Leach, *Roots of Conflict: British Armed Forces and Colonial Americans, 1677–1763* (1986), sets the war in a broad context. See also Guy Frégault, *Canada: The War of the Conquest* (1969); George F. G. Stanley, *New France: The Last Phase, 1744–1760* (1968); and Fred Anderson, *A People's Army: Massachusetts Soldiers and Society in the Seven Years' War* (1984). Richard White, *The Middle Ground* (1991), and Francis Jennings, *Empire of Fortune: Crown, Colonies, and Tribes in the Seven Years' War* (1988), describe the crucial role played by Indians in the conflict. See also Richard Aquila, *The Iroquois Restoration: Iroquois Diplomacy on the Colonial Frontier, 1701–1754* (1983), and David H. Corkran, *The Cherokee Frontier: Conflict and Survival, 1740–1762* (1966).

Gary M. Walton and James F. Shepherd, *The Economic Rise of Early America* (1979), trace the growing importance of commerce. See also Paul G. E. Clemens, *The Atlantic Economy and Colonial Maryland's Eastern Shore: From Tobacco to Grain* (1980).

On backcountry political agitation see Richard D. Brown, *The South Carolina Regulators* (1963), and Alfred Young, ed., *The American Revolution: Essays in the History of American Radicalism* (1976). See also W. Stitt Robinson, *The Southern Colonial Frontier, 1607–1763* (1979), and Rachel N. Klein, *Unification of a Slave State: The Rise of the Planter Class in the South Carolina Backcountry, 1660–1808* (1994).

Chapter 5: Toward Independence: Years of Decision, 1763–1775

Jack P. Greene and J. R. Pole, eds., *The Blackwell Encyclopedia of the American Revolution* (1991), illuminates both obscure and well-known aspects of the Revolutionary era, as do the personal testimonies in Barbara DeWolfe, *Discoveries of America: Personal Accounts of British Emigrants to North America during the Revolutionary Era* (1997). A good interpretive synthesis is Edward Countryman, *The American Revolution* (1985); for a British perspective, see Colin Bonwick, *The American Revolution* (1991). Lester D. Langley, *The Americas in the Age of Revolution, 1750–1850* (1996), provides a valuable comparative analysis. The Web site of the National Gallery of Art <http://www.nga.gov/> has an interesting section devoted to American paintings of the colonial and revolutionary periods, including a detailed analysis of a work by Jonathan Copley, and in the "Index of American Design" a collection of eighteenth-century German American folk art.

The Imperial Reform Movement, 1763–1765

For the state of the empire in 1763, see Alison Gilbert Olson, *Making the Empire Work: London and the American Interest Groups, 1690–1790* (1992); and Jack P. Greene, *Peripheries and Center: Constitutional Development in the Extended Polities of the British Empire and the United States, 1607–1788* (1986). The impact of the Seven Years' War is traced in the classic study by Lawrence H. Gipson, *The Coming of the Revolution, 1763–1775* (1954), and in Richard Middleton, *The Bells of*

Victory: The Pitt-Newcastle Ministry and the Conduct of the Seven Years' War, 1757–1762 (1985); Howard H. Peckham, *Pontiac and the Indian Uprising* (1947); and Joseph A. Ernst, *Money and Politics in America, 1755–1775* (1973). Marc Egnal, *A Mighty Empire: The Origins of the Revolution* (1988), shows the links to western expansion.

British politics and imperial reform can be traced in John Brewer, *Party Ideology and Popular Politics at the Accession of George III* (1976); P. D. G. Thomas, *British Politics and the Stamp Act Crisis: The First Phase of the American Revolution, 1763–1767* (1975); Thomas C. Barrow, *Trade and Empire: The British Customs Service in Colonial America, 1660–1775* (1967); John L. Bullion, *A Great and Necessary Measure: George Grenville and the Genesis of the Stamp Act, 1763–1765* (1982); Carl Ubbelohde, *The Vice-Admiralty Courts and the American Revolution* (1960); and Philip Lawson, *George Grenville* (1984).

The Dynamics of Rebellion, 1765–1766

For the American response to the British reform laws, see Edmund S. Morgan and Helen M. Morgan, *The Stamp Act Crisis* (1963); Pauline Maier, *From Resistance to Revolution: Colonial Radicals and the Development of Colonial Opposition to Britain, 1765–1776* (1972); and Gary B. Nash, *The Urban Crucible: Social Change, Political Consciousness, and the Origins of the American Revolution* (1979). Merrill Jensen, *The Founding of a Nation: A History of the American Revolution, 1763–1776* (1968), and Robert Middlekauff, *The Glorious Cause: The American Revolution, 1763–1789* (1982), provide detailed narratives of the Revolutionary era.

Studies of individual colonies capture the spirit of the resistance movement. See Woody Holton, *Forced Founders: Indians, Debtors, Slaves, and the Making of the American Revolution in Virginia* (1999); Joseph S. Tiedemann, *Reluctant Revolutionaries: New York City and the Road to Independence, 1963–1976* (1997); and Ronald Hoffman, *A Spirit of Dissension: Economics, Politics, and the Revolution in Maryland* (1973). The motives of Patriots are best addressed through biographies. See Francis Jennings, *Benjamin Franklin, Politician* (1996); Pauline Maier, *The Old Revolutionaries: Political Lives in the Age of Samuel Adams* (1980); Milton E. Flower, *John Dickinson, Conservative Revolutionary* (1983); Richard R. Beeman, *Patrick Henry: A Biography* (1974); John R. Alden, *George Washington: A Biography* (1984); Helen Hill Miller, *George Mason: Gentleman Revolutionary* (1975); and John Ferling, *John Adams: A Life* (1992).

The most important single study of Patriot ideology is Bernard Bailyn, *The Ideological Origins of the American Revolution* (1967), but see also Robert M. Calhoon, *Dominion and Liberty: Ideology in Anglo-American Political Thought, 1660–1801* (1994). Other works include Caroline Robbins, *The Eighteenth-Century Commonwealthman* (1959); Morton White, *The Philosophy of the American Revolution* (1978); Garry Wills, *Inventing America: Jefferson's Declaration of Independence* (1978); and H. T. Dickinson, *Liberty and Property: Political Ideology in Eighteenth-Century Britain* (1978). For a discussion of the legal tradition, see Charles H. McIlwain, *The American Revolution: A Constitutional Interpretation* (1923), and John Philip Reid's *Constitutional History of the American Revolution* (1986–1996).

The Growing Confrontation, 1767–1770

Peter D. G. Thomas, *The Townshend Duties Crisis: The Second Phase of the American Revolution, 1767–1773* (1987), is the most comprehensive treatment, but see also Colin Bonwick, *English Radicals and the American Revolution* (1977). On American resistance consult Richard Alan Ryerson, *The Revolution Is Now Begun: The Radical Committees of Philadelphia, 1765–1776* (1978); Peter Shaw, *American Patriots and the Rituals of Revolution* (1981); and Stanley Godbold Jr. and Robert W. Woody, *Christopher Gadsden* (1982). The military confrontation is covered in John Shy, *Toward Lexington: The Role of the British Army in the Coming of the American Revolution* (1965), and Hiller B. Zobel, *The Boston Massacre* (1970). *Liberty! The American Revolution* (6 hours), a six-part video available through PBS, provides a coherent narrative of the movement for independence. Contrasting firsthand accounts of the Boston Massacre are available on the Web site "From Revolution to Reconstruction" at the University of Groningen <http://odur.let.rug.nl/~usa/> which also contains other materials on the Revolutionary era.

The Road to War, 1771–1775

Benjamin Labaree, *The Boston Tea Party* (1964), is a stimulating account. See also Peter D. G. Thomas, *Tea Party to Independence* (1991); Bernard Donoughue, *British Politics and the American Revolution: The Path to War, 1773–75* (1972); and David Ammerman, *In the Common Cause: American Response to the Coercive Acts of 1774* (1968). A fine study of the resistance movement is Edward F. Countryman, *A People in Revolution: The American Revolution and Political Society in New York* (1983). On prewar Loyalism, see Bernard Bailyn, *The Ordeal of Thomas Hutchinson* (1974), and Janice Potter, *The Liberty We Seek: Loyalist Ideology in Colonial New York and Massachusetts* (1983). For the rising of the countryside, see David Hackett Fischer, *Paul Revere's Ride* (1994); Gregory H. Nobles, *Divisions throughout the Whole: Politics and Society in Hampshire County, Massachusetts, 1740–1775* (1983); and Richard Bushman, *King and People in Provincial Massachusetts* (1985). The transfer of authority is described in Jerrilyn Greene Marston, *King and Congress: The Transfer of Political Legitimacy, 1774–1776* (1987).

Chapter 6: War and Revolution, 1775–1783

Gordon Wood, *The Radicalism of the American Revolution* (1992), offers a fine overview. For contrasting interpretations, see the essays in Alfred F. Young, ed., *Beyond the American Revolution: Explorations in the History of American Radicalism* (1993). Jack P. Greene and J. R. Pole, eds., *The Blackwell Encyclopedia of the American Revolution* (1991), provides illuminating essays on important topics. Colin G. Calloway, *The American Revolution in Indian Country: Crisis and Diversity in Native American Communities* (1995), traces the Revolution's impact on the native peoples, while Robin Blackburn, *The Overthrow of Colonial Slavery, 1776–1848* (1988), shows how it aided the decline of racial bondage in the Western Hemisphere. *Liberty! The American Revolution* (PBS video; 6 hours) and the companion Web site

<http://www.pbs.org/ktca/liberty/> cover the war and the making of the Constitution.

Toward Independence, 1775–1776

Jerrilyn Greene Marston, *King and Congress: The Transfer of Political Legitimacy, 1774–1776* (1987), and Jack N. Rakove, *The Beginnings of National Politics* (1979), discuss the movement toward independence. See also Eric Foner, *Tom Paine and Revolutionary America* (1976); Jack Fruchtman Jr., *Thomas Paine: Apostle of Freedom* (1994); and Pauline Maier, *American Scripture: Making the Declaration of Independence* (1997). To explore the political philosophy of Thomas Jefferson, log on to "Quotations from the Writings of Thomas Jefferson" <http://etext.virginia.edu/jefferson/quotations/>, which are conveniently arranged by topic. On Loyalism, read William N. Nelson, *The American Tory* (1961), and the essays collected in Robert M. Calhoon et al., eds., *Loyalists and Community in North America* (1994).

The Trials of War, 1776–1778

The military history of the war is covered in James L. Stokesbury, *A Short History of the American Revolution* (1991), and Piers Mackesy, *The War for America, 1775–1783* (1964). Don Higginbotham, *George Washington and the American Military Tradition* (1985), and Ronald Hoffman and Peter Albert, eds., *Arms and Independence: The Military Character of the American Revolution* (1984), offer a more analytical perspective. Mark V. Kwasny, *Washington's Partisan War, 1775–1783* (1997), stresses Washington's increasing use of the militia. The war in the North can be followed in Ira D. Gruber, *The Howe Brothers and the American Revolution* (1972), and Richard J. Hargrove Jr., *General John Burgoyne* (1983). "Virtual Marching Tour of the Philadelphia Campaign 1777" <http://www.ushistory.org/march/index.html> offers a multimedia view of Howe's attack on Philadelphia and subsequent events.

Studies of ordinary soldiers include Rodney Attwood, *The Hessians* (1980); Sylvia R. Frey, *The British Soldier in America* (1981); Robert K. Wright Jr., *The Continental Army* (1983); Charles P. Neimeyer, *America Goes to War: A Social History of the Continental Army* (1996); and John C. Dann, ed., *The Revolution Remembered: Eyewitness Accounts of the War for Independence* (1980). For the military bureaucracy, see R. Arthur Bowler, *Logistics and the Failure of the British Army in America, 1775–1783* (1975), and E. Wayne Carp, *To Starve the Army at Pleasure: Continental Army Administration and American Political Culture, 1775–1783* (1984).

Local studies include Jean Butenhoff Lee, *The Price of Nationhood: The American Revolution in Charles County* (1994); David Hackett Fischer, *Paul Revere's Ride* (1994); Richard Buel Jr., *Dear Liberty: Connecticut's Mobilization for the Revolutionary War* (1980); and Donald Wallace White, *A Village at War: Chatham, New Jersey, and the American Revolution* (1979).

African American participation in the war is discussed in Sidney Kaplan, *The Black Presence in the Era of the American Revolution* (rev. ed., 1989), and Gary B. Nash, *Race and Revolution* (1990). A fine, data-rich source on the black experience is "Africans in America: Revolution" <http://www.pbs.org/wgbh/aia/part2/title.html>; other parts of this Web site cover the entire African American experience. The Native American response is described in Colin G. Calloway, *The American*

Revolution in Indian Country (1995); Barbara Graymont, *The Iroquois in the American Revolution* (1972); Isabel T. Kelsey, *Joseph Brant, 1743–1807* (1984); and James H. O'Donnell III, *Southern Indians in the American Revolution* (1973).

A classic discussion of the fiscal problems created by the war is E. James Ferguson, *The Power of the Purse* (1961); a more recent study is William G. Anderson, *The Price of Liberty: The Public Debt of the American Revolution* (1983).

The Path to Victory, 1778–1783

Bradford Perkins, *The Creation of a Republican Empire, 1776–1865* (1993), and Jonathan R. Dull, *A Diplomatic History of the American Revolution* (1985), provide good overviews. More specialized studies include James H. Hutson, *John Adams and the Diplomacy of the American Revolution* (1980); Richard B. Morris, *The Peacemakers: The Great Powers and American Independence* (1965); and Ronald Hoffman and Peter J. Albert, eds., *Peace and the Peacemakers: The Treaty of 1783* (1986).

For the southern campaign, consult W. Robert Higgins, ed., *The Revolutionary War in the South* (1979); Ronald Hoffman, Thad W. Tate, and Peter J. Albert, eds., *An Uncivil War: The Southern Backcountry during the American Revolution* (1985); and Jeffrey J. Crow and Larry E. Tise, eds., *The Southern Experience in the American Revolution* (1978). Studies of military action include Hugh F. Rankin, *Francis Marion: The Swamp Fox* (1973), and John S. Pancake, *The Destructive War, 1780–1782* (1985).

Republicanism Defined and Challenged

Milton M. Klein et al., *The Republican Synthesis Revisited* (1992), explores the debate over the importance of republican thought. See also Charles Royster, *A Revolutionary People at War: The Continental Army and American Character, 1775–1783* (1979). On women's lives, see Ronald Hoffman and Peter J. Albert, eds., *Women in the Age of the American Revolution* (1989); Mary Beth Norton, *Liberty's Daughters: The Revolutionary Experience of American Women, 1750–1800* (1980); and Joy Day Buel and Richard Buel Jr., *The Way of Duty: A Woman and Her Family in Revolutionary America* (1984).

On the black experience, consult Sylvia R. Frey, *Water from the Rock: Black Resistance in a Revolutionary Age* (1991); Ira Berlin and Ronald Hoffman, eds., *Slavery and Freedom in the Age of the American Revolution* (1983); and Gary B. Nash, *Forging Freedom: The Formation of Philadelphia's Black Community, 1720–1840* (1988). See also James W. St. G. Walker, *The Black Loyalists: The Search for a Promised Land in Nova Scotia and Sierra Leone, 1783–1870* (1976), and Shane White, *Somewhat More Independent: The End of Slavery in New York City, 1770–1810* (1991).

On changes in American religion, see Dee E. Andrews, *The Methodists and Revolutionary America, 1760–1800* (2000); Ronald Hoffman and Peter J. Albert, eds., *Religion in a Revolutionary Age* (1994); Rhys Isaac, *The Transformation of Virginia, 1740–1790* (1982); Fred Hood, *Reformed America, 1783–1837* (1980); and Nathan O. Hatch, *The Democratization of American Christianity* (1989). The spiritual roots of a new secular religion are traced by Catharine Albanese, *Sons of the Fathers: The Civil Religion of the American Revolution* (1976), and Ruth Bloch, *Visionary Republic: Millennial Themes in American Thought* (1985).

Chapter 7: The New Political Order, 1776–1800

Jack N. Rakove, *Original Meaning: Politics and Ideas in the Making of the Constitution* (1996), and Richard B. Bernstein and Kym S. Rice, *Are We to Be a Nation? The Making of the Constitution* (1987), are the best recent overviews of the creation of a national republic. Stanley Elkins and Eric McKitrick, *The Age of Federalism: The Early Republic, 1788–1800* (1993), offers a comprehensive assessment of the 1790s. Three interesting cultural studies of political life are Simon P. Newman, *Parades and the Politics of the Street: Festive Culture in the Early American Republic* (1997); David Waldstreicher, *In the Midst of Perpetual Fetes: The Making of American Nationalism, 1776–1820* (1997); and Len Travers, *Celebrating the Fourth: Independence Day and the Rise of Nationalism in the Early Republic* (1997).

Creating Republican Institutions, 1776–1787

Elisha P. Douglass, *Rebels and Democrats* (1965), documents the struggle for equal political rights while Gordon Wood, *The Creation of the American Republic, 1776–1790* (1965), provides a magisterial analysis of state and national constitutional development. For a contrary view, see Thomas Pangle, *The Spirit of Modern Republicanism: The Moral Vision of the American Founder and the Philosophy of Locke* (1988). See also Merrill Jensen, *The New Nation* (1950), and Jackson T. Main, *The Sovereign States, 1775–1783* (1973). Important studies of state constitutions include Willi Paul Adams, *The First American Constitutions* (1980); Edward F. Countryman, *A People in Revolution: The American Revolution and Political Society in New York, 1760–1790* (1981); and Donald Lutz, *Popular Consent and Popular Control: Whig Political Theory in the Early State Constitutions* (1980).

On women and republicanism, see Linda K. Kerber, *Women of the Republic* (1980), and *No Constitutional Right to Be Ladies: Women and the Obligations of Citizenship* (1999). Fine in-depth studies include Ronald Hoffman and Peter J. Albert, eds., *Women in the Age of the American Revolution* (1989); Rosemarie Zagarri, *A Woman's Dilemma: Mercy Otis Warren and the American Revolution* (1995); Judith Sargent Murray, *The Gleaner*, ed. Nina Baym (1992); and Lynn Withey, *Dearest Friend: A Life of Abigail Adams* (1982).

Important works on the 1780s include Peter S. Onuf, *The Origins of the Federal Republic: Jurisdictional Controversies in the United States, 1775–1787* (1983); Roger H. Brown, *Redeeming the Republic: Federalists, Taxation, and the Origins of the Constitution* (1993); Richard B. Morris, *The Forging of the Union, 1781–1789* (1987); and Robert A. Gross, ed., *In Debt to Shays* (1993).

The Constitution of 1787

In 1913 two studies initiated the modern analysis of the Constitution: Charles A. Beard, *An Economic Interpretation of the Constitution of the United States*, and Max Farrand, *The Framing of the Constitution*, which presented a detailed analysis of the Philadelphia convention. For critiques of Beard's work, see Leonard Levy, ed., *Essays on the Making of the Constitution* (rev. ed., 1987); for an update of Farrand, read Christopher Collier and James L. Collier, *Decision in Philadelphia* (1987).

Other significant works include Forrest McDonald, *Novus Ordo Seculorum: The Intellectual Origins of the Constitution* (1985); Edmund S. Morgan, *Inventing the People: The Rise of Popular Sovereignty in England and America* (1988); and Michael Kammen, *A Machine That Would Go by Itself: The Constitution in American Culture* (1986). Three fine collections of essays are Richard R. Beeman et al., eds., *Beyond Confederation: Origins of the Constitution and American National Identity* (1987); Ellen Frankel Paul and Howard Dickman, eds., *Liberty, Property and the Foundations of the American Constitution* (1989); and Herman Belz et al., eds., *To Form a More Perfect Union: The Critical Ideas of the Constitution* (1992).

On the Antifederalists and ratification, see Saul Cornell, *The Other Founders: The Antifederalists and the American Dissenting Tradition* (1999); Patrick T. Conley and John P. Kaminiski, eds., *The Constitution and the States* (1988); Stephen L. Schechter, *The Reluctant Pillar: New York and the Adoption of the Federal Constitution* (1985); and Herbert Storing, *The Antifederalists* (1985). Two insightful studies of the Federalist papers are David F. Epstein, *The Political Theory of "The Federalist"* (1984), and Charles R. Kesler, ed., *Saving the Revolution* (1987).

R. A. Rutland, *The Birth of the Bill of Rights, 1776–1791* (rev. ed., 1983), offers the basic narrative; more analytic treatments include Michael J. Lacey and Knud Haakonssen, *A Culture of Rights* (1991), and Joyce Lee Malcolm, *To Keep and Bear Arms: The Origins of an Anglo-American Right* (1993). Akhil Reed Amar, *The Bill of Rights: Creation and Reconstruction* (1998), offers a persuasive "republican" interpretation.

The Political Crisis of the 1790s

Two good syntheses are John C. Miller, *The Federalist Age* (1957), and James Rogers Sharp, *American Politics in the Early Republic* (1993). Studies of important statesmen include Forrest McDonald, *Alexander Hamilton: A Biography* (1979), and two works by James T. Flexner, *George Washington and the New Nation, 1783–1793* (1970) and *George Washington: Anguish and Farewell, 1793–1799* (1972). William Martin wrote the documentary *George Washington—The Man Who Wouldn't Be King* (PBS video, 1 hour). Additional material, including Washington's published correspondence, is available online at "The Papers of George Washington" <http://www.virginia.edu/gwpapers/>. For Jeffersonian ideology, see Joyce Appleby, *Capitalism and a New Social Order: The Republican Vision of the 1790s* (1984); Drew McCoy, *The Elusive Republic: Political Economy in Jeffersonian America* (1982); Lance Banning, *The Jeffersonian Persuasion: The Evolution of a Party Ideology* (1978); and John R. Nelson Jr., *Liberty and Property: Political Economy and Policymaking in the New Nation, 1789–1812* (1987). For more information on Thomas Jefferson consult the PBS Web site, "Thomas Jefferson" <http://www.pbs.org/jefferson>, which contains information on the documentary (PBS video, 3 hours), transcripts of interviews with Jefferson scholars, and a collection of documents relating to Jefferson's personal and public life.

Richard Hofstadter, *The Idea of a Party System: The Rise of Legitimate Opposition in the United States, 1790–1840* (1969), offers an overview; see also John F. Hoadley, *Origins of American Political Parties, 1789–1803* (1993), and Thomas P. Slaughter, *The Whiskey Rebellion* (1986). On diplomatic and military history, consult Harry Ammon, *The Genêt*

Mission (1973); Jerald A. Combs, *The Jay Treaty* (1970); Richard H. Kohn, *Eagle and Sword* (1975); and Lawrence D. Cress, *Citizens in Arms: The Army and the Military to the War of 1812* (1982).

On Adams's administration, see Ralph Brown Adams, *The Presidency of John Adams* (1975). More specialized studies are William Sinchcombe, *The XYZ Affair* (1980); Leonard Levy, *The Emergence of a Free Press* (1985); and James M. Smith, *Freedom's Fetters: The Alien and Sedition Laws and American Civil Liberties* (rev. ed., 1966).

Good state histories include Patricia Watlington, *The Partisan Spirit: Kentucky Politics, 1779–1792* (1972); Richard R. Beeman, *The Old Dominion and the New Nation, 1788–1801* (1972); and Mary K. Bonsteel Tachau, *Federal Courts in the Early Republic: Kentucky, 1789–1816* (1978).

Chapter 8: Dynamic Change: Western Settlement and Eastern Capitalism, 1790–1820

Gregory Evans Dowd, *A Spirited Resistance: The North American Indian Struggle for Unity, 1745–1815* (1992), presents a fine survey of the Indian peoples, while Gregory Nobles, *American Frontiers: Cultural Encounters and Continental Conquest* (1997), traces the course of western expansion. Donald R. Hickey, *The War of 1812: A Forgotten Conflict* (1989), places the conflict in an economic and diplomatic context. R. Kent Newmyer, *The Supreme Court under Marshall and Taney* (1968), concisely analyzes early constitutional development, and Jack Larkin, *The Reshaping of Everyday Life, 1790–1840* (1989), demonstrates the impact of economic change on material culture.

Westward Expansion

For studies of white policy toward Native Americans, see Bernard Sheehan, *Seeds of Extinction: Jeffersonian Philanthropy and the American Indian* (1973); Reginald Horsman, *Expansion and American Indian Policy, 1783–1812* (1967); Richard Slotkin, *Regeneration through Violence* (1973); and Dorothy Jones, *License for Empire: Colonialism by Treaty in Early America* (1982). Works dealing with the impact of Christian missions include William W. Fitzhugh, ed., *Cultures in Contact* (1985); William G. McLoughlin, *Cherokees and Missionaries, 1789–1839* (1984); and Earl P. Olmstead, *Blackcoats among the Delaware* (1991). Other analyses of cultural interaction are Theda Perdue, *Cherokee Women: Gender and Culture Change, 1700–1835* (1998); William G. McLoughlin, *Cherokee Renascence in the New Republic* (1986); J. Leitch Wright Jr., *Creeks and Seminoles: The Destruction and Regeneration of the Muscogulge People* (1986); and Kathryn E. Holland Braund, *Deerskins and Duffels* (1993). Two recent studies of white expansion are Eric Hinderaker, *Elusive Empires: Constructing Colonialism in the Ohio Valley, 1673–1800* (1999), and Claudio Saunt, *A New Order of Things: Property, Power, and the Transformation of the Creek Indians, 1733–1816* (1999). The "Chickasaw Historical Research Page" <http://home.flash.net/~kma/> compiled by K. M. Armstrong, contains a collection of letters written by or about Chickasaw Indians between 1792 and 1849; the texts of more than thirty treaties, and other documents.

On the activities of speculators and settlers in the Northeast, see two works by Alan Taylor: *Liberty Men and Great Proprietors* (1990) and *William Cooper's Town* (1995). For developments west of the Appalachians, read Malcolm J. Rohrbough, *The Trans-Appalachian Frontier: Peoples, Societies, and Institutions, 1775–1850* (1978); John Mack Faragher, *Sugar Creek: Life on the Illinois Prairie* (1986); and Andrew R. L. Cayton, *The Frontier Republic: Ideology and Politics in the Ohio Country, 1789–1812* (1986).

The Republicans' Political Revolution

Two good general accounts are Marshall Smelser, *The Democratic Republic, 1801–1815* (1968), and Ralph Ketcham, *Presidents above Party: The First American Presidency, 1789–1829* (1984). Detailed studies of Jefferson's presidency include Daniel Sisson, *The Revolution of 1800* (1974); Dumas Malone, *Jefferson the President* (2 vols., 1970 and 1974); and Richard E. Ellis, *The Jeffersonian Crisis: Courts and Politics in the New Republic* (1971). On the Louisiana Purchase, see James P. Ronda, *Lewis and Clark among the Indians* (1984) and Donald Jackson, *The Letters of the Lewis and Clark Expedition* (1963). *Lewis and Clark: The Journey of the Corps of Discovery* (PBS video, 4 hours) tells the story of the initial European exploration of the Louisiana Purchase; the companion Web site, <http://www.pbs.org/lewisandclark/> contains a rich body of material on the explorers and the Indian peoples of the region.

The activities of Aaron Burr are covered in Milton Lomask, *Aaron Burr* (1979). *The Duel* (PBS video, 1 hour) reenacts the confrontation between Alexander Hamilton and Aaron Burr. For the Federalists, see David Hackett Fischer, *The Revolution of American Conservatism: The Federalist Party in the Age of Jeffersonian Democracy* (1965), and James Banner, *To the Hartford Convention: The Federalists and the Origins of Party Politics in the Early Republic, 1789–1815* (1970). American attempts to avoid involvement in the Napoleonic Wars are traced in Lawrence Kaplan, *"Entangling Alliances with None": American Foreign Policy in the Age of Jefferson* (1987), and Bradford Perkins, *Prologue to War: England and the United States, 1805–1812* (1961). See also Clifford L. Egan, *Neither Peace nor War: Franco-American Relations, 1803–1812* (1983), and Doron S. Ben-Atar, *The Origins of Jeffersonian Commercial Policy and Diplomacy* (1993). On James Madison, see Robert A. Rutland, *The Presidency of James Madison* (1990); J. C. A. Stagg, *Mr. Madison's War: Politics, Diplomacy, and Warfare in the Early Republic, 1783–1830* (1983); and Drew McCoy, *The Last of the Fathers: James Madison and the Republican Legacy* (1989). For Native Americans and the War of 1812, consult R. David Edmunds, *Tecumseh and the Quest for Indian Leadership* (1984), and H. S. Halbert and T. H. Ball, *The Creek War of 1813 and 1814* (1970). "A Century of Lawmaking for a New Nation" <http://memory.loc.gov/ammem/amlaw/lawhome.html>, part of the Library of Congress's American Memory project, contains congressional documents and debates, including discussions of the Northwest Ordinance, the ban on slave imports, the Embargo of 1807, and the decision for war in 1812. The site also contains information and maps of Indian land cessions from 1784 to 1894.

On Spain's northern empire, see David Weber, *The Spanish Frontier in North America* (1992), and Walter La Feber, ed., *John Quincy Adams and American Continental Empire* (1965).

The Capitalist Commonwealth

Thomas M. Doerflinger, *A Vigorous Spirit of Enterprise: Merchants and Economic Development in Revolutionary Philadelphia* (1986); John Denis Haeger, *John Jacob Astor* (1991); and Stuart Bruchey, *Robert Oliver: Merchant of Baltimore* (1956), are fine studies of merchant enterprise. The standard history is Curtis R. Nettels, *The Emergence of a National Economy, 1775–1815* (1965). See also Ronald Hoffman, John J. McCusker, and Peter J. Albert, eds., *The Economy of Revolutionary America* (1987), and Daniel P. Jones, *The Economic and Social Transformation of Rhode Island, 1780–1850* (1992).

On banking, consult the classic study by Bray Hammond, *Banks and Politics in America* (1957), and Richard H. Timberlake, *Monetary Policy in the United States* (1992). Studies of manufacturing include Thomas C. Cochran, *Frontiers of Change: Early Industrialism in America* (1981), and David J. Jeremy, *Transatlantic Industrial Revolution: The Diffusion of Textile Technology between Britain and America, 1790–1830* (1981).

The classic studies of state mercantilism are Oscar Handlin and Mary Handlin, *Commonwealth: A Study of the Role of Government in the American Economy: Massachusetts, 1774–1861* (1947), and Louis Hartz, *Economic Policy and Democratic Thought: Pennsylvania, 1776–1860* (1948). State support for transportation can be traced in Carter Goodrich, *Government Promotion of American Canals and Railroads* (1960); Erik F. Hiates et al., *Western River Transportation: The Era of Early Internal Development, 1810–1860* (1975); and Harry N. Scheiber, *Ohio Canal Era: A Case Study of Government and the Economy* (1969). See also David Gilchrist, ed., *The Growth of the Seaport Cities, 1790–1825* (1967), and Winifred Barr Rothenberg, *From Market-Places to Market Economy: The Transformation of Rural Massachusetts, 1750–1850* (1994).

The legal implications of commonwealth ideology are analyzed in Leonard Levy, *The Law of the Commonwealth and Chief Justice Shaw* (1955), and Morton J. Horwitz, *The Transformation of American Law, 1780–1860* (1976). On the Supreme Court, see Robert K. Faulkner, *The Jurisprudence of John Marshall* (1968); Francis N. Stites, *John Marshall: Defender of the Constitution* (1981); Thomas C. Shevory, ed., *John Marshall's Achievement* (1989); and C. Peter McGrath, *Yazoo: Law and Politics in the New Republic* (1966). See also William J. Novak, *The People's Welfare: Law and Regulation in Nineteenth-Century America* (1996).

Chapter 9: The Quest for a Republican Society, 1790–1820

Two fine local studies—Alan Taylor, *William Cooper's Town: Power and Persuasion on the Frontier of the Early American Republic* (1995), and Laurel Thatcher Ulrich, *The Age of Homespun: Objects and Stories in the Creation of an American Myth* (2000)—capture the texture of northern life in the early republic. James Oakes, *The Ruling Race: A History of American Slaveholders* (1982), offers an important perspective on the expansion of slavery, while Nathan O. Hatch, *The Democratization of American Christianity* (1987), presents an interpretation of religious change.

Democratic Republicanism

Warren S. Tryon, *A Mirror for Americans: Life and Manners in the United States, 1790–1870, as Recorded by European Travelers* (3 vols., 1952), suggests the distinctive features of republican society. Clement Eaton, *Henry Clay and the Art of American Politics* (1957), perceptively describes the coming of political democracy, while more detailed studies are Ronald Formisano, *The Transformation of Political Culture: Massachusetts Parties, 1790s–1840s* (1983), and Chilton Williamson, *American Suffrage from Property to Democracy* (1960).

Michael Grossberg, *Governing the Hearth* (1985), discusses changing marriage rules. Catherine M. Scholten, *Childrearing in American Society, 1650–1850* (1985), should be supplemented by Philip Greven's pathbreaking analysis, *The Protestant Temperament: Patterns of Childrearing, Religious Experience, and the Self in Early America* (1977). On sentimentalism, see Shirley Samuels, *The Culture of Sentiment: Race, Gender, and Sentimentality in Nineteenth-Century America* (1992). Other important works include Daniel Blake Smith, *Inside the Great House: Planter Family Life in Eighteenth-Century Chesapeake Society* (1980); Bernard W. Wishy, *The Child and the Republic* (1970); and Jan Lewis, *The Pursuit of Happiness: Family and Values in Jefferson's Virginia* (1983).

Aristocratic Republicanism and Slavery, 1780–1820

On the expansion of slavery, see Ira Berlin, *Many Thousands Gone: The First Two Centuries of Slavery in North America* (1999), and the essays in Berlin and Ronald Hoffman, eds., *Slavery and Freedom in the Age of the American Revolution* (1983). Other important studies of pre-1820 slavery include Robert McColley, *Slavery and Jeffersonian Virginia* (2nd ed., 1973); Donald L. Robinson, *Slavery in the Structure of American Politics, 1765–1820* (1971); Joyce E. Chaplin, *Agricultural Innovation and Modernity in the Lower South, 1730–1815* (1993); and Peter A. Coclanis, *The Shadow of a Dream: Economic Life and Death in the South Carolina Low Country, 1670–1920* (1988). Other works that include material on this period are Charles Joyner, *Down by the Riverside: A South Carolina Slave Community* (1984), and Jacqueline Jones, *Labor of Love, Labor of Sorrow: Black Women, Work, and the Family from Slavery to the Present* (1986). The complex religious lives of African Americans are treated in Albert Raboteau, *Slave Religion* (1968); Mechal Sobel, *Trabelin' On: The Slave Journey to an Afro Baptist Faith* (1979) and Margaret Washington Creel, *"A Peculiar People," Slave Religion and Community-Culture among the Gullahs* (1988).

For slave revolts, consult Douglas R. Egerton, *Gabriel's Rebellion* (1993); James Sidbury, *Ploughs into Swords: Race, Rebellion, and Identity in Gabriel's Virginia, 1730–1810* (1997); Douglas R. Egerton, *He Shall Go Out Free: The Lives of Denmark Vesey* (1999). On the ambiguous position of free blacks in a slave society, consult Ira Berlin, *Slaves without Masters: The Free Negro in the Antebellum South* (1974). For blacks in the northern states, see Gary B. Nash, *Forging Freedom: Philadelphia's Black Community, 1720–1840* (1988). For primary documents that illustrate the ways in which African Americans acquired and transformed the doctrines and beliefs of Protestant Christianity, log on to Documenting the

American South, "The Church in the Southern Black Community" <http://metalab.unc.edu/docsouth/>.

Glover Moore, *The Missouri Compromise* (1953), provides a detailed analysis of that crisis. See also Merton L. Dillon, *Slavery Attacked: Southern Slaves and Their Allies, 1619–1865* (1990).

Protestant Christianity as a Social Force

Perry Miller, *The Life of the Mind in America* (1966), offers a good overview of the Second Great Awakening. For revivalism, see Stephen A. Marini, *Radical Sects of Revolutionary New England* (1982); Bernard A. Weisberger, *They Gathered at the River* (1958); John B. Boles, *The Great Revival, 1787–1805* (1972); and Paul Conkin, *Cane Ridge: America's Pentecost* (1990). The course of religious thought in New England is traced in Daniel Walker Howe, *The Unitarian Conscience* (1970).

Recent studies focusing on evangelical religion include Christine L. Heyrman, *Southern Cross: The Beginnings of the Bible Belt* (1997); Diana Hockstedt Butler, *Standing against the Whirlwind: Evangelical Episcopalians in Nineteenth-Century America* (1995); Randy J. Sparks, *On Jordan's Stormy Banks: Evangelicalism in Mississippi, 1773–1876* (1994); John G. West Jr., *The Politics of Revelation and Reason: Religion and Civic Life in the New Nation* (1996); and Ian H. Murray, *Revival and Revivalism: The Making and Marring of American Evangelicalism, 1750–1858* (1994).

For women's lives, see Susan Juster, *Disorderly Women: Sexual Politics and Evangelicalism in Revolutionary New England* (1994); Harriet B. Applewhite and Darline G. Levy, eds., *Women and Politics in the Age of Democratic Revolution* (1990); and Linda Kerber, *Women of the Republic: Intellect and Ideology in Revolutionary America* (1980). Specialized studies include Joan M. Jensen, *Loosening the Bonds: Mid-Atlantic Farm Women, 1750–1850* (1986); Jeanne Boydston, *Home and Work* (1990); and Laurel Thatcher Ulrich, *A Midwife's Tale: The Life of Martha Ballard, Based on Her Diary, 1785–1812* (1990), which has also been made into a PBS dramatic documentary, *A Midwife's Tale* (1.5 hours). Additional materials on Ballard's experiences and women's lives are available on the Web at <http://www.pbs.org/amex/midwife> and <http://www.DoHistory.org>.

Women's religious initiatives are discussed in Mary P. Ryan, *Cradle of the Middle Class* (1981); Barbara Epstein, *The Politics of Domesticity: Women, Evangelism, and Temperance* (1978); and Keith Melder, *Beginnings of Sisterhood: The American Women's Rights Movement, 1800–1850* (1977), which also traces the growth of female academies.

Chapter 10: The Economic Revolution, 1820–1860

Three important studies of the economic revolution and its consequences are Stuart Bruchey, *Enterprise: The Dynamic Economy of a Free People* (1990); Charles G. Sellers Jr., *The Market Revolution: Jacksonian America, 1815–1840* (1991); and Stuart M. Blumin, *The Emergence of the Middle Class: Social Experience in the American City, 1760–1900* (1989). See also Carolyn Merchant, *Ecological Revolutions: Nature, Gender, and Science in New England* (1989).

The Coming of Industry: Northeastern Manufacturing

Surveys of the Industrial Revolution in America include W. Elliot Brownlee, *Dynamics of Ascent: A History of the American Economy* (1979), and Thomas C. Cochran, *Frontiers of Change: Early Industrialism in America* (1981). See also the pioneering work in economic geography by Donald W. Meinig, *The Shaping of America: A Geographical Perspective, Vol. 2: Continental America, 1800–1867* (1993). Good regional studies are Peter J. Coleman, *The Transformation of Rhode Island* (1963), and Anthony F. C. Wallace, *Rockdale: The Growth of an American Village in the Early Industrial Revolution* (1978).

Books on technological change include Judith A. McGaw, ed., *Early American Technology* (1994); Gary Cross and Rick Szostak, *Technology and American Society: A History* (1995); David Freeman Hawke, *Nuts and Bolts of the Past: A History of American Technology, 1776–1860* (1988); David A. Hounshell, *From the American System to Mass Production, 1800–1932: The Development of Manufacturing Technology in the United States* (1984); and Barbara M. Tucker, *Samuel Slater and the Origins of the American Textile Industry* (1984).

On American workers during this period, see Mary H. Blewett, *Men, Women, and Work: Class, Gender, and Protest in the New England Shoe Industry, 1780–1910* (1990); Alan Dawley, *Class and Community: The Industrial Revolution in Lynn* (1976); Jonathan Prude, *The Coming of Industrial Order: Town and Factory Life in Rural Massachusetts* (1983); Jeanne Boydston, *Home and Work: Housework, Wages, and the Ideology of Labor in the Early Republic* (1990); and Thomas Dublin, *Transforming Women's Work: New England Lives in the Industrial Revolution* (1994). Other useful analyses are Paul A. Gilje and Howard B. Rock, eds., *Keepers of the Revolution: New Yorkers at Work in the Early Republic* (1992) and Paul Faler, *Mechanics and Manufacturers in the Early Industrial Revolution* (1983).

The Expansion of Markets

For the development of the Midwest, see Stephen Aron, *How the West Was Lost: The Transformation of Kentucky from Daniel Boone to Henry Clay* (1996); Andrew R. L. Cayton and Peter S. Onuf, *The Midwest and the Nation* (1990); and John Mack Faragher, *Sugar Creek: Life on the Illinois Prairie* (1986). On agricultural expansion, consult Paul W. Gates, *The Farmer's Age: Agriculture, 1815–1860* (1960). For the settlement of the Great Lakes region, log on to "Pioneering the Upper Midwest: Books from Michigan, Minnesota, and Wisconsin, 1820–1910" <http://memory.loc.gov/ammem/umhtml/umhome.html>, which offers the full text of first-person accounts, biographies, and promotional literature from the collections of the Library of Congress. An excellent tool for tracking social changes is the United States Historical Census Data Browser <http://fisher.lib.virginia.edu/census>, which has mined the censuses (especially the rich returns for 1850 and 1860) for information on race, slavery, immigration, religion, and other topics.

For urban development, see the classic study by R. G. Albion, *The Rise of New York Port, 1815–1860* (1939), and the fine analysis of Chicago by William Cronon, *Nature's Metrop-*

olis (1992). Also consult Richard C. Wade, *The Urban Frontier: Pioneer Life in Early Pittsburgh, Cincinnati, Lexington, Louisville, and St. Louis* (1964).

A comprehensive study of the role of transportation is presented in George R. Taylor, *The Transportation Revolution, 1815–1860* (1951). On canals, consult Carol Sheriff, *The Artificial River: The Erie Canal and the Paradox of Progress, 1817–1862* (1996); Peter Way, *Common Labour: Workers and the Digging of North American Canals* (1993); and Ronald E. Shaw, *Canals for a Nation: The Canal Era in the United States, 1790–1860* (1990). On the growth of railroads, consult Albert Fishlow, *American Railroads and the Transformation of the Ante-Bellum Economy* (1965). For the contribution of the law to the economic revolution, see Morton J. Horwitz, *The Transformation of American Law, 1780–1860* (1977) and Christopher L. Tomlins, *Law, Labor and Ideology in the Early American Republic* (1993).

Changes in the Social Structure

For the distribution of wealth and income in the early nineteenth century, see Frederic C. Jaher, *The Urban Establishment: Upper Strata in Boston, New York, Charleston, Chicago, and Los Angeles* (1982), and Edward Pessen, *Riches, Class, and Power before the Civil War* (1973). For the distinctive features of the new middle class, see John S. Gilkeson Jr., *Middle-Class Providence, 1820–1940* (1986).

Some of the disruptive effects of economic change are addressed in Karen Haltunen, *Confidence Men and Painted Women: A Study of Middle-Class Culture in America, 1830–1870* (1982); W. J. Rorabaugh, *The Alcoholic Republic: An American Tradition* (1979); and Christine Stansell, *City of Women: Sex and Class in New York, 1789–1860* (1986). For a stimulating discussion of the effects of markets and manufacturing on the countryside, see Christopher Clark, *The Roots of Rural Capitalism: Western Massachusetts, 1789–1860* (1990). See also Suzanne Lebsock, *The Free Women of Petersburg* (1987).

The concept of the business class is developed in Michael Katz et al., *The Social Organization of Early Industrial Capitalism* (1982). Surveys of reform movements closely linked to the Second Great Awakening include Alice F. Tyler, *Freedom's Ferment* (1944), and Ronald G. Walters, *American Reformers, 1815–1860* (1978). Studies of religious evangelism and social reform are particularly abundant for New York State. See Paul E. Johnson, *A Shopkeeper's Millennium: Society and Revivals in Rochester, New York, 1815–1837* (1978), and Mary Ryan, *Cradle of the Middle Class: The Family in Oneida County, New York, 1790–1865* (1981). On the relationship between religion and labor protest, see Jama Lazerow, *Religion and the Working Class in Antebellum America* (1996). For more general studies of religious ferment in the early republic, see John Butler, *Awash in a Sea of Faith: Christianizing the American People* (1990), and R. Lawrence Moore, *Selling God: American Religion in the Marketplace of Culture* (1994).

On European immigration, consult Philip Taylor, *The Distant Magnet: European Immigration to the U.S.A.* (1971), and Oscar Handlin, *Boston's Immigrants: A Study in Acculturation* (1979). See also Kathleen Neils Conzen, *Immigrant Milwaukee, 1836–1860* (1976); Dale T. Knobel, *Paddy and the Republic* (1985); and Bruce Laurie, *Working People in Philadelphia, 1800–1850* (1980).

Chapter 11: A Democratic Revolution, 1820–1844

Two fine surveys of the Jacksonian era are Charles Sellers, *The Market Revolution: Jacksonian America, 1814–1846* (1992), and Harry L. Watson, *Liberty and Power: The Politics of Jacksonian America* (1990). See also Daniel Feller, *The Jacksonian Promise: America, 1815–1840* (1995) and Robert J. Conley, *Mountain Windsong: A Novel of the Trail of Tears*, which brings to life the effects of Jackson's Indian removal policy. Alexis de Tocqueville's classic, *Democracy in America* (1835), should be sampled for its insights into the character of American society and political institutions. The book is available on line, accompanied by an excellent exhibit explaining Tocqueville's trip to the United States and a collection of essays complementing his study, at <http://xroads.virginia.edu/~HYPER/DETOC/home.html>.

The Rise of Popular Politics, 1820–1829

The classic study of American politics between 1815 and 1828 is George Dangerfield, *The Era of Good Feelings* (1952). More recent studies include James Sterling Young, *The Washington Community, 1800–1828* (1966); Harry Ammon, *James Monroe: The Quest for National Identity* (1971); and Merrill Peterson, *The Great Triumvirate: Webster, Clay, and Calhoun* (1987). The political innovations of Martin Van Buren are traced in John Niven, *Martin Van Buren: The Romantic Age of American Politics* (1983), and Robert V. Remini, *Martin Van Buren and the Making of the Democratic Party* (1959). See also Norman Risjord, *The Old Republicans* (1965); Amy Bridges, *A City in the Republic: Antebellum New York and the Origins of Machine Politics* (1984); and Chilton Williamson, *American Suffrage from Property to Democracy, 1760–1860* (1960).

For John Quincy Adams and his administration, see Samuel Flagg Bemis, *John Quincy Adams and the Union* (1956); Leonard L. Richards, *The Life and Times of Congressman John Quincy Adams* (1986); and Mary Hargreaves, *The Presidency of John Quincy Adams* (1985). For foreign policy, see Ernest R. May, *The Making of the Monroe Doctrine* (1975).

The Jacksonian Presidency, 1829–1837

Arthur M. Schlesinger Jr., *The Age of Jackson* (1945), initiated the modern reexamination of Andrew Jackson and his significance. Among the most provocative subsequent studies are Lee Benson, *The Concept of Jacksonian Democracy: New York as a Test Case* (1961); Marvin Meyers, *The Jacksonian Persuasion: Politics and Belief* (1957); and John William Ward, *Andrew Jackson: Symbol for an Age* (1962). For a comprehensive view of Jackson's life, see four works by Robert V. Remini: *The Election of Andrew Jackson* (1963); *Andrew Jackson and the Course of American Freedom, 1822–1833* (1977); *Andrew Jackson and the Course of American Democracy, 1833–1845* (1984); and *The Life of Andrew Jackson* (1988). Other studies include Donald Cole, *The Presidency of Andrew Jackson* (1992), and Leonard D. White, *The Jacksonians: A Study in Administrative History, 1828–1861* (1954). For a brief treatment of the life of Andrew Jackson and some of his important state papers, log on to the "Revolution to Reconstruction" site at the University of Groningen in the Netherlands: <http://odur.let.rug.nl/~usa/P/aj7/aj7.htm>.

On the politics of the bank war, see Robert V. Remini, *Andrew Jackson and the Bank War* (1967); Thomas P. Govan, *Nicholas Biddle: Nationalist and Public Banker, 1786–1844* (1959); and John M. McFaul, *The Politics of Jacksonian Finance*. On the nullification crisis, see Richard E. Ellis, *The Union at Risk* (1987); Merrill D. Peterson, *Olive Branch and Sword: The Compromise of 1833* (1982); and two studies by William W. Freehling, *Prelude to Civil War* (1966) and *The Road to Disunion, Vol. 1: Secessionists at Bay, 1776–1854* (1990).

Works treating Jackson's Indian policy include Michael D. Green, *The Politics of Indian Removal* (1982); William G. McLoughlin, *Cherokee Renascence in the New Republic* (1986); Gary E. Moulton, *John Ross: Cherokee Chief* (1978); Francis P. Prucha, *American Indian Policy in the Formative Years* (1962) and *American Indian Treaties: The History of a Political Anomaly* (1994); and Ronald N. Satz, *American Indian Policy in the Jacksonian Era* (1975). For additional material on the Cherokees, go to the Web sites prepared by Ken Martin, a tribal member of the Cherokee Nation of Oklahoma, <http://cherokeehistory.com/index.html> and by Golden Ink in North Georgia <http://ngeorgia.com/history/findex.html>.

For a fine study of Jackson's successor, consult Major J. Wilson, *The Presidency of Martin Van Buren* (1984); see also James C. Curtis, *The Fox at Bay* (1970). Biographies of the leading Whig opponents of Jackson include Richard N. Current, *John C. Calhoun* (3 vols., 1944–1951); Irving H. Bartlett, *Daniel Webster* (1978); and Robert V. Remini, *Henry Clay: Statesman for the Union* (1991).

Class, Culture, and the Second Party System

A rich literature describes the emergence of the Whigs in the context of a changing political culture and the creation of the Second Party System. Books that deal broadly with these topics include John Ashworth, *"Agrarians" and "Aristocrats": Party Political Ideology in the United States, 1837–1846* (1983); Richard Hofstadter, *The Idea of a Party System* (1972); Daniel W. Howe, *The Political Culture of the American Whigs* (1979); and Michael Holt, *The Rise and Fall of the American Whig Party* (1991). Also see Stephen C. Bullock, *Revolutionary Brotherhood: Freemasonry and the Transformation of the American Social Order, 1730–1840* (1994); Lawrence F. Kohl, *The Politics of Individualism: Parties and the American Character in the Jacksonian Era* (1989); Richard P. McCormick, *The Second American Party System: Party Formation in the Jacksonian Era* (1966); and Joel H. Silbey, *The Partisan Imperative: The Dynamics of American Politics before the Civil War* (1985).

More specialized studies include Paul Bourke and Donald DeBats, *Washington County: Politics and Community in Antebellum America* (1995); Thomas Brown, *Politics and Statesmanship: Essays on the American Whig Party* (1985); Ronald P. Formisano, *The Birth of Mass Political Parties: Michigan, 1827–1861* (1972), and *The Transformation of Political Culture: Massachusetts Parties, 1790s–1840s* (1983); William G. Shade, *Banks or No Banks: The Money Issue in Western Politics, 1832–1865* (1972); Harry L. Watson, *Jacksonian Politics and Community Conflict: The Emergence of the Second Party System in Cumberland County, North Carolina* (1981); and Daniel S. Dupre, *Transforming the Cotton Frontier: Madison County, Alabama, 1800–1840* (1997). For the presidency of John Tyler, see Robert J. Morgan, *A Whig Embattled* (1954).

For the impact of the Panic of 1837 on workers, see Mary H. Blewett, *Men, Women, and Work: Class, Gender, and Protest in the New England Shoe Industry, 1780–1910* (1988); Paul G. Faler, *Mechanics and Manufacturers in the Early Industrial Revolution* (1981); Ronald Schultz, *The Republic of Labor: Philadelphia Artisans and the Politics of Class* (1993); and Sean Wilentz, *Chants Democratic: New York City and the Rise of the American Working Class, 1788–1850* (1984). See also Christopher L. Tomlins, *Law, Labor, and Ideology in the Early American Republic* (1993).

Chapter 12: Religion and Reform, 1820–1860

General surveys of antebellum reform movements include Robert H. Abzug, *Cosmos Crumbling: American Reform and the Religious Imagination* (1994); C. S. Griffen, *The Ferment of Reform, 1830–1860* (1967); and Ronald G. Walters, *American Reformers, 1815–1860* (1978). Two studies that explore the ties between religious reform and politics are Curtis D. Johnson, *Redeeming America: Evangelicals and the Road to the Civil War* (1993) and Richard J. Carwardine, *Evangelicals and Politics in Antebellum America* (1993).

Individualism

The leading study linking transcendentalism and reform is Ann C. Rose, *Transcendentalism as a Social Movement, 1830–1850* (1981). See also Phyllis Cole, *Mary Moody Emerson and the Origins of Transcendentalism: A Family History* (1998), and Catherine L. Albanese, *Corresponding Motion: Transcendental Religion and the New America* (1977). Studies that relate literary developments to reform themes and cultural history include Harold Kaplan, *Democratic Humanism and American Literature* (1972); David S. Reynolds, *Beneath the American Renaissance: The Subversive Imagination in the Age of Emerson and Melville* (1988) and *Walt Whitman's America: A Cultural Biography* (1995); and Larzer Ziff, *Literary Democracy: The Declaration of Cultural Independence in America* (1981). On Margaret Fuller, see Charles Capper, *Margaret Fuller: An American Romantic Life* (1992), and Joan von Mehren, *Minerva and the Muse: A Life of Margaret Fuller* (1995).

Communalism

On communitarian experiments, see Arthur Bestor Jr., *Backwoods Utopias: The Sectarian and Owenite Phases of Communitarian Life in America* (1970); Lawrence Foster, *Religion and Sexuality: Three American Communal Experiments of the Nineteenth Century* (1981); Jean McMahon Humez, ed., *Gifts of Power: The Writings of Rebecca Jackson, Black Visionary, Shaker Eldress* (1981); Louis J. Kern, *An Ordered Love: Sex Roles and Sexuality in Victorian Utopias—The Shakers, the Mormons, and the Oneida Community* (1981); Spencer Klaw, *Without Sin: The Life and Death of the Oneida Community* (1995); and Stephen J. Stein, *The Shaker Experience in America* (1992).

On the Mormon experience, see Leonard J. Arrington, *Brigham Young: American Moses* (1985) and *The Mormon Experience: A History of the Latter-Day Saints* (1992); John L. Brooke, *The Refiner's Fire: The Making of Mormon Cosmology, 1644–1844* (1994); Grant Underwood, *The Millennarian*

World of Early Mormonism (1993); and Kenneth H. Winn, *Exiles in a Land of Liberty: Mormons in America, 1830–1846* (1989). On the linkages between religion and the utopians, see Paul E. Johnson and Sean Wilentz, *The Kingdom of Matthias: A Story of Sex and Salvation in Nineteenth-Century America* (1995); and Timothy L. Smith, *Revivalism and Social Reform: American Protestantism on the Eve of the Civil War* (1980).

Abolitionism

Two interesting new studies of abolitionism are James Oliver Horton and Lois E. Horton, *In Hope of Liberty: Culture, Community, and Protest among Northern Free Blacks, 1700–1860* (1996), and Paul Goodman, *Of One Blood: Abolitionism and the Origins of Racial Equality* (1998). Other important works include Robert H. Abzug, *Passionate Liberator: Theodore Dwight Weld and the Dilemma of Reform* (1980); David Brion Davis, *The Problems of Slavery in the Age of Revolution, 1770–1823* (1975); Stanley Harrold, *The Abolitionists and the South, 1831–1861* (1995); Leon F. Litwack, *North of Slavery: The Negro in the Free States, 1790–1860* (1961); Lewis Perry, *Childhood, Marriage, and Reform: Henry Clarke Wright, 1797–1870* (1980); James B. Stewart, *Holy Warriors: The Abolitionists and American Slavery* (1976); and John L. Thomas, *The Liberator: William Lloyd Garrison* (1963). Important studies of Frederick Douglass include Nathan I. Huggins, *Slave and Citizen: The Life of Frederick Douglass* (1980), and William S. McFeely, *Frederick Douglass* (1991); for Douglass's own accounts, read the *Narrative of the Life of Frederick Douglass, an American Slave* (1845) and *Life and Times of Frederick Douglass, Written by Himself* (1881).

For the role of women in the antislavery movement, consult Julie Roy Jeffrey, *The Great Silent Army of Abolitionism: Ordinary Women in the Antislavery Movement* (1998); Dorothy Sterling, *Ahead of Her Time: Abby Kelley and the Politics of Anti-Slavery* (1991); Blanche Hersh, *The Slavery of Sex: Female Abolitionists in Nineteenth-Century America* (1978); and Gerda Lerner, *The Grimké Sisters from South Carolina: Pioneers for Women's Rights and Abolition* (1967). On northern hostility to abolition, see Leonard L. Richards, *"Gentlemen of Property and Standing": Anti-Abolition Mobs in Jacksonian America* (1970).

The Women's Rights Movement

The most comprehensive history of women in the United States is Nancy Woloch, *Women and the American Experience* (1992). On the social history of women, see Nancy F. Cott, *The Bonds of Womanhood: "Women's Sphere" in New England, 1780–1835* (1977); Carl N. Degler, *At Odds: Women and the Family in America from the Revolution to the Present* (1980); and Mary P. Ryan, *Cradle of the Middle Class: The Family in Oneida County, New York, 1790–1865* (1981). The most complete discussion of women in education and benevolent reform is Keith Melder, *Beginnings of Sisterhood: The American Women's Rights Movement, 1800–1850* (1977). For studies of specific aspects of women's involvement in reform, see Barbara J. Berg, *The Remembered Gate: Origins of American Feminism: The Woman and the City, 1800–1860* (1978); Estelle B. Freedman, *Their Sisters' Keepers: Women's Prison Reform in America, 1830–1860* (1981); Lori D. Ginzberg, *Women and the*

Work of Benevolence: Morality, Politics, and Class in the Nineteenth-Century United States (1990); Nancy A. Hewitt, *Women's Activism and Social Change: Rochester, New York, 1822–1872* (1984); and Jean F. Yellin, *Women and Sisters: The Antislavery Feminists in American Culture* (1989). But see also Jeanne Boydston et al., *The Limits of Sisterhood: The Beecher Sisters on Women's Rights and Woman's Sphere* (1990).

On Dorothea Dix, see David Gollaher, *Voice for the Mad: The Life of Dorothea Dix* (1995); and Charles M. Snyder, *The Lady and the President: The Letters of Dorothea Dix and Millard Fillmore* (1975). The leading studies of the early women's rights movement include Kathleen Barry, *Susan B. Anthony—A Biography: A Singular Feminist* (1988); Ellen Du Bois, *Feminism and Suffrage: The Emergence of an Independent Women's Movement, 1848–1869* (1978); and Nancy Isenberg, *Sex and Citizenship in Antebellum America* (1998). See also Elizabeth R. Varon, *We Mean to Be Counted: White Women and Politics in Antebellum Virginia* (1996). "Women and Social Movements in the United States, 1830–1930," prepared by Kathryn Kish Sklar and Thomas Dublin <http://womhist.binghamton.edu./> provides a fine introductory essay and an extensive selection of primary documents. Additional source materials (newspapers and periodicals, with an index to articles and contributors) for the period 1830 to 1877 are available through Cornell University's "Making of America" project <http://moa.cit.cornell.edu/> and its companion site at the University of Michigan <http://moa.umdl.umich.edu/>.

Chapter 13: The Crisis of the Union, 1844–1860

Histories that trace the disruption of the Union between the time of the Mexican War and the election of Lincoln are rare. The best is David M. Potter, *The Impending Crisis, 1848–1861* (1976), but see also Michael A. Morrison, *Slavery and the American West: The Eclipse of Manifest Destiny and the Coming of the Civil War* (1995), and the relevant sections of William W. Freehling, *The Road to Disunion: Secessionists at Bay, 1776–1854* (1990), and Leonard L. Richards, *The Slave Power: The Free North and Southern Domination, 1780–1860* (2000). A fine social history that sheds light on the coming of the war is Stephanie McCurry, *Masters of Small Worlds: Yeoman Households, Gender Relations, and the Political Culture of the Antebellum South Carolina Low Country* (1995).

Manifest Destiny

Peter Kolchin, *American Slavery, 1619–1877* (1993), traces the expansion of the cotton South, while the essays in Ira Berlin and Philip D. Morgan, eds., *Cultivation and Culture: Labor and the Shaping of Slave Life* (1993), suggest the distinct characteristics of the cotton regime. See also Robert W. Fogel, *Without Consent or Contract: The Rise and Fall of American Slavery* (1989). Important studies of slave owners include James Oakes, *The Ruling Race: A History of American Slaveholders* (1982), Eugene D. Genovese, *The Political Economy of Slavery*, 2nd ed. (1989), and J. Mills Thornton III, *Politics and Power in a Slave Society: Alabama, 1800–1860* (1978). For slaveholding women, see Catherine Clinton, *The Plantation Mistress* (1983), and Elizabeth Fox-Genovese, *Within the Plantation Household: Black and White Women of the Old South* (1988).

Slave life is treated in Lawrence W. Levine, *Black Culture and Black Consciousness* (1977); Eugene Genovese, *Roll, Jordan, Roll* (1974); and Dena J. Epstein, *Sinful Tunes and Spirituals: Black Folk Music to the Civil War* (1977). On slave revolts, see Stephen B. Oates, *The Fires of Jubilee: Nat Turner's Fierce Rebellion* (1975). The culture of the planter class and non-slaveholding whites can be explored in O. Vernon Burton, *In My Father's House Are Many Mansions: Family and Community in Edgefield, South Carolina* (1985), and J. William Harris, *Plain Folk and Gentry in a Slave Society: White Liberty and Black Slavery in Augusta's Hinterlands* (1985). "Uncle Tom's Cabin and American Culture: A Multi-Media Archive" <http://jefferson.village.virginia.edu/utc/> is an extremely rich Web site that explores the literary and cultural context of the time through essays, original documents, and recordings of minstrel music.

Historians have recently focused attention on the trans-Appalachian West. See Gregory N. Nobles, *American Frontiers* (1996); Nicole Etcheson, *The Emerging Midwest: Upland Southerners and the Political Culture of the Old Northwest, 1787–1861* (1996); William Cronon, *Nature's Metropolis* (1992); and Malcolm J. Rohrbough, *The Trans-Appalachian Frontier: People, Societies, and Institutions, 1775–1850* (1978). A fine video documentary on *The West* (6 hours) by Ken Burns and Stephen Ives has a useful Web site, "New Perspectives on the West" <http://www.pbs.org/thewest>, that includes a good collection of maps, biographical essays, original documents, and images.

The ideology of Manifest Destiny is discussed in Norman Graebner, *Empire on the Pacific: A Study of American Continental Expansion* (1955), and Reginald Horsman, *Race and Manifest Destiny: The Origins of American Racial Anglo-Saxonism* (1981).

New approaches to the history of the trans-Mississippi West include Patricia Nelson Limerick, *The Legacy of Conquest: The Unbroken Past of the Unbroken West* (1987); David J. Weber, *The Mexican Frontier, 1821–1846* (1982); and Richard White, *"It's Your Misfortune and None of My Own": A History of the American West* (1991). This newer scholarship presents a more complete view of women. See Susan Armitage and Elizabeth Jameson, eds., *The Women's West* (1987); John Mack Faragher, *Women and Men on the Overland Trail* (1979); and Julie R. Jeffrey, *Frontier Women: The Trans-Mississippi West, 1840–1860* (1979).

War, Expansion, and Slavery, 1846–1850

Study of expansionism in the 1840s should begin with Frederick Merk, *The Monroe Doctrine and American Expansion, 1843–1849* (1972), and William J. Cooper, *The South and the Politics of Slavery, 1828–1856* (1978). On the coming of the Mexican War, consult Paul H. Bergeron, *The Presidency of James K. Polk* (1987); David Pletcher, *The Diplomacy of Annexation: Texas, Oregon, and the Mexican War* (1973); and Charles G. Sellers, *James K. Polk: Continentalist, 1843–1846* (1966). On the fighting of the war, see K. Jack Bauer, *The Mexican War, 1846–1848* (1974), and John S. D. Eisenhower, *So Far from God: The U.S. War with Mexico, 1846–1848* (1989). Richard Bruce Winders, *Mr. Polk's Army* (1977), discusses the experience of American soldiers. For the impact of the war on American expansionists, see Robert W. Johannsen, *To the Halls of the Montezumas: The Mexican War in the American Imagination* (1985). For the Mexican viewpoint, see Gene M. Brack, *Mexico Views Manifest Destiny, 1821–1846: An Essay on the Origins of the Mexican War* (1975). The PBS documentary *The U.S.-Mexican War* (4 hours) and its Web site <http://www.pbs.org/usmexicanwar> view the war both from the American and the Mexican perspective, drawing upon the expertise of historians from each country.

On congressional politics during the 1840s, see Chaplain Morrison, *Democratic Politics and Sectionalism: The Wilmot Proviso Controversy* (1967); Merrill Peterson, *The Great Triumvirate: Webster, Clay, and Calhoun* (1987); and Richard H. Sewell, *Ballots for Freedom: Antislavery Politics in the United States, 1837–1860* (1976). Holman Hamilton, *Prologue to Conflict: The Crisis and Compromise of 1850* (1964), covers the outcome of the political debate.

The End of the Second Party System, 1850–1858

An older but still valuable study of sectional conflict is Avery O. Craven, *The Growth of Southern Nationalism, 1848–1861* (1953). On the Fugitive Slave Act, consult Stanley W. Campbell, *The Slave Catchers* (1970). For the politics of southern expansionism, read Robert E. May, *The Southern Dream of a Caribbean Empire, 1854–1861* (1973).

On the development of the Republican Party, see Eric Foner, *Free Soil, Free Labor, Free Men: The Ideology of the Republican Party before the Civil War* (1970), and William E. Gienapp, *The Origins of the Republican Party, 1852–1856* (1987). The crisis over Kansas is discussed in James A. Rawley, *Race and Politics: Bleeding Kansas and the Coming of the Civil War* (1969), and Gerald W. Wolff, *The Kansas-Nebraska Bill: Party, Section, and the Coming of the Civil War* (1977). On the Buchanan administration, see Kenneth M. Stampp, *America in 1857: A Nation on the Brink* (1990), and Philip S. Klein, *President James Buchanan* (1962). On Dred Scott, see Don E. Fehrenbacher, *The Dred Scott Case: Its Significance in American Law and Politics* (1978). Good biographies include Robert W. Johannsen, *Stephen A. Douglas* (1973), and Stephen Oates, *To Purge This Land with Blood: A Biography of John Brown* (1970).

Abraham Lincoln and the Republican Triumph, 1858–1860

Abraham Lincoln has inspired a host of biographies. See Benjamin P. Thomas, *Abraham Lincoln: A Biography* (1952); Stephen B. Oates, *With Malice toward None* (1977); Mark E. Neely Jr., *The Last Best Hope of Earth* (1993); and David Herbert Donald, *Lincoln* (1995). On Lincoln's formative political years see Don E. Fehrenbacher, *Prelude to Greatness: Lincoln in the 1850s* (1962), and George B. Forgie, *Patricide and the House Divided* (1979). The fate of the Democratic Party is discussed in Michael Holt, *The Political Crisis of the 1850s* (1978).

Chapter 14: Two Societies at War, 1861–1865

The best up-to-date, comprehensive one-volume survey of the Civil War is James M. McPherson, *Battle Cry of Freedom: The Civil War Era* (1988), while Charles P. Roland, *An American Iliad:*

The Story of the Civil War (1991) is an excellent brief study. For the Confederacy, see George C. Rable, *The Confederate Republic* (1994). Charles Royster, *The Destructive War* (1991) explores the increasing dynamic of military violence. Two award-winning Web sites treat the events of these years. "The Valley of the Shadow" <http://jefferson.village.virginia.edu/vshadow2/> traces the experiences of two communities—one northern, one southern—during the prewar era using a multitude of hyperlinked sources—newspapers, letters, diaries, photographs, maps, etc. "The Freedmen and Southern Society Project" <http://www.inform.umd.edu/ARHU/Depts/History/Freedman/home.html> captures the drama of war and emancipation in the words of the participants: liberated slaves and defeated masters, soldiers and civilians, common folk and leaders.

Secession and Military Stalemate, 1861–1862

Classic studies of the secession crisis include Richard N. Current, *Lincoln and the First Shot* (1963); David M. Potter, *Lincoln and His Party in the Secession Crisis, 1860–61* (1962); and Kenneth M. Stampp, *And the War Came: The North and the Secession Crisis, 1860–61* (1950). Histories of the secession of the Deep South include William L. Barney, *The Secessionist Impulse: Alabama and Mississippi in 1860* (1974), and Michael P. Johnson, *Toward a Patriarchal Republic: The Secession of Georgia* (1977). On the Upper South, see Daniel Crofts, *Reluctant Confederates: Upper South Unionists in the Secession Crisis* (1989).

Toward Total War

To study northern society and politics during the war, consult Iver Bernstein, *The New York City Draft Riots* (1990); Gabor S. Boritt, ed., *Lincoln the War President: The Gettysburg Lectures* (1992); George M. Fredrickson, *The Inner Civil War: Northern Intellectuals and the Crisis of Union* (2nd ed., 1993); J. Matthew Gallman, *The North Fights the Civil War: The Home Front* (1994); Mark E. Neely Jr., *The Fate of Liberty: Abraham Lincoln and Civil Liberties* (1991); Phillip S. Paludan, *The Presidency of Abraham Lincoln* (1994); Joel Silbey, *A Respectable Minority: The Democratic Party in the Civil War Era* (1977); Hans Trefousse, *The Radical Republicans* (1969); and Garry Wills, *Lincoln at Gettysburg* (1992).

Important biographies of Union leaders include Michael Fellman, *Citizen Sherman: A Life of William Tecumseh Sherman* (1995); Jean Edward Smith, *Ulysses S. Grant* (2001); Stephen B. Oates, *With Malice toward None: A Life of Abraham Lincoln* (1977); Stephen W. Sears, *George B. McClellan: The Young Napoleon* (1988); and the Abraham Lincoln studies cited in Chapter 13.

Important studies of the Confederacy include Emory M. Thomas, *The Confederate Nation: 1861–1865* (1979), and Douglas B. Ball, *Financial Failure and Confederate Defeat* (1980). Good biographies of leading Confederates include William J. Cooper Jr., *Jefferson Davis, American* (2000); Emory M. Thomas, *Robert E. Lee, A Biography* (1997); and Thomas E. Schott, *Alexander H. Stephens of Georgia: A Biography* (1988). Three significant works on women are Drew Gilpin Faust,

Mothers of Invention: Southern Slaveholding Women in the Civil War (1996); Catherine Clinton and Nina Silber, eds., *Divided Houses: Gender and the Civil War* (1992); and Jeanie Artie, *Patriotic Toil: Northern Women and the American Civil War* (1998).

Other probing books on the Confederacy are Paul Escott, *After Secession: Jefferson Davis and the Failure of Southern Nationalism* (1978); Drew Gilpin Faust, *The Creation of Confederate Nationalism: Ideology and Identity in the Civil War* (1988); and Philip S. Paludan, *Victims: A True History of the Civil War* (1981).

The Turning Point: 1863

Studies of wartime emancipation include Ira Berlin, Barbara Fields, et al. *Slaves No More: Three Essays on Emancipation and the Civil War* (1992); Clarence R. Mohr, *On the Threshold of Freedom: Masters and Slaves in Civil War Georgia* (1986); and Willie Lee Rose, *Rehearsal for Reconstruction: The Port Royal Experiment* (1964). See also James M. McPherson, *The Struggle for Equality: Abolitionists and the Negro in the Civil War and Reconstruction* (1964). The best scholarship on the lives of slaves and black soldiers during the war is found in Ira Berlin et al., eds., *Freedom: A Documentary History of Emancipation, 1861–1867*, series 1, vol. 1: *The Destruction of Slavery* (1985), series 1, vol. 3: *The Wartime Genesis of Free Labor: The Lower South* (1990), and series 2: *The Black Military Experience* (1982).

The Union Victorious, 1864–1865

The most useful introduction to the military aspects of the war is T. Harry Williams, *The History of American Wars* (1981). On the experiences of Civil War soldiers, consult Albert Castel, *Decision in the West: The Atlanta Campaign* (1992); Gerald F. Linderman, *Embattled Courage: The Experience of Combat in the American Civil War* (1987); James M. McPherson, *What They Fought For, 1861–1865* (1994); and Reid Mitchell, *The Vacant Chair: The Northern Soldier Leaves Home* (1993) and Earl J. Hess, *The Union Soldier in Battle: Enduring the Ordeal of Combat* (1997). On the participation of African Americans in the war, see Noah Andre Trudeau, *Like Men of War: Black Troops in the Civil War, 1862–1865*. For Confederate military tactics, refer to Grady McWhiney and Perry D. Jamieson, *Attack and Die: Civil War Military Tactics and the Southern Heritage* (1982), and Steven E. Woodworth, *Jefferson Davis and His Generals: The Failure of Confederate Command in the West* (1990). For graphic accounts of two crucial battles, see Stephen W. Sears, *Landscape Turned Red: The Battle of Antietam* (1983), and Michael Shaara's novel, *Killer Angels* (1974). On the Civil War in the Far West, consult Alvin M. Josephy Jr., *The Civil War in the American West* (1991). For insightful analyses of the war's outcome, see William W. Freehling, *The South vs. the South : How Anti-Confederate Southerners Shaped the Course of the Civil War* (2001); Richard E. Beringer et al., *Why the South Lost the Civil War* (1986); Herman Hattaway and Archer Jones, *How the North Won: A Military History of the Civil War* (1983); and Archer Jones, *Civil War Command and Strategy: The Process of Victory and Defeat* (1992).

Absorbing firsthand accounts of the war years include C. Vann Woodward, ed., *Mary Chesnut's Civil War* (1981); David Donald, ed., *Inside Lincoln's Cabinet: The Civil War Diaries of Salmon P. Chase* (1959); T. W. Higginson, *Army Life in a Black Regiment* (1867); and W. T. Sherman, *Memoirs* (1990).

Chapter 15: Reconstruction, 1865–1877

The starting point for the study of Reconstruction is Eric Foner's major synthesis, *Reconstruction: America's Unfinished Revolution, 1863–1877* (1988), which is also available in a shorter version. Two older surveys that provide useful introductions are John Hope Franklin, *Reconstruction: After the Civil War* (1961), and Kenneth M. Stampp, *The Era of Reconstruction* (1965). *Black Reconstruction in America* (1935), by the black activist and scholar W. E. B. Du Bois, deserves attention as the first book to challenge traditional racist interpretations of Reconstruction as carpetbagger rule unjustly imposed on the defeated South by radical Republicans. The Web site <http://lcweb2.loc.gov/ammem/aaohtml/exhibit/aopart5 .html> provides Library of Congress documents and illustrations on African Americans during Reconstruction.

Presidential Reconstruction

For important studies of presidential efforts to rebuild the Union, see the books on Abraham Lincoln listed in Chapter 14 and the following works on Andrew Johnson: Albert Castel, *The Presidency of Andrew Johnson* (1979); Eric L. McKitrick, *Andrew Johnson and Reconstruction* (1960); and James Sefton, *Andrew Johnson and the Uses of Constitutional Power* (1979). On the radical resistance to presidential Reconstruction, see James M. McPherson, *The Struggle for Equality: Abolitionists and the Negro in the Civil War and Reconstruction* (1965). Books that focus on Congress include LaWanda Cox and John H. Cox, *Politics, Principle, and Prejudice, 1865–1867* (1963); David Donald, *The Politics of Reconstruction, 1863–1867* (1965); and William B. Brock, *An American Crisis: Congress and Reconstruction, 1865–1867* (1963). For insight into developments in the South, see Dan T. Carter, *When the War Was Over: The Failure of Self-Reconstruction in the South, 1865–1867* (1985). Michael Perman, *Reunion without Compromise: The South and Reconstruction, 1865–1868* (1973), stresses the South's relations with Johnson. On the freedmen, see Willie Lee Rose, *Rehearsal for Reconstruction: The Port Royal Experiment* (1964); Peter Kolchin, *First Freedom: The Responses of Alabama's Blacks to Emancipation and Reconstruction* (1972); and Leon F. Litwack, *Been in the Storm So Long: The Aftermath of Slavery* (1979). More recent emancipation studies emphasize slavery as a labor system: Barbara Fields, *Slavery and Freedom on the Middle Ground: Maryland during the Nineteenth Century* (1985); Julie Saville, *The Work of Reconstruction: From Slave to Wage Laborer in South Carolina, 1860–1870* (1994); Ira Berlin et al., *Slaves No More: Three Essays on Emancipation and the Civil War* (1992); and Amy Dru Stanley, *From Bondage to Contract: Wage Labor, Marriage, and the Market in the Age of Slave Emancipation* (1999), which ex-

pands the discussion to show what the onset of wage labor meant for freedwomen. Other books that deal with the impact of emancipation on black women are Jacqueline Jones, *Labor of Love, Labor of Sorrow: Black Women, Work, and the Family from Slavery to the Present* (1985), a pioneering work, and an important case study, Leslie A. Schwalm, *A Hard Fight for We: Women's Transition from Slavery to Freedom in South Carolina* (1997). For a Web site that explores how white northern women attempted to assist freed people during Reconstruction, see <http:// womhist.binghamton.edu/aid/intro.htm>. Eric Foner, *Nothing But Freedom: Emancipation and Its Legacy* (1983), helpfully places emancipation in a comparative context.

Radical Reconstruction

For Congress's role in radical Reconstruction, see Michael Les Benedict, *A Compromise of Principle: Congressional Republicans and Reconstruction* (1974), and Hans L. Trefousse, *Impeachment of a President: Andrew Johnson, the Blacks, and Reconstruction* (1975). William S. McFeely, *Grant: A Biography* (1981), deftly explains the politics of Reconstruction. Also helpful is Brooks D. Simpson, *Let Us Have Peace: Ulysses S. Grant and the Politics of War and Reconstruction, 1861–1868* (1991). State studies of Reconstruction include Richard Lowe, *Republicans and Reconstruction in Virginia, 1856–1870* (1991), and Otto Olsen, ed., *Reconstruction and Redemption in the South* (1980). The best account of carpetbaggers is Richard N. Current, *Those Terrible Carpetbaggers: A Reinterpretation* (1988). On blacks during radical Reconstruction, see Joel Williamson, *After Slavery: The Negro in South Carolina during Reconstruction, 1861–1877* (1965); Robert Cruden, *The Negro in Reconstruction* (1969); John Blassingame, *Black New Orleans, 1860–1880* (1973); Thomas Holt, *Black over White: Negro Political Leadership in South Carolina during Reconstruction* (1977); and Barry A. Crouch, *The Freedmen's Bureau and Black Texans* (1992). The emergence of the sharecropping system is explored in Roger L. Ransom and Richard Sutch, *One Kind of Freedom: The Economic Consequences of Emancipation* (1977); Jay Mandle, *The Roots of Black Poverty: The Southern Plantation Economy after the Civil War* (1978); Gavin Wright, *Old South, New South: Revolutions in the Southern Economy since the Civil War* (1986); Edward Royce, *The Origins of Southern Sharecropping* (1993); Harold Woodman, *New South, New Law: The Legal Foundations of Credit and Labor Relations in the Postbellum Agricultural South* (1995).

The Undoing of Reconstruction

The most thorough study of the Ku Klux Klan is Allen W. Trelease, *White Terror: The Ku Klux Klan Conspiracy and Southern Reconstruction* (1972), and on its founder, Brian S. Wills, *A Battle from the Start: The Life of Nathan Bedford Forrest* (1992). To survey Reconstruction politics in the South, consult Michael Perman, *The Road to Redemption: Southern Politics, 1869–1879* (1984). On politics in the North, see James Mohr, ed., *The Radical Republicans in the North: State Politics during Reconstruction* (1976), and William Gillette, *Retreat from Reconstruction, 1863–1879* (1979). Laura F. Edwards, *Gendered Strife and Confusion: The Political Culture of Reconstruction*

(1997) is an innovative study that explores the gendered dimension of Reconstruction politics in a North Carolina county. Equally illuminating as a more traditional political narrative is Jonathan M. Bryant, *How Curious a Land: Conflict and Change in Greene County, Georgia, 1850–1885* (1996). For the impact of Reconstruction on the national state, see Morton Keller, *Affairs of State: Public Life in Late Nineteenth-Century America* (1977), and Richard F. Bensel, *Yankee Leviathan: The Origins of Central State Authority in America, 1859–1877* (1990). On political corruption, see Mark W. Summers, *The Era of Good Stealings* (1993). On the Compromise of 1877, see C. Vann Woodward's classic *Reunion and Reaction* (1956), and K. I. Polakoff, *The Politics of Inertia: The Election of 1876 and the End of Reconstruction* (1973).

Chapter 1

American Voices: Friar Bernardino de Sahagun, "Aztec Elders Describe the Spanish Conquest." Excerpt from *The Florentine Codex: General History of the Things of New Spain*, translated by Arthur J. Anderson and Charles E. Dibble. Copyright © 1975 by the University of Utah Press and the School of American Research. Reprinted courtesy of the University of Utah Press.

Chapter 2

Table 2.2. "Environment, Disease, and Death in Virginia, 1618–1624." Adapted from table 3 in *The Chesapeake in the Seventeenth Century* by Thad W. Tate and David L. Ammerman, eds. Published by W. W. Norton (1979). Copyright © University of North Carolina Press. Reprinted by permission.

Chapter 4

American Voices: Gottlieb Mittelberger, "The Perils of Migration." Excerpt from "The Crossing to Pennsylvania" in *Journey to Pennsylvania* by Gottlieb Mittelberger, edited and translated by Oscar Handlin and John Clive, pp. 11–21: The Belknap Press of Harvard University Press. Copyright © 1960 by the President and Fellows of Harvard College. Reprinted by permission of the publisher.

American Voices: Nathan Cole, "The Power of a Preacher." Excerpt from *The Great Awakening: Documents on the Revival of Religion, 1740–1745*, edited by Richard L. Bushman. Copyright © 1979 by Richard L. Bushman. Used by permission of the University of North Carolina Press.

Voices from Abroad: Louis Antonine de Bougainville, "The Defense of Canada." From *Adventure in the Wilderness: The American Journals of Lewis Antonine de Bougainville*, edited and translated by Edward P. Hamilton. Copyright © 1964 by Edward P. Hamilton. Reprinted by permission of the University of Oklahoma Press.

Table 4.2. "Estimated European Migration to the British Mainland Colonies, 1700–1780." Adapted (and altered from) *The Journal of Interdisciplinary History*, XXII (1992), 628, with the permission of the editors of *The Journal of Interdisciplinary History* and The MIT Press, Cambridge, MA. Copyright © 1992 by the Massachusetts Institute of Technology and The Journal of Interdisciplinary History, Inc.

Chapter 5

American Voices: "Anonymous Broadside, May 18, 1775, To the Associators of the City of Philadelphia." Letter to the Library Company of Philadelphia from *Pennsylvania History*, vol. 52 (October 1985): 255–56. Courtesy of Pennsylvania State University, Dept. of History.

Chapter 6

American Voices: Benjamin Banneker, "On Jefferson and Natural Rights." Excerpt from Benjamin Banneker's letter to Thomas Jefferson in 1791, as it appears on pp. 102–5 in *Founding the Republic: A Documentary History* by John J. Patrick,

editor. Copyright © 1995 by John J. Patrick. Reprinted with permission of Greenwood Publishing Group, Inc., Westport, CT.

Chapter 7

American Voices: Abigail and John Adams, "The Status of Women." Excerpt from *The Adams Family Correspondence* by Lyman H. Butterfield, editor. Copyright © 1963 by the Massachusetts Historical Society. Reprinted by permission of the publisher, Harvard University Press.

Fig. 7.1. "Middling Men Enter the Halls of Government, 1765–1790." Adapted from "Government by the People: The American Revolution and the Democratization of the Legislature" by Jackson T. Main. From *William and Mary Quarterly*, 3rd series, vol. 23 (1996). Reprinted by permission of the Omohundro Institute of Early American History and Culture.

Chapter 8

Voices from Abroad: Alexis de Tocqueville, "Law and Lawyers in the United States." From *Democracy in America* by Alexis de Tocqueville, translated by Henry Reeve. Copyright © 1945 and renewed 1973 by Alfred A. Knopf, a division of Random House, Inc. Used by permission of Alfred A. Knopf, a division of Random House, Inc.

Chapter 9

Fig. 9.1. "Movement of Slaves from Upper South to Lower South, 1790–1850." Adapted from fig. 12 in *Time on the Cross* by Robert William Fogel and Stanley Engerman. Copyright © 1974 by Robert William Fogel and Stanley Engerman. Reprinted by permission.

Table 9.1. "Number of Lawyers in Three Selected States to 1820." Adapted from data on p. 49 in *Law in the New Republic: Private Law and the Public Estate* by George Dargo. Copyright © 1980 by George Dargo. Reprinted by permission.

Table 9.2. "African Slaves Imported into North America by Ethnicity, 1776–1809." Adapted from table A6, "From Slaves, Convicts and Servants to Free Passengers" as published in the *Journal of American History* 85 (June 1998). Reprinted by permission.

Chapter 10

Table 10.1. "Leading Branches of Manufacture, 1860." Adapted from data (p. 26) published in *Economic Growth of the U.S. 1790–1860* by Douglas C. North. Copyright © Douglas C. North. Reprinted by permission of Pearson Education, Inc., Upper Saddle River, NJ.

Table 10.2. "Government Investment in Canals in Three States." Adapted from data (p. 54) published by Roger Ransom in *American Economic Review*, vol. 54 (1964). Reprinted by permission of the American Economic Association.

Chapter 11

Voices from Abroad: Alexis de Tocqueville, "Parties in the United States." From *Democracy in America* by Alexis de

A note about the index: Names of individuals appear in boldface; biographical dates are included for major historical figures. Letters in parentheses following pages refer to: *(f)* figures, including charts and graphs; *(i)* illustrations, including photographs and artifacts; *(m)* maps; and *(t)* tables.

Southgate, Eliza, 254
Southwest, Old (Alabama, Mississippi, Louisiana)
    migration to, 262–263, 263(i), 263(f), 264(m), 265(t), 296, 297(m), 313
Spain
    Cuba and, 375
    vs. England, 33, 35, 40–41, 95, 98
    expansionist foreign policy of, 387
    vs. France, 40–41
    Islam in, 17
    maritime expansion of, 19, 22, 22(m)
    Mexican independence from, 370
    missions of, 41, 47
    Napoleon and, 231
    peace talks with, 182–184
    Portugal and, 33
    vs. Protestantism, 33
    in Revolutionary War, 177, 182
    rulers of (1474–1598), 29(t)
    territorial disputes with, 230
    Texas and, 369–370
    wars with, 89, 95–97
    the West and, 198, 240(m), 374
Spanish Armada, 33
Spanish colonization, 19, 22, 22(m), 40–44, 40(t), 41(m), 76, 134(m), 138(m), 267
    Carolinas and, 70
    Catholicism and, 27–28, 41–42, 44, 65, 67
    conquest of Aztecs and Incas, 9, 12, 24–28, 25(m), 27(i), 30–31, 37
    Florida and, 70–71
    gold and, 24, 27, 33, 35, 37, 40
    Louisiana and, 125, 198
    in Mexico, 24–26, 30–31, 37
    in North America, 102, 121, 122(m), 125, 136, 138(m), 151(m), 184(m), 240(m)
    in Texas, 241, 249
Spanish Netherlands, 33. See also Dutch colonization
specie, 324
Specie Circular (1836), 333
spinning, 242
spoils system, 330, 338
Spotsylvania Court House, battle of, 420
squatter sovereignty, 383
Staël, Madame de, 207
Stamp Act (1765), 134, 138–143, 146, 149, 155(t), 159, 177, 201
    repeal of, 144–145, 167
    resistance to, 140–144
Stamp Act Congress (1765), 140, 143, 155(t), 159
Stanley, Ann Lee (Mother Ann), 346–347
Stanton, Edward M., 437
Stanton, Elizabeth Cady, 357, 362, 381, 439
    Seneca Falls and, 363–364
Staple Act (1663), 72(t)

states
    constitutions of, 194–196, 219, 330, 437, 453
    formation and Indian cessions, 223(m)
    governments of, 244
    reform of government of, 329–330
    slave vs. free, 382–384, 391, 395
    women's rights and, 363
states' rights, 269, 280, 328, 331, 338
    Calhoun on, 323
    Fugitive Slave Act and, 386
    Indian removal and, 326
    interstate commerce and, 300
    Second Bank and, 324
Statute of Wills, 102
steam power
    manufacturing and, 286–287, 313
    steamboats and, 297, 300, 302
Stephens, Alexander, 402, 415, 424, 431
Steuben, Baron von, 175
Stevens, Thaddeus, 389, 413, 436
Stewart, Maria W., 359
Stiles, Ezra, 130, 194
Stoddard, Solomon, 116–117
Stone, Lucy, 357, 439
Stone, Samuel, 253
Stono Rebellion (1739), 89, 96
Story, Joseph, 246, 248, 321
Stowe, Harriet Beecher, 362, 370, 386
Strachey, Richard, 183
Stroyer, Jacob, 266–267
Stuyvesant, Peter, 48
suffrage. See voting rights
sugar
    duties on, 136–138, 154
    Molasses Act and, 98
    plantations and, 78, 80
    planter-merchant elite and, 79
    related industries and, 79
    slavery and, 69, 71, 76–78, 77(m), 77(t), 80, 84, 88, 125, 134(m), 137
    in the South, 262–263, 265, 265(m), 266(i)
    South Atlantic system and, 99
    West Indies trade and, 91, 93(m), 97(i), 105, 105(f), 106, 125, 134(m), 136–137, 138(m), 154
Sugar Act (1764), 136–138, 140, 143, 145, 155(t), 159, 177
Sullivan, John, 177(m)
A Summary View of the Rights of British America (Jefferson), 169
Summer, Sally, 152
Sumner, Charles, 367, 413, 436, 439, 449
Supreme Court, 204, 209, 218, 230, 249, 438
    constitutionality of Civil Rights Bill (1870) and, 449
    Dred Scott and, 391, 393

Fugitive Slave Act and, 386
Gibbons v. Ogden, 300
John Marshall and, 245–246, 246(t)
Native American cases and, 328
Roger Taney and, 328–329
slavery and, 393
Susquehanna Company, 128
Susquehannock Indians, 55, 64
Sutter, John A., 383
Swamp Fox. *See* Marion, Francis
Sweden, 40(t), 48

Taino Indians, 24
Tallender, Lydia, 256
Talleyrand, Charles, 216
Tallmadge, James, 269
Taney, Roger B., 321, 328–329
    Dred Scott and, 391
    Fugitive Slave Act and, 386
    Second Bank and, 324
Tappan, Arthur, 309, 354, 357
Tappan, Lewis, 309, 354, 357
Tariff of Abominations, 319(i), 320, 322
tariffs, 201, 205–206, 212, 331
    of 1816, 319
    of 1828, 319, 339
    during Adams's administration, 318–319, 319(i)
    in Civil War, 409, 411
    Jackson and, 320–323, 323(i)
    for manufacturing, 290–291
    nullification of, 321–323
    protective, 332, 335, 338
    Tocqueville on, 325
taverns
    as political centers, 142
    woman-run, 104(i)
taxation, 137(f). See also Shays's Rebellion
    in Civil War, 411, 413, 427
    in colonial America, 134–150, 154–155, 159
    colonial assemblies and, 94
    Confederacy and, 198, 200, 413
    excise levies and, 136, 303
    hidden currency, 186, 191
    Jefferson and, 230, 249
    land, 369
    in New England colonies, 73
    occupation tax, 252
    political rights and, 93
    poll tax, 252
    power of, 246
    property, 441
    rebellion and, 71
    in Reconstruction, 441
    religion and, 190, 453
    rise in, 74
    self-government and, 251
    smuggling and, 136–137, 149
    Southern gentry and, 90
    of stocks and bonds, 332
    of wealthy, 332

CANADA

MINNESOTA

Lake Superior

MICHIGAN

Duluth

WISCONSIN

Lake Huron

Lake Michigan

St. Paul
Minneapolis
Mississippi R.
Wisconsin R.
Milwaukee
Madison
Lansing ★
Detroit

IOWA
Sioux Falls
Chicago
Gary
Toledo
Cleveland
Lake Erie

Des Moines ★
Omaha
Lincoln

ILLINOIS
Illinois R.
Springfield
St. Louis
Wabash R.

INDIANA
Indianapolis

OHIO
Columbus
Wheeling
Ohio R.
Cincinnati

Lake Ontario

NEW YORK
Buffalo

MAINE
Augusta
Burlington
Montpelier
VT.
Albany
Hudson R.
N.H.
Concord
Manchester
Portland

MASS.
Hartford
Boston
Providence
RHODE ISLAND
CONNECTICUT

St. Lawrence R.

Newark
New York
Trenton
NEW JERSEY
Philadelphia

PENNSYLVANIA
Allegheny R.
Harrisburg
Pittsburgh

Baltimore
Dover
MD.
DELAWARE
Washington, D.C.
Annapolis
Potomac R.

WEST VIRGINIA
Charleston

Frankfort
Louisville

KENTUCKY
Cumberland R.

VIRGINIA
Richmond
Norfolk
Roanoke R.

APPALACHIAN MOUNTAINS

Topeka
Kansas City
Jefferson City
Missouri R.

MISSOURI

Knoxville
Nashville ★

TENNESSEE
Tennessee R.

NORTH CAROLINA
Raleigh
Charlotte
Cape Fear R.

Tulsa
Oklahoma City
Canadian R.

ARKANSAS
Arkansas R.
Little Rock
Memphis

SOUTH CAROLINA
Columbia
Santee R.
Charleston

Birmingham

ATLANTIC OCEAN

Fort Worth
Dallas
Trinity R.
Sabine R.
Red R.
Brazos R.

LOUISIANA

MISSISSIPPI
Jackson
Mississippi R.

ALABAMA
Montgomery
Alabama R.

GEORGIA
Atlanta
Chattahoochee R.
Altamaha R.
Savannah

Houston
Baton Rouge ★
New Orleans
Mobile
Tallahassee

Jacksonville

FLORIDA

Gulf of Mexico

Tampa

Miami

BAHAMAS

Elevation

Feet	Meters
9,843	3,000
6,562	2,000
3,281	1,000
1,640	500
656	200
0	0
Below sea level	Below sea level

67°W   66°W
ATLANTIC OCEAN
San Juan
PUERTO RICO
Ponce
18°N
Caribbean Sea

0   25   50 miles
0   25   50 kilometers

0   200   400 miles
0   200   400 kilometers

CUBA

95°W   90°W   85°W   80°W   75°W

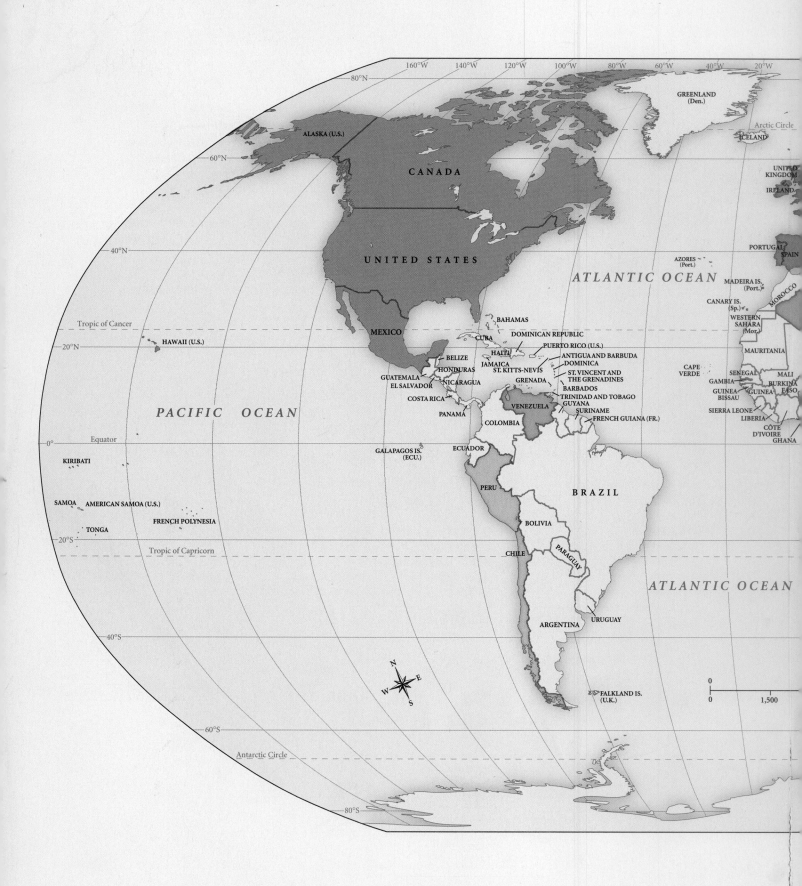

Political divisions as of April 2003